DIFFERENTIAL EQUATIONS

DIFFERENTIAL EQUATIONS
Matrices and Models

PAUL BUGL

University of Hartford

PRENTICE HALL, Englewood Cliffs, New Jersey 07632

Library of Congress Cataloging-in-Publication Data

Bugl, Paul.
   Differential equations : matrices and models / Paul Bugl.
     p. cm.
   Includes bibliographical references and index.
   ISBN 0-02-316540-5
   1. Differential equations. 2. Matrices. I. Title.
QA372.B874 1995
515'.35—dc20   94-31812
                                CIP

Acquisitions Editor: George Lobell
Editorial Production: Electronic Publishing Services Inc.
Cover Designer: Lee Goldstein

ⓒ1995 by Prentice Hall, Inc.
A Simon & Schuster Company
Englewood Cliffs, New Jersey 07632

Printed in the United States of America

10 9 8 7 6 5 4 3 2 1

ISBN 0-02-316540-5

Prentice Hall International (UK) Limited, *London*
Prentice Hall of Australia Pty. Limited, *Sydney*
Prentice Hall Canada Inc., *Toronto*
Prentice Hall Hispanoamericana, S.A., *Mexico*
Prentice Hall of India Private Limited, *New Delhi*
Prentice Hall of Japan, Inc., *Tokyo*
Simon & Schuster Asia Pte. Ltd., *Singapore*
Editora Prentice Hall do Brasil, Ltda., *Rio de Janeiro*

CONTENTS

Chapter 7   Nonlinear ODE's   443

PREFACE

Historically, the study of differential equations was a major driving force in the development of the ideas of the calculus. Models of physical problems were formulated in terms of differential equations whose solution often gave rise to new areas of study in both mathematics and the sciences. Problems worthy of study have become ever more difficult for the classical techniques. Reasonably accurate models frequently require the use of several dependent variables and a utilization of the power of matrix algebra.

Previously, the study of differential equations was a collection of sometimes unrelated techniques. However, change is moving through the course. The use of computer algebra systems renders superfluous some of the elaborate techniques needed for special cases. More emphasis on systems of linear ordinary differential equations reflects greater realism and requires an early introduction to linear algebra. As material is removed from the course, more attention can and should be given to modeling; students must learn how to properly formulate the problems that they, in turn, should solve.

This book is intended to provide a modern study of differential equations in the spirit of reasonable, but overdue, reform. Matrix algebra is presented along with many of the elementary numerical techniques needed for the computer implementation of its procedures. The methods for the solution of differential equations appear only after models which generate the equations have been studied. The ultimate goal of the text is the use of matrix methods for the solution of systems of linear ordinary differential equations. The reader who comes away with an understanding of the power of the state-transition matrix approach will have achieved the aim of the book.

A large proportion of students taking a course in differential equations major in either engineering or the physical sciences. Such students will have taken two semesters of calculus-based physics and possibly both statics and dynamics and/or a first course in electrical circuits. For this reason, the models most frequently used are those of classical mechanics and network analysis. They have seen these before and are usually more comfortable with them. Any student who sees these models in another context will suffer no harm and repeated study can only reinforce concepts learned elsewhere. To make it easier for students, the Lagrangian approach is used for formulating mechanics problems, thus avoiding the difficulty of constructing the free body diagram.

Many of the classical solution methods are not presented in this book. Exact equations and other such are nowhere to be found. A method appears only if it is useful in solving equations arising from reasonable models. Undetermined coefficients is given short shrift. Some methods which seem not to be a common part of the curriculum have been included, e.g., the LU-decomposition, pivoting and scaling, ill-conditioned systems, boundary and initial value Green's functions, the matrix exponential, controllability, and observability. On the other hand, series solutions are discussed in detail because none of the usual computer algebra systems can generate the general form of a solution for a simple but arbitrary second order equation. It is also possible to use this book for a more traditional course, if that it the aim.

The matrix language Matlab is used as an adjunct to keep one from being overwhelmed by the details involved in programming languages like Pascal, C, or FORTRAN. Matlab's notation is rapidly becoming universally adopted. The use of a computer algebra system would be helpful, insofar as large parts of several chapters could be omitted. In that case, use could be made of the appropriate lab manual which accompanies this text.

An attempt has been made to provide the reader with a large number of detailed nontrivial examples to enhance self-study.

Some say a book is only as good as its problems. The exercise sets have been designed to be broad-based. There are some simple computational problems, verifications, many "thought" problems, and a large number of modeling applications. Each chapter ends with a set of supplementary and complementary problems which are designed to extend either the material in the text or the reader. These problems are meant to be more interesting.

Outline

The first two chapters can be covered in either order.

Sections are organized logically so as to completely cover a single subject area. For this reason, one section can rarely be covered in one fifty minute class. Instead, subsections may be the units of class time.

Chapter 1 covers the lion's share of complex matrix algebra. Systems of linear algebraic equations are solved using pivotal reduction (Gauss-Jordan elimination with partial pivoting). The ideas of leading and nonleading variables and their relation to the rank and nullity of the coefficient matrix and its row-reduced echelon form are emphasized. Inverses appear as theoretical constructs for the further study of linear equations. Determinants are defined in terms of elementary row operations and applied to solving systems of linear equations and finding inverses of square matrices. Computer solution of linear systems and the LU-decomposition are discussed as optional material.

Chapter 2 gives an introduction to models and differential equations. Graphical and numerical solutions are discussed before any analytical methods. First order equations are solved using either separation of variables or the integrating factor for linear equations. As an option, Runge-Kutta methods are derived as multistage methods.

Chapter 3 introduces the complementary concepts of linear spaces and linear transformations. Infinite dimensional spaces are not shunned. Proofs are given when they use the ideas of systems of linear equations or provide a method of solution. Many results are only stated. Induced matrix norms and condition numbers are discussed and used as an assessment of the computational solvability of a linear system. Optional sections on the Gram-Schmidt procedure and fundamental subspaces associated with a matrix rounds out the chapter.

Chapter 4 introduces linear ODE's in terms of differential operators and trial solutions. Some of the ideas of linear spaces are used. For the most part, the treatment is fairly classical, but the intention is that computer software be used to speed the presentation. Applications to mechanical and electrical systems are given. Boundary value Green's functions are introduced as an optional technique for reducing a nonhomogeneous problem to a quadrature. Most of this material could be omitted if the course will utilize a computer algebra system.

Chapter 5 develops the ideas of the Laplace transform in six relatively compact sections. The evaluation of the transform and the inverse transform are unified into a single section for each. The geometrical interpretation of the convolution product is given. Transforms are then applied to solving linear ODE's and finding Green's functions. Applications to elastic beam problems illustrate the solution of problems with discontinuous forcing functions. A computer algebra system would be a valuable tool to eliminate much of the algebraic tedium involved in many of the calculations.

Chapter 6 begins with models which require more than one dependent variable, after which systems of equations are reduced to standard matrix form. After the ideas of linear systems are developed, the matrix eigenvalue problem is studied in some detail, including the Jordan normal form. Linear systems solution methods are then presented. The state-transition matrix is introduced and functions of matrices are discussed. Several methods for the calculation of the matrix exponential are given and applied to solving homogeneous and nonhomogeneous linear systems of ODE's. Phase portraits of linear systems are studied in terms of the eigenvalues of the coefficient matrix. Initial value Green's functions and the ideas of controllability and observability of a system are also discussed, as are Laplace transform methods for linear systems.

Chapter 7 provides an overview of nonlinear systems. In addition to the usual discussion of phase plane analysis, stability, and limit cycles, there is an outline of regular perturbation methods. Brief introductions to singular perturbations and chaotic systems are also given.

Chapter 8 contains a fairly detailed coverage of series solutions to linear equations with variable coefficients including the method of Frobenius.

Chapter 9 closes things out with an optional survey of special functions.

A listing of the Matlab commands that a student might use are collected in the first appendix. Other appendices are included as reviews or brief discussions of complex numbers, complex functions, unit steps and impulses, partial fraction expansions, and infinite series.

Answers are provided to most of the odd-numbered problems.

Ancillary Material

In addition to the text, other materials are available for use in teaching a course from this book.

- Student version of Matlab 4.0 which includes the Maple kernel can be packaged with the text. This includes the valuable command reference book. There are Windows and Macintosh versions.

- A student solution manual contains the fairly complete solutions to most of the odd-numbered problems in the exercise sets in the book.

- An instructor's solutions manual contains solutions to almost all of the problems in the book, including the supplementary and complementary problems.

- A computer lab manual which provides the student with problems and projects for exploration and experimentation. It comes in three separate versions: Matlab 4.0, Maple, and Mathematica.

Acknowledgments

What seems like countless students have worked through various drafts of the manuscript. Their spirits did not appear to be dampened by what must surely be a law of Nature, the more you proof read anything, the more errors creep in. They found the errors and made many suggestions about the exposition and organization. Special thanks go to Mark Linnick who generated the figures and graphs and also to Jean-Marie Rennetaud whose eagle eye caught many errors in preliminary drafts.

Reviewers have had a pronounced effect on the final outcome. Their suggestions were extremely valuable and, with very few exceptions, included in the text. I wish to thank the following reviewers:

Terry Herdman, Virginia Polytechnic Institute

Dar-Vieg Ho, Georgia Institute of Technology

Karl Kosler, University of Wisconsin

Calvin Piston, John Brown University

Lawrence Runyan, Shoreline Community College

Michael Simon, Housatonic Community College

My thanks go to my latest editor George Lobell, whose constant prodding has resulted in a timely publication schedule. Amy Hendrickson of TeXnology Inc. deserves credit for the speedy composition and visually pleasing design of this book.

Last, and most surely not least, my wife Dae deserves a debt of gratitude that goes beyond what mere words can express.

Any errors are mine, and mine alone. All suggestions, comments, and criticisms are welcome and will be gratefully received. You can write (using o-mail) to me at the Department of Math/Physics/CS at the University of Hartford, West Hartford, CT 06117-1500 or use my (inordinately long) e-mail address:

bugl%uhavax.dnet@ipgate.hartford.edu,

although I have been known to receive messages sent to *bugl@hartford.edu.*

1

MATRIX ALGEBRA

1.1 PREVIEW

Matrices lie at the very foundation of applied mathematics. They are the bedrock on which many models are built. Whenever more than one dependent variable is involved, a problem can be phrased in the language of matrix theory so that a number of powerful methods can be brought to bear.

We begin with some linear multivariate models that can be simplified by the use of matrices. All of the necessary operations of matrix algebra and their properties are introduced. Special matrices are defined and studied. Most problems that can be formulated in the language of matrices eventually lead to the problem of solving a system of linear algebraic equations. Section 1.4 presents the method of pivotal reduction for arriving at a solution when one exists. It also discusses the forms and existence of solutions.

The inverse of a matrix is introduced as a formal alternative to the use of the method of pivotal reduction. We restrict our attention to square matrices and their reduction by elementary matrices. Some of the implications of invertibility are explored. Finally, a model of cascaded two-port networks is introduced and the inverse is used to construct solutions.

The concept of the determinant of a square matrix as an alternating multilinear functional is developed by way of elementary row operations. The expansion by cofactors is stated, as is Cramer's Rule for solving square systems. Then the adjugate matrix is used to compute the inverse of a nonsingular matrix.

Two optional sections deal with the computer implementation of techniques for solving systems of linear equations. The method of Gaussian elimination is compared with pivotal reduction with a discussion of pivoting and scaling. A simple example of an ill-conditioned system is given, and the effects of computer round-off are discussed. The methodology of the LU-decomposition is presented and applied to solving linear systems.

1.2   LINEAR MULTIVARIATE MODELS

Mathematical models often devolve upon solving systems of simultaneous equations. Frequently, these equations involve the unknowns raised to the first power and there are no products of unknowns. Such models pervade applied mathematics. What follows is but a small sample of them.

1.2.1   Steady State AC Electrical Circuits

An electrical **circuit** is a collection of resistors, inductors, and capacitors connected by idealized wires joined at **nodes**. When there is an alternating current source, each of the circuit elements can be thought of as having an **impedance**, Z, that satisfies the generalized **Ohm's Law**,

$$E = IZ,$$

where E is the voltage drop across the element and I is the current flowing through it. In a general alternating current circuit, the impedance Z is complex and has the form

$$Z = R + i\left(\omega L - \frac{1}{\omega C}\right),$$

where R is the resistance (measured in ohms Ω), L is the inductance (measured in henrys H), C is the capacitance (measured in farads F), and $f = \omega/2\pi$ is the frequency (measured in hertz Hz) of the AC source.

Most circuits are composed of several loops, each of which has several elements on it. One method of analyzing a circuit is to assign currents to each loop, write Ohm's Law separately for each element, and use the **Kirchhoff Voltage Law**, which says that the sum of the voltage drops around a loop must be zero.

This procedure has the advantage of always resulting in as many equations as there are unknowns.

■ **EXAMPLE 1.1**   The circuit in Figure 1.1 has five loops with unknown loop currents I_1, I_2, I_3, I_4, and I_5 drawn clockwise. If the voltage E is known, set up the linear equations that determine these currents.

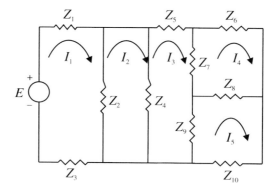

Fig. 1.1

Solution: Applying the Kirchhoff Voltage Law to each loop yields

$$Z_1 I_1 + Z_2 (I_1 - I_2) + Z_3 I_1 - E = 0,$$
$$Z_2 (I_2 - I_1) + Z_4 (I_2 - I_3) = 0,$$
$$Z_4 (I_3 - I_2) + Z_5 I_3 + Z_7 (I_3 - I_4) + Z_9 (I_3 - I_5) = 0,$$
$$Z_7 ((I_4 - I_3) + Z_6 I_4 + Z_8 (I_4 - I_5) = 0,$$
$$Z_9 (I_5 - I_3) + Z_8 (I_5 - I_4) + Z_{10} I_5 = 0.$$

These equations can be rewritten in the form

$$(Z_1 + Z_2 + Z_3) I_1 - Z_2 I_2 = E,$$
$$-Z_2 I_1 + (Z_2 + Z_4) I_2 - Z_4 I_3 = 0,$$
$$-Z_4 I_2 + (Z_4 + Z_5 + Z_7 + Z_9) I_3 - Z_7 I_4 - Z_9 I_5 = 0,$$
$$-Z_7 I_3 + (Z_6 + Z_7 + Z_8) I_4 - Z_9 I_5 = 0,$$
$$-Z_9 I_3 - Z_8 I_4 + (Z_8 + Z_9 + Z_{10}) I_5 = 0.$$

Thus the behavior of the entire circuit can be determined by solving five equations in five unknown currents. ■ ■ ■

Other steady state circuit problems can be handled in a similar manner.

1.2.2 Framework Models

A **framework** is an assembly of rigid or flexible members joined together either rigidly or with pins that allow rotation. Each member experiences either tension or compression. Flexible members can only be under tension. When studying rigid members, it is possible to calculate the total extension of the framework because **Hooke's Law** says the extension of a member is proportional to the internal force of the member. The complete analysis of a framework consists of applying Newton's Second Law at the points of contact between members and computing any extensions.

■ **EXAMPLE 1.2** A framework of rigid members forms a 3-4-5 triangle as drawn in Figure 1.2. Set up the force equations for static equilibrium.

Solution: The components of the external forces at support A are A_x and A_y, B_y is the external force at support B, F_{AB} is the internal force of the member joining supports A and B, F_{BC} is the internal force of the member joining supports B and C, and F_{AC} is the internal force of the member joining supports A and C. There is no force B_x because the support at B is a roller. Support C has an external force of 10 newtons acting downward and 5 newtons to the right. Because this is a static problem, the sum of the forces will be zero. Applying Newton's Second Law to the x- and y-components of the forces at A, B, and C, we have

$$
\begin{aligned}
A_x & & +F_{AB} & & & = 0, \\
& A_y & & +F_{AC} & & = 0, \\
& & -F_{AB} & & -\tfrac{4}{5}F_{BC} & = 0, \\
& B_y & & & +\tfrac{3}{5}F_{BC} & = 0, \\
& & & & +\tfrac{4}{5}F_{BC} & = -5, \\
& & & -F_{AC} & -\tfrac{3}{5}F_{BC} & = 10.
\end{aligned}
$$

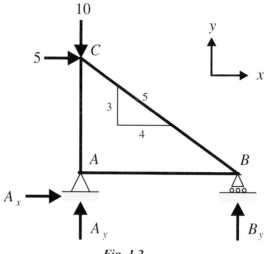

Fig. 1.2

The complete analysis of this framework requires the solution of six equations in as many unknowns and then the application of Hooke's Law, using the internal member forces to find their corresponding extensions. ■ ■ ■

In other types of statics problems it is possible to obtain additional equations by summing the moments. This is of use in pin-jointed frameworks where at least one member can rotate.

1.2.3 Linear Models for Experiments with Random Fluctuations

Many experiments consist of measurements taken to validate or derive some postulated equation relating variables that are under the control of the experimenter. The model in question contains several parameters that are to be determined from the experimental data.

No matter how careful the experimenter may be, there is always some error associated with whatever measurements are taken. Sometimes the errors are systematic, like those associated with an improperly calibrated instrument. More often than not they are purely random, due to the basic imprecision with which all measurements are taken. Perfect accuracy is never possible. For this reason it is common to take many more data points than there are parameters in the model.

■ **EXAMPLE 1.3** A chemical engineer is interested in determining the optimal combination of values of pressure P and temperature T necessary for maximizing the yield of a certain production process. The theoretical model that is postulated as representative of the effect of the these quantities on the yield Y is

$$Y = \beta_0 + \beta_1 P + \beta_2 T.$$

The unknown parameters are β_0, β_1, and β_2 and they appear linearly in the model equation. The experiment consists of analyzing previous years' manufacturing outputs wherein there were four different pressures and five different temperatures. The data consist of the values of the yield Y_{ijk} for the values of each of the various parameters.

The equation relating these data values is

$$Y_{ijk} = \beta_0 + \beta_1 P_i + \beta_2 T_j + e_{ijk},$$

where the quantities e_{ijk} have been added to account for the errors in the measurement and sampling processes. There are three subscripts on the yield Y because there may have been several readings at each combination of the varied quantities. The index i could range from one to four, j from one to five, and k may have different values at each combination because it is the number of replications, or repetitions, of each experimental setup. For simplicity, suppose that k ranged from one to three. The indexed equation describing the results of the experiment is really $4 \cdot 5 \cdot 3 = 60$ separate equations for the three parameters. Surely not all of these equations will result in exactly the same values for all of the β's. Because there are more equations than unknowns, we call this an **overdetermined system**. Since there is an inherent experimental error in each of the equations, we do not expect that the theoretical model should be satisfied exactly, but rather approximated somehow. The method of choice for doing this requires us to minimize the **square error** $\sum \sum \sum e_{ijk}^2$ with respect to the parameters β_0, β_1, and β_2, hence the name **method of least squares** is given to this procedure. ■ ■ ■

1.2.4 *Approximate Solutions of Partial Differential Equations*

All differential equations are relations between an unknown function or functions and their derivatives. Sometimes the measurement process that we use makes these unknown functions appear to be discrete insofar as we evaluate them only at finitely many points. In this case we may feel that a replacement of the differential equation by an equation relating the values we can measure is appropriate. As an example, we could replace the derivatives by the slope of the secant line:

$$f'(x) \doteq \frac{f(x+h) - f(x)}{h}, \quad f''(x) \doteq \frac{f(x+h) - 2f(x) + f(x-h)}{h^2}.$$

Thus an equation such as

$$\frac{\partial w}{\partial t} = \frac{\partial^2 w}{\partial x^2},$$

could be approximated by

$$\frac{w(x, t+\tau) - w(x,t)}{\tau} = \frac{w(x+h, t) - 2w(x,t) + w(x-h, t)}{h^2}.$$

Say we were given starting values of $w(x, 0)$ for $x = 0, h, 2h, \ldots, 1$ and boundary values of $w(0, t)$ and $w(1, t)$ for $t = 0, \tau, 2\tau, \ldots, 1$; then we would have a set of linear equations in the unknowns $w(0, 0)$, $w(h, 0), \ldots$, $w(1, 0)$, $w(0, \tau)$, $w(h, \tau), \ldots$, $w(1, \tau), \ldots$, $w(1, 1)$. If there were T subintervals on the t-axis and H subintervals on the x-axis, we would have $(T + 1)(H + 1)$ unknowns in the same number of equations.

It is especially interesting to notice that many of these models give rise to arrays that have a systematic structure. In particular, the nonzero elements tend to cluster along the line from upper left to lower right. This is only a hint of the usefulness of these models, which we will later call matrix models. Throughout the remainder of the book, other such models will arise at every turn.

1.2.5   *Exercise Set*

1. Set up the linear equations that govern the AC circuit in Figure 1.3.

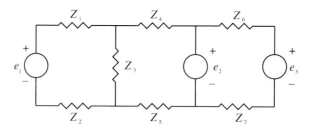

Fig. 1.3

2. The circuit in Figure 1.4.

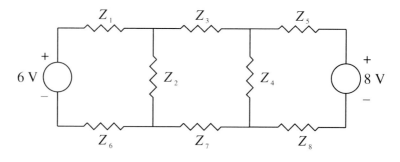

Fig. 1.4

3. Using Figure 1.5 set up the equations needed to determine the horizontal and vertical components of force at each of the pins A–E, if $\triangle ABF$ and $\triangle CDE$ are 30°-60°-90° triangles and the other nonright angles are 45°.

4. Use the difference quotient approximations given in this section to show that when we take equal stepsizes in the x- and y-directions, the equation

$$\frac{\partial^2 w}{\partial x^2} + \frac{\partial^2 w}{\partial y^2} = 0$$

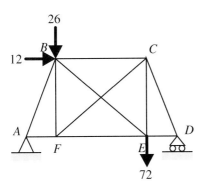

Fig. 1.5

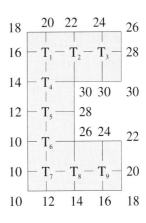

Fig. 1.6

translates into the requirement that the value of w at each interior node is equal to the average of the values at each of the four nearest neighbor nodes. Use this to write the equations which can be used to determine the values of w at the interior nodes of the grid shown in Figure 1.6.

1.3 MATRIX ALGEBRA

The goal of this section is to introduce the concept of a matrix and some of the algebraic structure that can be defined on the set of matrices.

An $m \times n$ (read m by n) **matrix A** is a rectangular array of mn objects chosen from a given set. For most of our needs, the given set of objects will be $\mathbb{C}$, the set of complex numbers; $\mathbb{C}[\lambda]$, the set of complex polynomials in the parameter λ; or $C[a, b]$, the set of functions continuous on the interval $[a, b]$. A matrix will usually be represented as the *filled* array

$$\begin{bmatrix} A_{11} & A_{12} & A_{13} & \cdots & A_{1k} & \cdots & A_{1n} \\ A_{21} & A_{22} & A_{23} & \cdots & A_{2k} & \cdots & A_{2n} \\ \vdots & \vdots & \vdots & & \vdots & & \vdots \\ A_{j1} & A_{j2} & A_{j3} & \cdots & A_{jk} & \cdots & A_{jn} \\ \vdots & \vdots & \vdots & & \vdots & & \vdots \\ A_{m1} & A_{m2} & A_{m3} & \cdots & A_{mk} & \cdots & A_{mn} \end{bmatrix}.$$

The quantity A_{jk} is the jk^{th} **entry** of the matrix $\mathbf{A}$, $j = 1 : m$, $k = 1 : n$. Each entry of $\mathbf{A}$ is a separate entity not related to any other. Think of post office boxes. The jk^{th} entry is located by starting at the upper left hand corner (above and to the left of the left bracket) and moving down j entries and over to the right k entries. As a convenience, and for later use, define the rows and columns of a matrix pictorially as

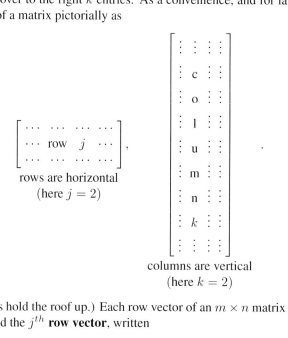

$$
\begin{bmatrix} \cdots & \cdots & \cdots & \cdots \\ \cdots & \text{row} & j & \cdots \\ \cdots & \cdots & \cdots & \cdots \end{bmatrix},
$$

rows are horizontal
(here $j = 2$)

columns are vertical
(here $k = 2$)

(If it helps: columns hold the roof up.) Each row vector of an $m \times n$ matrix is a $1 \times n$ matrix. The jth row is called the jth **row vector**, written

$$
\mathbf{row}_j(\mathbf{A}) := [A_{j1}, A_{j2}, \ldots, A_{jn}].
$$

Similarly, the kth column is an $m \times 1$ matrix, called the kth **column vector**, written

$$
\mathbf{col}_k(\mathbf{A}) = \begin{bmatrix} A_{1k} \\ A_{2k} \\ \vdots \\ A_{mk} \end{bmatrix}.
$$

Every $m \times n$ matrix $\mathbf{A}$ is completely described by either its m row vectors

$$
\{\mathbf{row}_1(\mathbf{A}), \mathbf{row}_2(\mathbf{A}), \ldots, \mathbf{row}_m(\mathbf{A})\}
$$

or its n column vectors

$$
\{\mathbf{col}_1(\mathbf{A}), \mathbf{col}_2(\mathbf{A}), \ldots, \mathbf{col}_n(\mathbf{A})\}.
$$

The jk^{th} entry of $\mathbf{A}$ lies at the intersection of $\mathbf{row}_j(\mathbf{A})$ and $\mathbf{col}_k(\mathbf{A})$.

The matrix software package Matlab uses the following notations to generate the row and column vectors of a matrix:

$$
\mathbf{row}_j(\mathbf{A}) = \mathbf{A}(j, :), \quad \mathbf{col}_k(\mathbf{A}) = \mathbf{A}(:, k).
$$

It also writes **zeros**(m, n), which will write as $\mathbf{0}$, and **ones**(m, n) for $m \times n$ matrices all of whose entries are zero or one, respectively.

We will adopt the single-line notation $\mathbf{col}_k(\mathbf{A}) = [A_{1k}; A_{2k}; \ldots; A_{mk}]$. The semicolon delimiter is used between rows of a matrix, whereas a comma or space are the only allowed delimiters for columns. With this notation we have

$$\mathbf{A} = [\mathbf{row}_1(\mathbf{A}); \mathbf{row}_2(\mathbf{A}); \ldots; \mathbf{row}_m(\mathbf{A})] = [\mathbf{col}_1(\mathbf{A}), \mathbf{col}_2(\mathbf{A}), \ldots, \mathbf{col}_n(\mathbf{A})].$$

The entries A_{11}, A_{22}, A_{33}, .. are called the **main diagonal entries** of $\mathbf{A}$. In Matlab, the operation $\mathbf{diag}(\mathbf{A})$ returns a column vector consisting of the diagonal entries of $\mathbf{A}$. If $\mathbf{x}$ is either an n-component row or column vector, then $\mathbf{diag}(\mathbf{x})$ returns an $n \times n$ matrix whose diagonal entries are the components of $\mathbf{x}$ and with all other entries zero. $\mathbf{diag}(\mathbf{A}, k)$ returns a column vector consisting of the kth diagonal of the matrix $\mathbf{A}$, where the main diagonal is referenced by $k = 0$, the $k = 1$ diagonal is the first diagonal *above* the main diagonal (called the **first superdiagonal**), the $k = -1$ diagonal is the first one *below* the main diagonal (called the **first subdiagonal**), and similarly for other diagonals.

■ **EXAMPLE 1.4** As an example of this notation, look at the following matrix:

$$\mathbf{A} = [1, 2, 3, 4; 3, 4, 5, 6; 6, 7, 8, 9] = \begin{bmatrix} 1 & 2 & 3 & 4 \\ 3 & 4 & 5 & 6 \\ 6 & 7 & 8 & 9 \end{bmatrix}.$$

$\mathbf{diag}(\mathbf{A}) = \mathbf{diag}(\mathbf{A}, 0) = [1; 4; 8]$, $\mathbf{diag}(\mathbf{A}, 1) = [2; 5; 9]$, $\mathbf{diag}(\mathbf{A}, -1) = [3; 7]$, $\mathbf{diag}(\mathbf{A}, 2) = [3; 6]$, $\mathbf{diag}(\mathbf{A}, -2) = [6]$, $\mathbf{diag}(\mathbf{A}, 3) = [4]$. ■ ■ ■

There are some very useful Matlab commands. In particular, the functions sum, abs, prod, mean, max, and min when applied to a vector return the sum of the entries, the absolute values or moduli of the entries, the product of the entries, the mean of the entries, the maximum of the entries, and the minimum of the entries, respectively. When applied to a matrix of size $m \times n$, when both m and n are at least two, each of the functions does its work separately on each column of the matrix and returns a row vector with the appropriate entries.

■ **EXAMPLE 1.5** The following are a few applications of the aforementioned Matlab functions. If we use $\mathbf{x} = [1, -2, 3]$ and $\mathbf{y} = [1+i, -i, 2-3i, 4]$, then $\mathrm{sum}(\mathbf{x}) = 2$, $\mathrm{prod}(\mathbf{x}) = -6$, $\mathrm{mean}(\mathbf{x}) = \frac{2}{3}$, $\max(\mathbf{x}) = 3$, $\min(\mathbf{x}) = -2$, $\mathrm{sum}(\mathbf{y}) = 7 - 3i$, $\max(\mathrm{abs}(\mathbf{y})) = 4$, $\min(\mathrm{abs}(\mathbf{y})) = 1$. Taking $\mathbf{A}$ to be the matrix of the previous example, we have

$$\begin{array}{cc} \mathrm{sum}(\mathbf{A}) = [10, 13, 16, 19], & \mathrm{prod}(\mathbf{A}) = [18, 56, 120, 216], \\ \max(\mathbf{A}) = [6, 7, 8, 9], & \min(\mathbf{A}) = [1, 2, 3, 4], \\ \mathrm{sum}\,(\mathrm{sum}(\mathbf{A})) = 58, & \mathrm{sum}\,(\mathrm{prod}(\mathbf{A})) = 410, \\ \mathrm{sum}\,(\max(\mathbf{A})) = 30, & \mathrm{sum}\,(\min(\mathbf{A})) = 10, \\ \max(\mathrm{sum}(\mathbf{A})) = 19, & \min(\mathrm{sum}(\mathbf{A})) = 10, \\ \max(\max(\mathbf{A})) = 9, & \min(\min(\mathbf{A})) = 1. \end{array}$$

■ ■ ■

The set of all $m \times n$ matrices with complex entries will be written as $\mathbb{C}_n^m$ (m rows and n columns). The notation $\mathbf{A} \in \mathbb{C}_n^m$ should be read as: $\mathbf{A}$ is an $m \times n$ matrix with complex entries. Its row vectors are elements of $\mathbb{C}_n := \mathbb{C}_n^1$ and its column vectors are elements of $\mathbb{C}^m := \mathbb{C}_1^m$.

Now we shall look at some of the structure on $\mathbb{C}_n^m$.

DEFINITION 1.1 *If* $\mathbf{A}, \mathbf{B} \in \mathbb{C}_n^m$ *and* $c \in \mathbb{C} = \mathbb{C}_1^1$, *then*

(a) *Two matrices,* $\mathbf{A} = \mathbf{B}$, *are* **equal** *if and only if*

$$A_{jk} = B_{jk}, \quad j = 1 : m, \ k = 1 : n;$$

i.e., all corresponding entries are equal.

(b) *The* **sum** *of two matrices is defined by*

$$(\mathbf{A} + \mathbf{B})_{jk} := A_{jk} + B_{jk}, \quad j = 1 : m, \ k = 1 : n;$$

i.e., add them entry by entry.

(c) *The* **scalar multiple** *of a matrix is defined by*

$$(c\mathbf{A})_{jk} := cA_{jk}, \quad j = 1 : m, \ k = 1 : n;$$

i.e., multiply each entry by that constant.

■ **EXAMPLE 1.6** A simple sum of constants times matrices follows.

$$(1 + i) \begin{bmatrix} 2 - i & -1 \\ i & 3 - 2i \end{bmatrix} - \begin{bmatrix} 1 & 2 \\ 2 & 1 \end{bmatrix} + i \begin{bmatrix} 1 - i & -i \\ i & 1 + i \end{bmatrix}$$

$$= \begin{bmatrix} 3 + i & -1 - i \\ -1 + i & 5 + i \end{bmatrix} + \begin{bmatrix} -1 & -2 \\ -2 & -1 \end{bmatrix} + \begin{bmatrix} 1 + i & 1 \\ -1 & -1 + i \end{bmatrix}$$

$$= \begin{bmatrix} 3 + 2i & -2 - i \\ -4 + i & 3 + 2i \end{bmatrix}.$$

■ ■ ■

DEFINITION 1.2 *If* $\{\mathbf{A}_{(1)}, \mathbf{A}_{(2)}, \ldots, \mathbf{A}_{(k)}\}$ *is a set of* $m \times n$ *matrices, then a* **linear combination** *of the* $\mathbf{A}_{(k)}$'s *is any matrix that can be written in the form:*

$$c_1 \mathbf{A}_{(1)} + c_2 \mathbf{A}_{(2)} + \cdots + c_k \mathbf{A}_{(k)}$$

for some complex constants $c_1, c_2, \ldots, c_k$.

■ **EXAMPLE 1.7** From the previous example, we see that the matrix

$$\mathbf{B} = \begin{bmatrix} 3 + 2i & -2 - i \\ -4 + i & 3 + 2i \end{bmatrix}$$

is a linear combination of the matrices

$$\mathbf{A}_{(1)} = \begin{bmatrix} 2 - i & -1 \\ i & 3 - 2i \end{bmatrix}, \quad \mathbf{A}_{(2)} = \begin{bmatrix} 1 & 2 \\ 2 & 1 \end{bmatrix}, \quad \mathbf{A}_{(3)} = \begin{bmatrix} 1 - i & -i \\ i & 1 + i \end{bmatrix},$$

because we constructed $\mathbf{B}$ as $\mathbf{B} = (1 + i)\mathbf{A}_{(1)} - \mathbf{A}_{(2)} + i\mathbf{A}_{(3)}$. ■ ■ ■

■ **EXAMPLE 1.8** If $\mathbf{A} \in \mathbb{C}_2^2$, then for any $a, b, c, d \in \mathbb{C}$ we have

$$\mathbf{A} = \begin{bmatrix} a & b \\ c & d \end{bmatrix} = a\begin{bmatrix} 1 & 0 \\ 0 & 0 \end{bmatrix} + b\begin{bmatrix} 0 & 1 \\ 0 & 0 \end{bmatrix} + c\begin{bmatrix} 0 & 0 \\ 1 & 0 \end{bmatrix} + d\begin{bmatrix} 0 & 0 \\ 0 & 1 \end{bmatrix}.$$

This equation can be rewritten as

$$\mathbf{A} = a\mathbf{E}_{(11;2,2)} + b\mathbf{E}_{(12;2,2)} + c\mathbf{E}_{(21;2,2)} + d\mathbf{E}_{(22;2,2)},$$

where

$$\mathbf{E}_{(11;2,2)} := \begin{bmatrix} 1 & 0 \\ 0 & 0 \end{bmatrix}, \quad \mathbf{E}_{(12;2,2)} := \begin{bmatrix} 0 & 1 \\ 0 & 0 \end{bmatrix},$$

$$\mathbf{E}_{(21;2,2)} := \begin{bmatrix} 0 & 0 \\ 1 & 0 \end{bmatrix}, \quad \mathbf{E}_{(22;2,2)} := \begin{bmatrix} 0 & 0 \\ 0 & 1 \end{bmatrix}.$$

Thus any 2×2 complex matrix can be written as a linear combination of the matrices in the set $\{\mathbf{E}_{(11;2,2)}, \mathbf{E}_{(12;2,2)}, \mathbf{E}_{(21;2,2)}, \mathbf{E}_{(22;2,2)}\}$. Notice the similarity in structure to the set of three dimensional vectors and the set of unit vectors $\{\mathbf{i}, \mathbf{j}, \mathbf{k}\}$ from either freshman physics or vector calculus. ■ ■ ■

Using the last example as a guide, we see that any $m \times n$ complex matrix can be written as a linear combination of the mn matrices

$$\{\mathbf{E}_{(11;m,n)}, \dots, \mathbf{E}_{(1n;m,n)}, \mathbf{E}_{(21;m,n)}, \dots, \mathbf{E}_{(2n;m,n)},$$
$$\dots, \mathbf{E}_{(m1;m,n)}, \dots, \mathbf{E}_{(mn;m,n)}\},$$

where $\mathbf{E}_{(jk;m,n)}$ has all its entries zero except the jk^{th} entry, which is one.

Many of the algebraic properties of addition and multiplication of complex numbers carry over to addition of matrices and multiplication of a matrix by a scalar. The following properties of these operations can be easily verified:

THEOREM 1.1 *If* **A**, **B**, **C** *are any complex* $m \times n$ *matrices and* c, c_1, *and* c_2 *are any complex constants, then the following hold:*

(MAdd1) $\mathbf{A} + \mathbf{B} = \mathbf{B} + \mathbf{A}$ *(matrix addition is commutative);*

(MAdd2) $\mathbf{A} + (\mathbf{B} + \mathbf{C}) = (\mathbf{A} + \mathbf{B}) + \mathbf{C}$ *(matrix addition is associative);*

(MAdd3) $\mathbf{A} + \mathbf{0} = \mathbf{A} = \mathbf{0} + \mathbf{A}$ $(\mathbf{0} = \mathbf{zeros}(m, n)$ *is the additive identity*$);$

(MAdd4) *If* $(-\mathbf{A})_{jk} = -(A_{jk})$ *for* $j = 1 : m$, $k = 1 : n$, *then*

$$\mathbf{A} + (-\mathbf{A}) = \mathbf{0} = (-\mathbf{A}) + \mathbf{A} \quad \text{(existence of an additive inverse);}$$

(MScMult1) $c(\mathbf{A} + \mathbf{B}) = c\mathbf{A} + c\mathbf{B};$

(MScMult2) $(c_1 + c_2)\mathbf{A} = c_1\mathbf{A} + c_2\mathbf{A};$

(MScMult3) $c_1(c_2\mathbf{A}) = c_2(c_1\mathbf{A}) = (c_1 c_2)\mathbf{A}\,.$ □

There are many possible and useful ways to multiply two matrices, not all of which lead to the same result. The utility of the standard seemingly mysterious choice will become clear after this next example.

■ **EXAMPLE 1.9**   Suppose that we have a system of linear equations of the form

$$ay_1 + by_2 = p_1,$$
$$cy_1 + dy_2 = p_2,$$

and we also have the following relation between the y's and x_1 and x_2:

$$y_1 = ex_1 + fx_2,$$
$$y_2 = gx_1 + hx_2.$$

If we eliminate the y's in favor of the x's in the original equation, we have

$$a(ex_1 + fx_2) + b(gx_1 + hx_2) = (ae + bg)x_1 + (af + bh)x_2 = p_1,$$
$$c(ex_1 + fx_2) + d(gx_1 + hx_2) = (ce + dg)x_1 + (cf + dh)x_2 = p_2.$$

Notice how the resulting system of equations couples the coefficients of each part together.

     ■ ■ ■

DEFINITION 1.3 *If* **a** *is an* n-*component row vector, an element of* $\mathbb{C}_n^1$, *and* **b** *is an* n-*component column vector, an element of* $\mathbb{C}_1^n$, *then we define the* **product** *of* **a** *and* **b** *to be the scalar*

$$\mathbf{ab} = [a_1, a_2, \ldots, a_n]\,[b_1; b_2; \ldots; b_n] := a_1 b_1 + a_2 b_2 + \cdots + a_n b_n.$$

If $\mathbf{A} \in \mathbb{C}_n^m$ *and* $\mathbf{B} \in \mathbb{C}_p^n$, *then the* **product** *of the matrices* $\mathbf{A}$ *and* $\mathbf{B}$ *is the* $m \times p$ *matrix* $\mathbf{C} = \mathbf{AB}$ *whose entries are defined by:*

$$(\mathbf{C})_{jk} = (\mathbf{AB})_{jk} = \mathbf{row}_j(\mathbf{A}) \, \mathbf{col}_k(\mathbf{B}).$$

We say $\mathbf{A}$ *is* **postmultiplied**, *or multiplied on the right, by* $\mathbf{B}$ *and* $\mathbf{B}$ *is* **premultiplied,** *or multiplied on the left, by* $\mathbf{A}$.

If $\mathbf{a}$ and $\mathbf{b}$ are either both either real column vectors or both real row vectors, we sometimes use the notation $\mathbf{a} \cdot \mathbf{b}$ to denote the scalar $a_1 b_1 + a_2 b_2 + \cdots + a_n b_n$. This is the so-called *dot product* you saw in vector calculus. For more detail you should consult your calculus book.

If we look at this definition a bit closer, we see that $A_{j\ell}$ is the ℓth entry of the jth row vector of $\mathbf{A}$, $[\mathbf{row}_j(\mathbf{A})]_\ell$. Similarly, $B_{\ell k}$ is the ℓth entry of the kth column vector of $\mathbf{B}$, $[\mathbf{col}_k(\mathbf{B})]_\ell$. Thus

$$(\mathbf{AB})_{jk} = \sum_{\ell=1}^{n} [\mathbf{row}_j(\mathbf{A})]_\ell [\mathbf{col}_k(\mathbf{B})]_\ell = \sum_{\ell=1}^{n} A_{j\ell} B_{\ell k}.$$

Except for the columnar representation of $\mathbf{col}_k(\mathbf{B})$, this sum of products of like components would be recognizable as the (dot) product of row j and column k. Of course, the rows of $\mathbf{A}$ and the columns of $\mathbf{B}$ must have the same number of components in order for the product of the row and column vectors to be meaningful. This accounts for the initial size requirements $\mathbf{A} \in \mathbb{C}_n^m$ and $\mathbf{B} \in \mathbb{C}_p^n$. A useful notational device to find the size of the product is:

$$\mathbf{AB} \in \mathbb{C}_n^m \mathbb{C}_p^n \rightarrow \mathbb{C}_p^m;$$

i.e., the n's "cancel" and the product is a complex $m \times p$ matrix.

▪ **EXAMPLE 1.10** Let's look at products of matrices that can be defined in both orders.

(a) We'll start with products of 2×2 matrices.

$$\mathbf{AB} = \begin{bmatrix} 1 & 2 \\ 3 & 4 \end{bmatrix} \begin{bmatrix} 2 & -3 \\ 2 & -1 \end{bmatrix}$$

$$= \begin{bmatrix} [1,2]\,[2;2] & [1,2]\,[-3;-1] \\ [3,4]\,[2;2] & [3,4]\,[-3;-1] \end{bmatrix}, \quad \mathbb{C}_2^2 \mathbb{C}_2^2 \rightarrow \mathbb{C}_2^2$$

$$\Rightarrow \quad \mathbf{AB} = \begin{bmatrix} 1(2)+2(2) & 1(-3)+2(-1) \\ 3(2)+4(2) & 3(-3)+4(-1) \end{bmatrix} = \begin{bmatrix} 6 & -5 \\ 14 & -13 \end{bmatrix}.$$

In the other order, we have

$$\mathbf{BA} = \begin{bmatrix} 2 & -3 \\ 2 & -1 \end{bmatrix} \begin{bmatrix} 1 & 2 \\ 3 & 4 \end{bmatrix} = \begin{bmatrix} [2,-3]\,[1;3] & [2,-3]\,[2;4] \\ [2,-1]\,[1;3] & [2,-1]\,[2;4] \end{bmatrix}$$

$$\Rightarrow \quad \mathbf{BA} = \begin{bmatrix} 2(1) + (-3)(3) & 2(2) + (-3)(4) \\ 2(1) + (-1)(3) & 2(2) + (-1)(4) \end{bmatrix}$$

$$= \begin{bmatrix} -7 & -8 \\ -1 & 0 \end{bmatrix}.$$

Not only are they not the same, no two entries are equal!

(b) If $\mathbf{a} = [1, 2, -1]$ and $\mathbf{b} = [3; 3; 4]$, then the usual matrix product is sometimes called an **inner product** of $\mathbf{a}$ and $\mathbf{b}$, which is

$$\mathbf{ab} = [1, 2, -1]\,[3; 3; 4] = 1(3) + 2(3) + (-1)(4) = 5.$$

On the other hand, the **outer product** of the column vectors $\mathbf{b}$ and $\mathbf{a}$ is

$$\mathbf{ba} = [3; 3; 4]\,[1, 2, -1] = \begin{bmatrix} 3 \\ 3 \\ 4 \end{bmatrix} [1, 2, -1]$$

$$= \begin{bmatrix} 3(1) & 3(2) & 3(-1) \\ 3(1) & 3(2) & 3(-1) \\ 4(1) & 4(2) & 4(-1) \end{bmatrix} = \begin{bmatrix} 3 & 6 & -3 \\ 3 & 6 & -3 \\ 4 & 8 & -4 \end{bmatrix}.$$

(c) If $\mathbf{1}_n = \mathbf{ones}(n, 1)$ and $\mathbf{A}$ is an arbitrary $m \times n$ matrix, then the product $\mathbf{1}_m^T \mathbf{A}$ is well-defined and the result is a $(1 \times m)(m \times n) \to 1 \times n$ matrix. The product is

$$\mathbf{1}_m^T \mathbf{A} = [1, 1, \ldots, 1][\mathbf{col}_1(\mathbf{A}), \mathbf{col}_2(\mathbf{A}), \ldots, \mathbf{col}_n(\mathbf{A})].$$

Looking at the kth entry, we see that

$$\left(\mathbf{1}_m^T \mathbf{A}\right)_k = [1, 1, \ldots, 1]\mathbf{col}_k(\mathbf{A}) = \mathrm{sum}\left(\mathbf{col}_k(\mathbf{A})\right).$$

Thus $\mathbf{1}_m^T \mathbf{A} = \mathrm{sum}(\mathbf{A})$. ■ ■ ■

The last example is a clear indication that *matrix multiplication is not commutative*. Generally, if $\mathbf{A} \in \mathbb{C}_n^m$ and $\mathbf{B} \in \mathbb{C}_p^n$, then although $\mathbf{AB}$ is defined, $\mathbf{BA}$ ($\mathbb{C}_p^n \mathbb{C}_n^m \to ?$) is not defined unless $m = p$. But even in this special case,

$$\mathbf{AB} \in \mathbb{C}_n^m \mathbb{C}_m^n \to \mathbb{C}_m^m, \quad \text{whereas} \quad \mathbf{BA} \in \mathbb{C}_m^n \mathbb{C}_n^m \to \mathbb{C}_n^n,$$

which, for $m \neq n$, will not even be the same size. Pay special attention to the difference in the cases of the inner and outer products of a pair of vectors. Now to some more numerical examples.

- **EXAMPLE 1.11**

  (a) $\mathbb{C}_3^3\mathbb{C}_1^3 \to \mathbb{C}_1^3$

$$\begin{bmatrix} 1+i & -1 & 0 \\ 2 & i & 3 \\ 0 & 1 & -1 \end{bmatrix} \begin{bmatrix} 1 \\ 2 \\ 3 \end{bmatrix} = \begin{bmatrix} (1+i)(1)+(-1)(2)+(0)(3) \\ 2(1)+i(2)+3(3) \\ 0(1)+1(2)+(-1)(3) \end{bmatrix}$$

$$= \begin{bmatrix} -1+i \\ 11+2i \\ -1 \end{bmatrix}.$$

  (b) $\mathbb{C}_3^1\mathbb{C}_2^3 \to \mathbb{C}_2^1$

$$[1, -1, 1] \begin{bmatrix} 2 & -1 \\ i & -i \\ -1 & 1 \end{bmatrix} = \begin{bmatrix} 1(2)-1(i)+1(-1) & 1(-1)-1(-i)+1(1) \end{bmatrix}$$

$$= \begin{bmatrix} 1-i & i \end{bmatrix}.$$

■ ■ ■

- **EXAMPLE 1.12** Now let's look at the pair of simultaneous linear equations from example 1.9. The first system of equations in the y variables

$$ay_1 + by_2 = p_1,$$
$$cy_1 + dy_2 = p_2,$$

could be written in the matrix form

$$\begin{bmatrix} a & b \\ c & d \end{bmatrix} \begin{bmatrix} y_1 \\ y_2 \end{bmatrix} = \begin{bmatrix} p_1 \\ p_2 \end{bmatrix}.$$

The equation for the y's in terms of the x's takes the form

$$\begin{matrix} y_1 = ex_1 + fx_2 \\ y_2 = gx_1 + hx_2 \end{matrix} \quad \Rightarrow \quad \begin{bmatrix} y_1 \\ y_2 \end{bmatrix} = \begin{bmatrix} e & f \\ g & h \end{bmatrix} \begin{bmatrix} x_1 \\ x_2 \end{bmatrix}.$$

Now using matrix multiplication we see that

$$\begin{bmatrix} a & b \\ c & d \end{bmatrix} \begin{bmatrix} y_1 \\ y_2 \end{bmatrix} = \begin{bmatrix} a & b \\ c & d \end{bmatrix} \begin{bmatrix} e & f \\ g & h \end{bmatrix} \begin{bmatrix} x_1 \\ x_2 \end{bmatrix}$$

$$= \begin{bmatrix} ae+bg & af+bh \\ ce+dg & cf+dh \end{bmatrix} \begin{bmatrix} x_1 \\ x_2 \end{bmatrix},$$

which is precisely what we obtained by substitution.

■ ■ ■

As a generalization of the last example, let's look at the matrix product equation $\mathbf{Ax} = \mathbf{b}$, when $\mathbf{A}$ is an $m \times n$ matrix, $\mathbf{x}$ is an $n \times 1$ matrix, and $\mathbf{b}$ is an $m \times 1$ matrix. We will see that it is more than it seems.

$$
\begin{bmatrix}
A_{11} & A_{12} & \cdots & A_{1k} & \cdots & A_{1n} \\
A_{21} & A_{22} & \cdots & A_{2k} & \cdots & A_{2n} \\
\vdots & \vdots & & \vdots & & \vdots \\
A_{j1} & A_{j2} & \cdots & A_{jk} & \cdots & A_{jn} \\
\vdots & \vdots & & \vdots & & \vdots \\
A_{m1} & A_{m2} & \cdots & A_{mk} & \cdots & A_{mn}
\end{bmatrix}
\begin{bmatrix}
x_1 \\ x_2 \\ \vdots \\ x_k \\ \vdots \\ x_n
\end{bmatrix}
$$

$$
=
\begin{bmatrix}
A_{11}x_1 + A_{12}x_2 + \cdots + A_{1k}x_k + \cdots + A_{1n}x_n \\
A_{21}x_1 + A_{22}x_2 + \cdots + A_{2k}x_k + \cdots + A_{2n}x_n \\
\vdots \\
A_{j1}x_1 + A_{j2}x_2 + \cdots + A_{jk}x_k + \cdots + A_{jn}x_n \\
\vdots \\
A_{m1}x_1 + A_{m2}x_2 + \cdots + A_{mk}x_k + \cdots + A_{mn}x_n
\end{bmatrix} .
$$

Hence the matrix product $\mathbf{Ax} = \mathbf{b}$ is equivalent to the following m simultaneous linear equations in n unknowns:

$$
\begin{aligned}
A_{11}x_1 + A_{12}x_2 + \cdots + A_{1k}x_k + \cdots + A_{1n}x_n &= b_1, \\
A_{21}x_1 + A_{22}x_2 + \cdots + A_{2k}x_k + \cdots + A_{2n}x_n &= b_2, \\
\vdots \qquad \vdots \qquad\qquad \vdots \qquad\qquad \vdots \\
A_{j1}x_1 + A_{j2}x_2 + \cdots + A_{jk}x_k + \cdots + A_{jn}x_n &= b_j, \\
\vdots \qquad \vdots \qquad\qquad \vdots \qquad\qquad \vdots \\
A_{m1}x_1 + A_{m2}x_2 + \cdots + A_{mk}x_k + \cdots + A_{mn}x_n &= b_m.
\end{aligned}
$$

We can reformat this system of linear equations so that we will have an alternate matrix representation of it. In particular, rewrite it by grouping terms with the same x coefficient as

$$
x_1 \begin{bmatrix} A_{11} \\ A_{21} \\ \vdots \\ A_{j1} \\ \vdots \\ A_{m1} \end{bmatrix}
+ x_2 \begin{bmatrix} A_{12} \\ A_{22} \\ \vdots \\ A_{j2} \\ \vdots \\ A_{m2} \end{bmatrix}
+ \cdots + x_k \begin{bmatrix} A_{1k} \\ A_{2k} \\ \vdots \\ A_{jk} \\ \vdots \\ A_{mk} \end{bmatrix}
+ \cdots + x_n \begin{bmatrix} A_{1n} \\ A_{2n} \\ \vdots \\ A_{jn} \\ \vdots \\ A_{mn} \end{bmatrix}
= \begin{bmatrix} b_1 \\ b_2 \\ \vdots \\ b_j \\ \vdots \\ b_m \end{bmatrix} .
$$

In matrix form, this is the linear combination of the columns of $\mathbf{A}$:

$$x_1\mathbf{col}_1(\mathbf{A}) + x_2\mathbf{col}_2(\mathbf{A}) + \cdots + x_n\mathbf{col}_n(\mathbf{A}) = \mathbf{b}.$$

The method for solving such a system will be the topic of the next section. The following is a listing of the properties of matrix multiplication.

THEOREM 1.2 *Whenever each of the following products is defined and c is a complex number, we have:*

(**MatProd1**) $\mathbf{A}(\mathbf{BC}) = (\mathbf{AB})\mathbf{C}$ *(matrix multiplication is associative);*

(**MatProd2**) $\mathbf{A}(\mathbf{B} + \mathbf{C}) = \mathbf{AB} + \mathbf{AC}$ *(multiplication distributes over addition);*

(**MatProd3**) $\mathbf{A}(c\mathbf{B}) = (c\mathbf{A})\mathbf{B} = c(\mathbf{AB})$;

(**MatProd4**) $c(\mathbf{A} + \mathbf{B}) = c\mathbf{A} + c\mathbf{B}.$

Proof Only (MatProd1) is not obvious. Take $\mathbf{A} \in \mathbb{C}_n^m$, $\mathbf{B} \in \mathbb{C}_p^n$, and $\mathbf{C} \in \mathbb{C}_q^p$; then we should have $\mathbf{A}(\mathbf{BC}) \in \mathbb{C}_n^m \mathbb{C}_p^n \mathbb{C}_q^p \to \mathbb{C}_q^m$. Look at the $i\ell^{th}$ entry of the product:

$$[\mathbf{A}(\mathbf{BC})]_{i\ell} = \sum_{j=1}^{n} A_{ij}(\mathbf{BC})_{j\ell} = \sum_{j=1}^{n} A_{ij} \left\{ \sum_{k=1}^{p} B_{jk}C_{k\ell} \right\}.$$

Because both sums are finite, there is no question of convergence, and the order of summation may be interchanged:

$$[\mathbf{A}(\mathbf{BC})]_{i\ell} = \sum_{k=1}^{p} \left\{ \sum_{j=1}^{n} A_{ij}B_{jk} \right\} C_{k\ell} = \sum_{k=1}^{p} (\mathbf{AB})_{ik}C_{k\ell} = [(\mathbf{AB})\mathbf{C}]_{i\ell}.$$

Since all the entries are equal, $\mathbf{A}(\mathbf{BC}) = (\mathbf{AB})\mathbf{C}$. □

In the problems you will be asked to verify the following two very useful identities:

$$\mathbf{AB} = [\mathbf{A}\,\mathbf{col}_1(\mathbf{B}), \mathbf{A}\,\mathbf{col}_2(\mathbf{B}), \ldots, \mathbf{A}\,\mathbf{col}_p(\mathbf{B})],$$

and

$$\mathbf{AB} = [\mathbf{row}_1(\mathbf{A})\,\mathbf{B}; \mathbf{row}_2(\mathbf{A})\,\mathbf{B}; \ldots; \mathbf{row}_m(\mathbf{A})\,\mathbf{B}].$$

■ **EXAMPLE 1.13** Matrix products involving the following vector will prove useful. Let $\mathbf{e}_{(k;n)}$ be an $n \times 1$ matrix, hence a column vector, whose only nonzero entry occurs in the kth row; then $\mathbf{e}_{(1;n)} = [1; 0; 0; \ldots; 0]$ and $\mathbf{e}_{(n;n)} = [0; \ldots; 0; 1]$. If A is an arbitrary $m \times n$ matrix, the product $\mathbf{Ae}_{(k;n)}$ can be written as

$$\mathbf{Ae}_{(k;n)} = [\mathbf{row}_1(\mathbf{A})\mathbf{e}_{(k;n)}; \mathbf{row}_2(\mathbf{A})\mathbf{e}_{(k;n)}; \ldots; \mathbf{row}_m(\mathbf{A})\mathbf{e}_{(k;n)}].$$

If we look at the jth entry, we see

$$\text{row}_j(\mathbf{A})\mathbf{e}_{(k;n)}$$

$$= [A_{j1}, A_{j2}, \ldots, A_{jk}, \ldots, A_{jn}][0; 0; \ldots; 0; \underbrace{1}_{k^{th}}; 0; \ldots; 0]$$

$$\text{entry}$$

$$= A_{jk}.$$

Thus we have $\mathbf{A}\mathbf{e}_{(k;n)} = [A_{1k}; A_{2k}; \ldots; A_{mk}] = \text{col}_k(\mathbf{A})$. You should verify that

$$\mathbf{e}_{(j;m)}^T \mathbf{e}_{k;n)} = \mathbf{E}_{(j,k;m,n)},$$

where $\mathbf{E}_{(j,k;m,n)}$ was defined following example 1.8. ■ ■ ■

There are several other operations on matrices that will be of use to us:

DEFINITION 1.4 *For any matrices, unless otherwise stated, we have:*

(a) *The* **complex conjugate** *of a matrix* $\mathbf{A}$ *is defined by*

$$\left(\bar{\mathbf{A}}\right)_{jk} := \overline{A_{jk}}, \quad j = 1 : m, \ k = 1 : n,$$

i.e., take the complex conjugate of each entry.

(b) *The* **transpose** *of an* $m \times n$ *matrix* $\mathbf{A}$ *is the* $n \times m$ *matrix* $\mathbf{A}^T$ *defined by*

$$\left(\mathbf{A}^T\right)_{jk} := A_{kj}, \quad j = 1 : m, \ k = 1 : n,$$

i.e., interchange rows and columns. (This is explained in detail following example 1.15.)

(c) *The* **Hermitian conjugate** *of the* $m \times n$ *matrix* $\mathbf{A}$ *is the* $n \times m$ *matrix* $\mathbf{A}^H$ *defined by*

$$\mathbf{A}^H := \left(\bar{\mathbf{A}}\right)^T = \overline{(\mathbf{A}^T)}.$$

(d) *If* $\mathbf{a} \in \mathbb{C}_1^n$, *then the* **length**, *or* **Euclidean norm**, *of* $\mathbf{a}$ *is defined to be*

$$\|\mathbf{a}\| := \sqrt{\mathbf{a}^H \mathbf{a}} = \sqrt{|a_1|^2 + |a_2|^2 + \cdots + |a_n|^2}.$$

Similarly for row vectors.

(e) *If* $\mathbf{A} \in \mathbb{C}_n^n$, *then the* **trace** *of* $\mathbf{A}$ *is defined to be*

$$\text{tr}(\mathbf{A}) := A_{11} + A_{22} + \cdots + A_{nn} = \text{sum}\left(\mathbf{diag}(\mathbf{A})\right).$$

■ **EXAMPLE 1.14** $\text{tr}(\mathbf{I}_n) = 1 + 1 + \cdots + 1 = n$, $\text{tr}(0_n) = 0 + 0 + \cdots + 0 = 0$,

$$\text{tr}\left(\begin{bmatrix} 1 & 2 \\ 3 & 4 \end{bmatrix}\right) = 1 + 4 = 5, \quad \text{tr}\left(\begin{bmatrix} 1-i & -i \\ i & 1+i \end{bmatrix}\right) = (1-i) + (1+i) = 2.$$

■ ■ ■

Some properties of the trace are given below.

THEOREM 1.3 *Whenever k is a complex number and all of the following matrices are square, the following hold:*

(**Trace1**) $\text{tr}(k\mathbf{A} + \mathbf{B}) = k\,\text{tr}(\mathbf{A}) + \text{tr}(\mathbf{B})$;

(**Trace2**) $\text{tr}(\mathbf{AB}) = \text{tr}(\mathbf{BA})$;

(**Trace3**) $\text{tr}(\mathbf{ABC}) = \text{tr}(\mathbf{BCA}) = \text{tr}(\mathbf{CAB})$.

Proof (Trace1)

$$\text{tr}(k\mathbf{A} + \mathbf{B}) = \sum_{j=1}^{n}(k\mathbf{A} + \mathbf{B})_{jj} = k\sum_{j=1}^{n}A_{jj} + \sum_{j=1}^{n}B_{jj}.$$

(Trace2) In this case we can have $\mathbf{A} \in \mathbb{C}_n^m$ and $\mathbf{B} \in \mathbb{C}_m^n$, so that the products $\mathbf{AB}$ and $\mathbf{BA}$ are both square, but not necessarily of the same size. Start with the left hand side:

$$\text{tr}(\mathbf{AB}) = \sum_{i=1}^{m}(\mathbf{AB})_{ii} = \sum_{i=1}^{m}\left\{\sum_{j=1}^{n}A_{ij}B_{ji}\right\}$$

$$= \sum_{j=1}^{n}\left\{\sum_{i=1}^{m}B_{ji}A_{ij}\right\} = \sum_{j=1}^{n}(BA)_{jj} = \text{tr}(\mathbf{BA}).$$

The proof of (Trace3) will be left to the problems.   □

When $\mathbf{a}$ is a column vector, an easy application of (Trace2) yields

$$\text{tr}\left(\mathbf{aa}^H\right) = \text{tr}(\mathbf{a}^H\mathbf{a}) = \text{tr}\left(\|\mathbf{a}\|^2\right) = \|\mathbf{a}\|^2.$$

■ **EXAMPLE 1.15** If

$$\mathbf{B} = \begin{bmatrix} i & 1 & 1+i \\ -1 & 2-i & 0 \end{bmatrix},$$

then

$$\bar{\mathbf{B}} = \begin{bmatrix} -i & 1 & 1-i \\ -1 & 2+i & 0 \end{bmatrix}, \quad \mathbf{B}^T = \begin{bmatrix} i & -1 \\ 1 & 2-i \\ 1+i & 0 \end{bmatrix},$$

$$\mathbf{B}^H = \begin{bmatrix} -i & -1 \\ 1 & 2+i \\ 1-i & 0 \end{bmatrix}.$$

■ ■ ■

The pattern of interchanging rows and columns under transposition can be visualized by sketch:

$$
\begin{bmatrix}
@ & \oslash & \oslash & \oslash & \oslash & \oslash \\
\bowtie & @ & \cdot & \cdot & \cdot & \cdot \\
\bowtie & \cdot & @ & \cdot & \cdot & \cdot \\
\bowtie & \cdot & \cdot & @ & \cdot & \cdot
\end{bmatrix}^T
=
\begin{bmatrix}
@ & \bowtie & \bowtie & \bowtie \\
\oslash & @ & \cdot & \cdot \\
\oslash & \cdot & @ & \cdot \\
\oslash & \cdot & \cdot & @ \\
\oslash & \cdot & \cdot & \cdot \\
\oslash & \cdot & \cdot & \cdot
\end{bmatrix}.
$$

The $45°$ line of @'s contains the entries $A_{11}, A_{22}, \ldots$ (which we called the diagonal entries of $\mathbf{A}$); it remains fixed, and the matrix is rotated in space $180°$ about it. There are several useful properties of these operations.

THEOREM 1.4 *If* $\mathbf{A}, \mathbf{C} \in \mathbb{C}_n^m$, $\mathbf{B} \in \mathbb{C}_p^n$ *and* $k \in \mathbb{C}$ *then the following hold:*

(1) $\overline{(\bar{\mathbf{A}})} = \mathbf{A};$ $\left(\mathbf{A}^T\right)^T = \mathbf{A};$ $\left(\mathbf{A}^H\right)^H = \mathbf{A}.$

(2) $\overline{(\mathbf{A} + \mathbf{C})} = \bar{\mathbf{A}} + \bar{\mathbf{C}};$ $(\mathbf{A} + \mathbf{C})^T = \mathbf{A}^T + \mathbf{C}^T;$ $(\mathbf{A} + \mathbf{C})^H = \mathbf{A}^H + \mathbf{C}^H.$

(3) $\overline{(k\mathbf{A})} = \bar{k}\,\bar{\mathbf{A}};$ $(k\mathbf{A})^T = k\,\mathbf{A}^T;$ $(k\mathbf{A})^H = \bar{k}\,\mathbf{A}^H.$

(4) $\overline{(\mathbf{A}\mathbf{B})} = \bar{\mathbf{A}}\,\bar{\mathbf{B}};$ $(\mathbf{A}\mathbf{B})^T = \mathbf{B}^T\mathbf{A}^T;$ $(\mathbf{A}\mathbf{B})^H = \mathbf{B}^H\mathbf{A}^H.$

Proof   Proving the second part of (4) will take care of most of the unobvious ones.

$$
\left[(\mathbf{A}\mathbf{B})^T\right]_{jk} = (\mathbf{A}\mathbf{B})_{kj} = \sum_{\ell=1}^n A_{k\ell} B_{\ell j} = \sum_{\ell=1}^n \left(\mathbf{B}^T\right)_{j\ell} \left(\mathbf{A}^T\right)_{\ell k} = \left[\mathbf{B}^T\mathbf{A}^T\right]_{jk}.
$$

□

The reversal of the order of multiplication under both transposition and Hermitian conjugation (and later under inversion) can be loosely thought of in terms of the input and output of a system. If $\mathbf{B} \in \mathbb{C}_n^m$, $\mathbf{x} \in \mathbb{C}_1^n$, $\mathbf{y} \in \mathbb{C}_1^m$, then $\mathbf{x}$ is the system input, $\mathbf{y}$ is the system output, and the system consists of matrix multiplication by $\mathbf{B}$. It can be visualized as shown below.

input $\mathbf{x}$ ⟹ $\boxed{\mathbf{B}}$ ⟹ $\mathbf{y} = \mathbf{B}\mathbf{x}$ output

If we cascaded two systems using $\mathbf{A} \in \mathbb{C}_m^p$, $\mathbf{z} \in \mathbb{C}_1^p$ then the appropriate visualization is shown below.

input $\mathbf{x}$ ⟹ $\boxed{\mathbf{B}}$ ⟹ $\mathbf{y} = \mathbf{B}\mathbf{x}$ ⟹ $\boxed{\mathbf{A}}$ ⟹ $\mathbf{z} = \mathbf{A}\mathbf{y} = \mathbf{A}(\mathbf{B}\mathbf{x}) = (\mathbf{A}\mathbf{B})\,\mathbf{x}$

For certain systems, transposition or Hermitian conjugation corresponds to reversing the input and output. Since $\mathbf{z} = (\mathbf{AB})\mathbf{x}$, then $\mathbf{x} = (\mathbf{AB})^T\mathbf{z}$ and the figure below shows this relation.

$$\mathbf{z} \Longrightarrow \boxed{\mathbf{A}^\mathrm{T}} \Longrightarrow \boxed{\mathbf{y} = \mathbf{A}^\mathrm{T}\mathbf{z}} \Longrightarrow \boxed{\mathbf{B}^\mathrm{T}} \Longrightarrow \mathbf{x} = \mathbf{B}^\mathrm{T}\mathbf{y} = \mathbf{B}^\mathrm{T}(\mathbf{A}^\mathrm{T}\mathbf{z}) = (\mathbf{B}^\mathrm{T}\mathbf{A}^\mathrm{T})\mathbf{z}$$

Using this point of view the reversal of order of the product is understandable: we encounter $\mathbf{B}$ first and then $\mathbf{A}$, but when going from right to left we encounter $\mathbf{A}$ reversed (in this case $\mathbf{A}^T$) followed by $\mathbf{B}$ reversed ($\mathbf{B}^T$).

We are not always forced to deal with the most general $n \times n$ matrices, but rather frequently encounter special types.

DEFINITION 1.5 *For square matrices:*

(a) *If* $\mathbf{A}^T = \mathbf{A}$, *then* $\mathbf{A}$ *is* **symmetric**.

(b) *If* $\mathbf{B}^H = \mathbf{B}$, *then* $\mathbf{B}$ *is* **Hermitian**.

(c) *If* $\mathbf{S}^T = -\mathbf{S}$, *then* $\mathbf{S}$ *is* **skew-symmetric**.

(d) *If* $\mathbf{K}^H = -\mathbf{K}$, *then* $\mathbf{K}$ *is* **skew-Hermitian**.

(e) *If* $U_{jk} = 0$ *for* $j > k$, *then* $\mathbf{U}$ *is* **upper triangular**. *If* $L_{jk} = 0$ *for* $j < k$, *then* $\mathbf{L}$ *is* **lower triangular**. *If* $\mathbf{T}$ *is triangular, meaning either upper triangular or lower triangular, with ones on its main diagonal, it is a* **unit triangular** *matrix*.

(f) *If* $D_{jk} = 0$ *for* $j \neq k$, *then* $\mathbf{D}$ *is* **diagonal**.

(g) $\mathbf{I}_n \in \mathbb{C}_n^n$ *is the* n^{th} *order* **identity matrix** *if* $(\mathbf{I}_n)_{jk} = 0$ *for* $j \neq k$ *and* $(\mathbf{I}_n)_{jj} = 1$.

It is customary to introduce a notation for the entries of the identity matrix. Define the **Kronecker delta function** by

$$\delta_{jk} := \begin{cases} 0, & j \neq k, \\ 1, & j = k. \end{cases}$$

In this notation the pq-entry of the matrix $\mathbf{E}_{(jk)}$ of example 1.8 is $\delta_{pj}\delta_{qk}$.

You should notice that symmetric, Hermitian, skew-symmetric, skew-Hermitian, and diagonal matrices must be square, otherwise their defining equations do not make sense. Matlab uses the notation $\mathbf{eye}(n)$ for the $n \times n$ identity. It also has two useful functions, $\mathbf{tril}$ and $\mathbf{triu}$. If, as before, we define the main diagonal of a matrix as the $k = 0$ diagonal, the diagonal above that as the $k = 1$ diagonal, the diagonal below the main diagonal as the $k = -1$ diagonal, then $\mathbf{tril}(\mathbf{A}, k)$ returns a matrix that has the entries of $\mathbf{A}$ on and *below* the kth diagonal and zeros elsewhere, while $\mathbf{triu}(\mathbf{A}, k)$ returns a matrix that has the entries of $\mathbf{A}$ on and *above* the

k^{th} diagonal and zeros elsewhere. The functions of a single variable $\mathbf{tril(A)}$ and $\mathbf{triu(A)}$ are read as having $k = 0$. Because the 0th, or main, diagonal is included in both $\mathbf{tril(A)}$ and $\mathbf{triu(A)}$, we have the identity

$$\mathbf{A = tril(A) + triu(A) - diag(diag(A))}.$$

▪ **EXAMPLE 1.16** Classify each of the following matrices.

(a) $\begin{bmatrix} 1+i & -1 \\ 1 & i \end{bmatrix}$ is square, not symmetric, not Hermitian, not triangular, not diagonal, not skew-symmetric, and not skew-hermitian.

(b) $\begin{bmatrix} 1+i & -1 \\ -1 & i \end{bmatrix}$ is symmetric only.

(c) $\begin{bmatrix} 0 & 1+i \\ -1-i & 0 \end{bmatrix}$ is skew-symmetric.

(d) $\begin{bmatrix} 2 & 1+i \\ 1-i & 3 \end{bmatrix}$ is Hermitian.

(e) $\begin{bmatrix} 3 & 0 \\ 0 & 2 \end{bmatrix}$ is symmetric, diagonal, and Hermitian.

(f) $\begin{bmatrix} 1-i & i \\ 0 & 3 \end{bmatrix}$ is upper triangular.

(g) $\begin{bmatrix} 3 & 0 \\ 0 & i \end{bmatrix}$ is symmetric, diagonal, and not Hermitian.

(h) $\begin{bmatrix} 0 & -4i \\ 4i & 0 \end{bmatrix}$ is skew-symmetric and Hermitian. ▪▪▪

It should be obvious that (a) every diagonal matrix is both upper and lower triangular, and (b) any triangular matrix with nonzero off-diagonal entries cannot be either symmetric or Hermitian.

Some of these special square matrices have the following general forms:

$$\underset{\text{upper triangular}}{\begin{bmatrix} A_{11} & * & \cdots & * \\ 0 & \ddots & \ddots & \vdots \\ \vdots & \ddots & \ddots & * \\ 0 & \cdots & 0 & A_{nn} \end{bmatrix}} \qquad \underset{\text{lower triangular}}{\begin{bmatrix} A_{11} & 0 & \cdots & 0 \\ * & \ddots & \ddots & \vdots \\ \vdots & \ddots & \ddots & 0 \\ * & \cdots & * & A_{nn} \end{bmatrix}}$$

$$\underset{\text{symmetric}}{\begin{bmatrix} A_{11} & & & & & \\ & \ddots & s & t & u & f & f \\ & s & \ddots & & & \\ & t & & \ddots & & \\ & u & & & \ddots & \\ & f & & & & \ddots & \\ & f & & & & & A_{nn} \end{bmatrix}} \qquad \underset{\text{skew-symmetric}}{\begin{bmatrix} 0 & & & & & \\ & \ddots & s & t & u & f & f \\ & -s & \ddots & & & \\ & -t & & \ddots & & \\ & -u & & & \ddots & \\ & -f & & & & \ddots & \\ & -f & & & & & 0 \end{bmatrix}}$$

$$\underset{\text{diagonal}}{\begin{bmatrix} d_1 & 0 & \cdots & \cdots & 0 \\ 0 & d_2 & 0 & & \vdots \\ \vdots & 0 & d_3 & \ddots & \vdots \\ \vdots & & \ddots & \ddots & 0 \\ 0 & \cdots & \cdots & 0 & d_n \end{bmatrix}} =: \mathbf{diag}\,(d_1, d_2, d_3, \ldots, d_n)$$

Using this last notation, $\mathbf{I}_n = \mathbf{diag}(1, 1, \ldots, 1) = \mathbf{diag}(\mathbf{ones}(n, 1))$. The identity matrices have the following very useful property: if $\mathbf{A} \in \mathbb{C}_n^m$, then

$$\mathbf{I}_m \mathbf{A} = \mathbf{A} \mathbf{I}_n = \mathbf{A}. \tag{1.1}$$

Every square matrix can be *uniquely* written as the sum of a symmetric and a skew-symmetric matrix:

$$\mathbf{A} = \frac{1}{2}\left(\mathbf{A} + \mathbf{A}^T\right) + \frac{1}{2}\left(\mathbf{A} - \mathbf{A}^T\right).$$

The first term is symmetric because

$$\left(\mathbf{A} + \mathbf{A}^T\right)^T = \mathbf{A}^T + \left(\mathbf{A}^T\right)^T = \mathbf{A}^T + \mathbf{A}.$$

Similarly, since

$$\left(\mathbf{A} - \mathbf{A}^T\right) = \mathbf{A}^T - \left(\mathbf{A}^T\right)^T = \mathbf{A}^T - \mathbf{A} = -\left(\mathbf{A} - \mathbf{A}^T\right),$$

the second term is skew-symmetric. A similar decomposition into the sum of a Hermitian and a skew-Hermitian matrix occurs in the obvious way.

Let $\mathcal{UT}_n$ and $\mathcal{LT}_n$ be the sets of upper and lower triangular $n \times n$ matrices, respectively, and $\mathcal{D}_n$ the set of diagonal matrices of order n. Then it can be shown $\mathcal{UT}_n$, $\mathcal{LT}_n$, and $\mathcal{D}_n$ are closed under multiplication, i.e., products of matrices of each type are of the same type. Furthermore, multiplication is commutative in $\mathcal{D}_n$.

Some matrices have very specific forms or patterns for their nonzero entries. Such matrices are said to be **patterned**. Matrices with relatively few nonzero entries are said to be **sparse**.

Diagonal matrices are sparse and patterned. Alternative forms of computer storage are available for sparse patterned matrices so that manipulation with them can be done more efficiently than for nonsparse matrices.

A matrix that has entries which are themselves matrices is said to be **partitioned**. Several special results hold for partitioned matrices. In particular, if the partitioning allows it, addition and multiplication is defined in the same way as if the entries were complex numbers; i.e.,

$$\begin{bmatrix} \mathbf{A} & \mathbf{B} \\ \mathbf{C} & \mathbf{D} \end{bmatrix} + \begin{bmatrix} \mathbf{P} & \mathbf{Q} \\ \mathbf{R} & \mathbf{S} \end{bmatrix} = \begin{bmatrix} \mathbf{A}+\mathbf{P} & \mathbf{B}+\mathbf{Q} \\ \mathbf{C}+\mathbf{R} & \mathbf{D}+\mathbf{S} \end{bmatrix},$$

when $\mathbf{A}, \mathbf{P} \in \mathbb{C}_n^m$, $\mathbf{B}, \mathbf{Q} \in \mathbb{C}_p^m$, $\mathbf{C}, \mathbf{R} \in \mathbb{C}_n^q$, and $\mathbf{D}, \mathbf{S} \in \mathbb{C}_p^q$, and

$$\begin{bmatrix} \mathbf{E} & \mathbf{F} \\ \mathbf{G} & \mathbf{H} \end{bmatrix} \begin{bmatrix} \mathbf{K} & \mathbf{L} \\ \mathbf{M} & \mathbf{N} \end{bmatrix} = \begin{bmatrix} \mathbf{EK}+\mathbf{FM} & \mathbf{EL}+\mathbf{FN} \\ \mathbf{GK}+\mathbf{HM} & \mathbf{GL}+\mathbf{HN} \end{bmatrix},$$

where $\mathbf{E} \in \mathbb{C}_n^m$, $\mathbf{F} \in \mathbb{C}_r^m$, $\mathbf{G} \in \mathbb{C}_n^q$, $\mathbf{H} \in \mathbb{C}_r^q$, $\mathbf{K} \in \mathbb{C}_p^n$, $\mathbf{L} \in \mathbb{C}_p^r$, $\mathbf{M} \in \mathbb{C}_s^n$, and $\mathbf{N} \in \mathbb{C}_s^r$. That is, the formulas are true as long as all the matrix additions and multiplications are defined.

1.3.1   *Exercise Set*

If

$$\mathbf{A} = \begin{bmatrix} 1 & 0 & 0 \\ 2 & i & 3 \\ -i & 2 & 2 \\ 0 & 0 & -i \end{bmatrix}, \quad \mathbf{B} = \begin{bmatrix} 3 & 5 & 6 & 0 \\ -1 & 1+i & 2 & 1 \\ 2 & 1 & -i & 0 \end{bmatrix}, \quad \mathbf{C} = \begin{bmatrix} -3 & 1 & 1+i \\ 2 & -2i & 3 \\ 1-i & 3 & -2 \end{bmatrix},$$

$$\mathbf{x} = \begin{bmatrix} 1 & 1 & 2 & -1 \end{bmatrix}, \quad \mathbf{y} = \begin{bmatrix} 2 & 1+i & -1 \end{bmatrix},$$

then find (or state that it is not computable):

1. $3\mathbf{A} + 2\mathbf{B}^T - \mathbf{B}^H$ 2. $\mathbf{BA} - \mathbf{A}^H\mathbf{B}^H$ 3. $4\mathbf{A}^H - 2\mathbf{B}$

4. $(\mathbf{AB})^H$ 5. $\mathbf{B}^H\mathbf{C} - \mathbf{A}$ 6. $(\mathbf{AB})^2$

7. $\mathbf{x}\mathbf{A}\mathbf{y}^H$ 8. $\mathbf{x}^H\mathbf{B}^H\mathbf{A}^H\mathbf{y}$ 9. $\mathbf{x}^H\mathbf{y} - \mathbf{A}$

10. $\mathbf{y}^H\mathbf{x} - \mathbf{B}$ 11. $\mathbf{y}(\mathbf{C} - \mathbf{BA})\mathbf{y}^H$ 12. $\mathbf{B}\mathbf{x}^T\mathbf{y}\mathbf{A}^T$

13. $\mathrm{tr}(\mathbf{AA}^T)$ 14. $\mathrm{tr}(\mathbf{BA} - \mathbf{C})$ 15. $\mathrm{tr}(\mathbf{x}^T\mathbf{y})$

16. $\mathbf{y} - \mathrm{diag}(\mathbf{C})$ 17. $\mathbf{C} - \mathrm{diag}(\mathbf{y})$ 18. $\mathrm{diag}(\mathbf{A} - \mathbf{x}^T\mathbf{y})$

19. If $\mathbf{e}_{(j;n)}$ is a n-entry column vector with a 1 in the jth row and all other entries zero, i.e., $\left(\mathbf{e}_{(j;n)}\right)_k = \delta_{jk}$, and $\mathbf{A}$ is an arbitrary $m \times n$ matrix, completely describe each of the following products:

(a) $\mathbf{e}_{(j;n)}^T \mathbf{e}_{(k;n)}$.   (b) $\mathbf{e}_{(j;m)}^T \mathbf{A}\mathbf{e}_{(j;n)}$.   (c) $\mathbf{e}_{(j;m)}^T \mathbf{A}\mathbf{e}_{(k;n)}$.

20. If $\mathbf{1}_n$ is an n-component column vector all of whose entries are one, i.e., $\mathbf{ones}(n, 1)$, and $\mathbf{A}$ is an arbitrary $m \times n$ matrix, write all the entries in each of the following products that are defined. You may want to express your answer in terms of the Matlab operator sum.

(a) $\mathbf{1}_n^T \mathbf{1}_n$. (b) $\mathbf{1}_n \mathbf{1}_n^T$. (c) $\mathbf{A} \mathbf{1}_n$.

(d) $\mathbf{1}_m^T \mathbf{A} \mathbf{A}^T \mathbf{1}_m$. (e) $\mathbf{A} \mathbf{1}_n \mathbf{1}_m^T \mathbf{A}$. (f) $\mathbf{1}_m^T \mathbf{A} \mathbf{1}_n$.

(g) $\mathbf{1}_n^T \mathbf{1}_m \mathbf{1}_m^T \mathbf{1}_n$.

21. Show that for any matrices $\mathbf{A}$ and $\mathbf{B}$,

(a) both $\mathbf{A}^T \mathbf{A}$ and $\mathbf{A} \mathbf{A}^T$ are symmetric. (b) both $\mathbf{B}^H \mathbf{B}$ and $\mathbf{B} \mathbf{B}^H$ are Hermitian.

22. If $\mathbf{U}$ is an $n \times n$ matrix all of whose entries are either $+1$ or -1, show that $\mathbf{diag}(\mathbf{diag}(\mathbf{U}\mathbf{U}^T)) = n\mathbf{I}$.

23. Prove property (Trace3).

24. A **permutation matrix P** is a matrix obtained from the identity by reordering its rows. Use either Matlab or a computer algebra system to generate five different 4×4 permutation matrices.

(a) If $\mathbf{A}$ is an arbitrary $4 \times n$ matrix, what is the effect of premultiplying by $\mathbf{P}$; i.e., what is $\mathbf{PA}$?

(b) If $\mathbf{B}$ is an arbitrary $m \times 4$ matrix, what is the effect of postmultiplying by $\mathbf{P}$; i.e., what is $\mathbf{BP}$?

(c) Convince yourself that the product of any two permutation matrices of the same size is another permutation matrix. Determine how the result is related to each of the factors.

25. If $\mathbf{A}$ and $\mathbf{B}$ are symmetric and of the same size, which of the following must be symmetric: $\mathbf{A} + \mathbf{B}$, $\mathbf{AB}$, $i(\mathbf{AB} - \mathbf{BA})$, $(\mathbf{AB} + \mathbf{BA})$, $\mathbf{A}^n$, $\mathbf{A} + i\mathbf{B}$, $\mathbf{A} - i\mathbf{B}$, $\mathbf{AB}^T$, $\mathbf{AB}^H$, $\mathbf{A}^T\mathbf{B} + \mathbf{B}^T\mathbf{A}$? For any which need not be symmetric, give a counterexample.

26. If $\mathbf{A}$ and $\mathbf{B}$ are Hermitian and of the same size, which of the following must be Hermitian: $\mathbf{A} + \mathbf{B}$, $\mathbf{AB}$, $i(\mathbf{AB} - \mathbf{BA})$, $(\mathbf{AB} + \mathbf{BA})$, $\mathbf{A}^n$, $\mathbf{A} + i\mathbf{B}$, $\mathbf{A} - i\mathbf{B}$, $\mathbf{AB}^T$, $\mathbf{AB}^H$, $\mathbf{A}^T\mathbf{B} + \mathbf{B}^T\mathbf{A}$? For any which need not be Hermitian, give a counterexample.

27. If $\mathbf{A} \in \mathbb{C}_n^n$, show that $\mathbf{A}$ can be written uniquely as $\mathbf{A} = \alpha\mathbf{I} + \mathbf{S} + \mathbf{K}$, where $\mathbf{S}$ is symmetric, $\mathbf{K}$ is skew-symmetric, and $\text{tr}(\mathbf{S}) = 0$. Do this by finding explicit formulas for α, $\mathbf{S}$, and $\mathbf{K}$. [Hint: Take the trace of both sides to start.]

If a and b are arbitrary complex constants and $\mathbf{A}$ is an $n \times n$ matrix whose entries are given below, what are the entries of $\mathbf{A}^2$?

28. $A_{jk} = a$ 29. $A_{jk} = a + (b - a)\delta_{jk}$

30. $A_{jk} = a\delta_{jk} + b\delta_{j,k-1}$ 31. $A_{jk} = a^{j+k}$

If $\mathbf{A}$ is $m \times n$, $\mathbf{B}$ is $n \times p$, and $\mathbf{C} = \mathbf{AB}$ then show that

32. $\mathbf{x}^T\mathbf{B} = \sum_1^n x_k \mathbf{row}_k(\mathbf{B})$.

33. $\mathbf{AB} = [\mathbf{Acol}_1(\mathbf{B}), \mathbf{Acol}_2(\mathbf{B}), \dots, \mathbf{Acol}_p(\mathbf{B})]$
    $= [\mathbf{row}_1(\mathbf{A})\mathbf{B}; \mathbf{row}_2(\mathbf{A})\mathbf{B}; \dots; \mathbf{row}_m(\mathbf{A})\mathbf{B}].$

34. $\mathbf{C} = \mathbf{AB} = \sum_{\ell=1}^{n} \mathbf{col}_\ell(\mathbf{A})\mathbf{row}_\ell(\mathbf{B})$. [This is an outer product.]

35. If $\mathbf{U}$ is the square matrix whose entries are $U_{jk} = \delta_{j,k-1}$ (1's on the $k = 1$ diagonal and zeros elsewhere), show that premultiplication of $\mathbf{A}$ by $\mathbf{U}$ shifts the rows of $\mathbf{A}$ upward, while postmultiplication shifts the columns to the right. If $\mathbf{L}$ has entries $L_{jk} = \delta_{j,k+1}$, prove an analogous result.

36. Prove the matrix properties (MatProd2) and (MatProd3).

37. A matrix $\mathbf{A}$ is said to be **idempotent** if $\mathbf{A}^2 = \mathbf{A}$. Give an example of a 2×2 idempotent matrix other than $\mathbf{0}$ or $\mathbf{I}_2$. Find the general form of all 2×2 idempotent matrices. What is the form of all real 3×3 skew-symmetric idempotent matrices (if there are any)?

38. We say $\mathbf{A} \in \mathbb{C}_{2n}^{2n}$ is **symplectic** if $\mathbf{A}^T \mathbf{J} \mathbf{A} = \mathbf{J}$ where

$$\mathbf{J} = \begin{bmatrix} 0 & -\mathbf{I}_n \\ \mathbf{I}_n & 0 \end{bmatrix}.$$

(a) Characterize all 2×2 symplectic matrices.

(b) In general, show that if $\mathbf{A}$ is symplectic then $\mathbf{A}^m$ is symplectic.

39. We say $\mathbf{N}$ is **nilpotent** of order k if $\mathbf{N}^k = \mathbf{0}$ and $\mathbf{N}^{k-1} \neq \mathbf{0}$.

(a) Find all 2×2 symmetric nilpotent matrices (if any).

(b) Show that the $n \times n$ matrix whose entries are

$$N_{jk} = a_1 \delta_{j,k-1} + a_2 \delta_{j,k-2} + a_3 \delta_{j,k-3} + \cdots + a_{n-1} \delta_{j,k-(n-1)}$$

is nilpotent of order no more than n for *any* choices of the a_k's.

40. A square matrix $\mathbf{S}$ is said to be **stochastic** if all its entries are nonnegative and the sum of the entries of each row vector is one. Writing the vector $\mathbf{1} := \mathbf{ones}(n, 1)$, convince yourself that if $\mathbf{S}$ is stochastic then $\mathbf{S1} = \mathbf{1}$. Show that the product of stochastic matrices is stochastic.

41. A square matrix $\mathbf{M}$ is said to be **doubly stochastic** if both $\mathbf{M}$ and $\mathbf{M}^T$ are stochastic. Show that if $\mathbf{M}$ is doubly stochastic, then $\mathbf{1}^T \mathbf{M1} = n$. Give an example of a matrix, other then the identity, that is doubly stochastic. Are products of doubly stochastic matrices doubly stochastic?

42. Let $\mathbf{A}$ and $\mathbf{B}$ be 2×2 matrices, and define the following seven terms:

$$T_1 := (A_{11} + A_{22})(B_{11} + B_{22}), \quad T_2 := (A_{21} + A_{22})B_{11},$$
$$T_3 := A_{11}(B_{12} - B_{22}), \quad T_4 := A_{22}(B_{21} - B_{11}),$$
$$T_5 := (A_{11} + A_{12})B_{22}, \quad T_6 := (A_{21} - A_{11})(B_{11} + B_{12}),$$
$$T_7 := (A_{12} - A_{22})(B_{21} + B_{22}).$$

(a) Show that the entries of the product $\mathbf{C} = \mathbf{AB}$ are given by

$$C_{11} = T_1 + T_4 - T_5 + T_7 \qquad C_{12} = T_3 + T_5$$
$$C_{21} = T_2 + T_4 \qquad C_{22} = T_1 + T_3 - T_2 + T_6$$

(b) Count the number of multiplications and additions required to implement this method and compare it with the standard definition for calculating the matrix product. This method is called the **Strassen algorithm**, and it can be implemented recursively for matrices larger than 2×2, in which case it can be shown that it requires $n^{\log_2 7} \approx n^{2.807}$ multiplications as opposed to the usual n^3 multiplications. Unfortunately, such "fast multipliers" are not always well-conditioned on every type of computer architecture.

1.4 SYSTEMS OF LINEAR EQUATIONS

Each of the linear multivariate models discussed in Section 1.2 resulted in a "system of simultaneous linear equations." This section will codify the terminology and provide an efficient method for hand calculation of the solutions of such equations.

DEFINITION 1.6 *A **linear equation** in the unknowns $x_1, x_2, \ldots, x_n$ is any equation of the form*

$$a_1 x_1 + a_2 x_2 + \cdots + a_n x_n = b,$$

*where $a_1, a_2, \ldots, a_n$, and b are complex constants. A **system of linear equations** in these n unknowns is m simultaneous linear equations,*

$$
\begin{aligned}
A_{11}x_1 &+ A_{12}x_2 &+ \cdots + A_{1k}x_k + \cdots + A_{1n}x_n &= b_1, \\
A_{21}x_1 &+ A_{22}x_2 &+ \cdots + A_{2k}x_k + \cdots + A_{2n}x_n &= b_2, \\
&\ \vdots & \vdots \qquad\qquad\qquad \vdots & \\
A_{j1}x_1 &+ A_{j2}x_2 &+ \cdots + A_{jk}x_k + \cdots + A_{jn}x_n &= b_j, \\
&\ \vdots & \vdots \qquad\qquad\qquad \vdots & \\
A_{m1}x_1 &+ A_{m2}x_2 &+ \cdots + A_{mk}x_k + \cdots + A_{mn}x_n &= b_m.
\end{aligned}
\tag{1.2}
$$

Solution: *A **solution** of the system of linear equations (1.2) is any $n \times 1$ vector expression for the unknowns; which may involve certain parameters $\alpha_1, \alpha_2, \ldots, \alpha_\nu$ where $\nu < n$, for which the system reduces to an identity. If a system has a solution, then it is said to be **consistent**; otherwise, it is **inconsistent**. If there are more equations than unknowns, the system is **overdetermined**, and if there are fewer equations than unknowns, the system is **underdetermined**.*

■ **EXAMPLE 1.17** The overdetermined system

$$
\begin{aligned}
x_1 &\quad &= 1, \\
&x_2 &= 0, \\
x_1 &+ x_2 &= 2
\end{aligned}
$$

is inconsistent, because the values from the first two equations do not satisfy the third equation; i.e., $1 + 0 \neq 2$. ■ ■ ■

■ **EXAMPLE 1.18** The overdetermined system

$$
\begin{aligned}
x_1 \quad\quad\quad - \ x_3 &= 1 \\
x_2 + \ x_3 &= 0 \\
x_1 + \ x_2 \quad\quad\quad &= 1 \\
x_1 + 2x_2 + \ x_3 &= 1
\end{aligned}
$$

is consistent because

$$
x_1 = \alpha + 1, \quad x_2 = -\alpha, \quad x_3 = \alpha
$$

is a solution with the single parameter α, which can take any complex value. This can be verified by inserting these values into the equations and showing that the result is an identity:

$$
\begin{aligned}
(\alpha + 1) \quad\quad\quad - \ \alpha &= 1 \ \Leftrightarrow \ 1 = 1, \\
(-\alpha) + \ \alpha &= 0 \ \Leftrightarrow \ 0 = 0, \\
(\alpha + 1) + \ (-\alpha) \quad\quad &= 1 \ \Leftrightarrow \ 1 = 1, \\
(\alpha + 1) + 2(-\alpha) + \ \alpha &= 1 \ \Leftrightarrow \ 1 = 1.
\end{aligned}
$$

Thus $\{[\alpha + 1; -\alpha; \alpha] : \alpha \in \mathbb{C}\}$ is a set of solutions to the linear system. ■ ■ ■

Any linear system can be written as a matrix product:

$$
\mathbf{Ax} = \mathbf{b},
$$

where $\mathbf{A}$ is called the **coefficient matrix** of the system. Every solution will take the form

$$
\mathbf{x} = \mathbf{x}(\alpha_1, \alpha_2, \ldots, \alpha_\nu),
$$

where the α_k are parameters. The set of all $\mathbf{x}$ defined this way is called the **solution set** of the linear system.

Looking back at example 1.18, we see that we had four equations in three unknowns. Not all of the equations were unrelated. The third equation was the sum of the first two, and the fourth was the first plus twice the second.

DEFINITION 1.7 *Any equation that can be written as a linear combination of other equations in the system is* **dependent**. *A system with at least one dependent equation is a* **dependent system**.

Since our goal is to find all solutions, or the solution set, of a linear system let's try an easy one.

■ **EXAMPLE 1.19** Solve the system

$$
\begin{aligned}
x_1 \quad\quad - \ x_3 &= 1, \\
x_2 + 2x_3 &= 5.
\end{aligned}
$$

Solution: Since this is a system of two equations in three unknowns we will not be able to find specific numerical values for x_1, x_2, and x_3. Instead, set $x_3 = \alpha$, an arbitrary parameter. Why put x_3 equal to the parameter rather than x_1 or x_2? Because x_3 is the only variable in terms of which the other two can each be written without additional algebra. The system is now two equations in the two unknowns, x_1 and x_2.

$$\begin{aligned} x_1 \quad - \quad \alpha &= 1 \\ x_2 + 2\alpha &= 5 \end{aligned}$$

or

$$\begin{aligned} x_1 &= \alpha + 1, \\ x_2 &= -2\alpha + 5. \end{aligned}$$

Thus the vector form of any vector in the solution set is

$$\mathbf{x} = \begin{bmatrix} \alpha + 1 \\ -2\alpha + 5 \\ \alpha \end{bmatrix} = \begin{bmatrix} \alpha \\ -2\alpha \\ \alpha \end{bmatrix} + \begin{bmatrix} 1 \\ 5 \\ 0 \end{bmatrix} = \alpha \begin{bmatrix} 1 \\ -2 \\ 1 \end{bmatrix} + \begin{bmatrix} 1 \\ 5 \\ 0 \end{bmatrix}.$$

Since α can be any complex number, there are infinitely many solution vectors $\mathbf{x}(\alpha)$ in the solution set. ■ ■ ■

There are only three possibilities for the solution set to $\mathbf{A}\mathbf{x} = \mathbf{b}$:

(a) The system is inconsistent; there are no solution vectors, and the solution set is empty.

(b) The system is consistent and the solution vector does not contain a parameter. There is exactly one solution vector, and the solution set is called a singleton.

(c) The system is consistent and the solution vector contains at least one parameter. There are infinitely many solution vectors in the solution set.

We'd like to systematize our method of solving a linear system. In order to do that we must know what it is we seek. The simplest possible system has the form:

$$\begin{aligned} x_1 \qquad &= \text{value of } x_1, \\ x_2 \qquad &= \text{value of } x_2, \\ x_3 \quad &= \text{value of } x_3, \\ \ddots \qquad &\quad \vdots \\ x_n &= \text{value of } x_n. \end{aligned}$$

The corresponding coefficient matrix would be

$$
\begin{bmatrix}
1 & 0 & \cdots & \cdots & 0 \\
0 & 1 & 0 & & \vdots \\
\vdots & 0 & 1 & \ddots & \vdots \\
\vdots & & \ddots & \ddots & 0 \\
0 & \cdots & \cdots & 0 & 1 \\
0 & \cdots & \cdots & \cdots & 0 \\
\vdots & & & & \vdots \\
0 & \cdots & \cdots & \cdots & 0
\end{bmatrix}.
$$

If the original system had $m > n$ equations, then we would need to have $m - n$ rows of zeros. Thus a good final form of a system is one containing a large number of regularly placed zeros. More specifically, as many columns as possible should contain only one nonzero entry and all rows of only zeros should lie below all nonzero rows.

When solving a system of linear equations we usually employ only three different operations called **elementary row operations** (because each row represents one equation):

(ERO1) Multiply an equation (row) by a nonzero constant.

(ERO2) Add a multiple of one equation (row) to another.

(ERO3) Interchange equations (rows).

Elementary row operations do not change the solution set of a linear system.

In each of these operations, which are repeated many times in the course of finding a solution, a great deal of effort is expended in writing the labels for the unknowns. For this reason we'll use a shorthand notation that suppresses the variable labels in a unique way. Corresponding to the system $\mathbf{Ax} = \mathbf{b}$ we will write its **augmented matrix**:

$$
[\mathbf{A}|\mathbf{b}] =
\left[
\begin{array}{cccccc|c}
A_{11} & A_{12} & A_{13} & \cdots & A_{1k} & \cdots & A_{1n} & b_1 \\
A_{21} & A_{22} & A_{23} & \cdots & A_{2k} & \cdots & A_{2n} & b_2 \\
\vdots & \vdots & \vdots & & \vdots & & \vdots & \vdots \\
A_{j1} & A_{j2} & A_{j3} & \cdots & A_{jk} & \cdots & A_{jn} & b_k \\
\vdots & \vdots & \vdots & & \vdots & & \vdots & \vdots \\
A_{m1} & A_{m2} & A_{m3} & \cdots & A_{mk} & \cdots & A_{mn} & b_m
\end{array}
\right].
\tag{1.3}
$$

The coefficient matrix $\mathbf{A}$ is concatenated laterally with the column vector $\mathbf{b}$, and the vertical line represents the equal signs. The kth column of $\mathbf{A}$ contains the coefficients of x_k; e.g., the third column consists of the coefficients of x_3 and the $(n+1)^{st}$ column contains the constants from the right hand side of the system of equations. The rows of $[\mathbf{A}|\mathbf{b}]$ correspond to the equations of the system.

We'll apply the elementary row operations (ERO1), (ERO2), and (ERO3) to the rows of $[\mathbf{A}|\mathbf{b}]$ in a systematic manner to change the coefficients of many of the variables in each of the equations to zero. The procedure is called the **method of pivotal reduction** or **Gauss-Jordan elimination** with pivoting.

To proceed, look through the first nonzero column of $[\mathbf{A}|\mathbf{b}]$ until you find a **pivot entry** that will be used to eliminate other coefficients in that column. A pivot must be nonzero (otherwise we wouldn't be able to use it to cancel the coefficients of that variable in other rows). If we are using hand computation, then we want a small integer, preferably $+1$. The row containing the first pivot will be designated the first **pivot row**. Start by moving the first pivot row to the first row and pushing all other rows down. Remember, these are the *entire* rows of $[\mathbf{A}\,|\mathbf{b}]$, not just the coefficient rows! By adding multiples of the pivot row to each of the other rows, our goal is to **sweep out**, or make all of the *remaining* entries in the first working column equal to zero. [Some authors (and most programs) interchange the first row with the pivot row, thus leaving the other rows in the same positions. Additionally, it is numerically advantageous to write a program that chooses the pivot with largest modulus in order to reduce round-off error.]

■ **EXAMPLE 1.20** In the interests of applying this strategy say that

$$[\mathbf{A}|\mathbf{b}] = \begin{bmatrix} 2 & \# & \# & \# & \# & | & @ \\ -1 & \# & \# & \# & \# & | & @ \\ -3 & \# & \# & \# & \# & | & @ \\ 0 & \# & \# & \# & \# & | & @ \end{bmatrix} \begin{matrix} (1) \\ (2) \\ (3) \\ (4) \end{matrix}$$

Since we're only working on the first column, everything else has been suppressed. The parenthesized numbers to the right of the augmented matrix are labels for the rows on which we are to operate.

Of the entries in the first column, the 0 prohibits us from using row (4) as a pivot row. The -1 in row (2) is probably the best choice for a pivot, so pick row (2) as the pivot row. Now for our first partial step, we must move row (2) to the top and push the other rows down (in this case, this is equivalent to swapping rows (1) and (2)).

$$\begin{matrix} (2) \\ (1) \\ (3) \\ (4) \end{matrix} \begin{bmatrix} -1 & \# & \# & \# & \# & | & @ \\ 2 & \# & \# & \# & \# & | & @ \\ -3 & \# & \# & \# & \# & | & @ \\ 0 & \# & \# & \# & \# & | & @ \end{bmatrix} \begin{matrix} \text{First Pivot Row} \\ (2) \\ (3) \\ (4) \end{matrix}$$

To complete the first step, we want to create a zero where the 2 is in row (1). We will do this by adding a multiple of the pivot row (2) to row (1). The required operation is $(1) + 2(2)$. To create a zero where the -3 is requires $(3) - 3(2)$. Nothing need be done about (4) because there is already a zero there. Thus the proper "second" step is

$$\begin{matrix} (2) \\ (1) + 2(2) \\ (3) - 3(2) \\ (4) \end{matrix} \begin{bmatrix} -1 & \# & \# & \# & \# & | & @ \\ 0 & \#' & \#' & \#' & \#' & | & @ \\ 0 & \#' & \#' & \#' & \#' & | & @' \\ 0 & \# & \# & \# & \# & | & @ \end{bmatrix} \begin{matrix} \text{First Pivot Row} \\ (2)' \\ (3)' \\ (4) \end{matrix}$$

Only the pivot row and the old row (4), which had a zero in its first entry, are unchanged.

■ ■ ■

More generally, if the pivot row is (1), we can sweep out the first column as follows:

$$
\begin{array}{r}
(1) \\
(2) - (A_{21}/A_{11})(1) \\
(3) - (A_{31}/A_{11})(1) \\
\vdots \\
(m) - (A_{m1}/A_{11})(1)
\end{array}
\left[
\begin{array}{cccc|c}
A_{11} & A_{12} & \cdots & A_{1n} & b_1 \\
0 & \multicolumn{2}{c}{\text{Once}} & & b'_2 \\
0 & \multicolumn{2}{c}{\text{Revised}} & & b'_3 \\
\vdots & \multicolumn{2}{c}{\text{Stuff}} & & \vdots \\
0 & & & & b'_m
\end{array}
\right]
\begin{array}{r}
\text{new row labels} \\
(1) \\
(2) \\
(3) \\
\vdots \\
(m)
\end{array}
$$

The $m - 1$ equations represented by the rows below the first pivot row constitute a linear system of one less equation in one fewer unknown.

Now we must work on the next column. We cannot use the same pivot row as before because as we sweep out the second column we'd destroy the special character of column 1, which has already been swept; we'd unsweep it, if you will. Thus we must choose the next pivot from among the new rows (2) through (m). Once we've chosen the second pivot row, we move it into the second position and sweep out the second column. This means we must sweep out the second entry in the first pivot row too, because it may have a nonzero entry in the second column which is not in the second pivot row. The next step (when (2) is the second pivot row) is

$$
\begin{array}{r}
(1) - (A_{12}/A_{22})(2) \\
(2) \\
(3) - (A_{32}/A_{22})(2) \\
\vdots \\
(m) - (A_{m2}/A_{22})(2)
\end{array}
\left[
\begin{array}{ccc|c}
A_{11} & 0 & \# & @' \\
0 & A_{22} & \# & @'' \\
0 & 0 & \text{Twice} & \vdots \\
\vdots & \vdots & \text{Revised} & \vdots \\
0 & 0 & \text{Stuff} & @''
\end{array}
\right]
$$

The row labels (1), $(2),\ldots, (m)$ refer to the matrix of the preceding step, *not* to the original matrix. Writing the operations performed in front of the reduced matrix is useful for checking hand calculations and is highly recommended. It further points out that each row, if changed, is changed only by the addition of multiples of the pivot row. Sometimes, it may be convenient to multiply the pivot row by a nonzero constant to either eliminate a factor common to every entry of that row or to change the sign of that row.

A standard notation for the multipliers used in the reduction process, when we choose the pivots to be the diagonal entries, of the jth column is

$$
m_{ij} := \frac{A_{ij}}{A_{jj}}, \quad i = 2 : n.
$$

At this stage, the pattern of attack should be clear. We must choose the next pivot row from among those rows not yet used as pivots. Then we must sweep out the corresponding column. We continue this sequence of operations until we have no more rows on which to pivot. This can occur in only one of three ways:

- We can run out of columns to sweep out before we reach the last row. This is the case of more equations than unknowns (the overdetermined system). The final form of the augmented matrix $[\mathbf{A}|\mathbf{b}]$ is then

$$\left[\begin{array}{ccccc|c} \# & 0 & \cdots & 0 & & @ \\ 0 & \# & & \ddots & & \vdots \\ \vdots & \ddots & \ddots & & & \vdots \\ 0 & \cdots & 0 & \# & & @ \\ 0 & \cdots & 0 & 0 & & \vdots \\ \vdots & & & \vdots & & \vdots \\ 0 & \cdots & 0 & 0 & & @ \end{array}\right].$$

The coefficient side of $[\mathbf{A}|\mathbf{b}]$ must have all zeros at the bottom because we've swept out every column. If these zero rows at the bottom do not have zeros to the right of the vertical bar (equal signs), then the system is inconsistent because these equations look like

$$0 \cdot x_1 + 0 \cdot x_2 + \cdots + 0 \cdot x_n = \text{some nonzero value,}$$

which cannot be true for any complex x's. Thus in this case a consistent system must have full zero rows at the bottom.

- We can run out of rows before we reach the vertical bar. The final form of $[\mathbf{A}|\mathbf{b}]$ is then

$$\left[\begin{array}{ccccccc|c} \# & 0 & 0 & \cdots & 0 & & & @ \\ 0 & \# & 0 & & \vdots & & & \vdots \\ 0 & 0 & \# & \ddots & \vdots & \text{Stuff} & & @ \\ \vdots & & \ddots & \ddots & 0 & & & \vdots \\ 0 & \cdots & \cdots & 0 & \# & & & @ \end{array}\right].$$

Here we have more unknowns than equations (the underdetermined system), and we'll have to introduce parameters into the solution, one parameter for each column in the "stuff."

- Last but not least, we can get a final form that is a combination of the first two cases, and it can be handled similarly.

After pivotal reduction, all dependent rows have been changed to zero rows, when the system is consistent. The first nonzero entry in any row of a reduced matrix is called the **leading entry** of that row.

DEFINITION 1.8   *Suppose that for a matrix* **R***:*

(EchForm1)   *All zero rows lie below any nonzero rows.*

(EchForm2)   *All entries below a leading entry in a column are zero.*

(EchForm3)   *If the leading entry in row* k *occurs in column* j_k*, then*

$$j_1 < j_2 < j_3 < \cdots \ ,$$

i.e., leading entries move down and to the right.

If these three requirements are satisfied, then **R** *is said to be in* **echelon form***.*

(EchForm4)   *If, in addition to (EF1)–(EF3), each leading entry is a one, the matrix* **R** *is said to be in* **row echelon form***.*

(EchForm5)   *If a matrix is in row echelon form and additionally all entries above a leading entry in each column are also zero, the matrix* **R** *is said to be in* **row-reduced echelon form***.*

We will abbreviate row-reduced echelon form as rref. We will use $\mathrm{rref}(\mathbf{A})$ to represent the function on the set of matrices that returns the rref of the matrix $\mathbf{A}$. This is a Matlab function. A square matrix in echelon form, row echelon form, or rref is at least upper triangular. A square matrix in row echelon form, with no rows of zeros, is unit upper triangular, because of the ones on the main diagonal.

▪ **EXAMPLE 1.21**   Put the augmented matrix for the following system in row-reduced echelon form.

$$
\begin{aligned}
4x + 5y + 6z &= 0, \\
7x + 8y + 9z &= 1, \\
x + 2y + 3z &= 1.
\end{aligned}
$$

Solution: First construct the augmented matrix by suppressing the variable labels and replacing the equal signs by the vertical bar:

$$
[\mathbf{A}|\mathbf{b}] =
\begin{bmatrix}
4 & 5 & 6 & 0 \\
7 & 8 & 9 & 1 \\
1 & 2 & 3 & 1
\end{bmatrix}
\begin{matrix}
(1) \\
(2) \\
(3)
\end{matrix}
$$

Scanning the first column, it appears that row (3) will make the best pivot row. The pivot row moves to the first position and the others move down. Sweeping out column 1, we have

$$
\begin{matrix}
(3) \\
(1) - 4(3) \\
(2) - 7(3)
\end{matrix}
\begin{bmatrix}
1 & 2 & 3 & 1 \\
0 & -3 & -6 & -4 \\
0 & -6 & -12 & -6
\end{bmatrix}
\begin{matrix}
\text{First Pivot } (1) \\
(2) \\
(3)
\end{matrix}
$$

The new row labels have been written to the extreme right. Either the new row (2) or (3) could be the next pivot. Choose (2) and sweep out the second column. Remember, when rewriting the augmented matrix, copy this pivot row first because all of the other rows will be modified by sweeping with it:

$$\begin{array}{c} (1) + \frac{2}{3}(2) \\ (2) \\ (3) - 2(2) \end{array} \left[\begin{array}{ccc|c} 1 & 0 & -1 & -\frac{5}{3} \\ 0 & -3 & -6 & -4 \\ 0 & 0 & 0 & 2 \end{array} \right] \quad \text{Second Pivot}$$

The augmented matrix is now in echelon form (although we needn't have swept out the A_{12} entry). The corresponding rref is

$$\left[\begin{array}{ccc|c} 1 & 0 & -1 & -\frac{5}{3} \\ 0 & 1 & 2 & \frac{4}{3} \\ 0 & 0 & 0 & 2 \end{array} \right].$$

Since the last equation is $0 = 2$, this system is inconsistent. ■ ■ ■

In order to solve many consistent systems we will be required to introduce arbitrary parameters into the solution. In the rref of the augmented matrix, the column in which the leading entry lies corresponds to the **leading variable**. Any column not containing a leading entry corresponds to a **nonleading variable**.

As a matter of practice all nonleading variables will be set equal to arbitrary parameters because the leading variables can always be written in terms of them.

■ **EXAMPLE 1.22** For the system whose augmented matrix $\mathbf{R}$ has the echelon form

$$\left[\begin{array}{ccccc|c} \mathbf{2} & 1 & 0 & 0 & 9 & 6 \\ 0 & 0 & \mathbf{3} & 0 & -5 & 7 \\ 0 & 0 & 0 & \mathbf{4} & -1 & 8 \\ 0 & 0 & 0 & 0 & 0 & 0 \end{array} \right]$$

we see the system is consistent because the zero row in the coefficient part is completed by a zero. Since $\mathbf{2} = R_{11}$, $\mathbf{3} = R_{23}$, and $\mathbf{4} = R_{34}$ are the first nonzero entries in the first three rows, they are the leading entries. x_1 (because $\mathbf{2}$ is in column 1), x_3 (because $\mathbf{3}$ is in column 3), and x_4 (because $\mathbf{4}$ is in column 4) are leading variables. Therefore, x_2 and x_5 are nonleading variables and should be set equal to parameters. Putting $x_2 = \alpha$ and $x_5 = \beta$ the equations are

$$\begin{array}{rl} 2x_1 + \alpha & +9\beta = 6, \\ 3x_3 & -5\beta = 7, \\ 4x_4 & -\beta = 8. \end{array}$$

Thus

$$\begin{array}{rl} x_1 = & -\frac{1}{2}\alpha -\frac{9}{2}\beta +3, \\ x_3 = & \frac{5}{3}\beta +\frac{7}{3}, \\ x_4 = & \frac{1}{4}\beta +2, \end{array}$$

and a typical solution vector is,

$$\mathbf{x} = \begin{bmatrix} -\frac{1}{2}\alpha - \frac{9}{2}\beta + 3 \\ \alpha \\ \frac{5}{3}\beta + \frac{7}{3} \\ \frac{1}{4}\beta + 2 \\ \beta \end{bmatrix} = \alpha \begin{bmatrix} -\frac{1}{2} \\ 1 \\ 0 \\ 0 \\ 0 \end{bmatrix} + \beta \begin{bmatrix} -\frac{9}{2} \\ 0 \\ \frac{5}{3} \\ \frac{1}{4} \\ 1 \end{bmatrix} + \begin{bmatrix} 3 \\ 0 \\ \frac{7}{3} \\ 2 \\ 0 \end{bmatrix}.$$

Since α and β are arbitrary, they could be replaced by

$$\alpha = 2\delta \quad \text{and} \quad \beta = \mathrm{lcm}(2,3,4)\gamma = 12\gamma$$

to remove some of the fractions. Then

$$\mathbf{x} = \delta \begin{bmatrix} -1 \\ 2 \\ 0 \\ 0 \\ 0 \end{bmatrix} + \gamma \begin{bmatrix} -54 \\ 0 \\ -20 \\ 3 \\ 12 \end{bmatrix} + \begin{bmatrix} 3 \\ 0 \\ \frac{7}{3} \\ 2 \\ 0 \end{bmatrix}$$

would be an arbitrary vector of the solution set. ■ ■ ■

■ **EXAMPLE 1.23** Solve

$$\begin{array}{rcrcrcl} x_1 & + & 3x_2 & - & 4x_3 & = & -2, \\ 2x_2 & - & x_2 & + & 2x_3 & = & 6, \\ 4x_1 & - & 6x_2 & + & x_3 & = & 9. \end{array}$$

Solution: The augmented matrix is

$$[\mathbf{A}|\mathbf{b}] = \begin{bmatrix} 1 & 3 & -4 & | & -2 \\ 2 & -1 & 2 & | & 6 \\ 4 & -6 & 1 & | & 9 \end{bmatrix} \begin{matrix} (1) \\ (2) \\ (3) \end{matrix} \quad \text{Choose (1) as pivot row.}$$

$$\begin{matrix} (1) \\ \hookrightarrow \quad (2) - 2(1) \\ (3) - 4(1) \end{matrix} \begin{bmatrix} 1 & 3 & -4 & | & -2 \\ 0 & -7 & 10 & | & 10 \\ 0 & -18 & 17 & | & 17 \end{bmatrix} \quad \begin{matrix} \text{Choose (2) as the lesser} \\ \text{of two evils.} \end{matrix}$$

$$\begin{matrix} 7(1) + 3(2) \\ \hookrightarrow \quad (2) \\ 7(3) - 18(2) \end{matrix} \begin{bmatrix} 7 & 0 & 2 & | & 16 \\ 0 & -7 & 10 & | & 10 \\ 0 & 0 & -61 & | & -61 \end{bmatrix} \quad \begin{matrix} \text{Rather than } (1) + \frac{3}{7}(2) \\ \\ \text{Rather than } (3) - \frac{18}{7}(2) \end{matrix}$$

The curved arrow means that elementary row operations have been used to arrive at the next matrix. Notice the avoidance of fractions in the hand calculation of new rows (1) and (3).

Only (3) remains as a possible pivot; divide it by -61 for simplicity:

$$\begin{array}{c} (1) + \frac{2}{61}(3) \\ \hookrightarrow \quad (2) + \frac{10}{61}(3) \\ -\frac{1}{61}(3) \end{array} \left[\begin{array}{ccc|c} 7 & 0 & 0 & 14 \\ 0 & -7 & 0 & 0 \\ 0 & 0 & 1 & 1 \end{array}\right] \hookrightarrow \begin{array}{c} \frac{1}{7}(1) \\ -\frac{1}{7}(2) \\ (3) \end{array} \left[\begin{array}{ccc|c} 1 & 0 & 0 & 2 \\ 0 & 1 & 0 & 0 \\ 0 & 0 & 1 & 1 \end{array}\right].$$

This is the row-reduced echelon form; the unique solution is

$$\begin{array}{c} x_1 = 2 \\ x_2 = 0 \\ x_3 = 1 \end{array} \quad \text{or} \quad \mathbf{x} = \left[\begin{array}{c} 2 \\ 0 \\ 1 \end{array}\right].$$

■ ■ ■

■ **EXAMPLE 1.24** Solve the system

$$\begin{array}{rrrrr} 2x_1 & + & x_2 & + & 3x_3 & = & 5, \\ x_1 & - & 2x_2 & + & 4x_3 & = & -5. \end{array}$$

Solution:

$$[\mathbf{A}|\mathbf{b}] = \left[\begin{array}{ccc|c} 2 & 1 & 3 & 5 \\ 1 & -2 & 4 & -5 \end{array}\right] \hookrightarrow \begin{array}{c} (2) \\ (1) - 2(2) \end{array} \left[\begin{array}{ccc|c} 1 & -2 & 4 & -5 \\ 0 & 5 & -5 & 15 \end{array}\right]$$

$$\hookrightarrow \begin{array}{c} (1) + \frac{2}{5}(2) \\ \frac{1}{5}(2) \end{array} \left[\begin{array}{ccc|c} 1 & 0 & 2 & 1 \\ 0 & 1 & -1 & 3 \end{array}\right].$$

The variables x_1 and x_2 are leading and x_3 is nonleading, so set $x_3 = \alpha$ to get the solution vector

$$\begin{array}{c} x_1 = -2\alpha + 1 \\ x_2 = \alpha + 3 \\ x_3 = \alpha \end{array} \quad \text{or} \quad \mathbf{x} = \left[\begin{array}{c} -2\alpha + 1 \\ \alpha + 3 \\ \alpha \end{array}\right] = \alpha\left[\begin{array}{c} -2 \\ 1 \\ 1 \end{array}\right] + \left[\begin{array}{c} 1 \\ 3 \\ 0 \end{array}\right].$$

■ ■ ■

■ **EXAMPLE 1.25** Solve

$$\begin{array}{rrrrrrrr} a & - & b & + & 2c & - & d & = & 1 \\ 2a & - & 2b & + & 3c & - & d & = & 2 \\ 3a & - & 3b & + & 5c & + & 2d & = & 7 \end{array}$$

This system will be slightly different.

Solution: Write the augmented matrix and use the first pivot row to sweep the first column:

$$\left[\begin{array}{cccc|c} 1 & -1 & 2 & -1 & 1 \\ 2 & -2 & 3 & -1 & 2 \\ 3 & -3 & 5 & 2 & 7 \end{array}\right] \hookrightarrow \begin{array}{c} (1) \\ (2) - 2(1) \\ (3) - 3(1) \end{array} \left[\begin{array}{cccc|c} 1 & -1 & 2 & -1 & 1 \\ 0 & 0 & -1 & 1 & 0 \\ 0 & 0 & -1 & 5 & 4 \end{array}\right].$$

It was a bit unusual that the use of the first pivot row swept out the first and second columns. There is no way to use either the second or third row as a pivot to sweep out the -1 from the A'_{12} position. Nothing more can be done for the second column. We must move to sweeping the third and fourth columns:

$$
\begin{matrix}
(1) + 2(2) \\
-(2) \\
(3) - (2)
\end{matrix}
\left[\begin{array}{cccc|c}
1 & -1 & 0 & 1 & 1 \\
0 & 0 & 1 & -1 & 0 \\
0 & 0 & 0 & 4 & 4
\end{array}\right]
\hookrightarrow
\begin{matrix}
(1) - \frac{1}{4}(3) \\
(2) + \frac{1}{4}(3) \\
\frac{1}{4}(3)
\end{matrix}
\left[\begin{array}{cccc|c}
1 & -1 & 0 & 0 & 1 \\
0 & 0 & 1 & 0 & 1 \\
0 & 0 & 0 & 1 & 1
\end{array}\right].
$$

We see that x_2 is the only nonleading variable, so set it equal to the parameter α, yielding $x_1 = \alpha + 1$, $x_3 = 1$, and $x_4 = 1$. An arbitrary vector in the solution set is the set of all x of the form

$$
\mathbf{x} = \begin{bmatrix} \alpha + 1 \\ \alpha \\ 1 \\ 1 \end{bmatrix} = \alpha \begin{bmatrix} 1 \\ 1 \\ 0 \\ 0 \end{bmatrix} + \begin{bmatrix} 1 \\ 0 \\ 1 \\ 1 \end{bmatrix}.
$$

■ ■ ■

Notice that the leading entries in the row-reduced echelon form of the last example move down and to the right, although not necessarily along the diagonal. The last example illustrates the possibility of the move down the diagonal with a jump to the right.

Suppose we are asked to solve $\mathbf{Ax} = \mathbf{b}_{(j)}$ for each $j = 1 : k$ and we are given all k of the b vectors at the outset. If we were to do each case separately, we would form the k augmented matrices $\left[\mathbf{A}|\mathbf{b}_{(j)}\right]$ and row reduce each of them. But it should be clear that in each case we would be doing precisely the same elementary row operations because it is the form of $\mathbf{A}$ drives that choice. To save a great deal of time we could augment the augmented matrix by appending all of the b's to $\mathbf{A}$ to form $\left[\mathbf{A}|\mathbf{b}_{(1)}, \mathbf{b}_{(2)}, \ldots, \mathbf{b}_{(k)}\right]$ and row reduce that. Then we could read off the solution to each of the separate systems by looking at each of the rightmost columns separately.

Now to some final remarks about linear systems:

DEFINITION 1.9 *The number of nonzero rows in the row-reduced echelon form of a matrix* **A** *is called the* **row rank** *of* **A***, written* $\text{rank}(\mathbf{A})$.

The row rank of **A** is also equal to the number of leading variables in the linear system $\mathbf{Ax} = \mathbf{b}$. The **nullity** of **A**, written $\text{null}(\mathbf{A})$, is the number of nonleading variables in the system, hence the number of arbitrary parameters in the solution. If $\mathbf{A} \in \mathbb{C}_n^m$, then there are n variables in the linear system $\mathbf{Ax} = \mathbf{b}$ and every variable is either leading or nonleading, so we must have

$$
\text{rank}(\mathbf{A}) + \text{null}(\mathbf{A}) = n. \tag{1.4}
$$

DEFINITION 1.10 *A linear system written in the form* $\mathbf{Ax} = \mathbf{b}$ *is said to be* **homogeneous** *if* $\mathbf{b} \equiv \mathbf{0}$ *and* **nonhomogeneous** *otherwise.*

For a homogeneous system the augmented matrix is $[\mathbf{A}|\mathbf{0}]$, and we may omit the rightmost column $\mathbf{0}$ because any linear combinations of 0's is again 0. Homogeneous systems are *always consistent* because $\mathbf{x} = \mathbf{0}$ is always a solution, called the **trivial solution**. If $\mathrm{rank}(\mathbf{A}) = n$, then $\mathbf{x} = \mathbf{0}$ is the only solution, whereas if $\mathrm{rank}(\mathbf{A}) < n$ the solution set contains infinitely many vectors. If $\mathrm{null}(\mathbf{A}) = n - \mathrm{rank}(\mathbf{A}) = \nu$, then any solution vector can be written in terms of ν parameters as

$$\mathbf{x} = \alpha_1 \mathbf{x}_1 + \alpha_2 \mathbf{x}_2 + \cdots + \alpha_\nu \mathbf{x}_\nu,$$

for any complex α_j, where $\mathbf{A}\mathbf{x}_j = \mathbf{0}$, $j = 1 : \nu$.

It is also true that any linear combination of solutions to a homogeneous equation is itself a solution. This can be seen by the following argument. Assume $\mathbf{x}_1, \mathbf{x}_2, \ldots, \mathbf{x}_k$ are any solutions to the homogeneous system $\mathbf{A}\mathbf{x} = \mathbf{0}$ and $c_1, c_2, \ldots, c_k$ are any constants. Then

$$\mathbf{A}(c_1 \mathbf{x}_1 + c_2 \mathbf{x}_2 + \cdots + c_k \mathbf{x}_k) = c_1(\mathbf{A}\mathbf{x}_1) + c_2(\mathbf{A}\mathbf{x}_2) + \cdots + c_k(\mathbf{A}\mathbf{x}_k) = \mathbf{0},$$

because $\mathbf{A}\mathbf{x}_j = \mathbf{0}$ for each $j = 1 : k$.

DEFINITION 1.11 *For the nonhomogeneous system* $\mathbf{A}\mathbf{x} = \mathbf{b}$ $(\neq \mathbf{0})$, *a solution of the corresponding homogeneous system* $\mathbf{A}\mathbf{x}_c = \mathbf{0}$ *is called a* **complementary solution** *and any solution of the nonhomogeneous system* $\mathbf{A}\mathbf{x} = \mathbf{b}$ *is called a* **particular solution**.

If $\mathbf{x}_{p_1}$ and $\mathbf{x}_{p_2}$ are two particular solutions then

$$\mathbf{A}\left(\mathbf{x}_{p_1} - \mathbf{x}_{p_2}\right) = \mathbf{A}\mathbf{x}_{p_1} - \mathbf{A}\mathbf{x}_{p_2} = \mathbf{b} - \mathbf{b} = \mathbf{0},$$

so that $\mathbf{x}_{p_1} - \mathbf{x}_{p_2}$ is a solution of the homogeneous system; thus we must have $\mathbf{x}_{p_1} - \mathbf{x}_{p_2}$ as a complementary solution. We may conclude that, when it exists, a particular solution is unique only to within the addition of a complementary solution. The general solution of the system $\mathbf{A}\mathbf{x} = \mathbf{b}$ can be written in the form

$$\mathbf{x} = \mathbf{x}_c + \mathbf{x}_p.$$

In words,

$$\text{general solution} = \text{complementary solution} + \text{particular solution}.$$

This decomposition of solutions will recur when we study linear differential equations. The easiest way to form this decomposition is to choose $\mathbf{x}_p$ to be that part of the solution without any arbitrary parameters.

Referring back to example 1.24, we had

$$\text{complementary solution} = \mathbf{x}_c = \alpha[-2; 1; 1],$$

$$\text{particular solution} = \mathbf{x}_p = [1; 3; 0],$$

$$\text{general solution} = \mathbf{x} = \mathbf{x}_c + \mathbf{x}_p = [-2\alpha + 1; \alpha + 3; \alpha].$$

DEFINITION 1.12 *If* **A** *is a complex* $n \times n$ *matrix with* $\mathrm{rank}(\mathbf{A}) = n$, *then* **A** *is said to be* **nonsingular**; *otherwise it is* **singular**.

From $\mathrm{rank}(\mathbf{A}) + \mathrm{null}(\mathbf{A}) = n$, we see that when **A** is nonsingular, $\mathbf{Ax} = \mathbf{b}$ is always consistent and has a unique solution because

$$\mathrm{null}(\mathbf{A}) = n - \mathrm{rank}(A) = n - n = 0 = \text{number of parameters in the solution.}$$

When **A** is nonsingular, Matlab can efficiently find the solution of $\mathbf{Ax} = \mathbf{b}$ by using the "back-division" operator, $\mathbf{x} = \mathbf{A} \backslash \mathbf{b}$.

We may use the concept of rank to determine the consistency of a nonhomogeneous system. Suppose the augmented matrix $[\mathbf{A}|\mathbf{b}]$ reduced to a row of zeros to the left of the vertical bar. Then we know the system was consistent only if the row of zeros extended across the vertical bar to the **b** part of the augmented matrix. Otherwise we'd have an equation of the form $0 = b' \neq 0$, which cannot be true. Therefore the row-reduced forms of **A** and $[\mathbf{A}|\mathbf{b}]$ had to have the same number of rows of zeros. This leads to the following result:

THEOREM 1.5 *The system* $\mathbf{Ax} = \mathbf{b}$ *is consistent if and only if*

$$\mathrm{rank}(\mathbf{A}) = \mathrm{rank}\left([\mathbf{A}|\mathbf{b}]\right).$$

□

This allows us to solve an inverse sort of problem, wherein we are asked to find all vectors **b** for which $\mathbf{Ax} = \mathbf{b}$ is consistent.

■ **EXAMPLE 1.26** When

$$\mathbf{A} = \begin{bmatrix} 1 & -2 & 1 \\ 2 & -3 & 1 \\ 1 & 0 & -1 \end{bmatrix}$$

for what vectors **b** is the system $\mathbf{Ax} = \mathbf{b}$ consistent?

Solution: Form the general augmented matrix.

$$[\mathbf{A}|\mathbf{b}] = \begin{bmatrix} 1 & -2 & 1 & a \\ 2 & -3 & 1 & b \\ 1 & 0 & -1 & c \end{bmatrix} \quad \begin{array}{l} \text{Pick (3) as the first} \\ \text{pivot row since it has} \\ \text{a zero in column 2.} \end{array}$$

$$\hookrightarrow \begin{array}{r} (3) \\ (1) - (3) \\ (2) - 2(3) \end{array} \begin{bmatrix} 1 & 0 & -1 & c \\ 0 & -2 & 2 & a - c \\ 0 & -3 & 3 & b - 2c \end{bmatrix}$$

$$\hookrightarrow \begin{array}{r} (1) \\ (2) \\ 3(2) - 2(3) \end{array} \begin{bmatrix} 1 & 0 & -1 & c \\ 0 & -2 & 2 & a - c \\ 0 & 0 & 0 & 3a - 2b + c \end{bmatrix}.$$

Therefore, the system will be consistent whenever $3a - 2b + c = 0$ for the column vector $\mathbf{b} = [a; b; c]$.   ■ ■ ■

By using problem 1.2.32, which says that the product $\mathbf{Ax}$ is a linear combination of the columns of $\mathbf{A}$, we could make the general statement: the system $\mathbf{Ax} = \mathbf{b}$ will be consistent if and only if $\mathbf{b}$ can be written as a linear combination of the columns of $\mathbf{A}$. Additional material on pivotal reduction and linear systems will be explored in the problems. Throughout a major portion of this book the solution of systems of linear equations will play a vital role.

If we return to the model of the framework in static equilibrium given in example 1.2, we find the augmented matrix is

$$
\left[
\begin{array}{cccccc|c}
1 & 0 & 0 & 1 & 0 & 0 & 0 \\
0 & 1 & 0 & 0 & 1 & 0 & 0 \\
0 & 0 & 0 & -1 & 0 & -\frac{4}{5} & 0 \\
0 & 0 & 1 & 0 & 0 & \frac{3}{5} & 0 \\
0 & 0 & 0 & 0 & 0 & \frac{4}{5} & -5 \\
0 & 0 & 0 & -1 & 0 & -\frac{3}{5} & 10
\end{array}
\right]
\hookrightarrow
\left[
\begin{array}{cccccc|c}
1 & 0 & 0 & 0 & 0 & 0 & -5 \\
0 & 1 & 0 & 0 & 0 & 0 & -\frac{25}{4} \\
0 & 0 & 1 & 0 & 0 & 0 & \frac{15}{4} \\
0 & 0 & 0 & 1 & 0 & 0 & 5 \\
0 & 0 & 0 & 0 & 1 & 0 & \frac{25}{4} \\
0 & 0 & 0 & 0 & 0 & 1 & -\frac{25}{4}
\end{array}
\right],
$$

from which we may conclude that $A_x = -5$, $A_y = -\frac{25}{4}$, $B_y = \frac{15}{4}$, $F_{AB} = 5$, $F_{AC} = \frac{25}{4}$, and $F_{BC} = -\frac{25}{4}$.

If we use the computer to row reduce the augmented matrix for the electrical circuit in example 1.2.1, we arrive at an unbelievably complicated expression involving E and the Z_k, $k = 1 : 10$. With the extreme simplification that all the impedances are equal to Z, you should verify that the unique solution is $I_1 = \frac{5E}{12Z}$, $I_2 = \frac{E}{4Z}$, $I_3 = \frac{E}{12Z}$, $I_4 = \frac{E}{24Z}$, and $I_5 = \frac{E}{24Z}$. Hand calculation of the general case would have been completely out of the question.

1.4.1 Exercise Set

1. Which of the following coefficient matrices are in rref? For each matrix that is in rref, give its nullity and write the most general form of the solution to the homogeneous system $\mathbf{Ax} = \mathbf{0}$.

(a)
$$
\left[
\begin{array}{ccccc}
1 & 0 & 2 & 1 & -1 \\
0 & 0 & 0 & 1 & 0 \\
0 & 0 & 0 & 0 & 2
\end{array}
\right]
$$

(b)
$$
\left[
\begin{array}{ccccc}
0 & 1 & 5 & 0 & 2 \\
0 & 0 & 0 & 1 & 1 \\
0 & 0 & 0 & 0 & 0 \\
0 & 0 & 0 & 0 & 0
\end{array}
\right]
$$

$$(c) \quad \begin{bmatrix} 1 & 0 & -3 & 0 & 5 \\ 0 & 1 & 2 & 0 & -2 \\ 0 & 0 & 0 & 1 & -1 \\ 0 & 0 & 0 & 0 & 0 \end{bmatrix}$$

$$(d) \quad \begin{bmatrix} 2 & 0 & 0 & 1 & 2 & 0 & 0 \\ 0 & 1 & 0 & 1 & 2 & 0 & 0 \\ 0 & 0 & 1 & 1 & 2 & 0 & 0 \\ 0 & 0 & 0 & 0 & 0 & 1 & 0 \\ 0 & 0 & 0 & 0 & 0 & 0 & 2 \end{bmatrix}$$

$$(e) \quad \begin{bmatrix} 1 & 0 & 0 & 2 & -1 & 0 & 0 \\ 0 & 1 & -3 & -2 & 4 & 0 & 0 \\ 0 & 0 & 0 & 0 & 0 & 1 & 0 \\ 0 & 0 & 0 & 0 & 0 & 0 & 1 \end{bmatrix}$$

2. List all possible row-reduced echelon forms of

    (a) a 2×3 coefficient matrix. [There are 7 cases.]

    (b) a 3×3 coefficient matrix. [There are 8 cases.]

    (c) a 3×4 coefficient matrix. [There are 15 cases.]

Find *all* possible solutions for each of the following linear systems that are consistent, writing the solutions to nonhomogeneous problems as a complementary plus a particular solution. Use either Matlab or a computer algebra system to find the rref of the augmented matrix.

3. $2x_1 + 2x_2 + x_3 + 4x_4 = 0$

4. $\quad 5x_1 + 2x_2 + 6x_3 = 0$
$$-2x_1 + x_2 + 3x_3 = 0$$

5. $\quad \begin{aligned} x_1 &+ 2x_2 &- 4x_3 &= 2 \\ x_2 &- 2x_3 &= -1 \\ x_3 &= 2 \end{aligned}$

6. $\quad \begin{aligned} x_1 &- 2x_2 &+ x_3 &- 4x_4 &= 1 \\ x_1 &+ 3x_2 &+ 7x_3 &+ 2x_4 &= 2 \\ x_1 &- 12x_2 &- 11x_3 &- 16x_4 &= -1 \end{aligned}$

7. $\quad \begin{aligned} 2x_1 + 2x_2 &- x_3 && + x_5 &= 0 \\ -x_1 - x_2 &+ 2x_3 &- 3x_4 &+ x_5 &= 0 \\ x_1 + x_2 &- 2x_3 && - x_5 &= 0 \\ & x_3 &+ x_4 &+ x_5 &= 0 \end{aligned}$

8. $\quad \begin{aligned} 3x_1 + 2x_2 &- x_3 &= -15 \\ 5x_1 + 3x_2 &+ 2x_3 &= 0 \\ 3x_1 + x_2 &+ 3x_3 &= 11 \\ 11x_1 + 7x_2 && = -30 \end{aligned}$

9. $\quad \begin{aligned} x_1 &- 2x_2 &+ x_3 &- 4x_4 &= 1 \\ x_1 &+ 3x_2 &+ 7x_3 &+ 2x_4 &= 2 \\ 2x_1 &+ x_2 &+ 8x_3 &- 2x_4 &= 3 \end{aligned}$

10. $\quad \begin{aligned} x_1 &- x_2 &+ x_3 &+ x_4 &= 1 \\ 2x_1 &- 2x_2 &- 3x_3 &- 3x_4 &= 17 \\ -x_1 &+ x_2 &+ 2x_3 &+ 2x_4 &= -10 \end{aligned}$

11.
$$\begin{aligned}
x_1 + x_2 - 2x_3 + x_4 + 3x_5 &= 1 \\
3x_1 + 2x_2 - 4x_3 - 3x_4 - 9x_5 &= 3 \\
2x_1 - x_2 + 2x_3 + 2x_4 + 6x_5 &= 2 \\
6x_1 + 2x_2 - 4x_3 &= 6 \\
2x_2 - 4x_3 - 6x_4 - 18x_5 &= 0
\end{aligned}$$

12.
$$\begin{aligned}
x_1 - x_3 + 2x_4 &= 3 \\
x_1 + x_2 + x_3 - x_4 &= 0 \\
- x_2 - 2x_3 + 3x_4 &= 3 \\
5x_1 + 2x_2 - x_3 + 4x_4 &= 9 \\
-x_1 + 2x_2 + 5x_3 - 8x_4 &= -9
\end{aligned}$$

13.
$$\begin{aligned}
x_1 + 2x_2 - x_3 + x_4 - 2x_5 &= 0 \,, \quad 2 \,, \quad 6 \\
2x_1 + 5x_2 - 3x_3 - x_4 + x_5 &= 0 \,, \quad -1 \,, \quad 7
\end{aligned}$$

14. $x_1 + x_2 = 1, \quad x_2 + x_3 - 1, \quad x_3 + x_4 = 1, \quad x_1 - x_2 + 3x_3 - 4x_4 = -1.$

15. For the system

$$\begin{aligned}
2x_1 + 2x_2 + 2x_3 - x_4 - 2x_5 &= a, \\
2x_1 + 2x_2 - 3x_3 - 13x_4 + 2x_5 &= b, \\
x_1 + x_2 - x_3 - 5x_4 + x_5 &= c, \\
x_1 + x_2 + x_3 + x_4 + x_5 &= d
\end{aligned}$$

   (a) Find a relation among a, b, c, d for which the system is consistent.

   (b) Put $\mathbf{b} = [1; 1; 1; 3]$ and write the general solution in terms of its complementary and particular parts.

16. For what values of k is the following system consistent?

$$\begin{aligned}
x_1 + 3x_2 + 2x_3 &= 4, \\
2x_1 + x_2 - x_3 &= 1, \\
3x_1 - 2x_2 + x_3 &= k.
\end{aligned}$$

17. Solve the system

$$\begin{aligned}
ax_1 + bx_2 + cx_3 &= 1, \\
a^2 x_1 + b^2 x_2 + c^2 x_3 &= 1, \\
a^3 x_1 + b^3 x_2 + c^3 x_3 &= 1,
\end{aligned}$$

   if $a, b,$ and c are distinct. Generalize this to the $n \times n$ case.

18. A matrix $\mathbf{A} \in \mathbb{C}^m_n$ is said to be of **full rank** if $\mathrm{rank}(\mathbf{A}) = n$.

   (a) Give four examples of nonsquare matrices that are of full rank.

   (b) Argue that if $\mathbf{A}$ is of full rank, then $\mathbf{A}^H \mathbf{A}$ must be nonsingular.

19. If a, b, c, and d are known solve for w, x, y, and z:

$$\begin{aligned}
w + ax + a^2y + a^3z + a^4 &= 1, \\
w + bx + b^2y + b^3z + b^4 &= 1, \\
w + cx + c^2y + c^3z + c^4 &= 1, \\
w + dx + d^2y + d^3z + d^4 &= 1.
\end{aligned}$$

20. Use the Kirchhoff Voltage Law to write the equations that relate the loop currents in the circuit in Figure 1.7.

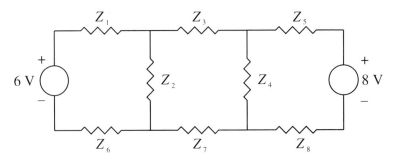

Fig. 1.7

(a) Find the voltage across Z_2, if $Z_1 = Z_2 = Z_3 = Z_5 = Z_6 = Z_7 = Z_8 = 1\Omega$ and $Z_2 = Z_4 = (2 + i)\Omega$.

(b) Find the voltages across Z_3 and Z_7 if they are 5Ω resistors and all the other elements have impedance 2Ω.

(c) Find the loop currents if $Z_k = k\Omega$, $k = 1 : 8$.

21. Find the value of the current through each of the impedances for the circuit in Figure 1.8 if $Z_1 = Z_2 = Z_3 = Z_4 = 4 + 3i$, $Z_5 = Z_6 = Z_7 = 2i$, and $Z_8 = Z_9 = 3 + 2i$.

22. The steady state temperature distribution in the interior of a region insulated from its exterior satisfies what is called "Laplace's equation." If we discretize the region, this equation translates into the simple requirement that the temperature at any given interior point is the average of the temperatures of all the points nearest to it. Suppose that a pipe has the following rectangular shape and boundary temperatures shown in Figure 1.9(a). Find the temperatures at all interior points.

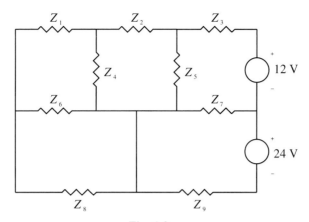

Fig. 1.8

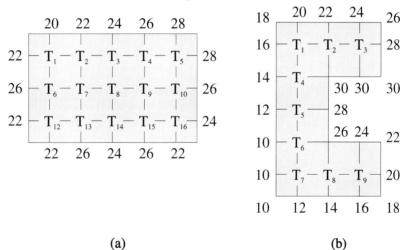

(a)   (b)

Fig. 1.9

23. Find the steady state heat distribution at the interior points for the region shown in Figure 1.9(b).

24. Classify all systems for which $\mathbf{x} = [\alpha - 2; \alpha + \beta + 1; \alpha; 2\beta - 3; \beta; \beta]$ for $\alpha, \beta \in \mathbb{C}$ is a general solution.

The function given by

$$w = f(z) = \frac{az + b}{cz + d}$$

is called a **Möbius**, or **bilinear transformation**, of the complex plane into itself. Find the Möbius transformations that map the following z triples into the given w triples. [Hint: Write $az + b - w(cz + d) = 0$, and solve for a, b, c, d.]

25. $z : 0, 1, -1 \;\rightarrow\; w : 0, -1, 1$ 26. $z : 0, 1, 2 \;\rightarrow\; w : 0, i, 1$

27. $z : 1, i, 0 \ \rightarrow \ w : 1, 2, 0$

28. $z : 1, i, -1 \ \rightarrow \ w : -1, i, 1$

29. Under what conditions do the n lines $a_k x + b_k y = c_k$, $k = 1 : n$, intersect in a single point?

30. Show that the matrix outer product $\mathbf{ab}^T$, sometimes called a **dyad**, is of rank one whenever $\mathbf{a}$ and $\mathbf{b}$ are n component column vectors. Further, show that any square rank one matrix can be written this way.

31. By generating several 5×5 matrices of ranks $0 : 5$, test the truth of each of the following statements. Be careful, just because it is true for your example doesn't guarantee it is always true. But if it's false for your example, that *does* prove the statement's falsity.

   (a) $\text{rank}(\mathbf{A} + \mathbf{B}) = \min\{\text{rank}(\mathbf{A}), \text{rank}(\mathbf{B})\}$

   (b) $\text{rank}(\mathbf{A} + \mathbf{B}) \leq \min\{\text{rank}(\mathbf{A}), \text{rank}(\mathbf{B})\}$

   (c) $\text{rank}(\mathbf{AB}) = \min\{\text{rank}(\mathbf{A}), \text{rank}(\mathbf{B})\}$

   (d) $\text{rank}(\mathbf{AB}) \leq \min\{\text{rank}(\mathbf{A}), \text{rank}(\mathbf{B})\}$

32. Computer solutions of linear equations can be very sensitive to deviations in the coefficients. Such systems are said to be **ill-conditioned**. Even arbitrarily small changes in a single coefficient can radically alter a system, changing its rank. To see this, solve the system

$$\begin{aligned}
(1 - 10^{-n}) x_1 & - & x_2 & + & x_3 & - & x_4 & = & -3, \\
x_1 & - & x_2 & + & x_3 & - & x_4 & = & -2, \\
x_1 & - & x_2 & & & & & = & -1, \\
x_1 & & & & & - & x_4 & = & -3.
\end{aligned}$$

Show that the unperturbed system (i.e.,without the 10^{-n}) is inconsistent but the perturbed system has a solution that grows as the perturbation decreases.

Find all square matrices that commute with the given matrices.

33. $\begin{bmatrix} 0 & 0 & 1 \\ 0 & 1 & 0 \\ 1 & 0 & 0 \end{bmatrix}$

34. $\begin{bmatrix} 1 & 0 & 1 \\ 0 & 1 & 0 \\ 1 & 0 & 1 \end{bmatrix}$

35. $\begin{bmatrix} a & 0 & c \\ 0 & e & 0 \\ c & 0 & a \end{bmatrix}$.

Find all 3×2 matrices $\mathbf{G}$ for which $\mathbf{AGA} = \mathbf{A}$ if

36. $\mathbf{A} = \begin{bmatrix} 1 & 0 & 1 \\ 0 & 1 & 0 \end{bmatrix}$

37. $\mathbf{A} = \begin{bmatrix} 1 & -1 & 0 \\ 0 & 1 & -1 \end{bmatrix}$

1.5 INVERSES

To solve the single consistent equation $ax = b$, we simply multiply both sides by $1/a = a^{-1}$, the reciprocal or inverse of a. This idea can be extended to some matrix systems $\mathbf{Ax} = \mathbf{b}$, so that their solutions can be written in the form $\mathbf{x} = \mathbf{A}^{-1}\mathbf{b}$. Surely we are not interested in inconsistent systems since they won't have solutions.

1.5.1 Invertible Square Matrices

DEFINITION 1.13 *If for $\mathbf{A} \in \mathbb{C}_n^n$ there is a matrix $\mathbf{B} \in \mathbb{C}_n^n$ such that*

$$\mathbf{BA} = \mathbf{I}_n \quad and \quad \mathbf{AB} = \mathbf{I}_n,$$

then $\mathbf{A}$ is said to be **invertible** *with* **inverse** $\mathbf{B}$. *We'll usually write $\mathbf{B} = \mathbf{A}^{-1}$ (read $\mathbf{A}$-inverse).*

If $\mathbf{A}$ has an inverse it must be unique, i.e., containing no parameters. To see that this is so, suppose $\mathbf{B}$ and $\mathbf{C}$ are inverses of $\mathbf{A}$; then

$$\mathbf{B} = \mathbf{BI} = \mathbf{B}(\mathbf{AC}) = (\mathbf{BA})\mathbf{C} = \mathbf{IC} = \mathbf{C}.$$

Verifying that a matrix is an inverse of another is merely a matter of applying the definition.

■ **EXAMPLE 1.27** Show that $\mathbf{B}$ is the inverse of $\mathbf{A}$ if

$$\mathbf{A} = \begin{bmatrix} 1 & 1 & 1 \\ 1 & 2 & 1 \\ 1 & 1 & 2 \end{bmatrix} \quad and \quad \mathbf{B} = \begin{bmatrix} 3 & -1 & -1 \\ -1 & 1 & 0 \\ -1 & 0 & 1 \end{bmatrix}.$$

Solution: We must form both products $\mathbf{AB}$ and $\mathbf{BA}$ and be sure we get the identity:

$$\mathbf{AB} = \begin{bmatrix} 1 & 1 & 1 \\ 1 & 2 & 1 \\ 1 & 1 & 2 \end{bmatrix} \begin{bmatrix} 3 & -1 & -1 \\ -1 & 1 & 0 \\ -1 & 0 & 1 \end{bmatrix} = \begin{bmatrix} 1 & 0 & 0 \\ 0 & 1 & 0 \\ 0 & 0 & 1 \end{bmatrix},$$

$$\mathbf{BA} = \begin{bmatrix} 3 & -1 & -1 \\ -1 & 1 & 0 \\ -1 & 0 & 1 \end{bmatrix} \begin{bmatrix} 1 & 1 & 1 \\ 1 & 2 & 1 \\ 1 & 1 & 2 \end{bmatrix} = \begin{bmatrix} 1 & 0 & 0 \\ 0 & 1 & 0 \\ 0 & 0 & 1 \end{bmatrix}.$$

Thus $\mathbf{B}$ is the inverse of $\mathbf{A}$. ■ ■ ■

■ **EXAMPLE 1.28** More general cases can be handled in the same way. If $\mathbf{u}$ is a real $n \times 1$ vector for which $\|\mathbf{u}\|^2 = \mathbf{u}^T\mathbf{u} = 1$, then $\mathbf{P} = \mathbf{I} - 2\mathbf{uu}^T$ is called a **Householder matrix**. Show that $\mathbf{P}$ is its own inverse.

Solution: Again, all we need do is apply the definition.

$$\begin{aligned} \mathbf{PP} &= \left(\mathbf{I} - 2\mathbf{uu}^T\right)\left(\mathbf{I} - 2\mathbf{uu}^T\right) \\ &= \mathbf{I}^2 - 2\mathbf{uu}^T - 2\mathbf{uu}^T + 4\left(\mathbf{uu}^T\right)\left(\mathbf{uu}^T\right) \\ &= \mathbf{I} - 4\mathbf{uu}^T + 4\mathbf{u}\left(\mathbf{u}^T\mathbf{u}\right)\mathbf{u}^T \\ &= \mathbf{I} - 4\mathbf{uu}^T + 4\mathbf{u}(1)\mathbf{u}^T = \mathbf{I}. \end{aligned}$$

Notice the use (once again) of the associativity of matrix multiplication. ■ ■ ■

Several properties of the inverse follow immediately.

THEOREM 1.6 *If* **A** *and* **B** *are invertible, then*

(Inv1) $\left(\mathbf{A}^{-1}\right)^{-1} = \mathbf{A}$;

(Inv2) $\left(k\mathbf{A}\right)^{-1} = \frac{1}{k}\mathbf{A}^{-1}$ *when* $k \neq 0$;

(Inv3) $\left(\mathbf{AB}\right)^{-1} = \mathbf{B}^{-1}\mathbf{A}^{-1}$;

(Inv4) $\left(\mathbf{A}^{T}\right)^{-1} = \left(\mathbf{A}^{-1}\right)^{T}$ *and* $\left(\mathbf{A}^{H}\right)^{-1} = \left(\mathbf{A}^{-1}\right)^{H}$.

Proof   The first is a consequence of the defining equations

$$\mathbf{A}\mathbf{A}^{-1} = \mathbf{I} = \mathbf{A}^{-1}\mathbf{A}.$$

Thus if $\mathbf{A}^{-1}$ is the inverse of $\mathbf{A}$, then $\mathbf{A}$ is the inverse of $\mathbf{A}^{-1}$. The second is obvious, and the third follows from the associative property of matrix multiplication:

$$\left(\mathbf{AB}\right)\left(\mathbf{B}^{-1}\mathbf{A}^{-1}\right) = \mathbf{A}\left(\mathbf{BB}^{-1}\right)\mathbf{A}^{-1} = \mathbf{AIA}^{-1} = \mathbf{AA}^{-1} = \mathbf{I},$$
$$\left(\mathbf{B}^{-1}\mathbf{A}^{-1}\right)\left(\mathbf{AB}\right) = \mathbf{B}^{-1}\left(\mathbf{A}^{-1}\mathbf{A}\right)\mathbf{B} = \mathbf{B}^{-1}\mathbf{IB} = \mathbf{B}^{-1}\mathbf{B} = \mathbf{I}.$$

(Inv3) should be recognized in terms of input and output reversal just as we saw in transposition and Hermitian conjugation. As for (Inv4),

$$\mathbf{A}^{T}\left(\mathbf{A}^{T}\right)^{-1} = \left[\left(\mathbf{A}^{-1}\right)\mathbf{A}\right]^{T} = \left[\mathbf{I}\right]^{T} = \mathbf{I} \quad \Rightarrow \quad \left(\mathbf{A}^{T}\right)^{-1} = \left(\mathbf{A}^{-1}\right)^{T},$$

and the result for Hermitian conjugation follows similarly.   □

No simple relation holds for the inverse of a sum. Indeed, a sum of invertible matrices need not be invertible; e.g., $\mathbf{A} + (-\mathbf{A}) = \mathbf{0}$ is not invertible. The Matlab function $\mathbf{inv}(\mathbf{A})$ efficiently returns the inverse of $\mathbf{A}$. Returning to a linear system $\mathbf{Ax} = \mathbf{b}$, if $\mathbf{A}$ is invertible we can multiply both sides by $\mathbf{A}^{-1}$ to get

$$\mathbf{A}^{-1}(\mathbf{Ax}) = (\mathbf{A}^{-1}\mathbf{A})\mathbf{x} = \mathbf{Ix} \quad \Rightarrow \quad \mathbf{x} = \mathbf{A}^{-1}\mathbf{b}.$$

When using Matlab, this would be entered as $\mathbf{x} = \mathbf{inv}(\mathbf{A}) * \mathbf{b}$. As was mentioned in the last section, a more efficient computational scheme is available by using the backdivision notation $\mathbf{x} = \mathbf{A}\backslash\mathbf{b}$. The latter will involve many fewer operations than the former. More detail will be given in Section 1.7.

1.5.2 Elementary Matrices

To determine when a matrix is invertible let's return to pivotal reduction, but from a different viewpoint. Let $e(\mathbf{A})$ be the matrix resulting from a single elementary row operation applied to $\mathbf{A}$. Applying a sequence of N such operations, $\mathbf{A}$ may be reduced to its echelon form $\mathbf{R}$ via

$$e_N\left(e_{N-1}\left(\cdots\left(e_1(\mathbf{A})\right)\cdots\right)\right) = \mathbf{R}.$$

Each of the elementary row operations is invertible and can be put in the form of a matrix multiplication. We can show that

$$e(\mathbf{A}) = e(\mathbf{I}\mathbf{A}) = e(\mathbf{I})\mathbf{A},$$

where $e(\mathbf{I}) =: \mathbf{E}$ is the result of applying an elementary row operation to the identity and is defined to be an **elementary matrix**, i.e., a matrix obtained from the identity by the application of a *single* elementary row operation.

Suppose $e(\cdot)$ consists of multiplying the first row by the nonzero constant k. Writing $\mathbf{A}$ in terms of its row vectors, we have

$$e(\mathbf{A}) = e\left(\begin{bmatrix} \mathbf{row}_1(\mathbf{A}) \\ \mathbf{row}_2(\mathbf{A}) \\ \vdots \\ \mathbf{row}_n(\mathbf{A}) \end{bmatrix}\right) = \begin{bmatrix} k\,\mathbf{row}_1(\mathbf{A}) \\ \mathbf{row}_2(\mathbf{A}) \\ \vdots \\ \mathbf{row}_n(\mathbf{A}) \end{bmatrix}$$

and

$$e(\mathbf{I})\mathbf{A} = \begin{bmatrix} k & 0 & \cdots & 0 \\ 0 & 1 & \ddots & \vdots \\ \vdots & \ddots & \ddots & 0 \\ 0 & \cdots & 0 & 1 \end{bmatrix} \begin{bmatrix} \mathbf{row}_1(\mathbf{A}) \\ \mathbf{row}_2(\mathbf{A}) \\ \vdots \\ \mathbf{row}_n(\mathbf{A}) \end{bmatrix} = \begin{bmatrix} k\,\mathbf{row}_1(\mathbf{A}) \\ \mathbf{row}_2(\mathbf{A}) \\ \vdots \\ \mathbf{row}_n(\mathbf{A}) \end{bmatrix}.$$

Similarly, if $e(\cdot)$ replaces the first row by the first row plus k times the second, then

$$e(\mathbf{A}) = e\left(\begin{bmatrix} \mathbf{row}_1(\mathbf{A}) \\ \mathbf{row}_2(\mathbf{A}) \\ \vdots \\ \mathbf{row}_n(\mathbf{A}) \end{bmatrix}\right) = \begin{bmatrix} \mathbf{row}_1(\mathbf{A}) + k\,\mathbf{row}_2(\mathbf{A}) \\ \mathbf{row}_2(\mathbf{A}) \\ \vdots \\ \mathbf{row}_n(\mathbf{A}) \end{bmatrix}$$

and

$$e(\mathbf{I})\mathbf{A} = \begin{bmatrix} 1 & k & \cdots & 0 \\ 0 & 1 & \ddots & \vdots \\ \vdots & \ddots & \ddots & 0 \\ 0 & \cdots & 0 & 1 \end{bmatrix} \begin{bmatrix} \mathbf{row}_1(\mathbf{A}) \\ \mathbf{row}_2(\mathbf{A}) \\ \vdots \\ \mathbf{row}_n(\mathbf{A}) \end{bmatrix} = \begin{bmatrix} \mathbf{row}_1(\mathbf{A}) + k\,\mathbf{row}_2(A) \\ \mathbf{row}_2(\mathbf{A}) \\ \vdots \\ \mathbf{row}_n(\mathbf{A}) \end{bmatrix}.$$

The interchange of two rows is treated in a similar fashion.

The echelon form can now be written as the product

$$\mathbf{E}_N\mathbf{E}_{N-1}\cdots\mathbf{E}_2\mathbf{E}_1\mathbf{A} = \mathbf{R}. \tag{1.5}$$

Let's see how this can be done with a simple numerical example.

■ **EXAMPLE 1.29**   Write the following matrix as a product of elementary matrices and verify the result:

$$\mathbf{A} = \begin{bmatrix} 1 & -2 & -3 \\ -3 & 5 & 7 \\ 3 & 1 & 5 \end{bmatrix}.$$

Solution: Start by reducing $\mathbf{A}$:

$$\mathbf{A} \hookrightarrow \begin{matrix} (1) \\ (2)+3(1) \\ (3)-3(1) \end{matrix} \begin{bmatrix} 1 & -2 & -3 \\ 0 & -1 & -2 \\ 0 & 7 & 14 \end{bmatrix} \hookrightarrow \begin{matrix} (1)-2(2) \\ -(2) \\ (3)+7(2) \end{matrix} \begin{bmatrix} 1 & 0 & 1 \\ 0 & 1 & 2 \\ 0 & 0 & 0 \end{bmatrix}.$$

Now that we have $\mathbf{A}$ in echelon form we can go back and count the number of elementary row operations used; that will be the number of elementary matrices we will need in the factorization. Altogether there are five operations. Listing the elementary matrices with their corresponding operations, we see that

$$\mathbf{E}_1 = \begin{bmatrix} 1 & 0 & 0 \\ 3 & 1 & 0 \\ 0 & 0 & 1 \end{bmatrix} \begin{matrix} (1) \\ (2)+3(1) \, ; \\ (3) \end{matrix} \qquad \mathbf{E}_2 = \begin{bmatrix} 1 & 0 & 0 \\ 0 & 1 & 0 \\ -3 & 0 & 1 \end{bmatrix} \begin{matrix} (1) \\ (2) \, ; \\ (3)-3(1) \end{matrix}$$

$$\mathbf{E}_3 = \begin{bmatrix} 1 & -2 & 0 \\ 0 & 1 & 0 \\ 0 & 0 & 1 \end{bmatrix} \begin{matrix} (1)-2(2) \\ (2) \, ; \\ (3) \end{matrix} \qquad \mathbf{E}_4 = \begin{bmatrix} 1 & 0 & 0 \\ 0 & -1 & 0 \\ 0 & 0 & 1 \end{bmatrix} \begin{matrix} (1) \\ -(2) \, ; \\ (3) \end{matrix}$$

$$\mathbf{E}_5 = \begin{bmatrix} 1 & 0 & 0 \\ 0 & 1 & 0 \\ 0 & 7 & 1 \end{bmatrix} \begin{matrix} (1) \\ (2) \, . \\ (3)+7(2) \end{matrix}$$

It is worth noting that since both $\mathbf{E}_1$ and $\mathbf{E}_2$ were part of the reduction that swept out different rows of the first column, they commute $\mathbf{E}_1\mathbf{E}_2 = \mathbf{E}_2\mathbf{E}_1$. Similarly for $\mathbf{E}_3$, $\mathbf{E}_4$, and $\mathbf{E}_5$. The required factorization is

$$\begin{bmatrix} 1 & 0 & 0 \\ 0 & 1 & 0 \\ 0 & 7 & 1 \end{bmatrix} \begin{bmatrix} 1 & 0 & 0 \\ 0 & -1 & 0 \\ 0 & 0 & 1 \end{bmatrix} \begin{bmatrix} 1 & -2 & 0 \\ 0 & 1 & 0 \\ 0 & 0 & 1 \end{bmatrix}$$

$$\times \begin{bmatrix} 1 & 0 & 0 \\ 0 & 1 & 0 \\ -3 & 0 & 1 \end{bmatrix} \begin{bmatrix} 1 & 0 & 0 \\ 3 & 1 & 0 \\ 0 & 0 & 1 \end{bmatrix} \begin{bmatrix} 1 & -2 & -3 \\ -3 & 5 & 7 \\ 3 & 1 & 5 \end{bmatrix} = \begin{bmatrix} 1 & 0 & 1 \\ 0 & 1 & 2 \\ 0 & 0 & 0 \end{bmatrix}$$

It will be left to the reader to verify that this is a valid decomposition.   ■ ■ ■

If $\text{rank}(\mathbf{A}) = n$, then $\text{rref}(\mathbf{A}) = \mathbf{R} = \mathbf{I}$ and $\mathbf{E}_N \mathbf{E}_{N-1} \cdots \mathbf{E}_1 \mathbf{A} = \mathbf{I}$, so that by definition of $\mathbf{A}^{-1}$, equation (1.5) allows us to write

$$\mathbf{A}^{-1} = \mathbf{E}_N \mathbf{E}_{N-1} \cdots \mathbf{E}_1.$$

If $\text{rank}(\mathbf{A}) < n$ then $\mathbf{R}$ has a row of zeros. Because the product $\mathbf{A}^{-1}\mathbf{A}$ cannot have rank greater than $\text{rank}(\mathbf{A})$ and because $\text{rank}(\mathbf{I}) = n$, the equation $\mathbf{A}^{-1}\mathbf{A} = \mathbf{I}$ cannot be valid. Therefore $\mathbf{A}$ will be invertible if and only if it is nonsingular.

Since we know that

$$\mathbf{A}^{-1} = \mathbf{E}_N \mathbf{E}_{N-1} \cdots \mathbf{E}_1 = e_N\left(e_{N-1}\left(\cdots e_2\left(e_1(\mathbf{I})\right)\cdots\right)\right),$$

we have an immediate computational scheme for finding $\mathbf{A}^{-1}$. The sequence $e_2, e_2, \ldots, e_N$ of elementary row operations is exactly the sequence that reduces $\mathbf{A}$ to the identity, its echelon form when nonsingular. The same sequence that is applied to reduce $\mathbf{A}$ can be applied to $\mathbf{I}$ to generate $\mathbf{A}^{-1}$. Thus, we should augment $\mathbf{I}$ to $\mathbf{A}$ to form $[\mathbf{A}\,|\mathbf{I}]$ and reduce it by selecting our pivots as we would for reducing $\mathbf{A}$. In particular,

$$e_N\left(e_{N-1}\left(\cdots e_2\left(e_1\left([\mathbf{A}|\mathbf{I}]\right)\right)\cdots\right)\right) = \left[\mathbf{I}|\mathbf{A}^{-1}\right].$$

Schematically we could write this as $[\mathbf{A}|\mathbf{I}] \hookrightarrow \left[\mathbf{I}|\mathbf{A}^{-1}\right]$, where the hooked arrow indicates pivotal reduction has occurred, in this case to row-reduced echelon form.

■ **EXAMPLE 1.30** Find the inverse of the general 2×2 matrix,

$$\mathbf{A} = \begin{bmatrix} a & b \\ c & d \end{bmatrix}.$$

Solution: Form the augmented matrix and row-reduce it:

$$[\mathbf{A}\,|\mathbf{I}] = \left[\begin{array}{cc|cc} a & b & 1 & 0 \\ c & d & 0 & 1 \end{array}\right] \hookrightarrow \begin{array}{c} (1) \\ a(2) - c(1) \end{array} \left[\begin{array}{cc|cc} a & b & 1 & 0 \\ 0 & ad-bc & -c & a \end{array}\right].$$

If $ad - bc \neq 0$, then $\text{rank}(\mathbf{A}) = 2$ and $\mathbf{A}$ will be nonsingular, hence invertible.

$$\hookrightarrow \begin{array}{c} (ad-bc)(1) - b(2) \\ (2) \end{array} \left[\begin{array}{cc|cc} a(ad-bc) & 0 & ad & -ab \\ 0 & ad-bc & -c & a \end{array}\right]$$

$$\hookrightarrow \begin{array}{c} \frac{1}{a}(1) \\ (2) \end{array} \left[\begin{array}{cc|cc} ad-bc & 0 & d & -b \\ 0 & ad-bc & -c & a \end{array}\right] \quad \text{when } a \neq 0.$$

From this we see that $\mathbf{A}$ will be invertible if and only if $ad - bc \neq 0$. Dividing by $ad - bc$ we have

$$\begin{bmatrix} a & b \\ c & d \end{bmatrix}^{-1} = \frac{1}{ad-bc}\begin{bmatrix} d & -b \\ -c & a \end{bmatrix}, \qquad \begin{array}{l} \text{which is a very} \\ \text{useful result.} \end{array}$$

Notice: At the third stage we used the operation $(1)/a$, which would be undefined if $a = 0$. In that case, we could not have used (1) as the first pivot and an alternative reduction would have been employed. Nevertheless, the formula for the inverse remains unchanged. ■ ■ ■

Now to something more numerical.

■ **EXAMPLE 1.31** Find the inverse of

$$\mathbf{B} = \begin{bmatrix} 1 & 2 & 3 \\ 2 & 3 & 5 \\ 0 & 1 & 2 \end{bmatrix}.$$

Solution:

$$[\mathbf{B}\,|\,\mathbf{I}] = \begin{bmatrix} 1 & 2 & 3 & | & 1 & 0 & 0 \\ 2 & 3 & 5 & | & 0 & 1 & 0 \\ 0 & 1 & 2 & | & 0 & 0 & 1 \end{bmatrix} \hookrightarrow \begin{matrix} (1) \\ (2)-2(1) \\ (3) \end{matrix} \begin{bmatrix} 1 & 2 & 3 & | & 1 & 0 & 0 \\ 0 & -1 & -1 & | & -2 & 1 & 0 \\ 0 & 1 & 2 & | & 0 & 0 & 1 \end{bmatrix}$$

$$\hookrightarrow \begin{matrix} (1)+2(2) \\ -(2) \\ (3)+(2) \end{matrix} \begin{bmatrix} 1 & 0 & 1 & | & -3 & 2 & 0 \\ 0 & 1 & 1 & | & 2 & -1 & 0 \\ 0 & 0 & 1 & | & -2 & 1 & 1 \end{bmatrix}$$

$$\hookrightarrow \begin{matrix} (1)-(3) \\ (2)-(3) \\ (3) \end{matrix} \begin{bmatrix} 1 & 0 & 0 & | & -1 & 1 & -1 \\ 0 & 1 & 0 & | & 4 & -2 & -1 \\ 0 & 0 & 1 & | & -2 & 1 & 1 \end{bmatrix}$$

$$\Rightarrow \begin{bmatrix} 1 & 2 & 3 \\ 2 & 3 & 5 \\ 0 & 1 & 2 \end{bmatrix}^{-1} = \begin{bmatrix} -1 & 1 & -1 \\ 4 & -2 & -1 \\ -2 & 1 & 1 \end{bmatrix}.$$

It's a good idea to multiply these together to verify that their product is indeed the identity. That will be left to the reader. ■ ■ ■

Of course, most matrices do not have such numerically simple inverses. If you generate a random matrix—the Matlab command is $\mathbf{A} = \mathbf{rand}(n)$—and find its inverse using the command $\mathbf{inv}(\mathbf{A})$, you will see that the entries need not be integers. Also, most randomly generated square matrices will be nonsingular.

1.5.3 Implications of Invertibility

Returning to the system of linear equations $\mathbf{Ax} = \mathbf{b}$, if $\mathbf{A}$ is nonsingular then premultiplying by $\mathbf{A}^{-1}$ we found

$$\mathbf{A}^{-1}\mathbf{Ax} = \mathbf{A}^{-1}\mathbf{b} \quad \Rightarrow \quad \mathbf{x} = \mathbf{A}^{-1}\mathbf{b}$$

to be the unique solution. If we have $\mathbf{b} = \mathbf{0}$ for the homogeneous system then

$$\mathbf{x} = \mathbf{A}^{-1}\mathbf{0} = \mathbf{0}$$

is the unique solution; i.e., the following is true.

THEOREM 1.7 *If* **A** *is nonsingular then the homogeneous system* $\mathbf{Ax} = \mathbf{0}$ *has* only *the trivial solution* $\mathbf{x} = \mathbf{0}$. □

Thus we see that nonsingularity and invertibility are one and the same.

Many of the results of the last two sections can be summarized by the following theorem.

THEOREM 1.8 *If* $\mathbf{A} \in \mathbb{C}_n^n$, *the following statements are equivalent (that means that if any one of these statements is true, all of the others are also true):*

(a) $\text{rank}(\mathbf{A}) = n$.

(b) $\text{null}(\mathbf{A}) = 0$.

(c) **A** *is row reducible to* $\mathbf{I}_n$.

(d) **A** *can be written as the product of elementary matrices.*

(e) **A** *is invertible.*

(f) *The system* $\mathbf{Ax} = \mathbf{0}$ *has only the trivial solution* $\mathbf{x} = \mathbf{0}$.

(g) *The system* $\mathbf{Ax} = \mathbf{b}$ *is consistent and has a unique solution for* all $\mathbf{b} \in \mathbb{C}^n$.

Proof To prove all these are equivalent we only need prove the following chain of implications:

$$(a) \Rightarrow (b) \Rightarrow (c) \Rightarrow (d) \Rightarrow (e) \Rightarrow (f) \Rightarrow (g) \Rightarrow (a).$$

If $\text{rank}(\mathbf{A}) = n$, then **A** has n leading entries and no zero rows. Hence, $\text{null}(\mathbf{A}) = 0$. Since all leading entries are 1's and there are no rows of 0's, **A** must reduce to $\mathbf{I}_n$. Since we know that **A** can be written as a product of elementary matrices times its echelon form, which in this case is $\mathbf{I}_n$, **A** can be written as a product of elementary matrices alone. Because it is the product of invertible matrices, it too is invertible. Since **A** is invertible, the system $\mathbf{Ax} = \mathbf{0}$ has the unique solution $\mathbf{x} = \mathbf{A}^{-1}\mathbf{0} = \mathbf{0}$. Similarly, $\mathbf{Ax} = \mathbf{b}$ is consistent with unique solution $\mathbf{x} = \mathbf{A}^{-1}\mathbf{b}$, for any column vector **b**. Since the system is consistent for all $\mathbf{b} \in \mathbb{C}^n$, there are no rows of zeros in the echelon form of **A**, so that $\text{rank}(\mathbf{A}) = n$. □

This theorem is often rephrased in terms of the so-called **Fredholm alternative**:

THEOREM 1.9 *If* $\mathbf{A} \in \mathbb{C}_n^n$, *then either (a)* $\mathbf{Ax} = \mathbf{0}$ *has a nontrivial solution or (b)* $\mathbf{Ax} = \mathbf{b}$ *has a unique solution for all* $\mathbf{b} \in \mathbb{C}^n$, *but not both.* □

1.5.4   Inverses of Special Matrices

Nonsingular diagonal matrices are easy to invert:

$$(\mathbf{diag}(d_1, d_2, \ldots, d_n)) = \mathbf{diag}(d_1^{-1}, d_2^{-1}, \ldots, d_n^{-1}),$$

because $d_k \neq 0$ for $k = 1 : n$, when the matrix is nonsingular.

There are many other special classes of matrices that have very simple inverses.

DEFINITION 1.14   *If $\mathbf{A}$ is nonsingular, then:*

(a) $\mathbf{A}$ *is* **unitary** *if and only if $\mathbf{A}^{-1} = \mathbf{A}^H$.*

(b) $\mathbf{A}$ *is* **orthogonal** *if and only if $\mathbf{A}^{-1} = \mathbf{A}^T$.*

(c) $\mathbf{A}$ *is an* **involution** *if and only if $\mathbf{A}^{-1} = \mathbf{A}$.*

Clearly, $\mathbf{I}_n$ is unitary, orthogonal, and an involution.

■ **EXAMPLE 1.32**

(a) $\mathbf{B} = \frac{1}{\sqrt{2}} \begin{bmatrix} 1 & i \\ i & 1 \end{bmatrix}$ is unitary because

$$\mathbf{BB}^H = \frac{1}{\sqrt{2}} \begin{bmatrix} 1 & i \\ i & 1 \end{bmatrix} \frac{1}{\sqrt{2}} \begin{bmatrix} 1 & -i \\ -i & 1 \end{bmatrix} = \frac{1}{2} \begin{bmatrix} 1 - i^2 & 0 \\ 0 & 1 - i^2 \end{bmatrix} = \begin{bmatrix} 1 & 0 \\ 0 & 1 \end{bmatrix}.$$

(b) $\mathbf{C} = \begin{bmatrix} \cos\theta & \sin\theta \\ -\sin\theta & \cos\theta \end{bmatrix}$ is orthogonal for any θ because

$$\begin{aligned}
\mathbf{CC}^T &= \begin{bmatrix} \cos\theta & \sin\theta \\ -\sin\theta & \cos\theta \end{bmatrix} \begin{bmatrix} \cos\theta & -\sin\theta \\ \sin\theta & \cos\theta \end{bmatrix} \\
&= \begin{bmatrix} \cos^2\theta + \sin^2\theta & -\cos\theta\sin\theta + \sin\theta\cos\theta \\ -\sin\theta\cos\theta + \cos\theta\sin\theta & \cos^2\theta + \sin^2\theta \end{bmatrix} = \mathbf{I}.
\end{aligned}$$

(c) $\mathbf{J} = \begin{bmatrix} \mathbf{0} & \mathbf{I} \\ \mathbf{I} & \mathbf{0} \end{bmatrix}$ is an involution because

$$\mathbf{J}^2 = \begin{bmatrix} \mathbf{0} & \mathbf{I} \\ \mathbf{I} & \mathbf{0} \end{bmatrix} \begin{bmatrix} \mathbf{0} & \mathbf{I} \\ \mathbf{I} & \mathbf{0} \end{bmatrix} = \begin{bmatrix} \mathbf{0}^2 + \mathbf{I}^2 & \mathbf{I0} + \mathbf{0I} \\ \mathbf{0I} + \mathbf{I0} & \mathbf{I}^2 + \mathbf{0}^2 \end{bmatrix} = \mathbf{I}.$$

■ ■ ■

1.5.5 A Matrix Model for Two-Port Networks

Within any electrical system Ohm's law can be generalized to a matrix form

$$\mathbf{E} = \mathbf{ZI},$$

where $\mathbf{E}$ is the column vector of voltages, $\mathbf{I}$ is the column vector of currents, and $\mathbf{Z}$ is the **impedance matrix** of the system. When there is an AC source driving the system, the time dependence is $e^{i\omega t}$, where $f = \omega/2\pi$ is the **frequency** of the current. Within the simple RLC circuit, we have scalar quantities and the complex impedance is defined in terms of the inductance L, the resistance R, and the capacitance C as

$$Z = R + i\left(\omega L - \frac{1}{\omega C}\right).$$

A **two-port network** is one with two input and two output terminals as shown in Figure 1.10.

Fig. 1.10

Everything between the input and output terminals can be treated as a black box for now. Writing $\mathbf{x}_n := [E_n; I_n]$, we can define the **transmission matrix** $\mathbf{T}$ of the network by

$$\mathbf{x}_1 = \mathbf{T}\mathbf{x}_2.$$

When networks are cascaded, as shown in Figure 1.11,

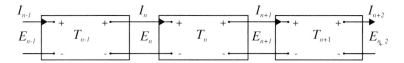

Fig. 1.11

we have

$$\mathbf{x}_{n-1} = \mathbf{T}_{n-1}\mathbf{x}_n = \mathbf{T}_{n-1}\mathbf{T}_n\mathbf{x}_{n+1} = \mathbf{T}_{n-1}\mathbf{T}_n\mathbf{T}_{n+1}\mathbf{x}_{n+2}.$$

Many networks have the special property that when their input and output terminals are interchanged the resulting current and voltage distributions is unchanged. Such networks are said to be **symmetric**. Since $\mathbf{x}_1 = \mathbf{T}\mathbf{x}_2$, reversing the terminals reverses the sign of the currents, so that

$$\tilde{\mathbf{x}} = \begin{bmatrix} 1 & 0 \\ 0 & -1 \end{bmatrix} \mathbf{x} =: \mathbf{R}\mathbf{x}$$

is the reversed vector. Since the reversal matrix $\mathbf{R}$ is an involution, we have

$$\mathbf{x}_1 = \mathbf{T}\mathbf{x}_2 \quad \text{and} \quad \mathbf{x}_2 = \mathbf{T}\mathbf{x}_1 \quad \Leftrightarrow \quad \mathbf{x}_2 = \mathbf{R}\mathbf{T}\mathbf{R}\mathbf{x}_1,$$

from which it follows that

$$\mathbf{x}_1 = \mathbf{T}\mathbf{R}\mathbf{T}\mathbf{R}\mathbf{x}_1 \quad \Leftrightarrow \quad \mathbf{T}\mathbf{R}\mathbf{T}\mathbf{R} = \mathbf{I}_2.$$

Upon performing the multiplication and solving the resulting equations, we are lead to the following form for the transmission matrix for a symmetric network:

$$\mathbf{T} = \begin{bmatrix} a & b \\ c & a \end{bmatrix}.$$

We can write the transmission matrices for several simple networks.

(a) Series impedance: see Figure 1.12.

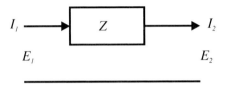

Fig. 1.12

Since the voltage is conserved, $E_1 = E_2$. The sum of the currents requires

$$I_1 = ZE_1 + I_2 = I_2 + ZE_1.$$

Thus

$$\mathbf{T} = \begin{bmatrix} 1 & Z \\ 0 & 1 \end{bmatrix}.$$

(b) Shunt impedance: see Figure 1.13.

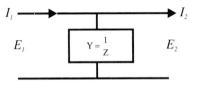

Fig. 1.13

For a shunt with admittance $Y = 1/Z$, the current flow is unimpeded, and $I_1 = I_2$. But voltages add: $E_1 = E_2 + YI_1 = E_2 + YI_2$. Thus

$$\mathbf{T} = \begin{bmatrix} 1 & 0 \\ Y & 1 \end{bmatrix}.$$

(c) Transmission line: see Figure 1.14.

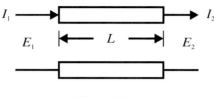

Fig. 1.14

For a transmission line of length L with characteristic impedance of Z_0 and wave number k, the transmission matrix is

$$T = \begin{bmatrix} \cosh kL & Z_0 \sinh kL \\ \frac{1}{Z_0} \sinh kL & \cosh kL \end{bmatrix}.$$

(d) For an ideal transformer with $r := N_1/N_2$: see Figure 1.15.

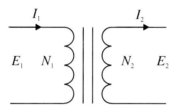

Fig. 1.15

$$\mathbf{T} = \begin{bmatrix} \frac{1}{r} & 0 \\ 0 & r \end{bmatrix}.$$

(e) Coupled inductors with a mutual inductance M and self-inductances of L_1 and L_2: see Figure 1.16.

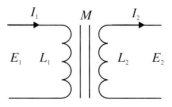

Fig. 1.16

$$\mathbf{T} = \frac{1}{M} \begin{bmatrix} L_1 & i\omega \left(L_1 L_2 - M^2 \right) \\ -\frac{i}{\omega} & L_2 \end{bmatrix}.$$

Computation of the transmission matrix for a cascade of n networks is merely a matter of matrix multiplication because

$$\mathbf{x}_1 = \mathbf{T}_1\mathbf{T}_2\cdots\mathbf{T}_n\mathbf{x}_{n+1}$$

so that

$$\mathbf{T}_{\text{equivalent}} = \mathbf{T}_1\mathbf{T}_2\cdots\mathbf{T}_n.$$

If we have n cascaded impedances, the transmission matrix is

$$\mathbf{T}_1\mathbf{T}_2\cdots\mathbf{T}_n = \begin{bmatrix} 1 & Z_1 \\ 0 & 1 \end{bmatrix}\begin{bmatrix} 1 & Z_2 \\ 0 & 1 \end{bmatrix}\cdots\begin{bmatrix} 1 & Z_n \\ 0 & 1 \end{bmatrix} = \begin{bmatrix} 1 & \sum Z_k \\ 0 & 1 \end{bmatrix},$$

which is a verification of the following result: The impedance of a sequence of elements arranged in series is the sum of their impedances. Similarly for parallel circuits, the admittance of a sequence is the sum of the admittances. For n identical impedances terminated by a transformer,

$$\mathbf{T}_{\text{equivalent}} = \begin{bmatrix} 1 & nZ \\ 0 & 1 \end{bmatrix}\begin{bmatrix} \frac{1}{r} & 0 \\ 0 & r \end{bmatrix} = \begin{bmatrix} \frac{1}{r} & nrZ \\ 0 & r \end{bmatrix}.$$

Were this particular subunit to be repeated m times

$$T = \begin{bmatrix} \frac{1}{r} & nrZ \\ 0 & r \end{bmatrix}^m = \begin{bmatrix} \frac{1}{r^2} & nZ(1+r) \\ 0 & r^2 \end{bmatrix}\begin{bmatrix} \frac{1}{r} & nrZ \\ 0 & r \end{bmatrix}^{m-2}$$

$$= \begin{bmatrix} \frac{1}{r^m} & nZ\frac{r^{m+1}-r^{-m+1}}{r-\frac{1}{r}} \\ 0 & r^m \end{bmatrix}.$$

1.5.6   Exercise Set

Find the inverse of each of the following matrices that are nonsingular.

1.
$$A = \begin{bmatrix} i & 2 & 1 \\ -i & 3 & 3 \\ i & 3 & 4 \end{bmatrix}$$

2.
$$B = \begin{bmatrix} 1 & 2 & 3 \\ 2 & 5 & 3 \\ 1 & 0 & 8 \end{bmatrix}$$

3.
$$C = \begin{bmatrix} 2 & 2 & 2 \\ 2 & 2 & -8 \\ -4 & 2 & 2 \end{bmatrix}$$

4.
$$D = \begin{bmatrix} 1 & 2 & 1 \\ 2 & 5 & 2 \\ 1 & 3 & 3 \end{bmatrix}$$

5.
$$E = \begin{bmatrix} 1 & 2 & 1 \\ 1 & 3 & 3 \\ 1 & 3 & 4 \end{bmatrix}$$

6.
$$F = \begin{bmatrix} -3 & 2 & -11 \\ 3 & -4 & 6 \\ 4 & -8 & 13 \end{bmatrix}$$

7.
$$G = \begin{bmatrix} -1 & -2 & 0 & 2 \\ 2 & -1 & 3 & 1 \\ 3 & 2 & 1 & 3 \\ 2 & -1 & 0 & -3 \end{bmatrix}$$

8.
$$H = \begin{bmatrix} 1 & -1 & 3 & 1 \\ 2 & 0 & 2 & 4 \\ 3 & 0 & 2 & -1 \\ 4 & 2 & 1 & 16 \end{bmatrix}$$

9.
$$M = \begin{bmatrix} 1 & 1+2i & 2+10i \\ 1+i & 3i & -5+14i \\ 1+i & 5i & -8+20i \end{bmatrix}$$

10.
$$N = \begin{bmatrix} 1 & 0 & 0 & 0 & 0 & 1 \\ 1 & 1 & 0 & 0 & 0 & -1 \\ -1 & 1 & 1 & 0 & 0 & 1 \\ 1 & -1 & 1 & 1 & 0 & -1 \\ -1 & 1 & -1 & 1 & 1 & 1 \\ 1 & -1 & 1 & -1 & 1 & -1 \end{bmatrix}$$

11. Write the matrix **E** in problem 5 as a product of elementary matrices and a matrix in row-reduced echelon form.

12. Write the matrix **F** in problem 6 as a product of elementary matrices and a matrix in row-reduced echelon form.

13. Give an argument that all permutation matrices are invertible. Also argue that the inverse of any permutation matrix is also a permutation matrix. How would you find the permutation that generates the inverse if you know the permutation of the original matrix?

14. If **A** is **idempotent**, i.e., $\mathbf{A} = \mathbf{A}^2$, and α and β are nonzero complex numbers, show that $\mathbf{B} = \alpha\mathbf{A} + \beta(\mathbf{I} - \mathbf{A})$ is nonsingular and

$$\mathbf{B}^{-1} = \frac{1}{\alpha}\mathbf{A} + \frac{1}{\beta}(\mathbf{I} - \mathbf{A}).$$

15. Let **a** and **b** be complex column vectors.

(a) Verify the **Sherman-Morrison formula**:

$$(\mathbf{I} + \mathbf{a}\mathbf{a}^H)^{-1} = \mathbf{I} - (1 + \mathbf{a}^H\mathbf{a})^{-1}\mathbf{a}\mathbf{a}^H.$$

[Hint: $\mathbf{a}^H\mathbf{a}$ is a number.]

(b) Show that
$$(\mathbf{I} + \mathbf{a}\mathbf{b}^H)^{-1} = \mathbf{I} - (1 + \mathbf{b}^H\mathbf{a})^{-1}\mathbf{a}\mathbf{b}^H, \quad \text{for} \quad \mathbf{b}^H\mathbf{a} \neq -1.$$

(c) Show that the inverse of the Householder matrix (see example 1.28) can be derived from the result of the previous problem by appropriate choices of the vectors **a** and **b**.

16. If $\mathbf{A}$ is an invertible $n \times n$ matrix and $\mathbf{x}$ and $\mathbf{y}$ are n-component column vectors, show that

$$\left(\mathbf{A} + \mathbf{x}\mathbf{y}^T\right)^{-1} = \mathbf{A}^{-1} - \frac{\mathbf{A}^{-1}\mathbf{x}\mathbf{y}^T\mathbf{A}^{-1}}{1 + \mathbf{y}^T\mathbf{A}^{-1}\mathbf{x}}.$$

17. If $\mathbf{J}$ is an $n \times n$ matrix all of whose entries are 1, i.e., $\mathbf{ones}(n)$, and $\mathbf{L} = \lambda\mathbf{I} + \mathbf{J}$, write $\mathbf{L}^{-1}$ as $(\mathbf{I} + c\mathbf{J})/\lambda$ and determine the value of the constant c.

18. Show that products of orthogonal matrices are orthogonal. Do the same for unitary matrices.

19. Under what conditions is a product of involutions an involution?

20. If $\mathbf{A}$ is $n \times n$ with entries $A_{jk} = 1 + \delta_{jk}$, find $\mathbf{A}^{-1}$.

21. If $\mathbf{S}$ is skew-symmetric, then, assuming $\mathbf{I}+\mathbf{S}$ is nonsingular, show that the product $(\mathbf{I}-\mathbf{S})(\mathbf{I}+\mathbf{S})^{-1}$ is orthogonal.

22. If $\mathbf{A}$, $\mathbf{B}$, and $\mathbf{A} + \mathbf{B}$ are nonsingular, show that

$$(\mathbf{A} + \mathbf{B})^{-1} = \mathbf{A}^{-1}(\mathbf{A}^{-1} + \mathbf{B}^{-1})\mathbf{B}^{-1} = \mathbf{B}^{-1}(\mathbf{A}^{-1} + \mathbf{B}^{-1})\mathbf{A}^{-1}.$$

23. It is possible to establish a relationship between the set of complex numbers and certain 2×2 matrices. In particular

$$a + ib \leftrightarrow \begin{bmatrix} a & b \\ -b & a \end{bmatrix}.$$

   (a) Show that the relationship is preserved under addition and multiplication.

   (b) Show that the relation is preserved under the operation of taking reciprocals of complex numbers and inverses of the corresponding matrices, and that the condition for invertibility of the matrix is the same as that for complex numbers.

Find the transmission matrix for each of the following networks:

24. An impedance Z_1 followed by a shunt with admittance Y followed by an impedance Z_2. See Figure 1.17.

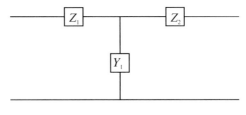

Fig. 1.17

25. A transmission line of length L_1 and characteristic impedance Z_1 followed by a line of length L_2 and impedance Z_2. See Figure 1.18.

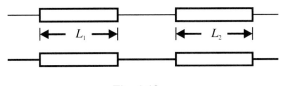

Fig. 1.18

26. An impedance Z followed by a transformer with a ratio of r for left to right windings followed by another impedance Z. See Figure 1.19.

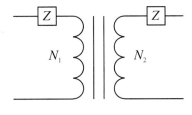

Fig. 1.19

27. A sequence of n units each of which consists of an impedance Z followed by an admittance Y. See Figure 1.20.

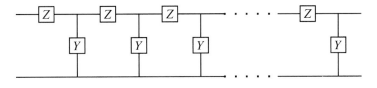

Fig. 1.20

If the matrix $\mathbf{A}$ is a function of t and D is differentiation with respect to the variable t, show that

28. $D\mathbf{A}^2 = \mathbf{A}(D\mathbf{A}) + (D\mathbf{A})\mathbf{A}$.

29. $D\mathbf{A}^{-1} = -\mathbf{A}^{-1}(D\mathbf{A})\mathbf{A}^{-1}$.

30. An $n \times n$ matrix $\mathbf{A}$ is said to be **strictly diagonally dominant** if

$$|A_{jj}| > \sum_{\substack{k=1 \\ k \neq j}}^{n} |A_{jk}| \quad \text{for } j = 1:n.$$

Give a convincing argument that all strictly diagonally dominant matrices are invertible. Is this result true for nonstrict (replace $>$ by $\geq$) diagonal dominance? Give an example to substantiate your claim.

1.6   DETERMINANTS

Although the calculation of a determinant may be familiar to you from previous work, this section will develop the concept in the context of elementary row operations. The determinant is a single complex number associated with a square matrix.

1.6.1   Definition of the Determinant

Since row reduction has played a fundamental role in our discussion of linear systems, it is only fitting that our definition of the determinant should be made in terms of elementary row operations.

DEFINITION 1.15   *The **determinant** of* $\mathbf{A} \in \mathbb{C}_n^n$ *is a function* $\det$ *from* $\mathbb{C}_n^n$ *into* $\mathbb{C}$ *defined on the row vectors* $\mathbf{A}_1 = \mathbf{row}_1(\mathbf{A})$, $\mathbf{A}_2 = \mathbf{row}_2(\mathbf{A})$,..., $\mathbf{A}_n = \mathbf{row}_n(\mathbf{A})$ *of* $\mathbf{A}$ *that satisfies:*

(Det1) $\det(\mathbf{A}) = 0$ *if any two row vectors of* $\mathbf{A}$ *are equal,*

(Det2) $\det$ *is linear in each row, i.e.,*

$$\det(\mathbf{A}_1; \ldots; c\mathbf{A}_k + \mathbf{B}_k; \ldots; \mathbf{A}_n)$$
$$= c\det(\mathbf{A}_1; \ldots; \mathbf{A}_k; \ldots; \mathbf{A}_n) + \det(\mathbf{A}_1; \ldots; \mathbf{B}_k; \ldots; \mathbf{A}_n),$$

(Det3) $\det(\mathbf{I}_n) = 1$.

Since $\det(\mathbf{A})$ is linear in each row of $\mathbf{A}$ and maps into $\mathbb{C}$, $\det$ is said to be a **multilinear functional**. We'll use the notations $\det(\mathbf{A}) = |\mathbf{A}|$ interchangeably.

▪ **EXAMPLE 1.33**   Evaluate each of the following determinants.

(a) $|\mathbf{diag}\ (2, 3, 4, 5)| = 2\,|\mathbf{diag}(1, 3, 4, 5)| = 2 \cdot 3\,|\mathbf{diag}(1, 1, 4, 5)|$
$$= 2 \cdot 3 \cdot 4\,|\mathbf{diag}(1, 1, 1, 5)| = 2 \cdot 3 \cdot 4 \cdot 5\,|\mathbf{diag}(1, 1, 1, 1)|$$
$$= 120\,|I_4| = 120.$$

(b) $\det(2I_n) = \det(\mathbf{diag}(2, 2, .., 2))$
$$= 2^n \det(I_n), \text{ since each of } n \text{ rows contains a factor of } 2 \qquad \blacksquare\,\blacksquare\,\blacksquare$$
$$= 2^n.$$

The following additional properties further tie the determinant to elementary row operations.

THEOREM 1.10

(Det4) $\det(\mathbf{A}_1; \ldots; c\mathbf{A}_k; \ldots; \mathbf{A}_n) = c \det(\mathbf{A}_1; \ldots; \mathbf{A}_k; \ldots; \mathbf{A}_n)$,

(Det5) *If any row of* $\mathbf{A}$ *is* $\mathbf{0}$ *then* $\det(\mathbf{A}) = 0$,

(Det6) $\det(\mathbf{A})$ *changes sign if any two rows of* $\mathbf{A}$ *are interchanged,*

(Det7) *If* e_k *is the elementary row operation that replaces row* k *by row* k *plus* c *times row* j, *for* $j \neq k$, *i.e.,*

$$e_k(\mathbf{A}) = e_k(\mathbf{A}_1; \ldots; \mathbf{A}_k; \ldots; \mathbf{A}_n) := [\mathbf{A}_1; \ldots; \mathbf{A}_k + c\mathbf{A}_j; \ldots; \mathbf{A}_n],$$

then $\det(e_k(\mathbf{A})) = \det(\mathbf{A})$ *for* $j \neq k$.

Properties (Det4), (Det6), and (Det7) show the effects of each of the elementary row operations on $\det(\mathbf{A})$. In particular, when we use (ERO1) and multiply a row by a constant c, we must introduce a factor of $1/c$ to keep the value of the determinant unchanged. When using (ERO2), no matter what multiple of another row we add to the given row, the determinant does not change. Swapping two rows as in (ERO3) results in a change of sign.

Because of (Det6), $\det(\mathbf{A})$ is said to be an **alternating multilinear functional**.

Proof   (Det4) follows from (Det2) by putting $\mathbf{B}_k = \mathbf{0}$. (Det5) follows from (Det4) by putting $c = 0$. To prove (Det6), start with the first two rows and put $\mathbf{B} = \mathbf{A}_1 + \mathbf{A}_2$; then

$$\begin{aligned}
0 &= \det(\mathbf{B}; \mathbf{B}; \ldots) = \det(\mathbf{A}_1 + \mathbf{A}_2; \mathbf{A}_1 + \mathbf{A}_2; \ldots) \\
&= \det(\mathbf{A}_1; \mathbf{A}_1; \ldots) + \det(\mathbf{A}_1; \mathbf{A}_2; \ldots) \\
&\quad + \det(\mathbf{A}_2; \mathbf{A}_1; \ldots) + \det(\mathbf{A}_2; \mathbf{A}_2; \ldots),
\end{aligned}$$

by virtue of (Det2). The first and last terms are zero because of (Det1); thus

$$\det(\mathbf{A}_1; \mathbf{A}_2; \ldots) = -\det(\mathbf{A}_2; \mathbf{A}_1; \ldots).$$

If we have rows $\mathbf{A}_j$ and $\mathbf{A}_{j+k}$ to be interchanged, first move $\mathbf{A}_j$ down k places. That pushes $\mathbf{A}_{j+k}$ up one place, and so it must be moved up $k-1$ places altogether, hence there are $2k-1$ interchanges in all giving a grand total sign change of $(-1)^{2k-1} = -1$.

Lastly, adding multiples of a row:

$$\begin{aligned}
|e_k(\mathbf{A})| &= \det(\mathbf{A}_1; \ldots; \mathbf{A}_k + c\mathbf{A}_j; \ldots; \mathbf{A}_n) \\
&= \det(\mathbf{A}_1; \ldots; \mathbf{A}_k; \ldots; \mathbf{A}_n) + c\det(\mathbf{A}_1; \ldots; \mathbf{A}_j; \ldots; \mathbf{A}_n).
\end{aligned}$$

In the second term $\mathbf{A}_j$ appears in row k and row j, and so by property (Det1) it is zero. $\square$

Now we can use the last theorem to apply pivotal reduction to the evaluation of determinants.

▪ **EXAMPLE 1.34** Evaluate

$$\det\left(\begin{bmatrix} 2 & 1 & 4 & -7 \\ 0 & -3 & 2 & 9 \\ 0 & 0 & 5 & -11 \\ 0 & 0 & 0 & 6 \end{bmatrix}\right).$$

Solution: Our goal is to reduce this to diagonal form because then the determinant is obviously the product of the diagonal elements. Rather than apply pivotal reduction, sweeping out columns from left to right, let's proceed from right to left and keep track of any factors introduced from (ERO1) operations and factors of -1 from (ERO3) interchanges:

$$\det\left(\begin{bmatrix} 2 & 1 & 4 & -7 \\ 0 & -3 & 2 & 9 \\ 0 & 0 & 5 & -11 \\ 0 & 0 & 0 & 6 \end{bmatrix}\right) = \det\left(\begin{matrix} (1) + \frac{7}{6}(4) \\ (2) - \frac{9}{6}(4) \\ (3) + \frac{11}{6}(4) \\ (4) \end{matrix}\begin{bmatrix} 2 & 1 & 4 & 0 \\ 0 & -3 & 2 & 0 \\ 0 & 0 & 5 & 0 \\ 0 & 0 & 0 & 6 \end{bmatrix}\right).$$

There were no extra factors because we used only (ERO2) type operations.

$$= \det\left(\begin{matrix} (1) - \frac{4}{5}(3) \\ (2) - \frac{2}{5}(3) \\ (3) \\ (4) \end{matrix}\begin{bmatrix} 2 & 1 & 0 & 0 \\ 0 & -3 & 0 & 0 \\ 0 & 0 & 5 & 0 \\ 0 & 0 & 0 & 6 \end{bmatrix}\right).$$

Again we used only (ERO2) operations.

$$= \det\left(\begin{matrix} (1) + \frac{1}{3}(2) \\ (2) \\ (3) \\ (4) \end{matrix}\begin{bmatrix} 2 & 0 & 0 & 0 \\ 0 & -3 & 0 & 0 \\ 0 & 0 & 5 & 0 \\ 0 & 0 & 0 & 6 \end{bmatrix}\right) = 2(-3)(5)(6) = -180.$$

▪ ▪ ▪

The lesson to be learned from this example is stated in the following theorem.

THEOREM 1.11 *The determinant of a triangular matrix is the product of its diagonal elements.* ☐

From this result we see that we need not use full pivotal reduction to the row-reduced echelon form to evaluate the determinant, but rather we only need to sweep out the columns below *or* above the pivot rows to reduce to upper or lower triangular form.

▪ **EXAMPLE 1.35** Use row reduction to triangular form to evaluate each of the following determinants.

(a) $\det \begin{bmatrix} 1 & 2 & 5 \\ 9 & 1 & 3 \\ 2 & 3 & 4 \end{bmatrix} = \det \left(\begin{matrix} (1) \\ (2) - 9(1) \\ (3) - 2(1) \end{matrix} \begin{bmatrix} 1 & 2 & 5 \\ 0 & -17 & -42 \\ 0 & -1 & 6 \end{bmatrix} \right)$

$$= -\det \left(\begin{matrix} (1) \\ (3) \\ (2) - 17(3) \end{matrix} \begin{bmatrix} 1 & 2 & 5 \\ 0 & -1 & -42 \\ 0 & 0 & 60 \end{bmatrix} \right)$$

$$= -(-1)(-1)(60) = 60.$$

(b) $\det \begin{bmatrix} 8 & 0 & 3 & 0 \\ 2 & 4 & 2 & 1 \\ 0 & 1 & 1 & 1 \\ -1 & 2 & 2 & 0 \end{bmatrix}$

$$= (-1)^2 \det \left(\begin{matrix} (4) \\ (3) \\ (2) + 2(4) \\ (1) + 8(4) \end{matrix} \begin{bmatrix} -1 & 2 & 2 & 0 \\ 0 & 1 & 1 & 1 \\ 0 & 8 & 6 & 1 \\ 0 & 16 & 19 & 0 \end{bmatrix} \right)$$

The $(-1)^2$ comes from the two interchanges $1 \rightleftharpoons 4$ and $2 \rightleftharpoons 3$.

$$\det \left(\begin{matrix} (1) \\ (2) \\ (3) - 8(2) \\ (4) - 16(2) \end{matrix} \begin{bmatrix} -1 & 2 & 2 & 0 \\ 0 & 1 & 1 & 1 \\ 0 & 0 & -2 & -7 \\ 0 & 0 & 3 & -16 \end{bmatrix} \right)$$

$$= \frac{1}{2} \det \left(\begin{matrix} (1) \\ (2) \\ (3) \\ 2(4) + 3(3) \end{matrix} \begin{bmatrix} -1 & 2 & 2 & 0 \\ 0 & 1 & 1 & 1 \\ 0 & 0 & -2 & -7 \\ 0 & 0 & 0 & -53 \end{bmatrix} \right)$$

The factor of $\frac{1}{2}$ compensates for the 2 times row (4) in the last step. The final answer is

$$\frac{1}{2}(-1)(1)(-2)(-53) = -53.$$

■ ■ ■

The following theorem will be very useful.

THEOREM 1.12 *For any $n \times n$ matrices $\mathbf{A}$ and $\mathbf{B}$, the determinant of their product is the product of their determinants, i.e.,*

$$\det(\mathbf{AB}) = \det(\mathbf{A})\det(\mathbf{B}).$$

□

Proof   Given $\mathbf{A}$, the matrix $\mathbf{B}$ can either be singular or nonsingular. If it is singular, then so is $\mathbf{AB}$. All singular matrices reduce to an rref with at least one row of zeros, hence they all have zero determinant, and the result follows trivially.

If $\mathbf{B}$ is fixed and nonsingular, define the function

$$\mathcal{D}(\mathbf{A}) = \frac{\det(\mathbf{AB})}{\det(\mathbf{B})}.$$

If any two rows of $\mathbf{A}$ are equal, two rows of $\mathbf{AB}$ will be equal. Looking at (Det2) we see that

$$\mathcal{D}(\mathbf{A}_1; \ldots; c\mathbf{A}_k + \mathbf{C}_k; \ldots; \mathbf{A}_n)$$
$$= \det\left((\mathbf{A}_1; \ldots; c\mathbf{A}_k + \mathbf{C}_k; \ldots; \mathbf{A}_n)\mathbf{B}\right) / \det(\mathbf{B})$$
$$= \det(\mathbf{A}_1\mathbf{B}; \ldots; c\mathbf{A}_k\mathbf{B} + \mathbf{C}_k\mathbf{B}; \ldots; \mathbf{A}_n\mathbf{B}) / \det(\mathbf{B}).$$

But $\mathbf{A}_k\mathbf{B}$ is the kth row vector of the product $\mathbf{AB}$, so that $\mathcal{D}$ is multilinear:

$$\mathcal{D}(\mathbf{A}_1; \ldots; c\mathbf{A}_k + \mathbf{C}_k; \ldots; \mathbf{A}_n)$$
$$= c\mathcal{D}(\mathbf{A}_1; \ldots; \mathbf{A}_k; \ldots; \mathbf{A}_n) + \mathcal{D}(\mathbf{A}_1; \ldots; \mathbf{C}_k; \ldots; \mathbf{A}_n).$$

Lastly, $\mathcal{D}(\mathbf{I}) = \det(\mathbf{IB}) / \det(\mathbf{B}) = 1$. Thus $\mathcal{D}(A)$ satisfies the axioms for $\det(\mathbf{A})$, and the theorem is proven.   □

Evaluating a determinant of a matrix in terms of its row vectors yields the same result as evaluating it in terms of its column vectors. This follows from:

THEOREM 1.13 $\det(\mathbf{A}) = \det(\mathbf{A}^T)$.   □

The proof of this theorem requires us to look at the details of the rearrangements or permutations of the row vectors and will not be given here. Any explicit formula we might derive for the determinant function would not be a computationally useful device compared with pivotal reduction to triangular form (there are $n!$ possible permutations of n row vectors and each permutation would give rise to a term, each of which would require $n - 1$ multiplications to evaluate. That many terms is still a lot of terms compared with $n^3/3$ multiplications).

Other related results are:

THEOREM 1.14   *Let* $\mathbf{A}$, $\mathbf{B}$, *and* $\mathbf{U}$ *be square matrices*

(a) *If* $\mathbf{A}$ *is nonsingular, then* $\det(\mathbf{A}^{-1}) = (\det(\mathbf{A}))^{-1}$.

(b) *If* $\mathbf{B}$ *is orthogonal, then* $\det(\mathbf{B}) = \pm 1$.

(c) *If* $\mathbf{U}$ *is unitary, then* $|\det(\mathbf{U})| = 1$.

(d) *Similar matrices have the same determinant.*

Proof   (a) $\mathbf{A}\mathbf{A}^{-1} = \mathbf{I} \quad \Rightarrow \quad |\mathbf{A}\mathbf{A}^{-1}| = |\mathbf{A}|\,|\mathbf{A}^{-1}| = |\mathbf{I}| = 1 \quad \Rightarrow \quad |\mathbf{A}^{-1}| = 1/|\mathbf{A}|.$

(b) $\mathbf{B}\mathbf{B}^T = \mathbf{I} \quad \Rightarrow \quad |\mathbf{B}\mathbf{B}^T| = |\mathbf{B}|\,|\mathbf{B}^T| = |\mathbf{B}|^2 = 1 \quad \Rightarrow \quad |\mathbf{B}| = \pm 1.$

(c) $\mathbf{U}\mathbf{U}^H = \mathbf{I} \quad \Rightarrow \quad |\mathbf{U}\mathbf{U}^H| = |\mathbf{U}|\,|\bar{\mathbf{U}}^T| = |\mathbf{U}|\,|\bar{\mathbf{U}}| = |\mathbf{U}|\,\overline{|\mathbf{U}|} = 1.$

Thus $\det(\mathbf{U})$ must have modulus unity; i.e.,

$$|\det(\mathbf{U})| = 1 \quad \Rightarrow \quad \det(\mathbf{U}) = e^{i\phi}.$$

(d) Recall that if $\mathbf{A}$ and $\mathbf{B}$ are similar, then $\mathbf{A} = \mathbf{P}^{-1}\mathbf{B}\mathbf{P}$ for some nonsingular matrix $\mathbf{P}$. Taking determinants of both sides and using the determinant of a product as the product of the determinants and part (a),

$$|\mathbf{A}| = |\mathbf{P}^{-1}\mathbf{B}\mathbf{P}| = |\mathbf{P}^{-1}|\,|\mathbf{B}|\,|\mathbf{P}| = |\mathbf{B}|. \qquad \Box$$

1.6.2   *Minors and Cofactors*

Row reduction to triangular form for the evaluation of $\det(\mathbf{A})$ is really first reducing an $n \times n$ matrix, then reducing an $(n-1) \times (n-1)$ matrix, and so on. A similar dimension reducing algorithm is available for the evaluation of $\det(\mathbf{A})$.

DEFINITION 1.16 *The* **minor** *of the jk^{th} entry of* $\mathbf{A}$*, written* $\mathrm{Minor}(A_{jk})$*, is the determinant of the $(n-1) \times (n-1)$ submatrix obtained from* $\mathbf{A}$ *by deleting row j and column k.*

$$\mathrm{Minor}(A_{jk}) := \det \begin{bmatrix} & A_{1k} & \\ & \vdots & \\ A_{j1} & \cdots & A_{jk} & \cdots & A_{jn} \\ & \vdots & \\ & A_{nk} & \end{bmatrix} \begin{matrix} \cdot \\ \cdot \\ \text{row } j \\ \cdot \\ \cdot \end{matrix}$$
$$\text{column } k$$

The **cofactor** *of the entry A_{jk}, written* $\mathrm{Cof}(A_{jk})$*, is*

$$\mathrm{Cof}(A_{jk}) := (-1)^{j+k}\,\mathrm{Minor}(A_{jk}).$$

Before we go to the theorem that generates the dimension reducing algorithm, we'll need to reintroduce the Kronecker delta function,

$$\delta_{jk} = \begin{cases} 0, & j \neq k, \\ 1, & j = k. \end{cases}$$

THEOREM 1.15 *If $A \in \mathbb{C}_n^n$, then*

$$\delta_{jk} \det(A) = \sum_{\ell=1}^{n} A_{\ell j}\,\mathrm{Cof}(A_{\ell k}) = \sum_{\ell=1}^{n} A_{j\ell}\,\mathrm{Cof}(A_{k\ell}). \qquad \Box$$

For the case when $j = k$, the first sum is the **column expansion** by cofactors of the determinant and the second is the **row expansion** by cofactors. Once again, the proof deals with the mechanics of permutations and will be omitted. The expansion by cofactors of the determinant of an $n \times n$ matrix consists of writing $\det(\mathbf{A})$ as a linear combination of at most n separate smaller $(n-1) \times (n-1)$ cofactors, each of which can be written as a linear combination of $(n-1)$ separate $(n-2) \times (n-2)$ cofactors, and eventually, all the way down to 2×2 cofactors. Then we can use

$$\det \begin{bmatrix} a & b \\ c & d \end{bmatrix} = ad - bc.$$

Unfortunately, for $n > 2$, there are $\frac{1}{2}n!$ different 2×2 determinants to be evaluated. At every stage we must choose either a row or column on which to expand. Since each term in the expansion is an entry times its cofactor we should *choose the row or column with the largest number of zeros*. For each zero there will be one less cofactor to evaluate.

■ **EXAMPLE 1.36** Redo example 1.35(b) using cofactors.

Solution: $\det \begin{bmatrix} 8 & 0 & 3 & 0 \\ 2 & 4 & 2 & 1 \\ 0 & 1 & 1 & 1 \\ -1 & 2 & 2 & 0 \end{bmatrix}$ Expand on the *first row* or fourth column, because they both have two zeros.

$$= (-1)^{1+1}8 \begin{vmatrix} 4 & 2 & 1 \\ 1 & 1 & 1 \\ 2 & 2 & 0 \end{vmatrix} + 0 \cdot \mathrm{Cof}(A_{12}) + (-1)^{1+3}3 \begin{vmatrix} 2 & 4 & 1 \\ 0 & 1 & 1 \\ -1 & 2 & 0 \end{vmatrix} + 0 \cdot \mathrm{Cof}(A_{14})$$

$$= 8 \left\{ (-1)^{1+3}1 \begin{vmatrix} 1 & 1 \\ 2 & 2 \end{vmatrix} + (-1)^{2+3}1 \begin{vmatrix} 4 & 2 \\ 2 & 2 \end{vmatrix} \right\}$$
expanded on the third column

$$+3 \left\{ (-1)^{2+2}1 \begin{vmatrix} 2 & 1 \\ -1 & 0 \end{vmatrix} + (-1)^{2+3} \begin{vmatrix} 2 & 4 \\ -1 & 2 \end{vmatrix} \right\}$$
expanded on the second row

$$= 8\{0 - (8-4)\} + 3\{(0+1) - (4+4)\} = 8(-4) + 3(-7) = -53.$$

■ ■ ■

It doesn't take much imagination to see that the cofactor expansion of the determinant of a large matrix with no zero entries will be quite lengthy. In fact, it is never used for evaluating determinants of large matrices with numerical entries.

1.6.3 *Determinantal Solutions of Linear Systems*

Now let's look at the determinantal solution of a system of n equations in n unknowns, $\mathbf{Ax} = \mathbf{b}$.

Notation: Use $\mathbf{A}(k \leftarrow \mathbf{b})$ to denote the matrix obtained from $\mathbf{A}$ by replacing its kth column, $\mathbf{col}_k(\mathbf{A})$, by the vector $\mathbf{b}$.

THEOREM 1.16 (Cramer's Rule) *If* $\mathbf{A}$ *is nonsingular, i.e.,* $\det(\mathbf{A}) \neq 0$, *then the* k^{th}
component of the solution vector $\mathbf{x}$ *of the system* $\mathbf{Ax} = \mathbf{b}$ *is given by*

$$x_k = \frac{\det\left(\mathbf{A}(k \leftarrow \mathbf{b})\right)}{\det(\mathbf{A})}, \quad k = 1 : n.$$

$\square$

Proof Write $\mathbf{Ax} = \mathbf{b}$ in component form as $\sum_k A_{jk} x_k = b_j$, and then multiply by $\mathrm{Cof}(A_{j\ell})$
and sum over j:

$$\sum_{j=1}^{n} \mathrm{Cof}(A_{j\ell}) \sum_{k=1}^{n} A_{jk} x_k = \sum_{j=1}^{n} \mathrm{Cof}(A_{j\ell}) b_j$$

$$= \sum_{k=1}^{n} \left\{ \sum_{j=1}^{n} A_{jk}\, \mathrm{Cof}(A_{j\ell}) \right\} x_k = \sum_{k=1}^{n} \delta_{k\ell} \left(\det(\mathbf{A})\right) x_k.$$

By the last theorem

$$\Rightarrow \quad x_\ell \det(\mathbf{A}) = \sum_{j=1}^{n} b_j\, \mathrm{Cof}(A_{j\ell}).$$

The right hand side is the usual expansion of $\det(\mathbf{A})$ except for the replacement of $A_{j\ell} = j^{th}$
component of column ℓ of $\mathbf{A}$ by b_j, i.e., $\mathbf{col}_\ell(\mathbf{A}) \leftarrow \mathbf{b}$. The stated result follows. $\square$

■ **EXAMPLE 1.37** Solve $2x - 3y = 11$, $5x + 7y = 14$ using Cramer's Rule.

Solution:

$$x = \frac{\begin{vmatrix} 11 & -3 \\ 14 & 7 \end{vmatrix}}{\begin{vmatrix} 2 & -3 \\ 5 & 7 \end{vmatrix}} = \frac{77 + 52}{14 + 15} = \frac{129}{29}, \qquad y = \frac{\begin{vmatrix} 2 & 11 \\ 5 & 14 \end{vmatrix}}{\begin{vmatrix} 2 & -3 \\ 5 & 7 \end{vmatrix}} = \frac{28 - 55}{29} = -\frac{27}{29}.$$

■ ■ ■

Although Cramer's rule is computationally tedious (using cofactors), it has certain theoretical advantages, especially since it provides an explicit formula for the solution. Solving
linear systems in which the coefficients may be variables whose values are not known at the
outset is best handled by Cramer's Rule.

1.6.4 Computing Inverses Using Determinants

DEFINITION 1.17 *The* **adjugate** *of* $\mathbf{A}$, *written* $\mathrm{adj}\,(\mathbf{A})$, *is defined by*

$$[\mathrm{adj}(\mathbf{A})]_{jk} := \mathrm{Cof}(A_{kj}), \quad j, k = 1 : n,$$

i.e., the transpose of the matrix of cofactors of $\mathbf{A}$.

Using Theorem 1.15 we have

$$\delta_{jk}\left(\det(\mathbf{A})\right) = \sum_{\ell=1}^{n} A_{\ell j}\,\mathrm{Cof}(A_{\ell k}) = \sum_{\ell=1}^{n} A_{\ell j}\left[\mathrm{adj}^{\mathbf{T}}(\mathbf{A})\right]_{\ell k}$$

$$= \sum_{\ell=1}^{n}\left[\mathrm{adj}(\mathbf{A})\right]_{k\ell} A_{\ell j} = \left[\mathrm{adj}(\mathbf{A})\,\mathbf{A}\right]_{kj}$$

$$\Rightarrow \left(\det(\mathbf{A})\right)\mathbf{I} = \mathrm{adj}\left((\mathbf{A})\right)\mathbf{A}.$$

We have just derived the result of the following theorem.

THEOREM 1.17 *If* $\mathbf{A}$ *is an invertible matrix, then*

$$\mathbf{A}^{-1} = \frac{\mathrm{adj}\,(\mathbf{A})}{\det(\mathbf{A})}.$$

□

If $\mathbf{A}$ is a noninvertible (singular) square matrix, then

$$\left(\mathrm{adj}(\mathbf{A})\right)\mathbf{A} = \mathbf{0}.$$

Use of the adjugate representation further reinforces the need for nonsingularity (à la determinants) in defining the inverse.

Note: One often sees the adjugate called the classical adjoint of the matrix. On the other hand, some authors refer to the Hermitian conjugate as the adjoint. Needless confusion! Better to use other terms.

■ **EXAMPLE 1.38** The use of the adjugate provides us with an alternative derivation of the inverse of a 2×2 matrix.

$$\mathrm{adj}\begin{bmatrix} a & b \\ c & d \end{bmatrix} = \begin{bmatrix} \mathrm{Cof}(a) & \mathrm{Cof}(b) \\ \mathrm{Cof}(c) & \mathrm{Cof}(d) \end{bmatrix}^{T} = \begin{bmatrix} d & -c \\ -b & a \end{bmatrix}^{T}.$$

Multiplying the adjugate by the reciprocal of the determinant yields

$$\begin{bmatrix} a & b \\ c & d \end{bmatrix}^{-1} = \frac{1}{ad - bc}\begin{bmatrix} d & -b \\ -c & a \end{bmatrix},$$

which is the same result we got using row reduction. ■ ■ ■

If we were to compute the solution of a system of n equations in n unknowns using Cramer's Rule we would have to evaluate $n + 1$ determinants each of size n. Because the evaluation ^{c} each determinant, when done the long way, involves $n!$ terms, each of which consists of -1 multiplications, there are a total of $(n + 1)(n!)(n - 1)$ multiplications to be executed in the solution of this system. To within the factor of $n - 1$ this is $(n + 1)!$ multiplications. In Section 1.7 it will be shown that the use of pivotal reduction to triangular form for this problem requires about $n^3/3$ multiplications. A comparison of the computational complexity of the two methods is in order. To be on the safe side, assume a computer can do 10^9 multiplications per second (this is as fast as the fastest machines presently available, 8/94). The table below shows the approximate number of multiplications (m's) and the CPU time required for each method at various values of n:

n	**Full Cramer's Rule**	**Pivotal Reduction**
2	6 m's $= 6 \times 10^{-9}$ sec	3 m's $= 3 \times 10^{-9}$ sec
3	24 m's $= 2.4 \times 10^{-8}$ sec	9 m's $= 9 \times 10^{-9}$ sec
5	720 m's $= 7.2 \times 10^{-6}$ sec	50 m's $= 5 \times 10^{-8}$ sec
9	3,628,800 m's $= 0.0036$ sec	300 m's $= 3 \times 10^{-7}$ sec
15	2.09×10^{13} m's $= 5.805$ hours	1200 m's $= 1.2 \times 10^{-6}$ sec
30	8.22×10^{33} m's $= 2.605 \times 10^{17}$ years	9000 m's $= 9 \times 10^{-6}$ sec
100	9.43×10^{159} m's $= 2.99 \times 10^{152}$ years	350,000 m's $= 0.00035$ sec

When compared with lifespans on the order of 10^2 years, Cramer's Rule seems particularly hopeless. Perhaps this points out the need for extremely efficient computational schemes when modern problems modeling the dynamics of a planetary atmosphere have resulted in systems of more than 250,000 equations in as many unknowns. For values of n of this magnitude, even pivotal reduction will take an inordinate amount of time.

1.6.5 Exercise Set

Separately use pivotal reduction and cofactors to evaluate the determinant of each of the following matrices.

1.
$$\begin{bmatrix} 1+i & 2i & 3-i \\ 2 & -2 & 2i \\ 0 & 1-3i & 2+3i \end{bmatrix}$$

2.
$$\begin{bmatrix} 1 & 2 & 4 \\ 3 & 1 & 4 \\ 5 & 2 & 7 \end{bmatrix}$$

3.
$$\begin{bmatrix} 3 & 2 & 3 \\ 4 & -6 & 5 \\ 1 & 2 & 2 \end{bmatrix}$$

4.
$$\begin{bmatrix} -1 & 2 & 0 & 2 \\ 2 & 1 & 3 & 1 \\ 3 & -2 & 1 & 3 \\ 2 & 1 & 0 & -3 \end{bmatrix}$$

5.
$$\begin{bmatrix} 1 & i & -1 & -i \\ i & -1 & -i & 1 \\ -1 & -i & 1 & i \\ -i & 1 & i & -1 \end{bmatrix}$$

6.
$$\begin{bmatrix} 1 & 3 & -2 & 4 \\ 1 & 4 & 3 & 0 \\ 1 & 5 & 5 & 4 \\ 1 & 6 & -2 & -3 \end{bmatrix}$$

7.
$$\begin{bmatrix} 1-i & i & 1+i & 1 \\ i & 1+i & 1 & 1-i \\ 1 & 1-i & i & 1+i \\ 1+i & 1 & 1-i & i \end{bmatrix}$$

8.
$$\begin{bmatrix} 2+3i & 2-2i & i & i-1 \\ i & 2 & i & -3 \\ 1+i & 2i & i-3 & 4 \\ i-1 & 5 & -2 & i \end{bmatrix}$$

Find $\det(\mathbf{A})$ if $\mathbf{A}$ is the $n \times n$ matrix whose jk^{th} entries are given below.

9. $A_{jk} = a^{j+k}$

10. $A_{jk} = a + (b-a)\delta_{jk}$

11. Find the determinant of

$$\begin{bmatrix} & & & & & 1 \\ & & & & & 2 \\ & \mathbf{I}_{n-1} & & & & 3 \\ & & & & & \vdots \\ & & & & & n-1 \\ 1 & 2 & 3 & \cdots & n-1 & n \end{bmatrix}.$$

12. Find the adjugate of each of the following matrices.

(a) $\begin{bmatrix} 2 & 3 & 1 \\ 1 & 2 & 1 \\ 1 & 1 & 2 \end{bmatrix}$

(b) $\begin{bmatrix} 1 & 4 & 7 \\ 2 & 5 & 8 \\ 3 & 6 & 9 \end{bmatrix}$

(c) $\begin{bmatrix} 1+i & i & i \\ 1 & 1+i & i \\ 1 & 1 & 1-i \end{bmatrix}$

13. Find *all* values of z for which each of the following is singular.

(a) $\begin{bmatrix} z & 1 & 1 \\ 1 & z & 1 \\ 1 & 1 & z \end{bmatrix}$

(b) $\begin{bmatrix} 1 & z & 1 \\ z & 1 & 1 \\ 1 & 1 & z \end{bmatrix}$

(c) $\begin{bmatrix} z & i & 0 \\ i & z & i \\ 0 & i & z \end{bmatrix}$

14. We say $\mathbf{A}$ is a **proper orthogonal matrix** if $\det(\mathbf{A}) = 1$ and $\mathbf{A}\mathbf{A}^T = \mathbf{I} = \mathbf{A}^T\mathbf{A}$. Show that if $\mathbf{A}$ is a proper orthogonal matrix of odd order n, then $\det(\mathbf{A} - \mathbf{I}) = 0$. What is the corresponding conclusion (if any) when n is even?

15. Show that when $\mathbf{x}$ and $\mathbf{y}$ are n-component column vectors, $\left|\mathbf{I} + \mathbf{x}\mathbf{y}^T\right| = 1 + \mathbf{y}^T\mathbf{x}$.

16. Show that when $\mathbf{A}$ is an $n \times n$ nonsingular matrix and $\mathbf{x}$ and $\mathbf{y}$ are n-component column vectors,

$$\left|\mathbf{A} + \mathbf{x}\mathbf{y}^T\right| = |\mathbf{A}|\left(1 + \mathbf{y}^T\mathbf{A}^{-1}\mathbf{x}\right).$$

What happens when $\mathbf{A}$ is singular with rank less than $n - 1$?

17. If $\mathbf{A}$ is skew-Hermitian, show that $|\mathbf{A}| = (-1)^n\overline{|\mathbf{A}|}$. What conclusion can you draw when n is even? When n is odd? Repeat this for a Hermitian matrix. What changes if we replace skew-Hermitian by skew-symmetric?

18. If $\mathbf{H} = \mathbf{A} + i\mathbf{B}$ is Hermitian, $\mathbf{A}$ is nonsingular, and both $\mathbf{A}$ and $\mathbf{B}$ are real, show that

$$|\det(\mathbf{H})|^2 = [\det(\mathbf{A})]^2[\det(\mathbf{I} + \mathbf{A}^{-1}\mathbf{B}\mathbf{A}^{-1}\mathbf{B})].$$

19. Show that the equation of the line passing through the points (x_1, y_1) and (x_2, y_2) is

$$\det \begin{bmatrix} x & y & 1 \\ x_1 & y_1 & 1 \\ x_2 & y_2 & 1 \end{bmatrix} = 0.$$

Prove a similar result for the equation of a plane passing through three noncollinear points. How does noncollinearity enter the picture?

20. Prove the determinant of a Householder matrix is $\det\left(\mathbf{I} - 2\mathbf{u}\mathbf{u}^T\right) = -1$.

21. The **Vandermonde matrix** is defined by

$$\mathbf{V}(x_1, x_2, \ldots, x_n) := \begin{bmatrix} 1 & 1 & 1 & \cdots & 1 \\ x_1 & x_2 & x_3 & \cdots & x_n \\ x_1^2 & x_2^2 & x_3^2 & \cdots & x_n^2 \\ \vdots & \vdots & \vdots & \ddots & \vdots \\ x_1^{n-1} & x_2^{n-1} & x_3^{n-1} & \cdots & x_n^{n-1} \end{bmatrix}.$$

Show that

$$|\mathbf{V}(x_1, x_2, \ldots, x_n)| = \prod_{1 \le j < k \le n} (x_j - x_k).$$

22. If $\mathbf{A}$ is the $n \times n$ matrix

$$\begin{bmatrix} 0 & 1 & 0 & \cdots & \cdots & \cdots & 0 \\ \vdots & 0 & 1 & 0 & & & 0 \\ \vdots & & 0 & 1 & 0 & & \vdots \\ \vdots & & & \ddots & 1 & \ddots & \vdots \\ \vdots & & & & \ddots & \ddots & 0 \\ 0 & \cdots & \cdots & \cdots & \cdots & 0 & 1 \\ -p_0 & -p_1 & -p_2 & -p_3 & \cdots & -p_{n-2} & -p_{n-1} \end{bmatrix},$$

show that

$$\det\left(\lambda \mathbf{I} - \mathbf{A}\right) = \lambda^n + p_{n-1}\lambda^{n-1} + p_{n-2}\lambda^{n-2} + \cdots + p_1\lambda + p_0.$$

A is called the **companion matrix** of the polynomial $\det\left(\lambda\mathbf{I} - \mathbf{A}\right)$.

23. We normally compute the rank of a matrix by counting the number of nonzero rows in its row-reduced or row echelon form. In general, this computation involves the use of floating point arithmetic, even if the entries of the matrix are integers. The following is an outline of an alternative algorithm due to L.J. Gerstein. Its strength lies in its nonuse of division. First arrange the rows and/or columns of **A** so that $A_{11} \neq 0$. For $j = 2 : m$, $k = 2 : n$, define D_{jk} to be the determinant of the 2×2 submatrix that lies at the intersections of rows 1 and j with columns 1 and k. Thus

$$D_{jk} := \begin{vmatrix} A_{11} & A_{1k} \\ A_{j1} & A_{jk} \end{vmatrix} = A_{11}A_{jk} - A_{j1}A_{1k}.$$

Our goal is to show that when $A_{11} \neq 0$,

$$\text{rank}(\mathbf{A}) = 1 + \text{rank}\left(\begin{bmatrix} D_{22} & \cdots & D_{2n} \\ \vdots & \ddots & \vdots \\ D_{m2} & \cdots & D_{mn} \end{bmatrix}\right).$$

(a) Multiply all but row one of **A** by A_{11} and then form $(j) - A_{j1}(1)$ for $j = 2 : m$. From this, prove the algorithm works.

(b) Apply the algorithm to the matrices

$$\begin{bmatrix} 1 & 2 & 3 \\ 4 & 5 & 6 \\ 7 & 8 & 9 \end{bmatrix}, \quad \begin{bmatrix} 3 & 1 & -1 & 2 \\ 2 & 1 & 2 & 3 \\ 7 & 2 & -2 & 6 \\ 5 & 1 & 2 & 3 \end{bmatrix}, \quad \text{and} \quad \begin{bmatrix} 1 & -i & -1 & i \\ i & 1 & i & -1 \\ 1 & i & 1 & i \\ i & 1 & -i & 1 \end{bmatrix}.$$

1.7 COMPUTER SOLUTION OF LINEAR SYSTEMS

1.7.1 Gaussian Elimination

Since our goal is the solution of the system of n linear equations in n unknowns, represented by the vector equation

$$\mathbf{A}\mathbf{x} = \mathbf{b},$$

we might just wonder why not always use the pivotal reduction scheme that worked so well when done by hand. One major problem is the vagaries of floating point arithmetic. The fewer floating point **operations** (flops) we do, the better the accuracy of our solution. The difficulty is that full reduction sweeping above and below the pivot row to the echelon form uses more operations than necessary. For the kth pivot there are $n - k + 1$ columns to work on and $n - 1$

rows. Thus $(n-1)(n-k+1)$ multiplications and additions are required. As k ranges from 1 to $n-1$ the number of flops is about

$$\sum_{k=1}^{n-1}(n-1)(n-k+1) = \frac{1}{2}n^3 + O(n^2).$$

Approximately $n^3/2$ flops are required. On the other hand, had we swept out only those rows *below* the diagonal, reduced to upper triangular form, and backsubstituted to find the solution, we would have swept out only $(n-k)$ rows, rather than $(n-1)$ and thus the number of flops would be about

$$\sum_{k=1}^{n-1}(n-k)(n-k+1) = \frac{1}{3}n^3 + O(n^2).$$

We would have used about $n^3/3$ flops for this partial reduction. Such a reduction to upper triangular form is called **Gaussian elimination** and is clearly computationally more efficient than full reduction to row-reduced echelon form.

■ **EXAMPLE 1.39**   We can solve the system

$$\begin{array}{rrrrr} x_1 & - & x_2 & + & x_3 & = & 1, \\ 2x_1 & + & x_2 & - & x_3 & = & 2, \\ x_1 & + & x_2 & + & 3x_3 & = & 5 \end{array}$$

by Gaussian elimination as follows:

$$\begin{bmatrix} 1 & -1 & 1 & | & 1 \\ 2 & 1 & -1 & | & 2 \\ 1 & 1 & 3 & | & 5 \end{bmatrix} \hookrightarrow \begin{array}{c} (1) \\ (2)-2(1) \\ (3)-(1) \end{array} \begin{bmatrix} 1 & -1 & 1 & | & 1 \\ 0 & 3 & -3 & | & 0 \\ 0 & 2 & 2 & | & 4 \end{bmatrix}$$

$$\hookrightarrow \begin{array}{c} (1) \\ (2) \\ (3)-\frac{2}{3}(2) \end{array} \begin{bmatrix} 1 & -1 & 1 & | & 1 \\ 0 & 3 & -3 & | & 0 \\ 0 & 0 & 4 & | & 4 \end{bmatrix}.$$

The third equation, $4x_3 = 4$, tells us that $x_3 = 1$. Substituting this into the second equation, we find $3x_2 - 3 = 0 \Rightarrow x_2 = 1$. When these results are used in the first equation, we have

$$x_1 - x_2 + x_3 = 1 \quad \Rightarrow \quad x_1 - 1 + 1 = 1 \quad \Rightarrow \quad x_1 = 1.$$

Thus the solution is $x_1 = x_2 = x_3 = 1$. The final elimination procedure wherein the value of the last variable is found and used in the second to last equation to find the next to last variable and so forth up to the first variable, is called **backsubstitution**.   ■ ■ ■

It has been proven that any general method that relies solely on row or column operations cannot do better than $n^3/3$ flops for general matrices. Strassen has presented an arithmetic method based on a fast matrix multiplication algorithm that uses $O(n^{2.8})$ flops (see problem

(1.4.43)). Recent work has brought the exponent down near 2.5, but the constant associated with the big-O is quite large.

Based on purely economic grounds for number of computations and the ease of programming, Gaussian elimination is superior to full reduction. As such, it should be our first choice for computer implementation.

1.7.2 *Pivoting*

The "good" entry for a hand calculated pivot may not be acceptable for machine computation. In fact, we can decrease the machine error by always choosing the pivot row by looking for the *column* entry with largest magnitude. Such a choice of pivot is referred to as **partial pivoting**:

$$
\begin{bmatrix}
\# & \cdots & \cdots & \cdots & & \# & \# & \cdots & \# \\
0 & \# & & & & \# & \# & & \vdots \\
\vdots & 0 & \ddots & & & \vdots & \vdots & & \vdots \\
\vdots & & \ddots & \# & & \# & \# & \cdots & \# \\
\vdots & & & 0 & & \vdots & \vdots & & \\
\vdots & & & \vdots & & \vdots & \vdots & \text{stuff} & \\
0 & 0 & \cdots & 0 & & \# & \# & \cdots & \#
\end{bmatrix}
$$

$$\Uparrow$$
$$\text{Search}$$
$$\text{here}$$
$$\text{for}$$
$$\text{pivot}$$

The alternative is to choose the entry below and to the right of the reduced part of the matrix that has largest magnitude. This is called **complete**, or **maximal**, **pivoting**.

$$
\begin{bmatrix}
\# & & & & & & & \\
0 & \# & & & & & & \\
\vdots & \ddots & & & & & & \\
\vdots & & 0 & \# & \# & \cdots & \# & \\
\vdots & \vdots & & \text{Search} & \text{in} & \text{here} & & \\
\vdots & \vdots & & \text{for} & \text{next} & \text{pivot} & & \\
0 & \cdots & 0 & & & & &
\end{bmatrix}
$$

Complete pivoting at the kth column requires a search of each of the $(n-k)^2$ remaining entries and an interchange of variable labels; it is seldom worth the extra effort required.

The recommended strategy for the solution of most linear systems is to use Gaussian elimination with partial pivoting. One possible form of the algorithm is:

Gaussian Elimination with Partial Pivoting
$n = \text{size}(A)$;
$\text{aug} = [A, b]$; $x = \text{zeros}(n, 1)$;
for $k = 1 : n - 1$ $p = k$;
   for $i = k : n$
     if $\text{abs}\,(\text{aug}(p, k)) < \text{abs}\,(\text{aug}(i, k))$
       $p = i$;
     end
     if $\text{aug}(p, k) == 0$
       display('matrix is singular')
     end
     if $p \sim= k$
       $\text{temp} = \text{aug}(p, :)$;
       $\text{aug}(p, :) = \text{aug}(k, :)$;
       $\text{aug}(k, :) = \text{temp}$;
     end
       for $i = (k + 1) : n$
         $\text{aug}(i, :) = \text{aug}(i, :) - \text{aug}(i, k) / \text{aug}(k, k) * \text{aug}(k, :)$;
       end % now tril(aug) will be all zeros
if $\text{aug}(n, n) == 0$
   display('no solution exists')
end
for $j = n : -1 : 1$
   $x(j) = (\text{aug}(j, n + 1) - \text{aug}(j, 1 : n) * x) / \text{aug}(j, j)$;
end
x % this prints the solution

One reasonable check of accuracy when solving any linear system is the computation of the **residual vector** $\mathbf{r} := \mathbf{b} - \mathbf{A}\mathbf{x}$ and its length, $\|\mathbf{r}\|^2 = \sqrt{\mathbf{r}^H \mathbf{r}}$. This should be done in double precision. Gaussian elimination with partial pivoting is fairly certain to yield low residuals $\|\mathbf{r}\|$. In this sense, it provides a good approximation to the true solution.

1.7.3 Scaling

Something we should worry about is the relative magnitude of the numbers we are subtracting and/or dividing—floating point arithmetic is not associative. We would prefer to be working with numbers that are of about the same magnitude. If one row of the augmented matrix is either several orders of magnitude smaller or larger than the others, it should be a simple matter to use (ERO1) to multiply the row by a nonzero constant to bring it into line. In theory any multiple of an equation has the same solutions as the equation, and so this should have absolutely no effect on the computed solution. In a similar vein, if the entries of any one column of $\mathbf{A}$ were disproportionately sized with respect to the other columns we could replace the variable corresponding to that column by a multiple of itself that would restore the relative similarity of size. Such maneuvering is called **scaling**.

More specifically, we could use the diagonal matrices

$$\mathbf{D}_r := \mathbf{diag}\left(\beta^{r_1}, \beta^{r_2}, \ldots, \beta^{r_n}\right),$$
$$\mathbf{D}_c := \mathbf{diag}\left(\beta^{c_1}, \beta^{c_2}, \ldots, \beta^{c_n}\right),$$

where β is the base of the machine arithmetic and the r's and c's are integers. Replace the system $\mathbf{Ax} = \mathbf{b}$ by the fully scaled system

$$(\mathbf{D}_r^{-1}\mathbf{AD}_c)\mathbf{y} = \mathbf{D}_r^{-1}\mathbf{b}.$$

The matrix $\mathbf{D}_r$ is chosen to scale the rows (equations) of $\mathbf{A}$ and $\mathbf{D}_c$ the columns (variables) because $\mathbf{x} = \mathbf{D}_c\mathbf{y}$. In **simple row scaling** we take $\mathbf{D}_c = \mathbf{I}$ and choose the r_i so that each row has about the same size (one possibility is to have the entry of largest magnitude scaled to 1, but we won't discuss the precise meaning of that). The combination of row and column scaling is often called **equilibration**. At present, there is no clear-cut or theoretically reasonable way to equilibrate a general square matrix.

As theoretically nice as scaling may seem, its appropriateness for computation is not recommended. Examples have been given where scaling *reduces* the accuracy of the solution.

The final advice is that if scaling is to be done, use only row scaling and either

(a) use scaling implicitly as a means of choosing the pivot row without actually changing the numerical values of the row entries, or

(b) use scale factors rounded to the nearest power of β and actually change the row entries. Multiplication or division by β will only change the exponent and leave the mantissa of the entry unchanged, and this process can be performed without error, except for possible overflow or underflow for which a flag should be provided.

1.7.4 Ill-conditioning

When solving n equations in n unknowns, we know that there will be a unique solution whenever the coefficient matrix reduces to the identity, which is equivalent to insisting that it have rank n. This is a go/no-go condition: a matrix either has rank n or it doesn't, at least theoretically. In practice, when row-reducing $\mathbf{A}$ there could be a truncation error introduced that prevents us from telling at any given stage whether two rows are multiples of each other or, for that matter, whether we have a row of zeros or not.

To illustrate the problem, let's study the system

$$
\begin{aligned}
x_1 - x_2 + x_3 - x_4 &= -3, \\
x_1 - x_2 + x_3 - x_4 &= -2, \\
x_1 - x_2 &= -1, \\
x_1 - x_4 &= -3.
\end{aligned}
$$

As it stands, this is an inconsistent system because the first two coefficient rows are the same but $-3 \neq -2$. No amount of (legitimate) reduction or manipulation could generate a solution. But suppose that in inputting the system a small error was introduced. It could come about as a read error, a floating point approximation to a true coefficient value, or during some other operation. Further suppose that the only error is in the coefficient of x_1 in the first equation:

$$
\begin{aligned}
(1 - 10^{-n})\,x_1 - x_2 + x_3 - x_4 &= -3 \\
x_1 - x_2 + x_3 - x_4 &= -2 \\
x_1 - x_2 &= -1 \\
x_1 - x_4 &= -3
\end{aligned}
$$

Since n could be as large as we want, the deviation between this system and the true system can be made arbitrarily small. Despite the seeming proximity between the two systems, the second has a solution while the first does not. On this score they are essentially "infinitely far" apart. The solution of the second is

$$
x_1 = 10^n, \quad x_2 = 10^n + 1, \quad x_3 = 10^n + 2, \quad x_4 = 10^n + 3.
$$

Had we omitted the first equation from the original system, the result would have been consistent with the solution

$$
x_1 = \alpha, \quad x_2 = \alpha + 1, \quad x_3 = \alpha + 2, \quad x_4 = \alpha + 3.
$$

Geometrically, this is the equation of a line that lives in four dimensions. The point on the line that is a solution to the system with the perturbed first equation corresponds to $\alpha = 10^n$. For n large, this point is *very far* from the origin. A small perturbation has moved the solution a large distance.

The perturbed system given above is an example of an **ill-conditioned system**. For such systems, small changes in the coefficients lead to large changes in the solution. Solution of such systems requires special care and methods that fall beyond the scope of this book.

One special matrix illustrates the problems associated with this phenomenon. The **Hilbert segment** of order n, $\mathbf{H}_{(n)}$ is defined to be the $n \times n$ matrix whose jk^{th} entry is $1/(j+k-1)$. If we use Matlab to compute $\mathbf{inv}(\mathbf{H}(n))$, form the product $\mathbf{E} := \mathbf{H}(n) * \mathbf{inv}(\mathbf{H}(n))$, and then extract the smallest and largest entries from $\mathbf{E}$ (which should be 0 and 1, respectively), we find the following very surprising results:

n	$\min\left(\min(\mathbf{E})\right)$	$\max\left(\max(\mathbf{E})\right)$
10	-0.0016	1.0000
11	-0.0362	1.0077
12	-1.4361	1.6803
13	-22.487	22.156
14	-47.376	49.265
15	$-41,200$	357.14
16	-657.68	519.54
17	$-14,716$	1,755
18	$-14,050$	1,452
19	$-4,544$	3,823
20	$-114,940$	82,314

The degree to which $\mathbf{E}$ differs from the identity matrix is amazing. This is a result of the inexactness of floating point arithmetic. As an added tidbit, the minimum entry in $\mathbf{H}_{(10)}^{-1}$ is $-2,121,035,716,800$ and the maximum is $44,914,183,600$. This is especially astounding when you consider that the entries of $\mathbf{H}_{(10)}$ itself go from a low of $\frac{1}{19}$ up to a high of 1.

1.7.5 Exercise Set

Write a program to solve a system of n linear equations in n unknowns using Gaussian elimination with partial pivoting. Analyze each of the following test systems in both single and double precision arithmetic. Write an additional subprogram to compute the residuals.

1. $\begin{aligned}
33x_1 + 16x_2 + 72x_3 &= -359 \\
-24x_1 + 10x_2 - 57x_3 &= 281 \\
-8x_1 - 4x_2 - 17x_3 &= 85
\end{aligned}$

2. $\begin{aligned}
x_1 + (1+2i)x_2 + (2+10i)x_3 &= 5+5i \\
(1+i)x_1 + 3ix_2 - (5-4i)x_3 &= 6+3i \\
(1+i)x_1 + 5ix_2 - (8-20i)x_3 &= -2
\end{aligned}$

3. $\begin{aligned}
x_1 - 2x_2 + 3x_3 + x_4 &= 3 \\
-2x_1 + x_2 - 2x_3 - x_4 &= -4 \\
3x_1 - 2x_2 + x_3 + 5x_4 &= 7 \\
x_1 - x_2 + 5x_3 + 3x_4 &= 8
\end{aligned}$

4. $\begin{aligned} x_1 + x_2 + x_3 + x_4 &= 217 \\ x_1 + 2x_2 + 3x_3 + 4x_4 &= 326 \\ x_1 + 3x_2 + 6x_3 + 10x_4 &= -592 \\ x_1 + 4x_2 + 10x_3 + 20x_4 &= 714 \end{aligned}$

5. $\begin{aligned} (0.9561E - 4)x_1 &= .00009561 \\ 0.7123x_1 + (0.9125E - 4)x_2 &= .71239125 \\ 0.8316x_1 + 0.9017x_2 \\ + (0.8563E - 4)x_3 &= 1.73338563 \\ 0.7231x_1 + 0.8178x_2 \\ + 0.6519x_3 \\ + (0.8867E - 4)x_4 &= 2.19288867 \end{aligned}$

6. $\begin{aligned} x_1 \qquad\qquad\qquad + x_{30} &= 2 \\ x_2 \qquad\qquad\quad + 2x_{30} &= 3 \\ x_3 \qquad\quad + 3x_{30} &= 4 \\ \ddots \qquad \vdots \quad\vdots \quad\vdots \\ x_{29} + 29x_{30} &= 30 \\ x_1 + 2x_2 + 3x_3 + \cdots + 29x_{29} + 30x_{30} &= 435 \end{aligned}$

7. Construct the system $\mathbf{H}\mathbf{1} = \mathbf{b}$, where $\mathbf{1} = \mathbf{ones}(n)$, and $\mathbf{H}$ is the Hilbert segment of order n–in Matlab it's $\mathbf{hilb}(n)$. Write a program, or use Matlab's backslash operator $\mathbf{A} \backslash \mathbf{b}$, to evaluate $\mathbf{b}$ for $n = 5 : 5 : 30$. Use these values and your program to solve the system and compute the residuals $\mathbf{r} = \mathbf{1} - \tilde{\mathbf{x}}$, where $\tilde{\mathbf{x}}$ is the computed solution of the system $\mathbf{H}\mathbf{x} = \mathbf{b}$. Also compute the norms of the residuals. Compare this quantity with n. At which value of n does your program no longer give you meaningful results?

1.8 LU-DECOMPOSITION

There are times when Gaussian elimination has unacceptable relative efficiency for either sparse or patterned matrices, so that we should look for another algorithm. To develop a more efficient scheme requires us to think about what constitutes an "easy" system to solve. In point of fact, if we could start with an upper triangular system, then backsubstitution would be all that was needed for solution. We know that backsubstitution requires about $1 + 2 + 3 + \cdots + n \approx n^2/2$ flops, which is a significant reduction over $n^3/3$ for large n. Of course, Gaussian elimination using elementary matrices will reduce $\mathbf{A}$ to upper triangular form. In addition, the product of the elementary matrices that perform this reduction, whenever we choose the natural order of pivots (i.e., there are no interchanges), will be lower triangular. Thus there is a factorization of $\mathbf{A}$ into

$$\mathbf{A} = \mathbf{L}\mathbf{U},$$

where $\mathbf{L}$ is lower triangular and $\mathbf{U}$ is upper triangular.

■ **EXAMPLE 1.40** For the following matrix we have the elementary matrix factorization $\mathbf{R} = \mathbf{E}_2 \mathbf{E}_1 \mathbf{A}$:

$$
\mathbf{R} = \begin{bmatrix} 1 & -1 & 1 \\ 0 & 3 & -3 \\ 0 & 0 & 4 \end{bmatrix} = \begin{bmatrix} 1 & 0 & 0 \\ 0 & 1 & 0 \\ 0 & -\frac{2}{3} & 1 \end{bmatrix} \begin{bmatrix} 1 & 0 & 0 \\ -2 & 1 & 0 \\ -1 & 0 & 1 \end{bmatrix} \begin{bmatrix} 1 & -1 & 1 \\ 2 & 1 & -1 \\ 1 & 1 & 3 \end{bmatrix}.
$$

The inverse relation $\mathbf{A} = \mathbf{E}_1^{-1} \mathbf{E}_2^{-1} \mathbf{R}$ is

$$
\mathbf{A} = \begin{bmatrix} 1 & -1 & 1 \\ 2 & 1 & -1 \\ 1 & 1 & 3 \end{bmatrix} = \begin{bmatrix} 1 & 0 & 0 \\ 2 & 1 & 0 \\ 1 & 0 & 1 \end{bmatrix} \begin{bmatrix} 1 & 0 & 0 \\ 0 & 1 & 0 \\ 0 & \frac{2}{3} & 1 \end{bmatrix} \begin{bmatrix} 1 & -1 & 1 \\ 0 & 3 & -3 \\ 0 & 0 & 4 \end{bmatrix}.
$$

Therefore, one possible LU-decomposition is

$$
\mathbf{A} = \begin{bmatrix} 1 & 0 & 0 \\ 2 & 1 & 0 \\ 1 & \frac{2}{3} & 1 \end{bmatrix} \begin{bmatrix} 1 & -1 & 1 \\ 0 & 3 & -3 \\ 0 & 0 & 4 \end{bmatrix}.
$$

■ ■ ■

Looking at the last example provides us with a clue as to how to compute the lower triangular matrix $\mathbf{L}$. Since the echelon form or even just the upper triangular form obtained from Gaussian elimination can be written as

$$
\mathbf{U} = \mathbf{E}_N \mathbf{E}_{N-1} \cdots \mathbf{E}_2 \mathbf{E}_1 \mathbf{A},
$$

we can write

$$
\mathbf{A} = \mathbf{E}_1^{-1} \mathbf{E}_2^{-1} \cdots \mathbf{E}_N^{-1} \mathbf{U}.
$$

The matrix $\mathbf{U}$ will be upper triangular and $\mathbf{L} = \mathbf{E}_1^{-1} \mathbf{E}_2^{-1} \cdots \mathbf{E}_N^{-1}$ will be lower triangular whenever there are no interchanges. We can compute $\mathbf{L}$ by using the inverse of each of the noninterchange elementary row operations that reduce $\mathbf{A}$ to triangular form. If we write $\mathbf{L}_1$ for the lower triangular matrix that combines the elementary matrices that sweep out the first column, write $\mathbf{P}_1$ for the permutation matrix that interchanges rows in that first sweep (possibly the identity), and proceed similarly, then the reduction will take the form

$$
\mathbf{U} = \mathbf{L}_{n-1} \mathbf{P}_{n-1} \mathbf{L}_{n-2} \mathbf{P}_{n-2} \cdots \mathbf{L}_2 \mathbf{P}_2 \mathbf{L}_1 \mathbf{P}_1 \mathbf{A}.
$$

The permutations merely tell us the order in which the rows of $\mathbf{A}$ should have been so that we could have performed the reduction without interchanges. Hence, we could reorder the rows of $\mathbf{A}$ at the outset by using

$$
\mathbf{P} = \mathbf{P}_{n-1} \mathbf{P}_{n-2} \cdots \mathbf{P}_2 \mathbf{P}_1.
$$

Then the simplest decomposition would be

$$
\mathbf{PA} = \mathbf{LU},
$$

when $\mathbf{L} = \mathbf{L}_1^{-1}\mathbf{L}_2^{-1}\cdots\mathbf{L}_{n-1}^{-1}\mathbf{L}_n^{-1}$. If we write

$$\mathbf{L}_1 = \begin{bmatrix} 1 & 0 & \cdots & \cdots & 0 \\ m_{21} & 1 & 0 & & \vdots \\ m_{31} & 0 & 1 & \ddots & \vdots \\ \vdots & \vdots & \ddots & \ddots & 0 \\ m_{n1} & 0 & \cdots & 0 & 1 \end{bmatrix},$$

then $\mathbf{L}_1^{-1}$ can be obtained by simply reversing the signs of all the m's, corresponding to the inverse elementary row operations.

■ **EXAMPLE 1.41** Let's compute the factorization for a matrix that does not require any interchanges to be reduced to upper triangular form.

$$\mathbf{A} = \begin{bmatrix} 1 & 2 & 3 \\ 4 & 5 & 6 \\ 7 & 8 & 9 \end{bmatrix} \begin{array}{c} (1) \\ \hookrightarrow (2)-4(1) \\ (3)-7(1) \end{array} \begin{bmatrix} 1 & 2 & 3 \\ 0 & -3 & -6 \\ 0 & -6 & -12 \end{bmatrix}$$

$$\hookrightarrow \begin{array}{c} (1) \\ (2) \\ (3)-2(2) \end{array} \begin{bmatrix} 1 & 2 & 3 \\ 0 & -3 & -6 \\ 0 & 0 & 0 \end{bmatrix}$$

Thus one possible upper triangular form is

$$\mathbf{U} = \begin{bmatrix} 1 & 2 & 3 \\ 0 & -3 & -6 \\ 0 & 0 & 0 \end{bmatrix}.$$

The inverses of the row operations $(2)-4(1)$ and $(3)-7(1)$, which sweep out the first column, are $(2)+4(1)$ and $(3)+7(1)$, respectively. We may write

$$\mathbf{L} = \begin{bmatrix} 1 & 0 & 0 \\ 4 & 1 & 0 \\ 7 & \# & 1 \end{bmatrix}.$$

The inverse of $(3)-2(2)$, which completes the sweep of the second column, is $(3)+2(2)$, so that we have

$$\mathbf{L} = \begin{bmatrix} 1 & 0 & 0 \\ 4 & 1 & 0 \\ 7 & 2 & 1 \end{bmatrix}.$$

Therefore, we can write the decomposition in the form

$$\mathbf{A} = \begin{bmatrix} 1 & 2 & 3 \\ 4 & 5 & 6 \\ 7 & 8 & 9 \end{bmatrix} = \begin{bmatrix} 1 & 0 & 0 \\ 4 & 1 & 0 \\ 7 & 2 & 1 \end{bmatrix} \begin{bmatrix} 1 & 2 & 3 \\ 0 & -3 & -6 \\ 0 & 0 & 0 \end{bmatrix} = \mathbf{LU}.$$

■ ■ ■

Generally, if we could efficiently find such a decomposition then the system could be rewritten as the pair of linear systems

$$\mathbf{Ax = b} \quad \Leftrightarrow \quad \mathbf{LUx = b} \quad \Leftrightarrow \quad \mathbf{Ux = y} \text{ and } \mathbf{Ly = b}.$$

As you can see, all that remains is the solution of two triangular systems, the first for $\mathbf{y}$ and the second for $\mathbf{x}$, which should involve a total of $2n^2$ flops, still much less than $n^3/3$ for large n. When interchanges are required, then we must use

$$\mathbf{PAx = Pb} =: \tilde{\mathbf{b}} \quad \Leftrightarrow \quad \mathbf{LUx} = \tilde{\mathbf{b}} \quad \Leftrightarrow \quad \mathbf{Ux = y} \text{ and } \mathbf{Ly} = \tilde{\mathbf{b}}.$$

In practice we need not compute the permutation matrix $\mathbf{P}$ but rather only keep a record of the interchanges that need to be applied.

■ **EXAMPLE 1.42** Suppose the system $\mathbf{Ax = b}$ can be decomposed into

$$\begin{bmatrix} 1 & 0 & 0 \\ -1 & 3 & 0 \\ 2 & 1 & 1 \end{bmatrix} \begin{bmatrix} 1 & 2 & 3 \\ 0 & -2 & 1 \\ 0 & 0 & 4 \end{bmatrix} \mathbf{x} = \begin{bmatrix} 7 \\ -22 \\ 13 \end{bmatrix}.$$

The system $\mathbf{Ly = b}$ can be solved by forward substitution:

$$\begin{bmatrix} 1 & 0 & 0 \\ -1 & 3 & 0 \\ 2 & 1 & 1 \end{bmatrix} \mathbf{y} = \begin{bmatrix} 7 \\ -22 \\ 13 \end{bmatrix} \quad \Rightarrow \quad \begin{matrix} y_1 = 7 \\ -7 + 3y_2 = -5 \quad \Rightarrow \quad y_2 = -5 \\ 14 - 5 + y_3 = 13 \quad \Rightarrow \quad y_3 = 4 \end{matrix}$$

The system $\mathbf{Ux = y}$ can be solved by backsubstitution:

$$\begin{bmatrix} 1 & 2 & 3 \\ 0 & -2 & 1 \\ 0 & 0 & 4 \end{bmatrix} \mathbf{x} = \begin{bmatrix} 7 \\ -5 \\ 4 \end{bmatrix} \quad \Rightarrow \quad \begin{matrix} x_3 = 1 \\ -2x_2 + 1 = -5 \quad \Rightarrow \quad x_2 = 3 \\ x_1 + 6 + 3 = 7 \quad \Rightarrow \quad x_1 = -2 \end{matrix}$$

■ ■ ■

There are several variants on this LU-decomposition:

- **Crout Reduction**: $\mathbf{U}$ has ones along its main diagonal.

- **Doolittle Reduction**: $\mathbf{L}$ has ones along its main diagonal.

- **Cholesky Reduction**: $\mathbf{U = L}^T$ and $\mathbf{L}$ has positive entries on its main diagonal.

Cholesky reduction can only be implemented for what are called positive definite matrices, but that will be left to the references, such as Golub and van Loan.

■ **EXAMPLE 1.43** For the matrix $[1, 2, 1; 2, 13, 2; 1, 2, 2]$, some of the various LU-decompositions are

$$
\begin{bmatrix} 1 & 0 & 0 \\ 2 & 9 & 0 \\ 1 & 0 & 1 \end{bmatrix} \begin{bmatrix} 1 & 2 & 1 \\ 0 & 1 & 0 \\ 0 & 0 & 1 \end{bmatrix} = \begin{bmatrix} 1 & 0 & 0 \\ 2 & 1 & 0 \\ 1 & 0 & 1 \end{bmatrix} \begin{bmatrix} 1 & 2 & 1 \\ 0 & 9 & 0 \\ 0 & 0 & 1 \end{bmatrix}
$$

$$
\underset{\text{Crout Reduction}}{} \qquad \underset{\text{Doolittle Reduction}}{}
$$

$$
= \begin{bmatrix} 1 & 0 & 0 \\ 2 & 3 & 0 \\ 1 & 0 & 1 \end{bmatrix} \begin{bmatrix} 1 & 2 & 1 \\ 0 & 3 & 0 \\ 0 & 0 & 1 \end{bmatrix}.
$$

$$
\underset{\text{Cholesky Reduction}}{}
$$

■ ■ ■

Neither the Crout nor the Doolittle decompositions are unique. You could use a different reduction scheme to generate an alternative form of each of the results shown above. The Cholesky decomposition (when it exists) is unique. The LU-decomposition's strong point is that once **A** is decomposed into **LU**, the solution of the system $\mathbf{Ax} = \mathbf{b}$ involves n^2 flops for each new **b**, no matter how many there are and when they are given. On the other hand, Gaussian elimination must be performed anew, using $n^3/3$ flops for each new **b** given after the solution of the initial system, if this decomposition is not used.

For nonpatterned matrices the Crout and Doolittle Reductions have smaller round-off error than Gaussian elimination whenever the computer has a $2p$ bit accumulator; otherwise, there is no advantage. All methods shown so far can be used to find the inverse of a nonsingular matrix **A** by solving the n linear systems represented by

$$\mathbf{AX} = \mathbf{I}.$$

Gaussian elimination can handle the problem in one pass with the augmented matrix $[\mathbf{A}|\mathbf{I}]$. The LU-decomposition is equally effective insofar as once the decomposition is found, **L** and **U** can be stored and any system $\mathbf{AX} = \mathbf{B}$ can be solved later by using forward substitution on $\mathbf{LY} = \mathbf{B}$ and backsubstitution on $\mathbf{UX} = \mathbf{Y}$.

1.8.1 Exercise Set

Find an LU-decomposition (by hand) of each of the following matrices.

1.
$$
\begin{bmatrix} 1 & 2 & 3 \\ 4 & 5 & 6 \\ 7 & 8 & 8 \end{bmatrix}
$$

2.
$$
\begin{bmatrix} 1 & 1 & 1 \\ 1 & 2 & 1 \\ 2 & 2 & 3 \end{bmatrix}
$$

3.
$$
\begin{bmatrix} i & 1 & i \\ -i & 2 & i \\ i & 1 & i \end{bmatrix}
$$

4. Use an LU-decomposition program–the command in Matlab is $[\mathbf{L}, \mathbf{U}] = \mathbf{lu}(\mathbf{A})$–to find the inverses of the first 10 Hilbert segments. Compare your results with the exact value of the inverse of the nth order segment, whose jk^{th} entry is

$$\frac{(-1)^{j+k}(n-j+1)!(n+k-1)!}{(j+k-1)\left((j-1)!(k-1)!\right)^2 (n-j)!(n-k)!}.$$

5. Wilkinson has given the following example of a well-conditioned nonsymmetric matrix:

$$\mathbf{W} = \begin{bmatrix} 1 & 0 & 0 & 0 & 0 & 1 \\ 1 & 1 & 0 & 0 & 0 & -1 \\ -1 & 1 & 1 & 0 & 0 & 1 \\ 1 & -1 & 1 & 1 & 0 & -1 \\ -1 & 1 & -1 & 1 & 1 & 1 \\ 1 & -1 & 1 & -1 & 1 & -1 \end{bmatrix}.$$

Show that the inverse has the transpose of the zero pattern of $\mathbf{W}$ with largest element $1/2$ and smallest element $1/32$. Use either the LU-decomposition or hand calculation with pivotal reduction.

6. By hand, find the Crout and Doolittle decompositions of the matrix

$$\begin{bmatrix} 16 & 4 & 8 \\ 4 & 5 & -4 \\ 8 & -4 & 22 \end{bmatrix}.$$

1.8.2 Notes and References

There are many areas of matrix algebra that are of current research interest. In particular, the development of better algorithms for calculation continues. Also, applications to partial differential equations require the solution of extremely large linear systems when the coefficient matrix has a special structure, such as tridiagonal. Often when a matrix has a special form, a great deal of saving can be effected by utilizing the pattern of nonzero elements. The interested reader is invited to consult current issues of **SIAM Review** for relevant expository articles written at a level that will require some effort but are not impossible.

No account of matrices and linear algebra would be complete without mention of the vast amount of high quality software currently available for all types of computer implementation of efficient algorithms. ASYST, IMSL, MathAdvantage, and the NAG library are large collections of algorithms and polyalgorithms for implementation on mini or mainframe computers. All are what you would call state of the art. LINPACK is a large public domain package for solving linear systems.

Microcomputers have not been neglected. GAUSS and PC-Matlab are but two examples of the advanced software packages available. Both implement all the algorithms discussed in this chapter and many more. Speed, advanced graphics capabilities, and relative user friendliness are the norm for such packages. Even easy to use languages, such as True Basic, have built-in matrix operations such as $\mathbf{inv}(\mathbf{A})$ and $\det(\mathbf{A})$. Most computer algebra systems have extensive matrix capabilities, although the command syntax varies from system to system.

- Gantmacher, **Matrix Theory**: An older but encyclopedic coverage of matrix algebra.

- Golub & van Loan, **Matrix Computations, 2nd ed.**: Up to date coverage of numerical linear algebra at an advanced level.

- Hoffman & Kunze, **Linear Algebra, 2nd ed.**: A more theoretical approach to the subject. It is considered to be a classic in the field.

- Horn & Johnson, **Matrix Analysis**: An advanced, theoretical, and fairly complete account of many aspects of the subject.

- Jennings, **Matrix Computations for Engineers and Scientists, 2nd ed.**: An intermediate level book dealing with some of the nitty-gritty issues of implementing many of the numerical algorithms used in matrix algebra.

- Noble & Daniel, **Applied Linear Algebra, 3rd ed.**: A comprehensive and readable account of the subject with many applications and frequent references to PC-Matlab.

- Rice, **Numerical Methods: Software and Analysis**: A working person's guide to numerical methods.

- Stewart, **Introduction to Matrix Computations**: A clear introduction to numerical methods in linear algebra.

- Varga, **Matrix Iterative Analysis**: One of the first books on the subject and a classic in the field.

- Watkins, **Fundamentals of Matrix Computations**: An intermediate to advanced level book with a complete coverage of numerical methods.

1.9 SUPPLEMENTARY AND COMPLEMENTARY PROBLEMS

1. What is the minimum number of *real* parameters needed to completely specify a complex $n \times n$ symmetric matrix? Hermitian matrix? Skew-symmetric matrix? Skew-Hermitian matrix?

2. Define the **commutator** of the square matrices $\mathbf{A}$ and $\mathbf{B}$ by $[\mathbf{A}, \mathbf{B}] := \mathbf{AB} - \mathbf{BA}$.

   (a) Show that $[\mathbf{A}, \mathbf{BC}] = [\mathbf{A}, \mathbf{B}]\mathbf{C} + \mathbf{B}[\mathbf{A}, \mathbf{C}]$.

   (b) Show that if $\mathbf{B}$ commutes with its commutator with $\mathbf{A}$, i.e., $[\mathbf{B}, [\mathbf{A}, \mathbf{B}]] = \mathbf{0}$ then for any positive integer n we have $[\mathbf{A}, \mathbf{B}^n] = n\mathbf{B}^{n-1}[\mathbf{A}, \mathbf{B}]$. [Hint: Use mathematical induction.]

3. If we define the **anticommutator** of $\mathbf{A}$ and $\mathbf{B}$ by $\{\mathbf{A}, \mathbf{B}\} := \mathbf{AB} + \mathbf{BA}$, is there an analogous result to the previous problem? If so, prove it.

4. Is it possible to have $[\mathbf{A}, \mathbf{B}] = a\mathbf{I}$ for matrices in $\mathbb{C}_n^n$? [Hint: Look at the trace of both sides.]

   This is an extremely relevant question because for the infinite matrices encountered in the Heisenberg formulation of quantum mechanics, one finds $[\mathbf{X}, \mathbf{P}] = i\hbar\mathbf{I}$, where $\mathbf{X}$ and $\mathbf{P}$ are the matrices corresponding to position and momentum and $\hbar$ is a constant. Because of this commutation relation, position and momentum are not simultaneously measurable, which is the statement of the **Heisenberg Uncertainty Principle**.

5. If $\mathbf{A} = \mathbf{B} + \mathbf{C}$, $\mathbf{C}^2 = \mathbf{0}$, and $[\mathbf{B}, \mathbf{C}] = \mathbf{0}$, show that for any natural number m, $\mathbf{A}^{m+1} = \mathbf{B}^m[\mathbf{B} + (m+1)\mathbf{C}]$.

6. The **Pauli spin matrices**, σ_0, σ_1, σ_2, and σ_3, are defined by

$$\sigma_0 = \mathbf{I}, \quad \sigma_1 = \begin{bmatrix} 0 & 1 \\ 1 & 0 \end{bmatrix}, \quad \sigma_2 = \begin{bmatrix} 0 & -i \\ i & 0 \end{bmatrix}, \quad \sigma_3 = \begin{bmatrix} 1 & 0 \\ 0 & -1 \end{bmatrix}.$$

Show that:

   (a) $\sigma_0^2 = \sigma_1^2 = \sigma_2^2 = \sigma_3^2 = \mathbf{I} = \sigma_0$.

   (b) $\sigma_1\sigma_2 = i\sigma_3$, $\sigma_2\sigma_3 = i\sigma_1$, $\sigma_3\sigma_1 = i\sigma_2$.

   (c) $[\sigma_1, \sigma_2] = 2i\sigma_3$, $[\sigma_2, \sigma_3] = 2i\sigma_1$, $[\sigma_3, \sigma_1] = 2i\sigma_2$, where $[\mathbf{A}, \mathbf{B}] := \mathbf{AB} - \mathbf{BA}$ is the commutator of $\mathbf{A}$ and $\mathbf{B}$.

   (d) $\{\sigma_1, \sigma_2\} = 0$, $\{\sigma_2, \sigma_3\} = 0$, $\{\sigma_3, \sigma_1\} = 0$, where $\{\mathbf{A}, \mathbf{B}\} := \mathbf{AB} + \mathbf{BA}$ is the anticommutator of $\mathbf{A}$ and $\mathbf{B}$.

   (e) If we write $\boldsymbol{\sigma} := [\sigma_1, \sigma_2, \sigma_3]$, which of these identities is contained in the formula $\boldsymbol{\sigma} \times \boldsymbol{\sigma} = 2i\boldsymbol{\sigma}$, where $\times$ is the vector cross product?

7. Following the vector notation of the previous problem, for an arbitrary complex 2×2 matrix write $\mathbf{A} = a_0\sigma_0 + \mathbf{a} \cdot \boldsymbol{\sigma}$ (where $\mathbf{a} \cdot \boldsymbol{\sigma} = a_1\sigma_1 + a_2\sigma_2 + a_3\sigma_3$ is the "scalar product" of two vectors) and find a_0 and $\mathbf{a}$ in terms of the entries of $\mathbf{A}$.

8. If we associate an arbitrary complex vector $\mathbf{a} = a_1\mathbf{i} + a_2\mathbf{j} + a_3\mathbf{k}$ with the complex matrix $\mathbf{A} = a_1\sigma_1 + a_2\sigma_2 + a_3\sigma_3$, show that under matrix multiplication of two such matrices we will have $\mathbf{AB} = \mathbf{a} \cdot \mathbf{b}\sigma_0 + i\mathbf{C}$, where $\mathbf{C}$ is the matrix associated with the vector $\mathbf{c} = \mathbf{a} \times \mathbf{b}$.

9. Let us write a complex 2×2 matrix as a linear combination of the Pauli spin matrices:

$$\mathbf{A} = a_0\sigma_0 + a_1\sigma_1 + a_2\sigma_2 + a_3\sigma_3.$$

Show that $|\mathbf{A}| = a_0^2 - a_1^2 - a_2^2 - a_3^2$.

10. The **Dirac matrices** can be defined in terms of the Pauli spin matrices in several ways. One possibility is the following partitioned form:

$$\gamma_k := \begin{bmatrix} 0 & -i\sigma_k \\ i\sigma_k & 0 \end{bmatrix}, \quad k = 1:3, \quad \gamma_4 := \begin{bmatrix} I & 0 \\ 0 & -I \end{bmatrix}.$$

Using γ_μ, $\mu = 1:4$, to denote these matrices, show that

(a) $\gamma_\mu^2 = I_4$.

(b) All of the γ_μ are Hermitian.

(c) $\{\gamma_\mu, \gamma_\nu\} = 0$ for $\mu \neq \nu$.

(d) If we define $\gamma_5 := \gamma_1\gamma_2\gamma_3\gamma_4$, then show that $\{\gamma_\mu, \gamma_5\} = 0$.

11. If we write $w = \exp(-2\pi i/n)$ for the complex conjugate of the first nonreal n^{th} root of unity, then define the **Fourier matrix F** by

$$F_{jk} := \frac{1}{\sqrt{n}} w^{(j-1)(k-1)}, \quad j, k = 1:n.$$

Show that:

(a) All Fourier matrices are symmetric.

(b) All Fourier matrices are unitary.

(c) $\mathbf{F}^2 = [\mathbf{e}_1, \mathbf{e}_n, \mathbf{e}_{n-1}, \ldots, \mathbf{e}_3, \mathbf{e}_2]$, where $\mathbf{e}_k = \mathbf{col}_k(\mathbf{I}_n)$.

(d) $\mathbf{F}^4 = \mathbf{I}_n$.

   If we write a Fourier matrix in terms of its real and imaginary parts as $\mathbf{F} = \mathbf{C} + i\mathbf{S}$, show that:

(e) $[\mathbf{C}, \mathbf{S}] = 0$.

(f) $\mathbf{C}^2 + \mathbf{S}^2 = \mathbf{I}$.

12. Two different "flipping" operations can be defined on matrices, row-flipping and column-flipping. In particular,

$$\mathbf{flipr}(\mathbf{A}) := [\mathbf{row}_m(\mathbf{A}); \mathbf{row}_{m-1}(\mathbf{A}); \ldots; \mathbf{row}_1(\mathbf{A})]$$
$$\mathbf{flipc}(\mathbf{A}) := [\mathbf{col}_n(\mathbf{A}), \mathbf{col}_{n-1}(\mathbf{A}), \ldots, \mathbf{col}_1(\mathbf{A})].$$

Matlab calls these flipud (up-down) and fliplr (left-right), respectively. Show that:

(a) $\mathbf{flipr}(\mathbf{AB}) = \mathbf{flipr}(\mathbf{A})\mathbf{B}$.

(b) $\mathbf{flipc}(\mathbf{AB}) = \mathbf{A}\,\mathbf{flipc}(\mathbf{B})$.

(c) $\mathbf{flipr}(\mathbf{flipc}(\mathbf{A})) = \mathbf{flipc}(\mathbf{flipr}(\mathbf{A}))$.

13. If $\mathbf{A}$ is invertible, show that:

    (a) $(\mathbf{flipr}(\mathbf{A}))^{-1} = \mathbf{flipc}(\mathbf{A}^{-1})$.
    (b) $(\mathbf{flipc}(\mathbf{A}))^{-1} = \mathbf{flipr}(\mathbf{A}^{-1})$.

14. There is a matrix rotation available in Matlab. In particular, $\mathbf{rot90}(\mathbf{A}, k)$ rotates the matrix $\mathbf{A}$ by $90 * k$ degrees counterclockwise, for integral k. Which of the identities from the previous two problems carry over to matrix rotation? Perhaps a computer experiment, using square matrices of even and odd size, is in order.

The **cross transpose** of an $m \times n$ matrix is the $n \times m$ matrix $\mathbf{AB}$ defined by

$$\mathbf{A}^{\ddagger} := \mathbf{flipc}\left(\left(\mathbf{flipc}(\mathbf{A})\right)^{T}\right).$$

15. Reformulate $\mathbf{A}^{\ddagger}$ in terms of $\mathbf{flipr}$, and write the entries of $\mathbf{A}^{\ddagger}$ in terms of the entries of $\mathbf{A}$.

16. If $\mathbf{E} = \mathbf{flipr}(\mathbf{I})$, show that $\mathbf{A}^{\ddagger} = \mathbf{E}\mathbf{A}^{T}\mathbf{E}$.

17. Show that: (a) $(\mathbf{A}^{\ddagger})^{\ddagger} = \mathbf{A}$, (b) $(c\mathbf{A} + \mathbf{B})^{\ddagger} = c\mathbf{A}^{\ddagger} + \mathbf{B}^{\ddagger}$, (c) $(\mathbf{AB})^{\ddagger} = \mathbf{B}^{\ddagger}\mathbf{A}^{\ddagger}$.

18. A square matrix is said to be **cross-symmetric** if $\mathbf{A}^{\ddagger} = \mathbf{A}$ and **skew-cross-symmetric** if $\mathbf{A}^{\ddagger} = -\mathbf{A}$. How many real parameters are needed to completely specify a complex cross-symmetric matrix? A complex skew-cross-symmetric matrix? A real cross-symmetric matrix? A real skew-cross-symmetric matrix? A complex symmetric and cross-symmetric matrix?

19. A square matrix is said to be **round** if it is invariant with respect to rotations by $90 * k$ degrees, $k = 1 : 3$. Give examples of round matrices of even and odd size for $n > 2$. How many real parameters are needed to completely specify a round matrix of order n? What about a round symmetric matrix? A round, symmetric, and cross-symmetric matrix? Is there redundancy in the previous question?

Two other matrix products arise in applications: the **Schur-Hadamard** or **entrywise product** of two matrices of the same size is defined by

$$[\mathbf{A} \circ \mathbf{B}]_{jk} := A_{jk}B_{jk}.$$

Surely, this product is commutative, associative, and the $m \times n$ matrix of all ones, $\mathbf{ones}(m, n)$, serves the same function as the identity does for the standard matrix product. Schur-Hadamard powers are also easily defined by

$$\mathbf{A}^{\circ k} := \underbrace{\mathbf{A} \circ \mathbf{A} \circ \cdots \circ \mathbf{A}}_{k\text{-factors}}.$$

20. If $\mathbf{x}, \mathbf{y}, \mathbf{z}$, and $\mathbf{w}$ are n-component column vectors and $\mathbf{A}$ and $\mathbf{B}$ are $n \times n$ matrices, show that:

(a) $(\mathbf{x}\mathbf{y}^H) \circ (\mathbf{z}\mathbf{w}^H) = (\mathbf{x} \circ \mathbf{z})(\mathbf{y} \circ \mathbf{w})^H.$

(b) $(\mathbf{x}\mathbf{y}^H) \circ \mathbf{A} = \mathbf{diag}(\mathbf{x})\,\mathbf{A}\,\mathbf{diag}(\mathbf{y})^H.$

(c) $\mathbf{y}^H(\mathbf{A} \circ \mathbf{B})\mathbf{x} = \mathrm{tr}\left(\mathbf{diag}(\mathbf{y})^H\mathbf{A}\,\mathbf{diag}(\mathbf{x})\mathbf{B}^T\right).$

    Note: Matlab uses the notation $\mathbf{A}.*\mathbf{B}$ for the Schur-Hadamard product.

21. Formulate conditions under which an $m \times n$ $\mathbf{A}$ has an inverse under the Schur-Hadamard product. What if we insist on a *unique* inverse? For an invertible matrix $\mathbf{A}$, find its Schur-Hadamard inverse, $\mathbf{A}^{-\circ 1}$.

If $\mathbf{A}$ is an $m \times n$ matrix and $\mathbf{B}$ is a $p \times q$ matrix, the **Kronecker product** or, **tensor product**, of $\mathbf{A}$ and $\mathbf{B}$ is the $mp \times nq$ partitioned matrix defined by

$$[\mathbf{A} \otimes \mathbf{B}] := [A_{jk}\mathbf{B}] = \begin{bmatrix} A_{11}\mathbf{B} & A_{12}\mathbf{B} & \cdots & A_{1n}\mathbf{B} \\ A_{21}\mathbf{B} & A_{22}\mathbf{B} & \cdots & A_{2n}\mathbf{B} \\ \vdots & \vdots & & \vdots \\ A_{m1}\mathbf{B} & A_{m2}\mathbf{B} & \cdots & A_{mn}\mathbf{B} \end{bmatrix}.$$

More formally, $[\mathbf{A} \otimes \mathbf{B}]_{p(j-1)+r,q(k-1)+s} = A_{jk}B_{rs}$ where $j = 1:m$, $k = 1:n$, $r = 1:p$, and $s = 1:q$.

22. If

$$\mathbf{A} = \begin{bmatrix} 1 & 1+i \\ -i & -2 \end{bmatrix},$$

then compute $\mathbf{A}^{\circ k}$ and $\mathbf{A} \otimes \mathbf{A}$.

23. Give examples to show that the Kronecker product is neither commutative nor associative. What corresponds to $\mathbf{I}$ for the Kronecker product?

24. Show that if both $\mathbf{A}$ and $\mathbf{B}$ are either diagonal, symmetric, or Hermitian, then $\mathbf{A} \otimes \mathbf{B}$ also has this property.

25. For the more theoretically oriented (and diligent) reader, show that if $\mathbf{A}$ and $\mathbf{C}$ are $m \times m$ and $\mathbf{B}$ and $\mathbf{D}$ are $p \times p$:

(a) $\mathbf{A} \otimes \mathbf{B} = (\mathbf{A} \otimes \mathbf{I}_m)(\mathbf{I}_p \otimes \mathbf{B}).$

(b) $(\mathbf{A}\mathbf{C}) \otimes (\mathbf{B}\mathbf{D}) = (\mathbf{A} \otimes \mathbf{B})(\mathbf{C} \otimes \mathbf{D}).$

(c) If $\mathbf{A}$ and $\mathbf{B}$ are nonsingular, then $(\mathbf{A} \otimes \mathbf{B}) = \mathbf{A}^{-1} \otimes \mathbf{B}^{-1}.$

(d) $\mathrm{tr}\,(\mathbf{A} \otimes \mathbf{B}) = \mathrm{tr}(\mathbf{A})\,\mathrm{tr}(\mathbf{B}).$

(e) $\mathrm{rank}\,(\mathbf{A} \otimes \mathbf{B}) = \mathrm{rank}(\mathbf{A})\,\mathrm{rank}(\mathbf{B}).$

(f) $\det(\mathbf{A} \otimes \mathbf{B}) = (\det \mathbf{A})^m (\det \mathbf{B})^p.$

(g) the submatrix of $\mathbf{A} \otimes \mathbf{B}$ lying at the intersection of columns $1, n+2, 2n+3, 3n+4, \ldots,$ $(n-1)n + n = n^2$ and rows $1, m+2, 2m+3, \ldots, (m-1)m + m = m^2$ is $\mathbf{A} \circ \mathbf{B}$.

26. A **magic square** is a square matrix whose row sums and column sums are all the same (that value is called the **magic sum**). Matlab will generate an $n \times n$ magic square as $\mathbf{M} = \mathbf{magic}(n)$. The entries of $\mathbf{M}$ can be reordered to form the set $1 : n^2$.

   (a) What is the magic sum s_n of a Matlab-generated magic square of size n?

   (b) How can you change a magic square into a doubly stochastic matrix?

   (c) Given one magic square, how many others can you generate from it by only using Matlab operations to rearrange things?

   (d) A **special magic square** has the additional property that its trace and the sum of its cross-diagonal entries are also equal to the magic sum. How many of the magic squares you generated are also special magic squares?

   (e) Are products of magic squares also magic squares? Replace magic squares by special magic squares and answer the same question.

   (f) Which magic squares are invertible?

   (g) Are inverses of invertible magic squares also magic squares? Replace magic squares by special magic squares and answer the same question.

   (h) Are Schur-Hadamard products of magic squares also magic squares?

   (i) Are Kronecker products of magic squares also magic squares?

27. Classify all systems for which

$$\mathbf{x} = [2\alpha; -\alpha + \beta; 3\alpha + 2\beta + \gamma - \delta; \gamma; 2\gamma - \delta; \delta; \alpha - \gamma; \beta + 2\delta],$$

for $\alpha, \beta, \gamma, \delta \in \mathbb{C}$, is a general solution. [Be careful, this is not trivial!]

28. Matrices $\mathbf{A}$ and $\mathbf{B}$ are said to be **congruent**, written $\mathbf{A} \cong \mathbf{B}$, if there exist nonsingular matrices $\mathbf{P}$ and $\mathbf{Q}$ such that $\mathbf{B} = \mathbf{PAQ}$.

   (a) Show that congruence is an equivalence relation.

   (b) Show that any two matrices of the same size and rank are congruent and in so doing construct $\mathbf{P}$ and $\mathbf{Q}$ in terms of elementary matrices.

29. Matrices $\mathbf{A}$ and $\mathbf{B}$, both $n \times n$, are said to be **similar**, written $\mathbf{A} \sim \mathbf{B}$, if there is an $n \times n$ nonsingular matrix $\mathbf{P}$ such that $\mathbf{A} = \mathbf{P}^{-1}\mathbf{B}\mathbf{P}$.

   (a) Show that if $\mathbf{A} \sim \mathbf{B}$, then $\mathbf{B} \sim \mathbf{A}$.

   (b) Show that if $\mathbf{A} \sim \mathbf{B}$ and $\mathbf{B} \sim \mathbf{C}$, then $\mathbf{A} \sim \mathbf{C}$.

   (c) Show that if $\mathbf{A} \sim \mathbf{B}$, then $\mathrm{tr}(\mathbf{A}) = \mathrm{tr}(\mathbf{B})$.

   (d) Show that if $\mathbf{A} \sim \mathbf{B}$, then $\det \mathbf{A} = \det \mathbf{B}$.

   (e) Show that if $\mathbf{A} \sim \mathbf{B}$, then $\mathrm{rref}(\mathbf{A}) = \mathrm{rref}(\mathbf{B})$ and $\mathrm{rank}(\mathbf{A}) = \mathrm{rank}(\mathbf{B})$.

30. Show that the following $n \times n$ matrix, whose entries are binomial coefficients, except for the alternation in sign, is its own inverse:

$$
\mathbf{B} = \begin{bmatrix}
1 & 0 & \cdots & \cdots & \cdots & 0 \\
1 & -\binom{1}{1} & 0 & & & \vdots \\
1 & -\binom{2}{1} & \binom{2}{2} & \ddots & & \vdots \\
1 & -\binom{3}{1} & \binom{3}{2} & -1 & \ddots & \vdots \\
\vdots & \vdots & \vdots & \vdots & \ddots & 0 \\
1 & -\binom{n}{1} & \binom{n}{2} & -\binom{n}{3} & \cdots & (-1)^n \binom{n}{n}
\end{bmatrix}.
$$

Additionally, if $\mathbf{A} = \mathbf{B}^T \mathbf{B}$, show that $\mathbf{A}^{-1} = \mathbf{B}\mathbf{B}^T$.

31. There are not many formulas for the inverse of the sum of matrices, here are two.

   (a) For any matrices $\mathbf{A}$ and $\mathbf{B}$ for which the following products and inverses are defined, prove **Woodbury's formula**,

   $$(\mathbf{I} + \mathbf{AB})^{-1} = \mathbf{I} - \mathbf{A}(\mathbf{I} + \mathbf{BA})^{-1}\mathbf{B}.$$

   (b) Put $\mathbf{U} = \mathbf{C}^{-1}\mathbf{A}$ and $\mathbf{V} = \mathbf{BC}^2$ to derive

   $$(\mathbf{C} + \mathbf{UV})^{-1} = \mathbf{C}^{-1} - \mathbf{C}^{-1}\mathbf{U}(\mathbf{I} + \mathbf{VC}^{-1}\mathbf{U})^{-1}\mathbf{VC}^{-1}.$$

32. Write $\mathbf{Q}$ and $\mathbf{Q}^{-1}$ in partitioned form as

$$
\mathbf{Q} = \begin{bmatrix} \mathbf{A} & \mathbf{B} \\ \mathbf{C} & \mathbf{D} \end{bmatrix} \quad \text{and} \quad \mathbf{Q}^{-1} = \begin{bmatrix} \mathbf{E} & \mathbf{F} \\ \mathbf{G} & \mathbf{H} \end{bmatrix}
$$

and show that when $\mathbf{A}$ and $\mathbf{D}$ and other matrices, as indicated, are nonsingular:

   (a) $\mathbf{E} = (\mathbf{A} - \mathbf{BD}^{-1}\mathbf{C})^{-1}$.
   (b) $\mathbf{H} = (\mathbf{D} - \mathbf{CA}^{-1}\mathbf{B})^{-1}$.
   (c) $\mathbf{F} = -(\mathbf{A} - \mathbf{BD}^{-1}\mathbf{C})^{-1}\mathbf{BD}^{-1} = -\mathbf{A}^{-1}\mathbf{B}(\mathbf{D} - \mathbf{CA}^{-1}\mathbf{B})^{-1}$.
   (d) $\mathbf{G} = -(\mathbf{D} - \mathbf{CA}^{-1}\mathbf{B})^{-1}\mathbf{CA}^{-1} = -\mathbf{D}^{-1}\mathbf{C}(\mathbf{A} - \mathbf{BD}^{-1}\mathbf{C})^{-1}$.
   (e) Use the uniqueness of $\mathbf{Q}^{-1}$ to show that

   $$(\mathbf{A} - \mathbf{BD}^{-1}\mathbf{C})^{-1} = \mathbf{A}^{-1} + \mathbf{A}^{-1}\mathbf{B}(\mathbf{D} - \mathbf{CA}^{-1}\mathbf{B})^{-1}\mathbf{CA}^{-1}.$$

33. We say $\mathbf{G}$ is a **generalized inverse** of $\mathbf{A}$ if $\mathbf{AGA} = \mathbf{A}$. Write

$$
\boldsymbol{\Delta} = \mathbf{PAQ} = \begin{bmatrix} \mathbf{D} & \mathbf{0} \\ \mathbf{0} & \mathbf{0} \end{bmatrix}
$$

where $\mathbf{P}$ and $\mathbf{Q}$ are respectively the products of elementary matrices that row and column reduce $\mathbf{A}$, and $\mathbf{D}$ is a nonsingular diagonal matrix. Define

$$\boldsymbol{\Delta}^- := \begin{bmatrix} \mathbf{D}^{-1} & \mathbf{0} \\ \mathbf{0} & \mathbf{0} \end{bmatrix}.$$

(a) Show that $\mathbf{G} = \mathbf{Q}\boldsymbol{\Delta}^-\mathbf{P}$ is a generalized inverse of $\mathbf{A}$.

(b) If $\mathbf{A}\mathbf{x} = \mathbf{b}$, show that $\mathbf{x} = \mathbf{G}\mathbf{b} + (\mathbf{G}\mathbf{A} - \mathbf{I})\mathbf{z}$ is the general solution of the system when $\mathbf{z}$ is a vector of arbitrary parameters and $\mathbf{G}$ is a generalized inverse of $\mathbf{A}$.

(c) If $\mathbf{A} \in \mathcal{C}_n^m$ and $\mathbf{H} = \mathbf{G}\mathbf{A}$, where $\mathbf{G}$ is a generalized inverse of $\mathbf{A}$, then show that $\mathbf{H}$ is idempotent, meaning $\mathbf{H}^2 = \mathbf{H}$. Also show that $\mathrm{rank}(\mathbf{H}) = \mathrm{rank}(\mathbf{A}) = r \Rightarrow \mathrm{rank}(\mathbf{I} - \mathbf{H}) = n - r$.

(d) Show that $\mathbf{P}\mathbf{X}^T\mathbf{X} = \mathbf{Q}\mathbf{X}^T\mathbf{X} \Rightarrow \mathbf{P}\mathbf{X}^T = \mathbf{Q}\mathbf{X}^T$.
[Hint: Show $\mathbf{X}^T\mathbf{X} = \mathbf{0} \Rightarrow \mathbf{X} = \mathbf{0}$ and apply this to
$(\mathbf{P}\mathbf{X}^T\mathbf{X} - \mathbf{Q}\mathbf{X}^T\mathbf{X})(\mathbf{P} - \mathbf{Q})^T$
$= (\mathbf{P}\mathbf{X}^T - \mathbf{Q}\mathbf{X}^T)(\mathbf{P}\mathbf{X}^T - \mathbf{Q}\mathbf{X}^T)^T = \mathbf{0}$.]

(e) Show that if $\mathbf{G} = (\mathbf{X}^T\mathbf{X})^-$, then $\mathbf{G}^T = \mathbf{G}$ and $\mathbf{X}\mathbf{G}\mathbf{X}^T\mathbf{X} = \mathbf{X}$.

(f) Find the generalized inverses of

$$\begin{bmatrix} 1 & 2 \\ 1 & 2 \end{bmatrix} \quad \text{and} \quad \begin{bmatrix} 1 & 0 & -1 \\ 0 & 1 & 1 \end{bmatrix}.$$

34. If $\mathbf{A}$ and $\mathbf{B}$ are strictly diagonally dominant, then which of the following are strictly diagonally dominant: $\mathbf{A}^T$, $\mathbf{A} + \mathbf{B}$, $\mathbf{A} - \mathbf{B}$, $\mathbf{A}^{-1}$, $c\mathbf{A}$, $\mathbf{A}\mathbf{B}^{-1}$, $[\mathbf{A}, \mathbf{B}] = \mathbf{A}\mathbf{B} - \mathbf{B}\mathbf{A}$, $\{\mathbf{A}, \mathbf{B}\} = \mathbf{A}\mathbf{B} + \mathbf{B}\mathbf{A}$?

35. The following problem explores some of the properties of the adjugate matrix.

(a) Show that $\mathbf{adj}(c\mathbf{A}) = c^{n-1}\mathbf{adj}(\mathbf{A})$.

(b) If $\mathbf{A}$ is nonsingular, find an expression for $\mathbf{adj}(\mathbf{adj}(\mathbf{A}))$.

(c) How does your result from part (b) change if $\mathbf{A}$ is singular?

(d) Find $\det(\mathbf{adj}(\mathbf{A}))$ in terms of $\det(\mathbf{A})$.

(e) If $\mathbf{A}$ is nonsingular, find an expression for $(\mathbf{adj}(\mathbf{A}))^{-1}$.

36. Verify the following result:

$$\det\left(a\delta_{jk} + b\left(\delta_{j,k-1} + \delta_{j,k+1}\right)\right) = \frac{(a+s)^{n+1} - (a-s)^{n+1}}{2^{n+1}s},$$

when the matrix is $n \times n$ and $s := \sqrt{a^2 - 4b^2}$.

Prove the following results involving partitioned matrices.

37. $\begin{vmatrix} \mathbf{A} & \mathbf{0} \\ \mathbf{C} & \mathbf{I} \end{vmatrix} = |\mathbf{A}|$

38. $\begin{vmatrix} \mathbf{A} & \mathbf{0} \\ \mathbf{C} & \mathbf{D} \end{vmatrix} = |\mathbf{A}|\,|\mathbf{D}|$ $\left[\text{Hint:} \quad \begin{bmatrix} \mathbf{A} & \mathbf{0} \\ \mathbf{C} & \mathbf{D} \end{bmatrix} = \begin{bmatrix} \mathbf{A} & \mathbf{0} \\ \mathbf{C} & \mathbf{I} \end{bmatrix} \begin{bmatrix} \mathbf{I} & \mathbf{0} \\ \mathbf{0} & \mathbf{D} \end{bmatrix}. \right]$

39. $\begin{vmatrix} \mathbf{A} & \mathbf{B} \\ \mathbf{C} & \mathbf{D} \end{vmatrix} = \begin{cases} |\mathbf{A}|\,|\mathbf{D} - \mathbf{C}\mathbf{A}^{-1}\mathbf{B}| & \text{if} \quad |\mathbf{A}| \neq 0 \\[2ex] |\mathbf{D}|\,|\mathbf{A} - \mathbf{B}\mathbf{D}^{-1}\mathbf{C}| & \text{if} \quad |\mathbf{D}| \neq 0 \end{cases}$

    [Hint: Factor the matrix as above.]

40. If $\mathbf{A} \in \mathbb{C}_n^m$, $\mathbf{B} \in \mathbb{C}_m^n$, show that $|\mathbf{I}_m - \mathbf{A}\mathbf{B}| = |\mathbf{I}_n - \mathbf{B}\mathbf{A}|$.

    $\left[\text{Hint: Consider} \quad \begin{vmatrix} \mathbf{I}_m & \mathbf{A} \\ \mathbf{B} & \mathbf{I}_n \end{vmatrix}. \right]$

2

ORDINARY DIFFERENTIAL EQUATIONS

2.1 PREVIEW

Ordinary differential equations (ODE's) have wide applicability in science and engineering models. They are often fairly accurate representations of reality and some can be easily solved, thus helping to illuminate the dominant mechanisms in a process. This is the first of several chapters devoted to the various aspects of this well-developed subject.

We begin with several physical situations that can be appropriately modeled by ordinary differential equations. The problems lead to linear and nonlinear univariate models. Although one such example will be given, multivariate models will be discussed more fully in Chapter 6.

Some of the theory behind ordinary differential equations is introduced. A solution is defined as are initial and boundary value problems. A theorem is stated for the existence and uniqueness of a solution to an ODE. Many ODE's are not amenable to analytic solution, so that some form of machine computation is required. Both graphical and elementary numerical methods are presented. The idea of stability of an ODE-solving algorithm is defined and three simple archetypical algorithms are discussed. After that we will look at the fundamentals of Runge-Kutta algorithms.

A few classes of first order ODE's are easily solvable. In particular, methods for separable and linear equations are developed. These methods are then applied to several physical problems that can be modeled by the methods of this chapter.

2.2 DIFFERENTIAL EQUATION MODELS

An **ordinary differential equation** is an equation relating an unknown function (or functions) of a *single* independent variable to its (or their) derivatives. The equation is said to be of **order** n if the highest derivative present is of order n. If the values of the unknown function and its derivatives of order less than n are specified at a single value of the independent variable, then these are called **initial conditions**; specifications of values at two or more values of the independent variable are called **boundary conditions**. Not all differential equations need be accompanied by either initial conditions or boundary conditions.

Many continuous processes (and even some discrete ones) in science and engineering can be accurately modeled using ordinary differential equations. All modeling is a cyclic process: The problem is first approximated by a model that is (usually) amenable to solution. The computed results are compared with actual experimental measurements, and the model is adjusted to more accurately reflect the responsible mechanisms that drive the process. Then the entire procedure is repeated. The examples presented are but a few and only involve the first step of the modeling process.

■ **EXAMPLE 2.1** If $Q(t)$ is the quantity of bacteria at time t, then $\dot{Q}(t) = dQ(t)/dt$ is the rate of growth (with respect to time) and $\dot{Q}/Q$ is the **relative growth rate**. For population models the units of relative growth rate are often births or deaths per thousand. Given an unlimited supply of food and an absence of toxic substances or deleterious ambient conditions, the relative growth rate of bacteria may be taken to be a positive constant. An equation that models the situation of constant relative growth rate is

$$\frac{\dot{Q}(t)}{Q(t)} = k \quad \Rightarrow \quad \dot{Q}(t) = kQ(t).$$

Together with the initial condition $Q(0) = Q_0$, which specifies the initial quantity of bacteria, this constitutes the **exponential growth model**, so called because of the form of its solution.

If the food supply were finite, we might expect negative effects due to crowding and competition. The more bacteria, the greater this effect. A possible model would assume a linear decrease in the relative growth rate:

$$\frac{\dot{Q}(t)}{Q(t)} = k\left(\ell - Q(t)\right) \quad \Rightarrow \quad \dot{Q}(t) = kQ(t)\left(\ell - Q(t)\right).$$

This is a **logistic growth model**. It admits a useful interpretation insofar as $\dot{Q}/Q$ should be equal to the birth rate minus the death rate, measured in the fraction of lives. This model takes the birth rate to be constant, $k\ell$, and the death rate to be increasing linearly with population as $kQ(t)$. ■ ■ ■

■ **EXAMPLE 2.2 Newton's Law of Cooling** states that the time rate of change of temperature of a body depends on

(a) the difference between the temperature of the body and that of the ambient, or surrounding, medium;

(b) the amount of surface area of the body that is in contact with the medium; and

(c) the rate of flow (when the medium is a liquid or a gas) of the medium across the body.

As our first approximation to this problem, let $T(t)$ be the temperature of the body at time t and T_{amb} be the temperature of the ambient medium. Start with a linear approximation to (a):

$$\frac{dT(t)}{dt} = k\left(T(t) - T_{amb}\right), \quad T(0) = T_0 = \text{initial temperature,}$$

where $k\left(T(t) - T_{amb}\right)$ is a first approximation to some unknown functional dependence $g(T - T_{amb})$. What about the constant k? If $T > T_{amb}$, the body is hotter than the medium and the Second Law of Thermodynamics says it must lose heat to the medium, meaning $\dot{T} < 0$. Thus, we must have $k < 0$ for a physically meaningful model.

Several assumptions are implicit here. One is that the temperature of the entire body changes at the same time. Our experience is that when we heat the outside of a large body, it takes a while for the interior to warm up. Furthermore, for a cooling body if the ambient medium is not flowing fairly rapidly, it will not be able to dissipate heat at a rate needed to keep its temperature at a predetermined level. Other problems arise, but under some conditions, this is a fairly accurate model.   ■ ■ ■

■ **EXAMPLE 2.3** An industrial process requires flushing a large vat that contains chemicals dissolved in a solvent. Say it is a 1000 liter vat of solvent containing 200 kilograms of chemical A and it is being stirred continuously. See Figure 2.1.

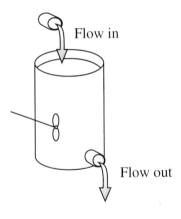

Flow in

Flow out

Fig. 2.1

To refresh the tank, pure solvent is poured into the top at a rate of 50 liters/minute and the well-stirred mixture is extracted at a rate of 50 liters/min from the bottom. An engineer has decided that the vat can be reused when only 1 kg of the chemical remains in the vat. How long must the flush operation continue?

Solution: Since 50 liters/min of solvent enters and 50 liters/min leaves, the volume balance equation is

$$\frac{dV(t)}{dt} = (\text{Volume Flow Rate In}) - (\text{Volume Flow Rate Out}) = 0$$

where $V(t)$ = volume of the mixture in liters at time t, measured in minutes. Initially $V(0) = 1000$ liters, so that $V(t) = 1000$ liters. Had the inflow and outflow rates not balanced, $V(t)$ would not have been constant.

Writing $A(t)$ for the amount of chemical A, in kilograms, and assuming that the presence of the chemical does not change the density of the solvent, the chemical balance equation is

$$\frac{dA(t)}{dt} = (A \text{ Flow Rate In}) - (A \text{ Flow Rate Out}).$$

The flow rate is specified so that

$$\begin{aligned} (A \text{ Flow Rate In}) &= [\text{Concentration of } A] \, (\text{Volume Flow Rate In}) \\ &= [0 \text{ kg/liter}] \, (50 \text{ liters/min}) = 0 \text{ kg/min}, \end{aligned}$$

because pure solvent flows in, and

$$(A \text{ Flow Rate Out}) = \left[\frac{A}{1000} \text{ kg/liter} \right] (50 \text{ liters/ min}) = \frac{A}{20} \text{ kg/min},$$

because the concentration of A is the ratio of the mass of A to the volume, which in this case is a constant 1000 liters. Thus the chemical balance equation is

$$\frac{dA(t)}{dt} = -\frac{A}{20}, \quad A(0) = 200.$$

All that remains is to solve this equation, set $A(t_1) = 1$, and solve for t_1.   ■ ■ ■

Many problems that arise from the study of the dynamics of particles and rigid bodies can be accurately modeled by ODE's. Newton's Laws will play a fundamental role in the process.

■ **EXAMPLE 2.4** Suppose a body of mass m is released at a height h above the surface of the earth. Formulate the equations that describe its fall.

Solution: Assume h is not so great and the object releasing the mass is not traveling so fast that it would be in orbit around the earth. Consider only the motion perpendicular to the surface of the earth. Call $z(t)$ the height of the object above the earth at time t; then $z(0) = h$. See Figure 2.2.

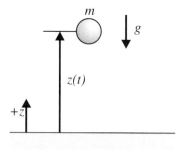

Fig. 2.2

Newton's Second Law tells us that

$$\frac{d}{dt}\left(m\frac{dz(t)}{dt}\right) = -F_{\mathrm{g}} + F_{\mathrm{r}},$$

where F_{g} is the force of gravity and F_{r} is the force resisting the motion. Since z increases upward, away from the surface of the earth, gravity acts downward, and F_{r} opposes the downward motion, the signs of the forces are as indicated when we take the forces to be positive. The Law of Gravitation tells us that

$$F_{\mathrm{g}} = \frac{GM_e m}{(R+z)^2},$$

where R and M_{e} are the radius and mass of the earth. Because $z(t)$ is of the order (in size) of h, z/R can be neglected in the Taylor expansion of $(R+z)^{-2}$ about $z = 0$, and we have

$$F_{\mathrm{g}} = \frac{GM_e m}{(R+z)^2} = \frac{GM_e m}{R^2}\frac{1}{(1+z/R)^2} = \frac{GM_e m}{R^2}\left[1 - 2\left(\frac{z}{R}\right) + \left(\frac{z}{R}\right)^2 - \cdots\right]$$

$$\approx \frac{GM_e m}{R^2} =: mg, \quad \text{by definition of } g.$$

The resistive force F_{r} is usually a function of the speed of the mass $v = \dot{z}(t)$, and it need not be a simple function. For small values of v, $F_{\mathrm{r}} = kv$, but as v increases, $F_{\mathrm{r}} = kv^{\alpha(v)}$ with $\alpha(v)$ an empirically derived increasing function of v. This approximation continues until v is the speed of sound. Let's take the simplest case:

$$m\frac{d^2 z(t)}{dt^2} = -mg + k\frac{dz(t)}{dt},$$

whenever the mass of the body is constant. This can be reduced from a second order ODE to a first order equation by using $v = \dot{z}$:

$$m\frac{dv(t)}{dt} = -mg + kv(t).$$

If the body started from rest, the initial conditions are $v(0) = 0$, because there is no initial velocity, and $z(0) = h$, the initial height.

If, in the course of solving this equation, we find values of v that exceed 200 meters/second, then our model would have been inappropriate because the assumption of linear velocity dependence for the resistive force is inaccurate at such speeds. We'd then have to go back and discard the $\alpha = 1$ value of the resisting force exponent in favor of an alternate functional form $\alpha(v)$, determined from experiment.

If, in addition, the object were propelled by the ejection of burned fuel moving at velocity u, then the system to be considered would be the object together with the expended fuel. The differential of force due to the change in velocity v of the object is $m\,dv$ while that of the ejected mass element would be $(v-u)\,dm$. If we write $c := v - u$ for the relative velocity of the expended propellant, the equation of motion would be

$$m\dot{v} + c\dot{m} = kv^{\alpha(v)} - mg.$$

■ ■ ■

■ **EXAMPLE 2.5** If a solid beam is supported between two posts (see Figure 2.3), it will undergo deflection due to its own weight $W = mg$. The question arises, if the beam is arbitrarily supported and has an additional load, what is the equation from which we can determine its deflection as a function of position?

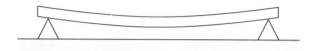

Fig. 2.3

Solution: The physical characteristics that will govern this deflection are Young's modulus E, the density ρ of the beam material, and the shape of the cross section of the beam.

Assume the neutral axis of the beam lies along the x-axis and all cross sections of the beam are parallel to the yz-plane. An arbitrary cross section will feel a force F and a bending moment M due to all external forces (see Figure 2.4).

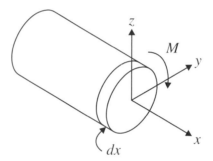

Fig. 2.4

All moments will be measured with respect to the center of gravity of a cross section. The x-component of the force F_1 acts along the beam axis and is called the **axial thrust**; F_2 and F_3 act at right angles to the axis and are called the **shearing forces**; M_1 is the **twisting moment**; M_2 and M_3 are the **bending moments** about the y- and z-axes.

Assume the beam cross section is symmetric with respect to the xz-plane and the effects of all forces are directed parallel to the z-axis. This will allow us to set $F_1 = F_2 = 0$ and $M_1 = M_3 = 0$. For simplicity of notation, set $F_3 = F$ and $M_2 = M$. Measure the deflection $u(x)$ positive in the downward direction, F positive upward, and M positive clockwise, as shown in Figure 2.4 The cross section of a cylindrical beam showing the directions and twisting moment.

If we denote the load per unit length by $w(x)$, then Newton's Second Law for the forces in the z-direction is

$$\frac{dF}{dx}\, dx + w(x)\, dx = 0.$$

The sum of the moments acting on the beam element is

$$\frac{dM}{dx}\,dx - F\,dx = 0.$$

From this we immediately conclude that $F = dM/dx$, $w(x) = -dF/dx$, and, finally, $w(x) = -d^2M/dx^2$.

Hooke's Law states that the deformation is related to the moment via the equation

$$EI = MR,$$

where I is the moment of inertia of a cross section with respect to the y-axis and R is the radius of curvature of the neutral axis of the beam at the cross section.

The radius of curvature is related to the deflection via a formula from calculus:

$$\frac{1}{R} = -\frac{u''(x)}{\left[1 + (u'(x))^2\right]^{3/2}} \approx -u''(x),$$

where primes indicate derivatives with respect to x. Using this approximation we can write the moment as $M(x) = EIu''$ and the force as $F(x) = (EIu'')'$. Thus the equations of the beam are approximately $u''(x) = -M/EI$, or upon differentiating twice to eliminate M, we have

$$\frac{d^2}{dx^2}\left(EI\frac{d^2u(x)}{dx^2}\right) = w(x).$$

Although our equation includes only the load per unit length, this can be extended to point loads by the use of impulses; in particular, $\delta(x - a)$ is a unit point load at $x = a$. For more information on step functions and impulses consult Appendix D.

Because the deflection at both ends of the beam must have some restrictions, we will have a boundary value problem. There are three possible types of end support: free, hinged, and clamped.

(a) For a **free end**, both the bending moment and shear force must be zero. Therefore,

$$EI\frac{d^2u}{dx^2} = M(\text{end}) = 0 \quad \text{and} \quad \frac{d}{dx}\left(EI\frac{d^2u}{dx^2}\right) = F(\text{end}) = 0.$$

(b) A **hinged**, or **simply supported**, **end** will have zero deflection and zero bending moment at the end:

$$u = 0 \quad \text{and} \quad EI\frac{d^2u}{dx^2} = M(\text{end}) = 0.$$

(c) A **clamped end** (sometimes called an **embedded** or **welded** end) will have zero deflection and be parallel to the x-axis there:

$$u = 0 \quad \text{and} \quad u' = 0.$$

■ ■ ■

■ **EXAMPLE 2.6** The theory of electrical networks is quite well developed. The **lumped parameter model** treats a **circuit** as an array of elements called resistors, inductors, and capacitors interconnected by idealized elements denoted by lines or curves. Any closed polygon or curve is called a **loop** of the circuit, and any point where more than two lines or curves intersect is called a **node**. Every circuit has two fundamental measurable quantities: the **voltage drop**, measured in volts, between any two points or nodes on a line or curve, denoted by E, and the **current**, measured in amperes, through an element, denoted by I. There are basic empirical constitutive equations, forms of **Ohm's Law**, relating voltages and currents across each type of idealized element:

(a) across an inductor of inductance L henrys,

$$L\frac{dI}{dt} = E.$$

(b) across a resistor of resistance R ohms ($R\,\Omega$),

$$RI = E.$$

(c) across a capacitor of capacitance C farads,

$$\frac{1}{C}\int I\,dt = E.$$

If we introduce the **charge** q (in coulombs), then the current is the time rate of change of the charge:

$$I = \frac{dq}{dt},$$

and the constitutive relation for a capacitor can be written $E = q/C$. The two fundamental laws of circuit analysis are:

1. **Kirchhoff Voltage Law** (KVL)

$$\sum_{\text{loop}} E = 0;$$

   i.e., the sum of the voltages around a loop is zero.

2. **Kirchhoff Current Law** (KCL)

$$\sum_{\text{node}} I = 0;$$

   i.e., the sum of the currents at a node is zero.

Taken together, these equations are sufficient to fairly accurately model the behavior of most low frequency (when the source is AC), low voltage, and low current systems. The schematic representation will be:

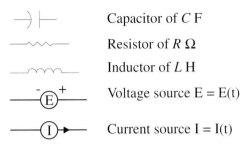

Capacitor of C F

Resistor of R Ω

Inductor of L H

Voltage source E = E(t)

Current source I = I(t)

The simplest circuit has one loop and its elements can be combined or lumped into a resistance, an inductance, and/or a capacitance (see Figure 2.5).

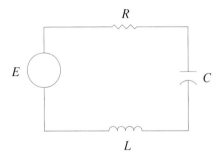

Fig. 2.5

Applying KVL to this loop yields

$$L\frac{dI(t)}{dt} + RI(t) + \frac{1}{C}\int I(t)\,dt = E(t)$$

Replacing $I(t)$ by $\dot{q}$, this equation becomes

$$L\frac{d^2q(t)}{dt^2} + R\frac{dq(t)}{dt} + \frac{1}{C}q(t) = E(t).$$

∎ ∎ ∎

Many mechanical systems without any dissipation can be modeled without the direct use of Newton's Laws by using the so-called Lagrangian approach to mechanics. Define the **Lagrangian** of the system to be the kinetic energy minus the potential energy:

$$L := \mathrm{KE} - \mathrm{PE}.$$

If the Lagrangian is a function of the coordinate q, its derivative with respect to time $\dot{q}$, and possibly time, then the equation describing the system is

$$\frac{d}{dt}\left(\frac{\partial L}{\partial \dot{q}}\right) - \frac{\partial L}{\partial q} = 0. \tag{2.1}$$

If there is any damping present, it can usually be added to these equations in an obvious way. Let's apply this method.

■ **EXAMPLE 2.7**   Apply the Lagrangian approach to the following systems.

(a) Let the system be a block of mass m resting on a smooth horizontal plane between two walls. The block is attached to each wall by a spring with force constant k. Let x be the displacement of the block to the right measured from a position of equilibrium. The Lagrangian of the system is

$$L = \frac{1}{2}m\dot{x}^2 - \frac{1}{2}k\left(x^2 + (-x)^2\right) = \frac{1}{2}m\dot{x}^2 - kx^2.$$

The equation of motion is

$$\frac{d}{dt}\left(\frac{\partial L}{\partial \dot{x}}\right) - \frac{\partial L}{\partial x} = \frac{d}{dt}(m\dot{x}) - (-2kx) = m\ddot{x} + 2kx = 0.$$

(b) We can add a little to the previous problem to make it more interesting. Instead of a block, put a cylindrical solid of mass m that rolls on a rough surface. Attach the springs from each wall to an axle on the cylinder. Now the Lagrangian must take into account the rotation of the cylinder in addition to its lateral motion. If we measure its lateral displacement by x, again measured from equilibrium, then we will also need to specify the angle of displacement θ. Since the cylinder must roll on the rough surface, we must have the arclength relation $x = R\theta$, where R is the radius of the cylinder. The only change is to the kinetic energy; there must be a term for the horizontal displacement and one for the rotation motion: $\text{KE} = \frac{1}{2}m\dot{x}^2 + \frac{1}{2}I\dot{\theta}^2$, where $I = \frac{1}{2}mR^2$ is the moment of inertia of the solid cylinder. Thus

$$\text{KE} = \frac{1}{2}m(R\dot{\theta})^2 + \frac{1}{2}\left(\frac{1}{2}mR^2\dot{\theta}^2\right) = \frac{3}{4}mR^2\dot{\theta}^2.$$

Thus the Lagrangian is $L = \frac{3}{4}mR^2\dot{\theta}^2 - kR^2\theta^2$. The equation of motion is

$$\frac{d}{dt}\left(\frac{\partial L}{\partial \dot{\theta}}\right) - \frac{\partial L}{\partial \theta} = \frac{d}{dt}\left(\frac{3}{2}mR^2\dot{\theta}\right) + kR^2\theta = \frac{3}{2}mR^2\ddot{\theta} + kR^2\theta = 0.$$

■ ■ ■

The cyclic nature of modeling a problem is so important that it deserves restatement. All of these models must be considered to be first approximations to reality. After comparison of theoretical and experimental data, further refinements of the model are usually required. These may entail additional terms in any power series expansions, reinstatement of neglected forces, additional variables, or a whole host of other things. The model may fit the problem over only a narrow range of the parameters in question. For example, if in example 2.2 the temperature

$T(t)$ takes values high enough to cause a phase change in the body or the surrounding medium, then the mechanism of heat exchange is not one that faithfully follows Newton's Law of Cooling and major revision is in order. On the other hand, if you're a coroner and you only use this model to determine the time of death, then the added burden a more general model requires you to bear is just so much unnecessary baggage.

A general rule of thumb for mathematical modeling is that if a phenomenon can be adequately explained by several models, choose the simplest model. This is often called the **Rule of Parsimony**.

One further note: the models discussed thus far are **deterministic**, i.e., there are no random fluctuations involved. In point of fact, most accurate large scale models require some degree of randomness. The growth of bacteria and the formation of stars in the universe have many things in common but uniformity is not one of them. The presence of granulation or clumping in the density can often be attributed to random factors. Similarly, temperature is defined in terms of the average of the apparently random motions of atoms and molecules. The assumption of uniform mixing in the industrial process is patently absurd and should be supplemented by random fluctuations in concentration. This should not be taken as a sign that all models should have random factors, but rather that the introduction of randomness may be intrinsic to the model or it may serve as a simplification of much more complex deterministic mechanisms.

2.2.1 Exercise Set

1. A mass driver launches a projectile from the surface of the earth toward the moon. The forces acting on the projectile are those of gravitation due to the moon and the earth. Using the form of the acceleration in polar coordinates, $\left(\ddot{r} - r\dot{\theta}^2 \right) \mathbf{e}_r + \left(2\dot{r}\dot{\theta} + r\ddot{\theta} \right) \mathbf{e}_\theta$, write the equations of motion. Take the origin to be the center of mass of the system, which can be assumed to be the center of the earth.

2. Pure water flows into a 200 liter tank at a rate of 20 liters/minute. The tank initially contains 100 liters of a 30% solution of dye. The well-stirred mixture is being pumped out at a rate of 30 liters/minute. Write the equation and initial conditions that model this system.

3. There are two tanks, one containing 200 liters of pure water and the other containing 200 liters of pure dye. Water from the first tank is pumped into the second tank at a rate of 20 liters/minute, and the well-stirred mixture is then pumped back into the first tank at the same rate. Write the equations and initial conditions that will allow us to determine when both tanks have the same dye concentration to within 2%.

4. A homogeneous cylinder is placed at the top of a rough plane inclined at an angle of θ with the horizontal. At $t = 0$, it is released. Set up the ODE and side conditions that will allow us to determine its position along the plane as a function of time.

5. A rectangular homogeneous beam is placed on an elastic foundation (one that opposes its deflection at every point proportional to the deflection there). Set up the equation for the deflection as a function of position due to the foundation and the beam's mass.

6. Set up the ODE for the current in the circuit shown in Figure 2.6.

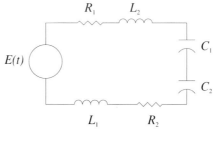

Fig. 2.6

7. Set up the equations for the displacement of the mass in the system shown in Figure 2.7, if the dashpot provides a resistive damping force of $b\dot{x}$ which opposes the motion.

Fig. 2.7

8. A system consists of a homogeneous solid wheel of radius R and mass m that is free to rotate about its center of mass, which is rigidly attached to an overhead frame. A rough strap extends over the top of the wheel and is attached on either side to a spring, each of which has been stretched by an amount x (see Figure 2.8). If the wheel is initially turned through a small angle θ and released, find the equation of motion and appropriate initial conditions.

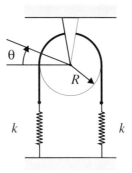

Fig. 2.8

9. A system consists of two homogeneous solid wheels each of radius R and mass m that are free to roll along a rough horizontal flat surface between two walls. They are constrained to move together by a horizontal rigid bar of mass M that is attached to the axle of each wheel. The bar is attached to *each* wall by a spring each with force constant k (see Figure 2.9). If the system is moved x_0 units to the right and released, find the equation of motion and the initial conditions needed to completely specify the subsequent motion.

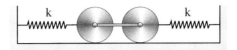

Fig. 2.9

10. The Lorentz force that a charged particle feels when moving in an electric field $\mathbf{E}$ and a magnetic field $\mathbf{B}$ is given by $\mathbf{F} = q(\mathbf{E} + \mathbf{v} \times \mathbf{B})$. If the fields are parallel to each other, write the equations of motion of the particle under the assumption that the fields remain constant. What if the fields are orthogonal to each other?

2.3 ORDINARY DIFFERENTIAL EQUATIONS

2.3.1 Solutions of Ordinary Differential Equations

Any n^{th} order ODE in the unknown function $y(t)$ can be written in the **implicit form**

$$F\left(t, y(t), y'(t), \ldots, y^{(n)}(t)\right) = 0. \tag{2.2}$$

If we can solve for the highest derivative of the unknown function $y^{(n)}(t)$ in (2.2), then the equation can be put into the **explicit form**

$$y^{(n)}(t) = f\left(t, y(t), y'(t), \ldots, y^{(n-1)}(t)\right).$$

An nth order equation that has the special form

$$y^{(n)}(t) + p_{n-1}(t)y^{(n-1)}(t) + \cdots + p_2(t)y''(t) + p_1(t)y'(t) + p_0(t)y(t) = g(t)$$

is said to be **linear**. Any equation that cannot be put into this form is **nonlinear**.

■ **EXAMPLE 2.8** The first order ODE $t^2 (y(t))^2 - (y'(t))^2 = \sin(y')$ is in implicit form and it *cannot* be put into explicit form because it is not possible to analytically solve for $y'(t)$ in terms of t and $y(t)$. The equation

$$y''(t) + 2 (y'(t))^3 - e^{y(t)} \sin t = \cos (ty(t))$$

can be put into explicit form by solving for y'' getting

$$y''(t) = -2\left(y'(t)\right)^3 + e^{y(t)}\sin t + \cos\left(ty(t)\right).$$

Both equations are nonlinear. ▪ ▪ ▪

DEFINITION 2.1 *The function $y = \phi(t)$ is said to be an* **explicit solution** *of equation (2.2) on the interval $[a, b]$ if*

(a) $\phi(t)$ *is differentiable n times on $[a, b]$, and*

(b) $F\left(t, \phi(t), \phi'(t), \ldots, \phi^{(n)}(t)\right) = 0$ *is an identity for all $t \in [a, b]$.*

If $g(t, y) = 0$ represents a curve that defines a solution of (2.2), then it is an **implicit solution** *and defines a* **solution curve**.

▪ **EXAMPLE 2.9** Verify each of the following are explicit solutions of the given equations.

(a) If in example 2.4 (falling body) we take the force of air resistance to be proportional to v^2, then the equation of motion takes the form of the initial value problem

$$m\dot{v}(t) = -mg + kv^2(t), \quad v(0) = 0, \ z(0) = h.$$

Using $v_0 := \sqrt{(mg/k)}$, the explicit form of the solution is known to be

$$z(t) = h - \frac{v_0^2}{g}\ln\left[\cosh\left(\frac{gt}{v_0}\right)\right].$$

This can be seen by differentiation:

$$v = \dot{z} = -v_0\tanh\left(\frac{gt}{v_0}\right) \qquad \Rightarrow \qquad \dot{v} = -g\,\mathrm{sech}^2\left(\frac{gt}{v_0}\right)$$

and

$$m\dot{v} = -mg\,\mathrm{sech}^2\left(\frac{gt}{v_0}\right) = -mg\left[1 - \tanh^2\left(\frac{gt}{v_0}\right)\right]$$

$$= -mg\left[1 - \left(\frac{v}{v_0}\right)^2\right]$$

$$\Rightarrow \quad m\dot{v} = -mg + kv^2.$$

Since $z(0) = h$ and $v(0) = 0$, this is a solution.

(b) A solution of the linear equation

$$x''(t) - 2x'(t) + x(t) = 0$$

is

$$x(t) = \phi(t) = (1 + 2t)e^t.$$

This can be seen by substituting back into the equation

$$
\begin{aligned}
[(1+2t)e^t]'' &- 2\left[(1+2t)e^t\right]' + \left[(1+2t)e^t\right] \\
&= \left[(3+2t)e^t\right]' - 2\left[(3+2t)e^t\right] + \left[(1+2t)e^t\right] \\
&= \left[(5+2t)e^t\right] - 2\left[(3+2t)e^t\right] + \left[(1+2t)e^t\right] \\
&= \left[(5+2t) - 2(3+2t) + (1+2t)\right]e^t \equiv 0.
\end{aligned}
$$

This solution is valid for all real values of t.

(c) A solution of the linear equation

$$x^2 w''(x) + x w'(x) - w(x) = 3x^2$$

is

$$w(x) = \phi(x) = x + x^2 + \frac{3}{x}.$$

The verification follows:

$$
\begin{aligned}
x^2 &\left[x + x^2 + \frac{3}{x}\right]'' + x\left[x + x^2 + \frac{3}{x}\right]' - \left[x + x^2 + \frac{3}{x}\right] \\
&= x^2\left[1 + 2x - \frac{3}{x^2}\right]' + x\left[1 + 2x - \frac{3}{x^2}\right] - \left[x + x^2 + \frac{3}{x}\right] \\
&= x^2\left[0 + 2 + \frac{6}{x^3}\right] + x\left[1 + 2x - \frac{3}{x^2}\right] - \left[x + x^2 + \frac{3}{x}\right] \\
&= 2x^2 + \frac{6}{x} + x + 2x^2 - \frac{3}{x} - x - x^2 - \frac{3}{x} = 3x^2, \ x \neq 0.
\end{aligned}
$$

Since the term $3/x$ is undefined when $x = 0$, this solution is valid only over an interval *not* containing 0. The two largest such intervals are $(-\infty, 0)$ and $(0, \infty)$.

(d) The nonlinear equation $y'(x) = (x/y(x))^2$ has the implicit solution

$$x^3 - y^3 = C.$$

To see this, differentiate both sides:

$$3x^2 - 3y^2(x)y'(x) = 0,$$

which is precisely the equation in question. ■ ■ ■

Knowing that an nth order ODE contains n differentiations, we might expect a solution to contain no more than n constants of integration. We must be careful when counting such constants. Consider

$$w(t) = c_1 e^t + c_2 e^{-t} + c_3 \cosh t + c_4 \sinh t.$$

If we use the definitions of the hyperbolic functions,

$$\cosh t := \frac{1}{2}\left(e^t + e^{-t}\right) \quad \text{and} \quad \sinh t := \frac{1}{2}\left(e^t - e^{-t}\right),$$

the function $w(t)$ can be written entirely in terms of exponentials as

$$w(t) = \left(c_1 + \frac{1}{2}c_3 + \frac{1}{2}c_4\right)e^t + \left(c_2 + \frac{1}{2}c_3 - \frac{1}{2}c_4\right)e^{-t}.$$

This is *not* a function containing four constants of integration but rather only the two constants k_1 and k_2, where

$$k_1 = c_1 + \frac{1}{2}c_3 + \frac{1}{2}c_4, \quad k_2 = c_2 + \frac{1}{2}c_3 - \frac{1}{2}c_4.$$

Henceforth, whenever we talk about m arbitrary constants we'll mean m independent constants (at this point we will take this in the intuitive sense and defer formalizing the concept of independence until the next chapter).

DEFINITION 2.2 *A solution of an nth order ODE that contains n independent arbitrary constants is called a* **general solution**. *Any solution that can be obtained from a general solution by assigning at least one of the constants a numerical value is called a* **specific solution**. *Any solution that* cannot *be obtained from a general solution by assigning numerical values to constants in a general solution is called a* **singular solution**.

■ **EXAMPLE 2.10** The function

$$x(t) = c_1 + c_2 e^{-t} + c_3 e^{2t} - t$$

is a general solution of the equation

$$x'''(t) - x''(t) - 2x'(t) = 2.$$

On the other hand, $x_1(t) = 2 - t$, $x_2(t) = c_1 + 3e^{-t}$, $x_3(t) = 1 - c_2 e^{2t} - t$, and $x_4(t) = 2e^{-t} - 3e^{2t}$ are all specific solutions of the equation. ■ ■ ■

■ **EXAMPLE 2.11** The general solution of $1 - y^2 = (yy')^2$ is

$$(x - c)^2 + y^2 = 1,$$

which is a family of circles of radius 1 centered at the point $(c, 0)$ on the x-axis (see Figure 2.10).

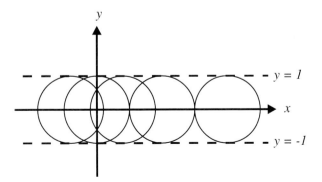

Fig. 2.10

Putting $c = 0$ we get one specific solution, $x^2 + y^2 = 1$. Both the functions $y = 1$ and $y = -1$ are singular solutions because no value of c will generate these solutions (we can't put $c = x$ to get $y^2 = 1$ because we can only assign a single *numerical* value to the constant of integration). Geometrically, these lines are the only lines that are tangent to every circle in the family. This is very much like the wavefronts in Huyghen's construction of optical wave motion. ■ ■ ■

2.3.2 *Initial and Boundary Value Problems*

DEFINITION 2.3 *An nth order* **linear** *ODE is one of the form*

$$y^{(n)}(t) + p_{n-1}(t)y^{(n-1)}(t) + \cdots + p_2(t)y''(t) + p_1(t)y'(t) + p_0(t)y(t) = g(t).$$

If $g(t) \equiv 0$ then the equation is **homogeneous**; *otherwise it is* **nonhomogeneous**. *An nth order ODE together with the n initial conditions*

$$y(t_0) = y_0, \ y'(t_0) = y_1, \ \ldots, \ y^{(n-1)}(t_0) = y_{n-1}$$

where the y_k are preassigned constants, is called an **initial value problem**. *If some of the side conditions specify the values of y and/or its derivatives at $t = a$ and the others are at $t = b (\neq a)$, then we have a* **boundary value problem**.

■ **EXAMPLE 2.12**

(a) The equation of motion of a horizontal mass-spring-dashpot system (see Figure 2.11)

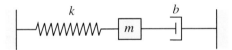

Fig. 2.11

is

$$m\ddot{x}(t) + b\dot{x}(t) + kx(t) = F(t).$$

This equation together with the initial conditions $x(0) = x_0$, $\dot{x}(0) = v_0$ form an initial value problem.

(b) The equation of motion of a string vibrating at an frequency $f = \omega/2\pi$ with vertical displacement $u(x)$ (see Figure 2.12)

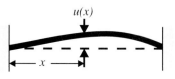

Fig. 2.12

is

$$u''(x) + \omega^2 u(x) = 0.$$

Together with the conditions of *fixed ends*: $u(0) = 0 = u(L)$, this forms a boundary value problem.   ■ ■ ■

2.3.3   *Existence and Uniqueness of Solutions to ODE's*

We now would like to know when a first order system has a solution. More specifically, under what conditions does the first order initial value problem

$$x'(t) = g(t, x(t)), \quad x(t_0) = x_0, \tag{2.3}$$

have a unique solution?

Even under relatively stringent conditions applied to the initial value problem (2.3), it will be possible to state only a local theorem, i.e., one not necessarily valid for all t and x.

THEOREM 2.1 *Suppose the function $g(t, x)$ is defined and continuous on the closed rectangle defined by $|x - x_0| \le K$, $|t - t_0| \le T$ and its partial derivative with respect to x is also continuous there; let $M = \max(|g(t, x)|)$, where the maximum is taken over all t and x in the rectangle; then the initial value problem (2.3) has a unique solution defined on the interval $|t - t_0| \le \min(T, K/M)$.*

For the proof you should refer to Birkhoff & Rota. Pictorially, if $g(t, x)$ is a function of t and x, then we can visualize it as a surface above the tx-plane. Figure 2.13 shows the surface and the rectangle in which the solution is defined.

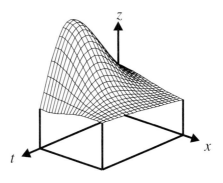

Fig. 2.13

All we need to check to determine existence and uniqueness of a solution is the continuity of the functions $g(t, x)$ and $\partial g(t, x)/\partial x$. Remember, the solution is only guaranteed to exist and be unique "near" the time $t = t_0$. We can stretch the "nearness" only if $g(t, x)$ is a very well-behaved function because, in general, increasing K and T will also increase M, keeping $\min(T, K/M)$ small. Fortunately, in practice $g(t, x)$ is often as smooth as we need and K/M and T will be large enough for our purposes.

▪ **EXAMPLE 2.13** Apply the Existence and Uniqueness Theorem to each of the following equations.

(a) The scalar equation

$$\frac{dx}{dt} = \frac{1 - x}{t}$$

has a $g(t, x)$ that is not continuous at $t = 0$, and so we cannot use that time value to start our solution. But $(1 - x)/t$ is analytic for $t > 0$ and for all values of x. Therefore, the initial value problem

$$\frac{dx}{dt} = \frac{1 - x}{t}, \quad x(1) = 2$$

has a unique solution "near" $t = 1$. "Near" means no further than the distance to $t = 0$ which is one unit away.

(b) $x'(t) = t\sqrt{x(t)}$ is a system where $g(t, x) = t\sqrt{x}$ is continuous for $x \geq 0$ but the partial derivative

$$\frac{\partial g}{\partial x} = \frac{t}{2\sqrt{x}}$$

is *not continuous* at $x = 0$. Thus an initial value problem of the form $x(t_0) = 0$ need not generate a unique solution. In fact, if $t_0 = 0$ then $x(t) \equiv 0$ and $x(t) = (t^2/4)^2$ are both solutions, thus contradicting the uniqueness part. ▪ ▪ ▪

2.3.4   *Exercise Set*

Verify that each of the following is a solution of the indicated ODE and if possible, classify it as a general, specific, or singular solution.

1. $y(t) = 2\cosh 2t - 3\sinh 2t, \quad y''(t) - 4y(t) = 0$

2. $(x - a)^2 + (y - b)^2 = c^2, \quad \left(1 + (y')^2\right)^3 = (cy'')^2$

3. $w(x) = x, \quad x^2 w''(x) + xw'(x) - w(x) = 0$

4. $w(s) = e^s(1 + \ln s), \quad sw''(s) + (1 - s)w'(s) - w(s) = e^s$

5. $u(s) = e^{2s}(5s - 4), \quad u''(s) + u(s) = 25se^{2s}$

6. $x^2 + y^2 = a^2, \quad y(x) = xy'(x) + a\sqrt{1 + (y'(x))^2}$

7. $z^2 = cy^2 + c^2, \quad y^2\left(z(y) - yz'(y)\right) = z(y)\left(z'(y)\right)^2$

8. $v(x) = \exp(x^2/2)\cos x, \quad v''(x) - 2xv'(x) + x^2v(x) = 0$

9. $r(\theta) = \cos\theta\cot\theta - \sin\theta, \quad r''(\theta) + 2r'(\theta)\cot\theta + 3r(\theta) = 0$

10. $w(\theta) = A\sec\theta + B(\sin\theta + \theta\sec\theta), \quad w''(\theta) - (1 + 2\tan^2\theta)w(\theta) = 0$

Given a general solution, it is possible to derive the form of its ODE. The basic idea is to isolate each of the arbitrary constants and differentiate the resulting expressions to obtain a set of simultaneous equations from which the arbitrary constants can be eliminated. The relations will involve derivatives of orders up to the number of arbitrary constants. For each of the following general solutions, derive the form of the corresponding ODE.

11. $x(t) = c_1\cos 3t + c_2\sin 3t$

12. $u(x) = c_1 + c_2 x + c_3 x^2$

13. $u(s) = A\cosh s + B\sinh s + s$

14. $x^2 + y^2 + 2c_1 x + 2c_2 y + c_3 = 0$

15. $y(t) = ct + c - c^3$

16. $w(\theta) = A\sin\theta + \cos\theta$

17. $u(s) = c_1\cos 2s + c_2\sin 2s + c_3\cosh 2s + c_4\sinh 2s$

Classify each of the following ODE's as linear or nonlinear and find their order. If an equation is linear tell whether it is homogeneous or nonhomogeneous and what the dependent variable is, when possible.

18. $y'(1 + y) - y''(1 + x) = x^2$

19. $(x + 2xy)dx + (3x - 2y)dy = 0$

20. $(y - 1)dx + (x + y - 2)dy = 0$

21. $\ddot{u} - 2\dot{u} + 3u = 6et$

22. $y' - xy = 2x/y^2$

23. $y'(y'')^2 = [1 - (y')^3]^2$

24. $(1 + u)\ddot{u} - u\dot{u} + u^2 = u$

25. $x^2 v'' + xv' + (x^2 - 4)v = 0$

26. $f'' + xf = x$

Classify each of the following as initial or boundary value problems.

27. $u'' + u = 0, \quad u(-2) = 0 = u(5)$

28. $u'' - 2u' + 7u = 6, \quad u(-2) = 0 = u'(-2)$

29. $x^2 u'' + xu' + x^2 u = 0, \quad u(1) = 0 = u'(1)$

30. $x^2 u'' + xu' + x^2 u = 0, \quad u(1) = 3, \ u'(1) = 4$

31. $x^2 u'' + xu' + x^2 u = 0, \quad u(1) = 3, \ u'(4) = 1$

32. $\left[1 + (y')^2\right]^3 = (2y'')^2, \quad y(2) = 3, \ y''(3) = 2$

Find the largest possible region in which an initial point could lie so that the following ODE's would be guaranteed to have a unique solution near it.

33. $y' = \sqrt{1 - (x^2 + 2xy + y^2)}$ 34. $(1 - t^2)u'' - 2tu' + 6u = 0$

35. $y' = \ln[1 - \mathrm{Atan}(y/x)]$ 36. $y' = \mathrm{Asin}(x^2 - y^2)$ 37. $w = w^2 - t^2$

2.4 GRAPHICAL SOLUTIONS OF ODE'S

The general form of the initial value problem for which we wish to find a numerical solution is

$$x' = g(t, x), \quad x(t_0) = x_0. \tag{2.4}$$

The Existence and Uniqueness Theorem from the previous section assures that there is a unique solution whenever g and $\partial g / \partial x$ are continuous in a region containing the point (t_0, x_0). We could obtain an approximate graphical solution by sketching the so-called **direction fields**.

If we wanted an approximate graph of the solution of the initial value problem of equation (2.4), one possibility is to draw line segments of slope $m = g(t, x)$ at each lattice point (t, x). Curves on which a solution has constant slope are called **isoclines**. As we start the solution at the initial point (t_0, x_0) all we would then need to do is follow a curve that had the slope of the line segment on which it lay. This is very nearly what computer software for plotting the solution curves would do. Given an initial value, the plotter pen would move to that point. Then the computer would calculate the value of the slope of a solution curve so that it could correctly set the direction of the pen. The pen would then move a distance prescribed by the degree of resolution required. The computer would recalculate the slope and readjust the pen motion. Continuing this process would result in a solution curve passing through the given initial point.

If we study the equation

$$x' = x(x - 2)^2(x + 3),$$

then the so-called **equilibrium solution curves** will occur where $x' = 0$. The horizontal lines at $x = -3$, $x = 0$, and $x = 2$ are equilibrium solution curves of the equation, which from Theorem 2.1 we know to be unique. Thus the tx-plane is divided into four regions I: $x < -3$, II: $-3 < x < 0$, III: $0 < x < 2$, and IV: $2 < x$. The aforementioned horizontal lines are the boundaries of these regions. No solution curve that begins in one of these regions can pass into any other region, because if they intersected but were not tangent to the boundary lines, x' would have two values there. It is a simple matter to determine the sign of x' in each region by looking at the function $g(x) = x(x-2)^2(x+3)$. We find

$$
\begin{aligned}
\text{I}: & & x < -3 & : x' > 0, \\
\text{II}: & & -3 < x < 0 & : x' < 0, \\
\text{III}: & & 0 < x < 2 & : x' > 0, \\
\text{IV}: & & 2 < x & : x' > 0.
\end{aligned}
$$

By using the Chain Rule we can compute the second derivative of x to be

$$
x'' = (x+2)(4x-3)(x-2)x' = x(x+3)(x+2)(4x-3)(x-2)^3.
$$

Hence, solution curves will have points of inflection where they cross the lines $x = -2$ and $x = 3/4$. We needn't include $x = 2$ or those x's where $x' = 0$ because they lie at the boundaries of the regions, which cannot be crossed. Taken together, this gives rise to the family of solution curves drawn in Figure 2.14.

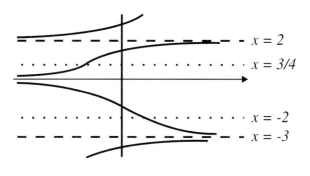

Fig. 2.14

Notice that solution curves on both sides of the line $x = -3$ move toward the line as t increases. For this reason that solution curve is said to be **stable**. On the other hand, solution curves on *both* sides of $x = 0$ move away from it. We say $x = 0$ is **unstable**. The uppermost horizontal solution curve $x = 2$ has the solution curves above it moving away and those below moving toward it and is said to be **semistable**.

The same information about the solution curves could have been obtained from what is called the **phase plane** description of the equation. In this case we graph x versus $v := x'$ to obtain the quartic curve of $g(x)$ shown in Figure 2.15.

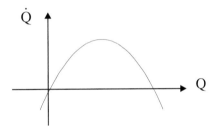

Fig. 2.15

From this we see where x' is positive and where it is negative. The solution curves will be concave upward where x' is increasing and concave downward where it is decreasing.

No solution curves can ever be vertical, because $g(x) = x(x-2)^2(x+3)$ is always finite.

We could have gotten a more detailed picture of the solution curves by plotting $g(x) = x(x-2)^2(x+3) = m$ for various values of m. The family of curves that are solutions to a differential equation are called its **integral curves**.

Because our goal is to compute numerical values for $x(t)$ in (2.4) at various values of t, we must quantify this graphical procedure quite a bit.

2.4.1 Exercise Set

Find the equilibrium solutions of each of the following equations and classify them as asymptotically stable, unstable, or semistable.

1. $x' = a^2 - x^2$
2. $x' = x(x^2 - a^2)$
3. $x = x^2(x^2 - a^2)$
4. $x' = \sin \pi x$
5. $x' = x + |x|$
6. $x' = x(x + |x|)$

2.5 INTRODUCTION TO NUMERICAL METHODS

2.5.1 Approximations

The true solution of the initial value problem $x' = g(t, x)$, $x(t_0) = x_0$, will be denoted by $x(t)$. We will want to evaluate the true solution at a set of equally spaced (for convenience) discrete points

$$t_n := t_0 + nh, \quad n = 0 : N;$$

h is called the **stepsize**. In particular, for an initial value problem beginning at t_0 we will want to compute the values of the solution from t_0 to some final time t_f. In theory, the smaller the stepsize, the better the resolution of the integral curve.

Denote the computed solution evaluated at t_n by X_n. The **local error** at t_n is defined to be

$$e_n := x(t_n) - X_n,$$

the difference between the true and the computed values at a given point. An equation relating the quantities $X_{n-r}, X_{n-r+1}, \ldots, X_{n-2}, X_{n-1}$, and X_n is called an rth order **recurrence equation**. For instance, $X_{n+1} = X_n + hg(t_n, X_n)$ is a first order recurrence equation and $X_{n+1} = X_{n-1} + 2hg(t_n, X_n)$ is a second order equation. Sometimes the rth order equation is said to be an r-**step** equation.

Our goal is to calculate the value of X_{n+1} based on the values of the previous X's. If we require m separate equations to do this, then we have an m-**stage** algorithm. If an algorithm can be written as $X_{n+1} = f(X_{n+1}, X_n, \ldots)$, then it is said to be **implicit** or **closed**. A closed algorithm will require that we solve for X_{n+1} using numerical methods (or if the original equation happens to be linear or something equally nice, we could solve it analytically). An algorithm that is not closed is said to be **open** or **explicit**, in which case it looks like $X_{n+1} = f(X_n, \ldots)$. Open algorithms can be iterated directly because at each step you are finding the value of X_{n+1} based only on previously calculated X's.

There are many ways to approximate the solution to $x' = g(t, x)$, but all of them hinge on the method we choose to approximate the derivative. Probably the simplest method is obtained by approximating x' by the slope of some "secant line." Considering that we want to evaluate the derivative at the point t_n, we have at least three possible t-values to use: t_{n-1}, t_n, t_{n+1}. We could use any of the lines joining the points $(t_{n+1}, x(t_{n+1})), (t_n, x(t_n))$, and $(t_{n-1}, x(t_{n-1}))$. Which line we use will determine how we construct our solution algorithm. We have at least three immediate choices: (a) forward differences, (b) backward differences, and (c) centered differences.

In **forward differences**, we will approximate the derivative at the point t_n by the slope of the secant line joining the points $(t_{n+1}, x(t_{n+1}))$ and $(t_n, x(t_n))$ as follows:

$$x'(t_n) \approx \frac{x(t_{n+1}) - x(t_n)}{t_{n+1} - t_n} = \frac{x(t_{n+1}) - x(t_n)}{h}. \tag{2.5}$$

If we use the secant line joining the points $(t_n, x(t_n))$ and $(t_{n-1}, x(t_{n-1}))$, we have the **backward difference** approximation to the derivative:

$$x'(t_n) \approx \frac{x(t_n) - x(t_{n-1})}{t_n - t_{n-1}} = \frac{x(t_n) - x(t_{n-1})}{h}. \tag{2.6}$$

We could just as easily use a weighted average of these two approximations. If θ is a number between 0 and 1, we could take $1 - \theta$ times the forward difference plus θ times the backward difference to get the **weighted difference**

$$x'(t_n) \approx \frac{(1 - \theta)x(t_{n+1}) + (2\theta - 1)x(t_n) - \theta x(t_{n-1})}{h}. \tag{2.7}$$

For the value $\theta = 1/2$, the weighted difference is the slope of the secant line joining the points $(t_{n+1}, x(t_{n+1}))$ and $(t_{n-1}, x(t_{n-1}))$,

$$x'(t_n) \approx \frac{x(t_{n+1}) - x(t_{n-1})}{2h}, \tag{2.8}$$

which is sometimes called the **centered difference**. More complicated (and also more accurate) approximations are available that use more than just these three points.

The simplest way to derive an algorithm for numerically "solving" our ODE is to replace the first derivative by an approximation to it while using the computed values of the solution. Using forward differences, we can immediately write the form of the **forward Euler method**:

$$\frac{X_{n+1} - X_n}{h} = g(t_n, X_n) \quad \Rightarrow \quad X_{n+1} = X_n + hG_n, \tag{2.9}$$

where $G_n := g(t_n, X_n)$. This equation will be iterated to obtain the sequence $\{X_n\}$. The sequence will be started by the initial condition $x(t_0) = x_0 = X_0$. We can find all the values of X_n by writing a program with a single loop. At each step we will compute the next value of X_n. Forward Euler is an open self-starting method. **Self-starting** refers to the fact that it is a first order recurrence equation and we have one initial value that completely specifies the right hand side of (2.9) for the lowest value of n. No second or higher order recurrence equation with a single initial value could be self-starting because X_{n+1} would depend on a value other than just X_n.

The algorithm for implementing this method is fairly straightforward. In Matlab it can be written as

$$\mathbf{X} = [x(0)]; \; x = x(0);$$
$$\textbf{for } t = h : h : t_{\mathrm{f}}$$
$$\qquad \mathbf{X} = [\mathbf{X}, x + h * g(t, x)];$$
$$\textbf{end}$$

■ **EXAMPLE 2.14** Apply the forward Euler method to the equation $x' = -x^2$, $x(0) = 1$, whose solution is $x(t) = 1/(t+1)$.

Solution: The form of the algorithm is

$$X_{n+1} = X_n + hG_n = X_n - X_n^2 h. \tag{2.10}$$

If we use various values of the stepsize h, we can get a handle on the merit of the method. The calculation will use $t_0 = 0$ and $t_f = 10$. In the following table all values are given to three decimal places and reported at every one unit of time. Values not reported are not calculated for the particular choice of h. The exact solution is given in the rightmost column.

t_n	$h = 0.25$	$h = 0.50$	$h = 1.00$	$h = 2.00$	$h = 5.00$	$x(t_n)$
0.0	1.000	1.000	1.000	1.000	1.000	1.000
1.0	0.449	0.375	0			0.500
2.0	0.300	0.258	0	-1		0.333
3.0	0.227	0.199	0			0.250
4.0	0.183	0.163	0	-3		0.200
5.0	0.153	0.138	0		-4	0.166
6.0	0.132	0.120	0	-21		0.142
7.0	0.116	0.107	0			0.125
8.0	0.104	0.096	0	-903		0.111
9.0	0.094	0.087	0			0.100
10.0	0.085	0.080	0	-163,172	-84	0.090

For $h = 0.25$, Euler's method is not too bad, although, in this case, it is always low. Larger values of h do not generate very good approximations to the true solution, with $h = 1$ being unusual because it causes the right hand side of (2.10) to be identically zero for this initial condition. ∎ ∎ ∎

If we use backward differences to approximate the derivative, we arrive at

$$X_n = X_{n-1} + hG_n.$$

Shifting all the n's up by one (so that it will be comparable with the forward Euler equation), we have the **backward Euler method:**

$$X_{n+1} = X_n + hG_{n+1}, \tag{2.11}$$

where $G_{n+1} = g(t_{n+1}, X_{n+1})$, in keeping with the previous notation. This is a self-starting closed method, because at each step we must solve for X_{n+1}.

Using centered differences we get the **centered Euler method**:

$$X_{n+1} = X_{n-1} + 2hG_n. \tag{2.12}$$

We now have a second order recurrence equation that is *not* self-starting, but it is open. To initiate this algorithm we will need the values of $x(t_0)$ and $x(t_1) = x(t_0 + h)$.

■ **EXAMPLE 2.15** Write the form of the backward and centered Euler methods for the equation $x' = -x^2$, $x(0) = 1$.

Solution: Since $g(t, x) = -x^2$, the backward Euler method is

$$X_{n+1} = X_n - hX_{n+1}^2,$$

which must be solved for X_{n+1}. Once again $h = 1$ causes trouble when $X_0 = 1$. The centered Euler method is

$$X_{n+1} = X_{n-1} - 2hX_n^2,$$

which gives X_{n+1} explicitly in terms of earlier X's. ■ ■ ■

We can also use a weighted average of the forward and backward Euler methods:

$$X_{n+1} = (1 - \theta)\left(X_n + hG_n\right) + \theta\left(X_n + hG_{n+1}\right).$$

This simplifies to the **weighted Euler method**:

$$X_{n+1} = X_n + h\left((1 - \theta)G_n + \theta G_{n+1}\right). \tag{2.13}$$

This is a closed self-starting method. For $\theta = \frac{1}{2}$ this becomes

$$X_{n+1} = X_n + \frac{h}{2}\left(G_n + G_{n+1}\right).$$

A slightly different approach to deriving this last result is available to us if we convert the differential equation $x' = g(t, x)$ to an integral equation. This can be done by simply integrating both sides from t_n to t_{n+1}:

$$x(t_{n+1}) - x(t_n) = \int_{t_n}^{t_{n+1}} g(t, x)\, dt.$$

Now the algorithm to solve the ODE has been transformed into an algorithm for evaluating an integral. One of the better simple approximations to the value of the integral is obtained from the trapezoid rule. With it, we can write

$$X_{n+1} = X_n + \frac{h}{2}\left(g(t_n, X_n) + g(t_{n+1}, X_{n+1})\right) = X_n + \frac{h}{2}\left(G_n + G_{n+1}\right), \tag{2.14}$$

which we will call the **trapezoid method**. This method is self-starting, but it is not open because X_{n+1} appears on both sides of the equation. The only ways to obtain a solution is either to solve (2.14) for X_{n+1} (analytically if possible, or numerically if not) or provide some form of approximation to X_{n+1}. One possible way to get a first approximation to X_{n+1} is to use the forward Euler algorithm. In this case, we will be left with a two-stage algorithm; the first is usually called the **predictor** for X_{n+1}, and the second is the **corrector**, hence the name **predictor-corrector method**:

$$X_n^* = X_n + hG_n,$$

$$X_{n+1} = X_n + \frac{h}{2}\left(G_n + G_n^*\right),$$

where $G_n^* := g(t_{n+1}, X_n^*)$. This is sometimes called the **corrected Euler method**. Implementing this algorithm in Matlab is straightforward:

$$\mathbf{X} = [x(0)]; \, x = x(0);$$
$$\textbf{for } t = h : h : t_f$$
$$x^* = x + h * g(t, x)$$
$$\mathbf{X} = [\mathbf{X}, x = x + .5 * h * (g(t, x) + g(t + h, x^*))];$$
$$\textbf{end}$$

2.5.2 Size of the Local Error

All the algorithms we have seen so far involve some form of iteration. We defined e_n as the error at the nth iteration. We say that error behaves **linearly** in the number of steps n if

$$e_n \approx An.$$

The error is of **order** k if

$$e_n \approx An^k.$$

It is **exponential** if

$$e_n \approx A\,r^n, \quad \text{for } r > 1.$$

An error sequence converges to 0 with **order** r if

$$\lim_{n \to \infty} \left| \frac{e_{n+1}}{e_n^r} \right| = A > 0.$$

The number r is roughly the number of decimal places of accuracy gained per iteration.
Two error sequences e_n and E_n are said to be of the **same order** if

$$\left| \frac{e_n}{E_n} \right| \approx A \neq 0,$$

and we can write $e_n = O(E_n)$. If e_n decreases faster than E_n, then

$$\lim_{n \to \infty} \left| \frac{e_n}{E_n} \right| = 0,$$

and we can write $e_n = o(E_n)$. Using this notation, the error sequence is of order k if $e_n = O(n^k)$ and it is exponential if $e_n = O(r^n)$. These definitions are virtually identical with that given in Appendix F, except that deals with functions and this with sequences.

We can get a handle on the magnitude of the local error for the Euler and related methods by expanding the function $x(t + h)$ in a Taylor series with a remainder:

$$x(t + h) = x(t) + hx'(t) + \frac{1}{2}h^2 x''(\tau), \quad \tau \in (t, t + h).$$

Taking $t = t_n$ and subtracting (2.5) from this, we have

$$e_{n+1} = x(t_{n+1}) - X_{n+1} = \frac{1}{2}h^2 x''(\tau)$$

Thus the local error at each time step is $O(h^2)$ whenever the second derivative of $x(t)$ is bounded. Halving the stepsize will reduce the error by a factor of one quarter. The overall or global error will turn out to be bounded not by h^2 but rather by h because of the accumulation due to the total number of time steps, which is proportional to $1/h$.

The value x_1 needed to start the centered Euler method could be obtained from Euler's forward method, in which case only t_0, h, g, and x_0 would be needed as input. A bound on the local error can be gotten by expanding both functions $x(t + h)$ and $x(t - h)$ in a Taylor series:

$$x(t + h) = x(t) + h\,x'(t) + \frac{1}{2}h^2\,x''(\xi), \quad \xi \in (t, t + h),$$

$$x(t - h) = x(t) - h\,x'(t) + \frac{1}{2}h^2\,x''(\eta), \quad \eta \in (t - h, t).$$

Subtracting these equations, we have

$$x(t + h) - x(t - h) = 2h\,x'(t) + \frac{1}{2}h^2\left(x''(\xi) - x''(\eta)\right).$$

The local error at each time step for the centered Euler method is at least $O(h^2)$ whenever x'' is bounded, the same as that for Euler's forward method.

More accurate methods are discussed in Section 2.6. For each of the foregoing algorithms termination criteria should include

(a) a final value for t, and

(b) a check for either overflow or underflow.

2.5.3 Stability

When doing any form of numerical calculation on a digital computer, we must always seek methods that

(a) use the fewest possible floating point operations, and

(b) perform all computations in the most accurate manner possible.

Some calculations will change character radically as computed values get near either the machine maximum or the machine minimum. Such calculations are said to be **ill-conditioned**. Additionally, a problem at hand may contain some form of "instability."

■ **EXAMPLE 2.16** If we look at the so-called recurrence equation for the **Fibonacci numbers**

$$F_n = F_{n-1} + F_{n-2},$$

you can see that if $F_1 = 1$ and $F_2 = 1$, then the resulting sequence is

$$1, 1, 2, 3, 5, 8, 13, 21, 34, 55, 89, \ldots .$$

It can be shown that for any starting values of F_1 and F_2 the general term of the sequence satisfying the recurrence equation is

$$F_n = c_1 \left(\frac{1 - \sqrt{5}}{2} \right)^n + c_2 \left(\frac{1 + \sqrt{5}}{2} \right)^n.$$

The values of c_1 and c_2 are entirely determined by the initial conditions, meaning the values of F_0 and F_1 or F_1 and F_2. Suppose we insist that the value of c_2 must be zero and that of c_1 one. The appropriate conditions are

$$F_0 = 1, \ F_1 = \frac{1 - \sqrt{5}}{2}.$$

In this case, part of the full solution, $\left(\frac{1-\sqrt{5}}{2} \right)^n$, will oscillate toward zero as $n \to \infty$ because $\frac{1-\sqrt{5}}{2} = -0.6180$. What happens if we choose to solve the problem directly using the floating point arithmetic of the computer? The results are not what we would expect. All the numbers following were obtained using single precision arithmetic and are chopped to three significant figures for presentation. Keep your eye on n and the relative error, $\text{RelError} = |F_n - \hat{F}_n|/|F_n|$, where $\hat{F}_n$ is the computed value from the true solution.

n	$\hat{F}_n$	$\left(\frac{1-\sqrt{5}}{2} \right)^n$	RelError
5	$1.458E - 01$	$1.459E - 01$	$4.085E - 07$
10	$-1.315E - 02$	$-1.315E - 02$	$4.226E - 05$
15	$1.180E - 03$	$1.186E - 03$	$5.217E - 03$
16	$-7.413E - 04$	$-7.331E - 03$	$1.365E - 02$
17	$4.369E - 04$	$4.531E - 04$	$3.575E - 02$
18	$-3.062E - 04$	$-2.800E - 04$	$9.361E - 02$
19	$1.306E - 04$	$1.730E - 04$	$2.450E - 01$
20	$-1.755E - 04$	$-1.069E - 04$	$6.416E + 00$
21	$4.494E - 05$	$6.610E - 05$	$1.679E + 00$
22	$-2.205E - 04$	$-4.085E - 05$	$4.397E + 00$
23	$-2.654E - 04$	$2.525E - 05$	$3.014E + 01$
24	$-4.860E - 04$	$-1.560E - 05$	$7.891E + 01$
25	$-7.514E - 04$	$9.644E - 06$	$2.066E + 02$
30	$-8.844E - 03$	$-8.696E - 07$	$3.707E + 03$

The second root $\frac{1+\sqrt{5}}{2} = 1.618 > 1$, called the **parasitic root**, forces the solution to be "unstable" and increase without bound even though $c_2 = 0$ in our example. This is so because the condition $F_1 = \frac{1-\sqrt{5}}{2}$ *cannot* be met exactly using floating point arithmetic. Suppose its error of realization is

$$\tilde{F}_1 = F_1(1 + \delta),$$

where $\tilde{F}_1$ is the machine represented value and F_1 is the true value. Then the actual solution of the recurrence equation will be

$$F_n = \left(\frac{1 - \sqrt{5}}{2}\right)^n + \delta \left(\frac{1 - \sqrt{5}}{2\sqrt{5}}\right) \left[\left(\frac{1 - \sqrt{5}}{2}\right)^2 + \left(\frac{1 + \sqrt{5}}{2}\right)^n\right].$$

Thus no matter how small δ is, the machine value will eventually be dominated by the term containing the factor $\left(\frac{1+\sqrt{5}}{2}\right)^n$. So even the most straightforward and seemingly best algorithms can deviate significantly from their theoretical values. Remember, even if we go to higher precision, all that will do is make δ smaller, meaning that it will take a higher value of n to make F_n start to deviate from the true value and increase, thus only postponing the inevitable.   ■ ■ ■

We can now address the question of stability of an algorithm for solving ODE's, which can be phrased as the question, "Does an algorithm maintain the size of its local error as the number of iterations increases?" Limiting cases can affect the behavior of algorithms in at least two ways:

1. As we increase the distance of the final time from the initial time, do we get a meaningful solution? Those algorithms that give meaningful solutions, in the sense that $|x(t_n) - X_n|$ remains bounded, are said to be **stable**.

2. If we want to improve the accuracy with which we approximate a solution, we must decrease the size of the time step h. Algorithms whose accuracy improves as we decrease the stepsize are said to **converge**.

The Fibonacci problem of the last example is not stable with respect to the initial data. Stability with respect to the initial data means that small changes in the input lead to only small changes in the output. Even stable and convergent algorithms may get caught in the problems of floating point arithmetic and have our algorithm deliver nonsense. The order of convergence of an algorithms has already been defined.

In order to get a feeling for the problem of stability, we will insist that any method we employ must work on a certain benchmark equation that we commonly encounter. Probably the most frequent first order initial value problem to be solved is that generated by the simplest decay model,

$$x' = -x/T, \quad x(0) = 1; \tag{2.15}$$

$T > 0$ is called the **decay time**. Since the true solution is $x(t) = \exp(-t/T)$, the computed solution should approximate this to some degree of accuracy. We will show that the local error for the forward Euler method is $O(h^2)$, that for the centered Euler method is $O(h^2)$, and the trapezoid or corrected Euler method leads to a $O(h^3)$ error, when h is the stepsize.

Aside: The benchmark equation we have chosen may seem arbitrary but it can be shown that for the general equation $x' = g(x, t)$ an expansion of $g(x, t)$ about $x = 0$ will give an equation that is approximated by (2.15).

We can apply each algorithm to our benchmark initial value problem. The result will be recurrence equations relating the elements of the sequence of computed values to each other.

Forward Euler Method

The recurrence equation for the benchmark equation is

$$X_{n+1} = X_n - \frac{h}{T}X_n.$$

Its *exact* solution can be shown to be

$$X_n = (1 - \lambda)^n$$

where $\lambda := h/T$ is a positive constant. The evaluation of X_n is now straightforward; and we have no reason to suspect that as h gets smaller there will be any problems, because when $\lambda < 1$ the value of X_n will decrease. Also, the local error will decrease as h decreases. To see this, write

$$
\begin{aligned}
e_n &= x(nh) - X_n = e^{-nh/T} - (1 - \lambda)^n = e^{-n\lambda} - (1 - \lambda)^n \\
&= \left(1 - n\lambda + \tfrac{1}{2}n^2\lambda^2 - \cdots\right) - \left(1 - n\lambda + \tfrac{1}{2}n(n - 1)\lambda^2 - \cdots\right) \\
&= \tfrac{1}{2}n\lambda^2 - \cdots.
\end{aligned}
$$

Thus e_n is linear in the number of steps n and quadratic in the stepsize h. Such behavior means that the forward Euler method is stable for $0 < \lambda < 1$.

Backward Euler Method

The recurrence equation for the benchmark equation is

$$X_{n+1} = X_n - \frac{h}{T}X_{n+1} \quad \Rightarrow \quad X_{n+1} = (1 + \lambda)^{-1}X_n.$$

The exact solution is
$$X_n = (1 + \lambda)^{-n},$$

which, for positive λ, is always converging to zero. Hence, the backward Euler method is stable when $\lambda > 0$.

Centered Euler Method

The recurrence equation for the benchmark ODE is

$$X_{n+1} = X_{n-1} - 2\lambda X_n,$$

again with $\lambda = h/T$. It can be shown that the exact solution is

$$X_n = c_1 \left(-\lambda + \sqrt{1 + \lambda^2} \right)^n + c_2 \left(-\lambda - \sqrt{1 + \lambda^2} \right)^n.$$

Unfortunately, the second term in the parentheses is greater than one in absolute value. Unless the computer always evaluates $c_2 \equiv 0$, the behavior of the solution will be dominated by this growing term. Thus this algorithm is unstable.

Corrected Euler, or Trapezoid, Method

Here the benchmark equation is transformed into the recurrence equation

$$X_{n+1} = X_n - \frac{\lambda}{2} \left(X_n + X_{n+1} \right).$$

The exact solution is the decreasing function

$$X_n = \left(\frac{2 - \lambda}{2 + \lambda} \right)^n.$$

Thus the corrected Euler, or trapezoid, method is always stable.

Due to its inherent instability, the use of the centered Euler method is not recommended for large numbers of small stepsizes, because as the number of time steps increases, the size of the increasing term becomes dominant and accuracy can deteriorate significantly.

None of these three methods would normally be used for long times, because there are more efficient algorithms available. This does not eliminate them as quick and dirty first tries where their programming simplicity gives them an edge. The question of how well they compare can only be decided by running them on several benchmark ODE's. The following example shows their relative performance on an equation whose exact solution can be calculated by other means. We'll look at an equation whose solution grows quite rapidly:

$$x' = -2(t - 2)x, \quad x(0) = 1 \quad \Rightarrow \quad x(t) = e^{4t - t^2}.$$

We'll compute the solution from $t = 0$ to $t = 3$ in steps of 0.5 using Matlab (precision is 16 decimal places) and list the computed value, chopped to three places, for each of the methods. For the centered Euler, the first calculated Euler method value was used to start the algorithm.

t_n	Forward Euler	Centered Euler	Trapezoid	Exact
0.0	1.000	1.000	1.000	1.000
0.5	3.000	3.000	5.000	5.754
1.0	7.500	5.500	18.125	20.085
1.5	15.000	8.500	45.312	42.521
2.0	22.500	9.750	73.632	54.598
2.5	22.500	8.500	73.632	42.521
3.0	11.250	5.500	46.020	20.085

Had we used a smaller stepsize, and consequently a larger number of steps, the instability of the midpoint method would have shown itself. Nevertheless, when used over a small number of steps, it is a perfectly adequate method for many equations.

2.5.4 Exercise Set

1. (a) As an example of a pathological ODE, consider the equation whose solution has higher order poles just off the real axis. Take the solution to be

$$x(t) = \frac{1}{(t^2 + \epsilon^2)^n}$$

for $n > 1$. Show that $x(t)$ is a solution of the ODE

$$x' = -2ntx^{1+1/n}.$$

(b) Write a program to compute the solution of this equation when $\epsilon = 0.1, 0.01,$ and 0.0001 using Euler, centered Euler, and trapezoid methods computing the relative error at each time step as t ranges from -1 to 1 in steps of $0.1, 0.01,$ and 0.001. Do this for $n = 2, 3,$ and 10. Use the initial condition $x(-1) = (1 + \epsilon^2)^{-n}$ as a starting value.

(c) Redo (b) with the "nice" ODE

$$x' + x = 1 + t, \quad x(-1) = e^{-1} - 1,$$

and compare it with the exact solution, $x(t) = t + e^{-t}$.

2. The Euler methods are the first of the class of Taylor series methods.

(a) For the equation $x' = g(t, x)$, show that

$$x'' = g_t + gg_x, \quad x''' = g_{tt} + g_t g_x + gg_x^2 + 2gg_{tx} + g^2 g_{xx}.$$

(b) Use the Taylor series expansion

$$x(t + h) = x(t) + hx'(t) + \frac{h^2}{2!} x''(t) + \frac{h^3}{3!} x'''(t) + \cdots$$

to derive the form of the second and third order Taylor series algorithms.

(c) Argue that the nth order Taylor method has error $O(h^{n+1})$.

3. Derive the centered Euler method by integrating the differential equation $x' = g(t, x)$ from t_{n-1} to t_{n+1} and approximating the integral by the height at the midpoint of the interval.

Use whatever method you want to find the solutions for 10 units beyond the initial time of each of the following benchmark equations. At each step compare the computed solution with the actual solution and compute the absolute and relative errors.

4. $t^2(1-x)x' + (1-t)x = 0$, $\quad x(1) = 1$, $\quad x = t\exp(x - 2 + 1/t)$

5. $(2 + 3t - tx)x' + x = 0$, $\quad x(1) = 0$, $\quad tx^3 = 2x^2 + 4x + 4 - 10e^{x-1}$

6. $(x^3 + y^3)y' + x^2(\pi x + 3y) = 0$, $\quad y(0) = 1$, $\quad \pi x^4 + 4x^3 y + y^4 = 1$

7. $2(x - y^4)y' = y$, $\quad y(0) = 1$, $\quad x + y^4 = y^2$

8. $x' + 2tx(1 + 4t^2 x^2) = 0$, $\quad x(0) = 1$, $\quad 2x^{-2} = 4\exp(2t^2) - 2(1 + 2t^2)$

9. $y' + x(\sin 2y - x^2 \cos 2y) = 0$, $\quad y(0) = 0$, $\quad 2\tan y + 1 - x^2 = \exp(-x^2)$

2.6 FIRST ORDER ODE'S

Since all first order equations involve a first derivative of the unknown function, the solution of these equations is often an exercise in unusual methods of integration. Just as there are many methods of integration, there are many methods for solving various forms of first order ODE's. In fact, some nineteenth century mathematicians made it their full time job to solve new and unusual forms of these equations. One treatise on the subject is by Murphy, although there is a recent volume by Zwillinger.

We'll limit ourselves to the forms of equations that arise most often in models that we'll encounter. Others will be relegated to the problems.

The simplest possible ODE has the form

$$\frac{dw}{dt} = 0,$$

and its immediate solution is

$$w(t) = C,$$

where C is an arbitrary constant that can only be determined by using additional information. The next easiest equation is

$$\frac{dw}{dt} = g(t). \tag{2.16}$$

Equation (2.16) can be rewritten in the differential form

$$dw = g(t)\, dt. \tag{2.17}$$

This is the basic problem of integral calculus: Find the function whose derivative is given. All we need do is integrate both sides of (2.17) to get

$$w(t) = \int g(t)\, dt + C,$$

where again C is an arbitrary constant.

Throughout this section we'll try to reduce all equations to the simple forms of equations (2.16) or (2.17), thus reducing all problems to a quadrature, i.e., an integration.

2.6.1 Separable Equations

The most frequently encountered and perhaps the easiest to solve is the following class of easily recognized equations. You may recognize the form as the differential in a line integral.

DEFINITION 2.4 *A first order ODE of the form*

$$M(x, y)\, dx + N(x, y)\, dy = 0 \tag{2.18}$$

is said to be **separable** *if* $M(x, y) = M_1(x)M_2(y)$ *and* $N(x, y) = N_1(x)N_2(y)$.

The "separate" in separable equation means to separate $M(x, y)$ and $N(x, y)$ into their *factors*, each of which depends on only one variable. Dividing a separable (2.18) by $N_1(x)M_2(y)$ and setting

$$f(x) := \frac{M_1(x)}{N_1(x)} \quad \text{and} \quad g(y) := \frac{N_2(y)}{M_2(y)},$$

we can transform it into the form

$$f(x)\, dx + g(y)\, dy = 0,$$

which is immediately integrable. Using the notation

$$F(x) := \int f(x)\, dx \quad \text{and} \quad G(y) := \int g(y)\, dy,$$

the general solution can be written in the form

$$F(x) + G(y) = C.$$

Of course, the most difficult part of this procedure is performing the integrations to obtain $F(x)$ and $G(y)$, so don't hesitate to use a computer algebra system whenever necessary.

■ **EXAMPLE 2.17** Solve each of the following ODE's.

(a) $\dfrac{dw}{dx} = e^{x+w}$, $w(1) = 4$. Multiply both sides by $e^{-w}\, dx$ to get the separated equation

$$e^{-w}\, dw = e^{x}\, dx.$$

Integrate: $\int e^{-w}\, dw = \int e^{x}\, dx \;\Rightarrow\; -e^{-w} = e^{x} + C$. Use the initial conditions to find C by setting $x = 1$ and $w = 4$:

$$-e^{-4} = e^{1} + C \quad \Rightarrow \quad C = -(e + e^{-4}).$$

The unique solution is

$$e^{x} + e^{-w} = e + e^{-4},$$

which is valid for all real x and w.

(b) $(1 + a + b + ab)\, da + db = 0$. We need to recognize the factors

$$1 + a + b + ab = (1 + a)(1 + b);$$

then the separation is easy:

$$(1 + a)\, da + \frac{db}{1 + b} = 0.$$

Integrating: $a + \frac{1}{2}a^{2} + \ln|1 + b| = C$ is the general solution. The solution is valid for all real a and $b \neq -1$. This divides the ab-plane into two regions in which solution curves can lie, the sides of the line $b = -1$.

(c) The equation $(\sin r)(\cos\theta)\, dr + (\cos r)\, d\theta = 0$ is immediately separated by multiplying by $1/(\cos\theta\cos r)$ to get

$$\tan r\, dr + \sec\theta\, d\theta = 0.$$

An integration yields

$$\ln|\sec r| + \ln|\sec\theta + \tan\theta| = C.$$

An equally acceptable, but more convenient, choice of arbitrary constant would be $C = \ln K$ where $K > 0$. This is allowed because $\ln K$ can be negative, zero, or positive as K is $< 1, = 1$, or > 1. Thus the solution takes the form

$$\ln|\sec r| + \ln|\sec\theta + \tan\theta| = \ln K.$$

Using the fact that $\ln(AB) = \ln(A) + \ln(B)$, this becomes

$$\ln |\sec\theta\,(\sec\theta + \tan\theta)| = \ln K.$$

Exponentiating both sides yields

$$\sec\theta\,(\sec\theta + \tan\theta) = K$$

as the general solution. With this solution we are restricted to values of both r and θ that are not odd multiples of $\pi/2$. If r and θ are the standard polar coordinates, the plane is divided into regions consisting of quarter annuli in which solution curves must live. ■ ■ ■

Warning: Nonseparated equations cannot be integrated because terms like $\int y\,dx \neq yx$, inasmuch as y is an *unknown* function of x. You should be especially careful not to fall into this trap.

For those of you who might feel the need for a more concrete criterion for determining separability, the following result (due to D. Scott, **American Mathematical Monthly 92**, 422–423 (1985)) should prove comforting.

THEOREM 2.2 *If the functions g, g_t, g_x, and g_{tx} are continuous on some region $\mathcal{D}$ in the tx-plane, g is never zero on $\mathcal{D}$, and $gg_{tx} = g_t g_x$ on $\mathcal{D}$, then the ODE $x' = g(t,x)$ is separable.*

2.6.2 Linear Equations

The general form of the first order linear equation is

$$y'(t) + p_0(t)y(t) = g(t).$$

Dropping the subscript on $p_0(t)$, we have the form

$$y'(t) + p(t)y(t) = g(t). \tag{2.19}$$

This equation is said to be **homogeneous** when $g(t) \equiv 0$; otherwise, it is **nonhomogeneous**.

The Existence and Uniqueness Theorem tells us that if both $p(t)$ and $g(t)$ are continuous functions in some region $\mathcal{R}$, then we are guaranteed a unique solution to (2.19) with an appropriate initial condition in $\mathcal{R}$. As with all linear equations (algebraic or differential), we begin by solving the homogeneous equation,

$$y' + p(t)y = 0,$$

which is separable:

$$\frac{dy}{y} + p(t)\,dt = 0.$$

The solution of the homogeneous equation, written $y_c(t)$, is called the **complementary solution**. An integration yields

$$y_c(t) = Ce^{-\int p(t)\,dt}.$$

■ **EXAMPLE 2.18** Solve the homogeneous linear ODE: $t^2 y'(t) - (1 + t^2)y(t) = 0$.

Solution: The equation is linear and separable to

$$\frac{dy}{y} - \frac{1 + t^2}{t^2} dt = 0 \Rightarrow \ln|y| + \frac{1}{t} - t = C \Rightarrow y_{\mathrm{c}}(t) = \exp\left(t - \frac{1}{t} + C\right).$$

■ ■ ■

Any solution $y_{\mathrm{p}}(t)$ to the nonhomogeneous equation (it need not contain an arbitrary constant) is called a **particular solution**. The general solution will be the sum of the complementary solution and any particular solution.

There is a method that will produce the general solution in one fell swoop.

Our goal is to put the equation (2.19) into the form of equation (2.17), i.e., $dw/dt = g(t)$. The problem is to find the proper function $w(t)$. We would be naive to expect $w(t)$ to be $y(t) := y_{\mathrm{c}}(t)$, so let's settle for next best and assume that $w(t)$ is a multiple of $y(t)$ as

$$w(t) = \mu(t)\, y(t).$$

The function $\mu(t)$ is called the **integrating factor** of the equation. Since $y(t)$ is not the answer and $w(t)$ is, then we can think of $\mu(t) = w(t)/y(t)$ as a fudge factor, the right answer divided by the wrong answer. Multiplying the linear equation by $\mu(t)$, we have

$$\mu \frac{dy}{dt} + \mu\, py = \mu g.$$

The left hand side of this equation could be equal to dw/dt if it took the form of a Product Rule differentiation. Then it would have to look like

$$\mu \frac{dy}{dt} + y \frac{d\mu}{dt} = \mu g.$$

In order for this to be true, the second terms on the left hand sides of the last two equations must be the same and $\mu(t)$ must satisfy

$$\frac{d\mu(t)}{dt} = \mu(t)\, p(t).$$

Since this equation is separable, an immediate solution is

$$\mu(t) = e^{\int p(t)\, dt}. \tag{2.20}$$

Be careful, this exponent has a plus sign, as opposed to the minus sign in the equation for $y_{\mathrm{c}}(t)$.

Multiplying (2.19) by $\mu(t)$, using the differential equation it satisfies, and the Product Rule for differentiation, we have

$$\mu y' + \mu py = \mu g \quad \Rightarrow \quad \mu y' + \mu' y = \mu g \quad \Rightarrow \quad (\mu y)' = \mu g. \tag{2.21}$$

This last equation has the form of the simple equation (2.17); thus all we need do is integrate both sides

$$\mu(t)y(t) = \int \mu(t)g(t)\, dt,$$

and solve for $y(t)$.

Remember, the equation must be in the form $y' + p(t)y = g(t)$ to start. Once in this form, we can find the integrating factor $\mu(t)$. Then we can immediately write the final form of the equation given in (2.21) and integrate both sides.

▪ **EXAMPLE 2.19**   Solve each of the following first order ODE's.

(a) The equation $zu'(z) + 2u(z) = 5z^3$ is linear in the dependent variable $u(z)$. Since the equation is not in proper first order linear form, we must multiply by $1/z$ to get

$$u'(z) + \frac{2}{z}u(z) = 5z^2.$$

Now we may write the integrating factor as

$$\mu(z) = e^{\int p(z)\, dz} = e^{\int \frac{2}{z}\, dz} = e^{2\ln z} = e^{\ln z^2} = z^2.$$

Multiplying the equation in standard form by $\mu(z) = z^2$, we have

$$z^2 u'(z) + 2zu(z) = 5z^4.$$

The right hand side always takes the form of a Product Rule differentiation, so that it can be written as

$$\left(z^2 u\right)' = 5z^4.$$

One quick integration yields

$$z^2 u(z) = z^5 + C.$$

Solving for $u(z)$ leads us to the general solution:

$$u(z) = z^3 + \frac{C}{z^2}.$$

The complementary solution is $u_c(z) = C/z^2$ and a particular solution is $u_p(z) = z^3$. You should verify that $zu_c'(z) + 2u_c(z) = 0$ and $zu_p'(z) + 2u_p(z) = 5z^3$.

(b) $y(1 + y)\, dt + [t - 2y(1 + y)2]\, dy = 0$. This equation is not linear in the dependent variable y because of the presence of the terms

$$y^2, \quad y\, dy, \quad \text{and} \quad y^3\, dy.$$

It is, however, linear in the variable t. This is no problem because, as written, the equation treats t and y equally; either could be the independent variable, and the other would be dependent. The standard form will now be $t'(y) + p(y)t(y) = g(y)$, where the prime indicates a derivative with respect to y.

$$y(1 + y)\frac{dt}{dy} + \left[t - 2y(1 + y)^2\right] = 0$$

$$\Rightarrow \frac{dt}{dy} + \frac{1}{y(1 + y)}t = 2(1 + y).$$

Now we have

$$p(y) = \frac{1}{y(1 + y)} = \frac{1}{y} - \frac{1}{1 + y} \quad \text{(using partial fractions)}$$

and $g(y) = 2(1 + y)$. The integrating factor is

$$\mu(y) = e^{\int p(y)\, dy} = e^{\int \left(\frac{1}{y} - \frac{1}{1+y}\right) dy}$$

$$= e^{\ln|y| - \ln|1 + y|} = e^{\ln\left|\frac{y}{1+y}\right|} = \frac{y}{1 + y}.$$

Multiplying by $\mu(y)$, we immediately arrive at the form $(\mu t)' = \mu g$:

$$\left(\frac{ty}{1 + y}\right)' = 2\left(\frac{y}{1 + y}\right)(1 + y) = 2y \quad \Rightarrow \quad \frac{ty}{1 + y} = y^2 + C.$$

The explicit form of the general solution is

$$t(y) = \frac{1 + y}{y}\left(y^2 + C\right),$$

which will be valid away from $y = 0$. The quantity $C(1 + y)/y$ is the complementary solution and $y^2(1 + y)/y = y(1 + y)$ is a particular solution.

(c) $r'(\theta) + (\cot \theta)r(\theta) = \csc \theta$, $r(\pi/2) = 3$. This equation is in standard form, and so the integrating factor is

$$\mu(\theta) = e^{\int \cot \theta\, d\theta} = e^{\ln|\sin \theta|} = \sin \theta.$$

Multiplying by $\mu(\theta)$, we have the final form:

$$(\mu r)' = (r \sin \theta)' = \sin \theta \csc \theta = 1 = \mu g.$$

An integration yields

$$r \sin \theta = \theta + C \quad \Rightarrow \quad r(\theta) = (\theta + C) \csc \theta.$$

The complementary solution is $r_c(\theta) = C \csc \theta$ and a particular solution is $r_p(\theta) = \theta \csc \theta$. Setting $\theta = \pi/2$ and $r = 3$, we find

$$3 = \left(\frac{\pi}{2} + C\right) 1 \quad \Rightarrow \quad C = 3 - \frac{\pi}{2} = 1.492\ldots,$$

and the unique specific solution to the initial value problem is

$$r(\theta) = \left[\theta + \left(3 - \frac{\pi}{2}\right)\right] \csc \theta.$$

$\blacksquare\ \blacksquare\ \blacksquare$

2.6.3 *Applications of First Order ODE's*

Now we'll apply some of the methods of this section to the solution of some of the model equations of Section 2.2.

■ **EXAMPLE 2.20** The simplest growth/decay model had a constant relative growth rate. The ODE for this model is

$$Q'(t) = kQ(t), \quad Q(0) = Q_0.$$

Since k is constant, this can be immediately separated and integrated to yield

$$\frac{dQ}{Q} = k\,dt \quad \Rightarrow \quad \ln Q = kt + \ln Q_0 \quad \Rightarrow \quad Q(t) = Q_0 e^{kt}.$$

The phase plane view of this equation is a straight line of slope k. When $k > 0$, we have a **growth model**, and for $k < 0$, a **decay model**. When $k = 0$, the population $Q(t)$ is constant at the initial value Q_0. If we are modeling population growth, then this result is unrealistic because unimpeded growth is not possible. There are always factors present that will cause a decrease in the relative growth rate. The assumption of a constant growth model was that the birth and mortality rates are equal. If we refine our model by assuming a relative mortality rate proportional to the population, we arrive at the logistic growth model that is governed by the equation

$$Q' = kQ(L - Q), \quad Q(0) = Q_0.$$

If k and L are both constant, this equation is separable, and

$$\frac{dQ}{kQ(L-Q)} = \frac{1}{kL}\left(\frac{1}{Q} + \frac{1}{L-Q}\right)dQ = dt$$

is the separated form after we have performed a partial fraction decomposition. After an integration, an unusual choice of arbitrary constant (for convenience), and insertion of the initial condition, we find

$$\frac{1}{kL}\left(\ln|Q| - \ln|L-Q|\right) = t + \frac{1}{kL}\ln C \quad\Rightarrow\quad \frac{L-Q}{Q} = Ce^{-kLt}$$

$$\Rightarrow\quad Q(t) = \frac{L}{1 + Ce^{-kLt}}, \quad \text{where} \quad C = \frac{L-Q_0}{Q_0}.$$

Looking at either the equation or the solution, we can see that if $Q_0 > L$ then the population will decrease asymptotically toward $Q = L$, whereas if $Q_0 < L$ it will increase asymptotically toward $Q = L$ following an S-shaped curve called an **ogive** or **sigmoid** (see Figure 2.16).

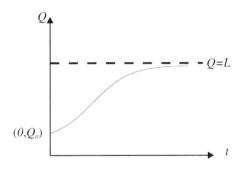

Fig. 2.16

For this reason L is sometimes called the **loading population**. The phase plane picture of the logistic growth model is the parabola shown in Figure 2.17.

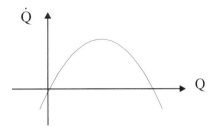

Fig. 2.17

Thus the solution will be asymptotically increasing when $0 \le Q \le L$ and asymptotically decreasing otherwise. The horizontal lines $Q = 0$ and $Q = L$ are unstable and stable, respectively, as could be seen from the previous graph of the solution.

Although our initial model was one of bacterial growth where reproduction is asexual, this model could be applied to human population growth. Historically, Verhulst proposed this equation as a model of such growth. ■ ■ ■

In 1925 Pearl and Reed applied the logistic growth model to the United States. Since there are three parameters Q_0, L, and k, to be determined, three base years must be taken for a proper fit. They choose 1790, 1850, and 1910 to fit the model and found $L = 197,000,000$. Unfortunately, the present U.S. population exceeds this by more than 25% and is still growing. There is a need for at least one more cycle to adequately model this process. At the very least the next step should distinguish between the populations of men and women. In fact, most actuaries do not refine this model but rather jump to the so-called **life table model**.

An elementary extended discussion of simple population growth models is given by D.A.Smith, Human Population Growth in **Mathematics Magazine 50**, 186–197 (1977). The constant relative growth/decay model that led to an exponential solution can be applied to radioactive decay which is treated through a more complete model in Chapter 5.

■ **EXAMPLE 2.21** The equation modeling Newton's Law of Cooling for small temperatures changes was given in example 2.2 and is

$$\frac{dT}{dt} = -\lambda\left(T - T_{\text{amb}}\right), \quad T(0) = T_0$$

with $\lambda > 0$. This equation can be rewritten in the standard linear form

$$\dot{T}(t) + \lambda T(t) = \lambda T_{\text{amb}}.$$

Using the integrating factor approach under the assumption of constant ambient temperature T_{amb},

$$\frac{d}{dt}\left(e^{\lambda t}T(t)\right) = \lambda T_{\text{amb}}e^{\lambda t}$$

$$\Rightarrow \quad e^{\lambda t}T(t) = T_{\text{amb}}e^{\lambda t} + C \quad \Rightarrow \quad T(t) = T_{\text{amb}} + Ce^{-\lambda t}.$$

Applying the initial condition, we have $T_0 = T_{\text{amb}} + C$, so that

$$T(t) = T_{\text{amb}} + (T_0 - T_{\text{amb}})e^{-\lambda t}.$$

Here, too, if $T_0 > T_{\text{amb}}$ (a hot object being cooled) we have an asymptotic decrease to $T = T_{\text{amb}}$ and if $T_0 < T_{\text{amb}}$ (a cool object being warmed) an asymptotic increase to $T = T_{\text{amb}}$ (see Figure 2.18).

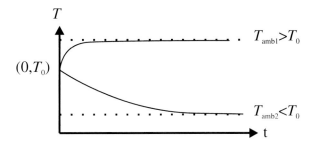

Fig. 2.18

If T_{amb} were a function of time and the temperature of the body were equal to T_{amb} at some time t, then our model would predict $T(t) = T_{amb}(t)$ for all later time. Unless $T_{amb}(t)$ is a slowly varying function and the temperature could redistribute itself throughout the body in a short time, the original model would be inaccurate and require revision. A possible refinement that accounts for a constant delay in temperature distribution is discussed in Chapter 5. ■ ■ ■

■ **EXAMPLE 2.22** The first approximation to the problem of the falling body was the pair of equations

$$m\frac{dv}{dt} = -mg - kv \quad \text{and} \quad \frac{dz}{dt} = v$$

with the initial conditions $v(0) = 0$ and $z(0) = h$. Although this is a first order system as described in Section 2.2, it is a simple one insofar as the first equation involves only v and t and is linear. Thus

$$\dot{v} + \frac{k}{m}v = -g \quad \Rightarrow \quad \frac{d}{dt}\left(ve^{-kt/m}\right) = -ge^{-kt/m}$$

$$\Rightarrow \quad v(t) = \frac{mg}{k}e^{-kt/m} + C.$$

Using $v(0) = 0$, we have

$$v(t) = \frac{mg}{k}\left(e^{-kt/m} - 1\right).$$

The velocity $v(t)$ is negative because the object is moving down, which is the direction of decreasing z. If the initial height h is sufficiently large for $e^{-kt/m}$ to become negligibly small, then the body will attain a maximum speed, called the **terminal velocity**:

$$v_T := \frac{mg}{k}.$$

Of course, if the body started falling at this speed, then $\dot{v} = 0$ and it would continue to move with speed v_T. Sky divers utilize this fact, and the actual dependence of v_T on the area the object presents normal to the direction of fall, to estimate their distance traveled before their parachute opens. The value of v_T for humans is as high as 200 mph.

Getting back to the problem, we must use $\dot{z} = v$ and integrate once more:

$$\dot{z} = \frac{mg}{k}\left(e^{-kt/m} - 1\right) \quad \Rightarrow \quad z(t) = -\frac{m^2g}{k^2}e^{-kt/m} - \frac{mgt}{k} + C.$$

Putting $z = h$ when $t = 0$ yields the height above the ground as a function of time:

$$z(t) = \frac{m^2g}{k^2}\left(1 - e^{-kt/m}\right) - \frac{mgt}{k} + h.$$

■ ■ ■

■ **EXAMPLE 2.23**   A body ejected (without losing mass) from a planet at the so-called **escape velocity** v_e will be able to travel infinitely far away from the planet. If it is ejected at a lower velocity, it must return. Ejection at a higher velocity will send it to "infinity" so that it has a positive velocity there. To calculate the escape velocity, let's model the process.

Solution: Assume the mass is ejected radially out from the surface of the planet, which we assume is a stationary sphere of radius R. Thus our initial conditions are: when $t = 0$, $r = R$, and $v = v_e$, where r is the distance from the center of the planet. The equation of motion is Newton's Second Law together with the Law of Universal Gravitation, i.e.,

$$\frac{dv}{dt} = -\frac{GMm}{r^2}.$$

Since $v = dr/dt$, this becomes a second order ODE, which we do not as yet know how to solve. With both v and r in the equation we cannot do any separation. We need to write a first order equation so that not all three variables t, r, and v are present, but only two of them. To achieve this, change the independent variable from t to r. This is reasonable, because when moving to infinity the mass will not come back and for every time t there will be one and only one distance r. It also has the advantage of using a phase space analysis of the problem. To effect this change, we must use the Chain Rule in the form

$$\frac{dv}{dt} = \frac{dv}{dr}\frac{dr}{dt} = v\frac{dv}{dr}.$$

Now the first order separable equation of motion and its solution are

$$mv\frac{dv}{dr} = -\frac{GMm}{r^2} \quad \Rightarrow \quad \frac{1}{2}mv^2 = \frac{GMm}{r} + C.$$

You should recognize this equation as the statement of conservation of energy. Using the initial condition that $v = v_e$ when $r = R$, we have

$$\frac{1}{2}mv^2 - \frac{GMm}{r} = \frac{1}{2}mv_e^2 - \frac{GMm}{R}.$$

The requirement for the escape velocity was that the object would have just enough energy to make it to infinity. Thus as $r \to \infty$ we must have $v \to 0+$. Thus the left hand side of the energy equation is zero, and we can solve for v_e in terms of the known quantities G, M, and R. We find

$$v_e = \sqrt{\frac{2GM}{R}}.$$

There is an alternative way to write this if we define the acceleration due to gravity at the surface to be mg, where g is different on each planet. From the Law of Gravitation, we have

$$mg = \frac{GMm}{R^2} \quad \Rightarrow \quad 2gR = \frac{2GM}{R} \quad \Rightarrow \quad v_e = \sqrt{2gR}.$$

As a handy reference, here are some data for the main planets, with distances given in km and speeds in km/sec:

	R (km)	g/g_e	M/M_e	v_e (km/sec)
Mercury	2,433	0.39	0.053	4.172
Venus	6,053	0.91	0.816	10.365
Earth	6,371	1.00	1.000	11.179
Mars	3,380	0.38	0.170	5.028
Jupiter	69,758	2.64	317.929	60.238
Saturn	58,219	1.13	95.066	36.056
Uranus	23,470	1.07	14.521	22.194
Neptune	22,716	1.41	17.177	24.536

Notice that Saturn's escape velocity is quite high even though its mass density is a paltry 0.688 gm/cm^3, i.e., it floats. ∎∎∎

■ **EXAMPLE 2.24** A one-stage rocket is composed of a payload, fuel, and a structure to encase everything. Normally only the mass of the fuel changes during the flight. Thus the total mass m as a function of time is

$$m(t) = m_p + m_f(t) + m_s,$$

where m_p is the mass of the payload, $m_f(t)$ the mass of the fuel, and m_s the mass of the structure. In a first approximation, the fuel is expended at a constant rate, so that $\dot{m}_f = -k$; hence $m_f(t) = m_f(0) - kt$. Firing will cease when all fuel is expended at the time $t = T := m_f(0)/k$. If the total initial mass is $m_0 := m(0) = m_p + m_f(0) + m_s$, then $m(t) = m_0 - kt$. If the fuel is expelled at a velocity of c backward relative to the rocket, the equation of motion is

$$m\dot{v} + c\dot{m} = -mg \quad \Rightarrow \quad (m_0 - kt)\dot{v} - kc = -(m_0 - kt)g, \quad v(0) = 0.$$

Air resistance has been neglected because the rocket will feel its effect over only a small fraction of its journey. Also, we assume that the change in gravitational force with height is negligible because the typical orbit is only several hundred kilometers as compared with the 6371 km radius of the earth. The equation is separable and easily integrated to yield

$$v(t) = -c \ln \left(1 - \frac{kt}{m_0} \right) - gt.$$

At burnout the velocity takes its maximum value at $t = T = m_f(0)/k$:

$$v(T) = -c \ln \left(1 - \frac{m_f(0)}{m_0} \right) - \frac{g}{k} m_f(0).$$

If $v(T)$ doesn't exceed the required satellite injection velocity, then the rocket will not place the payload into orbit.

The **thrust** T of a rocket is the force of the burning fuel, which is $c\dot{m} = ck$. The specific impulse I is the thrust per unit weight of fuel burned, and so $I = T/\dot{m}g = c/g$. The value of the specific impulse can vary from 250 sec for solid fuel to 400+ sec for some of the more exotic liquid fuels. In a typical orbital rocket, $m_p = m_0/100$ and $m_f(0)/m_0 = 0.8$. Using values of $I = 300$, $m_0 = 10^5$ kg, and $k = 5 \times 10^3$ kg/sec, we find that $v(T) = 4.6$ km/sec, well below the value needed to put a payload into a reasonable orbit.

By the way, the gravitational term has the value of 0.16 km/sec, so that we may neglect the effects of gravity with little loss in accuracy.

The previous numbers indicate that a single-stage rocket will not be adequate. For this reason, we should move up to consider a two-stage rocket. Suppose the masses of the stages are m_1 and m_2. The total mass is now

$$m(t) = m_p + m_1(t) + m_2(t).$$

Further suppose that both stages are composed of the same fraction f of fuel. Thus the mass of the unfueled rocket will be $m_s = m_p + (1 - f)(m_1 + m_2)$ and the mass of the fuel is $(m_1 + m_2)f$. If both stages burn at the same constant rate k, then

$$m(t) = m_s + \begin{cases} (fm_1 - kt) + fm_2, & 0 \le t \le fm_1/k, \\ fm_2 - kt, & fm_1/k \le t \le f(m_1 + m_2)/k. \end{cases}$$

Neglecting gravity, we can use the previous result to write the velocity of the rocket at completion of the first stage as

$$v_1 := v(T = fm_1/k) = -c \ln \left(1 - \frac{fm_1}{m_1 + m_2 + m_p} \right).$$

Using this and $v_2 := v\left(f(m_1 + m_2)/k \right)$, the relative increase in velocity due to the second stage burn is

$$v_2 - v_1 = -c \ln \left(1 - \frac{fm_2}{m_2 + m_p} \right).$$

Writing $M := m_1 + m_2$, $\mu := m_2/M$, and $p := m_p/M$, we can write the final velocity in the form

$$v_2 = -c \left\{ \ln \left(1 - \frac{f(1 - \mu)}{1 + p} \right) + \ln \left(1 - \frac{f\mu}{\mu + p} \right) \right\}.$$

An immediate question arises: what should the relative sizes of the two stages be to maximize the final velocity v_2? If M is fixed, then we must maximize v_2 with respect to μ. Differentiating with respect to μ, setting to zero, and simplifying, we find the requirement

$$f(1 - f)\left(\mu^2 + 2p\mu - p\right) = 0.$$

Neither $f = 0$ (no fuel) nor $f = 1$ (all fuel) are reasonable, and so we must have

$$\mu = -p + \sqrt{p^2 + p}.$$

Since p is small, we can factor out $\sqrt{p}$ and expand $\sqrt{1 + p}$ in a Taylor series to get

$$\mu_* = -p + \sqrt{p}\sqrt{1 + p} = -p + \sqrt{p}\left(1 + \frac{1}{2}p - \frac{1}{8}p^2 + \cdots\right)$$

$$= \sqrt{p} - p + \frac{1}{2}p^{3/2} + \cdots .$$

In the lowest order approximation we have $\mu_* \approx \sqrt{p}$, or

$$\frac{m_2}{m_1 + m_2} \approx \sqrt{\frac{m_p}{m_1 + m_2}}.$$

Typically $m_{\mathrm{p}}/M = 0.01$ so that we should choose $m_2/M = 0.10$ and the ratio of the masses of the stages should be $m_1 : m_2 = 9 : 1$.

A similar, albeit more algebraically difficult, analysis can be performed for an n-stage rocket. The interested reader should consult Burghes & Downes, **Modern Introduction to Classical Mechanics & Control**.　■ ■ ■

■ **EXAMPLE 2.25** Whether we look at an RL or an RC circuit with an AC voltage source, the form of the equation will be the same. Both involve a single loop (see Figure 2.19).

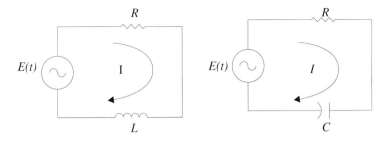

Fig. 2.19

An AC voltage source can be described by

$$E(t) = E_0 \cos \omega t,$$

where $f = \omega/2\pi$ is the **frequency of oscillation** and E_0 is the **amplitude of oscillation**. KVL for the RL circuit is

$$LI' + RI = E(t),$$

while for an RC circuit it is

$$RI + \frac{1}{C}\int I \, dt = E(t).$$

Upon differentiation, the latter becomes

$$RI' + \frac{1}{C}I = E'(t),$$

or when written in terms of the charge using $q' = I$, the original equation is

$$Rq + \frac{1}{C}q = E(t)$$

All of these equations are linear. Since R, L, and C are usually constant over the range of currents, voltages, and charges normally encountered, we may use an integrating factor on either form (RL) or (RC):

$$\frac{d}{dt}\left(I(t)\,e^{Rt/L}\right) = \frac{E_0}{L}e^{Rt/L}\cos\omega t.$$

An integration yields

$$I(t)\,e^{Rt/L} = \frac{E_0}{L}\frac{e^{Rt/L}}{\omega^2 + (R/L)^2}\left(\frac{R}{L}\cos\omega t + \omega\sin\omega t\right) + C.$$

Assuming zero initial current, $I(0) = 0$, we have

$$I(t) = \frac{E_0}{\omega^2 L^2 + R^2}\left(R\cos\omega t + \omega L\sin\omega t\right) - \frac{E_0 R}{\omega^2 L^2 + R^2}e^{-Rt/L}.$$

The oscillatory part of $I(t)$ is usually referred to as the **steady state**, or **equilibrium**, **solution** and the decaying part is the **transient solution**. We could define a **relaxation time** of the circuit by $\tau := L/R$. The transient solution would have decayed to 5% ($\approx e^{-3}$) of its original value after 3τ seconds. ∎ ∎ ∎

2.6.4   Exercise Set

Solve each of the following ODE's and determine in what regions the solutions are well-defined.

1. $\dot{x} + x\cot t = 2t\csc t$ 2. $(3ab + 3b - 4)da + (a + 1)^2 db = 0$

3. $dr = b(\cos\theta\, dr + r\sin\theta\, d\theta)$

4. $(b\ln a)(\ln b)\, da + db = 0$

5. $(\cos^2 x)y' + y = \tan x$

6. $(uv^2 + u + v^2 + 1)\, du + (v-1)\, dv = 0$

7. $2w^2 t\, dt - 3w(t^2 - 1)\, dw = 0$

8. $(t^2 + 1)\, dw + t(2w - 1)\, dt = 0$

9. $a\, db + (2b + ab - 4)\, da = 0$

10. $x^2\, dy + y^2\, dx = y\, dx + dy$

11. $(a + b\alpha + c\beta)\, d\alpha = d\beta$

12. $(2 + 2\alpha + 3\beta)\beta' = 1 - 2\alpha - 3\beta$

13. $y' = \cos x - y\sec x, \quad x = 0, y = 1$

14. $x\cos 2y\, dx + \tan y\, dy = 0$

15. $xy' + y = 2x^2 y, \quad x = 1, \ y = 1$

16. $3x^3 y' = 2y(y - 3)$

17. $m\, dn = (2m + 1)(dm - dn)$

18. $x^2 y' + y = xy, \quad x = 2, y = 1$

19. $(5 + 2m - 4n)m' = 3 + m - 2n$

20. $u(1 - v)v' + (1 - u)v = 0$

21. $2a^2 b' = 3b(b - 2)$

22. $v\, du = (e^v + 2uv - 2u)\, dv$

23. $tz' + t + z = 0, \quad t = 1, \ z = 2$

24. $tz' + t^2 - z = 0, \quad t = 2, \ z = 3$

25. $y' = e^{2x-y}$

26. $y' = e^x(a + be^{-y})$

27. $y' + y(\ln x)(\ln y) = 0$

28. $y' = y(y - 2), \quad y(1) = 1$

29. $r' - r\tan\theta = \cos 2\theta, \quad r(\pi/6) = \sqrt{3/2}$

30. $yy'(1 - 2x) = 1$

31. $r' - 3r\tan\theta = 3\tan^3\theta, \quad r(0) = 1$

32. $r' + \tan\theta\sec\theta\cos^2 r = 0$

33. $r' - \sec^2\theta\cot r\cos r = 0$

34. $(\sin\theta)\, r' = -1 - 2r\cos\theta, \quad r(\pi/2) = 1$

35. $r'\tan\theta + r = \csc\theta, \quad r(\pi/4) = 2$

36. $2s(t^2 - t)\, ds + (s^2 - 1)\, dt = 0, \quad s = 2, \ t = 3$

37. $(1 + t^2)\, ds + 2t[st^2 - 3(1 + t^2)^2]\, dt = 0, \quad s = 2, \ t = 0$

38. (a) Assuming a constant relative decay rate of $-\lambda$, model the process of decay of a mass $Q(t)$ of a radioactive substance. (b) The half-life T of a radioactive substance is defined to be the time it takes for the substance to decay to one half of its original mass. Derive the relation between the decay constant λ and the half-life. (c) Write an expression for $Q(t)$ in terms of the initial mass and the half-life.

39. If the radioactive half-life of the radionuclides 152-EU is 4700 days, how long will it take for 100 grams to decay to 1 gram?

40. The radionuclide 141-CE has a half-life of 320 days. Its soluble form normally accumulates in the liver, the permissible quarterly oral intake is $180\ \mu$curies. Suppose for every μcurie of cesium taken in that decays, there is a corresponding 2 μgram destruction of the liver. How much cesium must one ingest at once in order to account for a 50 gram cumulative loss of tissue in a single quarter?

41. One bit/megabyte of memory is destroyed for every hour that a computer operates at each 10% voltage reduction. Suppose that the computer center is forced to operate at a voltage that is normal at all times except between 8 AM and 6 PM, wherein the voltage decreases linearly to 25 volts

below normal at 1 PM and then increases linearly to normal. Model the loss in a single day for a machine with 50 megabytes of main memory.

42. It is not unreasonable to assume that a mothball losses mass by evaporation from its surface. Suppose that the rate of loss of mass is proportional to the surface area to the power α. Find the lifetime of the mothball in terms of the initial volume and α. The evaporation rate depends on the amount of surface area, and the mothball is not a perfect sphere but rather is quite rough and uneven. Additionally, we expect the degree of roughness to increase as the size of the ball decreases. How might these factors be taken into account?

43. Find the escape velocity for the central force field $F(r) = -km/r^n$, where m is the mass of the escaping body. What happens when $n = 1$?

44. Some planets have relatively extensive ring systems that affect the force of gravitational attraction. Within a reasonable approximation the usual $1/r^2$ force is modified to behave like $(ke^{-m/r})/r^2$. Find the escape velocity for a planet with such a gravitational force field.

45. If a particle encounters a resistive force $F_r = mk(e^v - 1)$, which is much stronger than a simple linear resistance, it will achieve a terminal velocity in free fall. Find v_T.

46. In a typical ballistics test, a gun is fired into a material that will offer a resistance proportional to speed but will do little damage to the bullet. If we write $F_r = a|v|$, how far will the bullet penetrate if it has an initial velocity of v_0?

47. A projectile is fired straight up. It encounters a resistive force of $F_r = a|v|$. If its initial velocity is v_0 upward, what is the maximum height it will attain?

48. A projectile with an initial velocity of 10 meters/second feels a resistive force of $10v^2$. At what time will it be traveling at 1 meter/second?

49. If a particle moves through a field that resists its motion with a force of ke^{av}, find its velocity as a function of time and the initial velocity.

50. A body at a temperature of $2000°C$ cools in air at a temperature of $200°C$. If its temperature drops to $1000°C$ in 10 minutes, how long will it take to cool to $400°C$?

51. At time $t = 0$, a body of temperature T_0 (> 0) is immersed in a medium whose ambient temperature increases linearly with time from 0, i.e., $T_{amb} = at$. Find the time it takes for the body to cool down to the ambient temperature. Find the time until the body returns to its initial temperature.

52. A family of curves $G(x, y) = C$ is an **orthogonal trajectory** of the family $F(x, y) = K$ if the two families intersect orthogonally. Convince yourself that if $y(x)$ is the functional representation of the orthogonal curves, then $y' = -1/m(x)$, where $m(x)$ is the slope of the curves in the other family. As an example, the trajectories orthogonal to the circles $x^2 + y^2 = a^2$ are the radial lines $y = mx$. Find the orthogonal trajectories to the family $y^3 = cx^2$. [Hint: Solve for c; then differentiate to find $m(x)$.]

53. In an RL circuit with an inductance of 2 henrys, a resistance of $10\,\Omega$, and zero initial current, find the current after 10 seconds if the voltage is a constant 20 volts.

54. The voltage source in an RL circuit from a battery that is losing its charge can be approximated by $E(t) = E_0 e^{-at}$. Find the current as a function of time if there is no initial current.

55. A nonohmic RL circuit with a DC voltage source has a constant inductance and a resistance that is proportional to the current; i.e., $R = kI$. Show the circuit is **current limited**, i.e., the current cannot exceed a maximum value.

56. Show that a nonohmic RL circuit with a constant resistance and an inductance proportional to current is current limited.

57. Brine containing 5 kg/liter of salt flows at a rate of 5 liter/min into a 200 liter tank that is half full of pure water. The well-stirred mixture drains out at a rate of 3 liter/min. Calculate the concentration of the solution in the tank at the moment of overflow.

58. A tank contains a 200 liter solution of nitric acid at a concentration 4 gm/liter. Pure water enters at a rate of 2 liter/min and the well-stirred mixture leaves at the same rate. How long will it take for the concentration to drop to 1% of its original level?

59. Suppose that the relative population growth of a single species was quadratically related to the population by $\dot{Q}/Q = a^2 - b^2 Q^2$, where a and b are positive constants. Find Q as a function of time and compare the result with the logistic growth model. Find the equilibrium solutions and classify them as asymptotically stable, unstable, or semistable. How would these results change if there were a quartic dependence of the form $\dot{Q}/Q = a^4 - b^4 Q^4$?

2.7   RUNGE-KUTTA METHODS

The general form of the initial value problem for which we wish to find a numerical solution is

$$x' = g(t, x), \quad x(t_0) = x_0.$$

We know there is a unique solution whenever both $g(t, x)$ and $\partial g/\partial x$ are continuous in a region containing the point (t_0, x_0), which we will assume is true for the equation we want to solve.

In this section we will study the general idea of Runge-Kutta methods, including RKF45. These algorithms are all more accurate than the elementary methods discussed in Section 2.5. As before, the true solution will be denoted by $x(t)$.

The general idea of the Runge-Kutta family of methods is to take a series of "partial steps" away from the point (t_n, x_n) and evaluate x' at each of them. To obtain the estimate for x_{n+1} we take a linear combination of each of these estimates. The general form of a Runge-Kutta method with m slopes is

$$K_j = hg\left(t_n + c_j h, \ X_n + \sum_{\ell=1}^{j-1} a_{j\ell} K_\ell\right), \quad c_1 = 0, \ j = 1 : m,$$

and the weighted linear combination of the K_j slopes obtained from the partial steps is

$$X_{n+1} = X_n + \sum_{j=1}^{m} w_j K_j$$

The coefficients $c_2, c_3, \ldots, c_m, a_{21}, a_{31}, a_{32}, \ldots, a_{m,m-1}, w_1, \ldots, w_m$ are to be determined by the conditions we place on the algorithm. Together with the m-partial steps and the evaluation of x_{n+1}, this constitutes an $(m + 1)$-stage algorithm.

If we write out the $m = 2$ method, things should be a bit clearer:

$$K_1 = hg(t_n, X_n), \quad K_2 = hg(t_n + c_2 h, \ X_n + a_{21} K_1),$$

$$X_{n+1} = X_n + w_1 K_1 + w_2 K_2.$$

Notice that each K_j may need all the previous K's to be evaluated.

We could derive the form of the equations that the coefficients must satisfy by expanding everything in sight in a Taylor series and equating all terms of the same order in h. Even with this there remains some arbitrariness in the choice of the coefficients, so that there will be several methods of the same order of accuracy. To make life simpler, we'll only look at the $m = 2$ case.

Start by expanding the function $x(t_{n+1})$ in a Taylor series as

$$x(t_{n+1}) = x(t_n) + hx'(t_n) + \frac{h^2}{2!}x''(t_n) + \frac{h^3}{3!}x'''(t_n) + \cdots$$

where we must use a multivariate Chain Rule because $x' = g(t, x)$. Performing these differentiations, we get

$$x'' = g_t + gg_x, \quad x''' = g_{tt} + 2gg_{tx} + g_{xx}g^2 + g_x(g_t + gg_x).$$

Now expand K_1 and K_2 about the point (t_n, x_n):

$$K_1 = hg(t_n, X_n) =: hG_n,$$

$$\begin{aligned}
K_2 &= hg(t_n + c_2 h, X_n + a_{21} h) \\
&= h\{G_n + (c_2 h g_t + a_{21} h g_x) \\
&\quad + \tfrac{1}{2!}\left(c_2^2 h^2 g_{tt} + 2c_2 a_{21} h^2 G_n g_{tx} + a_{21}^2 h^2 G_n^2 g_{xx}\right) + \cdots \\
&= hG_n + h^2\left(c_2 g_t + a_{21} G_n g_x\right) \\
&\quad + \tfrac{1}{2!}h^3\left(c_2^2 h^2 g_{tt} + 2c_2 a_{21} h^2 G_n g_{tx} + a_{21}^2 h^2 G_n^2 g_{xx}\right) + \cdots
\end{aligned}$$

$$\Rightarrow \quad X_{n+1} = X_n + (w_1 + w_2) hG_n + h^2 \left(w_2 c_2 G_n + w_2 a_{21} G_n g_x\right) + \cdots .$$

Equating both sides leads to the following restrictions on the parameters of the algorithm:

$$w_1 + w_2 = 1, \quad w_2 c_2 = \frac{1}{2}, \quad w_2 a_{21} = \frac{1}{2},$$

which imply that

$$a_{21} = c_2, \quad w_2 = \frac{1}{2c_2}, \quad w_1 = 1 - \frac{1}{2c_2}.$$

The Taylor series for X_{n+1} is

$$X_{n+1} = X_n + hG_n + \frac{1}{2!}h^2 \left(g_t + G_n g_x\right) + \frac{1}{4}c_2 h^3 \left(g_{tt} + 2G_n g_{tx} + G_n^2 g_{xx}\right) + \cdots$$

Subtracting the last two results, we find the error to be

$$\begin{aligned} e_n &= x(t_{n+1}) - X_{n+1} \\ &= h^3 \left\{ \left(\tfrac{1}{6} - \tfrac{c_2}{4}\right) \left(g_{tt} + 2G_n g_{tx} + G_n^2 g_{xx}\right) + \tfrac{1}{6}g_x \left(g_t + g g_x\right) \right\} + \cdots. \end{aligned}$$

No choice of c_2 can make the entire error term of order h^3 equal to zero. The size of the multiplier depends on the value of the solution together with the values of g and its derivatives. The constant c_2 is usually chosen to lie in the interval $[0, 1]$. Various choices are made to optimize certain externally imposed criteria. Thus there are many Runge-Kutta algorithms of each order. If we choose $c_2 = 1$, we are back at the trapezoid method.

$$K_1 = hg(t_n, X_n), \quad K_2 = hg(t_n + h, X_n + K_1),$$

$$X_{n+1} = X_n + \frac{1}{2} \left(K_1 + K_2\right).$$

The **classical Runge-Kutta method** has a local error that is $O(h^5)$. It is given by

$$K_1 = hg\left(t_n, X_n\right), \quad K_2 = hg\left(t_n + \frac{h}{2}, \ X_n + \frac{K_1}{2}\right),$$

$$K_3 = hg\left(t_n + \frac{h}{2}, \ X_n + \frac{K_2}{2}\right), \quad K_4 = hg\left(t_n + h, \ X_n + K_3\right),$$

$$X_{n+1} = X_n + \frac{1}{6} \left(K_1 + 2K_2 + 2K_3 + K_4\right).$$

Notice that it is an open, five-stage, self-starting method. It is also stable. Unfortunately, in this form it is hard to get a handle on the size of the error at a time step. To alleviate this difficulty, Fehlberg suggested an alternative form using two separate Runge-Kutta schemes, a fourth and a fifth order method whereby the error bound could be estimated as the difference of the values of the two methods. The explicit form of the K's in RKF45 (Runge-Kutta-Fehlberg of orders 4 and 5) is

$$K_1 = hg(t_n, X_n), \quad K_2 = hg\left(t_n + \frac{1}{4}h, \ X_n + \frac{1}{4}K_1\right),$$

$$K_3 = hg\left(t_n + \frac{3}{8}h, \ X_n + \frac{3}{32}K_1 + \frac{9}{32}K_2\right),$$

$$K_4 = hg\left(t_n + \frac{12}{13}h, \; X_n + \frac{1932}{2197}K_1 - \frac{7200}{2197}K_2 + \frac{7296}{2197}K_3\right),$$

$$K_5 = hg\left(t_n + h, \; X_n + \frac{439}{216}K_1 - 8K_2 + \frac{3680}{513}K_3 - \frac{845}{4104}K_4\right),$$

$$K_6 = hg\left(t_n + \frac{1}{2}h, \; X_n - \frac{8}{27}K_1 + 2K_2 - \frac{3544}{2565}K_3 + \frac{1859}{4104}K_4 - \frac{11}{40}K_5\right).$$

The weighted sum of slopes for the order 5 method is $\tilde{X}_n$, which is used as an estimation of the local error of an order 4 method:

$$\tilde{X}_{n+1} = X_n + \frac{16}{135}K_1 + \frac{6,656}{12,825}K_3 + \frac{28,561}{56,430}K_4 - \frac{9}{50}K_5 + \frac{2}{55}K_6,$$

$$X_{n+1} = X_n + \frac{25}{216}K_1 + \frac{1408}{2565}K_3 + \frac{2197}{4104}K_4 - \frac{1}{5}K_5.$$

The error control built into this method comes about by calculating the multiplier m, where

$$m = \sqrt[4]{\frac{\epsilon h}{2\left|\tilde{X}_{n+1} - X_{n+1}\right|}}.$$

The desired error tolerance is ϵ. The choice of increasing or decreasing the stepsize should be made as m varies. The design is to choose a stepsize of mh, although recalculating the stepsize at every time step is not a good idea. Usually one would change h only if m or $1/m$ exceed a fixed factor, say 2, 4, or 10. At no time should you exceed your maximum stepsize or fall below a minimum stepsize (based on the smallest number representable by your machine).

IMSL has implementations of several different differential equation solvers including the RKF45. There is also a procedure for so-called stiff systems. Anyone who needs to solve ODE's numerically using this software package should have a copy of the appropriate IMSL documentation together with Rice's book, which is an invaluable reference. Kahaner, Moler, & Nash include a copy of the subroutine SDRIV2, which is part of a class of routines, that implements a so-called multivalue method.

2.7.1 Exercise Set

1. Use the trial solution $X_n = c\alpha^n$ in the classical Runge-Kutta method applied to $x' = -x/T$ and solve for α in terms of $\lambda = h/T$. Show that the value of α differs from the Taylor series expansion for $e^{-\lambda}$ only for terms of order h^5 or higher.

2. Use the trial solution $x_n = ca_n$ in the fourth order predictor-corrector method applied to $x' = -x/T$ and solve for a in terms of $\lambda = h/T$. Show that the value of a differs from the Taylor series expansion for $e^{-\lambda}$ only for terms of order h^5 or higher.

Use either RK23 and RK45 in Matlab to find the solutions of each of the following benchmark equations. At each step compare the computed solution with the actual solution and compute the absolute and relative errors.

3. $x^2(1-y)y' + (1-x)y = 0$, $\quad y(1) = 1$, $\quad y = x\exp(y - 2 + 1/x)$

4. $(2 + 3x - xy)y' + y = 0$, $\quad y(1) = 0$, $\quad xy^3 = 2y^2 + 4y + 4 - 10e^{y-1}$

5. $(x^3 + y^3)y' + x^2(\pi x + 3y) = 0$, $\quad y(0) = 1$, $\quad \pi x^4 + 4x^3y + y^4 = 1$

6. $2(x - y^4)y' = y$, $\quad y(0) = 1$, $\quad x + y^4 = y^2$

7. $y'' - (1 + 2x)y' - (1 - x - x^2)y = 0$, $\quad y(0) = 1 + \sqrt{e}$, $\quad y'(0) = \sqrt{e}$,
   $y(x) = \exp(x^2/2) + \exp\{(x+1)^2/2\}$

8. $y'' + 4xy' + 2(1 + 2x^2)y = 0$, $\quad y(0) = 2$, $\quad y'(0) = 3$,
   $y(x) = (2 + 3x)\exp(-x^2)$

9. $y'' + 2y'\tan x + 3y = 0$, $\quad y(\pi) = -1$, $\quad y'(\pi) = 3$,
   $y(x) = \cos 3x - \sin x(1 + 2\cos 2x)$

10. $xy'' - y' + 4x^3y = 0$, $\quad y(\sqrt{\pi}) = 1$, $\quad y'(\sqrt{\pi}) = 0$, $\quad y(x) = \cos x^2$

11. $y'' - e^x(y')^2 = 0$, $\quad y(0) = 1 + \ln 2$, $\quad y'(0) = -1/2$,
    $y(x) = 1 - x + \ln(1 + e^x)$

12. $xy'' = x(y')^2 + y'$, $\quad y(1) = 2$, $\quad y'(1) = 1$, $\quad y(x) = 2 - \ln(1 - \ln x)$

2.7.2 Notes and References

Much current software exists for generating graphical solutions to ODE's, such as MDEP (Midshipmen's Differential Equation Program, available from the US Naval Academy), Phaser, MacMath, Models, and many others. All of them incorporate some form of numerical method or methods for generating the solutions. Matlab includes .m files for implementing some more sophisticated methods.

There are volumes written on the solution of ODE's with more methods than you can imagine. Each new and unusual equation spawned a new and unusual method. Here are two good references.

- Celia and Gray, **Numerical Methods for Differential Equations: Fundamental Concepts for Scientific and Engineering Applications**: An integrated presentation of methods for both ordinary and partial differential equations.

- Kahaner, Moler, and Nash, **Numerical Methods and Software**: An applied and computer oriented approach to the subject.

- Murphy, **Ordinary Differential Equations and Their Solutions**: An extensive collection of equations, classification and transformation schemes, and methods of solution.

- Zwillinger, **Handbook of Differential Equations**: The name says it all.

2.8   SUPPLEMENTARY AND COMPLEMENTARY PROBLEMS

A first order equation $M(x, y)\, dx + N(x, y)\, dy = 0$ that can be put into the form

$$\frac{dy}{dx} = F\left(\frac{y}{x}\right)$$

is amenable to simple solution after the change of dependent variable to $v = y/x$ or $y = xv$ which forces $dy = x\, dv + v\, dx$.

1. Show that the equation is separable after this change of variable, being sure to change dy to dv.

2. Use this technique to solve: $(x + y)\, dx + (x - y)\, dy = 0$.

3. Solve $(2xy - y^2)\, dx + (x^2 + 3xy + y^2)\, dy = 0$.

An equation of the form

$$y'(t) + P(t)y(t) = Q(t)y^n$$

is called a **Bernoulli equation**. Although it is nonlinear, it can be made linear by the change of dependent variable

$$u(t) = y^{1-n}(t).$$

4. Show that the original equation becomes

$$u'(t) + (1 - n)P(t)u(t) = (1 - n)Q(t),$$

which is linear in $u(t)$.

5. Solve: $ty' + y = y^2$.

6. Solve: $ty' + 2y = ty^3$.

7. Solve: $y\, dt - t(t - y - 1)\, dy = 0$.

8. A piece of spacejunk of mass m is attracted by a body of much larger mass M according to the Law of Gravitation. If the larger mass is a uniform sphere of radius R and the spacejunk is initially a distance D from the center of the body, how long will it take the smaller mass to contact the larger mass?

9. A sky diver is dropped from a plane flying at an altitude of 2000 meters. She falls in the spread formation so that her deceleration due to air resistance is triple her velocity. At 1000 meters she opens her parachute and the air resistance becomes double the square of her velocity. If she and her gear weigh 75 kilograms, how long will she be in the air?

10. A particle is projected vertically upward in a uniform gravitational field subject to a resistive force mbv^2. The particle has equal upward and downward speeds at heights z and w, respectively. If h is the maximum height attained by the particle, show that

$$\exp\left(2b(h-z)\right) + \exp\left(-2b(h-w)\right) = 2.$$

[For a generalization of this, see **Mathematics Magazine 63**, 197 (1990)]

11. A hot air balloon of weight W lifts off while dragging along one end of a rope that was coiled on the ground. The heated air exerts a lifting force F, gravity acts downward, and there is a resistive force $F_{\text{resist}} = -k\dot{x}^2$. The weight per unit length of the rope is ρ. Suppose the balloon was initially at rest at a height z_0. Find its speed of ascent up until the time when the entire rope is lifted into the air.

12. To show that the requirement of $g(t,x) \neq 0$ cannot be dropped from the statement of Theorem 2.2, define the function
$$g(t,x) = \begin{cases} t^2 e^{2x}, & x \le 0, \\ t^2 e^x, & 0 < x. \end{cases}$$

Show that $gg_{tx} = g_t g_x$ on $\mathbb{R}$. Also show that $g(t,x)$ doesn't factor on $\mathbb{R}$.

3

LINEAR SPACES AND TRANSFORMATIONS

3.1 PREVIEW

Many of the topics we have studied (and will study) have a common structure. This structure admits several concepts fundamental to the understanding to a large area of mathematics. We begin by defining linear spaces and subspaces. Through many examples we will be able to see their extensive applicability. Delving deeper into the innards of a linear space will force us to consider special classes of sets within the space, in particular, spanning sets and linearly independent sets. We will then consider the special case when a set is both a spanning set and linearly independent. In this case there are certain fundamental properties that will allow us to categorize all vectors in terms of the elements of such sets, called bases of the space. This categorization will allow us to represent any element of a linear space as a column vector, something with which we should be quite familiar. At this point we will add the notion of relative and absolute measurement to the structure of a linear space by introducing inner products and norms. We will see how the norm of a vector can induce a norm on a matrix. The induced matrix norm will then be applied to deriving bounds on the relative error in a system of linear equations and this bound will be written in terms of the condition number of the coefficient matrix. Following this will be an optional discussion of the linear spaces associated with a matrix and the relationship among those spaces.

Using all the previous material, we will study a special class of functions acting on a linear space, the set of linear transformations. As special visual examples we will look at (literally) the actions of rotations in two and three dimensions. We will show that any linear transformation can be represented as a matrix.

3.2 LINEAR SPACES

The set of $m \times n$ matrices, $\mathbb{C}_n^m$, is closed under addition, meaning sums of $m \times n$ matrices are $m \times n$ matrices, and closed under multiplication by complex numbers: complex multiples of $m \times n$ matrices are $m \times n$ matrices. In addition, these operations satisfied several of the *usual* properties of algebra. Taken together, these qualities are characteristic of a great many sets that we encounter when applying mathematical techniques.

3.2.1 Linear Spaces and Subspaces

DEFINITION 3.1 *The nonempty set $\mathcal{V}$ is a* **linear space**, *or* **vector space**, *over the set of complex numbers if when* $\mathbf{x}, \mathbf{y}, \mathbf{z}, \ldots$ *are elements of $\mathcal{V}$, called* **vectors**, *and* $c, c_1, c_2, \ldots$ *are complex numbers, called* **scalars**, *the following are true:*

(Closure1) *Whenever* $\mathbf{x}, \mathbf{y} \in \mathcal{V}$, *we have* $\mathbf{x} + \mathbf{y} \in \mathcal{V}$.

(Closure2) *Whenever* $\mathbf{x} \in \mathcal{V}$ *and* $c \in \mathbb{C}$, *we have* $c\mathbf{x} \in \mathcal{V}$.

(Add1) $\mathbf{x} + \mathbf{y} = \mathbf{y} + \mathbf{x}$.

(Add2) $\mathbf{x} + (\mathbf{y} + \mathbf{z}) = (\mathbf{x} + \mathbf{y}) + \mathbf{z}$.

(Add3) *There is an element* $\mathbf{0} \in \mathcal{V}$ *such that* $\mathbf{0} + \mathbf{x} = \mathbf{x}$.

(Add4) *For each* $\mathbf{x} \in \mathcal{V}$, *there is an element* $(-\mathbf{x}) \in \mathcal{V}$ *such that* $\mathbf{x} + (-\mathbf{x}) = \mathbf{0}$.

(ScMult1) $c_1(c_2\mathbf{x}) = (c_1 c_2)\mathbf{x}$.

(ScMult2) $(c_1 + c_2)\mathbf{x} = c_1\mathbf{x} + c_2\mathbf{x}$.

(ScMult3) $c(\mathbf{x} + \mathbf{y}) = c\mathbf{x} + c\mathbf{y}$.

(ScMult4) $1\mathbf{x} = \mathbf{x}$.

The last, seemingly trivial, property must be included lest we be forced to include sets on which are defined pathological multiplications. If we replace the set of complex numbers $\mathbb{C}$ by the set of real numbers $\mathbb{R}$ in the preceding definition, we have a linear space over the set of real numbers, or a real linear space, as opposed to a complex linear space.

Properties (Closure1) and (Closure2) refer to the fact that a linear space is **closed** under addition of vectors and also closed under multiplication of a vector by a scalar.

From the definition we can infer several simple results:

- There is only one $\mathbf{0}$ vector in $\mathcal{V}$. If $\mathbf{0}'$ were another such,

$$\mathbf{0} = \mathbf{0} + \mathbf{0}' = \mathbf{0}'.$$

- For each $\mathbf{x}$ in $\mathcal{V}$, its additive inverse $-\mathbf{x}$ is unique. To see this, suppose $\mathbf{y}$ and $\mathbf{z}$ are vectors satisfying (Add4); then

$$\mathbf{y} = \mathbf{y} + \mathbf{0} = \mathbf{y} + (\mathbf{x} + \mathbf{z}) = (\mathbf{y} + \mathbf{x}) + \mathbf{z} = \mathbf{0} + \mathbf{z} = \mathbf{z}.$$

- For each x in $\mathcal{V}$, $0x = 0$. We have $0x = (0 + 0)x = 0x + 0x$ and adding $-(0x)$ to both sides yields the desired result.

- For every scalar c, we have $c0 = 0$. We have

$$c0 + c0 = (c + c)0 = (2c)0 = c(20) = c(0 + 0) = c0,$$

and again adding $-(c0)$ to both sides yields $c0 = 0$.

- For each x in $\mathcal{V}$, $-x = (-1)x$. This follows because

$$0 = (1 + (-1))x = 1x + (-1)x = x + (-1)x,$$

and the vector $-x$ is unique.

Examples of linear spaces are everywhere:

■ **EXAMPLE 3.1** The following sets with the indicated operations are linear spaces.

(a) Complex n-space $\mathbb{C}_n := \mathbb{C}_n^1$ with the usual operations,

$$[x_1, x_2, \ldots, x_n] + [y_1, y_2, \ldots, y_n] := [x_1 + y_1, x_2 + y_2, \ldots, x_n + y_n],$$

$$c[x_1, x_2, \ldots, x_n] := [cx_1, cx_2, \ldots, cx_n]$$

is a complex linear space.

(b) For exactly the same reasons as in part (a), the set of all complex column vectors $\mathbb{C}^n$ is also a complex linear space. If we restrict ourselves to multiplication by real scalars, then both $\mathbb{C}_n$ and $\mathbb{C}^n$ are real linear spaces.

(c) If we restrict ourselves to real numbers only, then $\mathbb{R}^n$ and $\mathbb{R}_n$ are both linear spaces.

(d) The set of $m \times n$ matrices, $\mathbb{C}_n^m$, with the usual definitions of matrix addition and multiplication by a complex scalar is a complex linear space.

(e) The set of real-valued functions continuous on the interval $[a, b]$, written $C[a, b]$, with the usual addition and multiplication by a scalar:

$$(f + g)(t) := f(t) + g(t), \quad (cf)(t) := cf(t),$$

is a real linear space because it is closed under addition and multiplication by a scalar.

(f) The set of all real-valued functions whose derivatives up to and including those of order n are continuous on the interval $[a, b]$, denoted by $C^n[a, b]$ is a real linear space: The properties (Add1)–(Add4) and (ScMult1)–(ScMult4) are satisfied because they are true for all real-valued functions, and (Closure1) and (Closure2) are true because sums of and scalar multiples of functions in $C^n[a, b]$ are again in $C^n[a, b]$. If we looked at complex-valued functions over the set of complex numbers, we'd have a complex linear space.

(g) The set of all complex polynomials in the variable t of degree n or less, denoted by $\mathbb{C}_n[t]$, with the usual definitions of addition and multiplication by a complex scalar, is a complex linear space.

(h) The set of p-integrable functions on (a, b), denoted by $L^p(a, b)$, is the set of functions satisfying

$$\int_a^b |f(x)|^p \, dx < \infty.$$

This is a linear space when $p \geq 1$ because of the inequality

$$|f(x) + g(x)|^p \leq 2^p \max\left\{|f(x)|^p, |g(x)|^p\right\}.$$

The integral of the right hand side is finite if both f and g are in $L^p(a, b)$, so that we must have $f + g$ in $L^p(a, b)$.

(i) The set of all sequences $x := (x_1, x_2, \ldots)$ such that

$$\sum_{k=1}^{\infty} |x_k|^p < \infty$$

is a linear space when $p \geq 1$, called ℓ_p, by the same sort of argument used in part (g).

(j) The set of complex numbers $\mathbb{C}$ is a complex linear space. It is also a real linear space because every complex number can be written as $a + ib$ where a and b are real. ∎ ∎ ∎

DEFINITION 3.2 *Any subset $\mathcal{W}$ of a linear space $\mathcal{V}$ that is also a linear space with the same operations is called a* **subspace** *of $\mathcal{V}$.*

If $\mathcal{W} \subseteq \mathcal{V}$ then the algebraic properties (Add1)–(Add4) and (ScMult1)–(ScMult4) are still valid, so all we need check is closure under both operations. This can be done in a single step.

THEOREM 3.1 *If $\mathbf{x}, \mathbf{y} \in \mathcal{W} \subseteq \mathcal{V}$ implies that $c\mathbf{x} + \mathbf{y}$ is element of $\mathcal{W}$ for any complex number c, then $\mathcal{W}$ is a subspace of $\mathcal{V}$.* □

▪ **EXAMPLE 3.2** Determine which of the following subsets are subspaces.

(a) Let $\mathcal{W}_a := \{\mathbf{x} \in \mathbb{C}^3 : x_1 + x_2 + x_3 = 0\}$. Since

$$x_1 + x_2 + x_3 = \mathbf{1}^T \mathbf{x}, \quad \text{where} \quad \mathbf{1} := \mathbf{ones}(3, 1),$$

and

$$\mathbf{1}^T(c\mathbf{x} + \mathbf{y}) = c(\mathbf{1}^T\mathbf{x}) + \mathbf{1}^T\mathbf{y} = c(0) + 0 = 0$$

whenever $\mathbf{x}, \mathbf{y} \in \mathcal{W}_a$ and $c \in \mathbb{C}$, we may conclude that $\mathcal{W}_a$ is a subspace of $\mathbb{C}^3$.

(b) Let $W_b := \{\mathbf{x} \in \mathbb{C}^4 : x_1 + x_2 + x_3 + x_4 = 1\}$. Then when we consider the linear combination $c\mathbf{x} + \mathbf{y}$, we have

$$\mathbf{1}^T(c\mathbf{x} + \mathbf{y}) = c(\mathbf{1}^T\mathbf{x}) + \mathbf{1}^T\mathbf{y} = c(1) + 1 \neq 1$$

for an arbitrary complex constant c. Thus W_b is *not* a subspace of $\mathbb{C}^4$. Another tack would have been to notice that $\mathbf{0} \notin W_b$.

(c) Let $W_c := \{\mathbf{A} \in \mathbb{C}_n^n : \mathrm{tr}(\mathbf{A}) = 0\}$. Using the properties of the trace operation, we have

$$\mathrm{tr}(c\mathbf{A} + \mathbf{B}) = c\,\mathrm{tr}(\mathbf{A}) + \mathrm{tr}(\mathbf{B}) = c(0) + 0 = 0,$$

whenever $\mathbf{A}, \mathbf{B} \in W_c$ and $c \in \mathbb{C}$. Thus W_c is a subspace of $\mathbb{C}_n^n$.

(d) Take $W_d := \{f(x) \in C[0,1] : f(0) = 0 = f(1)\}$. Then since

$$(cf + g)(x) = cf(x) + g(x),$$

we have $(cf + g)(0) = cf(0) + g(0) = 0$ and $(cf + g)(1) = cf(1) + g(1) = 0$, so that when $f, g \in W_d$, $cf + g \in W_d$ for any complex c. Thus W_d is a subspace of $C[0,1]$.

(e) If $\mathbf{A}$ is a given $m \times n$ matrix, then consider $\{\mathbf{x} : \mathbf{A}\mathbf{x} = \mathbf{0}\}$. If $\mathbf{x}, \mathbf{y}$ satisfy this homogeneous system, then

$$\mathbf{A}(c\mathbf{x} + \mathbf{y}) = c(\mathbf{A}\mathbf{x}) + (\mathbf{A}\mathbf{y}) = c(\mathbf{0}) + \mathbf{0} = \mathbf{0}.$$

Hence the set is a subspace of $\mathbb{C}^n$. It is called the **solution space** of the homogeneous system $\mathbf{A}\mathbf{x} = \mathbf{0}$, or the **null space** of $\mathbf{A}$, written $\mathrm{NullSp}(\mathbf{A})$.

(f) Again specifying $\mathbf{A}$, write $F_{\mathbf{A}} := \{\mathbf{x} : \mathbf{A}\mathbf{x} = \mathbf{b}\}$ for some $\mathbf{b} \neq \mathbf{0}$. The set $F_{\mathbf{A}}$ is *not* a subspace of $\mathbb{C}^n$, because if $\mathbf{x}, \mathbf{y} \in F_{\mathbf{A}}$ and c is an arbitrary complex constant, then

$$\mathbf{A}(c\mathbf{x} + \mathbf{y}) = c(\mathbf{A}\mathbf{x}) + (\mathbf{A}\mathbf{y}) = c\mathbf{b} + \mathbf{b} = (c + 1)\mathbf{b} \neq \mathbf{b}.$$

Once again there is an easier way to see this isn't a subspace. Just look at the zero vector: $\mathbf{A}\mathbf{0} \neq \mathbf{b}$.

(g) The smallest possible subspace is the one containing the zero vector only, $\{\mathbf{0}\}$, because any multiple of the zero vector is still zero.

(h) If $C^2[a, b]$ is the linear space of functions that are twice continuously differentiable and $\mathcal{S} := \{f(t) \in C^2[a, b] : f''(t) + pf'(t) + qf(t) = 0\}$ where p and q are specified complex numbers, then $\mathcal{S}$ is a subspace. This follows because the arbitrary linear combination of functions in $\mathcal{S}$, $cf(t) + g(t)$, satisfies the equation specifying $\mathcal{S}$:

$$\begin{aligned}
(cf(t) + g(t))'' &+ p\,(cf(t) + g(t))' + q\,(cf(t) + g(t)) \\
&= c\,(f''(t) + pf'(t) + qf(t)) + (g''(t) + pg'(t) + qg(t)) \\
&= c(0) + 0 = 0.
\end{aligned}$$

(i) The set of real numbers is a subspace of the linear space of complex numbers over the reals. But $\mathbb{R}$ is *not* a subspace of $\mathbb{C}$ over the complex numbers over $\mathbb{C}$, because $cr + s$, where r and s are real and c is complex, need not be real.   ■ ■ ■

DEFINITION 3.3 *The* **span** *of a set of vectors* $S = \{\mathbf{x}_1, \mathbf{x}_2, \ldots, \mathbf{x}_m\}$ *is the set of all possible linear combinations of the elements of* S, *i.e.*,

$$\text{Span}(S) := \{c_1\mathbf{x}_1 + c_2\mathbf{x}_2 + \cdots + c_m\mathbf{x}_m : c_k \in \mathbb{C}\}.$$

We make the additional convention that $\text{Span}(\emptyset) = \{\mathbf{0}\}$.

■ **EXAMPLE 3.3**   The following are examples of spanning sets.

(a) $\text{Span}\{[1; 0; 0]\} = \{[c; 0; 0] : c \in \mathbb{C}\}$, which is the set of coordinate vectors to all points on the x_1-axis.

(b) $\text{Span}\{\mathbf{I}_n\} = \{c\mathbf{I}_n : c \in \mathbb{C}\}$ is the set of **scalar matrices** in $\mathbb{C}_n^n$.

(c) $\text{Span}\{1, t\} = \mathbb{C}_1[t]$, the set of all complex polynomials of degree one or less in the variable t.

(d) If the base set is the set of real numbers and we have $\mathcal{E} = \{[1; 0; 0], [0; 1; 0], [0; 0; 1]\}$, then $\text{Span}(\mathcal{E}) = \mathbb{R}^3$.

(e) When viewed as a linear space over the reals, $\text{Span}\{1, i\} = \mathbb{C}$.

(f) If $\mathcal{W} = \text{Span}\{[1, 0; 0, 0], [0, 1; 1, 0], [0, 0; 0, 1]\}$, then an arbitrary element in $\mathcal{W}$ has the form

$$\alpha \begin{bmatrix} 1 & 0 \\ 0 & 0 \end{bmatrix} + \beta \begin{bmatrix} 0 & 1 \\ 1 & 0 \end{bmatrix} + \gamma \begin{bmatrix} 0 & 0 \\ 0 & 1 \end{bmatrix} = \begin{bmatrix} \alpha & \beta \\ \beta & \gamma \end{bmatrix}.$$

This is the form of a general 2×2 symmetric matrix. Similarly, the linear space $\text{Span}\{[0, 1; -1, 0]\}$ is the space of all 2×2 skew-symmetric matrices.   ■ ■ ■

The last example suggests that $\text{Span}(S)$ is a subspace of $\mathcal{V}$.

THEOREM 3.2   *If* $S = \{\mathbf{x}_1, \mathbf{x}_2, \ldots, \mathbf{x}_m\}$ *is a subset of a linear space* $\mathcal{V}$, *then* $\text{Span}(S)$ *is a subspace of* $\mathcal{V}$.

Proof Suppose $\mathbf{a}, \mathbf{b} \in \mathrm{Span}(S)$. Then there must be complex numbers $a_1, a_2, \ldots, a_m$ and $b_1, b_2, \ldots, b_m$ such that

$$\mathbf{a} = a_1\mathbf{x}_1 + a_2\mathbf{x}_2 + \cdots + a_m\mathbf{x}_m$$

and

$$\mathbf{b} = b_1\mathbf{x}_1 + b_2\mathbf{x}_2 + \cdots + b_m\mathbf{x}_m.$$

Hence

$$c\mathbf{a} + \mathbf{b} = (ca_1 + b_1)\mathbf{x}_1 + (ca_2 + b_2)\mathbf{x}_2 + \cdots + (ca_m + b_m)\mathbf{x}_m \in \mathrm{Span}(S).$$

$\square$

3.2.2 *Linearly Independent Sets*

We would like to find the smallest set S such that $\mathrm{Span}(S) = \mathcal{V}$. To this end, we introduce the concept of linear independence so that we can determine when we have the minimum number of vectors to completely determine any vector in $\mathcal{V}$.

DEFINITION 3.4 *Any finite linear combination of the vectors* $\mathbf{x}_1, \mathbf{x}_2, \ldots, \mathbf{x}_k$ *that is zero, i.e.,*

$$c_1\mathbf{x}_1 + c_2\mathbf{x}_2 + \cdots + c_k\mathbf{x}_k = \mathbf{0},$$

is called a **linear relation** *among the vectors. If* $c_1 = c_2 = \cdots = c_k = 0$*, then this is a* **trivial linear relation***. If at least one of the* c_j *is nonzero, then it is a* **nontrivial linear relation***. A set* S *is said to be* **linearly dependent** *if there is a nontrivial linear relation among its elements. A set that is not linearly dependent is* **linearly independent***.*

Suppose the set $S = \{\mathbf{x}_1, \mathbf{x}_2, \ldots, \mathbf{x}_k\}$ is linearly dependent and

$$c_1\mathbf{x}_1 + c_2\mathbf{x}_2 + \cdots + c_k\mathbf{x}_k = \mathbf{0}$$

is a nontrivial linear relation on S with $c_1 \neq 0$ (if $c_1 = 0$, rearrange the $\mathbf{x}$'s so that $c_1 \neq 0$). Then we can solve for $\mathbf{x}_1$:

$$\mathbf{x}_1 = \left(-\frac{c_2}{c_1}\right)\mathbf{x}_2 + \left(\frac{c_3}{c_1}\right)\mathbf{x}_3 + \cdots + \left(\frac{c_k}{c_1}\right)\mathbf{x}_k.$$

We may conclude that when S is linearly dependent, one of the vectors in S can be written as a linear combination of the other vectors in S. Hence, S contains at least one vector that "depends" on the others.

■ **EXAMPLE 3.4** The set $\{[1; 1; 0], [1; 0; 1], [0; 1; 1], [1; 1; 1]\}$ is linearly dependent because there is a nontrivial linear relation among its elements. In particular, we have

$$[1; 1; 0] + [1; 0; 1] + [0; 1; 1] - 2[1; 1; 1] = [0; 0; 0].$$

■ ■ ■

Testing for linear dependence of a set of vectors in $\mathbb{C}^n$ is the same as solving a homogeneous system of linear equations. In particular,

$$c_1 \mathbf{x}_1 + c_2 \mathbf{x}_2 + \cdots + c_k \mathbf{x}_k = [\mathbf{x}_1, \mathbf{x}_2, \ldots, \mathbf{x}_k][c_1; c_2; \ldots; c_k] =: \mathbf{X}\mathbf{c} = \mathbf{0}.$$

Previous results on systems of linear equation from Section 1.4 tell us that there will be a nontrivial solution for the constants c_j if and only if

$$\text{rank}([\mathbf{x}_1, \mathbf{x}_2, \ldots, \mathbf{x}_k]) = \text{rank}(\mathbf{X}) < k,$$

because in that case $k - \text{rank}(\mathbf{X}) = \text{null}(\mathbf{X}) > 0$ and there will be a parameter in the solution. Thus we may state the following requirement for linear independence of a set of column vectors.

THEOREM 3.3 *The set $\mathcal{S} = \{\mathbf{x}_1, \mathbf{x}_2, \ldots, \mathbf{x}_k\} \subseteq \mathcal{C}^n$ is linearly independent if and only if*

$$\text{rank}([\mathbf{x}_1, \mathbf{x}_2, \ldots, \mathbf{x}_k]) = \text{rank}(\mathbf{X}) = k.$$

$\square$

As a corollary we see that, any nonempty subset of a linearly independent set is linearly independent, because the nullity of the test matrix $\mathbf{X} = [\mathbf{x}_1, \mathbf{x}_2, \ldots, \mathbf{x}_k]$ cannot increase by deleting a column. At best it can decrease, but for a linearly independent set it is already zero.

■ **EXAMPLE 3.5** Test each of the following sets for linear independence.

(a) The set $\mathcal{A} = \{[1, 2], [2, -1], [3, 2]\}$ is clearly linearly dependent because the test matrix

$$\begin{bmatrix} 1 & 2 & 3 \\ 2 & -1 & 2 \end{bmatrix}$$

can have at most rank of two and not three as required by the last theorem.

(b) To test the set

$$\mathcal{B} = \{[1; 0; 1; 0], [1; 2; 3; 4], [0; 1; 0; 1], [1; -1; 1; -1]\}$$

for independence, form the test matrix $\mathbf{X}$ whose columns are these vectors, and then reduce $\mathbf{X}$ to row echelon or row-reduced echelon form:

$$\mathbf{X} = \begin{bmatrix} 1 & 1 & 0 & 1 \\ 0 & 2 & 1 & -1 \\ 1 & 3 & 0 & 1 \\ 0 & 4 & 1 & -1 \end{bmatrix} \hookrightarrow \begin{bmatrix} 1 & 0 & 0 & 1 \\ 0 & 1 & 0 & 0 \\ 0 & 0 & 1 & -1 \\ 0 & 0 & 0 & 0 \end{bmatrix}.$$

We have $\text{rank}(\mathbf{X}) = 3 < 4$, and so there are nontrivial linear relations among the vectors of $\mathcal{B}$ (in particular, we have $-\mathbf{x}_1 + 0 \cdot \mathbf{x}_2 + \mathbf{x}_3 + \mathbf{x}_4 = \mathbf{0}$) and the set is linearly dependent.

(c) The set $\mathcal{C} = \{1 - x - x^2, x + x^3, 1 - x^3\}$ can be tested by associating each polynomial with a column vector in the form

$$ax^3 + bx^2 + cx + d \quad \leftrightarrow \quad [a; b; c; d].$$

This should be clear because

$$ax^3 + bx^2 + cx + d = [x^3, x^2, x, 1][a; b; c; d].$$

From this we have

$$
\begin{aligned}
1 - x - x^2 &= 0x^3 - 1x^2 - 1x + 1 &\leftrightarrow& \quad [0; -1; -1; 1] \\
x + x^3 &= 1x^3 + 0x^2 + 1x + 0 &\leftrightarrow& \quad [1; 0; 1; 0] \\
1 - x^3 &= -1x^3 + 0x^2 + 0x + 1 &\leftrightarrow& \quad [-1; 0; 0; 1].
\end{aligned}
$$

In this case, the test matrix is

$$
\mathbf{X} = \begin{bmatrix} 0 & 1 & -1 \\ -1 & 0 & 0 \\ -1 & 1 & 0 \\ 1 & 0 & 1 \end{bmatrix} \hookrightarrow \begin{bmatrix} 1 & 0 & 0 \\ 0 & 1 & 0 \\ 0 & 0 & 1 \\ 0 & 0 & 0 \end{bmatrix}.
$$

Since the rank of the test matrix is equal to the number of vectors in the set, we may conclude that $\mathcal{C}$ is linearly independent. ∎ ∎ ∎

As a general rule, when testing sets in $\mathbb{C}^n$ for linear independence, everything depends on the character of the test matrix $\mathbf{X} = [\mathbf{x}_1, \mathbf{x}_2, \ldots, \mathbf{x}_k]$. If we are testing a set of k vectors, then $\mathbf{X}$ will be $n \times k$. The set will be linearly independent if and only if $\mathrm{rank}(\mathbf{X}) = k$. Thus if $k > n$ we must have $\mathrm{rank}(\mathbf{X}) \leq n < k$ and the set will be linearly dependent. We can have a linearly independent set only if we have n or fewer vectors. The quantity $\mathrm{rank}(\mathbf{X})$ is the number of linearly independent rows of $\mathbf{X}$. It can be shown that $\mathrm{rank}(\mathbf{X}^T) = \mathrm{rank}(\mathbf{X})$. Thus $\mathrm{rank}(\mathbf{X})$ is also the number of linearly independent columns of $\mathbf{X}$.

The space $\mathbb{C}^n$ has sets of at most n linearly independent vectors. In fact,

$$\mathcal{E} := \{\mathbf{e}_1, \mathbf{e}_2, \ldots, \mathbf{e}_n\} = \{[1; 0; \ldots; 0], [0; 1; 0; \ldots; 0], \ldots, [0; \ldots; 0; 1]\}$$

is such a set. The set $\mathcal{E}$ consists of the columns of the $n \times n$ identity matrix. On the other hand, ℓ_1 can have infinitely many vectors in a linearly independent set. For example,

$$\{\mathbf{e}_k : k = 1 : \infty\}$$

where

$$\mathbf{e}_k := (0, 0, \ldots, 0, \underset{\underset{k^{th} \text{ place}}{\uparrow}}{1}, 0, 0, \ldots)$$

is such a set.

3.2.3   Bases and Dimension

DEFINITION 3.5 *Any linearly independent set of vectors that spans the linear space* $\mathcal{V}$ *is said to be a* **basis** *of* $\mathcal{V}$.

■ **EXAMPLE 3.6**   The following sets are examples of bases of the indicated linear spaces.

(a) $\mathcal{E} = \{[1; 0; \ldots; 0], \ldots, [0; \ldots; 0; 1]\}$ is a basis, called the **standard basis** of $\mathbb{C}^n$.

(b) If we define the $m \times n$ matrices $\mathbf{E}_{(jk;m,n)}$ by

$$\left[\mathbf{E}_{(jk;m,n)}\right]_{rs} = \delta_{jr}\delta_{ks}$$

then each $\mathbf{E}_{(jk;m,n)}$ is a "unit matrix" insofar as it has only one 1 (in the jk^{th} position) and all the other entries are 0. There are mn of these $\mathbf{E}_{(jk;m,n)}$. If we think of a matrix $\mathbf{A} \in \mathbb{C}_n^m$ as one long vector made by attaching each column vector to the bottom of its predecessor, which we denote as $\mathbf{A}(:)$, then it would look like an element of $\mathbb{C}^{mn}$ and $\mathbf{E}_{(jk;m,n)}$ would look like the unit vector $\mathbf{e}_{j+(n-1)k}$ in the standard basis for $\mathbb{C}^{mn}$. Thus $\mathcal{B} = \{\mathbf{E}_{(jk;m,n)} : j = 1 : m, \ k = 1 : n\}$ is a linearly independent spanning set and hence a basis of $\mathbb{C}_n^m$.

(c) The set $\{1, t, t^2, t^3, \ldots, t^m\}$ is a basis of $\mathbb{C}_m[t]$, the set of polynomials of degree less than or equal to m in the variable t.

(d) For the set of summable infinite sequences ℓ_p, see example 3.1(c), the set $\{e_k : k = 1 : \infty\}$ is linearly independent, and it can be shown that it is a basis.

(e) The *real* linear space $\mathbb{C}$ is spanned by the set $\{1, i\}$ which is clearly independent, since no nontrivial real linear combination of 1 and i can be zero.

(f) A basis of the space of all 2×2 symmetric matrices is

$$\left\{ \begin{bmatrix} 1 & 0 \\ 0 & 0 \end{bmatrix}, \begin{bmatrix} 0 & 1 \\ 1 & 0 \end{bmatrix}, \begin{bmatrix} 0 & 0 \\ 0 & 1 \end{bmatrix} \right\}.$$

■ ■ ■

Suppose that a basis of a linear space $\mathcal{V}$ consists of a finite number of vectors. Can another basis have a different number of vectors? The answer is no! All bases must have the same number of vectors.

THEOREM 3.4 *If the set* $\mathcal{X} = \{\mathbf{x}_1, \mathbf{x}_2, \ldots, \mathbf{x}_n\}$ *is a basis of* $\mathbb{C}^n$ *and the set* $\mathcal{Y} = \{\mathbf{y}_1, \mathbf{y}_2, \ldots, \mathbf{y}_m\}$ *is a linearly independent set in* $\mathbb{C}^n$, *then we must have* $m \leq n$.

Proof Suppose that $m > n$; we'll see if we can arrive at a contradiction. Since $\mathcal{Y}$ is linearly independent, the linear relation

$$c_1\mathbf{y}_1 + c_2\mathbf{y}_2 + \cdots + c_m\mathbf{y}_m = \mathbf{0}$$

has only the trivial solution $c_1 = c_2 = \cdots = c_m$. Since $\mathcal{X}$ is a basis of $\mathbb{C}^n$, it is also a spanning set, and each of the $\mathbf{y}_i$ can be written as a linear combination of the $\mathbf{x}_j$ as

$$\mathbf{y}_i = A_{i1}\mathbf{x}_1 + A_{i2}\mathbf{x}_2 + \cdots + A_{in}\mathbf{x}_n,$$

for $i = 1 : m$. If we insert this into the linear relation on the $\mathbf{y}$'s, we have, in compressed notation,

$$\sum_{i=1}^{m} c_i \sum_{j=1}^{n} A_{ij}x_j = \sum_{j=1}^{n} \left(\sum_{i=1}^{m} c_i A_{ij} \right) x_j = 0.$$

Since $\mathcal{X}$ is linearly independent, this linear relation must be trivial. That is, we have

$$\sum_{i=1}^{m} c_i A_{ij} = 0$$

This is a set of n equations in the m unknowns $c_1, c_2, \ldots, c_m$. But $m > n$, and so there must be at least one nonleading variable, and therefore a nontrivial solution for the c's. This is a contradiction! Thus we must have $m \leq n$. $\qquad\square$

Suppose $\mathcal{X}$ and $\mathcal{Y}$ were both bases. By the previous theorem applied to $\mathcal{X}$ as the basis, we have $m \leq n$. If we apply the theorem to the basis $\mathcal{Y}$, then we'd have $n \geq m$, and we are forced to conclude that $m = n$:

THEOREM 3.5 *Every finite basis of a linear space has the same number of elements.* $\qquad\square$

We often refer to a basis whose vectors are considered to be in a specific order as an **ordered basis**. Since the number of vectors in any finite basis is the same, we can define the following unique number:

DEFINITION 3.6 *The **dimension** of a linear space $\mathcal{V}$, written $\dim(\mathcal{V})$, is the number of vectors in any basis of $\mathcal{V}$. If a basis of $\mathcal{V}$ has infinitely many vectors, we say that $\mathcal{V}$ is **infinite dimensional**. By standard convention $\dim(\{\mathbf{0}\}) = 0$.*

■ **EXAMPLE 3.7** For many subspaces the dimensions are easily found from the bases given in a previous example.

(a) $\dim(\mathbb{C}_n^m) = mn$.

(b) $\dim(\mathbb{C}_m[t]) = m + 1$. (Remember $1 = t^0$ is the first element.)

(c) $\dim(\ell_p)$ is infinite, as is $\dim(L^p(a,b))$.

(d) As a real vector space $\dim(\mathbb{C}) = 2$ with basis $\{1, i\}$, but as a complex vector space, $\dim(\mathbb{C}) = 1$ with basis $\{1\}$.

(e) The dimension of the space of all 2×2 symmetric matrices is 2. You should verify that the dimension of all $n \times n$ symmetric matrices is $1 + 2 + \cdots + n = \binom{n+1}{2} = \frac{1}{2}n(n+1)$.

∎ ∎ ∎

Intuitively, the "dimension" of a linear space $\mathcal{V}$ is the number of linearly independent vectors in $\mathcal{V}$, because each such vector corresponds to a "different direction" in $\mathcal{V}$. With $\mathcal{W}_1 = \{[c; 0; 0] : c \in \mathbb{C}\}$, which is the x_1-axis, we associate one dimension, whereas the "$x_1 x_2$-plane" $\mathcal{W}_2 = \{[c; d; 0] : c, d \in \mathbb{C}\}$ would be two-dimensional.

We called the subspace of $\mathbb{C}^n$, $\{\mathbf{x} : \mathbf{Ax} = \mathbf{0}\}$, the **null space** of the matrix $\mathbf{A}$, and we wrote it as $\text{NullSp}(\mathbf{A})$. We know that we solve the homogeneous system by row reducing $\mathbf{A}$, assigning arbitrary parameters to the nonleading variables, and reading off the solution. From the solution we were able to separate out a set of $\text{null}(\mathbf{A})$ vectors in terms of which the solution was written as a linear combination. In fact, these vectors form a basis of $\text{NullSp}(\mathbf{A})$.

THEOREM 3.6 *If $\mathbf{A}$ is an $m \times n$ matrix, then $\dim(\text{NullSp}(\mathbf{A})) = \text{null}(\mathbf{A})$ and a basis of the null space is the set of vectors derived from the $\text{rref}(\mathbf{A})$.*   □

∎ **EXAMPLE 3.8** If we have

$$\text{rref}(\mathbf{A}) = \begin{bmatrix} 1 & -2 & 0 & 4 & -5 & 0 \\ 0 & 0 & 1 & 3 & 6 & 0 \\ 0 & 0 & 0 & 0 & 0 & 1 \\ 0 & 0 & 0 & 0 & 0 & 0 \end{bmatrix},$$

then $\text{null}(\mathbf{A}) = 3$. If we set $x_2 = \alpha$, $x_4 = \beta$, and $x_5 = \gamma$, then the solution is

$$\mathbf{x} = \begin{bmatrix} 2\alpha - 4\beta + 5\gamma \\ \alpha \\ -3\beta - 6\gamma \\ \beta \\ \gamma \\ 0 \end{bmatrix} = \alpha \begin{bmatrix} 2 \\ 1 \\ 0 \\ 0 \\ 0 \\ 0 \end{bmatrix} + \beta \begin{bmatrix} -4 \\ 0 \\ -3 \\ 1 \\ 0 \\ 0 \end{bmatrix} + \gamma \begin{bmatrix} 5 \\ 0 \\ -6 \\ 0 \\ 1 \\ 0 \end{bmatrix}.$$

Thus the set $\{[2; 1; 0; 0; 0; 0], [-4; 0; -3; 1; 0; 0], [5; 0; -6; 0; 1; 0]\}$ is a basis of the null space of $\mathbf{A}$.   ∎ ∎ ∎

A summary of the properties of spanning sets, linearly independent sets, and bases is contained in the following theorem.

THEOREM 3.7 *If V is a linear space of finite dimension n, then*

(a) *every basis of V contains exactly n elements;*

(b) *every set that spans V contains at least n elements;*

(c) *every linearly independent set in V has at most n elements;*

(d) *every set containing the zero vector is linearly dependent;*

(e) *any nonempty subset of a linearly independent set is linearly independent;*

(f) *any superset of a linearly dependent set is linearly dependent.* □

The quantity $n = \dim V$ is the number of vectors at which one crosses over from being linearly independent to being linearly dependent or from a set that cannot span V to a set that could span V. Schematically:

$$\text{\# of vectors } \underbrace{1 \ \ 2 \ \ 3 \ \ 4 \ldots\ldots\ldots n-1 \ \ n}_{\text{possibly independent}} = \underbrace{n \ \ n+1 \ \ n+2 \ \ n+3 \ldots\ldots\ldots}_{\text{possibly spanning}}$$

When $\dim V$ is infinite, the quantitative difference between $\dim V$ and $(\dim V) + 1$ is lost, and so parts (a), (b), and (c) of the previous theorem are no longer true. As an example,

$$\mathcal{E} := \{e_{2k} : k = 1 : \infty\}$$

is a linearly independent set in ℓ_1 with infinitely many elements, but it does not span ℓ_1 (it misses all the odd subscripted elements of the sequences).

3.2.4 Exercise Set

Determine which of the following sets are subspaces. For those that are, find the dimension when finite and a basis.

1. $\{\mathbf{x} \in \mathbb{C}^2 : x_1 - 2x_2 = 0\}$ 2. $\{\mathbf{x} \in \mathbb{C}^2 : x_1 - 2x_2 = 1\}$ 3. $\{p(x) \in \mathbb{C}_2[x] : p(0) = 0\}$

4. $\{p(x) \in \mathbb{C}_2[x] : p(0) = 1\}$ 5. $\{\mathbf{A} \in \mathbb{C}_2^2 : \operatorname{tr}(\mathbf{A}) = 0\}$ 6. $\{\mathbf{A} \in \mathbb{C}_2^2 : \operatorname{tr}(\mathbf{A}) = 1\}$

7. $\{p(x) \in \mathbb{C}[x] : \deg(f) \text{ is odd}\}$ 8. $\{\mathbf{x} \in \mathbb{C}_4 : x_1 = 2x_2 + x_3 - x_4\}$

9. $\{\mathbf{A} \in \mathbb{C}_n^n : \mathbf{A}^2 = \mathbf{A}\}$ 10. $\{\mathbf{A} \in \mathbb{C}_n^n : \operatorname{rank}(\mathbf{A}) = n\}$

11. $\{x_n \in \ell_1 : |x_n| < \frac{1}{n^2}\}$ 12. $\{\mathbf{x} \in \mathbb{C}^n : \|\mathbf{x}\| \leq 1\}$

13. $\{p \in \mathbb{C}_4[t] : p(a) = 0 = p(b)\}$

14. $\{\mathbf{x} \in \mathbb{C}_4 : \mathbf{x} = [a + 2b - c, a + b - c, 2a + b, a - b + c]$ for $a, b, c \in \mathbb{C}\}$

15. $\left\{\mathbf{x} \in \mathbb{C}_2 : \mathbf{x} = \left[\frac{a}{b} - \frac{c}{d}, 2\frac{a}{b} + 3\frac{c}{d}\right], \ a, b, c, d \in \mathbb{C}\right\}$

16. $\{[x, x + y, y, 2x + 3y] : x, y \in \mathbb{C}\}$

17. $\{\mathbf{A} \in \mathbb{C}_n^n : A_{jk}$ are rational$\}$

18. $\{f(z) : f$ has finitely many simple poles in the finite z-plane$\}$

19. $\{f \in C[a, b] : f(a) - f(b) = 1\}$

20. $\{\mathbf{A} \in \mathbb{C}_n^n : [\mathbf{A}, \mathbf{B}] = \mathbf{AB} - \mathbf{BA} = \mathbf{0}$ for a given $\mathbf{B} \in \mathbb{C}_n^n\}$

21. $\{f(z)$ analytic: $f''(z) + f(z) = 0\}$

By using a test matrix determine which of the following sets are linearly independent. [Hint: For some of these problems no row reduction is needed.]

22. $\{[1, 2], [3, 4]\}$ in $\mathbb{C}_2$

23. $\{[1; 2], [3; 4], [5; 6]\}$ in $\mathbb{C}^2$

24. $\{[1, 2], [3, -1], [4, 6], [-1, 2]\}$ in $\mathbb{C}_2$

25. $\{[1, 2, 3], [4, 5, 6]\}$ in $\mathbb{C}_3$

26. $\{[1; 2; 3], [4; 5; 6], [7; 8; 9]\}$ in $\mathbb{C}^3$

27. $\{[2, 1, 3], [4, 2, 1], [1, 0, 1], [4, -3, 2]\}$ in $\mathbb{C}_3$

28. $\{(2i - 3x)^2, (3 + 2x)^2, (2i + 3x)^2\}$ in $\mathbb{C}_3[x]$

29. $\{x^3 - 6x^2 + 2, 7x^2 + 7ix - 3, ix^2 + 6, 8x^3, (1 + 2i) - ix^2 + (1 - i)x^3\}$ in $\mathbb{C}_3[x]$

30. $\{1 + 2i, 2 + 3i\}$ in $\mathbb{C}$

31. $\{2 - 3i, 4 + 5i, 6 - 7i\}$ in $\mathbb{C}$

32. $\{2\mathbf{e}_1 + \mathbf{e}_2 - 3\mathbf{e}_3 + 5\mathbf{e}_4, 4\mathbf{e}_1 + \mathbf{e}_2 + \mathbf{e}_3 - \mathbf{e}_4, \mathbf{e}_1 + 2\mathbf{e}_3 - 2\mathbf{e}_4, 12\mathbf{e}_1 + 5\mathbf{e}_2 - 11\mathbf{e}_3 + 19\mathbf{e}_4\}$ in any linear space of dimension 4 or greater when $\{\mathbf{e}_1, \mathbf{e}_2, \ldots, \mathbf{e}_n\}$ is a basis.

33. $\left\{\cos\theta, \sin\theta, \cos^2(\theta/2), \sin^2(\theta/2)\right\}$ in $C(-\infty, \infty)$.

34. Prove that any set containing the zero vector must be linearly dependent.

35. Prove that any superset of a linearly dependent set is linearly dependent.

36. Prove that any nonempty subset of a linearly independent set is linearly independent.

37. If $\mathcal{V}$ is a linear space and $\{\mathbf{x}, \mathbf{y}, \mathbf{z}\}$ is a linearly independent set, then show that $\{\mathbf{x}+\mathbf{y}, \mathbf{y}+\mathbf{z}, \mathbf{z}+\mathbf{x}\}$ is linearly independent. Can this be generalized to $\{\mathbf{x}_1, \mathbf{x}_2, \ldots, \mathbf{x}_n\}$ and $\{\mathbf{x}_1+\mathbf{x}_2, \mathbf{x}_2+\mathbf{x}_3, \ldots, \mathbf{x}_n+\mathbf{x}_1\}$? [Hint: Watch the value of n.] What about the set $\{\mathbf{x} - \mathbf{y}, \mathbf{y} - \mathbf{z}, \mathbf{z} - \mathbf{x}\}$? How about $\{\mathbf{x}_1 - \mathbf{x}_2, \mathbf{x}_2 - \mathbf{x}_3, \mathbf{x}_3 - \mathbf{x}_4, \ldots, \mathbf{x}_n - \mathbf{x}_1\}$?

3.3   REPRESENTATIONS OF A VECTOR

Most of arguments given so far were based on the use of column vectors. It turns out that the vectors in any linear space can be thought of as column vectors. If $B = \{x_1, x_2, \ldots, x_n\}$ is an ordered basis of an n-dimensional linear space V, then for any vector $y \in V$ there are complex constants c_k for which we can write

$$y = c_1 x_1 + c_2 x_2 + \cdots + c_n x_n. \tag{3.1}$$

We call the column vector

$$[y]^B = [c_1; c_2; \ldots; c_n]$$

the **representation** of the vector y in the basis B. The constants c_k are called the **components**, or **coordinates**, of the vector y with respect to the basis B. Thus any vector in any linear space can be represented by a column vector in $\mathbb{C}^n$. The components c_k are unique: If we had the alternative representation

$$y = d_1 x_1 + d_2 x_2 + \cdots + d_n x_n,$$

then by subtracting the two representations we could conclude that

$$(c_1 - d_1)x_1 + (c_2 - d_2)x_2 + \cdots + (c_n - d_n)x_n = 0.$$

Since B, the set of x's, is a basis, it is linearly independent and the only linear relation on the set is the trivial one. Therefore,

$$c_1 - d_1 = 0, \ c_2 - d_2 = 0, \ \ldots, \ c_n - d_n = 0.$$

The vectors in the basis need to be ordered so that the matrix representation is a uniquely defined vector.

■ **EXAMPLE 3.9**   Find the representation of each vector in the given basis.

(a) The set $B_1 = \{[1, 0, 0], [1, 1, 0], [1, 1, 1]\}$ is a basis of $\mathbb{C}_3$. The representation of the row vector $a = [6, 5, 3]$ is a column vector $[c_1; c_2; c_3]$; the components satisfy the equation

$$c_1[1, 0, 0] + c_2[1, 1, 0] + c_3[1, 1, 1] = [6, 5, 3].$$

The augmented matrix can be written and reduced to obtain

$$\begin{bmatrix} 1 & 1 & 1 & | & 6 \\ 0 & 1 & 1 & | & 5 \\ 0 & 0 & 1 & | & 3 \end{bmatrix} \hookrightarrow \begin{bmatrix} 1 & 0 & 0 & | & 1 \\ 0 & 1 & 0 & | & 2 \\ 0 & 0 & 1 & | & 3 \end{bmatrix}$$

$$\Rightarrow \quad [a]^B = \begin{bmatrix} c_1 \\ c_2 \\ c_3 \end{bmatrix} = \begin{bmatrix} 1 \\ 2 \\ 3 \end{bmatrix}.$$

(b) The set $\mathcal{B}_2 = \{1+t, 1-t, (1+t)^2\}$ is a basis of $\mathbb{C}_2[t]$. The matrix representation of $p(t) = 1 - 2(1+i)t - t^2$ satisfies

$$c_1(1+t) + c_2(1-t) + c_3(1+t)^2 = 1 - 2(1+i)t - t^2.$$

Equating like decreasing powers of t, forming the augmented matrix, and row reducing, we have

$$\left[\begin{array}{ccc|c} 1 & 1 & 1 & 1 \\ 1 & -1 & 2 & -2(1+i) \\ 0 & 0 & 1 & -1 \end{array}\right] \quad \Rightarrow \quad [p(t)]^\mathcal{B} = \left[\begin{array}{c} 1-i \\ 1+i \\ -1 \end{array}\right].$$

■ ■ ■

Changing the representation of the vector $\mathbf{x} \in \mathbb{C}^n$ from an ordered basis $\mathcal{B}$ to an ordered basis $\mathcal{B}'$ is straightforward. Construct the square matrices $\mathbf{B}$ and $\mathbf{B}'$ whose columns are the standard basis representations of the vectors of the bases $\mathcal{B}$ and $\mathcal{B}'$, respectively. Referring back to the basis $\mathcal{B}_1$ of example 3.9, we have

$$\mathbf{B}_1 = \left[\begin{array}{ccc} 1 & 1 & 1 \\ 0 & 1 & 1 \\ 0 & 0 & 1 \end{array}\right].$$

Using the notation $[\mathbf{x}]$ for the representation of $\mathbf{x}$ in the standard basis and a result established in Section 1.2, we can write equation (3.1) in the form

$$[\mathbf{x}] = \mathbf{B}\,[\mathbf{x}]^\mathcal{B} = \mathbf{B}'\,[\mathbf{x}]^{\mathcal{B}'}. \tag{3.2}$$

Notice, from this equation we also get $[\mathbf{x}]^\mathcal{B} = \mathbf{B}^{-1}[\mathbf{x}]$. Since $\mathbf{B}$ and $\mathbf{B}'$ must be nonsingular, we can write

$$[\mathbf{x}]^\mathcal{B} = \mathbf{B}^{-1}[\mathbf{x}] = \mathbf{B}^{-1}\mathbf{B}'[\mathbf{x}]^{\mathcal{B}'} = \mathbf{P}^\mathcal{B}_{\mathcal{B}'}[\mathbf{x}]^{\mathcal{B}'}, \tag{3.3}$$

where $\mathbf{P}^\mathcal{B}_{\mathcal{B}'} = \mathbf{B}^{-1}\mathbf{B}'$, which is also nonsingular. It is customary to refer to $\mathbf{P}$ as the **transition matrix** from the ordered basis $\mathcal{B}'$ to the ordered basis $\mathcal{B}$. Inverting equation (3.3), we can write

$$[\mathbf{x}]^{\mathcal{B}'} = \left(\mathbf{P}^\mathcal{B}_{\mathcal{B}'}\right)^{-1}[\mathbf{x}]^\mathcal{B}. \tag{3.4}$$

Calculating $\mathbf{P}^\mathcal{B}_{\mathcal{B}'}$ is also straightforward: Form the augmented matrix $[\mathbf{B}|\mathbf{B}']$ and row reduce to $\left[\mathbf{I}|\mathbf{P}^\mathcal{B}_{\mathcal{B}'} = \mathbf{B}^{-1}\mathbf{B}'\right]$. From equation (3.4) it should be obvious that

$$\left(\mathbf{P}^\mathcal{B}_{\mathcal{B}'}\right)^{-1} = \mathbf{P}^{\mathcal{B}'}_\mathcal{B}; \tag{3.5}$$

i.e., the inverse of the transition matrix from the basis $\mathcal{B}'$ to $\mathcal{B}$ is the transition matrix from the basis $\mathcal{B}$ to $\mathcal{B}'$.

■ **EXAMPLE 3.10** Transform the representation of each vector by using the transition matrix between the given bases.

(a) The vector $\mathbf{a} = [1; 2; 3]$ can be represented in the basis

$$\mathcal{B} = \{[0; 0; 1], [0; 1; 1], [1; 1; 1]\}$$

as $[\mathbf{a}]^{\mathcal{B}} = [1; 1; 1]$ because

$$[1; 2; 3] = 1[0; 0; 1] + 1[0; 1; 1] + 1[1; 1; 1].$$

The transition matrix from the standard basis $\mathcal{E}$ to the basis $\mathcal{B}$ is $\mathbf{P}_{\mathcal{E}}^{\mathcal{B}} = \mathbf{B}^{-1}\mathbf{I}$. As a verification of the representation we have

$$\mathbf{P}_{\mathcal{E}}^{\mathcal{B}} \begin{bmatrix} 1 \\ 2 \\ 3 \end{bmatrix} = \begin{bmatrix} 0 & 0 & 1 \\ 0 & 1 & 1 \\ 1 & 1 & 1 \end{bmatrix}^{-1} \begin{bmatrix} 1 \\ 2 \\ 3 \end{bmatrix}$$

$$= \begin{bmatrix} 0 & -1 & 1 \\ -1 & 1 & 0 \\ 1 & 0 & 0 \end{bmatrix} \begin{bmatrix} 1 \\ 2 \\ 3 \end{bmatrix} = \begin{bmatrix} 1 \\ 1 \\ 1 \end{bmatrix}.$$

If we want to change from the basis $\mathcal{B}$ to the basis

$$\mathcal{B}' = \{[1; 0; 1], [0; 1; 0], [-1; 0; 1]\},$$

we must use the transition matrix $\mathbf{P}_{\mathcal{B}}^{\mathcal{B}'} = (\mathbf{B}')^{-1}\mathbf{B}$, which is

$$\mathbf{P}_{\mathcal{B}}^{\mathcal{B}'} = \begin{bmatrix} 1 & 0 & -1 \\ 0 & 1 & 0 \\ 1 & 0 & 1 \end{bmatrix}^{-1} \begin{bmatrix} 0 & 0 & 1 \\ 0 & 1 & 1 \\ 1 & 1 & 1 \end{bmatrix}$$

$$= \frac{1}{2} \begin{bmatrix} 1 & 0 & 1 \\ 0 & 2 & 0 \\ -1 & 0 & 1 \end{bmatrix} \begin{bmatrix} 0 & 0 & 1 \\ 0 & 1 & 1 \\ 1 & 1 & 1 \end{bmatrix} = \frac{1}{2} \begin{bmatrix} 1 & 1 & 2 \\ 0 & 2 & 2 \\ 1 & 1 & 0 \end{bmatrix}.$$

Thus we have,

$$[\mathbf{a}]^{\mathcal{B}'} = \mathbf{P}_{\mathcal{B}}^{\mathcal{B}'} [\mathbf{a}]^{\mathcal{B}} = \frac{1}{2} \begin{bmatrix} 1 & 1 & 2 \\ 0 & 2 & 2 \\ 1 & 1 & 0 \end{bmatrix} \begin{bmatrix} 1 \\ 1 \\ 1 \end{bmatrix} = \begin{bmatrix} 2 \\ 2 \\ 1 \end{bmatrix}.$$

We can verify the validity of this in several ways, one of which is by going back to the representation in the standard basis;

$$[\mathbf{a}] = \mathbf{B}' [\mathbf{a}]^{\mathcal{B}'} = \begin{bmatrix} 1 & 0 & -1 \\ 0 & 1 & 0 \\ 1 & 0 & 1 \end{bmatrix} \begin{bmatrix} 2 \\ 2 \\ 1 \end{bmatrix} = \begin{bmatrix} 1 \\ 2 \\ 3 \end{bmatrix}.$$

(b) In the vector space $\mathbb{C}_2^2$ we'll use the bases

$$\mathcal{B} = \left\{ \begin{bmatrix} 1 & 0 \\ 0 & 1 \end{bmatrix}, \begin{bmatrix} 0 & 1 \\ 1 & 0 \end{bmatrix}, \begin{bmatrix} 0 & -i \\ i & 0 \end{bmatrix}, \begin{bmatrix} 1 & 0 \\ 0 & -1 \end{bmatrix} \right\}$$

and

$$\mathcal{B}' = \left\{ \begin{bmatrix} 1 & 0 \\ 0 & 0 \end{bmatrix}, \begin{bmatrix} 1 & 1 \\ 0 & 0 \end{bmatrix}, \begin{bmatrix} 1 & 1 \\ 1 & 0 \end{bmatrix}, \begin{bmatrix} 1 & 1 \\ 1 & 1 \end{bmatrix} \right\}.$$

The element of $\mathbb{C}_2^2$ we will use is the complex matrix

$$\mathbf{M} = \begin{bmatrix} 1-i & 0 \\ 2i & 1+i \end{bmatrix}.$$

The representation of $\mathbf{M}$ in the basis $\mathcal{B}$ satisfies

$$\mathbf{B}\,[\mathbf{M}]^{\mathcal{B}} = \mathbf{M}(:) \quad \Rightarrow \quad \begin{bmatrix} 1 & 0 & 0 & 1 \\ 0 & 1 & i & 0 \\ 0 & 1 & -i & 0 \\ 1 & 0 & 0 & -1 \end{bmatrix} [\mathbf{M}]^{\mathcal{B}} = \begin{bmatrix} 1-i \\ 2i \\ 0 \\ 1+i \end{bmatrix}$$

where $\mathbf{M}(:) = [\mathbf{col}_1(\mathbf{M}); \mathbf{col}_2(\mathbf{M}); \ldots; \mathbf{col}_n(\mathbf{M})]$ (for this notation, see Section 1.2). After some row reduction we find

$$[\mathbf{M}]^{\mathcal{B}} = [1; i; -1; -i].$$

The transition matrix from $\mathcal{B}'$ to $\mathcal{B}$ comes from row reducing $[\mathbf{B}\,|\mathbf{B}']$, and it is

$$\mathbf{P}_{\mathcal{B}'}^{\mathcal{B}} = \frac{1}{2} \begin{bmatrix} 1 & 1 & 1 & 2 \\ 0 & 1 & 2 & 2 \\ 0 & i & 0 & 0 \\ 1 & 1 & 1 & 0 \end{bmatrix}.$$

Inverting $\mathbf{P}_{\mathcal{B}'}^{\mathcal{B}}$ immediately leads to $[\mathbf{M}]^{\mathcal{B}'} = \left(\mathbf{P}_{\mathcal{B}'}^{\mathcal{B}} \right)^{-1} [\mathbf{M}]^{\mathcal{B}}$. On the other hand, we could have solved $\mathbf{B}'\,[\mathbf{M}]^{\mathcal{B}'} = \mathbf{M}(:)$. In either case we find

$$[\mathbf{M}]^{\mathcal{B}'} = [1+i; 2i; -1-i; 1-i].$$

■ ■ ■

3.3.1 Exercise Set

1. Find the representation of $(x-2)(2x+1)$ in terms of the basis $\mathcal{B} = \left\{ x-1, x+2, x^2 \right\}$.

2. Find the representation of $[1, 2; 3, 4]$ in terms of the basis

$$\mathcal{B} = \left\{ \begin{bmatrix} 1 & -1 \\ -1 & 1 \end{bmatrix}, \begin{bmatrix} 1 & 1 \\ 1 & 1 \end{bmatrix}, \begin{bmatrix} 0 & 1 \\ 1 & 1 \end{bmatrix}, \begin{bmatrix} 1 & 0 \\ 1 & 0 \end{bmatrix} \right\}.$$

3. Find the representation of an arbitrary 2×2 Hermitian matrix in terms of the Pauli spin matrices

$$\left\{ \begin{bmatrix} 1 & 0 \\ 0 & 1 \end{bmatrix}, \begin{bmatrix} 0 & 1 \\ 1 & 0 \end{bmatrix}, \begin{bmatrix} 0 & -i \\ i & 0 \end{bmatrix}, \begin{bmatrix} 1 & 0 \\ 0 & -1 \end{bmatrix} \right\}.$$

4. Show that $\{[2, 2, -1], [2, -1, 2], [-1, 2, 2]\}$ is a basis of $\mathbb{C}_3$ and find the coordinates of $[2, 1, 3]$ with respect to this basis.

3.4   INNER PRODUCT SPACES

So far we have no apparatus in place for performing any measurements in a linear space. We will need a construct to find the length of a vector and the angle between two vectors.

3.4.1   *Inner Products and Norms*

DEFINITION 3.7   *A complex linear space $\mathcal{V}$ is:*
(a) a **complex inner product space** *if there is a function of two vectors, written $\langle \mathbf{x}, \mathbf{y} \rangle$, called an* **inner product**, *satisfying*

(InProd1) $\langle \mathbf{x}, \mathbf{x} \rangle \geq 0, = 0$ *only if* $\mathbf{x} = \mathbf{0}$;

(InProd2) $\langle \mathbf{x}, \mathbf{y} \rangle = \overline{\langle \mathbf{y}, \mathbf{x} \rangle}$;

(InProd3) $\langle \mathbf{x}, c\mathbf{y} + \mathbf{z} \rangle = c \langle \mathbf{x}, \mathbf{y} \rangle + \langle \mathbf{x}, \mathbf{z} \rangle$;

for all $c \in \mathcal{C}$ and all $\mathbf{x}, \mathbf{y}, \mathbf{z} \in \mathcal{V}$.
(b) a **normed linear space** *if there is a function, $\|\mathbf{x}\|$, called a* **norm** *of a single vector, satisfying*

(Norm1) $\|\mathbf{x}\| \geq 0, = 0$ *only if* $\mathbf{x} = \mathbf{0}$;

(Norm2) $\|c\mathbf{x}\| = |c| \|\mathbf{x}\|$;

(Norm3) $\|\mathbf{x} + \mathbf{y}\| \leq \|\mathbf{x}\| + \|\mathbf{y}\|$ *(the* **Triangle Inequality***)*.

The "dot product" from the calculus of real vectors is an example of a real inner product on the space of real vectors. All complex inner product spaces are normed spaces; we can take the norm to be $\|\mathbf{x}\| = \sqrt{\langle \mathbf{x}, \mathbf{x} \rangle}$. In general, the converse is not true; there are norms that are not derivable from inner products.

If we look only at real linear spaces, both definitions can be restricted to the real case. The only major difference occurs in (InProd2), where the complex conjugate is omitted, i.e., $\langle \mathbf{x}, \mathbf{y} \rangle = \langle \mathbf{y}, \mathbf{x} \rangle$. Everything else remains the same.

■ **EXAMPLE 3.11** There are many examples of inner product spaces.

(a) $\mathbb{C}^n := \mathbb{C}^n_1$ has several possible inner products. The standard, or Euclidean, inner product is

$$\langle \mathbf{x}, \mathbf{y} \rangle := \bar{x}_1 y_1 + \bar{x}_2 y_2 + \cdots + \bar{x}_n y_n = \mathbf{x}^H \mathbf{y}$$

and $\|\mathbf{x}\| = \sqrt{\langle \mathbf{x}, \mathbf{x} \rangle} = \sqrt{|x_1|^2 + |x_2|^2 + \cdots + |x_n|^2}$, is the corresponding norm. Other norms can be defined, for example

$$\begin{aligned}
\|\mathbf{x}\|_1 &:= |x_1| + |x_2| + \cdots + |x_n|, & \ell_1 \text{ norm,} \\
\|\mathbf{x}\|_p &:= (|x_1|^p + |x_2|^p + \cdots + |x_n|^p)^{1/p}, & \ell_p \text{ norm,} \\
\|\mathbf{x}\|_\infty &:= \max\{|x_k|,\ k = 1 : n\}, & \ell_\infty \text{ norm.}
\end{aligned}$$

Neither the ℓ_1 nor the ℓ_∞ norm can be generated from an inner product. It can also be shown that for $p \geq 1$, $\|\mathbf{x}\|_p$ is a decreasing function of p.

(b) $\mathbb{C}^m_n$ can be made into an inner product space in several ways. One possibility is

$$\langle \mathbf{A}, \mathbf{B} \rangle := \sum_{j=1}^n \sum_{k=1}^n \overline{(A_{jk})} B_{jk} = \operatorname{tr}\left(\mathbf{A}^H \mathbf{B}\right),$$

with corresponding norm

$$\|\mathbf{A}\| = \sqrt{\sum_{j=1}^n \sum_{k=1}^n |A_{jk}|^2}.$$

This inner product can also be computed as $\sqrt{\mathbf{A}(:)^H \mathbf{B}(:)}$. To show this is an inner product we will need to verify it satisfies (InProd1), (InProd2), and (InProd3). $\langle \mathbf{A}, \mathbf{A} \rangle = \operatorname{tr}\left(\mathbf{A}^H \mathbf{B}\right) = \sum\sum |A_{jk}|^2$ is clearly nonnegative and zero only when $\mathbf{A}$ is the zero matrix. Also, by virtue of the fact that $\operatorname{tr}(\mathbf{C}) = \operatorname{tr}(\mathbf{C}^T)$ and trace property (Tr2) from Section 1.5

$$\langle \mathbf{A}, \mathbf{B} \rangle = \operatorname{tr}\left(\mathbf{A}^H \mathbf{B}\right) = \operatorname{tr}\left(\mathbf{B} \mathbf{A}^H\right) = \operatorname{tr}\left(\mathbf{B}^T \bar{\mathbf{A}}\right)$$

$$= \overline{\operatorname{tr}\left(\mathbf{B}^H \mathbf{A}\right)} = \overline{\langle \mathbf{B}, \mathbf{A} \rangle}.$$

Lastly we can use property (Tr1) of the trace to write

$$\langle \mathbf{A}, c\mathbf{B} + \mathbf{C} \rangle = \operatorname{tr}\left(\mathbf{A}^H (c\mathbf{B} + \mathbf{C})\right) = c\operatorname{tr}\left(\mathbf{A}^H \mathbf{B}\right) + \operatorname{tr}\left(\mathbf{A}^H \mathbf{C}\right)$$

$$= c\langle \mathbf{A}, \mathbf{B} \rangle + \langle \mathbf{A}, \mathbf{C} \rangle.$$

(c) $C[a, b]$ has a possible inner product of the form

$$\langle f, g \rangle_w := \int_a^b w(x) \, \overline{f(x)} \, g(x) \, dx,$$

where $w(x)$ is continuous on the interval (a, b) and positive for all but at most finitely many points in $[a, b]$. This inner product is very much like the one used in $\mathbb{C}^3$; take the product of like components $\bar{a}_k b_k$ (as opposed to $\overline{f(x)g(x)}$) and sum them (an integral is a special form of summation). The function $w(x)$ is included as a positive scale factor for weighting different x-values.

(d) ℓ_∞ has a possible norm $\|x\|_\infty := \sup \{|x_k| : k = 1 : \infty\}$ for sequences, and this is *not* derivable from an inner product.

(e) $L^p(a, b)$ has the norm

$$\|f\| := \left\{ \int_a^b |f(x)|^p \, dx \right\}^{1/p}.$$

Because of subtleties involved with the definition of the integral on the right hand side, we'll assume all functions are relatively smooth.

(f) You should verify that the following two Matlab functions generate norms on the set of complex $n \times n$ matrices:

$$\max \left(\max \left(\mathrm{abs}(\mathbf{A}) \right) \right), \quad \max \left(\mathrm{sum} \left(\mathrm{abs}(\mathbf{A}) \right) \right).$$

Which norms are they?   ■ ■ ■

Because we will often be dealing with inner product spaces, it will be convenient to utilize some special properties available to us when choosing a basis.

DEFINITION 3.8 *The vectors* $\mathbf{x}$ *and* $\mathbf{y}$ *are said to be* **orthogonal** *if* $\langle \mathbf{x}, \mathbf{y} \rangle = 0$. *A set* $S = \{\mathbf{x}_1, \mathbf{x}_2, \ldots\}$ *is an* **orthogonal set** *if* $\langle \mathbf{x}_j, \mathbf{x}_k \rangle = 0$ *for* $j \neq k$, *i.e., every vector in* S *is orthogonal to every other vector in* S. *An orthogonal set* $\{\mathbf{u}_1, \mathbf{u}_2, \ldots\}$ *is said to be an* **orthonormal set** *if* $\langle \mathbf{u}_j, \mathbf{u}_j \rangle = 1$ *for all* j, *i.e., an orthogonal set of unit vectors (of norm, or length, one). Two sets* $\mathcal{A}$ *and* $\mathcal{B}$ *are orthogonal if every element of* $\mathcal{A}$ *is orthogonal to every element of* $\mathcal{B}$. *We will write this as* $\mathcal{A} \perp \mathcal{B}$.

The criterion for an orthonormal set can be written compactly if we use the Kronecker delta function. The set $\{\mathbf{u}_1, \mathbf{u}_2, \ldots\}$ is orthonormal if and only if

$$\langle \mathbf{u}_j, \mathbf{u}_k \rangle = \delta_{jk}. \tag{3.6}$$

■ **EXAMPLE 3.12** Verify each of the following is an orthogonal set with respect to the standard inner product.

(a) $\mathcal{S} = \{[1; 2; 2], [2; -2; 1], [2; 1; -2]\}$ is an orthogonal set. To verify this all we need do is compute the three possible inner products:

$$[1; 2; 2]^H [2; -2; 1] = 2 - 4 + 2 = 0,$$

$$[1; 2; 2]^H [2; 1; -2] = 2 + 2 - 4 = 0,$$

$$[2; -2; 1]^H [2; 1; -2] = 4 - 2 - 2 = 0.$$

Since

$$\|[1; 2; 2]\| = \|[2; -2; 1]\| = \|[2; 1; -2]\| = 3,$$

if we multiplied each vector in $\mathcal{S}$ by $1/3$ the resulting set would be orthonormal.

(b) $\mathcal{E} = \{e^{inx} : n = -\infty : \infty\}$ is an orthogonal set in $C[-\pi, \pi]$ if we use the unweighted inner product

$$\langle f, g \rangle := \int_{-\pi}^{\pi} \overline{f(x)}\, g(x)\, dx$$

because

$$\langle e^{imx}, e^{inx} \rangle = \int_{-\pi}^{\pi} e^{-imx} e^{inx}\, dx$$

$$= \frac{1}{i(n-m)} \left[e^{i(n-m)x} \right]_{-\pi}^{\pi} = \begin{cases} 0, & m \neq n, \\ 2\pi, & m = n. \end{cases}$$

(c) The set of Pauli spin matrices is

$$\mathcal{P} = \left\{ \boldsymbol{\sigma}_0 = \mathbf{I}_2,\ \boldsymbol{\sigma}_1 = \begin{bmatrix} 0 & 1 \\ 1 & 0 \end{bmatrix},\ \boldsymbol{\sigma}_2 = \begin{bmatrix} 0 & -i \\ i & 0 \end{bmatrix},\ \boldsymbol{\sigma}_3 = \begin{bmatrix} 1 & 0 \\ 0 & -1 \end{bmatrix} \right\}.$$

They are of use in the quantum mechanics of systems with half-integral spin. If we use the inner product

$$\langle \mathbf{A}, \mathbf{B} \rangle = \operatorname{tr}\left(\mathbf{A}^H \mathbf{B} \right) = \sum_{j=1}^{n} \sum_{k=1}^{n} \overline{A_{jk}}\, B_{jk},$$

then $\mathcal{S}$ is an orthogonal set. As a check of one inner product,

$$\langle \boldsymbol{\sigma}_1, \boldsymbol{\sigma}_2 \rangle = \operatorname{tr}(\boldsymbol{\sigma}_1^H \boldsymbol{\sigma}_2) = \operatorname{tr}(\boldsymbol{\sigma}_1 \boldsymbol{\sigma}_2) = \operatorname{tr}(i\boldsymbol{\sigma}_3) = 0.$$

■ ■ ■

Any orthogonal set of nonzero vectors can be made into an orthonormal set by multiplying each vector by the reciprocal of its length. Any orthogonal set of $n = \dim \mathcal{V}$ nonzero vectors is a basis of $\mathcal{V}$ because of the following theorem.

THEOREM 3.8 *An orthogonal set of nonzero vectors is linearly independent.*

Proof Form a linear relation on the set of vectors $\{\mathbf{x}_1, \mathbf{x}_2, \ldots, \mathbf{x}_k\}$:

$$c_1 \mathbf{x}_1 + c_2 \mathbf{x}_2 + \cdots + c_k \mathbf{x}_k = \mathbf{0}.$$

Take the inner product of both sides with $\mathbf{x}_j$:

$$c_1 \langle \mathbf{x}_j, \mathbf{x}_1 \rangle + c_2 \langle \mathbf{x}_j, \mathbf{x}_2 \rangle + \cdots + c_k \langle \mathbf{x}_j, \mathbf{x}_k \rangle = 0.$$

By virtue of orthogonality the only inner product that is not zero is $\langle \mathbf{x}_j, \mathbf{x}_j \rangle$; hence

$$c_j \langle \mathbf{x}_j, \mathbf{x}_j \rangle = c_j \| \mathbf{x}_j \|^2 = 0 \quad \Rightarrow \quad c_j = 0$$

for $j = 1 : k$, and the theorem is proven. $\square$

When $\dim \mathcal{V} = n$, any orthonormal set of n nonzero vectors will form an orthonormal basis. We'll use the notation $\mathcal{B} = \{\mathbf{u}_1, \mathbf{u}_2, \ldots\}$ for a generic orthonormal basis. Since $\mathcal{B}$ spans $\mathcal{V}$, for any $\mathbf{x} \in \mathcal{V}$ there are complex constants x_j such that

$$\mathbf{x} = \sum_{j=1}^{n} x_j \mathbf{u}_j.$$

The x_j are the components of $\mathbf{x}$ in the basis $\mathcal{B}$. If $\mathcal{B}$ is orthonormal, we can take the inner product of both sides with an arbitrary $\mathbf{u}_k$ to get

$$\langle \mathbf{u}_k, \mathbf{x} \rangle = \left\langle \mathbf{u}_k, \sum_{j=1}^{n} x_j \mathbf{u}_j \right\rangle = \sum_{j=1}^{n} x_j \langle \mathbf{u}_k, \mathbf{u}_j \rangle = \sum_{j=1}^{n} x_j \delta_{kj} = x_k,$$

so that

$$\mathbf{x} = \sum_{k=1}^{n} \langle \mathbf{u}_k, \mathbf{x} \rangle \mathbf{u}_k. \tag{3.7}$$

Thus the representation of $\mathbf{x}$ in the orthonormal basis $\mathcal{B}$ can be written in the form

$$[\mathbf{x}]^{\mathcal{B}} = [\langle \mathbf{u}_1, \mathbf{x} \rangle ; \langle \mathbf{u}_2, \mathbf{x} \rangle ; \ldots ; \langle \mathbf{u}_n, \mathbf{x} \rangle]. \tag{3.8}$$

■ **EXAMPLE 3.13** Using previously discussed bases, we can find the representations of various vectors.

(a) Writing

$$\mathbf{u}_1 = \frac{1}{3}[1; 2; 2], \quad \mathbf{u}_2 = \frac{1}{3}[2; -2; 1], \quad \mathbf{u}_3 = \frac{1}{3}[2; 1; -2],$$

we have seen that $\mathcal{B} = \{\mathbf{u}_1, \mathbf{u}_2, \mathbf{u}_3\}$ is orthonormal with respect to the standard inner product. For any $\mathbf{x} \in \mathbb{C}^3$ we have

$$\mathbf{x} = \langle \mathbf{u}_1, \mathbf{x} \rangle \, \mathbf{u}_1 + \langle \mathbf{u}_2, \mathbf{x} \rangle \, \mathbf{u}_2 + \langle \mathbf{u}_3, \mathbf{x} \rangle \, \mathbf{u}_3.$$

If $\mathbf{x} = [1; 0; 0]$, then $\langle \mathbf{u}_1, \mathbf{x} \rangle = \frac{1}{3}$, $\langle \mathbf{u}_2, \mathbf{x} \rangle = \frac{2}{3}$, and $\langle \mathbf{u}_3, \mathbf{x} \rangle = \frac{2}{3}$, so that

$$[1; 0; 0] = \frac{1}{3}\mathbf{u}_1 + \frac{2}{3}\mathbf{u}_2 + \frac{2}{3}\mathbf{u}_3$$

and

$$[\mathbf{x}]^{\mathcal{B}} = \left[\frac{1}{3}; \frac{2}{3}; \frac{2}{3} \right].$$

(b) If we write $\mathbf{E}_1 = \frac{1}{\sqrt{2}}\boldsymbol{\sigma}_0$, $\mathbf{E}_2 = \frac{1}{\sqrt{2}}\boldsymbol{\sigma}_1$, $\mathbf{E}_3 = \frac{1}{\sqrt{2}}\boldsymbol{\sigma}_2$, $\mathbf{E}_4 = \frac{1}{\sqrt{2}}\boldsymbol{\sigma}_3$, then the $\mathbf{E}$'s form an orthonormal basis $\mathcal{S}$ of $\mathbb{C}_2^2$ with respect to the inner product $\langle \mathbf{A}, \mathbf{B} \rangle = \mathrm{tr}(\mathbf{A}^H \mathbf{B})$, written in terms of the Pauli spin matrices; for any $\mathbf{A} \in \mathbb{C}_2^2$, we may write

$$\mathbf{A} = \langle \mathbf{E}_1, \mathbf{x} \rangle \, \mathbf{E}_1 + \langle \mathbf{E}_2, \mathbf{x} \rangle \, \mathbf{E}_2 + \langle \mathbf{E}_3, \mathbf{x} \rangle \, \mathbf{E}_3 + \langle \mathbf{E}_4, \mathbf{x} \rangle \, \mathbf{E}_4.$$

Using

$$\mathbf{A} = \begin{bmatrix} a & b \\ c & d \end{bmatrix},$$

we have

$$\langle \mathbf{E}_1, \mathbf{x} \rangle = \frac{1}{\sqrt{2}}(a + d), \quad \langle \mathbf{E}_2, \mathbf{x} \rangle = \frac{1}{\sqrt{2}}(b + c),$$

$$\langle \mathbf{E}_3, \mathbf{x} \rangle = \frac{i}{\sqrt{2}}(b - c), \quad \langle \mathbf{E}_4, \mathbf{x} \rangle = \frac{1}{\sqrt{2}}(a - d),$$

so that

$$\mathbf{A} = \frac{1}{\sqrt{2}} \left((a + d)\mathbf{E}_1 + (b + c)\mathbf{E}_2 + i(b - c)\mathbf{E}_3 + (a - d)\mathbf{E}_4 \right),$$

or

$$\mathbf{A} = \frac{1}{2} \left((a + d)\boldsymbol{\sigma}_0 + (b + c)\boldsymbol{\sigma}_1 + i(b - c)\boldsymbol{\sigma}_2 + (a - d)\boldsymbol{\sigma}_3 \right).$$

Thus the representation of an arbitrary 2×2 matrix in the orthonormal basis $\{\mathbf{E}_1, \mathbf{E}_2, \mathbf{E}_3, \mathbf{E}_4\}$ is

$$[\mathbf{A}] = \frac{1}{\sqrt{2}} [a + d; b + c; i(b - c); a - d].$$

(c) $\mathcal{F} = \left\{ \frac{1}{\sqrt{2\pi}} e^{inx} : n = -\infty : \infty \right\}$ is an orthonormal set in the linear space $C[-\pi, \pi]$, with respect to the inner product of example 3.12(b), where the weight function of example 3.11(c) $w(x)$ is one. If $f(x)$ is any function continuous on the interval $[-\pi, \pi]$, then an infinite dimensional version of (3.7) says

$$f(x) = \sum_{n=-\infty}^{\infty} f_n e^{inx}, \tag{3.9}$$

where

$$f_n = \left\langle e^{inx}, f \right\rangle = \frac{1}{2\pi} \int_{-\pi}^{\pi} f(x) e^{-inx} \, dx.$$

The question of convergence of (3.9) will not be discussed here.

(d) If $\mathbf{P}$ is a real orthogonal matrix, i.e., $\mathbf{P}^T \mathbf{P} = \mathbf{I} = \mathbf{P} \mathbf{P}^T$, then the set of row (or column) vectors of $\mathbf{P}$ forms an orthonormal basis of $\mathbb{R}_n$ (or $\mathbb{R}^n$) with respect to the standard inner product. This can be seen by looking at the jk^{th} entry in the product $(\mathbf{P} \mathbf{P}^T)$, which is

$$\left(\mathbf{P} \mathbf{P}^T\right)_{jk} = \mathbf{row}_j(\mathbf{P}) \, \mathbf{col}_k(\mathbf{P}^T) = \mathbf{row}_j(\mathbf{P}) \, (\mathbf{row}_k(\mathbf{P}))^T = \delta_{jk}.$$

Similarly, the set of row (or column) vectors of a unitary matrix, $\mathbf{U}^H \mathbf{U} = \mathbf{I} = \mathbf{U} \mathbf{U}^H$, forms an orthonormal basis of $\mathbb{C}_n$ (or $\mathbb{C}^n$) with respect to the standard inner product.

■ ■ ■

3.4.2 *Induced Matrix Norms*

Using the fact that a matrix is a vector in a linear space, finding a norm is only a matter of finding its representation with respect to some basis and then finding the norm of that column vector. Unfortunately, the value of any such norm will depend on the choice of basis. Also, the value of those norms need have no relation to any corresponding norms of a vector, because the matrices and vectors live in different linear spaces. We would prefer a norm of $\mathbf{A}$ that was, in some sense, inherited from the norm of the vector $\mathbf{x}$. This more reasonable approach is available to us.

If $\mathbf{A} \in \mathbb{C}_n^m$, then by premultiplication it sends column vectors $\mathbf{x}$ from $\mathbb{C}^n$ into $\mathbb{C}^m$; we can induce a norm on $\mathbb{C}_n^m$ from the norm on $\mathbb{C}^n$ as follows:

DEFINITION 3.9 *The* **norm** *of a matrix* $\mathbf{A} \in \mathbb{C}_n^m$ **induced** *by, or* **consistent** *with, the associated vector norm* $\|\mathbf{x}\|$ *is defined by*

$$\|\mathbf{A}\| := \max\{\|\mathbf{Ax}\| : \|\mathbf{x}\| = 1\}.$$

The maximum is taken over all possible directions of the unit vector **x**.

Since a unit vector can be obtained from any nonzero vector by multiplying by the reciprocal of its length, and since multiplication by $\mathbf{A}$ is linear as a map from $\mathbb{C}^n$ to $\mathbb{C}^m$, an equivalent definition is

$$\|\mathbf{A}\| = \max_{\mathbf{x} \neq \mathbf{0}} \left\{ \frac{\|\mathbf{Ax}\|}{\|\mathbf{x}\|} \right\}.$$

An immediate consequence of the latter defining equation is obtained by multiplying both sides by $\|\mathbf{x}\|$ and noting that any quantity is less than its maximum:

$$\|\mathbf{Ax}\| \leq \|\mathbf{A}\|\,\|\mathbf{x}\|. \tag{3.10}$$

Also, it should be obvious that for any induced norm we must have $\|\mathbf{I}\| = 1$.

Not all matrix norms need be induced by a vector norm. As a simple example,

$$\|\mathbf{A}\| := \sum_{j=1}^{m} \sum_{k=1}^{n} |A_{jk}|^2 \tag{3.11}$$

is not induced by any vector norm. This can be seen by employing the following theorem.

THEOREM 3.9 *If* $\|\cdot\|$ *is an induced matrix norm on* $\mathbb{C}_n^m$, *then*

(IndMatNorm1) $\|\mathbf{A}\| \geq 0, = 0$ *only if* $\mathbf{A} = \mathbf{0}$;

(IndMatNorm2) $\|c\mathbf{A}\| = |c|\,\|\mathbf{A}\|$;

(IndMatNorm3) $\|\mathbf{A} + \mathbf{B}\| \leq \|\mathbf{A}\| + \|\mathbf{B}\|$;

(IndMatNorm4) $\|\mathbf{AB}\| \leq \|\mathbf{A}\|\,\|\mathbf{B}\|$.

Proof Since the first three properties are those of any norm, nothing needs to be proven there since $\|\mathbf{A}\|$ is generated by a vector norm. (IndMatNorm4) follows from setting $\mathbf{x} = \mathbf{By}$ in (3.10):

$$\|\mathbf{ABy}\| \leq \|\mathbf{A}\|\,\|\mathbf{By}\| \leq \|\mathbf{A}\|\,\|\mathbf{B}\|\,\|\mathbf{y}\| \quad \Rightarrow \quad \|\mathbf{AB}\| \leq \|\mathbf{A}\|\,\|\mathbf{B}\|.$$

$\square$

Two induced matrix norms are particularly easy to calculate.

THEOREM 3.10   *The vector norm* $\|\cdot\|_1$ *on* $\mathbb{C}^n$ *induces the matrix norm*

$$\|\mathbf{A}\|_1 = \max_{k=1:n} \left\{ \sum_{j=1}^{n} |A_{jk}| \right\} = \max\left(\mathrm{sum}(\mathrm{abs}(\mathbf{A}))\right).$$

Before we prove this, let's look at what it means. The sum is over j, the row index. Within the curly braces we have the sum of moduli of the entries in the kth column of the matrix. The maximum picks out the largest such column sum.

Proof   Suppose $\|\mathbf{x}\|_1 = 1$; then

$$\|\mathbf{A}\mathbf{x}\|_1 = \sum_{j=1}^{n} \left| \sum_{k=1}^{n} A_{jk} x_k \right| \leq \sum_{j=1}^{n} \sum_{k=1}^{n} |A_{jk}| \, |x_k|$$

$$= \sum_{k=1}^{n} \left(|x_k| \sum_{j=1}^{n} |A_{jk}| \right) \leq \max_{k=1:n} \left\{ \sum_{j=1}^{n} |A_{jk}| \right\} \sum_{\ell=1}^{n} |x_\ell|.$$

The right hand side is the aforementioned norm. Choosing $\mathbf{x}$ so that $x_\ell = 1$, where ℓ is the index of the maximum magnitude column of $\mathbf{A}$, we have

$$\|\mathbf{A}\mathbf{x}\|_1 = \sum_{j=1}^{n} |A_{j\ell}|.$$

Thus the maximum is attained, as required.   □

The ℓ_1 induced matrix norm $\|\mathbf{A}\|_1$ is the largest of the sums of the moduli of the column vectors. Similarly, the ℓ_∞ norm induces the **maximum row sum norm** on $\mathbb{C}_n^n$:

$$\|\mathbf{A}\|_\infty = \max_{j=1:n} \left\{ \sum_{k=1}^{n} |A_{jk}| \right\} = \max\left(\mathrm{sum}(\mathrm{abs}(\mathbf{A}^H))\right).$$

The proof is similar to that of the previous theorem. No general size relation holds between the ℓ_1 and ℓ_∞ norms that is valid for both finite and infinite dimensional spaces. Surely, of all norms available to us, the induced ℓ_1 and ℓ_∞ norms are by far the easiest to calculate.

Relative Error in the Solution of a Linear System

Ordinarily the linear system $\mathbf{A}\mathbf{x} = \mathbf{b}$ would not be perfectly representable in floating point arithmetic. Additionally, parameters present in either the coefficient matrix $\mathbf{A}$ or the input vector $\mathbf{b}$ may not be known exactly. Consequently, the system being solved would be something of the form $\tilde{\mathbf{A}}\tilde{\mathbf{x}} = \tilde{\mathbf{b}}$, where the tilde indicates an inexactly known quantity. It is possible to analyze this inexact system in full generality, but the algebra tends to obscure the basic idea. Luck has it that we can assume that only the output vector $\mathbf{x}$ and the input vector $\mathbf{b}$ are known inexactly and arrive at roughly the same result.

Begin with the exact system

$$\mathbf{Ax} = \mathbf{b} \tag{3.12}$$

and the inexact system adjusted to make it a true equality, i.e., use $\tilde{\mathbf{b}} = \mathbf{b} - \mathbf{r}$,

$$\mathbf{A\tilde{x}} = \mathbf{b} - \mathbf{r}, \tag{3.13}$$

where the vector $\mathbf{r}$ is called the **residual** (the sign is chosen for convenience). We assume the exact system has a unique solution, which must be

$$\mathbf{x} = \mathbf{A}^{-1}\mathbf{b}. \tag{3.14}$$

Define the **error** in the computation of the output vector to be $\mathbf{e} := \mathbf{x} - \tilde{\mathbf{x}}$. If we subtract the inexact system from the exact system, we have

$$\mathbf{Ax} - \mathbf{A\tilde{x}} = \mathbf{A}(\mathbf{x} - \tilde{\mathbf{x}}) = \mathbf{Ae} = \mathbf{b} - (\mathbf{b} - \mathbf{r}) = \mathbf{r} \quad \Rightarrow \quad \mathbf{Ae} = \mathbf{r}. \tag{3.15}$$

Since $\mathbf{A}$ is invertible, we can write the error in terms of the residual as

$$\mathbf{e} = \mathbf{A}^{-1}\mathbf{r}. \tag{3.16}$$

The question to be answered is, if a system has a small residual (that is easily calculated) does it necessarily follow that it also has a small error? To answer this, we can apply the inequality from (IndMatNorm4) to each of the equations (3.12), (3.14), (3.15), and (3.16). Taking norms of (3.12), we have

$$\|\mathbf{b}\| = \|\mathbf{Ax}\| \leq \|\mathbf{A}\| \, \|\mathbf{x}\| \,,$$

where $\|\mathbf{A}\|$ is the matrix norm induced by the vector norm. Taking the norm of (3.14) yields

$$\|\mathbf{x}\| = \left\|\mathbf{A}^{-1}\mathbf{b}\right\| \leq \left\|\mathbf{A}^{-1}\right\| \|\mathbf{b}\| \,.$$

We can combine these as inequalities on $\|\mathbf{x}\|$ and write

$$\frac{\|\mathbf{b}\|}{\|\mathbf{A}\|} \leq \|\mathbf{x}\| \leq \left\|\mathbf{A}^{-1}\right\| \|\mathbf{b}\| \,.$$

Since the equation relating the error and the residual is precisely the same as that relating the exact solution to the input vector, we have the associated inequality for $\|\mathbf{e}\|$:

$$\frac{\|\mathbf{r}\|}{\|\mathbf{A}\|} \leq \|\mathbf{e}\| \leq \left\|\mathbf{A}^{-1}\right\| \|\mathbf{r}\| \,.$$

We can combine these into a single inequality for what are called the **relative error** $\|\mathbf{e}\| \, / \, \|\mathbf{x}\|$ and the **relative residual** $\|\mathbf{r}\| \, / \, \|\mathbf{b}\|$, but we must be careful because dividing inequalities can only be accomplished if we reverse their order. The result is

$$\frac{1}{\|\mathbf{A}\| \, \|\mathbf{A}^{-1}\|} \left(\frac{\|\mathbf{r}\|}{\|\mathbf{b}\|}\right) \leq \frac{\|\mathbf{e}\|}{\|\mathbf{x}\|} \leq \|\mathbf{A}\| \, \|\mathbf{A}^{-1}\| \left(\frac{\|\mathbf{r}\|}{\|\mathbf{b}\|}\right) \,.$$

The similarity of both extremes of the inequalities suggests we define the **condition number** of a matrix $\mathbf{A}$ by

$$\text{cond}(\mathbf{A}) = \|\mathbf{A}\| \, \|\mathbf{A}^{-1}\|\,. \tag{3.17}$$

This allows us to rewrite the inequalities in the form

$$\frac{1}{\text{cond}(\mathbf{A})} \left(\frac{\|\mathbf{r}\|}{\|\mathbf{b}\|} \right) \leq \frac{\|\mathbf{e}\|}{\|\mathbf{x}\|} \leq \text{cond}(\mathbf{A}) \left(\frac{\|\mathbf{r}\|}{\|\mathbf{b}\|} \right). \tag{3.18}$$

Since we know $\|\mathbf{I}\| = 1$ implies $\|\mathbf{I}\| = \|\mathbf{A}\mathbf{A}^{-1}\| \leq \|\mathbf{A}\| \, \|\mathbf{A}^{-1}\|$, it follows that $\text{cond}(\mathbf{A}) \geq 1$. From this we see that the larger the condition number of the coefficient matrix, the wider is our bound on the relative error as multiples of the relative residual. Generally speaking, large condition numbers mean that the floating point solution of the linear system may be susceptible to wide discrepancies, even when we have small residuals. A rule of thumb is if $\text{cond}(\mathbf{A}) = O(10^d)$, then in the worst case scenario we will lose d decimal places to round-off (relative to the accuracy of $\mathbf{A}$) when solving $\mathbf{A}\mathbf{x} = \mathbf{b}$. In particular, the Hilbert segment of order n, $\mathbf{H}^{(n)}$, has a condition number that is approximately proportional to $e^{3.5n}$. Thus for n as small as 6, our calculation for the solution could go awry by as many as 7 decimal places (that is more than single precision). The troublesome aspect of all this is that $\mathbf{H}^{(n)}$ arises naturally in least square fits of polynomial equations (which is something that we do quite often). Even worse, there are useful matrices with even higher condition numbers!

There are alternative representations of the condition number that help in understanding its significance as a bound. The first is

$$\text{cond}(\mathbf{A}) = \frac{\max\{\|\mathbf{A}\mathbf{x}\| : \|\mathbf{x}\| = 1\}}{\min\{\|\mathbf{A}\mathbf{x}\| : \|\mathbf{x}\| = 1\}}.$$

If we multiply $\mathbf{A}$ times a vector on the "unit circle," the result will be an "ellipse" and the condition number will be the ratio of the largest to the smallest semi-axis. Well-conditioned matrices leave the unit circle fairly circular, while ill-conditioned matrices change it into a long and thin ellipse. In the extreme, the long thin ellipse becomes a line, in which case the coefficient matrix $\mathbf{A}$ is singular.

The second representation is written in terms of the reciprocal of the condition number as

$$\frac{1}{\text{cond}(\mathbf{A})} = \min \left\{ \frac{\|\mathbf{E}\|}{\|\mathbf{A}\|} : \mathbf{A} + \mathbf{E} \text{ singular} \right\}.$$

Since $\mathbf{E}$ is a matrix that when added to the nonsingular $\mathbf{A}$ makes it singular, its norm is an inverse measure of the distance $\mathbf{A}$ is from being singular. Large condition numbers are reserved for matrices that are close to being singular, while low condition numbers go to matrices that are far from being singular. Since $\text{cond}(\mathbf{I}) = 1$, we may conclude that the identity matrix is as far from being singular as you can get.

A natural question arises concerning the calculation of the condition number as a function of p when we use a p norm to induce the matrix norm. Are the results very different for various values of p? The answer is no, because of the following relations, which are valid for real $n \times n$ matrices:

$$\begin{aligned}
\tfrac{1}{n} \operatorname{cond}_2(A) &\leq \operatorname{cond}_1(A) \leq n \operatorname{cond}_\infty(A), \\
\tfrac{1}{n} \operatorname{cond}_\infty(A) &\leq \operatorname{cond}_2(A) \leq n \operatorname{cond}_\infty(A), \\
\tfrac{1}{n^2} \operatorname{cond}_1(A) &\leq \operatorname{cond}_\infty(A) \leq n^2 \operatorname{cond}_1(A).
\end{aligned}$$

At first glance, the computation of the condition number according to the defining equation (3.17) requires the full computation of the inverse of $\mathbf{A}$, something we think may not always be accurately computed. But suffice it to say there are robust methods for computing $\operatorname{cond}(\mathbf{A})$, so let's let that pass. For further information you should consult Golub and van Loan.

3.4.3 Gram-Schmidt Orthogonalization Procedure

Orthonormal bases are not just anomalies in the grand scheme of things. *Any* basis can be used to generate an orthonormal basis by utilizing the **Gram-Schmidt orthogonalization procedure**. It proceeds as follows:

(a) Take any basis $\{\mathbf{x}_1, \mathbf{x}_2, \ldots\}$ of $\mathcal{V}$ to start.

(b) To form the orthogonal basis $\{\mathbf{u}_1, \mathbf{u}_2, \ldots\}$ choose $\mathbf{u}_1 = \mathbf{x}_1$. Then set

$$\mathbf{u}_2 = \mathbf{x}_2 - \mathbf{u}_1 k_{12}$$

and impose the first orthogonality condition,

$$\langle \mathbf{u}_1, \mathbf{u}_2 \rangle = \langle \mathbf{u}_1, \mathbf{x}_2 \rangle - \langle \mathbf{u}_1, \mathbf{u}_1 \rangle k_{12} = 0,$$

from which we find k_{12} to be

$$k_{12} = \frac{\langle \mathbf{u}_1, \mathbf{x}_2 \rangle}{\|\mathbf{u}_1\|^2}.$$

(c) Continue by setting

$$\mathbf{u}_3 = \mathbf{x}_3 - \mathbf{u}_1 k_{13} - \mathbf{u}_2 k_{23}.$$

Requiring

$$\langle \mathbf{u}_1, \mathbf{u}_3 \rangle = 0 = \langle \mathbf{u}_2, \mathbf{u}_3 \rangle$$

forces

$$k_{13} = \frac{\langle \mathbf{u}_1, \mathbf{x}_3 \rangle}{\|\mathbf{u}_1\|^2}, \quad k_{23} = \frac{\langle \mathbf{u}_2, \mathbf{x}_3 \rangle}{\|\mathbf{u}_2\|^2}.$$

(d) In general

$$\mathbf{u}_\ell = \mathbf{x}_\ell - \sum_{j=1}^{\ell-1} \mathbf{u}_j \, k_{j\ell},$$

where

$$k_{j\ell} = \frac{\langle \mathbf{u}_j, \mathbf{x}_\ell \rangle}{\|\mathbf{u}_j\|^2}.$$

All that remains is to multiply each $\mathbf{u}_\ell$ by $1/\|\mathbf{u}_\ell\|$ to form the desired orthonormal set.

■ **EXAMPLE 3.14** Using the standard inner product, apply the Gram-Schmidt procedure to each of the following nonorthogonal bases.

(a) $\{[1;1;1],[1;2;0],[2;1;0]\}$ is a basis of $\mathbb{C}^3$ because

$$\text{rank}\left(\begin{bmatrix} 1 & 1 & 2 \\ 1 & 2 & 1 \\ 1 & 0 & 0 \end{bmatrix}\right) = 3.$$

Using $\mathbf{u}_1 = [1;1;1]$ to start, we find

$$\mathbf{u}_2 = \mathbf{x}_2 - \mathbf{u}_1 k_{12} = [1;2;0] - \frac{\langle [1;1;1],[1;2;0]\rangle}{\|[1;1;1]\|^2}[1;1;1]$$

$$\Rightarrow \quad \mathbf{u}_2 = [1;2;0] - [1;1;1] = [0;1;-1].$$

Proceeding to the next step:

$$\mathbf{u}_3 = \mathbf{x}_3 - \frac{\langle \mathbf{u}_1, \mathbf{x}_3\rangle}{\|\mathbf{u}_1\|^2}\mathbf{u}_1 - \frac{\langle \mathbf{u}_2, \mathbf{x}_3\rangle}{\|\mathbf{u}_2\|^2}\mathbf{u}_2$$

$$= [2;1;0] - [1;1;1] = \frac{1}{2}[0;1;-1] = \frac{1}{2}[2;-1;-1].$$

Thus

$$\left\{\frac{1}{\sqrt{3}}[1;1;1], \frac{1}{\sqrt{2}}[0;1;-1], \frac{1}{\sqrt{6}}[2;-1;-1]\right\}$$

is an orthonormal basis of $\mathbb{C}^3$.

(b) Using the real unweighted inner product

$$\langle f, g\rangle = \int_{-1}^{1} f(x)\,g(x)\,dx,$$

on $\mathbb{R}_n[x]$ and the basis $\{1, x, x^2, \dots, x^n\}$, let's generate the first few elements of an orthogonal basis. Start with $u_1(x) = 1$; then

$$u_2(x) = x - \frac{\langle 1, x\rangle}{\|1\|^2}1 = x - \frac{\int_{-1}^{1} \xi\, d\xi}{\int_{-1}^{1} 1^2\, d\xi}1 = x - \frac{0}{2}1 = x,$$

$$u_3(x) = x^2 - \frac{\langle 1, x^2\rangle}{\|1\|^2}1 - \frac{\langle x, x^2\rangle}{\|x\|^2}x = x^2 - \frac{\int_{-1}^{1} \xi^2\, d\xi}{\int_{-1}^{1} 1^2\, d\xi}1 - \frac{\int_{-1}^{1} \xi^3\, d\xi}{\int_{-1}^{1} \xi^2\, d\xi}x$$

$$\Rightarrow \quad u_3(x) = x^2 - \frac{(2/3)}{2}1 - 0 = \frac{1}{3}\left(3x^2 - 1\right).$$

The functions $1, x, \frac{1}{3}\left(3x^2 - 1\right)$ are proportional to the first three **Legendre polynomials**, which are important in models utilizing spherical geometry. ■ ■ ■

The Gram-Schmidt procedure outlined above often leads to ill-conditioned calculations. For this reason an alternative formulation of the method is preferred. Details can be found in the Anton.

3.4.4 Exercise Set

Using the norm derived from the standard inner product, find the length of each of the following vectors.

1. $\mathbb{R}_2$: $[1, 2], [2, 3], [\pi, e]$

2. $\mathbb{R}_3$: $\mathbf{i} - 2\mathbf{j} + 3\mathbf{k}$, $\frac{2}{3}\mathbf{i} - \frac{1}{3}\mathbf{j} + \frac{2}{3}\mathbf{k}$, $6\mathbf{i} - 4\mathbf{k}$, $\mathbf{i} + \mathbf{j} - 4\mathbf{k}$, if $\mathbf{i} = [1, 0, 0]$, $\mathbf{j} = [0, 1, 0]$, and $\mathbf{k} = [0, 0, 1]$

3. $\mathbb{C}_3$: $[1, i, -1], [1 - i, 1 + i, 1], [2, 1, 2], [2i, 1, -2i]$

4. $C[0, 1]$ with $w(x) = 1$: $\sin x$, $\cos x$, e^{-x}, e^x, $2x + 3$, 1

5. $C[0, 1]$ with $w(x) = e^x$: $\sin x$, $\cos x$, e^{-x}, e^x, $2x + 3$, 1

6. $\mathbb{C}[x]_n^n$ with $\langle \mathbf{A}, \mathbf{B} \rangle = \mathrm{tr}(\mathbf{A}^H \mathbf{B})$: $A_{jk} = x^{j+k}$, $B_{jk} = j - k$, $C_{jk} = D^j x^k$

Which of the following are inner products on the linear spaces indicated? For those which are not, show they do not satisfy at least one of the requirements of an inner product.

7. $\langle \mathbf{a}, \mathbf{b} \rangle := a_1 b_2 + 2a_2 b_1 + 3a_3 b_3$, on $\mathbb{C}^3$

8. $\langle \mathbf{a}, \mathbf{b} \rangle := a_1 b_2 + a_2 b_3 + a_3 b_4 + \cdots + a_{n-1} b_n + a_n b_1$, on $\mathbb{C}^n$

9. $\langle p(x), q(x) \rangle := p(-1)q(-1) + p(0)q(0) + p(1)q(1)$, on $\mathbb{C}_2[z]$

10. $\langle p(x), q(x) \rangle := p(1)q(1) + p(2)q(2) + \cdots + p(n)q(n)$, on $\mathbb{C}_n[z]$

11. $\langle \mathbf{A}, \mathbf{B} \rangle := \det(\mathbf{AB})$, on $\mathbb{C}_n^n$

12. $\langle \mathbf{A}, \mathbf{B} \rangle := (\mathbf{A}(:))^H (\mathbf{B}(:))$ on $\mathbb{C}_n^m$

13. Construct two 3×3 matrices, whose transposes and Hermitian conjugates share *no* common entries, for which $\|\mathbf{A}\|_1 < \|\mathbf{B}\|_1$ and $\|\mathbf{A}\|_\infty > \|\mathbf{B}\|_\infty$.

14. Show that the norm $\|\mathbf{A}\|_\infty := \max\{|A_{jk}|, \; j, k = 1 : n\}$ satisfies $\|\mathbf{AB}\|_\infty \leq n \|\mathbf{A}\|_\infty \|\mathbf{B}\|_\infty$.

15. Show that the **Euclidean**, or **Frobenius**, **norm** defined by $\|\mathbf{A}\|_E := \sqrt{\mathrm{tr}(\mathbf{A}^H \mathbf{A})}$ is not an induced norm.

16. Show that in a real inner product space the **Parallelogram Law** is true:

$$\|\mathbf{x} + \mathbf{y}\|^2 + \|\mathbf{x} - \mathbf{y}\|^2 = 2 \|\mathbf{x}\|^2 + 2 \|\mathbf{y}\|^2.$$

As an aside: A norm can be derived from an inner product if and only if the Parallelogram Law holds. That inner product is defined in the following problems.

17. Show that in a real inner product space the **Polarization Identity** is true:

$$4 \langle \mathbf{x}, \mathbf{y} \rangle = \|\mathbf{x} + \mathbf{y}\|^2 - \|\mathbf{x} - \mathbf{y}\|^2 .$$

18. Show that in a complex inner product space,

$$4 \langle \mathbf{y}, \mathbf{x} \rangle = \|\mathbf{x} + \mathbf{y}\|^2 + i \|\mathbf{x} + i\mathbf{y}\|^2 - \|\mathbf{x} - \mathbf{y}\|^2 - i \|\mathbf{x} - i\mathbf{y}\|^2 .$$

19. Using the inner product $\langle \mathbf{A}, \mathbf{B} \rangle = \mathrm{tr}(\mathbf{A}^H \mathbf{B})$, apply the Gram-Schmidt orthogonalization procedure to the following basis of $\mathbb{C}_2^2$:

$$\left\{ \begin{bmatrix} 1 & 0 \\ 0 & 1 \end{bmatrix}, \begin{bmatrix} 1 & 0 \\ 1 & 1 \end{bmatrix}, \begin{bmatrix} 1 & 1 \\ 0 & 1 \end{bmatrix}, \begin{bmatrix} 1 & 1 \\ 1 & 0 \end{bmatrix} \right\}.$$

20. Using the weighted inner product $\langle f, g \rangle := \int_0^\infty e^{-t} f(t) g(t) \, dt$, construct an orthogonal basis from the standard basis of $\mathbb{C}_3[t]$: $\{1, t, t^2, t^3\}$.

21. If $\mathbf{D}$ is an arbitrary diagonal $n \times n$ matrix, find its condition numbers derived from the 1-norm, the ∞-norm, and the Euclidean norm (see problem 15). Compare the value of the determinant with that of the condition number as an indication of possible ill-conditioning. Then simplify everything by looking at the subcase where all the diagonal entries are equal.

22. Numerical approximations to many problems can often be represented by linear systems $\mathbf{Ax} = \mathbf{b}$ where the coefficient matrix has relatively few nonzero entries. The better the approximation, the larger the size of $\mathbf{A}$. For each of the following coefficient matrices, find the condition numbers for $n = 10 : 30$ and formulate a conjecture about the effectiveness of the solution to the approximation.

(a) 4 along the $k = 0$ diagonal and -1 along the $k = 1$ and $k = -1$ diagonals, except $A_{11} = A_{nn} = 1$.

(b) 2 along the $k = 0$ diagonal and -1 along the $k = 1$ and $k = -1$ diagonals.

(c) 4 along the $k = 0$ diagonal, -1 along the $k = 1$, $k = 4$, $k = -1$, and $k = -4$ diagonals.

(d) 0.7 along the $k = 0$ diagonal, 0.3 along the $k = 1$ diagonal, and 0.1 along the $k = -2$ diagonal.

(e) 30 along the $k = 0$ diagonal, -15 along the $k = 1$ and $k = -1$ diagonals, and 1 along the $k = 2$ and $k = -2$ diagonals.

(f) 30 along the $k = 0$ diagonal, -15 along the $k = 1$ and $k = -1$ diagonals, and 2 along the $k = 2$ and $k = -2$ diagonals.

3.5   FUNDAMENTAL SUBSPACES OF A MATRIX

With every matrix $\mathbf{A}$ we can associate four fundamental subspaces that tell us a great deal about its character. There is also an amazing relation amongst these subspaces.

DEFINITION 3.10   *If* $\mathbf{A} \in \mathbb{C}_n^m$, *then the* **null space** *of* $\mathbf{A}$, *written* $\mathrm{NullSp}(\mathbf{A})$, *is the subset of* $\mathbb{C}^n$ *defined by*

$$\mathrm{NullSp}(\mathbf{A}) := \{\mathbf{x} \in \mathbb{C}^n : \mathbf{A}\mathbf{x} = \mathbf{0}\}.$$

The **row space** *of* $\mathbf{A}$, *written* $\mathrm{RowSp}(\mathbf{A})$, *is the subset of* $\mathbb{C}_n$ *defined by*

$$\mathrm{RowSp}(\mathbf{A}) := \mathrm{Span}\{\mathbf{row}_j(\mathbf{A}), \; j = 1 : m\}.$$

The **column space** *of* $\mathbf{A}$, *written* $\mathrm{ColSp}(\mathbf{A})$, *is the subset of* $\mathbb{C}^m$ *defined by*

$$\mathrm{ColSp}(\mathbf{A}) := \mathrm{Span}\{\mathbf{col}_k(\mathbf{A}), \; k = 1 : n\}.$$

By Theorem 3.2, both $\mathrm{RowSp}(\mathbf{A})$ and $\mathrm{ColSp}(\mathbf{A})$ are linear spaces. By example 3.2(e), $\mathrm{NullSp}(\mathbf{A})$ is also a linear space. If $\mathbf{R}$ is either the row echelon or row-reduced echelon form of $\mathbf{A}$, then the rows of $\mathbf{R}$ are linear combinations of the set of linearly independent rows of $\mathbf{A}$. Thus

$$\mathrm{RowSp}(\mathbf{A}) = \mathrm{RowSp}(\mathbf{R}).$$

Therefore, the nonzero rows of the row-reduced echelon form of a matrix constitute a basis for its row space. An immediate consequence of this is

$$\dim(\mathrm{RowSp}(\mathbf{A})) = \mathrm{rank}(\mathbf{A}). \tag{3.19}$$

It should be obvious that

$$(\mathrm{RowSp}(\mathbf{A}))^H = \mathrm{ColSp}(\mathbf{A}^H), \tag{3.20}$$

where $(\mathrm{RowSp}(\mathbf{A}))^H$ means the space of column vectors obtained by taking the Hermitian conjugates of the vectors in $\mathrm{RowSp}(\mathbf{A})$. This tells us that we can find a basis of $\mathrm{ColSp}(\mathbf{A})$ by reducing $\mathbf{A}^H$ to row echelon or row-reduced echelon form, taking the Hermitian conjugate, and reading off the nonzero columns. Alternatively, a basis of $\mathrm{ColSp}(\mathbf{A})$ can be gotten from $\mathrm{rref}(\mathbf{A})$ by selecting column vectors of $\mathbf{A}$ corresponding to the leading variables. Also, because the number of leading variables is the same when reducing $\mathbf{A}$ or $\mathbf{A}^H$, we have

$$\dim(\mathrm{ColSp}(\mathbf{A})) = \mathrm{rank}(\mathbf{A}). \tag{3.21}$$

We could also utilize the symmetry of equation (3.20) to look at $\mathrm{NullSp}(\mathbf{A}^H)$ with the hope of extending the pattern. This fourth subspace is sometimes called the **left null space** of $\mathbf{A}$ because $\mathbf{A}^H\mathbf{y} = \mathbf{0} \iff \mathbf{y}^H\mathbf{A} = \mathbf{0}$.

An amazing geometric relation holds between the subspaces $\mathrm{NullSp}(\mathbf{A})$ and $\mathrm{ColSp}(\mathbf{A}^H)$ and between $\mathrm{NullSp}(\mathbf{A}^H)$ and $\mathrm{ColSp}(\mathbf{A})$ beyond that of equation (3.20), as will be seen in the next example.

■ **EXAMPLE 3.15** Let's find each of the fundamental subspaces of

$$\mathbf{B} = \begin{bmatrix} 1 & 0 & -1 \\ 0 & 1 & 2 \\ 1 & 1 & 1 \\ 2 & -1 & -4 \end{bmatrix}. \quad \text{We have} \quad \mathbf{R} = \mathrm{rref}(\mathbf{B}) = \begin{bmatrix} 1 & 0 & -1 \\ 0 & 1 & 2 \\ 0 & 0 & 0 \\ 0 & 0 & 0 \end{bmatrix}.$$

From this we can immediately write a basis of the row space:

$$\mathcal{B}_{\mathrm{row}} = \{[1, 0, -1], [0, 1, 2]\}.$$

Because of the form of $\mathbf{R}$, we see that any two nonparallel and nonzero rows of $\mathcal{B}$ form a linearly independent set. Thus we could have chosen $\mathcal{B}_{\mathrm{row}}$ as any pair of the row vectors of the original matrix $\mathbf{B}$. Solving the homogeneous system $\mathbf{Bx} = \mathbf{0}$, we introduce one parameter for the nonleading variable x_3 to find that

$$\mathrm{NullSp}(\mathbf{B}) = \mathrm{Span}\{[1; -2; 1]\}.$$

From this it is clear that, with respect to the standard inner product, $\mathrm{NullSp}(\mathbf{B}) \perp \mathrm{ColSp}(\mathbf{B}^H) = (\mathrm{RowSp}(\mathbf{B}))^H$. To get a basis of $\mathrm{ColSp}(\mathbf{B})$, we could either reduce $\mathbf{B}^H$ and use the fact that any two columns form a linearly independent set, or pick the first two columns of $\mathbf{B}$ because the first two variables are leading. Hence, one possible basis is

$$\mathcal{B}_{\mathrm{col}} = \{[1; 0; 1; 2], [0; 1; 1; -1]\}$$

$$\Rightarrow \quad \mathrm{ColSp}(\mathbf{B}) = \mathrm{Span}\{[1; 0; 1; 2], [0; 1; 1; -1]\}.$$

It can be verified that

$$\mathrm{NullSp}(\mathbf{B}^H) = \mathrm{Span}\{[-1; -1; 1; 0], [-2; 1; 0; 1]\},$$

from which it is easily seen that, with respect to the standard inner product, $\mathrm{NullSp}(\mathbf{B}^H) \perp \mathrm{ColSp}(\mathbf{B})$. ■ ■ ■

In the last example we took what appeared to be an inner product between a row vector and a column vector. Strictly speaking, that wasn't an inner product, since inner products are defined on a single linear space. Hence the notation of orthogonality is incorrect (although appealing). For this reason, many authors call such a relation **biorthogonality** because it works between two spaces. We will adopt this term and allow the notation $\perp$ to stand for both orthogonality and biorthogonality.

THEOREM 3.11 *If $\mathbf{A}$ is an $m \times n$ matrix, then the following hold:*

(a) $\mathrm{NullSp}(\mathbf{A}) \perp \mathrm{ColSp}(\mathbf{A}^H) = \mathrm{RowSp}(\mathbf{A})$;

(b) $\mathrm{NullSp}(\mathbf{A}^H) \perp \mathrm{ColSp}(\mathbf{A}) = \mathrm{RowSp}(\mathbf{A}^H)$;

(c) *If $\mathcal{B}_{\mathrm{null}}$ is a basis of $\mathrm{NullSp}(\mathbf{A})$ and $\mathcal{B}_{\mathrm{col}\,'}$ is a basis of $\mathrm{ColSp}(\mathbf{A}^H)$, then $\mathcal{B}_{\mathrm{null}} \cup \mathcal{B}_{\mathrm{col}\,'}$ is a basis of $\mathbb{C}^n$.*

(d) *If $\mathcal{B}_{\mathrm{null}'}$ is a basis of $\mathrm{NullSp}(\mathbf{A}^H)$ and $\mathcal{B}_{\mathrm{col}}$ is a basis of $\mathrm{ColSp}(\mathbf{A})$, then $\mathcal{B}_{\mathrm{null}'} \cup \mathcal{B}_{\mathrm{col}}$ is a basis of $\mathbb{C}^m$.*

Proof   Starting with $\mathbf{x} \in \mathrm{NullSp}(\mathbf{A})$, we have

$$\mathbf{Ax} = [\mathbf{row}_1(\mathbf{A})\mathbf{x}; \mathbf{row}_2(\mathbf{A})\mathbf{x}; \ldots; \mathbf{row}_m(\mathbf{A})\mathbf{x}] = \mathbf{0},$$

thus every row vector of $\mathbf{A}$ is biorthogonal to every vector in the null space of $\mathbf{A}$. Therefore $\mathrm{NullSp}(\mathbf{A}) \perp \mathrm{ColSp}(\mathbf{A}^H)$. By a similar argument, if $\mathbf{y} \in \mathrm{NullSp}(\mathbf{A}^H)$ we have

$$\mathbf{y}^H \mathbf{A} = [\mathbf{y}^H \mathbf{col}_1(\mathbf{A}), \mathbf{y}^H \mathbf{col}_2(\mathbf{A}), \ldots, \mathbf{y}^H \mathbf{col}_n(\mathbf{A})] = \mathbf{0},$$

and thus every column vector of $\mathbf{A}$ is biorthogonal to every vector in the left null space of $\mathbf{A}$. Therefore, $\mathrm{NullSp}(\mathbf{A}^H) \perp \mathrm{ColSp}(\mathbf{A})$. Further, since

$$\dim(\mathrm{NullSp}(\mathbf{A})) = \mathrm{null}(\mathbf{A}),$$
$$\dim(\mathrm{ColSp}(\mathbf{A}^H)) = \dim(\mathrm{RowSp}(\mathbf{A}))^H = \mathrm{rank}(\mathbf{A}),$$

and $\mathrm{rank}(\mathbf{A}) + \mathrm{null}(\mathbf{A}) = n$, every vector in $\mathbb{C}^n$ can be written uniquely as a vector from $\mathrm{NullSp}(\mathbf{A})$ and a vector from $\mathrm{ColSp}(\mathbf{A}^H)$. A similar result holds for the other pair $\mathrm{NullSp}(\mathbf{A}^H)$ and $\mathrm{ColSp}(\mathbf{A})$ as a so-called **direct sum decomposition** of $\mathbb{C}^m$.   □

The symmetry of the relations between the fundamental subspaces of $\mathbf{A}$ is truly striking. Associated with the linear system $\mathbf{Ax} = \mathbf{b}$ is the so-called **adjoint system**, $\mathbf{A}^H \mathbf{y} = \mathbf{g}$. Because $\mathrm{NullSp}(\mathbf{A}^H) \perp \mathrm{ColSp}(\mathbf{A})$, the complementary solutions of the adjoint system must be biorthogonal to particular solutions of the original system. $\mathrm{NullSp}(\mathbf{A}) \perp \mathrm{ColSp}(\mathbf{A}^H)$ means that complementary solutions of the original system are biorthogonal to particular solutions of the adjoint system.

THEOREM 3.12   *The linear system* $\mathbf{Ax} = \mathbf{b}$ *has a solution if and only if* $\mathbf{b} \perp \mathrm{NullSp}(\mathbf{A}^H)$.

□

We can use the ideas associated with the fundamental subspaces of a matrix to add to the statement of Theorem 1.8.

THEOREM 3.13   *If* $\mathbf{A} \in \mathbb{C}_n^n$, *then the following statements are equivalent:*

(a) $\mathrm{ColSp}(\mathbf{A}) = \mathbb{C}^n$.

(b) *The columns of* $\mathbf{A}$ *are linearly independent.*

(c) $\mathrm{RowSp}(\mathbf{A}) = \mathbb{C}^n$.

(d) *The rows of* $\mathbf{A}$ *are linearly independent.*

(e) $\mathrm{NullSp}(\mathbf{A}) = \{\mathbf{0}\}$.

(f) $\mathbf{A}$ *is nonsingular.*

3.5.1   *Exercise Set*

Find bases for the row space, column space, and null space of each of the following matrices and verify the statement of Theorem 3.11 in each case.

1. $\begin{bmatrix} 0 & 1 & 1 & 1 & 0 \\ 1 & 1 & 2 & 1 & 1 \\ 1 & 0 & 1 & 1 & 0 \end{bmatrix}$

2. $\begin{bmatrix} i & 1 & i & 2 \\ 1 & i & 1-i & 1 \\ i & 1 & i & 2 \end{bmatrix}$

3.6 LINEAR TRANSFORMATIONS

The linear transformation is all pervasive in mathematical models, both linear and nonlinear. Such universal operations as differentiation and integration are linear. The study of these transformations will show a great similarity between them and matrix multiplication. Many corresponding properties can be extended to even more general operations that will be of use to us in later chapters.

DEFINITION 3.11 *A* **linear transformation** *from the linear space V into the linear space W is a function T mapping V to W, written $T : V \rightarrow W$, such that*

$$T\left(c\mathbf{x} + \mathbf{y}\right) = cT\left(\mathbf{x}\right) + T\left(\mathbf{y}\right)$$

for any complex number c and any vectors $\mathbf{x}$ and $\mathbf{y}$ in V. A linear transformation from V to itself is called a **linear operator**.

■ **EXAMPLE 3.16**   Which of the following functions is a linear transformation?

(a) If $\mathbf{A} \in \mathbb{C}_n^m$ is a specified matrix, then $T_\mathbf{A} : \mathbb{C}^n \rightarrow \mathbb{C}^m$ defined by

$$T_\mathbf{A}\left(\mathbf{x}\right) := \mathbf{A}\mathbf{x},$$

for $\mathbf{x} \in \mathbb{C}^n$, is a linear transformation because

$$T_\mathbf{A}\left(c\mathbf{x} + \mathbf{y}\right) = \mathbf{A}(c\mathbf{x} + \mathbf{y}) = c(\mathbf{A}\mathbf{x}) + (\mathbf{A}\mathbf{y}) = cT_\mathbf{A}\left(\mathbf{x}\right) + T_\mathbf{A}\left(\mathbf{y}\right).$$

Later in this section we will see that $T_\mathbf{A}$ is the prototype for *all* linear transformations.

(b) If $\mathbf{S} \in \mathbb{C}_n^n$ is a specified nonsingular matrix, then the transformation $\mathbf{Sim_S} : \mathbb{C}_n^n \rightarrow \mathbb{C}_n^n$ defined by

$$\mathbf{Sim_S}\left(\mathbf{A}\right) := \mathbf{S}^{-1}\mathbf{A}\mathbf{S}$$

is linear because

$$\mathbf{Sim_S} \left(c\mathbf{A} + \mathbf{B} \right) = \mathbf{S}^{-1}(c\mathbf{A} + \mathbf{B})\mathbf{S} = c(\mathbf{S}^{-1}\mathbf{AS}) + (\mathbf{S}^{-1}\mathbf{BS})$$
$$= c\mathbf{Sim_S}\left(\mathbf{A}\right) + \mathbf{Sim_S}\left(\mathbf{B}\right).$$

We call $\mathbf{Sim_S}$ a **similarity transformation**.

(c) If $\mathbb{C}_n[t]$ is the linear space of all polynomials of degree n or less in the variable t with complex coefficients, and D is differentiation with respect to t, then D is a linear transformation from $\mathbb{C}_n[t]$ to $\mathbb{C}_n[t]$ because

$$D(cf + g) = cDf + Dg.$$

More specifically, D maps $\mathbb{C}_n[t]$ to $\mathbb{C}_{n-1}[t]$.

(d) Using $C[a,b]$ for the inner product space of real functions that are continuous on the interval $[a,b]$ and $g(t)$ as a specified continuous function, then, for each g,

$$T_g\left(f\right) := \langle f, g \rangle_2 = \int_a^b f(t)\,g(t)\,dt$$

is a linear transformation because the integral of a sum is the sum of the integrals and the integral of a constant times a function is the constant times the integral of the function.

(e) Suppose a particle moves along the x_1-axis at velocity $v = \beta c$, where c is the speed of light, and its motion is measured with respect to two inertial frames, xt and $x't'$. The postulates of special relativity are as follows:

(**SpRel1**) The velocity of light in a vacuum is the same in all inertial frames.

(**SpRel2**) The laws of physics remain unchanged under transformations between inertial frames.

From these postulates it is possible to derive the following Lorentz transformation equations for motion parallel to the x_1-axis:

$$\begin{aligned}
x_1' &= \gamma\left(x_1 + i\beta x_4\right), \\
x_2' &= x_2, \\
x_3' &= x_3, \\
x_4' &= \gamma\left(-i\beta x_1 + x_4\right),
\end{aligned}$$

where $x_4 = ict$ and $\gamma = \left(1 - \beta^2\right)^{-1/2}$. Representing the space-time point $(\mathbf{x}, ict)$ by a column vector, we can write the transformation as

$$\begin{bmatrix} x_1' \\ x_2' \\ x_3' \\ x_4' \end{bmatrix} = \begin{bmatrix} \gamma & 0 & 0 & i\beta\gamma \\ 0 & 1 & 0 & 0 \\ 0 & 0 & 1 & 0 \\ -i\beta\gamma & 0 & 0 & \gamma \end{bmatrix} \begin{bmatrix} x_1 \\ x_2 \\ x_3 \\ x_4 \end{bmatrix},$$

which is of the form of the matrix multiplication transformation in part (a) of this example and is therefore linear.

(f) The operation of taking the trace is a linear transformation from $\mathbb{C}_n^n$ to the set of complex numbers $\mathbb{C}$, because

$$\mathrm{tr}(c\mathbf{A} + \mathbf{B}) = c\,\mathrm{tr}(\mathbf{A}) + \mathrm{tr}(\mathbf{B}).$$

(g) The determinant is *not* a linear transformation on $\mathbb{C}_n^n$ for $n > 1$, because

$$\det(c\mathbf{A}) = c^n \det(\mathbf{A})$$

and

$$\det(\mathbf{A} + \mathbf{B}) \neq \det(\mathbf{A}) + \det(\mathbf{B}).$$

Specifically,

$$-2 = \begin{vmatrix} 1 & 2 \\ 3 & 4 \end{vmatrix} = \det\left(\begin{bmatrix} 4 & 1 \\ 1 & 3 \end{bmatrix} + \begin{bmatrix} -3 & 1 \\ 2 & 1 \end{bmatrix} \right)$$

$$\neq \begin{vmatrix} 4 & 1 \\ 1 & 3 \end{vmatrix} + \begin{vmatrix} -3 & 1 \\ 2 & 1 \end{vmatrix} = 6.$$

(h) If ℓ is the linear space of all complex sequences $x = \{x_n\}$, then the transformation that gives the Nth partial sum of the series $\sum x_n$ is linear because

$$S_N\,(cx + y) = \sum_{n=0}^{N} (cx_n + y_n) = c \sum_{n=0}^{N} x_n + \sum_{n=0}^{N} y_n$$
$$= cS_N\,(x) + S_N\,(y).$$

(i) Evaluation of a continuous function at a point P, defined by $\delta_P[f] := f(P)$, is also a linear transformation. ▪▪▪

We call a linear transformation from a linear space $\mathcal{V}$ to the space of complex numbers a **linear functional**. In the last example, part (a), if $\mathbf{A} \in \mathbb{C}_n^1$ then $T_\mathbf{A}$ is a linear functional. Also T_g, tr, S_N and δ_P are linear functionals. Getting back to the general case of linear transformations:

DEFINITION 3.12 *The* **range** *(or* **image***) of a linear transformation* $T : \mathcal{V} \to \mathcal{W}$ *is the set*

$$\mathrm{range}(T) := \{T\,(\mathbf{x}) : \mathbf{x} \in \mathcal{V}\}.$$

The **kernel** *of* T *is*

$$\ker(T) := \{\mathbf{x} : T\,(\mathbf{x}) = \mathbf{0}\}.$$

■ **EXAMPLE 3.17** Find the image and kernel of each of the following linear transformations.

(a) Using $T_\mathbf{A}(\mathbf{x}) = \mathbf{A}\mathbf{x}$, we can find $\text{range}(T)$ by finding all possible $\mathbf{y}$ such that $\mathbf{A}\mathbf{x} = \mathbf{y}$ is a consistent system. This requires

$$\text{rank}(\mathbf{A}) = \text{rank}\left([\mathbf{A}|\mathbf{b}]\right).$$

Because $\mathbf{A}\mathbf{x}$ is a linear combination of the columns of $\mathbf{A}$, we have $\text{range}(T_\mathbf{A}) = \text{ColSp}(\mathbf{A})$. The kernel of $T_\mathbf{A}$ is the solution space of $\mathbf{A}\mathbf{x} = \mathbf{0}$, that is, $\text{NullSp}(\mathbf{A})$.

(b) For what matrix $\mathbf{A}$ does $\mathbf{Sim_S}(\mathbf{A}) = \mathbf{S}^{-1}\mathbf{A}\mathbf{S} = \mathbf{0}$? Premultiplying by $\mathbf{S}$ and post-multiplying by $\mathbf{S}^{-1}$ yields $\mathbf{A} = \mathbf{0}$. Thus $\ker(\mathbf{Sim_S}) = \{\mathbf{0}\}$. If $\mathbf{B} \in \text{range}(\mathbf{Sim_S})$, then $\mathbf{B} = \mathbf{S}^{-1}\mathbf{A}\mathbf{S}$. Thus the range of $\mathbf{Sim_S}$ consists of all matrices to which $\mathbf{A}$ is similar.

(c) It should be obvious that if D is the differentiation operation on polynomials of degree n or less, then $\text{im}(D) = \mathbb{C}_{n-1}[t]$ and $\ker(D) = \{c\}$, the set of all constant polynomials.

■ ■ ■

THEOREM 3.14 *If* $T : \mathcal{V} \to \mathcal{W}$, *then* $\text{im}(T)$ *is a subspace of* $\mathcal{W}$ *and* $\ker(T)$ *is a subspace of* $\mathcal{V}$.

Proof If $T(\mathbf{x}), T(\mathbf{y}) \in \text{range}(T)$, then

$$cT(\mathbf{x}) + T(\mathbf{y}) = T(c\mathbf{x} + \mathbf{y}) \in \text{range}(T).$$

If $\mathbf{x}, \mathbf{y} \in \ker(T)$, then

$$T(c\mathbf{x} + \mathbf{y}) = cT(\mathbf{x}) + T(\mathbf{y}) = c(\mathbf{0}) + \mathbf{0} = \mathbf{0} \quad \Rightarrow \quad c\mathbf{x} + \mathbf{y} \in \ker(T).$$

□

We bring over the notation and terminology from matrix multiplication, motivated by the fact that $T_\mathbf{A}(\mathbf{x}) = \mathbf{A}\mathbf{x}$ is a linear transformation:

DEFINITION 3.13 *If* T *is a linear transformation, we define*

$$\dim(\text{range}(T)) =: \text{rank}(T) \text{ *to be the* **rank** *of* } T,$$
$$\dim(\ker(T)) =: \text{null}(T) \text{ *to be the* **nullity** *of* } T.$$

There is a subtle difference between the rank of a matrix and that of a linear transformation. The last subsection will be devoted to showing the relation between linear transformations and matrices that will allow us to blur this distinction. Remember, $\mathrm{rank}(\mathbf{A})$ is the number of linearly independent rows of $\mathbf{A}$, and $\mathrm{null}(\mathbf{A})$ is the number of nonleading variables in the general solution of the homogeneous system $\mathbf{A}\mathbf{x} = \mathbf{0}$. Thus $\mathbf{A}\mathbf{x} = \mathbf{0}$ had $\mathrm{null}(\mathbf{A})$ linearly independent solutions, one corresponding to each arbitrary parameter, and $\mathbf{A}\mathbf{x} = \mathbf{y}$ was consistent for $\mathrm{rank}(\mathbf{A})$ linearly independent choices of the vector $\mathbf{y}$.

3.6.1 Exercise Set

Which of the following are linear transformations? For those which are linear, find bases of $\mathrm{range}(T)$ and $\ker(T)$ when both are finite dimensional. For those which are not, show why they are not.

1. $T_1 [x_1, x_2] := [x_1 - ix_2, 2x_1 + ix_2]$

2. $T_2[x_1, x_2] := [x_2, ix_1]$

3. $T_3 (p(x)) := x^2 D^2 p(x)$ for $p \in \mathbb{C}_n[x]$

4. $T_4 (p(x)) := p(1) - p(-1),\ p(x) \in \mathbb{C}_3[x]$

5. $T_5 (p(x)) := p(x) - p(-x),\ p(x) \in \mathbb{C}_n[x]$

6. $T_6 (p(x)) := p(x) - p(-1),\ p(x) \in \mathbb{C}_n[x]$

7. $T_7[x_1, x_2, x_3, x_4, x_5] := ix_1 - x_2 + ix_3 - x_4 + ix_5$

8. $T_8[x_1, x_2, x_3] := [3x_1 - 2x_2 + x_3, 2x_2 - x_1, 2x_3 - x_1 - 2x_2]$

9. $T_9[x_1, \ldots, x_n] := [x_1, x_1 + x_2, \ldots, x_1 + x_2 + \ldots + x_n]$

10. $T_{10}[\mathbf{A}] := \mathbf{A}^{-1}$ when $\mathbf{A} \in \mathbb{C}_n^n$ is invertible and $\mathbf{0}$ otherwise

11. $T_{11}[\mathbf{A}] := \mathrm{tr}(\mathbf{A}^H \mathbf{B})$, when $\mathbf{B} = \mathbf{diag}(1 : n)$ and $\mathbf{A} \in \mathbb{C}_n^n$

3.7 ROTATIONS IN THE PLANE AND SPACE

There is a class of linear operators on $\mathbb{R}^2$ and $\mathbb{R}^3$ that have special geometric significance. We'll start with the transformation of the plane into itself by a rotation about a line orthogonal to the plane. Take x_1 and x_2 to be the coordinates in the original plane and x_1' and x_2' the coordinates in the rotated plane. Thus, the x_1 and x_1' axes make an angle of θ with each other as do the x_2 and x_2' axes. The rotation will move the axes but leave the points unchanged. The points, however, will have different coordinate representations with respect to the changed axes.

Suppose the point P has coordinates (x_1, x_2) in the unrotated system and (x_1', x_2') in the rotated system (see Figure 3.1).

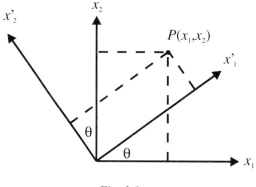

Fig. 3.1

The coordinates are related by the equations

$$\begin{array}{rcl} x_1' &=& x_1\cos\theta \;+\; x_2\sin\theta, \\ x_2' &=& -x_1\sin\theta \;+\; x_2\cos\theta. \end{array}$$

If we want to think of this as part of a three dimensional picture, then we would add the transformation equation for the other coordinate: $x_3' = x_3$. In matrix form the rotation is

$$\begin{bmatrix} x_1' \\ x_2' \\ x_3' \end{bmatrix} = \begin{bmatrix} \cos\theta & \sin\theta & 0 \\ -\sin\theta & \cos\theta & 0 \\ 0 & 0 & 1 \end{bmatrix} \begin{bmatrix} x_1 \\ x_2 \\ x_3 \end{bmatrix}. \tag{3.22}$$

This matrix represents a rotation about the x_3 axis through an angle θ. Denote it by $\mathbf{Rot}[\theta; x_3]$. Analogously, we can write the forms of $\mathbf{Rot}[\theta; x_1]$ and $\mathbf{Rot}[\theta; x_2]$.

It should be clear that rotations of the $x_1 x_2$-plane commute. This can be seen by performing the matrix multiplication.:

$$\mathbf{Rot}[\theta; x_3]\mathbf{Rot}[\phi; x_3] = \begin{bmatrix} \cos\theta & \sin\theta & 0 \\ -\sin\theta & \cos\theta & 0 \\ 0 & 0 & 1 \end{bmatrix} \begin{bmatrix} \cos\phi & \sin\phi & 0 \\ -\sin\phi & \cos\phi & 0 \\ 0 & 0 & 1 \end{bmatrix}$$

$$= \begin{bmatrix} \cos\theta\cos\phi - \sin\theta\sin\phi & \cos\theta\sin\phi + \sin\theta\cos\phi & 0 \\ -\sin\theta\cos\phi - \cos\theta\sin\phi & \cos\theta\cos\phi - \sin\theta\sin\phi & 0 \\ 0 & 0 & 1 \end{bmatrix}$$

$$= \begin{bmatrix} \cos(\theta+\phi) & \sin(\theta+\phi) & 0 \\ -\sin(\theta+\phi) & \cos(\theta+\phi) & 0 \\ 0 & 0 & 1 \end{bmatrix} = \mathbf{Rot}[\theta+\phi; x_3].$$

Since $\mathbf{Rot}[\theta+\phi; x_3] = \mathbf{Rot}[\phi+\theta; x_3]$ we have established commutativity.

When moving from the plane into space, this commutativity of rotations no longer need hold. To see that this is so, we need only construct one case (and there are infinitely many) where commutativity fails. Let's look at the following sequence of three rotations. First rotate by $\pi/2$ about x_3, then by π about x_1, and finally by π about x_2. Visually we see the result drawn in Figure 3.2.

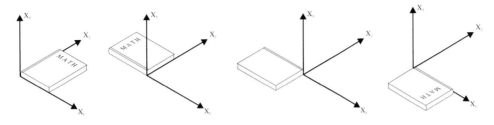

Fig. 3.2

Now look at a different order: π about x_1, followed by $\pi/2$ about x_3, and finally π about x_2. The result is shown in Figure 3.3.

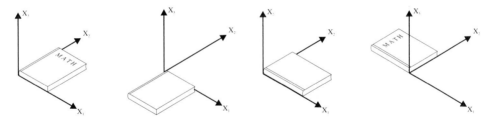

Fig. 3.3

Clearly the two sets of operations do not yield the same result.

To specify the general rotation in $\mathbb{R}^3$, the first question that needs to be answered is, how many rotation angles do we need to specify a rotation about an arbitrary axis? We start by determining the axis of rotation. Any line determines three direction angles, only two of which are independent because a unit vector can be used to determine its direction. That together with the angle of rotation makes three angles needed to completely specify an arbitrary rotation in $\mathbb{R}^3$.

Euler suggested the following scheme (see Figure 3.4):

(a) Rotate about the x_3- or z-axis through an angle of ϕ. Thus $\mathbf{Rot}[\phi; x_3]$ will take $x_1x_2x_3$ into the system $x_1'x_2'x_3'$ with $x_3' = x_3$.

(b) Rotate about the x_1'- or x'-axis through an angle of θ. Thus $\mathbf{Rot}[\theta; x_1']$ takes the system $x_1'x_2'x_3'$ into an $x_1''x_2''x_3''$ system with $x_1'' = x_1'$.

(c) Lastly rotate about the x_3''- or z''-axis through an angle ψ. The matrix $\mathbf{Rot}[\psi; x_3'']$ brings us to the final form.

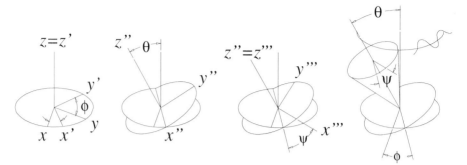

Fig. 3.4 The Euler angles of rotation and the motion of a spinning top with one point fixed.

Each of the rotation matrices is easy to write. They are

$$\mathbf{Rot}[\phi; x_3] = \begin{bmatrix} \cos\phi & \sin\phi & 0 \\ -\sin\phi & \cos\phi & 0 \\ 0 & 0 & 1 \end{bmatrix},$$

$$\mathbf{Rot}[\theta; x_1'] = \begin{bmatrix} 1 & 0 & 0 \\ 0 & \cos\theta & \sin\theta \\ 0 & -\sin\theta & \cos\theta \end{bmatrix},$$

$$\mathbf{Rot}[\psi; x_3''] = \begin{bmatrix} \cos\psi & \sin\psi & 0 \\ -\sin\psi & \cos\psi & 0 \\ 0 & 0 & 1 \end{bmatrix}.$$

We call ϕ, θ, and ψ the **Euler angles** of the rotation. The total rotation matrix is the product

$$\mathbf{Rot}[\psi; x_3'']\mathbf{Rot}[\theta; x_1']\mathbf{Rot}[\phi; x_3]. \tag{3.23}$$

These angles are natural for studying the rotation of a rigid body about some pivot point. The quantity $\dot{\psi}$ is the angular velocity of a body rotated about its axis through the pivot point. The quantity $\dot{\phi}$ is the angular velocity of precessional motion, which is the motion of the axis of the body when it is acted on by a torque. Lastly, $\dot{\theta}$ is the angular velocity of the deviations of the precessional axis from a fixed angle. This last motion is called nutation.

Think of the spinning top shown in the rightmost panel of Figure 3.4. As the top spins, its line of symmetry precesses about the vertical. If you were to push down on the rotational axis, you would feel a force resisting you. Thus as the body axis dropped below its equilibrium, it would move back up and continue to oscillate about that position, tracing out a curve similar to the one shown. In general, if the body rotated with an angular frequency vector ω, then in the body's coordinate system (call it abc rather than $x_1'''x_2'''x_3'''$ for simplicity) its components would be

$$\begin{aligned} \omega_a &= \dot{\phi}\sin\theta\sin\psi + \dot{\theta}\cos\psi, \\ \omega_b &= \dot{\phi}\sin\theta\cos\psi - \dot{\theta}\sin\psi, \\ \omega_c &= \dot{\phi}\cos\theta + \dot{\psi}. \end{aligned} \tag{3.24}$$

All rotation matrices share a very special property. The inverse operation to a rotation about an axis through an angle of θ is also a rotation about the same axis but through an angle of $-\theta$. This turns everything back to the original position. In matrix notation,

$$\mathbf{Rot}^{-1}[\theta; \xi] = \mathbf{Rot}[-\theta; \xi].$$

Looking at the forms of the rotation matrices, we see that

$$\mathbf{Rot}[-\theta; \xi] = \mathbf{Rot}^{T}[\theta; \xi].$$

Thus, the inverse of a rotation matrix is its transpose. Generally speaking any matrix whose inverse is its transpose is said to be orthogonal (see Section 1.5.E). The rows of an orthogonal matrix form a real orthonormal set, and so do its columns. Not all orthogonal matrices are rotations.

3.7.1   *Exercise Set*

1. Write out the form of a rotation through the Euler angles ϕ, θ, and ψ in full by multiplying the rotation matrices given in this section.

2. Draw the results of the three rotations $\mathbf{Rot}(\pi/2; x)$, $\mathbf{Rot}(\pi; z)$, and $\mathbf{Rot}(-3\pi/2; y)$ applied in *all* possible orders where the axis of rotation is the designated axis of the initial frame. Redo this problem with the same rotations, instead using the axes of each new frame. You may want to physically perform these rotations on your book so the end result will be clear.

3. Show that rotations need not commute under multiplication by providing another example of a pair of such rotations in $\mathbb{R}^3$. Provide an example of a pair of rotations about different axes that do commute.

3.8   REPRESENTATIONS OF LINEAR TRANSFORMATIONS

The analogy between matrices and linear transformations can be made complete by showing that for every linear transformation between two linear spaces there corresponds a unique matrix. If $T : \mathcal{V} \to \mathcal{W}$, $\mathcal{E} = \{\mathbf{e}_1, \mathbf{e}_2, \ldots, \mathbf{e}_n\}$ is an ordered basis of $\mathcal{V}$, and $\mathcal{F} = \{\mathbf{f}_1, \mathbf{f}_2, \ldots, \mathbf{f}_m\}$ is an ordered basis of $\mathcal{W}$, then for $\mathbf{x} = \sum_1^n x_k \mathbf{e}_k \in \mathcal{V}$ we have (by linearity)

$$T(\mathbf{x}) = T\left(\sum_{k=1}^{n} x_k \mathbf{e}_k\right) = \sum_{k=1}^{n} x_k T(\mathbf{e}_k).$$

Since $T(\mathbf{e}_k) \in \mathcal{W}$, it can be written as a linear combination of the $\mathcal{F}$-basis vectors:

$$T(\mathbf{e}_k) = \sum_{j=1}^{m} T_{jk} \mathbf{f}_j.$$

Thus

$$T\left(\mathbf{x}\right) = \sum_{j=1}^{m}\left\{\sum_{j=1}^{m}T_{jk}x_{k}\right\}\mathbf{f}_{j}.$$

In component form, this is

$$y_{j} := \left[T\left(\mathbf{x}\right)\right]_{j} = \sum_{j=1}^{m}T_{jk}x_{k}.$$

If we write $\left[x_{1};x_{2};\ldots;x_{n}\right] = \left[\mathbf{x}\right]^{\mathcal{E}}$ and $\left[y_{1};y_{2};\ldots;y_{m}\right] = \left[\mathbf{y}\right]^{\mathcal{F}}$ then

$$\left[\mathbf{y}\right]^{\mathcal{F}} = \left[T\right]^{\mathcal{F}}_{\mathcal{E}}\left[\mathbf{x}\right]^{\mathcal{E}}, \tag{3.25}$$

where the $m \times n$ matrix $\left[T\right]^{\mathcal{F}}_{\mathcal{E}}$ is called the **representation** of the linear transformation T with respect to the bases $\mathcal{E}$ of $\mathcal{V}$ and $\mathcal{F}$ of $\mathcal{W}$. There is a certain mnemonic convenience to this notation: notice the "cancellation" of $\mathcal{E}$ in equation (3.25). The superscript refers to the row entries and the subscript to the column entries; so $\left[\mathbf{x}\right]^{\mathcal{E}}$ is a column vector whereas $\left[\mathbf{x}\right]_{\mathcal{E}}$ would be a row vector.

The calculation of the representation of a linear transformation merely follows the steps of the derivation.

- **EXAMPLE 3.18** Find the representations of the following linear transformations.

  (a) It should be clear that when using the standard bases for $\mathbb{C}^{m}$ and $\mathbb{C}^{n}$ for $T_{\mathbf{A}}\left(\mathbf{x}\right) := \mathbf{A}\mathbf{x}$,

  $$\left[T_{\mathbf{A}}\right] = \mathbf{A},$$

  where the superscripts and subscripts have been suppressed because we are in the standard bases.

  (b) Choosing the standard basis $\mathcal{B} = \left\{1, t, t^{2}, \ldots, t^{n}\right\}$ of $\mathbb{C}_{n}[t]$, we have

  $$D\left(\sum_{k=0}^{n}c_{k}t^{k}\right) = \sum_{k=1}^{n}kc_{k}t^{k-1},$$

  which is a linear combination of the basis vectors. Thus

  $$\left[D\right]^{\mathcal{B}}_{\mathcal{B}} = \left[\left[D\left(1\right)\right]^{\mathcal{B}}, \left[D\left(t\right)\right]^{\mathcal{B}}, \ldots, \left[D\left(t^{n}\right)\right]^{\mathcal{B}}\right]$$

  $$= \begin{bmatrix} 0 & 1 & 0 & \ldots & 0 \\ 0 & 0 & 2 & \ddots & \vdots \\ 0 & 0 & 0 & \ddots & 0 \\ \vdots & \vdots & \vdots & \ddots & n \\ 0 & 0 & 0 & \ldots & 0 \end{bmatrix}.$$

In component form,

$$\left[[D]_{\mathcal{B}}^{\mathcal{B}} \right]_{jk} = j\delta_{j,k-1}.$$

From the representation that is in row echelon form, we see that $\mathrm{rank}(D) = n$ and $\mathrm{null}(D) = 1$.

(c) Again we'll look at the linear space $\mathbb{C}_n[t]$. The pth order **Euler differential operator** is defined by

$$E_p(f) := t^p D^p(f),$$

where D is differentiation with respect to t. Look at the typical standard basis element:

$$E_p(t^k) = t^p D^p t^k = \begin{cases} k(k-1)\cdots(k-p+1)t^k & , & k \geq p, \\ 0 & , & k < p. \end{cases}$$

Thus

$$[E_p]_{\mathcal{B}}^{\mathcal{B}} = \mathbf{diag}\left(\underbrace{0, 0, \ldots, 0}_{p-1 \text{ zeros}}, \frac{(p+1)!}{1!}, \frac{(p+2)!}{2!}, \ldots, \frac{n!}{(n-p)!} \right),$$

because $k(k-1)\cdots(k-p+1) = k!/(k-p)!$. We can also read off $\mathrm{null}(E_p) = p-1$ and $\mathrm{rank}(E_p) = n+1-p$. $\blacksquare\blacksquare\blacksquare$

THEOREM 3.15 *If T_1 and T_2 map $\mathcal{U}$ into $\mathcal{V}$, T_3 maps $\mathcal{V}$ into $\mathcal{W}$, and $\mathcal{E}$, $\mathcal{F}$, and $\mathcal{G}$ are bases for $\mathcal{U}$, $\mathcal{V}$, and $\mathcal{W}$, respectively, then the following hold:*

(a) $[T_1 + T_2]_{\mathcal{E}}^{\mathcal{F}} = [T_1]_{\mathcal{E}}^{\mathcal{F}} + [T_2]_{\mathcal{E}}^{\mathcal{F}}$;

(b) $[cT_1]_{\mathcal{E}}^{\mathcal{F}} = c[T_1]_{\mathcal{E}}^{\mathcal{F}}$ for any complex c;

(c) $[T_3 T_1]_{\mathcal{E}}^{\mathcal{G}} = [T_3]_{\mathcal{F}}^{\mathcal{G}} [T_1]_{\mathcal{E}}^{\mathcal{F}}$.

The proof can be found in Hoffman and Kunze.

From the last relation in the last theorem and the fact that all diagonal matrices commute under matrix multiplication, we can infer that Euler differential operators commute. This will be of use in the study of a certain class of linear ordinary differential equations, called appropriately enough **Euler equations**.

3.8.1 Exercise Set

Find the representation with respect to the standard bases for each of the following linear transformations.

1. $A[x, y, z] = [x - y + z, y - z, z - x]$

2. $B[\mathbf{A}] = \operatorname{tr}(\mathbf{A})$, $\mathbf{A} \in \mathbb{C}_3^3$

3.
$$C \begin{bmatrix} a & b \\ c & d \end{bmatrix} = \begin{bmatrix} a + b & c \\ b & a - d \end{bmatrix}$$

4. $D[\mathbf{x}] = \langle \mathbf{x}, \mathbf{a} \rangle \mathbf{a}$

5. $G[\mathbf{A}] = \mathbf{A}^T$, $\mathbf{A} \in \mathbb{C}_3^2$

6.
$$H \begin{bmatrix} a & b & c \\ d & e & f \end{bmatrix} = \begin{bmatrix} a + d & e - f \\ b - c & d + f \end{bmatrix}$$

7. $J[\mathbf{x}] = \mathbf{x}\mathbf{a}^H$ for any $\mathbf{x} \in \mathbb{C}_1^n$ and a specific $\mathbf{a} \in \mathbb{C}_1^n$

8. T is a transformation from $\mathbb{R}^3$ into $\mathbb{R}^3$ whose matrix representation in the standard basis $\mathcal{E}$ is

$$[T]_{\mathcal{E}}^{\mathcal{E}} = \begin{bmatrix} -1 & -2 & 2 \\ 1 & -1 & 1 \\ 2 & -1 & 1 \end{bmatrix}.$$

Find a basis for $\ker(T)$ and a basis for $\operatorname{range}(T)$.

9. If $\mathcal{V} = \operatorname{Span}\{\cos x, \sin x, \cos 2x, \sin 2x\}$ is a subspace of $C[-\pi, \pi]$ and we define the transformation

$$T[f] := \int_{-\pi}^{\pi} f(\xi) \sin(x - \xi)\, d\xi,$$

show that T is linear. Find $[T]_{\mathcal{B}}^{\mathcal{B}}$ if $\mathcal{B} = \{\cos x, \sin x, \cos 2x, \sin 2x\}$. Find bases for $\ker(T)$ and $\operatorname{range}(T)$.

10. If T is defined to be $T(\mathbf{x}) = [3x_1 + x_3, -2x_1 + x_2, -x_1 + 2x_2 + 4x_3]$ and $\mathcal{F} = \{[1; 0; 1], [-1; 2; 1], [2; 1; 1]\}$, find $[T]_{\mathcal{F}}^{\mathcal{F}}$.

11. If $\mathbf{x} \in \mathbb{C}^n$ and $T(\mathbf{x}) := \mathbf{U}\mathbf{x}$ where $\mathbf{U}$ is unitary, show that for the standard ℓ_2-norm, $\|\mathbf{x}\| = \|T(\mathbf{x})\|$.

3.8.2 Notes and References

There is a vast literature on the subject of linear spaces and linear transformations that falls under the rubric of linear algebra. Most undergraduate texts restrict themselves to finite dimensional linear spaces. The complete set of extensions to infinite dimensions has applications far and wide.

- Anton, **Elementary Linear Algebra, 7th ed.**: This a standard undergraduate text.

- Hoffman & Kunze, **Linear Algebra, 2nd ed.**: A more theoretical approach to the subject, considered to be a classic in the field.

3.9 SUPPLEMENTARY AND COMPLEMENTARY PROBLEMS

1. A matrix is **cross-symmetric** if it is unchanged by a rotation about its cross diagonal (which extends from A_{n1} up to A_{1n}). Show that the set $\mathcal{SCS}_n$ of all $n \times n$ matrices that are both symmetric and cross-symmetric is a subspace of $\mathbb{C}_n^n$. Find $\dim(\mathcal{SCS}_n)$ for $n = 2, 3, 4, 5$. Generalize this.

2. Under what conditions on the set $\{\mathbf{a}_1, \mathbf{a}_2, \ldots, \mathbf{a}_k\}$ of real column vectors is the matrix

$$\mathbf{A} = \mathbf{a}_1 \mathbf{a}_1^T + \mathbf{a}_2 \mathbf{a}_2^T + \cdots + \mathbf{a}_k \mathbf{a}_k^T$$

   invertible? Orthogonal?

3. The **Gram matrix** of a set of vectors $\mathcal{A} = \{\mathbf{a}_1, \mathbf{a}_2, \ldots, \mathbf{a}_m\}$ in an inner product space is defined by $[\mathbf{G}]_{jk} := \langle \mathbf{a}_j, \mathbf{a}_k \rangle$. Show that $\mathbf{x}^H \mathbf{G} \mathbf{x} \geq 0$ and is equal to zero only if $\mathbf{x} = \mathbf{0}$. By considering a linear relation on the set $\mathcal{A}$, show that $\mathcal{A}$ is linearly dependent if and only if $\det \mathbf{G} = 0$.

4. In special relativity a space-time point $x = (\mathbf{x}, ct)$, where c is the speed of light. Distance is measured using the so-called "metric"

$$\text{dist}\,(x_1, x_2) := \sqrt{\|\mathbf{x}_1 - \mathbf{x}_2\|^2 - c^2\,(t_1 - t_2)^2}.$$

   The presence of the minus sign within the square root is unlike anything we have seen before. The **light cone** is defined to be the set $\mathcal{C} = \left\{\|\mathbf{x}\|^2 - c^2 t^2 = 0\right\}$. The set of **timelike** points is the set $\mathcal{T} = \left\{\|\mathbf{x}\|^2 - c^2 t^2 < 0\right\}$, and the set of **spacelike** points is $\mathcal{S} = \left\{\|\mathbf{x}\|^2 - c^2 t^2 > 0\right\}$. Which of these sets is a linear space?

If $\{\mathbf{u}_1, \mathbf{u}_2, \ldots, \mathbf{u}_n\}$ is an orthonormal basis of a finite dimensional linear space $\mathcal{V}$, then show that:

5. $\left\| \sum_1^n c_k \mathbf{u}_k \right\|^2 = \sum_1^n |c_k|^2$, for all scalars c_k.

6. $\langle \mathbf{a}, \mathbf{b} \rangle = \sum_1^n \langle \mathbf{a}, \mathbf{u}_k \rangle \langle \mathbf{u}_k, \mathbf{b} \rangle$, for all $\mathbf{a}, \mathbf{b} \in \mathcal{V}$.

7. $\|\mathbf{a}\|^2 = \sum_1^n |\langle \mathbf{u}_k, \mathbf{a} \rangle|^2$, for all $\mathbf{a} \in \mathcal{V}$.

8. Using the norm defined by $\|\mathbf{x}\|^2 = \mathbf{x}^T \mathbf{x}$ on $\mathcal{R}^n$, find the value of ϑ that minimizes the quantity $\|\mathbf{x} - \vartheta \mathbf{y}\|^2$. Show that for this value ϑ, we have $\mathbf{y}$ orthogonal to $\mathbf{x} - \vartheta \mathbf{y}$ and $\|\mathbf{x}\|^2 = \|\vartheta \mathbf{y}\|^2 + \|\mathbf{x} - \vartheta \mathbf{y}\|^2$, which is the Pythagorean Theorem. You might want to draw a picture to see what is happening here.

9. Suppose $\mathcal{W} = \mathrm{Span}\{e^{at}\cos\omega t, e^{at}\sin\omega t\} =: \mathrm{Span}(\mathcal{B})$, which is a subspace of $C(\mathcal{R})$, and D is differentiation with respect to t. Find $\mathbf{D} := [D]_{\mathcal{B}}^{\mathcal{B}}$. Theorem 3.15 tells us that $\mathbf{D}^{-1}$ is the representation of the integration operator (the inverse of differentiation). Use this to find

$$\int e^{at}\cos\omega t\, dt \quad \text{and} \quad \int e^{at}\sin\omega t\, dt.$$

10. Suppose $\mathcal{W} = \mathrm{Span}\{e^{st}, te^{st}, \ldots, t^n e^{st}\} =: \mathrm{Span}(\mathcal{B})$, which is a subspace of $C(\mathcal{R})$. Following the idea of the previous problem, find the values of the integrals

$$\int t^k e^{st}\, dt, \quad k = 0:n.$$

11. Show that the transformation for relativistic motion along the x_1-axis from example 3.16(e) can be written as a rotation in the $x_1 x_4$-plane with a complex angle; find the angle.

4

LINEAR DIFFERENTIAL EQUATIONS

4.1 PREVIEW

In this chapter we will develop the ideas behind the methods for solving linear ordinary differential equations, with special emphasis on equations with constant coefficients. At first, the fundamental ideas of ODE's and their solutions will be presented together with the ideas of linearly independent sets of solutions and the real form of complex solutions to real equations. Then methods of solution based on the idea of trial solution functions will be developed and applied to linear time invariant homogeneous ODE's. These methods will then be applied to the models of free oscillations of systems with one degree of freedom.

Two methods for solving nonhomogeneous equations will be presented, the more general method of variation of parameters and the more restrictive method of undetermined coefficients. Both will suffice for time invariant differential operators. The only difference will be whether you want to differentiate and do algebra, or do algebra and then integrate. These methods will be applied to models of forced oscillations of systems.

Lastly, we will look at an alternative method for solving nonhomogeneous equations together with boundary values. This will define the boundary value Green's function, which once known will allow us to find the solution to the original problem by evaluating a single integral.

4.2 ELEMENTS OF LINEAR DIFFERENTIAL EQUATIONS

In Section 2.2 we defined an nth order **linear differential equation** to be any ODE that can be put into the form

$$y^{(n)}(t) + p_{n-1}(t)y^{(n-1)}(t) + \cdots + p_1(t)y'(t) + p_0(t)y(t) = g(t), \qquad (4.1)$$

If $g(t) \equiv 0$, then the equation is **homogeneous**; otherwise, it is **nonhomogeneous**. The function $g(t)$ is called the **input** to the system described by the equation. The function $y(t)$ is called the **output**.

If we use the differential operator notation $D := d/dt$, then

$$L := D^n + p_{n-1}(t)D^{n-1} + \cdots + p_1(t)D + p_0(t), \tag{4.2}$$

and we call L the **differential operator** of the equation (4.1). This linear differential equation can be rewritten in the compact operator form as

$$L[y(t)] = g(t).$$

The linear differential operator L can be written as a polynomial in the differentiation operator D:

$$L = \phi(D) \quad \Rightarrow \quad L[y(t)] = \phi(D)y(t).$$

We will make use of this fact later.

By definition of a linear operator, L satisfies the following two fundamental equations:

(**LinTr1**) $L[u(t) + v(t)] = L[u(t)] + L[v(t)]$;

(**LinTr2**) $L[cu(t)] = cL[u(t)]$, for any constant c.

It can be shown that:

THEOREM 4.1 *If L is the nth order linear differential operator of equation (4.1), then the following are true:*

(a) *L is a linear transformation on the set of n times differentiable functions.*

(b) *Linear combinations of solutions to the homogeneous equation $L[u] = 0$ are also solutions.*

(c) *The set of all functions w for which $L[w] = 0$, called the kernel of L and written $\ker(L)$, is a linear space.*

(d) *$\dim(\ker(L)) = n$, the order of the operator.*

(e) *If the set $\{u_1, u_2, \ldots, u_n\}$ is a basis of the solution space of $L[u] = 0$, then the general solution of the homogeneous equation can be written as an arbitrary linear combination*

$$c_1 u_1(t) + c_2 u_2(t) + \cdots + c_n u_n(t). \qquad \square$$

Result (b) is called the **Principle of Superposition for Outputs**. A solution of the homogeneous equation is called a **complementary**, or **zero-input, solution**.

There is a version of the Existence and Uniqueness Theorem for linear equations.

THEOREM 4.2 *If each of the functions $p_{n-1}(t)$, $p_{n-2}(t)$, $\ldots$, $p_1(t)$, $p_0(t)$, and $g(t)$ are continuous on the interval $[a, b]$, and $y_0, y_1, y_2, \ldots, y_{n-1}$ are given constants, then the initial value problem consisting of the linear differential equation*

$$y^{(n)} + p_{n-1}(t)y^{(n-1)}(t) + \cdots + p_2(t)y''(t) + p_1(t)y'(t) + p_0(t)y(t) = g(t) \tag{4.3}$$

and the initial conditions

$$y(t_0) = y_0, \ y'(t_0) = y_1, \ y''(t_0) = y_2, \ldots, \ y^{(n-1)}(t_0) = y_{n-1}$$

will have a unique solution whenever $t_0 \in (a, b)$. $\square$

4.2.1 Real Form of Complex Solutions

If the linear equation (4.1) has real coefficients, then it is unchanged by complex conjugation. Thus, if $y(t)$ is a solution, $\bar{y}(t)$ is also a solution. We may take linear combinations, using

$$\text{Re}(y) = \frac{1}{2}(y + \bar{y}), \quad \text{Im}(y) = \frac{1}{2i}(y - \bar{y}),$$

and the linearity of L to infer that:

THEOREM 4.3 *The real and imaginary parts of a complex solution of a real linear ODE are also solutions.* $\square$

■ **EXAMPLE 4.1** Applications of Theorem 4.3.

(a) If $w(t) = e^{(a+ib)t}$ is a solution to a real homogeneous linear ODE, then

$$\text{Re}(w) = \text{Re}\left(e^{(a+ib)t}\right) = \text{Re}\left(e^{at}(\cos bt + i \sin bt)\right) = e^{at} \cos bt$$

and

$$\text{Im}\left(e^{(a+ib)t}\right) = e^{at} \sin bt$$

are both solutions, and the corresponding real part of the general solution would be

$$Ae^{at} \cos bt + Be^{at} \sin bt.$$

(b) If $y(x) = x^{a+ib}$ were one solution to a real homogeneous linear ODE, then

$$\text{Re}(y) = \text{Re}\left[x^a(\cos(b \ln x) + i \sin(b \ln x)\right] = x^a \cos(b \ln x)$$

and

$$\text{Im}(y) = x^a \sin(b \ln x)$$

would also be solutions. Thus the real part of the general solution corresponding to the function x^{a+ib} would be the sum of real terms:

$$Ax^a \cos(b \ln x) + Bx^a \sin(b \ln x).$$

(c) If a and b are real, t is a real variable, and $y(t) = (a + it)/(t - ib)$ is a solution to a real homogeneous linear ODE, then

$$\frac{a + it}{t - ib} \cdot \frac{t + ib}{t + ib} = \frac{(a - b)t + i(t^2 + ab)}{t^2 + b^2}.$$

The real form of that corresponding part of the general solution is then

$$c_1 \frac{(a - b)t}{t^2 + b^2} + c_2 \frac{t^2 + ab}{t^2 + b^2}.$$

■ ■ ■

4.2.2   Linearly Independent Sets of Solutions

When solving linear equations of order n, Theorem 4.1 told us that n functions will be required in the general solution of the homogeneous equation. How can we decide when we have enough of the right kind of functions? Not any n functions will do. For instance, the functions 1, t, and $1 + t$ are not all really different and will not suffice as parts of the general solution of a third order equation. Since the set of solutions of a homogeneous equation is a linear space, we must seek a basis of this linear space.

As a reminder, let's review a definition.

DEFINITION 4.1 *A set of functions $\{w_1(t), w_2(t), \ldots, w_n(t)\}$ is said to be* **linearly independent** *on the interval $[a, b]$ if the functional equation*

$$c_1 w_1(t) + c_2 w_2(t) + .. + c_n w_n(t) = 0 \quad \text{for all } t \in [a, b]$$

is valid only when $c_1 = c_2 = \cdots = c_n = 0$.

The following result is fundamental to the solution of linear ODE's.

THEOREM 4.4 *Any linearly independent set of n nonzero solutions to an nth order linear ODE will be a basis of the solution space of $L[w(t)] = 0$.* □

When dealing with n^{th} order ODE's, the functions in a set to be tested for linear independence will be n times differentiable since they are solutions, so that we can use derivatives of the linear relation in the definition to generate $n - 1$ other equations to, hopefully, arrive at a consistent homogeneous system of n linear algebraic equations in the n unknown constants $c_1, c_2, \ldots, c_n$. In particular,

$$
\begin{aligned}
c_1 w_1(t) &+ c_2 w_2(t) &+ \cdots + c_n w_n(t) &= 0 \\
c_1 w_1'(t) &+ c_2 w_2'(t) &+ \cdots + c_n w_n'(t) &= 0 \\
c_1 w_1''(t) &+ c_2 w_2''(t) &+ \cdots + c_n w_n''(t) &= 0 \\
&\vdots \\
c_1 w_1^{(n-1)}(t) &+ c_2 w_2^{(n-1)}(t) &+ \cdots + c_n w_n^{(n-1)}(t) &= 0.
\end{aligned}
\tag{4.4}
$$

From the theory of linear algebraic systems (see Theorem 1.7) we know that there will be only a trivial solution (all of the c's zero) if the coefficient matrix is nonsingular. This is equivalent to saying that the determinant of the coefficient matrix is nonzero. This determinant is usually called the **Wronskian** W of the set of functions:

$$W(w_1, w_2, \ldots, w_n; t) := \begin{vmatrix} w_1(t) & w_2(t) & \cdots & w_n(t) \\ w_1'(t) & w_2'(t) & \cdots & w_n'(t) \\ w_1''(t) & w_2''(t) & \cdots & w_n''(t) \\ \vdots & \vdots & & \vdots \\ w_1^{(n-1)}(t) & w_2^{(n-1)}(t) & \cdots & w_n^{(n-1)}(t) \end{vmatrix}.$$

The following theorem summarizes this result.

THEOREM 4.5 *The set of solutions* $\{w_1, w_2, \ldots, w_n\}$ *to an* n^{th} *order linear ODE with continuous coefficients is linearly independent on the interval* $[a, b]$ *if and only if its Wronskian is nonzero on* $[a, b]$. $\qquad\square$

An important point: If we remove the condition that these functions be solutions to an ODE with continuous coefficients, then the nonvanishing of the Wronskian becomes a sufficient but not necessary condition for linear independence. Thus a nonzero Wronskian guarantees linear independence. On the other hand, there are sets of functions whose Wronskian is zero that are linearly independent and are not solutions of linear ODE's. An example due to Peano is explored in the next example. For a more complete discussion you should consult M. Krusemeyer, Why Does the Wronskian Work? in the **American Mathematical Monthly 95**, 46–49 (1988).

■ **EXAMPLE 4.2** Use the previous theorem to test each of the following sets of functions for linear independence over the largest possible interval.

(a) The set $\{\cos \omega t, \sin \omega t\}$, for ω nonzero, is a solution set for the linear ODE

$$u'' + \omega^2 u = 0.$$

It is linearly independent for all real t because its Wronskian is nonzero everywhere:

$$W(t) = \begin{vmatrix} \cos \omega t & \sin \omega t \\ -\omega \sin \omega t & \omega \cos \omega t \end{vmatrix} = \omega \left(\cos^2 \omega t + \sin^2 \omega t\right) = \omega \neq 0.$$

(b) The set $\{1, t, t^2, \ldots, t^n\}$ is the solution set of

$$D^{n+1} w = 0.$$

It is linearly independent on $\mathbb{R}$ because its Wronskian is nonzero:

$$W(t) = \begin{vmatrix} 1 & t & t^2 & t^3 & \cdots & & t^n \\ 0 & 1 & 2t & 3t^2 & \cdots & & nt^{n-1} \\ 0 & 0 & 2 & 3 \cdot 2t & \cdots & & n(n-1)t^{n-2} \\ 0 & 0 & 0 & 3! & & & \vdots \\ \vdots & \vdots & \vdots & & \ddots & & \vdots \\ 0 & 0 & 0 & \cdots & & 0 & n! \end{vmatrix}$$

$$= 1! \, 2! \, 3! \cdots n! \neq 0.$$

(c) When a, b, and c are *distinct* (possibly complex) constants, the set $\{e^{at}, e^{bt}, e^{ct}\}$ is the solution set of the linear equation

$$(D - a)(D - b)(D - c)u = u''' - (a + b + c)u'' + (ab + bc + ca)u' - abcu$$
$$= 0.$$

It is linearly independent for all real t because its Wronskian is

$$W(t) = e^{(a+b+c)t} \begin{vmatrix} 1 & 1 & 1 \\ a & b & c \\ a^2 & b^2 & c^2 \end{vmatrix} = (a - b)(b - c)(c - a)e^{(a+b+c)t} \neq 0.$$

(d) The set $\{e^t, e^{-t}, \cosh t, \sinh t\}$ is a solution set of the linear homogeneous fourth order ODE

$$w^{(iv)} - w = 0.$$

Its Wronskian is zero:

$$W(t) = \begin{vmatrix} e^t & e^{-t} & \cosh t & \sinh t \\ e^t & -e^{-t} & \sinh t & \cosh t \\ e^t & e^{-t} & \cosh t & \sinh t \\ e^t & -e^{-t} & \sinh t & \cosh t \end{vmatrix} = 0$$

(its first and third (and second and fourth) rows are equal). Thus the set is not linearly independent. If we use the definitions of the hyperbolic functions

$$\cosh t = \frac{1}{2}\left(e^t + e^{-t}\right) \quad \text{and} \quad \sinh t = \frac{1}{2}\left(e^t - e^{-t}\right),$$

then we can write at least two nontrivial linear relations among this set of functions. In particular,

$$e^t - \cosh t - \sinh t = 0,$$
$$e^{-t} - \cosh t + \sinh t = 0.$$

(e) The set $\{t^2, t\,|t|\}$ is linearly independent for all real t even though $t\,|t|$ is not twice differentiable at $t = 0$. We cannot use the Wronskian test here (unless we restrict the interval to either $(-\infty, 0)$ or $(0, \infty)$) because these are not solutions to any second order ODE that is defined at zero. Instead, we must go to the defining equation

$$c_1 t^2 + c_2 t\,|t| = 0.$$

We can get two equations from these by writing the $t < 0$ and $t > 0$ versions of it. They are

$$c_1 t^2 + c_2 t^2 = 0, \quad \text{for } t > 0,$$
$$c_1 t^2 - c_2 t^2 = 0, \quad \text{for } t < 0.$$

The solution to these is $c_1 = c_2 = 0$ for $t \neq 0$, so that the set $\{t^2, t\,|t|\}$ is linearly independent. Notice that if we looked at an interval totally contained in either $(-\infty, 0]$ or $[0, \infty)$, then the set would not be linearly dependent there because then the functions are multiples of each other. ■ ■ ■

It is possible to derive a relation between the Wronskian of the solutions of a homogeneous linear ODE and its coefficients. To simplify matters, let's look at the second order equation

$$L[y(t)] = y''(t) + p(t)y'(t) + q(t)y(t) = 0. \tag{4.5}$$

Suppose $y_1(t)$ and $y_2(t)$ are solutions. Their Wronskian is

$$W(t) = \begin{vmatrix} y_1(t) & y_2(t) \\ y_1'(t) & y_2'(t) \end{vmatrix} = y_1 y_2' - y_1' y_2.$$

Now differentiate $W(t)$ using the Product Rule:

$$W' = (y_1 y_2' - y_1' y_2)' = (y_1' y_2' - y_1' y_2') + (y_1 y_2'' - y_1'' y_2).$$

Since both $y_1(t)$ and $y_2(t)$ are solutions of (4.5), we have

$$y_1'' = -p y_1' - q y_1 \quad \text{and} \quad y_2'' = -p y_2' - q y_2.$$

Substituting these values for the second derivatives into the expression for W' leads to

$$W' = -p\,(y_1 y_2' - y_1' y_2) = -pW.$$

This is a first order separable (also linear) ODE whose solution can be written in the form

$$W(t) = W(t_0) \exp\left\{ -\int_{t_0}^{t} p(\tau)\, d\tau \right\}. \tag{4.6}$$

Equation (4.6) is called **Abel's Formula**. For well-behaved $p(t)$, the exponential will never be zero. Thus $W(t)$ can only be zero if it is zero at some point t_0.

THEOREM 4.6 *If $p(t)$ in (4.5) is continuous, then a set of solutions is linearly independent on an interval (a, b) if and only if its Wronskian is nonzero at some point t_0 in (a, b).*   □

The basic inference to be made from this is that linear independence of a set of solutions is a large scale, or global, property and cannot change unless at least one of the functions in the set fails to be defined or the equation itself is undefined there.

■ **EXAMPLE 4.3** Verify Abel's Formula for each of the following solutions sets.

(a) When $a \neq b$, the set $\{e^{at}, e^{bt}\}$ is a solution basis of the equation

$$(D - a)(D - b)y(t) = y''(t) - (a + b)y'(t) + aby(t) = 0.$$

The set is linearly independent for all real t and its Wronskian is

$$W(t) = \begin{vmatrix} e^{at} & e^{bt} \\ ae^{at} & be^{bt} \end{vmatrix} = (b - a)e^{(a+b)t} = W_0 \exp\left\{ \int_0^t (a + b) \, d\tau \right\},$$

as expected.

(b) When $a \neq b$, the set $\{x^a, x^b\}$ is a solution basis of the equation

$$x^2 y''(x) - (a + b - 1)xy'(x) + aby(x) = 0.$$

The set is linearly independent on any interval not containing the origin. Its Wronskian is

$$W(x) = \begin{vmatrix} x^a & x^b \\ ax^{a-1} & bx^{b-1} \end{vmatrix} = (b - a)x^{a+b-1}.$$

For this differential equation we need to be a bit careful because it is not in the general form of (4.5). We need to divide by x^2 to make the coefficient of the highest derivative term equal to one. Then $p(x) = -\frac{a+b-1}{x}$, and Abel's formula is

$$\begin{aligned} W(x) &= W_0 \exp\left\{ \int_1^x \frac{a+b-1}{\xi} \, d\xi \right\} \\ &= W_0 \exp\left\{ (a + b - 1)\ln x \right\} = W_0 x^{a+b-1}, \end{aligned}$$

as expected. Notice that $W(0) = 0$. This is no problem because the ODE itself is undefined at the point $x = 0$.   ■ ■ ■

4.2.3 Nonhomogeneous Linear Equations

For the nonhomogeneous linear equation $L[u] = g(t)$, we can also use the results of Chapter 3. If $g(t)$ can be written as a linear combination, say

$$g(t) = g_1(t) + g_2(t) + \cdots + g_r(t)$$

and $w_k(t)$ is a solution of $L[w_k(t)] = g_k(t)$, $k = 1 : r$, then we have

$$\begin{aligned} L[w_1(t) + \cdots + w_r(t)] &= L[w_1(t)] + \cdots + L[w_r(t)] \\ &= g_1(t) + \cdots + g_r(t). \end{aligned} \tag{4.7}$$

Since the $g_k(t)$ are the inputs to the system and the $w_k(t)$ the outputs, this last result is called the **Principle of Superposition for Inputs** for nonhomogeneous equations. This means that the output due to a sum of inputs is the sum of the corresponding outputs. When solving a linear nonhomogeneous equation, we can separately solve for the output due to each nonhomogeneity and sum the results.

The solution to the nonhomogeneous equation that has all initial values equal to zero is usually called the **zero-state solution**.

■ **EXAMPLE 4.4** Knowing that $y_1(t) = 4$ is a particular solution of

$$y''(t) + y(t) = 4,$$

$y_2(t) = 2t$ is a particular solution of

$$y''(t) + y(t) = 2t,$$

and $y_3(t) = t \sin t$ is a particular solution of

$$y''(t) + y(t) = 2 \cos t,$$

we can infer that a particular solution of the equation

$$y''(t) + y(t) = 12 - 10t + 4 \cos t$$

is

$$y(t) = 3(4) - 5(2t) + 2(t \sin t) = 12 - 10t + 2t \sin t.$$

■ ■ ■

The Principle of Superposition for Inputs also tells us that the set of solutions to a nonhomogeneous equation does *not* form a subspace: not every linear combination of solutions is a solution, only certain linear combinations. In the last example $-5(2t)$ is *not* a solution to the original equation, $y''(t) + y(t) = 2t$, even though $2t$ is.

4.2.4 Exercise Set

1. Show that $y_1(z) = \exp(z^2)$ and $y_2(z) = z$ are solutions of the equation

$$(1 - 2z^2)y''(z) + (2 + 4z^2)(zy'(z) - y(z)) = 0$$

and that any linear combination of them is also a solution.

2. Show that $w_1(x) = 1$ and $w_2(x) = x^2$ are separately solutions of the equation $xww'' + x(w')^2 = 3ww'$, but no linear combination of these, with both coefficients nonzero, is a solution. Further show that $w^2(x) = c_1 + c_2 x^4$ is a solution. Is $w^2(x) = (c_1 + c_2 x^2)^2$ a solution? Why might this be?

3. Show that $v_1(x) = 1/\sqrt{x}$ and $v_2(x) = x^2$ are separately solutions of the nonlinear equation $x^2 vv'' + (xv' - v)^2 = 3v^2$, but no linear combination of them is a solution, although $v(x) = \sqrt{(c_1 + c_2 x^5)}/x$ is a solution. This cannot happen for a linear equation.

4. For what values of n is $w(t) = t^n e^t$ a solution of the equation

$$D^5 w - 5D^4 w + 10D^3 w - 10D^2 w + 5Dw - w = 0?$$

5. For what values of m is $z(x) = x^m$ a solution of the equation

$$\left(x^4 D^4 - 4x^3 D^3 + 12x^2 D^2 - 24xD + 24\right) z(x) = 0?$$

6. Verify that $w(t) = c_1 e^{2t} + c_2 e^{-3t}$ is the general solution of the equation $w'' + w' - 6w = 0$, and find the specific solution that satisfies $w(0) = 1$ and $w'(0) = 12$.

7. Verify that $v(t) = c_1 e^t + c_2 \cos t + c_3 \sin t$ is the general solution of $v'''(t) - v''(t) + v'(t) - v(t) = 0$, and find the specific solution that satisfies $v(0) = 0$, $v'(0) = 3$, $v''(0) = 2$.

8. Verify that $y(t) = c_1 t e^t + c_2 \cosh t + c_3 \sinh t$ is the general solution of $(D^3 - D^2 - D + 1)y(t) = 0$, and find the specific solution that satisfies $y(0) = 3$, $y'(0) = 4$, $y''(0) = -1$.

9. Given that $w(t) = c_1 \cos t + c_2 \sin t + c_3 \cosh t + c_4 \sinh t$ is the general solution of the equation $(D^4 - 1)w(t) = 0$, find the specific solution that satisfies $w(0) = 3$, $w'(0) = 8$, $w''(0) = 1$, and $w'''(0) = -2$.

Show that each of the following sets is a basis of the solution space of the indicated linear ODE, and tell over what interval it is linearly independent.

10. $\{t, 1/t\}, \quad t^2 \ddot{w}(t) + t\dot{w}(t) - w(t) = 0$

11. $\{e^t, te^t, t^2 e^t\}, \quad (D^3 - 3D^2 + 3D - 1)w(t) = 0$

12. $\{\cosh \mu x, \sinh \mu x\}, \quad y''(x) - \mu^2 y(x) = 0$

13. $\{\cos{(2\ln x)}, \sin{(2\ln x)}\}, \quad x^2 v''(x) + x v'(x) - 4v(x) = 0$

14. $\{e^z, e^z \ln z\}, \quad z y''(z) + (1 - 2z)y'(z) + (z - 1)y(z) = 0$

15. $\{z^2, z\cos z, z\sin z\},$
    $$\left(z^3 D^3 - 4z^2 D^2 + z(8 + z^2)D - 2(4 + z^2)\right) w(z) = 0$$

16. $\left\{\dfrac{1}{x}, \dfrac{1}{x\sqrt{1 - x^2}}, \dfrac{A\sin x}{x\sqrt{1 - x^2}}\right\},$
    $$\left[x(1 - x^2)D^3 + (3 - 8x^2)D^2 - 14xD - 4\right] y(x) = 0$$

17. $\{\cos t, \sin t, \cosh t, \sinh t\}, \quad \left(D^4 - 1\right) w(t) = 0$

18. $\{1, t, e^t, te^t\}, \quad \left(D^4 - 2D^3 + D^2\right) v(t) = 0$

What is the largest interval of the real line over which the Existence and Uniqueness Theorem guarantees each of the following linear equations to have a unique solution?

19. $y''(t) + 4y'(t) + 4y(t) = t^4$

20. $x^2 y''(x) + x y'(x) + y(x) = x^4$

21. $(1 - x^2)y''(x) - 2xy'(x) + \lambda y(x) = 0$

22. $y''(t) + \omega^2 y(t) = \tan t$

23. $x(4 - x)y''(x) - (2x - 1)y(x) = \ln x$

24. $(D^4 - 1)w(t) = \sin 2t - \cos 2t$

25. $(1 - z^2)(9 - z^2)v''(z) - (2z - \cot z)v'(z) + \left(1 - \sqrt{z + 2}\right) v(z) = \ln|\sec z + \tan z|$

4.3   HOMOGENEOUS, LINEAR, TIME INVARIANT ODE'S

First approximations to models of mass-spring-dashpot systems and RLC circuits involve linear, homogeneous, constant coefficient ODE's. Many other applications generate such equations, which are easily solved. A homogeneous equation is **time invariant** if it does not change form under the replacement $t \leftarrow t - t_0$. This can occur only if all of the coefficients are constant. The simplest linear, homogeneous, time invariant equation is first order:

$$y'(t) + Py(t) = 0,$$

where P is a constant. Either by separating variables or using an integrating factor, we immediately find

$$y(t) = Ce^{-Pt}.$$

For the nth order linear homogeneous equation

$$y^{(n)} + p_{n-1}y^{(n-1)} + p_{n-2}y^{(n-2)} + \cdots + p_2 y'' + p_1 y' + p_0 y = 0 \qquad (4.8)$$

with all the p's constant, we know that there will be a solution valid for all t. The question is: What one form of function is defined for all t and has derivatives that are linear combinations of itself and its lower order derivatives? From the solution of the first order problem it should be clear that exponential functions of the form e^{st}, with s constant, are likely to do the trick.

If we substitute the **trial solution** $y(t) = e^{st}$ into (4.8), we obtain

$$\left(s^n + p_{n-1} s^{n-1} + p_{n-2} s^{n-2} + \cdots + p_2 s^2 + p_1 s + p_0 \right) e^{st} = 0,$$

which is to be valid for all t. Because e^{st} is never zero, we are left with the **auxiliary equation** (sometimes called the characteristic equation, but in this book that term will be reserved for the eigenvalue problems studied in Section 6.2)

$$s^n + p_{n-1} s^{n-1} + p_{n-2} s^{n-2} + \cdots + p_2 s^2 + p_1 s + p_0 = 0. \tag{4.9}$$

This is an nth degree polynomial equation, so the Fundamental Theorem of Algebra guarantees the existence of n (possibly complex) roots, counting multiplicities. If the coefficients are real, then any complex roots must occur in complex conjugate pairs. As is mentioned in Appendix C, there are formulas for the roots of quadratic, cubic, and quartic equations but not for equations of degree five or higher. It might be a good idea to check the manual for the computer algebra system that you use for factoring polynomials. Factoring the auxiliary polynomial is akin to factoring the polynomial representation of the linear differential operator

$$L = D^n + p_{n-1} D^{n-1} + p_{n-2} D^{n-2} + \cdots + p_2 D^2 + p_1 D + p_0$$

Aside: The factorization of a differential operator is consistent with our experience with algebraic factors only if the operator factors commute. Operators with nonconstant coefficients need not commute: e.g., if $L = tD$ and $M = D$, then $LM = tD^2$ but $ML = tD^2 + D$.

If the operator L is factored into the form

$$L = (D - s_1)(D - s_2) \cdots (D - s_n),$$

then $y(t)$ will be a solution of $L[y(t)] = 0$ whenever $y(t)$ is solution of the equation $(D - s_k)y(t) = 0$ for some value of k. Such a $y(t)$ will be a constant multiple of $\exp(s_k t)$. Therefore, if the roots of the auxiliary equation are $s_1, s_2, \ldots, s_n$, a set of solutions will be

$$\left\{ e^{s_1 t}, e^{s_2 t}, \ldots, e^{s_n t} \right\}.$$

A simple extension of example 4.2(c) tells us that if all the s's are distinct, this set is also linearly independent. The set contains n functions; consequently, it is a basis of the solution space, and any solution can be written as a linear combination

$$y(t) = c_1 e^{s_1 t} + c_2 e^{s_2 t} + \cdots + c_n e^{s_n t}. \tag{4.10}$$

If the auxiliary equation has real coefficients, then any roots that are complex must occur in conjugate pairs $s = a \pm ib$. Then

$$e^{st} = e^{(a+ib)t} = e^{at} \left(\cos bt + i \sin bt \right) \tag{4.11}$$

and the real form of the solution of an equation with real coefficients corresponding to the complex conjugate pair $s = a + ib$ and $s = a - ib$ is a linear combination of the real and imaginary parts of (4.11). This segment of the general solution takes the real form

$$c_1 e^{at} \cos bt + c_2 e^{at} \sin bt.$$

If the root is repeated, say $s = s_0$ occurs k-times, then we will not have k different, much less linearly independent, solutions. The differential term $(D - s_0)^k$ will be a factor of the linear operator L. Assuming a solution of the form $v(t)e^{s_0 t}$, we want to solve

$$(D - s_0)^k \left(v(t)e^{s_0 t} \right) = 0$$

for $v(t)$. It is an exercise in mathematical induction to show that

$$(D - s_0)^k \left(v(t)e^{s_0 t} \right) = e^{s_0 t} D^k v(t).$$

Setting the latter equation to zero, we can integrate k times to get

$$v(t) = c_1 + c_2 t + c_3 t^2 + \cdots + c_{k-1} t^{k-2} + c_k t^{k-1}.$$

Thus the linearly independent solution set corresponding to $s = s_0$ repeated k-times is

$$\left\{ e^{s_0 t}, t e^{s_0 t}, t^2 e^{s_0 t}, \ldots, t^{k-2} e^{s_0 t}, t^{k-1} e^{s_0 t} \right\},$$

and the corresponding contribution to the general solution is the linear combination

$$\left(c_1 + c_2 t + c_3 t^2 + \cdots + c_{k-1} t^{k-2} + c_k t^{k-1} \right) e^{s_0 t}. \tag{4.12}$$

A similar polynomial factor could be used for $e^{at} \cos bt$ and $e^{at} \sin bt$ when there are k-fold repeated complex conjugate pairs $s = a \pm ib$. Once we have the auxiliary equation, factor it, and find its roots, it just a matter of following the recipe dictated by equations (4.10), (4.11), and (4.12) to write the solution.

■ **EXAMPLE 4.5** Each of the following are sets of roots to the auxiliary equation of time invariant homogeneous ODE's. Write their general solutions.

(a) $\mathcal{S}_a = \{\pm 1, 2, 2 \pm \pi i\}$. Because there are five roots, this must have originated from a fifth order homogeneous linear time invariant ODE. The general solution of that equation is

$$y(t) = c_1 e^{-t} + c_2 e^{+t} + c_3 e^{2t} + c_4 e^{2t} \cos \pi t + c_5 e^{2t} \sin \pi t.$$

Notice that there are as many different arbitrary constants as the order of the equation, which is also the same as the number of roots.

(b) $S_b = \{-3, -2, -1, 0, 0, 0, 1, 2, 5, 5, -1 \pm 2i, -1 \pm 2i, \pm 3i, \pm 3i, \pm 3i\}$. Since there are 20 roots, they must have come from a 20th order ODE, and we must end up with a solution containing 20 different arbitrary constants. Each repeated root will need an extra term with a multiple of t, up to one lower power than the multiplicity, according to equation (4.12). The solution to the ODE will be

$$
\begin{aligned}
y(t) = \; & c_1 e^{-3t} + c_2 e^{-2t} + c_3 e^{-t} + \left(c_4 + c_5 t + c_6 t^2\right) e^{0t} \\
& + c_7 e^t + c_8 e^{2t} + \left(c_9 + c_{10} t\right) e^{5t} + \left(c_{11} + c_{12} t\right) e^{-t} \cos 2t \\
& + \left(c_{13} + c_{14} t\right) e^{-t} \sin 2t + \left(c_{15} + c_{16} t + c_{17} t^2\right) e^{0t} \cos 3t \\
& + \left(c_{18} + c_{19} t + c_{20} t^2\right) e^{0t} \sin 3t.
\end{aligned}
$$

Of course, this simplifies slightly by using $e^{0t} = 1$. ■ ■ ■

There is an alternative way to write the solution when we have real pairs of roots of the auxiliary equation of the form $s = \pm b$. Then the solution

$$
Ae^{bt} + Be^{-bt}
$$

can be rewritten in terms of hyperbolic functions by using the identity

$$
e^{\pm bt} = \cosh bt \pm \sinh bt.
$$

Thus

$$
\begin{aligned}
Ae^{bt} + Be^{-bt} &= A\left(\cosh bt + \sinh bt\right) + B\left(\cosh bt - \sinh bt\right) \\
&= (A + B)\cosh bt + (A - B)\sinh bt.
\end{aligned}
$$

Relabeling our constants allows us to write the solution in the form

$$
k_1 \cosh bt + k_2 \sinh bt.
$$

This is frequently more convenient because

$$
\cosh 0 = 1, \quad \sinh 0 = 0, \quad \frac{d}{dt}\cosh t = \sinh t, \quad \frac{d}{dt}\sinh t = \cosh t,
$$

thus making the evaluation of constants in initial value problems somewhat easier.

■ **EXAMPLE 4.6** To solve each of the following equations, first substitute the trial solution $y = e^{st}$ to obtain the auxiliary equation, solve the auxiliary equation to find all the values of s, and construct the solution.

(a) $y'' + 4y' + 13y = 0$. The auxiliary equation is gotten by setting $y = e^{st}$, which replaces each differentiation by a power of s. Thus we have a quadratic for which we can complete the square:

$$
s^2 + 4s + 13 = (s + 2)^2 + 3^2 = 0
$$

$$\Rightarrow \quad s = -2 \pm 3i.$$

Using the real form of the solution, with $s = a \pm ib$ and $a = -2$ and $b = 3$, we have

$$y(t) = c_1 e^{-2t} \cos 3t + c_2 e^{-2t} \sin 3t.$$

(b) $D^3 w = 0$. Setting $w = e^{st}$ results in the simple cubic

$$s^3 = 0 \quad \Rightarrow \quad s = 0, 0, 0.$$

Since the root is triply repeated we must use the function $e^{0t} = 1$ and then introduce multiplicative factors of t and t^2 for the solution

$$w(t) = c_1 + c_2 t + c_3 t^2.$$

This is precisely the solution we would have gotten by integrating 0 three times.

(c) $z'' + \omega^2 z = 0$. This ubiquitous equation, called the **harmonic oscillator equation**, has the corresponding auxiliary equation

$$s^2 + \omega^2 = 0 \quad \Rightarrow \quad s = \pm i\omega.$$

Using the real form of the solution with $a \pm ib = 0 \pm i\omega$, we have

$$z(t) = c_1 \cos \omega t + c_2 \sin \omega t.$$

(d) $(D^3 - D)y(t) = 0$. This equation seems to have a factor of D common to the left hand side. This will manifest itself in a common factor of s in the auxiliary equation:

$$s^3 - s = s(s+1)(s-1) = 0 \quad \Rightarrow \quad s = 0, -1, 1$$

$$\Rightarrow \quad y(t) = c_1 + c_2 e^{-t} + c_3 e^t, \quad \text{or} \quad y(t) = k_1 + k_2 \cosh t + k_3 \sinh t.$$

Suppose we impose the initial conditions $y(0) = 3$, $y'(0) = 3$, $y''(0) = 2$. Then the linear system for c_1, c_2, and c_3 using the exponential form of the solution is

$$y(0) = (c_1 + c_2 e^{-t} + c_3 e^t)_{t=0} = c_1 + c_2 + c_3 = 3,$$

$$y'(0) = (c_1 + c_2 e^{-t} + c_3 e^t)'_{t=0} = -c_2 + c_3 = 3,$$

$$y''(0) = (c_1 + c_2 e^{-t} + c_3 e^t)''_{t=0} = c_2 + c_3 = 2.$$

Compare this with the linear system for k_1, k_2, and k_3 using the form of the solution with the hyperbolic functions:

$$
\begin{aligned}
y(0) &= (k_1 + k_2 \cosh t + k_3 \sinh t)_{t=0} \\
&= k_1 + k_2 &= 3, \\
y'(0) &= (k_1 + k_2 \cosh t + k_3 \sinh t)'_{t=0} \\
&= k_3 &= 3, \\
y''(0) &= (k_1 + k_2 \cosh t + k_3 \sinh t)''_{t=0} \\
&= k_2 &= 2.
\end{aligned}
$$

The first system has the solutions

$$c_1 = 1, \quad c_2 = -\frac{1}{2}, \quad c_3 = \frac{5}{2},$$

with corresponding solution to the original equation of

$$y(t) = 1 - \frac{1}{2}e^{-t} + \frac{5}{2}e^t.$$

On the other hand, the solution to the second system is more easily computed to be

$$k_1 = 1, \quad k_2 = 2, \quad k_3 = 3,$$

and the corresponding unique solution to the initial value problem is

$$y(t) = 1 + 2\cosh t + 3\sinh t,$$

which is identical with the previous solution as can be seen by substituting in the defining equations for $\cosh t$ and $\sinh t$.

(e) $\left(D^4 + 2D^3 + 2D^2 + 2D + 1\right) w(t) = 0$ gives us the quartic polynomial

$$s^4 + 2s^3 + 2s^2 + 2s + 1 = 0.$$

If you don't have access to computer software to do the job, this can be factored: it can be seen that $s = -1$ is one root, and we can use synthetic division to reduce the order of the auxiliary equation and find the other roots. The correct factorization is

$$s^4 + 2s^3 + 2s^2 + 2s + 1 = (s+1)^2(s^2+1) \quad \Rightarrow \quad s = -1, -1, \pm i$$

$$\Rightarrow \quad w(t) = (c_1 + c_2 t)e^{-t} + c_3 \cos t + c_4 \sin t.$$

(f) $x^{(iv)} + x = 0 \quad \Rightarrow \quad s^4 + 1 = 0$. Since $s^4 = -1$, we need to compute the fourth roots of -1, which are

$$s = (-1)^{1/4} = \pm \frac{1}{\sqrt{2}} (1 \pm i).$$

$$\Rightarrow \quad x(t) = c_1 e^{t/\sqrt{2}} \cos\left(\frac{t}{\sqrt{2}}\right) + c_2 e^{t/\sqrt{2}} \sin\left(\frac{t}{\sqrt{2}}\right)$$

$$+ c_3 e^{-t/\sqrt{2}} \cos\left(\frac{t}{\sqrt{2}}\right) + c_4 e^{-t/\sqrt{2}} \sin\left(\frac{t}{\sqrt{2}}\right).$$

(g) $y'' + iy' + 2y = 0 \Rightarrow s^2 + is + 2 = (s - i)(s + 2i) \Rightarrow s = i, -2i$

$$\Rightarrow \quad y(t) = c_1 e^{it} + c_2 e^{-2it}.$$

Because this equation does *not* have real coefficients, the complex roots of the auxiliary equation were *not* complex conjugates. Also, the real and imaginary parts of the solution are not themselves solutions; e.g., $\cos t = \text{Re}(e^{it})$ but

$$(\cos t)'' + i(\cos t)' + 2\cos t = -\cos t - i\sin t + 2\cos t \neq 0.$$

Similarly for $\sin t = \text{Im}(e^{it})$:

$$(\sin t)'' + i(\sin t)' + 2\sin t = -\sin t + i\cos t + 2\sin t \neq 0.$$

■ ■ ■

4.3.1 Euler Equations

There is a class of useful variable coefficient linear differential equations that can easily be transformed into constant coefficient equations.

DEFINITION 4.2 *Any homogeneous equation of the form*

$$x^n y^{(n)}(x) + b_{n-1} x^{n-1} y^{(n-1)}(x) + \cdots + b_2 x^2 y''(x) + b_1 x y'(x) + b_0 y(x) = 0,$$

where all the b's are constant, is called an **Euler equation***.*

A general term in an Euler equation is

$$x^k D^k y(x).$$

The power of x is the same as the order of the derivative.

If we were to change the units in which x is measured, then x would change by a constant scale factor, say $x = \sigma z$, and

$$x^k \left(\frac{d}{dx} \right)^k y(x) = (\sigma z)^k \left(\frac{d}{d(\sigma z)} \right)^k y(\sigma z) = z^k \left(\frac{d}{dz} \right)^k y(\sigma z).$$

From this we see that an Euler equation is unchanged by a change of units in the independent variable. In fact, the units of the general term are

$$\left[x^k D^k y(x) \right] = [x]^k \frac{[y]}{[x]^k} = [y].$$

Thus all terms in an Euler equation have the same units when the b's are dimensionless. Compare this with the typical time invariant equation; when the independent variable t is time, $y'' + p_1 y' + p_0 y = 0$, wherein $[p_1] = (\text{time})^{-1}$ and $[p_0] = (\text{time})^{-2}$.

Just as constant coefficient differential operators commuted, $D^k D^\ell = D^\ell D^k$, so too do Euler operators commute:

$$\left(x^k D^k\right)\left(x^\ell D^\ell\right) = \left(x^\ell D^\ell\right)\left(x^k D^k\right),$$

but showing this is left to the problems. This means that a solution to a first order Euler equation will give us the form of the appropriate trial solution. Let's find that solution of a first order homogeneous Euler equation.

$$xy' + by = 0 \quad \Rightarrow \quad y' + \frac{b}{x}y = 0; \quad \mu = e^{\int \frac{b}{x}\,dx} = e^{b\ln x} = x^b$$

$$\Rightarrow \quad \left(x^b y\right)' = 0 \quad \Rightarrow \quad y(x) = Cx^{-b}.$$

Constant coefficient equations had solutions that were linear combinations of powers of e^t, because $(e^t)^s = e^{st}$. We see that the solution of an Euler equation is a power of x.

A good guess for the trial solution of the homogeneous n^{th} order Euler equation would be $y(x) = x^m$, where m is a constant that is to be determined. Then the kth order Euler term would become

$$\begin{aligned}
x^k D^k\left(x^m\right) &= m(m-1)(m-2)\cdots(m-k+1)x^k \cdot x^{m-k} \\
&= m(m-1)(m-2)\cdots(m-k+1)x^m.
\end{aligned}$$

Very much in the style of the constant coefficient case, if we substitute the trial solution $y = x^m$ into the ODE, there will be a factor of x^m multiplying every term of the equation. Since we can take either $x > 0$ or $x < 0$, $x^m \neq 0$ and we will obtain an auxiliary equation consisting of a polynomial in m.

As an example, take the second order case: $ax^2 y'' + bxy' + cy = 0$ for $x > 0$. Putting $y = x^m$, we get the simple quadratic equation

$$\left(am(m-1) + bm + c\right)x^m = 0.$$

Consequently, the auxiliary equation is

$$am(m-1) + bm + c = 0.$$

If the roots are distinct, then we expect the solution of the equation to be

$$y(x) = c_1 x^{m_1} + c_2 x^{m_2}.$$

If $m = a \pm ib$ and the equation is real, then since

$$x^{a+ib} = x^a\, x^{ib} = x^a\, e^{ib\ln x} = x^a\left(\cos(b\ln x) + i\sin(b\ln x)\right),$$

the real form of the solution would be

$$y(x) = c_1 x^a \cos(b\ln x) + c_2 x^a \sin(b\ln x).$$

In order to determine the form of the solution for the case of repeated roots of the auxiliary equation, it will be convenient to follow a slightly different tack.

Writing $x^m = e^{m \ln x}$ makes the solution look like e^{mt}, but with $t = \ln x$. What if we make this change of independent variable? We must use the Chain Rule to transform the derivatives:

$$x\frac{dy}{dx} = x\frac{dy}{dt}\frac{dt}{dx} = x\left(\frac{1}{x}\frac{dy}{dt}\right) = \frac{dy}{dt},$$

$$x^2\frac{d^2y}{dx^2} = x^2\frac{d}{dx}\left(\frac{1}{x}\frac{dy}{dt}\right) = x^2\left(\frac{1}{x}\frac{d}{dx}\left[\frac{dy}{dt}\right] - \frac{1}{x^2}\frac{dy}{dt}\right)$$

$$= x^2\left(\frac{1}{x^2}\frac{d^2y}{dt^2} - \frac{1}{x^2}\frac{dy}{dt}\right) = \frac{d^2y}{dt^2} - \frac{dy}{dt}.$$

There are two things worth noting here:

- The substitution $x = e^t \Leftrightarrow t = \ln x$ reduces the Euler equation to a constant coefficient equation.

- When putting $y(x) = x^m$ in the Euler term $x^k D^k y$, we get the same coefficient $m(m-1)\cdots(m-k+1)$ we would get from putting $y(t) = e^{mt}$ into the transformed term.

The last observation allows us to find the transformed equation without using the Chain Rule: set $y = x^m$ in the Euler equation to find the auxiliary equation, and then replace each m by d/dt and $t = \ln x$ or $x = e^t$ to get the transformed equation.

▪ **EXAMPLE 4.7** Transform each of the following Euler equations to time invariant form.

(a) $x^2y + 5xy' - 2y = 0$. When we use the trial solution $y = x^m$, we get the auxiliary equation

$$m(m-1) + 5m - 2 = m^2 + 4m - 2 = 0.$$

Replacing m by a derivative with respect to time and denoting d/dt by an overdot, the transformed equation is

$$\ddot{y} + 4\dot{y} - 2y = 0.$$

(b) $x^4y^{(iv)} - 3x^3y''' + 5x^2y'' - 7y = 0$. Again, use the trial solution $y = x^m$ to get the auxiliary equation

$$m(m-1)(m-2)(m-3) - 3m(m-1)(m-2) + 5m(m-1) - 7 = 0.$$

Upon simplification this becomes

$$m^4 - 9m^3 + 25m^2 - 17m - 7 = 0,$$

and the associated time invariant equation is

$$\frac{d^4y}{dt^4} - 9\frac{d^3y}{dt^3} + 25\frac{d^2y}{dt^2} - 17\frac{dy}{dt} - 7y = 0.$$

■ ■ ■

Since the change of variables is $t = \ln x$, or equivalently $x = e^t$, the identity $x^m = e^{mt} = (e^t)^m$ allows us to transform our constant coefficient equation solution rules to Euler equation solution rules. If the roots of the auxiliary equation are distinct, then the solution of the transformed equation is

$$y(t) = c_1 e^{m_1 t} + c_2 e^{m_2 t} + \cdots + c_n e^{m_n t},$$

while the solution of the original Euler equation is

$$y(x) = c_1 x^{m_1} + c_2 x^{m_2} + \cdots + c_n x^{m_n}. \tag{4.13}$$

If $m = m_0$ is a k-fold repeated root, the solution of the transformed equation is

$$\left(c_1 + c_2 t + c_3 t^2 + \cdots + c_k t^{k-1}\right) e^{m_0 t},$$

and that of the original Euler equation is

$$\left(c_1 + c_2 \ln x + c_3 (\ln x)^2 + \cdots + c_k (\ln x)^{k-1}\right) x^{m_0}. \tag{4.14}$$

When $m = a \pm ib$ as the roots to a real auxiliary equation, the solution of the transformed equation is

$$c_1 e^{at} \cos bt + c_2 e^{at} \sin bt,$$

and that of the original Euler equation is

$$c_1 x^a \cos(b \ln x) + c_2 x^a \sin(b \ln x). \tag{4.15}$$

■ **EXAMPLE 4.8** Suppose the roots of the auxiliary equation for an Euler equation were

$$-3, -1, -1, 0, 0, 2, 2, 2, \pm i, \pm i, -1 \pm 2i, 2 \pm 3,$$

write the form of the solution.

Solution: Following the recipe given by equations (4.13), (4.14), and (4.15), and noting that $2 \pm 3 = -1, 5$, we can immediately write

$$
\begin{aligned}
y(x) &= c_1 x^{-3} + x^{-1}\left(c_2 + c_3 \ln x + c_4 (\ln x)^2\right) + x^0 \left(c_5 + c_6 \ln x\right) \\
&\quad + x^2 \left(c_7 + c_8 \ln x + c_9 (\ln x)^2\right) + c_{10} x^5 \\
&\quad + \left(c_{11} \cos(\ln x) + c_{12} \sin(\ln x)\right) \\
&\quad + (\ln x)\left(c_{13} \cos(\ln x) + c_{14} \sin(\ln x)\right) \\
&\quad + x^{-1}\left(c_{15} \cos(2 \ln x) + c_{16} \sin(2 \ln x)\right).
\end{aligned}
$$

■ ■ ■

■ **EXAMPLE 4.9** Solve each of the following Euler equations.

(a) $x^2 y'' + 5xy' + 13y = 0$. Put $y = x^m$ to get the quadratic auxiliary equation

$$m(m - 1) + 5m + 13 = 0 \quad \Rightarrow \quad (m + 2)^2 + 3^2 = 0,$$

which has the roots $m = -2 \pm 3i$. The solution is

$$y(x) = c_1 x^{-2} \cos(3 \ln x) + c_2 x^{-2} \sin(3 \ln x).$$

(b) $(x^3 D^3 + 3x^2 D^2 + xD)y = 0$ has the auxiliary equation

$$m(m - 1)(m - 2) + 3m(m - 1) + m = m^3 = 0,$$

with roots $m = 0, 0, 0$. The solution is then

$$y(x) = c_1 + c_2 \ln x + c_3 (\ln x)^2.$$

(c) $(x^3 D^3 + 3x^2 D^2)y = 0$. The auxiliary equation is

$$m(m - 1)(m - 2) + 3m(m - 1) = m(m + 1)(m - 1) = 0.$$

From the factored form we see that the roots are $m = 0, -1, 1$. Thus the solution is

$$y(x) = c_1 + c_2 x^{-1} + c_3 x.$$

(d) $x^2 y'' - 3xy' + 3y = 0 \Rightarrow$

$$m(m - 1) - 3m + 3 = m^2 - 4m + 3 = (m - 1)(m - 3) = 0 \Rightarrow m = 1, 3$$

$$\Rightarrow \quad y(x) = c_1 x + c_2 x^3.$$

(e) $(x^4 D^4 + 3x^2 D^2 - 5xD + 5)y = 0$

$$\Rightarrow \quad m(m - 1)(m - 2)(m - 3) + 3m(m - 1) - 5m + 5 = 0$$

$$\Rightarrow \quad m^4 - 6m^3 + 14m^2 - 14m + 5 = (m - 1)^2[(m - 2)^2 + 1]$$
$$\Rightarrow \quad m = 1, 1, 2 \pm i$$

$$\Rightarrow y(x) = (c_1 + c_2 \ln x)x + (c_3 \cos(\ln x) + c_4 \sin(\ln x)) x^2.$$

■ ■ ■

4.3.2 Exercise Set

If the roots of the auxiliary equation are as listed, write the solution of the homogeneous linear constant coefficient equation $L[y] = 0$.

1. $0, 0, 2, 3$

2. $i, 2i, 1, 2$

3. $1, 2, \pm 3$

4. $\pm 1, \pm 2, 3$

5. $1, 2i, 3$

6. $1 \pm 2i, 3$

7. $\pm i, 2, \pm 3$

8. π, π^2

9. $e, e, e, 3, 3, 2e$

10. $\pm e, \pm e, \pm 3, \pm 3$

11. $\pm 1, \pm 1, 2 \pm 3i$

12. $-1, -1, 1, 0, 2, 2 - 3i, 2 + 4i$

13. $-3, -2, -1, 0, 1, 1, i, 2i$

14. $-\pi, -\pi, 1, \pi, \pi, \pi + i$

15. m 0's and n 1's

16. $\pm i$, each n times

Solve each of the following homogeneous equations.

17. $y' + 2y = 0, \ y(0) = -6$

18. $3y' - 2y = 0, \ y(0) = \pi$

19. $y' + 2y = 0, \ y(2) = -6$

20. $3y' - 2y = 0, \ y(-3) = \pi$

21. $y'' + 8y' + 25y = 0$

22. $y'' + 3y' + 2y = 0$

23. $2y'' + 5y' - 12y = 0$

24. $4y'' - 12y' + 9y = 0$

25. $2y'' + 3y' - 4y = 0$

26. $9y'' - 9y' + 4y = 0$

27. $u'' + 2u' + 5u = 0$

28. $5u'' - 10u' + 11u = 0$

29. $w'' - 9w' + 20w = 0$

30. $w'' + 7w' + 12w = 0$

31. $3w'' + 2w' - w = 0$

32. $2w'' - w' - 6w = 0$

33. $4w'' - 4w' + w = 0$

34. $4w'' - 4w' + 5w = 0$

35. $\ddot{x} + 4\dot{x} + 5x = 0$

36. $\ddot{x} - (2 - i)\dot{x} - 2ix = 0$

37. $\ddot{x} + i\dot{x} + 6x = 0$

38. $(12D^3 - 4D^2 - 3D + 1)y = 0$

39. $(D^3 + 2D^2 - D - 2)y = 0$

40. $(D^3 + 5D^2 + 6D + 2)y = 0$

41. $(D^3 + 8D^2 + 21D + 18)y = 0$

42. $(D^3 - 3D^2 + 3D - 9)y = 0$

43. $y^{(iv)} + 4y''' + 6y'' - 4y' - 7y = 0$

44. $(D^4 - D^3 - 3D^2 + 5D - 2)y = 0$

45. $(D^4 + 2D^3 - 2D - 1)y = 0$

46. $(D^4 - 2D^3 + 2D^2 - 2D + 1)y = 0$

47. $(D^4 + 2D^3 + 3D^2 + 2D + 1)y = 0$

48. $(4D^4 - 12D^3 + 11D^2 - 3D)y = 0$

49. $(D^4 + 6D^3 + 15D^2 + 18D + 10)y = 0$

50. $x^3 y''' + 5x^2 y'' - 6xy' - 18y = 0$

51. $x^2 y'' + 5xy' + 5y = 0$

52. $x^2 y'' + 5xy' + 4y = 0$

53. $3x^2 u'' + 5xu' - u = 0$

54. $2x^2 u'' + xu' - 6u = 0$

55. $4z^2 u'' - 4u = 0$

56. $4z^2 u'' + u = 0$

57. $z^2 u'' + 3zu' + 3u = 0$

58. $9z^2 w'' + 15zw' + w = 0$

59. $4x^2 v'' - 8xv' + 9v = 0$

60. $x^3 D^3 y + 2x^2 D^2 y - 10xDy - 8y = 0$

61. $z^3 D^3 w + 4z^2 D^2 w - 8zDw + 8w = 0$

62. $x^3 y''' + 2x^2 y'' + xy' - y = 0$

63. $y'' - 3y' - 4y = 0, \quad y(0) = 1, \ y'(0) = 9$

64. $y'' + 4y' + 4y = 0, \quad y(1) = 1, \ y'(1) = 2$

65. $y'' - 16y = 0, \quad y(\pi) = 4, \ y'(\pi) = 0$

66. $w'' + 4w' + 4w = 0, \quad w(0) = e^{-1}, \ w(1) = 0$

67. $w'' - 6w' + 8w = 0, \quad w(1) = 3, \ w'(1) = 8$

68. $u'' + 2u' + 2u = 0, \quad u(0) = 1, \ u'(0) = 0$

69. $u'' - 6u' + 9u = 0, \quad u(0) = 0, \ u'(0) = 18$

70. $(D^3 + D^2 + 4D + 4)y = 0, \quad y(0) = 0, \ y'(0) = -1, \ y''(0) = 5$

71. $2y^2 w'' + yw' - w = 0, \quad w(1) = 3, \ w'(1) = 0$

72. $z^2 u'' + 7zu' + 13u = 0, \quad u(1) = 3, \ u'(1) = 11$

73. Show that the equation $ay'' + by' + cy = 0$ with initial conditions $y(0) = y_0$ and $y'(0) = v_0$ and with $b^2 - 4ac = 0$ has a decreasing solution for $t > t_0$ and find t_0.

74. For the equation $y'' - 2y' \cot 2x - 3y \tan^2 x = 0$, change the independent variable using $z = \cos x$, and solve the resulting equation.

75. For the equation $xy'' - 2(a + bx)y' + b(2a + bx)y = 0$, change the dependent variable by setting $y(x) = e^{bx} w(x)$, and solve the resulting equation to get a solution to the original equation.

76. For the equation $y'' + 2ay' \cot ax + (b^2 - a^2)y = 0$, change the dependent variable by setting $u(x) = y(x) \sin ax$, and solve the resulting equation to get a solution to the original equation.

77. For the equation $y'' + ay' + b^2 e^{2ax} y = 0$, change the dependent variable by setting $y(x) = e^{-ax} u(x)$. Also change the independent variable by setting $z = e^{ax}$. Solve the resulting equation, thereby solving the original equation.

78. If the roots of the auxiliary equation for a constant coefficient ODE are $0, 0, -1 \pm 2i$, what is the equation? Redo this for an Euler equation.

79. Write the homogeneous time invariant or Euler equation whose complementary solution is:

(a) $a(b) = c_1 + c_2 e^{2b} + c_3 e^{-3b}$.

(b) $z(y) = c_1 + c_2 y^2 + c_3 y^4 + c_4 y^6$.

(c) $x(t) = c_1 2^{3t} + c_2 3^{2t}$.

(d) $w(t) = \left(c_1 + c_2 t + c_3 t^2 \right) e^{-\pi t} \cos \Omega t + \left(c_4 + c_5 t + c_6 t^2 \right) e^{-\pi t} \sin \Omega t$.

4.4 FREE OSCILLATIONS OF SYSTEMS

4.4.1 Undamped Systems

The simplest undamped mechanical system is the mass-spring system shown in Figure 4.1.

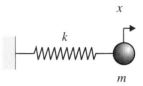

Fig. 4.1

The system is so simple that we need not use the Lagrangian approach to find the equation of motion.

The indicated variable x is the displacement of the mass m from its equilibrium position. Using the linear approximation to Hooke's Law—the force exerted by the spring is proportional to the displacement—the equation of motion is simply

$$m\ddot{x} + kx = 0. \tag{4.16}$$

Putting $x = e^{st}$ as a trial solution we get the auxiliary equation $ms^2 + k = 0$. If we define

$$\omega_0 := \sqrt{\frac{k}{m}},$$

then $s = \pm i\omega_0$, and the solution satisfying the initial conditions $x(0) = x_0$, $x'(0) = v_0$ is

$$x(t) = x_0 \cos \omega_0 t + \frac{v_0}{\omega_0} \sin \omega_0 t. \tag{4.17}$$

Equation (4.17) is a sinusoid that can be written in terms of its **amplitude** A and **phase angle** ϕ by looking at the triangle in Figure 4.2.

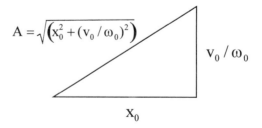

Fig. 4.2

Then

$$x_0 = A \cos \phi \quad \text{and} \quad \frac{v_0}{\omega_0} = A \sin \phi$$

where

$$\tan\phi = \frac{(v_0/\omega_0)}{x_0}.$$

Substituting these into the left hand side of (4.17) yields

$$x(t) = A\cos\omega_0 t\cos\phi + A\sin\omega_0 t\sin\phi \Rightarrow x(t) = A\cos(\omega_0 t - \phi). \qquad (4.18)$$

The **natural frequency** of oscillation is $f_0 := \omega_0/2\pi$, and the **period** is $T = 2\pi/\omega_0 = 1/f_0$. The response is shown in Figure 4.3.

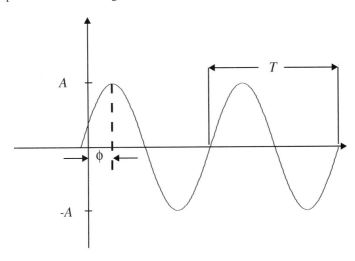

Fig. 4.3 The displacement of the simple mass-spring system as a function of time, showing the amplitude, phase, and period of oscillation.

Many other systems can be cast in a form similar to (4.16), whereupon it will be a simple matter to read off the value of ω_0 and the complete form of the specific solution.

■ **EXAMPLE 4.10** For each of the following systems, find the natural frequency.

(a) The system shown in Figure 4.4 consists of a homogeneous solid pulley in the form of a wheel of radius R and mass m that is free to rotate about its center of mass, which is rigidly attached to an overhead frame. A rough strap extends over the pulley and is attached on either side to springs of spring constant k, each of which has been stretched by an amount x. If the pulley is initially turned through a small angle θ and released, find the equation of motion.

Solution: Because the pulley rotates through an angle θ, the left hand spring is stretched by $x + R\theta$ and the right hand spring is stretched by $x - R\theta$. The moment of inertia of the wheel is $I = \frac{1}{2}mR^2$, so that the equation of motion is

$$\frac{1}{2}mR^2\ddot{\theta} = -kR(x + R\theta) + kR(x - R\theta)$$

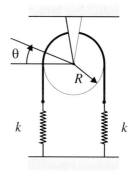

Fig. 4.4

$$\Rightarrow \quad \ddot{\theta} + \frac{4k}{m}\theta = 0.$$

From this we see that the angular frequency is

$$\omega_0 = \sqrt{\frac{4k}{m}}.$$

In terms of the initial angular displacement θ_0 and the initial angular velocity $\dot{\theta}_0$, we can write the angular displacement as a function of time:

$$\theta(t) = \theta_0 \cos\left(\sqrt{\frac{4k}{m}}t\right) + \dot{\theta}_0\sqrt{\frac{m}{4k}}\sin\left(\sqrt{\frac{4k}{m}}t\right).$$

(b) A wheel rolls along the ground as it is pulled by a horizontal spring that is initially extended x_0 beyond its equilibrium length but otherwise its right end does not move (see Figure 4.5).

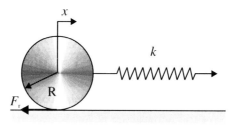

Fig. 4.5

The equation of motion is

$$m\ddot{x} = k\left(x_0 - x\right) - F_{\mathrm{r}},$$

where F_r is a frictional force that resists the motion. Taking moments about the center of mass, we have

$$\frac{1}{2}mR^2\ddot{\theta} = F_r R.$$

Using the constraint of pure rolling which says that the distance traveled must be equal to the arclength along the circular edge,

$$x = R\theta \quad \Leftrightarrow \quad \ddot{x} = R\ddot{\theta},$$

allows us to solve for F_r in the second equation, obtaining

$$F_r = \frac{1}{2}mR\ddot{\theta} = \frac{1}{2}m\ddot{x}.$$

Substituting this into the first equation, we have

$$m\ddot{x} = k\left(x_0 - x\right) - \frac{1}{2}m\ddot{x} \quad \Rightarrow \quad \frac{3}{2}m\ddot{x} + kx = kx_0.$$

It follows that the natural angular frequency is

$$f_0 = \frac{\omega_0}{2\pi} = \frac{1}{2\pi}\sqrt{\frac{2k}{3m}}.$$

(c) The LC circuit shown in Figure 4.6 has a single loop.

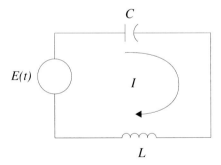

Fig. 4.6

Applying the Kirchhoff Voltage Law (KVL), we have

$$\frac{q}{C} + L\frac{dI}{dt} = E(t).$$

Replacing I by $\dot{q}$, this becomes

$$L\ddot{q} + \frac{1}{C}q = E(t),$$

from which it follows that the natural angular frequency is

$$f_0 = \frac{\omega_0}{2\pi} = \frac{1}{2\pi} \frac{1}{\sqrt{LC}}.$$

(d) A uniform circular cylinder of height h, radius R, and mass m floats in a liquid of density ρ_0 (see Figure 4.7).

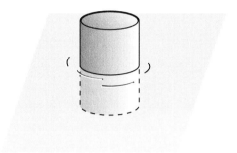

Fig. 4.7

When pushed down, it bobs back up and begins to oscillate.

Before we try to find ω_0, we need to know the equilibrium position of the cylinder so that we can measure displacements with respect to it. Suppose the cylinder is covered by the liquid to a height h_0. Archimedes' Principle tells us that the downward gravitational force of the cylinder must be counterbalanced by the buoyancy force of the liquid. Thus

$$mg = \rho_0 \left(\pi R^2 h_0 \right) g.$$

Solving for h_0 and using $m = \rho(\pi R^2 h)$ for the mass of the solid cylinder, we have

$$h_0 = \left(\frac{\rho}{\rho_0} \right) h.$$

Knowing the cylinder floats means $\rho_0 > \rho$, so that $h_0 < h$. If the cylinder is pushed downward x units (see Figure 4.8),

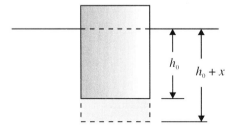

Fig. 4.8

then the equation of motion is

$$m\ddot{x} = mg - \rho_0 \left(\pi R^2 (h_0 + x) \right) g.$$

After a little algebra, this can be written as

$$\rho \left(\pi R^2 h \right) \ddot{x} + \rho_0 \left(\pi R^2 h \right) gx = 0,$$

so that the natural frequency is

$$f_0 = \frac{\omega_0}{2\pi} = \frac{1}{2\pi} \sqrt{\frac{\rho_0 g}{\rho h}}.$$

■ ■ ■

4.4.2 *Damped Systems*

A series RLC-circuit, as shown in Figure 4.9,

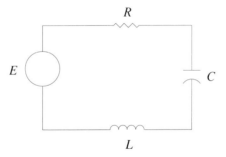

Fig. 4.9

is one of the simplest damped systems. Every damped system loses energy through some form of dissipative mechanism. In the RLC circuit, the resistor dissipates energy by converting electrical to thermal energy, which it gives off. Furthermore, the resistance of a conductive material is approximately a linear function of temperature over a fairly wide range.

KVL tells us the system equation is

$$L\dot{I} + RI + \frac{q}{C} = E(t), \tag{4.19}$$

or, written entirely in terms of the charge q on the capacitor, we have

$$L\ddot{q} + R\dot{q} + \frac{q}{C} = E(t). \tag{4.20}$$

To see that the resistor dissipates energy by way of the term $R\dot{q}$, multiply equation (4.20) by q and recognize the identities

$$\dot{q}\ddot{q} = \frac{1}{2}\frac{d}{dt}\left(\dot{q}^2\right) \quad \text{and} \quad q\dot{q} = \frac{1}{2}\frac{d}{dt}\left(q^2\right),$$

then (4.20) can be written in the form

$$\frac{1}{2}\frac{d}{dt}\left(L\dot{q}^2 + \frac{1}{C}q^2\right) + R\dot{q}^2 = \dot{q}E(t).$$

Since $\dot{q} = I$, the right hand side is $I(t)E(t)$, which is the power loss in the circuit. Because the quantity $L\dot{q}^2 + q^2/C$ can be either increasing or decreasing, the first quantity can either gain or lose energy. But the quantity $R\dot{q}^2 = RI^2$ is always nonnegative; hence a resistor can only *lose* energy.

The auxiliary equation corresponding to equation (4.20) is

$$Ls^2 + Rs + \frac{1}{C} = 0,$$

which gives rise to three possible solutions depending on the value of the discriminant $\Delta := R^2 - 4L/C$. The quantity Δ is a measure of the difference in the energy lost to damping versus that stored in the inductor and capacitor.

Case 1: $R^2 - 4L/C > 0$. Such a system is said to be **overdamped** because more energy is lost to the damping in the resistor than is stored. The roots of the auxiliary equation are

$$s_{1,2} = -\frac{R}{2L} \pm \sqrt{\left(\frac{R}{2L}\right)^2 - \frac{1}{LC}} =: -\alpha \pm \beta.$$

Since R, L, and C are positive and

$$\left(\frac{R}{2L}\right)^2 - \frac{1}{LC} < \left(\frac{R}{2L}\right)^2 \quad \Rightarrow \quad \sqrt{\left(\frac{R}{2L}\right)^2 - \frac{1}{LC}} < \frac{R}{2L},$$

both roots s_1 and s_2 are negative. The zero-input solution is

$$q(t) = k_1 e^{s_1 t} + k_2 e^{s_2 t},$$

or

$$q(t) = e^{-\alpha t}\left(c_1 \cosh \beta t + c_2 \sinh \beta t\right).$$

If the initial conditions are $q(0) = q_0$ and $q(0) = I_0$, then this becomes

$$q(t) = e^{-\alpha t}\left(q_0 \cosh \beta t + \left(\frac{I_0 + \alpha q_0}{\beta}\right)\sinh \beta t\right).$$

Although such a solution may initially increase (depending on the values of q_0 and I_0), the overall behavior is one of exponential decay back to equilibrium at least as fast as $e^{(-\alpha+\beta)t}$ (see Figure 4.10).

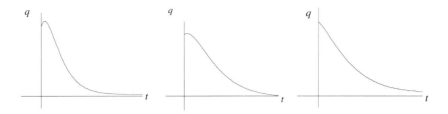

Fig. 4.10 Possible graphs of the charge on the capacitor in an overdamped series RLC circuit.

The phase portrait of the solution is a curve moving toward the origin (see Figure 4.11).

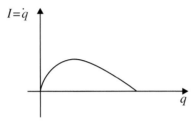

Fig. 4.11 The phase portrait of the solution is a curve moving toward the origin.

Case 2: $R^2 - 4L/C = 0$. Such a system is said to be **critically damped**, because its energy loss and energy storage are in precise balance. Because of the improbable nature of achieving exact equality, except by design, critical damping is infrequently observed. Now the auxiliary equation has multiple roots $s = -\alpha, -\alpha$, where $\alpha = \frac{R}{2L}$, and the zero-input solution that satisfies the initial conditions is

$$q(t) = q_0 e^{-\alpha t} + (\alpha q_0 + I_0) t e^{-\alpha t}.$$

This has roughly the same graphical form as the overdamped case. The solution returns to equilibrium exponentially rapidly (see Figure 4.12).

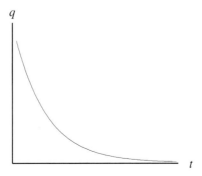

Fig. 4.12 One possible response for a critically damped system.

Case 3: $R^2 - 4L/C < 0$. Such a system is **underdamped** because more energy is stored in the inductor and capacitor than is being dissipated by the resistor. The roots of the auxiliary equation are

$$s_\pm = -\frac{R}{2L} \pm i\sqrt{\frac{1}{LC} - \left(\frac{R}{2L}\right)^2} =: -\alpha \pm i\omega_1.$$

Because the roots are complex conjugate pairs, the solution will be oscillatory. The natural frequency of the underdamped system is $f_0 = \omega_1/2\pi$. With $\omega_0 = 1/\sqrt{LC}$, we see that

$$\omega_1^2 = \frac{1}{LC} - \left(\frac{R}{2L}\right)^2 = \omega_0^2 - \alpha^2 < \omega_0^2.$$

The new "frequency" of oscillation is less than that of the corresponding undamped system.

$$q(t) = e^{-\alpha t}\left(k_1 \cos \omega_1 t + k_2 \sin \omega_1 t\right),$$

is the zero-input solution or, in terms of the initial conditions,

$$q(t) = e^{-\alpha t}\left(q_0 \cos \omega_1 t + \left(\frac{\alpha q_0 + I_0}{\omega_1}\right)\sin \omega_1 t\right). \qquad (4.21)$$

The behavior of the system is oscillatory but with exponentially decaying amplitude (see Figure 4.13).

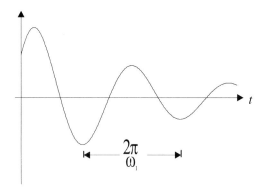

Fig. 4.13   Response for an underdamped system.

Using $T = 2\pi/\omega_1$ as the "period" of oscillation and measuring the amplitude at points T units apart, we can compute the degree of damping per period. Say

$$q_1 = q(t_1) \quad \text{and} \quad q_2 = q(t_2) = q(t_1 + T);$$

then

$$\frac{q_1}{q_2} = \frac{e^{-\alpha t_1}}{e^{-\alpha(t_1+T)}} = e^{\alpha T}.$$

Define the **logarithmic decrement**, δ, of the system to be the natural logarithm of these successive amplitudes;

$$\delta := \ln\left(\frac{q_1}{q_2}\right) = \alpha T = \frac{2\pi\alpha}{\omega_1} = \frac{2\pi\alpha}{\sqrt{\omega_0^2 - \alpha^2}}. \tag{4.22}$$

In actual practice one seldom takes successive amplitudes, but rather points n "periods" apart, i.e., q_1 and $q_{n+1} = q(t_1 + nT)$, because the relative decrease in amplitude over one unit of T may be too small to measure accurately. In that case, $q_n = e^{-n\alpha T}$, so that

$$\delta_n = \frac{1}{n} \ln\left(\frac{q_1}{q_{n+1}}\right) = \frac{2\pi\alpha}{\sqrt{\omega_0^2 - \alpha^2}}. \tag{4.23}$$

Equation (4.23) may be solved for α yielding

$$\alpha = \frac{\omega_0\delta_n}{\sqrt{4\pi^2 + 1}} = \frac{1}{n}\frac{\omega_0}{\sqrt{4\pi^2 + 1}} \ln\left(\frac{q_1}{q_{n+1}}\right). \tag{4.24}$$

In this way, both the frequency of oscillation $\omega_1/2\pi$ and the damping factor can be calculated from the system response.

The phase portrait of the underdamped system will be a curve spiraling in toward the origin (see Figure 4.14).

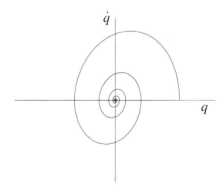

Fig. 4.14 The phase portrait for an underdamped system.

4.4.3 *Exercise Set*

1. A spring of relaxed length 50 cm stretches 10 cm when a 250 gram mass is attached. If the mass is pulled down an additional 10 cm and released, what is the subsequent motion?

2. A particle performs harmonic oscillations as $x(t) = A \sin \omega t$. If when $x = x_k$ its velocity is $v = v_k$, $k = 1 : 2$, find A and ω in terms of x_1, x_2, v_1, and v_2.

3. A mass-spring system is underdamped and passes through its equilibrium position every 8 seconds. If the spring has a force constant of 4 newtons per meter and the mass is 6 kilograms, what is the value of the damping constant in MKS units. In CGS units? What is the value of the logarithmic decrement?

4. What should the initial displacement and velocity be so that a critically damped system will attain its maximum displacement after $t = 0$?

5. Into what range should the initial displacement and velocity fall to guarantee that the mass of a mass-spring system returns to its equilibrium position?

6. Find the rate at which energy is dissipated as a function of time in an RLC circuit with $R = 50\Omega$, $L = 4$H, and $C = 10^{-6}$F if the initial charge on the capacitor is 0.1 coulomb and the initial current passing through the resistor is 1 ampere.

7. Find the natural frequency of the circuit of problem 2.27 and Figure 2.6.

8. Consider a pendulum of length L with a mass m attached to the lower end as shown in Figure 4.15(a).

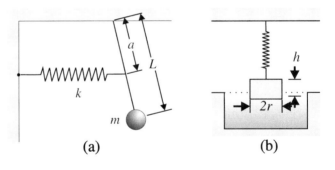

(a)   (b)

Fig. 4.15

If the spring has force constant k and is attached to the massless pendulum arm at a distance a ($< L$) from the pivot, find the frequency of small oscillations.

9. A cylinder of radius r, height h, and weight $W = mg$ is attached to an upper support by a spring of force constant k. At equilibrium the cylinder is immersed in water to a depth of half its height (see Figure 4.15(b)). The system is set into motion by pushing the cylinder into the water so that two thirds of its height is immersed and releasing it. Find its subsequent motion in terms of the density of water ρ_0. Redo the problem so that at equilibrium it is immersed a fraction f of the way and motion is initiated by pushing it down f^* of the way.

10. Find the system equation for the mass m attached to a pulley of radius R and mass M as drawn in Figure 4.16(a).

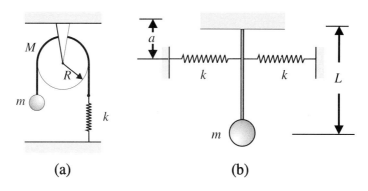

(a)   (b)

Fig. 4.16

If the spring has force constant k and the mass is pulled down a distance D and released, find its subsequent motion. Redo this problem when the pulley feels a resistive force proportional to the angular velocity of rotation.

11. Coulomb studied the viscosity of liquids by suspending a thin rectangular plate of total surface area (both sides) $2S$ in the liquid from a spring. He measured the period of oscillation to be T_1 in air and T_2 in the liquid. He postulated the force between the plate and the liquid to be $2S\mu v$, where μ is the coefficient of viscosity and v is the velocity of the plate. Assuming there is no viscosity between air and the plate, find an expression for μ if the mass of the plate is m.

12. A pendulum consists of a rigid rod of length L, pivoted at its upper end and carrying a mass m at its lower end. Two springs each with force constant k are attached to the rod at a distance a from the pivot and their other ends are rigidly attached to a wall (see Figure 4.16(b)). Set up the equation of motion of the pendulum and find its period of small oscillations. Reverse the geometry so that the pendulum is upside down, with its lower end pivoted and the mass attached to its upper end. The two springs are attached as before. Now what is the period of small oscillations?

13. A simple, old-fashioned, nonelectronic metronome consisted of a vertical pendulum pivoted at its lower end and a sliding mass m (see Figure 4.17(a)). As the mass is moved, the moment of inertia of the system changes. Suppose that the mass of the pendulum alone is M and the center of mass of the pendulum alone is a distance x_0 above the pivot. If the distance from the pivot to the adjustable mass is x and the moment of inertia of the pendulum about its pivot is I_0, find the period of small oscillations of the metronome.

14. A system consists of two homogeneous geared wheels as shown in Figure 4.17(b). Each is made of the same material. The upper wheel has radius r and is connected to a torsional spring of torque constant k, and the lower wheel has radius R and is connected to a viscous rotary damper of damping constant b. If the upper shaft experiences a torque τ_1 as drawn and the lower shaft feels a loading torque τ_2, find the equation of motion of the upper shaft. What is its undamped

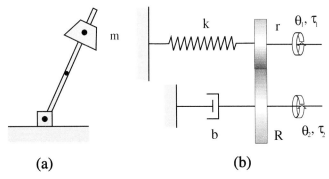

(a)   (b)

Fig. 4.17

natural frequency of oscillation? What are the conditions for overdamped, critically damped, and underdamped motion? Show that the lower shaft has the same equation of motion except for the driving torque, which is r/R times that of the upper shaft.

15. Find the natural frequency of the mass-spring(s) system shown in Figure 4.18(a).

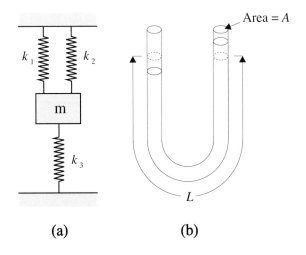

(a)   (b)

Fig. 4.18

16. The typical mercury barometer consists of a U-shaped tube as shown in Figure 4.18(b). The tube is assumed to have uniform cross-sectional area A. The total length of mercury is L. If the column is pushed down and released, it will oscillate about its equilibrium position. Show that the angular frequency of the oscillation is given by $\omega = \sqrt{2g/L}$.

17. Within the rings of a particle accelerator there is a constant magnetic field directed radially inward. Particles move in circular orbits, so that the field is always orthogonal to their direction of motion. Write Newton's Second Law with the Lorentz force and show that the particles move along the

ring with a period of $T = 2\pi m/qB$ seconds, where B is the magnetic field strength, m is the mass, and q the charge of the particle, all measured in MKS units.

18. The mass in each system in Figure 4.19 is free to oscillate with a natural angular frequency $\omega = \sqrt{k/m}$.

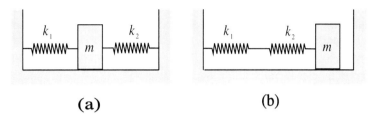

(a)   (b)

Fig. 4.19

(a) Show that $k = k_1 + k_2$ for the system of Figure 4.19(a).

(b) Show that $\frac{1}{k} = \frac{1}{k_1} + \frac{1}{k_2}$ for the system of Figure 4.19(b).

(c) What are the analogous electrical systems?

19. An oscillating system loses 10% of its energy in each cycle. After how many cycles will the system have lost at least half of its initial energy? 99% of its initial energy? In each case, by how much has the amplitude decreased?

20. The following is an experiment to determine the value of g at your location. A spring of force constant k hangs from the ceiling. A weight W_1 is attached to the lower end of the spring, causing it to stretch a distance L_1. An additional weight W_2 is attached to the same end of the spring, and the total stretch is L_2. Both weights are removed. The first weight is attached, and the period of small oscillations T_1 is measured. Then the second weight is attached, and the period T_2 is measured. We need to use two experiments so that we can account for the weight of the spring (That's a hint!). Find an expression for g.

4.5 NONHOMOGENEOUS EQUATIONS

We will discuss two methods that are of use in the solution of nonhomogeneous linear ODE's: the method of variation of parameters and the so-called method of undetermined coefficients.

4.5.1 *Variation of Parameters*

We begin with *any* nonhomogeneous linear ODE in operator form:

$$L[y(t)] = g(t). \tag{4.25}$$

The equation may have constant or variable coefficients. In order to start, we must know the complementary solution $y_c(t)$. To simplify matters we'll work with the second order equation

$$a(t)y''(t) + b(t)y'(t) + c(t)y(t) = g(t) \qquad (4.26)$$

and indicate the extension to the nth order case.

Write the complementary solution in the form

$$y_c(t) = c_1 y_1(t) + c_2 y_2(t)$$

and assume the particular solution to be of the form

$$y_p(t) = k_1(t)y_1(t) + k_2(t)y_2(t), \qquad (4.27)$$

where $k_1(t)$ and $k_2(t)$ are functions to be determined, the so-called "parameters" to be "varied."

Our goal is to convert (4.26) into a system of *two* algebraic equations in the unknowns $k_1'(t)$ and $k_2'(t)$. Once that is done, all we need do is solve for $k_1'(t)$ and $k_2'(t)$ in terms of some known functions, integrate, and insert the results back into (4.27). The ODE will give us one of the equations, and so we'll have to look elsewhere for the other equation. Start by using the Product Rule to compute $y_p'(t)$:

$$y_p' = k_1 y_1' + k_2 y_2' + \left(k_1' y_1 + k_2' y_2\right).$$

Now differentiate this again:

$$y_p'' = k_1 y_1'' + k_2 y_2'' + 2\left(k_1' y_1' + k_2' y_2'\right) + \left(k_1'' y_1 + k_2'' y_2\right).$$

Now insert the results for y_p, y_p', and y_p'' into (4.26):

$$\begin{aligned}
g(t) &= a(t)y_p''(t) + b(t)y_p'(t) + c(t)y_p \\[1em]
&= k_1 \left[a(t)y_1''(t) + b(t)y_1'(t) + c(t)y_1\right] \\
&\quad + k_2 \left[a(t)y_2''(t) + b(t)y_2'(t) + c(t)y_2\right] \\
&\quad + a(t)\left[k_1'' y_1 + k_1' y_1' + k_2'' y_2 + k_2' y_2' + k_1' y_1' + k_2' y_2'\right] \\
&\quad + b(t)\left[k_1' y_1 + k_2' y_2\right] \\[1em]
&= a(t)\left[k_1'' y_1 + k_1' y_1'\right] + a(t)\left[k_2'' y_2 + k_2' y_2'\right] + b(t)\left[k_1' y_1 + k_2' y_2\right] \\
&\quad + a(t)\left[k_1' y_1' + k_2' y_2'\right] \\[1em]
&= a(t)\left[k_1' y_1 + k_2' y_2\right]' + b(t)\left[k_1' y_1 + k_2' y_2\right] + a(t)\left[k_1' y_1' + k_2' y_2'\right],
\end{aligned}$$

where we have used the fact that y_1 and y_2 are solutions of the homogeneous equation to drop the bracketed terms multiplying k_1 and k_2. Notice that if we set

$$k_1' y_1 + k_2' y_2 = 0,$$

then two of the three terms are zero and the nonhomogeneous equation reduces to

$$a(t)\left[k_1' y_1' + k_2' y_2'\right] = g(t),$$

which together with the prior equation forms a linear system of algebraic equations in the unknowns k_1' and k_2' that can be easily solved. The two equations in the two unknowns k_1' and k_2' we wanted are now

$$
\begin{aligned}
y_1 k_1' + y_2 k_2' &= 0, \\
y_1' k_1' + y_2' k_2' &= \frac{g(t)}{a(t)}.
\end{aligned}
$$

(4.28)

This linear system can be written in matrix form as

$$
\begin{bmatrix} y_1 & y_2 \\ y_1' & y_2' \end{bmatrix} \begin{bmatrix} k_1' \\ k_2' \end{bmatrix} = \begin{bmatrix} 0 \\ g(t)/a(t) \end{bmatrix}.
$$

(4.29)

The coefficient matrix of this system is

$$
\mathbf{W} = \begin{bmatrix} y_1 & y_2 \\ y_1' & y_2' \end{bmatrix},
$$

the Wronski matrix. Knowing that $c_1 y_1 + c_2 y_2$ is the complementary solution tells us that the set $\{y_1, y_2\}$ is a basis of the solution space, and so $\mathbf{W}$ is nonsingular and there is a unique solution for $\mathbf{k}' := [k_1'; k_2']$.

Denoting the Wronskian by $W(t) = |\mathbf{W}(t)|$, we can use Cramer's Rule to solve for k_1' and k_2', getting

$$
k_1'(t) = \frac{1}{W(t)} \begin{vmatrix} 0 & y_2(t) \\ g(t)/a(t) & y_2'(t) \end{vmatrix}, \quad k_2'(t) = \frac{1}{W(t)} \begin{vmatrix} y_1(t) & 0 \\ y_1'(t) & g(t)/a(t) \end{vmatrix}.
$$

All that remains is two integrations, which may be quite difficult. In particular,

$$
k_1(t) = \int \frac{1}{W(t)} \begin{vmatrix} 0 & y_2(t) \\ g(t)/a(t) & y_2'(t) \end{vmatrix} dt,
$$

$$
k_2(t) = \int \frac{1}{W(t)} \begin{vmatrix} y_1(t) & 0 \\ y_1'(t) & g(t)/a(t) \end{vmatrix} dt.
$$

These functional forms for the k_i must then be inserted into (4.27). We need not keep the constants of integration in the form of the k_i's because we are only interested in y_p, which need not contain any arbitrary constants.

When doing a problem by variation of parameters, there is no need to go through the entire derivation each time. Rather, once $y_c(t)$ is found we can immediately write the matrix form of the system (4.29) for k_1' and k_2'. This method can be extended to an nth order linear nonhomogeneous ODE and the result is summarized in the following theorem.

THEOREM 4.7 *For the general n^{th} order nonhomogeneous linear equation*

$$
y^{(n)}(t) + p_{n-1}(t) y^{(n-1)}(t) + \cdots + p_1(t) y'(t) + p_0(t) y(t) = g(t)
$$

with complementary solution

$$y_c(x) = c_1 y_1(t) + c_2 y_2(t) + \cdots + c_n y_n(t),$$

the particular solution can be written in the form

$$y_p(t) = k_1(t) y_1(t) + \cdots + k_n(t) y_n(t),$$

where the functions $k_i'(t)$ satisfy the linear algebraic system

$$\begin{bmatrix} y_1 & y_2 & \cdots & y_n \\ y_1' & y_2' & \cdots & y_n' \\ \vdots & \vdots & \ddots & \vdots \\ y_1^{(n-1)} & y_2^{(n-1)} & \cdots & y_n^{(n-1)} \end{bmatrix} \begin{bmatrix} k_1' \\ k_2' \\ \vdots \\ k_n' \end{bmatrix} = \begin{bmatrix} 0 \\ 0 \\ \vdots \\ g(t) \end{bmatrix}. \tag{4.30}$$

□

Warning: The result given in equation (4.30) presupposes that the nonhomogeneous linear ordinary differential equation has been put into standard form, so that the coefficient of the highest derivative is *one*. If not, we need to divide $g(t)$ by that coefficient.

■ **EXAMPLE 4.11** Use the method of variation of parameters to solve each of the following equations.

(a) $y'' + y = \tan t$. First we need to find $y_c(t)$. Put $y = e^{st}$ to get

$$s^2 + 1 = 0 \quad \Rightarrow \quad s = \pm i$$

$$\Rightarrow \quad y_c(t) = c_1 \cos t + c_2 \sin t.$$

Using $y_1(t) = \cos t$, $y_2(t) = \sin t$, $a(t) = 1$, and $g(t) = \tan t$, (4.29) becomes

$$\begin{bmatrix} \cos t & \sin t \\ -\sin t & \cos t \end{bmatrix} \begin{bmatrix} k_1' \\ k_2' \end{bmatrix} = \begin{bmatrix} 0 \\ \tan t \end{bmatrix};$$

and the Wronskian is

$$W(t) = \begin{vmatrix} \cos t & \sin t \\ -\sin t & \cos t \end{vmatrix} = 1.$$

Now use Cramer's Rule to solve for k_1' and k_2'. Integrating:

$$k_1' = \frac{1}{1} \begin{vmatrix} 0 & \sin t \\ \tan t & \cos t \end{vmatrix} = -\sin t \tan t$$

$$= -\frac{\sin^2 t}{\cos t} = \frac{\cos^2 t - 1}{\cos t} = \cos t - \sec t,$$

$$k_2' = \frac{1}{1} \begin{vmatrix} \cos t & 0 \\ -\sin t & \tan t \end{vmatrix} = \cos t \tan t = \sin t.$$

Integrating,

$$k_1 = \int (\cos t - \sec t)\, dt = \sin t - \ln|\sec t + \tan t|,$$

$$k_2 = \int \sin t\, dt = -\cos t.$$

Now put this into $y_p(t) = k_1(t)\cos t + k_2(t)\sin t$ to get

$$y_p(t) = [\sin t - \ln|\sec t + \tan t|]\cos t + [-\cos t]\sin t$$

$$\Rightarrow \quad y_p(t) = -\cos t \ln|\sec t + \tan t|.$$

The general solution is the complementary plus a particular solution:

$$y(t) = y_c(t) + y_p(t) = c_1 \cos t + c_2 \sin t - \cos t \ln|\sec t + \tan t|.$$

(b) $z^2 y'' - 2zy' + 2y = 12z^3$. This is a nonhomogeneous Euler equation. To find $y_c(z)$, put $y = z^m$, getting

$$m(m-1) - 2m + 2 = m^2 - 3m + 2$$
$$= (m-1)(m-2) = 0 \Rightarrow m = 1, 2.$$

Thus $y_c(z) = c_1 z + c_2 z^2$; so assume

$$y_p(z) = k_1(z)z + k_2(z)z^2.$$

Using $y_1(z) = z$, $y_2(z) = z^2$, $a(z) = z^2$, and $g(z) = 12z^3$, (4.29) adjusted for the coefficient of the highest derivative is

$$\begin{bmatrix} z & z^2 \\ 1 & 2z \end{bmatrix}\begin{bmatrix} k_1' \\ k_2' \end{bmatrix} = \begin{bmatrix} 0 \\ 12z^3/z^2 \end{bmatrix}; \quad W(z) = \begin{vmatrix} z & z^2 \\ 1 & 2z \end{vmatrix} = z^2.$$

Again, use Cramer's Rule and integrate:

$$k_1'(z) = \frac{1}{z^2}\begin{vmatrix} 0 & z^2 \\ 12z & 2z \end{vmatrix} = -\frac{12z^3}{z^2} = -12z \quad \Rightarrow \quad k_1(z) = -6z^2,$$

$$k_2'(z) = \frac{1}{z^2}\begin{vmatrix} z & 0 \\ 1 & 12z \end{vmatrix} = \frac{12z^2}{z^2} = 12 \quad \Rightarrow \quad k_2(z) = 12z.$$

Thus

$$y_p(z) = (-6z^2)z + (12z)z^2 = -6z^3 + 12z^3 = 6z^3,$$

and the general solution is

$$y(z) = y_c(z) + y_p(z) = c_1 z + c_2 z^2 + 6z^3.$$

(c) Suppose that we are told that the complementary solution to the equation

$$yw''(y) - (1+y)w'(y) + w(y) = y^2$$

is $w_c(y) = c_1(1+y) + c_2 e^y$. With this precious bit of information we can find the particular solution by using variation of parameters. We can immediately write the matrix form of the equations for the k''s:

$$\begin{bmatrix} 1+y & e^y \\ 1 & e^y \end{bmatrix} \begin{bmatrix} k_1' \\ k_2' \end{bmatrix} = \begin{bmatrix} 0 \\ y^2/y \end{bmatrix}.$$

You should verify that the Wronskian is ye^y and

$$k_1'(y) = -1 \quad \Rightarrow \quad k_1(y) = -y$$

and

$$k_2'(y) = (1+y)e^{-y} \quad \Rightarrow \quad k_2(y) = -(2+y)e^{-y}.$$

The particular solution is then

$$w_p(y) = k_1(1+y) + k_2 e^y = -y(1+y) - (2+y)e^{-y}e^y = -2(1+y) - y^2.$$

The term $-2(1+y)$ is a multiple of $w_1(y)$ and can be incorporated into the complementary solution. Thus

$$w(y) = c_1(1+y) + c_2 e^y - y^2$$

is the general solution.   ■ ■ ■

4.5.2   *Method of Undetermined Coefficients*

The assumptions needed to make the method of undetermined coefficients work are considerably more restrictive than those for the rather general approach of variation of parameters. The restrictions are as follows:

When solving $L[y(t)] = g(t)$, L *must* be a constant coefficient linear differential operator and $g(t)$ *must* be a specific solution to some constant coefficient homogeneous linear differential equation, $M[g(t)] = 0$. The operator M is called the **annihilator** of $g(t)$.

Since L and M are both constant coefficient operators, they commute, i.e., $ML = LM$. If we know the annihilator M of $g(t)$, then we can apply M to the nonhomogeneous equation $L[y(t)] = g(t)$ to get

$$ML[y(t)] = M[g(t)] = 0.$$

This leaves us with a higher order homogeneous equation $ML[y] = 0$ to solve. Since the general solution is the complementary plus a particular solution, $y(t) = y_c(t) + y_p(t)$, if we delete the terms in $y(t)$ corresponding to $y_c(t)$, we are left with those terms corresponding to $y_p(t)$. Only the specific constants are undetermined (hence the name). Finding the coefficients is only a matter of using $L[y_p(t)] = g(t)$, equating coefficients of linearly independent functions, and solving for the coefficients. Surely, we want M to be of the lowest order possible.

■ **EXAMPLE 4.12** To solve $y'' + y' = 2e^t$, we need to find the annihilator of $2e^t$. What operator M will force $M[2e^t] = 0$?

Solution: Since we are looking for a linear time invariant operator, the presence of the constant factor of 2 will not affect us; because of linearity we have

$$M[2e^t] = 2M[e^t].$$

We get a solution of e^t to the equation $M[y] = 0$ if a root of the corresponding auxiliary equation is $s = 1$, meaning that $s - 1$ is a factor of the auxiliary polynomial. Since s replaced a differentiation, the ODE is $(D - 1)e^t = 0$ and the annihilator is $M = D - 1$. The original operator is $L = D^2 + D$, so that

$$ML = (D - 1)(D^2 + D) = D(D - 1)(D + 1).$$

Thus $y_p(t)$ must satisfy

$$D(D - 1)(D + 1)y_p(t) = 0.$$

The corresponding auxiliary equation is

$$s(s - 1)(s + 1) = 0.$$

The roots are $s = 0, -1, 1$, and the solution is

$$y_p(t) = k_1 + k_2 e^{-t} + k_3 e^t.$$

Since $y_c(t) = c_1 + c_2 e^{-t}$, we may discard all but the last term in $y_p(t)$. This leaves us with

$$y_p(t) = k_3 e^t.$$

Inserting that into $L[y_p(t)] = 2e^t$, we have

$$D(D + 1)(k_3 e^t) = 2k_3 e^t = 2e^t.$$

Hence $k_3 = 1$ and $y_p(t) = e^t$. The general solution is

$$y(t) = y_c(t) + y_p(t) = c_1 + c_2 e^{-t} + e^t.$$

■ ■ ■

There are certain properties of the annihilators that will be helpful:

- The annihilator of a linear combination of functions is the product of the annihilators of each function.

- If several functions have the same annihilator, then it is the annihilator of their sum, and we need not form a product.

An example of these properties can be seen by looking at

$$g(t) = 2 - 3t + 4t^2 - e^{3t}.$$

The annihilator for 2 is D. The annihilator of $-3t$ is D^2, that of $4t^2$ is D^3, and that of e^{3t} is $D - 3$. Thus D^3 annihilates $2 - 3t + 4t^2$ and $D^3(D - 3)$ annihilates $g(t)$. Also this annihilator is of lowest possible order.

The annihilator of $\cos \omega t$ is $D^2 + \omega^2$, because $\cos \omega t$ is a specific solution of the equation $y'' + \omega^2 y = 0$. For the same reason $D^2 + \omega^2$ is also an annihilator of $\sin \omega t$. Rather than grinding through this procedure for every problem, there is a simple one-pass algorithm that can be followed for constructing $y_\mathrm{p}(t)$.

Algorithm for Constructing $y_\mathrm{p}(t)$

1. If $g(t)$ contains a term of the form $t^m e^{\lambda t}$, where m is the largest nonnegative integer value present, then put

$$y_\mathrm{p}(t) = (k_1 + k_2 t + \cdots + k_{m+1} t^m) \, e^{\lambda t}.$$

2. If $g(t)$ contains a term of the form $t^m e^{at} \cos bt$ or $t^m e^{at} \sin bt$, where m is the largest such nonnegative integer power, then put

$$y_\mathrm{p}(t) = (A_1 + A_2 t + \cdots + A_{m+1} t^m) \, e^{at} \cos bt$$

$$+ (B_1 + B_2 t + \cdots + B_{m+1} t^m) \, e^{at} \sin bt.$$

3. If any set of terms in $y_\mathrm{p}(t)$ duplicates a similar set of terms in $y_\mathrm{c}(t)$, then multiply those terms in your choice of $y_\mathrm{p}(t)$ by t to a power one higher than the highest power of t in that $y_\mathrm{c}(t)$ term.

4. Use the Principle of Superposition to write $y_\mathrm{p}(t)$ as the sum of the choices for each term, deleting any terms that are totally contained in another set of terms.

■ **EXAMPLE 4.13** If we are given the complementary solution

$$y_c(t) = c_1 + c_2 t + c_3 et + (c_4 + c_5 t)e^{-t} \cos t + (c_6 + c_7 t)e^{-t} \sin t,$$

and

$$g(t) = 6 - 12t^2 - 6 \cosh t + 8 \sin t - 7e^{-t} \sin t,$$

then construct $y_\mathrm{p}(t)$.

Solution: Proceed term by term:

(a) 6 and $-12t^2$ are of the form $t^m e^{0t}$, and so we need only look at the term with the higher power, $-12t^2$. Here $m = 2$ so try $k_1 + k_2 t + k_3 t^2$. Two of these terms duplicate terms in $y_c(t)$ so multiply by t^2, since 2 is one higher than the power of 1 in $y_c(t)$, to get

$$y_{p_1}(t) = t^2 \left(k_1 + k_2 t + k_3 t^2\right) = k_1 t^2 + k_2 t^3 + k_3 t^4.$$

(b) By definition, $-6\cosh t = -3e^t - 3e^{-t}$, which is sum of two different types of terms. $-3e^t$ repeats one term in $y_c(t)$, and so we must multiply by t to get

$$y_{p_2}(t) = k_4 t e^t.$$

$-3e^{-t}$ does not repeat any term in $y_c(t)$, so that

$$y_{p_3}(t) = k_5 e^{-t}.$$

(c) $8\sin t$ requires *both* $\cos t$ and $\sin t$ in $y_p(t)$. Since this term does not exactly repeat any $y_c(t)$ terms (the $e^{-t}\sin t$ in $y_c(t)$ is not a repeat; it came from the root of the auxiliary equation $s = -1 \pm i$, whereas $\sin t$ came from $s = \pm i$), we have

$$y_{p_4}(t) = k_6 \cos t + k_7 \sin t.$$

(d) $-7e^{-t}\sin t$ requires something of the form

$$k_8 e^{-t}\cos t + k_9 e^{-t}\sin t.$$

But, these terms repeat terms in $y_c(t)$. Since $y_c(t)$ contains t times our suggested form, we must multiply by t^2. Thus

$$y_{p_5}(t) = t^2 \left(k_8 e^{-t}\cos t + k_9 e^{-t}\sin t\right).$$

Now we can use superposition for inputs to write the final form of $y_p(t)$:

$$\begin{aligned} y_p(t) = \; & k_1 t^2 + k_2 t^3 + k_3 t^4 + k_4 t e^t + k_5 e^{-t} \\ & + k_6 \cos t + k_7 \sin t + t^2 \left(k_8 e^{-t}\cos t + k_9 e^{-t}\sin t\right). \end{aligned}$$

■ ■ ■

Note: (a) If we do not include the necessary t^m multiplier when there are repeated terms between $y_c(t)$ and $y_p(t)$, then we will not be able to solve for the k's because what we have tried for $y_p(t)$ is part of the solution of the homogeneous equation—when inserted into the equation it will yield zero.

(b) If we inadvertently include terms with lower powers of t as multipliers in addition to those required, they too are part of $y_c(t)$ and will vanish when inserted into the equation, thus preventing the determination of their coefficients.

■ **EXAMPLE 4.14** Solve each of the following equations using the method of undetermined coefficients.

(a) $y'' + 3y' + 2y = 8e^{-3t}t$, $y(0) = 4$, $y'(0) = -11$. First find $y_c(t)$:

$$s^2 + 3s + 2 = (s+1)(s+2) = 0 \quad \Rightarrow \quad s = -1, -2$$

$$\Rightarrow \quad y_c(t) = c_1 e^{-t} + c_2 e^{-2t}.$$

Construct $y_p(t)$: e^{-3t} does not repeat a term in $y_c(t)$ so set

$$y_p(t) = ke^{-3t}.$$

Solve for k:

$$(ke^{-3t})'' + 3(ke^{-3t})' + 2(ke^{-3t}) = k(9 - 9 + 2)e^{-3t} = 8e^{-3t}$$

$$\Rightarrow \quad k = 4 \quad \Rightarrow \quad y_p(t) = 4e^{-3t}.$$

General solution:

$$y(t) = y_c(t) + y_p(t) = c_1 e^{-t} + c_2 e^{-2t} + 4e^{-3t}.$$

Initial conditions can be applied only to the general solution. Use these to solve for c_1 and c_2:

$$\begin{aligned} y(0) &= & c_1 &+ & c_2 &+ & 4 &= & 4, \\ y'(0) &= & -c_1 &- & 2c_2 &- & 12 &= & -11 \end{aligned}$$

$$\Rightarrow \quad c_1 = 1 \quad \text{and} \quad c_2 = -1.$$

Specific solution: $y(t) = e^{-t} - e^{-2t} + 4e^{-3t}$.

(b) $y'' + y = 2\cos t$. Find $y_c(t)$:

$$s^2 + 1 = 0 \quad \Rightarrow \quad s = \pm i$$

$$\Rightarrow \quad y_c(t) = c_1 \cos t + c_2 \sin t.$$

Construct $y_p(t)$: $\cos t$ repeats a term in $y_c(t)$, so set

$$y_p(t) = t(A\cos t + B\sin t).$$

Solve for A and B:

$$\begin{aligned} (At\cos t + Bt\sin t)'' &+ (At\cos t + Bt\sin t) \\ &= [A(-2\sin t - t\cos t) + B(2\cos t - t\sin t)] \\ &\quad + (At\cos t + Bt\sin t) \\ &= -2A\sin t + 2B\cos t \\ &= 2\cos t \end{aligned}$$

$$\Rightarrow \quad -2A = 0, \ 2B = 2 \quad \Rightarrow \quad A = 0, \ B = 1$$

$$\Rightarrow \quad y_{\mathrm{p}}(t) = t \sin t.$$

General solution: $y(t) = y_c(t) + y_{\mathrm{p}}(t) = c_1 \cos t + c_2 \sin t + t \sin t.$

(c) If the complementary solution of the ODE is

$$y_c(t) = (c_1 + c_2 t)e^{-3t} + (c_3 + c_4 t)e^{-t} \cosh 2t$$
$$+(c_5 + c_6 t)e^{-t} \sinh 2t$$

and the forcing function is

$$g(t) = 3t \cos \pi t - 2t^2 e^{-3t} + 7t^3,$$

then we could construct the form of the particular solution term by term. Since there is no $\cos \pi t$ or $\sin \pi t$ in $y_c(t)$, that part of the particular solution will be

$$(A_1 + A_2 t) \cos \pi t + (B_1 + B_2 t) \sin \pi t.$$

Before we go on to the next term, it would be a good idea to notice that $e^{-t} \cosh 2t$ and $e^{-t} \sinh 2t$ are linear combinations of $e^{-t}e^{2t} = e^t$ and $e^{-t}e^{-2t} = e^{-3t}$. The $t^2 e^{-3t}$ term duplicates two terms in $y_c(t)$, so that part of $y_{\mathrm{p}}(t)$ will be

$$t^2(k_1 + k_2 t + k_3 t^2)e^{-3t}.$$

The last term, $7t^3$, does not duplicate any part of $y_c(t)$, so that part of $y_{\mathrm{p}}(t)$ is

$$k_4 + k_5 t + k_6 t^2 + k_7 t^3.$$

Taken together, the choice for $y_{\mathrm{p}}(t)$ is

$$(A_1 + A_2 t) \cos \pi t + (B_1 + B_2 t) \sin \pi t$$
$$+t^2(k_1 + k_2 t + k_3 t^2)e^{-3t} + (k_4 + k_5 t + k_6 t^2 + k_7 t^3).$$

■ ■ ■

In summary: The method of variation of parameters will work for any linear nonhomogeneous ODE for which you can find (or are told) the complementary solution. It requires as many integrations as the order of the equation and finding closed form answers for these may limit this method. On the other hand, the method of undetermined coefficients works only on constant coefficient linear nonhomogeneous ODE's that are driven by forcing functions that are specific solutions of some other constant coefficient homogeneous linear ODE. When both methods apply, you have a choice between (a) doing algebra and integrating (a procedure that can be fairly easily implemented on any computer algebra system) or (b) differentiating and then doing some algebra.

4.5.3   *Exercise Set*

Solve each of the following nonhomogeneous equations

1. $y'' - 4y' + 3y = 2\cos t + 4\sin t + 6$

2. $y'' - 3y' + 2y = (1 + e^{-t})^{-1}$

3. $v'' + 2v' + v = \dfrac{e^{-t}}{t^2}$

4. $2y'' + 3y' - 2y = 6e^t + 4$

5. $y'' + y = \sec^2 t \csc t$

6. $y'' + 4y' + 9y = 84\cosh t + 18t - 1$

7. $(D^3 + D^2)w(t) = 4$

8. $(z^3 D^3 + 2z^2 D^2 - 10zD - 8)x(z) = 16$

9. $w'' + 2w' + w = 7 + 75\sin 2t$

10. $\ddot{x} + 4\dot{x} + 5x = 10, \quad x(0) = 0, \ \dot{x}(0) = 0$

11. $(y^3 D^3 + 4y^2 D^2 + 5yD - 5)x(y) = \ln y$

12. $\ddot{r} - 2\dot{r} + r = e^{2t}(e^t + 1)^{-2}$

13. $\ddot{x} + 3x = -18t, \quad x(0) = 0, \ \dot{x}(0) = 5$

14. $2y'' + 3y' - 2y = 6e^t + 5 - 6t$

15. $g'' + g = \tan t \sec t$

16. $y'' + 4y' + 4y = \ln t$

17. $g'' - 3g' - 4g = \cos t$

18. $r''(\theta) + r(\theta) = \sin\theta\cos\theta$

19. $z^2 w'' + 5zw' + 4w = \ln z$

20. $y'' + 4y = 3e^{2z} - \cos z$

21. $y'' + y' - 2y = 6e^z - 3z + 4\cos z$

22. $w'' + w = \cot z \csc z$

23. $u'' + 2u' + 2u + \sin z + 2\cos z = 0$

24. $(D^3 + 3D^2 + 3D + 1)x(z) = ze^{-z}$

25. $(z^3 D^3 + 4z^2 D^2 - 8zD + 8)w(z) = 16 + \dfrac{38}{z}$

26. $z^2 y'' + 5zy' + 5y = 10 + \dfrac{4}{z^2}$

27. $r''(\theta) + r'(\theta) - 2r(\theta) = 2\theta - 4\cos 2\theta$

28. $y^2 x'' + x' - x = 9y\ln y$

29. $z^2 y'' + zy' - 4y = z$

30. $(z^3 D^3 + 5z^2 D^2 + 4zD)w(z) = \ln z$

31. $x^3 y''' + 6x^2 y'' - 12y = 12x - 24\ln x - 20$

32. $(x^3 D^3 + 7x^2 D^2 + 11xD + 4)w(x) = 30x - \dfrac{4}{x}$

33. $u^3 w'''(u) + 5u^2 w''(u) - 6uw'(u) - 18w(u) = 18u - 36\ln u - 72$

34. $z^2 y'' + zy' - y = (1 + z^2)^{-1}$

35. $z^2 y'' - 6y = \ln z, \quad y(1) = \frac{1}{6}, \ y'(1) = -\frac{1}{6}$

36. If $(x^2 + 1)y'' - 2xy' + 2y = x^2 + 1$, show that the complementary solution is $y_c(x) = c_1 x + c_2(x^2 - 1)$, and use this to find the general solution.

37. Show that $y_c(x) = c_1 + c_2 \ln[(1 + x)/(1 - x)]$, and use this to find the general solution of
$$(1 - x^2)y'' - 2xy' = 2x.$$

38. Show that the problem $y'' + y = 6 \cos t$, $y(0) = 0 = y(2\pi)$, has infinitely many solutions. How do you reconcile this with the Existence and Uniqueness Theorem of Section 4.2?

39. Find the constant coefficient ODE whose general solution is

$$y(t) = (c_1 + c_2 t)e^t + c_3 \cos t + c_4 \sin t + t^2 - 3.$$

40. Write the lowest order ODE whose general solution is

$$y(z) = z(c_1 + c_2 \ln z) - z^2.$$

4.6   FORCED OSCILLATIONS OF SYSTEMS

4.6.1   Undamped Systems

Let's look at an LC circuit driven by an AC voltage source. The system equation is

$$L\ddot{q} + \frac{1}{C}q = E_0 \cos(\omega t - \alpha),$$

and the general solution is

$$q(t) = k_1 \cos \omega_0 t + k_2 \sin \omega_0 t + \frac{E_0}{L\left(\omega_0^2 - \omega^2\right)} \cos\left(\omega t - \psi\right), \tag{4.31}$$

where $\omega_0^2 = \frac{1}{LC} \neq \omega^2$. The zero-state solution (i.e., $q(0) = 0$ and $\dot{q}(0) = 0$) is

$$q(t) = \frac{E_0}{L\left(\omega_0^2 - \omega^2\right)} \left[\cos\left(\omega t - \psi\right) - \cos\left(\omega_0 t - \psi\right)\right].$$

A standard trigonometric identity allows us to write this in the form

$$q(t) = \frac{2E_0}{L\left(\omega_0^2 - \omega^2\right)} \sin\left(\frac{\omega_0 - \omega}{2}t\right) \sin\left(\frac{\omega_0 - \omega}{2}t - 2\psi\right). \tag{4.32}$$

If the forcing frequency is near the natural frequency, say $\omega + 2\epsilon = \omega_0$ where ϵ is small, then the first sine term oscillates at the "slow" frequency $\epsilon/2\pi$ and period $2\pi/\epsilon$, which would be large. The second sine will oscillate with period $2\pi/2(\omega_0 - \epsilon) \approx \pi/\omega_0 \ll \pi/\epsilon$. The slower sine wave modulates the amplitude of the faster one as shown in Figure 4.20.

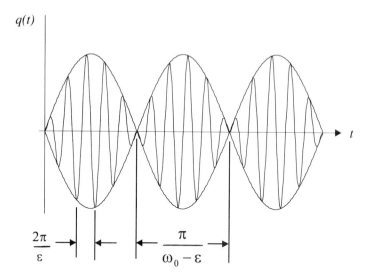

Fig. 4.20 A slow sinusoid modulating a faster sinusoid.

This gives rise to the phenomenon of **beats**: as two pure tones of nearly equal frequency are sounded, one can hear a tone of lower frequency equal to their difference.

When the input frequency equals the natural frequency, the form of the solution in (4.31) is no longer valid. Instead we have

$$q(t) = k_1 \cos \omega_0 t + k_2 \sin \omega_0 t + \frac{E_0}{2L\omega_0} t \sin \left(\omega_0 t - \alpha\right).$$

The graph of this zero-state solution has increasing amplitude (see Figure 4.21).

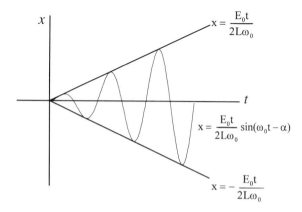

Fig. 4.21 The zero-state solution of a forced undamped system when the forcing frequency equals the natural frequency of the system.

This is an example of the phenomenon of **resonance**, wherein there is constructive interference between the forcing function and the natural oscillation. After reasonably short times the solution usually violates the assumptions of the original model and a different system equation is required. A simple way to avoid this form of resonance is to introduce some damping into the system.

4.6.2 *Damped Systems*

If the RLC-circuit drawn in Figure 4.22

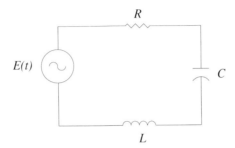

Fig. 4.22 An RLC circuit with an AC source.

(An RLC circuit with an AC source.) is driven by an AC source, the system equation is

$$L\ddot{q} + R\dot{q} + \frac{1}{C}q = E_0 \cos \omega t.$$

No matter whether the system is overdamped, critically damped, or underdamped, just as long as there is some nonzero damping, there will be no repeat between the complementary solution and the assumed particular solution. Thus the zero-state response can be shown to be

$$q_\mathrm{p}(t) = \frac{E_0}{L} \frac{\left(\omega_0^2 - \omega^2\right) \cos \omega t + 2\alpha\omega \sin \omega t}{\left(\omega_0^2 - \omega^2\right)^2 + 4\alpha^2\omega^2}, \tag{4.33}$$

where $\omega_0 = \frac{1}{\sqrt{LC}}$ and $\alpha := \frac{R}{2L}$. This is valid whenever $\alpha \neq 0$. We need only concern ourselves with $q_\mathrm{p}(t)$ because so long as the values of the system parameters R, L, and C are nonnegative, the zero-input solution will decay exponentially. A decaying zero-input solution is often referred to as a **transient solution**, and its corresponding zero-state solution is a **steady state solution**.

The steady state solution in (4.33) can be rewritten in terms of its amplitude and phase shift as

$$q_\mathrm{p}(t) = \frac{E_0}{L\sqrt{\left(\omega_0^2 - \omega^2\right)^2 + 4\alpha^2\omega^2}} \cos(\omega t - \psi),$$

where

$$\tan \psi = \frac{\alpha\omega}{\omega_0^2 - \omega^2}.$$

In "tunable" circuits, the capacitance C can be varied. One usually wants to maximize the amplitude of the output, $q_\mathrm{p}(t)$. This will occur at the value of ω where $\left(\omega_0^2 - \omega^2\right)^2 + 4\alpha^2\omega^2$ is minimum. This is called the **resonance value**, ω_R, of ω. It is a simple calculus problem to show that

$$\omega_\mathrm{R}^2 = \omega_0^2 - 2\alpha^2 = \omega_1^2 - \alpha^2.$$

The geometric relation between ω_0^2, ω_1^2, and ω_R^2 is worth noting (see Figure 4.23).

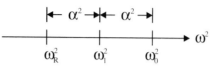

Fig. 4.23

It is possible that $\omega_\mathrm{R}^2 < 0$ so that resonance will not occur. The amplitude and phase of $q_\mathrm{p}(t)$ as a function of the input frequency ω are shown in Figures 4.24 and 4.25.

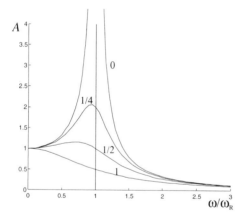

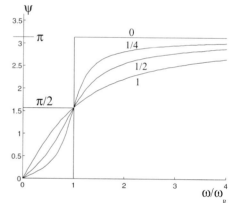

Fig. 4.24 The amplitude of the steady state solution for various values of the input frequency.

Fig. 4.25 The phase of the steady state solution for various values of the input frequency.

An exactly analogous procedure can be followed for the mass-spring-dashpot system (see Figure 4.26)

Fig. 4.26 A mass-spring-dashpot system.

with governing equation

$$m\ddot{x} + b\dot{x} + kx = F(t). \tag{4.34}$$

The natural frequency is

$$f_0 = \frac{\omega_0}{2\pi} = \frac{1}{2\pi}\sqrt{\frac{k}{m}},$$

while the frequency of oscillation is

$$f_1 = \frac{\omega_1}{2\pi} = \frac{1}{2\pi}\sqrt{\omega_0^2 - \left(\frac{b}{2m}\right)^2},$$

and the damping constant is

$$\alpha = \frac{b}{2m}.$$

Resonance occurs at

$$\omega_R = \sqrt{\omega_1^2 - \alpha^2} = \sqrt{\frac{k}{m} - 2\left(\frac{b}{2m}\right)^2}.$$

Generally speaking, we can establish an analogy between series electrical circuits and series mechanical systems, called the **force-voltage analogy**. Included in the following table is a section for rotary motion.

Force-Voltage Analogy		
Linear Mechanical	**Rotary Mechanical**	**Electrical**
Force F	Torque τ	Voltage E
Displacement x	Angular displacement θ	Charge q
Velocity $v = \dot{x}$	Angular velocity $\omega = \dot{\theta}$	Current $I = \dot{q}$
Mass m	Moment of inertia I	Inductance L
Linear damping b	Angular damping b	Resistance R
Spring constant k	Torsion spring constant k	(Capacitance)$^{-1}$ $1/C$

If instead, we begin with the parallel RLC circuit in Figure 4.27,

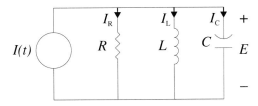

Fig. 4.27 A parallel RLC circuit.

then we must apply KCL to get

$$\frac{E}{R} + \frac{1}{L}\int I\,dt + C\dot{E} = I(t). \tag{4.35}$$

Using the relation between the magnetic flux linkage, Φ, and the voltage $\dot{\Phi} = E$, equation (4.35) is

$$C\ddot{\Phi} + \frac{1}{R}\dot{\Phi} + \frac{1}{L}\Phi = I(t). \tag{4.36}$$

Comparing (4.36) and (4.34), we are led to the **force-current analogy**:

Force-Current Analogy		
Linear Mechanical	**Rotary Mechanical**	**Electrical**
Force F	Torque τ	Current I
Displacement x	Angular displacement θ	Magnetic flux linkage Φ
Velocity $v = \dot{x}$	Angular velocity $\omega = \dot{\theta}$	Voltage E
Mass m	Moment of inertia I	Capacitance C
Linear damping b	Angular damping b	(Resistance)$^{-1}$ $1/R$
Spring constant k	Torsion spring constant k	(Inductance)$^{-1}$ $1/L$

Both analogies are valid only within those values of the dependent variables for which the dynamic equations (4.34), (4.35), and (4.36) adequately describe the state of the system.

4.6.3   Exercise Set

1. A particle of charge q is injected into an electric field with field vector E. If the initial velocity is v_0 parallel to the field, find the subsequent motion.

2. An RLC circuit is driven by a battery whose voltage is given by $E(t) = E_0 e^{-kt}$, where k is very small. If the system is underdamped, find the voltage across the resistor as a function of time. If you take the limit as $k \to 0$, do you get the same result you would have gotten by using a battery with a constant voltage?

3. A solid cylindrical yo-yo of mass m and radius r has its cord attached to the ceiling. The axis of the cylinder is initially horizontal, and the yo-yo is released at $t = 0$. Show that when gravity is the only external force acting and the string remains vertical, the equation of motion is $\frac{1}{2}m\ddot{s} = mg$, where s is the length of string that has unwound. If the total length of string was L, how long will it take for the yo-yo to unwind? [Be careful to pay attention to the initial configuration of the string.]

4. An undamped torsional pendulum consists of a cylindrical solid of moment of inertia I hanging from a long metal bar. The cylinder is free to rotate and the bar remains vertical. The bar exerts a restoring force of $k\theta$, where θ is the angle of deflection of the pendulum from its equilibrium position. If the upper end of the bar experiences an angular oscillation with frequency Ω, discuss the ensuing motion as a function of time.

5. A mass m is initially at rest in a frictionless groove in a horizontal plane. It is connected to two springs, also in the groove, each with force constant k. If the mass is driven by an offset cam so that it feels a force $F(t) = 3 \cos \Omega t - 4 \sin \Omega t$, find its motion. Also, construct both the force-voltage and force-current analogous electrical circuits.

6. The point of suspension of a pendulum of length L performs horizontal harmonic oscillations about a fixed point. If $x(t)$ is the horizontal distance of the pivot from the fixed point, then $x(t) = A \sin \Omega t$. If the pendulum is initially at rest in the vertical position, find its subsequent motion under the assumption of small oscillations.

7. A bob of mass m is attached to the lower end of a spring of natural length L and force constant k. The upper end of the spring is moved vertically as $A \sin \Omega t$. If the bob also feels a resistive force of $m\gamma$ times its speed, show that the vertical displacement of the mass, $z(t)$, satisfies $m\ddot{z} + m\gamma\dot{z} + \frac{k}{L}x = A\Omega (\Omega \sin \Omega t - \gamma \cos \Omega t)$. Find the amplitude and phase angle of the motion. What happens in the special case $\gamma = \Omega$ and $k = mL\Omega^2$?

4.7 BOUNDARY VALUE GREEN'S FUNCTIONS

In this section we will discuss a method for solving boundary value problems with nonhomogeneous ODE's and homogeneous boundary conditions using a method that will incorporate the boundary conditions into the calculation as we go as opposed to applying them onto the end of the problem as constraint equations that determine the arbitrary constants. Boundary value problems are different from initial value problems insofar as we have no existence and uniqueness theorem for them.

We'll restrict our attention to what are called **self-adjoint** nonhomogeneous second order equations, which are those of the form

$$L[u(x)] := \frac{d}{dx}\left(p(x)\frac{du(x)}{dx}\right) + q(x)u(x) = f(x), \tag{4.37}$$

where $p(x) > 0$, $p'(x)$, and $q(x)$ are continuous on some closed interval $[a, b]$. The general form of the homogeneous boundary conditions will be assumed to be

$$\begin{aligned} B_{\mathrm{L}}[u(x)] &:= \ell_1 u(a) + \ell_2 u'(a) = 0, \\ B_{\mathrm{R}}[u(x)] &:= r_3 u(b) + r_4 u'(b) = 0. \end{aligned} \tag{4.38}$$

L and ℓ are used for the left endpoint and R and r for the right endpoint.

DEFINITION 4.3 *The* **boundary value Green's function** *of a linear differential operator L is the function $G(x, \xi)$ satisfying*

$$L[G(x, \xi)] = \delta(x - \xi) \tag{4.39}$$

together with the boundary conditions in (4.38). $G(x, \xi)$ is the response to the impulsive source at the arbitrary point $x = \xi$.

In order to find a form for the solution of the general nonhomogeneous equation $L[w(x)] = f(x)$, proceed by multiplying (4.39) by $f(\xi)$ and integrating over ξ from a to b:

$$L\left[\int_a^b G(x,\xi)f(\xi)\,d\xi\right] = \int_a^b f(\xi)\delta(x-\xi)\,d\xi = f(x).$$

Therefore,

$$u(x) = \int_a^b G(x,\xi)f(\xi)\,d\xi \tag{4.40}$$

is the solution of the boundary value problem of (4.39) and (4.38). It should be clear that the right hand side of equation (4.40) satisfies the boundary conditions on x because $G(x,\xi)$ does. Be especially careful to notice that (4.40) is the form of the solution to a given boundary value problem only when $f(x)$ is taken from the *self-adjoint* form of the ODE.

We can find the form of the Green's function if we write the equation (4.39) in full and integrate from $\xi-$ to $\xi+$:

$$\int_{\xi-}^{\xi+}\left[\frac{d}{dx}\left(p(x)\frac{dG(x,\xi)}{dx}\right) + q(x)G(x,\xi)\right]dx = \int_{\xi-}^{\xi+}\delta(x-\xi)\,dx = 1.$$

If we assume that $G(x,\xi)$ is a continuous function then the second term in the left hand integral will be zero. Integrating the first term leaves us with

$$\left[p(x)\frac{dG(x,\xi)}{dx}\right]_{\xi-}^{\xi+} = 1.$$

Having assumed that $p(x)$ is continuous means that $p(\xi-) = p(\xi+)$, so that we can write this as

$$\left[\frac{dG(x,\xi)}{dx}\right]_{\xi-}^{\xi+} = \frac{1}{p(\xi)}. \tag{4.41}$$

This last equation specifies the jump in the discontinuity of the first derivative of $G(x,\xi)$. Thus $G(x,\xi)$ is continuous at ξ but its derivative has a jump discontinuity there.

Suppose we can solve the homogeneous equation $L[u(x)] = 0$ and find two solutions $u_L(x)$ and $u_R(x)$ satisfying the left and right hand boundary conditions, respectively, i.e.

$$L[u_L(x)] = 0, \; B_L[u_L(x)] = 0 \quad \text{and} \quad L[u_R(x)] = 0, \; B_R[u_R(x)] = 0.$$

Since $G(x,\xi)$ must satisfy the boundary conditions, we can write

$$G(x,\xi) = \begin{cases} k_1(\xi)u_L(x), & a \le x \le \xi \le b, \\ k_2(\xi)u_R(x), & a \le \xi \le x \le b. \end{cases}$$

Because $G(x,\xi)$ must be continuous at $x = \xi$, the limits from the left and the right must be equal:

$$k_2(\xi)u_R(\xi) - k_1(\xi)u_L(\xi) = 0.$$

Applying the jump condition on $G'(x, \xi)$, (4.41) yields

$$k_2(\xi)u_{\mathrm{R}}'(\xi) - k_1(\xi)u_{\mathrm{L}}'(\xi) = \frac{1}{p(\xi)}.$$

Solving these last two algebraic equations for $k_1(\xi)$ and $k_2(\xi)$, we find

$$k_1(\xi) = \frac{u_{\mathrm{R}}(\xi)}{p(\xi)W(\xi)}, \quad k_2(\xi) = \frac{u_{\mathrm{L}}(\xi)}{p(\xi)W(\xi)},$$

where

$$W(\xi) := \begin{vmatrix} u_{\mathrm{L}}(\xi) & u_{\mathrm{R}}(\xi) \\ u_{\mathrm{L}}'(\xi) & u_{\mathrm{R}}'(\xi) \end{vmatrix} = u_{\mathrm{L}}(\xi)u_{\mathrm{R}}'(\xi) - u_{\mathrm{L}}'(\xi)u_{\mathrm{R}}(\xi)$$

is the Wronskian of $\{u_{\mathrm{L}}(\xi), u_{\mathrm{R}}(\xi)\}$. Thus

$$G(x, \xi) = \frac{1}{p(\xi)W(\xi)} \begin{cases} u_{\mathrm{L}}(x)u_{\mathrm{R}}(\xi), & a \le x \le \xi \le b, \\ u_{\mathrm{L}}(\xi)u_{\mathrm{R}}(x), & a \le \xi \le x \le b. \end{cases} \qquad (4.42)$$

If we use the notation $x_< := \min(x, \xi)$ and $x_> := \max(x, \xi)$, then

$$G(x, \xi) = \frac{u_{\mathrm{L}}(x_<)u_{\mathrm{R}}(x_>)}{p(\xi)W(\xi)}. \qquad (4.43)$$

As a further simplification, it can be shown (see the problems) that for the special self-adjoint form of equation (4.37), the quantity $p(\xi)W(\xi)$ is constant.

■ **EXAMPLE 4.15** Find the Green's function for the simple boundary value problem

$$u''(x) = 0, \quad u(0) = 0 = u'(L).$$

Solution: The general solution of the ODE is

$$u(x) = c_1 + c_2 x.$$

This solution will be to build the Green's function that satisfies

$$G''(x, \xi) = \delta(x - \xi), \quad G(0, \xi) = 0 = G'(L, \xi).$$

For the left boundary condition we have

$$u_{\mathrm{L}}(0) = c_1 = 0 \quad \Rightarrow \quad u_{\mathrm{L}}(x) = x,$$

as a possible solution. (Since we have only one boundary condition for each of the solutions, we will not necessarily get a unique answer.) Similarly, the right boundary condition yields,

$$u'(L) = c_2 = 0 \quad \Rightarrow \quad u_{\mathrm{R}}(x) = 1.$$

In this case we have $p(x) = 1$, $q(x) = 0$, and

$$W(\xi) = \begin{vmatrix} \xi & 1 \\ 1 & 0 \end{vmatrix} = -1.$$

Thus $G(x, \xi) = -x_< = -\min(x, \xi)$.

If we want to solve the nonhomogeneous boundary value problem

$$u''(x) = 2, \quad u(0) = 0 = u'(L),$$

we could use equation (4.40) to write

$$u(x) = \int_0^L G(x, \xi) f(\xi)\, d\xi = -\int_0^x \xi \cdot 2\, d\xi - \int_x^L x \cdot 2\, d\xi = x^2 - 2Lx.$$

You should verify that this is the correct solution. ▪▪▪

▪ **EXAMPLE 4.16** It can be shown that if $u(x)$ is the vertical displacement of a string of length L vibrating with known frequency $f = \omega/2\pi$ whose ends are fixed, then the corresponding boundary value problem is

$$u''(x) + \omega^2 u(x) = 0, \quad u(0) = 0 = u(L).$$

Find the boundary value Green's function for this problem.

Solution: The general solution of the ODE is

$$u(x) = c_1 \cos \omega x + c_2 \sin \omega x.$$

Since $u_L(0) = 0$ we could choose

$$u_L(x) = \sin \omega x.$$

Similarly, $u_R(L) = c_1 \cos \omega L + c_2 \sin \omega L = 0$ yields

$$u_R(x) = \sin \omega L \cos \omega x - \cos \omega L \sin \omega x = \sin \omega (L - x)$$

as a possibility. Since $p(x) = 1$ and

$$W(\xi) = \begin{vmatrix} \sin \omega \xi & \sin \omega(L - \xi) \\ \omega \cos \omega \xi & -\omega \cos \omega(L - \xi) \end{vmatrix} = -\omega \sin \omega L,$$

when $\omega L \neq n\pi$, we have

$$G(x, \xi) = -\frac{\sin \omega x_< \sin \omega(L - x_>)}{\omega \sin \omega L}$$

$$= \frac{1}{\omega \sin \omega L} \begin{cases} \sin \omega x \sin \omega(L - \xi), & 0 \leq x \leq \xi, \\ \sin \omega \xi \sin \omega(L - x), & \xi \leq x \leq L. \end{cases}$$

▪▪▪

Looking back at (4.39), we might expect that

$$G(x, \xi) = G(\xi, x).$$

This is a form of the **Reciprocity Principle** that says that the response at x due to an impulsive source at ξ is the same as the response at ξ due to an impulsive source at x. Further discussion of this is left to the references.

4.7.1 Exercise Set

For each of the following boundary value problems, find its Green's function.

1. $u''(x) = 0,\quad u(0) = 0 = u(L)$

2. $u''(x) = 0,\quad u(-1) = 0 = u(1)$

3. $u''(x) + \omega^2 u(x) = 0,\quad u(0) = 0 = u(L)$

4. $u''(x) + \omega^2 u(x) = 0,\quad u'(0) = 0 = u(L)$

5. $u''(x) + \omega^2 u(x) = 0,\quad u'(a) = 0 = u'(b)$

6. $u''(x) - \mu^2 u(x) = 0,\quad u(0) = 0 = u(1)$

7. $u''(x) + \omega^2 u(x) = 0,\quad u'(a) - u(a) = 0 = u(b)$

8. $xu''(x) + u'(x) = 0,\quad u(0) < \infty,\ u(1) = 0$

9. $u''(x) + \omega^2 u(x) = 0,\quad u(0) = u'(0),\ u(1) = u'(1)$

10. $\left(x^{-2}u'(x)\right)' + 2x^{-4}u(x) = 0,\quad u(-1) = 0 = u(1)$

11. $(1 - x^2)u''(x) - 2xu'(x) = 0,\quad u'(0) = 0 = u(b),\ b < 1$

12. Show that for an equation of the form $(p(x)u'(x))' + q(x)u(x) = 0$, $p(x)W(x)$ is constant when $W(x)$ is the Wronskian of the solution set $\{u_{\mathrm{L}}(x), u_{\mathrm{R}}(x)\}$.

13. Show that the second order ODE $a_2(x)u''(x) + a_1(x)u'(x) + a_0(x)u(x) = 0$ can be put into self-adjoint form by multiplying by the "integrating factor"

$$\mu(x) = \frac{1}{a_2(x)} \exp\left\{\int \frac{a_1(x)}{a_2(x)}\, dx\right\},$$

and find the form of $p(x)$ and $q(x)$ in terms of $a_2(x)$, $a_1(x)$, and $a_0(x)$.

4.7.2 Notes and References

The study of differential equations is a field unto itself. Many of the original categories of equations we have studied were first pursued because they served as models for physical systems of interest at the time. This chapter was only an introduction to the subject. More will be said in the remaining chapters.

- Birkhoff & Rota, **Ordinary Differential Equations, 4th ed.:** This is a very popular classic upper level text that is fairly theoretical.

- Borelli & Coleman, **Differential Equations: A Modeling Approach**: A very broad coverage of the subject with many unusual applications.

- Boyce & diPrima, **Elementary Differential Equations and Boundary Value Problems, 4th ed.:** One of the more popular texts in this area, with an extensive discussion of qualitative solutions of nonlinear equations.

- Celia & Gray, **Numerical Methods for Differential Equations**: A complete integrated discussion of methods for solving both ordinary and partial differential equations numerically.

4.8 SUPPLEMENTARY AND COMPLEMENTARY PROBLEMS

1. If $y(t) = c_1 y_1(t) + c_2 y_2(t) + \cdots + c_n y_n(t)$ is the general solution of an nth order homogeneous linear ODE, give an argument that the equation is given by

$$\det \begin{bmatrix} y_1(x) & y_2(x) & \ldots & y_n(x) & y(x) \\ y_1'(x) & y_2'(x) & \ldots & y_n'(x) & y'(x) \\ \vdots & \vdots & & \vdots & \vdots \\ y_1^{(n)}(x) & y_2^{(n)}(x) & \ldots & y_n^{(n)}(x) & y^{(n)}(x) \end{bmatrix} = 0.$$

Use the result of the previous problem to find the equations whose solutions are given below:

2. $y(t) = c_1 + c_2 t$

3. $y(t) = c_1 e^t + c_2 e^{2t}$

4. $y(t) = c_1 t + c_2 e^t$

5. $y(t) = c_1 \cos t + c_2 \sin 2t$

6. $y(t) = c_1 t + c_2 t^2 + c_3 e^t$

7. $y(t) = c_1 t + c_2 \cos \omega t + c_3 \sin \omega t$

8. $y(t) = c_1 + c_2 t + c_3 t^2 + c_4 t^4 + c_5 t^5$

9. $y(t) = c_1 \cos at + c_2 \sin bt + c_3 \cosh at + c_4 \sinh bt$. [This is *much* worse than it looks!!]

Construct the lowest order homogeneous constant coefficient linear ODE and the associated initial conditions for which a specific solution is:

10. $u(t) = (4 + 3t^2) \cosh 2t + (2t + 5t^2) \sinh 2t$

11. $u(t) = \pi e^{-\pi t} + e^{-\pi t}(\cos \pi t - 2 \sin \pi t)$

12. $u(t) = \cosh 2t \sin 2t$

13. $u(t) = \cosh 2t \cos 2t - \sinh 2t \sin 2t$

Construct the lowest order homogeneous Euler equation and the associated initial conditions for which a specific solution is

14. $w(x) = x + 2x^2 - 3x^3$

15. $w(x) = (3x - 6)/\sqrt{x}$

16. $w(x) = (2\cos(\ln x) + 1)/x^2$

17. $w(x) = \cosh(3 \ln x) - x \sinh(3 \ln x)$

18. Suppose the auxiliary polynomial for a constant coefficient equation is $\phi(s)$. Show that if $\phi(s)$ has a multiple zero of order m at $s = a$, then $\phi^{(k)}(a) = 0$ for $k = 0 : m - 1$. Also show that $(D_s)^k e^{st}$ is a solution of the original equation $L[y(t)] = \phi(D)y(t) = 0$. Thus infer the general form of that part of the solution associated with the multiple root, which was derived another way in the text.

19. Show that $(D - s_0)^k [v(t)e^{s_0 t}] = e^{s_0 t} D^k v(t)$, $k = 1 : \infty$.

20. Suppose that it were possible to drill a cylindrical hole through the center of our assumed homogeneous spherical planet. Further suppose that a mass m could move through this hole without encountering any resistive forces. If initially dropped into the hole it would oscillate. Find the frequency of oscillation.

21. Two cars of masses m_1 and m_2 are connected by a spring of force constant k. They are free to roll along the horizontal axis (see Figure 4.28(a)).

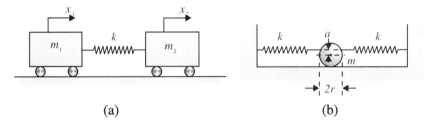

(a)   (b)

Fig. 4.28

Set up the equations of motion for each car. Let X be the distance between them and use these equations to derive an equation for X. What is the natural frequency of oscillation?

22. A long uniform cylinder of radius r and mass m is free to roll without sliding on a horizontal plane. Midway along the length of the cylinder are attached two springs, each with force constant k. They are attached to the periphery of the cylinder at a height a above the central axis and the other ends are rigidly fastened to the two opposing walls (see Figure 4.28(b)). Set up the equations of motion and find the period of small oscillations.

23. A pendulum consists of a rigid massless rod with a mass m_2 attached to its end and an additional mass m_1 attached a distance a higher along the rod (see Figure 4.29(a)).

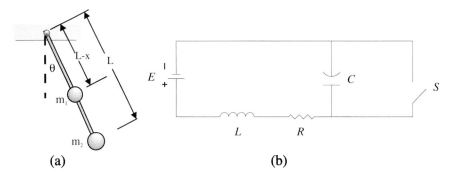

(a)   (b)

Fig. 4.29

How far from the lower mass should the pivot of the pendulum be in order to minimize the period of small oscillations?

24. In the circuit shown in Figure 4.29(b), when the switch is open, the capacitor is charged to a potential E and discharged at $t = 0$. Find the charge on the capacitor as a function of time.

25. Using the circuit from the previous problem, suppose that a steady current is flowing and at $t = 0$ the switch is opened. Find the current as a function of time.

26. For the circuit shown in Figure 4.30,

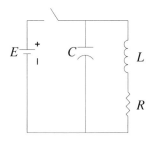

Fig. 4.30

the switch at S has been closed for a time T. At $t = 0$ the switch at S is opened. Find the current as a function of time.

27. Find the constant coefficient second order initial value problem whose unique solution is $w(t) = (1 + t)\cos t - \sin t$. What if we replace second order with fourth order?

28. The technique of **reduction of order** consists of finding the general solution of a linear nonhomogeneous ODE given one solution to the homogeneous equation. If $y_0(t)$ is part of the complementary

solution, then assume the form of the general solution is $y(t) = y_0(t)u(t)$. Insert this into the equation $a(t)y''(t) + b(t)y'(t) + c(t)y(t) = g(t)$, and derive the ODE that $u(t)$ must satisfy. This should be a second order linear equation *without* a $u(t)$ term. Let $v(t) = u'(t)$, and show that this converts the u-equation to a *first order* linear equation in $v(t)$. Thus we can solve for $v(t)$, integrate the result to find $u(t)$, and multiply by $y_0(t)$ to find the general solution. Write an expression for the general solution.

29. Show that $y(t) = \exp(t^2/2)\cos t$ is part of the complementary solution of $y''(t) - 2ty'(t) + t^2 y(t) = t^2$, and use reduction of order to find the general solution.

30. Show that $y(z) = e^{az}\sec z$ is part of the complementary solution of $y''(z) - 2y'(z)\tan z - (1 + a^2)y(z) = \sin z$, and use reduction of order to find the general solution.

5

LAPLACE TRANSFORMS

5.1 PREVIEW

Many mathematical techniques employ a transformation whereby one problem is changed into another that is more tractable. This chapter will introduce the concept of a linear integral transform. A derivation will show that transforms based on an exponential kernel will simplify the solution of time invariant ODE initial value problems.

The Laplace transform will be defined and most of its simple properties derived and then used for transforming functions. Special emphasis will be placed on functions that are piecewise smooth and can be expressed in terms of step functions. Such functions are discussed in Appendix D.

A theorem will be stated that assures us the transformation is invertible, and its inverse will be studied. The concept of a convolution product of functions will be introduced and the Convolution Theorem for Laplace transforms proven. Using the properties of the transform and its inverse, ODE's will be solved. Special attention will be given to nonhomogeneous equations with discontinuous forcing functions. The solution of boundary value problems will be approached through the study of the deflection of an elastic beam. Finally, Laplace transform techniques will be applied to finding boundary value Green's functions.

5.2 INTRODUCTION TO TRANSFORMS

A fundamental approach to problem solving is the use of transformations, which consists of translating one problem into another that is more amenable to solution, solving the transformed problem, and then translating the solution back into the original formulation.

This approach is utilized in many areas of mathematics:

- Involved geometric arguments can often be simplified by utilizing the coordinate representations for points and curves and applying algebraic techniques to derive principles of geometry.

- The indefinite integral of a rational function is computed by using the method of substitution to reduce the integrand to a more easily integrated function.

- The solution of a time invariant homogeneous ODE is obtained by using the trial solution $x(t) = e^{st}$, thus transforming the problem into an algebraic equation, known as the auxiliary equation, finding the roots, and using these to generate the solution $y(t)$.

- The solution of an Euler ODE is obtained by setting $y(x) = x^m$ to obtain the polynomial equation for the values of m that generate the solution.

- A function of a diagonalizable matrix can be computed by first evaluating the function of its diagonal form and then using the inverse similarity transform (more of this in Section 6.6 and Appendix G).

- The solution $y(x)$ of a variable coefficient ODE as a power series about an ordinary point can be obtained after transforming the ODE into a recurrence equation for the coefficients a_k of the power series, that generates $y(x)$ (See Chapter 8).

This chapter will deal with a special case of the general class of integral transforms of the form

$$\mathcal{T}\{f; \lambda\} := \int_a^b f(t) K(t, \lambda) \, dt, \tag{5.1}$$

where $K(t, \lambda)$ is called the **transform kernel**. $\mathcal{T}\{f; \lambda\}$ is the function of λ obtained by transforming the function $f(t)$.

One of the fundamental properties of most transforms, which is automatically satisfied by those defined by equation (5.1), is that of linearity:

$$\mathcal{T}\{cf + g; \lambda\} = c\mathcal{T}\{f; \lambda\} + \mathcal{T}\{g; \lambda\}, \quad \text{for constant } c.$$

This holds because the integral of a sum is the sum of the integrals and the integral of a constant multiple of a function is the constant multiple of the integral (where questions of convergence are avoided). The linearity of the integral transform will make it a powerful tool for the analysis of linear problems.

We must also have the integral transform defined on a sufficiently rich class of functions that all possible input and output functions in which we are interested can be transformed. Furthermore, if we write

$$\mathcal{T}\{f; \lambda\} =: F(\lambda),$$

then we should like the operator $\mathcal{T}$ to be invertible on our class of functions so that an inverse can be computed to return the original function:

$$f(t) = \mathcal{T}^{-1}\{F(\lambda)\}.$$

Since $\mathcal{T}$ is linear, if it is invertible, its inverse will be linear; i.e.,

$$\mathcal{T}^{-1}\{cF(\lambda) + G(\lambda)\} = c\mathcal{T}^{-1}\{F(\lambda)\} + \mathcal{T}^{-1}\{G(\lambda)\}.$$

We assume the inverse transform has the form

$$\mathcal{T}^{-1}\{F; t\} = f(t) := \int_c^d F(\lambda) H(t, \lambda) \, d\lambda. \tag{5.2}$$

This forces a restriction on the kernels $K(t, \lambda)$ and $H(t, \lambda)$ because, by definition of the inverse, we must have

$$\mathcal{T}^{-1}\{\mathcal{T}\{f(t)\}\} = f(t),$$

which has the integral form

$$f(t) = \int_c^d \int_a^b f(\tau) K(\tau, \lambda) H(t, \lambda) \, d\tau \, d\lambda. \tag{5.3}$$

Equation (5.3) is usually called the **Fourier Integral Theorem** for the transform in question.

There are many possible integral transforms, only one of which will be covered in this chapter. To most effectively utilize integral transforms let us summarize the conditions that should be met:

- A large class of functions should be *easily* transformed.

- A large class of *useful* problems should be simplified upon transformation.

- Solutions of transformed problems should be transformable back into the original class of functions.

Since our goal is the simplification of ODE's, we would also like the transform of a derivative to take a simple form, preferably in terms of the transform of the original function. Integration by parts will play a fundamental role, as can be seen from

$$\mathcal{T}\{f'(t)\} = \int_a^b f'(t) K(t, \lambda) \, dt = [f(t) K(t, \lambda)]_a^b - \int_a^b f(t) \frac{\partial K(t, \lambda)}{\partial t} \, dt.$$

This implies

$$\mathcal{T}\{f'(t)\} = f(b) K(b, \lambda) - f(a) K(a, \lambda) - \int_a^b f(t) \frac{\partial K(t, \lambda)}{\partial t} \, dt.$$

If we are to maintain the form of our transform, we must have

$$\frac{\partial K(t, \lambda)}{\partial t} = g(\lambda) K(t, \Psi(\lambda))$$

for some functions $g(\lambda)$ and $\Psi(\lambda)$. When this is true and $F(\lambda) = \mathcal{T}\{f(t)\}$, then

$$\mathcal{T}\{f'(t)\} = f(b) K(b, \lambda) - f(a) K(a, \lambda) - g(\lambda) F(\Psi(\lambda)).$$

Thus the transform of a derivative will be expressible in terms of the transform of the function. The simplest useful case occurs when $g(\lambda) = c\lambda$, for some constant c, and $\Psi(\lambda) = \lambda$. Then

$$\mathcal{T}\{f'(t)\} = f(b) K(b, \lambda) - f(a) K(a, \lambda) - cF(\lambda).$$

This occurs only if

$$\frac{\partial K(t, \lambda)}{\partial t} = c\lambda K(t, \lambda),$$

from which it follows by a partial integration that

$$K(t, \lambda) = m(\lambda)e^{c\lambda t}. \tag{5.4}$$

Equation (5.4) is valid for both the Laplace and Fourier transforms, wherein c takes the values of -1 and $-i$, respectively. The remainder of this chapter will deal with Laplace transforms and their use in solving ODE's.

5.3   LAPLACE TRANSFORMS

Just as we transformed an Euler differential equation to a constant coefficient linear ODE by changing variables, so too can we change a time invariant constant coefficient ODE to an *algebraic* equation by taking the Laplace transform of it. This will greatly extend the class of linear differential equations we can readily solve.

5.3.1   Basic Properties

Every function can be written as the sum of two functions, one that is zero for $t < \tau$ and the other that is zero for $t \geq \tau$. A function that is zero on $(-\infty, \tau)$ is said to be **causal**, whereas a function zero on $[\tau, \infty)$ is **anticausal**. We usually take $\tau = 0$. The Laplace transform will be applied only to causal functions. If we define the **unit step function** at $t = \tau$ by

$$u(t - \tau) = \begin{cases} 0, & t - \tau < 0, \\ 1, & t - \tau \geq 0, \end{cases}$$

then functions written as $f(t)$ should be understood to be $f(t)u(t)$, thus forcing them to be causal.

DEFINITION 5.1   *The (**one-sided**) **Laplace transform** of the function $f(t)$ is the linear integral transformation*

$$\mathcal{L}\{f(t)\} := F(s) = \int_0^\infty f(t)e^{-st}\,dt. \tag{5.5}$$

It can be shown that if $f(t)$ is **piecewise smooth** on $[0, \infty)$, i.e. continuously differentiable everywhere except at finitely many points in any finite interval at each of which the function can have at worst a finite jump discontinuity, and **exponentially bounded**, meaning

$$|f(t)| \leq Ae^{mt}$$

where A and m are positive real constants, then the transformed function $F(s)$ will be analytic for $\mathrm{Re}(s) > m$. Furthermore, the Laplace transform operator will be invertible on this class of functions.

Polynomials $p(t)$, exponentials $e^{\alpha t}$, sinusoids, and their sums and products are all exponentially bounded and continuously differentiable, hence transformable. On the other hand, $\exp(at^2)$ is not exponentially bounded for $\operatorname{Re}(a) > 0$. So, not all smooth functions are transformable.

If t has units of time, then s has units of reciprocal time and can be thought of as a frequency. Thus the Laplace transform maps a time domain function $f(t)$ into the frequency domain function $F(s)$. Because the integral of the difference of two functions that differ at no more than countably many points is zero, the Laplace transform of a function and any function differing from it by a finite amount at countably many points will be the same. The most important thing to notice at this stage is that the Laplace transform is a linear transformation carrying with it all the useful baggage that entails. In particular:

(**LinTr1**) $\mathcal{L}\{f(t) + g(t)\} = \mathcal{L}\{f(t)\} + \mathcal{L}\{g(t)\}$;

(**LinTr2**) $\mathcal{L}\{cf(t)\} = c\mathcal{L}\{f(t)\}$, for any complex constant c.

Several Laplace transforms can be obtained from the evaluation of a single simple integral.

■ **EXAMPLE 5.1** Start with the integral defining $\mathcal{L}\{e^{\alpha t}\}$:

$$\mathcal{L}\{e^{\alpha t}\} = \int_0^\infty e^{\alpha t} e^{-st}\, dt = \int_0^\infty e^{-(s-\alpha)t}\, dt = \frac{1}{s - \alpha}. \tag{5.6}$$

Notice that the resulting frequency domain function is analytic for $s > \alpha$, as expected. Putting $\alpha = i\omega$, we have

$$\mathcal{L}\{e^{i\omega t}\} = \mathcal{L}\{\cos \omega t + i \sin \omega t\} = \frac{1}{s - i\omega}\frac{s + i\omega}{s + i\omega} = \frac{s + i\omega}{s^2 + \omega^2}.$$

Equating real and imaginary parts yields two new transforms:

$$\mathcal{L}\{\cos \omega t\} = \frac{s}{s^2 + \omega^2} \quad \text{and} \quad \mathcal{L}\{\sin \omega t\} = \frac{\omega}{s^2 + \omega^2}. \tag{5.7}$$

Setting $\omega = i\mu$, and using $\cos(i\mu) = \cosh \mu$ and $\sin(i\mu) = i \sinh \mu$, we have

$$\mathcal{L}\{\cosh \mu t\} = \frac{s}{s^2 - \mu^2} \quad \text{and} \quad \mathcal{L}\{\sinh \mu t\} = \frac{\mu}{s^2 - \mu^2}. \tag{5.8}$$

■ ■ ■

The importance of this example lies in the power of linearity of the Laplace transform, the only property besides the one elementary integration used to derive these results. As our concern is the solution of constant coefficient ODE's, we need to know the transform of polynomials (associated with repeated roots of the auxiliary equation) or, more simply (because of linearity), the transform of t^n. Writing the integral for the transform and substituting $u = st$ leaves us with an integral depending only on n divided by s^{n+1}. This will force us to define a new function in terms of that integral as follows:

$$\mathcal{L}\{t^n\} = \int_0^\infty t^n e^{-st}\, dt = \int_0^\infty \left(\frac{u}{s}\right)^n e^{-u}\frac{du}{s} =: \frac{\Gamma(n + 1)}{s^{n+1}}. \tag{5.9}$$

$\Gamma(n+1)$ is the **gamma function**. Thus we may write

$$\Gamma(n+1) = \int_0^\infty u^n e^{-u} du. \tag{5.10}$$

When n is a nonnegative integer, it can be shown that $\Gamma(n+1) = n!$. The **fundamental recurrence relation** for the gamma function, which can be derived by an integration by parts of (5.10) (see Section 9.2) is

$$\Gamma(n+1) = n\Gamma(n). \tag{5.11}$$

You can see the validity of equation (5.11) in terms of the factorial for $n = 5$ by looking at

$$\begin{aligned}
\Gamma(5) &= 4 \cdot \Gamma(4) = 4 \cdot 3 \cdot \Gamma(3) \\
&= 4 \cdot 3 \cdot 2 \cdot \Gamma(2) = 4 \cdot 3 \cdot 2 \cdot 1 \cdot \Gamma(1) \\
&= 4 \cdot 3 \cdot 2 \cdot 1 = 24.
\end{aligned}$$

Additionally, one simple value of $\Gamma(n)$ for nonintegral n is known:

$$\Gamma\left(\frac{1}{2}\right) = \sqrt{\pi}. \tag{5.12}$$

The values $\Gamma\left(\frac{3}{2}\right) = \left(\frac{1}{2}\right)\Gamma\left(\frac{1}{2}\right) = \frac{\sqrt{\pi}}{2}, \Gamma\left(\frac{5}{2}\right) = \left(\frac{3}{2}\right)\left(\frac{1}{2}\right)\Gamma\left(\frac{1}{2}\right) = \frac{3\sqrt{\pi}}{4}$, etc. can be obtained by applying the fundamental recurrence relation.

■ **EXAMPLE 5.2** Let's apply the few simple properties of the Laplace transform that we have derived to the evaluation of the transforms of several functions.

(a) $\mathcal{L}\left\{2t^3 - 6t^2 + 8t + 7\right\} = 2\dfrac{3!}{s^4} - 6\dfrac{2!}{s^3} + 8\dfrac{1!}{s^2} + 7\dfrac{0!}{s^1} = \dfrac{12}{s^4} - \dfrac{12}{s^3} + \dfrac{8}{s^2} + \dfrac{7}{s}.$

(b) Using $\Gamma(1/2) = \sqrt{\pi}$ and the fundamental recurrence relation for the gamma function, $\Gamma(n+1) = n\Gamma(n)$, we have

$$\mathcal{L}\left\{\sqrt{t}\right\} = \frac{\Gamma\left(\frac{3}{2}\right)}{s^{3/2}} = \frac{1}{2}\Gamma\left(\frac{1}{2}\right)\frac{1}{s^{3/2}} = \frac{\sqrt{\pi}}{2s^{3/2}}.$$

To get other half-integral powers, proceed similarly:

$$\mathcal{L}\{t^{3/2}\} = \frac{\Gamma(5/2)}{s^{5/2}} = \left(\frac{3}{2}\right)\left(\frac{1}{2}\right)\frac{\Gamma(1/2)}{s^{5/2}} = \frac{3\sqrt{\pi}}{4s^{5/2}}.$$

(c) We can find the transform of a piecewise smooth function by direct integration. Suppose the piecewise defined function of interest is

$$g(t) = \begin{cases} 1, & 0 \le t < 2, \\ 2, & 2 \le t < 3, \\ 0, & \text{elsewhere.} \end{cases}$$

Then its transform can be written as the sum of integrals

$$\mathcal{L}\{g(t)\} = \int_0^\infty g(t)e^{-st}\,dt$$

$$= \int_0^2 g(t)e^{-st}\,dt + \int_2^3 g(t)e^{-st}\,dt + \int_3^\infty g(t)e^{-st}\,dt.$$

Since $g(t) = 0$ when $t \geq 3$, the last integral is zero. Substituting the values of $g(t)$ in the intervals over which the first two integrals range, we have

$$\mathcal{L}\{g(t)\} = \int_0^2 1 \cdot e^{-st}\,dt + \int_2^3 2 \cdot e^{-st}\,dt$$

$$= \frac{1 - e^{-2s}}{s} + 2\frac{e^{-2s} - e^{-3s}}{s}.$$

■ ■ ■

The following fundamental theorem lists several useful properties of the Laplace transform.

THEOREM 5.1   *If $F(s) := \mathcal{L}\{f(t)\}$ is analytic for $\mathrm{Re}(s) > m$, then*

(LapTr1) First Shifting Theorem: $\mathcal{L}\{e^{\alpha t}f(t)\} = F(s - \alpha)$ *for* $\mathrm{Re}(s - \alpha) > m$.

(LapTr2) $\mathcal{L}\{f'(t)\} = sF(s) - f(0)$,

$$\mathcal{L}\{f'(t)\} = s^2 F(s) - sf(0) - f'(0),$$
$$\mathcal{L}\{f^{(n)}(t)\} = s^n F(s) - s^{n-1}f(0) - \cdots - sf^{(n-2)}(0) - f^{(n-1)}(0).$$

(LapTr3) $\mathcal{L}\left\{\displaystyle\int_0^t f(\tau)\,d\tau\right\} = \dfrac{F(s)}{s}$.

(LapTr4) $\mathcal{L}\{tf(t)\} = -\dfrac{d}{ds}F(s), \quad \mathcal{L}\{t^n f(t)\} = \left(-\dfrac{d}{ds}\right)^n F(s)$.

(LapTr5) $\mathcal{L}\left\{\dfrac{f(t)}{t}\right\} = \displaystyle\int_s^\infty F(\sigma)\,d\sigma$,

$$\mathcal{L}\left\{\frac{f(t)}{t^n}\right\} = \int_s^\infty \int_{\sigma_n}^\infty \cdots \int_{\sigma_2}^\infty F(\sigma_1)\,d\sigma_1\,d\sigma_2 \cdots d\sigma_n.$$

Proof To prove (LapTr1), just write out the left hand side:

$$\mathcal{L}\left\{e^{\alpha t} f(t)\right\} = \int_0^\infty e^{\alpha t} f(t) e^{-st}\, dt = \int_0^\infty f(t) e^{-(s-\alpha)t}\, dt = F(s-\alpha).$$

(LapTr2): Using integration by parts,

$$\mathcal{L}\{f'(t)\} = \left[f(t)e^{-st}\right]_0^\infty - \int_0^\infty f(t)(-s)e^{-st}\, dt = -f(0) + sF(s)$$

The value of $\lim_{t\to\infty} f(t)e^{-st} = 0$ because $|f(t)| \le Ae^{mt}$ and $\mathrm{Re}(s) > m$.

To prove (LapTr3) define $G(t) := \int_0^t f(\tau)\, d\tau$. Then $G(0) = 0$ and $G'(t) = f(t)$. Using (LapTr2), $\mathcal{L}\{G'(t)\} = s\mathcal{L}\{G(t)\} - 0 \Rightarrow \mathcal{L}\{G'(t)\} = F(s) = s\mathcal{L}\{G(t)\}$, and the result follows by dividing by s.

(LapTr4): Here we will need to recognize the effect of a derivative with respect to s:

$$\mathcal{L}\{tf(t)\} = \int_0^\infty tf(t)e^{-st}\, dt = -\int_0^\infty f(t)\frac{\partial}{\partial s}\left(e^{-st}\right) dt = -\frac{d}{ds}F(s).$$

(LapTr5): Using (LapTr4),

$$\mathcal{L}\{f(t)\} = \mathcal{L}\left\{t\frac{f(t)}{t}\right\} = -\frac{d}{ds}\mathcal{L}\left\{\frac{f(t)}{t}\right\} = F(s)$$

$$\Rightarrow \quad \mathcal{L}\left\{\frac{f(t)}{t}\right\} = \int_s^\infty F(\sigma)\, d\sigma \quad \text{because } \lim_{s\to\infty} F(s) = 0.$$

□

Quite often, several methods are available for the evaluation of the transform of a given function. Such is the power of the method.

■ **EXAMPLE 5.3** Again, let's evaluate the transform of several functions, but now we'll use the results of the last theorem.

(a) $\mathcal{L}\{t^n e^{\alpha t}\} = \mathcal{L}\{t^n\}|_{s\leftarrow s+\alpha} = \left.\dfrac{\Gamma(n+1)}{s^{n+1}}\right|_{s\leftarrow s-\alpha} = \dfrac{\Gamma(n+1)}{(s-\alpha)^{n+1}}$ using the First

Shifting Theorem. We have used the standard notation for the **assignment operator**,; in particular, $s \leftarrow s-\alpha$ means s is assigned, or replaced, by the value $s-\alpha$. Alternatively, if n is a positive integer, then

$$\mathcal{L}\{t^n e^{\alpha t}\} = \left(-\frac{d}{ds}\right)^n \mathcal{L}\{e^{\alpha t}\} = \left(-\frac{d}{ds}\right)^n \frac{1}{s-\alpha}$$

$$= \frac{n!}{(s-\alpha)^{n+1}} = \frac{\Gamma(n+1)}{(s-\alpha)^{n+1}}.$$

Even if n were not a positive integer, this result would still be valid if we defined the **fractional derivative** of $(s - \alpha)^{-1}$ by

$$\left(\frac{d}{ds}\right)^n (s - \alpha)^{-1} := (-1)^n \Gamma(n + 1)(s - \alpha)^{-n-1}.$$

(b) Similar results can be gotten with cosines or sines:

$$\mathcal{L}\{e^{\alpha t} \cos \omega t\} = \mathcal{L}\{\cos \omega t\}|_{s \leftarrow s - \alpha}$$

$$= \left.\frac{s}{s^2 + \omega^2}\right|_{s \leftarrow s - \alpha} = \frac{s - \alpha}{(s - \alpha)^2 + \omega^2},$$

by virtue of the First Shifting Theorem.

(c) In a similar manner we can use the last part of the theorem.

$$\mathcal{L}\left\{\frac{\sin \omega t}{t}\right\} = \int_s^\infty \mathcal{L}\{\sin \omega t\}|_{s \leftarrow \sigma} \, d\sigma$$

$$= \int_s^\infty \frac{\omega}{\sigma^2 + \omega^2} \, d\sigma$$

$$= \left.\text{Atan}\left(\frac{\sigma}{\omega}\right)\right|_s^\infty$$

$$= \frac{\pi}{2} - \text{Atan}\left(\frac{s}{\omega}\right)$$

$$= \text{Acot}\left(\frac{s}{\omega}\right).$$

■ ■ ■

Whenever you use the First Shifting Theorem in finding $\mathcal{L}\{\cdot\}$ it is usually best to apply it first.

5.3.2 *Transforms of Periodic Functions*

As a last application of the methods of finding transforms, we'll look at the transform of a periodic function, which we assume to be of exponential order. If $f(t)$ is **periodic** with **period** T, then

$$f(t) = f(t + nT),$$

for any integer n and T is the smallest positive number for which this is true. We'll use this property in the integral defining the transform to break it up into infinitely many integrals, each over one period. Then we'll apply the definition of periodicity and use the geometric series to obtain the final result.

Aside: No causal function can be periodic. Periodic functions must be defined over the entire real line save a *countable* set of points; e.g., $\tan t$ is not defined at $\pm\pi/2$, $\pm 3\pi/2, \pm 5\pi/2,\ldots$. So when talking about periodic functions in the context of Laplace transforms, we mean those functions for which the defining equation is true when the arguments of both sides, t and $t + nT$, are both nonnegative.

Start with the defining integral written as a sum of integrals over each period:

$$\mathcal{L}\{f(t)\} = \int_0^\infty f(t)e^{-st}dt = \sum_{n=0}^\infty \int_{nT}^{(n+1)T} f(t)e^{-st}\,dt.$$

Translate the last integral by making the substitution $t = \tau + nT \Rightarrow dt = d\tau$:

$$\mathcal{L}\{f(t)\} = \sum_{n=0}^\infty \int_0^T f(\tau + nT)e^{-s(\tau+nT)}\,d\tau = \sum_{n=0}^\infty e^{-snT} \int_0^T f(\tau)e^{-s\tau}\,d\tau.$$

The interchange of the order of summation and integration is allowed because both the integral and the series converge uniformly. Since the integral does not depend on n, we can sum the geometric series to the result in the following theorem.

THEOREM 5.2 *If $f(t)$ is periodic of period T, then its Laplace transform is given by*

$$\mathcal{L}\{f(t)\} = \frac{1}{1 - e^{-sT}} \int_0^T f(\tau)e^{-s\tau}\,d\tau. \tag{5.13}$$

$\square$

■ **EXAMPLE 5.4** The classic **sawtooth function** of period T is defined by

$$\mathrm{Saw}(t; T) := \begin{cases} t, & 0 \le t < T, \\ t - 2T, & T \le t < 2T, \\ t - 3T, & 2T \le t < 3T, \\ \text{etc.} \end{cases}$$

Its graph is sketched in Figure 5.1.

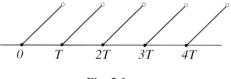

$$0 \qquad T \qquad 2T \qquad 3T \qquad 4T$$

Fig. 5.1

To find its transform all we need do is evaluate the integral in equation (5.13):

$$\int_0^T \tau e^{-s\tau}\,d\tau = \frac{1}{s^2} - \frac{e^{-sT}}{s}\left(T + \frac{1}{s}\right).$$

Dividing by $1 - e^{-sT}$ we have

$$\mathcal{L}\{\text{Saw}(t;T)\} = \frac{1}{s^2} - \frac{Te^{-sT}}{s\left(1 - e^{-sT}\right)}.$$

■ ■ ■

5.3.3   *Step Functions and the Second Shifting Theorem*

We have already applied the Laplace transform to a function with a jump discontinuity. It required breaking the integral into pieces each of which had to be integrated separately. An alternative approach is available that uses step functions (see Appendix D). Begin with the simplest type of piecewise defined function:

$$f(t) = \begin{cases} g(t), & t < a, \\ h(t), & a \le t. \end{cases}$$

If $g(a) \neq h(a)$ then $f(t)$ will have a jump discontinuity at $t = a$. Using the unit step function

$$u(t - a) := \begin{cases} 0, & t < a, \\ 1, & a \le t, \end{cases}$$

the function $f(t)$ can be written in the form

$$f(t) = g(t) + [h(t) - g(t)]u(t - a).$$

Think of $f(t)$ as consisting of $g(t)$ until the time $t = a$, when we *turn on* the difference $[h(t) - g(t)]$ that is to be added to what we already have. The net result is $g(t) + [h(t) - g(t)] = h(t)$. If $g(t)$ and $h(t)$ are both continuous, then the added piece $[h(t) - g(t)]$ has value zero at $t = a$ and $f(t)$ is at least piecewise continuous.

■ **EXAMPLE 5.5** Write each of the following functions in terms of unit steps.

(a) The **rectangular window** is defined by (see Figure 5.2)

$$w(t; a, b) := \begin{cases} 1, & a \le t < b, \\ 0, & \text{elsewhere.} \end{cases}$$

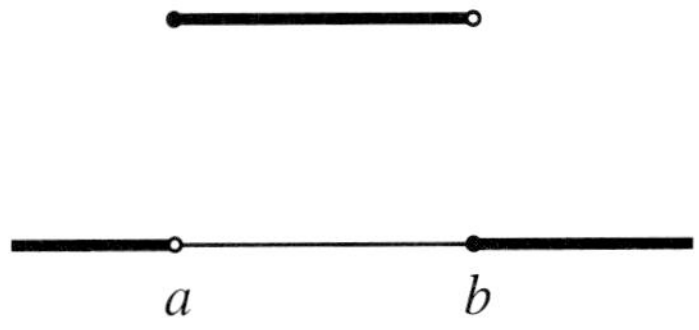

$$a \qquad\qquad b$$

Fig. 5.2

The step $u(t - a)$ will *turn the function on* at $t = a$ and $u(t - b)$ can be made to *turn the function off* at $t = b$. Thus

$$w(t; a, b) = 1 \cdot u(t - a) + (0 - 1) \cdot u(t - b) = u(t - a) - u(t - b).$$

We can use this window function and the idea of *turning a signal on and off* as a prototype for all other piecewise smooth functions. A window from a to ∞ is one that is opened but never closed, so that

$$w(t; a, \infty) = u(t - a)$$

(b) The sawtooth function was defined by

$$\text{Saw}(t; T) := t \quad \text{for } 0 \le t < T,$$

and $\text{Saw}(t; T) = \text{Saw}(t + T; T)$ is periodic with period T. Since the Laplace transform only looks at the interval $[0, \infty)$, we can neglect the noncausal part of $\text{Saw}(t; T)$. What we need is appropriate $45°$ lines times rectangular windows of width T, like

$$tw(t; 0, T) = t[u(t - 0) - u(t - T)],$$

which represents the first *tooth* of $\text{Saw}(t; T)$. The tooth that begins at $t = nT$ is

$$(t - nT)w(t; nT, (n + 1)T) = (t - nT)[u(t - nT) - u(t - (n + 1)T)],$$

turned on at $t = nT$ and *turned off* at $t = (n+1)T$. Taken together we have $\text{Saw}(t; T)$ as a sum of lines times rectangular windows:

$$\text{Saw}(t; T) = \sum_{n=0}^{\infty} (t - nT)w(t; nT, (n + 1)T).$$

After some manipulation, this can be rewritten in the form

$$\text{Saw}(t; T) = tu(t) - \sum_{n=1}^{\infty} Tu(t - nT).$$

This formula affords us an alternative interpretation of the sawtooth see Figure 5.3).

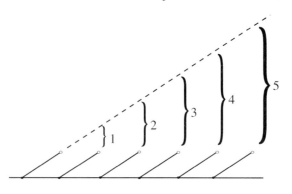

Fig. 5.3

The first term is t for $t \geq 0$, and every T units we subtract an additional T to move it back down toward the t-axis.

(c) If we define a piecewise function

$$f(t) = \begin{cases} t, & 0 \leq t < 1, \\ t^2, & 1 \leq t < 2, \\ 4, & 2 \leq t, \end{cases}$$

then we can write $f(t)$ as a combination of three rectangular windows, the first from 0 to 1, the second from 1 to 2, and the third starts at $t = 2$:

$$f(t) = tw(t; 0, 1) + t^2 w(t; 1, 2) + 4w(t; 2, \infty)$$

In terms of unit steps, this takes the form

$$f(t) = t[u(t - 0) - u(t - 1)] + t^2[u(t - 1) - u(t - 2)]$$

$$+4[u(t - 2)].$$

The last term involves only one step function because it is never *turned off*; the function is equal to 4 for all $t \geq 2$. If we combine similar terms, we have

$$f(t) = tu(t) + (t^2 - t)u(t - 1) + (4 - t^2)u(t - 2).$$

Notice that the coefficient of each step function is zero when the step *turns on*, indicating $f(t)$ is in fact continuous on $[0, \infty)$.

(d) If $g(t)$ is as shown in Figure 5.4,

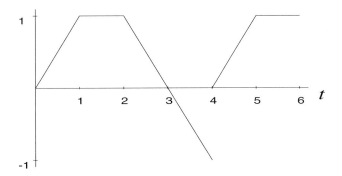

Fig. 5.4

let's write it in terms of step functions. We'll need five rectangular windows.

$$tw(t; 0, 1) = t[u(t - 0) - u(t - 1)]$$

will take care of the first ramp;

$$1 \cdot w(t; 1, 2) = 1 \cdot [u(t - 1) - u(t - 2)]$$

is the horizontal step. The decreasing ramp is a $45°$ line through $t = 3$, and so its equation is $3 - t$ and it starts at $t = 2$ and finishes at $t = 4$, thus

$$(3 - t)w(t; 2, 3) = (3 - t)[u(t - 2) - u(t - 4)]$$

will do the trick. The increasing ramp is

$$(t - 4)w(t; 4, 5) = (t - 4)[u(t - 4) - u(t - 5)]$$

and the last step is

$$w(t; 5, 6) = 1 \cdot [u(t - 5) - u(t - 6)]$$

Therefore,

$$g(t) = tw(t; 0, 1) + w(t; 1, 2) + (3 - t)w(t; 2, 4)$$

$$+(t - 4)w(t; 4, 5) + w(t; 5, 6),$$

or in terms of unit steps,

$$g(t) = tu(t) - (t - 1)u(t - 1) - (t - 2)u(t - 2)$$

$$+(2t - 7)u(t - 4) - (t - 5)u(t - 5) - u(t - 6).$$

Only the coefficients of the steps *turning on* at $t = 4$ and $t = 6$ are nonzero at those respective times. Hence, as seen in the figure, these are the only jump discontinuities of $g(t)$. ∎∎∎

The evaluation of the transform of the two-part piecewise defined function

$$f(t) = g(t) + [h(t) - g(t)]u(t - a)$$

can be accomplished by the following integration:

$$\mathcal{L}\{g(t)u(t - a)\} = \int_0^\infty g(t)u(t - a)e^{-st} \, dt$$

$$= \int_a^\infty g(t)e^{-st} \, dt$$

$$= \int_0^\infty g(\tau + a)e^{-s(\tau + a)} \, d\tau \quad \text{(using } t = \tau + a\text{)}$$

$$= e^{-sa} \int_0^\infty g(\tau + a)e^{-s\tau} \, d\tau.$$

This establishes the Second Shifting Theorem:

THEOREM 5.3 (Second Shifting Theorem) *If $F(s) = \mathcal{L}\{f(t)\}$ and $u(t - a)$ is the unit step at $t = a$, then*

$$\mathcal{L}\{g(t)u(t - a)\} = e^{-sa}\mathcal{L}\{g(t + a)\}, \tag{5.14}$$

which can be rewritten in the alternative form

$$\mathcal{L}\{f(t - a)u(t - a)\} = e^{-sa}\mathcal{L}\{f(t)\} = e^{-sa}F(s). \tag{5.15}$$

□

In principle, the application of this result is straightforward, but it seldom seems so in practice. First, every discontinuous function must be written in terms of unit steps so that we can apply the Second Shifting Theorem in either form (5.14) or (5.15). Since the example that started this subsection was left unfinished, let's apply the Second Shifting Theorem to it:

$$\mathcal{L}\{g(t) + [h(t) - g(t)]u(t - a)\} = G(s) + \mathcal{L}\{h(t + a) - g(t + a)\}e^{-sa}.$$

When using the Second Shifting Theorem to evaluate transforms, the first form (5.14) will be more convenient at points of discontinuity, whereas the second form (5.15) may be better at points of continuity. In either case, it will be easier if we have combined all steps that turn on at the same time.

■ **EXAMPLE 5.6** Let's find the transform of each of the functions in the previous example.

(a) $\mathcal{L}\{w(t; a, b)\} = \mathcal{L}\{u(t - a) - u(t - b)\} = e^{-sa}\mathcal{L}\{1\} - e^{-sb}\mathcal{L}\{1\}$

$$= \frac{1}{s}\left(e^{-sa} - e^{-sb}\right).$$

(b) The sawtooth function has been entirely written in terms of steps so that the Second Shifting Theorem can be used:

$$\mathcal{L}\{\text{Saw}(t; T)\} = \mathcal{L}\left\{tu(t) - \sum_{n=1}^{\infty} Tu(t - nT)\right\}$$

$$= e^{-s \cdot 0}L\{t\} - T\sum_{n=1}^{\infty} e^{-snT}L\{1\}$$

$$= \frac{1}{s^2} - \frac{T}{s} \cdot \sum_{1}^{\infty} \left(e^{-sT}\right)^n$$

$$= \frac{1}{s^2} - \frac{T}{s} \cdot \frac{e^{-sT}}{1 - e^{-sT}},$$

where the last term comes from summing the geometric series. This is precisely the same result we obtained by applying the procedure for periodic functions.

(c) $\mathcal{L}\{f(t)\} = \mathcal{L}\{tu(t) + (t^2 - t)u(t - 1) + (4 - t^2)u(t - 2)\}$. Since $t^2 - t$ is not of the form $h(t - 1)$, which is necessary because the step is at $t = 1$, and $4 - t^2$ is not of the form of $k(t - 2)$, the first form of the Shifting Theorem (5.14) will be more useful:

$$\begin{aligned} \mathcal{L}\{f(t)\} &= e^{-s \cdot 0}\mathcal{L}\{t\} + e^{-s \cdot 1}\mathcal{L}\{(t + 1)^2 - (t + 1)\} \\ &\quad + e^{-s \cdot 2}\mathcal{L}\{4 - (t + 2)^2\} \\ &= \frac{1}{s^2} + e^{-s}\mathcal{L}\{t^2 + t\} + e^{-2s}\mathcal{L}\{-t^2 - 4t\} \\ &= \frac{1}{s^2} + e^{-s}\left(\frac{2}{s^3} + \frac{1}{s^2}\right) - e^{-2s}\left(\frac{2}{s^3} + \frac{4}{s^2}\right). \end{aligned}$$

(d) $\mathcal{L}\{g(t)\} = \mathcal{L}\{tu(t) - (t - 1)u(t - 1) - (t - 2)u(t - 2) + (2t - 7)u(t - 4)\}$
$$\qquad\qquad\qquad - \mathcal{L}\{(t - 5)u(t - 5) - u(t - 6)\}$$

$$\Rightarrow \mathcal{L}\{g(t)\} = e^{-s \cdot 0}\mathcal{L}\{t\} - e^{-s \cdot 1}\mathcal{L}\{t\} - e^{-s \cdot 2}\mathcal{L}\{t\}$$

$$+ e^{-s4}\mathcal{L}\{2(t + 4) - 7\} - e^{-s \cdot 5}\mathcal{L}\{t\} - e^{-s \cdot 6}\mathcal{L}\{1\}$$

Finally we have

$$\mathcal{L}\{g(t)\} = \frac{1}{s^2} - \frac{1}{s^2}e^{-s} - \frac{1}{s^2}e^{-2s} + \left(\frac{2}{s^3} + \frac{1}{s^2}\right)e^{-4s}$$

$$- \frac{1}{s^2}e^{-5s} + \frac{1}{s^2}e^{-6s}.$$

■ ■ ■

■ **EXAMPLE 5.7** Of course, we can find formal transforms of generalized functions or impulses as well.

(a) We will need to use the integral relation for the Dirac-δ function:

$$\mathcal{L}\{\delta(t - a)\} = \int_0^\infty \delta(t - a)e^{-st}\,dt = \begin{cases} 0, & a < 0, \\ e^{-sa}, & a > 0. \end{cases}$$

(b) $\mathcal{L}\{\delta(t - a)f(t)\} = \displaystyle\int_0^\infty \delta(t - a)f(t)e^{-st}\,dt = \begin{cases} 0, & a < 0, \\ f(a)e^{-sa}, & a > 0. \end{cases}$

(c) $\mathcal{L}\{\delta'(t - a)f(t)\} = \displaystyle\int_0^\infty \delta'(t - a)f(t)e^{-st}\,dt = -\frac{d}{dt}\left[f(t)e^{-st}\right]_{t=a}$
$$= [sf(a) - f'(a)]\,e^{-sa}, \text{ for } a > 0.$$

■ ■ ■

5.3.4 Exercise Set

Find the Laplace transform of each of the following functions.

1. $(e^t - 1)^2$
2. $(t - 1)^2$
3. $(2t - 1)e^{3t}$
4. $t^2 e^{-2t}$

5. $e^{2t} \cosh 3t$
6. $\sin \pi t \cos \pi t$
7. $3t \sin 2t$
8. $(2t - 3)^2$

9. $\sin at \sinh at$
10. $\sinh at - \sin at$
11. $t^3 e^{-4t}$
12. $t^3 \sin 2t$

13. $te^{at} \cos \omega t$
14. $e^{at} \sin(\omega t + \phi)$
15. $\dfrac{\sin \omega t}{t}$
16. $\dfrac{(t^2 + 2t)^2}{t^2}$

17. $\cosh^2 3t$
18. $(e^t - t)^2$
19. $\sin^3 \omega t$
20. $(t^3 - 3)e^{-3t}$

21. $f(t) = \sin \omega_1 t \sin \omega_2 t$, when $\omega_1 \neq \omega_2$

22. $\begin{cases} \sin t, & 0 < t \leq \pi/2 \\ 1, & \pi/2 < t \end{cases}$

23. $\begin{cases} \sin t, & t < \pi/2 \\ 1 - \cos t, & \pi/2 \leq t \end{cases}$

24. $\dfrac{t+1}{\sqrt{t}} e^{-4t}$

25. $\left(t - 2\sqrt{t}\right)^2$
26. $(t + 1)^2 e^{-2t}$
27. $(t + 1)^2 \cos \omega t$
28. $\cosh^3 \mu t$

29. $2^t - 3^t$
30. $t \cosh \mu t$
31. $\sqrt{t}(t - 2)e^{-3t}$
32. $t\delta(t - 1)$

33. $t^2 e^t \cosh t$
34. $(t - 2)\delta(t - 2)$
35. $e^{at} \delta(t - a)$
36. $at - \sin at$

37. $\sin at - at \cos at$
38. $\sin 2t \, w(t; 0, \pi/2)$
39. $e^{-at} \cos^2 \omega t$
40. $t \sinh t$

41. $\cos^4(\omega t)$
42. $\displaystyle\int_1^\infty e^{-xt} \dfrac{dx}{x}$

43. $\begin{cases} t^2, & 0 \leq t < 1 \\ \sin(\pi t/2), & 1 \leq t \end{cases}$

44. $\begin{cases} 2t - 1, & 0 \leq t < 1 \\ t, & 1 \leq t < 2 \\ 3t - 4, & 2 \leq t < 3 \\ 8 - t, & 3 \leq t \end{cases}$

45. $\begin{cases} 1 - 2t, & 0 \leq t < 2 \\ 0, & 2 \leq t < 3 \\ 1, & 3 \leq t < 5 \\ \sin \pi t, & 5 \leq t \end{cases}$

46. $\begin{cases} t^2 - 1, & 1 \leq t < 4 \\ 3t - 1, & 4 \leq t < 9 \\ 2t - t^2, & 9 \leq t \end{cases}$

47. $\begin{cases} \sin \pi t, & 0 \leq t < 1 \\ \cos \pi t, & 1 \leq t < 2 \\ \sin \pi t, & 2 \leq t < 3 \end{cases}$

48. $f(t)$ as drawn in Figure 5.5.

49. $g(t)$ as drawn in Figure 5.6.

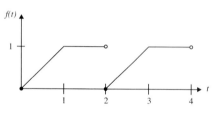

Fig. 5.5

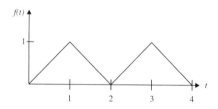

Fig. 5.6

50. $(t-1)^2 e^{-2t} \delta(t-3)$

51. $\sin 3(t-1) u(t-2) \delta(t-3)$

52. $u(t-2) u(t-4)$

53. $u(t-3) \delta(t-4)$

54. $\delta(t-2) \delta(t-3)$

55. $u(|t-3|-1)$

56. $u(\sin \pi t)$

57. $u(\sin \pi t) u(\sin 2\pi t)$

58. $\sin \pi t \, u(\sin \pi t)$

59. $|\sin \pi t| u(\sin \pi t)$

60. $\dfrac{e^{-at}(1-at)}{\sqrt{\pi t}}$

61. $\dfrac{e^{-bt} - e^{-at}}{\sqrt{\pi t^3}}$

62. $(\lfloor t \rfloor - t)^2$, where $\lfloor t \rfloor$ is the largest integer less than or equal to t.

63. $(\lceil t \rceil - \lfloor t \rfloor)^2$, where $\lceil t \rceil$ is the smallest integer greater than or equal to t.

64. $t \cdot \mathrm{Saw}(t; T)$

65. $\mathrm{Saw}(t; 2) - \mathrm{Saw}(t; 1)$

66. $\mathrm{Saw}^2(t; T)$

67. $\sin(\mathrm{Saw}(t; \pi))$

68. If $f(t)$ is periodic with period $2T$, show that the **half-wave rectification** of $f(t)$ (every other half period deleted) is given by

$$f(t) \sum_{n=0}^{\infty} (-1)^n u(t - nT),$$

and find its Laplace transform.

5.4 INVERSE LAPLACE TRANSFORMS

By restricting ourselves to the set of exponentially bounded piecewise smooth (meaning at least differentiable) functions, we can be assured that $\mathcal{L}$ is an invertible transformation. This follows from the following theorem, due to Lerch.

THEOREM 5.4 *If $f(t)$ and $g(t)$ are piecewise continuous functions, they are of exponential order on $[0, \infty)$, and $\mathcal{L}\{f\} = \mathcal{L}\{g\}$, then $f(t) = g(t)$ for $t \geq 0$, except possibly at their points of discontinuity.* □

We may conclude that for all practical purposes–only to within its values at its points of discontinuity–the inverse is unique. Thus on the set of continuous and exponentially bounded functions, the Laplace transform is invertible. Our goal now is to evaluate $\mathcal{L}^{-1}\{F(s)\}$ for as many frequency domain functions $F(s)$ as feasible. Since $\mathcal{L}$ acted only on causal functions, when we perform an inversion to get $f(t)$, we really mean $f(t)u(t)$, where $u(t)$ is the unit step at zero. The actual inversion integral is defined for complex s and requires knowledge of contour integration. We will seek an alternative (and for the problems we'll encounter, easier) approach.

5.4.1 Properties of Inverse Transforms

The easiest way to proceed is to refer to Table 1 in Appendix G which lists a number of Laplace transforms, and *read it backwards*. Of course, no table can be complete, and so some manipulation will be in order to bring an $F(s)$ into recognizable form. Fortunately, most problems will only require us to complete the square of a quadratic factor of the denominator or perform a partial fraction expansion. For the latter technique, you should refer to Appendix E.

An important thing to remember is that the inverse of a linear transformation is linear, so that

$$\mathcal{L}^{-1}\{cF(s) + G(s)\} = c\mathcal{L}^{-1}\{F(s)\} + \mathcal{L}^{-1}\{G(s)\}$$

for any complex number c. Most of the properties of the Laplace transform $\mathcal{L}$ can be translated into properties of the inverse transform $\mathcal{L}^{-1}$.

THEOREM 5.5 *If $f(t) = \mathcal{L}^{-1}\{F(s)\}$, then the following hold:*

(LapInv1) $\mathcal{L}^{-1}\{F(s - a)\} = e^{at}f(t)$ (**First Shifting Theorem**).

(LapInv2) $\mathcal{L}^{-1}\{F'(s)\} = -tf(t) \quad and \quad \mathcal{L}^{-1}\{F^{(n)}(s)\} = (-t)^n f(t).$

(LapInv3) $\mathcal{L}^{-1}\left\{\dfrac{F(s)}{s}\right\} = \displaystyle\int_0^t f(\tau)\, d\tau.$

(LapInv4) $\mathcal{L}^{-1}\left\{\displaystyle\int_s^\infty F(\sigma)\, d\sigma\right\} = \dfrac{f(t)}{t}.$

(LapInv5) $\mathcal{L}^{-1}\{e^{-as}F(s)\} = f(t - a)u(t - a)$ (**Second Shifting Theorem**).

(LapInv6)

$$\mathcal{L}^{-1}\{s^{-n}\} = \frac{t^{n-1}}{\Gamma(n)}, \quad \mathcal{L}^{-1}\left\{\frac{1}{s - a}\right\} = e^{at},$$

$$\mathcal{L}^{-1}\left\{\frac{s}{s^2 + \omega^2}\right\} = \cos(\omega t), \quad \mathcal{L}^{-1}\left\{\frac{\omega}{s^2 + \omega^2}\right\} = \sin(\omega t).$$

□

Much the same as for finding transforms, there are often several ways to approach a problem.

▪ **EXAMPLE 5.8** Some applications of the previous theorem follow.

(a) $\mathcal{L}^{-1}\{1/s^2\} = t^{2-1}/\Gamma(2) = t/1! = t$ using (LapInv6), or

$$\mathcal{L}^{-1}\left\{\frac{1}{s} \cdot \frac{1}{s}\right\} = \int_0^t L^{-1}\{1/s\}d\tau = \int_0^t 1 \cdot d\tau = t$$

using (LapInv3). Or we could try

$$\mathcal{L}^{-1}\left\{\frac{1}{s^2}\right\} = -L^{-1}\left\{\frac{d}{ds}\frac{1}{s}\right\} = -(-t)L^{-1}\left\{\frac{1}{s}\right\} = t \cdot 1 = t,$$

which followed from (LapInv2) of the theorem.

(b) Now let's use a partial fraction expansion:

$$\mathcal{L}^{-1}\left\{\frac{3s^2 + 8s - 4}{s^3 - s^2 - 2s}\right\} = \mathcal{L}^{-1}\left\{\frac{3s^2 + 8s - 4}{s(s + 1)(s - 2)}\right\}$$

$$= \mathcal{L}^{-1}\left\{\frac{2}{s} - \frac{3}{s + 1} + \frac{4}{s - 2}\right\}$$

$$= 2 - 3e^{-t} + 4e^{2t}.$$

All that was needed beyond the partial fraction expansion was the basic formula for the transform of an exponential.

(c) To use the inverse form of the First Shifting Theorem, we will need to complete the square:

$$\mathcal{L}^{-1}\left\{\frac{2s + 1}{s^2 + 2s + 5}\right\} = \mathcal{L}^{-1}\left\{\frac{2s + 1}{(s + 1)^2 + 4}\right\}$$

$$= e^{-t}\mathcal{L}^{-1}\left\{\frac{2(s - 1) + 1}{s^2 + 4}\right\}$$

$$= e^{-t}\mathcal{L}^{-1}\left\{2\frac{s}{s^2 + 4} - \frac{1}{s^2 + 4}\right\}$$

$$= e^{-t}\left(2\cos 2t - \frac{1}{2}\sin 2t\right).$$

(d) Sometimes higher order partial fraction expansions must be used:

$$\mathcal{L}^{-1}\left\{\frac{5}{s^2(s^2+1)}\right\} = \mathcal{L}^{-1}\left\{\frac{5}{s^2} - \frac{5}{s^2+1}\right\} = 5(t-\sin t).$$

(e)

$$\mathcal{L}^{-1}\left\{\frac{(s+2)e^{-s}}{s^2+4s+3}\right\} = \mathcal{L}^{-1}\left\{\frac{s+2}{(s+1)(s+3)}e^{-s}\right\}$$

$$= \mathcal{L}^{-1}\left\{\left(\frac{1/2}{s+1} + \frac{1/2}{s+3}\right)e^{-s}\right\}$$

$$= \frac{1}{2}\mathcal{L}^{-1}\left\{\frac{1}{s+1}e^{-s}\right\} + \frac{1}{2}\mathcal{L}^{-1}\left\{\frac{1}{s+3}e^{-s}\right\}$$

$$= \frac{1}{2}\left.e^{-t}\right|_{t\leftarrow t-1} u(t-1) + \frac{1}{2}\left.e^{-3t}\right|_{t\leftarrow t-1} u(t-1)$$

$$= \tfrac{1}{2}\left(e^{-(t-1)} + e^{-3(t-1)}\right)u(t-1).$$

This time a partial fraction expansion of the rational part of the function was followed by the use of the inverse form of the Second Shifting Theorem with its *shift and step*.

(f) Some functions require more work than others:

$$\mathcal{L}^{-1}\left\{e^s\frac{\operatorname{sech} s}{s}\right\} = \mathcal{L}^{-1}\left\{\frac{1}{s} \cdot \frac{2e^s}{e^s + e^{-s}}\right\}$$

$$= \mathcal{L}^{-1}\left\{\frac{1}{s} \cdot \frac{2}{1+e^{-2s}}\right\}$$

$$= 2\mathcal{L}^{-1}\left\{\frac{1}{s}\sum_0^\infty \left(-e^{-2s}\right)^n\right\}$$

$$= 2\mathcal{L}^{-1}\left\{\frac{1}{s}\sum_0^\infty (-1)^n e^{-2ns}\right\}$$

$$= 2\sum_0^\infty (-1)^n \mathcal{L}^{-1}\left\{\frac{1}{s} \cdot e^{-2ns}\right\}$$

$$= 2\sum_0^\infty (-1)^n u(t-2n).$$

The graph of this function is drawn in Figure 5.7.   ■ ■ ■

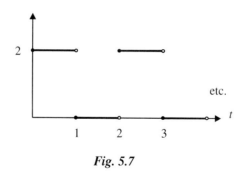

Fig. 5.7

. . .

Warning: Remember that a partial fraction expansion can be applied only to a rational function, i.e., a ratio of polynomials. Thus any exponential factors, e^{-sa}, do not enter into the partial fraction expansion but rather are carried along to be used to shift and step as in $\mathcal{L}^{-1}\{e^{-as}F(s)\} = f(t-a)u(t-a)$.

So far, all transformed functions $F(s)$ have involved denominators with higher powers of s than the numerators. When this is not the case, the result will be an impulse or its derivatives.

▪ **EXAMPLE 5.9** Inverses can result in impulses.

(a) $\mathcal{L}^{-1}\left\{\dfrac{s^2+1}{s^2-1}e^{-sa}\right\} = \mathcal{L}^{-1}\left\{\left(1+\dfrac{2}{s^2-1}\right)e^{-sa}\right\}$

$$= \delta(t-a) + 2\sinh(t-a)u(t-a).$$

(b) $\mathcal{L}^{-1}\{se^{-sa}\} = \delta'(t-a)$.

▪ ▪ ▪

5.4.2 *Convolution Theorem*

Unfortunately, there still remain some rather elementary $F(s)$ that cannot be inverted without resort to some rather involved algebraic trickery. A simple example is $F(s) = (s^2+1)^{-2}$, which arises very naturally in partial fraction expansions with repeated quadratic factors. You could argue that since $s^2+1 = (s+i)(s-i)$ this could be handled by the usual formulas and you'd be correct. As an alternative, let's introduce a new concept.

DEFINITION 5.2 *The* **convolution product** *of the time domain functions $f(t)$ and $g(t)$, when they are absolutely integrable (which means those functions for which $\int |f(t)|\,dt < \infty$) is defined by*

$$(f*g)(t) := \int_{-\infty}^{\infty} f(\tau)g(t-\tau)\,d\tau. \tag{5.16}$$

It is a straightforward, albeit tedious, matter to show that the following results are true.

THEOREM 5.6 *For all absolutely integrable functions:*

(ConvPr1) $f * (cg + h) = cf * g + f * h$ *for any constant c.*

(ConvPr2) $f * g = g * f.$

(ConvPr3) $f * (g * h) = (f * g) * h.$

(ConvPr4) $\delta_a * f = f(t - a),$ *where* $\delta_a(t) = \delta(t - a).$

All of our Laplace transform analyses dealt with causal functions, meaning the integrand of the convolution integral, which is $f(\tau)g(t - \tau)$, is nonzero when the arguments of *both* functions are nonnegative, to wit

$$\tau \geq 0 \quad \text{and} \quad t - \tau \geq 0 \quad \Rightarrow \quad 0 \leq \tau \leq t.$$

For this reason you'll usually use the convolution product, in the context of Laplace transforms, defined by

$$(f * g)(t) = \int_0^t f(\tau)g(t - \tau)\, d\tau \tag{5.17}$$

subject to the understanding that $f * g$ itself is causal, i.e., $(f * g)(t) = 0$ for $t < 0$. Now to evaluate some convolution products using (5.17).

■ **EXAMPLE 5.10** Most of the manipulation should be done using a computer algebra system, but the explicit results will be shown here.

(a) $e^{at} * e^{bt} = \displaystyle\int_0^t e^{a\tau} e^{b(t-\tau)}\, d\tau = e^{bt} \int_0^t e^{(a-b)\tau}\, d\tau = \dfrac{e^{at} - e^{bt}}{a - b}$ for $a \neq b$. It is a
simple matter to verify that when $a = b$, we have $e^{at} * e^{at} = te^{at}$.

(b) Now to an easy integral:

$$1 * t = \int_0^t 1 \cdot (t - \tau)\, d\tau = t * 1 = \int_0^t \tau \cdot 1\, d\tau = \frac{1}{2} t^2.$$

(c) In the following case a computer algebra system may return rather meaningless results:

$$t^m * t^n = \int_0^t \tau^m (t - \tau)^n\, d\tau = t^{m+n+1} \int_o^1 u^m (1 - u)^n\, du.$$

If you haven't declared the variables m and n to be integers, then the last integral will be evaluated as a beta function (see Section 9.2.3), in particular $B(m+1, n+1)$. The beta function takes familiar values for integer values of its arguments; in particular,

$$t^m * t^n = t^{m+n+1} B(m + 1, n + 1) = t^{m+n+1} \frac{m!n!}{(m + n + 1)!}.$$

The only noninteger values for which you can get a closed form answer are those where m and n are multiples of $1/2$. ■ ■ ■

The graphical interpretation of $f * g$ is of interest. For simplicity take the special case where $g(\tau)$ is the triangular window,

$$g(\tau) = \frac{\tau}{T} w(\tau; 0, T) = \frac{\tau}{T} [u(\tau) - u(\tau - T)].$$

The window and its folding are shown in Figure 5.8.

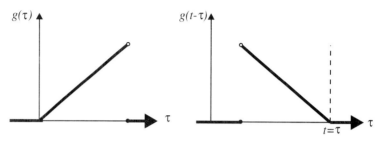

Fig. 5.8

Then

$$g(t - \tau) = \frac{t - \tau}{T} w(t - \tau; 0, T) = \frac{(t - \tau)[u(t - \tau) - u(t - \tau - T)]}{T}$$

is the mirror image of $g(t)$ about the line $t = \tau$. Thus the integrand is the product $f(\tau)g(t-\tau)$. See Figure 5.9.

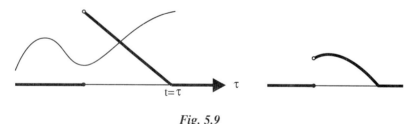

Fig. 5.9

At any time t, the convolution product gives the average of $f(t)$ weighted by the window $g(t)$ folded over the line $t = \tau$. If $f(t)$ were a light intensity, then the convolution of f with g would be the total intensity seen through the folded window $g(t - \tau)$ as a function of t. For this reason, the convolution is called *Faltung* (which means folding) in German.

This graphical interpretation affords us an alternative method of calculating some convolutions.

■ **EXAMPLE 5.11** Graphically compute the convolution product of two rectangular windows, one of width 1 and the other of width 2.

Solution: In particular, in terms of unit steps we have

$$f(t) = u(t) - u(t - 1) \quad \text{and} \quad g(t) = u(t) - u(t - 2).$$

Since both windows are symmetric about their center lines, the folding has absolutely no effect. We can visualize the smaller window moving from left to right toward a stationary window of width 2, as shown below.

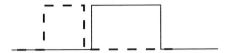

At first, the square window lies entirely to the left of the rectangular window. Their product is zero. Or, if you will, neither can see through the other. Thus for $t < 0$, $f * g = 0$.

As the square window crosses into the other, the amount of viewing area increases proportional to t.

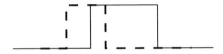

In the region $0 \leq t \leq 1$ we have $f * g = t$. Up until $t = 2$, the two windows overlap completely and the total output is the output from the smaller window.

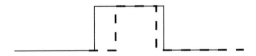

Thus for $1 \leq t \leq 2$, we have $f * g = 1$. Then the moving window passes outside the stationary one.

The net output must drop linearly from 1 to 0 as t increases from 2 to 3. Hence, on $[2, 3]$ we have $f * g = 3 - t$. After $t = 3$, there is no longer any overlap and $f * g = 0$.

We can combine these results using unit steps as follows:

$$\begin{aligned}
(f * g)(t) &= tw(t; 0, 1) + w(t; 1, 2) + (3 - t)w(2, 3) \\
&= t[u(t - 0) - u(t - 1)] + [u(t - 1) - u(t - 2)] \\
&\quad + (3 - t)[u(t - 2) - u(t - 3)] \\
&= t\, u(t) - (t - 1)u(t - 1) - (t - 2)u(t - 2) + (t - 3)u(t - 3).
\end{aligned}$$

The graph of the convolution product is shown in Figure 5.10. ∎

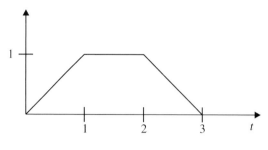

Fig. 5.10

■ ■ ■

■ **EXAMPLE 5.12** Now let's take the convolution product of a rectangular window with an exponential function: $\exp(-at) * w(t; 0, 1)$.

Solution: Since the convolution product is commutative, we can fold either factor. Surely it will be easier to fold the window over the exponential. When $t < 0$, there is no overlap and $(f * g)(t) = 0$. For $t \in (0, 1)$, the window only partially overlaps the exponential as shown in Figure 5.11.

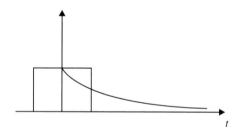

Fig. 5.11

In this region we have

$$(f * g)(t) = \int_0^t e^{-a\tau} \, d\tau = \frac{1}{a} \left(1 - e^{-at} \right).$$

As soon as $t > 1$, the window is completely within the exponential and

$$(f * g)(t) = \int_{t-1}^t e^{-a\tau} \, d\tau = \frac{1}{a} \left(e^{-a(t-1)} - e^{-at} \right).$$

Combining these, we can write

$$(f * g)(t) = \frac{1}{a} \left(1 - e^{-at} \right) w(t; 0, 1) + \frac{1}{a} \left(e^{-a(t-1)} - e^{-at} \right) u(t - 1).$$

After some manipulation, this can be rewritten as

$$(f * g)(t) = \frac{1}{a}\left(1 - e^{-at}\right) - \frac{1}{a}\left(1 - e^{-a(t-1)}\right)u(t-1).$$

■ ■ ■

The power of the convolution concept is contained in the following theorem.

THEOREM 5.7 (Convolution Theorem) *If $f(t)$ and $g(t)$ are transformable, then $(f * g)(t)$ is transformable and*

$$\mathcal{L}\{f * g\} = \mathcal{L}\{f\}\mathcal{L}\{g\} = F(s)G(s). \tag{5.18}$$

Thus the convolution product in the time domain is mapped into the standard product in s-space (the frequency domain) under the Laplace transform.

Proof Write the product $F(s)G(s)$ as a product of integrals and use Fubini's Theorem:

$$F(s)G(s) = \int_0^\infty f(a)e^{-sa}\,da \int_0^\infty g(b)e^{-sb}\,db$$

$$= \int_0^\infty \int_0^\infty f(a)g(b)e^{-s(a+b)}\,da\,db.$$

Now make the substitution $t = a + b$, $\tau = a$. The inverse is $a = \tau$, $b = t - \tau$. The region of integration is $0 \le t < \infty$ and $0 \le t - \tau < \infty$ which is the same as $0 \le \tau \le t$ and $0 \le t < \infty$ and is mapped into the region shown in Figure 5.12.

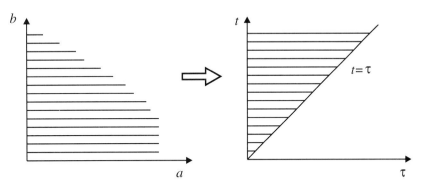

Fig. 5.12 The old and new regions of integration.

The Jacobian of this transformation is one so that $da\,db = d\tau\,dt$. Thus

$$F(s)G(s) = \int_0^\infty \int_0^\infty f(\tau)g(t - \tau)e^{-st}\,d\tau\,dt$$

$$= \int_0^\infty \left(\int_0^t f(\tau)g(t - \tau)\,d\tau\right)e^{-st}\,dt = \mathcal{L}\{f * g\}.$$

□

The inverse form of the Convolution Theorem is

$$\mathcal{L}^{-1}\{F(s)G(s)\} = (f * g)(t), \tag{5.19}$$

and this can be used to invert some of the more recalcitrant functions of s.

■ **EXAMPLE 5.13** Here are some problems that are amenable to solution using the Convolution Theorem.

(a) Let's look at a higher order partial fraction expansion term first:

$$\mathcal{L}^{-1}\left\{\frac{1}{(s^2+1)^2}\right\} = \mathcal{L}^{-1}\left\{\frac{1}{s^2+1} \cdot \frac{1}{s^2+1}\right\}$$

We'll use $\mathcal{L}^{-1}\{1/(s^2+1)\} = \sin t$ and the Convolution Theorem in the form (5.19) to write

$$\mathcal{L}^{-1}\left\{\frac{1}{(s^2+1)^2}\right\} = \sin t * \sin t = \frac{1}{2}\left(\sin t - t\cos t\right),$$

where the convolution was evaluated by computer.

(b) We can use the Convolution Theorem as an alternative avenue for evaluating convolution products of piecewise smooth functions. Going back to example 5.11, we can write

$$\mathcal{L}\{w(t; 0, 1) * w(t; 0, 2)\} = \mathcal{L}\{u(t) - u(t-1)\} \cdot \mathcal{L}\{u(t) - u(t-2)\}$$

Evaluating the right hand side, we find

$$\mathcal{L}\{f * g\} = \frac{1}{s}\left(1 - e^{-s}\right)\frac{1}{s}\left(1 - e^{-s}\right) = \frac{1}{s^2}\left(1 - e^{-s} - e^{-2s} + e^{-3s}\right).$$

The inversion is a straightforward application of the Second Shifting Theorem and gives us the same result obtained before. ■ ■ ■

5.4.3 *Exercise Set*

Find the inverse transform of each of the following.

1. $\dfrac{(s+1)^2}{s\left(s^2+1\right)}$

2. $\dfrac{s^2+6s+10}{s\left(s^2-1\right)\left(s+3\right)}$

3. $\dfrac{s+3}{s^2+8s+16}$

4. $\dfrac{2s+1}{s^2+6s+13}$

5. $\dfrac{1}{\left(s^2+1\right)^3}$

6. $\dfrac{s}{s^2+4s+4}$

7. $\dfrac{1}{(s^2 - 1)(s^2 + 4)}$

8. $\dfrac{1}{s(s^2 + 9)}$

9. $\dfrac{2s + 3}{(s + 4)^3}$

10. $s^{-7/2}$.

11. $\dfrac{s}{(s + a)^2 + b^2}$

12. $\dfrac{1}{s^2}\left(1 - e^{-2s}\right)\left(1 - 3e^{-2s}\right)$

13. $\dfrac{12s}{s^4 - 1}$

14. $\dfrac{s^2 + s + 1}{s^3 - s}$

15. $\dfrac{\tanh s}{s}$

16. $\dfrac{\operatorname{sech} 2s}{s}$

17. $\dfrac{s^2 + 9}{s(s^2 - 9)}$

18. $\dfrac{e^{-2s}}{s^2 + 1}$

19. $\dfrac{e^{-2s} \cosh s}{s^2}$

20. $\dfrac{4}{s^2} e^{-3s} \sinh 2s$

21. $e^{-2s}\left(1 - \dfrac{3}{s}\right)$

22. $\dfrac{se^{-s} - s^2 e^{-2s} + s^3 e^{-3s}}{s(s^2 + 1)}$

23. $\displaystyle\int_s^\infty e^{-2\sigma}\, d\sigma$

24. $\dfrac{e^{-3s}}{(s + 1)^3}$

25. Show that

$$\mathcal{L}^{-1}\left\{\frac{1}{\sqrt{s + a} + \sqrt{s + b}}\right\} = \frac{e^{-bt} - e^{-at}}{a - b} \cdot \frac{t^{-3/2}}{2\sqrt{\pi}}.$$

26. If $\mathcal{L}\{f(t)\} = F(s)$, then show that

$$\mathcal{L}^{-1}\{F(a + bs)\} = \frac{1}{b} e^{-at/b}\, \mathcal{L}^{-1}\{F(s)\}\big|_{t \leftarrow t/b}.$$

Find each of the following convolution products.

27. $t * e^{at}$

28. $\sin t * \sin t$

29. $t * u(t - 5)$

30. $u(t - 2) * u(t - 4)$

31. $u(t - 2) * u(2 - t)$

32. $u(t - 2) * \delta(t - 1)$.

Find each of the following by using the Convolution Theorem.

33. $\mathcal{L}^{-1}\{1/[(s - 2)(s + 3)]\}$

34. $\mathcal{L}\left\{\displaystyle\int_0^t e^{-\tau} \sin(t - \tau)\, d\tau\right\}$

35. $\mathcal{L}\left\{\displaystyle\int_0^t (t - \tau)\, 3e^{-2\tau} \cos \tau\, d\tau\right\}$

Evaluate the following integrals:

36. $\displaystyle\int_0^t \tau u(\tau - 1)\delta(t - \tau - 2)\, d\tau$

37. $\displaystyle\int_0^t \tau e^{-\tau} u(\tau - 1) \sin(t - \tau)\, d\tau$

38. If $f(t) = tw(t; 0, 1)$, use the Convolution Theorem to evaluate the function $g(t) = (f * f)(t)$. Also, graph $g(t)$.

5.5   SOLVING ODE'S WITH TRANSFORMS

5.5.1   *Initial Value Problems*

We'll start with an easy problem, a second order constant coefficient (time invariant) ODE:

$$y'' + py' + qy = g(t). \tag{5.20}$$

Writing $y_0 := y(0)$ and $v_0 := y'(0)$, the transform of this initial value problem is

$$[s^2 Y(s) - sy_0 - v_0] + p[sY(s) - y_0] + qY(s) = G(s).$$

After rearranging, we get

$$(s^2 + ps + q)Y(s) = sy_0 + (py_0 + v_0) + G(s).$$

Notice, the coefficient of $Y(s)$ is the auxiliary polynomial of the original equation, and it is this that determines the functional form of the complementary solution. Solving for $Y(s)$, we find

$$Y(s) = \frac{sy_0 + (py_0 + v_0)}{s^2 + ps + q} + \frac{G(s)}{s^2 + ps + q}. \tag{5.21}$$

This decomposition of $Y(s)$ illustrates the systems terminology for ODE's. The function $g(t)$ is the **system input** and $y(t)$ is the **system output**. If there is no input, $g(t) \equiv 0$, then the complementary solution

$$y_c(t) = \mathcal{L}^{-1} \left\{ \frac{sy_0 + (py_0 + v_0)}{s^2 + ps + q} \right\} \tag{5.22}$$

is called the **zero-input response**. If the initial state is zero, $y_0 = 0$ and $v_0 = 0$, then the particular solution

$$y_p(t) = \mathcal{L}^{-1} \left\{ \frac{G(s)}{s^2 + ps + q} \right\} \tag{5.23}$$

is called the **zero-state response**. This can be represented as the convolution product

$$y_p(t) = \mathcal{L}^{-1} \left\{ \frac{1}{s^2 + ps + q} \right\} * g(t). \tag{5.24}$$

For what problems will Laplace transforms be preferable to either the method of variation of parameters or undetermined coefficients applied to nonhomogeneous time invariant ODE's? For smooth $g(t)$ there may be no advantage. But for piecewise defined inputs or those with jump discontinuities the transform approach will be far preferable. The following examples will illustrate this.

■ **EXAMPLE 5.14** Solve $y'' - 2y' - 3y = 8e^t + 12$, $y(0) = 8$, $y'(0) = -4$.

Solution: First transform the equation:

$$[s^2 Y(s) - s(8) - (-4)] - 2[sY(s) - 8] - 3Y(s) = \frac{8}{s-1} + \frac{12}{s}.$$

Collect terms:

$$(s^2 - 2s - 3)\, Y(s) = (8s - 20) + \frac{8}{s-1} + \frac{12}{s}.$$

Solve for $Y(s)$:

$$Y(s) = \frac{8s - 20}{(s-3)(s+1)} + \frac{8}{(s-1)(s-3)(s+1)} + \frac{12}{s(s-3)(s+1)}.$$

Use partial fractions on each term:

$$Y(s) = \left[\frac{1}{s-3} + \frac{7}{s+1} \right] + \left[\frac{-2}{s-1} + \frac{1}{s-3} + \frac{1}{s+1} \right]$$

$$+ \left[-\frac{4}{s} + \frac{1}{s-3} + \frac{3}{s+1} \right]$$

Combine like terms:

$$Y(s) = -\frac{4}{s} - \frac{2}{s-1} + \frac{3}{s-3} + \frac{11}{s+1}.$$

Finally, invert:

$$y(t) = -4 - 2e^t + 3e^{3t} + 11e^{-t}.$$

■■■

■ **EXAMPLE 5.15** Solve the harmonic oscillator problem $y'' + \omega^2 y = g(t)$ with initial values $y(0) = y_0$, $y'(0) = v_0$.

Solution: We use the same steps as before:

$$[s^2 Y(s) - sy_0 - v_0] + \omega^2 Y(s) = G(s)$$

$$\Rightarrow \quad Y(s) = \frac{sy_0 + v_0}{s^2 + \omega^2} + \frac{1}{\omega}\left(\frac{\omega}{s^2 + \omega^2} \right) G(s).$$

Inverting and using the Convolution Theorem we obtain

$$y(t) = y_0 \cos \omega t + \frac{v_0}{\omega} \sin \omega t + \frac{1}{\omega} \int_0^t g(\tau) \sin \omega(t - \tau)\, d\tau,$$

which is the usual convolution integral solution.

■■■

▪ **EXAMPLE 5.16** This example will model a chain of radioactive disintegrations by a recursive set of ODE's. Every radioactive substance decays by the emission of alpha particles, which are helium nuclei consisting of two protons and two neutrons. The parent, or initial substance, decays into a daughter substance of lower atomic number, which may or may not be radioactive. By the same token, the daughter substance can decay into yet another substance. Once a decay product is the element lead, the sequence stops. Thus the chain of events is of finite length.

Solution: Denote the quantity of parent matter by $Q_1(t)$. Then the law of radioactive decay states that

$$Q_1'(t) = -\lambda_1 Q_1(t),$$

where $\lambda_1 > 0$ is the **parent disintegration constant**. The quantity of daughter substance, $Q_2(t)$ will grow at the same rate λ_1 proportional to the quantity of the parent remaining and, if the daughter is radioactive, it will decay at a rate proportional to its remaining quantity of matter. Thus

$$Q_2'(t) = \lambda_1 Q_1(t) - \lambda_2 Q_2(t).$$

The quantity $\lambda_2 > 0$ is called the **daughter disintegration constant**. A similar mechanism prevails until the first stable element, say the nth product, is reached, which will grow at the same rate as its parent decays. Thus we have the system of equations

$$
\begin{aligned}
Q_1' &= -\lambda_1 Q_1 \\
Q_{k+1}' &= \lambda_k Q_k - \lambda_{k+1} Q_{k+1}, \, k = 1 : n-1 \\
Q_{n+1}' &= \lambda_n Q_n.
\end{aligned}
$$

A reasonable set of initial conditions would be one that begins with only the parent present in its pure form, i.e.,

$$Q_1(0) = Q_0, Q_2(0) = Q_3(0) = \cdots = Q_{n+1}(0) = 0.$$

Transforming the equations and using the notation $\hat{Q}_k(s) := \mathcal{L}\{Q_k(t)\}$, we have the system

$$
\begin{aligned}
(s + \lambda_1)\hat{Q}_1(s) &= Q_0, \\
(s + \lambda_{k+1})\hat{Q}_{k+1}(s) &= \lambda_k \hat{Q}_k, \\
s\hat{Q}_{n+1}(s) &= \lambda_n \hat{Q}_n.
\end{aligned}
$$

Iterating on these, we find

$$
\begin{aligned}
\hat{Q}_1 &= \frac{Q_0}{s + \lambda_1}, \\
\hat{Q}_{k+1} &= \frac{Q_0}{\lambda_{k+1}}\left(\frac{\lambda_{k+1}}{s + \lambda_{k+1}}\right)\left(\frac{\lambda_k}{s + \lambda_k}\right)\cdots\left(\frac{\lambda_1}{s + \lambda_1}\right), \\
\hat{Q}_{n+1} &= \frac{Q_0}{s}\left(\frac{\lambda_n}{s + \lambda_n}\right)\left(\frac{\lambda_{n-1}}{s + \lambda_{n-1}}\right)\cdots\left(\frac{\lambda_1}{s + \lambda_1}\right).
\end{aligned}
$$

Inverting these is only a matter of partial fraction expansions. Let's look at some simple cases:

Case 1: One by-product, $n = 1$. Then

$$\hat{Q}_1(s) = \frac{Q_0}{s + \lambda_1} \quad \Rightarrow \quad Q_1(t) = Q_0 e^{-\lambda_1 t},$$

$$\hat{Q}_2(s) = \frac{Q_0}{s} \cdot \frac{\lambda_1}{s + \lambda_1} = \frac{Q_0}{s} - \frac{Q_0}{s + \lambda_1} \quad \Rightarrow \quad Q_2(t) = Q_0 \left(1 - e^{-\lambda_1 t}\right).$$

Graphically, we have the situation shown in Figure 5.13.

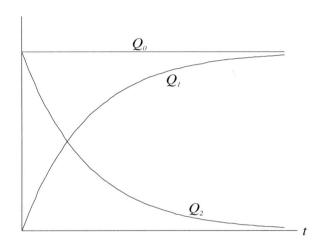

Fig. 5.13

Case 2: Two by-products, $n = 2$. Then

$$\hat{Q}_1(s) = \frac{Q_0}{s + \lambda_1} \quad \Rightarrow \quad Q_1(t) = Q_0 e^{-\lambda_1 t},$$

$$\hat{Q}_2(s) = \frac{Q_0}{\lambda_2} \left(\frac{\lambda_2}{s + \lambda_2}\right) \left(\frac{\lambda_1}{s + \lambda_1}\right) = \frac{Q_0 \lambda_1}{\lambda_1 - \lambda_2} \left(\frac{1}{s + \lambda_2} - \frac{1}{s + \lambda_1}\right),$$

$$\Rightarrow \quad Q_2(t) = \frac{Q_0 \lambda_1}{\lambda_1 - \lambda_2} \left(e^{-\lambda_2 t} - e^{-\lambda_1 t}\right).$$

$$\hat{Q}_3(s) = \frac{Q_0}{s} \left(\frac{\lambda_2}{s + \lambda_2}\right) \left(\frac{\lambda_1}{s + \lambda_1}\right) = \frac{Q_0}{s} + \frac{Q_0}{\lambda_1 - \lambda_2} \left(\frac{\lambda_2}{s + \lambda_1} - \frac{\lambda_1}{s + \lambda_2}\right)$$

$$\Rightarrow \quad Q_3(t) = Q_0 \left(1 + \frac{\lambda_2}{\lambda_1 - \lambda_2} e^{-\lambda_1 t} - \frac{\lambda_1}{\lambda_1 - \lambda_2} e^{-\lambda_2 t}\right).$$

Graphically the situation is shown in Figure 5.14. ■ ■ ■

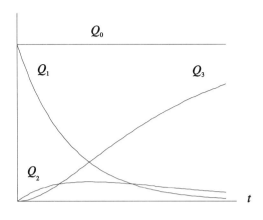

Fig. 5.14

∎ ∎ ∎

Now let's look at a problem with discontinuous inputs, where the Laplace transform method shines.

▪ **EXAMPLE 5.17** A simple RLC circuit with $L = 1$, $R = 2$, and $C = 1/5$ is energized by a T second pulse of a q_0 coulomb charge on the capacitor. Find the zero-state response.

Solution: When $q(t)$ is the charge on the capacitor, the derivative of Kirchhoff's Voltage Law yields
$$q'' + 2q' + 5q = q_0[u(t) - u(t - T)].$$
Transforming and using $q(0) = 0 = q'(0)$ we have

$$\left(s^2 + 2s + 5\right) Q(s) = \frac{q_0}{s} \left(1 - e^{-sT}\right)$$

$$\Rightarrow Q(s) = \frac{q_0 \left(1 - e^{-sT}\right)}{s\left[(s+1)^2 + 4\right]}$$

$$= \frac{q_0 \left(1 - e^{-sT}\right)}{5s} - \frac{s+2}{5\left[(s+1)^2 + 4\right]} q_0 \left(1 - e^{-sT}\right).$$

Inversion using a *shift and step* yields

$$q(t) = \frac{q_0}{5} \left[(1 - u(t - T)) - e^{-t} \left(\cos 2t + \frac{1}{2} \sin 2t \right) \right.$$

$$\left. + e^{-(t-T)} \left(\cos 2(t - T) + \frac{1}{2} \sin 2(t - T) \right) u(t - T) \right].$$

∎ ∎ ∎

■ **EXAMPLE 5.18** Let's find the output of a simple RC circuit that is driven by a half-wave rectified sine wave of frequency $\Omega/2\pi$.

Solution: The system equations are given by

$$L\ddot{q}(t) + \frac{1}{C}q(t) = f(t),$$

where $f(t)$ is the half-wave rectified sine, which could be written as $\sin(\Omega t)\,\mathrm{sgn}(\sin(\Omega t))$. (Think about this.) The forcing function is periodic of period $2\pi/\Omega$, so that we can apply equation (5.13) when we transform. Let's look for the zero-state response so that we need not be bothered by initial conditions. The transform of the equation is

$$\left(Ls^2 + \frac{1}{C}\right)Q(s) = \frac{\Omega}{s^2 + \Omega^2} \cdot \frac{1}{\left(1 - e^{-\pi s/\Omega}\right)}.$$

Write $Ls^2 + (1/C) =: L(s^2 + \omega^2)$, where $\omega = 1/\sqrt{LC}$. If we solve for $Q(s)$, use partial fractions, and expand the factor $1/[1 - \exp(-\pi s/\Omega)]$ in a geometric series, we have

$$Q(s) = \frac{L}{\omega\,(\Omega^2 - \omega^2)}\left[\frac{\omega}{s^2 + \omega^2}\Omega - \frac{\Omega}{s^2 + \Omega^2}\omega\right]\sum_{n=0}^{\infty}\left(e^{-\pi s/\Omega}\right)^n.$$

The inversion is now fairly easy using the Second Shifting Theorem:

$$q(t) = \frac{L}{\omega\,(\Omega^2 - \omega^2)}\sum_{n=0}^{\infty}\left(\Omega\sin\omega\left(t - \frac{n\pi}{\Omega}\right) - \omega\sin\Omega\left(t - \frac{n\pi}{\Omega}\right)\right)u\left(t - \frac{n\pi}{\Omega}\right).$$

Just as we expect, when $\Omega = \omega$, the right hand side is indeterminate and there could be resonance. In that limiting case, we have

$$Q(s) = \frac{\omega}{s^2 + \omega^2}\frac{1}{\left(1 - e^{-\pi s/\omega}\right)}.$$

An inversion yields

$$q(t) = \frac{L}{2\omega^2}\sum_{n=0}^{\infty}\left(\sin(\omega t - n\pi) - (\omega t - n\pi)\cos(\omega t - n\pi)\right)u\left(t - \frac{n\pi}{\omega}\right).$$

The factor of $\omega t - n\pi$ indicates the presence of resonance.

As an interesting exercise, you should plot the system response for a *slow* half-wave rectified driver, i.e., $\Omega = k\omega$ with $k < 1$, and also for a *fast* driver, $\omega = k\Omega$ with $k > 1$. Odd things can happen. ■ ■ ■

Laplace transforms can be used to solve systems of equations with more than one dependent variable.

■ **EXAMPLE 5.19** Suppose we have particles of mass $3m$, $4m$, and $3m$ connected by four springs, each of which has a force constant k. Assume the apparatus lies in a horizontal plane, so that there are no deflections in the springs. The system is in static equilibrium. Suddenly an impulse I is delivered to the center particle so that it moves parallel to the line of equilibrium. What happens to the system?

Solution: We will take the coordinates as drawn in Figure 5.15.

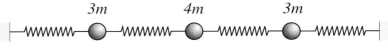

Fig. 5.15

It will be left to the reader to show that the equations of motion are given by

$$3\ddot{x}_1(t) + \omega^2\left(2x_1(t) - x_2(t)\right) = 0,$$
$$4\ddot{x}_2(t) + \omega^2\left(2x_2(t) - x_1(t) - x_3(t)\right) = 0,$$
$$3\ddot{x}_3(t) + \omega^2\left(2x_3(t) - x_2(t)\right) = 0,$$

where $\omega^2 = k/m$. The initial conditions must reflect the equilibrium situation together with the impulse applied to the middle particle of mass $4m$. Thus, at $t = 0$, we have

$$x_1 = x_2 = x_3 = 0, \quad \dot{x}_1 = 0, \quad \dot{x}_2 = \frac{I}{4m}, \quad \dot{x}_3 = 0.$$

The transformed equations are

$$\left(3s^2 + 2\omega^2\right)X_1(s) - \omega^2 X_2(s) = 0,$$
$$-\omega^2 X_1(s) + \left(4s^2 + 2\omega^2\right)X_2(s) - \omega^2 X_3(s) = \frac{I}{4m},$$
$$-\omega^2 X_2(s) + \left(3s^2 + 2\omega^2\right)X_3(s) = 0.$$

If we apply Cramer's Rule, we find the factored determinant of the coefficient matrix to be

$$D = 2(s^2 + \omega^2)(3s^2 + 2\omega^2)(6s^2 + \omega^2).$$

The transformed solution vector $\mathbf{X}(s)$ is then found to be

$$\mathbf{X}(s) = \frac{I}{mD}\left(3s^2 + 2\omega^2\right)\begin{bmatrix} \omega^2 \\ 3s^2 + 2\omega^2 \\ \omega^2 \end{bmatrix}.$$

After using a partial fraction expansion, this can be written in the form

$$\mathbf{X}(s) = \frac{I}{10m}\left\{\frac{1}{s^2 + \omega^2}\begin{bmatrix} -1 \\ 1 \\ -1 \end{bmatrix} + \frac{1}{6s^2 + \omega^2}\begin{bmatrix} 6 \\ 9 \\ 6 \end{bmatrix}\right\}.$$

Now it is a straightforward matter to write the solution:

$$x_1(t) = \frac{I}{10m\omega}\left[-\sin\omega t + \frac{1}{\sqrt{6}}\sin\omega t\right]$$

$$x_2(t) = \frac{I}{10m\omega}\left[\sin\omega t + \frac{9}{\sqrt{6}}\sin\frac{\omega t}{\sqrt{6}}\right]$$

$$x_3(t) = \frac{I}{10m\omega}\left[-\sin\omega t + \frac{1}{\sqrt{6}}\sin\omega t\right]$$

The subsequent motion has the two smaller masses moving together. ■ ■ ■

■ **EXAMPLE 5.20** Several of the physical situations that we modeled using first order ODE's in Section 2.1 involved an assumption of instantaneous change. In particular, in problems of mixing chemicals in solution we assumed that the chemical was absorbed into solution in zero time when in fact there would be a delay while mixing occurred. Similarly, in Newton's Law of Cooling we expect a delay in the distribution of temperature throughout the body.

A more accurate model would involve the incorporation of a delay τ that we will assume to be constant. An equation to model this would be

$$\frac{d}{dt}T(t) = -\lambda\left(T(t-\tau) - T_{\text{amb}}\right), \quad T(0) = T_0.$$

Such ODE's are called **differential-delay equations**. Since τ is assumed to be constant, we can use Laplace transforms and apply the Second Shifting Theorem. The transform of this equation is

$$s\hat{T}(s) - T_0 = -\lambda\left(e^{-s\tau}\hat{T}(s) - \frac{T_{\text{amb}}}{s}\right),$$

where $T(s) = \mathcal{L}\{T(t)\}$ and T_{amb} is assumed to be constant. Therefore,

$$\hat{T}(s) = \frac{T_0}{s + \lambda e^{-s\tau}} + \frac{\lambda T_{\text{amb}}}{s\left(s + \lambda e^{-s\tau}\right)}.$$

Formally expanding in a geometric series, we have

$$\hat{T}(s) = \sum_{n=0}^{\infty}(-\lambda)^n e^{-ns\tau}\left(\frac{T_0}{s^{n+1}} + \frac{\lambda T_{\text{amb}}}{s^{n+2}}\right).$$

Using the Second Shifting Theorem to invert yields

$$T(t) = \sum_{n=0}^{\infty}(-\lambda)^n\left(T_0\frac{(t-n\tau)^n}{n!} + \lambda T_{\text{amb}}\frac{(t-n\tau)^{n+1}}{(n+1)!}\right)u(t-n\tau).$$

It is instructive to study this solution to determine the effect of the delay. To simplify matters, take the case where $T_{\text{amb}} = 0$. The solution of the equation without delay is $T(t) = T_0 e^{-\lambda t}$. The formal solution of the delay model is

$$T(t) = T_0\left\{u(t) - \lambda(t-\tau)u(t-\tau) + \frac{\lambda^2}{2!}(t-2\tau)^2 u(t-2\tau) + \cdots\right\}.$$

After onset and before $t = \tau$, we have $T(t) = T_0$. For the next t seconds, the solution is $T(t) = T_0[1 - \lambda(t - \tau)]$, and for the following t seconds $T(t) = T_0[1 - \lambda(t - \tau) + \lambda^2(t - 2\tau)^2/2!]$, etc. The graphs of $e^{-\lambda t}$ and $T(t)$ are shown in Figure 5.16. Since $T(t)$ becomes increasing, we may conclude that this is not an acceptable model; insofar as it violates the Second Law of Thermodynamics. ■ ■ ■

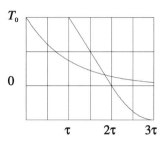

Fig. 5.16

Were we not in such a hurry to invert the transformed solution $Y(s)$ of the ODE $L[y(t)] = g(t)$, we could have studied the zero-state response written as the product

$$Y(s) = H(s)G(s). \tag{5.25}$$

The function $H(s)$ is called the **transfer function** of the system represented by the original differential equation. Were we to further take $y(t)$ to be the input to another system with transfer function $K(s)$, then

$$Z(s) = K(s)Y(s),$$

and we could combine these equations to form a higher order system whose input was $G(s)$, whose output was $Z(s)$, and whose transfer function was $K(s)H(s)$:

$$Z(s) = K(s)H(s)Y(s).$$

Such a process of concatenating systems could be continued for any finite number of steps.

The response of the system is totally determined by the transfer function. In fact, if we wrote

$$H(s) = \frac{N(s)}{D(s)}, \tag{5.26}$$

then $N(s)$ and $D(s)$ would be polynomials in s for all the systems we have studied. Further, the poles of $H(s)$ would be the zeros of $D(s)$. Thus the system would be stable, i.e., its zero-state or transient response would tend to zero as time increased, if all the zeros of $D(s)$ had negative real parts.

Suppose we form a system consisting of two subsections as drawn in Figure 5.17.

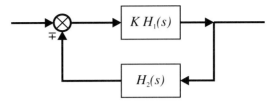

Fig. 5.17

Then $H_1(s)$ is the transfer function for the upper subsystem and $H_2(s)$ is the transfer function for the lower subsystem. The quantity $K(s)$ is called the **gain**, and we assume that it can be adjusted. The idea is to take the outgoing signal from the upper system, pass it through the lower subsystem and use it as a correcting input to the upper subsystem. This is called a **feedback loop**. If the feedback signal is added to the input we have **positive feedback**; otherwise, it is **negative feedback**. The transfer function for the entire system is

$$H(s) = \frac{KH_1(s)}{1 \pm KH_1(s)H_2(s)}. \tag{5.27}$$

The goal of most control systems problems is to vary the gain K and study the resulting output. The details will be left to the references.

5.5.2 *Variable Coefficient ODE's*

Now we need to leave the time invariant case and see what can be done with variable coefficient (time dependent) ODE's. In order to get anywhere, we'll need a formula for $\mathcal{L}\{p(t)y(t)\}$ where $p(t)$ is a coefficient in the ODE. For general functions $p(t)$, no such result exists. (Be careful! The Convolution Theorem cannot be applied here. It refers to multiplication in s-space, not t-space.) For positive integral powers of t, we do have

$$\mathcal{L}\{t^n y(t)\} = \left(-\frac{d}{ds}\right)^n Y(s).$$

This is not quite what we wanted, because terms like $t^3 y(t)$ in a first order ODE will be transformed into third derivatives in s. Only equations involving low powers of t, like t^1 or t^2, will be amenable to simple solution.

■ **EXAMPLE 5.21** The second order equation $t\ddot{y} + \dot{y} + ty = 0$ is called the **zero order Bessel equation**. We would like to find the Laplace transform of the regular part of its solution.

Solution: The general solution of the equation is

$$y(t) = c_1 J_0(t) + c_2 Y_0(t),$$

where $J_0(t)$ and $Y_0(t)$ are the **Bessel functions of order zero of the first and second kinds**, respectively. The function $Y_0(t)$ is not defined at $t = 0$, but $J_0(0) = 1$ and $J_0'(0) = 0$. To find the transform of $J_0(t)$, we proceed as follows:

$$\mathcal{L}\{t\ddot{y}\} + [sY(s) - 1] + \mathcal{L}\{ty(t)\} = 0$$

$$\Rightarrow \quad -\frac{d}{ds}[s^2Y(s) - s(1) - 0] + [sY(s) - 1] - \frac{d}{ds}Y(s) = 0.$$

Using primes for derivatives with respect to s, we find

$$(s^2 + 1)Y'(s) + sY(s) = 0.$$

This equation is separable (and first order linear) and can be immediately solved to obtain

$$Y(s) = \frac{c}{\sqrt{s^2 + 1}} = \frac{1}{s} \cdot \frac{c}{\sqrt{1 + s^{-2}}}.$$

We can find the value of the constant c by using the assumption that $y(t)$, $y'(t)$, and $y''(t)$ are all transformable, in which case we must have $\lim \mathcal{L}\{y'(t)\} = 0$ as $s \to \infty$. Thus it follows that $c = 1$. Therefore,

$$\mathcal{L}\{J_0(t)\} = \frac{1}{\sqrt{s^2 + 1}}.$$

■ ■ ■

Other variable coefficient or nonlinear ODE's do not get any easier than this last example. More information about Bessel functions can be found in Section 9.4.

5.5.3 Boundary Value Problems

We are not restricted to initial value problems when using Laplace transforms. Boundary value problems can be handled by setting the initial values to y_0 and v_0, solving the problem, and then substituting into the boundary conditions to obtain values for y_0 and v_0.

The combination of boundary values and discontinuous inputs occurs frequently in elastic beam deflection problems. If $y(x)$ is the vertical deflection of the beam x units from the left end (see Figure 5.18),

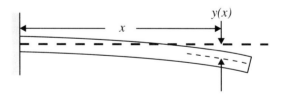

Fig. 5.18

then Hooke's law is

$$EI\, y^{(iv)}(x) = W(x), \tag{5.28}$$

where $W(x)$ is the loading along the beam, E is Young's modulus, and I is the moment of inertia of a cross section to the neutral axis. The ends can be either clamped (embedded in a rigid support), hinged (simply supported), or free. The associated boundary conditions are

$$\begin{aligned} y &= 0 = y' &&\text{horizontally clamped,} \\ y &= 0 = y'' &&\text{hinged,} \\ y'' &= 0 = y''' &&\text{free.} \end{aligned} \qquad (5.29)$$

Point loads can be represented by δ-functions and piecewise varying loads with step functions.

■ **EXAMPLE 5.22** Find the deflection of a beam of length $2L$ due to a point load of W_0 at the midpoint if one end is horizontally clamped and the other is free.

Solution: The boundary value problem is

$$EI\,y^{(iv)} = W_0 \delta(x - L), \quad y(0) = y'(0) = 0 = y''(2L) = y'''(2L).$$

For convenience, set

$$J := \frac{W_0}{EI}, \quad y''(0) = A, \quad y'''(0) = B.$$

We have to carry along the second and third derivatives of the deflection because our conditions are boundary conditions and half of them are given at the right end, $x = 2L$. Transforming, we have

$$s^4 Y(s) - s^3(0) - s^2(A) - B = Je^{-sL}$$

$$\Rightarrow \quad Y(s) = \frac{As + B}{s^4} + \frac{J}{s^4}e^{-sL} = \frac{A}{s^3} + \frac{B}{s^4} + \frac{J}{s^4}e^{-sL}.$$

Inverting, we find

$$y(x) = \frac{1}{2}Ax^2 + \frac{1}{6}Bx^3 + \frac{1}{6}J(x - L)^3 u(x - L).$$

In order to apply the boundary conditions at $x = 2L$, we need the form of $y''(x)$ and $y'''(x)$ there. Beyond $x = L$ the step $u(x - L)$ has turned on and the last term in $y(x)$ is included thus

$$y''(2L) = [A + Bx + J(x - L)]_{x=2L} = A + 2BL + JL = 0,$$

$$y'''(2L) = [0 + B + J]_{x=2L} = B + J = 0.$$

Solving for A and B in terms of the known constant J, we find

$$A = JL, \quad B = -J.$$

The deflection in the beam as a function of x is

$$y(x) = \frac{W_0}{EIL^3}\left[\frac{1}{2}\left(\frac{x}{L}\right)^2 - \frac{1}{6}\left(\frac{x}{L}\right)^3 + \frac{1}{6}\left(\frac{x}{L} - 1\right)^3 u(x - L)\right].$$

The deflection at the end of the beam is

$$y(2L) = \frac{5W_0}{12EIL^3}.$$

■ ■ ■

5.5.4 Exercise Set

Solve each of the following initial value problems using Laplace transforms.

1. $x' + x = u(t - \pi) - u(t - 2\pi), \quad x(0) = 0$

2. $x' - x = u(t - \pi), \quad x(0) = 1$

3. $x' + 2x = 1 - u(t - 1), \quad x(0) = 2$

4. $x' + 2x = 1 - \delta(t - 1), \quad x(0) = 0$

5. $x'' + 2x' - 3x = \delta(t - 1) - u(t - 2), \quad x(0) = 0, \; x'(0) = 0$

6. $x'' + x = \sin t, x(0) = 1, \; x'(0) = 0$

7. $x'' - x = \cosh^2 t, \quad x(0) = 1, \; x'(0) = 0$

8. $x'' - 4x = e^{2t}, \quad x(0) = 2, \; x(0) = 4$

9. $x'' + x = \sin t, \quad x(0) = 1/16, \; x'(0) = 0$

10. $x'' + 3x' + 2x = 1 + t + t^2, \quad x(0) = 1, \; x'(0) = -2$

11.
$$(D^3 - D^2 - 6D)v = \begin{cases} 0, & t < 1, \\ e^{-t}, & 1 \le t, \end{cases} \quad v(0) = 0, \; v'(0) = 2, \; v''(0) = -6$$

12. $\ddot{v} + 3\dot{v} + 2v = 1 - u(t - 1), \quad v(0) = 1, \; v'(0) = 1$

13. $y'' + 3y' + 2y = u(t - 1) - u(t - 2), \quad y(0) = 1, \; y'(0) = 2$

14. $\ddot{x} - 8\dot{x} + 16x = u(t - 1) - u(t - 2), \quad x(0) = 0, \; x'(0) = 1$

15. $\ddot{x} + 4\dot{x} - 5x = u(t) - u(t - \pi/2), \quad x(0) = 0, \; x'(0) = 1$

16. $y'' + 3y' + 2y = \sin t[1 - u(t - \pi)], \quad y(0) = 1, \; y'(0) = 0$

17.
$$\ddot{x} + x = \sum_1^\infty \delta(t - n\pi), \quad x(0) = 0, \; x'(0) = 1$$

Solve each of the following boundary value problems using Laplace transforms.

18. $v'' + v = u(t - 1), \quad v'(0) = 0, \; v(2) = 0$

19. $v'' + 2\sigma v' + (\sigma^2 + \omega^2)v = u(t - \tau), \quad v(0) = 0, \ v(T) = 0, \ \tau \in (0, T)$

20. $y'' + 5y' + 4y = 0, \quad y(0) = 1, \ y(2) = 3$

21. $y'' + y = 0, \quad y(0) = 0, \ y(\pi) = 0$ [What's wrong here?]

22. $y'' + 4y' + 13y = 0, \quad y(0) = 0, \ y(\pi) = 10$

23. A cam follower of mass m is inserted in a tube in such a way that it is connected to the upper end of the tube by a spring with force constant k_1. The lower end of the mass is attached to a spring with force constant k_2, the other end of which connects to a small piece, the cam, which is free to move in a smaller tube (see Figure 5.19).

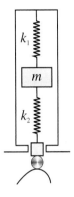

Fig. 5.19

As the larger tube moves across a surface, the cam follows the contour of the surface and the mass and two springs move in reaction to it. If the cam follows an arched protuberance described by $z = a\,(1 - \cos \Omega t)\, w(t; 0, 2\pi/\Omega)$ on an otherwise flat surface, find the motion of the mass m.

24. A weight $W = mg$ suspended by a spring is initially acted upon by a constant force F. After a time τ, the force ceases. If the force constant of the spring is k, find the motion of the weight for $t > 0$. Redo the problem if the force increases linearly from a value of zero at $t = 0$ to its full value F at $t = \tau$, at which time it ceases. What are the amplitude and period of the oscillations that follow the application of the force?

25. Suppose we are still looking at a weight $W = mg$ attached to a spring with force constant k, only this time the weight is being driven by a force $F(t) = F_0 \,|\sin \Omega t|$. Determine the form of the oscillations that have the same frequency as the driving force.

26. In the Lagrangian formulation of models for traffic flow, the location of each car is specified and followed. In particular, $x_n(t)$ is the location of the nth car as a function of time, $v_n(t) := \dot{x}_n(t)$ is its velocity, and we assume that all cars were initially moving at a constant speed, so that $v_n(t) = v_0$ for $t \le 0$. The idea is to model the flow of traffic after $t = 0$. To eliminate v_0 from the problem, set $u_n(t) := v_n(t) - v_0$, so that $u_n(t)$ is causal. A first approximation to the motion of any one car

is that its acceleration (or deceleration) is proportional to its speed relative to the car in front of it; i.e., $\dot{u}_n(t) = k\,(u_{n-1}(t) - u_n(t))$, $n = 2 : N$, where N is the number of cars in the queue. The corresponding initial conditions are $u_n(0) = 0$, $n = 2 : N$. Once we specify the speed of the lead car as a function of time, these equations can be solved. By the way, a plausible value of k is 0.35.

(a) Suppose the lead car moves at a sinusoidal speed $u_0(t) = \sin \omega t$. Use Laplace transforms to find the speed of the second and third cars.

(b) Argue that $|u_n(t)| \leq w^{n-1}$, where $w = k/\sqrt{k^2 + \omega^2} < 1$, and use this to argue that $u_n(t)$ decreases as n increases. Thus the effect of the lead car does not propagate along the queue, which is clearly unrealistic (as anyone who has sat in traffic will know).

27. In an attempt to improve the previous model of traffic flow, introduce a constant lag in the response of each of the follower cars by using the model equation

$$\dot{u}_n(t) = k\,(u_{n-1}(t - T) - u_n(t - T)), \ t > T, \ n = 2 : N.$$

(a) Use Laplace transforms to find $U_n(s)$.

(b) Again take the case where $u_1(t) = \sin \omega t$, and find $U_2(s)$ and $U_n(s)$.

(c) Use a computer algebra system to find $u_2(t) = \mathcal{L}^{-1}\{U_2(s)\}$. Plot this function and tell what the response of the second car is to the oscillatory behavior of the first car. It can be shown that the behavior of the queue will be stable for "small" values of kT.

28. An elastic beam of length 4 is simply supported at both ends, and a uniform load of mass 1 and length 2 is centered on the beam. Find the resulting deflection as a function of position. Also, find the deflection of the beam at the center.

29. An elastic beam of length $2L$ is clamped at the $x = 0$ end and simply supported at the other. A point load W_0 is placed at $x = L$. Find the deflection as a function of position, and in particular at the center.

30. A beam of length L is clamped at both ends. If there is a unit point load at $x = a$, find the deflection in the beam as a function of the distance from the left end.

31. A uniform beam of length L has a load of Wx per unit length on its left half and a load of $W(L-x)$ per unit length on its right half. If the left end is clamped and the right end is simply supported, find the deflection as a function of distance from the left end.

32. A mass-spring system with natural period T is given an impulse of magnitude one at time zero and every T seconds thereafter. Find the displacement as a function of time and show that the system is in resonance.

33. Suppose the circuit shown in Figure 5.20 has zero initial current and zero initial charge on the capacitor. Can the inductive effect of the resistive coil be neutralized by shunting with a resistance and a capacitor as shown?

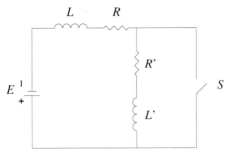

Fig. 5.20

5.6 BOUNDARY VALUE GREEN'S FUNCTIONS VIA TRANSFORMS

The last section of the previous chapter introduced the idea of the boundary value Green's function as the response to an impulsive input. Our experience so far indicates that Laplace transforms are a powerful tool for solving ODE's with discontinuous inputs.

Solving $L[G(x,\xi)] = \delta(x - \xi)$ using transforms will be easiest when $\mathcal{L}$ is a constant coefficient linear differential operator. In fact, if a, b, and c are constants and the boundary conditions are applied at $x = 0$ and $x = L$, the second order equation for $G(x,\xi)$ can be written as

$$aG''(x,\xi) + bG'(x,\xi) + cG(x,\xi) = \delta(x - \xi). \tag{5.30}$$

Denoting the Laplace transform of $G(x,\xi)$ by $\hat{G}(s,\xi)$, this equation can be transformed into

$$(as^2 + bs + c)\hat{G}(s,\xi) = e^{-s\xi} + asG(0,\xi) + (aG'(0,\xi) + bG(0,\xi)).$$

If $w_0(x) = \mathcal{L}^{-1}\left\{\left(as^2 + bs + c\right)^{-1}\right\}$, then we can use inversion and the Convolution Theorem to write the Green's function as the sum

$$G(x,\xi) = w_0(x - \xi)u(x - \xi) - aG(0,\xi)\delta'_\xi * w_0 + (aG'(0,\xi) + bG(0,\xi))\,w_0(x). \tag{5.31}$$

■ **EXAMPLE 5.23** Use Laplace transforms to solve the following simple problem.

$$w''(x) = 0, \quad w(0) = 0 = w'(L).$$

Solution: The transform of the Green's function satisfies

$$s^2\hat{G}(s,\xi) = e^{-s\xi} + G'(0,\xi).$$

Inversion yields

$$G(x,\xi) = (x - \xi)u(x - \xi) + xG'(0,\xi).$$

Since $G'(0, \xi)$ is not given, we must use the right boundary condition to find it:

$$G'(L, \xi) = 1 + 1 \cdot G'(0, \xi) = 0.$$

From this we can write

$$G(x, \xi) = (x - \xi)u(x - \xi) - x.$$

It is left as an exercise to show this is the same as the result obtained in the previous chapter.

■ ■ ■

■ **EXAMPLE 5.24** Find the Green's function for the harmonic oscillator equation with fixed ends by using transforms.

Solution: The equation is

$$G''(x, \xi) + \omega^2 G(x, \xi) = \delta(x - \xi), \quad G(0, \xi) = 0 = G(L, \xi).$$

After transforming, it becomes

$$(s^2 + \omega^2)\hat{G}(s, \xi) = e^{-sc} + G'(0, \xi).$$

Inversion leads to

$$G(x, \xi) = \frac{\sin \omega(x - \xi)}{\omega}u(x - \xi) + G'(0, \xi)\frac{\sin \omega x}{\omega}.$$

Using $G(L, \xi) = 0$ to solve for $G'(0, \xi)$, we must remember that the point at which the impulse is applied, ξ, lies between 0 and L. Thus the unit step is turned on and

$$G(x, L) = \frac{\sin \omega(x - L)}{\omega} + G'(0, L)\frac{\sin \omega L}{\omega} = 0.$$

This brings us to the final result:

$$G(x, \xi) = \frac{\sin \omega L \sin \omega(x - \xi)u(x - \xi) - \sin \omega(L - \xi)\sin \omega x}{\omega \sin \omega L}.$$

Once again it is a nontrivial task to verify that the form of this Green's function is the same as that derived in the previous chapter, and so it is left to the problems.

■ ■ ■

5.6.1 *Exercise Set*

Use Laplace transforms to find the Green's functions for each of the following boundary value problems.

1. $u'' + \omega^2 u = 0$, $\quad u(0) = 0 = u'(L)$ 2. $u'' + \omega^2 u = 0$, $\quad u'(0) = 0 = u(L)$

3. $u'' + \omega^2 u = 0$, $\quad u'(a) = 0 = u'(b)$ 4. $u'' - \mu^2 u = 0$, $\quad u(0) = 0 = u(1)$

5. $u'' + \omega^2 u = 0$, $\quad u(0) = u(1), \ u'(0) = u'(1)$

6. $D^4 u = 0, \quad u(0) = u'(0) = 0 = u(L) = u'(L)$

7. $(D^4 - 1)u = 0, \quad u(0) = u''(0) = 0 = u(L) = u''(L)$

8. $(D^4 - 1)u = 0, \quad u(0) = u'(0) = 0 = u(L) = u'(L)$

5.6.2   Notes and References

Not all functions $F(s)$ that we will see can be inverted by the methods of this chapter. For that reason the subject must be revisited in courses in complex analysis wherein more powerful techniques can be brought to bear. Most differential equations texts have chapters covering Laplace transforms at about the same level as this chapter. More advanced work in the subject is usually called *operational mathematics*.

- Churchill, *Operational Mathematics*: The first part of the book deals with Laplace transforms.

5.7   SUPPLEMENTARY AND COMPLEMENTARY PROBLEMS

1. The Laguerre polynomials can be defined by the formula

$$L_n(t) = \frac{1}{n!} e^t \left(\frac{d}{dt}\right)^n \left(t^n e^{-t}\right).$$

Show that the Laplace transform of $L_n(t)$ is

$$\frac{1}{s}\left(\frac{s-1}{s}\right)^n.$$

Assuming all operations are allowed, use the power series representations of the s-space functions to verify each of the following identities.

2. $\mathcal{L}^{-1}\left\{\log\left(1 + \dfrac{a^2}{s^2}\right)\right\} = 2 - \dfrac{2\cos at}{t}$

3. $\mathcal{L}^{-1}\left\{\log\left(\dfrac{s+a}{s+b}\right)\right\} = \dfrac{1}{t}\left(e^{-bt} - e^{-at}\right)$

4. $\mathcal{L}^{-1}\left\{\dfrac{e^{-a\sqrt{s}}}{\sqrt{s}}\right\} = \dfrac{1}{\sqrt{\pi t}} e^{-a^2/(4t)}$

5. Assuming all integrals are as well behaved as necessary, show that if $\mathcal{L}\{f(t)\} = F(s)$, then

$$\int_0^\infty F(s)\, ds = \int_0^\infty \frac{f(t)}{t}\, dt.$$

Use the result of problem 5 to evaluate each of the following integrals:

6. $\displaystyle\int_0^\infty \frac{\sin \alpha t}{t}\, dt$

7. $\displaystyle\int_0^\infty \frac{e^{-\alpha t} - e^{-\beta t}}{t}\, dt$

Evaluate each of the following integrals by transforming them and inverting.

8. $\displaystyle\int_0^\infty \exp(-tz^2)\, dz$

9. $\displaystyle\int_0^\infty \frac{\cos(tz)}{1 + z^2}\, dz$

10. The nth **convolution power** is defined by

$$(f(t))^{*n} := \underbrace{(f * f * .. * f)}_{n\text{-factors}} (t).$$

(a) Show that

$$(u(t - T))^{*n} = \frac{(t - nT)^{n-1}}{(n-1)!} u(t - nT).$$

(b) What is $(\delta(t - T))^{*n}$?

(c) What is $(\delta'(t - T))^{*n}$?

11. If $a(t)$, $f(t)$, and $k(t)$ are known functions, then the integral equation

$$a(t)\phi(t) - \lambda \int_0^t k(t - \tau)\phi(\tau)\, d\tau = f(t)$$

satisfied by the unknown function $f(t)$ is called a **Volterra integral equation**. By taking Laplace transforms, show that when $a(t) = 1$ (this is not a restriction unless $a(t)$ is zero),

$$\phi(t) = \mathcal{L}^{-1}\{\Phi(s)\} = \mathcal{L}^{-1}\left\{\frac{F(s)}{1 - \lambda K(s)}\right\}.$$

Use the last problem to solve each of the following Volterra integral equations:

12. $\phi(t) - \beta \displaystyle\int_0^t \phi(\tau) \sin \beta(t - \tau)\, d\tau = \alpha \sin t.$

13. $\phi(t) - \displaystyle\int_0^t \phi(\tau) e^{-\beta(t-\tau)}\, d\tau = 1.$

14. $\displaystyle\int_0^t \phi(\tau) e^{-\beta(t-\tau)}\, d\tau = t.$ In this case $a(t) = 0$, and so you'll have to start from scratch.

15. By transforming the equation directly (and *not* changing to time invariant form), use Laplace transforms to find the Green's function for the following boundary value problem:

$$x^2 y'' + xy' + y = 0, \quad y(1) = 0 = y(e).$$

6

SYSTEMS OF LINEAR ODE'S

6.1 PREVIEW

Many physical problems have more than one dependent variable to be considered. Models of such problems can give rise to systems of equations. This chapter will concern itself with systems of simultaneous linear ordinary differential equations. We will begin with an overview of linear systems of ODE's. It will be shown that all linear systems can be put into the form of a first order ODE whose unknown function is a vector function. Just as for scalar equations, the understanding of the concept of a linearly independent set of functions will be crucial to assuring us that we have a general solution.

In order to know how to use an appropriate form for a trial solution, we will need to digress slightly to the study of the matrix eigenvalue problem. This will begin with a discussion of the form of a matrix under a change of basis. Eigenvalues and eigenvectors will be defined, and we will see that the eigenvalues of a matrix satisfy the so-called characteristic equation. Once the eigenvalues are known, it will be a simple matter of solving homogeneous systems of linear algebraic equations to find the corresponding eigenvectors. Upon a change to the "eigenbasis," a certain class of matrices takes a diagonal form. A special approach is necessary for matrices that do not fall into this class, and hence the more general Jordan normal form needs to be considered.

Two distinct solution methods will be developed for the equivalent of constant coefficient equations. In the first, a trial solution vector function will be inserted into the system, converting it into a matrix eigenvalue problem whose solution will be used to construct the general solution. The second method will avoid the use of eigenvectors altogether. Examples of oscillations of multidegree of freedom systems and a model for a one-dimensional lattice vibrations will be given.

An analog to the method of variation of parameters will be derived and applied to nonhomogeneous linear systems. The theory of linear systems will be generalized by the introduction of the state-transition matrix for a system. It will be shown that knowing the state-transition matrix leads to the solution of the homogeneous and nonhomogeneous systems. For homogeneous autonomous systems, the state-transition matrix is the exponential of the coefficient matrix times $t - t_0$, where t_0 is the starting time. We will take a small detour to develop methods for evaluating functions of a square matrix.

As a change of pace, we then look at phase plane analysis of time invariant linear systems. Fixed points are defined and classified in terms of the eigenvalues of the coefficient matrix. Solution curves near the fixed points are drawn and the trajectories are studied. This will serve as a prelude to the analysis of nonlinear systems in the next chapter.

Linear systems with initial conditions can be solved by defining the response matrix or initial value Green's function for the system. The solution can then be written as a convolution integral of the forcing function and the Green's function. A brief introduction to the concepts of controllability, observability, and stability of systems is given. Lastly, the Laplace transform techniques are applied to linear systems to convert them to algebraic systems that can then be solved and inverted.

6.2 MULTIVARIATE ODE MODELS

A model with more than one unknown function can be formulated as a system of equations. We saw that for systems in equilibrium the resulting set of equations was algebraic. When our model includes the possibility of change, we will arrive at systems of differential equations.

■ **EXAMPLE 6.1** As an extension of the simple RLC circuits from Chapter 2, consider the more involved circuit shown in Figure 6.1.

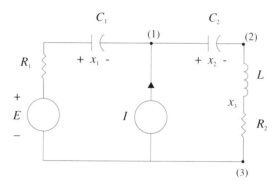

Fig. 6.1

Solution: Let $x_1(t)$ and $x_2(t)$ be the voltage drops across the capacitors C_1 and C_2, and let $x_3(t)$ be the current from the inductor toward the resistor. The current from C_1 to the right is $C_1\dot{x}_1$; the current to the right from C_2 is $C_2\dot{x}_2$; the voltage across L is $L\dot{x}_3$; the voltage across R_2 is R_2x_3; and the voltage across R_1 is $R_1C_1\dot{x}_1$. If we apply the KVL to the outer loop, we get

$$-E(t) + R_1C_1\dot{x}_1(t) + x_1(t) + x_2(t) + L\dot{x}_3(t) + R_2x_3(t) = 0.$$

KCL at nodes (1) and (2) yields

$$C_1\dot{x}_1(t) + I(t) - C_2\dot{x}_2(t) = 0,$$
$$C_2\dot{x}_2(t) - x_3(t) = 0.$$

If the output $y(t)$ of the system is the voltage across nodes (2) and (3), then

$$
\begin{aligned}
y(t) &= L\dot{x}_3(t) + R_2 x_3(t) \\
&= x_1(t) + x_2(t) - (R_1 + R_2) x_3(t) + u_1(t) + R_1 u_2(t) + R_2 x_3(t) \\
&= x_1(t) + x_2(t) - R_1 x_3(t) + R_1 u_2(t),
\end{aligned}
$$

where $u_1(t) := E(t)$ and $u_2(t) := I(t)$. This can be put into the matrix form:

$$
\dot{\mathbf{x}}(t) =
\begin{bmatrix}
0 & 0 & 1/C_1 \\
0 & 0 & 1/C_2 \\
1/L & 1/L & -(R_1 + R_2)/L
\end{bmatrix}
\mathbf{x}(t) +
\begin{bmatrix}
0 & -1/C_1 \\
0 & 0 \\
1/L & R_1/L
\end{bmatrix}
\mathbf{u}(t),
$$

with output

$$y(t) = [1, 1, -R_1]\mathbf{x}(t) + [1, R_1]\mathbf{u}(t),$$

where the vectors $\mathbf{x}(t)$ and $\mathbf{u}(t)$ are defined in the obvious way. An alternative form using loop currents will be explored in the problems. ■ ■ ■

■ **EXAMPLE 6.2** Find the equations of motion of a satellite of mass $m = 1$ (in the appropriate choice of units) that is orbiting the earth.

Solution: From Newton's Law of Gravitation we have

$$\ddot{\mathbf{r}} = -G\frac{M_e}{r^3}\mathbf{r} =: -\frac{k}{r^3}\mathbf{r}, \tag{6.1}$$

where $G = 6.67 \times 10^{-11}$ Nm^2/kg^2 is the universal constant of gravitation and M_e is the mass of the earth (5.98×10^{24} kg). Using the vector equations

$$\mathbf{r} = r\mathbf{e}_r = r(\cos\theta\mathbf{i} + \sin\theta\mathbf{j}) \quad \text{and} \quad \mathbf{e}_\theta = -\sin\theta\mathbf{i} + \cos\theta\mathbf{j},$$

equation (6.1) can be transformed into

$$\left(\ddot{r} - r\dot{\theta}^2\right)\mathbf{e}_r + \left(2\dot{r}\dot{\theta} + r\ddot{\theta}\right)\mathbf{e}_\theta = -\frac{k}{r^2}\mathbf{e}_r.$$

Equating components, the equations of motion of the satellite are

$$\ddot{r} = r\dot{\theta}^2 - \frac{k}{r^2}, \quad \ddot{\theta} = -\frac{2\dot{r}\dot{\theta}}{r},$$

when there are no inputs to the system. Suppose the satellite is fitted with retro rockets that provide thrust u_1 in the radial and u_2 in the tangential directions. Then the equations of motion become

$$\ddot{r} = r\dot{\theta}^2 - \frac{k}{r^2} + u_1, \quad \ddot{\theta} = -\frac{2\dot{r}\dot{\theta}}{r} + \frac{u_2}{r}.$$

This is clearly two simultaneous ordinary differential equations in the unknown functions $r(t)$ and $\theta(t)$. When there are no thrusters, it can be verified that

$$r(t) = r_0 \quad \text{and} \quad \theta(t) = \omega t$$

are solutions for $r_0^3 \omega^2 = k$ (which is Kepler's Third Law). This is exactly a circular orbit. These equations can be put this into matrix form by setting

$$x_1 := r - r_0, \quad x_2 := \dot{r}, \quad x_3 := r_0(\theta - \omega t), \quad x_4 := r_0(\dot{\theta} - \omega);$$

linearizing (multiplying everything out and keeping only terms involving the x's to the first power and dropping all products of x's) and choosing our units so that $r_0 = 1$, we have

$$\dot{\mathbf{x}}(t) = \begin{bmatrix} 0 & 1 & 0 & 0 \\ 3\omega^2 & 0 & 0 & 2\omega \\ 0 & 0 & 0 & 1 \\ 0 & -2\omega & 0 & 0 \end{bmatrix} \mathbf{x}(t) + \begin{bmatrix} 0 & 0 \\ 1 & 0 \\ 0 & 0 \\ 0 & 1 \end{bmatrix} \mathbf{u}(t).$$

Not only do we want to know the trajectory of the satellite as a function of time, but there are other fundamental questions to be answered. Using the thrusters can the satellite be maneuvered into an orbit that takes it through a given point? What if one of the thrusters fails to function; how does that change the answer to the previous question? ∎ ∎ ∎

Finding the equations of motion of a system without dissipative forces can be facilitated by using the so-called Euler-Lagrange equations. The Lagrangian of the system is $L = \text{KE} - \text{PE}$, kinetic minus potential energy. If L is a function of the coordinates q_k and their derivatives with respect to time $\dot{q}_k$, $k = 1 : n$, then the Euler-Lagrange equations are

$$\frac{d}{dt} \left(\frac{\partial L}{\partial \dot{q}_k} \right) - \frac{\partial L}{\partial q_k} = 0, \quad k = 1 : n.$$

Use of the Euler-Lagrange equations allows us to avoid the complexities of the free body diagram.

■ **EXAMPLE 6.3** Find the equations of small oscillations of the double pendulum system shown in Figure 6.2.

Solution: Were we to try to draw a free body diagram for the lower mass we'd be in deep trouble because its pivot is accelerating and we would be in a noninertial reference frame. Instead, we can easily find the Lagrangian. If θ_1 and θ_2 are the angular deflections from the vertical for the upper and lower pendulum arms, respectively, then the coordinate vector to the masses would be

$$\mathbf{r}_1 = (L_1 \sin \theta_1)\, \mathbf{i} - (L_1 \cos \theta_1)\, \mathbf{j}$$

and

$$\mathbf{r}_2 = (L_1 \sin \theta_1 + L_2 \sin \theta_2)\, \mathbf{i} - (L_1 \cos \theta_1 + L_2 \cos \theta_2)\, \mathbf{j},$$

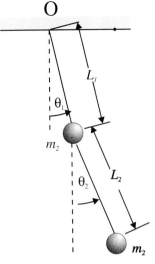

Fig. 6.2

where the x-axis points to the right and the y-axis points upward. Since the kinetic energy is

$$\frac{1}{2}m_1\left\|\mathbf{r}_1\right\|^2 + \frac{1}{2}m_2\left\|\mathbf{r}_2\right\|^2,$$

we can write the Lagrangian as

$$L = \frac{1}{2}m_1 L_1^2\dot{\theta}_1^2 + \frac{1}{2}m_2\left(L_1\dot{\theta}_1^2 + L_2\dot{\theta}_2^2 + 2L_1L_2\dot{\theta}_1\dot{\theta}_2\cos(\theta_1-\theta_2)\right)$$

$$+ m_1 g L_1\cos\theta_1 + m_2 g\left(L_1\cos\theta_1 + L_2\cos\theta_2\right).$$

The equations of motion are

$$\frac{d}{dt}\left(m_1 L_1^2\dot{\theta}_1 + m_2 L_1^2\dot{\theta}_1 + m_2 L_1 L_2\dot{\theta}_2\cos(\theta_1-\theta_2)\right) + (m_1+m_2)gL_1\sin\theta_1 = 0,$$

$$\frac{d}{dt}\left(m_2 L_2^2\dot{\theta}_2 + m_2 L_1 L_2\dot{\theta}_1\cos(\theta_1-\theta_2)\right) + m_2 g L_2\sin\theta_2 = 0.$$

Performing the differentiation:

$$(m_1+m_2)L_1^2\ddot{\theta}_1 + m_2 L_1 L_2\left(\ddot{\theta}_2\cos(\theta_1-\theta_2) - \dot{\theta}_2(\dot{\theta}_1-\dot{\theta}_2)\sin(\theta_1-\theta_2)\right)$$
$$+ (m_1+m_2)gL_1\sin\theta_1 = 0,$$
$$m_2 L_2^2\ddot{\theta}_2 + m_2 L_1 L_2\left(\ddot{\theta}_1\cos(\theta_1-\theta_2) - \dot{\theta}_1(\dot{\theta}_1-\dot{\theta}_2)\sin(\theta_1-\theta_2)\right)$$
$$+ m_2 g L_2\sin\theta_2 = 0.$$

If we assume small oscillations, then $\sin\theta \approx \theta$, $\cos\theta \approx 1$, and we can neglect products of θ's. The final equations are

$$(m_1 + m_2)L_1^2\ddot{\theta}_1 + m_2L_1L_2\ddot{\theta}_2 + (m_1 + m_2)gL_1\theta_1 = 0,$$

$$m_2L_2^2\ddot{\theta}_2 + m_2L_1L_2\ddot{\theta}_1 + m_2gL_2\theta_2 = 0.$$

Without a doubt, this was much easier than the alternative.

■ ■ ■

6.2.1 Exercise Set

1. A system consists of two identical blocks, each of mass m, which are free to slide along a smooth horizontal floor between two vertical walls. Between the blocks and attached from the wall to each block are springs, each with force constant k (See Figure 6.3).

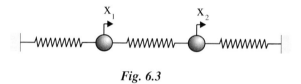

Fig. 6.3

Write the equations of motion of the system. Redo the problem if there are three blocks and four springs.

2. A pendulum consists of a bob of mass m attached to a pivot by a rigid and (relatively) massless bar of length L. The pivot, which is the axle of a homogeneous solid wheel of radius R and mass M, is free to roll horizontally in a rough keyway (See Figure 6.4(a)).

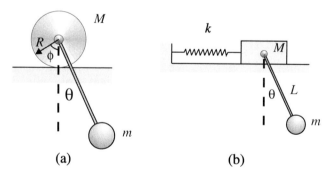

Fig. 6.4

Find the equations of motion of the system.

3. A pendulum consists of a bob of mass m attached to a pivot by a rigid and (relatively) massless bar of length L. The pivot is attached to a block of mass M that is free to slide along a horizontal rail. The block is attached to a wall to the left by a spring with force constant k (see Figure 6.4(b)). Find the equations of motion.

4. An electrical circuit consists of four loops as shown in Figure 6.5.

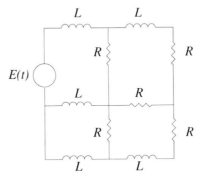

Fig. 6.5

Find the dynamical equations for the circuit.

5. A chemical reactor consists of four tanks. The first three each contain different reagents and the fourth contains pure water. Tanks $1 : 3$ are interconnected so that there is a flow of 5% of the volume of each tank between each other tank each minute. As a form of mixing, the second and third tanks have 10% of their volume drawn off from their bottoms and pumped back into the top each minute. Pure water is added to the first and second tanks at a rate of 5 liters per minute. If the capacity of each tank is 1000 liters and they are all initially half full with a 25%, 25%, 50%, and 35% concentration of reagents in each, respectively, set up the equations that will determine what the volumes and concentrations in each tank are as a function of time.

6.3   SYSTEMS OF LINEAR ODE'S

6.3.1   *Introduction to Systems of ODE's*

As an indication of the power of the mathematics associated with systems of ODE's, every equation of order n that can be written in explicit form as

$$w^{(n)} = f\left(t, w, w', w'', \ldots, w^{(n-1)}\right)$$

can be put into matrix form by the following procedure. Define the vector function $\mathbf{x}(t) = [x_1(t) ; x_2(t) ; \ldots ; x_n(t)]$. Then set

$$x_1(t) = w(t), \quad x_2(t) = w'(t), \quad x_3(t) = w''(t), \quad \ldots, \quad x_n(t) = w^{(n-1)}(t). \qquad (6.2)$$

Differentiating $\mathbf{x}$, we have

$$\mathbf{x}' = \left[w'; w''; \ldots; w^{(n)}\right] = \left[x_2; x_3; \ldots; x_n; f(t, x_1, x_2, \ldots, x_n)\right].$$

This can be rewritten as the first order vector ODE

$$\mathbf{x}'(t) = \begin{bmatrix} x_2 \\ x_3 \\ \vdots \\ f(t, x_1, x_2, \ldots, x_n) \end{bmatrix} =: \mathbf{f}(t, \mathbf{x}).$$

We will call this the **standard matrix form** of the equation.

A system that has no explicit dependence on time is said to be **autonomous**, i.e., it has the form

$$\mathbf{x}' = \mathbf{f}(\mathbf{x}). \tag{6.3}$$

Unfortunately, it is not always a trivial matter to convert a system of ODE's to a first order system. The key point is that we need to use a vector whose components contain the unknown functions and their derivatives up to one order lower than the highest orders that appear in the system. An example or two should clarify this.

■ **EXAMPLE 6.4** For each of the following equations or systems of equations, convert to the standard matrix form.

(a) The forced damped harmonic oscillator equation can be written in the form

$$y'' + 2\beta y' + \omega^2 y = g(t).$$

Because there is only one dependent variable and the equation is second order we need to introduce a vector variable whose components are y and y'. In particular $\mathbf{x} := [y; y']$. Then

$$\mathbf{x}' = [y'; y''] = \left[y'; -\omega^2 y - 2\beta y' + g(t)\right]$$
$$= \left[x_2; -\omega^2 x_1 - 2\beta x_2 + g(t)\right].$$

This can be put into standard matrix form as

$$\mathbf{x}' = \begin{bmatrix} 0 & 1 \\ -\omega^2 & -2\beta \end{bmatrix} \mathbf{x} + \begin{bmatrix} 0 \\ g(t) \end{bmatrix}.$$

(b) The system governed by the pair of equations

$$u'' + u' + 2v' - 3u + v = t,$$
$$u' + 4v' + 5u - 6v = 2t$$

has the dependent variables u and v, with u appearing as a second order term but v occurring as at most a first order term. Thus the vector should contain u, u', and v, with $\mathbf{x} := [u; u'; v]$ as one possible choice. In terms of the components of x, the system is

$$
\begin{aligned}
x_1' - x_2 &= 0, \\
x_2' + x_2 + 2x_3' - 3x_1 + x_3 &= t, \\
x_2 + 4x_3' + 5x_1 - 6x_3 &= 2t
\end{aligned}
$$

$$
\Rightarrow \quad
\begin{aligned}
x_1' &= & x_2, \\
x_2' + 2x_3' &= & 3x_1 & -x_2 & -x_3 & +t, \\
4x_3' &= & -5x_1 & -x_2 & +6x_3 & +2t.
\end{aligned}
$$

Putting this into matrix form, we have

$$
\begin{bmatrix} 1 & 0 & 0 \\ 0 & 1 & 2 \\ 0 & 0 & 4 \end{bmatrix} \mathbf{x}'(t) = \begin{bmatrix} 0 & 1 & 0 \\ 3 & -1 & -1 \\ -5 & -1 & 6 \end{bmatrix} \mathbf{x}(t) + \begin{bmatrix} 0 \\ t \\ 2t \end{bmatrix}.
$$

At this stage we should invert the matrix multiplying $\mathbf{x}'(t)$ to put the system in the standard nonautonomous form

$$
\mathbf{x}'(t) = \frac{1}{4} \begin{bmatrix} 0 & 4 & 0 \\ 22 & -2 & -16 \\ -5 & -1 & 6 \end{bmatrix} \mathbf{x}(t) + \frac{1}{2} \begin{bmatrix} 0 \\ 0 \\ t \end{bmatrix}.
$$

(c) Consider the nonlinear system

$$
\begin{aligned}
u'' + 3u'v - 2\sin v &= t, \\
v'' - uv' + 3\cos u &= 1.
\end{aligned}
$$

Because both u and v occur as second derivatives, one appropriate unknown vector function is $\mathbf{x} := [u; u'; v; v']$. In terms of the components of $\mathbf{x}$, the system can be written as

$$
\begin{aligned}
x_2' + 3x_2 x_3 - 2\sin x_3 &= t, \\
x_4' - x_1 x_4 + 3\cos x_1 &= 1.
\end{aligned}
$$

The standard matrix form of the nonautonomous system is

$$
\mathbf{x}'(t) = \begin{bmatrix} x_2 \\ -3x_2 x_3 + 2\sin x_3 + t \\ x_4 \\ x_1 x_4 - 3\cos x_1 + 1 \end{bmatrix}.
$$

■ ■ ■

In addition to coming from scalar equations, systems arise naturally in multidegree of freedom problems like those given in example 6.1. For the purposes of this chapter, we will be concerned with linear systems.

DEFINITION 6.1 *If* $\mathbf{A}(t) \in \mathbb{C}_n^n$, $\mathbf{x}(t), \mathbf{b}(t) \in \mathbb{C}^n$, *then a system is said to be* **linear** *if it can be put into the form*

$$\mathbf{x}'(t) = \mathbf{A}(t)\mathbf{x}(t) + \mathbf{b}(t), \tag{6.4}$$

where $\mathbf{b}(t)$ *is the* **forcing**, *or* **input**, **vector** *and* $\mathbf{A}(t)$ *is the* **coefficient matrix**. *We call* $\mathbf{x}(t)$ *the* **state** *of the system.*

The systems in parts (a) and (b) of the last example are linear systems, whereas part (c) is a nonlinear system.

6.3.2 *Linearly Independent Sets of Vector Functions*

Just as we did with scalar linear equations, we will solve the homogeneous system

$$\mathbf{x}'(t) = \mathbf{A}(t)\mathbf{x}(t) \tag{6.5}$$

first. As we accumulate solution vector functions, we will need to know when we have enough of them. This is equivalent to knowing when we have found a basis of the solution space of the equation. The notion of linear independence of vector functions is a bit more subtle than it was for sets of constant vectors.

DEFINITION 6.2 *A set of vector functions* $\mathcal{B} = \{\mathbf{x}_1(t), \mathbf{x}_2(t), \ldots, \mathbf{x}_k(t)\}$ *is said to be* **linearly independent** *on the interval* (a, b) *if the only linear relation among the elements of* $\mathcal{B}$ *that holds for every* $t \in (a, b)$ *is the trivial one. This requires that the linear relation*

$$c_1\mathbf{x}_1(t) + c_2\mathbf{x}_2(t) + \cdots + c_k\mathbf{x}_k(t) = \mathbf{0},$$

defined for all t *between* a *and* b, *be true only when* $c_1 = c_2 = \cdots = c_k = 0$.

This may not appear to be very different from the definitions in either Section 3.2.2 or 4.2.2 but the following example should illustrate the difference.

■ **EXAMPLE 6.5** Let's study the linear independence of the set of vector functions

$$\mathcal{B} = \left\{ \mathbf{x}_1(t) = \left[e^{3t}; e^{3t}\right], \mathbf{x}_2(t) = \left[2e^{-5t}; 2e^{-5t}\right] \right\}.$$

If we look at these two vector functions at a particular point, say $t = t_0$, the linear relation is

$$c_1 \left[e^{3t_0}; e^{3t_0}\right] + c_2 \left[2e^{-5t_0}; 2e^{-5t_0}\right] = [0; 0].$$

This can be rewritten in the form

$$\left(c_1 e^{3t_0}\right)[1; 1] + \left(c_2 e^{-5t_0}\right)[2; 2] = [0; 0].$$

This is a linear relation on the *set of constant vectors* $\{[1; 1], [2; 2]\}$. This set is clearly not linearly independent because the vectors are multiples of each other. Thus the constants $c_1 e^{3t_0}$

and $c_2 e^{-5t_0}$ could be nonzero. Knowing that e^z is never zero, for all finite z, allows us to conclude that

$$c_1 = -c_2 e^{-8t_0}.$$

Hence the vectors are linearly dependent at the point $t = t_0$, for any value of t_0. But for t ranging throughout the interval $(-\infty, \infty)$ we have another matter. Form the linear relation that must hold for all real t:

$$c_1 \left[e^{3t}; e^{3t} \right] + c_2 \left[2e^{-5t}; 2e^{-5t} \right] = [0; 0].$$

Knowing that the functions are the important aspects of this relation, write this linear relation in the form

$$\left(c_1 e^{3t} + c_2 e^{-5t} \right) [1; 1] = [0; 0].$$

We know that the vector equation will be true if and only if both of its component equations are true. Each component equation is

$$c_1 e^{3t} + c_2 e^{-5t} = 0.$$

This is the linear relation that we would use to test for linear independence of the set of scalar *functions* $\left\{ e^{3t}, e^{-5t} \right\}$. But we know this set is linearly independent on the real line, so that we must have $c_1 = c_2 = 0$. Thus the set of vector functions, $\{\mathbf{x}_1(t), \mathbf{x}_2(t)\}$, is linearly independent on the interval $(-\infty, \infty)$. ∎ ∎ ∎

This last example shows that linear independence of vector functions on an interval is quite different from that of constant vectors. A set of vector functions can be linearly independent on an interval even if it is linearly dependent at various points on the interval.

If we form the linear relation on a set of vector functions

$$\{\mathbf{x}_1(t), \mathbf{x}_2(t), \ldots, \mathbf{x}_n(t)\}$$

in $\mathbb{C}^n$ all of which are differentiable on the interval (a, b), then we have

$$c_1 \mathbf{x}_1(t) + c_2 \mathbf{x}_2(t) + \cdots + c_n \mathbf{x}_n(t) = \mathbf{0}.$$

We can rewrite this in matrix form as

$$[\mathbf{x}_1(t), \mathbf{x}_2(t), \ldots, \mathbf{x}_n(t)] \begin{bmatrix} c_1 \\ c_2 \\ \vdots \\ c_n \end{bmatrix} = \mathbf{0}.$$

Denote the coefficient matrix by $\mathbf{X}$, whose determinant we call the **Wronskian**, and the column vector of constants by $\mathbf{c}$. The system $\mathbf{Xc} = \mathbf{0}$ will have a nontrivial solution if and only if $\det(\mathbf{X}) = 0$. Let's further insist that the vector functions $\mathbf{x}_i(t)$ are all solutions of the homogeneous system, $\mathbf{x}_i'(t) = \mathbf{A}(t)\mathbf{x}_i(t)$. Then when we can differentiate $\det(\mathbf{X})$ (which will involve the use of the Product Rule for a product of n factors, one from each column vector of $\mathbf{X}$), we will have

$$\frac{d}{dt} \det(\mathbf{X}) = |\mathbf{x}_1', \mathbf{x}_2, \ldots, \mathbf{x}_n| + |\mathbf{x}_1, \mathbf{x}_2', \ldots, \mathbf{x}_n| + \cdots + |\mathbf{x}_1, \mathbf{x}_2, \ldots, \mathbf{x}_n'|.$$

Looking at a typical term in this sum and using the differential equation yields

$$|\mathbf{x}_1, \ldots, \mathbf{x}_i', \ldots, \mathbf{x}_n| = |\mathbf{x}_1, \ldots, \mathbf{A}\mathbf{x}_i, \ldots, \mathbf{x}_n|.$$

Now write out the product $\mathbf{A}\mathbf{x}_i$ in entry form:

$$(\mathbf{A}\mathbf{x}_i)_j = \sum_{k=1}^n \mathbf{A}_{jk} (\mathbf{x}_i)_k .$$

Thus the ith column of the determinant is a linear combination of the other columns. Using pivotal reduction we can reduce the determinant to eliminate all row terms except the ith, leaving us with

$$|\mathbf{x}_1, \ldots, A_{ii}\mathbf{x}_i, \ldots, \mathbf{x}_n| = A_{ii} |\mathbf{x}_1, \ldots, \mathbf{x}_i, \ldots, \mathbf{x}_n|.$$

Summing these for $i = 1 : n$, we have

$$\frac{d}{dt} \det(\mathbf{X}) = \text{tr}(\mathbf{X}) \det(\mathbf{X}),$$

which is a first order linear (or separable) ODE. It can be solved to yield

$$\det (\mathbf{X}(t)) = \det (\mathbf{X}(t_0)) \exp \left\{ \int_{t_0}^t \text{tr} (\mathbf{A}(\tau)) \, d\tau \right\}. \qquad (6.6)$$

Equation (6.6) is called **Abel's formula** for linear systems. This proves the following theorem.

THEOREM 6.1 *The Wronskian of the system (6.5) is nonzero for all values of t where* $\text{tr} (\mathbf{A}(t))$ *is continuous if and only if it is nonzero for some t_0. If a solution set of vector functions is linearly independent at a single value of t, then it is linearly independent for all t in some interval for which the equation is defined.* $\qquad \square$

■ **EXAMPLE 6.6** Show the linear system

$$\mathbf{x}'(t) = \begin{bmatrix} 3 & -2 \\ 4 & -3 \end{bmatrix} \mathbf{x}(t)$$

has the linearly independent solutions

$$\mathbf{x}_1(t) = [1; 1] \, e^t \quad \text{and} \quad \mathbf{x}_2(t) = [1; 2] \, e^{-t}.$$

Solution: This is true because

$$\mathbf{x}_1'(t) = \begin{bmatrix} 1 \\ 1 \end{bmatrix} e^t \quad \text{and} \quad \mathbf{A}\mathbf{x}_1(t) = \begin{bmatrix} 3 & -2 \\ 4 & -3 \end{bmatrix} \begin{bmatrix} 1 \\ 1 \end{bmatrix} e^t = \begin{bmatrix} 1 \\ 1 \end{bmatrix} e^t.$$

Also,

$$\mathbf{x}_2'(t) = \begin{bmatrix} -1 \\ -2 \end{bmatrix} e^{-t} \quad \text{and} \quad \mathbf{A}\mathbf{x}_2(t) = \begin{bmatrix} 3 & -2 \\ 4 & -3 \end{bmatrix} \begin{bmatrix} 1 \\ 2 \end{bmatrix} e^t = \begin{bmatrix} -1 \\ -2 \end{bmatrix} e^{-t}.$$

The Wronskian of the solution set is

$$\det\left(\mathbf{X}(t)\right) = \begin{vmatrix} e^t & e^{-t} \\ e^t & 2e^{-t} \end{vmatrix} = 2e^{-t}e^t - e^te^{-t} = 1 \neq 0.$$

Thus we may conclude the set $\{\mathbf{x}_1(t), \mathbf{x}_2(t)\}$ is linearly independent for all real t.   ■ ■ ■

We call the $n \times n$ matrix $\mathbf{X}(t)$ whose linearly independent columns are solutions of $\mathbf{x}'(t) = \mathbf{A}(t)\mathbf{x}(t)$ a **fundamental matrix** of the system. Obtaining a solution of a general linear system of ODE's is usually a daunting task. If we subdivide the problem into two cases, nonautonomous and autonomous systems, we will see the difficulties associated with the former.

■ **EXAMPLE 6.7**   Solve the following nonautonomous system:

$$\mathbf{x}' = \begin{bmatrix} 0 & 1 \\ 0 & -2t \end{bmatrix} \mathbf{x}, \quad \mathbf{x}(T) = \begin{bmatrix} a \\ b \end{bmatrix}.$$

Solution: Not having developed any appropriate methodology, our only option is to write this system as the following two simultaneous ODE's.

$$\begin{aligned} x_1' &= x_2, & x_1(T) &= a, \\ x_2' &= -2tx_2, & x_2(T) &= b. \end{aligned}$$

The first equation couples x_1 and x_2, but the second equation involves only x_2. Hence, the second is amenable to solution by separation of variables; we immediately find

$$x_2(t) = b\exp\left(-t^2 + T^2\right).$$

The first equation is now

$$x_1' = b\exp\left(-t^2 + T^2\right),$$

whose solution can be written in terms of the integral

$$x_1(t) = a + b\int_T^t \exp\left(-\tau + T^2\right) d\tau.$$

Considering what a simple system this was, it was not the easiest problem to solve.   ■ ■ ■

The moral of the last example is that nonautonomous systems do not usually have simple or straightforward solutions. It turns out that for linear autonomous systems we can generate solutions in a straightforward manner. In order to develop a complete methodology, we will need to take a detour of at least one section.

6.3.3 Exercise Set

Convert each of the following linear systems (equations) to the standard matrix form, $\mathbf{x}'(t) = \mathbf{A}(t)\mathbf{x}(t)$.

1. $u'' + 2u' - 3v' = u - 2v, \quad v'' + u' + v' - u + 3v = t$

2. $a' = 2a - 3b + c, \quad b' = a + b + c, \quad c' = 3a + c$

3. $u'' + v'' - u' - v = 0, \quad u'' - v'' + v' + 3u = 0$

4. $(D^3 - 2D^2 + 7D - 8)u = 0$

Which of the following sets of vector functions are linearly independent at a point and which are linearly independent over some interval? For those sets which are linearly independent over an interval, find the largest such interval.

5. $\left\{ \left[1; t; t^2\right], \left[t; t^2; 1\right], \left[t^2; t; 1\right] \right\}$

6. $\left\{ \left[e^t; \cos t; \sin t\right], \left[0; \cos t; \sin t\right], \left[e^t; 0; \sin t\right] \right\}$

7. $\left\{ \left[1 + t; t; 1 - t\right], \left[2t; t; t - 3\right], \left[t; 2 - 3t; t\right] \right\}$

8. $\left\{ \left[e^t; e^t; e^t\right], \left[te^t; te^t; te^t\right], \left[t^2e^t; t^2e^t; t^2e^t\right] \right\}$

6.4 THE EIGENVALUE PROBLEM

After seeing how vectors transform under a change of basis, a natural question arises. How do matrices transform under a change of basis? Once we know the answer to that question, we might continue our search for particularly simple forms for matrices, e.g., the row-reduced echelon form, which played such an important role in the solution of systems of simultaneous linear equations. But first things first.

6.4.1 Change of Basis for Matrices

Let's begin by looking at the matrix form of the typical linear system, $\mathbf{A}\mathbf{x} = \mathbf{y}$. This can be written in either of two ways, in the basis $\mathcal{B}$ or the basis $\mathcal{B}'$:

$$[\mathbf{A}\mathbf{x}]^{\mathcal{B}} = [\mathbf{y}]^{\mathcal{B}} \quad \text{or} \quad [\mathbf{A}\mathbf{x}]^{\mathcal{B}'} = [\mathbf{y}]^{\mathcal{B}'}.$$

From a Chapter 3 we have the two equivalent forms of the change of basis result for vectors:

$$[\mathbf{x}]^{\mathcal{B}'} = \mathbf{P}^{-1}[\mathbf{x}]^{\mathcal{B}} \quad \text{or} \quad [\mathbf{x}]^{\mathcal{B}} = \mathbf{P}[\mathbf{x}]^{\mathcal{B}'},$$

where $\mathbf{P}$ is the transition matrix from the basis $\mathcal{B}'$ to the basis $\mathcal{B}$. If we define the representation of the matrix, $[\mathbf{A}]$, by

$$[\mathbf{Ax}] = [\mathbf{A}][\mathbf{x}],$$

then we can apply the change of basis results to the vectors $\mathbf{x}$ and $\mathbf{y}$ separately. Let's abbreviate our notation somewhat and write $\mathbf{x}$ for $[\mathbf{x}]^{\mathcal{B}}$, $\mathbf{x}'$ for $[\mathbf{x}]^{\mathcal{B}'}$, $\mathbf{A}$ for the form of $\mathbf{A}$ in the basis $\mathcal{B}$, and $\mathbf{A}'$ for the form of $\mathbf{A}$ in the basis $\mathcal{B}'$. Then we have

$$\mathbf{Ax} = \mathbf{y} \quad \Rightarrow \quad \mathbf{APx}' = \mathbf{Py}' \quad \Rightarrow \quad \mathbf{P}^{-1}\mathbf{APx}' = \mathbf{y}'. \tag{6.7}$$

Since the last part of equation (6.7) must be valid for all possible vectors $\mathbf{x}'$, a comparison with $\mathbf{A}'\mathbf{x}' = \mathbf{y}'$ leads us to conclude that

$$\mathbf{A}' = \mathbf{P}^{-1}\mathbf{AP}. \tag{6.8}$$

By premultiplying by $\mathbf{P}$ and postmultiplying by $\mathbf{P}^{-1}$ we can rewrite this as an equation for $\mathbf{A}$ in terms of $\mathbf{A}'$:

$$\mathbf{A} = \mathbf{PA}'\mathbf{P}^{-1}. \tag{6.9}$$

Thus we see that the forms of a matrix in different bases must be *similar*.

6.4.2 *Eigenvalues and Eigenvectors*

Now let's return to the question of finding a simple form for the matrix $\mathbf{A}$ in the new basis. Surely, the simplest possible form would be for $\mathbf{A}'$ to be a multiple of the identity, i.e., the scalar matrix $\lambda\mathbf{I}$. Is that possible? Using equation (6.9) would allow us to find all matrices that could be reduced to that form. In particular, they must be

$$\mathbf{A} = \mathbf{P}\left(\lambda\mathbf{I}\right)\mathbf{P}^{-1} = \lambda\left(\mathbf{PI}\right)\mathbf{P}^{-1} = \lambda\left(\mathbf{PP}^{-1}\right) = \lambda\mathbf{I}.$$

No luck! Only a multiple of the identity itself will have that simple form in a new (or, for that matter, any) basis. If $\mathbf{A}$ were of that special form, we would have had $\mathbf{Ax} = \lambda\mathbf{x}$ for *all* vectors $\mathbf{x}$.

Shedding one of our requirements, we could insist that rather than having $\mathbf{A}'$ behave like a scalar multiplier for all possible column vectors, perhaps it could behave like a scalar multiplier with different scalars for vectors lying in different subspaces of $\mathbb{C}^n$. Thus vectors in those subspaces would not have their direction changed under matrix multiplication, only their length. Since the zero subspace is seldom of interest to us, we should insist this be true for nonzero vectors.

DEFINITION 6.3 *The column vector* $\mathbf{x}$ *is said to be an* **eigenvector** *or* **characteristic vector** *of the matrix* $\mathbf{A} \in \mathbb{C}_n^n$ *corresponding to the* **eigenvalue** *or* **characteristic value** $\lambda \in \mathbb{C}$ *if* *(a)* $\mathbf{x} \neq \mathbf{0}$. *Nontrivial vectors only!*

(b) $\mathbf{Ax} = \lambda \mathbf{x}$.

The set of eigenvalues of a matrix is called its **spectrum**, *written* $\lambda(\mathbf{A})$. *The magnitude of the eigenvalue of largest modulus is the* **spectral radius** *of* $\mathbf{A}$, *written* $\rho(\mathbf{A})$. *An ordered pair* $(\lambda, \mathbf{x})$ *that satisfies (a) and (b) is called an* **eigenpair** *of* $\mathbf{A}$.

Eigenvalues are also known as latent roots, secular roots, normal frequencies, principal moments of inertia, principal components of stress, etc. Eigenvectors are sometimes called normal modes, principal directions, principal axes, etc. We start with an example.

■ **EXAMPLE 6.8** It is merely a matter of applying the definition to verify that a given set of vectors are the eigenvectors of a matrix corresponding to the specified eigenvalues. For instance, if we are told that $\mathbf{x}_1 = [1; -1]$ and $\mathbf{x}_2 = [1; 1]$ are the eigenvectors of the matrix

$$\mathbf{A} = \begin{bmatrix} -1 & -3 \\ -3 & -1 \end{bmatrix},$$

then matrix multiplication will tell us the eigenvalues:

$$\mathbf{Ax}_1 = \begin{bmatrix} -1 & -3 \\ -3 & -1 \end{bmatrix} \begin{bmatrix} 1 \\ -1 \end{bmatrix} = 2 \begin{bmatrix} 1 \\ -1 \end{bmatrix}$$

and

$$\text{and } \mathbf{Ax}_2 = \begin{bmatrix} -1 & -3 \\ -3 & -1 \end{bmatrix} \begin{bmatrix} 1 \\ 1 \end{bmatrix} = -4 \begin{bmatrix} 1 \\ 1 \end{bmatrix}.$$

Thus $(2, \mathbf{x}_1)$ and $(-4, \mathbf{x}_2)$ are eigenpairs of $\mathbf{A}$. The spectrum of $\mathbf{A}$ is $\{2, -4\}$, and the spectral radius is 4.   ■ ■ ■

By using the definition of eigenvalues and eigenvectors, we can generate a couple of easy results:

- Nonzero scalar multiples of eigenvectors are also eigenvectors corresponding to the same eigenvalue, because

$$\mathbf{A}(c\mathbf{x}) = c(\mathbf{Ax}) = c(\lambda \mathbf{x}) = \lambda(c\mathbf{x}).$$

- Sums of eigenvectors corresponding to the same eigenvalue are also eigenvectors, because

$$\mathbf{A}(\mathbf{x} + \mathbf{y}) = (\mathbf{Ax}) + (\mathbf{Ay}) = (\lambda \mathbf{x}) + (\lambda \mathbf{y}) = \lambda(\mathbf{x} + \mathbf{y}).$$

Taking the last two results together with the fact that $\mathbf{A}(0\mathbf{x}) = \mathbf{0}$, we may conclude that what we will call the **eigenspace** $\mathcal{E}_\lambda = \{\mathbf{x} : \mathbf{Ax} = \lambda \mathbf{x}\}$ of the matrix $\mathbf{A}$ associated with the eigenvalue λ is indeed a subspace of $\mathbb{C}^n$.

Before looking at the simple form a matrix may take when changing bases, let's look at properties of the eigenvalues and eigenvectors in more detail. Consider the set of all matrices for which $\lambda = 0$ is an eigenvalue. The eigenvector $\mathbf{x}$ must be a nontrivial solution of $\mathbf{Ax} = \mathbf{0}$. This can occur if and only if the row-reduced echelon form of $\mathbf{A}$ contains at least one row of zeros, in which case $\mathbf{A}$ is singular. Thus we may add to Theorem 1.8.

THEOREM 6.2 *If* $A \in \mathbb{C}_n^n$, *the following conditions are equivalent:*

(a) $\det(\mathbf{A}) \neq 0$.

(b) $\mathbf{Ax} = \mathbf{0}$ *has only the trivial solution.*

(c) $\mathbf{Ax} = \mathbf{b}$ *is consistent for any* $\mathbf{b} \in \mathbb{C}^n$.

(d) *The echelon form of* $\mathbf{A}$ *has no rows of zeros.*

(e) $\mathbf{A}$ *is invertible.*

(f) $\mathbf{A}$ *can be written as a product of elementary matrices.*

(g) $\mathrm{rank}(\mathbf{A}) = n$.

(h) $\mathrm{RowSp}(\mathbf{A}) = \mathbb{C}_n$.

(i) *The set of row vectors of* $\mathbf{A}$ *is linearly independent.*

(j) $\mathrm{null}(\mathbf{A}) = 0$.

(k) $\mathrm{NullSp}(\mathbf{A}) = \{\mathbf{0}\}$.

(l) $\mathrm{ColSp}(\mathbf{A}) = \mathbb{C}^n$.

(m) *The set of column vectors of* $\mathbf{A}$ *is linearly independent.*

(n) *Zero is not an eigenvalue of* $\mathbf{A}$.   □

■ **EXAMPLE 6.9** Some matrices have a simple eigenvalue structure.

(a) Since $\mathbf{Ix} = 1\mathbf{x}$ for all $\mathbf{x} \in \mathbb{C}^n$, the number 1 is the only eigenvalue of $\mathbf{I}$ and *any* nonzero vector is an eigenvector of $\mathbf{I}$.

(b) $\mathbf{0x} = 0\mathbf{x}$ tells us that 0 is the only eigenvalue of $\mathbf{0}$ and *any* nonzero vector is an eigenvector of $\mathbf{0}$.

(c) If $\mathbf{D} = \mathbf{diag}\,(d_1, d_2, \ldots, d_n)$, then $\mathbf{De}_{(j;n)} = d_j\mathbf{e}_{(j;n)}$ where $\mathbf{e}_{(j;n)}$ is the jth vector in the standard basis, i.e., $\left(\mathbf{e}_{(j;n)}\right)_k = \delta_{jk}$. Thus $\mathbf{e}_{(j;n)}$ is the eigenvector of $\mathbf{D}$ corresponding to the eigenvalue d_j.   ■ ■ ■

The computation of the eigenvalues and eigenvectors can be achieved by employing the following device of inserting an identity matrix appropriately:

$$\mathbf{Ax} = \lambda\mathbf{x} = \lambda\mathbf{Ix} \quad \Rightarrow \quad (\lambda\mathbf{I} - \mathbf{A})\,\mathbf{x} = \mathbf{0} \tag{6.10}$$

Because we are searching for nontrivial solutions of (6.10), Theorem 6.2(a), (b) tells us that they will exist if and only if

$$\phi_{\mathbf{A}}(\lambda) := \det(\lambda \mathbf{I} - \mathbf{A}) = 0. \tag{6.11}$$

Equation (6.11) is called the **characteristic equation** of $\mathbf{A}$, and $\phi_{\mathbf{A}}(\lambda)$ is the **characteristic polynomial** of $\mathbf{A}$. The eigenvalues of $\mathbf{A}$ are the zeros of the characteristic polynomial. Eigenvalues which are simple zeros of the characteristic equation are called **simple eigenvalues**.

Let's look at the form of $\phi_{\mathbf{A}}(\lambda)$ in more detail:

$$|\lambda \mathbf{I} - \mathbf{A}| = \det \begin{bmatrix} \lambda - A_{11} & -A_{12} & \cdots & -A_{1n} \\ -A_{21} & \lambda - A_{22} & \cdots & -A_{2n} \\ \vdots & \vdots & \ddots & \vdots \\ -A_{n1} & -A_{n2} & \cdots & \lambda - A_{nn} \end{bmatrix}.$$

Since one of the $n!$ terms in this expansion is the product of the diagonal entries,

$$(\lambda - A_{11})(\lambda - A_{22}) \cdots (\lambda - A_{nn}),$$

which is a polynomial (as anticipated by our naming of $\phi_{\mathbf{A}}(\lambda)$) in λ of degree n, and all other terms are of lower degree, we may conclude:

THEOREM 6.3 *If $\mathbf{A} \in \mathbb{C}_n^n$, then the characteristic equation $\det(\lambda \mathbf{I} - \mathbf{A}) = 0$ is an nth degree polynomial equation with complex coefficients, and it has n complex roots; i.e., every complex square matrix of order n has n complex (and possibly repeated) eigenvalues.* □

The statement that there are always n roots is really the Fundamental Theorem of Algebra. Repeated roots are counted by their multiplicity. Simple eigenvalues have multiplicity one. We can state this more formally.

DEFINITION 6.4 *If for m as large as possible, $(\lambda - \lambda_0)^m$ is a factor of the characteristic polynomial $\phi_{\mathbf{A}}(\lambda) := \det(\lambda \mathbf{I} - \mathbf{A})$, then λ_0 is said to be an* **eigenvalue of order** *m.*

■ **EXAMPLE 6.10** Let's return to the matrices of the previous example and find their characteristic polynomials.

(a) If $\mathbf{A} = \mathbf{I}$, then the characteristic equation is

$$|\lambda \mathbf{I} - \mathbf{I}| = |(\lambda - 1)\mathbf{I}| = (\lambda - 1)^n |\mathbf{I}| = (\lambda - 1)^n = 0.$$

Thus $\lambda = 1$ is an eigenvalue of multiplicity n.

(b) $|\lambda \mathbf{I} - \mathbf{0}| = |\lambda \mathbf{I}| = \lambda^n |\mathbf{I}| = \lambda^n = 0$. Thus $\lambda = 0$ is the only eigenvalue of $\mathbf{0}$ and it has multiplicity n.

(c) Consider the 4×4 upper triangular matrix

$$\mathbf{A} = \begin{bmatrix} 1 & 2 & 0 & 0 \\ 0 & 1 & 0 & 0 \\ 0 & 0 & -2 & 1 \\ 0 & 0 & 0 & -2 \end{bmatrix}.$$

The characteristic equation is

$$\det (\lambda \mathbf{I} - \mathbf{A}) = \det \begin{bmatrix} \lambda - 1 & -2 & 0 & 0 \\ 0 & \lambda - 1 & 0 & 0 \\ 0 & 0 & \lambda + 2 & -1 \\ 0 & 0 & 0 & \lambda + 2 \end{bmatrix}$$

$$= (\lambda - 1)^2 (\lambda + 2)^2.$$

Thus $\lambda = 1$ and $\lambda = -2$ are both eigenvalues of multiplicity 2. ∎∎∎

Looking at the last example and the form of the characteristic equation leads to:

THEOREM 6.4 *If the square matrix* $\mathbf{A}$ *is triangular, then its eigenvalues are its diagonal entries.* □

An especially simple formula holds for the 2×2 case.

■ **EXAMPLE 6.11** If

$$\mathbf{A} = \begin{bmatrix} a & b \\ c & d \end{bmatrix}, \quad \text{then} \quad \lambda \mathbf{I} - \mathbf{A} = \begin{bmatrix} \lambda - a & -b \\ -c & \lambda - d \end{bmatrix}$$

and

$$|\lambda \mathbf{I} - \mathbf{A}| = \lambda^2 - (a + d)\,\lambda + (ad - bc) = \lambda^2 - (\text{tr}(\mathbf{A}))\,\lambda + \det(\mathbf{A}).$$

∎∎∎

The result of the last example can be generalized somewhat. If

$$\phi_{\mathbf{A}}(\lambda) = (\lambda - \lambda_1)(\lambda - \lambda_2) \cdots (\lambda - \lambda_n),$$

then we can write

$$\phi_{\mathbf{A}}(\lambda) = \lambda^n - c_1 \lambda^{n-1} + c_2 \lambda^{n-2} + \cdots + (-1)^n c_n.$$

From the theory of equations it is known that

$$c_1 = \sum_1^n \lambda_j, \quad c_2 = \sum \sum_{j \neq k} \lambda_j \lambda_k, \quad \ldots, \quad c_n = \lambda_1 \lambda_2 \cdots \lambda_n.$$

In words, c_k is the sum of the products of the roots (eigenvalues) taken k at a time. For instance, if $\mathbf{A}$ is 3×3, in terms of its eigenvalues its characteristic polynomial can be written in the form

$$\lambda^3 - (\lambda_1 + \lambda_2 + \lambda_3)\,\lambda^2 + (\lambda_1\lambda_2 + \lambda_2\lambda_3 + \lambda_1\lambda_3)\,\lambda - \lambda_1\lambda_2\lambda_3.$$

It can be shown that for an $n \times n$ matrix,

$$|\lambda\mathbf{I} - \mathbf{A}| = \lambda^n - (\mathrm{tr}(\mathbf{A}))\,\lambda^{n-1} + \cdots + (-1)^n\,(\det(\mathbf{A})).$$

▪ **EXAMPLE 6.12** Find the eigenvalues of the following three matrices.

(a) If the first matrix is

$$\mathbf{A} = \begin{bmatrix} 2 & 1 \\ -1 & 2 \end{bmatrix}, \quad \text{then} \quad \lambda\mathbf{I} - \mathbf{A} = \begin{bmatrix} \lambda - 2 & -1 \\ 1 & \lambda - 2 \end{bmatrix}$$

and

$$\det(\lambda\mathbf{I} - \mathbf{A}) = (\lambda - 2)^2 + 1 = 0 \Rightarrow \lambda = 2 \pm i$$

are the eigenvalues of $\mathbf{A}$. Notice that this is a *real* matrix with complex eigenvalues.

(b) The second matrix will be

$$\mathbf{B} = \begin{bmatrix} 4 & 2 \\ 1 & 3 \end{bmatrix}; \quad \text{then} \quad \lambda\mathbf{I} - \mathbf{B} = \begin{bmatrix} \lambda - 4 & -2 \\ -1 & \lambda - 3 \end{bmatrix}$$

and $\det(\lambda\mathbf{I} - \mathbf{B}) = \lambda^2 - 7\lambda + 10 = (\lambda - 2)(\lambda - 5) = 0$. Thus $\lambda = 2, 5$ are the eigenvalues of $\mathbf{B}$.

(c) The last matrix will be a bit messier. Although we could (and should) use a computer algebra system to evaluate the characteristic polynomial, all of the algebra will be shown here. When

$$\mathbf{C} = \begin{bmatrix} -9 & 4 & 4 \\ -8 & 3 & 4 \\ -16 & 8 & 7 \end{bmatrix},$$

we have

$$\lambda\mathbf{I} - \mathbf{C} = \begin{bmatrix} \lambda + 9 & -4 & -4 \\ 8 & \lambda - 3 & -4 \\ 16 & -8 & \lambda - 7 \end{bmatrix}.$$

Using a cofactor expansion on the first column,

$$\det\left(\lambda\mathbf{I}-\mathbf{C}\right) = (\lambda+9)\begin{vmatrix} \lambda-3 & -4 \\ -8 & \lambda-7 \end{vmatrix} - 8\begin{vmatrix} -4 & -4 \\ -8 & \lambda-7 \end{vmatrix}$$

$$+16\begin{vmatrix} -4 & -4 \\ \lambda-3 & -4 \end{vmatrix}$$

$$= (\lambda+9)\left((\lambda-3)(\lambda-7)-32\right)$$
$$-8\left(-4\lambda+28-32\right)+16\left(16+4\lambda-12\right)$$

$$= (\lambda+9)(\lambda+1)(\lambda-11)$$
$$+32(\lambda+1)+64(\lambda+1)$$

$$= (\lambda+1)\left((\lambda+9)(\lambda-11)+96\right)$$
$$= (\lambda+1)^2(\lambda-3) = 0,$$

and we see that $\lambda = -1, -1, 3$ are the eigenvalues of $\mathbf{C}$. ∎∎∎

Once the eigenvalues of $\mathbf{A}$ are known, we must solve the linear system

$$\mathbf{A}\mathbf{x} = \lambda\mathbf{x} \quad \Leftrightarrow \quad (\lambda\mathbf{I}-\mathbf{A})\,\mathbf{x} = \mathbf{0}$$

for $\mathbf{x}$, and we must do this once for *each* distinct eigenvalue. When $\mathbf{A}$ is $n \times n$ this means we may have as many as n $n \times n$ homogeneous linear systems to solve:

$$(\lambda_k\mathbf{I}-\mathbf{A})\,x_k = 0, \quad k = 1:n.$$

Remember, the characteristic equation, $\det\left(\lambda\mathbf{I}-\mathbf{A}\right) = 0$, forced each coefficient matrix, $\lambda_k\mathbf{I}-\mathbf{A}$, to be reducible to at least one row of zeros, so that there *must* be a nontrivial solution $\mathbf{x}_k \neq \mathbf{0}$ for each of these systems.

■ **EXAMPLE 6.13** Find the eigenvectors for each of the matrices in the previous example.

(a) If $\mathbf{A} = \begin{bmatrix} 2 & 1 \\ -1 & 2 \end{bmatrix}$, then $\lambda = 2 \pm i$. For $\lambda = 2 + i$, we have

$$(2+i)\,\mathbf{I}-\mathbf{A} = \begin{bmatrix} (2+i)-2 & -1 \\ 1 & (2+i)-2 \end{bmatrix} = \begin{bmatrix} i & -1 \\ 1 & i \end{bmatrix}.$$

With complex entries it may not always be obvious that $\lambda\mathbf{I}-\mathbf{A}$ will reduce to at least one row of zeros. In the 2×2 case, this means the row vectors must be multiples of each other. Here $\mathrm{row}(1) = i\,\mathrm{row}(2)$, so that

$$(2+i)\,\mathbf{I}-\mathbf{A} = \begin{bmatrix} i & -1 \\ 1 & i \end{bmatrix} \overset{(2)}{\underset{(1)-i(2)}{\hookrightarrow}} \begin{bmatrix} 1 & i \\ 0 & 0 \end{bmatrix}$$

$$\Rightarrow \mathbf{x}_{(1)} = \begin{bmatrix} -i \\ 1 \end{bmatrix}$$

is one possible form of the solution. When $\lambda = 2 - i$, we have

$$(2 - i)\,\mathbf{I} - \mathbf{A} = \begin{bmatrix} -i & -1 \\ 1 & -i \end{bmatrix} \underset{(1)+i(2)}{\overset{(2)}{\hookrightarrow}} \begin{bmatrix} 1 & -i \\ 0 & 0 \end{bmatrix}$$

$$\Rightarrow \mathbf{x}_{(2)} = \begin{bmatrix} i \\ 1 \end{bmatrix}.$$

It is no accident that we were able to choose $\mathbf{x}_1 = \bar{\mathbf{x}}_2$.

(b) If $\mathbf{B} = \begin{bmatrix} 4 & 2 \\ 1 & 3 \end{bmatrix}$, then $\lambda = 2, 5$. For $\lambda = 2$, we have

$$2\mathbf{I} - \mathbf{B} = \begin{bmatrix} 2 - 4 & -2 \\ -1 & 2 - 3 \end{bmatrix} = \begin{bmatrix} -2 & -2 \\ -1 & -1 \end{bmatrix}$$

$$\underset{(1)-2(2)}{\overset{-(2)}{\hookrightarrow}} \begin{bmatrix} 1 & 1 \\ 0 & 0 \end{bmatrix} \Rightarrow \mathbf{x}_{(1)} = \begin{bmatrix} 1 \\ -1 \end{bmatrix}.$$

Using $\lambda = 5$, we have

$$5\mathbf{I} - \mathbf{B} = \begin{bmatrix} 5 - 4 & -2 \\ -1 & 5 - 3 \end{bmatrix} = \begin{bmatrix} 1 & -2 \\ -1 & 2 \end{bmatrix}$$

$$\underset{(2)+(1)}{\overset{(1)}{\hookrightarrow}} \begin{bmatrix} 1 & -2 \\ 0 & 0 \end{bmatrix} \Rightarrow \mathbf{x}_{(2)} = \begin{bmatrix} 2 \\ 1 \end{bmatrix}.$$

(c) If $\mathbf{C} = \begin{bmatrix} -9 & 4 & 4 \\ -8 & 3 & 4 \\ -16 & 8 & 7 \end{bmatrix}$, then $\lambda = -1, -1, 3$. When $\lambda = 3$, we have

$$3\mathbf{I} - \mathbf{C} = \begin{bmatrix} 3 + 9 & -4 & -4 \\ 8 & 3 - 3 & -4 \\ 16 & -8 & 3 - 7 \end{bmatrix} = \begin{bmatrix} 12 & -4 & -4 \\ 8 & 0 & -4 \\ 16 & -8 & -4 \end{bmatrix}$$

$$\underset{\substack{(1)-\frac{3}{2}(2) \\ (3)-2(2)}}{\overset{\frac{1}{4}(2)}{\hookrightarrow}} \begin{bmatrix} 2 & 0 & -1 \\ 0 & -4 & 2 \\ 0 & -8 & 4 \end{bmatrix}$$

$$\underset{\substack{\frac{1}{2}(2) \\ (3)-2(2)}}{\overset{(1)}{\hookrightarrow}} \begin{bmatrix} 2 & 0 & -1 \\ 0 & 2 & -1 \\ 0 & 0 & 0 \end{bmatrix} \Rightarrow \mathbf{x}_{(1)} = \begin{bmatrix} 1 \\ 1 \\ 2 \end{bmatrix}$$

is the eigenvector corresponding to the simple eigenvalue. Using the multiple eigenvalue $\lambda = -1$, we have

$$-\mathbf{I} - \mathbf{C} = \begin{bmatrix} -1 + 9 & -4 & -4 \\ 8 & -1 - 3 & -4 \\ 16 & -8 & -1 - 7 \end{bmatrix} = \begin{bmatrix} 8 & -4 & -4 \\ 8 & -4 & -4 \\ 16 & -8 & -8 \end{bmatrix}$$

$$\hookrightarrow \quad \begin{matrix} \frac{1}{4}(1) \\ (2) - (1) \\ (3) - 2(2) \end{matrix} \quad \begin{bmatrix} 2 & -1 & -1 \\ 0 & 0 & 0 \\ 0 & 0 & 0 \end{bmatrix}.$$

Since $\text{null}(-\mathbf{I} - \mathbf{C}) = 2$, we must use 2 parameters, and thus we will get two linearly independent eigenvectors corresponding to $\lambda = -1$. Put $x_2 = 2\alpha$ and $x_3 = 2\beta$ to get $x_1 = \alpha + \beta$. Then a solution vector is

$$\begin{bmatrix} \alpha + \beta \\ 2\alpha \\ 2\beta \end{bmatrix} = \alpha \begin{bmatrix} 1 \\ 2 \\ 0 \end{bmatrix} + \beta \begin{bmatrix} 1 \\ 0 \\ 2 \end{bmatrix}.$$

The corresponding eigenspace is two dimensional. Two possible eigenvectors (which form a basis of the eigenspace) are gotten by setting $\alpha = 1$, $\beta = 0$ and $\alpha = 0$, $\beta = 1$:

$$\mathbf{x}_{(2)} = \begin{bmatrix} 1 \\ 2 \\ 0 \end{bmatrix}, \quad \mathbf{x}_{(3)} = \begin{bmatrix} 1 \\ 0 \\ 2 \end{bmatrix}.$$

■ ■ ■

The last example leads us to two important points:

- If $\mathbf{A}$ is a *real* $n \times n$ matrix, then $\det(\lambda\mathbf{I} - \mathbf{A})$ will be a polynomial with real coefficients. Then taking complex conjugates of the characteristic equation yields

$$|\lambda\mathbf{I} - \mathbf{A}| = 0 \quad \Rightarrow \quad |\bar{\lambda}\mathbf{I} - \mathbf{A}| = 0$$

Thus both λ and $\bar{\lambda}$ must be roots of the equation; i.e., complex eigenvalues of *real* matrices must occur in complex conjugate pairs.

- Now to the corresponding eigenvectors of real matrices with complex conjugate eigenvalues. Say

$$\lambda_+ = a + ib \quad \text{and} \quad \lambda_- = a - ib$$

are the complex eigenvalue pair. We further assume λ_+ and λ_- are simple eigenvalues with corresponding eigenvectors $\mathbf{x}_{(+)}$ and $\mathbf{x}_{(-)}$. Then

$$\mathbf{A}\mathbf{x}_{(+)} = \lambda_+\mathbf{x}_{(+)} \quad \text{and} \quad \mathbf{A}\mathbf{x}_{(-)} = \lambda_-\mathbf{x}_{(-)}.$$

Taking the complex conjugate of the second equation, we have the pair

$$\mathbf{A}\mathbf{x}_{(+)} = \lambda_+\mathbf{x}_{(+)} \quad \text{and} \quad \mathbf{A}\bar{\mathbf{x}}_{(-)} = \bar{\lambda}_-\bar{\mathbf{x}}_{(-)} = \lambda_+\bar{\mathbf{x}}_{(-)}.$$

But the second equation is the defining equation for λ_+ and $\mathbf{x}_{(+)}$, so that the solutions of each of the equations must be multiples of each other, since λ_+ is a simple eigenvalue. We have

$$\mathbf{x}_{(+)} = c\bar{\mathbf{x}}_{(-)},$$

where c is any complex constant. Since multiples of eigenvectors are still eigenvectors, we could set $c = 1$ without loss of generality. Hence we are allowed to save some effort by choosing $\mathbf{x}_{(+)} = \bar{\mathbf{x}}_{(-)}$, which is the same as $\mathbf{x}_{(-)} = \bar{\mathbf{x}}_{(+)}$. Although we have assumed that λ_+ and λ_- are simple eigenvalues, the same result—if $\mathbf{x}$ is an eigenvector for λ_+, then $\bar{\mathbf{x}}$ is an eigenvector for λ_-—holds even if λ_+ and λ_- are multiple eigenvalues.

Therefore, when working with real matrices with complex eigenvalues we need only find eigenvectors $\mathbf{x}_{(+)}$ for λ_+. Their complex conjugates will be eigenvectors corresponding to λ_-.

THEOREM 6.5 *A set of eigenvectors, each corresponding to distinct eigenvalues is linearly independent.*

Proof   This can be seen by forming the linear relation

$$c_1 \mathbf{x}_{(1)} + c_2 \mathbf{x}_{(2)} + \cdots + c_k \mathbf{x}_{(k)} = \mathbf{0},$$

and successively premultiplying by $\prod (\mathbf{A} - \lambda_i \mathbf{I})$, where the product is taken over all $i \neq j$ for $j = 1 : k$:

$$c_j \prod (\lambda_j - \lambda_i) \mathbf{x}_{(j)} = \mathbf{0} \;\Rightarrow\; c_j = 0,$$

which tells us the c's are all zero and the set of eigenvectors is linearly independent.   □

Only if $\text{null}(\lambda_0 \mathbf{I} - \mathbf{A}) = m$ will there be m linearly independent eigenvectors of $\mathbf{A}$ corresponding to the eigenvalue λ_0 of multiplicity m. In that case the corresponding eigenspace $\mathcal{E}_\lambda$ will be m dimensional.

An $n \times n$ matrix that does not have a full set of n linearly independent eigenvectors is said to be **defective**. A matrix that does have a full set of n linearly independent eigenvectors is said to be **simple** or **nondefective**. We'll defer the study of defective matrices until the next section. The matrices of examples 6.12 and 6.13 were simple.

Aside: There is an easy relation between the spectral radius of a matrix and all of its induced norms. Looking back at the defining equation for the matrix induced norm in Section 3.4.2, take $\mathbf{x}$ to be a unit eigenvector of $\mathbf{A}$. Then we have

$$\|\mathbf{A}\mathbf{x}\| = \|\lambda \mathbf{x}\| = |\lambda|\,\|\mathbf{x}\| \leq \|\mathbf{A}\|\,\|\mathbf{x}\| \leq \|\mathbf{A}\|\,.$$

Thus we may conclude that $|\lambda| \leq \|\mathbf{A}\|$ for *any* eigenvalue of $\mathbf{A}$ and any induced norm. We have proven the following theorem.

THEOREM 6.6 *For any induced matrix norm $\|\cdot\|$ we have*

$$\rho(A) \leq \|\mathbf{A}\|\,,$$

where $\rho(A) = \max\{|\lambda_k|,\; k = 1 : n\}$ is the spectral radius of $\mathbf{A}$.   □

We'll end this discussion with a rather important theorem.

THEOREM 6.7 (Cayley-Hamilton) *If $A \in \mathbb{C}_n^n$ and $\phi(\lambda) := \det(\lambda \mathbf{I} - \mathbf{A})$, then $\phi(\mathbf{A}) = 0$;*
i.e., $\mathbf{A}$ satisfies its own characteristic equation.   □

Although there are many proofs known, none of them are particularly transparent or illu-
minating. For a proof you should consult any of the theoretical references, such as Hoffman
and Kunze or Horn and Johnson. You're probably wondering why we can't just plug $\mathbf{A}$ in for
λ in the terms of

$$\det(\lambda \mathbf{I} - \mathbf{A})$$

to get the result. Unfortunately, this is not valid because the determinant can be defined only
over the set of matrices whose entries are complex polynomials which $\lambda - A_{kk}$ is but the
undefined "thing" $\mathbf{A} - A_{kk}$ is not.

The utility of the theorem becomes apparent when we raise matrices to powers. Suppose
$\mathbf{A} \in \mathbb{C}_2^2$ and $\det(\lambda \mathbf{I} - \mathbf{A}) = \lambda^2 - \lambda + 5$; then $\mathbf{A}^2 - \mathbf{A} + 5\mathbf{I} = 0$, so that $\mathbf{A}^2 = \mathbf{A} - 5\mathbf{I}$. To
find higher powers we only need multiply and use this result to reduce everything to a linear
combination of $\mathbf{A}$ and $\mathbf{I}$:

$$\mathbf{A}^3 = \mathbf{A}\left(\mathbf{A}^2\right) = \mathbf{A}\left(\mathbf{A} - 5\mathbf{I}\right) = \mathbf{A}^2 - 5\mathbf{A} = (\mathbf{A} - 5\mathbf{I}) - 5\mathbf{A} = -4\mathbf{A} - 5\mathbf{I},$$

$$\mathbf{A}^4 = \mathbf{A}\left(-4\mathbf{A} - 5\mathbf{I}\right) = -4\mathbf{A}^2 - 5\mathbf{A} = -4\left(\mathbf{A} - 5\mathbf{I}\right) - 5\mathbf{A} = -9\mathbf{A} + 20\mathbf{I}.$$

Because $\mathbf{A} - \mathbf{A}^2 = 5\mathbf{I}$, we can write $\mathbf{A}^{-1} = \frac{1}{5}\left(\mathbf{I} - \mathbf{A}\right)$ and

$$\mathbf{A}^{-2} = \left(\frac{1}{5}\left(\mathbf{I} - \mathbf{A}\right)\right)^2 = \frac{1}{25}\left(\mathbf{I} - 2\mathbf{A} + \mathbf{A}^2\right) = -\frac{1}{25}\left(4\mathbf{I} + \mathbf{A}\right).$$

Let $m(\lambda)$ be a polynomial for which $m(\mathbf{A}) = 0$. Such a polynomial may have degree
greater than, equal to, or even less than $\phi(\lambda)$. We call $m(\lambda)$ the **minimal polynomial** of $\mathbf{A}$ if
it is of lowest possible degree and its coefficient of the highest power of λ is 1. It can be shown
that if $\deg(m(\lambda)) = n$, then $\mathbf{A}$ is simple. Additionally, we have the following theorem, which
is a rewording of previous results.

THEOREM 6.8 *The $n \times n$ matrix $\mathbf{A}$ is simple if and only if the multiplicity of each eigenvalue*
is equal to the dimension of the corresponding eigenspace.   □

Now let's get back to the special forms $\mathbf{A}$ can take.

6.4.3 *Diagonalizable Matrices*

Since the forms of a matrix in different bases are similar, we need to know the relation between
eigenvalues and eigenvectors of similar matrices.

THEOREM 6.9 *If $\mathbf{A}' = \mathbf{P}^{-1}\mathbf{A}\mathbf{P}$ for some nonsingular matrix $\mathbf{P}$, then*
(a) $\mathbf{A}'$ and $\mathbf{A}$ have the same characteristic polynomial, and
(b) if $(\lambda, \mathbf{x}')$ is an eigenpair of $\mathbf{A}'$, then $(\lambda, \mathbf{P}\mathbf{x}')$ is an eigenpair of $\mathbf{A}$.

Proof If we prove that $\mathbf{A}'$ and $\mathbf{A}$ have the same characteristic polynomial, then we'll know that they have the same set of eigenvalues. The characteristic polynomial of $\mathbf{A}'$ is

$$
\begin{aligned}
\phi_{\mathbf{A}'}(\lambda) &= \det\left(\lambda\mathbf{I} - \mathbf{A}'\right) = \det\left(\lambda\mathbf{I} - \mathbf{P}^{-1}\mathbf{A}\mathbf{P}\right) \\
&= \det\left(\lambda\mathbf{P}^{-1}\mathbf{I}\mathbf{P} - \mathbf{P}^{-1}\mathbf{A}\mathbf{P}\right) \\
&= \det\left(\mathbf{P}^{-1}\left(\lambda\mathbf{I} - \mathbf{A}\right)\mathbf{P}\right) \\
&= \det\left(\mathbf{P}^{-1}\right)\det\left(\lambda\mathbf{I} - \mathbf{A}\right)\det(\mathbf{P}) \\
&= \det\left(\lambda\mathbf{I} - \mathbf{A}\right) = \phi_{\mathbf{A}}(\lambda).
\end{aligned}
$$

Now that we know they have the same set of eigenvalues, write

$$
\mathbf{A}'\mathbf{x}' = \lambda\mathbf{x}' \;\Rightarrow\; \mathbf{P}^{-1}\mathbf{A}\mathbf{P}\mathbf{x}' = \lambda\mathbf{x}' \;\Rightarrow\; \mathbf{A}\left(\mathbf{P}\mathbf{x}'\right) = \lambda\left(\mathbf{P}\mathbf{x}'\right),
$$

which was to be shown. □

From example 6.9(c) and the previous theorem we have the following useful result.

COROLLARY 6.1 *If* $\mathbf{A}$ *is similar to a diagonal matrix* $\mathbf{D}$*, then the diagonal elements of* $\mathbf{D}$ *are the eigenvalues of* $\mathbf{A}$*.*

The question is, when will $\mathbf{A}$ be similar to a diagonal matrix?

DEFINITION 6.5 *A matrix* $\mathbf{A} \in \mathbb{C}^n_n$ *is said to be* **diagonalizable** *if it is similar to a diagonal matrix in some basis.*

Suppose $\mathbf{A}$ is simple and therefore has n linearly independent eigenvectors $\mathbf{x}_{(1)}, \mathbf{x}_{(2)}, \ldots,$ $\mathbf{x}_{(n)}$. Form the nonsingular matrix $\mathbf{P}$ whose columns are the eigenvectors:

$$
\mathbf{P} = \left[\mathbf{x}_{(1)}, \mathbf{x}_{(2)}, \ldots, \mathbf{x}_{(n)}\right].
$$

By definition of the inverse of $\mathbf{P}$, we have

$$
\begin{aligned}
\mathbf{P}^{-1}\mathbf{P} &= \mathbf{P}^{-1}\left[\mathbf{x}_{(1)}, \mathbf{x}_{(2)}, \ldots, \mathbf{x}_{(n)}\right] = \left[\mathbf{P}^{-1}\mathbf{x}_{(1)}, \mathbf{P}^{-1}\mathbf{x}_{(2)}, \ldots, \mathbf{P}^{-1}\mathbf{x}_{(n)}\right] \\
&= [\mathbf{e}_1, \mathbf{e}_2, \ldots, \mathbf{e}_n] = \mathbf{I}.
\end{aligned}
$$

Thus if we use $\mathbf{P}^{-1}\mathbf{x}_k = \mathbf{e}_k$ when forming the product for change of basis, we have

$$
\begin{aligned}
\mathbf{P}^{-1}\mathbf{A}\mathbf{P} &= \mathbf{P}^{-1}\mathbf{A}\left[\mathbf{x}_{(1)}, \mathbf{x}_{(2)}, \ldots, \mathbf{x}_{(n)}\right] = \mathbf{P}^{-1}\left[\mathbf{A}\mathbf{x}_{(1)}, \mathbf{A}\mathbf{x}_{(2)}, \ldots, \mathbf{A}\mathbf{x}_{(n)}\right] \\
&= \mathbf{P}^{-1}\left[\lambda_1\mathbf{x}_{(1)}, \lambda_2\mathbf{x}_{(2)}, \ldots, \lambda_n\mathbf{x}_{(n)}\right] \\
&= \left[\lambda_1\mathbf{P}^{-1}\mathbf{x}_{(1)}, \lambda_2\mathbf{P}^{-1}\mathbf{x}_{(2)}, \ldots, \lambda_n\mathbf{P}^{-1}\mathbf{x}_{(n)}\right] \\
&= [\lambda_1\mathbf{e}_1, \lambda_2\mathbf{e}_2, \ldots, \lambda_n\mathbf{e}_n] = \mathbf{diag}\left(\lambda_1, \lambda_2, \ldots, \lambda_n\right).
\end{aligned}
$$

Therefore, if $\mathbf{A}$ is simple, then it is diagonalizable.

THEOREM 6.10 *The matrix* $\mathbf{A}$ *is diagonalizable if and only if there is set of* n *linearly independent vectors that are eigenvectors of* $\mathbf{A}$*.*

Proof   The previous argument showed that if $\mathbf{A}$ had n linearly independent eigenvectors, then it was diagonalizable. The converse remains to be shown. Suppose $\mathbf{A}$ is similar to the diagonal matrix $\mathbf{\Lambda}$ via the nonsingular matrix $\mathbf{S}$, i.e., $\mathbf{S}^{-1}\mathbf{A}\mathbf{S} = \mathbf{\Lambda}$. By premultiplying by $\mathbf{S}$ we have $\mathbf{A}\mathbf{S} = \mathbf{S}\mathbf{\Lambda}$. If the kth column of $\mathbf{S}$ is denoted by $\mathbf{x}_k$, then looking at the kth columns of both sides of the last equation we have

$$\mathbf{A}\left[\mathbf{x}_{(1)}, \mathbf{x}_{(2)}, \ldots, \mathbf{x}_{(n)}\right] = \left[\mathbf{x}_{(1)}, \mathbf{x}_{(2)}, \ldots, \mathbf{x}_{(n)}\right]\mathbf{\Lambda}.$$

This is the same as $\mathbf{A}\mathbf{x}_{(k)} = \lambda_k \mathbf{x}_{(k)}$ because $\mathbf{\Lambda} = \mathbf{diag}\,(\lambda_1, \lambda_2, \ldots, \lambda_n)$. $\square$

COROLLARY 6.2   *A matrix* $\mathbf{P}$ *whose columns are linearly independent eigenvectors of a diagonalizable matrix* $\mathbf{A}$ *is a similarity transformation that diagonalizes* $\mathbf{A}$, *i.e.,* $\mathbf{D} = \mathbf{P}^{-1}\mathbf{A}\mathbf{P}$.

Surely, if $\mathbf{A}$ has n distinct eigenvalues, then from Theorem 6.5, we know that it is simple and has a set of n linearly independent eigenvectors. A set of n linearly independent eigenvectors will be called an **eigenbasis** of $\mathbb{C}^n$.

COROLLARY 6.3   *If* $\mathbf{A}$ *has* n *distinct eigenvalues, then it is diagonalizable.*

Notice that example 6.13(c), which showed a diagonalizable matrix with repeated eigenvalues, shows the converse of this corollary is not true: i.e., diagonalizable matrices need not have distinct eigenvalues.

▪ **EXAMPLE 6.14**   In each of the following, diagonalize the matrix.

(a) $\mathbf{A} = \begin{bmatrix} 2 & 1 \\ 1 & 2 \end{bmatrix} \Rightarrow \phi(\lambda) = \lambda^2 - 4\lambda + 3 = (\lambda - 1)(\lambda - 3) = 0 \Rightarrow \lambda = 1, 3.$

$$\mathbf{I} - \mathbf{A} = \begin{bmatrix} -1 & -1 \\ -1 & -1 \end{bmatrix} \Rightarrow \mathbf{x}_{(1)} = \begin{bmatrix} 1 \\ -1 \end{bmatrix},$$

$$3\mathbf{I} - \mathbf{A} = \begin{bmatrix} 1 & -1 \\ -1 & 1 \end{bmatrix} \Rightarrow \mathbf{x}_{(2)} = \begin{bmatrix} 1 \\ 1 \end{bmatrix}.$$

Forming $\mathbf{P} = \left[\mathbf{x}_{(1)}, \mathbf{x}_{(2)}\right] = \begin{bmatrix} 1 & 1 \\ -1 & 1 \end{bmatrix}$, we have $\mathbf{P}^{-1} = \frac{1}{2}\begin{bmatrix} 1 & -1 \\ 1 & 1 \end{bmatrix}$ and

$$\mathbf{P}^{-1}\mathbf{A}\mathbf{P} = \frac{1}{2}\begin{bmatrix} 1 & -1 \\ 1 & 1 \end{bmatrix}\begin{bmatrix} 2 & 1 \\ 1 & 2 \end{bmatrix}\begin{bmatrix} 1 & 1 \\ -1 & 1 \end{bmatrix} = \begin{bmatrix} 1 & 0 \\ 0 & 3 \end{bmatrix}.$$

(b) Consider the matrix representing a rotation through an angle θ about the $\mathbf{e}_3$ axis:

$$\mathbf{R} = \begin{bmatrix} \cos\theta & \sin\theta & 0 \\ -\sin\theta & \cos\theta & 0 \\ 0 & 0 & 1 \end{bmatrix}$$

$$\Rightarrow \phi(\lambda) = (\lambda - 1)\left[(\lambda - \cos\theta)^2 + \sin^2\theta\right].$$

Thus the eigenvalues are $\lambda = 1, \cos\theta \pm i \sin\theta = e^{\pm i\theta}$. For $\lambda = 1$,

$$\mathbf{I} - \mathbf{R} = \begin{bmatrix} 1 - \cos\theta & -\sin\theta & 0 \\ \sin\theta & 1 - \cos\theta & 0 \\ 0 & 0 & 0 \end{bmatrix}.$$

Since

$$\begin{vmatrix} 1 - \cos\theta & -\sin\theta \\ \sin\theta & 1 - \cos\theta \end{vmatrix} = (1 - \cos\theta)^2 + \sin^2\theta = 2(1 - \cos\theta),$$

which is nonzero except when $\theta = 0$, $\text{rank}(\mathbf{I}-\mathbf{R}) = 2$ and we may choose $\mathbf{x}_{(1)} = \mathbf{e}_3 = [0; 0; 1]$. This is eminently reasonable: the axis of rotation should not change direction under a rotation about it. Because $\mathbf{R}$ is real, we need only look at $\lambda_+ = \cos\theta + i \sin\theta$.

$$(\cos\theta + i \sin\theta)\mathbf{I} - \mathbf{R} = \begin{bmatrix} i \sin\theta & \sin\theta & 0 \\ -\sin\theta & i \sin\theta & 0 \\ 0 & 0 & \cos\theta + i \sin\theta - 1 \end{bmatrix}$$

$$\hookrightarrow \begin{bmatrix} i & 1 & 0 \\ 0 & 0 & 1 \\ 0 & 0 & 0 \end{bmatrix}.$$

Thus $\mathbf{x}_{(+)} = [1; -i; 0]$ and $\mathbf{x}_{(-)} = [1; i; 0]$ are eigenvectors. Using

$$\mathbf{P} = \begin{bmatrix} 0 & 1 & 1 \\ 0 & -i & i \\ 1 & 0 & 0 \end{bmatrix},$$

we have (after some algebra)

$$\mathbf{D} = \mathbf{P}^{-1}\mathbf{R}\mathbf{P}$$

$$= \begin{bmatrix} 0 & 1 & 1 \\ 0 & -i & i \\ 1 & 0 & 0 \end{bmatrix}^{-1} \begin{bmatrix} \cos\theta & \sin\theta & 0 \\ -\sin\theta & \cos\theta & 0 \\ 0 & 0 & 1 \end{bmatrix} \begin{bmatrix} 0 & 1 & 1 \\ 0 & -i & i \\ 1 & 0 & 0 \end{bmatrix}$$

$$= \begin{bmatrix} 1 & 0 & 0 \\ 0 & e^{i\theta} & 0 \\ 0 & 0 & e^{-i\theta} \end{bmatrix}.$$

The complex entries corresponding to $\mathbf{x}_{(+)}$ and $\mathbf{x}_{(-)}$ are intuitively appealing because in a rotation of the plane no *real* vector in the plane is left unchanged in direction, unless of course $\theta = 0$, which is the case we've eliminated. ∎

Hermitian and unitary matrices have especially nice eigenvalue and eigenvector properties.

THEOREM 6.11

  (a) *If* **A** *is Hermitian, it has real eigenvalues.*

  (b) *If* **A** *is unitary, its eigenvalues lie on the unit circle in the complex λ-plane, $|\lambda| = 1$.*

  (c) *If* **A** *is either Hermitian or unitary, eigenvectors corresponding to different eigenvalues are orthogonal with respect to the inner product $\langle \mathbf{x}, \mathbf{y} \rangle = \mathbf{x}^H \mathbf{y}$.*

  (d) *If* **A** *is Hermitian or unitary, it is unitarily similar to a diagonal matrix, that is, there is a unitary matrix* **U** *such that* $\mathbf{U}^H \mathbf{A} \mathbf{U}$ *is diagonal.*

Proof   (a) Use $\mathbf{A} = \mathbf{A}^H$ and form the the eigenvector equations

$$\mathbf{A}\mathbf{x} = \lambda\mathbf{x}, \tag{6.12}$$

$$\mathbf{A}\mathbf{y} = \mu\mathbf{y}. \tag{6.13}$$

Take the Hermitian conjugate of (6.12):

$$(\mathbf{A}\mathbf{x})^H = \mathbf{x}^H \mathbf{A}^H = (\lambda\mathbf{x})^H = \bar{\lambda}\mathbf{x}^H \quad \Rightarrow \quad \mathbf{x}^H \mathbf{A} = \bar{\lambda}\mathbf{x}. \tag{6.14}$$

Now take the combination $(6.14)\mathbf{y} - \mathbf{x}^H(6.13)$:

$$\mathbf{x}^H \mathbf{A}\mathbf{y} - \mathbf{x}^H \mathbf{A}\mathbf{y} = \bar{\lambda}\mathbf{x}^H\mathbf{y} - \mu\mathbf{x}^H\mathbf{y} = \left(\bar{\lambda} - \mu \right)\mathbf{x}^H\mathbf{y},$$

which implies that

$$\left(\bar{\lambda} - \mu \right)\mathbf{x}^H\mathbf{y} = 0.$$

If $\mathbf{x} = \mathbf{y}$, then $\lambda = \mu$, and we have

$$\left(\bar{\lambda} - \lambda \right)\|\mathbf{x}\|^2 = 0 \quad \Rightarrow \quad \bar{\lambda} = \lambda,$$

so that all the eigenvalues must be real.

  (b) **A** being unitary means $\mathbf{A}^{-1} = \mathbf{A}^H$. Since **A** is invertible it cannot have zero as an eigenvalue. Starting with (6.12) and (6.13), (6.14) is

$$\mathbf{x}^H \mathbf{A}^H = \mathbf{x}^H \mathbf{A}^{-1} = \bar{\lambda}\mathbf{x}^H. \tag{6.15}$$

Multiplying (6.15) on the right by (6.13), we have

$$\mathbf{x}^H \mathbf{A}^{-1} \mathbf{A}\mathbf{y} = \bar{\lambda}\mu\mathbf{x}^H\mathbf{y} \quad \Rightarrow \quad \mathbf{x}^H\mathbf{y} = \bar{\lambda}\mu\mathbf{x}^H\mathbf{y}.$$

If $\lambda = \mu$, then $\mathbf{x} = \mathbf{y}$ and $\mathbf{x}^H\mathbf{y} = \mathbf{x}^H\mathbf{x} = \|\mathbf{x}\|^2 > 0$, so that

$$\bar{\lambda}\lambda = |\lambda|^2 = 1,$$

as required. When $\lambda \neq \mu$, we have

$$\left(\bar{\lambda}\mu - 1 \right)\mathbf{x}^H\mathbf{y} = 0.$$

Either $\bar{\lambda}\mu = 1$ or $\mathbf{x}^H\mathbf{y} = 0$, the latter of which is the desired orthogonality condition. We must show the former condition cannot be met. Suppose $\lambda \neq \mu$. Since $|\lambda| = |\mu| = 1$, we can write $\lambda = e^{i\alpha}$ and $\mu = e^{i\beta}$ to get

$$\bar{\lambda}\mu = e^{-i\alpha}e^{i\beta} = e^{i(\beta-\alpha)} = 1.$$

This is true if and only if $\beta - \alpha = 0$ (or a multiple of 2π), so that $\lambda = \mu$, contrary to our assumption.

(c) Going back to (6.15), we have

$$(\lambda - \mu)\mathbf{x}^H\mathbf{y} = 0.$$

If $\lambda \neq \mu$, then we must have $\mathbf{x}^H\mathbf{y} = 0$; i.e., eigenvectors corresponding to different eigenvalues are orthogonal.

The proof of (d) proceeds by using mathematical induction and will be left to the references. □

If a unitary or Hermitian matrix has multiple eigenvalues, we can separately apply the Gram-Schmidt orthonormalization procedure to the set of eigenvectors corresponding to each multiple eigenvalue. If we do this for all sets of multiple eigenvalues, the resulting set of eigenvectors will be orthonormal. Thus the diagonalizing matrix whose columns are the eigenvectors will be unitary.

If we restrict our attention to real matrices, then $\mathbf{A}^H = \mathbf{A}^T$, so that a real Hermitian matrix is symmetric and a real unitary matrix is orthogonal.

COROLLARY 6.4 *Real symmetric matrices are orthogonally similar to real diagonal matrices, and eigenvectors corresponding to different eigenvalues are orthogonal under the inner product* $\mathbf{x}^T\mathbf{y}$.

■ **EXAMPLE 6.15** Let's use the results of the previous theorem to diagonalize the following matrices.

(a) $\mathbf{A} = \begin{bmatrix} 2 & 1 \\ 1 & 2 \end{bmatrix}$ has the real eigenvalues 1 and 3. Choosing unit eigenvectors, we have the orthogonal matrix

$$\mathbf{P} = \frac{1}{\sqrt{2}}\begin{bmatrix} 1 & 1 \\ -1 & 1 \end{bmatrix},$$

which will diagonalize $\mathbf{A}$ by way of

$$\mathbf{D} = \mathbf{P}^T\mathbf{A}\mathbf{P} = \frac{1}{\sqrt{2}}\begin{bmatrix} 1 & -1 \\ 1 & 1 \end{bmatrix}\begin{bmatrix} 2 & 1 \\ 1 & 2 \end{bmatrix}\frac{1}{\sqrt{2}}\begin{bmatrix} 1 & 1 \\ -1 & 1 \end{bmatrix}$$

$$= \begin{bmatrix} 1 & 0 \\ 0 & 3 \end{bmatrix}.$$

(b) $\mathbf{B} = \begin{bmatrix} 1 & 1 & 1 \\ 1 & 2 & 0 \\ 1 & 0 & 2 \end{bmatrix}$ is also symmetric, with $\phi(\lambda) = \lambda(\lambda - 2)(\lambda - 3)$, so that the

eigenvalues are $\lambda = 0, 2, 3$. The corresponding orthonormal eigenvectors are

$$\frac{1}{\sqrt{6}} \begin{bmatrix} 2 \\ -1 \\ -1 \end{bmatrix} , \quad \frac{1}{\sqrt{2}} \begin{bmatrix} 0 \\ 1 \\ -1 \end{bmatrix} , \quad \frac{1}{\sqrt{3}} \begin{bmatrix} 1 \\ 1 \\ 1 \end{bmatrix} .$$

(c) $\mathbf{R} = \begin{bmatrix} \cos\theta & \sin\theta & 0 \\ -\sin\theta & \cos\theta & 0 \\ 0 & 0 & 1 \end{bmatrix}$ is unitary (and orthogonal). Had we normalized the eigen-

vectors to

$$\mathbf{x}_{(0)} = [0; 0; 1] , \quad \mathbf{x}_{(+)} = \frac{1}{\sqrt{2}} [1; -i; 0] , \quad \mathbf{x}_{(-)} = \frac{1}{\sqrt{2}} [1; i; 0] ,$$

then $\mathbf{P}$ would have been unitary. Surely the eigenvalues $1, e^{i\theta}, e^{-i\theta}$ all lie on the unit circle in the complex plane. ■ ■ ■

It is interesting to revisit systems of linear equations with the added perspective of diagonalizability. The matrix form of the system could be written in one of two ways,

$$\mathbf{Ax} = \mathbf{b} \quad \text{or} \quad \mathbf{A'x'} = \mathbf{b'},$$

where the first form is given in the standard basis and the second in a new basis $\mathcal{B'}$. Suppose that new basis is an eigenbasis of $\mathbf{A}$, which is assumed to be diagonalizable. Then in that basis, $\mathbf{A}$ has the diagonal form $\mathbf{D} = \mathbf{P}^{-1}\mathbf{AP} = \mathbf{A'}$, where $\mathbf{P}$ is the transition matrix from the eigenbasis $\mathcal{B'}$ to the standard basis $\mathcal{E}$. Thus our system takes the form

$$\mathbf{Dx'} = \mathbf{b'}.$$

Since $\mathbf{D}$ is diagonal in the eigenbasis, each of these equations has been decoupled from the others, and their form is

$$\lambda_k x'_k = b'_k.$$

If $\mathbf{A}$ is invertible, then all of the eigenvalues are nonzero, and each of these equations can be solved by dividing by the corresponding eigenvalue. What could be simpler? Unfortunately, the computational requirements of effecting such a change of basis are prohibitive.

If $\mathbf{A}$ is diagonalizable, then the set of its eigenvectors $\{\mathbf{x}_{(1)}, \mathbf{x}_{(2)}, \dots, \mathbf{x}_{(n)}\}$ forms a basis of $\mathbb{C}^n$. Thus any vector $\mathbf{z} \in \mathbb{C}^n$ can be written as a linear combination of the $\mathbf{x}$'s as

$$\mathbf{z} = z_1\mathbf{x}_{(1)} + z_2\mathbf{x}_{(2)} + \cdots + z_n\mathbf{x}_{(n)}.$$

In this basis we know that $\mathbf{A}$ has the diagonal representation

$$\mathbf{diag}(\lambda_1, \lambda_2, \dots, \lambda_n) .$$

The action of $\mathbf{A}$ on $\mathbf{z}$ is

$$\mathbf{A}\mathbf{z} = z_1\lambda_1\mathbf{x}_{(1)} + z_2\lambda_2\mathbf{x}_{(2)} + \cdots + z_n\lambda_n\mathbf{x}_{(n)}.$$

When seen in this eigenbasis, the effect of $\mathbf{A}$ is to multiply each component of $\mathbf{z}$ by a scale factor that is the eigenvalue corresponding to that basis vector. This is precisely the form conjectured at the outset of this section.

There is an interesting theorem for representing diagonalizable matrices as a sum of outer products. It is called the **spectral theorem**.

THEOREM 6.12 *If* $\mathbf{A}$ *is diagonalizable with eigenpairs* $(\lambda_k, \hat{\mathbf{x}}_{(k)})$, $k = 1 : n$, *and each eigenvector has unit length,* $\left\| \hat{\mathbf{x}}_{(k)} \right\|_2^2 = \hat{\mathbf{x}}_{(k)}^H \hat{\mathbf{x}}_{(k)} = 1$, *then*

$$\mathbf{A} = \sum_{k=1}^{n} \lambda_k \hat{\mathbf{x}}_{(k)} \hat{\mathbf{x}}_{(k)}^H. \qquad (6.16)$$

$\square$

Geometrically, this can be easily visualized in a special case by taking $\mathbf{A}$ to be the matrix representing a reflection through the plane whose normal vector is $\mathbf{n}$. As an eigenbasis we can choose $\{\mathbf{m}_1, \mathbf{m}_2, \mathbf{n}\}$ where $\mathbf{m}_1$ and $\mathbf{m}_2$ are orthogonal to $\mathbf{n}$ and to each other, hence they lie *in* the reflection plane (see Figure 6.6).

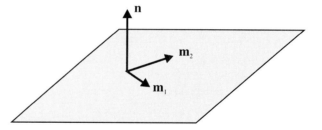

Fig. 6.6 The reflection plane spanned by the set $\{\mathbf{m}_1, \mathbf{m}_2\}$ and the vector $\mathbf{n}$ is normal to the plane.

Clearly, by definition of the action of a reflection,

$$\mathbf{A}\mathbf{n} = -\mathbf{n} \quad \text{and} \quad \mathbf{A}\mathbf{m}_k = \mathbf{m}_k, \quad k = 1 : 2,$$

because only vectors orthogonal to the plane are reflected. Converting the vectors $\mathbf{m}_1$, $\mathbf{m}_2$, and $\mathbf{n}$ to unit vectors (again denoted by hats), the spectral theorem allows us to write

$$\mathbf{A} = \hat{\mathbf{m}}_1 \hat{\mathbf{m}}_1^T + \hat{\mathbf{m}}_2 \hat{\mathbf{m}}_2^T - \hat{\mathbf{n}} \hat{\mathbf{n}}^T.$$

On the other hand, we could use the diagonalizability results. In the basis $\{\mathbf{m}_1, \mathbf{m}_2, \mathbf{n}\}$, $\mathbf{A}$ has the representation

$$\mathbf{D} = \mathbf{diag}(1, 1, -1).$$

The transformation matrix to this basis is

$$\mathbf{P} = [\mathbf{m}_1, \mathbf{m}_2, \mathbf{n}],$$

so that

$$\mathbf{D} = \mathbf{P}^{-1}\mathbf{A}\mathbf{P} \quad \Rightarrow \quad \mathbf{A} = \mathbf{P}\mathbf{D}\mathbf{P}^{-1},$$

where $\mathbf{P}^{-1} = \mathbf{P}^T$ if $\mathbf{m}_1, \mathbf{m}_2$, and $\mathbf{n}$ are unit vectors. This enables us to read off the reflection matrix without any elaborate geometrical constructions. Nevertheless, the spectral theorem proved to be the more powerful tool.

Following the same argument, we can find a basis of the null space of $\mathbf{A}$ by taking the eigenvectors corresponding to the zero eigenvalues.

A general diagonalizability result is the following:

THEOREM 6.13 *The matrix $\mathbf{A} \in \mathbb{C}_n^n$ is* **normal**, *meaning $\mathbf{A}^H\mathbf{A} = \mathbf{A}\mathbf{A}^H$, if and only if it is unitarily similar to a diagonal matrix, meaning that there is a unitary matrix $\mathbf{U}$ such that $\mathbf{U}^H\mathbf{A}\mathbf{U}$ is diagonal.* □

Details of the proof can be found in Horn and Johnson.

6.4.4 Exercise Set

Find the eigenvalues and eigenvectors of each of the following matrices, and diagonalize any that are diagonalizable.

1. $\begin{bmatrix} 0.45 & 0.55 \\ 0.25 & 0.75 \end{bmatrix}$

2. $\begin{bmatrix} 4 & -1 \\ 1 & 2 \end{bmatrix}$

3. $\dfrac{1}{2} \begin{bmatrix} 1+i & -1+i \\ 1+i & 1-i \end{bmatrix}$

4. $\begin{bmatrix} 2 & 2 \\ 3 & 3 \end{bmatrix}$

5. $\begin{bmatrix} -17 & 18 & -6 \\ -18 & 19 & -6 \\ -9 & 9 & -2 \end{bmatrix}$

6. $\begin{bmatrix} 4 & 2 & -2 \\ -5 & 3 & 2 \\ -2 & 4 & 1 \end{bmatrix}$

7. $\begin{bmatrix} 1 & 2 & 0 \\ 2 & 2 & 2 \\ 0 & 2 & 3 \end{bmatrix}$

8. $\begin{bmatrix} -6 & 4 & 2 \\ -14 & 9 & 4 \\ 6 & -3 & 0 \end{bmatrix}$

9. $\begin{bmatrix} z & 1 & 0 \\ 1 & z & 0 \\ 0 & 0 & z \end{bmatrix}$

10.
$$\begin{bmatrix} -3 & 0 & 4 \\ 6 & 2 & 5 \\ 4 & 0 & 3 \end{bmatrix}$$

11.
$$\begin{bmatrix} a & 0 & b \\ 0 & c & 0 \\ b & 0 & a \end{bmatrix}$$

12.
$$\begin{bmatrix} 1 & 2 & -1 \\ 2 & 1 & 1 \\ -1 & 1 & 0 \end{bmatrix}$$

13.
$$\begin{bmatrix} 2 & -i & 0 \\ i & 2 & 0 \\ 0 & 0 & 3 \end{bmatrix}$$

14.
$$\begin{bmatrix} 5 & 0 & 0 & -3 \\ 0 & 5 & -1 & 0 \\ 0 & -1 & 5 & 0 \\ -3 & 0 & 0 & 5 \end{bmatrix}$$

15.
$$\begin{bmatrix} 0 & 0 & 1 & 0 \\ 0 & 0 & 0 & 1 \\ 2 & 4 & -1 & -2 \\ 1 & 2 & -1 & -2 \end{bmatrix}$$

16.
$$\begin{bmatrix} 0 & 1 & 0 & 0 \\ -1 & 0 & 0 & -2 \\ 0 & 0 & 0 & 1 \\ 0 & 0 & -2 & -3 \end{bmatrix}$$

17.
$$\begin{bmatrix} -2 & 2 & 2 & 2 \\ -3 & 3 & 2 & 2 \\ -2 & 0 & 4 & 2 \\ -1 & 0 & 0 & 5 \end{bmatrix}$$

18.
$$\begin{bmatrix} 5 & 4 & 1 & 1 \\ 4 & 5 & 1 & 1 \\ 1 & 1 & 4 & 2 \\ 1 & 1 & 2 & 4 \end{bmatrix}$$

19.
$$\begin{bmatrix} 6 & 4 & 4 & 1 \\ 4 & 6 & 1 & 4 \\ 4 & 1 & 6 & 4 \\ 1 & 4 & 4 & 6 \end{bmatrix}$$
[Hint: This matrix has a multiple eigenvalue, so orthogonalize the eigenvectors.]

20.
$$\begin{bmatrix} 5+9i & 5+5i & -6-6i & -7-7i \\ 3+3i & 6+10i & -5-5i & -6-6i \\ 2+2i & 3+3i & -1+3i & -5-5i \\ 1+i & 2+2i & -3-3i & 4i \end{bmatrix}$$

21. If $\mathbf{J} = \mathbf{ones}(n)$ and $\mathbf{1} = \mathbf{ones}(n,1)$, show that $\mathbf{1}$ is an eigenvector of $\mathbf{J}$ corresponding to the eigenvalue $\lambda = n$. Also show that $\mathbf{J}$ has $n-1$ zero eigenvalues with eigenvectors $\mathbf{1} - n\mathbf{e}_{(k;n)}$, $k = 1 : n-1$, where the $\mathbf{e}_{(k;n)}$ are the standard basis vectors in $\mathbb{C}^n$. Further show that $\mathbf{e}_{(n;n)} - \mathbf{e}_{(k;n)}$, $k = 1 : n-1$ are also eigenvectors of the eigenvalue zero.

Find the eigenvalues and eigenvectors of each of the following $n \times n$ matrices if their entries are:

22. $A_{jk} = a + (b-a)\delta_{jk}$

23. $B_{jk} = a\delta_{jk} + b(\delta_{j,k-1} + \delta_{j,k+1})$ [This should be approached as a computer experiment that may not have an entirely satisfactory solution.]

24. If $(\lambda_k, \mathbf{x}_{(k)})$ are the eigenpairs of $\mathbf{A}$, show the following

(a) $(\lambda_k^n, \mathbf{x}_{(k)})$ are the eigenpairs of $\mathbf{A}^n$.

(b) If $\mathbf{A}$ is nonsingular, then the eigenpairs of $\mathbf{A}^{-1}$ are $(\lambda_k^{-1}, \mathbf{x}_{(k)})$.

25. Show that **u** is an eigenvector of the Householder matrix that is defined by $\mathbf{H} = \mathbf{I} - 2\mathbf{uu}^T$ and find its corresponding eigenvalue. Give a geometric interpretation for **H**.

26. If $\mathbf{A} \in \mathbb{C}_n^m$, show that the eigenvalues of $\mathbf{A}^H \mathbf{A}$ must be nonnegative and there are $n - \mathrm{rank}(\mathbf{A})$ positive eigenvalues.

27. The eigenvector of a rotation matrix corresponding to the eigenvalue $\lambda = 1$ will be the axis of rotation. Find the axis of rotation of the product $\mathbf{Rot}(\pi; x'')\mathbf{Rot}(\pi/2; y')\mathbf{Rot}(\pi; z)$.

28. Find the eigenvalues and eigenvectors of the dyad $\mathbf{aa}^T$ where **a** is an n-component column vector. Do the same for the rank one matrix $\mathbf{ab}^T$.

29. Derive the form of the matrix $\mathbf{Rot}(\alpha; \mathbf{a})$, representing a rotation through an angle α about the axis parallel to the vector **a**. Start by using **a** as the eigenvector of $\mathbf{Rot}(\alpha; \mathbf{a})$ corresponding to the eigenvalue 1. The other two eigenvectors will be orthogonal to **a** with eigenvalues $e^{\pm i\alpha}$. Construct the diagonalizing transform and transform backward.

6.5 JORDAN NORMAL FORM

Recall that an $n \times n$ matrix was said to be defective, or nondiagonalizable, if it did not have a full set of n linearly independent eigenvectors. This could only occur if at least one eigenvalue λ_1 had multiplicity $m_1 > 1$ and $\mathrm{null}(\lambda_1 \mathbf{I} - \mathbf{A}) < m_1$, resulting in fewer than m_1 eigenvectors corresponding to λ_1. We know there are such matrices; the question is, what is the simplest form to which they can be reduced?

The plan is to define a **chain of generalized eigenvectors** for each multiple eigenvalue with insufficient eigenvectors. The special relation between generalized eigenvectors will generate the **Jordan normal form**. Proceed as follows: If the characteristic polynomial of **A** is

$$\phi(\lambda) := \det(\lambda \mathbf{I} - \mathbf{A}) = (\lambda - \lambda_1)^{m_1}(\lambda - \lambda_2)^{m_2} \cdots (\lambda - \lambda_k)^{m_k},$$

with $m_1 + m_2 + \cdots + m_k = n$, then the Cayley-Hamilton Theorem tells us that $\phi(\mathbf{A}) = \mathbf{0}$. For a simple eigenvalue λ_0, the equation $(\lambda_0 \mathbf{I} - \mathbf{A})\mathbf{x}_{(0)} = \mathbf{0}$ yields its eigenvector. To find an m_1 dimensional subspace corresponding to the m_1-fold eigenvalue λ_1, the factorization of $\phi(\lambda)$ and the Cayley-Hamilton Theorem suggest that we look at the equation

$$(\lambda_1 \mathbf{I} - \mathbf{A})^{m_1} \mathbf{x} = \mathbf{0}.$$

If $\mathbf{x}_{(1)}$ is an eigenvector, we actually have $(\lambda_1 \mathbf{I} - \mathbf{A})\mathbf{x}_{(1)} = \mathbf{0}$.

DEFINITION 6.6 *We say **u** is a **generalized eigenvector** of **A** of order k associated with the eigenvalue λ_0 if*

$$(\lambda_0 \mathbf{I} - \mathbf{A})^k \mathbf{u} = \mathbf{0} \quad and \quad (\lambda_0 \mathbf{I} - \mathbf{A})^{k-1} \mathbf{u} \neq \mathbf{0}.$$

If $\mathbf{u}$ *is a generalized eigenvector of* $\mathbf{A}$ *of order* k, *then the* **chain of generalized eigenvectors** $\{\mathbf{v}_{(1)}, \mathbf{v}_{(2)}, \ldots, \mathbf{v}_{(k)}\}$ *associated with* $\mathbf{u}$ *is given by the equations*

$$
\begin{aligned}
\mathbf{v}_{(k)} &:= \mathbf{u}, \\
\mathbf{v}_{(k-1)} &:= (\mathbf{A} - \lambda_0\mathbf{I})\mathbf{u} &&= (\mathbf{A} - \lambda_0\mathbf{I})\mathbf{v}_{(k)}, \\
\mathbf{v}_{(k-2)} &:= (\mathbf{A} - \lambda_0\mathbf{I})^2\mathbf{u} &&= (\mathbf{A} - \lambda_0\mathbf{I})\mathbf{v}_{(k-1)}, \\
&\;\;\vdots &&\;\;\vdots \\
\mathbf{v}_{(1)} &:= (\mathbf{A} - \lambda_0\mathbf{I})^{k-1}\mathbf{u} &&= (\mathbf{A} - \lambda_0\mathbf{I})\mathbf{v}_{(2)}.
\end{aligned}
$$

It's easy to see that such a chain is linearly independent. Form a linear relation

$$
c_1\mathbf{v}_{(1)} + c_2\mathbf{v}_{(2)} + \cdots + c_k\mathbf{v}_{(k)} = \mathbf{0}.
$$

Apply $(\mathbf{A} - \lambda_0\mathbf{I})^{k-1}$ to both sides. All that remains is

$$
c_k(\mathbf{A} - \lambda_0\mathbf{I})^{k-1}\mathbf{v}_{(k)} = \mathbf{0},
$$

from which it follows that $c_k = 0$. Premultiplying by $(\mathbf{A} - \lambda_0\mathbf{I})^{k-i}$ for $i = k-1 : -1 : 1$ yields $c_k = c_{k-1} = \cdots = c_1 = 0$.

An alternative to this *top-down* approach is to choose $\mathbf{u}_{(1)}$ as an eigenvector of $\mathbf{A}$, $\mathbf{u}_{(2)}$ to satisfy $(\mathbf{A} - \lambda_0\mathbf{I})\mathbf{u}_{(2)} = \mathbf{u}_{(1)}$, $\mathbf{u}_{(3)}$ to satisfy $(\mathbf{A} - \lambda_0\mathbf{I})\mathbf{u}_{(3)} = \mathbf{u}_{(2)}$, etc. This is called a *bottom-up* approach.

■ **EXAMPLE 6.16** Find chains of generalized eigenvectors using *both* a bottom-up and a top-down approach for

$$
\mathbf{A} = \begin{bmatrix} 1 & 1 & 0 \\ 0 & 0 & 1 \\ 0 & 0 & 1 \end{bmatrix}
$$

Solution: Since $\mathbf{A}$ is upper triangular, we can read off the eigenvalues from its diagonal entries as $\lambda = 1, 0, 1$. It can be easily verified that the eigenvector corresponding to $\lambda = 0$ is $\mathbf{x}_1 = [1; -1; 0]$. If we look at $\lambda = 1$, then

$$
\mathbf{A} - \mathbf{I} = \begin{bmatrix} 0 & 1 & 0 \\ 0 & -1 & 1 \\ 0 & 0 & 0 \end{bmatrix} \quad \Rightarrow \quad \mathbf{x} = \begin{bmatrix} 1 \\ 0 \\ 0 \end{bmatrix}
$$

is an eigenvector of $\mathbf{A}$. Following a bottom-up approach, set $\mathbf{u}_{(1)} = \mathbf{x}$. Then

$$
\left[\mathbf{A} - \mathbf{I} \,\middle|\, \mathbf{u}_{(1)}\right] = \begin{bmatrix} 0 & 1 & 0 & 1 \\ 0 & -1 & 1 & 0 \\ 0 & 0 & 0 & 0 \end{bmatrix} \quad \Rightarrow \quad \mathbf{u}_{(2)} = \begin{bmatrix} 0 \\ 1 \\ 1 \end{bmatrix}
$$

is one possible solution. Thus we have $\{[1; 0; 0], [0; 1; 1]\}$ as a bottom-up chain of generalized eigenvectors corresponding to $\lambda = 1$. Alternatively, a top-down approach yields

$$
(\mathbf{A} - \mathbf{I})^2\mathbf{v} = \begin{bmatrix} 0 & -1 & 1 \\ 0 & 1 & -1 \\ 0 & 0 & 0 \end{bmatrix} \mathbf{v} = \mathbf{0}
$$

and

$$(\mathbf{A} - \mathbf{I})\mathbf{v} = \begin{bmatrix} 0 & -1 & 0 \\ 0 & 1 & -1 \\ 0 & 0 & 0 \end{bmatrix} \mathbf{v} \neq \mathbf{0},$$

which has $\mathbf{v} = [0; 1; 1]$ as a possible solution. Then

$$(\mathbf{A} - \mathbf{I})\mathbf{v} = \begin{bmatrix} 0 & -1 & 0 \\ 0 & 1 & -1 \\ 0 & 0 & 0 \end{bmatrix} \begin{bmatrix} 0 \\ 1 \\ 1 \end{bmatrix} = \begin{bmatrix} -1 \\ 0 \\ 0 \end{bmatrix},$$

and $\{[-1; 0; 0], [0; 1; 1]\}$ is one possible required top-down chain. Notice that both chains span the same subspace.   ■ ■ ■

The form of the matrix in the basis consisting of generalized eigenvectors (which will be genuine eigenvectors when there are no multiple eigenvalues) can be computed by looking at each chain separately. Written recursively, the top-down chain satisfies

$$\begin{aligned} \mathbf{v}_{(k)} &= \mathbf{u}, \\ \mathbf{v}_{(k-1)} &= (\mathbf{A} - \lambda_0 \mathbf{I})\mathbf{v}_{(k)}, \\ \mathbf{v}_{(k-2)} &= (\mathbf{A} - \lambda_0 \mathbf{I})\mathbf{v}_{(k-1)}, \\ &\vdots \qquad\qquad \vdots \\ \mathbf{v}_{(1)} &= (\mathbf{A} - \lambda_0 \mathbf{I})\mathbf{v}_{(2)}. \end{aligned}$$

Thus in the basis of the chain, the matrix representation of $\mathbf{A}$ in the subspace spanned by the chain is the **Jordan block**:

$$\mathbf{J} = \begin{bmatrix} \lambda_0 & 1 & 0 & \cdots & 0 \\ 0 & \lambda_0 & 1 & \ddots & \vdots \\ 0 & 0 & \lambda_0 & \ddots & 0 \\ \vdots & \vdots & \ddots & \ddots & 1 \\ 0 & 0 & \cdots & 0 & \lambda_0 \end{bmatrix}.$$

The **Jordan normal form** of a matrix is

$$\begin{bmatrix} \mathbf{J}_1 & \mathbf{0} & \cdots & \mathbf{0} \\ \mathbf{0} & \mathbf{J}_2 & \ddots & \vdots \\ \vdots & \ddots & \ddots & \mathbf{0} \\ \mathbf{0} & \cdots & \mathbf{0} & \mathbf{J}_k \end{bmatrix},$$

where each $\mathbf{J}_i$ is a Jordan block.

The computation of the Jordan normal form is somewhat tedious and is often unnecessary. Actual problems do not often have repeated eigenvalues. In point of fact, the elements of a matrix are seldom known with infinite precision. The eigenvalues are continuous functions of the matrix entries A_{jk}, and small changes in the entries thus will lead to correspondingly small changes in the locations of the eigenvalues in the complex plane, usually splitting any multiple eigenvalues. Nevertheless, the Jordan normal form has great theoretical importance because some physical models lead to a multiple eigenvalue which remains even under small perturbations.

▪ **EXAMPLE 6.17** Find the Jordan normal form of

$$A = \begin{bmatrix} 1 & 0 & 0 \\ 1 & 1 & 0 \\ 0 & 3 & 2 \end{bmatrix}.$$

Solution: The characteristic polynomial is $\phi(\lambda) = (\lambda - 1)^2(\lambda - 2)$. The eigenvector corresponding to $\lambda = 2$ is $[0; 0; 1]$. A possible eigenvector for $\lambda = 1$ is $[0; 1; -3]$. Using

$$(\mathbf{A} - \mathbf{I})\mathbf{v}_{(2)} = \begin{bmatrix} 0 \\ 1 \\ -3 \end{bmatrix} \Rightarrow \begin{bmatrix} 0 & 0 & 0 & | & 0 \\ 1 & 0 & 0 & | & 1 \\ 0 & 3 & 1 & | & -3 \end{bmatrix} \Rightarrow \mathbf{v}_{(2)} = \begin{bmatrix} 1 \\ -1 \\ 0 \end{bmatrix},$$

we have $\{[0; 1; -3], [1; -1; 0]\}$ as a chain. A basis of generalized eigenvectors is then

$$\{[0; 0; 1], [0; 1; -3], [1; -1; 0]\}$$

and the corresponding Jordan normal form is

$$\mathbf{J} = \begin{bmatrix} 0 & 0 & 1 \\ 0 & 1 & -1 \\ 1 & -3 & 0 \end{bmatrix}^{-1} \begin{bmatrix} 1 & 0 & 0 \\ 1 & 1 & 0 \\ 0 & 3 & 2 \end{bmatrix} \begin{bmatrix} 0 & 0 & 1 \\ 0 & 1 & -1 \\ 1 & -3 & 0 \end{bmatrix} = \begin{bmatrix} 2 & 0 & 0 \\ 0 & 1 & 1 \\ 0 & 0 & 1 \end{bmatrix},$$

which has the required block structure. ▪▪▪

Looking back at the structure of a Jordan block, we can write each block as

$$\mathbf{J} = \lambda\mathbf{I} + \mathbf{N},$$

where $\mathbf{N}$ is nilpotent of order k, meaning there is a positive integer k such that $\mathbf{N}^k = \mathbf{0}$ and $\mathbf{N}^{k-1} \neq \mathbf{0}$. The $k \times k$ matrix $\mathbf{N}$ can be put in the special form

$$\mathbf{N} = \begin{bmatrix} 0 & 1 & 0 & \cdots & 0 \\ 0 & 0 & 1 & \ddots & \vdots \\ 0 & 0 & 0 & \ddots & 0 \\ \vdots & \vdots & \vdots & \ddots & 1 \\ 0 & 0 & 0 & \cdots & 0 \end{bmatrix}$$

If the eigenvalue λ has multiplicity m, then $\mathbf{N}$ is nilpotent of order no greater than m. This approach is employed for evaluating functions of matrices in Section 6.9.

The most general result that can be stated is that the Jordan normal form will be

$$\mathbf{J} = \mathbf{D} + \mathbf{N},$$

where $\mathbf{D}$ is diagonalizable with the same eigenvalues as $\mathbf{A}$, $\mathbf{N}$ is nilpotent of order no higher than $n - 1$, and $\mathbf{DN} = \mathbf{ND}$.

The article by Hill and Bechtel, Eigenvectors and Jordan Bases Using Symbolic Programs (**College Math Journal 23**, 59–63) discusses a method for using the symbolic algebra system Derive to find the generalized eigenvectors and Jordan normal form for matrices. It is worth consulting if you have access to the software.

6.5.1 Exercise Set

Find the Jordan normal form of each of the following matrices.

1. $\begin{bmatrix} 1 & 0 & 1 \\ 0 & 1 & 0 \\ 0 & 0 & 1 \end{bmatrix}$

2. $\begin{bmatrix} 1 & 0 & 0 \\ 1 & 1 & 0 \\ 1 & 1 & 1 \end{bmatrix}$

3. $\begin{bmatrix} 2 & 1 & 2 \\ 0 & 2 & 1 \\ 0 & 0 & 2 \end{bmatrix}$

4. $\begin{bmatrix} -3 & 6 & 2 \\ -1 & 3 & 0 \\ -6 & 8 & 5 \end{bmatrix}$

5. $\begin{bmatrix} 8 & -4 & -1 \\ 13 & -6 & -2 \\ 3 & -3 & 1 \end{bmatrix}$

6. $\begin{bmatrix} 1 & 0 & 0 \\ -1 & 1 & 0 \\ 0 & -1 & 1 \end{bmatrix}$

6.6 SOLVING AUTONOMOUS LINEAR SYSTEMS

6.6.1 Solving Linear Systems Using Eigenvectors

Homogeneous autonomous systems must have the form $\mathbf{x}'(t) = \mathbf{Ax}(t)$, where $\mathbf{A}$ is a *constant* matrix. Our goal will be to use the eigenvalue structure of $\mathbf{A}$ to greatly simplify the problem. We'll start with the simplest nontrivial type of matrix for $\mathbf{A}$, a constant diagonalizable matrix. The constant matrix $\mathbf{P}$ of eigenvectors of $\mathbf{A}$ will diagonalize it; i.e., $\mathbf{P}^{-1}\mathbf{AP} = \mathbf{D}$ will be diagonal with the eigenvalues of $\mathbf{A}$ along the diagonal in the order in which the eigenvectors appear in the columns of $\mathbf{P}$. Thus the linear system becomes

$$\mathbf{x}'(t) = \mathbf{Ax}(t) = \mathbf{PDP}^{-1}\mathbf{x}(t) \; \Rightarrow \; \mathbf{P}^{-1}\mathbf{x}'(t) = \mathbf{D}\left(\mathbf{P}^{-1}\mathbf{x}(t)\right).$$

If we make the change of dependent variable $\mathbf{y}(t) := \mathbf{P}^{-1}\mathbf{x}(t)$, then we have

$$\mathbf{y}'(t) = \mathbf{Dy}(t) = \mathbf{diag}(\lambda_1, \lambda_2, \dots, \lambda_n)\mathbf{y}(t).$$

Although, in general, a system couples equations in different variables, when the coefficient matrix is diagonalizable, the system can be decoupled into n separate scalar first order equations, each of the form

$$y'_k(t) = \lambda_k y_k(t), \quad k = 1 : n. \tag{6.17}$$

The immediate solution of the kth equation is

$$y_k(t) = c_k e^{\lambda_k t}. \tag{6.18}$$

■ **EXAMPLE 6.18** The idea of coupling of equations can be better understood by looking at the mass-spring system drawn in Figure 6.7.

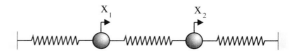

Fig. 6.7 A coupled mass-spring system with two degrees of freedom.

You can see that as the left mass moves to the right, $x_1(t)$ increases and the center spring is compressed. This compression exerts a force on the right mass, so that $x_2(t)$ is also forced to change. The $x_1 x_2$ coordinates are coupled. ■ ■ ■

For any constant coefficient matrix $\mathbf{A}$, it would be worth using a trial solution of the system that has the form $\mathbf{x}(t) = e^{\lambda t}\mathbf{x}$ where $\mathbf{x}$ is a constant vector. Putting this into the equation $\mathbf{x}'(t) = \mathbf{A}\mathbf{x}(t)$, we have

$$\lambda \mathbf{x} e^{\lambda t} = \mathbf{A}\mathbf{x} e^{\lambda t} \quad \Rightarrow \quad (\lambda \mathbf{I} - \mathbf{A})\mathbf{x} = 0,$$

which is the equation for the eigenvalue problem for $\mathbf{A}$.

When $\mathbf{A}$ is diagonalizable, there will be n eigenpairs $(\lambda_k, \mathbf{x}_{(k)})$ and each will give rise to a solution of the form $\mathbf{x}_{(k)} e^{\lambda_k t}$. The n solutions so obtained must be linearly independent. More specifically, the Wronski matrix of the solutions is

$$\mathbf{W}(t) = \left[\mathbf{x}_{(1)} e^{\lambda_1 t}, \mathbf{x}_{(2)} e^{\lambda_2 t}; \ldots, \mathbf{x}_{(n)} e^{\lambda_n t} \right].$$

The Wronskian is

$$W(t) = \det\left(\mathbf{W}(t)\right) = \det\left[\mathbf{x}_{(1)}, \mathbf{x}_{(2)}, \ldots, \mathbf{x}_{(n)} \right] e^{(\lambda_1 + \lambda_2 + \ldots + \lambda_n)t}.$$

The exponential factor is never zero, and the determinant is nonzero because

$$\mathbf{P} = \left[\mathbf{x}_{(1)}, \mathbf{x}_{(2)}, \ldots, \mathbf{x}_{(n)} \right]$$

is the nonsingular matrix of eigenvectors. This leads to the following theorem.

THEOREM 6.14 *Whenever* $\mathbf{A}$ *is diagonalizable with eigenvalues* $\lambda_1, \lambda_2, \ldots, \lambda_n$ *and corresponding eigenvectors* $\mathbf{x}_{(1)}, \mathbf{x}_{(2)}, \ldots, \mathbf{x}_{(n)}$, *the general solution of the linear system* $\mathbf{x}'(t) = \mathbf{A}\mathbf{x}(t)$ *will be*

$$\mathbf{x}(t) = c_1 e^{\lambda_1 t} \mathbf{x}_{(1)} + c_{(2)} e^{\lambda_2 t} \mathbf{x}_2 + \cdots + c_n e^{\lambda_n t} \mathbf{x}_{(n)}. \tag{6.19}$$

$\square$

■ **EXAMPLE 6.19** Solve the system

$$\mathbf{x}'(t) = \begin{bmatrix} -1 & 1 & 0 & 0 \\ 1 & -1 & 0 & 0 \\ 0 & 0 & -3 & 2 \\ 0 & 0 & 1 & -2 \end{bmatrix} \mathbf{x}.$$

Solution: We must find the eigenvalues and eigenvectors of the coefficient matrix, which should be fairly easy since it is in so-called *block diagonal* form. The characteristic equation is

$$\det \begin{bmatrix} \lambda + 1 & -1 & 0 & 0 \\ -1 & \lambda + 1 & 0 & 0 \\ 0 & 0 & \lambda + 3 & -2 \\ 0 & 0 & -1 & \lambda + 2 \end{bmatrix} = \lambda(\lambda + 1)(\lambda + 2)(\lambda + 4).$$

Thus, the eigenvalues are $\lambda = 0, -1, -2, -4$. For each value of λ we must form $\lambda \mathbf{I} - \mathbf{A}$, row reduce it, and read off the eigenvectors:

$$0\mathbf{I} - \mathbf{A} = \begin{bmatrix} 1 & -1 & 0 & 0 \\ -1 & 1 & 0 & 0 \\ 0 & 0 & 3 & -2 \\ 0 & 0 & -1 & 2 \end{bmatrix} \hookrightarrow \begin{bmatrix} 1 & -1 & 0 & 0 \\ 0 & 0 & 1 & 0 \\ 0 & 0 & 0 & 1 \\ 0 & 0 & 0 & 0 \end{bmatrix}$$

$$\Rightarrow \mathbf{x}_{(1)} = [1; 1; 0; 0],$$

$$-2\mathbf{I} - \mathbf{A} = \begin{bmatrix} -1 & -1 & 0 & 0 \\ -1 & -1 & 0 & 0 \\ 0 & 0 & 1 & -2 \\ 0 & 0 & -1 & 0 \end{bmatrix} \hookrightarrow \begin{bmatrix} 1 & 1 & 0 & 0 \\ 0 & 0 & 1 & 0 \\ 0 & 0 & 0 & 1 \\ 0 & 0 & 0 & 0 \end{bmatrix}$$

$$\Rightarrow \mathbf{x}_{(2)} = [1; -1; 0; 0],$$

$$-\mathbf{I} - \mathbf{A} = \begin{bmatrix} 0 & -1 & 0 & 0 \\ -1 & 0 & 0 & 0 \\ 0 & 0 & 2 & -2 \\ 0 & 0 & -1 & 1 \end{bmatrix} \hookrightarrow \begin{bmatrix} 1 & 0 & 0 & 0 \\ 0 & 1 & 0 & 0 \\ 0 & 0 & 1 & -1 \\ 0 & 0 & 0 & 0 \end{bmatrix}$$

$$\Rightarrow \mathbf{x}_{(3)} = [0; 0; 1; 1],$$

$$-4\mathbf{I} - \mathbf{A} = \begin{bmatrix} -3 & -1 & 0 & 0 \\ -1 & -3 & 0 & 0 \\ 0 & 0 & -1 & -2 \\ 0 & 0 & -1 & -2 \end{bmatrix} \hookrightarrow \begin{bmatrix} 1 & 0 & 0 & 0 \\ 0 & 1 & 0 & 0 \\ 0 & 0 & 1 & 2 \\ 0 & 0 & 0 & 0 \end{bmatrix}$$

$$\Rightarrow \mathbf{x}_{(4)} = [0; 0; 2; -1].$$

Thus, the general solution is

$$\mathbf{x}(t) = c_1 \begin{bmatrix} 1 \\ 1 \\ 0 \\ 0 \end{bmatrix} e^{0t} + c_2 \begin{bmatrix} 1 \\ -1 \\ 0 \\ 0 \end{bmatrix} e^{-2t} + c_3 \begin{bmatrix} 0 \\ 0 \\ 1 \\ 1 \end{bmatrix} e^{-t} + c_4 \begin{bmatrix} 0 \\ 0 \\ 2 \\ -1 \end{bmatrix} e^{-4t}.$$

∎ ∎ ∎

Real Form of the Solution for Complex Eigenvalues

If $\mathbf{A}$ is a *real* matrix with complex eigenvalues, then we know that these eigenvalues must occur in complex conjugate pairs of the form $\lambda_\pm = a \pm ib$. The corresponding eigenvectors can also be chosen to be conjugate pairs $\mathbf{x}_{(\pm)} = \mathbf{u} \pm i\mathbf{v}$. The complex form of the solution for one such pair is

$$c_+ e^{\lambda_+ t} \mathbf{x}_{(+)} + c_- e^{\lambda_- t} \mathbf{x}_{(-)},$$

which must be a real function. Hence, the constants $c_\pm$ must also be complex conjugates.

Just as in the scalar case, the real and imaginary parts of a complex solution of a real equation are also solutions. Thus the vector functions

$$\begin{aligned} \mathrm{Re}\left[e^{(a+ib)t}(\mathbf{u} + i\mathbf{v})\right] &= e^{at}\,\mathrm{Re}\left[(\cos bt + i\sin bt)(\mathbf{u} + i\mathbf{v})\right] \\ &= e^{at}\,\mathrm{Re}\left[(\mathbf{u}\cos bt - \mathbf{v}\sin bt) + i\,(\mathbf{u}\sin bt + \mathbf{v}\cos bt)\right] \\ &= e^{at}\,(\mathbf{u}\cos bt - \mathbf{v}\sin bt) \end{aligned}$$

and

$$\mathrm{Im}\left[e^{(a+ib)t}(\mathbf{u} + i\mathbf{v})\right] = e^{at}\,(\mathbf{u}\sin bt + \mathbf{v}\cos bt)$$

are solutions. We have proven the following theorem.

THEOREM 6.15 *The real form of part of the solution of the real linear system $\mathbf{x}'(t) = \mathbf{A}\mathbf{x}(t)$ associated with the complex eigenvalue pair $\lambda_\pm = a \pm ib$ with corresponding complex eigenvector pair $\mathbf{x}_{(\pm)} = \mathbf{u} \pm i\mathbf{v}$ is*

$$k_1 e^{at}(\mathbf{u}\cos bt - \mathbf{v}\sin bt) + k_2 e^{at}(\mathbf{u}\sin bt + \mathbf{v}\cos bt), \tag{6.20}$$

where the constants k_1 and k_2 are real.   □

■ **EXAMPLE 6.20** Solve the linear system

$$\mathbf{x}' = \begin{bmatrix} -1 & 2 \\ -2 & -1 \end{bmatrix} \mathbf{x}, \quad \mathbf{x}(0) = \begin{bmatrix} 3 \\ 2 \end{bmatrix}.$$

Solution: Set up the characteristic equation:

$$\det(\lambda\mathbf{I} - \mathbf{A}) = \det \begin{bmatrix} \lambda+1 & -2 \\ 2 & \lambda+1 \end{bmatrix} = (\lambda+1)^2 + 4 \;\Rightarrow\; \lambda = -1 \pm 2i.$$

The one complex eigenvector we need is gotten by solving $(\lambda_+\mathbf{I} - \mathbf{A})\mathbf{x}_{(+)} = 0$:

$$(-1+2i)\mathbf{I} - \mathbf{A} = \begin{bmatrix} 2i & -2 \\ 2 & 2i \end{bmatrix} \;\hookrightarrow\; \begin{bmatrix} 1 & i \\ 0 & 0 \end{bmatrix}$$

$$\Rightarrow\; \mathbf{x}_{(+)} = \begin{bmatrix} -i \\ 1 \end{bmatrix} = \begin{bmatrix} 0 \\ 1 \end{bmatrix} + i \begin{bmatrix} -1 \\ 0 \end{bmatrix}.$$

Thus we have $\mathbf{u} = [0; 1]$ and $\mathbf{v} = [-1; 0]$. The general solution of the system is

$$\mathbf{x}(t) = c_1 e^{-t} \left\{ \begin{bmatrix} 0 \\ 1 \end{bmatrix} \cos 2t - \begin{bmatrix} -1 \\ 0 \end{bmatrix} \sin 2t \right\}$$

$$+ c_2 e^{-t} \left\{ \begin{bmatrix} 0 \\ 1 \end{bmatrix} \sin 2t + \begin{bmatrix} -1 \\ 0 \end{bmatrix} \cos 2t \right\}$$

Applying the initial conditions leads to the algebraic system

$$c_1 \begin{bmatrix} 0 \\ 1 \end{bmatrix} + c_2 \begin{bmatrix} -1 \\ 0 \end{bmatrix} = \begin{bmatrix} 3 \\ 2 \end{bmatrix} \;\Rightarrow\; c_1 = 2, \; c_2 = -3.$$

The specific solution is

$$\mathbf{x}(t) = 2e^{-t} \begin{bmatrix} \sin 2t \\ \cos 2t \end{bmatrix} - 3e^{-t} \begin{bmatrix} -\cos 2t \\ \sin 2t \end{bmatrix} = e^{-t} \begin{bmatrix} 3\cos 2t + 2\sin 2t \\ 2\cos 2t - 3\sin 2t \end{bmatrix}.$$

■ ■ ■

■ **EXAMPLE 6.21** Find the general solution of the linear system

$$\mathbf{x}' = \begin{bmatrix} 0 & 1 & 0 & 0 \\ 0 & 1 & 1 & -1 \\ 0 & 0 & 0 & 1 \\ 1 & 2 & 1 & -1 \end{bmatrix} \mathbf{x}.$$

Solution: It can be verified that

$$\det(\lambda \mathbf{I} - \mathbf{A}) = \begin{bmatrix} \lambda & -1 & 0 & 0 \\ 0 & \lambda - 1 & -1 & 1 \\ 0 & 0 & \lambda & -1 \\ -1 & -2 & -1 & \lambda + 1 \end{bmatrix} = (\lambda + 1)(\lambda - 1)(\lambda^2 + 1).$$

Thus, the eigenvalues are $\lambda = \pm 1, \pm i$. The eigenpairs are calculated to be

$$\begin{aligned} \lambda = 1 : & \quad \mathbf{x}_{(1)} = [1; 1; 3; 3], \\ \lambda = -1 : & \quad \mathbf{x}_{(2)} = [-1; 1; -1; 1], \\ \lambda = i : & \quad \mathbf{x}_{(+)} = [1; i; -i; 1]. \end{aligned}$$

Separating $\mathbf{x}_{(+)} = \mathbf{u} + i\mathbf{v}$, we have $\mathbf{u} = [1; 0; 0; 1]$ and $\mathbf{v} = [0; 1; -1; 0]$. The general solution is

$$\mathbf{x}(t) = c_1 e^t \begin{bmatrix} 1 \\ 1 \\ 3 \\ 3 \end{bmatrix} + c_2 e_1^{-t} \begin{bmatrix} -1 \\ 1 \\ -1 \\ 1 \end{bmatrix} + c_3 \begin{bmatrix} \cos t \\ -\sin t \\ \sin t \\ \cos t \end{bmatrix} + c_4 \begin{bmatrix} \sin t \\ \cos t \\ -\cos t \\ \sin t \end{bmatrix}.$$

■ ■ ■

Solutions for Doubly Repeated Eigenvalues

When the coefficient matrix is defective, we cannot find n linearly independent eigenvectors and, therefore, cannot construct the general solution, $\mathbf{x}(t)$, using the above procedure. The use of generalized eigenvectors is called for. But what solution should be associated with them?

Repeated roots in the scalar case mandated the introduction of extra factors of t in the solution. We will look at the case of *doubly* repeated eigenvalues with a single eigenvector $x_{(0)}$. Try a solution of the form

$$\mathbf{x}(t) = (t\mathbf{x}_{(0)} + \mathbf{z})e^{\lambda_0 t}, \tag{6.21}$$

where $\mathbf{z}$ is a constant vector added to the solution to take care of any effects due to the coupling of the variables. Substituting into the differential equation, we find

$$\mathbf{x}'(t) = \left(\lambda_0(t\mathbf{x}_{(0)} + \mathbf{z}) + \mathbf{x}_{(0)}\right)e^{\lambda_0 t} = \mathbf{A}(t\mathbf{x}_{(0)} + \mathbf{z})e^{\lambda_0 t} = \mathbf{A}\mathbf{x}(t)$$

$$\Rightarrow \quad (\mathbf{A} - \lambda_0 \mathbf{I})\mathbf{z} = \mathbf{x}_{(0)} + t(\mathbf{A} - \lambda_0 \mathbf{I})\mathbf{x}_{(0)}.$$

But $(\mathbf{A} - \lambda_0 \mathbf{I})\mathbf{x}_0 = \mathbf{0}$, because $\mathbf{x}_0$ is an eigenvector of $\mathbf{A}$ corresponding to the eigenvalue λ_0. Thus

$$(\mathbf{A} - \lambda_0 \mathbf{I})\mathbf{z} = \mathbf{x}_{(0)}; \tag{6.22}$$

that is, $\mathbf{z}$ is the generalized eigenvector of $\mathbf{A}$ corresponding to λ_0. Therefore, we have the following theorem.

THEOREM 6.16 *The part of the solution of* $\mathbf{x}'(t) = \mathbf{A}\mathbf{x}(t)$ *corresponding to the doubly repeated eigenvalue* λ_0 *with single eigenvector* $\mathbf{x}_{(0)}$, *meaning* $\mathbf{A}\mathbf{x}_{(0)} = \lambda_0\mathbf{x}_{(0)}$, *and generalized eigenvector* $\mathbf{z}$, *meaning* $(\mathbf{A} - \lambda_0\mathbf{I})\mathbf{z} = \mathbf{x}_{(0)}$, *is*

$$c_1\mathbf{x}_{(0)}e^{\lambda_0 t} + c_2(t\mathbf{x}_{(0)} + \mathbf{z})e^{\lambda_0 t}. \tag{6.23}$$

$\square$

■ **EXAMPLE 6.22** Solve the linear system

$$\mathbf{x}'(t) = \begin{bmatrix} 5 & -2 \\ 2 & 1 \end{bmatrix}\mathbf{x}(t), \quad \mathbf{x}(0) = \begin{bmatrix} 3 \\ 1 \end{bmatrix}.$$

Solution: Find the eigenvalues:

$$\det(\mathbf{B} - \lambda\mathbf{I}) = \det\begin{bmatrix} 5 - \lambda & -2 \\ 2 & 1 - \lambda \end{bmatrix} = (\lambda - 3)^2 \Rightarrow \lambda = 3, 3.$$

The single eigenvector is gotten from

$$\mathbf{B} - 3\mathbf{I} = \begin{bmatrix} 2 & -2 \\ 2 & -2 \end{bmatrix} \hookrightarrow \begin{bmatrix} 1 & -1 \\ 0 & 0 \end{bmatrix} \Rightarrow \mathbf{x}_{(0)} = \begin{bmatrix} 1 \\ 1 \end{bmatrix}.$$

Solving for the generalized eigenvector, one possible solution is

$$[\mathbf{B} - 3\mathbf{I}|\mathbf{x}_0] = \begin{bmatrix} 2 & -2 & | & 1 \\ 2 & -2 & | & 1 \end{bmatrix} \Rightarrow \mathbf{z} = \begin{bmatrix} \frac{1}{2} \\ 0 \end{bmatrix}.$$

The general solution is

$$\mathbf{x}(t) = c_1 e^{3t}\begin{bmatrix} 1 \\ 1 \end{bmatrix} + c_2 e^{3t}\left\{ t\begin{bmatrix} 1 \\ 1 \end{bmatrix} + \begin{bmatrix} \frac{1}{2} \\ 0 \end{bmatrix} \right\}.$$

Applying the initial conditions, we find the specific solution to be

$$\mathbf{x}(t) = e^{3t}\begin{bmatrix} 3 + 4t \\ 1 + 4t \end{bmatrix}.$$

■ ■ ■

Comment: Since $\text{rank}(\mathbf{A} - \lambda_0\mathbf{I}) < n$, the system

$$(\mathbf{A} - \lambda_0\mathbf{I})\mathbf{z} = \mathbf{x}_{(0)}$$

does not have a unique solution. The complementary solution must satisfy $(\mathbf{A} - \lambda_0\mathbf{I})\mathbf{z}_c = \mathbf{0}$, so that the complementary solution is $\mathbf{z}_c = \mathbf{x}_{(0)}$ to within a constant multiple. Thus $\mathbf{z}$ can be determined only to within an added multiple of $\mathbf{x}_{(0)}$. This causes no problem: the constant of the solution

$$c_2 \mathbf{z}_c e^{\lambda_0 t} = c_2 \mathbf{x}_{(0)} e^{\lambda_0 t}$$

can be incorporated into the term $c_1 \mathbf{x}_{(0)} e^{\lambda_0 t}$ by adjusting the value of the arbitrary constant c_1.

Triply repeated roots add further complications because of the two possible Jordan forms

$$\begin{bmatrix} \lambda & 1 & 0 \\ 0 & \lambda & 1 \\ 0 & 0 & \lambda \end{bmatrix} \quad \text{and} \quad \begin{bmatrix} \lambda & 1 & 0 \\ 0 & \lambda & 0 \\ 0 & 0 & \lambda \end{bmatrix}.$$

This case is best handled by using the methods of the Jordan normal form in the calculation of the exponential matrix.

We can use this methodology to return to $\mathbf{X}(t)$, a fundamental matrix of the system. We defined the kth column of a fundamental matrix to be

$$\mathbf{col}_k \left(\mathbf{X}(t) \right) = \mathbf{x}_k(t),$$

the kth solution vector. Thus the columns of $\mathbf{X}(t)$ are linearly independent solutions of the system; i.e.,

$$\left(\mathbf{col}_k \left(\mathbf{X}(t) \right) \right)' = \mathbf{A} \, \mathbf{col}_k \left(\mathbf{X}(t) \right).$$

This is just the kth column of the matrix equation

$$\mathbf{X}'(t) = \mathbf{A}\mathbf{X}(t).$$

Once we've solved a linear system, writing a fundamental matrix is no problem.

■ **EXAMPLE 6.23** By looking at the examples in this section, write a fundamental matrix for each system.

(a) A fundamental matrix for the system

$$\mathbf{x}'(t) = \begin{bmatrix} -1 & 1 & 0 & 0 \\ 1 & -1 & 0 & 0 \\ 0 & 0 & -3 & 2 \\ 0 & 0 & 1 & -2 \end{bmatrix} \mathbf{x(t)}$$

can be read off from the solution given in example 6.19. It is

$$\mathbf{X}(t) = \begin{bmatrix} 1 & e^{-2t} & 0 & 0 \\ 1 & -e^{-2t} & 0 & 0 \\ 0 & 0 & e^{-t} & 2e^{-4t} \\ 0 & 0 & e^{-t} & -e^{-4t} \end{bmatrix}.$$

(b) The system

$$\mathbf{x}'(t) = \begin{bmatrix} -1 & 2 \\ -2 & -1 \end{bmatrix} \mathbf{x}(t)$$

of example 6.20 has a fundamental matrix

$$\mathbf{X}(t) = \begin{bmatrix} e^{-t}\cos 2t & e^{-t}\sin 2t \\ -e^{-t}\sin 2t & e^{-t}\cos 2t \end{bmatrix}.$$

(c) The system

$$\mathbf{x}'(t) = \begin{bmatrix} 0 & 1 & 0 & 0 \\ 0 & 1 & 1 & -1 \\ 0 & 0 & 0 & 1 \\ 1 & 2 & 1 & -1 \end{bmatrix} \mathbf{x}(t)$$

of example 6.21 has as a possible fundamental matrix

$$\mathbf{X}(t) = \begin{bmatrix} e^t & -e^{-t} & \cos t & \sin t \\ e^t & e^{-t} & -\sin t & \cos t \\ 3e^t & -e^{-t} & \sin t & -\cos t \\ 3e^t & e^{-t} & \cos t & \sin t \end{bmatrix}.$$

(d) The system

$$\mathbf{x}'(t) = \begin{bmatrix} 5 & -2 \\ 2 & 1 \end{bmatrix} \mathbf{x}(t)$$

of example 6.22 has as a possible fundamental matrix

$$\mathbf{X}(t) = \begin{bmatrix} e^{3t} & \left(t + \frac{1}{2}\right)e^{3t} \\ e^{3t} & te^{3t} \end{bmatrix}.$$

Since any linearly independent solution vectors could be used, choose twice the second solution vector to eliminate fractions. Another fundamental matrix is

$$\mathbf{X}(t) = e^{3t}\begin{bmatrix} 1 & 2t+1 \\ 1 & 2t \end{bmatrix}.$$

■ ■ ■

6.6.2 *Solving Linear Systems Without Using Eigenvectors*

An alternative method to solving the linear system $\mathbf{x}' = \mathbf{A}\mathbf{x}$ for constant coefficient matrices is available that does not use the eigenvectors of the coefficient matrix. The method is due to B. van Rootselaar, How to Solve the System $\mathbf{x}' = \mathbf{A}\mathbf{x}$, **American Mathematical Monthly 92**, p.321–326 (May 1985). It has some distinct advantages.

We proceed by finding the characteristic polynomial of $\mathbf{A}$, which we wrote as

$$\phi_{\mathbf{A}}(\lambda) = \det(\lambda\mathbf{I} - \mathbf{A}) = \lambda^n + a_1\lambda^{n-1} + \cdots + a_n. \tag{6.24}$$

The roots of $\phi_{\mathbf{A}}(\lambda)$ are the eigenvalues of $\mathbf{A}$. By the Cayley-Hamilton Theorem we know that $\mathbf{A}$ satisfies its characteristic equation, i.e.,

$$\mathbf{A}^n + a_1 \mathbf{A}^{n-1} + \cdots + a_n \mathbf{I} = 0.$$

Because this matrix equation is identically zero, we can multiply on the right by any vector $\mathbf{x}$ and it will still be zero:

$$\mathbf{A}^n \mathbf{x} + a_1 \mathbf{A}^{n-1} \mathbf{x} + \cdots + a_n \mathbf{x} = 0. \tag{6.25}$$

We would like to use this form of the theorem to help us solve our linear system. The basic idea is to convert it to a set of simple scalar equations and somehow rearrange the solutions in a useful way. To do that, start with the basic system $\mathbf{x}'(t) = \mathbf{A}\mathbf{x}(t)$ and successively differentiate. The first differentiation gives us $\mathbf{x}''(t) = (\mathbf{A}\mathbf{x}(t))' = \mathbf{A}\mathbf{x}'(t) = \mathbf{A}(\mathbf{A}\mathbf{x}(t)) = \mathbf{A}^2 \mathbf{x}(t)$, because $\mathbf{A}$ is a constant matrix. Clearly this pattern generalizes to $\mathbf{x}^{(k)}(t) = \mathbf{A}^k \mathbf{x}(t)$. If we insert these terms into the left hand side of (6.25), we see that any solution of $\mathbf{x}' = \mathbf{A}\mathbf{x}$ must also be a solution of the vector equation

$$\mathbf{x}^{(n)} + a_1 \mathbf{x}^{(n-1)} + \cdots + a_{n-1} \mathbf{x}' + a_n \mathbf{x} = 0. \tag{6.26}$$

Each component of this vector equation is the same scalar ODE. If we write the characteristic polynomial in factored form as

$$\phi_{\mathbf{A}}(\lambda) = (\lambda - \lambda_1)^{m_1} (\lambda - \lambda_2)^{m_2} \cdots (\lambda - \lambda_r)^{m_r},$$

then each component of $\mathbf{x}$ satisfies the equation

$$(D - \lambda_1)^{m_1} (D - \lambda_2)^{m_2} \cdots (D - \lambda_r)^{m_r} x_i = 0, \quad i = 1 : n. \tag{6.27}$$

For the eigenvalue λ_i, the corresponding scalar equation is

$$(D - \lambda_i)^{m_i} x = 0.$$

From Chapter 4, we know the linearly independent set of solutions of this equation can be written as

$$\left\{ f_{i,m_i-1}(t) = \frac{t^{m_i-1}}{(m_i-1)!} e^{\lambda_i t}, \ f_{i,m_i-2}(t) = \frac{t^{m_i-2}}{(m_i-2)!} e^{\lambda_i t}, \ldots, \ f_{i,0}(t) = e^{\lambda_i t} \right\}.$$

The reciprocal factorials were added to make life easier later on (think of the inverse Laplace transform of s^{-k}). Now arrange these *descending* power solutions for each eigenvalue to form the column vector

$$\mathbf{f}(t) = [f_{1,m_1-1}(t); f_{1,m_1-2}(t); \ldots; f_{1,0}(t); \ldots; f_{r,m_r-1}(t); \ldots; f_{r,0}(t)]. \tag{6.28}$$

Because $\mathbf{f}(t)$ is constructed from solutions of (6.27), it is a solution of equation (6.26). Thus a general solution of (6.26) can be written in the form

$$\mathbf{x}(t) = \mathbf{C}\mathbf{f}(t), \tag{6.29}$$

where $\mathbf{C}$ is an $n \times n$ constant matrix. This will also be a solution of our original linear system $\mathbf{x}' = \mathbf{A}\mathbf{x}$ if

$$\mathbf{C}\mathbf{f}'(t) = \mathbf{A}\mathbf{C}\mathbf{f}(t).$$

The question remains, how do we find a solution of $\mathbf{x}' = \mathbf{A}\mathbf{x}$ subject to the initial conditions $\mathbf{x}(0) = \mathbf{x}_0$? Notice that setting $t = 0$ for the initial condition is no restriction, because the system is time invariant. Start by constructing a "Wronski-like" matrix obtained from the solution vector $\mathbf{x}(t)$:

$$\mathbf{W}(t) := \left[\mathbf{x}(t), \mathbf{x}'(t), \ldots, \mathbf{x}^{(n-1)}(t)\right].$$

Analogously, form the matrix $\mathbf{F}(t)$ from the solution vector $\mathbf{f}(t)$:

$$\mathbf{F}(t) := \left[\mathbf{f}(t), \mathbf{f}'(t), \ldots, \mathbf{f}^{(n-1)}(t)\right].$$

Now we need to tie together the solution vector $\mathbf{x}(t)$ of the original linear system and $\mathbf{f}(t)$ of the nth order vector equation. To this end, we'll use the implication $\mathbf{x}' = \mathbf{A}\mathbf{x} \Rightarrow \mathbf{x}^{(k)} = \mathbf{A}^k\mathbf{x}$ and reduce $\mathbf{W}(t)$ to the matrix obtained from these powers:

$$\mathbf{P}(\mathbf{x}(t)) = \left[\mathbf{x}(t), \mathbf{A}\mathbf{x}(t), \ldots, \mathbf{A}^{n-1}\mathbf{x}(t)\right]. \tag{6.30}$$

In order to derive the required relation, start with (6.29) and iterate:

$$\begin{aligned}
\mathbf{x}(t) &= \mathbf{C}\mathbf{f}(t), \\
\mathbf{x}'(t) &= \mathbf{C}\mathbf{f}'(t) &\Rightarrow& \quad \mathbf{A}\mathbf{x}(t) = \mathbf{C}\mathbf{f}'(t), \\
&\vdots & \vdots & \\
\mathbf{x}^{(n-1)}(t) &= \mathbf{C}\mathbf{f}^{(n-1)}(t) &\Rightarrow& \quad \mathbf{A}^{n-1}\mathbf{x}(t) = \mathbf{C}\mathbf{f}^{(n-1)}(t).
\end{aligned}$$

From this we can immediately infer the relation

$$\mathbf{P}(\mathbf{x}(t)) = \mathbf{C}\mathbf{F}(t). \tag{6.31}$$

When $t = 0$, this becomes

$$\mathbf{P}(\mathbf{x}_0) = \mathbf{C}(\mathbf{x}_0)\mathbf{F}(0) \quad \Rightarrow \quad \mathbf{C}(\mathbf{x}_0) = \mathbf{P}(\mathbf{x}_0)\mathbf{F}^{-1}(0).$$

Therefore, the solution to $\mathbf{x}' = \mathbf{A}\mathbf{x}$ with $\mathbf{x}(0) = \mathbf{x}_0$ is

$$\mathbf{x}(t) = \mathbf{C}(\mathbf{x}_0)\mathbf{f}(t). \tag{6.32}$$

To get $\mathbf{C}(\mathbf{x}_0)$, we need to calculate $\mathbf{F}(0)$. There are m_i rows in the matrix $\mathbf{F}(t)$ corresponding to the eigenvalue λ_i; they are

$$\mathbf{row}_{\mu+1}(\mathbf{F}(0)) = \left[f_{i,m_i-1}(0), f'_{i,m_i-1}(0), \ldots, f^{(n-1)}_{i,m_i-1}(0)\right],$$

$$\vdots \qquad\qquad \vdots$$

$$\mathbf{row}_{\mu+m_i}(\mathbf{F}(0)) = \left[f_{i,0}(t), f'_{i,0}(t), \ldots, f^{(n-1)}_{i,0}(t)\right],$$

where $\mu = \sum_1^{i-1} m_j$. Since

$$f_{i,j}(t) = \frac{t^j}{j!} e^{s_i t} = \frac{t}{j} \left\{ \frac{t^{j-1}}{(j-1)!} e^{s_i t} \right\} = \frac{t}{j} f_{i,j-1}(t),$$

we can write a relation among the derivatives of the f's as

$$f_{i,j}^{(k)}(0) = D^{k-1} D \left(\frac{t}{j} f_{i,j-1}(t) \right)_{t=0} = D^{k-1} \left(\frac{1}{j} f_{i,j-1}(t) + \frac{t}{j} f'_{i,j-1}(t) \right)_{t=0}$$

$$= \frac{k}{j} f_{i,j-1}^{(k-1)}(0), \quad j > 0, \ k > 0.$$

When $k = 0$ and $j = 0$ matters change slightly and we have

$$f_{i,j}^{(0)}(0) = \left(\frac{t^j}{j!} e^{s_i t} \right)_{t=0} = 0, \quad j > 0, \quad \text{and} \quad f_{i,0}^{(k)}(0) = \left(\left(\frac{d}{dt} \right)^k e^{s_i t} \right)_{t=0} = s_i^k.$$

These equations have a relatively simple solution. They generate the following infinite upper triangular "table" matrix of coefficients:

$$\mathbf{T} = \begin{bmatrix} 1 & \lambda & \lambda^2 & \lambda^3 & \lambda^4 & \lambda^5 & \lambda^6 & \lambda^7 & \cdots \\ 0 & 1 & 2\lambda & 3\lambda^2 & 4\lambda^3 & 5\lambda^4 & 6\lambda^5 & 7\lambda^6 & \cdots \\ 0 & 0 & 1 & 3\lambda & 6\lambda^2 & 10\lambda^3 & 15\lambda^4 & 21\lambda^5 & \cdots \\ 0 & 0 & 0 & 1 & 4\lambda & 10\lambda^2 & 20\lambda^3 & 35\lambda^4 & \cdots \\ 0 & 0 & 0 & 0 & 1 & 5\lambda & 15\lambda^2 & 35\lambda^3 & \cdots \\ 0 & 0 & 0 & 0 & 0 & 1 & 6\lambda & 21\lambda^2 & \cdots \\ 0 & 0 & 0 & 0 & 0 & 0 & 1 & 7\lambda & \cdots \\ \vdots & \vdots & \vdots & \vdots & \vdots & \vdots & & 0 & 1 & \ddots \end{bmatrix}. \tag{6.33}$$

The pattern is eminently "binomial-like" because

$$\mathrm{sum}(\mathbf{T}) = \left[(\lambda + 1)^0, (\lambda + 1)^1, (\lambda + 1)^2, (\lambda + 1)^3, \ldots \right].$$

To handle the eigenvalue λ_i we use the first m_i rows of $\mathbf{T}$ to generate solutions and read "up"; i.e., **flipr** $(\mathbf{T}(1 : m_i, 1 : n))$. Thus if $\lambda = 3$ is a fivefold repeated root and $\lambda = 2$ is a doubly repeated root, then we need the upper left 5×7 submatrix row-flipped with $\lambda = 3$ and the upper left 2×7 submatrix row-flipped with $\lambda = 2$ to get

$$\mathbf{F}(0) = \begin{bmatrix} 0 & 0 & 0 & 0 & 1 & 5 \cdot 3 & 15 \cdot 3^2 \\ 0 & 0 & 0 & 1 & 4 \cdot 3 & 10 \cdot 3^2 & 20 \cdot 3^3 \\ 0 & 0 & 1 & 3 \cdot 3 & 6 \cdot 3^2 & 10 \cdot 3^3 & 15 \cdot 3^4 \\ 0 & 1 & 2 \cdot 3 & 3 \cdot 3^2 & 4 \cdot 3^3 & 5 \cdot 3^4 & 6 \cdot 3^5 \\ 1 & 3 & 3^2 & 3^3 & 3^4 & 3^5 & 3^6 \\ 0 & 1 & 2 \cdot 2 & 3 \cdot 2^2 & 4 \cdot 2^3 & 5 \cdot 2^4 & 6 \cdot 2^5 \\ 1 & 2 & 2^2 & 2^3 & 2^4 & 2^5 & 2^6 \end{bmatrix}.$$

■ **EXAMPLE 6.24** Find the specific solution of the following initial value problem of example 6.21:

$$\mathbf{x}' = \begin{bmatrix} 0 & 1 & 0 & 0 \\ 0 & 1 & 1 & -1 \\ 0 & 0 & 0 & 1 \\ 1 & 2 & 1 & -1 \end{bmatrix} \mathbf{x}, \quad \mathbf{x}(0) = \begin{bmatrix} -1 \\ 4 \\ 0 \\ 3 \end{bmatrix}.$$

Solution: You can verify that the characteristic polynomial is

$$\det(\lambda \mathbf{I} - \mathbf{A}) = (\lambda + 1)(\lambda - 1)(\lambda^2 + 1).$$

The eigenvalues of $\lambda = \pm 1, \pm i$ allow us to write

$$\mathbf{f}(t) = [e^t; e^{-t}; e^{it}; e^{-it}].$$

Computing $\mathbf{F}(0)$ is not difficult, we need only use the first row of $\mathbf{T}$ with *each* value of λ because of the distinct roots. We find

$$\mathbf{F}(0) = \begin{bmatrix} 1 & 1 & 1 & 1 \\ 1 & -1 & 1 & -1 \\ 1 & i & -1 & -i \\ 1 & -i & -1 & i \end{bmatrix} \quad \Rightarrow \quad \mathbf{F}^{-1}(0) = \frac{1}{4} \begin{bmatrix} 1 & 1 & 1 & 1 \\ 1 & -1 & -i & i \\ 1 & 1 & -1 & -1 \\ 1 & -1 & i & -i \end{bmatrix}.$$

Using $\mathbf{x}(0) = [-1; 4; 0; 3]$ we can generate the matrix of powers:

$$\mathbf{P}(\mathbf{x}_0) = \begin{bmatrix} -1 & 4 & 1 & 0 \\ 4 & 1 & 0 & -1 \\ 0 & 3 & 4 & 5 \\ 3 & 4 & 5 & 0 \end{bmatrix}.$$

Using this, we (meaning the computer) find

$$\mathbf{C}(\mathbf{x}_0) = \mathbf{P}(\mathbf{x}_0)\mathbf{F}^{-1}(0) = \frac{1}{2} \begin{bmatrix} 2 & -2 & -1 - 2i & -1 + 2i \\ 2 & 2 & 2 - i & 2 + i \\ 6 & -2 & -2 + i & -2 - i \\ 6 & 2 & -1 - 2i & -1 + 2i \end{bmatrix}.$$

The unique solution is then

$$\mathbf{x}(t) = \mathbf{C}(\mathbf{x}_0)f(t) = \begin{bmatrix} 2\sinh t - \cos t + 2\sin t \\ 2\cosh t + 2\cos t + \sin t \\ 2\cosh t + 4\sinh t - 2\cos t - \sin t \\ 4\cosh t + 2\sinh t - \cos t + 2\sin t \end{bmatrix}.$$

■ ■ ■

▪ **EXAMPLE 6.25** Use this method to find the complementary solution of the linear system

$$\mathbf{x}'(t) = \begin{bmatrix} 1 & 1 & 0 \\ 0 & 1 & 0 \\ 0 & 0 & 2 \end{bmatrix} \mathbf{x}(t).$$

Solution: Since $\mathbf{A}$ is triangular, we can immediately write the characteristic polynomial:

$$\det(\lambda \mathbf{I} - \mathbf{A}) = (\lambda - 1)^2(\lambda - 2).$$

Solutions of the scalar equation $(D-1)^2 x(t) = 0$ are te^t and e^t. A solution of $(D-2)x(t) = 0$ is e^{2t}. From this we can avoid using the table matrix and write $\mathbf{f}(t)$ and the full matrix obtained from it, $\mathbf{F}(t) = [\mathbf{f}(t), \mathbf{f}'(t), \mathbf{f}''(t)]$:

$$\mathbf{f}(t) = \begin{bmatrix} te^t \\ e^t \\ e^{2t} \end{bmatrix} \qquad \Rightarrow \qquad \mathbf{F}(t) = \begin{bmatrix} te^t & (t+1)e^t & (t+2)e^t \\ e^t & e^t & e^t \\ e^{2t} & 2e^{2t} & 4e^{2t} \end{bmatrix}.$$

Evaluating and then inverting $\mathbf{F}(0)$ is straightforward:

$$\mathbf{F}(0) = \begin{bmatrix} 0 & 1 & 2 \\ 1 & 1 & 1 \\ 1 & 2 & 4 \end{bmatrix} \qquad \Rightarrow \qquad \mathbf{F}^{-1}(0) = \begin{bmatrix} -2 & 0 & 1 \\ 3 & 2 & -2 \\ -1 & -1 & 1 \end{bmatrix}.$$

Notice that generating the first two rows of $\mathbf{F}$ came from the table matrix $\mathbf{T}$ with $\lambda = 1$ and the last row came from $\mathbf{T}(1,1:3)$ with $\lambda = 2$. If we take an arbitrary starting vector $\mathbf{x}_0 = [c_1; c_2; c_3]$, then

$$\mathbf{P}(\mathbf{x}_0) = \begin{bmatrix} \mathbf{x}_0, \mathbf{A}\mathbf{x}_0, \mathbf{A}^2\mathbf{x}_0 \end{bmatrix} = \begin{bmatrix} c_1 & c_1 + c_2 & c_1 + 2c_2 \\ c_2 & c_2 & c_2 \\ c_3 & 2c_3 & 4c_3 \end{bmatrix}$$

and

$$\mathbf{C}(\mathbf{x}_0) = \mathbf{P}(\mathbf{x}_0)\mathbf{F}^{-1}(0) = \begin{bmatrix} c_2 & c_1 & 0 \\ 0 & c_2 & 0 \\ 0 & 0 & c_3 \end{bmatrix}.$$

Thus the required solution is

$$\mathbf{x}(t) = \mathbf{C}(\mathbf{x}_0)\mathbf{f}(t) = \begin{bmatrix} c_2 & c_1 & 0 \\ 0 & c_2 & 0 \\ 0 & 0 & c_3 \end{bmatrix} \begin{bmatrix} te^t \\ e^t \\ e^{2t} \end{bmatrix} = \begin{bmatrix} (c_1 + c_2 t)e^t \\ c_2 e^t \\ c_3 e^{2t} \end{bmatrix}.$$

▪ ▪ ▪

■ **EXAMPLE 6.26** Now let's try another 4×4 matrix. To solve

$$\mathbf{x}' = \begin{bmatrix} 1 & 1 & 2 & -2 \\ 0 & 1 & 2 & -2 \\ 0 & 0 & 2 & -1 \\ 0 & 0 & 1 & 0 \end{bmatrix} \mathbf{x},$$

we can write the characteristic polynomial as

$$\det(\lambda \mathbf{I} - \mathbf{A}) = (\lambda - 1)^4.$$

We can immediately use $\mathbf{T}$ to write

$$\mathbf{F}(0) = \begin{bmatrix} 0 & 0 & 0 & 1 \\ 0 & 0 & 1 & 3 \\ 0 & 1 & 2 & 3 \\ 1 & 1 & 1 & 1 \end{bmatrix} \quad \Rightarrow \quad \mathbf{F}^{-1}(0) = \begin{bmatrix} -1 & 1 & -1 & 1 \\ 3 & -2 & 1 & 0 \\ -3 & 1 & 0 & 0 \\ 1 & 0 & 0 & 0 \end{bmatrix}.$$

The full matrix (only the first column of which we actually need) is not so simple. $\mathbf{F}(t)$ is given by

$$\begin{bmatrix} \frac{1}{6}t^3 e^t & \frac{1}{6}(t^3 + 3t^2)e^t & \frac{1}{6}(t^3 + 6t^2 + 6t)e^t & \frac{1}{6}(t^3 + 9t^2 + 18t + 6)e^t \\ \frac{1}{2}t^2 e^t & \frac{1}{2}(t^2 + 2t)e^t & \frac{1}{2}(t^2 + 4t + 2)e^t & \frac{1}{2}(t^2 + 6t + 6)e^t \\ te^t & (t+1)e^t & (t+2)e^t & (t+3)e^t \\ e^t & e^t & e^t & e^t \end{bmatrix}.$$

Again using an arbitrary starting vector $\mathbf{x}_0 = [c_1; c_2; c_3; c_4]$ we find the matrix of powers to be $\mathbf{P}(\mathbf{x}_0) = \begin{bmatrix} \mathbf{x}_0, \mathbf{A}\mathbf{x}_0, \mathbf{A}^2\mathbf{x}_0, \mathbf{A}^3\mathbf{x}_0 \end{bmatrix}$ or

$$\begin{bmatrix} c_1 & c_1 + c_2 + 2c_3 - 2c_4 & c_1 + 2c_2 + 6c_3 - 6c_4 & c_1 + 3c_2 + 12c_3 - 12c_4 \\ c_2 & c_2 + 2c_3 - 2c_4 & c_2 + 4c_3 - 4c_4 & c_2 + 6c_3 - 6c_4 \\ c_3 & 2c_3 - c_4 & 3c_3 - 2c_4 & 4c_3 - 3c_3 \\ c_4 & c_3 & 2c_3 - c_4 & 3c_3 - 2c_4 \end{bmatrix}.$$

Next, we get

$$\mathbf{C}(\mathbf{x}_0) = \mathbf{P}(\mathbf{x}_0)\mathbf{F}^{-1}(0) = \begin{bmatrix} 0 & 2c_3 - 2c_4 & c_2 + 2c_3 - 2c_4 & c_1 \\ 0 & 0 & 2c_3 - 2c_4 & c_2 \\ 0 & 0 & c_3 - c_4 & c_3 \\ 0 & 0 & c_3 - c_4 & c_4 \end{bmatrix}.$$

Last, but not least, we have the full solution

$$\mathbf{x}(t) = \mathbf{C}(\mathbf{x}_0)\mathbf{f}(t) = e^t \begin{bmatrix} c_1 + c_2 t + c_3(t^2 + 2t) - c_4(t^2 + 2t) \\ c_2 + 2c_3 t - 2c_4 t \\ c_3(t+1) - c_4 t \\ c_3 t + c_4(1-t) \end{bmatrix}.$$

■ ■ ■

The most important thing to notice about this technique is how easily it can be implemented on a computer algebra system. Generating $\mathbf{F}(0)$ by using $\mathbf{T}$ is actually unnecessary since we know $\mathbf{f}(t)$ and can form the full matrix $\mathbf{F}(t)$ quite easily using differentiation and concatenation commands.

6.6.3 Exercise Set

For each of the following systems of linear ODE's, find a general or specific solution, as appropriate, and write a fundamental matrix.

1.
$$\mathbf{x}'(t) = \begin{bmatrix} 3 & -2 \\ 4 & -1 \end{bmatrix} \mathbf{x}(t)$$

2.
$$\mathbf{x}'(t) = \begin{bmatrix} -1 & -4 \\ 1 & -1 \end{bmatrix} \mathbf{x}(t)$$

3.
$$\mathbf{x}'(t) = \begin{bmatrix} 3 & -4 \\ 1 & -1 \end{bmatrix} \mathbf{x}(t)$$

4.
$$\mathbf{x}'(t) = \begin{bmatrix} 1 & 1+i \\ 1-i & 1 \end{bmatrix} \mathbf{x}(t)$$

5.
$$\mathbf{x}'(t) = \begin{bmatrix} -7 & -4 \\ 8 & 1 \end{bmatrix} \mathbf{x}(t), \quad \mathbf{x}(0) = \begin{bmatrix} -2 \\ 1 \end{bmatrix}$$

6.
$$\mathbf{x}'(t) = \begin{bmatrix} -9 & -2 \\ 17 & 1 \end{bmatrix} \mathbf{x}(t), \quad \mathbf{x}(0) = \begin{bmatrix} 2 \\ 4 \end{bmatrix}$$

7.
$$\mathbf{x}'(t) = \begin{bmatrix} -4 & 5 \\ -1 & -2 \end{bmatrix} \mathbf{x}(t), \quad \mathbf{x}(0) = \begin{bmatrix} 1 \\ 3 \end{bmatrix}$$

8.
$$\mathbf{x}'(t) = \begin{bmatrix} 4 & 1 \\ -1 & 2 \end{bmatrix} \mathbf{x}(t), \quad \mathbf{x}(0) = \begin{bmatrix} 4 \\ -2 \end{bmatrix}$$

9.
$$\mathbf{x}'(t) = \begin{bmatrix} -3 & 3 \\ 2 & 2 \end{bmatrix} \mathbf{x}(t), \quad \mathbf{x}(0) = \begin{bmatrix} -6 \\ 2 \end{bmatrix}$$

10.
$$\mathbf{x}'(t) = \begin{bmatrix} 8 & -3 \\ 16 & -8 \end{bmatrix} \mathbf{x}(t), \quad \mathbf{x}(0) = \begin{bmatrix} 5 \\ 12 \end{bmatrix}$$

11.
$$\mathbf{x}'(t) = \begin{bmatrix} 4 & 1 \\ -8 & 8 \end{bmatrix} \mathbf{x}(t), \quad \mathbf{x}(0) = \begin{bmatrix} 1 \\ 0 \end{bmatrix}$$

12.
$$\mathbf{x}'(t) = \begin{bmatrix} 4 & 1 \\ -4 & 8 \end{bmatrix} \mathbf{x}(t), \quad \mathbf{x}(0) = \begin{bmatrix} 1 \\ 1 \end{bmatrix}$$

13.
$$\mathbf{x}'(t) = \begin{bmatrix} 3 & 2 \\ 0 & 1 \end{bmatrix} \mathbf{x}(t), \quad \mathbf{x}(0) = \begin{bmatrix} 1 \\ 1 \end{bmatrix}$$

14.
$$\mathbf{x}'(t) = \begin{bmatrix} 5 & -2 \\ 2 & 1 \end{bmatrix} \mathbf{x}(t), \quad \mathbf{x}(0) = \begin{bmatrix} 3 \\ 1 \end{bmatrix}$$

15.
$$\mathbf{x}'(t) = \begin{bmatrix} 1 & -3 & 3 \\ -3 & 1 & 3 \\ 3 & -3 & 1 \end{bmatrix} \mathbf{x}(t)$$

16.
$$\mathbf{x}'(t) = \begin{bmatrix} -6 & 4 & 2 \\ -14 & 9 & 4 \\ 6 & -3 & 0 \end{bmatrix} \mathbf{x}(t)$$

17.
$$\mathbf{x}'(t) = \begin{bmatrix} -3 & 0 & 2 \\ 1 & -1 & 0 \\ -2 & -1 & 0 \end{bmatrix} \mathbf{x}(t)$$

18.
$$\mathbf{x}'(t) = \begin{bmatrix} 1 & 1 & 1 \\ 2 & 1 & -1 \\ 0 & -1 & 1 \end{bmatrix} \mathbf{x}(t)$$

19.
$$\mathbf{x}'(t) = \begin{bmatrix} -1 & 1 & 4 \\ 3 & 1 & -4 \\ -1 & 0 & 3 \end{bmatrix} \mathbf{x}(t), \quad \mathbf{x}(0) = \begin{bmatrix} 2 \\ -3 \\ 3 \end{bmatrix}$$

20.
$$\mathbf{x}'(t) = \begin{bmatrix} 1 & 2 & -1 \\ 2 & 1 & 1 \\ -1 & 1 & 0 \end{bmatrix} \mathbf{x}(t), \quad \mathbf{x}(0) = \begin{bmatrix} 1 \\ 1 \\ -3 \end{bmatrix}$$

21.
$$\mathbf{x}'(t) = \begin{bmatrix} 1 & 0 & 0 \\ 2 & 1 & -2 \\ 3 & 2 & 1 \end{bmatrix} \mathbf{x}(t), \quad \mathbf{x}(0) = \begin{bmatrix} 2 \\ -2 \\ 1 \end{bmatrix}$$

22.
$$\mathbf{x}'(t) = \begin{bmatrix} -5 & 0 & 12 \\ 0 & 2 & 0 \\ -4 & 0 & 9 \end{bmatrix} \mathbf{x}(t), \quad \mathbf{x}(0) = \begin{bmatrix} 9 \\ 2 \\ 3 \end{bmatrix}$$

23.
$$\mathbf{x}'(t) = \begin{bmatrix} 0 & 1 & 1 & 1 \\ 1 & 0 & 1 & 1 \\ 1 & 1 & 0 & 1 \\ 1 & 1 & 1 & 0 \end{bmatrix} \mathbf{x}(t)$$

24.
$$\mathbf{x}'(t) = \begin{bmatrix} 2 & 0 & 1 & 0 \\ 0 & 0 & 0 & 1 \\ -1 & 0 & 2 & 0 \\ 0 & -1 & 0 & 0 \end{bmatrix} \mathbf{x}(t)$$

25.
$$\mathbf{x}'(t) = \begin{bmatrix} 0 & 0 & 1 & 0 \\ 0 & 0 & 0 & 1 \\ 2 & 4 & -1 & -2 \\ 1 & 2 & -1 & -2 \end{bmatrix} \mathbf{x}(t), \quad \mathbf{x}(0) = \begin{bmatrix} 1 \\ 0 \\ 0 \\ 1 \end{bmatrix}$$

26.
$$\mathbf{x}'(t) = \begin{bmatrix} 2 & 0 & 1 & 0 \\ 0 & 2 & 0 & 1 \\ 0 & 0 & 2 & 0 \\ 0 & -1 & 0 & 2 \end{bmatrix} \mathbf{x}(t), \quad \mathbf{x}(0) = \begin{bmatrix} 1 \\ 1 \\ 1 \\ 1 \end{bmatrix}$$

27.
$$\mathbf{x}'(t) = \begin{bmatrix} -3 & 0 & 4 & 0 \\ 0 & 2 & 0 & 5 \\ 4 & 0 & 3 & 0 \\ 0 & 1 & 0 & -2 \end{bmatrix} \mathbf{x}(t), \quad \mathbf{x}(0) = \begin{bmatrix} 0 \\ 2 \\ 5 \\ 4 \end{bmatrix}$$

28.
$$\mathbf{x}'(t) = \begin{bmatrix} 1 & 0 & 1 & 0 \\ 0 & 0 & 0 & 1 \\ 0 & 0 & 1 & 0 \\ 0 & -1 & 0 & 0 \end{bmatrix} \mathbf{x}(t), \quad \mathbf{x}(0) = \begin{bmatrix} 1 \\ 2 \\ 3 \\ 4 \end{bmatrix}$$

6.7 APPLICATIONS OF LINEAR SYSTEMS

We have any number of systems we can model using multivariate methods. To be democratic, we'll study one of each: a multiloop circuit, a mixing model, and a multiple mass-spring system. After those we will look at the so-called modal analysis of mechanical systems. Then a model of the oscillations of a crystalline solid will be studied.

■ **EXAMPLE 6.27** Model a system of RL circuit loops coupled by a mutual inductance if the primary loop is energized by a constant voltage E (see Figure 6.8).

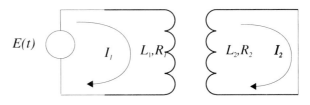

Fig. 6.8

Solution: If the kth loop has resistance, inductance, and current R_k, L_k, and I_k, then the system equations are

$$L_1 \dot{I}_1 + R_1 I_1 + M \dot{I}_2 = E,$$
$$M \dot{I}_1 + L_2 \dot{I}_2 + R_2 I_2 = 0,$$

where M is the mutual inductance; it is known that $L_1 L_2 - M^2 \geq 0$. The case of equality is called *perfect coupling*. We will assume strict inequality for reasons that will become obvious. Writing $\mathbf{I} := [I_1; I_2]$, the system can be reformulated as

$$\begin{bmatrix} L_1 & M \\ M & L_2 \end{bmatrix} \dot{\mathbf{i}} = \begin{bmatrix} -R_1 & 0 \\ 0 & -R_2 \end{bmatrix} \mathbf{I} + \begin{bmatrix} E \\ 0 \end{bmatrix}.$$

In order to convert to standard matrix form we will need to invert the matrix premultiplying $\dot{\mathbf{I}}$. Doing this leads to

$$\dot{\mathbf{i}} = \frac{1}{L_1 L_2 - M^2} \left\{ \begin{bmatrix} -L_2 R_1 & M R_2 \\ M R_1 & -L_1 R_2 \end{bmatrix} \mathbf{I} + \begin{bmatrix} L_2 E \\ -M E \end{bmatrix} \right\}.$$

The characteristic equation for the coefficient matrix is

$$\lambda^2 + \frac{1}{L_1 L_2 - M^2} \left(L_2 R_1 + L_1 R_2 \right) \lambda + \frac{R_1 R_2}{L_1 L_2 - M^2} = 0.$$

To make life *much* simpler, let's assume that $L_1 = L_2$ and $R_1 = R_2$. Since we must have $L_1 L_2 - M^2 = L^2 - M^2 = (L - M)(L + M) > 0$, we must have $L - M > 0$. The characteristic equation is now

$$\frac{\left(L^2 - M^2 \right) \lambda^2 + 2LR\lambda + R^2}{L^2 - M^2} = 0.$$

If we call the roots λ_+ and λ_-, the signs corresponding to the $\pm$ signs in the quadratic formula, the solution is

$$\lambda_\pm = \frac{R}{L^2 - M^2} \left(-L \pm M \right) =: \beta \left(-L \pm M \right),$$

where both roots are real and negative. The eigenpairs can be shown to be

$$\left(\lambda_+, [1; 1] \right) \quad \text{and} \quad \left(\lambda_-, [1; -1] \right).$$

Thus the complementary solution is

$$\mathbf{I}_c(t) = c_1 \begin{bmatrix} 1 \\ 1 \end{bmatrix} e^{-\beta(L-M)t} + c_2 \begin{bmatrix} 1 \\ -1 \end{bmatrix} e^{-\beta(L+M)t}.$$

It can be shown that the particular solution is

$$\mathbf{I}_p(t) = \frac{E}{R} \begin{bmatrix} 1 \\ 0 \end{bmatrix}.$$

Thus the general solution is

$$\mathbf{I}(t) = c_1 \begin{bmatrix} 1 \\ 1 \end{bmatrix} e^{-\beta(L-M)t} + c_2 \begin{bmatrix} 1 \\ -1 \end{bmatrix} e^{-\beta(L+M)t} + \frac{E}{R} \begin{bmatrix} 1 \\ 0 \end{bmatrix}.$$

Since the voltage is energized at $t = 0$, the initial current in each loop should be zero. From this, we find the specific solution to be

$$\mathbf{I}(t) = \frac{E}{2R} \left\{ \begin{bmatrix} -1 \\ -1 \end{bmatrix} e^{-\beta(L-M)t} + \begin{bmatrix} -1 \\ 1 \end{bmatrix} e^{-\beta(L+M)t} + \begin{bmatrix} 2 \\ 0 \end{bmatrix} \right\}.$$

Therefore, the current in the secondary loop is given by

$$I_2(t) = -\frac{E}{R} e^{-\beta L t} \sinh(\beta M t),$$

and the current in the primary loop is

$$I_1(t) = \frac{E}{R} \left(1 - e^{-\beta L t} \cosh(\beta M t) \right).$$

A similar analysis of this circuit with an AC source will be deferred to the problems. ■ ■ ■

■ **EXAMPLE 6.28** Suppose we can model a system by a mixing model using three tanks (see Figure 6.9).

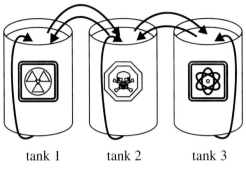

tank 1   tank 2   tank 3

Fig. 6.9

Tank 1 pumps fluid from its bottom into tank 2 at a rate of 1% of the volume per hour and also into its top at a rate of 1% of the volume per hour. The second tank pumps into itself, tank 1, and tank 3, all at a rate of 2% of its volume per hour. Tank 3 pumps into tank 2 at a rate of 2% of its volume per hour and back into itself at rate of 3% of its volume per hour. Find the changes in volume of fluid in each tank as function of time if the initial volumes were 23,000, 1000, and 1000 liters, respectively.

Solution: If we denote the volume of tank k by x_k, the system of ODE's in matrix form is

$$\dot{\mathbf{x}}(t) = \frac{1}{100} \begin{bmatrix} 1 & 2 & 0 \\ 2 & 2 & 2 \\ 0 & 2 & 3 \end{bmatrix} \mathbf{x}(t).$$

The eigenpairs of the symmetric coefficient matrix are

$$(-0.01, [2; -2; 1]), \quad (0.02, [2; 1; -2]), \quad (0.05, [1; 2; 2]).$$

We can write the solution in the form

$$\mathbf{x}(t) = c_1 e^{-0.01t} \begin{bmatrix} 2 \\ -2 \\ 1 \end{bmatrix} + c_2 e^{0.02t} \begin{bmatrix} 2 \\ 1 \\ -2 \end{bmatrix} + c_3 e^{0.05t} \begin{bmatrix} 1 \\ 2 \\ 2 \end{bmatrix}.$$

Using the initial conditions, we find

$$c_1 \begin{bmatrix} 2 \\ -2 \\ 1 \end{bmatrix} + c_2 \begin{bmatrix} 2 \\ 1 \\ -2 \end{bmatrix} + c_3 \begin{bmatrix} 1 \\ 2 \\ 2 \end{bmatrix} = \begin{bmatrix} 23000 \\ 1000 \\ 1000 \end{bmatrix} \Rightarrow \begin{array}{l} c_1 = 5000, \\ c_2 = 5000, \\ c_3 = 3000. \end{array}$$

The mathematics of the model will fail to represent reality when the volume of any tank becomes negative. If this is to happen at time T, then T will be the smallest root of the following set of (nonsimultaneous) equations (divided through by 1000):

$$10e^{-0.01T} + 10e^{0.02T} + 3e^{0.05T} = 0,$$
$$-10e^{-0.01T} + 5e^{0.02T} + 6e^{0.05T} = 0,$$
$$5e^{-0.01T} - 10e^{0.02T} + 6e^{0.05T} = 0.$$

It will be left to the reader to show that only the second equation has any real roots and those are negative. Hence the model is never invalidated for purely mathematical reasons.   ■ ■ ■

■ **EXAMPLE 6.29** The mechanical system shown in Figure 6.10 consists of three identical springs with force constant k, connected to two masses each of mass m, both of which are constrained to move in a straight line.

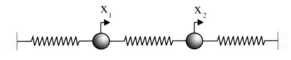

Fig. 6.10

If the left mass remains in its equilibrium position and the right mass is initially moved one unit to the right and released, find the subsequent motion.

Solution: If we denote the displacements of the masses by the coordinates y_1 and y_2, both measured to the right, then the Lagrangian is

$$L = \frac{1}{2}m\left(\dot{y}_1^2 + \dot{y}_2^2\right) - \frac{1}{2}k\left(y_1^2 + (y_1 - y_2)^2 + y_2^2\right),$$

the equations of motion are

$$m\ddot{y}_1 + 2ky_1 - ky_2 = 0,$$
$$m\ddot{y}_2 - ky_1 + 2ky_2 = 0,$$

and the initial conditions are $y_1(0) = 0$, $y_2(0) = 1$, $\dot{y}_1(0) = 0$, and $\dot{y}_2(0) = 0$. We begin by putting the system in standard matrix form. Use the vector $\mathbf{x} = [x_1; x_2; x_3; x_4]$ with $x_1 = y_1$, $x_2 = \dot{y}_1$, $x_3 = y_2$, and $x_4 = \dot{y}_2$. The system takes the form

$$\dot{\mathbf{x}} = \begin{bmatrix} 0 & 1 & 0 & 0 \\ -2\omega^2 & 0 & \omega^2 & 0 \\ 0 & 0 & 0 & 1 \\ \omega^2 & 0 & -2\omega^2 & 0 \end{bmatrix} \mathbf{x},$$

where $\omega^2 := k/m$. The characteristic equation of the coefficient matrix is

$$\left(\lambda^2 + \omega^2\right)\left(\lambda^2 + 3\omega^2\right) = 0 \quad \Rightarrow \quad \lambda = \pm i\omega, \pm i\sqrt{3}\omega.$$

The eigenvectors corresponding to $\lambda = +i\omega$ and $+i\sqrt{3}\omega$ are

$$[1; i\omega; 1; i\omega] = [1; 0; 1; 0] + i\,[0; \omega; 0; \omega],$$

$$\left[-1; -i\omega\sqrt{3}; 1; i\omega\sqrt{3}\right] = [-1; 0; 1; 0] + i\left[0; -\omega\sqrt{3}; 0; \omega\sqrt{3}\right].$$

Using this, we can write the general form of the solution as

$$\mathbf{x}(t) = c_1 \begin{bmatrix} \cos\omega t \\ -\omega\sin\omega t \\ \cos\omega t \\ -\omega\sin\omega t \end{bmatrix} + c_2 \begin{bmatrix} \sin\omega t \\ \omega\cos\omega t \\ \sin\omega t \\ \omega\cos\omega t \end{bmatrix}$$

$$+ c_3 \begin{bmatrix} -\cos\left(\sqrt{3}\omega t\right) \\ \omega\sqrt{3}\sin\left(\sqrt{3}\omega t\right) \\ \cos\left(\sqrt{3}\omega t\right) \\ -\omega\sqrt{3}\sin\left(\sqrt{3}\omega t\right) \end{bmatrix} + c_4 \begin{bmatrix} -\sin\left(\sqrt{3}\omega t\right) \\ -\omega\sqrt{3}\cos\left(\sqrt{3}\omega t\right) \\ \sin\left(\sqrt{3}\omega t\right) \\ \omega\sqrt{3}\cos\left(\sqrt{3}\omega t\right) \end{bmatrix}.$$

Applying the initial conditions, we have

$$\mathbf{x}(0) = c_1 \begin{bmatrix} 1 \\ 0 \\ 1 \\ 0 \end{bmatrix} + c_2 \begin{bmatrix} 0 \\ \omega \\ 0 \\ \omega \end{bmatrix} + c_3 \begin{bmatrix} -1 \\ 0 \\ 1 \\ 0 \end{bmatrix} + c_4 \begin{bmatrix} 0 \\ -\omega\sqrt{3} \\ 0 \\ \omega\sqrt{3} \end{bmatrix} = \begin{bmatrix} 0 \\ 0 \\ 1 \\ 0 \end{bmatrix},$$

from which we immediately find $c_1 = c_2 = \frac{1}{2}$, $c_3 = c_4 = 0$. Thus the vector solution is

$$\mathbf{x}(t) = \frac{1}{2} \begin{bmatrix} \cos\omega t - \cos\left(\sqrt{3}\omega t\right) \\ -\omega\sin\omega t + \omega\sqrt{3}\sin\left(\sqrt{3}\omega t\right) \\ \cos\omega t + \cos\left(\sqrt{3}\omega t\right) \\ -\omega\sin\omega t - \omega\sqrt{3}\sin\left(\sqrt{3}\omega t\right) \end{bmatrix}.$$

All that remains is to return to the original coordinates:

$$y_1(t) = \frac{1}{2}\left(\cos\omega t - \cos\left(\sqrt{3}\omega t\right)\right), \quad y_2(t) = \frac{1}{2}\left(\cos\omega t + \cos\left(\sqrt{3}\omega t\right)\right).$$

It is easy to see that the components x_2 and x_4 are merely the derivatives of x_1 and x_3, just as we expected. ■ ■ ■

6.7.1 *Modal Analysis*

Many applied problems with no energy loss mechanism can be cast in the form of the second order system

$$\mathbf{M\ddot{x}} + \mathbf{Kx} = \mathbf{F}(t). \tag{6.34}$$

One option we have is to introduce new dependent variables so that (6.34) can be written as a first order system of twice the dimension of the original system. Instead, we'll try an alternative approach.

In most applications, $\mathbf{M}$ and $\mathbf{K}$ are real, symmetric, and **positive definite** (for real symmetric matrices, this means that all of their eigenvalues are positive). In that case it can be shown that the solution vector $\mathbf{x}(t)$ will be oscillatory. Rather than $\mathbf{x}(t) = \mathbf{x}_0 e^{\lambda t}$, a more appropriate choice for an oscillatory trial solution would be $\mathbf{x}(t) = \mathbf{x}_0 e^{i\omega t}$. Substituting this into the homogeneous version of (6.34), we must solve for ω and $\mathbf{x}_0$ in the algebraic system

$$(\mathbf{K} - \mathbf{M}\omega^2)\mathbf{x}_0 = \mathbf{0}.$$

There will be a nontrivial solution for $\mathbf{x}_0$ if and only if

$$\det(\mathbf{K} - \mathbf{M}\omega^2) = 0. \tag{6.35}$$

Thus there will be n values of ω^2, where these ω_k are called **normal frequencies** of the system. A further simplification is available because it is often the case that the matrices $\mathbf{M}$ and $\mathbf{K}$ are symmetric. This means there will be n linearly independent eigenvectors $\mathbf{x}_1, \mathbf{x}_2, \ldots, \mathbf{x}_n$, which are called the **normal modes** of the system, corresponding to the normal frequencies ω^2.

If $\mathbf{M}$ were positive definite, then it would be invertible; therefore, the equation $(\mathbf{K} - \mathbf{M}\omega^2)\mathbf{x}_0 = \mathbf{0}$ could be premultiplied by $-\mathbf{M}^{-1}$, so that

$$(\omega^2\mathbf{I} - \mathbf{M}^{-1}\mathbf{K})\mathbf{x}_0 = \mathbf{0}.$$

The squares of the normal frequencies of the system are the eigenvalues of the matrix $\mathbf{M}^{-1}\mathbf{K}$ and the normal modes are its corresponding eigenvectors. An alternative approach is to use the positive definiteness of $\mathbf{M}$ (see problem 5 in Section 6.14), which guarantees the existence of the square root of $\mathbf{M}$, and premultiply (6.35) by $\det(\mathbf{M}^{1/2})$ and postmultiply by its inverse to obtain

$$\det\left(\mathbf{M}^{1/2}\mathbf{K}\mathbf{M}^{-1/2} - \omega^2\mathbf{I}\right) = 0$$

as the characteristic equation. The advantage of this formulation is the matrix $\mathbf{M}^{1/2}\mathbf{K}\mathbf{M}^{-1/2}$ is symmetric and positive-definite, whereas $\mathbf{M}^{-1}\mathbf{K}$ need not be symmetric unless $\mathbf{M}$ is diagonal. In either case, the orthogonality relation for the eigenvectors now involves a weight, i.e., $\langle \mathbf{x}, \mathbf{y} \rangle := \mathbf{x}^T\mathbf{M}\mathbf{y}$.

■ **EXAMPLE 6.30** Find the normal frequencies and normal modes of the coupled pendulum system shown in Figure 6.11.

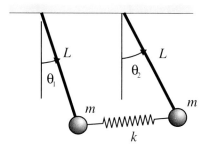

Fig. 6.11

Solution: We assume the arms are massless, inextensible, and of length L. Also, assume the spring is massless, in equilibrium when $\theta_1 = 0 = \theta_2$, and does not sag. The Lagrangian of the system is

$$\frac{1}{2}mL^2 \left(\dot{\theta}_1^2 + \dot{\theta}_2^2 \right) - \frac{1}{2}k \left((L \sin \theta_1) - (L \sin \theta_2) \right)^2 + mgL \left(\cos \theta_1 + \cos \theta_2 \right).$$

The equations of motion are

$$\frac{d}{dt} \left(mL^2 \dot{\theta}_1 \right) + kL \cos \theta_1 \left((L \sin \theta_1) - (L \sin \theta_2) \right) + mgL \sin \theta_1 = 0,$$

$$\frac{d}{dt} \left(mL^2 \dot{\theta}_2 \right) - kL \cos \theta_2 \left((L \sin \theta_1) - (L \sin \theta_2) \right) + mgL \sin \theta_2 = 0.$$

For small angular deviations, they are

$$mL^2 \ddot{\theta}_1 + mgL\theta_1 + kL^2(\theta_1 - \theta_2) = 0,$$
$$mL^2 \ddot{\theta}_2 + mgL\theta_2 - kL^2(\theta_1 - \theta_2) = 0,$$

or in matrix form

$$\begin{bmatrix} mL & 0 \\ 0 & mL \end{bmatrix} \begin{bmatrix} \ddot{\theta}_1 \\ \ddot{\theta}_2 \end{bmatrix} + \begin{bmatrix} mg + kL & -kL \\ -kL & mg + kL \end{bmatrix} \begin{bmatrix} \theta_1 \\ \theta_2 \end{bmatrix} = \mathbf{0}.$$

Dividing by mL and writing $\omega_p^2 := g/L$ and $\omega_s^2 := k/m$, we have

$$\ddot{\theta} + \begin{bmatrix} \omega_p^2 + \omega_s^2 & -\omega_s^2 \\ -\omega_s^2 & \omega_p^2 + \omega_s^2 \end{bmatrix} \theta = \mathbf{0}.$$

In this form, $\mathbf{M} = \mathbf{I}$. Setting $\theta(t) = \theta_0 e^{i\omega t}$ we arrive at

$$\det \left(\mathbf{K} - \mathbf{M}\omega^2 \right) = \begin{vmatrix} \left(\omega_p^2 + \omega_s^2 \right) - \omega^2 & -\omega_s^2 \\ -\omega_s^2 & \left(\omega_p^2 + \omega_s^2 \right) - \omega^2 \end{vmatrix} = 0.$$

The resulting characteristic equation for ω^2 is

$$\left[(\omega_p^2 + \omega_s^2) - \omega^2\right]^2 - \omega_s^4 = 0.$$

It follows that

$$\omega^2 = (\omega_p^2 + \omega_s^2) \pm \omega_s^2 = \begin{cases} \omega_p^2 + 2\omega_s^2 \\ \omega_p^2 \end{cases}$$

The normal mode for $\omega^2 = \omega_p^2 + 2\omega_s^2$ satisfies

$$\left[\mathbf{K} - (\omega_p^2 + 2\omega_s^2)\,\mathbf{M}\right]\theta = \begin{bmatrix} -\omega_s^2 & -\omega_s^2 \\ -\omega_s^2 & -\omega_s^2 \end{bmatrix}\theta = 0$$

$$\Rightarrow \theta_1 = [1; -1]$$

and for $\omega^2 = \omega_p^2$ is,

$$\left[\mathbf{K} - \omega_p^2\mathbf{M}\right]\theta = \begin{bmatrix} \omega_s^2 & -\omega_s^2 \\ -\omega_s^2 & \omega_s^2 \end{bmatrix}\theta = 0$$

$$\Rightarrow \theta_2 = [1; 1].$$

When $\theta_1 = \theta_2$, the system moves so that the spring is neither compressed nor extended. This then looks like two independent uncoupled pendulums each moving together with the angular frequency $\omega_p = \sqrt{g/L}$ of a simple pendulum (see Figure 6.11). But when $\theta_1 = -\theta_2$, the masses move opposite to each other, thus effectively doubling the spring effect from the case when one mass is fixed (see Figure 6.12).

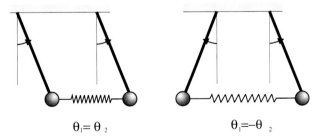

$$\theta_1 = \theta_2 \qquad\qquad \theta_1 = -\theta_2$$

Fig. 6.12

The spring remains horizontal in both normal modes. The complex form of the general solution of the system is a linear combination of the normal motions, so that

$$\theta(t) = c_1 \begin{bmatrix} 1 \\ -1 \end{bmatrix} e^{i\omega_p t} + c_{21} \begin{bmatrix} 1 \\ 1 \end{bmatrix} e^{i\sqrt{\omega_p^2 + 2\omega_s^2}\,t}.$$

■ ■ ■

■ **EXAMPLE 6.31** Many materials have a crystalline form whereby the atoms in the solid are arranged in a regular and highly symmetric configuration. The equilibrium positions of the atoms are called the lattice points. Brillouin modeled the diatomic crystal by replacing the solid by a linear array of atoms as shown in Figure 6.13.

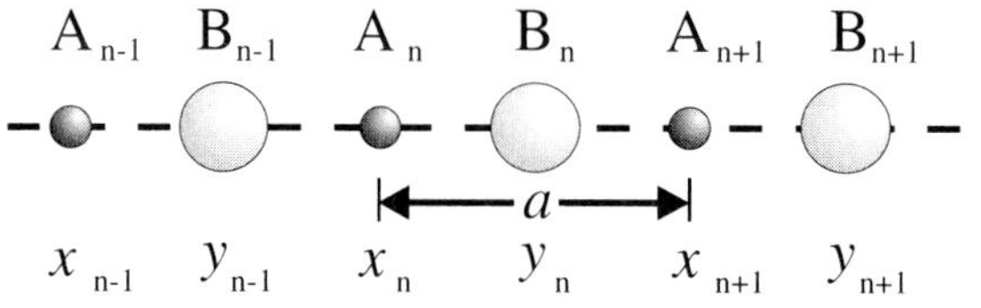

Fig. 6.13

He assumed the interaction between atoms, in the simplest case, could be characterized by spring-type forces, with alternating spring constants K and K', between nearest neighbor particles. If we look at the nth pair of atoms, the equations of motion are

$$mx'' = K(y_n - x_n) - K'(x_n - y_{n-1}),$$
$$My'' = K(x_{n+1} - y_n) - K'(y_n - x_n),$$

when the A atoms have mass m and the B atoms have mass M. If all the spring constants are the same, $K = K'$, we may rewrite this as

$$mx_n'' = K(y_{n-1} - 2x_n + y_n),$$
$$My_n'' = K(x_n - 2y_n + x_{n+1}),$$

which is an infinite system of simultaneous ODE's. As in the system of the previous example, we expect oscillatory solutions, but we must also take into account the spacing for the atoms. Geometrically, this infinite chain of atoms looks the same no matter on which AB pair we focus our attention. We should be able to include a periodicity along the lattice in our calculations. Try the periodic oscillatory solutions

$$x_n = Ae^{i(kna - \omega t)}, \ y_n = Be^{i(kna - \omega t)},$$

where ω is the angular frequency and $k = 2\pi/\lambda$ is called the **wave number**. The constant a could be taken as a measure of interatomic spacing. Some simple arithmetic shows that

$$x_{n+1} = e^{ika}x_n, \ y_{n+1} = e^{ika}y_n.$$

This forces the nth A and the nth B atoms to move as a pair but with possibly different amplitudes. As special cases:

(a) If $\lambda = \infty$ (no wave motion), we have $k = 0$ and $x_{n+1} = x_n$, $y_{n+1} = y_n$.

(b) If $\lambda = a$, we have $ka = 2\pi$, and so again we have $x_{n+1} = x_n$ and $y_{n+1} = y_n$.

   In both of these cases, the nodes of the wave have the same spacing as do like atoms; thus there is no motion along the lattice.

(c) If $\lambda = 2a$, we have $ka = \pi$, so that $x_{n+1} = -x_n$ and $y_{n+1} = -y_n$.

Alternate atoms of the same type move in opposite directions.

Substituting the forms of x_n and y_n into the ODE's, we find

$$\begin{bmatrix} 2K - m\omega^2 & -K\left(1 + e^{ika}\right) \\ -K\left(1 + e^{ika}\right) & 2K - m\omega^2 \end{bmatrix} \begin{bmatrix} A \\ B \end{bmatrix} = \mathbf{0}.$$

The characteristic equation is

$$mM\omega^4 - 2K(m + M)\omega^2 + 2K^2(1 - \cos ka) = 0.$$

Using a half-angle identity and solving, we find

$$\omega^2 = \frac{K}{mM}\left[(m + M) \pm \sqrt{(m + M)^2 - 4mM\sin^2\left(\tfrac{ka}{2}\right)}\right]$$

$$=: \frac{K}{mM}\left[(m + M) \pm \Delta\right].$$

There are two allowed frequencies. The higher frequency $(+)$ is called the **optical mode** and the lower $(-)$ is the **acoustic mode**. The corresponding ratio of amplitudes is

$$\frac{A}{B} = -\frac{M\left(1 + e^{ika}\right)}{m - M \pm \Delta}.$$

Using the restriction $|\lambda| \le 2a$ or $|k| \le \pi/a$, the graph of ω versus k, called a **dispersion relation**, looks like that in Figure 6.14.

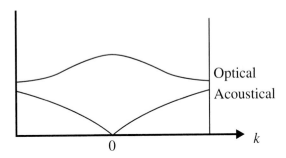

Fig. 6.14

The nonlinear dispersion relation manifests itself in the propagation of waves along the lattice. The phase velocity ω/k and the group velocity $d\omega/dk$ of a wave are no longer the same, and waves of different wavelengths move at different wavespeeds.

We can get an idea of the form of the curves near $k = 0$ by expanding ω^2 in a Taylor series about $k_0 = 0$ and keeping low order terms. We get

$$\omega^2 \doteq \begin{cases} \dfrac{Ka^2}{m + M} \cdot \dfrac{1}{2}k^2 & \text{acoustic,} \\[3mm] \dfrac{2(m + M)K}{mM} & \text{optical} \end{cases}.$$

■ ■ ■

A more detailed (but no more difficult) analysis of this problem is carried out in the first five chapters of Brillouin, **Wave Propagation in Periodic Structures**.

6.7.2 Exercise Set

Where possible, use the Euler-Lagrange equations to find the equations of motion.

1. Redo the coupled pendulum problem for the case of different masses, write $M = \alpha m$ and look at the limiting cases $\alpha \to 0$ and $\alpha \to \infty$.

2. Find the normal frequencies and normal modes of the double pendulum system when $m_1 = m_2 = m$ and $L_1 = L_2 = L$. [Hint: Don't be afraid of having square roots in your answer.]

3. Suppose three subway cars, of masses m_1, m_2, and m_3, are coupled together so that between the first and second cars there is spring with force constant k_1 and between the second and third there is a spring with force constant k_2 (see Figure 6.15).

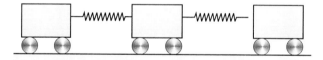

Fig. 6.15

Using modal analysis, find the characteristic equation for the normal frequencies. Take all the masses equal and both force constants equal, and find the normal modes of oscillation.

4. The pendulum shown in Figure 6.16(a)

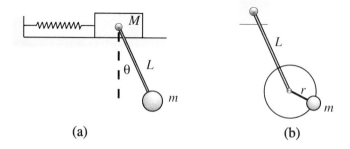

(a)   (b)

Fig. 6.16

consists of a slider of mass M and a bob of mass m connected by a rigid rod of length L. The slider can move horizontally without friction, while the rod is free to oscillate about an axis at the center of mass of the slider. To add to this, a spring of force constant k is attached to the slider and to the wall to its left. If x is the lateral displacement of the slider and θ is the angular deviation of the pendulum from the vertical, write the equations of motion and solve them for the case of small oscillations.

5. A rod of length L is free to swing in a vertical plane about a frictionless pivot attached to the ceiling. A uniform circular disk of radius r and mass M is free to rotate about a horizontal axle attached to the bottom of the bar. Attached to the outer edge of the wheel is a particle of mass m (see Figure 6.16(b)). If the mass of the rod is negligible, find the frequencies of small oscillations of this contraption.

6. A homogeneous flat rectangular plate measuring $2a$ by $2b$ and of mass m is supported by four identical springs, each with force constant k, at its corners. If the springs are constrained to remain vertical, find the frequencies of small oscillations.

7. Some triatomic molecules can be modeled by a linear chain of three equal masses connected by two springs as shown in Figure 6.17.

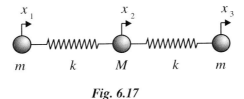

Fig. 6.17

Find the normal frequencies. Consider the limiting cases, $M \to 0$ and $M \to \infty$.

8. Redo the linear triatomic molecule with equal masses when the outer masses are coupled with an additional spring of force constant K (see Figure 6.18).

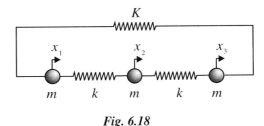

Fig. 6.18

Study the limiting cases of small and large K.

9. Find the current in each of the resistors in Figure 6.19 as a function of time.

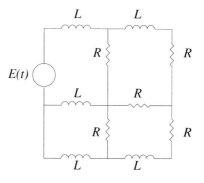

Fig. 6.19

6.8   NONHOMOGENEOUS LINEAR SYSTEMS

Our goal in this section is to find the solution of the nonhomogeneous linear system

$$\mathbf{x}'(t) = \mathbf{A}\mathbf{x}(t) + \mathbf{b}(t). \tag{6.36}$$

We'll use the method of variation of parameters, which (as in the scalar case) will work if $\mathbf{A}$ is either time dependent or time independent.

Suppose we have a complementary solution to (6.36) written as a linear combination of n linearly independent solution vectors:

$$\mathbf{x}_c(t) = c_1 \mathbf{x}_1(t) + c_2 \mathbf{x}_2(t) + \cdots + c_n \mathbf{x}_x(t).$$

Just as we did in the scalar case, assume the particular solution can be written in the form

$$\mathbf{x}_p(t) = k_1(t)\mathbf{x}_1(t) + k_2(t)\mathbf{x}_2(t) + \cdots + k_n(t)\mathbf{x}_n(t), \tag{6.37}$$

where $k_1(t), k_2(t), \ldots, k_n(t)$ are functions that are to be determined.

Inserting (6.37) into (6.36) yields

$$[k_1(t)\mathbf{x}_1'(t) + \cdots + k_n(t)\mathbf{x}_n'(t)] + [k_1'(t)\mathbf{x}_1(t) + \cdots + k_n'(t)\mathbf{x}_n(t)]$$

$$= \mathbf{A}\left[k_1(t)\mathbf{x}_1(t) + \cdots + k_n(t)\mathbf{x}_n(t)\right] + \mathbf{b}(t).$$

Each of the vector functions $\mathbf{x}_j(t)$ is a solution of the homogeneous linear system $\mathbf{x}_j'(t) = \mathbf{A}\mathbf{x}_j(t)$, so after n canceling pairs of terms we are left with

$$k_1'(t)\mathbf{x}_1(t) + \cdots + k_n'(t)\mathbf{x}_n(t) = \mathbf{b}(t).$$

The left hand side can be written in matrix form as

$$[\mathbf{x}_1(t), \mathbf{x}_2(t), \ldots, \mathbf{x}_n(t)] \begin{bmatrix} k_1'(t) \\ k_2'(t) \\ \vdots \\ k_n'(t) \end{bmatrix} = \mathbf{b}(t);$$

or in shorthand notation,

$$\mathbf{X}(t)\mathbf{k}'(t) = \mathbf{b}(t), \tag{6.38}$$

where $\mathbf{X}(t)$ is the matrix whose column vectors are the linearly independent solution vectors, i.e., a fundamental matrix of the system. Since $\mathbf{X}(t)$ is of full rank, it is invertible and

$$\mathbf{k}'(t) = \mathbf{X}^{-1}(t)\mathbf{b}(t).$$

All that remains is integration. This is very similar to the scalar case.

■ **EXAMPLE 6.32** Solve the nonhomogeneous linear system

$$\mathbf{x}'(t) = \begin{bmatrix} 8 & -3 \\ 16 & -8 \end{bmatrix} \mathbf{x}(t) + \begin{bmatrix} 23 \\ 59 \end{bmatrix} e^t, \quad \mathbf{x}(0) = \begin{bmatrix} -3 \\ 7 \end{bmatrix}.$$

Solution: It can be shown that

$$\mathbf{x}_c(t) = c_1 \begin{bmatrix} 1 \\ 4 \end{bmatrix} e^{-4t} + c_2 \begin{bmatrix} 3 \\ 4 \end{bmatrix} e^{4t}.$$

We can immediately write (6.38) as

$$\begin{bmatrix} e^{-4t} & 3e^{4t} \\ 4e^{-4t} & 4e^{4t} \end{bmatrix} \begin{bmatrix} k_1' \\ k_2' \end{bmatrix} = \begin{bmatrix} 23e^t \\ 59e^t \end{bmatrix}.$$

Cramer's Rule can be used to solve for k_1' and k_2', but first we need to evaluate the Wronskian

$$|\mathbf{X}(t)| = \begin{vmatrix} e^{-4t} & 3e^{4t} \\ 4e^{-4t} & 4e^{4t} \end{vmatrix} = 4 - 12 = -8.$$

Continuing:

$$k_1'(t) = -\frac{1}{8} \begin{vmatrix} 23e^t & 3e^{4t} \\ 59e^t & 4e^{4t} \end{vmatrix} = -\frac{1}{8} \left(92e^{5t} - 177e^{5t} \right) = \frac{85}{8} e^{5t},$$

$$k_2'(t) = -\frac{1}{8} \begin{vmatrix} e^{-4t} & 23e^t \\ 4e^{-4t} & 59e^t \end{vmatrix} = -\frac{1}{8} \left(59e^{-3t} - 92e^{-3t} \right) = \frac{33}{8} e^{-3t}.$$

A pair of quick integrations yields

$$k_1(t) = \frac{17}{8} e^{5t}, \quad k_2(t) = -\frac{11}{8} e^{-3t}.$$

Thus the particular solution is

$$\mathbf{x}_p(t) = k_1 \begin{bmatrix} 1 \\ 4 \end{bmatrix} e^{-4t} + k_2 \begin{bmatrix} 3 \\ 4 \end{bmatrix} e^{4t}$$

$$= \tfrac{17}{8} e^{5t} \begin{bmatrix} 1 \\ 4 \end{bmatrix} e^{-4t} - \tfrac{11}{8} e^{-3t} \begin{bmatrix} 3 \\ 4 \end{bmatrix} e^{4t} = \begin{bmatrix} -2 \\ 3 \end{bmatrix} e^t,$$

and the general solution is

$$\mathbf{x}(t) = \mathbf{x}_c(t) + \mathbf{x}_p(t) = c_1 \begin{bmatrix} 1 \\ 4 \end{bmatrix} e^{-4t} + c_2 \begin{bmatrix} 3 \\ 4 \end{bmatrix} e^{4t} + \begin{bmatrix} -2 \\ 3 \end{bmatrix} e^t.$$

Apply the initial conditions to the general solution:

$$\mathbf{x}(0) = c_1 \begin{bmatrix} 1 \\ 4 \end{bmatrix} + c_2 \begin{bmatrix} 3 \\ 4 \end{bmatrix} + \begin{bmatrix} -2 \\ 3 \end{bmatrix} = \begin{bmatrix} -3 \\ 7 \end{bmatrix}$$

$$\Rightarrow \begin{bmatrix} 1 & 3 & \big| & -1 \\ 4 & 4 & \big| & 4 \end{bmatrix} \Rightarrow \begin{cases} c_1 = 2 \\ c_2 = -1. \end{cases}$$

The specific solution is

$$\mathbf{x}(t) = 2 \begin{bmatrix} 1 \\ 4 \end{bmatrix} e^{-4t} - \begin{bmatrix} 3 \\ 4 \end{bmatrix} e^{4t} + \begin{bmatrix} -2 \\ 3 \end{bmatrix} e^t$$

$$= \begin{bmatrix} -\cosh 4t - 5 \sinh 4t - 2e^t \\ 4 \cosh 4t - 12 \sinh 4t + 3e^t \end{bmatrix}.$$

■ ■ ■

Although this method is straightforward, it hides the dynamics of the system. For this reason, the state-transition matrix approach of the next section is preferable for nonhomogeneous systems.

6.8.1 Exercise Set

Solve each of the following nonhomogeneous linear systems by using the method of variation of parameters as outlined in this section.

1.
$$\mathbf{x}'(t) = \begin{bmatrix} 18 & -30 \\ 10 & -17 \end{bmatrix} \mathbf{x}(t) + \begin{bmatrix} 13 \\ 8 \end{bmatrix} e^t$$

2.
$$\mathbf{x}'(t) = \begin{bmatrix} 2 & -1 \\ 3 & -2 \end{bmatrix} \mathbf{x}(t) + \begin{bmatrix} e^t \\ t \end{bmatrix}$$

3.
$$\mathbf{x}'(t) = \begin{bmatrix} 2 & -5 \\ 1 & -2 \end{bmatrix} \mathbf{x}(t) + \begin{bmatrix} -\cos t \\ \sin t \end{bmatrix}$$

4.
$$\mathbf{x}'(t) = \begin{bmatrix} 2 & -5 \\ 1 & -2 \end{bmatrix} \mathbf{x}(t) + \begin{bmatrix} \csc t \\ \sec t \end{bmatrix}$$

5.
$$\mathbf{x}'(t) = \begin{bmatrix} 2 & 1 \\ -4 & 2 \end{bmatrix} \mathbf{x}(t) + \begin{bmatrix} t \\ -1 \end{bmatrix} e^{2t}$$

6.
$$\mathbf{x}'(t) = \begin{bmatrix} 2 & -1 \\ 5 & -2 \end{bmatrix} \mathbf{x}(t) + \begin{bmatrix} \cos t \\ \sin t \end{bmatrix}$$

7.
$$\mathbf{x}'(t) = \begin{bmatrix} 1 & 1 & 1 \\ 0 & 2 & 1 \\ 0 & 0 & 3 \end{bmatrix} \mathbf{x}(t) - \begin{bmatrix} 2t \\ t+2 \\ 3t \end{bmatrix}$$

8.
$$\mathbf{x}'(t) = \begin{bmatrix} 1 & 0 & 1 \\ 0 & -2 & 0 \\ 4 & 0 & 1 \end{bmatrix} \mathbf{x}(t) + \begin{bmatrix} -3 \\ 6 \\ -4 \end{bmatrix} e^t$$

9.
$$\mathbf{x}'(t) = \begin{bmatrix} 1 & 0 & 1 \\ 0 & 1 & 0 \\ 1 & 0 & 0 \end{bmatrix} \mathbf{x}(t) + \begin{bmatrix} 1 \\ 1 \\ 1 \end{bmatrix} e^t, \quad \mathbf{x}(0) = \begin{bmatrix} 4 \\ 2 \\ 0 \end{bmatrix}$$

10. If $\mathbf{x}_c(t) = c_1 \begin{bmatrix} 1 \\ 1 \end{bmatrix} e^t + c_2 \begin{bmatrix} -1 \\ 1 \end{bmatrix} e^{-t}$ and $\mathbf{b}(t) = \begin{bmatrix} e^t \\ e^{-t} \end{bmatrix}$, then find the particular solution $\mathbf{x}_p(t)$
and the coefficient matrix of the system when it is written in the form $\mathbf{x}'(t) = \mathbf{A}\mathbf{x}(t) + \mathbf{b}(t)$.

11. Convert the system
$$2\dot{u} + \dot{v} + u + 5v = 4t,$$
$$\dot{u} + \dot{v} + 2u + 2v = 2$$

to standard matrix form and find the general solution.

12. Redo the problem of the coupled pendulums of example 6.30 with different masses for each bob
when the left mass is driven by an offset cam that imparts a force $F_0 \cos \omega t$.

6.9 STATE-TRANSITION MATRIX

6.9.1 Basic Concepts

The homogeneous linear system

$$\mathbf{x}'(t) = \mathbf{A}(t)\mathbf{x}(t), \quad \mathbf{x}(t_0) = \mathbf{x}_0, \tag{6.39}$$

can be solved by the methods of Section 6.5 when $\mathbf{A}(t)$ is a constant matrix. In that case, and
even when $\mathbf{A}(t)$ is a function of t, the solution was expressible as a linear combination of n
linearly independent solution vectors:

$$\mathbf{x}(t) = c_1\mathbf{x}_1(t) + c_2\mathbf{x}_2(t) + \cdots + c_n\mathbf{x}_n(t). \tag{6.40}$$

It was then necessary to solve for the arbitrary constants $c_1, c_2, \ldots, c_n$ using the initial conditions. A conceptually easier method, although not necessarily computationally more efficient, is available to us for general time dependent coefficient matrices $\mathbf{A}(t)$. Instead of studying the solution vectors, we put our emphasis on the transformation that moves us along a solution curve.

DEFINITION 6.7 *The* **state-transition matrix** *of the system (6.39) is the matrix* $\boldsymbol{\Phi}(t, \tau)$ *that satisfies the equation*

$$\mathbf{x}(t) = \boldsymbol{\Phi}(t, \tau)\mathbf{x}(\tau), \tag{6.41}$$

where $\mathbf{x}(\tau)$ *and* $\mathbf{x}(t)$ *are solution vectors to the system (6.39) at the times* τ *and* t, *respectively.*

Multiplication by $\boldsymbol{\Phi}(t, \tau)$ is a linear transformation that takes the solution vector $\mathbf{x}$ at time τ on the trajectory and moves it to its proper position at time t. If $t > \tau$, the state-transition matrix moves the solution forward in time, whereas when $t < \tau$, it moves it backward in time.

The defining equation (6.41) can be used to advantage. Several properties of $\boldsymbol{\Phi}(t, \tau)$ follow easily.

- Set $\tau = t$ to get $\mathbf{x}(t) = \boldsymbol{\Phi}(t, t)\mathbf{x}(t)$ for any t. Hence, for any t we must have

$$\boldsymbol{\Phi}(t, t) = \mathbf{I}. \tag{6.42}$$

- Rewrite (6.41) with t and τ reversed. Then $\mathbf{x}(\tau) = \boldsymbol{\Phi}(\tau, t)\mathbf{x}(t)$. Combining this with (6.41), we have

$$\mathbf{x}(\tau) = \boldsymbol{\Phi}(\tau, t)\boldsymbol{\Phi}(t, \tau)\mathbf{x}(\tau),$$

so that $\boldsymbol{\Phi}(\tau, t)\boldsymbol{\Phi}(t, \tau) = \mathbf{I}$, and it follows that

$$\boldsymbol{\Phi}^{-1}(t, \tau) = \boldsymbol{\Phi}(\tau, t). \tag{6.43}$$

Thus the state-transition matrix from τ to t is nonsingular, and its inverse is the state-transition matrix from t to τ.

- Put $t = t_1$ and $\tau = t_0$ in (6.41), so that

$$\mathbf{x}(t_1) = \boldsymbol{\Phi}(t_1, t_0)\mathbf{x}(t_0).$$

Now write (6.41) with t replaced by t_2 and τ replaced by t_1:

$$\mathbf{x}(t_2) = \boldsymbol{\Phi}(t_2, t_1)\mathbf{x}(t_1).$$

Combining the two we have

$$\mathbf{x}(t_2) = \boldsymbol{\Phi}(t_2, t_1)\boldsymbol{\Phi}(t_1, t_0)\mathbf{x}(t_0),$$

so that

$$\boldsymbol{\Phi}(t_2, t_0) = \boldsymbol{\Phi}(t_2, t_1)\boldsymbol{\Phi}(t_1, t_0). \tag{6.44}$$

The state-transition matrix from t_0 to t_2 is the product of the state-transition matrices from t_0 to t_1 and from t_1 to t_2, for any time t_1, whether it is between t_0 and t_2 or not.

If we substitute (6.41) into (6.39), we have

$$\frac{d}{dt}\mathbf{x}(t) = \frac{d}{dt}\left(\mathbf{\Phi}(t, t_0)\mathbf{x}(t_0)\right) = \left(\frac{d}{dt}\mathbf{\Phi}(t, t_0)\right)\mathbf{x}(t_0)$$

$$= \mathbf{A}(t)\mathbf{x}(t) = \mathbf{A}(t)\mathbf{\Phi}(t, t_0)\mathbf{x}(t_0).$$

Since this must hold for any initial vector $\mathbf{x}(t_0)$, we can use the third and last terms to write the matrix ODE satisfied by $\mathbf{\Phi}(t, t_0)$ for fixed time t_0:

$$\frac{d}{dt}\mathbf{\Phi}(t, t_0) = \mathbf{A}(t)\mathbf{\Phi}(t, t_0).$$

We also have the initial condition $\mathbf{\Phi}(t_0, t_0) = \mathbf{I}$ from equation (6.42).

It remains to be shown that such a matrix can be found. In fact, (6.41) is equivalent to (6.19). Rewrite (6.19) as

$$\mathbf{x}(t) = [\mathbf{x}_1(t), \mathbf{x}_2(t), \ldots, \mathbf{x}_n(t)]\begin{bmatrix} c_1 \\ c_2 \\ \vdots \\ c_n \end{bmatrix} =: \mathbf{X}(t)\mathbf{c}, \tag{6.45}$$

where $\mathbf{X}(t)$ is a fundamental matrix. The columns of a fundamental matrix form a linearly independent set of solution vectors; hence it is invertible. The initial condition equation is easily solved for $\mathbf{c}$:

$$\mathbf{x}(t_0) = \mathbf{x}_0 = \mathbf{X}(t_0)\mathbf{c} \quad \Rightarrow \quad \mathbf{c} = \mathbf{X}^{-1}(t_0)\mathbf{x}_0. \tag{6.46}$$

Combining (6.45) and (6.46) yields

$$\mathbf{x}(t) = \mathbf{X}(t)\mathbf{X}^{-1}(t_0)\mathbf{x}_0, \tag{6.47}$$

so that the state-transition matrix is given in terms of *any* fundamental matrix by the equation

$$\mathbf{\Phi}(t, t_0) = \mathbf{X}(t)\mathbf{X}^{-1}(t_0). \tag{6.48}$$

For linear autonomous systems, we can use the usual shifting result to simplify matters:

$$\mathbf{\Phi}(t, t_0) = \mathbf{\Phi}(t - t_0, 0) = \mathbf{X}(t - t_0)\mathbf{X}^{-1}(0). \tag{6.49}$$

■ **EXAMPLE 6.33** Find the state transition matrix for the system

$$\mathbf{x}'(t) = \begin{bmatrix} 8 & -3 \\ 16 & -8 \end{bmatrix}\mathbf{x}(t), \quad \mathbf{x}(0) = \begin{bmatrix} 5 \\ 12 \end{bmatrix}.$$

Solution: The general solution was

$$\mathbf{x}(t) = c_1 \begin{bmatrix} 1 \\ 4 \end{bmatrix} e^{-4t} + c_2 \begin{bmatrix} 3 \\ 4 \end{bmatrix} e^{4t}.$$

Thus one possible fundamental matrix is

$$\mathbf{X}(t) = \begin{bmatrix} e^{-4t} & 3e^{4t} \\ 4e^{-4t} & 4e^{4t} \end{bmatrix},$$

and its inverse is

$$\mathbf{X}^{-1}(t) = -\frac{1}{8} \begin{bmatrix} 4e^{4t} & -3e^{4t} \\ -4e^{-4t} & e^{-4t} \end{bmatrix}.$$

Therefore, the state-transition matrix is

$$\mathbf{\Phi}(t, t_0) = \mathbf{X}(t)\mathbf{X}^{-1}(t_0) = \mathbf{X}(t - t_0)\mathbf{X}^{-1}(0)$$

$$= -\frac{1}{8} \begin{bmatrix} 4e^{-4\alpha} - 12e^{4\alpha} & 3\left(-e^{-4\alpha} + e^{4\alpha}\right) \\ 16\left(e^{-4\alpha} - e^{4\alpha}\right) & -12e^{-4\alpha} + 4e^{4\alpha} \end{bmatrix},$$

where $\alpha = t - t_0$. Thus $\mathbf{\Phi}$ is a function of $t - t_0$, the time elapsed since the starting time. Surely $\mathbf{\Phi}(t_0, t_0) = \mathbf{\Phi}(\alpha = 0) = \mathbf{I}$. The solution to the original system is

$$\mathbf{x}(t) = \mathbf{\Phi}(t, 0)\mathbf{x}(0) = \mathbf{\Phi}(t, 0) \begin{bmatrix} 5 \\ 12 \end{bmatrix} = \begin{bmatrix} 2e^{-4t} + 3e^{4t} \\ 8e^{-4t} + 4e^{4t} \end{bmatrix}.$$

■ ■ ■

It has been shown, in Section 6.3.2, that for any fundamental matrix $\mathbf{X}(t)$, we have Abel's Formula,

$$|\mathbf{X}(t)| = |\mathbf{X}(t_0)| \exp\left\{ \int_{t_0}^{t} \mathrm{tr}\left(\mathbf{A}(\tau)\right) d\tau \right\}. \tag{6.50}$$

Since $\left|\mathbf{X}^{-1}(t_0)\right| = |\mathbf{X}(t_0)|^{-1}$ and $\mathbf{\Phi}(t, t_0) = \mathbf{X}(t)\mathbf{X}^{-1}(t_0)$, we have

$$|\mathbf{\Phi}(t, t_0)| = \exp\left\{ \int_{t_0}^{t} \mathrm{tr}\left(\mathbf{A}(\tau)\right) d\tau \right\}. \tag{6.51}$$

Thus if $\mathbf{A}(t)$ is piecewise continuous on an interval containing t_0, $\mathbf{\Phi}(t, t_0)$ will be nonsingular there.

6.9.2 *Exponential of a Matrix*

The calculation of the state-transition matrix for time dependent systems is an extremely difficult task. On the other hand, the autonomous case is fairly straightforward. Let's push the limits of analogy by looking at the *scalar* equation

$$x' = Ax, \quad x(t_0) = x_0,$$

and solving it. That's easy because it's separable; the solution is immediately seen to be

$$x(t) = e^{A(t-t_0)}x_0.$$

This was arrived at by dividing by x, an operation that cannot be extended to vectors, and integrating. The end result is worth looking at in more detail. But first we need to take a detour to look at functions of matrices.

Functions of Matrices

Our goal is to define and evaluate arbitrary functions of a square matrix. The plan is to begin with polynomial functions. Next, we will say a few words about the convergence of infinite series of matrices. Then, we will define an analytic function of a matrix and derive computational schemes for its evaluation.

Polynomial Functions of a Matrix Argument   The basic equation that will take us quite far is derived as follows: Every matrix is similar to its Jordan normal form via the similarity transformation $\mathbf{J} = \mathbf{P}^{-1}\mathbf{A}\mathbf{P}$, which is equivalent to $\mathbf{A} = \mathbf{P}\mathbf{J}\mathbf{P}^{-1}$. Since $\mathbf{A}$ commutes with itself, the powers $\mathbf{A}^m$ for $m = 2 : \infty$ are all well defined and

$$\mathbf{A}^m = \underbrace{\mathbf{A}\mathbf{A}\cdots\mathbf{A}}_{m \text{ factors}} = \underbrace{(\mathbf{P}\mathbf{J}\mathbf{P}^{-1})(\mathbf{P}\mathbf{J}\mathbf{P}^{-1})\cdots(\mathbf{P}\mathbf{J}\mathbf{P}^{-1})}_{m \text{ triples of factors}}$$

$$= \mathbf{P}\mathbf{J}\underbrace{(\mathbf{P}^{-1}\mathbf{P})}_{\mathbf{I}}\mathbf{J}\underbrace{(\mathbf{P}^{-1}\mathbf{P})}_{\mathbf{I}}\mathbf{J}\cdots\mathbf{J}\underbrace{(\mathbf{P}^{-1}\mathbf{P})}_{\mathbf{I}}\mathbf{J}\mathbf{P}^{-1}.$$

Therefore,

$$\mathbf{A}^m = \mathbf{P}\mathbf{J}^m\mathbf{P}^{-1}. \tag{6.52}$$

Using (6.52) we can easily prove the following result:

THEOREM 6.17   *If $p(\mathbf{A})$ is any polynomial function of $\mathbf{A}$, then*

$$p(\mathbf{A}) = \mathbf{P}\, p(\mathbf{J})\mathbf{P}^{-1}, \tag{6.53}$$

where $\mathbf{P}\mathbf{J}\mathbf{P}^{-1} = \mathbf{A}$ and $\mathbf{J}$ is the Jordan normal form of $\mathbf{A}$.

The case when $\mathbf{A}$ is diagonalizable and each Jordan block is 1×1 deserves special attention.

COROLLARY 6.5   *If $\mathbf{A}$ is diagonalizable with eigenvalues $\lambda_1, \lambda_2, \ldots, \lambda_n$, and $\mathbf{P}$ is the matrix of corresponding eigenvectors, then*

$$p(\mathbf{A}) = \mathbf{P}\,\mathbf{diag}\,(p(\lambda_1), p(\lambda_2), \ldots, p(\lambda_n))\,\mathbf{P}^{-1}.$$

□

■ **EXAMPLE 6.34** Using $\mathbf{A} = \begin{bmatrix} 0 & 1 \\ -2 & -3 \end{bmatrix}$ we have $\lambda_1 = -1$, $\lambda_2 = 2$ and $\mathbf{x}_{(1)} = [1; -1]$, $\mathbf{x}_{(2)} = [-1; 2]$.
Therefore,

$$\mathbf{P} = \begin{bmatrix} 1 & -1 \\ -1 & 2 \end{bmatrix}, \quad \mathbf{P}^{-1} = \begin{bmatrix} 2 & 1 \\ 1 & 1 \end{bmatrix}, \quad \mathbf{J} = \begin{bmatrix} -1 & 0 \\ 0 & -2 \end{bmatrix},$$

so that

$$\mathbf{A}^m = \mathbf{P}\mathbf{J}^m\mathbf{P}^{-1} = \mathbf{P} \begin{bmatrix} (-1)^m & 0 \\ 0 & (-2)^m \end{bmatrix} \mathbf{P}^{-1}$$

$$= \begin{bmatrix} 2(-1)^m - (-2)^m & (-1)^m - (-2)^m \\ -2(-1)^m + 2(-2)^m & -(-1)^m + 2(-2)^m \end{bmatrix}.$$

It's a good idea to do an algebra check of the $m = 0$ and $m = 1$ cases for correctness! ■ ■ ■

When there are multiple eigenvalues, all is not so nice.

■ **EXAMPLE 6.35** Find the mth power of

$$\mathbf{B} = \begin{bmatrix} 0 & 1 & 0 \\ 0 & 0 & 1 \\ -2 & -5 & -4 \end{bmatrix}.$$

Solution: It can be shown that

$$\det(\lambda\mathbf{I} - \mathbf{B}) = (\lambda + 1)^2(\lambda + 2),$$

and when $\lambda = -2$ the eigenvector is $\mathbf{x}_{(1)} = [1; -2; 4]$. The eigenvalue $\lambda = -1$ has the associated chain

$$\{[1; -1; 1], [1; 0; -1]\}.$$

The required transformation matrices are given by

$$\mathbf{P} = \begin{bmatrix} 1 & 1 & 1 \\ -2 & -1 & 0 \\ 4 & 1 & -1 \end{bmatrix}, \quad \mathbf{P}^{-1} = \begin{bmatrix} 1 & 2 & 1 \\ -2 & -5 & -2 \\ 2 & 3 & 1 \end{bmatrix},$$

$$\mathbf{J} = \begin{bmatrix} -2 & 0 & 0 \\ 0 & -1 & 1 \\ 0 & 0 & -1 \end{bmatrix}.$$

Even at this stage, a great deal of algebra has been omitted. Next we will use $\mathbf{B}^m = \mathbf{P}\mathbf{J}^m\mathbf{P}^{-1}$, but what is $\mathbf{J}^m$? Look at the 2×2 Jordan block:

$$\begin{bmatrix} -1 & 1 \\ 0 & -1 \end{bmatrix} = \begin{bmatrix} -1 & 0 \\ 0 & -1 \end{bmatrix} + \begin{bmatrix} 0 & 1 \\ 0 & 0 \end{bmatrix} =: -\mathbf{I} + \mathbf{N}.$$

You should verify that $\mathbf{N}$ is nilpotent of order 2, i.e., $\mathbf{N}^2 = 0$. Thus

$$(-\mathbf{I} + \mathbf{N})^m = (-1)^m\mathbf{I} + m\mathbf{N}(-1)^{m-1}\mathbf{I} + \text{terms with } \mathbf{N}^2.$$

Then we have

$$\mathbf{J}^m = \begin{bmatrix} (-2)^m & 0 & 0 \\ 0 & 0 & 0 \\ 0 & 0 & 0 \end{bmatrix} + \begin{bmatrix} 0 & 0 & 0 \\ 0 & (-1)^m & 0 \\ 0 & 0 & (-1)^m \end{bmatrix} + \begin{bmatrix} 0 & 0 & 0 \\ 0 & 0 & m(-1)^{m-1} \\ 0 & 0 & 0 \end{bmatrix}$$

$$\Rightarrow \quad \mathbf{J}^m = \begin{bmatrix} (-2)^m & 0 & 0 \\ 0 & (-1)^m & m(-1)^{m-1} \\ 0 & 0 & (-1)^m \end{bmatrix}.$$

If we set $a := (-2)^m$ and $b := (-1)^m$, then

$$\mathbf{B}^m = \begin{bmatrix} a+b & 2a-2b-3m & a-b-m \\ -2a+2b+2m & -4a+5b+3m & -2a+2b+m \\ 4a-4b-2m & 8a-8b-3m & 4a-3b-m \end{bmatrix}.$$

■ ■ ■

Raising a Jordan block to the mth power involves separating $\mathbf{J}$ into a diagonalizable plus a nilpotent part, via

$$\mathbf{J} = \begin{bmatrix} \lambda & 1 & 0 & \cdots & 0 \\ 0 & \lambda & 1 & \ddots & \vdots \\ \vdots & \ddots & \lambda & \ddots & 0 \\ \vdots & & \ddots & \ddots & 1 \\ 0 & \cdots & \cdots & 0 & \lambda \end{bmatrix} = \lambda\mathbf{I} + \mathbf{N},$$

where

$$\mathbf{N}^2 = \begin{bmatrix} 0 & 0 & 1 & & \\ & 0 & 0 & \ddots & \\ & & 0 & \ddots & 1 \\ & & & \ddots & 0 \\ 0 & & & & 0 \end{bmatrix}.$$

As the power of $\mathbf{N}$ increases, the line of 1's moves up and away from the $k = 0$, or main, diagonal until $\mathbf{N}^k = 0$, when $\mathbf{N}$ is $k \times k$. Therefore,

$$\mathbf{J}^m = \lambda^m\mathbf{I} + \binom{m}{1}\mathbf{N} + \binom{m}{2}\mathbf{N}^2 + \cdots + \binom{m}{j}\mathbf{N}^j, \quad \text{where } j = \min\{m, k-1\}. \quad (6.54)$$

The computational complexity of this procedure, which requires at least $k - 1$ matrix multiplications, suggests a need for an alternative approach. Suppose $\mathbf{A}$ is diagonalizable and $\mathbf{A} = \mathbf{PDP}^{-1}$. Write

$$p(\mathbf{D}) = \sum_{j=1}^{n} p(\lambda_j) \mathbf{E}_{(j,j;n,n)}, \tag{6.55}$$

where $\left(\mathbf{E}_{(j,j;n,n)}\right)_{k\ell} = \delta_{jk}\delta_{j\ell}$. This is a valid decomposition because the set $\{\mathbf{E}_{(j,j;n,n)}, \ j = 1 : n\}$ is a basis of the space of all diagonal matrices. Premultiply (6.55) by $\mathbf{P}$, postmultiply by $\mathbf{P}^{-1}$, and put $\mathbf{Z}_{(j0)} := \mathbf{PE}_{(j,j;n,n)}\mathbf{P}^{-1}$. Then

$$p(\mathbf{A}) = \sum_{j=1}^{n} p(\lambda_j) \mathbf{Z}_{(j0)}. \tag{6.56}$$

If we could find the $\mathbf{Z}_{(j0)}$ without computing either $\mathbf{P}$ or $\mathbf{P}^{-1}$, we'd be in business.

Since (6.56) must be true for all polynomials $p(\xi)$, choose some specific ones. Put $p(\lambda) = 1 \Leftrightarrow p(\mathbf{A}) = \mathbf{I}$; then, we have the equation

$$\mathbf{I} = \sum_{j=1}^{n} \mathbf{Z}_{(j0)}.$$

When $p(\lambda) = \lambda \Leftrightarrow p(\mathbf{A}) = \mathbf{A}$, and

$$\mathbf{A} = \sum_{j=1}^{n} \lambda_j \mathbf{Z}_{(j0)}.$$

This suggests trying $p_k(\lambda) = (\lambda_k - \lambda) \Leftrightarrow p_k(\mathbf{A}) = (\lambda_k \mathbf{I} - \mathbf{A})$:

$$p_k(\mathbf{A}) = \lambda_k \mathbf{I} - \mathbf{A} = \sum_{j=1}^{n} \left(\lambda_k - \lambda_j\right) \mathbf{Z}_{(j0)}, \quad k = 1 : n.$$

It can be shown that a unique solution of these equations is

$$\mathbf{Z}_{(j0)}(\mathbf{A}) = \prod_{\substack{k=1 \\ k \neq j}}^{n} \left\{ \frac{\mathbf{A} - \lambda_k \mathbf{I}}{\lambda_j - \lambda_k} \right\}. \tag{6.57}$$

These are called the **Lagrange interpolation polynomials**. It can be shown that $\mathbf{Z}_{(j0)}(\mathbf{A})$ is the projection operator onto the eigenspace of λ_j.

■ **EXAMPLE 6.36** Redo example 6.34 using the Lagrange interpolation polynomials.

Solution: We had

$$\mathbf{A} = \begin{bmatrix} 0 & 1 \\ -2 & -3 \end{bmatrix} \quad \text{with} \quad \lambda = -1, -2.$$

The **Z**'s are

$$\mathbf{Z}_{(10)} = \frac{\mathbf{A} - \lambda_2 \mathbf{I}}{\lambda_1 - \lambda_2} = \frac{\mathbf{A} + 2\mathbf{I}}{-1 - (-2)} = \mathbf{A} + 2\mathbf{I} = \begin{bmatrix} 2 & 1 \\ -2 & -1 \end{bmatrix}$$

$$\mathbf{Z}_{(20)} = \frac{\mathbf{A} - \lambda_1 \mathbf{I}}{\lambda_2 - \lambda_1} = \frac{\mathbf{A} + \mathbf{I}}{-2 - (-1)} = -\mathbf{A} - \mathbf{I} = \begin{bmatrix} -1 & -1 \\ 2 & 2 \end{bmatrix}.$$

Thus

$$\mathbf{A}^m = \sum_{j=1}^{2} \lambda_j^m \mathbf{Z}_{(j0)} = (-1)^m \mathbf{Z}_{(10)} + (-2)^m \mathbf{Z}_{(20)} = \begin{bmatrix} 2a - b & a - b \\ -2a + 2b & -a + 2b \end{bmatrix},$$

where $a := (-1)^m$ and $b := (-2)^m$.　　　　　　　　　　　■ ■ ■

When **J** is *not* diagonal, we can use (6.54) in the form

$$\mathbf{J}^m = \begin{bmatrix} \lambda^m & m\lambda^{m-1} & \cdots & \binom{m}{k}\lambda^{m-k} \\ 0 & \lambda^m & \ddots & \vdots \\ \vdots & \ddots & \ddots & m\lambda^{m-1} \\ 0 & \cdots & 0 & \lambda^m \end{bmatrix}.$$

Knowing that

$$\binom{m}{j}\lambda^{m-j} = \frac{1}{j!}\left(\frac{d}{d\lambda}\right)^j \lambda^m,$$

we see that when evaluating $p(\mathbf{J})$, the diagonal elements are $p(\lambda)$, the $k = 1$ diagonal elements are $p'(\lambda)/1!$, and the $k = j$ diagonal elements are $p^{(j)}(\lambda)/j!$. We are lead to the following extension of (6.56) when we use m_j as the multiplicity of λ_j for $j = 1 : k$:

$$p(\mathbf{A}) = \sum_{j=1}^{k} \sum_{k=0}^{m_j - 1} p^{(k)}(\lambda_j)\, \mathbf{Z}_{(jk)}. \tag{6.58}$$

If λ_j is a simple eigenvalue, the inner sum will be only one term and $\mathbf{Z}_{(j0)}$ will be the usual j^{th} Lagrange interpolation polynomial. Finding the other $\mathbf{Z}_{(jk)}$ is a matter of setting $p(\lambda) = 1$, $\lambda - \lambda_j$ for each j and $(\lambda - \lambda_j)^k$ for each j, and k and solving simultaneously.

■ **EXAMPLE 6.37** Apply this method to the 3×3 matrix

$$\mathbf{B} = \begin{bmatrix} 0 & 1 & 0 \\ 0 & 0 & 1 \\ -2 & -5 & -4 \end{bmatrix}.$$

Solution: From example 6.35 we know that

$$\mathbf{B} = \begin{bmatrix} 0 & 1 & 0 \\ 0 & 0 & 1 \\ -2 & -5 & -4 \end{bmatrix} \quad \text{with} \quad \lambda = -2, -1, -1.$$

We can write

$$p(\mathbf{A}) = p(-2)\mathbf{Z}_{(10)} + p(-1)\mathbf{Z}_{(20)} + p'(-1)\mathbf{Z}_{(21)}.$$

Setting $p(\lambda) = 1$, $\lambda + 1$, and $(\lambda + 1)^2$, we get

$$\mathbf{Z}_{(10)} + \mathbf{Z}_{(20)} = \mathbf{I} = \begin{bmatrix} 1 & 0 & 0 \\ 0 & 1 & 0 \\ 0 & 0 & 1 \end{bmatrix},$$

$$-\mathbf{Z}_{(10)} + \mathbf{Z}_{(21)} = \mathbf{B} + \mathbf{I} = \begin{bmatrix} 1 & 1 & 0 \\ 0 & 1 & 1 \\ -2 & -5 & -3 \end{bmatrix},$$

$$\mathbf{Z}_{(10)} = (\mathbf{B} + \mathbf{I})^2 = \begin{bmatrix} 1 & 2 & 1 \\ -2 & -4 & -2 \\ 4 & 8 & 4 \end{bmatrix}.$$

Backsubstituting yields

$$\mathbf{Z}_{(21)} = \begin{bmatrix} 2 & 3 & 1 \\ -2 & -3 & -1 \\ 2 & 3 & 1 \end{bmatrix}, \quad \mathbf{Z}_{(20)} = \begin{bmatrix} 0 & -2 & -1 \\ 2 & 5 & 2 \\ -4 & -8 & -3 \end{bmatrix}.$$

Thus

$$p(\mathbf{B}) = p(-2)\begin{bmatrix} 1 & 2 & 1 \\ -2 & -4 & -2 \\ 4 & 8 & 4 \end{bmatrix} + p(-1)\begin{bmatrix} 0 & -2 & -1 \\ 2 & 5 & 2 \\ -4 & -8 & -3 \end{bmatrix}$$

$$+ p'(-1)\begin{bmatrix} 2 & 3 & 1 \\ -2 & -3 & -1 \\ 2 & 3 & 1 \end{bmatrix}.$$

■ ■ ■

This completes the discussion of the polynomial case.

Convergence of Matrix Series Following the usual power series development, once a norm is defined on $\mathbb{C}_n^n$, the region of convergence $\|\mathbf{A}\| < R$ is meaningful and all the usual theory holds.

Suppose $f(\lambda)$ has a convergent power series about $\lambda = 0$:

$$f(\lambda) = \sum_{n=0}^{\infty} a_n \lambda^n.$$

Then the series converges for all λ such that $|\lambda| < R$, the radius of convergence. When $\mathbf{A} \in \mathbb{C}_n^n$, we may write

$$f(\mathbf{A}) = \sum_{n=0}^{\infty} a_n \mathbf{A}^n, \tag{6.59}$$

where $\|\mathbf{A}\| < R$. If all the eigenvalues lie within $|\lambda| < R$, then (6.59) will converge absolutely.

Evaluating Functions of Matrices Formally rewriting (6.58) for an analytic function $f(\cdot)$,

$$f(\mathbf{A}) = \sum_{j=1}^{k} \sum_{k=0}^{m_j-1} f^{(k)}(\lambda_j) \mathbf{Z}_{(jk)}. \tag{6.60}$$

We see that the right hand side of (6.60) is well defined whenever the eigenvalues of $\mathbf{A}$ lie within the circle of convergence of $f(\cdot)$. Hence (6.60) is valid for any function analytic on the spectrum of $\mathbf{A}$. We could also use the explicit series representation of $f(\cdot)$ if powers of $\mathbf{A}$ were known or easily calculated.

■ **EXAMPLE 6.38** Let

$$\mathbf{A} = \begin{bmatrix} 0 & 0 & 1 \\ 0 & 1 & 0 \\ 1 & 0 & 0 \end{bmatrix}.$$

Compute $e^{\mathbf{A}t}$, using several different methods.

(Method 1) First use the series expansion of the exponential function:

$$e^{\mathbf{A}t} = \sum_{n=0}^{\infty} \frac{t^n}{n!} \mathbf{A}^n.$$

Since $\mathbf{A}$ is a permutation matrix and $\mathbf{A}^2 = \mathbf{I}$, we have

$$\mathbf{A}^{2n} = \mathbf{I}, \quad \mathbf{A}^{2n+1} = \mathbf{A}^{2n}\mathbf{A} = \mathbf{A},$$

so that

$$e^{\mathbf{A}t} = \sum_0^\infty \frac{t^{2n}}{(2n)!} \mathbf{A}^{2n} + \sum_0^\infty \frac{t^{2n+1}}{(2n+1)!} \mathbf{A}^{2n+1}$$

$$= \mathbf{I} \sum_0^\infty \frac{t^{2n}}{(2n)!} + \mathbf{A} \sum_0^\infty \frac{t^{2n+1}}{(2n+1)!}.$$

The power series are those of $\cosh t$ and $\sinh t$; hence

$$\exp \left\{ \begin{bmatrix} 0 & 0 & 1 \\ 0 & 1 & 0 \\ 1 & 0 & 0 \end{bmatrix} t \right\} = \mathbf{I} \cosh t + \mathbf{A} \sinh t$$

$$= \begin{bmatrix} \cosh t & 0 & \sinh t \\ 0 & e^t & 0 \\ \sinh t & 0 & \cosh t \end{bmatrix}.$$

(Method 2) We need the eigenvalues of $\mathbf{A}$ to use a similarity transform to combine (6.52) and (6.59). We know that

$$(-1, [1; 0; -1]), \quad (1, [0; 1; 0]), \quad (1, [1; 0; 1])$$

are eigenpairs. Therefore, we can write

$$e^{\mathbf{A}t} = \mathbf{P} e^{\mathbf{D}t} \mathbf{P}^{-1}$$

$$= \begin{bmatrix} 1 & 0 & 1 \\ 0 & 1 & 0 \\ -1 & 0 & 1 \end{bmatrix} \begin{bmatrix} e^{-t} & 0 & 0 \\ 0 & e^t & 0 \\ 0 & 0 & e^t \end{bmatrix} \tfrac{1}{2} \begin{bmatrix} 1 & 0 & -1 \\ 0 & 1 & 0 \\ 1 & 0 & 1 \end{bmatrix}$$

$$= \begin{bmatrix} \cosh t & 0 & \sinh t \\ 0 & e^t & 0 \\ \sinh t & 0 & \cosh t \end{bmatrix}.$$

(Method 3) Lastly, using (6.60) we can write

$$f(\mathbf{A}) = f(-1)\mathbf{Z}_{(10)} + f(1)\mathbf{Z}_{(20)} + f'(1)\mathbf{Z}_{(30)},$$

because $\mathbf{A}$ is nondefective. Now put $f(\lambda) = 1, \lambda + 1, \lambda - 1$ to get

$$\begin{aligned} \mathbf{Z}_{(10)} + \mathbf{Z}_{(20)} + \mathbf{Z}_{(30)} &= \mathbf{I}, \\ 2\mathbf{Z}_{(20)} + 2\mathbf{Z}_{(30)} &= \mathbf{A} + \mathbf{I}, \\ -2\mathbf{Z}_{(10)} &= \mathbf{A} - \mathbf{I}, \end{aligned}$$

from which we have

$$f(\mathbf{A}) = \frac{1}{2} f(-1)(\mathbf{I} - \mathbf{A}) + \frac{1}{2} f(1)(\mathbf{I} + \mathbf{A}),$$

or

$$e^{\mathbf{A}t} = \tfrac{1}{2}e^{-t} \begin{bmatrix} 1 & 0 & -1 \\ 0 & 0 & 0 \\ -1 & 0 & 1 \end{bmatrix} + \tfrac{1}{2}e^{t} \begin{bmatrix} 1 & 0 & 1 \\ 0 & 2 & 0 \\ 1 & 0 & 1 \end{bmatrix}$$

$$= \begin{bmatrix} \cosh t & 0 & \sinh t \\ 0 & e^{t} & 0 \\ \sinh t & 0 & \cosh t \end{bmatrix}$$

which is precisely the result we got the other ways. ■ ■ ■

Expressions like $(s\mathbf{I} - \mathbf{A})^{-1}$ can be written in terms of the geometric series:

$$(s\mathbf{I} - \mathbf{A})^{-1} = \frac{1}{s} \left(\mathbf{I} - \frac{1}{s}\mathbf{A} \right)^{-1} = \frac{1}{s} \sum_{m=0}^{\infty} \mathbf{A}^{m} s^{-m} \text{ for } \|\mathbf{A}\| < |s| .$$

If the complex number s is taken far enough from the origin, the series will converge for any square matrix $\mathbf{A}$. This matrix function is called the **resolvent kernel** and is of use in the study of linear systems using Laplace transforms: see Section 6.13.

Back to the Exponential of a Matrix

To see that $e^{\mathbf{A}t}$ is the unique solution matrix for the system $\mathbf{X}' = \mathbf{A}\mathbf{X}$, $\mathbf{X}(t_0) = \mathbf{I}$, start with the infinite series representation

$$e^{\mathbf{A}(t-t_0)} = \sum_{n=0}^{\infty} \frac{1}{n!} \mathbf{A}^{n} (t - t_0)^{n}.$$

The series is well defined and uniformly convergent for all finite $t - t_0$. We can legitimately differentiate both sides with respect to t (with $t_0 = 0$ for convenience):

$$\frac{d}{dt} e^{\mathbf{A}t} = \sum_{n=0}^{\infty} \mathbf{A}^{n} \frac{nt^{n-1}}{n!} = \sum_{n=1}^{\infty} \mathbf{A}^{n} \frac{t^{n-1}}{(n-1)!} = \mathbf{A} \sum_{m=0}^{\infty} \mathbf{A}^{m} \frac{t^{m}}{m!} = \mathbf{A} e^{\mathbf{A}t}.$$

This was allowed because $\mathbf{A}$ commutes with $\mathbf{A}^{m}$ for any integer power m. Since $e^{\mathbf{A}t}\big|_{t=0} = \mathbf{I}$, $e^{\mathbf{A}t}$ is a solution of equation (6.39) with $t_0 = 0$, and we have

$$\mathbf{\Phi}(t, 0) = e^{\mathbf{A}t} \quad \text{and} \quad \mathbf{\Phi}(t, \tau) = e^{\mathbf{A}(t-\tau)}. \tag{6.61}$$

The exponential matrix function would *not* be a solution of (6.39) if $\mathbf{A}$ were time *dependent* because of terms in the derivative of the Taylor series expansion of $e^{\mathbf{A}t}$ like

$$\frac{d}{dt} \left(\mathbf{A}^{3} \right) = \mathbf{A}'\mathbf{A}^{2} + \mathbf{A}\mathbf{A}'\mathbf{A} + \mathbf{A}^{2}\mathbf{A}'$$

and the fact that $\mathbf{A}'$ need not commute with $\mathbf{A}$. A simple example should convince you this is true. Take $\mathbf{A} = [1, t; t^2, 0]$; then $\mathbf{A}' = [0, 1; 2t, 0]$, and

$$\mathbf{A}\mathbf{A}' = \begin{bmatrix} 1 & t \\ t^2 & 0 \end{bmatrix} \begin{bmatrix} 0 & 1 \\ 2t & 0 \end{bmatrix} = \begin{bmatrix} 2t^2 & 1 \\ 0 & t^2 \end{bmatrix}$$

$$\neq \begin{bmatrix} t^2 & 0 \\ 2t & 2t^2 \end{bmatrix} = \begin{bmatrix} 0 & 1 \\ 2t & 0 \end{bmatrix} \begin{bmatrix} 1 & t \\ t^2 & 0 \end{bmatrix} = \mathbf{A}'\mathbf{A}.$$

Several results about the matrix exponential can be stated.

THEOREM 6.18   *If* $\mathbf{A}$ *is a square matrix, then*

(a) $\left(e^{\mathbf{A}t}\right)^{-1} = e^{-\mathbf{A}t}$, *and*

(b) $e^{\mathbf{A}t}e^{\mathbf{B}t} = e^{(\mathbf{A}+\mathbf{B})t}$ *whenever* $\mathbf{A}\mathbf{B} = \mathbf{B}\mathbf{A}$. □

▪ **EXAMPLE 6.39**   Find the state-transition matrices for each of the following linear systems.

(a) $x_1' = 2x_1 + x_2$, $x_2' = -x_1 + 2x_2$. The coefficient matrix, its eigenvalues, and eigenvectors are

$$\mathbf{A} = \begin{bmatrix} 2 & 1 \\ -1 & 2 \end{bmatrix}, \quad \lambda_\pm = 2 \pm i, \quad \mathbf{x}_{(\pm)} = \begin{bmatrix} 1 \\ \pm i \end{bmatrix}.$$

Using equation (6.60), we have

$$e^{\mathbf{A}t} = e^{(2+i)t} \left(\frac{\mathbf{A} - (2-i)\mathbf{I}}{(2+i) - (2-i)} \right) + e^{(2+i)t} \left(\frac{\mathbf{A} - (2+i)\mathbf{I}}{((2-i) - (2+i))} \right)$$

$$= \frac{1}{2i} e^{(2+i)t} \begin{bmatrix} i & 1 \\ -1 & i \end{bmatrix} - \frac{1}{2i} e^{(2-i)t} \begin{bmatrix} -i & 1 \\ -1 & -i \end{bmatrix}$$

$$\Rightarrow e^{\mathbf{A}t} = e^{2t} \begin{bmatrix} \cos t & \sin t \\ -\sin t & \cos t \end{bmatrix}.$$

(b) $x_1' = -2x_1 + x_2$, $x_2' = -2x_2$. The coefficient matrix is defective (nondiagonalizable), but it can be decomposed into a diagonalizable plus a nilpotent part:

$$\mathbf{B} = \begin{bmatrix} -2 & 1 \\ 0 & -2 \end{bmatrix} = \begin{bmatrix} -2 & 0 \\ 0 & -2 \end{bmatrix} + \begin{bmatrix} 0 & 1 \\ 0 & 0 \end{bmatrix} := -2\mathbf{I} + \mathbf{N}.$$

Since $\mathbf{N}$ commutes with $\mathbf{I}$ and $\mathbf{N}^2 = \mathbf{0}$, we have

$$\mathbf{B}^n = (-2\mathbf{I} + \mathbf{N})^n = (-2)^n \mathbf{I} + n(-2)^{n-1} \mathbf{N}.$$

Thus

$$e^{\mathbf{B}t} = \sum_0^\infty \frac{1}{n!}\mathbf{B}^n t^n = \sum_0^\infty \frac{1}{n!}\left((-2)^n\mathbf{I} + n(-2)^{n-1}\mathbf{N}\right) t^n$$

$$= e^{-2t}(\mathbf{I} + t\mathbf{N}) = e^{-2t}\begin{bmatrix} 1 & t \\ 0 & 1 \end{bmatrix}.$$

(c) $x_1' = -9x_1 + 4x_2 + 4x_3$, $x_2' = -8x_1 + 3x_2 + 4x_3$, $x_3' = -16x_1 + 8x_2 + 7x_3$. The eigenvalues of the coefficient matrix are $3, -1, -1$, with corresponding eigenvectors

$$[1; 1; 2], \ [1; 2; 0], \ [1; 0; 2].$$

Using the diagonalizing transformation approach, $e^{\mathbf{C}t} = \mathbf{P}e^{\mathbf{D}t}\mathbf{P}^{-1}$ yields

$$e^{\mathbf{C}t} = \begin{bmatrix} -2e^{3t} + 3e^{-t} & e^{3t} - e^{-t} & e^{3t} - e^{-t} \\ -2e^{3t} + 2e^{-t} & e^{3t} & e^{3t} - e^{-t} \\ -4e^{3t} + 4e^{-t} & 2e^{3t} - 2e^{-t} & 2e^{3t} - e^{-t} \end{bmatrix}.$$

(d) We saw that the system

$$\mathbf{x}'(t) = \begin{bmatrix} 5 & -2 \\ 2 & 1 \end{bmatrix}\mathbf{x}(t),$$

had

$$\mathbf{X}(t) = e^{3t}\begin{bmatrix} 1 & 2t+1 \\ 1 & 2t \end{bmatrix}$$

as one possible fundamental matrix. Using either (6.48) or (6.49) we can write the state-transition matrix in the form

$$e^{\mathbf{A}t} = \mathbf{\Phi}(t,0) = \mathbf{X}(t)\mathbf{X}^{-1}(0) = e^{3t}\begin{bmatrix} 1 & 2t+1 \\ 1 & 2t \end{bmatrix}\begin{bmatrix} 0 & 1 \\ 1 & -1 \end{bmatrix}$$

$$= e^{3t}\begin{bmatrix} 2t+1 & 2t \\ 2t & 1-2t \end{bmatrix}.$$

(e) Again using equation (6.49) and the result of previous examples we can write the state-transition matrix for the system

$$\mathbf{x}'(t) = \begin{bmatrix} -1 & 1 & 0 & 0 \\ 1 & -1 & 0 & 0 \\ 0 & 0 & -3 & 2 \\ 0 & 0 & 1 & -2 \end{bmatrix}\mathbf{x}(t)$$

as

$$e^{\mathbf{A}t} = \mathbf{\Phi}(t,0) = \mathbf{X}(t)\mathbf{X}^{-1}(0)$$

$$= \begin{bmatrix} 1 & e^{-2t} & 0 & 0 \\ 1 & -e^{-2t} & 0 & 0 \\ 0 & 0 & e^{-t} & 2e^{-4t} \\ 0 & 0 & e^{-t} & -e^{-4t} \end{bmatrix} \mathbf{X}^{-1}(0)$$

$$\Rightarrow e^{\mathbf{A}t} = \mathbf{\Phi}(t,0)$$

$$= \frac{1}{6} \begin{bmatrix} 3\left(1+e^{-2t}\right) & 3\left(1-e^{-2t}\right) & 0 & 0 \\ 3\left(1-e^{-2t}\right) & e^{-2t} & 0 & 0 \\ 0 & 0 & 2\left(e^{-t}+2e^{-4t}\right) & 4\left(e^{-t}-e^{-4t}\right) \\ 0 & 0 & 2\left(e^{-t}-e^{-4t}\right) & 2\left(e^{-t}+2e^{-4t}\right) \end{bmatrix}.$$

(f) Even systems with complex eigenvalues are amenable to solution using equation (6.49). The system

$$\mathbf{x}'(t) = \begin{bmatrix} 0 & 1 & 0 & 0 \\ 0 & 1 & 1 & -1 \\ 0 & 0 & 0 & 1 \\ 1 & 2 & 1 & -1 \end{bmatrix} \mathbf{x}(t)$$

has a fundamental matrix

$$\mathbf{X}(t) = \begin{bmatrix} e^t & -e^{-t} & \cos t & \sin t \\ e^t & e^{-t} & -\sin t & \cos t \\ 3e^t & -e^{-t} & \sin t & -\cos t \\ 3e^t & e^{-t} & \cos t & \sin t \end{bmatrix}.$$

Therefore,

$$\mathbf{\Phi}(t,0) = \begin{bmatrix} e^t & -e^{-t} & \cos t & \sin t \\ e^t & e^{-t} & -\sin t & \cos t \\ 3e^t & -e^{-t} & \sin t & -\cos t \\ 3e^t & e^{-t} & \cos t & \sin t \end{bmatrix} \begin{bmatrix} 1 & -1 & 1 & 0 \\ 1 & 1 & 0 & 1 \\ 3 & -1 & 0 & -2 \\ 3 & 1 & 1 & 0 \end{bmatrix}^{-1}$$

$$\Rightarrow \quad \mathbf{\Phi}(t,0) = \begin{bmatrix} e^t & 0 & 0 & 0 \\ 0 & e^{-t} & 0 & 0 \\ 0 & 0 & \cos t & \sin t \\ 0 & 0 & -\sin t & \cos t \end{bmatrix}.$$

■ ■ ■

An Alternative Calculation of the Exponential of a Matrix

In terms of the state-transition matrix, the solution of the initial value problem $\mathbf{x}' = \mathbf{A}\mathbf{x}$, $\mathbf{x}(0) = \mathbf{x}_0$, is

$$\mathbf{x}'(t) = \mathbf{\Phi}(t, 0)\mathbf{x}(0) = e^{\mathbf{A}t}\mathbf{x}(0).$$

By looking at the set of linearly independent solutions to the original system, we can rewrite this as a matrix ODE in terms of a fundamental matrix $\mathbf{X}(t)$:

$$\mathbf{X}'(t) = \mathbf{A}\mathbf{X}(t).$$

If we put $\mathbf{X}(0) = \mathbf{I}$ and write $\mathbf{e}_k = \mathbf{col}_k(\mathbf{I})$, then from equation (6.32),

$$\mathbf{\Phi}(t, 0) = e^{\mathbf{A}t} = \left[\mathbf{C}(\mathbf{e}_1)\mathbf{f}(t), \mathbf{C}(\mathbf{e}_2)\mathbf{f}(t), \ldots, \mathbf{C}(\mathbf{e}_n)\mathbf{f}(t)\right],$$

and that solves the problem.

■ **EXAMPLE 6.40** Find the state-transition matrix for the system of example 6.25.

Solution: All we need to find is $\mathbf{C}(\mathbf{e}_k)\mathbf{f}(t)$ for $k = 1 : 3$. Setting $c_1 = 1$, $c_2 = c_3 = 0$, we have

$$\mathbf{C}(\mathbf{e}_1)\mathbf{f}(t) = \left[e^t; 0; 0\right].$$

Setting $c_2 = 1$, $c_1 = c_3 = 0$, we have

$$\mathbf{C}(\mathbf{e}_2)\mathbf{f}(t) = \left[te^t; e^t; 0\right].$$

Lastly, $c_3 = 1$, $c_1 = c_2 = 0$ gives us

$$\mathbf{C}(\mathbf{e}_3)\mathbf{f}(t) = \left[0; 0; e^{2t}\right].$$

From these we can write

$$\mathbf{\Phi}(t, 0) = e^{\mathbf{A}t} = \begin{bmatrix} e^t & te^t & 0 \\ 0 & e^t & 0 \\ 0 & 0 & e^{2t} \end{bmatrix}.$$

■ ■ ■

■ **EXAMPLE 6.41** Find the state-transition matrix for the 4×4 of example 6.26.

Solution: Setting $c_1 = 1$, $c_2 = c_3 = c_4 = 0$, we have

$$\mathbf{C}(\mathbf{e}_1)\mathbf{f}(t) = e^t[1; 0; 0; 0].$$

Setting $c_2 = 1$, $c_1 = c_3 = c_4 = 0$,

$$\mathbf{C}(\mathbf{e}_2)\mathbf{f}(t) = e^t[t; 1; 0; 0].$$

Setting $c_3 = 1$, $c_1 = c_2 = c_4 = 0$,

$$\mathbf{C}(e_3)\mathbf{f}(t) = e^t[t^2 + 2t; 2t; t + 1; t].$$

Setting $c_4 = 1$, $c_1 = c_2 = c_3 = 0$,

$$\mathbf{C}(e_4)\mathbf{f}(t) = e^t[-(t^2 + 2t); -2t; -t; 1 - t].$$

Therefore, the state transition matrix is

$$\boldsymbol{\Phi}(t, 0) = e^{\mathbf{A}t} = e^t \begin{bmatrix} 1 & t & t^2 + 2t & -(t^2 + 2t) \\ 0 & 1 & 2t & -2t \\ 0 & 0 & t + 1 & -t \\ 0 & 0 & t & 1 - t \end{bmatrix}.$$

■ ■ ■

6.9.3 *Nonhomogeneous Linear Systems*

Assuming we can evaluate the state-transition matrix, let's turn our attention to the problem with nonzero input. The dynamical system can be written as

$$\mathbf{x}'(t) = \mathbf{A}(t)\mathbf{x}(t) + \mathbf{B}(t)\mathbf{u}(t), \quad \mathbf{x}(t_0) = \mathbf{x}_0, \tag{6.62}$$

where $\mathbf{u}(t)$ is the **input** to the system. Starting with the form of the zero-input solution in terms of a fundamental matrix as given in (6.45),

$$\mathbf{x}(t) = \mathbf{X}(t)\mathbf{c},$$

we can make the usual variation of parameters assumption about the form of the particular solution:

$$\mathbf{x}_\mathrm{p}(t) = \mathbf{X}(t)\mathbf{k}(t).$$

Substituting this into (6.62), we have

$$\mathbf{x}_\mathrm{p}' = \mathbf{A}\mathbf{x}_\mathrm{p} + \mathbf{B}\mathbf{u} = \mathbf{X}'\mathbf{k} + \mathbf{X}\mathbf{k}' = \mathbf{A}\mathbf{X}\mathbf{k} + \mathbf{X}\mathbf{k}' = \mathbf{A}\mathbf{x}_\mathrm{p} + \mathbf{X}\mathbf{k}'.$$

Therefore,

$$\mathbf{k}'(t) = \mathbf{X}^{-1}(t)\mathbf{B}(t)\mathbf{u}(t).$$

Integrating this equation, we have

$$\mathbf{k}(t) = \int_{t_0}^t \mathbf{X}^{-1}(\tau)\mathbf{B}(\tau)\mathbf{u}(\tau)\, d\tau.$$

The general solution is then

$$\mathbf{x}(t) = \mathbf{x}_\mathrm{c}(t) + \mathbf{x}_\mathrm{p}(t) = \boldsymbol{\Phi}(t, t_0)\mathbf{x}(t_0) + \mathbf{X}(t)\int_{t_0}^t \mathbf{X}^{-1}(\tau)\mathbf{B}(\tau)\mathbf{u}(\tau)\, d\tau. \tag{6.63}$$

Because the integration is over τ, $\mathbf{X}(t)$ can be moved inside the integral and equation (6.48), $\mathbf{\Phi}(t, t_0) = \mathbf{X}(t)\mathbf{X}^{-1}(t_0)$, can be used to write

$$\mathbf{x}(t) = \mathbf{\Phi}(t, t_0)\mathbf{x}(t_0) + \int_{t_0}^{t} \mathbf{\Phi}(t, \tau)\mathbf{B}(\tau)\mathbf{u}(\tau)\, d\tau. \tag{6.64}$$

For constant $\mathbf{A}$, equation (6.64) takes the form

$$\mathbf{x}(t) = e^{\mathbf{A}(t-t_0)}\mathbf{x}(t_0) + \int_{t_0}^{t} e^{\mathbf{A}(t-\tau)}\mathbf{B}(\tau)\mathbf{u}(\tau)\, d\tau. \tag{6.65}$$

In equations (6.63), (6.64), and (6.65) the solution decomposes into a sum of the zero-input (the nonintegral part) plus the zero-state response (the integral part).

■ **EXAMPLE 6.42** Solve the linear system

$$x_1' = 3x_1 - 2x_2 + e^t,$$
$$x_2' = 4x_1 - x_2 + e^t$$

by converting to matrix form and finding the eigenvalues and eigenvectors.

Solution: The zero-input solution is

$$\mathbf{x}_c(t) = c_1 e^t \begin{bmatrix} \cos 2t \\ \cos 2t + \sin 2t \end{bmatrix} + c_2 e^t \begin{bmatrix} -\sin 2t \\ \sin 2t - \cos 2t \end{bmatrix}.$$

Rather than compute $e^{\mathbf{A}(t-\tau)}\mathbf{B}\mathbf{u}(\tau)$, it is easier to compute $e^{-\mathbf{A}\tau}\mathbf{B}\mathbf{u}(\tau)$ and then premultiply by $e^{\mathbf{A}t}$:

$$e^{\mathbf{A}t} \int_0^t e^{-\mathbf{A}\tau}\mathbf{B}\mathbf{u}(\tau)\, d\tau = e^{\mathbf{A}t} \int_0^t \begin{bmatrix} \cos 2\tau \\ \cos 2\tau + \sin 2\tau \end{bmatrix} d\tau$$

$$= \tfrac{1}{2} e^{\mathbf{A}t} \begin{bmatrix} \sin 2t \\ \sin 2t - \cos 2t + 1 \end{bmatrix}$$

$$= \tfrac{1}{2} e^t \begin{bmatrix} \sin 2t \\ 1 - \cos 2t + \sin 2t \end{bmatrix}$$

$$= \tfrac{1}{2} e^t \begin{bmatrix} 0 \\ 1 \end{bmatrix} - \tfrac{1}{2} e^t \begin{bmatrix} \sin 2t \\ \cos 2t - \sin 2t \end{bmatrix}.$$

This form of $\mathbf{x}_p(t)$ is slightly different from that which would have been obtained using the method of variation of parameters of the last section, because in this form $\mathbf{x}_p(0) = \mathbf{0}$, a truly zero-state solution. Variation of parameters generates a particular solution, which need not be a zero-state solution. The two results only differ by an addition of part of the zero-input solution, which in this case corresponded to $c_1 = 0$ and $c_2 = -1$. ■ ■ ■

■ **EXAMPLE 6.43** Solve the nonhomogeneous initial value problem

$$\mathbf{x}'(t) = \begin{bmatrix} 2 & 1 & 1 \\ 1 & 2 & 1 \\ 1 & 1 & 2 \end{bmatrix} \mathbf{x}(t) + \begin{bmatrix} 0 \\ t \\ 1 \end{bmatrix} e^t, \quad \mathbf{x}(0) = \begin{bmatrix} 0 \\ 0 \\ 1 \end{bmatrix}.$$

Solution: It is an easy matter to use the computer to find the eigenpairs,

$$(1, [1; -1; 0]), \quad (1, [1; 0; -1]), \quad (4, [1; 1; 1]).$$

From these we can immediately write a fundamental matrix:

$$\mathbf{X}(t) = \begin{bmatrix} e^t & e^t & e^{4t} \\ -e^t & 0 & e^{4t} \\ 0 & -e^t & e^{4t} \end{bmatrix}.$$

Using $e^{\mathbf{A}t} = \mathbf{X}(t)\mathbf{X}^{-1}(0)$, we have

$$e^{\mathbf{A}t} = \frac{1}{3} \begin{bmatrix} e^{4t} + 2e^t & e^{4t} - e^t & e^{4t} - e^t \\ e^{4t} - e^t & e^{4t} + 2e^t & e^{4t} - e^t \\ e^{4t} - e^t & e^{4t} - e^t & e^{4t} + 2e^t \end{bmatrix}.$$

Using equation (6.65), we can write

$$\mathbf{x}(t) = e^{\mathbf{A}t}\mathbf{x}(0) + \int_0^t e^{\mathbf{A}(t-\tau)}\mathbf{b}(\tau)\, d\tau$$

$$\Rightarrow \mathbf{x}(t) = \frac{1}{3} \begin{bmatrix} 2e^{4t} + e^t \\ 2e^{4t} - 2e^t \\ 2e^{4t} + e^t \end{bmatrix} + \int_0^t \begin{bmatrix} -2e^{4t-3\tau} \\ -2e^{4t-3\tau} \\ -2e^{4t-3\tau} \end{bmatrix} d\tau$$

$$\Rightarrow \mathbf{x}(t) = \frac{1}{3} \begin{bmatrix} e^{4t} - e^t \\ e^{4t} - e^t \\ e^{4t} + 2e^t \end{bmatrix} + \frac{1}{3} \begin{bmatrix} e^t - e^{4t} \\ (3t+1)e^t - e^{4t} \\ e^t - e^{4t} \end{bmatrix} = \begin{bmatrix} 0 \\ te^t \\ e^t \end{bmatrix}.$$

■ ■ ■

■ **EXAMPLE 6.44** Let's look at the time dependent linear system

$$\mathbf{x}'(t) = \begin{bmatrix} \dfrac{-1}{1+t} & 1+t \\ 0 & \dfrac{-2}{1+t} \end{bmatrix} \mathbf{x}(t) + \frac{1}{(1+t)^2} \begin{bmatrix} 0 \\ 1 \end{bmatrix}.$$

Solution: The only method by which we can evaluate $\mathbf{\Phi}(t, t_0)$ for a time dependent system is by explicitly solving the zero-input system,

$$\mathbf{x}'(t) = \begin{bmatrix} \dfrac{-1}{1+t} & 1+t \\ 0 & \dfrac{-2}{1+t} \end{bmatrix} \mathbf{x}(t).$$

Rewriting in component form,

$$x_2'(t) = -\frac{2}{1+t}x_2(t) \quad \Rightarrow \quad x_2(t) = \frac{1}{(1+t)^2}x_2(0)$$

and

$$\mathbf{x}_1'(t) = -\frac{1}{1+t}\mathbf{x}_1(t) + (1+t)\mathbf{x}_2(t) = -\frac{1}{1+t}\left(\mathbf{x}_1(t) + \mathbf{x}_2(0)\right)$$

$$\Rightarrow \quad x_1(t) = \frac{x_1(0) + tx_2(0)}{1+t}.$$

Therefore,

$$\mathbf{x}(t) = \mathbf{\Phi}(t,0)\mathbf{x}(0) = \begin{bmatrix} \dfrac{1}{1+t} & \dfrac{t}{1+t} \\[2ex] 0 & \dfrac{1}{(1+t)^2} \end{bmatrix}\mathbf{x}(0),$$

so that $\mathbf{\Phi}(t,t_0) = \mathbf{\Phi}(t,0)\mathbf{\Phi}(0,t_0) = \mathbf{\Phi}(t,0)\mathbf{\Phi}^{-1}(t_0,0)$ and

$$\mathbf{\Phi}(t,t_0) = \left(\frac{1+t}{1+t_0}\right)\begin{bmatrix} 1 & \dfrac{t-t_0}{1+t_0} \\[2ex] 0 & \dfrac{1+t_0}{1+t} \end{bmatrix}.$$

Then we have

$$\mathbf{x}(t) = \mathbf{\Phi}(t,0)\mathbf{x}(0) + \int_0^t \mathbf{\Phi}(t,\tau)\begin{bmatrix} 0 \\ 1 \end{bmatrix}\frac{d\tau}{(1+\tau)^2}$$

$$= \mathbf{\Phi}(t,0)\mathbf{x}(0) + \frac{1}{2(1+t)^2}\begin{bmatrix} t^2(1+t) \\ 2t \end{bmatrix}.$$

∎

6.9.4 Exercise Set

1. If $\mathbf{A}$ is a 2×2 matrix with distinct eigenvalues λ and μ, derive a general formula for $e^{\mathbf{A}t}$. Repeat this if there are repeated eigenvalues. Your result should not depend on the eigenvectors of $\mathbf{A}$.

2. Show that each of the matrices $\mathbf{Z}_{(j0)}$ is a projection matrix by showing that it is idempotent. Onto what subspaces do they project? Are the $\mathbf{Z}_{(jk)}$, for $k > 0$, projection matrices, and if they are, onto what subspaces do they project?

3. Find an expression for $f(\mathbf{B})$ and use it to evaluate $\mathbf{B}^m$ and $e^{\mathbf{B}t}$ if

$$\mathbf{B} = \begin{bmatrix} 5 & -4 \\ 4 & -3 \end{bmatrix}.$$

4. For the matrix

$$\mathbf{C} = \begin{bmatrix} 1 & 1 & 0 \\ 0 & 0 & 1 \\ 0 & 0 & 1 \end{bmatrix},$$

find $\mathbf{C}^m$, $e^{\mathbf{C}t}$, and $\sin \mathbf{C}t$.

5. If

$$\mathbf{E} = \begin{bmatrix} 0 & 4 & 3 \\ 0 & 20 & 16 \\ 0 & -25 & -20 \end{bmatrix},$$

then find $e^{\mathbf{E}t}$ by two *different* methods.

6. If

$$\mathbf{F} = \begin{bmatrix} -3 & 1 & 0 \\ -4 & 0 & 1 \\ -2 & 0 & 0 \end{bmatrix},$$

then find $e^{\mathbf{F}t}$ by two *different* methods.

7. If $\mathbf{J} = \mathbf{ones}(n)$, find $\mathbf{J}^m$ and $e^{\mathbf{J}t}$.

8. If $\mathbf{H}$ is the matrix whose entries are $H_{jk} = a + (b - a)\delta_{jk}$ for $a \neq b$, then find $\mathbf{H}^m$ and $e^{\mathbf{H}t}$.

Find the state-transition matrix for each of the following linear systems.

9.
$$\mathbf{x}'(t) = \begin{bmatrix} 5 & -2 \\ 2 & 1 \end{bmatrix} \mathbf{x}(t)$$

10.
$$\mathbf{x}'(t) = \begin{bmatrix} 4 & 1 \\ -4 & 8 \end{bmatrix} \mathbf{x}(t)$$

11.
$$\mathbf{x}'(t) = \begin{bmatrix} 4 & 1 \\ -8 & 8 \end{bmatrix} \mathbf{x}(t)$$

12.
$$\mathbf{x}'(t) = \begin{bmatrix} 8 & -3 \\ 16 & -8 \end{bmatrix} \mathbf{x}(t)$$

13.
$$\mathbf{x}'(t) = \begin{bmatrix} 1 & 1 & 1 \\ 2 & 1 & -1 \\ 0 & -1 & 1 \end{bmatrix} \mathbf{x}(t)$$

14.
$$\mathbf{x}'(t) = \begin{bmatrix} -1 & 1 & 4 \\ 3 & 1 & -4 \\ -1 & 0 & 3 \end{bmatrix} \mathbf{x}(t)$$

15.
$$\mathbf{x}'(t) = \begin{bmatrix} 1 & 1 & 1 \\ 1 & 1 & 1 \\ 1 & 1 & 1 \end{bmatrix} \mathbf{x}(t)$$

16.
$$\mathbf{x}'(t) = \begin{bmatrix} 4 & 2 & -2 \\ -5 & 3 & 2 \\ -2 & 4 & 1 \end{bmatrix} \mathbf{x}(t).$$

Solve each of the following nonhomogeneous linear systems using the state-transition matrix approach.

17.
$$\mathbf{x}'(t) = \begin{bmatrix} 18 & -30 \\ 10 & -17 \end{bmatrix} \mathbf{x}(t) + \begin{bmatrix} 13 \\ 8 \end{bmatrix} e^t$$

18.
$$\mathbf{x}'(t) = \begin{bmatrix} 2 & -1 \\ 3 & -2 \end{bmatrix} \mathbf{x}(t) + \begin{bmatrix} e^t \\ t \end{bmatrix}$$

19.
$$\mathbf{x}'(t) = \begin{bmatrix} 2 & -5 \\ 1 & -2 \end{bmatrix} \mathbf{x}(t) + \begin{bmatrix} -\cos t \\ \sin t \end{bmatrix}$$

20.
$$\mathbf{x}'(t) = \begin{bmatrix} 2 & -5 \\ 1 & -2 \end{bmatrix} \mathbf{x}(t) + \begin{bmatrix} \csc t \\ \sec t \end{bmatrix}$$

21.
$$\mathbf{x}'(t) = \begin{bmatrix} 2 & 1 \\ -4 & 2 \end{bmatrix} \mathbf{x}(t) + \begin{bmatrix} t \\ -1 \end{bmatrix} e^{2t}$$

22.
$$\mathbf{x}'(t) = \begin{bmatrix} 2 & -1 \\ 5 & -2 \end{bmatrix} \mathbf{x}(t) + \begin{bmatrix} \cos t \\ \sin t \end{bmatrix}$$

23.
$$\mathbf{x}'(t) = \begin{bmatrix} 1 & 1 & 1 \\ 0 & 2 & 1 \\ 0 & 0 & 3 \end{bmatrix} \mathbf{x}(t) - \begin{bmatrix} 2t \\ t+2 \\ 3t \end{bmatrix}$$

24.
$$\mathbf{x}'(t) = \begin{bmatrix} 1 & 0 & 1 \\ 0 & -2 & 0 \\ 4 & 0 & 1 \end{bmatrix} \mathbf{x}(t) + \begin{bmatrix} -3 \\ 6 \\ -4 \end{bmatrix} e^t$$

25.
$$\mathbf{x}'(t) = \begin{bmatrix} 1 & 0 & 2 \\ 0 & 1 & 0 \\ 1 & 0 & 0 \end{bmatrix} \mathbf{x}(t) + \begin{bmatrix} 1 \\ 1 \\ 1 \end{bmatrix} e^t, \quad \mathbf{x}(0) = \begin{bmatrix} 4 \\ 2 \\ 0 \end{bmatrix}$$

6.10   INITIAL VALUE GREEN'S FUNCTIONS

The Green's function for an ODE is of fundamental importance in studying the zero-state (particular) solution for an impulsive input. There are two types of Green's functions, those for initial value problems and those for boundary value problems (which you have seen in Chapters 4 and 5). Both are related to the method of variation of parameters. This section will deal exclusively with initial value Green's functions.

The nonhomogeneous vector ODE can be written in the form

$$\mathbf{x}'(t) = \mathbf{A}(t)\mathbf{x}(t) + \mathbf{b}(t). \tag{6.66}$$

The zero-state solution is

$$\mathbf{x}_p(t) = \int_{t_0}^{t} \mathbf{\Phi}(t, \tau)\mathbf{b}(\tau)\, d\tau, \tag{6.67}$$

where $\boldsymbol{\Phi}(t, \tau)$ is the state-transition matrix for the system. We know that $\boldsymbol{\Phi}(t, \tau)$ is the unique solution to the initial value problem

$$\frac{d}{dt}\boldsymbol{\Phi}(t, \tau) = \mathbf{A}(t)\boldsymbol{\Phi}(t, \tau), \quad \boldsymbol{\Phi}(t, t) = \mathbf{I} \text{ for fixed } t.$$

This allows us to solve (6.66) for any input $\mathbf{b}(t)$ once $\boldsymbol{\Phi}(t, \tau)$ is known.

DEFINITION 6.8 *The* **initial value Green's function**, $\mathbf{G}(t, \tau)$, *is the solution of*

$$\frac{d}{dt}\mathbf{G}(t, \tau) = \mathbf{A}(t)\mathbf{G}(t, \tau) + \mathbf{I}\delta(t - \tau), \tag{6.68}$$

for which $\mathbf{G}(t, \tau) = \mathbf{0}$ *for* $t < \tau$, *i.e.,* $\mathbf{G}(t, \tau)$ *is causal.*

If we integrate the defining equation (6.68) on t from $\tau-$ to $\tau+$, we find

$$\int_{\tau-}^{\tau+} \frac{d}{dt}\mathbf{G}(t, \tau)\, dt = \mathbf{G}(\tau+, \tau) - \mathbf{G}(\tau-, \tau) = \int_{\tau-}^{\tau+} \mathbf{A}(t)\mathbf{G}(t, \tau)\, dt + \mathbf{I}.$$

By causality $\mathbf{G}(\tau-, \tau) = \mathbf{0}$, and the integral on the right will be zero if both $\mathbf{A}(t)$ and $\mathbf{G}(t, \tau)$ are continuous, which we shall assume they are. This leaves us with the initial condition

$$\mathbf{G}(\tau+, \tau) = \mathbf{I}. \tag{6.69}$$

For $t > \tau$, the solution of (6.68) is

$$\mathbf{G}(t, \tau) = \boldsymbol{\Phi}(t, \tau).$$

Hence we may conclude that

$$\mathbf{G}(t, \tau) = \boldsymbol{\Phi}(t, \tau)u(t - \tau), \tag{6.70}$$

where $u(t - \tau)$ is the unit step *turning on* at $t = \tau$. As you can see, the initial value Green's function is nothing more than the state-transition matrix turned on at $t = \tau$. Nevertheless, it provides an alternative approach to obtaining (6.67).

Multiply (6.68) by $\mathbf{b}(t)$, which can be brought inside the derivative with respect to t as

$$\frac{d}{dt}[\mathbf{G}(t, \tau)\mathbf{b}(\tau)] = \mathbf{A}(t)\mathbf{G}(t, \tau)\mathbf{b}(\tau) + \mathbf{I}b(\tau)\delta(t - \tau).$$

Now integrate this with respect to t:

$$\frac{d}{dt}\left[\int_{-\infty}^{\infty} \mathbf{G}(t, \tau)\mathbf{b}(\tau)\, d\tau\right] = \mathbf{A}(t)\int_{-\infty}^{\infty} \mathbf{G}(t, \tau)\mathbf{b}(\tau)\, d\tau + \mathbf{I}\int_{-\infty}^{\infty} b(\tau)\delta(t - \tau)\, d\tau.$$

From the properties of the δ-function, it follows that

$$\frac{d}{dt}\left[\int_{-\infty}^{\infty} \mathbf{G}(t, \tau)\mathbf{b}(\tau)\, d\tau\right] = \mathbf{A}(t)\int_{-\infty}^{\infty} \mathbf{G}(t, \tau)\mathbf{b}(\tau)\, d\tau + \mathbf{b}(t).$$

Comparing this with (6.66), we are led to the conclusion

$$\mathbf{x}_p(t) = \int_{-\infty}^{\infty} \mathbf{G}(t,\tau)\mathbf{b}(\tau)\,d\tau. \tag{6.71}$$

Inserting the expression from (6.70), $\mathbf{G}(t,\tau) = \mathbf{\Phi}(t,\tau)u(t-\tau)$, leads to

$$\mathbf{x}_p(t) = \int_{-\infty}^{t} \mathbf{\Phi}(t,\tau)\mathbf{b}(\tau)\,d\tau. \tag{6.72}$$

Thus we have an explicit expression for the particular solution as an integral of the forcing function and no dependence on the initial time t_0.

It will be very useful to apply this to the scalar equation

$$L[G(t,\tau)] := G^{(n)} + p_{n-1}(t)G^{(n-1)} + \cdots + p_1(t)G' + p_0(t)G = \delta(t-\tau),$$

and put it into standard matrix form,

$$\frac{d}{dt}\begin{bmatrix} G \\ G' \\ G'' \\ \vdots \\ G^{(n-1)} \end{bmatrix} = \begin{bmatrix} 0 & 1 & 0 & \cdots & & 0 \\ 0 & 0 & 1 & \ddots & & \vdots \\ \vdots & \vdots & \ddots & \ddots & & 0 \\ 0 & 0 & \cdots & 0 & & 1 \\ -p_0 & -p_1 & \cdots & -p_{n-2} & -p_{n-1} \end{bmatrix}\begin{bmatrix} G \\ G' \\ G'' \\ \vdots \\ G^{(n-1)} \end{bmatrix} + \begin{bmatrix} 0 \\ 0 \\ \vdots \\ 0 \\ \delta(t-\tau) \end{bmatrix}.$$

Then we see that $\mathbf{G} := [G; G'; G''; \ldots; G^{(n-1)}]$ must satisfy the following initial conditions (because of its causality)

$$G = G' = G'' = \cdots = G^{(n-2)} = 0, \; G^{(n-1)} = 1 \text{ for } t = \tau \text{ with } t \text{ fixed},$$

together with the original ODE, $L[G(t,\tau)] = \delta(t-\tau)$.

The scalar function $G(t,\tau)$ is frequently called the **impulse response** of the linear differential operator $L[\cdot]$. The initial conditions require G to have its first $n-2$ derivatives continuous and its $(n-1)^{st}$ derivative discontinuous at $t=0$.

■ **EXAMPLE 6.45** For the underdamped harmonic oscillator

$$m\ddot{x} + b\dot{x} + kx = F(t),$$

the complementary solution is

$$x(t) = c_1 e^{-\beta t}\cos\omega_1 t + c_2 e^{-\beta t}\sin\omega_1 t,$$

where

$$\beta = \frac{b}{2m} \quad \text{and} \quad \omega_1^2 = \frac{k}{m} - \beta^2.$$

The impulse response satisfies

$$mG''(t, \tau) + bG'(t, \tau) + kG(t, \tau) = \delta(t - \tau).$$

For $t = \tau$, we may use the form of $x(t)$ given above because the equation is homogeneous. The initial conditions are $x(0) = 0$ and $\dot{x}(0) = 1$, resulting in the following two equations for c_1 and c_2:

$$c_1 e^{-\beta\tau} \cos \omega_1 \tau + c_2 e^{-\beta\tau} \sin \omega_1 \tau = 0,$$

$$c_1 \left(\beta \cos \omega_1 \tau + \omega_1 \sin \omega_1 \tau \right) e^{-\beta\tau} + c_2 \left(-\beta \sin \omega_1 \tau + \omega_1 \cos \omega_1 \tau \right) e^{-\beta\tau} = 1.$$

Solving, we find

$$c_1 = e^{-\beta\tau} \frac{\sin \omega_1 \tau}{\omega_1}, \quad c_2 = -e^{-\beta\tau} \frac{\cos \omega_1 \tau}{\omega_1},$$

so that the impulse response is

$$G(t, \tau) = e^{-\beta(t-\tau)} \frac{\sin \omega_1 (t - \tau)}{\omega_1} u(t - \tau).$$

Therefore a solution to the forced underdamped harmonic oscillator equation $m\ddot{x} + b\dot{x} + kx = F(t)$ can be written as

$$x_{\mathrm{p}}(t) = \int_0^t F(\tau) e^{-\beta(t-\tau)} \frac{\sin \omega_1 (t - \tau)}{\omega_1} \, d\tau.$$

■ ■ ■

For time invariant (constant coefficient) scalar systems, we must have

$$G(t, \tau) = G(t - \tau, 0),$$

so that G is only a function of the time difference $(t - \tau)$, as is the case in the last example. We may thus simplify the problem of finding the initial value Green's function by setting $\tau = 0$. Also, for the time invariant case, equation (6.71) takes the form

$$\mathbf{x}_{\mathrm{p}}(t) = \int_{-\infty}^t \mathbf{G}(t - \tau, 0)\mathbf{b}(\tau) \, d\tau,$$

which is the so-called **convolution integral**.

■ **EXAMPLE 6.46** Find the initial value Green's function for the fourth order linear differential operator

$$L[y(x)] := y^{(iv)}(x) - y(x).$$

Solution: We know the complementary solution is

$$G(x, 0) = c_1 \cos x + c_2 \sin x + c_3 \cosh x + c_4 \sinh x.$$

Applying the initial conditions

$$G = G' = G'' = 0, \quad G''' = 1 \text{ at } t = 0,$$

we find

$$c_1 = c_3 = 0 \quad \text{and} \quad c_2 = c_4 = \frac{1}{2},$$

so that

$$G(x, 0) = \frac{1}{2} (\sin x + \sinh x) \, u(x)$$

and

$$G(x, c) = \frac{1}{2} (\sin(x - \xi) + \sinh(x - \xi)) \, u(x - \xi).$$

Thus the zero-state solution of $y^{(iv)} - y = f(x)$ can be written as

$$y_{\mathrm{p}}(x) = \frac{1}{2} \int_0^x (\sin(x - \xi) + \sinh(x - \xi)) \, f(\xi) \, d\xi.$$

■ ■ ■

Warning: The convolution integrals generated by the Green's function solution for the zero-state problem are seldom easy to evaluate, even for computers (which are most certainly *not* infallible!)!

■ **EXAMPLE 6.47**   Find the initial value Green's function for the system

$$\mathbf{x}'(t) = \begin{bmatrix} 1 & 1 \\ 0 & 2 \end{bmatrix} \mathbf{x}(t).$$

Solution: The eigenpairs are

$$\lambda = 1, \ \mathbf{x}_1 = [1; 0]; \quad \lambda = 2, \ \mathbf{x}_2 = [1; 1].$$

The state-transition matrix is $\boldsymbol{\Phi}(t, \tau) = \mathbf{X}(t) \mathbf{X}^{-1}(\tau)$. Thus

$$\mathbf{X}(t) = \begin{bmatrix} e^t & e^{2t} \\ 0 & e^{2t} \end{bmatrix} \ \Rightarrow \ \boldsymbol{\Phi}(t, \tau) = \begin{bmatrix} e^{t-\tau} & e^{2(t-\tau)} - e^{t-\tau} \\ 0 & e^{2(t-\tau)} \end{bmatrix}.$$

Finally, the initial value Green's function is

$$\mathbf{G}(t, \tau) = \boldsymbol{\Phi}(t, \tau) u(t - \tau) = \begin{bmatrix} e^{t-\tau} & e^{2(t-\tau)} - e^{t-\tau} \\ 0 & e^{2(t-\tau)} \end{bmatrix} u(t - \tau).$$

■ ■ ■

6.10.1 Exercise Set

For each of the following ODE's, find the initial value Green's function.

1. $v'' + \omega^2 v = 0$

2. $v'' + 4v' + 4v = 0$

3. $v'' + 4v' + 5v = 0$

4. $v'' + 4v' + 3v = 0$

5. $v''' - v' = 0$

6. $v''' + 3v'' + 3v' + v = 0$

7. $y^{(iv)} - 2y'' + y = 0$

8. $y^{(iv)} - 5y'' + 4y = 0$

9.
$$\mathbf{x}'(t) = \begin{bmatrix} 3 & -2 \\ 4 & -1 \end{bmatrix} \mathbf{x}(t)$$

10.
$$\mathbf{x}'(t) = \begin{bmatrix} 3 & -4 \\ 1 & -1 \end{bmatrix} \mathbf{x}(t)$$

11.
$$\mathbf{x}'(t) = \begin{bmatrix} 1 & -3 & 3 \\ -3 & 1 & 3 \\ 3 & -3 & 1 \end{bmatrix} \mathbf{x}(t)$$

12.
$$\mathbf{x}'(t) = \begin{bmatrix} 1 & 1 & 1 \\ 2 & 1 & -1 \\ 0 & -1 & 1 \end{bmatrix} \mathbf{x}(t)$$

13.
$$\mathbf{x}'(t) = \begin{bmatrix} 0 & 1 & 1 & 1 \\ 1 & 0 & 1 & 1 \\ 1 & 1 & 0 & 1 \\ 1 & 1 & 1 & 0 \end{bmatrix} \mathbf{x}(t)$$

14.
$$\mathbf{x}'(t) = \begin{bmatrix} 1 & 0 & 1 & 0 \\ 0 & 0 & 0 & 1 \\ 0 & 0 & 1 & 0 \\ 0 & -1 & 0 & 0 \end{bmatrix} \mathbf{x}(t)$$

6.11 PHASE PLANE ANALYSIS OF LINEAR SYSTEMS

We will study second order linear ODE's by using the phase plane, which is the xv-coordinate plane with $v = \dot{x}$. This is related to the standard matrix form of the typical second order ODE. Let's begin with a simple example, the harmonic oscillator.

■ **EXAMPLE 6.48** If $x(t)$ is the displacement of the simple harmonic oscillator as a function of time, then the unforced equation of motion is $\ddot{x} + \omega^2 x = 0$. In order to bring the velocity $v = \dot{x}$ into the picture, we can make a change of independent variables from t to x as follows:

$$\frac{d^2 x}{dt^2} = \frac{d}{dt}\left(\frac{dx}{dt}\right) = \frac{dv}{dt} = \frac{dv}{dx}\frac{dx}{dt} = v\frac{dv}{dx}.$$

Now the second order equation for the system can be written as the first order equation

$$v\frac{dv}{dx} + \omega^2 x = 0.$$

Since ω is assumed to be constant, this equation is separable and can be easily integrated to yield

$$v\,dv + \omega^2 x\,dx = 0 \quad \Rightarrow \quad \frac{1}{2}v^2 + \frac{1}{2}\omega^2 x^2 = C.$$

To within a multiple of the mass m, we have already seen that this equation expresses the conservation of energy. We can analyze the motion by graphing the family of curves $v^2 + \omega^2 x^2 = 2C$ in the phase plane. The results are the ellipses shown in Figure 6.20.

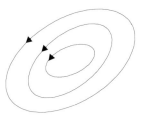

Fig. 6.20   Ellipses form the phase portraits of the harmonic oscillator equation $\ddot{x} + \omega^2 x = 0$.

Each has a semiaxis of length $\sqrt{2C}$ along x and $\sqrt{2C}/\omega$ along v. This is the so-called **phase portrait of the trajectory**

$$x(t) = A\cos(\omega t - \alpha).$$

As the mass follows this trajectory, it traces out its phase portrait. Parametrically the trajectory is given by

$$x(t) = A\cos(\omega t - \alpha)$$
$$v(t) = -\omega A\sin(\omega t - \alpha).$$

With $A > 0$ the motion starts at $t = 0$, with $x = A\cos(-\alpha) = A\cos a$. As time increases, the particle moves in the counterclockwise direction.   ■ ■ ■

If there were (over)damping present, then the equation of motion in terms of the independent variable x and dependent variable v would be

$$v\frac{dv}{dx} + 2\beta v + \omega^2 x = 0.$$

The equation is neither separable nor linear and cannot be simply integrated. Instead, we could look at the equation of the trajectory

$$x(t) = Ae^{-\beta t}\cos(\omega_1 t - \alpha),$$

where $\omega_1^2 = \omega^2 - \beta^2$. Graphing x versus v, we would have a spiral converging toward the origin in the phase plane as shown in Figure 6.21.

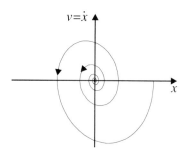

Fig. 6.21 Phase portrait of the damped harmonic oscillator $\ddot{x} + 2\beta\dot{x} + \omega^2 x = 0$.

Many linear and nonlinear systems can be fruitfully studied by analyzing their phase portraits. A qualitative picture of their behavior can be gotten by looking at the particular curves in the phase plane. Trajectories, alternatively called **paths** or **orbits**, are the curves along which the motion proceeds including the time dependence. Certain points can help to characterize these curves.

Points of equilibrium, or **fixed points**, of a system

$$\dot{\mathbf{x}} = \mathbf{f}(t, \mathbf{x}) \tag{6.73}$$

are the solutions $\mathbf{x}(t)$ of the system of equations $\mathbf{f}(t, \mathbf{x}) = \mathbf{0}$, essentially points where the speed is zero. The fixed point(s) can be a function of time. If the force vector function is independent of time, the system

$$\dot{\mathbf{x}} = \mathbf{f}(\mathbf{x}) \tag{6.74}$$

is said to be autonomous and the fixed points do not change with time. For autonomous systems, fixed points are solutions of the system. In the case of the homogeneous linear system

$$\dot{\mathbf{x}} = \mathbf{A}\mathbf{x}, \tag{6.75}$$

the origin is the only fixed point whenever $\mathbf{A}$ is nonsingular, which we will assume to be the case.

A system can have a finite or infinite number of fixed points. For instance, $\ddot{x} + \sin x = 0$ has fixed points at $x = n\pi$, $n = -\infty : \infty$, and $v = 0$.

Let's concentrate for the moment on a first order 2×2 linear system (6.75). Its qualitative behavior is completely determined by the eigenvalues of the matrix $\mathbf{A}$. There are only five possibilities:

    (a) two distinct eigenvalues of the same sign;

    (b) two eigenvalues of opposite signs;

    (c) one repeated eigenvalue with a single eigenvector;

    (d) a complex conjugate pair of eigenvalues with nonzero real parts;

(e) a complex conjugate pair of pure imaginary eigenvalues.

Let's look at each case separately.

(a) When both eigenvalues λ and μ are of the same sign, the solution can be written in the form

$$\mathbf{x}(t) = c_1 \mathbf{x}_{(1)} e^{\lambda t} + c_2 \mathbf{x}_{(2)} e^{\mu t},$$

where $\mathbf{x}_{(1)}$ and $\mathbf{x}_{(2)}$ are the eigenvectors corresponding to λ and μ, respectively. Thus all components of solutions $\mathbf{x}(t)$ are either increasing or decreasing functions of time. Such a fixed point is called a **node**. When both eigenvalues are positive, the solutions are increasing away from the origin and the node is unstable whereas when they are negative, the solutions are decreasing toward the origin and the node is stable. The two possible phase portraits are shown in Figure 6.22.

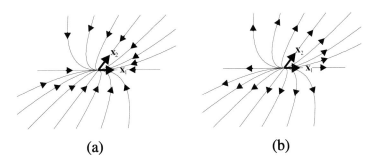

(a)   (b)

Fig. 6.22   Stable and unstable nodes along the eigenvectors $\mathbf{x}_1$ and $\mathbf{x}_2$.

(b) When the eigenvalues have opposite signs, say α and $-\beta$, with α and β both positive, the solution looks like

$$\mathbf{x}(t) = c_1 \mathbf{x}_{(1)} e^{\alpha t} + c_2 \mathbf{x}_{(2)} e^{-\beta t}.$$

Now a solution moving parallel to x_1 will increase with time, while that moving parallel to x_2 will decrease. The lines through the origin along the eigenvectors separate the solution curves into distinct classes, and for this reason each line is referred to as a **separatrix**. Such a fixed point is called a **saddle**. Figure 6.23 shows an example of this.

(c) When we have the repeated root λ with eigenvector $\mathbf{x}_{(1)}$ and cyclic vector $\mathbf{z}$, for which $(\mathbf{A} - \lambda \mathbf{I})\mathbf{z} = \mathbf{x}_{(1)}$, the solution is $\mathbf{x}(t) = c_1 \mathbf{x}_{(1)} e^{\lambda t} + c_2 \left(\mathbf{x}_{(1)} t + \mathbf{z} \right) e^{\lambda t}$. All trajectories will be asymptotic to the line through the origin parallel to the vector $\mathbf{x}_1$. The phase portrait is again a node, called an **improper node**, being stable or unstable as λ is negative or positive. The only difference between this and a regular node is that there may be a reversal of direction near the fixed point because of the $t e^{\lambda t}$ term. See Figure 6.24.

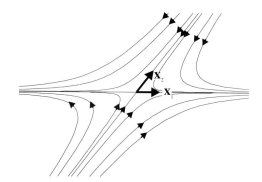

Fig. 6.23 A saddle that is increasing along one vector and decreasing along another.

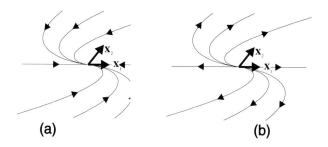

Fig. 6.24 Stable and unstable improper nodes.

(d) For complex conjugate eigenvalues with nonzero real parts, the solution vector is

$$\mathbf{x}(t) = c_1 e^{at} \left[\mathbf{u} \cos bt - \mathbf{v} \sin bt \right] + c_2 e^{at} \left[u \sin bt + v \cos bt \right],$$

where $\mathbf{x}_{(+)} := \mathbf{u} + i\mathbf{v}$ is the eigenvector corresponding to the eigenvalue $\lambda_+ = a + ib$. Were we to change to the $\{\mathbf{u}, \mathbf{v}\}$ basis and introduce the usual polar coordinates, we'd find that the original system is transformed to the new system

$$\dot{r}(t) = ar(t) \quad \text{and} \quad \dot{\theta}(t) = b.$$

This can be integrated to yield

$$r(t) = r_0 e^{at} \quad \text{and} \quad \theta(t) = bt + \theta_0,$$

which is an exponential spiral. Such a fixed point is called a **focus**. If $a > 0$, the trajectory spirals outward and we have an **unstable**, or **repelling**, **focus**; when $a < 0$, it spirals inward and we have a **stable**, or **attracting**, **focus**. Figure 6.25 shows this.

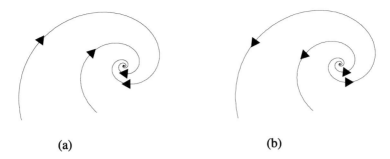

(a)   (b)

Fig. 6.25   A stable and an unstable focus.

(e) The only difference in the solution when the real part of the eigenvalues is zero
is that now $\dot{r} = 0 \Rightarrow r(t) = r_0$. Such a fixed point is called a **center** and all the
orbits are closed curves, not necessarily circles because the set $\{\mathbf{u}, \mathbf{v}\}$ need not be
orthonormal, which represent periodic motion. See Figure 6.26.

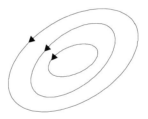

Fig. 6.26   A center.

Many ocean currents circulate about a fixed point that is a center. As plastic wastes are
discarded by coastal cities or ships at sea, they travel along closed orbits until reaching a land
mass lying in their path. The Caribbean island of Bonaire in the Lesser Antilles is one such
interrupting land mass. Beaches on the current side of the island are covered with as many as
135,000 plastic particles per square meter.

If asked to classify the origin as to the type of critical point for the 2×2 system

$$\dot{\mathbf{x}}(t) = \mathbf{A}\mathbf{x}(t) \quad \Leftrightarrow \quad \frac{d}{dt}\begin{bmatrix} x \\ v \end{bmatrix} = \begin{bmatrix} a & b \\ c & d \end{bmatrix}\begin{bmatrix} x \\ v \end{bmatrix}$$

then we would need to look at the characteristic equation for $\mathbf{A}$, which is

$$\lambda^2 - (\mathrm{tr}(\mathbf{A}))\,\lambda + \det(\mathbf{A}) = 0.$$

When $\mathbf{A}$ is real we see that if $\det(\mathbf{A}) = \det(\mathbf{PJP}^{-1}) = \det(\mathbf{J}) < 0$, where $\mathbf{J}$ is the Jordan normal form of $\mathbf{A}$, then there must be eigenvalues of opposite sign and the origin is a saddle. When $\det(\mathbf{A}) > 0$ and $\mathrm{tr}(\mathbf{A}) = 0$ there are imaginary roots and the origin is a center. Looking at the discriminant $(\mathrm{tr}(\mathbf{A}))^2 - 4\det(\mathbf{A})$ we see that when it is negative and $\mathrm{tr}(\mathbf{A})$ is not zero, there will be a focus. When it is positive or zero, there will be a node. Whether the node is a repeller or an attractor depends on whether $\mathrm{tr}(\mathbf{A})$ is positive or negative. In summary: if λ and μ are the eigenvalues, we have the following possibilities:

(a) λ and μ real with opposite signs: saddle.

(b) $\lambda = \mu$ equal eigenvalues

   i. $\lambda > 0$: unstable improper node.

   ii. $\lambda < 0$: stable improper node.

(c) λ and μ real, unequal, and of the same sign

   i. $\lambda, \mu > 0$: unstable node.

   ii. $\lambda, \mu < 0$: stable node.

(d) λ and μ are complex

   i. $\mathrm{Re}(\lambda) > 0$: unstable focus.

   ii. $\mathrm{Re}(\lambda) = 0$: center.

   iii. $\mathrm{Re}(\lambda) < 0$: stable focus.

▪ **EXAMPLE 6.49**   Classify the origin for each of the following linear systems.

(a) The system

$$\begin{aligned} \dot{x} &= 2x + v, \\ \dot{v} &= x + 2v \end{aligned}$$

has the characteristic equation $\lambda^2 - 4\lambda + 3 = (\lambda - 1)(\lambda - 3) \Rightarrow \lambda = 1, 3$. Thus the origin is an unstable node.

(b) For the system

$$\begin{aligned} \dot{x} &= 3x + 4v, \\ \dot{v} &= 4x + 3v, \end{aligned}$$

the characteristic equation is $\lambda^2 - \lambda + 25 = (\lambda - 3)^2 + 16 \Rightarrow \lambda = 3 \pm 4i$. Thus the origin is an unstable focus.

(c) For the system

$$\begin{aligned} \dot{x} &= 3x + 4v, \\ \dot{v} &= 4x - 3v, \end{aligned}$$

the characteristic equation is $\lambda^2 - 25 = (\lambda - 5)(\lambda + 5) \Rightarrow \lambda = \pm 5$. Thus the origin is a saddle.

(d) For the system
$$\begin{aligned} \dot{x} &= 3x - 5v, \\ \dot{v} &= 5x - 3v, \end{aligned}$$

the characteristic equation is $\lambda^2 + 16 = (\lambda + 4i)(\lambda - 4i) \Rightarrow \lambda = \pm 4i$. Thus the origin is a center.

(e) For the system
$$\begin{aligned} \dot{x} &= -3x + v, \\ \dot{v} &= x - 3v, \end{aligned}$$

the characteristic equation is $\lambda^2 + 6\lambda + 8 = (\lambda + 2)(\lambda + 4) \Rightarrow \lambda = -2, -4$. Thus the origin is a stable node.   ■ ■ ■

Were we to look at higher dimensional linear systems, the classification of the origin as a fixed point would depend on the possible Jordan normal forms of the coefficient matrix $\mathbf{A}$. All 1×1 or 2×2 blocks would have the same classification scheme as a two dimensional system. The only difference would be for the higher dimensional blocks. If the size of a block were $\nu \times \nu$, then the solutions would contain terms of the form $t^k e^{\lambda t}$, $k = 0 : \nu$. The overall long term behavior would remain the same; systems whose base response is decreasing to zero would also decrease to zero, and similarly for responses that are increasing.

6.11.1 *Exercise Set*

Classify the fixed point at the origin for each of the following linear systems.

1.
$$\dot{\mathbf{x}} = \begin{bmatrix} 3 & -2 \\ 4 & -1 \end{bmatrix} \mathbf{x}$$

2.
$$\dot{\mathbf{x}} = \begin{bmatrix} -1 & -4 \\ 1 & -1 \end{bmatrix} \mathbf{x}$$

3.
$$\dot{\mathbf{x}} = \begin{bmatrix} 3 & -4 \\ 1 & -1 \end{bmatrix} \mathbf{x}$$

4.
$$\dot{\mathbf{x}} = \begin{bmatrix} 4 & 1 \\ -1 & 2 \end{bmatrix} \mathbf{x}$$

5.
$$\dot{\mathbf{x}} = \begin{bmatrix} -3 & 3 \\ 2 & 2 \end{bmatrix} \mathbf{x}$$

6.
$$\dot{\mathbf{x}} = \begin{bmatrix} -4 & 5 \\ -1 & -2 \end{bmatrix} \mathbf{x}$$

7.
$$\dot{\mathbf{x}} = \begin{bmatrix} 1 & -3 & 3 \\ -3 & 1 & 3 \\ 3 & -3 & 1 \end{bmatrix} \mathbf{x}$$

8.
$$\dot{\mathbf{x}} = \begin{bmatrix} 1 & 1 & 1 \\ 2 & 1 & -1 \\ 0 & -1 & 1 \end{bmatrix} \mathbf{x}$$

9. Construct a 2×2 system for which the origin is an unstable node and the eigenvectors are orthogonal.

10. Explain what happens to the origin when the coefficient matrix $\mathbf{A}$ for the 2×2 system is singular. What is the shape of the trajectories?

11. Construct a plot in the td-plane, where t is the trace of $\mathbf{A}$ and d is its determinant, showing the regions of stability and instability. Indicate the regions where the origin is a node, a center, a focus, or a saddle.

12. Suppose the 2×2 linear system takes the form $\mathbf{M}\dot{\mathbf{x}} = \mathbf{A}\mathbf{x}$, where the matrix $\mathbf{M}$ may be singular. How might that change the stability and the trajectories?

6.12 INTRODUCTION TO CONTROLLABILITY AND OBSERVABILITY

The general system problem consists of a dynamic equation relating the state, $\mathbf{x}(t) \in \mathbb{C}^n$, of the system to the input, $\mathbf{u}(t)$, and a measurement equation relating the output, $\mathbf{y}(t) \in \mathbb{C}^m$ with $m < n$, to the state and the input. The so-called **state space formulation** of the system equations is

$$\begin{aligned} \mathbf{x}'(t) &= \mathbf{A}(t)\mathbf{x}(t) + \mathbf{B}(t)\mathbf{u}(t), \\ \mathbf{y}(t) &= \mathbf{C}(t)\mathbf{x}(t) + \mathbf{D}(t)\mathbf{u}(t). \end{aligned} \tag{6.76}$$

The first vector equation is called the **process model** and the second is the **measurement model** for the system.

There are several fundamental questions relating to the two model system equations (6.76).

1. **Controllability Question:** Can any initial state $\mathbf{x}(t_0)$ be transformed to any desired state x_1 in a finite time using an appropriate input $\mathbf{u}(t)$? More generally, to which states can an initial state be driven by varying the input?

2. **Observability Question:** Given the value of the input $\mathbf{u}(t)$ and output $\mathbf{y}(t)$ for all $t \in [t_0, t_1]$, is it possible to determine the initial state vector $\mathbf{x}(t_0)$?

3. **Stability Question:** Under what conditions is the solution of (6.76) asymptotically stable, meaning that the state vector approaches $\mathbf{0}$ with increasing time?

4. **Stabilization Question:** Does there exist a linear feedback signal, defined by $\mathbf{u}(t) = \mathbf{K}(t)\mathbf{y}(t)$, that will stabilize the system?

DEFINITION 6.9 *Any state that can be reached from the zero initial state is said to be* **controllable**. *If all states are controllable, then the system is* **controllable**; *otherwise, the system is* **uncontrollable**. *The state* $\mathbf{x}_0$ *is* **observable** *at a time* t_0 *if, for any later time* t_1, *knowledge of both the input* $\mathbf{u}(t)$ *and the output* $\mathbf{y}(t)$ *throughout the interval* $[t_0, t_1]$ *allows us to completely determine the initial state* $\mathbf{x}_0$. *If all initial states are observable, then the system is* **observable**; *otherwise, it is* **unobservable**.

6.12.1 *Controllability*

Controllability of a state has nothing to do with the output model. To simplify matters, let's look at a time independent system with a single input of the form

$$\mathbf{x}'(t) = \mathbf{A}\mathbf{x}(t) + \mathbf{b}u(t).$$

(Note: $u(t)$ is *not* a unit step here.) Since the system is time independent we can write the zero state response in terms of the matrix exponential:

$$\mathbf{x}(t) = \int_0^t e^{\mathbf{A}(t-\tau)}\mathbf{b}u(\tau)\,d\tau.$$

We can further simplify things if we shift the argument of the matrix exponential by setting $\alpha := t - \tau$, so that

$$\mathbf{x}(t) = \int_0^t e^{\mathbf{A}\alpha}\mathbf{b}u(t-\alpha)\,d\alpha. \tag{6.77}$$

Now write the series expansion for the exponential

$$e^{\mathbf{A}\alpha} = \sum_{k=0}^{\infty} \frac{1}{k!}\mathbf{A}^k\alpha^k.$$

We know from the Cayley-Hamilton Theorem that no matter what the eigenvalue structure of $\mathbf{A}$ is, we can always write any higher power of $\mathbf{A}$ in terms of $\mathbf{I} = \mathbf{A}^0$, $\mathbf{A}^1$, $\mathbf{A}^2$,..., and $\mathbf{A}^{n-1}$ by using the characteristic polynomial. Thus it is possible to reassemble this uniformly convergent series into only n terms as

$$e^{\mathbf{A}\alpha} = \sum_{k=0}^{n-1} f_k(\alpha)\mathbf{A}^k, \tag{6.78}$$

where the explicit form of the functions $f_k(\alpha)$ is determined by the eigenvalue structure of $\mathbf{A}$. We are assured that the subset $\{f_k(\alpha)\}$ of nonzero functions (the sum may not go all the way to $n-1$ when there are multiple eigenvalues) is linearly independent on the real line.

Inserting (6.78) into (6.77) yields

$$\mathbf{x}(t) = \sum_{k=0}^{n-1} \mathbf{A}^k\mathbf{b} \int_0^t f_k(\alpha)\,u(t-\alpha)\,d\alpha.$$

At any given time t the integral is a scalar that depends on the input $u(t)$. Thus we have written the state vector as a linear combination of the n column vectors

$$\mathbf{b}, \mathbf{A}\mathbf{b}, \mathbf{A}^2\mathbf{b}, \ldots, \mathbf{A}^{n-1}\mathbf{b}.$$

The set spanned by these vectors is the linear subspace of the space of all controllable vectors. That space will be all of $\mathbb{C}^n$ if and only if

$$\text{rank}[\mathbf{b}, \mathbf{A}\mathbf{b}, \ldots, \mathbf{A}^{n-1}\mathbf{b}] = n.$$

This result can be generalized to a multiple input system in the obvious way.

6.12.2 Observability

The question of observability can be answered using a similar argument. This time we must concentrate on the output equation

$$\mathbf{y}(t) = \mathbf{C}\mathbf{x}(t) + \mathbf{D}\mathbf{u}(t).$$

For a time independent system we can write this as

$$\mathbf{y}(t) = \mathbf{C}e^{\mathbf{A}t}\mathbf{x}(t_0) + \mathbf{C}\int_0^t e^{\mathbf{A}(t-\tau)}\mathbf{B}\mathbf{u}(\tau)\,d\tau + \mathbf{D}\mathbf{u}(\tau).$$

Since the input and output are assumed known, they can be combined into a single known vector $\mathbf{z}(t)$, which can be defined to be

$$\mathbf{z}(t) = \mathbf{y}(t) - \mathbf{C}\int_0^t e^{\mathbf{A}(t-\tau)}\mathbf{B}\mathbf{u}(\tau)\,d\tau - \mathbf{D}\mathbf{u}(\tau).$$

Then the initial state $\mathbf{x}(t_0)$ will be observable if and only if we can solve the equation

$$\mathbf{z}(t) = \mathbf{C}e^{\mathbf{A}t}\mathbf{x}(t_0) \tag{6.79}$$

for $\mathbf{x}(t_0)$. This will be possible only if the columns of $\mathbf{C}e^{\mathbf{A}t}$ are linearly independent, meaning that the matrix is of full rank. Once again we can rewrite the matrix exponential so the computation will devolve on at most n simple powers of $\mathbf{A}$ instead of all possible powers:

$$\mathbf{C}e^{\mathbf{A}t} = \sum_{k=0}^{n-1} f_k(t)\mathbf{C}\mathbf{A}^k.$$

Because we have $\mathbf{C}$ premultiplying $\mathbf{A}^k$, the rows of $\mathbf{C}\mathbf{A}^k$ determine whether or not we can solve equation (6.79). The matrix

$$[\mathbf{C}; \mathbf{C}\mathbf{A}; \mathbf{C}\mathbf{A}^2; \ldots; \mathbf{C}\mathbf{A}^{n-1}]$$

must be of full rank for the state to be observable. This is true for any initial state, so that this criterion determines observability of the system.

6.12.3 Stability

The question of stability can be answered fairly easily since we know that the matrix exponential can be written as a linear combination of polynomials in $\mathbf{A}$ times exponential functions $\exp(\lambda_k t)$, where the λ_k are the eigenvalues of $\mathbf{A}$. Using elementary calculus we can see that a zero state solution will approach zero if and only if all eigenvalues have negative real parts.

The question of stabilizability is beyond the scope of this book.

The following theorem summarizes all the previous results for the special case of time invariant systems.

THEOREM 6.19 *For the time invariant system governed by the system equations*

$$\begin{aligned}
\mathbf{x}'(t) &= \mathbf{A}(t)\mathbf{x}(t) + \mathbf{B}(t)\mathbf{u}(t), \\
\mathbf{y}(t) &= \mathbf{C}(t)\mathbf{x}(t) + \mathbf{D}(t)\mathbf{u}(t),
\end{aligned}$$

where $\mathbf{A} \in \mathbb{C}_n^n$, $\mathbf{B} \in \mathbb{C}_k^n$, $\mathbf{C} \in \mathbb{C}_n^m$, $\mathbf{D} \in \mathbb{C}_m^k$, *with* $m < n$, *the system is*

(a) *controllable if and only if* $\operatorname{rank}[\mathbf{B}, \mathbf{A}\mathbf{B}, \mathbf{A}^2\mathbf{B}, \dots, \mathbf{A}^{n-1}\mathbf{B}] = n$;

(b) *observable if and only if* $\operatorname{rank}[\mathbf{C}; \mathbf{C}\mathbf{A}; \mathbf{C}\mathbf{A}^2; \dots; \mathbf{C}\mathbf{A}^{n-1}] = m$;

(c) *asymptotically stable if and only if all the eigenvalues of the matrix* $\mathbf{A}$ *have negative real parts.* □

■ **EXAMPLE 6.50** The circuit drawn in Figure 6.27

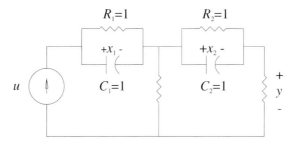

Fig. 6.27

has current input $u(t)$, and the state variables are the voltages across the capacitors as drawn. The output is $y(t)$, and the voltage across the resistance $R_4 = 1\Omega$. Find the state equations and determine if it is controllable, observable, and/or stable.

Solution: The state equation is

$$\mathbf{x}'(t) = \begin{bmatrix} -1 & 0 \\ 0 & -1 \end{bmatrix} \mathbf{x}(t) + \begin{bmatrix} 1 \\ \frac{1}{2} \end{bmatrix} u(t).$$

The output equation is

$$y(t) = \begin{bmatrix} 0, \dfrac{3}{2} \end{bmatrix} \mathbf{x}(t) + \frac{1}{2} u(t).$$

The controllability test matrix is

$$[\mathbf{B}, \mathbf{A}\mathbf{B}] = \begin{bmatrix} 1 & -1 \\ \frac{1}{2} & -\frac{1}{2} \end{bmatrix},$$

which clearly has rank one. Thus the system is *not controllable.* The observability test matrix is

$$\begin{bmatrix} \mathbf{C} \\ \mathbf{C}\mathbf{A} \end{bmatrix} = \begin{bmatrix} 0 & 0 \\ \frac{3}{2} & -\frac{3}{2} \end{bmatrix},$$

which also has rank one. The system is *not observable.*

Since $\mathbf{A} = -\mathbf{I}$, both eigenvalues of $\mathbf{A}$ are -1, and the system is asymptotically stable.

■ ■ ■

■ **EXAMPLE 6.51** Getting back to the problem of a satellite with radial and tangential thrusters (see example 6.2), we had the linearized system matrices

$$\mathbf{A} = \begin{bmatrix} 0 & 1 & 0 & 0 \\ 3\omega^2 & 0 & 0 & 2\omega \\ 0 & 0 & 0 & 1 \\ 0 & -2\omega & 0 & 0 \end{bmatrix}, \quad \mathbf{B} = \begin{bmatrix} 0 & 0 \\ 1 & 0 \\ 0 & 0 \\ 0 & 1 \end{bmatrix}.$$

The test for controllability uses $\text{rank}[\mathbf{B}, \mathbf{AB}, \mathbf{A}^2\mathbf{B}, \mathbf{A}^3\mathbf{B}]$:

$$\text{rank} \begin{bmatrix} 0 & 0 & 1 & 0 & 0 & 2\omega^2 & -\omega & 0 \\ 1 & 0 & 0 & 2\omega & -\omega^2 & 0 & 0 & -2\omega^3 \\ 0 & 0 & 0 & 1 & -2\omega^2 & 0 & 0 & -4\omega^2 \\ 0 & 1 & -2\omega & 0 & 0 & -4\omega^2 & 2\omega^3 & 0 \end{bmatrix} = 4.$$

This tells us that the system is controllable and can be driven to any given point (r_1, θ_1) using both thrusters. If the tangential thruster fails, $\mathbf{B} = [0; 1; 0; 0]$ and

$$\text{rank}[\mathbf{B}, \mathbf{AB}, \mathbf{A}^2\mathbf{B}, \mathbf{A}^3\mathbf{B}] = \text{rank} \begin{bmatrix} 0 & 1 & 0 & -\omega^2 \\ 1 & 0 & -\omega^2 & 0 \\ 0 & 0 & -2\omega & 0 \\ 0 & -2\omega & 0 & 2\omega^3 \end{bmatrix} = 3 \neq 4.$$

The system is no longer controllable. Thus, loss of the tangential thruster will prevent the satellite from reaching its specified rendezvous. When the radial thruster fails, $\mathbf{B} = [0; 0; 0; 1]$ and

$$\text{rank}[\mathbf{B}, \mathbf{AB}, \mathbf{A}^2\mathbf{B}, \mathbf{A}^3\mathbf{B}] = \begin{bmatrix} 0 & 0 & 2\omega & 0 \\ 0 & 2\omega & 0 & -2\omega^3 \\ 0 & 1 & 0 & -4\omega^2 \\ 1 & 0 & -4\omega^2 & 0 \end{bmatrix} = 4.$$

Because this reduced system is controllable, the radial thruster is irrelevant to the control of the satellite; but the tangential thruster is essential.

■ ■ ■

The following problem is a classic example used in the analysis of systems.

■ **EXAMPLE 6.52** The inverted pendulum problem involves a pendulum of mass m attached to a carriage of mass M. The distance of the carriage from a fixed reference point is measured as s to the right, and the angle of the pendulum with the vertical is θ measured positive clockwise (see Figure 6.28).

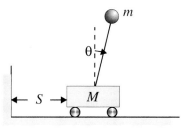

Fig. 6.28

The goal is to specify the scalar input, $u(t)$, that will keep the pendulum balanced in the vertical position. Writing $\beta := \frac{I}{mL} + L$ and $\alpha := \frac{mL}{Mb}$, the system equations can be shown to be

$$\mathbf{x}'(t) = \begin{bmatrix} 0 & 1 & 0 & 0 \\ 0 & 0 & -g & 0 \\ 0 & 0 & 0 & 1 \\ 0 & 0 & \frac{g(1+\alpha)}{\beta} & 0 \end{bmatrix} \mathbf{x}(t) + \frac{1}{m} \begin{bmatrix} 0 \\ 1 \\ 0 \\ -\frac{1}{\beta} \end{bmatrix} u(t),$$

$$\mathbf{y}(t) = \begin{bmatrix} 1 & 0 & 0 & 0 \\ 0 & 0 & 1 & 0 \end{bmatrix} \mathbf{x}(t),$$

with $\mathbf{x}(t) = [s; s'; \theta; \theta']$ and $\mathbf{y}(t) = [s; \theta]$. It will be left to the reader to show that this system is controllable and observable.   ∎ ∎ ∎

The design of an engineering system usually demands stable, controllable, and observable systems. If not stable, or at least stabilizable, the system will eventually self destruct or move out of the domain of linear operation in some way. If not controllable, once it begins there will be no way to get it to reach a preassigned state; this is an especially significant problem for a system that may have some random fluctuations that could work to prevent it from achieving its initial task. If the system is not observable, there is no hope for any form of correction to its (mis)behavior. Without knowing whence it came, it's difficult to return it there.

6.12.4   *Exercise Set*

1. Test example 6.52 for observability, controllability, and stability.

Determine which of the following systems are controllable and which are observable.

2.
$$\mathbf{x}'(t) = \begin{bmatrix} 0 & 1 & 0 \\ 0 & 0 & 1 \\ 0 & -1 & -1 \end{bmatrix} \mathbf{x}(t) + \begin{bmatrix} 0 \\ 0 \\ 1 \end{bmatrix} u(t), \quad y(t) = \begin{bmatrix} 1 & 0 & 0 \end{bmatrix} \mathbf{x}(t)$$

3.
$$\mathbf{x}'(t) = \begin{bmatrix} 0 & 1 & 0 \\ 0 & 0 & 1 \\ 0 & -1 & -1 \end{bmatrix} \mathbf{x}(t) + \begin{bmatrix} 0 \\ 1 \\ 0 \end{bmatrix} u(t), \quad y(t) = \begin{bmatrix} 0 & 1 & 0 \end{bmatrix} \mathbf{x}(t)$$

4.
$$\mathbf{x}'(t) = \begin{bmatrix} 0 & 1 & 0 \\ 0 & 0 & 1 \\ 0 & -1 & -1 \end{bmatrix} \mathbf{x}(t) + \begin{bmatrix} 1 \\ 0 \\ 1 \end{bmatrix} u(t), \quad y(t) = \begin{bmatrix} 1 & 0 & 1 \end{bmatrix} \mathbf{x}(t)$$

5.
$$\mathbf{x}'(t) = \begin{bmatrix} 0 & 1 & 0 \\ 0 & 0 & 1 \\ 0 & -1 & -1 \end{bmatrix} \mathbf{x}(t) + \begin{bmatrix} 1 & 0 \\ 0 & 0 \\ 0 & 1 \end{bmatrix} u(t), \quad y(t) = \begin{bmatrix} 0 & 1 & 1 \end{bmatrix} \mathbf{x}(t)$$

6.
$$\mathbf{x}'(t) = \begin{bmatrix} 0 & 1 & 0 \\ 0 & 0 & 1 \\ 0 & -1 & -1 \end{bmatrix} \mathbf{x}(t) + \begin{bmatrix} 1 & 0 \\ 0 & 0 \\ 0 & 1 \end{bmatrix} u(t), \quad \mathbf{y}(t) = \begin{bmatrix} 1 & 0 & 0 \\ 0 & 0 & 1 \end{bmatrix} \mathbf{x}(t)$$

7.
$$\mathbf{x}'(t) = \begin{bmatrix} 0 & 1 & 0 \\ 0 & 0 & 1 \\ 0 & -1 & -1 \end{bmatrix} \mathbf{x}(t) + \begin{bmatrix} 0 & 0 \\ 0 & -1 \\ 1 & 0 \end{bmatrix} u(t), \quad \mathbf{y}(t) = \begin{bmatrix} 0 & 1 & 0 \\ 0 & 0 & 1 \end{bmatrix} \mathbf{x}(t)$$

6.13   SOLVING LINEAR SYSTEMS WITH LAPLACE TRANSFORMS

The application of Laplace transforms to vector equations proceeds in much the same manner as that for scalar equations. A system of ODE's is transformed into a system of algebraic equations. In fact, several general results can be derived.

The state-transition matrix satisfies the equation

$$\mathbf{\Phi}'(t, t_0) = \mathbf{A}\mathbf{\Phi}(t, t_0), \quad \mathbf{\Phi}(t_0, t_0) = \mathbf{I}, \tag{6.80}$$

where the prime denotes a derivative with respect to the first argument of $\mathbf{\Phi}$. Taking $t_0 = 0$ and $\mathbf{A}$ to be a constant matrix, the transform of this equation is

$$s\hat{\mathbf{\Phi}}(s, 0) - \mathbf{I} = \mathbf{A}\hat{\mathbf{\Phi}}(s, 0).$$

Thus

$$\hat{\mathbf{\Phi}}(s, 0) = (s\mathbf{I} - \mathbf{A})^{-1}. \tag{6.81}$$

The matrix $(s\mathbf{I} - \mathbf{A})^{-1}$ is called the **resolvent kernel** of the equation (6.80). The poles of $\hat{\mathbf{\Phi}}(s, 0)$ are the eigenvalues of $\mathbf{A}$. We know the form of the state-transition matrix to be $\mathbf{\Phi}(t, 0) = e^{\mathbf{A}t}$, and so we must have

$$e^{\mathbf{A}t} = \mathcal{L}^{-1}\left\{(sI - A)^{-1}\right\}$$

The computation of the initial value Green's function is now straightforward. The defining equation is

$$\mathbf{G}'(t,\tau) = \mathbf{A}\mathbf{G}(t,\tau) + \mathbf{I}\delta(t-\tau).$$

Its Laplace transform with respect to t is

$$s\hat{\mathbf{G}}(s,\tau) = \mathbf{A}\hat{\mathbf{G}}(s,\tau) + \mathbf{I}e^{-s\tau};$$

thus

$$\hat{\mathbf{G}}(s,\tau) = (s\mathbf{I} - \mathbf{A})^{-1}e^{-s\tau}.$$

Therefore, according to the Second Shifting Theorem for Laplace transforms

$$\mathbf{G}(t,\tau) = e^{\mathbf{A}(t-\tau)}u(t-\tau),$$

which agrees with our previous results of Section 6.10.

Applying the transform to the standard state variable formulation of the system equations for constant $\mathbf{A}$, $\mathbf{B}$, $\mathbf{C}$, and $\mathbf{D}$:

$$\begin{aligned}
\mathbf{x}'(t) &= \mathbf{A}\mathbf{x}(t) + \mathbf{B}\mathbf{u}(t), \\
\mathbf{y}(t) &= \mathbf{C}\mathbf{x}(t) + \mathbf{D}\mathbf{u}(t),
\end{aligned} \tag{6.82}$$

where $\mathbf{u}(t)$ is the input, $\mathbf{y}(t)$ is the output, and $\mathbf{x}(t)$ is the state vector, we have

$$\begin{aligned}
s\mathbf{X}(s) - \mathbf{x}(0) &= \mathbf{A}\mathbf{X}(s) + \mathbf{B}\mathbf{U}(s), \\
\mathbf{Y}(s) &= \mathbf{C}\mathbf{X}(s) + \mathbf{D}\mathbf{U}(s).
\end{aligned}$$

These can be solved for $\mathbf{X}(s)$ to yield

$$\mathbf{X}(s) = (s\mathbf{I} - \mathbf{A})^{-1}\mathbf{x}(0) + \mathbf{C}(s\mathbf{I} - \mathbf{A})^{-1}\mathbf{B}\mathbf{U}(s) + \mathbf{D}\mathbf{U}(s).$$

The zero-state output is defined by

$$\hat{\mathbf{G}}(s)\mathbf{U}(s) := [\mathbf{C}(s\mathbf{I} - \mathbf{A})^{-1}\mathbf{B} + \mathbf{D}]\mathbf{U}(s),$$

where $\hat{\mathbf{G}}(s)$ is called the **transfer function matrix**. Inverting, we can write the result as a convolution product:

$$\mathbf{G}(t,0) = (\mathbf{C}e^{\mathbf{A}t}\mathbf{B} + \mathbf{D}) * \mathbf{u}(t).$$

This formalism is all well and good, but its utility depends on the computation of the resolvent kernel $(s\mathbf{I} - \mathbf{A})^{-1}$, which will be somewhat tedious since its entries will be rational functions of s.

■ **EXAMPLE 6.53** Solve the following linear system using Laplace transforms:

$$\mathbf{x}'(t) = \begin{bmatrix} 3 & -2 \\ 4 & -1 \end{bmatrix}\mathbf{x}(t), \quad \mathbf{x}(0) = \begin{bmatrix} 2 \\ 3 \end{bmatrix}$$

Solution: We immediately get

$$s\mathbf{X}(s) - \begin{bmatrix} 2 \\ 3 \end{bmatrix} = \begin{bmatrix} 3 & -2 \\ 4 & -1 \end{bmatrix} \mathbf{X}(s) \quad \Rightarrow \quad \mathbf{X}(s) = \begin{bmatrix} s-3 & 2 \\ -4 & s+1 \end{bmatrix}^{-1} \begin{bmatrix} 2 \\ 3 \end{bmatrix}.$$

It will be quickest to use the adjugate to invert $(s\mathbf{I} - \mathbf{A})$:

$$\begin{bmatrix} s-3 & -2 \\ 4 & s-3 \end{bmatrix}^{-1} = \frac{1}{(s-1)^2 + 4} \begin{bmatrix} s+1 & -2 \\ 4 & s-3 \end{bmatrix}.$$

Thus

$$\mathbf{X}(s) = \frac{1}{(s-1)^2 + 4} \begin{bmatrix} 2s-4 \\ 3s-1 \end{bmatrix} \quad \Rightarrow \quad \mathbf{x}(t) = e^t \begin{bmatrix} 2\cos t - \sin t \\ 3\cos t + \sin t \end{bmatrix}.$$

We also could have computed $e^{\mathbf{A}t}$ to be

$$e^{\mathbf{A}t} = e^t \begin{bmatrix} \cos t + \sin t & -\sin t \\ 2\sin t & \cos t - \sin t \end{bmatrix},$$

and worked from there.   ■ ■ ■

■ **EXAMPLE 6.54** For the circuit shown in Figure 6.29,

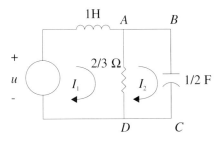

Fig. 6.29

use Laplace transforms to find the currents.

Solution: If we choose the state variables as the loop currents (measured positive clockwise) in each loop, then the state equations are

$$\text{KVL left loop:} \quad -u + \dot{I}_1 + \tfrac{2}{3}(I_1 - I_2) = 0,$$
$$\text{KVL right loop:} \quad \tfrac{2}{3}(I_2 - I_1) + 2\int I_2 \, dt = 0.$$

Choosing the state vector $\mathbf{x} = [I_1; I_2]$ and the output to be the voltage drop from B to C (which is the same as that from A to B), we have the usual form of the system equations with

$$\mathbf{A} = \frac{1}{3}\begin{bmatrix} -2 & 2 \\ -2 & -7 \end{bmatrix}, \quad \mathbf{B} = \begin{bmatrix} 1 \\ 1 \end{bmatrix}, \quad \mathbf{C} = \frac{2}{3}\begin{bmatrix} 1 & -1 \end{bmatrix}, \quad \mathbf{D} = \mathbf{0}.$$

The transfer function matrix (in this case a scalar) is

$$\hat{G}(s) = \mathbf{C}(s\mathbf{I} - \mathbf{A})^{-1}\mathbf{B} + \mathbf{D} = \frac{2}{3} \begin{bmatrix} 1 & -1 \end{bmatrix} \begin{bmatrix} s + \frac{2}{3} & -\frac{2}{3} \\ \frac{2}{3} & s + \frac{7}{3} \end{bmatrix}^{-1} \begin{bmatrix} 1 \\ 1 \end{bmatrix} + 0$$

$$\Rightarrow \hat{G}(s) = \frac{2/3}{s^2 + 3s + 2} \begin{bmatrix} 1 & -1 \end{bmatrix} \begin{bmatrix} s + \frac{7}{3} & \frac{2}{3} \\ -\frac{2}{3} & s + \frac{2}{3} \end{bmatrix} \begin{bmatrix} 1 \\ 1 \end{bmatrix} = \frac{2}{s^2 + 3s + 2}.$$

Of course, we could have chosen other state variables. As an alternative, choose x_1 to be the current from the inductor toward A and x_2 as the voltage drop across the capacitor (see Figure 6.30).

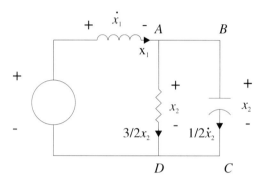

Fig. 6.30

Then the equations are

KVL left loop: $\dot{x}_1 + x_2 - u = 0$

KVL right loop: $-x_1 + \frac{1}{2}\dot{x}_2 + \frac{3}{2}x_2 = 0.$

For this formulation, the transfer function is

$$\hat{G}(s) = \mathbf{C}(s\mathbf{I} - \mathbf{A})^{-1}\mathbf{B} + \mathbf{D} = \begin{bmatrix} 0 & 1 \end{bmatrix} \begin{bmatrix} s & 1 \\ -2 & s + 3 \end{bmatrix}^{-1} \begin{bmatrix} 1 \\ 0 \end{bmatrix} = \frac{2}{s^2 + 3s + 2}.$$

Thankfully, this agrees with the previous result—as we expect that $\hat{G}(s)$ should be invariant with respect to the choice of state variables. ■ ■ ■

Problems in mechanical vibrations can be handled in a similar manner. If $\mathbf{q}$ is the vector of generalized coordinates (usually displacements or angles), then the dynamical equations can be put in the form

$$\mathbf{M}\ddot{\mathbf{q}} + \mathbf{B}\dot{\mathbf{q}} + \mathbf{K}\mathbf{q} = \mathbf{f}(t), \tag{6.83}$$

where $\mathbf{M}$ is called the **inertia matrix**, B the **damping matrix**, and K the **compliance matrix**.

Using $\mathbf{Q}(s) = \mathcal{L}\{\mathbf{q}(t)\}$, the transform of (6.83) is

$$\mathbf{M}\left(s^2\mathbf{Q}(s) - s\mathbf{q}(0) - \dot{\mathbf{q}}(0)\right) + \mathbf{B}\left(s\mathbf{Q}(s) - \mathbf{q}(0)\right) + \mathbf{K}\mathbf{Q}(s) = \mathbf{F}(s).$$

From this, it follows that

$$\mathbf{Q}(s) = \left(s^2\mathbf{M} + s\mathbf{B} + \mathbf{K}\right)^{-1}\left((s\mathbf{M} + \mathbf{B})\mathbf{q}(0) + \mathbf{M}\mathbf{q}(0)\right).$$

Just as in the systems case, the poles of the matrix function

$$\left(s^2\mathbf{M} + s\mathbf{B} + \mathbf{K}\right)^{-1}$$

are the normal "frequencies" of the damped motion.

6.13.1 Exercise Set

Solve each of the following linear systems by using Laplace transforms.

1. $\dot{a} = 4a - 2b$, $\dot{b} = a + b$, $a(0) = 1$, $b(0) = 0$

2. $\dot{a} = b$, $\dot{b} = c$, $\dot{c} = a$, $a(0) = 1$, $b(0) = 2$, $c(0) = 3$

3. $\ddot{a} - 3\dot{a} + 2a + \dot{b} - b = 0$, $a(0) = 0$, $\dot{a}(0) = 0$,
   $-\dot{a} + a + \ddot{b} - 5\dot{b} + 4b = 0$, $b(0) = 1$, $\dot{b}(0) = 0$

4. $2\ddot{a} - \dot{a} + 9a - \ddot{b} - \dot{b} - 3b = 0$, $a(0) = 1$, $\dot{a}(0) = 1$,
   $2\ddot{a} + \dot{a} + 7a - \ddot{b} + \dot{b} - 5b = 0$, $b(0) = 0$, $\dot{b}(0) = 0$

5. $\ddot{a} - 4a - \dot{b} - 2b + \dot{c} - 2c = \sin 2t$, $a(0) = 0$, $\dot{a}(0) = 0$,
   $2\dot{a} - \ddot{b} + 3b + \ddot{c} - 4c = 0$, $b(0) = 0$, $\dot{b}(0) = 0$,
   $\dot{a} - 2a - b + \ddot{c} - 4c = 0$, $c(0) = 0$, $\dot{c}(0) = 0$
   $\dot{x}_0 = -kx_0$, $x_0(0) = 1$,

6. $\dot{x}_n = -k\left(x_{n-1} - x_n\right)$, $x_n(0) = 0$, $n = 1 : \infty$

Find $e^{\mathbf{A}t}$ by inverting the resolvent kernel, i.e., finding $\mathcal{L}^{-1}\{(s\mathbf{I} - \mathbf{A})^{-1}\}$, for each of the following matrices.

7. $\begin{bmatrix} 5 & -4 \\ 4 & -3 \end{bmatrix}$

8. $\begin{bmatrix} 0 & -1 \\ 1 & -2 \end{bmatrix}$

9. $\begin{bmatrix} 1 & 1 & 0 \\ 0 & 0 & 1 \\ 0 & 0 & 1 \end{bmatrix}$

10. $\begin{bmatrix} 0 & 4 & 3 \\ 0 & 20 & 16 \\ 0 & -25 & -20 \end{bmatrix}$

11. $\begin{bmatrix} -3 & 1 & 0 \\ -4 & 0 & 1 \\ -2 & 0 & 0 \end{bmatrix}$

12. $\begin{bmatrix} 2 & -1 & 1 \\ 0 & 1 & 1 \\ -1 & 1 & 1 \end{bmatrix}.$

Solve using Laplace transforms.

13.
$$\dot{\mathbf{x}}(t) = \begin{bmatrix} 18 & -30 \\ 10 & -17 \end{bmatrix} \mathbf{x}(t) + \begin{bmatrix} 13 \\ 8 \end{bmatrix} e^t, \quad \mathbf{x}(0) = \begin{bmatrix} 1 \\ 0 \end{bmatrix}$$

14.
$$\dot{\mathbf{x}}(t) = \begin{bmatrix} 2 & -5 \\ 1 & -2 \end{bmatrix} \mathbf{x}(t) + \begin{bmatrix} -\cos t \\ \sin t \end{bmatrix}, \quad \mathbf{x}(0) = \begin{bmatrix} 3 \\ 1 \end{bmatrix}$$

15.
$$\dot{\mathbf{x}}(t) = \begin{bmatrix} 1 & 0 & 2 \\ 0 & 1 & 0 \\ 1 & 0 & 0 \end{bmatrix} \mathbf{x}(t) + \begin{bmatrix} 1 \\ 1 \\ 1 \end{bmatrix} e^t, \quad \mathbf{x}(0) = \begin{bmatrix} 4 \\ 2 \\ 0 \end{bmatrix}$$

As always seems to be the case, there is yet another method available for computing the exponential matrix using Laplace transforms. If $\mathbf{A}$ is an $n \times n$ matrix with eigenvalues $\lambda_1, \lambda_2, \ldots, \lambda_n$ (repeated or not), then define the following sequences of functions and matrices:

$$f_1(t) = e^{\lambda_1 t}, \quad f_k(t) = f_{k-1}(t) * e^{\lambda_k t};$$

$$\mathbf{B}_1 = \mathbf{I}, \quad \mathbf{B}_k = \mathbf{B}_{k-1} (\mathbf{A} - \lambda_{k-1}\mathbf{I}).$$

It can be shown that

$$e^{\mathbf{A}t} = \sum_{k=1}^{n} f_k(t)\mathbf{B}_k.$$

Use this method to find $e^{\mathbf{A}t}$ for each of the following matrices.

16.
$$\begin{bmatrix} 2 & -5 \\ 1 & -2 \end{bmatrix}$$

17.
$$\begin{bmatrix} 1 & 0 & 2 \\ 0 & 1 & 0 \\ 1 & 0 & 0 \end{bmatrix}$$

18.
$$\begin{bmatrix} 1 & 1 & 2 & -2 \\ 0 & 1 & 2 & -2 \\ 0 & 0 & 2 & -1 \\ 0 & 0 & 1 & 0 \end{bmatrix}$$

6.13.2 *Notes and References*

The literature for systems of ordinary differential equations is large and growing rapidly because of its extensive use in engineering. Most books pretty much begin either with a brief review or where this chapter has ended. Applications to discrete systems have been omitted here, but that is not because they are not useful—quite the contrary. With the increase in computer control, the need for discrete analyses can only grow.

- Gantmacher, **Matrix Theory**: An older but encyclopedic coverage of the subject.

- Hirsch & Smale, **Dynamic Systems**: A more modern treatment with detailed discussions of nonlinear systems.

- Hochstadt, **Differential Equations: A Modern Approach** : Although it says modern treatment, the book was originally published in 1964! Available in paperback.

- Luenberger, **Introduction to Dynamic Systems**: Broad and integrated coverage including difference models and equations.

- Mickens, **Difference Equations: Theory and Applications** : A fairly complete coverage of the subject of the title at an elementary to intermediate level, including the difference analog to this chapter.

6.14 SUPPLEMENTARY AND COMPLEMENTARY PROBLEMS

1. Show that if $\mathbf{A}$ and $\mathbf{B}$ are simple matrices with a common set of eigenvectors $\{\mathbf{x}_1, \mathbf{x}_2, \ldots, \mathbf{x}_n\}$, then the commutator $[\mathbf{A}, \mathbf{B}] = \mathbf{0}$. Is the converse true?

2. If $\phi_{\mathbf{A}}(\lambda)$ is the characteristic polynomial of $\mathbf{A}$, find the characteristic polynomial of $\operatorname{adj}(\mathbf{A})$ in terms of $\phi_{\mathbf{A}}(\lambda)$. [You should assume that $\mathbf{A}$ is nonsingular.]

3. Show that the spectral norm, defined by $\|\mathbf{A}\|_s := \sqrt{\rho\left(\mathbf{A}^H \mathbf{A}\right)}$, is induced by the ℓ_2 vector norm $\|\mathbf{x}\| = \sqrt{\mathbf{x}^H \mathbf{x}}$.

4. If $\mathbf{u} = [a; b; c] \in \mathbb{R}^3$ such that $\mathbf{u}^T \mathbf{u} = 1$ and

$$\mathbf{A} = \begin{bmatrix} 0 & -c & b \\ c & 0 & -a \\ -b & a & 0 \end{bmatrix},$$

then $\mathbf{A}$ is called the **dual** of $\mathbf{u}$.

 (a) Show that $e^{\mathbf{A}\alpha} = \mathbf{I}\cos\alpha + (1 - \cos\alpha)\mathbf{u}\mathbf{u}^T + \mathbf{A}\sin\alpha$.

 (b) Show that $\mathbf{u}$ is an eigenvector of $e^{\mathbf{A}\alpha}$ corresponding to the eigenvalue $+1$.

 (c) Show that $e^{\mathbf{A}\alpha}$ is orthogonal.

 (d) Show that $e^{\mathbf{A}\alpha}$ is a rotation through the angle α about the axis parallel to $\mathbf{u}$.

5. If $\mathbf{A}$ is real and symmetric (hence orthogonally diagonalizable to $\mathbf{D}$) with positive eigenvalues λ_k and $\mathbf{P}$ is the orthogonal matrix of normalized eigenvectors, then define the square root of $\mathbf{A}$ to be

$$\mathbf{A}^{1/2} := \mathbf{P}\mathbf{D}^{1/2}\mathbf{P}^T,$$

where $\mathbf{D}^{1/2} = \operatorname{diag}\left(\sqrt{\lambda_1}, \sqrt{\lambda_2}, \ldots, \sqrt{\lambda_n}\right)$. Show that:

 (a) $\mathbf{A}^{1/2}$ is symmetric.

 (b) $\mathbf{A}^{1/2}\mathbf{A}^{1/2} = \mathbf{A}$.

 (c) If $\mathbf{A}^{-1/2} := \mathbf{P}\mathbf{D}^{-1/2}\mathbf{P}^T$, then $\mathbf{A}^{1/2}\mathbf{A}^{-1/2} = \mathbf{I}$.

(d) $\mathbf{A}^{-1/2}\mathbf{A}^{-1/2} = \mathbf{A}^{-1}$.

(e) Find the square root of

$$\begin{bmatrix} 3 & 1 & 0 & 0 \\ 1 & 3 & 0 & 0 \\ 0 & 0 & 2 & 1 \\ 0 & 0 & 1 & 2 \end{bmatrix}.$$

6. It is possible to define something akin to eigenvalues and eigenvectors for nonsquare matrices. These problems will develop some of the theory of this singular value decomposition. If $\mathbf{A} \in \mathbb{C}^m_n$ and there is a number σ and vectors $\mathbf{u} \in \mathbb{C}^n$ and $\mathbf{v} \in \mathbb{C}^m$ such that

$$\mathbf{A}\mathbf{u} = \sigma\mathbf{v}, \quad \mathbf{v}^H\mathbf{A} = \bar{\sigma}\mathbf{u}^H,$$

then σ is a **singular value** of $\mathbf{A}$ and $\mathbf{u}$ and $\mathbf{v}$ are the **right** and **left singular vectors** of $\mathbf{A}$ corresponding to σ. Show that:

(a) The singular value problem can be written in the form

$$\begin{bmatrix} \mathbf{0} & \mathbf{A}^H \\ \mathbf{A} & \mathbf{0} \end{bmatrix} \begin{bmatrix} \mathbf{u} \\ \mathbf{v} \end{bmatrix} = \sigma \begin{bmatrix} \mathbf{u} \\ \mathbf{v} \end{bmatrix}.$$

(b) Use the previous part to show that σ must be real.

(c) Show that if $\mathbf{u},\mathbf{v}$ are right and left singular vectors corresponding to σ, then $-\mathbf{u},\mathbf{v}$ are right and left singular vectors corresponding to $-\sigma$. Conclude that singular values must occur in $\pm$ pairs.

(d) Show that $\mathbf{A}^H\mathbf{A}\mathbf{u} = \sigma^2\mathbf{u}$ and $\mathbf{A}\mathbf{A}^H\mathbf{v} = \sigma^2\mathbf{v}$.

Since $\mathbf{A}^H\mathbf{A}$ is Hermitian, it has an orthonormal set of $r = \text{rank}(\mathbf{A})$ eigenvectors $\{\mathbf{u}_{(1)}, \mathbf{u}_{(2)}, \ldots, \mathbf{u}_{(r)}\}$ corresponding to the positive eigenvalues $\{\sigma_1^2, \sigma_2^2, \ldots, \sigma_r^2\}$. Assuming $m < n$, define

$$\mathbf{v}_{(j)} := \frac{1}{\sigma_j}\mathbf{A}\mathbf{u}_{(j)}, \quad j = 1 : r.$$

(e) Show that the $\mathbf{v}_{(j)}$ form an orthonormal set of eigenvectors of $\mathbf{A}\mathbf{A}^H$ corresponding to the eigenvalues σ_j^2.

(f) Show that $\mathbf{u}_{(j)},\mathbf{v}_{(j)}$ are a pair of right and left singular vectors corresponding to the singular value σ_j.

(g) Find the singular values and singular vectors of

$$\mathbf{A} = \begin{bmatrix} 1 & 0 \\ 0 & i \\ 1 & 0 \end{bmatrix}.$$

7. An elliptic pendulum consists of a trolley of mass M that is free to move horizontally without friction, and a mass m attached to the trolley by a rod of length L that is free to rotate about the horizontal axle in the trolley (see Figure 6.31).

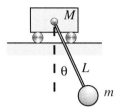

Fig. 6.31

If the mass of the rod is negligible, find the motion of the system.

8. A smooth tube is bent in the form of a circle. Three identical particles of mass m are constrained to move on the tube. Between each particle is an identical spring with force constant k (see Figure 6.32(a)).

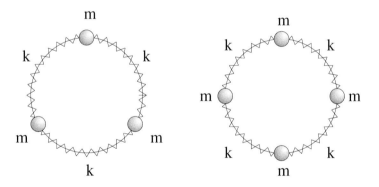

Fig. 6.32

Using s_k, $k = 1:3$, for the displacement of the kth particle along the tube, find and solve the equations of motion.

9. Use the same geometry as in the previous problem except that now there are four identical masses connected by four springs (see Figure 6.32(b)).

10. Redo the previous problem when opposing masses are the same, but adjacent masses are not. In particular, moving clockwise from the top, the masses are M, m, M, and m (see Figure 6.33).

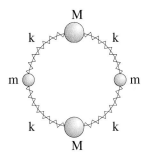

Fig. 6.33

11. What would happen to the acoustic and optical modes if the linear model of the solid (see example 6.31) had an atomic pattern like that in Figure 6.34?

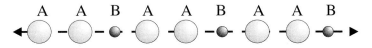

Fig. 6.34

12. Write the equations of motion for a two dimensional solid whose geometry is as shown in Figure 6.35)

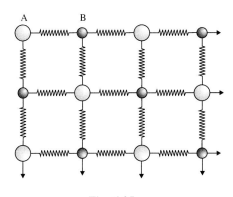

Fig. 6.35

if all springs have force constant K, the A particles have mass m and the B particles have mass M.

13. If we think of the state-transition matrix for a linear system as a function of two variables, then it satisfies the equation

$$\frac{\partial}{\partial t}\mathbf{\Phi}(t,\tau) = \mathbf{A}(t)\mathbf{\Phi}(t,\tau), \quad \mathbf{\Phi}(\tau,\tau) = \mathbf{I}.$$

(a) Show that

$$\frac{\partial}{\partial \tau} \mathbf{\Phi}^T(t, \tau) = -\mathbf{A}^T(\tau)\mathbf{\Phi}^T(t, \tau).$$

(b) Infer from part (a) that $\mathbf{\Phi}^T(t, \tau)$ is the state-transition matrix for the adjoint system defined by $\mathbf{y}'(t) = -\mathbf{A}^T(t)\mathbf{y}(t)$, so that we have $\mathbf{y}(t) = \mathbf{\Phi}^T(t, \tau)\mathbf{y}(t)$.

(c) If $\mathbf{y}(t)$ is a solution of the adjoint system and $\mathbf{x}(t)$ is a solution of the original system, show that $\mathbf{x}^T\mathbf{y}$ is constant.

14. If $\mathbf{\Phi_A}(t, t_0)$ is the state-transition matrix for the system

$$\mathbf{x}'(t) = \mathbf{A}(t)\mathbf{x}(t),$$

show that the matrix system

$$\mathbf{X}'(t) = \mathbf{A}(t)\mathbf{X}(t) + \mathbf{X}(t)\mathbf{B}^T(t), \quad \mathbf{X}(t_0) = \mathbf{X}_0$$

has the solution $\mathbf{X}(t) = \mathbf{\Phi_A}(t, t_0)\mathbf{X}_0\mathbf{\Phi}_{\mathbf{B}}^T(t, t_0)$.

15. If $\mathbf{Q}(t)$ is differentiable and invertible, start with the system $\mathbf{x}'(t) = \mathbf{A}(t)\mathbf{x}(t)$ and make the change of variable $\mathbf{z}(t) = \mathbf{Q}(t)\mathbf{x}(t)$. Show that the state-transition matrices for the $\mathbf{x}$ system and the $\mathbf{z}$ system are related as follows

$$\mathbf{\Phi_A}(t, \tau) = \mathbf{Q}^{-1}(t)\mathbf{\Phi}_{\mathbf{QAQ}^{-1}+\mathbf{Q}'\mathbf{Q}^{-1}}(t, \tau)\mathbf{Q}(\tau).$$

16. If $\mathbf{A}$ and $\mathbf{B}$ are constant $n \times n$ matrices, show that the system

$$\mathbf{x}'(t) = e^{-\mathbf{A}t}\mathbf{B}e^{\mathbf{A}t}\mathbf{x}(t)$$

has the state-transition matrix

$$\mathbf{\Phi}(t, \tau) = e^{-\mathbf{A}t}e^{(\mathbf{A}+\mathbf{B})(t-\tau)}e^{\mathbf{A}\tau}.$$

17. We would like to evaluate the integral

$$J = \int_0^\infty \mathbf{x}^T(\tau)\mathbf{Q}\mathbf{x}(\tau)\, d\tau,$$

where $\mathbf{x}'(t) = \mathbf{A}(t)\mathbf{x}(t)$. Define the scalar-valued function

$$V(t) := \int_t^\infty \mathbf{x}^T(\tau)\mathbf{Q}\mathbf{x}(\tau)\, d\tau = \mathbf{x}^T(t)\int_t^\infty \mathbf{\Phi}^T(\tau, t)\mathbf{Q}\mathbf{\Phi}(\tau, t)\, d\tau\, \mathbf{x}(t)$$
$$=: \mathbf{x}^T(t)\mathbf{M}(t)\mathbf{x}(t).$$

(a) Verify that $V(t)$ is as given by the second integral. Clearly, $V(0) = J = \mathbf{x}^T(0)\mathbf{M}(0)\mathbf{x}(0)$.

(b) Using the results on the adjoint system from problem 13, show that

$$\mathbf{M}'(t) + \mathbf{A}^T(t)\mathbf{M}(t) + \mathbf{M}(t)\mathbf{A}(t) + \mathbf{Q} = \mathbf{0}.$$

18. In the same situation as problem 17, when $\mathbf{A}(t) = \mathbf{A}$ and $\boldsymbol{\Phi}(t,\tau) = e^{\mathbf{A}(t-\tau)}$, show that

$$\mathbf{M}(t) = \int_0^\infty e^{\mathbf{A}^T\sigma}\mathbf{Q}e^{\mathbf{A}\sigma}\,d\sigma = \mathbf{M}$$

is constant and that this implies

$$\mathbf{A}^T\mathbf{M} + \mathbf{M}\mathbf{A} + \mathbf{Q} = \mathbf{0}.$$

19. Suppose that in the standard formulation of the state equations

$$\dot{\mathbf{x}} = \mathbf{A}\mathbf{x} + \mathbf{B}\mathbf{u},$$
$$\mathbf{y} = \mathbf{C}\mathbf{x} + \mathbf{D}\mathbf{u},$$

we make a change of basis so that $\mathbf{x} = \mathbf{P}\mathbf{a}$, $\mathbf{y} = \mathbf{P}\mathbf{b}$, and $\mathbf{u} = \mathbf{P}\mathbf{v}$, where $\mathbf{P}$ is a constant nonsingular matrix. Show that the transfer function matrix for the transformed system is $\mathbf{P}$ similar to that for the original system. How do things change if $\mathbf{x} = \mathbf{P}\mathbf{a}$, $\mathbf{y} = \mathbf{Q}\mathbf{b}$, and $\mathbf{u} = \mathbf{R}\mathbf{v}$, with $\mathbf{P}$, $\mathbf{Q}$, and $\mathbf{R}$ constant nonsingular matrices?

7

NONLINEAR ODE'S

7.1 PREVIEW

Our prior study of ODE's concentrated on linear equations. Only for certain special types of first order equations were we able to solve any nonlinear problems. This does not mean nonlinear problems are not important, rather they are hard, usually *very* hard. We begin with some models of simple physical systems for which a nonlinear equation is appropriate. Quite often, an approximation can be made that allows the system to be modeled by a linear equation. Sometimes the model will be intrinsically nonlinear, where no simple approximation that preserves the sense of the model can remove the nonlinearity.

It will be convenient to reintroduce the notion of the phase plane, wherein we study a trajectory in terms of x and $v := \dot{x}$ without reference to the time. The analysis of fixed points of linear systems that was begun in the last chapter will be extended to nonlinear systems. Limit cycles will be defined and related to the existence of periodic solutions. Some general theorems governing the behavior of solutions will be stated and applied to several examples.

Approximate forms for solutions to nonlinear equations will be obtained by using perturbation procedures whereby an expansion in a small parameter is performed and the equation is changed to an infinite system of linear equations that can be solved. Two regular perturbation schemes are presented, one using an expansion and the other using an averaging process. The area of singular perturbations will be briefly introduced. The chapter will end with an introductory discussion of chaotic dynamics, approached by way of iterated maps of the interval $(0, 1)$.

7.2 NONLINEAR ODE MODELS

The lion's share of previous chapters was devoted to the study of linear ODE's. There was a large foundation on which their solution could be based. The solution of nonlinear equations has not yet reached the state of mathematical development that linear equations now enjoy.

Much progress has been made in recent years, but much remains. Furthermore, nonlinear models have found ever wider application.

▪ **EXAMPLE 7.1**   The classic pendulum problem leads to a nonlinear model for large oscillations. We assume the pendulum has a bob of mass m connected by an inextensible massless rod to a frictionless pivot as shown in Figure 7.1.

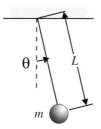

Fig. 7.1

The only force acting is gravity directed downward. Using the angle θ that the bar makes with the vertical, we see that the downward component of this force is $mg \sin \theta$ and the torque is $mgL \sin \theta$. Balancing moments, the equation of motion is

$$mL^2\ddot{\theta} + mgL \sin \theta = 0.$$

Since θ appears in a form of $\sin \theta$, the equation is nonlinear. But it is not intrinsically nonlinear, because for small oscillations we can make the usual small angle approximation whereby we replace $\sin \theta$ by θ to get the linearized equation

$$mL^2\ddot{\theta} + mgL\theta = 0.$$

The solution of this "reduced" equation displays a periodic "swinging" motion. We could attempt to solve the nonlinear equation by adjusting its linear solution $\theta(t) = \theta_0 \cos(\omega t - \alpha)$, but more of that later.   ▪ ▪ ▪

▪ **EXAMPLE 7.2**   The previous example can be made more complicated by insisting that the pendulum of length L and mass m be constrained to move in a plane rotating with angular velocity Ω about a vertical line through the pivot point. If $\theta(t)$ denotes the angular deviation of the pendulum from the vertical, the equation of motion can be shown to be

$$I\ddot{\theta} - m\Omega^2 L^2 \sin \theta \cos \theta + mgL \sin \theta = 0,$$

where I is the moment of inertia of the pendulum. Once again the use of the small angle approximation allows us to arrive at a reduced equation that is linear:

$$I\ddot{\theta} + \left(mgL - m\Omega^2 L^2\right)\theta = 0.$$

When $m\Omega^2 L^2 > mgL$, the solution to the reduced equation no longer displays swinging motion.   ▪ ▪ ▪

■ **EXAMPLE 7.3** Problems involving the dynamics of bodies moving in a resisting medium must be modeled by nonlinear equations when the resistive force is nonlinear. We know that F_{resist} is a function of the magnitude of the speed of the particle. Were the particle to be moving in two or three dimensions then we could have

$$F_{\text{resist}} = g\left(\sqrt{\dot{x}^2 + \dot{y}^2 + \dot{z}^2}\right),$$

which would lead to a nonlinear ODE for all but constant $g(\cdot)$. On the other hand, the force itself could be proportional to the square of the speed rather than just its magnitude. In either case the fundamental equations of motion are nonlinear. ■ ■ ■

■ **EXAMPLE 7.4** Our elementary model of population growth $\dot{Q}(t) = kQ(t)$ led to a solution of exponential growth that was clearly unrealistic. We modified the model by introducing the effects of competition via $\dot{Q}(t) = kQ(t) - \ell Q^2(t)$ which led to the nonlinear logistic growth model. Further improvements can be made.

In particular, suppose that the species in which we are interested is the prey of a predatory species. As an example consider an island on which the only mammals are foxes and rabbits. We assume that without the rabbits the foxes could not exist. Without the foxes the rabbit population would follow a logistic growth pattern limited only by the amount of vegetation on the island. An appropriate system of model equations for the number of rabbits $R(t)$ and the number of foxes $F(t)$ could be

$$\begin{aligned}
\dot{R}(t) &= kR(t) - lR^2(t) - aR(t)F(t), \\
\dot{F}(t) &= -bF(t) + cR(t)F(t),
\end{aligned}$$

if we neglect competition among the foxes (which is reasonable given their reproductive rate vis-à-vis rabbits). Intuitively we would expect that as the rabbit population increased so too would the fox population since their food source would be plentiful. Then as the rabbit population leveled off due to competition, the foxes would have an easy time of dispatching the rabbits so that their numbers would continue to increase while those of the rabbits would decrease. Then the fox population would start to decrease as the supply of rabbits drops off. This behavior could continue in a somewhat cyclical manner for quite a while, although there are certain peculiarities that could prevent such a recurrence. For example, the foxes could so completely decimate the rabbit population that they could not sustain themselves and become extinct, whereupon the foxes too are not long for the island. ■ ■ ■

■ **EXAMPLE 7.5** Many biological systems are driven by chemical reactions involving enzymes. The simplest reactions frequently proceed in two steps: the first takes the enzyme E plus the so-called substrate S into another short-lived quantity ES, which then breaks into the enzyme plus a final product P. As a chemical equation it can be written

$$E + S \rightleftharpoons ES \rightarrow E + P.$$

The first reaction $E + S \rightleftharpoons ES$ is reversible with reaction rate constant k_1 in the forward direction and constant k_{-1} in the backward direction. The second reaction $ES \rightarrow E + P$ is assumed to be irreversible with forward rate constant k_2. The **Michaelis-Menten Theory** of such reactions assumes the following:

1. Only initial reaction rates are considered, and the decrease in the reaction rate due to the decrease in the level of the substrate S can be ignored.

2. There is an excess of substrate in solution with the enzyme, so that there is no impediment to the initial reaction.

3. The rate constant k_2 is small compared with that of the backward initial reaction, i.e., $k_2 << k_{-1}$. Furthermore, the initial reaction reaches equilibrium in a short time, and that equilibrium is maintained throughout the remainder of the reaction.

4. The product ES is short-lived with respect to the rate of change for the substrate and product S and P. Thus the rate of formation and dissociation of ES is small with respect to k_1 and k_2.

With assumption (1) it is possible to use the Law of Mass Action to write dynamical equations for the rates of change of the reactants.

$$\frac{d}{dt}[S] = -k_1[E][S] + k_{-1}[ES],$$

$$\frac{d}{dt}[ES] = -(k_{-1} + k_2)[ES] + k_1[E][S],$$

$$\frac{d}{dt}[P] = k_2[ES],$$

where $[Q]$ is the concentration in molars of the quantity Q. There are also initial conditions and consequences of the other assumptions that can be brought to bear. The major idea here is that the system of equations we have is nonlinear. Nevertheless, they still represent a simplification of the mechanism involved in living cells. More often than not, there is not just one enzyme at work but rather several, leading to a cascade of enzymatically driven chemical reactions, each of which gives rise to equations of the form written above. ■ ■ ■

■ **EXAMPLE 7.6**   Suppose we study a simple LC circuit (Figure 7.2). Rather than treating the current as the dependent variable let's use the magnetic flux linkage Φ. The solenoid is the usual iron core inductor. If the capacitor has a capacitance of C farads and charge of q coulombs, then the circuit equation is

$$L\frac{d\Phi}{dt} + \frac{q}{C} = 0.$$

Differentiating this equation and using the relation of the current to the charge, $I = dq/dt$, we find

$$L\frac{d^2\Phi}{dt^2} + \frac{I}{C} = 0.$$

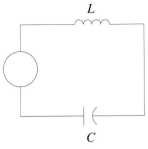

Fig. 7.2

In introductory treatments of network analysis the constitutive relation between flux linkage and current is assumed to be linear, $LI = \Phi$. But a more typical relation that models some core saturation is

$$I = a\Phi - b\Phi^2,$$

with $a, b > 0$. Now the nonlinear equation is

$$L\frac{d^2\Phi}{dt^2} + \frac{1}{C}\left(a\Phi - b\Phi^2\right) = 0.$$

■ ■ ■

■ **EXAMPLE 7.7** Suppose we want to analyze the orbit of an earth satellite. Choose the coordinate system so the origin is the center of mass of the earth. Newton's Second Law in a central force field $f(r)$ states that

$$m\ddot{\mathbf{r}} = f(r)\frac{\mathbf{r}}{r},$$

where $r := \|\mathbf{r}\| = \sqrt{x^2 + y^2}$. If we introduce the unit vectors $\mathbf{e}_r$ and $\mathbf{e}_\theta$, we can write $\mathbf{r} = r\mathbf{e}_r$ and

$$\ddot{\mathbf{r}} = (\ddot{r} - r\dot{\theta}^2)\mathbf{e}_r + (2\dot{r}\dot{\theta} + r\ddot{\theta})\mathbf{e}_\theta.$$

The component equations are then

$$\ddot{r} - r\dot{\theta}^2 = -f(r), \quad 2\dot{r}\dot{\theta} + r\ddot{\theta} = 0.$$

After multiplying by r the second equation can be integrated to yield

$$r^2\dot{\theta} = \frac{L}{m},$$

where L is the magnitude of the conserved angular momentum. This allows us to eliminate $\dot{\theta}$ from the r equation, getting

$$\ddot{r} - \frac{L^2}{m^2 r^3} = -f(r).$$

If we change the dependent variable r to $u = 1/r$, we find

$$\dot{r} = \frac{d}{dt}\left(\frac{1}{u}\right) = -\frac{1}{u^2}\frac{du}{d\theta}\frac{d\theta}{dt} = -r^2\dot{\theta}\frac{du}{d\theta} = -\frac{L}{m}\frac{du}{d\theta} \quad \Rightarrow \quad \ddot{r} = -u^2\frac{L^2}{m^2}\frac{d^2u}{d\theta^2}.$$

The equation of motion is now

$$\frac{d^2u}{d\theta^2} + u = \frac{m^2}{L^2}\frac{1}{u^2}f\left(\frac{1}{u}\right).$$

Were we to take $f(1/u) = u^2$ or u^3, the equation would be linear. But all other choices would lead to a nonlinear equation. Although the Universal Law of Gravitation tells us that each body attracts every other with a force proportional to $1/r^2 = u^2$, this does not take into account the sum of the external forces from all the other bodies in the universe. We know that there are significant contributions from more than one source; e.g., in the case of the differential attraction that causes the tides, the contribution from the moon predominates but that of the sun cannot be disregarded.   ■ ■ ■

■ **EXAMPLE 7.8** A slider of mass m is constrained to move in a slot and is held in place by two identical springs of force constant k, which are relaxed when θ, the angle between the slot and the spring, is $\pi/2$ (Figure 7.3).

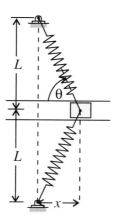

Fig. 7.3

Call the lateral displacement $x(t)$, measured positive to the right. Identical springs mean the forces in the vertical direction are balanced. Newton's Second Law applied to the horizontal direction is

$$m\ddot{x} = 2F\cos\theta + F_r,$$

where F is the force exerted along each spring and F_r is the frictional force. The geometry tells us that

$$\cos\theta = \frac{x}{\sqrt{L^2 + x^2}}.$$

The force exerted by each spring is

$$k * (\text{change in length}) = k \left[\sqrt{L^2 + x^2} - L \right].$$

The equation of motion is

$$m\ddot{x} = 2kx \left[1 - \frac{L}{\sqrt{L^2 + x^2}} \right] + F_r.$$

As a first approximation, we might neglect the resistive force and assume the motion occurs so that x/L is small. Then we could use the series expansion

$$\frac{1}{\sqrt{1 + w^2}} = 1 - \frac{1}{2}w + \frac{1 \cdot 3}{2 \cdot 4}w^2 - \dots$$

and neglect all terms of order 2 or higher in $w = x/L$. The approximate equation of motion is now

$$m\ddot{x} = \frac{kx^2}{L}.$$

Even in the first approximation, this model contains a term proportional to x^2. All first tries in similar problems led to linear equations. This physical process is intrinsically nonlinear. ■ ■ ■

■ **EXAMPLE 7.9** The spinning of an asymmetrical top leads to a nonlinear system of equations. Suppose the top is arranged so that its principal axes lie along the $x_1 x_2 x_3$-axes; i.e., the axes are the (orthogonal) directions of the eigenvectors of the (symmetric) inertia matrix. Suppose the top is oriented so the principal moments of inertia are related by the inequality

$$I_1 > I_2 > I_3.$$

Once the top is set in motion, the $x_1 x_2 x_3$-frame is no longer inertial. If ω is the angular velocity vector of the motion, then from equation (3.24) we have

$$\begin{aligned} \omega_1 &= \dot{\phi} \sin\theta \sin\psi + \dot{\theta} \cos\psi \\ \omega_2 &= \dot{\phi} \sin\theta \cos\psi - \dot{\theta} \sin\psi \\ \omega_3 &= \dot{\phi} \cos\theta + \dot{\psi}, \end{aligned}$$

where ϕ, θ, and ψ are the Euler angles of the rotating frame. To write the equations of motion, we must use the fact that the $x_1 x_2 x_3$-coordinates of the top are rotating with angular velocity ω with respect to an inertial frame. If $d\mathbf{A}/dt$ is the rate of change of the vector $\mathbf{A}$ with respect to the inertial frame and $d'\mathbf{A}/dt$ is its rate of change with respect to the moving frame, then we know that

$$\frac{d\mathbf{A}}{dt} = \frac{d'\mathbf{A}}{dt} + \omega \times \mathbf{A}.$$

Because the rate of change of momentum $\mathbf{p} = m\mathbf{v}$ is the applied force and the rate of change of angular momentum $\mathbf{L} = \mathbf{I}\omega$ is the applied torque, the equations of motion are

$$\frac{d'\mathbf{p}}{dt} + \omega \times \mathbf{p} = \mathbf{F}, \quad \frac{d'\mathbf{L}}{dt} + \omega \times \mathbf{L} = \tau,$$

where $\mathbf{F}$ is the external applied force and τ is the external applied torque. Since the differentiation in the equations of motion is performed in the rotating coordinate system, we may use the subscripts $1, 2, 3$ to refer to the components in the $x_1 x_2 x_3$-system. In this system, the components of $\mathbf{F}$ are mv_1, mv_2, and mv_3 and those of $\mathbf{L}$ are $I_1\omega_1$, $I_2\omega_2$, and $I_3\omega_3$. The momentum equations are

$$m(\dot{v}_1 + \omega_2 v_3 - \omega_3 v_2) = F_1,$$
$$m(\dot{v}_2 + \omega_3 v_1 - \omega_1 v_3) = F_2,$$
$$m(\dot{v}_3 + \omega_1 v_2 - \omega_2 v_1) = F_3.$$

The equations for the components of angular momentum are

$$I_1\dot{\omega}_1 + (I_3 - I_2)\,\omega_2\omega_3 = \tau_1,$$
$$I_2\dot{\omega}_2 + (I_1 - I_3)\,\omega_1\omega_3 = \tau_2, \qquad (7.1)$$
$$I_3\dot{\omega}_3 + (I_2 - I_1)\,\omega_1\omega_2 = \tau_3.$$

Although the momentum equations are linear, the equations for the angular velocity ω are clearly nonlinear. ∎ ∎ ∎

Many of the equations derived in this section were linearized by considering values of some quantity to be "small." It will turn out that the linearizability of a system will have important consequences for determining its behavior.

7.2.1   Exercise Set

1. Revise the rabbit-fox predator-prey model to account for different sexes of each animal. Arrange it so that the population will become extinct if there are only animals of a single sex. How might the model be revised to account for the finite life of both rabbits and foxes?

2. In the central field model, compute $f(r)$ when the mass in question is that of a satellite of the earth in a geosynchronous orbit (about 3×10^4 km above the earth's surface). Be sure to include the effects of both the earth and the moon and numerically compare their relative magnitude.

3. Suppose a mass m is attached to the midpoint of an extensible wire as shown in Figure 7.4. Assume the initial tension in the wire is T, the strain due to an extension is

$$\epsilon = \frac{\sqrt{a^2 + x^2} - a}{a},$$

and the tension after displacement is $T + AE\epsilon$ (where A is the wire's cross-sectional area and E is Young's modulus). Take the x-component of the restoring force and assume x is small to show that the approximate equation of motion is

$$m\ddot{x} + \frac{2T}{a}x + \frac{AE}{a^3}\left(1 - \frac{T}{AE}\right)x^3 = 0.$$

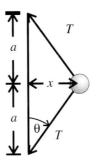

Fig. 7.4

7.3 PHASE PLANE ANALYSIS OF NONLINEAR SYSTEMS

We will study second order linear ODE's by using the phase plane, which is the xv-coordinate plane when $v = \dot{x}$. This will be shown to be related to the standard matrix form of the typical second order ODE. Let's begin with a simple example, the harmonic oscillator.

■ **EXAMPLE 7.10** If $x(t)$ is the displacement of the simple harmonic oscillator as a function of time, then the unforced equation of motion is

$$\ddot{x} + \omega^2 x = 0.$$

In order to bring the velocity $v = \dot{x}$ into the picture, we can make a change of independent variables from t to x as follows:

$$\frac{d^2 x}{dt^2} = \frac{d}{dt}\left(\frac{dx}{dt}\right) = \frac{dv}{dt} = \frac{dv}{dx}\frac{dx}{dt} = v\frac{dv}{dx}.$$

Now the second order equation for the system can be written as the first order equation

$$v\frac{dv}{dx} + \omega^2 x = 0.$$

Since ω is assumed to be constant, this equation is separable and can be easily integrated to yield

$$v\,dv + \omega^2 x\,dx = 0 \quad \Rightarrow \quad \frac{1}{2}v^2 + \frac{1}{2}\omega^2 x^2 = C.$$

To within a multiple of the mass m, we have already seen that this equation expresses the conservation of energy. We can analyze the motion by graphing the family of curves $v^2 + \omega^2 x^2 = 2C$ in the phase plane. The results are the ellipses shown in Figure 7.5.

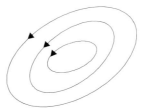

Fig. 7.5

Each has a semiaxis of length $\sqrt{2C}$ along x and $\sqrt{2C}/\omega$ along v. This is the so-called **phase portrait of the trajectory**

$$x(t) = A\cos(\omega t - \alpha).$$

As the mass follows this trajectory it traces out its phase portrait. Parametrically the trajectory is given by

$$\begin{aligned} x(t) &= A\cos(\omega t - \alpha), \\ v(t) &= -\omega A\sin(\omega t - \alpha). \end{aligned}$$

With $A > 0$ the motion starts at $t = 0$ with $x = A\cos(-\alpha) = A\cos a$. As time increases the particle moves in the counterclockwise direction.

If there were (over)damping present, then the equation of motion in terms of the independent variable x and dependent variable v would be

$$v\frac{dv}{dx} + 2\beta v + \omega^2 x = 0.$$

The equation is neither separable nor linear and cannot be simply integrated. Instead, we could look at the equation of the trajectory

$$x(t) = Ae^{-\beta t}\cos(\omega_1 t - \alpha),$$

where $\omega_1^2 = \omega^2 - \beta^2$. Graphing x versus v we would have a spiral converging toward the origin in the phase plane as shown in Figure 7.6. ∎∎∎

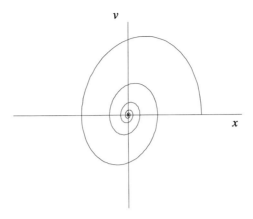

Fig. 7.6 Phase portrait for the damped harmonic oscillator equation.

Many linear and nonlinear systems can be fruitfully studied by analyzing their phase portraits. A qualitative picture of their behavior can be gotten by looking at the particular curves in the phase plane. Trajectories, alternatively called **paths** or **orbits**, are the curves along which the motion proceeds including the time dependence. Certain points can help to characterize these curves.

Points of equilibrium, or **fixed points**, of a system

$$\dot{\mathbf{x}} = \mathbf{f}(t, \mathbf{x}) \tag{7.2}$$

are the solutions of $\mathbf{f}(t, \mathbf{x}) = \mathbf{0}$, essentially points where the speed and force are zero. The fixed point(s) can be a function of time. If the force vector function is independent of time, the system

$$\dot{\mathbf{x}} = \mathbf{f}(\mathbf{x}) \tag{7.3}$$

is said to be **autonomous**, and the fixed points do not change with time. For autonomous systems, fixed points are solutions of the system. In the case of the homogeneous linear system

$$\dot{\mathbf{x}} = \mathbf{A}\mathbf{x}, \tag{7.4}$$

the origin is the only fixed point whenever $\mathbf{A}$ is nonsingular.

A system can have a finite or infinite number of fixed points. For instance, the equation $\ddot{x} + \sin x = 0$ has fixed points at $x = n\pi, n = -\infty : \infty$, and $v = 0$.

At this stage you may want to review the material on the stability of linear autonomous systems from the previous chapter.

Just as the phase plane analysis told us a great deal about the qualitative behavior of linear systems, much can be learned about nonlinear systems from their phase portraits and the classification of their fixed points. We shall begin by looking at the phase portraits of some specific nonlinear second order equations. The nonlinear equation

$$\ddot{x} + \omega^2 x + \beta x^3 = 0$$

is called the **Duffing equation**. Its matrix normal form is

$$\frac{d}{dt}\begin{bmatrix} x \\ v \end{bmatrix} = \begin{bmatrix} v \\ -\omega^2 x - \beta x^3 \end{bmatrix}.$$

The term βx^3 could be thought of as a small perturbation on the standard mass-spring harmonic oscillator equation. There is a fixed point where

$$-\omega^2 x - \beta x^3 = 0 \quad \Rightarrow \quad x = 0, \; \frac{\omega}{\sqrt{-\beta}}.$$

If we graph the spring force $-\omega^2 x - \beta x^3$ versus x for the cases $\beta < 0$, $\beta = 0$, and $\beta > 0$ we see the differences between a soft spring, an ideal spring, and a hard spring (Figure 7.7).

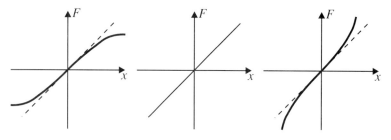

Fig. 7.7

A soft spring is easier to extend as it lengthens, whereas a hard spring becomes more difficult to extend.

The equation governing the phase portrait can be gotten by using the Chain Rule, $dv/dx = \dot{v}/\dot{x}$, to transform to the differential equation

$$\frac{dv}{dx} = -\left(\frac{\omega^2 x + \beta x^3}{v}\right).$$

This is separable and can be integrated to yield the first integral,

$$2\left(v^2 + \omega^2 x^2\right) + \beta x^4 = C.$$

The character of the phase portrait changes dramatically as β varies (Figure 7.8). For $\beta = 0$ it is an ellipse, for $\beta > 0$ it is a closed bounded curve, but for $\beta < 0$ it is no longer bounded.

The closed curves correspond to periodic solutions, because as the particle traverses them it must pass each point infinitely often at the same position and with the same velocity. For $\beta < 0$, there are open curves whereon the mass will move away from the origin. The curves corresponding to the solution lying between the bounded periodic solutions and the unbounded nonperiodic solutions are called the **separatrices** (plural of separatrix). Following the arrows we see that the separatrices need not be everywhere differentiable functions v of x. Such trajectories are said to be singular. There are three singular trajectories, the left downward moving curve, the center closed curve, and the right upward moving curve.

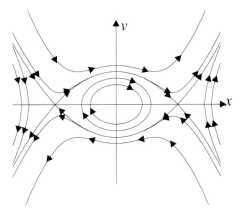

Fig. 7.8 The phase portrait of the Duffing equation $\ddot{x} + \omega^2 x + \beta x^3 = 0$.

A final form for the solution can be obtained by solving for v, using $v = dx/dt$, separating the equation of the first integral, and integrating. Unfortunately, the integral cannot be evaluated in closed form without using so-called elliptic functions.

A similar analysis can be applied (no more successfully) to the free undamped simple pendulum problem, where the equation is

$$\ddot{\theta} + \omega^2 \sin \theta = 0.$$

The equivalent matrix system is

$$\frac{d}{dt} \begin{bmatrix} \theta \\ \dot{\theta} \end{bmatrix} = \begin{bmatrix} \dot{\theta} \\ -\omega^2 \sin \theta \end{bmatrix}.$$

There are fixed points where

$$-\omega^2 \sin \theta = 0 \quad \Rightarrow \quad \theta = n\pi, \ n = -\infty : \infty, \text{ and } v = 0.$$

Eliminating t between the two component equations leads to the phase equation

$$\frac{dv}{d\theta} = -\omega^2 \frac{\sin \theta}{v}.$$

An integration yields

$$v^2 - 2\omega^2 \cos \theta = C.$$

The presence of the $\cos \theta$ term gives rise to infinitely many closed periodic singular trajectories separating the periodic and non-periodic motion, each of which surrounds a fixed point (Figure 7.9).

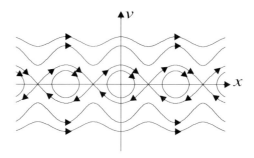

Fig. 7.9 The phase portrait for the simple pendulum problem, $\ddot{\theta} + \omega^2 \sin\theta = 0$.

Each orbit is determined by its total energy. Each closed curve about a fixed point has an equivalent companion at every other fixed point, and they both have the same energy. The closed orbits correspond to the usual oscillations of the pendulum. As the energy increases, we reach the situation wherein the kinetic energy at the bottom of the pendulum's swing will be exactly equal to the potential energy at the top of the swing. The bob will then come to rest at the top and continue swinging in the same direction. This motion corresponds to the two separatrices and is called *rotary* motion. The top separatrix in Figure 7.10 (with the solid line)

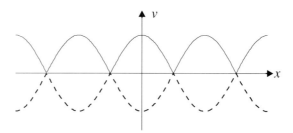

Fig. 7.10 The rotary motion separatrices of the simple pendulum phase portrait. The solid line corresponds to clockwise rotation and the dashed line to counterclockwise rotation.

corresponds to clockwise rotation and the bottom one (the broken line) to counterclockwise rotation. Any further increase in energy will give the mass a nonzero velocity at the top of its swing and the rotation will be smooth; so the corresponding orbits are smooth.

We can also find the actual time dependence of the solution by multiplying the equation of motion by $\dot{\theta}$:

$$\dot{\theta}\ddot{\theta} + \omega^2 \dot{\theta}\sin\theta = 0.$$

This can be immediately integrated to yield

$$\dot{\theta}^2 - \omega^2 \cos\theta = h.$$

Solving for $\dot{\theta} = d\theta/dt$, separating, and integrating, we find

$$t = \int_{\theta_0}^{\theta} \frac{d\phi}{\sqrt{h + \omega^2 \cos \phi}}.$$

Upon inverting this we would have an expression for the angle as a function of time. Unfortunately, the integral cannot be expressed in terms of elementary functions. Rather, we must use elliptic integral functions.

If damping were introduced into this system then continuous periodic motion about the pivot would be prevented because energy needed to move the bob repeatedly around its topmost point would be dissipated. Thus the angular excursion would have to decrease and the phase portrait would consist of the family of spirals shown in Figure 7.11.

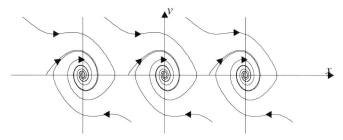

Fig. 7.11   The phase portrait of the damped simple pendulum, $\ddot{\theta} + \beta\dot{\theta} + \omega^2 \sin \theta = 0$.

Changing problems, the equations for the angular velocity of rotation of the free asymmetric top from equation (7.1) were

$$I_1\dot{\omega}_1 + (I_3 - I_2)\,\omega_2\omega_3 = 0,$$
$$I_2\dot{\omega}_2 + (I_1 - I_3)\,\omega_1\omega_3 = 0,$$
$$I_3\dot{\omega}_3 + (I_2 - I_1)\,\omega_1\omega_2 = 0.$$

We expect both energy and angular momentum to be conserved. To see that energy is conserved, we can multiply the ith equation by ω_i, add the results, and integrate to get

$$I_1\omega_1^2 + I_2\omega_2^2 + I_3\omega_3^2 = 2E.$$

Similarly, to show conservation of angular momentum, multiply the ith equation by $I_i\omega_i$, add the results, and integrate to get

$$(I_1\omega_1)^2 + (I_2\omega_2)^2 + (I_3\omega_3)^2 = \|\mathbf{L}\|^2.$$

Using the components of the angular momentum rather than the angular velocity, these two integrals of the equations of motion become

$$\frac{L_1^2}{I_1} + \frac{L_2^2}{I_2} + \frac{L_3^2}{I_3} = 2E,$$

$$L_1^2 + L_2^2 + L_3^2 = \|\mathbf{L}\|^2.$$

The first is the equation of an ellipsoid with semiaxes $\sqrt{2EI_1}$, $\sqrt{2EI_2}$, and $\sqrt{2EI_3}$, while the second is the equation of a sphere of radius $\|\mathbf{L}\|$, both centered at the origin. The orbits will be the curves lying at the intersection of these surfaces for various values of the constant energy and angular momentum. They can be pictured as curves lying on the ellipsoid or curves lying on the sphere (Figure 7.12).

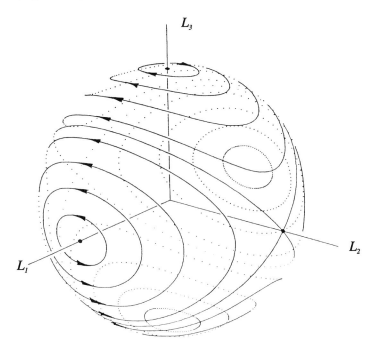

Fig. 7.12   The orbits of the asymmetric top are curves lying at the intersection of spheres and ellipsoids.

We are assured that there are such intersections because of the obvious inequality

$$2EI_1 > \|\mathbf{L}\|^2 > 2EI_3,$$

which follows from our assumption $I_1 > I_2 > I_3$. The angular momentum vector must move so that it extends from the origin to a point on an orbit. From the phase portrait we can see that the top, bottom, front, and back of the ellipsoid are centers of the motion. Thus motion about the axes with minimum and maximum moments of inertia is stable. But motion about the x_2-axis, of intermediate moment of inertia, is unstable because the fixed point is a saddle. Of course, these conclusions depend heavily on the picture. A more precise analysis will be given in teh next section.

We could proceed in the manner of the simple pendulum problem to find an expression for one of the coordinates of angular momentum in terms of time. To do this we will need to eliminate two components by using the conservation equations. In particular, if we are interested in the unstable motion about the x_2-axis, we would eliminate ω_1 and ω_3 using

$$\omega_1^2 = \frac{\left(-2EI_3 - \|\mathbf{L}\|^2\right) - I_2\left(I_3 - I_2\right)\omega_2^2}{I_1\left(I_3 - I_1\right)},$$

$$\omega_3^2 = \frac{\left(-2EI_1 - \|\mathbf{L}\|^2\right) - I_2\left(I_2 - I_1\right)\omega_2^2}{I_3\left(I_3 - I_1\right)}.$$

Thus the equation for ω_2 is

$$\frac{d\omega_2}{dt} = \frac{\sqrt{\left\{\left(-2EI_3 - \|\mathbf{L}\|^2\right) - I_2\left(I_3 - I_2\right)\omega_2^2\right\}\left\{\left(\|\mathbf{L}\|^2 - 2EI_1\right) - I_2\left(I_2 - I_1\right)\omega_2^2\right\}}}{I_2\sqrt{I_1 I_3}}.$$

Needless to say, this cannot be integrated in terms of elementary functions and requires the introduction of elliptic functions, too.

So far we have been able to find the fixed points of nonlinear systems and sketch some of their phase portraits. It remains to classify the fixed points and to determine if there is any periodic motion.

7.3.1 Exercise Set

1. A wire of length L carrying a current I is restrained by two identical springs, each with force constant k. Parallel to this wire and at a distance of a is an infinitely long wire carrying a current I_0.

   (a) Using $\lambda = 2I_0 IL/k$, show that the equation of motion of the short wire is

   $$m\ddot{x} + k\left(x - \frac{\lambda}{a - x}\right) = 0.$$

   (b) Show that the motion is conservative with potential energy

   $$U(x) = \frac{1}{2}kx^2 + k\lambda \ln(a - x).$$

   (c) Sketch the phase portraits and find the equations of the separatrices for the cases $4\lambda < a^2$ and $4\lambda = a^2$. You may disregard the case $4\lambda > a^2$.

7.4   QUALITATIVE BEHAVIOR OF NONLINEAR ODE'S

We have classified the fixed points of linear equations. Also, we have seen that when there are closed orbits, the systems have periodic solutions. It remains for us to classify the fixed points and determine their stability for nonlinear equations. Furthermore, for equations whose phase portraits are not readily found we need to find a way of determining if there are any periodic solutions.

7.4.1   Fixed Points of Nonlinear Systems

Because we want to build on our knowledge of linear systems we might try to approach a nonlinear system by looking at its Taylor series expansion about the fixed point $\mathbf{x}_0$ so that the autonomous system $\dot{\mathbf{x}} = \mathbf{f}(\mathbf{x})$ can be written in the form

$$\dot{\mathbf{x}} = \mathbf{J}(\mathbf{x}_0)\,(\mathbf{x} - \mathbf{x}_0) + \frac{1}{2} \sum_j \sum_k \frac{\partial^2 \mathbf{f}(\mathbf{x}_0)}{\partial x_j \partial x_k} (\mathbf{x} - \mathbf{x}_0)_j (\mathbf{x} - \mathbf{x}_0)_k + \cdots, \qquad (7.5)$$

where $\mathbf{J}(\mathbf{x}_0)$ is the **Jacobi matrix** evaluated at $\mathbf{x}_0$,

$$\mathbf{J}(\mathbf{x}) = \left[\frac{\partial f_j}{\partial x_k} \right] = \begin{bmatrix} \frac{\partial f_1}{\partial x_1} & \frac{\partial f_1}{\partial x_2} & \cdots & \frac{\partial f_1}{\partial x_n} \\ \frac{\partial f_2}{\partial x_1} & \frac{\partial f_2}{\partial x_2} & \cdots & \frac{\partial f_2}{\partial x_n} \\ \vdots & \vdots & \ddots & \vdots \\ \frac{\partial f_n}{\partial x_1} & \frac{\partial f_n}{\partial x_2} & \cdots & \frac{\partial f_n}{\partial x_n} \end{bmatrix}. \qquad (7.6)$$

This is equivalent to rewriting the system in terms of the **local variable** about the fixed point $\mathbf{x}_0$, $\mathbf{y} = \mathbf{x} - \mathbf{x}_0$. It now remains to be seen what the relationship is between the nonlinear autonomous system $\dot{\mathbf{x}} = \mathbf{f}(\mathbf{x})$ and its **linearization** at the fixed point $\mathbf{x}_0$, which is defined to be

$$\dot{\mathbf{x}} = \mathbf{J}(\mathbf{x}_0)(\mathbf{x} - \mathbf{x}_0) \quad \Rightarrow \quad \dot{\mathbf{y}} = \mathbf{J}(\mathbf{x}_0)\mathbf{y}. \qquad (7.7)$$

The phase portraits have both a global and a local character. Locally, near a specific point, two systems may have similar behavior but globally they still may differ. In particular, Figure 7.13 illustrates two systems each of which has a stable focus and a saddle.

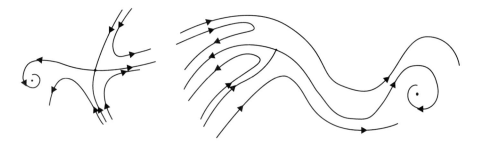

Fig. 7.13   The phase portraits of two systems each of whose fixed points are a focus and a saddle.

Both systems have different global behavior but near their fixed points they look very similar.

As a partial answer to the question of the relationship between the fixed points of the nonlinear system and its linearization, we have the following theorem.

THEOREM 7.1 *If $\mathbf{x}_0$ is a fixed point of the autonomous system $\dot{\mathbf{x}} = \mathbf{f}(\mathbf{x})$, with $\mathbf{f}(\mathbf{x})$ smooth, and $\mathbf{J}(\mathbf{x}_0)$, the Jacobi matrix of $\mathbf{f}(\mathbf{x})$ at $\mathbf{x}_0$, is nonsingular, then the local phase portrait of the linear and nonlinear system are the same except perhaps when $\mathbf{x}_0$ is a center.* □

An immediate corollary to this theorem allows us to classify the fixed points of the nonlinear system by analyzing those of the linear system except in the case when the linear system has a center. The only way we know to determine if a fixed point really is a center for a nonlinear system is to find the equation of the trajectories near it. If it's a center, they should be closed curves.

■ **EXAMPLE 7.11** For each of the following systems, find and classify the fixed points.

(a) $\dot{x}_1 = x_1^2 - x_2^2$, $\dot{x}_2 = x_2^2 - 5x_1 + 6$. Setting $\mathbf{f}(\mathbf{x})$ to zero we find $x_1 = \pm x_2$, so that we must solve

$$x^2 \mp 5x + 6 = 0$$

to find the fixed points. The only real solutions are 2 and 3, so that the fixed points are $(2, 2)$, $(2, -2)$, $(3, 3)$, and $(3, -3)$. In order to classify the fixed points, we must evaluate the Jacobi matrix at each point and find its eigenvalues there. It is

$$\mathbf{J}(x_1, x_2) = \begin{bmatrix} 2x_1 & -2x_2 \\ -5 & 2x_2 \end{bmatrix}.$$

At the point $(2, 2)$ its eigenvalues are $4 \pm \sqrt{20}$, so that is an unstable node. At $(2, -2)$ they are $\pm 2i$, yielding what *might* be a center. At $(3, 3)$ we have eigenvalues $6 \pm \sqrt{30}$ for another unstable node, whereas $(3, -3)$ gives us $\pm\sqrt{6}$, which means a saddle.

As an expansion of the idea of using local coordinates, let's transform the system to the coordinates local to the fixed point $(3, 3)$. This means we must make the substitution $\mathbf{y} = \mathbf{x} - [3; 3]$. Then $\dot{\mathbf{x}} = \dot{\mathbf{y}}$, and the system takes the form

$$\dot{y}_1 = (y_1 + 3)^2 - (y_2 + 3)^2 = y_1^2 - y_2^2 + 6y_1 - 6y_2,$$
$$\dot{y}_2 = (y_2 + 3)^2 - 5(y_1 + 3)\,6 = y_2^2 - 5y_1 + 6y_2.$$

The matrix of the linearized system (which can be read off from the coefficients of the linear terms) is

$$\begin{bmatrix} 6 & -6 \\ -5 & 6 \end{bmatrix},$$

which is precisely the Jacobi matrix evaluated at $(3, 3)$.

(b) $\dot{x}_1 = x_1 - x_2 + x_1 x_2$, $\dot{x}_2 = x_1 - x_2 - x_2^2$. It can be verified that the only fixed points are $(0,0)$ and $(2,-2)$. The Jacobi matrix is

$$\mathbf{J}(x_1, x_2) = \begin{bmatrix} 1 + x_2 & -1 + x_1 \\ 1 & -1 - 2x_2 \end{bmatrix}.$$

The matrix $\mathbf{F}(0,0)$ is singular, and the theorem cannot be applied. The eigenvalues of $\mathbf{J}(2,-2)$ are $1 \pm \sqrt{2}$, so that fixed point is a saddle. ■■■

■ **EXAMPLE 7.12** We can apply this analysis to the spinning asymmetric top. Since the surfaces that defined the trajectories were given in terms of the components of angular momentum, it might be more convenient to convert from equations in terms of ω to equations in terms of $\mathbf{L} = \mathbf{I}\omega$. The form of the equations is

$$\dot{L}_1 = \left(\frac{1}{I_3} - \frac{1}{I_2} \right) L_2 L_3,$$

$$\dot{L}_2 = \left(\frac{1}{I_1} - \frac{1}{I_3} \right) L_3 L_1,$$

$$\dot{L}_3 = \left(\frac{1}{I_2} - \frac{1}{I_1} \right) L_1 L_2.$$

For convenience we can choose $\|\mathbf{L}\|^2 = 1$. Then the fixed points in $L_1 L_2 L_3$-space will be $(\pm 1, 0, 0)$, $(0, \pm 1, 0)$, and $(0, 0, \pm 1)$. In order to classify them, we need to evaluate the Jacobi matrix at each of the fixed points. Starting with $(\pm 1, 0, 0)$, we have

$$\begin{bmatrix} 0 & 0 & 0 \\ 0 & 0 & \pm \left(\frac{1}{I_1} - \frac{1}{I_3} \right) \\ 0 & \left(\frac{1}{I_2} - \frac{1}{I_1} \right) & 0 \end{bmatrix}.$$

This matrix is clearly singular, so that the theorem does not apply. But, we can get around this by analyzing the motion in the $L_2 L_3$-plane. The submatrix of interest is

$$\begin{bmatrix} 0 & \pm \left(\frac{1}{I_1} - \frac{1}{I_3} \right) \\ \pm \left(\frac{1}{I_2} - \frac{1}{I_1} \right) & 0 \end{bmatrix}.$$

Its eigenvalues satisfy the equation

$$\lambda^2 - \left(\frac{1}{I_2} - \frac{1}{I_1} \right) \left(\frac{1}{I_1} - \frac{1}{I_3} \right) = 0.$$

Because of the assumption $I_1 > I_2 > I_3$, this gives rise to purely imaginary eigenvalues. Thus, the points $(\pm 1, 0, 0)$ may be centers, but further analysis is needed. At the points $(0, \pm 1, 0)$, the Jacobi matrix is also singular. The reduced system in the $L_1 L_3$-plane is

$$
\begin{bmatrix}
0 & \pm \left(\dfrac{1}{I_3} - \dfrac{1}{I_2} \right) \\
\pm \left(\dfrac{1}{I_2} - \dfrac{1}{I_1} \right) & 0
\end{bmatrix}.
$$

Its eigenvalues satisfy

$$
\lambda^2 - \left(\frac{1}{I_2} - \frac{1}{I_1} \right) \left(\frac{1}{I_3} - \frac{1}{I_2} \right) = 0.
$$

Thus, both eigenvalues are real and of opposite signs. The points $(0, \pm 1, 0)$ are both saddles. Lastly, the points $(0, 0, \pm 1)$ can be analyzed as a reduced system in the $L_1 L_2$-plane with matrix

$$
\begin{bmatrix}
0 & \pm \left(\dfrac{1}{I_3} - \dfrac{1}{I_2} \right) \\
\pm \left(\dfrac{1}{I_1} - \dfrac{1}{I_3} \right) & 0
\end{bmatrix}.
$$

The eigenvalues satisfy

$$
\lambda^2 - \left(\frac{1}{I_1} - \frac{1}{I_3} \right) \left(\frac{1}{I_3} - \frac{1}{I_2} \right) = 0.
$$

Thus both eigenvalues are purely imaginary and $(0, 0, \pm 1)$ may be centers.

We still need to verify that $(\pm 1, 0, 0)$ and $(0, 0, \pm 1)$ are indeed centers. To see this is true, we can look at the equations in their respective planes. The following equations can be easily verified:

$$
\frac{I_3 I_1}{I_1 - I_3} L_2 \dot{L}_2 + \frac{I_1 I_2}{I_1 - I_2} L_3 \dot{L}_3 = 0,
$$

$$
\frac{I_2 I_3}{I_2 - I_3} L_1 \dot{L}_1 + \frac{I_3 I_1}{I_1 - I_3} L_2 \dot{L}_2 = 0.
$$

Both equations are easily integrated to yield

$$
\frac{I_3 I_1}{I_1 - I_3} L_2^2 + \frac{I_1 I_2}{I_1 - I_2} L_3^2 = C_1,
$$

$$
\frac{I_2 I_3}{I_2 - I_3} L_1^2 + \frac{I_3 I_1}{I_1 - I_3} L_2^2 = C_2.
$$

Since each of the coefficients of the L_k's are positive, these are equations of elliptic cylinders in the $L_1 L_2 L_3$-space. Their intersection with either the sphere $L_1^2 + L_2^2 + L_3^2 = \|\mathbf{L}\|^2 = 1$

or the ellipsoid $(L_1^2/I_1) + (L_2^2/I_2) + (L_3^2/I_3) = 2E$ are closed curves about the L_1- and L_3-axes, respectively. Therefore, $(\pm 1, 0, 0)$ and $(0, 0, \pm 1)$ are centers.   ■ ■ ■

When we speak of a stable fixed point for a nonlinear system it may not be entirely clear what we mean.

DEFINITION 7.1   *A fixed point $\mathbf{x}_0$ of the autonomous system $\dot{\mathbf{x}} = \mathbf{f}(\mathbf{x})$ is said to be **asymptotically stable** if any trajectory that passes into a neighborhood $N_\epsilon(\mathbf{x}_0) := \{\mathbf{x} : \|\mathbf{x} - \mathbf{x}_0\| < \epsilon\}$ approaches $\mathbf{x}_0$ as t increases.*

We need to make the statement that the trajectory must pass into a neighborhood of $\mathbf{x}_0$ before approaching it, because the phase portrait need not have all trajectories coming close to the fixed point actually approaching it. Once we have such a trajectory, the condition of asymptotic stability is equivalent to

$$\lim_{t \to \infty} \mathbf{x}(t) = \mathbf{x}_0. \tag{7.8}$$

This leads to the following theorem.

THEOREM 7.2   *If x_0 is a fixed point of the autonomous system $\dot{\mathbf{x}} = \mathbf{f}(\mathbf{x})$, with $\mathbf{f}(\mathbf{x})$ smooth, and $\mathbf{J}(\mathbf{x}_0)$ is the Jacobi matrix of $\mathbf{f}(\mathbf{x})$ at $\mathbf{x}_0$, is nonsingular, then if all the eigenvalues of $\mathbf{J}(\mathbf{x}_0)$ have negative real part, $\mathbf{x}_0$ is asymptotically stable. If any eigenvalue has positive real part, then $\mathbf{x}_0$ is unstable.*   □

Trajectories can come close to a fixed point without approaching it in the limit of large t. Consider the system

$$\dot{x} = -y^3, \ \dot{y} = x^5.$$

Eliminating t using $y^3 \, dy + x^5 \, dx = 0$ we can see that all the trajectories are given by

$$2x^6 + 3y^2 = C.$$

If we take C small, then the entire path will lie in some neighborhood of the fixed point $(0, 0)$ but it will not approach it. Since this is a closed curve the motion will be periodic, and $(0, 0)$ is a center of the nonlinear system. Any attempt at linearizing this system and analyzing the result would have proved useless, because the linearized form is trivial: $\dot{x} = 0, \dot{y} = 0$.

On the other hand, for the system

$$\dot{x} = -x^3, \ \dot{y} = -y^5$$

the equation of the trajectories is

$$2y^4 = x^2 + Cx^2y^4.$$

Now every trajectory that enters a neighborhood of the origin will approach it.

For the last system, look at the function $V(x) = \|\mathbf{x}\|^2$ on a trajectory:

$$\dot{V} = \nabla V \cdot \dot{x} = [2x, 2y]\,[\dot{x}; \dot{y}] = [2x, 2y]\left[-x^3; -y^5\right] = -2\left(x^4 + y^6\right).$$

Since $\dot{V}$ is always negative, no matter what path we are on, V will decrease. Knowing that V is the square of the distance from the origin, we may conclude that distance is always decreasing along a trajectory. Thus we must approach the origin, and it is asymptotically stable.

This idea can be generalized by introducing the concept of a strong Liapunov function.

DEFINITION 7.2 *We say $V(x)$ is a **strong Liapunov function** at $\mathbf{x}_0$ if for $\mathbf{x}$ in a neighborhood of the fixed point $\mathbf{x}_0$,*

(a) *∇V exists and is a continuous vector field,*

(b) *$V(\mathbf{x}) > 0$ for $\mathbf{x} \neq \mathbf{x}_0$ and $V(\mathbf{x}_0) = 0$, and*

(c) *$\dot{V}(\mathbf{x}) < 0$ for $\mathbf{x} \neq \mathbf{x}_0$ and $\dot{V}(\mathbf{x}_0) = 0$.*

Conditions (b) and (c) are equivalent to saying that V is positive definite near $\mathbf{0}$ and $\dot{V}$ is negative definite there. This means that a strong Liapunov function has a local minimum at the fixed point. We saw that $V(\mathbf{x}) = \|\mathbf{x}\|^2$ is a strong Liapunov function for the system

$$\dot{x} = -x^3, \ \dot{y} = -y^5.$$

The following theorem explains the utility of the strong Liapunov function.

THEOREM 7.3 *If the system $\dot{\mathbf{x}} = \mathbf{f}(\mathbf{x})$ with a fixed point at $\mathbf{x}_0$ has a strong Liapunov function there, then $\mathbf{x}_0$ is asymptotically stable.* □

Applying this theorem depends on how successful we are in finding a strong Liapunov function. Of course we could always try $\|\mathbf{x}\|^2$ as a possibility because it is already positive away from $\mathbf{0}$. More generally, we might try $\mathbf{x}^T \mathbf{Q} \mathbf{x}$ where $\mathbf{Q}$ is positive definite (meaning that all of its eigenvalue are positive).

■ **EXAMPLE 7.13** Where possible, find Liapunov functions for each of the following nonlinear systems.

(a) The system

$$\dot{x}_1 = -x_2 - x_1^3, \ \dot{x}_2 = x_1 - x_2^3$$

has only one fixed point at $(0,0)$. For $V = \|\mathbf{x}\|^2$ we have

$$V(x_1, x_2) = [2x_1, 2x_2][-x_2 - x_1^3; x_1 - x_2^3] = -2(x_1^4 + x_2^4),$$

which is negative away from $(0,0)$. Thus $V(x_1, x_2)$ is a strong Liapunov function, and the origin is asymptotically stable.

Notice that linearization leads to the system

$$\dot{\mathbf{x}} = \begin{bmatrix} 0 & -1 \\ 1 & 0 \end{bmatrix} \mathbf{x}.$$

The eigenvalues are $\lambda = \pm i$, thus classifying the origin as a center, which is not consistent with the Liapunov function approach.

(b) The system

$$\dot{x}_1 = -x_1 \sin^2 x_1, \quad \dot{x}_2 = -x_2 - x_2^3$$

has its only fixed point at the origin. Again using $V = \|\mathbf{x}\|^2$, we have

$$V(x_1, x_2) = -x_1^2 \sin^2 2x_1 - x_2^2 - x_2^4,$$

which is negative in a neighborhood of the origin. Thus $(0,0)$ is asymptotically stable.

Again, linearization leads to the system

$$\dot{\mathbf{x}} = \begin{bmatrix} 0 & 0 \\ 0 & -1 \end{bmatrix} \mathbf{x}.$$

Since $\mathbf{J}(0,0)$ is singular, we get no information.

(c) $\dot{x}_1 = -x_1^3 + x_1 x_2^2, \quad \dot{x}_2 = -2x_1^2 x_2 - x_2^3$. Trying the general quadratic form

$$V(\mathbf{x}) = \mathbf{x}^T \mathbf{Q} \mathbf{x} = \mathbf{x}^T \begin{bmatrix} a & b \\ b & d \end{bmatrix} \mathbf{x} = ax_1^2 + 2bx_1 x_2 + dx_2^2,$$

we have

$$V(\mathbf{x}) = -2\left(ax_1^4 + dx_2^4 + (2d - a)x_1^2 x_2^2\right) + 3bx_1^2 x_2.$$

The requirements that $V > 0$ and $\dot{V} < 0$ can be satisfied with

$$b = 0, \quad 2d - a > 0, \quad a > 0, \quad \text{and} \quad d > 0.$$

Thus a and d are the positive eigenvalues of the diagonal matrix $\mathbf{Q}$. Hence the system is asymptotically stable. ■ ■ ■

Unfortunately, there is no simple method available for constructing a Liapunov function for the general nonlinear system.

7.4.2   Limit Cycles

The next best thing to having an asymptotically stable fixed point is to have all nearby trajectories approach a single closed path. Thus all such motion would approach periodic motion except that of the closed trajectory itself, which would be periodic.

DEFINITION 7.3 *An isolated closed trajectory is called a* **limit cycle**.

When we say a limit cycle is "isolated," we mean there are no other closed trajectories that are arbitrarily close to it. It represents an "island" in the phase portrait, on which the motion is periodic. Showing that a system has a limit cycle by explicitly exhibiting that closed trajectory is usually quite difficult. Some closed curves have fairly reasonable polar coordinate representations, so that such a change of coordinates is sometimes useful.

■ **EXAMPLE 7.14** The system

$$\dot{x}_1 = x_1(a^2 - x_1^2 - x_2^2) - x_2, \ \dot{x}_2 = x_2(a^2 - x_1^2 - x_2^2) + x_1$$

probably should be converted to polar coordinates. The presence of $x_1^2 + x_2^2$ is the key. Let

$$x_1 = r\cos\theta, \ x_2 = r\sin\theta.$$

Then we have

$$\dot{r}\cos\theta - r\dot{\theta}\sin\theta = (r\cos\theta)\left(a^2 - r^2\right) - r\sin\theta, \qquad \text{(a)}$$
$$\dot{r}\sin\theta + r\dot{\theta}\cos\theta = (r\sin\theta)\left(a^2 - r^2\right) + r\cos\theta \qquad \text{(b)}$$

Forming the new equations (a) $\cos\theta +$ (b) $\sin\theta$ and $-$(a) $\sin\theta +$ (b) $\cos\theta$ leads to the system

$$\dot{r} = r\left(a^2 - r^2\right), \ \dot{\theta} = 1. \qquad\qquad \text{(c)}$$

There is no question that the circle $r = a$ is a solution that is closed and therefore periodic. Thus a solution in terms of x_1 and x_2 is

$$x(t) = [a\cos(t + \theta_0); a\sin(t + \theta_0)].$$

If we look back at (c), we see that when $0 < r < a$ we have $\dot{r} > 0$, so that trajectories starting inside the circle move out toward it. When $r > a$ we have $\dot{r} < 0$, so that trajectories outside the circle move in toward it (Figure 7.14). ■ ■ ■

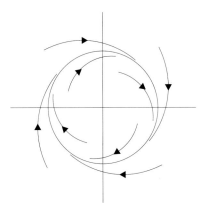

Fig. 7.14   A circle of radius a is a limit cycle. Trajectories starting within the circle move out toward it, and those starting outside it move in toward it.

Limit cycles toward which trajectories move are said to be **stable**, or **attracting**, whereas those away from which trajectories move are **unstable**, or **repelling**. It is possible that a limit cycle will be part of each type, if trajectories on one side move toward it and those on the other side move away. Such limit cycles are called **semistable**. See Figure 7.15.

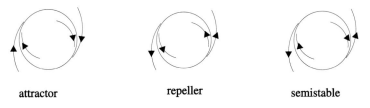

attractor   repeller   semistable

Fig. 7.15

■ **EXAMPLE 7.15** The system

$$\dot{r} = r(a - r)(b - r)(c - r)^2, \ \theta = 1,$$

with $0 < a < b < c$ has limit cycles at $r = a$, $r = b$, and $r = c$. Within $0 < r < a$ we have $\dot{r} > 0$, so that trajectories move out to the $r = a$ limit cycle. When $a \leq r \leq b$ we have $\dot{r} < 0$, and trajectories in this annulus move into the limit cycle $r = a$. Thus $r = a$ is an attractor. For $b \leq r \leq c$, $\dot{r} > 0$. Trajectories between $r = a$ and $r = b$ move toward $r = a$, but those between $r = b$ and $r = c$ move out toward $r = c$. Thus $r = b$ is a repeller that pushes the trajectories away from itself, out to $r = c$ and in to $r = a$. Outside $r = c$ we have $\dot{r} > 0$, so that limit cycle is semistable (Figure 7.16).

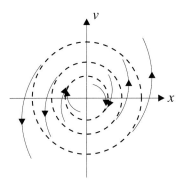

Fig. 7.16

Another way to see this is by looking at the phase plane analysis wherein we plot r versus $v = \dot{r} = f(r)$ (Figure 7.17).

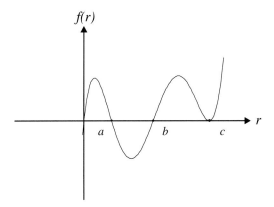

Fig. 7.17

From either analysis we have a rough idea of the phase portrait. ■ ■ ■

If a limit cycle is not a circle, which it seldom is outside of textbook problems, then we will not usually be able to determine much by the change to polar coordinates. Something more powerful is needed.

7.4.3 The Existence of Limit Cycles

In the general nonlinear system only certain things can happen. If we restrict our discussion to 2×2 systems, we can state a fairly deep theorem that contains all that our intuition tells us.

THEOREM 7.4 (Poincaré-Bendixson) *Suppose that a trajectory that begins at $t = t_0$ (which is sometimes called a **half-trajectory**) lies entirely within a closed bounded region* *of the plane containing no singular points (as defined in Chapter 8) of the system. Then the trajectory either*

(a) *is a closed path, and hence motion is periodic,*

(b) *approaches a limit cycle, or*

(c) *terminates at a fixed point of the system.*   □

If the region in question is free of fixed points, then any half-trajectory in it must either approach a limit cycle or be a closed curve, and so the region must contain a periodic solution. This is in distinction to the case of chaotic motion wherein there is no periodic solution and the trajectory wanders about aimlessly and randomly for all time (more about this in Section 7.7). We may conclude that there cannot be chaotic motion in two dimensions.

The closed path of part (a) of the theorem need not be a limit cycle, because it need not be isolated. If the trajectories are of the form $x^2 + y^2 = a^2$, then there are infinitely many closed paths in any closed bounded set about the origin.

One fairly general nonlinear second order ODE is **Lienard's equation**,

$$\ddot{x} + f(x, \dot{x})\dot{x} + g(x) = 0.$$

Some authors refer to such equations as **quasilinear** because the highest derivative appears only to the first power. Under certain very restrictive conditions, satisfied by many equations of interest in applications, this equation will have a limit cycle.

THEOREM 7.5 *If $f(x, v)$ and $g(x)$ in Lienard's equation are continuous functions that satisfy*

(a) $f(x, v) > 0$ *for* $x^2 + v^2 > a^2$ *for some positive a,*

(b) $f(0, 0) < 0$,

(c) $g(0) = 0$, $\operatorname{sgn}(g(x)) = \operatorname{sgn}(x)$,

(d) $G(x) := \int g(x)\, dx \to \infty$ *as* $x \to \infty$,

then $\ddot{x} + f(x, \dot{x})\dot{x} + g(x) = 0$ has at least one limit cycle.

The proof can be found in Jordan & Smith. Several well-known equations have limit cycles because of the theorem.

▪ **EXAMPLE 7.16** Apply the previous theorem to the following equations.

(a) The **van der Pol equation**

$$\ddot{x} + \epsilon(x^2 - 1)\dot{x} + x = 0, \ \epsilon > 0,$$

has a limit cycle because $f(x, v) = \epsilon(x^2 - 1)$, so that for $x > 1$, $f > 0$. Also, $f(0) = -\epsilon < 0$. Since $g(x) = x$, part (c) of the theorem is satisfied. Also, $G(x) = \int x \, dx = \frac{1}{2}x^2 \to \infty$ as $x \to \infty$. This guarantees that the van der Pol equation has a periodic solution.

(b) The **Rayleigh equation** is

$$\ddot{x} - \left(\dot{x} - \frac{1}{3}\dot{x}^3\right) + x = 0.$$

Here $f(x, v) = -1 + \frac{1}{3}v^2 = -\frac{1}{3}(3 - v^2)$. Thus for $0 < v < \sqrt{3}$, we have $f > 0$. Also $f(0, 0) = -1 < 0$. Because $g(x) = x$, the requirements of part (c) are satisfied. Also, $G(x) = \frac{1}{2}x^2 \to \infty$ as $x \to \infty$. You should notice the difference between the Rayleigh and van der Pol equations.   ▪ ▪ ▪

This is but one of a family of theorems that tell about the existence of limit cycles. Consult Jordan and Smith for more detail.

7.4.4 *Exercise Set*

Find and classify all fixed points of each of the following nonlinear systems.

1. $\dot{x} = 4x, \quad \dot{y} = 12y + 3y^2$

2. $\dot{x} = xy + y^2, \quad \dot{y} = 2x + xy - x^2$

3. $\dot{x} = 2x - xy, \quad \dot{y} = 3y - xy - 2y^2$

4. $\dot{x} = x(1 + y) - (x + y), \quad \dot{y} = 2 - x + 3y - xy + y^2$

5. $\dot{x} = y - x^2y, \quad \dot{y} = 2x - 3xy + xy^2$

7.5 REGULAR PERTURBATION SCHEMES

Closed form solutions to nonlinear ODE's are seldom available. Whenever the nonlinearity is present as a small perturbation on a linear equation, it *may* be possible to construct a solution that can be represented as a power series in a small parameter. If the equation does not change character when the parameter is set to zero, we can use a regular perturbation scheme. Duffing's equation,

$$\ddot{x} + \omega^2 x + \beta x^3 = F(t), \tag{7.9}$$

admits a regular perturbation solution in terms of the parameter β. Some equations undergo a change in character when the parameter is set to zero. A classic example is

$$\epsilon \ddot{x} + \alpha x = F(t).$$

If ϵ is set to zero, we no longer have a differential equation.

The fundamental idea of the regular perturbation schemes is to write the solution in the form of a series,

$$x(t) = \sum_{n=0}^{\infty} x_n(t)\, \epsilon^n. \tag{7.10}$$

The function $x_0(t)$ will be chosen to be the solution to the linear equation that results from setting ϵ to zero. The next step is to insert this expression into the equation and expand all quantities in a power series in ϵ. Then equate like powers of ϵ to obtain equations for each unknown function $x_n(t)$. It will turn out that the solution for each $x_n(t)$ may depend on the form of $x_0(t)$, $x_1(t)$, ..., and $x_{n-1}(t)$. You should compare this with the series techniques to be discussed in Chapter 8.

If we assume that $x(t, \epsilon)$ is an analytic function of ϵ, then we can use Taylor's Theorem to evaluate the terms of the power series as derivatives with respect to ϵ. We'll use

$$x(t, \epsilon) = x(t, 0) + \epsilon \frac{\partial x(t, 0)}{\partial \epsilon} + \frac{\epsilon^2}{2!} \frac{\partial^2 x(t, 0)}{\partial \epsilon^2} + \cdots. \tag{7.11}$$

In fact, this can usually be applied to the entire equation together with any initial conditions.

Let's try to derive a form for a periodic solution to the harmonically forced Duffing's equation, which is

$$\ddot{x} + \omega^2 x + \beta x^3 = F_0 \cos \Omega t. \tag{7.12}$$

We will look for a solution of period $T = 2\pi/\Omega$ because that is the same period as the forcing function. Assume that the equation has been converted to nondimensionalized form, so that all the constants are dimensionless and $\beta = \epsilon$. Inserting

$$x(t) = x_0(t) + \epsilon x_1(t) + \epsilon^2 x_2(t) + \cdots \tag{7.13}$$

into the equation, we have

$$\left[\ddot{x}_0 + \epsilon \ddot{x}_1 + \epsilon^2 \ddot{x}_2 + \cdots \right] + \omega^2 \left[x_0 + \epsilon x_1 + \epsilon^2 x_2 + \cdots \right]$$
$$+ \epsilon \left[x_0 + \epsilon x_1 + \epsilon^2 x_2 + \cdots \right]^3 = F_0 \cos \Omega t.$$

Taking appropriate derivatives with respect to ϵ, we find the ϵ^n, $n = 0 : 2$, version of equation (7.12) to be

$$
\begin{aligned}
\epsilon^0 : \quad & \ddot{x}_0 + \omega^2 x_0 = F \cos \Omega t, \\
\epsilon^1 : \quad & \ddot{x}_1 + \omega^2 x_1 + x_0^3 = 0, \\
\epsilon^2 : \quad & \ddot{x}_2 + \omega^2 x_2 + 3x_0^2 x_1 = 0,
\end{aligned}
$$

and the rest are quite messy. Since we seek a periodic solution with angular frequency Ω, use the particular solution $x_{0_{\mathrm{p}}} = K \cos \Omega t$. We get the general solution

$$
x_0(t) = A_0 \cos \omega t + B_0 \sin \omega t + \frac{F_0}{\omega^2 - \Omega^2} \cos \Omega t.
$$

If $\omega \neq \Omega$, then we must set $A_0 = 0 = B_0$ because those terms are not of the desired periodicity. Inserting this into the next equation, using the identity

$$
\cos^3 \theta = \frac{3}{4} \cos \theta + \frac{1}{4} \cos 3\theta,
$$

solving, and keeping only the terms of the correct periodicity, we find

$$
x_1(t) = \frac{3F_0^3}{4 \left(\omega^2 - \Omega^2\right)^4} \cos \Omega t + \frac{F_0^3}{4 \left(\omega^2 - \Omega^2\right)^3 \left(\omega^2 - 3\Omega^2\right)} \cos 3\Omega t.
$$

If we repeat this procedure and solve for $x_2(t)$, $\ldots$, we will find contributions from the harmonic terms $\cos 5\Omega t$, $\cos 7\Omega t$, etc. The solution is then

$$
\begin{aligned}
x(t) \;=\;& \frac{F_0}{\omega^2 - \Omega^2} \cos \Omega t \\
&+ \epsilon \left\{ \frac{3F_0^3}{4 \left(\omega^2 - \Omega^2\right)^4} \cos \Omega t + \frac{F_0^3}{4 \left(\omega^2 - \Omega^2\right)^3 \left(\omega^2 - 3\Omega^2\right)} \cos 3\Omega t \right\} + O(\epsilon^2).
\end{aligned}
$$

The solution derived by this method is not valid if $\omega^2 = n^2 \Omega^2$ for some whole number n, because then the particular solution for one of the $x_k(t)$ will contain a "secular" term of the form $t \cos(n\Omega t)$. Such a solution would display resonance, and its amplitude would increase as a function of time. Hence the original expansion in powers of ϵ would not be valid.

7.5.1 Lindstedt's Procedure

Were we to seek solutions of a free nonlinear equation, which arises from a conservative system with closed phase portraits, we know there would be periodic solutions but we may not know their period. In such cases a procedure due to Lindstedt must be used. Write not only x but also Ω as a perturbation series in powers of ϵ, i.e.,

$$
\begin{aligned}
x(t, \epsilon) &= x_0(t) + \epsilon x_1(t) + \cdots, \\
\Omega &= \omega + \omega \Omega_1 + \cdots.
\end{aligned}
\tag{7.14}
$$

Let's look at the so-called "**satellite equation**,"

$$\ddot{x} + x = \epsilon x^2.$$

We could just insert (7.13) into this equation and solve, but there is a more natural method. Because the angular frequency of the solution is unknown, we could remove it from within the functional dependence by changing the independent variable from t to $\tau = \Omega t$. In this case the new equation is

$$\Omega^2 x'' + x = \epsilon x^2,$$

and where primes denote derivatives with respect to τ. Now we will be looking for solutions with period 2π in τ. Inserting the perturbation expansions for $x(\tau)$ and Ω, we find

$$
\begin{aligned}
\epsilon^0 : & \quad x_0'' + x_0 = 0, \\
\epsilon^1 : & \quad x_1'' + x_1 = x_0^2 - \Omega_1 x_0'', \\
\epsilon^2 : & \quad x_2'' + x_2 = 2x_0 x_1 - \left(\Omega_1^2 + 2\Omega_2\right) x_0'' - 2\Omega_1 x_1''.
\end{aligned}
$$

The immediate solution for x_0 is $x_0(\tau) = A \cos \tau$, and the equation for $x_1(\tau)$ is

$$x_1'' + x_1 = \frac{1}{2}A^2 + 2\Omega_1 A \cos \tau + \frac{1}{2}A^2 \cos 2\tau.$$

If we don't have $\Omega_1 = 0$, then every solution to this equation will contain a secular term and lead to resonance. Forcing $\Omega_1 = 0$, we find

$$x_1(t) = \frac{1}{6}A^2(3 - 2\cos \tau - \cos 2\tau),$$

which has period 2π in τ, as required. The next order equation is

$$x_2'' + x_2 = \frac{1}{6}\left[(5A^3 + 12A\Omega_2)\cos \tau - A^3(2 + 2\cos 2\tau + \cos 3\tau)\right].$$

Similarly to the previous equation, there will be secular terms unless the coefficient of $\cos \tau$ is zero. We must require

$$\Omega_2 = -\frac{5}{12}A^2.$$

With this value, the solution for $x_2(t)$ is

$$x_2(t) = \frac{1}{144}A^3\left(-48 + 29\cos \tau + 16\cos 2\tau + 3\cos 3\tau\right).$$

So far, we have

$$\Omega = \omega - \frac{5}{12}A^2\epsilon^2 + O(\epsilon^3)$$

and

$$x(t) = A\cos\tau + \epsilon\frac{A^2}{6}\left(3 - 2\cos\tau - \cos 2\tau\right)$$

$$+\epsilon^2\frac{A^3}{144}\left(-48 + 29\cos\tau + 16\cos 2\tau + 3\cos 3\tau\right) + O(\epsilon^3).$$

Higher order corrections can be calculated.

7.5.2 *Method of Krylov-Bogoliubov*

There is an alternative technique available for solving autonomous systems like the free satellite equation. The idea is due to Krylov and Bogoliubov and consists of replacing one second order equation by two first order equations whose solution will be obtained by averaging them.

Suppose the equation whose solution we seek can be put in the form of a perturbation of the harmonic oscillator equation of the form

$$\ddot{u} + \omega^2 u = \epsilon g(u, \dot{u}). \tag{7.15}$$

The solution to the linear equation, when $\epsilon = 0$, is our old friend

$$u(t) = A\cos(\omega t - \alpha),$$

where A is the amplitude and α is the phase, both of which are constant. Now assume the solution to the full nonlinear equation still has this form but A and α are now time dependent. Very much in the style of the method of variation of parameters, we will also assume that the first derivative of $u(t)$ has the form it would have for the linear problem, to wit

$$\dot{u} = -A\omega\sin\theta, \quad \theta = \omega t - \alpha. \tag{7.16}$$

Since A and θ depend on t there will be two terms in the differentiation using the Product Rule that must be set to zero so this assumption will be valid. In particular, we must force

$$\dot{A}\cos\theta - A\dot{\theta}\sin\theta = 0.$$

Now compute the second derivative by differentiating (7.16):

$$\ddot{u} = -A\omega^2\cos\theta - \omega\dot{A}\sin\theta - A\omega\dot{\theta}\cos\theta.$$

Using this in (7.15), we have

$$\omega\dot{A}\sin\theta + A\omega\dot{\theta}\cos\theta = -\epsilon g(A\cos\theta, -A\omega\sin\theta).$$

Taking this equation together with the requirement that arose from the special form of u, inserting into (7.15), and solving for $\dot{A}$ and $\dot{\theta}$, we have the two equations

$$\frac{dA}{dt} = -\frac{\epsilon}{\omega}\sin\theta\, g(A\cos\theta, -A\omega\sin\theta),$$

$$\frac{d\theta}{dt} = -\frac{\epsilon}{A\omega}\cos\theta\, g(A\cos\theta, -A\omega\sin\theta).$$

The right hand sides of both equations are periodic of period $T = 2\pi/\omega$. They are also small because they are of order ϵ. We may conclude that both $A(t)$ and $\omega(t)$ are both slowly varying functions of time and they do not change much over one period. We could replace the equations by their average over one period. Such an average is obtained by integrating from 0 to T over t or from $-\pi$ to π over θ. Write

$$g_s(A) = \frac{1}{\pi} \int_{-\pi}^{\pi} g(A\cos\theta, -A\omega\sin\theta) \sin\theta \, d\theta,$$

$$g_c(A) = \frac{1}{\pi} \int_{-\pi}^{\pi} g(A\cos\theta, -A\omega\sin\theta) \cos\theta \, d\theta$$

Then g_s and g_c are the first Fourier sine and cosine coefficients in the full Fourier series expansion of $g(A\cos\theta, -A\omega\sin\theta)$. Since we are now interested in the averaged quantities $\bar{A} := \int A(t)\, dt/2\pi$ and $\bar{\theta} := \int \theta(t)\, dt/2\pi$, where both integrals extend from $-\pi$ to π, the averaged equations to be solved are

$$\frac{d\bar{A}}{dt} = -\frac{\epsilon}{2\omega} g_s(\bar{A}), \quad \frac{d\bar{\theta}}{dt} = -\frac{\epsilon}{2\bar{A}\omega} g_c(\bar{A}).$$

Applying this to Duffing's equation we have $g(u) = -u^3$, so that

$$g_s(\bar{A}) = \frac{1}{\pi} \int_{-\pi}^{\pi} \left(\bar{A}\cos\theta\right)^3 \sin\theta \, d\theta = 0,$$

$$g_c(\bar{A}) = \frac{1}{\pi} \int_{-\pi}^{\pi} \left(\bar{A}\cos\theta\right)^3 \cos\theta \, d\theta = -\frac{3}{4}\bar{A}^3.$$

The pair of averaged differential equations is

$$\frac{d\bar{A}}{dt} = 0, \quad \frac{d\bar{\theta}}{dt} = \frac{3\epsilon}{8\bar{A}\omega}\bar{A}^3.$$

We immediately see that $\bar{A} = A_0$, a constant, and

$$\bar{\theta}(t) = \frac{3\bar{A}^2\epsilon}{8\omega}t + \alpha_0.$$

Hence, an approximate solution is given by

$$u(t) = A\cos\left\{\omega t\left(1 + \frac{3\bar{A}^2\epsilon}{8\omega}\right) + \alpha_0\right\}.$$

Higher order corrections can be calculated.

There are many other methods available for solving nonlinear equations that can be written as perturbed linear systems. Throughout this discussion we have concentrated on solutions without secular terms. Thus the series expansion will be "uniformly" valid over a range of the independent variable. Sometimes it is not possible to construct a uniformly valid expansion. That is the subject of the next section.

7.5.3 *Exercise Set*

1. Write Duffing's equation in the form $\omega^2 x'' + x - \epsilon x^3 = 0$, where primes denote derivatives with respect to the dimensionless variable $\tau = \omega t$. Expand ω and x in perturbation series of the form

$$
\begin{aligned}
\omega &= 1 + \epsilon \omega_1 + \cdots, \\
x(\tau, \epsilon) &= x_0(\tau) + \epsilon x_1(\tau) + \cdots.
\end{aligned}
$$

Use Lindstedt's procedure to find solutions of period 2π to show that

$$
x(\tau, \epsilon) = A_0 \cos \omega t + \frac{1}{32} \epsilon A_0^3 (\cos \omega t - \cos 3\omega t) + O(\epsilon^2),
$$

where

$$
\omega = 1 - \frac{3}{8} \epsilon A_0^2 + O(\epsilon^2).
$$

2. Show that an approximation to the forced response of period 2π for the equation $x'' + 0.25x + \epsilon x^3 = \cos \tau$, where τ is dimensionless, is

$$
x(\tau, \epsilon) = -\frac{4}{3} \cos \tau - \epsilon \left(\frac{64}{27} \cos \tau + \frac{64}{945} \cos 3\tau \right) + O(\epsilon^2).
$$

7.6 SINGULAR PERTURBATIONS

When solving linear ODE's with variable coefficients, there are two cases to consider, solutions about ordinary points and solutions about singular points. Solutions about ordinary points were always expressible as Taylor series with nonzero radii of convergence. On the other hand, solutions about singular points need not have Taylor series, nor did they have to converge. Even when the singular points were regular, we need not have gotten a Taylor series because of the presence of the Fröbenius correction factor $(x - x_0)^\lambda$ or the possibility of roots of the indicial equation differing by an integer, whic could lead to the presence of a logarithmic term (for more detail, see Chapter 8).

Much the same situation holds for expansions of solutions of nonlinear equations. Some problems give rise to series in the small parameter ϵ that converge within some region, whereas others do not lead to convergent series but rather asymptotic series. Even worse, some problems give rise to "solutions" that in the limit as $\epsilon \to 0$ do not satisfy the limiting model equations. Such problems lead to so-called **singular perturbation expansions**. Usually, problems requiring such solutions experience a distinct change of character as ϵ goes to zero.

■ **EXAMPLE 7.17**   Suppose ϵ is a small parameter and we want to solve the simple quadratic equation

$$\epsilon x^2 + 4x + 4 = 0.$$

Our intuition and the results of Section 7.5 would tell us to look at the problem when $\epsilon = 0$, i.e.

$$4x + 4 = 0.$$

Thus our first "approximation" to a solution is $x = -1$. Of course we are in deep trouble because we solved a linear equation that has but one root whereas the original quadratic equation always has two roots, counting multiplicity. This change of character of the problem is a characteristic of problems requiring singular perturbations.

We might be tempted to use the fact that the product of the roots of the original equation is $4/\epsilon$. So if $x = -1$ is one root, then $x = -4/\epsilon$ should be the other. We also know that the sum of the roots is $-4/\epsilon$. But our roots total $-(1 + 4/\epsilon)$. One might argue that since ϵ is small, $4/\epsilon$ is much larger than 1 and so it dominates the sum. Such an argument drives us to neglect the one root we found directly, -1. If instead we use the sum of the roots to obtain the second root we get $x = 1 - 4/\epsilon$. Then the product of the roots is $-1 + 4/\epsilon$, and again we are faced with neglecting the zeroth order approximation -1 in favor of $4/\epsilon$.

If we took the easy route and used the quadratic formula, we would be able to get both roots. They are

$$\frac{-2 \pm 2\sqrt{1 - \epsilon}}{\epsilon}.$$

Putting $\epsilon = 0$ leads to an undefined expression for one of the roots. Were we to use the Binomial Theorem to expand the square root, we'd find

$$\frac{-2 \pm 2\left(1 - \frac{1}{2}\epsilon - \frac{1}{8}\epsilon^2 + \cdots\right)}{\epsilon} = \begin{cases} -1 - \frac{\epsilon}{4} + \cdots, \\[2mm] -\frac{4}{\epsilon} + 1 + \frac{\epsilon}{4} + \cdots. \end{cases}$$

Notice that as we neglect ϵ, one root is meaningful, whereas if we neglect terms other than $1/\epsilon$, the other is meaningful. Also -1, $-4/\epsilon$, and $1 - 4/\epsilon$ all appear as approximations to the roots. Here we have a problem in which there are at least two different scales of size with respect to the small parameter.   ■ ■ ■

Solving higher order polynomial equations containing a small parameter requires much work. One must employ a balancing procedure whereby various combinations of terms are assumed to be of the same order of magnitude and others can be neglected. Such an analysis is carried out in Bender & Orszag.

The last example indicated the significance of the multiple scales we must employ to find an expansion of the solution in terms of the small parameter. These are required because the expansion is not uniformly valid over a range of the parameter. There are several procedures available for such problems. One particular procedure is the **method of strained coordinates** due to Lighthill. The idea is to expand both dependent and independent variables in terms of the parameter as

$$x(t; \epsilon) = x_0(\tau) + \epsilon x_1(\tau) + \epsilon^2 x_2(\tau) + \cdots,$$

$$t(\tau; e) = \tau + \epsilon t_1(\tau) + \epsilon^2 t_2(\tau) + \cdots.$$

The difference between this and Lindstedt's procedure is that the independent variable is determined by a series of unknown functions, the $t_k(\tau)$, insofar as we need not arrive at periodic solutions. We do our analysis as if we are using the wrong kind of clock and it is our job to discover the correct time scale(s) along which events proceed. There might even be a need for multiple time scales to accommodate radically different categories of events.

Were the original problem a boundary value problem, we would need to use different time scales for near times and far times. These scales are separated by a **boundary layer**, further discussion of which is beyond the scope of the text. The following example is due to Lighthill.

■ **EXAMPLE 7.18** We wish to "solve" the first order equation

$$(\epsilon x + t)\frac{dx}{dt} + (2 + t)x = 0, \ x(t = 1) = e^{-1}.$$

To avoid the complications of division, we can rewrite the equation in differential form:

$$(\epsilon x + t)\, dx + (2 + t)\, x\, dt = 0.$$

Before inserting the series expansions for x and t we need to think about the initial condition at $t = 1$, which is very unlikely to correspond to $\tau = 1$. Suppose that $\tilde{\tau}$ corresponds to $t = 1$. The relation that we must solve to find $\tilde{\tau}$ is

$$1 = \tilde{\tau} + \epsilon t_1(\tilde{\tau}) + \epsilon^2 t_2(\tilde{\tau}) + \cdots.$$

Suppose $\tilde{\tau}$ is "near" 1 and this expansion can be inverted and recast in the simpler form

$$\tilde{\tau} = 1 + \epsilon \tilde{\tau}_1 + \epsilon^2 \tilde{\tau}_2 + \cdots.$$

Inserting this into the general expansion leads to

$$\tilde{\tau} = 1 - \epsilon t_1(1) - \epsilon^2 \left\{ t_2(1) - t_1(1)t_1'(1) \right\} + \cdots.$$

Now the boundary condition takes the form

$$e^{-1} = x_0(1) + \epsilon \left\{ x_1(1) - x_0'(1)t_1(1) \right\} + \cdots.$$

Equating powers of ϵ, we find

$$\epsilon^0 : \ x_0(1) = e^{-1},$$
$$\epsilon^1 : \ x_1(1) = x_0'(1)t_1(1), \quad \text{etc.}$$

Inserting the expansions in the equation, we find

$$\{\epsilon\,(x_0 + \epsilon x_1 + \cdots) + (\tau + \epsilon t_1 + \cdots)\}\,\{dx_0 + \epsilon\,dx_1 + \cdots\}$$
$$+ \{2 + (\tau + \epsilon t_1 + \cdots)\}\,\{x_0 + \epsilon x_1 + \cdots\}\,\{d\tau + \epsilon\,dt_1 + \cdots\} = 0.$$

Using primes for derivatives with respect to τ we have,

$$\tau x_0' + (2 + \tau)x_0 = 0,$$
$$\tau x_1' + (2 + \tau)x_1 = -(2 + \tau)x_0 t_1' - (x_0 + x_0')t_1 - x_0 x_0'.$$

The first order equation for $x_0(t)$ is easily solved, yielding

$$x_0(\tau) = \frac{1}{\tau^2}e^{-\tau},$$

where use has been made of the zeroth order approximation to the initial condition. The initial condition for the second order equation is

$$x_1(1) = x_0'(1)t_1(1) = e^{-1}t_1(1).$$

Since we have no restrictions on $t_1(\tau)$, it might seem that it can be chosen in any reasonable manner. Lighthill, however, found that to yield a uniformly valid solution, we must have $x_1(\tau)$ *no more singular* than $x_0(\tau)$. If we insert the value of $x_0(\tau)$ into the equation for x_1, we have

$$\tau x_1' + (2 + \tau)x_1 = \frac{1}{\tau}\left[\left(1 - \frac{2}{\tau}\right)e^{-\tau}t_1' + \frac{2}{\tau^2}t_1 + \left(\frac{2}{\tau^4} - \frac{1}{\tau^3}\right)e^{-2\tau}\right].$$

To ensure that x_1 is no more singular than x_0, we can choose t_1 so that we remove the worst singularity from the equation. Since the $e^{-\tau}t_1'$ term is not singular at $t = 0$, we need not consider it. The worst singularity on the right hand side is $(2/\tau^5)e^{-2\tau}$. Since we are worrying about the region where τ is nearly zero, the factors $e^{-\tau}$ and $e^{-2\tau}$ should both be nearly one. Thus it is not unreasonable to choose t_1 to satisfy the equation (multiplied through by τ^5)

$$-2\tau^3 t_1' + 2\tau^2 t_1 + 2 = 0.$$

This is a first order linear ODE and can be easily solved to yield the particular solution

$$t_1(\tau) = -\frac{1}{3\tau^2}.$$

Solving for $x_1(\tau)$, we are left with

$$x_1(\tau) = \frac{e^{-\tau}}{\tau^2}\left[\frac{2}{3\tau^3} + \frac{1}{3\tau^2} - \int_\tau^1 e^{-s}\left(\frac{2}{s^4} + \frac{1}{s^3}\right)ds\right].$$

Thus to within first order in ϵ, x is given by

$$x(\tau) = \frac{e^{-\tau}}{\tau^2}\left\{1 + \epsilon\left[\frac{2}{3\tau^3} + \frac{1}{3\tau^2} - \int_\tau^1 e^{-s}\left(\frac{2}{s^4} + \frac{1}{s^3}\right)ds\right]\right\} + O(\epsilon^2)$$

and

$$t = \tau - \frac{1}{3\tau^2}\epsilon + O(\epsilon^2).$$

Further analyses can be performed to attain greater accuracy. Unfortunately, other methods must be employed to deal with other forms of nonlinearities. The interested reader should consult Lin & Segel, Nayfeh, or Bender & Orszag. ■ ■ ■

7.7 INTRODUCTION TO CHAOTIC DYNAMICS

When computing the values of relevant variables along a trajectory, we must discretize our time variable and replace t by t_n. Doing this causes the trajectory to be replaced by a set of discrete points. Such a discrete set is related to the so-called Poincaré map of the trajectory. Any strange behavior demonstrated by the Poincaré map must also characterize the trajectory. Rather than looking at ODE's, in this section we will study two very simple forms of discrete sequences that lead to rather unusual behavior.

7.7.1 Poincaré Map

If $\dot{\mathbf{x}} = \mathbf{f}(\mathbf{x})$ is an autonomous system in $\mathbb{R}^n$, $\mathcal{S}$ is an $(n-1)$ dimensional surface that is nowhere tangent to a trajectory of the system, $\mathbf{x}_0$ is a point of intersection of the surface and the trajectory, and $\mathbf{x}_1$ is the first point on the trajectory that intersects $\mathcal{S}$, then the map P that sends $\mathbf{x}_0$ into $\mathbf{x}_1$ is called the **Poincaré map**, or **map of first return**.

■ **EXAMPLE 7.19** Find the Poincaré map of the first order equation $u' + 2u = \cos t + 2\sin t$.

Solution: The equation has as one possible solution

$$u(t) = e^{-2t} + \sin t.$$

We can construct a Poincaré map by looking at the intersections of the trajectory with the x_1-axis at the times $0, \pi/2, \pi, \ldots$. Thus the map of first return is $P(x(0)) = P(1) = e^{-\pi} + 1$, and $P^2(1) = e^{-2\pi}$. ■ ■ ■

7.7.2 Iterated Maps

We want to consider one dimensional maps defined by the functional sequence

$$x_{n+1} = f(x_n), \tag{7.17}$$

where $f(x)$ is a scalar function such as one we might get by implementing Euler's method for finding numerical solutions to an ODE or successive applications of the Poincaré map. We'll restrict our attention to sequences $x_0, x_1, x_2, \ldots$ generated by f that are bounded; i.e., there are finite numbers A and B such that $A < x_n < B$ for all $n = 0 : \infty$. A point ξ is said to be a **fixed point** of this map f if

$$f(\xi) = \xi.$$

Just as in previous sections, we will be interested in studying the stability of fixed points. One way to accomplish this is to write the sequence as $x_n = \xi + \delta_n$, where we will take the δ_n to be small. The iteration equation (7.17) takes the form

$$\xi + \delta_{n+1} = f(\xi + \delta_n).$$

Assume $f(x)$ is sufficiently well-behaved so that we can replace it by its linear approximation, getting

$$\xi + \delta_{n+1} = f(\xi) + f'(\xi)\delta_n = \xi + f'(\xi)\delta_n.$$

Solving for the ratio δ_{n+1}/δ_n, we find

$$\frac{\delta_{n+1}}{\delta_n} = f'(\xi).$$

Thus whenever $|f'(\xi)| < 1$, the fixed point is stable, and whenever $|f'(\xi)| > 1$, it is unstable.

We say that a function f that generates a sequence of points as defined by equation (7.17) is **chaotic** if it satisfies the following three properties:

(a) f has sensitive dependence on initial conditions: If we have two distinct initial points that are within $\Delta(0)$ of each other, then the distance $\Delta(n)$ between corresponding elements of the sequences they generate under repeated applications of f will behave like

$$\Delta(n) = k\Delta(0)e^{Ln};$$

$L > 0$ is called the **Lyapunov exponent**.

(b) Points of the sequence become uncorrelated as n increases. We interpret this in the following way. If we define the **average** of the sequence by

$$\bar{x} := \lim_{N \to \infty} \frac{1}{N} \sum_{n=1}^{N} x_n,$$

then the **correlation** is defined by

$$C(m) := \lim_{N \to \infty} \frac{1}{N} \sum_{n=1}^{N} (x_n - \bar{x})(x_{n+m} - \bar{x}).$$

We require that as $m \to \infty$ we must have $C(m) \to 0$. This is a technical requirement with which we will not deal.

(c) The sequence is nonperiodic.

Chaotic sequences are surely unusual insofar as nearby points tend to move apart and they seem to lose any memory of where they originated. Just how this can happen remains to be seen. Let's look at a particular map. Define

$$f(x) := a(1 - 2|x - 0.5|),$$

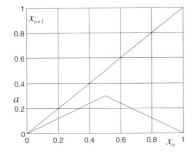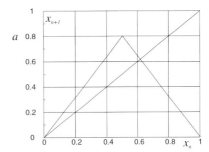

Fig. 7.18 The cases $0 < a \leq 0.5$ (left) and $0.5 < a \leq 1$ (right).

with the restriction that $0 < a \leq 1$. The hat-shaped graphs of $y = f(x)$ shown in Figure 7.18 clearly show that $f(x)$ is not differentiable at $x = 0.5$ and that it is a noninvertible function— that the equation $y = f(x)$ does not have a unique solution for x in terms of y. This exemplifies a major difference between sequences and ODE's; we can always integrate an ODE backward in time!

For points in the open interval $(0, 1)$, the result of the map $f(x)$ is also in the interval $(0, 1)$. There are two distinct cases to be considered, $0 < a < 0.5$ and $0.5 \leq a \leq 1$, which were illustrated in Figure 7.18. The $45°$ line $x_{n+1} = x_n$ was added to the graph of x_{n+1} versus x_n to facilitate the visualization of the functional iteration. For an x_n value on the horizontal axis, we move vertically up to the hat curve (a distance of $f(x_n) = x_{n+1}$); then we move horizontally to the $45°$ line (where $x_{n+1} = x_n$), after which we move vertically down to the axis, and then we repeat the procedure.

When $0 < a < 0.5$, the hat curve lies below the $45°$ line, and so the only fixed point is $x = 0$, and $f'(0) = a < 0.5$, so that zero is stable. Alternatively, notice that whenever we move horizontally, it is a movement to the left. Thus every $f(x_n)$ lies below the $45°$ line and x_n converges to zero.

Now consider the range $0.5 \leq a \leq 1$. The hat curve intersects the $45°$ line in two places, and those fixed points of the map are solutions of the equation

$$a(1 - 2\,|x - 0.5|) = x.$$

They are 0 and $2a/(2a+1)$. Since $f'(x) = -2a$, both fixed points are unstable. Something else can be extracted from the graph. If we start at $x_n = a$, then we find $f(x_n) = 2a(1-a)$. Since the peak of the hat is at $(0.5, a)$ no matter where we begin our sequence, we will eventually be locked between the values $2a(1 - a)$ and a. The claim is that the sequence will wander chaotically between these values. This can be illustrated by looking at the simple case $a = 1$, wherein the chaotic interval $(2a(1-a), a)$ becomes $(0, 1)$. Looking back at $f(x)$ when $a = 1$,

$$f(x) = 1 - 2\,|x - 0.5|,$$

we see that the function performs two actions: (a) it stretches the interval $(0, 1)$ to twice its original length (because of the factor of 2); then (b) it takes the stretched interval and folds it in half (because of the absolute value), so that the result has length one. It is precisely this folding property that causes $f(x)$ to be noninvertible. But it also keeps the sequence bounded.

In order for the distance between nearby points to grow exponentially, the map must increase the length of the interval, so that on average the interval is being stretched. Figure 7.19 illustrates the process of stretching and folding when a is between $1/2$ and 1.

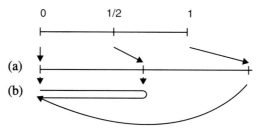

Fig. 7.19   The effects of the hat map as stretching followed by folding.

The top part of the figure shows that after a single application of f, there are no points in the interval $(a, 1)$. The bottom part of the figure shows that the interval $(0, 2a(1 - a))$ is stretched by a factor of a but nothing is folded back onto it, rather all the folding takes $(1/2, a)$ into $(2a(1 - a), a)$. Once a point in $(0, 2a(1 - a))$ leaves that interval, it never returns. Hence the sequence gets locked into the interval $(2a(1 - a), a)$ as claimed.

If we repeat the application of f twice, the resulting graph of x_{n+2} vs. x_n will still be polygonal, but now there will be two peaks, each of width $1/2$ and height a, as seen in Figure 7.20.

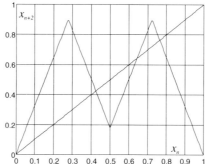

Fig. 7.20   The graph of x_{n+2} vs. x_n for the hat function.

Repeating the application m times and graphing x_{n+m} vs. x_n will cause the m hats to have width that is a multiple of 2^{-m}. To see this, the sequence in Figure 7.21 shows the case for $m = 3 : 5$. Now suppose that two initial points are within $\Delta(0)$ of each other; then after $m \approx \log_2 (1/\Delta(0))$ iterations of f, we will be unable to locate the image of one of the points knowing the image of the other. As an example, if $a = 1$, $\Delta(0) = 10^{-10}$, and then a mere $m \approx 34$ iterations will send the point anywhere on the hat, and following the geometric construction, almost anywhere in the interval $(0, a)$.

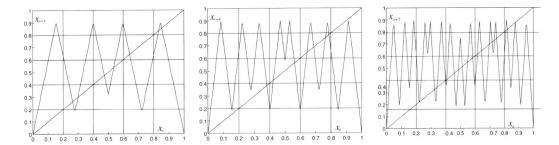

Fig. 7.21 The $m = 3 : 5$ iterates of the hat function.

7.7.3 *Period Doubling and the Transition to Chaos*

Now we will turn our attention to the so-called **logistic map**, defined by

$$F(x) = 4bx(1 - x),$$

where the factor of 4 has been included so that we can make the same restriction on b as we did on a, i.e., $0 < b \leq 1$. The fixed points of F are 0 and $x^* = 1 - 1/(4b)$, and so there is only one fixed point until $b = 1/4$. Since

$$F'(x) = 4b(1 - 2x),$$

the origin will be stable as long as b remains less than $1/4$. As b increases beyond $1/4$, the origin sheds its stability as the other fixed point is born. Since $F'(x^*) = 2 - 4b$, we see that x^* will be stable for $b \in (1/4, 3/4)$. Once b exceeds $3/4$, $F'(x^*)$ drops below -1, so that x^* sheds its stability. We should look at $x_{n+2} = F(F(x_n)) =: F^{[2]}(x_n)$. Graphs of x_{n+2} vs. x_n are given for $b = 0.7$ and $b = 0.8$ in Figure 7.22.

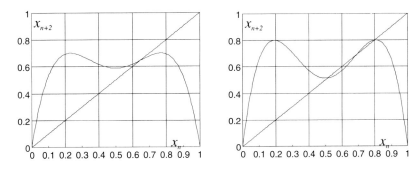

Fig. 7.22 x_{n+2} vs. x_n for $b = 0.7$ and $b = 0.8$.

For $b > 3/4$, $F^{[2]}$ has three nonzero fixed points (the intersections with the $45°$ line), but for $b < 3/4$ it has only one. Thus two new fixed points are born at $b = 3/4$.

Now sketch the graphs of F and $F^{[2]}$, along with the $45°$ line, on the same set of axes in Figure 7.23.

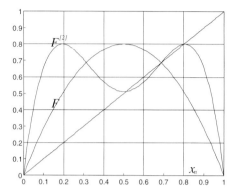

Fig. 7.23 Graphs of F and $F^{[2]}$ along with the $45°$ line.

Notice that there is a point x^* that is a fixed point of both F and $F^{[2]}$. That point occurs at $x^* \approx 0.6875$. Thus $x^* = F(x^*) = F^{[2]}(x^*)$. The claim is that in the sequence generated by $F(x)$, there must be a 2-cycle, meaning a set of alternating values $\alpha, \beta, \alpha, \beta, \ldots$, and both α and β must be fixed points of $F^{[2]}$. Additionally, we must have $\alpha = F(\beta)$ and $\beta = F(\alpha)$.

Now to the stability of α and β: Again set $x_n = \alpha + \delta_n$ and insert this into $F^{[2]}$ and linearize getting

$$\alpha + \delta_{n+2} = F^{[2]}(\alpha + \delta_n) = F^{[2]}(\alpha) + \delta_n(F^{[2]}(\alpha))' = \alpha + \delta_n F'(F(\alpha))F'(\alpha).$$

Because $\beta = F(\alpha)$, we are left with

$$\frac{\delta_{n+2}}{\delta_n} = F'(\alpha)F'(\beta).$$

Looking back at the graph of $F^{[2]}$, we see that as its slope exceeds one and the fixed point sheds its stability, two new fixed points are born. At birth, the slope of $F^{[2]}$ at both new fixed points is one and that slope decreases as β increases. We can conclude that the new fixed points are stable immediately after birth. But

$$\left(F^{[2]}(x)\right)' = 16b^2(1 - 2x)(8bx^2 - 8bx + 1)$$

will fall below -1 when $b \approx 0.862$, and the pair α, β will shed their stability as $4 = 2^2$ new fixed points are born. This foursome will form a 4-cycle. When these 4 points shed their stability, $8 = 2^3$ new fixed points will be born. Figure 7.24 shows $F^{[k]}$ for $k = 3 : 6$.

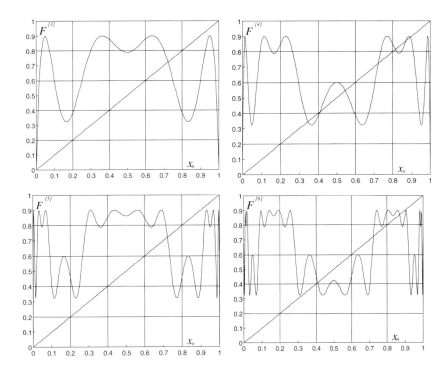

Fig. 7.24 The 3rd–6th iterates of the logistic map.

The procedure of shedding stability as new stable fixed points are born continues with some unexpected results. If b_k is the value of b at which a 2^k-cycle sheds its stability and a 2^{k+1}-cycle is born, it has been shown that

$$\lim_{k \to \infty} b_k = 0.892 \ldots,$$

and, even more amazingly, the limit of the ratio of the differences between these change points exists,

$$\lim_{k \to \infty} \frac{b_k - b_{k-1}}{b_{k+1} - b_k} = 4.669201 \ldots,$$

and is called the **Feigenbaum number**. The last limit remains valid for a surprisingly wide class of functions.

This process of period doubling is only one of the ways that motion can become chaotic. One thing to take away from this discussion is that only noninvertible one dimensional maps can become chaotic. Not so with two dimensional maps. In that case only invertible maps can become chaotic. It can be shown that the lowest dimensional system of ODE's that can become chaotic is three. Chaos cannot occur in the plane.

Surely, more needs to be said on this subject, but as they say, it is beyond the scope of the text. Please consult either Hale & Koçak or Jordan & Smith.

7.7.4 *Notes and References*

This chapter was meant as a brief introduction to a vast and rapidly growing area of mathematics. The current state of computer graphics has allowed easy visualization of very complex phenomena associated with nonlinear problems. See, for instance, MDEP, Phaser, Models, and a whole host of other packages. The whole area of bifurcations, period doubling, and chaotic dynamics is a subject of continuing scrutiny. Although much of the current research is at a high mathematical level, more accessible material is forthcoming.

The following is only a partial list of references because of the rate at which new material is being generated.

- Bender & Orszag, **Applied Mathematical Methods for Scientists and Engineers**: A major emphasis is the local and global analysis of nonlinear equations.

- Hale & Koçak, **Dynamics and Bifurcations**: The early chapters treat one dimensional systems in great detail before moving on to higher dimensional systems. The level increases rapidly.

- Ioos & Joseph, **Elementary Stability and Bifurcation Theory, 2nd ed.**: An aptly titled book that will introduce you to many of the currently interesting areas of the field.

- Jordan & Smith, **Nonlinear Ordinary Differential Equations, 2nd ed.**: A very nice presentation that is much more detailed than this chapter. Included is a more detailed introduction to bifurcations and chaotic dynamics.

- Lin & Segel, **Mathematics Applied to Deterministic Problems in the Natural Sciences**: A classic. Very interesting coverage of problems from the dynamics of a galaxy to the growth of slime mold. The *views on applied mathematics* compiled in Appendix 1.1 are a *must read* for everyone with an interest in the *controversy*.

- Nayfeh, **Perturbation Methods**: An older book that gives a detailed presentation of many of the methods used when it was written.

8

SERIES SOLUTIONS OF ODE'S

8.1 PREVIEW

This chapter will be devoted to the solution of the homogeneous linear second order ODE with variable coefficients,

$$a_2(x)y''(x) + a_1(x)y'(x) + a_0(x)y(x) = 0.$$

One example of a nonhomogeneous equation will be presented. Certain commonly occurring equations will be shown to give rise to new families of functions, some of which will be studied in the next chapter.

A point x in the complex plane can be ordinary or singular with respect to the given equation. The solution of a variable coefficient linear ODE can be expressed as a linear combination of power series expansions about an ordinary point. The next section will deal with the details of converting the ODE into an infinite system of algebraic equations, called a recurrence equation, for the unknown sequence of coefficients $\{a_n\}$ and its solution.

Singular points can be classified as being either regular or irregular. When forced to find a solution written as a series expansion about a regular singular point, we will be able to write the solution as a product of the solution about an ordinary point and an Euler equation solution. There are several possible complications. A theorem will tell us what to expect, and a method will be derived to utilize the theorem without solving the equation completely.

The method of Frobenius will be employed to obtain explicit power series solutions about regular singular points. There will be three cases to consider. We will concentrate our attention on the simplest case.

A special example of the breakdown of the method of Frobenius when applied to the solution of an equation about an irregular singular point will be given. It will lead to a noncausal coefficient sequence.

8.2 SERIES SOLUTIONS ABOUT AN ORDINARY POINT

We seek to solve the homogeneous linear second order ODE with variable coefficients,

$$a_2(x)y''(x) + a_1(x)y'(x) + a_0(x)y(x) = 0, \tag{8.1}$$

which after division by $a_2(x)$ can be rewritten in the form

$$y''(x) + p(x)y'(x) + q(x)y(x) = 0. \tag{8.2}$$

As we know from the Existence and Uniqueness Theorem of Chapter 4, a solution to equation (8.2) exists locally in a region about x_0 whenever $p(x)$ and $q(x)$ are both continuous near x_0. In this chapter we will insist $p(x)$ and $q(x)$ satisfy even stricter conditions so that we may obtain a solution.

Most solutions to (8.2) will not be any of the usual elementary functions such as polynomials, logs, exponentials, trig functions, or their inverses. In fact, just as we defined the natural logarithm as an integral that could not be evaluated using the standard formulas, so too can we define new functions as the solutions of variable coefficient differential equations. To study these new functions will require us to find and analyze their infinite series representations. So it is not the functions themselves that we will try to find but rather the coefficients of their Taylor series. For a quick review of power series, you should read Appendix F.

DEFINITION 8.1 *The point $x = x_0$ is said to be an* **ordinary point** *of the ODE (8.2) if both functions $p(x)$ and $q(x)$ are analytic at x_0. Any point that is not ordinary is said to be a* **singular point**; *i.e., if either $p(x)$ or $q(x)$ is not analytic at x_0, then it is a singular point.*

Remember (or look in the appendix), that a function is **analytic** at x_0 if it can be represented by a power series about the point $x = x_0$ with a nonzero radius of convergence. The analyticity of $p(x)$ and $q(x)$ is equivalent to analyticity of $a_2(x)$, $a_1(x)$, and $a_0(x)$ together with the nonvanishing of $a_2(x)$. For many of the equations we will study, $a_1(x)$ and $a_0(x)$ will be analytic for all finite complex x, so that singular points will occur only where $a_2(x) = 0$.

The plan of attack for solving (8.1) is to expand $y(x)$, $a_2(x)$, $a_1(x)$, and $a_0(x)$ in power series about x_0, perform all the required derivatives and algebra, collect like powers of $(x - x_0)$, and equate coefficients. This will lead to an infinite system of equations for the coefficients of the power series of the solution $y(x)$. For the moment we will defer discussing the method of solving such a system.

■ **EXAMPLE 8.1** For each of the following equations, find all singular points.

(a) **Legendre's equation** is $(1 - x^2)y'' - 2xy' + \lambda y = 0$. Thus,

$$p(x) = -\frac{2x}{1 - x^2}, \ q(x) = \frac{\lambda}{1 - x^2},$$

both of which are singular (not analytic) at $x = \pm 1$, because they have simple poles and hence are undefined there. Thus $x = \pm 1$ are the only singular points of the equation, and all other complex x are ordinary points.

(b) For the equation $(x^2 + 2x + 2)y'' + 3y' - e^x y = 0$, we have

$$p(x) = \frac{3}{x^2 + 2x + 2}, \; q(x) = \frac{-e^x}{x^2 + 2x + 2}.$$

Since e^x is analytic for all finite complex x and

$$x^2 + 2x + 2 = (x + 1)^2 + 1$$

is zero when $x = -1 \pm i$, the only singular points of this equation are $x = -1 \pm i$; all other complex numbers are ordinary points.

(c) Things are a bit more difficult for $(1 - \cosh x)y'' + (\tan x)y = 0$. Now

$$p(x) = 0, \; q(x) = \frac{\tan x}{1 - \cosh x}.$$

The numerator of $q(x)$, $\tan x$, has poles at odd multiples of $\pi/2$, i.e.,

$$x = (2n + 1)\pi/2, \; n = -\infty : \infty.$$

The denominator $1 - \cosh x$ can be rewritten as

$$1 - \cosh x = 1 - \cos(ix)$$

and $\cosh x = \cos(ix) = 1$ when $ix = 2m\pi$ or $x = -2mi\pi$ for $m : -\infty : \infty$. Drawing the complex plane and locating the singular points,

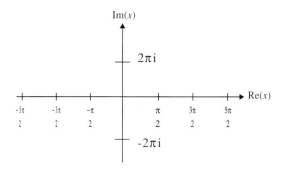

we see that all other complex points are ordinary points.　　　■ ■ ■

A theorem from basic complex analysis states that a power series can be differentiated any finite number of times and the result converges within the same circle of convergence. Also, the algebra of functions carries over to their power series. This assures us that our method of attack will work for any solution whose series has a nonzero radius of convergence. The following result gives us a lower bound on the radius of convergence based entirely on the behavior of $p(x)$ and $q(x)$.

THEOREM 8.1 *Every solution of a linear ODE whose coefficients are analytic at x_0 can be represented as a power series about the ordinary point $x = x_0$:*

$$y(x) = \sum_{n=0}^{\infty} a_n (x - x_0)^n. \tag{8.3}$$

Furthermore, the radius of convergence will be at least as large as the distance from x_0 to the nearest singular point of the equation.   □

The proof of this result can be found in Birkhoff & Rota. The theorem says "at least as large as," so the radius of convergence might be larger. If it is not equal to this distance, it will usually be infinite. This will occur when the series in (8.3) has finitely many rather than infinitely many nonzero terms.

■ **EXAMPLE 8.2**   Apply the previous theorem to each of the following ODE's.

(a) If we attempt to find a solution of Legendre's equation,

$$(1 - x^2)y'' - 2xy' + \lambda y = 0,$$

about $x_0 = 0$, we could expect a radius of convergence of at least one, because the singular points are at $x = \pm 1$. When $\lambda = 2$, one solution is $y(x) = x$, which is an "infinite" series all but one of whose coefficients are zero. This "series" has an infinite radius of convergence. The other solution will converge only for $|x| < 1$, the lower bound given by the theorem. Were we to expand the solution about $x_0 = 2 + i$, then $x = 1$ is the nearest singular point, and it is $\sqrt{2}$ units away.

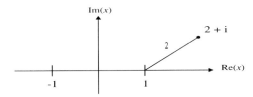

Thus we expect this solution to have a radius of convergence of at least $\sqrt{2}$; i.e., the region of convergence will be all complex x such that

$$|x - (2 + i)| < \sqrt{2}.$$

(b) A solution about $x_0 = 0$ of

$$(x^2 + 2x + 2)y''(x) + 3y'(x) - e^x y(x) = 0$$

will have a radius of convergence of at least

$$\text{dist}(0, -1 + i) = \sqrt{2},$$

whereas a solution about $2 + 2i$ will have (see Figure 8.1)

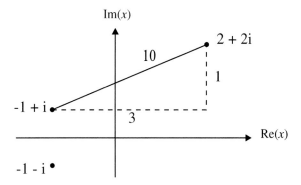

Fig. 8.1

$$R \geq |(2 + 2i) - (-1 + i)| = |3 + i| = \sqrt{10}.$$

(c) Expanding $y(x)$ about $x_0 = 0$ in the equation

$$(1 - \cosh x)y''(x) + (\tan x)y(x) = 0$$

will yield $R \geq \pi/2$, while using $x_0 = 2 + 2i$ will give us

$$\begin{aligned} R &\geq \min\{|2 + 2i - \pi/2|, |2 + 2i - 2\pi i|\} \\ &= \min\{2.0455, 4.7271\} = 2.0455, \end{aligned}$$

because $2 + 2i$ is nearest to $\pi/2$.   ■ ■ ■

8.2.1 *Possible Complications Using Series Expansions*

Looking back at equation (8.2),

$$y''(x) + p(x)y'(x) + q(x)y(x) = 0,$$

we see that $p(x)$ and $q(x)$ may be rational functions (ratios of polynomials) or contain transcendental functions, such as $\cos x$, $\sin x$, e^x, etc. So what, you may ask? Either of these possibilities could significantly increase the complexity of our problem. The most cumbersome case is when the coefficient functions are transcendental. In one of the examples there was a term $e^x y(x)$. The expansion of $y(x)$ about $x_0 = 0$ is

$$y(x) = \sum_{n=0}^{\infty} a_n (x - 0)^n = a_0 + a_1 x + a_2 x^2 + a_3 x^3 + \cdots,$$

and that of e^x is

$$e^x = \sum_{n=0}^{\infty} \frac{x^n}{n!} = 1 + x + \frac{1}{2!}x^2 + \frac{1}{3!}x^3 + \cdots.$$

Thus $e^x y(x)$ is a product of two infinite series:

$$e^x y(x) = a_0 \cdot 1 + (a_0 \cdot 1 + a_1 \cdot 1) x + \left(a_2 \cdot 1 + a_1 \cdot 1 + a_0 \cdot \frac{1}{2!} \right) x^2 + \cdots .$$

Notice, the result has none of the simplicity of either series.

This suggests that we should return to equation (8.1),

$$a_2(x) y''(x) + a_1(x) y'(x) + a_0(x) y(x) = 0,$$

and, for simplicity, restrict our attention to coefficient functions that are polynomials in x.

8.2.2   The Basic Method

An outline of the basic method for finding a solution as a power series about an ordinary point follows:

1. Set

$$y(x) = \sum a_n (x - x_0)^n$$

   for a solution about the ordinary point x_0. No limits of summation have been indicated because we assume n ranges over all integers, from $-\infty$ to ∞, with the proviso that any a_k with a negative subscript is identically zero; the terminology is that $\{a_k\}$ is a **causal sequence**. This will allow us to freely shift indices without worrying about the lower limit of summation until the end of the calculation. We needn't worry about the upper limit of summation, because any finite quantity added or subtracted from ∞ is still ∞.

2. Differentiate $y(x)$ termwise:

$$y'(x) = \sum n a_n (x - x_0)^{n-1}, \quad y''(x) = \sum n(n-1) a_n (x - x_0)^{n-2} .$$

   The similarity of what is being done here to solving an Euler equation should be evident. Only the coefficients and summations have been added. Remember, these series have the same circle of convergence as that of $y(x)$.

3. Insert $y(x)$, $y'(x)$, and $y''(x)$ into (8.1), multiply all coefficients, and collect like powers into separate summations.

4. Shift *down* the summation indices so that all the powers of $(x - x_0)$ agree with the lowest power.

5. By looking for the coefficients with the first nonnegative subscripts, set the lower index of each summation.

6. Separate all powers of $(x - x_0)$ not common to every summation and then combine all the summations.

7. Set coefficients of each power of $(x - x_0)$ to zero and solve the resulting infinite system of equations for the coefficients in $y(x)$, the a_n. You should have an arbitrary constant(s) in this solution (more of this later).

8. Separate the parts of $y(x)$ containing each arbitrary constant to get the linearly independent solutions.

Steps 4 through 8 probably seem a bit murky, but let's try an example to clarify matters.

■ **EXAMPLE 8.3** Find the solution of the first order ODE

$$L[y] := y' + 2xy = 0$$

as a power series about $x_0 = 0$.

Solution: The equation has no singular points, so that the series solution we obtain will converge for all complex x. Because $x_0 = 0$ is an ordinary point, according to Theorem 8.1 we should use

$$y(x) = \sum a_n (x - 0)^n, \ y'(x) = \sum n a_n (x - 0)^{n-1}.$$

Inserting these into the equation, we find

$$L[y(x)] = \sum n a_n x^{n-1} + 2x \sum a_n x^n.$$

Performing the multiplication in the second term yields

$$L[y(x)] = \sum n a_n x^{n-1} + 2 \sum a_n (x \cdot x^n) = \sum n a_n x^{n-1} + 2 \sum a_n x^{n+1}.$$

The two sums cannot be combined until

(a) they have the same reference power of x, and

(b) they have the same indices of summation.

To get the powers to agree we'll need to shift the summation index of the second sum down. This will require replacing n by $n - 2$ there to get

$$L[y(x)] = \sum n a_n x^{n-1} + 2 \sum a_{n-2} x^{n-1}.$$

We can determine the ranges of the summation indices by looking at the value of n for which the first coefficient is a_0. In the first sum that value is $n = 0$, while in the second sum it is $n = 2$, so that

$$L[y(x)] = \sum_{n=0}^{\infty} n a_n x^{n-1} + 2 \sum_{n=2}^{\infty} a_{n-2} x^{n-1}.$$

Since the two sums do not have the same ranges of summation, we need to remove the $n = 0$ and $n = 1$ terms from the first summation:

$$L[y(x)] = 0 \cdot a_0 x^{-1} + 1 \cdot a_1 x^0 + \sum_{n=2}^{\infty} n a_n x^{n-1} + 2 \sum_{n=2}^{\infty} a_{n-2} x^{n-1}.$$

The term where $n = 0$ is identically zero for *any* value of a_0, so that a_0 is an arbitrary constant. Combining the remaining sums, we have

$$L[y(x)] = a_1 + \sum_{n=2}^{\infty} n a_n x^{n-1} + 2 \sum_{n=2}^{\infty} a_{n-2} x^{n-1} = a_1 + \sum_{n=2}^{\infty} \left(n a_n + 2 a_{n-2} \right) x^{n-1}.$$

Since the only way a series can be zero is if all of the separate coefficients are zero, we must have $a_1 = 0$ and the equality

$$n a_n + 2 a_{n-2} = 0, \ n = 2 : \infty,$$

which is the **recurrence equation** for the elements of the sequence a_n. If we write the equation for the values of the first few coefficients we may be able to see a pattern, thereby solving this infinite system of linear equations for the infinitely many unknowns.

$$
\begin{aligned}
n = 2: \quad & 2a_2 + 2a_0 = 0, \\
n = 3: \quad & 3a_3 + 2a_1 = 0, \\
n = 4: \quad & 4a_4 + 2a_2 = 0, \\
n = 5: \quad & 5a_5 + 2a_3 = 0, \\
n = 6: \quad & 6a_6 + 2a_4 = 0, \\
n = 7: \quad & 7a_7 + 2a_5 = 0, \\
n = 8: \quad & 8a_8 + 2a_6 = 0, \ \text{etc.}
\end{aligned}
$$

Since $a_1 = 0$, the $n = 3$ equation tells us that $3a_3 + 0 = 0$, so that $a_3 = 0$. By the same token, the $n = 5$ equation says that

$$5a_5 + 2a_3 = 5a_5 + 0 = 0 \quad \Rightarrow \quad a_5 = 0.$$

Continuing, we can see that $a_7 = 0$, $a_9 = 0$, $a_{11} = 0$, and in fact *all* odd subscripted a_n will be zero. Thus we know half of the unknowns are zero and we only need look at the even subscripted a_n. To do this, set $n = 2k$. Since n began at 2, k will begin at 1 and the new recurrence equation will be

$$2k a_{2k} + 2 a_{2k-2} = 0, \ k = 1 : \infty.$$

Solving for a_{2k} in terms of a_{2k-2}, we find

$$a_{2k} = -\frac{1}{k} a_{2k-2}, \ k = 1 : \infty.$$

Evaluating the first several terms we see that

$$a_2 = -\frac{1}{1} a_0, \ a_4 = -\frac{1}{2} a_2, \ a_6 = -\frac{1}{3} a_4, \ a_8 = -\frac{1}{4} a_6.$$

Now we can use the value of a_2 from the first equation to find a_4 in terms of a_0, the value of a_4 thus obtained to find a_6 in terms of a_0, etc. In particular,

$$a_4 = -\frac{1}{2}a_2 = \left(-\frac{1}{2}\right)\left(-\frac{1}{1}\right)a_0,$$
$$a_6 = -\frac{1}{3}a_4 = \left(-\frac{1}{3}\right)\left(-\frac{1}{2}\right)\left(-\frac{1}{1}\right)a_0,$$
$$a_8 = -\frac{1}{4}a_6 = \left(-\frac{1}{4}\right)\left(-\frac{1}{3}\right)\left(-\frac{1}{2}\right)\left(-\frac{1}{1}\right)a_0.$$

The pattern is that there are as many factors as the value of k, each involving a minus sign. Recognizing the factorial function, we can write

$$a_{2k} = (-1)^k \frac{1}{k!}a_0.$$

Although the original recurrence equation was to hold for $k = 1 : \infty$, our solution is also valid for $k = 0$ because the result reduces to the identity $a_0 = a_0$ for this value. Usually, we will be forced to write the solution as $a_0 + \sum a_n x^n$, where the sum ranges from 1 to ∞. Here we can write the result as a single sum:

$$y(x) = \sum_{n \text{ even}} a_n x^n = a_0 \sum_{k=0}^{\infty} (-1)^k \frac{1}{k!} x^{2k}.$$

You should recognize this series as the power series expansion of the function $\exp(-x^2)$. If not, notice that the equation is separable and solve it that way to obtain the same result. ■ ■ ■

■ **EXAMPLE 8.4** Let's find a solution of the second order equation

$$L[y] := (1 - x^2)y'' - 5xy' + 5y = 0$$

as a power series about $x_0 = 0$.

Solution: Since the functions

$$p(x) = -\frac{5x}{1 - x^2} \quad \text{and} \quad q(x) = \frac{5}{1 - x^2}$$

are both singular at $x = \pm 1$, $x_0 = 0$ is an ordinary point and our solutions should converge at least within the disc $|x - 0| < 1$. Use

$$y(x) = \sum a_n x^n, \quad y'(x) = \sum n a_n x^{n-1}, \quad y''(x) = \sum n(n-1) a_n x^{n-2}.$$

Let's look at each term of the equation separately:

$$5y(x) = 5y(x) = 5 \sum a_n x^n, \quad \text{and nothing more need be done.}$$

$$-5xy'(x) = -5x \sum n a_n x^{n-1} = -5 \sum n a_n \left(x \cdot x^{n-1}\right) = -5 \sum n a_n x^n.$$

$$\begin{aligned}
\left(1 - x^2\right) y''(x) &= \left(1 - x^2\right) \sum n(n-1)a_n x^{n-2} \\
&= 1 \cdot \sum n(n-1)a_n x^{n-2} - x^2 \sum n(n-1)a_n x^{n-2} \\
&= \sum n(n-1)a_n x^{n-2} - \sum n(n-1)a_n \left(x^2 \cdot x^{n-2}\right) \\
&= \sum n(n-1)a_n x^{n-2} - \sum n(n-1)a_n x^n.
\end{aligned}$$

Now write everything together:

$$\begin{aligned}
L[y] &= (1 - x^2)y'' - 5xy' + 5y \\
&= \sum n(n-1)a_n x^{n-2} - \sum n(n-1)a_n x^n \\
&\quad -5 \sum n a_n x^n + 5 \sum a_n x^n = 0.
\end{aligned}$$

Notice that the last three summations all involve x^n, the same power with which we started. These terms correspond to the part of the equation

$$-x^2 y'' - 5xy' + 5y,$$

which is a sum of Euler-type operators. For this reason, these will be referred to as **Euler terms**. Now combine the Euler terms:

$$\begin{aligned}
&-\sum n(n-1)a_n x^n - 5 \sum n a_n x^n + 5 \sum a_n x^n \\
&= -\sum \left(n(n-1) + 5n - 5\right) a_n x^n \\
&= -\sum \left(n^2 + 4n - 5\right) a_n x^n = -\sum (n+5)(n-1)a_n x^n.
\end{aligned}$$

Whenever possible, at this stage *factor the separate coefficients into a product of linear terms.* The whole equation is

$$\left(1 - x^2\right) y'' - 5xy' + 5y = \sum n(n-1)a_n x^{n-2} - \sum (n+5)(n-1)a_n x^n = 0.$$

The powers of x are $n - 2$ and n, and so we should shift the index in the second sum *down* by 2, by replacing n by $n - 2$ everywhere that it appears:

$$\begin{aligned}
\sum (n+5)(n-1)a_n x^n &\longmapsto \sum (n-2+5)(n-2-1)a_{n-2} x^{n-2} \\
&= \sum (n+3)(n-3)a_{n-2} x^{n-2}.
\end{aligned}$$

Thus

$$\left(1 - x^2\right) y'' - 5xy' + 5y = \sum n(n-1)a_n x^{n-2} - \sum (n+3)(n-3)a_{n-2} x^{n-2}.$$

Now we must initialize the summations. The first involves a_n, and so $n = 0$ is the first nonnegative value of the subscript on the coefficient and the sum starts at $n = 0$. For the same reason, the second sum, involving a_{n-2}, starts at $n = 2$. The resulting right hand side is

$$\sum_{n=0}^{\infty} n(n-1)a_n x^{n-2} - \sum_{n=2}^{\infty} (n+3)(n-3)a_{n-2} x^{n-2} = 0.$$

The sums cannot be combined until they have the same power of x *and* the same range of summation. The first sum has two more terms, $n = 0$ and $n = 1$, than the second sum. Separate these terms, and then combine the sums.

$$\sum_{n=0}^{\infty} n(n-1)a_n x^{n-2} - \sum_{n=2}^{\infty}(n+3)(n-3)a_{n-2}x^{n-2}$$

$$= 0(-1)a_0 x^{-2} + 1(0)a_1 x^{-1} + \sum_{2}^{\infty} n(n-1)a_n x^{n-2}$$

$$- \sum_{2}^{\infty}(n+3)(n-3)a_{n-2}x^{n-2}$$

$$= \sum_{2}^{\infty} \left(n(n-1)a_n - (n+3)(n-3)a_{n-2} \right) x^{n-2} = 0.$$

The terms where $n = 0$ and $n = 1$ are identically zero for any values of a_0 and a_1 (as they should be, because they involve negative powers of x, which were not in our original solution). Thus a_0 and a_1 must be arbitrary constants; i.e., the nullity of this system is 2. The remaining a_n will be written in terms of a_0 and a_1.

The last sum can be zero only if each term is zero. This leads to the recurrence equation associated with the ODE:

$$n(n-1)a_n - (n+3)(n-3)a_{n-2} = 0, \ n = 2 : \infty.$$

This is valid only for $n = 2 : \infty$, because that is the range of the summation from which it was obtained. Solving for a_n, we obtain

$$a_n = \frac{(n+3)(n-3)}{n(n-1)}a_{n-2}, \ n = 2 : \infty.$$

This is an unusual second order recurrence equation because it involves only a second order shift. It can be said that the equation *steps by* 2, meaning that if $n = 10$, $n - 2 = 8$ and repeating, a_8 is a multiple of a_6; a_6 is a multiple of a_4; a_4 is a multiple of a_2, and a_2 is a multiple of the arbitrary constant a_0. Thus all a_n with even values of $n(= 2k)$ are multiples of a_0. By the same token, all a_n with odd $n(= 2k + 1)$ are multiples of a_1. This will always be the case for recurrence equations that step by 2.

Aside: Recurrence equations that step by three will divide into three cases:

(a) n divisible by three, $n = 3k$;

(b) n divisible by three with a remainder of one, $n = 3k + 1$; and

(c) n divisible by three with a remainder of two, $n = 3k + 2$.

Similarly for equations that step by larger amounts.

Let's evaluate a_n directly for even $n = 2k$:

$$a_{2k} = \frac{(2k+3)(2k-3)}{2k(2k-1)}a_{2k-2}, \ k = 1 : \infty.$$

We got $k \geq 1$ from $n = 2k \geq 2$. Put $k = 1$ (same as $n = 2$):

$$a_2 = \frac{5(-1)}{2 \cdot 1} a_0.$$

Put $k = 2$ (same as $n = 4$):

$$a_4 = \frac{7(1)}{4 \cdot 3} a_2 = \frac{7(1)}{4 \cdot 3} \cdot \frac{5(-1)}{2 \cdot 1} a_0 = \frac{[7(5)][1(-1)]}{4!} a_0.$$

Put $k = 3$ (same as $n = 6$):

$$a_6 = \frac{9(3)}{6 \cdot 5} a_4 = \frac{9(3)}{6 \cdot 5} \frac{[7(5)][1(-1)]}{4!} a_0 = \frac{[9 \cdot 7 \cdot 5][3 \cdot 1(-1)]}{6!} a_0.$$

If we work from the top down, i.e., going from k to $k - 1$, we have

$$a_{2(k-1)} = \frac{[2(k-1)+3][2(k-1)-3]}{2(k-1)[2(k-1)-1]} a_{2k-4} = \frac{(2k+1)(2k-5)}{(2k-2)(2k-3)} a_{2k-4}.$$

$$\Rightarrow \quad a_{2k} = \frac{[(2k+3)(2k+1)][(2k-3)(2k-5)]}{2k(2k-1)(2k-2)(2k-3)} a_{2k-4}.$$

A pattern is emerging. You should be able to see that

$$a_{2k} = \frac{[(2k+3)(2k+1)(2k-1) \cdots (7)(5)][(2k-3)(2k-5) \cdots (1)(-1)]}{(2k)!} a_0.$$

Now to the case of odd $n = 2k + 1$:

$$a_{2k+1} = \frac{(2k+4)(2k-2)}{(2k+1)(2k)} a_{2k-1} = \frac{2(k+2)(k-1)}{(2k+1)k} a_{2k-1}, \ k = 1 : \infty.$$

If we put $k = 1$, we immediately get

$$a_3 = \frac{2(3)(0)}{(3)(1)} a_1 = 0.$$

Setting $k = 2$ yields

$$a_5 = \frac{2(4)(1)}{5(2)} a_3 = 0, \text{ because } a_3 = 0.$$

Continuing, we'll get

$$0 = a_3 = a_5 = a_7 = a_9 = \cdots.$$

The part of the solution that is a multiple of a_1 will have only one term, $a_1 x$. This is a polynomial, not an infinite series; thus its radius of convergence is infinite.

Now combine terms to write the general solution:

$$y(x) = \sum_0^\infty a_n x^n = \sum_{\text{even}} a_n x^n + \sum_{\text{odd}} a_n x^n$$

$$= a_0 \left[1 + \sum_1^\infty \frac{[(2k+3)(2k+1)\cdots 5][(2k-3)(2k-5)\cdots(-1)]}{(2k)!} x^{2k} \right] + a_1 x,$$

and the separate functions are linearly independent.

It would be instructive to verify that the radius of convergence is as Theorem 8.1 says. Using the limit form of the Ratio Test, we have

$$\lim_{n\to\infty} \left| \frac{\dfrac{(2k+5)(2k+3)\cdots 5(2k-1)(2k-3)\cdots(-1)}{(2k+2)!} x^{2k+2}}{\dfrac{(2k+3)\cdots 5(2k-3)\cdots(-1)}{(2k)!} x^{2k}} \right|$$

$$= |x|^2 \lim_{n\to\infty} \frac{(2k+5)(2k-1)}{(2k+2)(2k+1)} = |x|^2.$$

We can conclude that $|x|^2 < 1 \Rightarrow |x| < 1$, just as predicted by the theorem.   ■ ■ ■

Aside: We know the factorial function is

$$n! := n(n-1)(n-2)(n-3)\cdots(3)(2)(1).$$

It would be nice if we had a notation for products that skip down by other than one. For this purpose, it is customary to introduce the **semifactorials**, defined by

$$(2k-1)!! := (2k-1)(2k-3)(2k-5)\cdots(5)(3)(1)$$

$$(2k)!! := (2k)(2k-2)(2k-4)\cdots(6)(4)(2).$$

Specifically,

$$7!! = 7\cdot 5\cdot 3\cdot 1 = 105, \ 8!! = 8\cdot 6\cdot 4\cdot 2 = 384, \ 3!! = 3, \ 2!! = 2.$$

Both the even and odd semifactorials, as defined, are products of k factors. Furthermore,

$$(2k)!! = 2(k)2(k-1)2(k-2)\cdots 2(3)2(2)2(1) \Rightarrow (2k)!! = 2^k k!.$$

and since $(2k)!$ is a product of all the even and odd positive integers up to $2k$, we can write

$$(2k)! = (2k)!! \, (2k-1)!!,$$

so that

$$(2k-1)!! = \frac{(2k)!}{2^k \, k!}.$$

Thus semifactorials add little new, because they can be written entirely in terms of factorials, but they are a convenience. We could define other kinds of "factorials" that are products of every third positive integer, etc., but it would complicate our already complicated notation. Besides, such beasts can be easily handled by the gamma function (see Section 9.2).

The terms in the even part of the solution of the last example can be rewritten as

$$(2k+3)(2k+1)\cdots 5\frac{3}{3} = (2k+3)(2k+1)\frac{(2k-1)!!}{3} = \frac{(2k+3)(2k+1)(2k)!}{3 \cdot 2^k \cdot k!}$$

and

$$(2k-3)(2k-5)\cdots(-1) = -(2k-3)!! = -\frac{(2k-1)!!}{2k-1} = -\frac{(2k)!}{(2k-1)\,2^k\,k!}.$$

Combining these terms, we can write the even part of the solution as

$$y_{\text{even}}(x) = 1 - \frac{1}{3}\sum_{k=1}^{\infty}\frac{(2k+3)(2k+1)(2k)!}{(2k-1)\,2^{2k}\,(k!)^2}x^{2k}.$$

This is only simpler insofar as there is an explicit formula for each term in the series.

Warning: The recurrence equation that will arise when substituting the power series for $y(x)$ into the ODE won't usually have the same special form we saw in the last example. In all likelihood we won't be able to guess the pattern for a_n. Of course, we shouldn't expect to, we have replaced a hard time dependent ODE by a hard recurrence equation. This may be true even if the original ODE has a reasonably simple solution.

■ **EXAMPLE 8.5** Find a solution of

$$(x^2 - 2x + 1)y'' + (1 - x^2)y' + 2(x-1)y = 0$$

as a power series about $x_0 = 0$.

Solution: Since

$$p(x) = \frac{1-x^2}{x^2 - 2x + 1} = \frac{(1-x)(1+x)}{(x-1)^2} = \frac{1+x}{1-x}$$

and

$$q(x) = \frac{2(x-1)}{x^2 - 2x + 1} = \frac{2(x-1)}{(x-1)^2} = \frac{2}{x-1}$$

are both analytic at $x_0 = 0$, we can set $y = \sum a_n x^n$. It would be a good idea to divide the whole equation by the common factor $(x-1)$, just as we did when reducing $p(x)$ and $q(x)$. Thus it takes the simpler form

$$(x-1)y'' - (x+1)y' + 2y = 0.$$

We should suspect something fishy here because there are Euler terms: xy' and $2y$; Euler less one: xy'' and y'; and Euler less two: y''. Three different types of terms!

Start with

$$y(x) = \sum a_n x^n, \quad y'(x) = \sum n a_n x^{n-1}, \quad y''(x) = \sum n(n-1)a_n x^{n-2}.$$

Then

$$(x-1)y'' - (x+1)y' + 2y$$
$$= (x-1)\sum n(n-1)a_n x^{n-2} - (x+1)\sum n a_n x^{n-1} + 2\sum a_n x^n$$
$$= \sum n(n-1)a_n x^{n-1} - \sum n(n-1)a_n x^{n-2}$$
$$- \sum n a_n x^n - \sum n a_n x^{n-1} + 2\sum a_n x^n = 0.$$

Combining terms with like powers, we have

$$\sum n(n-2)a_n x^{n-1} - \sum n(n-1)a_n x^{n-2} - \sum(n-2)a_n x^n = 0.$$

Shift down so all powers agree, and initialize the sums.

$$\sum_1^\infty (n-1)(n-3)a_{n-1}x^{n-2} - \sum_0^\infty n(n-1)a_n x^{n-2}$$
$$- \sum_2^\infty (n-4)a_{n-2}x^{n-2} = 0.$$

Pull out the $n = 0$ and $n = 1$ terms:

$$0 \cdot a_0 x^{-1} + \sum_2^\infty (n-1)(n-3)a_{n-1}x^{n-2} - 0 \cdot a_0 x^{-2} - 0 \cdot a_1 x^{-1}$$
$$- \sum_2^\infty n(n-1)a_n x^{n-2} - \sum_2^\infty (n-4)a_{n-2}x^{n-2} = 0.$$

Combine the sums and treat a_0 and a_1 as arbitrary constants:

$$\sum_2^\infty \left((n-1)(n-3)a_{n-1} - n(n-1)a_n - (n-4)a_{n-2} \right) x^{n-2} = 0.$$

The recurrence equation is

$$(n-1)(n-3)a_{n-1} - n(n-1)a_n - (n-4)a_{n-2} = 0, \ n = 2 : \infty,$$

or

$$a_n = \frac{(n-1)(n-3)a_{n-1} - (n-4)a_{n-2}}{n(n-1)}, \ n = 2 : \infty.$$

This is still a second order recurrence equation, but it does not step *only* by 2, and so direct evaluation is required. Start with $n = 2$ and work out as many terms as necessary:

$$a_2 = \frac{-a_1 + 2a_0}{2} = a_0 - \tfrac{1}{2}a_1, \quad a_3 = \tfrac{1}{6}a_1, \quad a_4 = \tfrac{3}{12}a_3 = \tfrac{3}{12} \cdot \tfrac{1}{6}a_1 = \tfrac{1}{24}a_1,$$

$$a_5 = \frac{8a_4 - a_3}{5 \cdot 4} = \tfrac{2}{5}a_4 - \tfrac{1}{20}a_3 = \tfrac{2}{5}\left(\tfrac{1}{24}a_1\right) - \tfrac{1}{20}\left(\tfrac{1}{6}a_1\right) = \tfrac{1}{120}a_1,$$

$$a_6 = \frac{15a_5 - 2a_4}{6 \cdot 5} = \tfrac{1}{2}a_5 - \tfrac{1}{15}a_4 = \tfrac{1}{2}\left(\tfrac{1}{120}a_1\right) - \tfrac{1}{15}\left(\tfrac{1}{24}a_1\right) = \tfrac{1}{720}a_1$$

A pattern seems to emerge:

$$a_k = \frac{1}{k!}, \ k = 3 : \infty;$$

Hence we can write the general form of the equation as

$$\begin{aligned}
y(x) &= a_0 + a_1 x + a_2 x^2 + a_3 x^3 + a_4 x^4 + \cdots \\
&= a_0 + a_1 x + \left(a_0 - \frac{1}{2}a_1\right)x^2 + \frac{1}{6}a_1 x^3 + \frac{1}{24}x^4 + \cdots \\
&= a_0\left(1 + x^2\right) + a_1\left(x - \frac{1}{2}x^2 + \frac{1}{3!}x^3 + \frac{1}{4!}x^4 + \cdots\right).
\end{aligned}$$

Although $y(x)$ is presently unrecognizable, it can be shown that for appropriate constants c_1 and c_2,

$$y(x) = c_1 e^x + c_2\left(1 + x^2\right). \qquad\qquad \blacksquare\;\blacksquare\;\blacksquare$$

8.2.3   *Initial Conditions*

Series solutions about an ordinary point x_0 together with initial conditions have a particularly simple interpretation because of Taylor's Theorem, which states: For a function analytic at $x = x_0$,

$$f(x) = f(x_0) + f'(x_0)(x - x_0) + \cdots.$$

For our solutions,

$$y(x) = a_0 + a_1(x - x_0) + \cdots.$$

Equating coefficients, we must have

$$a_0 = y(x_0) \quad \text{and} \quad a_1 = y'(x_0).$$

Thus if $y(x_0)$ and $y'(x_0)$ are both specified, so too are a_0 and a_1 in the expansion about $x = x_0$, and the result is the unique solution to the equation.

If we put $a_0 = c_1 + c_2$ and $a_1 = c_1$ in the solution of the last example, the two forms of the solution will agree completely.

8.2.4 *Solutions About Points Other than* $x_0 = 0$

When finding a solution about an x_0 other than 0, it is much more convenient to make the translation of coordinates

$$t = x - x_0.$$

Using the Chain Rule, we see that derivatives with respect to x are transformed into the same derivatives with respect to t,

$$\frac{dy}{dx} = \frac{dy}{dt}\frac{dt}{dx} = \frac{dy}{dt}1 = \frac{dy}{dt},$$

and the new coefficients are easily evaluated. What was $x = x_0$ is now the point $t = 0$, and we can find a solution about $t_0 = 0$ just as before.

■ **EXAMPLE 8.6** Were we to seek a solution of the equation

$$x(x + 2)y'' - (2x - 3)y' + (1 - x)y = 0$$

about the ordinary point $x = -1$, it would be best to let $t = x + 1$, which is equivalent to $x = t - 1$. The translated equation is then

$$(t - 1)[(t - 1) + 2]\ddot{y} - [2(t - 1) - 3]\dot{y} + [1 - (t - 1)]y = 0,$$

which is

$$\left(t^2 - 1\right)\ddot{y} - (2t - 5)\dot{y} + (2 - t)y = 0. \qquad \blacksquare\blacksquare\blacksquare$$

8.2.5 *Nonhomogeneous Equations*

The same series solution technique, although computationally more tedious, can be applied to nonhomogeneous equations. The major difference will be a nonhomogeneity in the recurrence equation.

■ **EXAMPLE 8.7** The following equation has been purposely constructed so that a simple form of the solution can be obtained with minimal manipulation:

$$L[y] = (1 - x)y'' - 2y' = -2.$$

The only singular point is $x = 1$, so a series solution about $x_0 = 0$ will have a radius of convergence of at least 1. As usual, set

$$y(x) = \sum a_n x^n, \; y'(x) = \sum n a_n x^{n-1}, \; y''(x) = \sum n(n - 1)a_n x^{n-2}.$$

Inserting this into the equation leads to

$$\sum n(n-1)a_n x^{n-2} - \sum n(n-1)a_n x^{n-1} - 2\sum na_n x^{n-1} = -2.$$

Collect terms with like powers, combine, and factor:

$$\sum n(n-1)a_n x^{n-2} - \sum n(n+1)a_n x^{n-1} = -2.$$

Shift the second term down by one and initialize:

$$\sum_0^\infty n(n-1)a_n x^{n-2} - \sum_1^\infty n(n-1)a_{n-1} x^{n-2} = -2.$$

Separate out the $n = 0$ term:

$$0 \cdot a_0 x^{-2} + \sum_1^\infty n(n-1)a_n x^{n-2} - \sum_1^\infty n(n-1)a_{n-1} x^{n-2} = -2.$$

Thus the constant a_0 is arbitrary. Combining the sums

$$\sum_1^\infty n(n-1)\left[a_n - a_{n-1}\right] x^{n-2} = -2.$$

The factor of $n(n-1)$ makes the $n = 1$ term identically zero. Thus the resulting recurrence equation is valid for $n = 2 : \infty$. The right hand side has only a coefficient for x_0, and so the sequence is $-2\delta_{n2}$ (this is the Kronecker delta function of Section 1.3): i.e., it is zero everywhere except $n = 2$ where it is equal to -2.

$$n(n-1)\left(a_n - a_{n-1}\right) = -2\delta_{n2}, \quad n = 2 : \infty.$$

It's probably easier to separate the $n = 2$ term.

$$2(2-1)\left(a_2 - a_1\right) = -2$$
$$n(n-1)\left(a_n - a_{n-1}\right) = 0, \quad n = 3 : \infty.$$

For $n = 3 : \infty$, we have $a_n = a_{n-1}$. The first equation yields $a_2 = a_1 - 1$, so that after $n = 1$ we have $a_n = a_1 - 1$. The resulting solution is

$$\begin{aligned}
y(x) &= a_0 + a_1 x + a_2 x^2 + a_3 x^3 + \cdots \\
&= a_0 + a_1 x + (a_1 - 1)\left(x^2 + x^3 + \cdots\right) \\
&= a_0 + a_1\left(x + x^2 + x^3 + \cdots\right) - \left(x^2 + x^3 + \cdots\right).
\end{aligned}$$

At this point, we can use the geometric series to find the closed form solution:

$$y(x) = a_0 + a_1\left(\frac{x}{1-x}\right) - \frac{x^2}{1-x}.$$

So that the solution will be simpler looking, choose $a_0 = c_1 + c_2$ and $a_1 = c_2 + 1$ (this will maintain two arbitrary constants). Then

$$y(x) = c_1 + c_2 \left(\frac{1}{1-x} \right) + x.$$

Hiding behind this elaborate machinery was the lowly function $f(x) = x$ as a particular solution. ■ ■ ■

Series methods for homogeneous equations do not yield a very good starting point for the method of variation of parameters, which is the only direct method we have available for finding the particular solution of a nonhomogeneous ODE with nonconstant coefficients. This is because of the difficulty in evaluating the Wronskian of the solution set.

The differential equations satisfied by many of the classical orthogonal polynomials (more about them in the next chapter) have ordinary points at $x_0 = 0$:

(a) Jacobi polynomials, $y(x) = P_n^{\alpha,\beta}(x)$:

$$\left(1 - x^2\right) y'' + [(\beta - \alpha) - (\alpha + \beta + 2)x]y' + n(n + \alpha + \beta + 1)y = 0.$$

(b) Gegenbauer polynomials, $y(x) = C_n^{\gamma}(x)$:

$$\left(1 - x^2\right) y'' - (2\gamma + 1)xy' + n(n + 2\gamma)y = 0.$$

(c) Chebyshev polynomials, $y(x) = T_n(x)$:

$$\left(1 - x^2\right) y'' - xy' + n^2 y = 0.$$

(d) Legendre polynomials, $y(x) = P_\ell(x)$:

$$\left(1 - x^2\right) y'' - 2xy' + \ell(\ell + 1)y = 0.$$

(e) Hermite polynomials, $y(x) = H_n(x)$:

$$y'' - xy' + ny = 0.$$

More will be said about some of these functions in Sections 9.3 and 9.5.

8.2.6 *Exercise Set*

Find all the singular points and the minimum radius of convergence of the power series solution of each of the following equations about each of the points $x_0 = 0$, 2, and $3 - 2i$:

1. $(x^2 - 9)y'' + (x + 1)y' - 2y = 0$

2. $(x^2 + 3x + 2)y'' + (x^2 - 1)y' = 0$

3. $5(\sin x)y'' + y = 0$ 4. $(1 + x^3)y'' + 4xy' + y = 0$

5. $(x^4 - 1)^2 y'' + (x^2 - x - 2)y' + x^2 y = 0$ 6. $(\cot x)y'' + (\tan x)y' - (\ln x)y = 0$

7. $(x^2 + 1)(x + 5)^3 y'' + (x + 5)^2 y' + 6y = 0$

8. For the equation $(1 + x^2)y'' + (2x + 1)y' + (x - 2)y = 0$

   (a) Derive the recurrence equation for a series solution about $x_0 = 0$.

   (b) If $y(0) = 1$ and $y'(0) = 2$, calculate a_2, a_3, and a_4.

For each of the following ODE's, find the recurrence equation for a series solution about $x_0 = 0$ and find the first five nonzero terms in the series expansion of the general solution.

9. $(2 - 3x)y'' + (1 + x^2)y' - xy = 0$ 10. $(1 + x)y'' - (3 - 5x)y' + (x + 3)y = 0$

11. $(1 + 2x + x^2)y'' + (3 + x)y' + (1 + x)y = 0$

For each of the following ODE's, find the form of the general solution as a linear combination of power series about $x_0 = 0$.

12. $(1 + x)y' + y = 0$ 13. $y' - 2xy = 0$ 14. $y'' + y = 0$

15. $y'' + xy = 0$ 16. $y'' - xy' + 2y = 0$ 17. $(1 - x^2)y'' + 2y = 0$

18. $(1 + x^2)y'' + 2xy' = 0$ 19. $(1 + x^2)y'' + 2xy' - 2y = 0$

20. $(1 + 4x^2)y'' + 2xy' - 12y = 0$ 21. $(1 - x^2)y'' + xy' + 15y = 0$

22. $(1 - x^2)y'' - xy' + 16y = 0$ 23. $(x^2 + 1)y'' + 8xy' + 12y = 0$

24. $(x^2 + 2)y'' - xy' + y = 0$ 25. $(1 + 2x^2)y'' + 3xy' - 3y = 0$

26. $(1 - x^2)y'' - 4xy' - 6y = 0$ 27. $2y'' - xy' - 2y = 0$

28. $(1 + x^2)y'' - xy' - 3y = 0$ 29. $(1 - x^2)y'' - 6xy' - 4y = 0$

30. $(1 - x^2)y'' + xy' + 3y = 0$ 31. $(1 + x^2)y'' - 6xy' + 12y = 0$

32. $(8 + x^3)y'' + x^2 y' - 4xy = 0$ 33. $(4 + x^2)y'' + 2xy' - 12y = 0$

Find a power series solution of each of the following equations about $x_0 = 1$.

34. $xy'' + y = 0$. Terms up through $(x - 1)^4$.

35. $y'' + y' + (x - 1)y = 0$. Terms up through $(x - 1)^5$.

36. $x(2 - x)y'' - 2y = 0$. General solution.

37. $2y = 0$. General solution.

38. Use the power series expansion of $y(x)$ to find the first four nonzero terms of the solution of the nonlinear equation $y' = y^2$.

Find the power series expansion about $x_0 = 0$ of the general solution of each of the following nonho-mogeneous equations.

39. $y' + y = x$

40. $y'' - y = 1$

41. $y'' + xy' + y = 2x$

42. For the equation $(1 + x^2)y'' - 8xy' + 20y = 0$

    (a) Find the minimum radius of convergence of a solution expanded about the point $x_0 = 3e^{i5\pi/6}$.

    (b) Find the specific solution of this equation for which $y(0) = 1$ and $y(1) = 0$.

43. For $\alpha = 0, 1, 2, 3,$ and 4, find the polynomial solutions of Hermite's equation,

$$y'' - 2xy' + 2\alpha y = 0.$$

44. For $\alpha = 0, 1, 2, 3,$ and 4, find the polynomial solutions of Chebyshev's equation,

$$(1 - x^2)y'' - xy' + \alpha^2 y = 0.$$

45. For $\ell = 0, 1, 2, 3,$ and 4, find the polynomial solutions of Legendre's equation,

$$(1 - x^2)y'' - 2xy' + \ell(\ell + 1)y = 0.$$

46. As derived when solving the linear harmonic oscillator problem in quantum mechanics, one finds the wave function is

$$\psi(x) = u(x)\exp(-x^2/2)$$

where $u(x)$ is a solution of the Hermite equation

$$u'' - 2xu' + \lambda u = 0,$$

where λ is an unknown constant. Derive the form of the recurrence equation for a power series solution about $x_0 = 0$ of $u(x)$ and show that for large values of n it is the same as the recurrence equation for $\exp(x^2/2)$. Conclude that the wave function $\psi(x)$ behaves like $\exp(x^2/2)$ for large $|x|$. Argue that if the requirement $\int |\psi(x)|^2\, dx < \infty$ is to hold, this cannot be the case. Thus conclude that λ must be chosen so that the series terminates. This condition gives the quantization rules for the harmonic oscillator.

8.3 SINGULAR POINTS

Recall that $x = x_0$ was a singular point of the equation

$$y''(x) + p(x)y'(x) + q(x)y(x) = 0$$

if either $p(x)$ or $q(x)$ failed to be analytic at $x = x_0$. We have already encountered a class of ODE's with a singular point for which a simple solution method is available: the Euler equation about $x = x_0$, which has the form

$$a(x - x_0)^2 y''(x) + b(x - x_0)y'(x) + cy(x) = 0, \tag{8.4}$$

where a, b, and c are constants. For the Euler equation (8.4) we have

$$p(x) = \frac{b}{a(x - x_0)} \quad \text{and} \quad q(x) = \frac{c}{a(x - x_0)^2}.$$

The function $p(x)$ has a simple pole at $x = x_0$, and $q(x)$ has a double pole there. Perhaps we could mimic the character of the Euler equation to arrive at a solution of (8.2) using a power series about $x = x_0$. To that end, let's classify singular points that are Euler-like.

DEFINITION 8.2 *In the complex plane, $x = x_0$ is a **regular singular point**, written RSP, of (8.2) if $p(x)$ has no worse than a simple pole there and $q(x)$ has no worse than a double pole there. Any singular point that is not an RSP is an **irregular singular point**, written ISP.*

Using the results in Appendix F, we can say $x = x_0$ is a RSP of (8.2) if *both*

$$(x - x_0)\, p(x) \quad \text{and} \quad (x - x_0)^2\, q(x)$$

are analytic at $x = x_0$.

■ **EXAMPLE 8.8** Find and classify the singular points of the following ODE's.

(a) $x^3(1 - x)^2 y'' - 2x(1 - x^2)y' + (6 - 4x)y = 0$. We have

$$p(x) = -\frac{2x(1 - x^2)}{x^3(1 - x)^2} = -\frac{2(1 + x)}{x^2(1 - x)}$$

and

$$q(x) = \frac{6 - 4x}{x^3(1 - x)^2},$$

so the equation has singular points at $x = 0$ and $x = 1$. We must check each singular point separately .

$x = 0$:

$$(x - 0)p(x) = x\left[-\frac{2(1 + x)}{x^2(1 - x)}\right] = -\frac{2(1 + x)}{x(1 - x)}$$

is undefined at $x = 0$ and is, thus, not analytic there. Therefore, we need not check $(x - 0)^2 q(x)$. We may conclude that $x = 0$ is an ISP.

$x = 1$:

$$(x - 1)p(x) = (x - 1)\left[-\frac{2(1 + x)}{x^2(1 - x)}\right] = \frac{2(1 + x)}{x^2},$$

which is analytic at $x = 1$ (it is not analytic at $x = 0$, but we're checking $x = 1$, so that doesn't matter to us). The function

$$(x-1)^2 q(x) = (x-1)^2 \left[\frac{6-4x}{x^3(1-x)^2} \right] = \frac{6-4x}{x^3}$$

is also analytic at $x = 1$. Since both conditions are satisfied, $x = 1$ is an RSP.

Alternatively, we could have analyzed the pole structure of these functions; i.e.,

$$p(x) = -\frac{2(1+x)}{x^2(1-x)}$$

has a double pole at $x = 0$ and a single pole at $x = 1$. Thus $x = 0$ is not an RSP. The function

$$q(x) = \frac{6-4x}{x^3(1-x)}$$

has a double pole at $x = 1$ and a triple pole at $x = 0$. Thus $x = 1$ is a RSP.

(b) $(\sin x)y'' + (x \cot x)y' - (\tan x)y = 0$. In this case,

$$p(x) = \frac{x \cot x}{\sin x} = \frac{x \cos x}{\sin^2 x}, \quad q(x) = -\frac{\tan x}{\sin x} = -\frac{1}{\cos x}.$$

We have singular points where $\sin^2 x = 0$ or $\cos x = 0$:

$$\sin x = 0 \Rightarrow x = n\pi, \; n = -\infty : \infty,$$

$$\cos x = 0 \Rightarrow x = (2m+1)\frac{\pi}{2}, \; m = -\infty : \infty.$$

These sets of singular points can be combined into

$$x_k = k\frac{\pi}{2}, \; k = -\infty : \infty.$$

Because of the factor of x in $p(x)$, let's separate the $k = 0$ case.

$x = 0$:

$$(x-0)p(x) = \frac{x^2 \cos x}{\sin^2 x} = \left(\frac{x}{\sin x} \right)^2 \cos x.$$

To determine the analyticity of $xp(x)$, look at

$$\frac{\sin x}{x} = \frac{1}{x} \left(x - \frac{x^3}{3!} + \frac{x^5}{5!} - \cdots \right) = 1 - \frac{x^2}{3!} + \frac{x^4}{5!} - \cdots$$

which is analytic at $x = 0$ and equal to one there, as is $\cos x$. Since $xp(x)$ is the ratio of analytic functions and the denominator is not zero at the point in question, it is analytic at $x = 0$.

$$(x - 0)^2 q(x) = -\frac{x^2}{\cos x}.$$

This is zero at $x = 0$, because $0^2/1 = 0$, which is well-defined, so $x^2 q(x)$ is analytic at $x = 0$. Thus $x = 0$ is an RSP.

Now take $k \neq 0$. We know that $p(x)$ has double poles at even multiples of $\pi/2$ and is analytic at odd multiples of $\pi/2$. Also, $q(x) = \sec x$ has simple poles at odd multiples of $\pi/2$. Therefore, $x = k\pi/2$ are ISP's for even values of k and RSP's for odd values of k.

(c) **Bessel's equation** of order α is defined to be

$$x^2 y'' + x y' + \left(x^2 - \alpha^2\right) y = 0.$$

Since

$$p(x) = \frac{1}{x} \quad \text{and} \quad q(x) = 1 - \frac{\alpha^2}{x^2},$$

the only finite singular point is $x = 0$. The analyticity of

$$xp(x) = 1 \quad \text{and} \quad x^2 q(x) = x^2 - \alpha^2$$

proves that $x = 0$ is an RSP. ∎ ∎ ∎

8.3.1   *The Point at Infinity*

So far nothing has been said about the point at infinity. One way to handle this is to map it into zero using the change of variables $x = 1/t$. Applying the Chain Rule to (8.2), we get the new equation

$$\frac{d^2 y}{dt^2} + r(t)\frac{dy}{dt} + s(t)y = 0, \tag{8.5}$$

where

$$r(t) := \frac{1}{t^2}\left(2t - p\left(\frac{1}{t}\right)\right) \quad \text{and} \quad s(t) = \frac{1}{t^4}q\left(\frac{1}{t}\right).$$

Thus $x = \infty$ will be a singular point of (8.2) if $t = 0$ is a singular point of (8.5). The complex point at ∞ will be an RSP if

$$tr(t) = 2 - \frac{1}{t}p\left(\frac{1}{t}\right) \quad \text{and} \quad t^2 s(t) = \frac{1}{t^2}q\left(\frac{1}{t}\right)$$

are both analytic at $t = 0$.

■ **EXAMPLE 8.9** Classify the point at infinity for Bessel's equation.

Solution: After substituting $x = 1/t$, Bessel's equation becomes

$$\frac{d^2y}{dt^2} + \frac{1}{t}\frac{dy}{dt} + \left(\frac{1 - \alpha^2 t^2}{t^4}\right) y = 0,$$

so that $t = 0$, which is the same as $x = \infty$, is a singular point. Checking for an RSP at $t = 0$ we find

$$t\,r(t) = 1 \quad \text{is analytic at } t = 0,$$

but

$$t^2\,s(t) = \frac{1}{t^2}\left(1 - \alpha^2 t^2\right) \quad \text{is not analytic at } t = 0.$$

Therefore, $x = \infty$ is an ISP of Bessel's equation. ■ ■ ■

To better study the solution of (8.2) near an RSP, we will rewrite the coefficient functions. If $p(x)$ has no worse than a simple pole at x_0, it can be rewritten in the form

$$p(x) = \frac{A(x)}{x - x_0},$$

where $A(x)$ is analytic at $x = x_0$. Similarly, if $q(x)$ has no worse than a double pole at x_0, it can be written as

$$q(x) = \frac{B(x)}{(x - x_0)^2},$$

where $B(x)$ is analytic at $x = x_0$. Thus (8.2) takes the Euler-like form

$$L[y] := (x - x_0)^2\,y'' + (x - x_0)\,A(x)y' + B(x)y = 0. \tag{8.6}$$

If $A(x)$ and $B(x)$ were constant functions, we could try a solution of the form $y = (x - x_0)^m$, an Euler solution. When one of the resulting values of m is negative, the solution itself will be singular at $x = x_0$. Furthermore, m need not be an integer, and so the solution could have what is called a branch point at x_0. These possibilities must be allowed for when trying a form of $y(x)$ for a solution to (8.2). One choice that encompasses all these possibilities is the product of an Euler solution and an ordinary point solution, i.e.,

$$y(x) = (x - x_0)^\lambda \sum_{n=0}^{\infty} a_n\,(x - x_0)^n = \sum_{n=0}^{\infty} a_n\,(x - x_0)^{n+\lambda}. \tag{8.7}$$

The constant λ is called the **exponent of singularity** and is unknown at the outset of the calculation. A solution of the form given in (8.7) will converge in the annulus $0 < |x - x_0| < R$, for some positive R. The point $x = 0$ has been deleted because if λ has a negative real part, then (8.7) is undefined there.

If we substitute (8.7) into (8.6) and use the analyticity of $A(x)$ and $B(x)$ to write

$$A(x) = \sum_{n=0}^{\infty} A_n\,(x - x_0)^n, \quad B(x) = \sum_{n=0}^{\infty} B_n\,(x - x_0)^n,$$

then we will find terms

$$L\left[\sum_{n=0}^{\infty} a_n (x - x_0)^{n+\lambda}\right]$$
$$= [\lambda(\lambda - 1) + A_0\lambda + B_0] a_0 (x - x_0)^\lambda + O\left((x - x_0)^{\lambda+1}\right)$$

where $A_0 = A(x_0)$ and $B_0 = B(x_0)$. Since all coefficients of powers of $(x - x_0)$ will be set equal to zero, we have for the coefficient of the lowest power of $(x - x_0)$ what is called the **indicial equation**:

$$\text{Ind}(\lambda) := \lambda(\lambda - 1) + A_0\lambda + B_0 = 0. \tag{8.8}$$

From this we can solve for the exponents of singularity. The coefficient of the next highest power of x, $x^{\lambda+1}$, will satisfy

$$[(\lambda + 1)\lambda + A_0(\lambda + 1) + B_0]a_1 + A_1\lambda + B_1 = 0. \tag{8.9}$$

Having used the indicial equation to find the values for λ, we must use this secondary equation to find a_1. From this we can continue recursively to solve for all the a_n, once for each value of λ. If we do this, we find ourselves solving the infinite system of equations

$$\text{Ind}(\lambda + n)a_n = -\sum_{k=0}^{n-1} [(\lambda + k)A_{n-k} + B_{n-k}] a_k, \quad n = 1 : \infty. \tag{8.10}$$

The only time our recursive technique will break down is when both $\text{Ind}(\lambda) = 0$ and $\text{Ind}(\lambda + m) = 0$ for some positive integer m. When this is the case, we will not be able to solve for a_m or any higher order a_p, $p > m$, which depend on it. This anomalous case arises only when λ and $\lambda + m$ are roots of the indicial equation, meaning that the difference of the roots is an integer. If we choose to solve the system (8.10) only for the exponent with the largest real part, then we would avoid the degeneration of the recursive system. This would guarantee us at least one solution.

Suppose, instead of looking for the solution of the ODE itself, we look for the function $y(x; \lambda)$ that satisfies the *non*homogeneous equation

$$L[y(x; \lambda)] = (x - x_0)^2 y''(x; \lambda) + (x - x_0)A(x)y'(x; \lambda) + B(x)y(x; \lambda)$$
$$= \text{Ind}(\lambda)a_0 x^\lambda.$$

This can be done by setting

$$y(x; \lambda) = \sum_{n=0}^{\infty} a_n (x - x_0)^{n+\lambda} \tag{8.11}$$

and requiring all of the recurrence equations in (8.10) to be satisfied *except* the indicial equation. When we use a value of λ that satisfies the indicial equation in $y(x; \lambda)$, we have a solution. For roots differing by an integer it is possible that we may not be able to generate two linearly independent solutions. At that point $y(x; \lambda)$ must be manipulated to obtain the full general solution. This is the basis of the method of Frobenius that will be the focus of the next section.

THEOREM 8.2 *If the ODE (8.2) has an RSP at $x = x_0$, then the following hold:*

(a) It has at least one solution of the form

$$y(x; \lambda) = \sum_{n=0}^{\infty} a_n (x - x_0)^{n+\lambda}$$

converging in the annulus $0 < |x - x_0| < R$ for some $R > 0$, where $\text{Ind}(\lambda) = 0$ and λ is the solution of the indicial equation with larger real part.

(b) It has the general solution

$$y(x) = c_1 y(x; \lambda_1) + c_2 y(x; \lambda_2)$$

when λ_1 and λ_2 are solutions of the indicial equation that do not differ by an integer, and the series for $y(x)$ converges in the annulus $0 < |x - x_0| < R$ for some $R > 0$. The radius R of the annulus will be at least the distance from the RSP x_0 to the nearest other singular point of the equation. □

The proof of this theorem is given in Birkhoff & Rota.

8.3.2 Finding the Exponents of Singularity

It would be useful to know the exponents of singularity without having to solve the entire equation, so that we might be able to assess the applicability of the previous theorem. To do this, it would be best to put the ODE in the form of equation (8.6) so that we could use the indicial equation (8.8).

■ **EXAMPLE 8.10** For each of the following equations, find the exponents of singularity.

(a) $xy'' - 2y' + 3y = 0$ has an RSP at $x = 0$. Multiply by x to put it in the form of (8.6):

$$x^2 y'' - 2xy' + 3xy = 0.$$

Thus $A(x) = -2$, $B(x) = 3x$ and $A_0 = A(0) = -2$, $B_0 = B(0) = 0$, so that the indicial equation is

$$\lambda(\lambda - 1) - 2\lambda + 0 = \lambda^2 - 3\lambda = \lambda(\lambda - 3) = 0.$$

The exponents of singularity are $\lambda = 0$ and $\lambda = 3$. Since these differ by an integer, the theorem does not guarantee that we will be able to generate the general solution.

(b) $2x^2 y'' - (\sin x)y' - 2e^x y = 0$ has an RSP at $x = 0$ and is in the proper form with

$$A(x) = -\frac{\sin x}{2x} \quad \text{and} \quad B(x) = -e^x.$$

Thus, $A_0 = A(0) = -1/2$ and $B_0 = B(0) = -1$, so that

$$\lambda(\lambda - 1) - \frac{1}{2}\lambda - 1 = \lambda^2 - \frac{3}{2}\lambda - 1 = \left(\lambda + \frac{1}{2}\right)(\lambda - 2) = 0.$$

$\lambda = -1/2$ and $\lambda = 2$ have a nonintegral difference, and so the theorem applies and the general solution may be found by substituting into (8.11). The solution corresponding to $\lambda = -1/2$ will *not* be analytic at $x = 0$, whereas the solution corresponding to $\lambda = 2$ will be analytic there.

(c) $x(1 - x)y'' + (2 - 3x)y' - (1 + x)y = 0$ has an RSP at $x = 1$. To put it in the proper form we must multiply by $(1 - x)/x$ to get

$$(x - 1)^2 y'' - \frac{(2 - 3x)(x - 1)}{x}y' - \frac{(1 - x^2)}{x}y = 0.$$

Since $A(x) = (3x - 2)/x$ and $B(x) = (x^2 - 1)/x$, we have $A(1) = 1$, $B(1) = 0$, and the indicial equation is

$$\lambda(\lambda - 1) + \lambda + 0 = \lambda^2 = 0 \quad \Rightarrow \quad \lambda = 0, 0.$$

■ ■ ■

8.3.3 Exercise Set

Find and classify all the finite singular points of each of the following equations:

1. $(1 + 4x^2)^2 y'' + 6x(1 + 4x^2)y' - 9y = 0$ 2. $x(x^2 - 1)y'' + 2(x + 1)y' + 3y = 0$

3. $x^2(4 - x^2)^2 y'' + 3(x + 2)y' - 4y = 0$ 4. $(\sin x)(y'' + y') + (e^x - 1)y = 0$

5. $x^2(x - 1)(x + 3)^2 y'' + x(x - 1)^2 y' + 5(x - 2)y = 0$

6. $(x^4 - 1)y'' + (x^2 - x - 2)y' + x^2 y = 0$ 7. $x^2 y'' - 2(\tan x)y' + (\cos x)y = 0$

8. $xy'' + (c - x)y' - ay = 0$ 9. $x(1 - x)y'' + [c - (a + b + 1)x]y' - aby = 0$

10. Find and classify the finite singular points of the following equations and find the minimum radius of convergence of a series solution about $x_0 = 2$.

(a) $(x^2 + 1)(x + 5)^3 y'' + (x + 5)^2 y' + 6y = 0.$ (b) $x^2(x^2 + 3)y'' + (x^2 + 3)y' + 4y = 0.$

11. Find and classify the finite singular points and find the minimum radius of convergence of a series solution about $x_0 = 1 + i$ of $x(x^2 - 1)y'' + 2(x + 1)y' + (1 + x)y = 0$.

12. Give an example of a linear variable coefficient ODE that has:

    (a) a RSP at $x = 0$, an ISP at $x = 1$, and all other finite points are ordinary. Is the point at ∞ an ISP or an RSP?

    (b) RSP's at $x = 0$ and $x = 1$, and an ISP at $x = -1$ and $x = 3$ with all other finite points ordinary. Is the point at infinity regular or irregular?

    (c) a RSP at ∞ and all other points ordinary.

13. Find and classify all finite singular points of

$$2x^2 y'' + 3(x + \sin x)y' + y = 0.$$

    What are the exponents of singularity?

14. Which of the equations in problems 1–9 have a singular point at ∞? For each of these equations, classify the singular point at infinity.

Find the exponents of singularity of each of the following equations about each of their finite RSP's.

15. $(1 + x^2)y'' + 3xy' - y = 0$

16. $(x^2 + 3x^3)y'' + (x - 2x^2)y' - (1 + x)y = 0$

17. $(2x^2 + x^3)y'' + (3x - x^2)y' + (x - 1)y = 0$

18. $(x^2 + 3x)y'' + (x + 4)y' + 3y = 0$

19. $(x-1)^2(x+1)^2 y'' + 2(x-2)y' + x(3+2x)y = 0$

20. $(x^2 + 1)y'' + 3xy' - y = 0$

21. $x^2(\cos x - 3x)y'' - (2x^2 - \sin x)y' - e^x y = 0$

22. $2x(\tan x - x)y'' - 3x(x - \cos x)y' - e^{-x}y = 0$

8.4   METHOD OF FROBENIUS

Following the discussion of the last section, we will use as the form of our solution the product of an Euler term and a power series. The **method of** Frobenius, part of which is contained in the statement of Theorem 8.2, tells us how to find the general solution of

$$y''(x) + p(x)y'(x) + q(x)y(x) = 0$$

as a series expansion about the RSP $x = x_0$. Proceed as follows: The form of the solution is taken to be

$$y(x; \lambda) = \sum_{n=0}^{\infty} a_n (x - x_0)^{n+\lambda},$$

where λ is to be found from the indicial equation: $\mathrm{Ind}(\lambda) = 0$.

Although there will be much in common, separate types of solution will be needed for each of the cases:

(a) $\lambda_1 - \lambda_2 \neq$ integer,

(b) $\lambda_1 - \lambda_2 = 0$,

(c) $\lambda_1 - \lambda_2 =$ integer$\neq 0$.

Case (a) falls directly under the rubric of Theorem 8.2. Cases (b) and (c) are referred to as **anomalous cases**, and they will be discussed in later subsections.

8.4.1 *Roots Not Differing by an Integer*

We must substitute (8.11) into (8.2) and choose the coefficients a_n for $n = 1 : \infty$ by satisfying all of the recurrence equations except the indicial equation. Then the general solution will be

$$y(x) = c_1 y(x; \lambda_1) + c_2 y(x; \lambda_2),$$

where λ_1 and λ_2 are the exponents of singularity (which do not differ by an integer) as determined from the indicial equation.

Just as in the ordinary point situation, all summations will be assumed to go from $-\infty$ to $+\infty$ with $a_m = 0$ for $m < 0$.

- **EXAMPLE 8.11** Solve $L[y] := 3x^2 y'' + 2xy' + x^2 y = 0$.

Solution: We see that

$$p(x) = \frac{2}{3x} \quad \text{has a simple pole at } x = 0$$

and

$$q(x) = \frac{1}{3} \quad \text{is analytic everywhere.}$$

Therefore, $x_0 = 0$ is the only finite singular point, and it is a regular singular point. Put

$$
\begin{aligned}
y(x; \lambda) &= \sum a_n x^{n+\lambda}, \\
y'(x; \lambda) &= \sum (n + \lambda) a_n x^{n+\lambda-1}, \\
y''(x; \lambda) &= \sum (n + \lambda)(n + \lambda - 1) a_n x^{n+\lambda-2}.
\end{aligned}
$$

Then we have

$$
\begin{aligned}
L[y(x; \lambda)] &= 3x^2 y''(x; \lambda) + 2xy'(x; \lambda) + x^2 y(x; \lambda) \\
&= 3x^2 \sum (n + \lambda)(n + \lambda - 1) a_n x^{n+\lambda-2} \\
&\quad + 2x \sum (n + \lambda) a_n x^{n+\lambda-1} + x^2 \sum a_n x^{n+\lambda} \\
&= 3 \sum (n + \lambda)(n + \lambda - 1) a_n x^{n+\lambda} \\
&\quad + 2 \sum (n + \lambda) a_n x^{n+\lambda} + \sum a_n x^{n+\lambda+2}.
\end{aligned}
$$

Combine like powers (of the Euler terms of the ODE):

$$L[y(x; \lambda)] = \sum (3(n + \lambda)(n + \lambda - 1) + 2(n + \lambda)) a_n x^{n+\lambda} + \sum a_n x^{n+\lambda+2}.$$

Now factor all higher degree polynomials into products of linear terms:

$$L[y(x; \lambda)] = \sum (n + \lambda)(3n + 3\lambda - 1) a_n x^{n+\lambda} + \sum a_n x^{n+\lambda+2}.$$

Shift the second sum down by two, so we have like powers, and initialize both sums:

$$L[y(x; \lambda)] = \sum_0^\infty (n + \lambda)(3n + 3\lambda - 1) a_n x^{n+\lambda} + \sum_2^\infty a_{n-2} x^{n+\lambda}.$$

Pull out the $n = 0$ and $n = 1$ terms from the first sum and combine the sums

$$L[y(x; \lambda)] = \lambda(3\lambda - 1) a_0 x^\lambda + (\lambda + 1)(3\lambda + 2) a_1 x^{\lambda+1}$$
$$+ \sum_2^\infty [(n + \lambda)(3n + 3\lambda - 1) a_n + a_{n-2}] x^{n+\lambda}.$$

The coefficient of the lowest power of x is

$$\lambda(3\lambda - 1) a_0 = 0, \quad \text{the indicial equation.}$$

The coefficient of the next lowest power of x is

$$(\lambda + 1)(3\lambda + 2) a_1 = 0, \quad \text{the secondary equation.}$$

The recurrence equation is

$$(n + \lambda)(3n + 3\lambda - 1) a_n + a_{n-2} = 0, \ n = 2 : \infty.$$

From the indicial equation, the exponents of singularity are

$$\lambda = 0, \ \frac{1}{3}.$$

Since these do not differ by an integer, we will be able to find the general solution in series form. Neither of these values of λ satisfies the secondary equation, and so we are forced to set $a_1 = 0$.

The recurrence equation has a special form that steps by two, so the cases of n even and n odd must be treated separately. The condition $a_1 = 0$ forces all odd n subscripted terms to be zero, and so we need only consider the recurrence equation for even $n = 2k$:

$$a_{2k} = \frac{-1}{(2k + \lambda)(6k + 3\lambda - 1)} a_{2k-2}, \ k = 1 : \infty.$$

Iterating, we find

$$a_{2k} = \frac{(-1)^k}{[(2k+\lambda)(2k+\lambda-2)\cdots(\lambda+2)][(6k+3\lambda-1)(6k+3\lambda-7)\cdots(3\lambda+5)]} a_0$$

for $k = 1 : \infty$. Thus

$$y(x; \lambda) = x^\lambda + \sum_1^\infty \frac{(-1)^k}{[(2k+\lambda)(2k+\lambda-2)\cdots(\lambda+2)][(6k+3\lambda-1)(6k+3\lambda-7)\cdots(3\lambda+5)]} x^{2k+\lambda}.$$

The constant a_0 has been set to 1 because Theorem 8.2 tells us how to construct the two linearly independent solutions. Now we can evaluate $y(x; \lambda)$ for $\lambda = 0$ and $\lambda = 1/3$ to obtain those solutions:

$$\begin{aligned}
y(x; 0) &= y_1(x) \\
&= 1 + \sum_1^\infty \frac{(-1)^k x^{2k}}{[(2k)(2k-2)\cdots 2][(6k-1)(6k-7)\cdots 5]} \\
&= 1 + \sum_1^\infty \frac{(-1)^k x^{2k}}{2^k k! [(6k-1)(6k-7)\cdots 5]},
\end{aligned}$$

$$\begin{aligned}
y(x; 1/3) &= y_2(x) \\
&= x^{1/3} + \sum_1^\infty \frac{(-1)^k x^{2k+1/3}}{[(2k+1/3)(2k-5/3)\cdots(7/3)][6k(6k-6)\cdots 6]} \\
&= x^{1/3} + \sum_1^\infty \frac{(-1)^k x^{2k+1/3}}{[(2k+1/3)(2k-5/3)\cdots(7/3)] 6^k k!}.
\end{aligned}$$

The general solution is then

$$y(x) = c_1 y_1(x) + c_2 y_2(x).$$

■ ■ ■

■ **EXAMPLE 8.12**   Solve the equation $2x(x+3)y'' - 3(x+1)y' + 2y = 0$.

Solution: The equation has an RSP at the point $x = 0$, because

$$p(x) = -\frac{3(x+1)}{2x(x+3)} \quad \text{has a simple pole at } x = 0,$$

and

$$q(x) = \frac{2}{2x(x+3)} \quad \text{has a simple pole there, too.}$$

Rewrite the equation as a sum of Euler and Euler less one terms:

$$2x(x+3)y'' - 3(x+1)y' + 2y = \underbrace{2x^2 y'' - 3xy + 2y}_{\text{Euler terms}} + \underbrace{6xy'' - 3y'}_{\text{Euler less one}}.$$

Putting $y(x; \lambda) = \sum a_n x^{n+\lambda}$, we can combine each set of terms:

$$\begin{aligned}
L[y(x; \lambda)] = &\sum \left(2(n+\lambda)(n+\lambda-1) - 3(n+\lambda) + 2\right) a_n x^{n+\lambda} \\
&+ \sum \left(6(n+\lambda)(n+\lambda-1) - 3(n+\lambda)\right) a_n x^{n+\lambda-1}.
\end{aligned}$$

These can be simplified to:

$$L[y(x; \lambda)] = \sum (n + \lambda - 2)(2n + 2\lambda - 1)a_n x^{n+\lambda}$$
$$+ \sum 3(n + \lambda)(2n + 2\lambda - 3)a_n x^{n+\lambda-1}.$$

Shift the first sum down by 1 and initialize:

$$L[y(x; \lambda)] = \sum_{1}^{\infty} (n + \lambda - 3)(2n + 2\lambda - 3)a_{n-1} x^{n+\lambda-1}$$
$$+ \sum_{0}^{\infty} 3(n + \lambda)(2n + 2\lambda - 3)a_n x^{n+\lambda-1}.$$

Pull out the $n = 0$ term from the second sum and combine:

$$3\lambda(2\lambda - 3)a_0 x^{\lambda-1} + \sum_{1}^{\infty} (2n + 2\lambda - 3)\left[(n + \lambda - 3)a_{n-1} + 3(n + \lambda)a_n\right] x^{n+\lambda-1}.$$

The indicial equation is

$$3\lambda(2\lambda - 3)a_0 = 0,$$

and the exponents of singularity are $\lambda = 0$ and $\lambda = 3/2$, which do not differ by an integer, and so the theorem applies. The multiple of $(2n + 2\lambda - 3)$ in the second sum has the value of

$$2n - 3 \text{ when } \lambda = 0 \quad \text{and} \quad 2n \text{ when } \lambda = 3/2,$$

neither of which are zero for $n = 1 : \infty$. Thus the recurrence equation is

$$(n + \lambda - 3)a_{n-1} + 3(n + \lambda)a_n = 0.$$

Rather than solving this in all generality, it will be easier to do each value of λ separately.
$\lambda = 0$: $(n - 3)a_{n-1} + 3na_n = 0$ for $n = 1 : \infty$;

$$a_n = -\frac{(n - 3)}{3n}a_{n-1}, \quad \text{which will terminate when } n = 3.$$

$$a_1 = -\frac{2}{3}a_0, \quad a_2 = -\frac{1}{6}a_1 = \left(-\frac{1}{6}\right)\left(-\frac{2}{3}\right)a_0 = \frac{1}{9}a_0.$$

The first solution is

$$y(x; 0) = y_1(x) = 1 - \frac{2}{3}x + \frac{1}{9}x^2.$$

$\lambda = \frac{3}{2}$:

$$
\begin{aligned}
a_n &= -\frac{(n - 3/2)}{3(n + 3/2)} a_{n-1} \\
&= (-1)^n \frac{(n - 3/2)(n - 5/2) \cdots (3/2)(1/2)(-1/2)}{3^n (n + 3/2)(n + 1/2)(n - 1/2)5/2)} a_0 \\
&= (-1)^n \frac{(3/2)(1/2)(-1/2)}{3^n (n + 3/2)(n + 1/2)(n - 1/2)} a_0 \\
&= (-1)^n \frac{-3}{3^n (2n + 3)(2n + 1)(2n - 1)} a_0, \quad n = 1 : \infty.
\end{aligned}
$$

The second solution is

$$
y(x; 3/2) = x^{3/2} + \sum_1^\infty (-1)^{n+1} \frac{x^{n+3/2}}{3^{n-1}(2n + 3)(2n + 1)(2n - 1)}.
$$

The general solution is a linear combination of these two,

$$
y(x) = c_1 y(x; 0) + c_2 y(x; 3/2).
$$

■ ■ ■

8.4.2 *Roots Differing by an Integer*

The solution for roots λ_1, λ_2 differing by an integer is straightforward, albeit tedious.

Equal Roots

To treat the anomalous cases, start with *equal* exponents of singularity, a difference of zero. When $\lambda_1 = \lambda_2$, $y(x; \lambda)$ satisfies the *non*homogeneous equation

$$
L[y(x; \lambda)] = \text{Ind}(\lambda) \, a_0 x^\lambda.
$$

Setting $\lambda_1 = \lambda_2 = \lambda_0$, this becomes

$$
L[y(x; \lambda)] = (\lambda - \lambda_0)^2 a_0 x^\lambda.
$$

Surely, $y(x; \lambda_0)$ will be one solution of the original equation. To get a second linearly independent solution we'll need to employ a trick. Take the partial derivative of both sides of the last equation with respect to λ; use the facts that the operator L does not depend on λ and a power series that converges uniformly within the circle of convergence, and so we can interchange the operator and the differentiation with respect to λ. Then

$$
\frac{\partial}{\partial \lambda} L[y(x; \lambda)] = L\left[\frac{\partial}{\partial \lambda} y(x; \lambda)\right] = 2(\lambda - \lambda_0)a_0 x^\lambda + (\lambda - \lambda_0)^2 a_0 x^\lambda \ln x.
$$

Putting $\lambda = \lambda_0$ in this equation results in

$$L\left[\frac{\partial}{\partial\lambda}y(x;\lambda)\bigg|_{\lambda=\lambda_0}\right] = 0.$$

Therefore, the general solution of the ODE for repeated exponents of singularity is

$$y(x) = c_1 y(x;\lambda_0) + c_2 \left[\frac{\partial}{\partial\lambda}y(x;\lambda)\right]_{\lambda=\lambda_0}.$$

If we write

$$y(x;\lambda) = \sum_0^\infty a_n(\lambda)(x-x_0)^{n+\lambda},$$

then we see that

$$\begin{aligned}
\frac{\partial}{\partial\lambda}y(x;\lambda)\bigg|_{\lambda=\lambda_0} &= \sum_0^\infty a_n'(\lambda_0)(x-x_0)^{n+\lambda_0} \\
&+ \sum_0^\infty a_n(\lambda_0)(x-x_0)^{n+\lambda_0}\ln|x-x_0| \\
&= y(x;\lambda_0)\ln|x-x_0| + \sum_0^\infty a_n'(\lambda_0)(x-x_0)^{n+\lambda_0}.
\end{aligned}$$

The only derivative we really need to compute is that of the coefficient $a_n(\lambda)$, which in itself will be quite nasty.

Now to an example.

■ **EXAMPLE 8.13** Solve $x^2 y'' - x(1+x)y' + (x+1)y = 0$.

Solution: The equation has an RSP at $x = 0$, because

$$p(x) = -\frac{1+x}{x} \quad \text{has a simple pole at } x = 0,$$

and

$$q(x) = \frac{x+1}{x^2} \quad \text{has a double pole at } x = 0.$$

Put $y(x;\lambda) = \sum a_n x^{n+\lambda}$, and combine Euler terms:

$$L[y(x;\lambda)] = \sum(n+\lambda-1)^2 a_n x^{n+\lambda} - \sum(n+\lambda-1)a_n x^{n+\lambda+1}.$$

Shift the index of the second sum down by 1:

$$L[y(x;\lambda)] = \sum(n+\lambda-1)^2 a_n x^{n+\lambda} - \sum(n+\lambda-2)a_{n-1}x^{n+\lambda}.$$

Initialize the sums, starting at 0 in the first and 1 in the second. Then pull out the $n = 0$ term from the first sum:

$$L[y(x; \lambda)] = (\lambda - 1)^2 a_0 x^\lambda + \sum_1^\infty \left[(n + \lambda - 1)^2 a_n - (n + \lambda - 2) a_{n-1} \right] x^{n+\lambda}.$$

The recurrence equation is

$$(n + \lambda - 1)^2 a_n - (n + \lambda - 2) a_{n-1} = 0, \ n = 1 : \infty,$$

or

$$a_n = \frac{(n + \lambda - 2)}{(n + \lambda - 1)^2} a_{n-1}, \ n = 1 : \infty.$$

Iterating, we find

$$a_n = \frac{(n + \lambda - 2)(n + \lambda - 3) \cdots \lambda(\lambda - 1)}{(n + \lambda - 1)^2 (n + \lambda - 2)^2 \cdots (\lambda)^2} a_0$$

$$= \frac{\lambda - 1}{(n + \lambda - 1)[(n + \lambda - 1)(n + \lambda - 2) \cdots \lambda]} a_0, \quad n = 1 : \infty.$$

Therefore,

$$y(x; \lambda) = x^\lambda + \sum_1^\infty \frac{\lambda - 1}{(n + \lambda - 1)[(n + \lambda - 1)(n + \lambda - 2) \cdots \lambda]} x^{n+\lambda}.$$

The indicial equation is $(\lambda - 1)^2 a_0 = 0$, and so $\lambda = 1$. When substituting this into $y(x; \lambda)$, the entire summation vanishes and only the first term remains:

$$y(x; 1) = x = y_1(x).$$

The only reasonable way to handle the differentiation of $a_n(\lambda)$ is by taking the natural logarithm of both sides and using the Chain Rule (Remember: $\ln(\text{product}) = \text{sum}(\ln's)$):

$$\ln a_n(\lambda) = \ln(\lambda - 1) - \ln(n + \lambda - 1) - \sum_{k=0}^{n-1} \ln(k + \lambda).$$

Differentiating with respect to λ,

$$\frac{\partial}{\partial \lambda} \ln a_n(\lambda) = \frac{a_n'(\lambda)}{a_n(\lambda)} = \frac{1}{\lambda - 1} - \frac{1}{n + \lambda - 1} - \sum_{k=0}^{n-1} \frac{1}{k + \lambda}.$$

$$\Rightarrow a_n'(\lambda) = \frac{\lambda - 1}{(n + \lambda - 1)[(n + \lambda - 1) \cdots \lambda]} \times \left[\frac{1}{\lambda - 1} - \frac{1}{n + \lambda - 1} - \sum_{k=0}^{n-1} \frac{1}{k + \lambda} \right]$$

$$\Rightarrow a_n'(\lambda) = \frac{1}{(n + \lambda - 1)[(n + \lambda - 1) \cdots \lambda]}$$

$$- \frac{\lambda - 1}{(n + \lambda - 1)[(n + \lambda - 1) \cdots \lambda]} \left[\frac{1}{n + \lambda - 1} + \sum_{k=0}^{n-1} \frac{1}{k + \lambda} \right].$$

Setting $\lambda = 1$, everything simplifies considerably:

$$a_n'(1) = \frac{1}{n \cdot n!}, \quad n = 1 : \infty.$$

Therefore, the second linearly independent solution is

$$y_2(x) = y_1(x) \ln|x| + \sum_1^{\infty} a_n'(1)\, x^{n+1}$$

$$\Rightarrow \quad y_2(x) = x \ln|x| + \sum_1^{\infty} \frac{x^{n+1}}{n \cdot n!}.$$

■ ■ ■

If it's any consolation, most problems *don't* work out as nicely as this one did!

Unequal Roots Differing by an Integer

When the roots of the indicial equation are real and differ by a nonzero integer, the method of Frobenius takes account of the two possibilities:

(a) If $\lambda_< := \min\{\lambda_1, \lambda_2\}$ and for some positive integer m the right hand side of (8.10) is zero, then the sequence of recurrence equations can be solved with no unusual difficulty (relatively speaking!). In this subcase, $y(x; \lambda_<)$ will generate *both* solutions because the secondary equation will *not* force a_1 to be zero.

(b) If the right hand side of (8.10) is not zero, then the expression for $a_n(\lambda)$ will involve a factor of $(\lambda - \lambda_<)^{-1}$. Then $(\lambda - \lambda_<) y(x; \lambda)$ evaluated at $\lambda = \lambda_<$ will be a multiple of $y(x; \lambda)$. Since

$$L\left[(\lambda - \lambda_<)\, y(x; \lambda) \right] = (\lambda - \lambda_<)^2 (\lambda - \lambda_>)\, a_0 x^{\lambda},$$

a derivative with respect to λ will generate the solution

$$\left[\frac{\partial}{\partial \lambda} [(\lambda - \lambda_<)\, y(x; \lambda)] \right]_{\lambda = \lambda_<},$$

which together with $y(x; \lambda_<)$ forms a basis for the solution space.

■ **EXAMPLE 8.14** $x(x^2 - 1)y'' + (x^2 + 2)y' - xy = 0$ will lead to an indicial equation with roots differing by an integer that will admit a general solution *without* differentiation.

Solution: Since

$$p(x) = \frac{x^2 + 2}{x\,(x^2 - 1)} \quad \text{and} \quad q(x) = \frac{-x}{x\,(x^2 - 1)},$$

we see $x = 0$ is a regular singular point. Using the usual form of the solution we arrive at

$$\lambda(\lambda - 3)a_0 x^{\lambda-1} + (\lambda + 1)(\lambda - 2)a_1 x^\lambda$$
$$+ \sum_2^\infty (n + \lambda - 3)\left[(n + \lambda - 1)a_{n-2} - (n + \lambda)a_n\right] x^{n+\lambda-1}.$$

The roots of the indicial equation are $\lambda = 0, 3$. Neither of these satisfy the secondary equation $(\lambda + 1)(\lambda - 2)a_1 = 0$, so that we are forced to take $a_1 = 0$. Though the recurrence equation steps by two, we *cannot* conclude that all odd subscripted a's are zero because of the presence of the factor $(n + \lambda - 3)$ in the recurrence equation. If we use the smaller root of the indicial equation, $\lambda = 0$, then $(n + \lambda - 3) = n - 3$, which is identically zero when $n = 3$. For this value of n, the terms in the square brackets are $2a_1 - 3a_3 = -3a_3$. Hence a_3 is arbitrary. Thus the odd subsequence starts at $n = 3$. When $n = 2k$ is even, we have

$$a_{2k} = \frac{(2k - 1)(2k - 3) \cdots (1)}{(2k)(2k - 2) \cdots (2 \cdot 2)} a_0 = \frac{(2k - 1)!!}{(2k)!!} a_0, \ k = 1 : \infty.$$

One solution is

$$y_1(x) = 1 + \sum_1^\infty \frac{(2k - 1)!!}{(2k)!!} x^{2k}.$$

Starting the odd subsequence at $n = 3$, we find

$$a_{2k+1} = \frac{(2k)(2k - 2) \cdots (2 \cdot 2)}{(2k + 1)(2k - 1) \cdots (5)} a_3 = \frac{3}{2} \frac{(2k)!!}{(2k + 1)!!} a_3, \ k = 2 : \infty,$$

with corresponding solution

$$y_2(x) = x^3 + \frac{3}{2} \sum_2^\infty \frac{(2k)!!}{(2k + 1)!!} x^{2k+1}.$$

■ ■ ■

An example where differentiation must be used will be deferred to Section 9.2. Looking back at the (often unrecognizable) solutions generated using the method of Frobenius, one is not highly motivated to frequently implement the procedure. This is as it should be, because numerical or asymptotic methods are often preferable. Nevertheless, we need to know the basic behavior of a solution as reflected by the exponents of singularity.

If we want to find an approximation to the true solution for large values of $|x|$ when ∞ is an ordinary point or RSP of the equation, we can change independent variables via $x = 1/t$. Then we can generate a series solution about $t = 0$. Keeping only the first few terms will lead to a reasonable approximation to $y(x)$ when x is far from the origin.

Fortunately, there is a rich class of ODE's that lead to certain "special functions" that are often encountered in applications. For this reason the next chapter will be devoted to the study of some of these functions.

8.4.3   Exercise Set

Use the Method of Frobenius to find the series solutions about $x_0 = 0$ of each of the following equations.

1. $2xy' - (2x + 1)y = 0$

2. $xy' + (2x - 1)y = 0$

3. $9x^2y'' + 9xy' - y = 0$

4. $2x^2y'' - 3x(1 - x)y' + 2y = 0$

5. $2x^2y'' - x(2x + 1)y' + (1 - 5x)y = 0$

6. $2x(x + 1)y'' + 3(x + 1)y' - y = 0$

7. $3x^2y'' + xy' + 3x^2y = 0$

8. $4x^2y'' + xy' + 4x^2y = 0$

9. $4xy'' + 3y' + 3y = 0$

10. $x^2(x + 2)y'' + 3xy' - 3y = 0$

11. $2xy'' - (1 + 2x^2)y' - xy = 0$

12. $2x^2y'' + 3xy' + (2x - 1)y = 0$

13. $2xy'' + (x + 1)y' + 3y = 0$

14. $2x^2y'' + x(2x + 1)y' + 2xy = 0$

15. $x^2(x + 3)y'' - 5xy' - 3(1 + 2x)y = 0$

16. $2x(1 - x)y'' + 3(1 - 3x)y' - 6y = 0$

17. $2x^2y'' + x(4x - 1)y' + 2(3x - 1)y = 0$

18. $x(3 - 2x^2)y'' + (8 - 4x^2)y' + 4xy = 0$

19. $2x(1 + x)y'' + (3 - 9x)y' - 6y = 0$

20. $3x^2y'' + (5x + 3x^3)y' + (3x^2 - 1)y = 0$

21. $2x^2(1 + x)y'' + 5x(x + 1)y' - 2(10x + 1)y = 0$

22. $(2x^2 - x^3)y'' + (7x - 6x^2)y' + (3 - 6x)y = 0$

The following equations involve the anomalous cases.

23. $9x^2y'' + 6xy' + (x^2 - 2)y = 0$

24. $4x^2y'' + 2x(2 - x)y' - (1 + 3x)y = 0$

25. $x^2(1 - x)y'' - 3xy' + 4y = 0$

26. $x^2y'' + 3xy' + (1 - 2x)y = 0$

27. $xy'' + (x^3 - 1)y' + x^2y = 0$

28. $x^2y'' - x(2 - x)y' + 2y = 0$

29. $x^2y'' - x^2y' + (x - 2)y = 0$

30. $9x^2y'' + 3xy' - 2y = 0$

31. $x^2y'' - xy' + y = 0$

32. $x(x - 1)y'' - 3y' - 2y = 0$

33. For $\alpha = 0, 1, 2$, and 3, find the polynomial solutions of the equation $xy'' + (1 - x)y' + 2\alpha y = 0$. By changing variables from x to $t = 1/x$, find solutions about $x = \infty$ of the following equations:

34. $4x^3y'' + 6x^2y' + y = 0$

35. $4x^4y'' + 4x^3y' - (x^2 - 1)y = 0$

8.5   SOLUTION ABOUT AN IRREGULAR SINGULAR POINT

Thus far we have used series expansions about ordinary and regular singular points of ODE's to find solutions. What about irregular singular points? Solutions about ordinary points were analytic within a circle of convergence, $|x - x_0| < R$, and solutions about RSP's were analytic within an annulus, $0 < |x - x_0| < R$.

Unlike RSP's which give rise to solutions that can have poles or branch points at $x = x_0$, an ISP can give rise to solutions with essential singularities (poles of *all* orders) at x_0. The difficulties that beset an ISP solution obtained from the method of Frobenius are best illustrated by an example.

■ **EXAMPLE 8.15** Let's find a series solution of

$$L[y] := x^3 y'' + x(x + 1)y' - y = 0$$

about $x_0 = 0$.

Solution: [*sic!*]: We immediately see that

$$p(x) = \frac{x + 1}{x^2} \quad \text{has a } double \text{ pole at } x_0 = 0$$

and

$$q(x) = -\frac{1}{x^3} \quad \text{has a } triple \text{ pole at } x_0 = 0.$$

Therefore, $x = 0$ is an ISP. Nevertheless, let's use the method of Frobenius and set

$$y(x; \lambda) = \sum_0^\infty a_n x^{n+\lambda}.$$

We have Euler plus one terms and Euler terms in the equation,

$$L[y(x; \lambda)] = \underbrace{x^3 y'' + x^2 y'}_{\text{Euler plus one}} + \underbrace{xy' - y}_{\text{Euler}}.$$

Combining like terms, we have

$$L[y(x; \lambda)] = \sum (n + \lambda)^2 a_n x^{n+\lambda+1} + \sum (n + \lambda - 1)a_n x^{n+\lambda}.$$

Shift the first sum down by 1:

$$L[y(x; \lambda)] = \sum (n + \lambda - 1)^2 a_{n-1} x^{n+\lambda} + \sum (n + \lambda - 1)a_n x^{n+\lambda}.$$

Initialize the sums and pull out the $n = 0$ term from the second(!!) sum:

$$L[y(x; \lambda)] = \sum_1^\infty (n + \lambda - 1)^2 a_{n-1} x^{n+\lambda} + (\lambda - 1)a_0 x^\lambda$$
$$+ \sum_1^\infty (n + \lambda - 1)a_n x^{n+\lambda}.$$

The indicial equation is

$$(\lambda - 1)a_0 = 0.$$

This is most unusual because the indicial equation of a second order ODE has *always* been a quadratic. We'll only get one root and one solution to the ODE, and so we might just as well set $\lambda = 1$ at the outset. The recurrence equation is

$$n^2 a_{n-1} + n a_n = 0, \; n = 1 : \infty,$$

or

$$a_n = -n a_{n-1}, \; n = 1 : \infty.$$

Iterating, we get

$$a_n = (-1)^n \, n! \, a_0.$$

So the solution is

$$y(x; 1) = \sum_0^\infty (-1)^n \, n! \, x^{n+1} \, a_0.$$

We have a problem! If we apply the Ratio Test for convergence to the series we have just obtained, we see that

$$\lim_{n \to \infty} \left| \frac{a_n}{a_{n-1}} \right| = |x| \lim_{n \to \infty} n = \infty, \quad \text{for } \textit{every} \text{ nonzero } x.$$

The series converges only at the point $x = 0$, where it takes the value zero! This is a truly unusual situation!

If we were to assume what was stated without proof—the solution about an ISP will have an essential singularity—then we should try a solution of the form

$$y(x) = \sum_{-\infty}^\infty a_n x^n$$

and *not* assume that $\{a_n\}$ is a causal sequence. If our example is any indication, the causal part of the series diverges, so that we could look for an anticausal sequence instead. Using $\lambda = 0$ in the recurrence equation,

$$(n - 1)[(n - 1)a_{n-1} + a_n] = 0.$$

Assuming an anticausal sequence, we can replace n by $-n$, and divide by $n - 1$, which is not zero, to get

$$a_{-(n+1)} = \frac{1}{n + 1} a_{-n}, \; n = 1 : \infty.$$

Iterating, we find

$$a_{-n} = \frac{1}{n!} a_0.$$

The final solution is

$$y(x) = \sum_0^\infty \frac{x^{-n}}{n!} = e^{1/x}.$$

Some simple algebra will verify that this is indeed a solution. ■ ■ ■

Not all irregular singular point solutions lead to causal sequences whose series diverge. The solution of the recurrence equation may be more difficult in such a case. As a rule, we will avoid ISP's! In the unfortunate circumstance when ∞ is an ISP, as in Bessel's equation, we will not be able to use the method of Frobenius to find a simple approximation to the solution for large $|x|$.

8.5.1 Exercise Set

1. For the differential equation $x^4 y'' + xy' + 2y = 0$

   (a) Show that $x = 0$ is an irregular singular point.

   (b) Using the trial solution $y(x) = \sum a_n x^{-2n}$, obtain *both* solutions to this equation.

   (c) Using the standard ordinary point trial solution $y(x) = \sum a_n x^n$, show that the resulting recurrence equation leads to a divergent series.

8.5.2 Notes and References

- Birkhoff & Rota, **Ordinary Differential Equations, 4th ed.**: A good follow-up to the ODE chapters, including proofs of all relevant results.

8.6   SUPPLEMENTARY AND COMPLEMENTARY PROBLEM

1. The **hypergeometric equation** is

$$x(1 - x)y'' + [c - (a + b + 1)x]y' - aby = 0.$$

Use the method of Frobenius to find the general solution expressed as a power series about $x_0 = 0$. Consider each of the following possibilities as special cases:

(a) $a = -n, \ n = 0 : \infty.$ (b) $a = -n, \ b = 1, \ c = 1.$

(c) $a = 1, \ b = 1, \ c = 2.$ (d) $a = 1/2, \ b = 1/2, \ c = 3/2.$

(e) $a = 1/2, \ b = 1, \ c = 3/2.$

9

SPECIAL FUNCTIONS

9.1 PREVIEW

Most of the functions that we will study in this chapter arise as solutions to ODE's with variable coefficients, so that their power series representations will play a major role. So that we might write closed form expressions for the power series coefficients, we will need to generalize the factorial function so that it can be defined for nonintegral values. This generalization is the gamma function. Its major characteristics will be derived and applied.

An ODE studied by Legendre gives rise to polynomial solutions that are especially useful in problems involving either cylindrical or spherical geometry. Some of the properties of these functions will be derived. The generalization of these polynomials to the spherical harmonic functions will be introduced.

Bessel's equation leads to a large class of functions, which are studied in some detail. Many results are simply stated, but some are proven. A generalization of Bessel's equation is given and used to solve variable coefficient ODE's that can be made to fit its form. The oscillations of a heavy chain, a problem first mentioned by Edgar Allan Poe, and the critical height of a beam will be studied using Bessel functions and their relatives.

Many of the properties of Legendre polynomials can be generalized to the family of orthogonal polynomials. There are three basic classes of such polynomials, and they are studied separately. The Chebyshev, Laguerre, and Hermite polynomials are the prototypes of each class.

9.2 GAMMA FUNCTION

DEFINITION 9.1 *The **gamma function**, written Γ, is defined by the integral*

$$\Gamma(z+1) := \int_0^\infty t^z e^{-t} dt. \tag{9.1}$$

The integral in (9.1) converges uniformly for $\text{Re}(z) \geq 0$. Later we will see that this restriction can be relaxed considerably. In order to identify $\Gamma(z+1)$ with a factorial function, we perform an integration by parts keeping $\text{Re}(z) > 0$:

$$\Gamma(z+1) = \left[-t^z e^{-t}\right]_0^\infty + \int_0^\infty z t^{z-1} e^{-t} dt = z \int_0^\infty t^{z-1} e^{-t} dt.$$

We recognize the rightmost integral to be the same as (9.1) but with z reduced by one. Thus we have the **fundamental recurrence relation** for $\Gamma(z+1)$:

$$\Gamma(z+1) = z\Gamma(z) \tag{9.2}$$

By direct evaluation, $\Gamma(1) = 1$: because

$$\Gamma(1) = \int_0^\infty t^0 e^{-t} dt = \left[-e^{-t}\right]_0^\infty = 1.$$

Iterating (9.2) k times we have

$$\Gamma(z+1) = z\Gamma(z), \ \Gamma(z) = (z-1)\Gamma(z-1), \dots,$$

$$\Gamma(z-k+1) = (z-k+1)\Gamma(z-k+1),$$

from which we can infer that

$$\Gamma(z+1) = z(z-1)(z-2)\cdots(z-k+1)\Gamma(z-k+1). \tag{9.3}$$

Looking at equation (9.3) and setting $z = n$, taking values in $1 : \infty$ and using $k = z = n$, we see that

$$\Gamma(n+1) = n(n-1)(n-2)\cdots(2)(1)\Gamma(1) = n!. \tag{9.4}$$

Thus $\Gamma(n+1)$ agrees with the factorial function on the set of nonnegative integers. Be careful of the shift by 1 on the left hand side of (9.4). $\Gamma(11) = 10!$ and $\Gamma(101) = 100!$.

Equation (9.3), together with some tabulated values from Abramowitz & Stegun, will allow us to evaluate the gamma function at many different arguments. Additionally, many scientific calculators will return values of gamma function through their factorial keys.

■ **EXAMPLE 9.1**   Using the values of Γ given, compute the values of $\Gamma(z)$ for the values of z specified.

Solution: Truncated to five decimals we have $\Gamma(1.200) = 0.91816$, so that we can write

$$\Gamma(4.2) = (3.2)(2.2)(1.2)\Gamma(1.2) = 7.75661.$$

Using $\Gamma(1.600) = 0.89351$, we have

$$\Gamma(1.6) = (0.6)(-0.4)(-1.4)(-2.4)\Gamma(-2.4) = 0.89351,$$

from which it follows by simple division that

$$\Gamma(-2.4) = -1.10802.$$

Even complex values are available since

$$\log\left(\Gamma(1+i)\right) = -0.65092 - 0.30164i,$$

from which it follows that

$$\Gamma(1+i) = e^{-0.65092 - 0.30164i} = 0.49802 - 0.15495i,$$

where $e^{a+ib} = e^a(\cos b + i \sin b)$ was used. Since $\Gamma(2+i) = (1+i)\Gamma(1+i)$, we have the end result

$$\Gamma(2+i) = (1+i)(0.49802 - 0.15495i) = 0.65297 + 0.34307i.$$

■ ■ ■

We can use the fundamental recurrence relation for $\Gamma(z+1)$ to define it for some values of z in the left half plane. Just divide (9.2) by z:

$$\Gamma(z) = \frac{\Gamma(z+1)}{z}. \tag{9.5}$$

Iterating, we have

$$\Gamma(z) = \frac{\Gamma(z+k)}{z(z+1)(z+2)\cdots(z+k-1)}, \quad k = 1 : \infty. \tag{9.6}$$

If we want, we can write

$$\Gamma(-\pi) = \frac{\Gamma(-\pi+4)}{(-\pi)(-\pi+1)(-\pi+2)(-\pi+3)}.$$

Since $-\pi + 4 > 0$, $\Gamma(-\pi + 4)$ is well defined and can be found to be approximately 1.04594, either by the numerical approximation, using your calculator or computer, or by looking in Abramowitz & Stegun.

Looking back at (9.6), we see that if z is zero or a negative integer, then no matter how large we choose k, one factor in the denominator will be zero. Thus $\Gamma(z)$ is undefined for $z = 0 : -1 : -\infty$; i.e., you can't find gamma of zero or a negative integer. $\Gamma(z)$ can be defined for all other complex values of z. The graph of $\Gamma(z)$ for real z is shown in Figure 9.1.

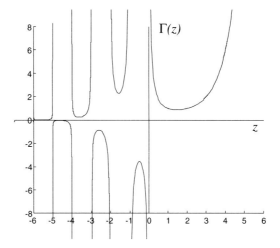

Fig. 9.1 The gama function $\Gamma(z)$ is defined for all real z except zero and negative integers.

Certain recurrence type products can be written in terms of the gamma function. For instance, since

$$\Gamma(5) = 4 \cdot 3 \cdot 2 \cdot 1 \cdot \Gamma(1),$$

we can divide to get

$$4 \cdot 3 \cdot 2 \cdot 1 = \frac{\Gamma(5)}{\Gamma(1)}.$$

Notice that the argument of the numerator is one higher than the highest factor 4 and the argument of the denominator is equal to the lowest factor 1. If we return to (9.6) and invert the relation, we see that this pattern holds in general:

$$\frac{\Gamma(z+k)}{\Gamma(z)} = (z+k-1)(z+k-2)\cdots(z+2)(z+1)z. \tag{9.7}$$

The recurrence equation

$$a_n = (n+\alpha)a_{n-1}, \; n = 1 : \infty$$

has the solution

$$a_n = (n+\alpha)(n+\alpha-1)(n+\alpha-2)\cdots(2+\alpha)(1+\alpha)a_0.$$

Using the gamma function and (9.7), we can write the solution to the recurrence equation as

$$a_n = \frac{\Gamma(n+\alpha+1)}{\Gamma(\alpha+1)}a_0. \tag{9.8}$$

Notice that the right hand side of equation (9.8) is equal to one when $n = 0$ even though the left hand side is undefined there. Thus the solution of the recurrence equation is valid for $n = 0 : \infty$. This is almost always true when using the gamma function.

Equation (9.7) can be applied to the solution of recurrence equations that step by one, two, or whatever, providing they involve only two terms.

■ **EXAMPLE 9.2** Use the gamma function to solve the recurrence equation $(2n + 3)a_n = -(5n - 7)a_{n-1}$.

Solution: To solve $(2n + 3)a_n = -(5n - 7)a_{n-1}$, first factor out all coefficients of n in every term, and then use (9.7):

$$a_n = -\frac{5}{2}\frac{\left(n - \frac{7}{5}\right)}{\left(n + \frac{3}{2}\right)}a_{n-1} = \left(-\frac{5}{2}\right)^n \frac{\Gamma\left(n - \frac{7}{5} + 1\right)\Gamma\left(\frac{5}{2}\right)}{\Gamma\left(-\frac{2}{5}\right)\Gamma\left(n + \frac{3}{2} + 1\right)}a_0.$$

■ ■ ■

No matter how complicated the polynomial coefficients may be, the method remains the same if the coefficients are available in factored form (which the Fundamental Theorem of Algebra guarantees, albeit not necessarily either easily or nicely).

■ **EXAMPLE 9.3** Solve each of the following two term recurrence equations.

(a) To solve

$$(n + 3)(2n - 1)(5n - 2)a_n = (n + 2)(3n - 2)a_{n-1}, n = 1 : \infty,$$

proceed as follows:

$$\begin{aligned}
a_n &= \frac{(n + 2)(3n - 2)}{(n + 3)(2n - 1)(5n - 2)}a_{n-1} \\
&= \left(\frac{1 \cdot 3}{1 \cdot 2 \cdot 5}\right)\frac{(n + 2)\left(n - \frac{2}{3}\right)}{(n + 3)\left(n - \frac{1}{2}\right)\left(n - \frac{2}{5}\right)}a_{n-1}
\end{aligned}$$

$$\Rightarrow \quad a_n = \left(\frac{1 \cdot 3}{1 \cdot 2 \cdot 5}\right)^n \frac{\dfrac{\Gamma(n + 3)}{\Gamma(3)}\dfrac{\Gamma(n + 1/3)}{\Gamma(1/3)}}{\dfrac{\Gamma(n + 4)}{\Gamma(4)}\dfrac{\Gamma(n + 1/2)}{\Gamma(1/2)}\dfrac{\Gamma(n + 3/5)}{\Gamma(3/5)}}a_0.$$

This can be simplified by using the fundamental recurrence equation in the form $\Gamma(n + 4) = (n + 3)\Gamma(n + 3)$ and $\Gamma(4) = 3\Gamma(3)$, so that

$$a_n = \left(\frac{3}{10}\right)^n \frac{3}{n + 3}\frac{\Gamma(1/2)}{\Gamma(n + 1/2)}\frac{\Gamma(3/5)}{\Gamma(n + 3/5)}\frac{\Gamma(n + 1/3)}{\Gamma(1/3)}a_0.$$

(b) To solve the equation

$$(2n + 1)a_n - na_{n-3} = 0,$$

which steps by three, we must separate the values of n into three subcases:

Subcase 1: $n = 3k$,

$$(6k + 1)a_{3k} - 3ka_{3k-3} = 0.$$

Solving for a_{3k} and factoring as before, we find

$$a_{3k} = \frac{1}{2} \frac{k}{(k + 1/6)} a_{3k-3} = \left(\frac{1}{2}\right)^k \frac{k!\, \Gamma(7/6)}{\Gamma(k + 7/6)} a_0.$$

Subcase 2: $n = 3k + 1$,

$$a_{3k+1} = \frac{1}{2} \frac{(k + 1/3)}{(k + 1/2)} a_{3k-2} = \left(\frac{1}{2}\right)^k \frac{\Gamma(3/2)}{\Gamma(k + 3/2)} \frac{\Gamma(k + 4/3)}{\Gamma(4/3)} a_1.$$

Subcase 3: $n = 3k + 2$,

$$a_{3k+2} = \frac{1}{2} \frac{(k + 2/3)}{(k + 5/6)} a_{3k-1} = \left(\frac{1}{2}\right)^k \frac{\Gamma(11/6)}{\Gamma(k + 11/6)} \frac{\Gamma(k + 5/3)}{\Gamma(5/3)} a_2.$$

These completely specify the sequence a_n. ∎ ■ ■ ■

If we define

$$0 =: \frac{1}{\Gamma(0)} = \frac{1}{\Gamma(-1)} = \frac{1}{\Gamma(-2)} = \cdots$$

then $1/\Gamma(z)$ will be an analytic function in the finite complex z-plane.

9.2.1 Semifactorials and the Gauss Duplication Formula

The semifactorial arises naturally from $\Gamma((2n + 1)/2)$ when n is a positive integer. In fact, using the fundamental recurrence relation (9.2), we have

$$\Gamma\left(\frac{2n + 1}{2}\right) = \left(\frac{2n - 1}{2}\right)\left(\frac{2n - 3}{2}\right) \cdots \left(\frac{1}{2}\right) \Gamma\left(\frac{1}{2}\right),$$

which implies

$$\Gamma\left(\frac{2n + 1}{2}\right) = \frac{(2n - 1)!!}{2^n} \Gamma\left(\frac{1}{2}\right). \tag{9.9}$$

To compute $\Gamma(1/2)$ and complete (9.9) we'll need to employ an ingenious device, which you may have seen before: Start with the defining integral

$$\Gamma\left(\frac{1}{2}\right) = \int_0^\infty t^{-1/2} e^{-t} dt.$$

Now put $t = x^2$ and $dt = 2x\, dx$ to get

$$\Gamma\left(\frac{1}{2}\right) = \int_0^\infty x^{-1} e^{-x^2} 2x\, dx = 2\int_0^\infty e^{-x^2} dx = \int_{-\infty}^\infty e^{-x^2} dx.$$

This integral cannot be evaluated using elementary techniques. Instead, square it (keeping in mind that although there are two integrals, the variable of integration in each can be whatever we want) and use Fubini's Theorem to write the iterated integrals as a double integral:

$$\Gamma^2\left(\frac{1}{2}\right) = \int_{-\infty}^\infty e^{-x^2} dx \int_{-\infty}^\infty e^{-y^2} dy = \int_{-\infty}^\infty \int_{-\infty}^\infty e^{-(x^2+y^2)} dx\, dy$$

The presence of the quantity $x^2 + y^2$ just cries out for a change to polar coordinates. We need to use the change in the element of area as $dx\, dy = r\, dr\, d\theta$. Then we have

$$\Gamma^2\left(\frac{1}{2}\right) = \int_{-\pi}^\pi \int_0^\infty e^{-r^2} r\, dr\, d\theta = -\pi \left[e^{-r^2}\right]_0^\infty = \pi.$$

Finally, we can take the square root of both sides:

$$\Gamma\left(\frac{1}{2}\right) = \sqrt{\pi}.$$

We can use the fundamental recurrence relation in either form (9.2) or (9.5) to generate other half-integral values, e.g.,

$$\Gamma\left(\frac{3}{2}\right) = \frac{1}{2}\Gamma\left(\frac{1}{2}\right) = \frac{\sqrt{\pi}}{2}, \qquad \Gamma\left(\frac{7}{2}\right) = \frac{5}{2} \cdot \frac{3}{2}\Gamma\left(\frac{3}{2}\right) = \frac{15\sqrt{\pi}}{8}.$$

Returning to semifactorials, we had

$$(2n)! = (2n)!!(2n-1)!! = 2^n n!(2n-1)!!.$$

Converting to gamma functions, this becomes

$$\Gamma(2n+1) = 2^n \Gamma(n+1) 2^n \Gamma(n+1/2)\sqrt{\pi},$$

from which it follows that

$$2n\Gamma(2n) = 2n \cdot 2^{2n-1}\Gamma(n)\Gamma(n+1/2)/\sqrt{\pi}.$$

Multiplying by $\sqrt{\pi}/2n$ we arrive at the **Gauss duplication formula**:

$$\sqrt{\pi}\,\Gamma(2n) = 2^{2n-1}\Gamma(n)\Gamma(n+1/2). \tag{9.10}$$

Equation (9.10) is valid for all complex n such that $2n$ is not a nonpositive integer, i.e., n other than $0, -1/2, -1, -3/2, \ldots$.

There is a useful approximation to $\Gamma(z)$ that is valid for large $|z|$. It is

$$\Gamma(z) \doteq \sqrt{2\pi}\,z^{z-1/2}e^{-z}\left(1 + \frac{1}{12z} + \frac{1}{288z^2} - \frac{139}{51480z^3} + \cdots\right). \tag{9.11}$$

If we translate this into the factorial function and take the first term, then we have the usual form of **Stirling's formula**:

$$n! \doteq \sqrt{2\pi n}\left(\frac{n}{e}\right)^n. \tag{9.12}$$

The relative size of the factorial should be apparent from this approximation. It increases as $n^{n+1/2}$ which is far larger than e^n for $n > 3$. In fact, some values for large n might give some perspective.

$$
\begin{aligned}
10! &= 3,628,800, \\
50! &= 3.04 \times 10^{64}, \\
100! &= 9.33 \times 10^{157}, \\
500! &= 1.22 \times 10^{1134}, \\
1000! &= 4.02 \times 10^{2567}.
\end{aligned}
$$

As a size reference,

$$\exp(100) = 2.68 \times 10^{43} \text{ and } \exp(1000) = 1.97 \times 10^{434}.$$

The factorial is a *very rapidly* growing function!

9.2.2 Derivatives of the Gamma Function

A relative of $\Gamma(z)$ that arises in the anomalous case of the method of Frobenius (exponents of singularity differing by an integer) is the digamma function (so named because of a now unused notation for it):

$$\psi(z) := \frac{d}{dz}\log\Gamma(z) = \frac{1}{\Gamma(z)}\frac{d}{dz}\Gamma(z). \tag{9.13}$$

If we take the natural logarithm of the fundamental recurrence relation for the gamma function, equation (9.2), and differentiate with respect to z, we have

$$\log\Gamma(z+1) = \log z + \log\Gamma(z) \quad \Rightarrow \quad \psi(z+1) = \frac{1}{z} + \psi(z).$$

Now define $\psi(1) := -\gamma$; it has been calculated that $\gamma = 0.5772156\ldots$, which is called **Euler's constant** and is defined by the limit

$$\gamma := \lim_{k\to\infty}\left(\ln k - H_k\right),$$

where H_k is the kth partial sum of the harmonic series (see Appendix F). The status of Euler's constant as a rational or irrational number is as yet *unknown*. For positive integers n,

$$\psi(n + 1) = -\gamma + 1 + \frac{1}{2} + \frac{1}{3} + \cdots + \frac{1}{n} = -\gamma + H_n. \tag{9.14}$$

9.2.3 Applications of the Gamma Function

The gamma function can be used for more than just solving the recurrence equations associated with variable coefficient ODE's. In fact, the anomalous cases in the method of Frobenius can be handled quickly by using $\Gamma(z)$ and its derivative. In addition, many problems in probability demand the use of this function.

■ **EXAMPLE 9.4** Suppose we have the recurrence equation from a time dependent ODE with equal exponents of singularity, $\lambda = b$:

$$a_n = \frac{1}{bn + \lambda} a_{n-1}, \; n = 1 : \infty.$$

Factoring out b and applying (9.7) we have

$$a_n = \frac{\Gamma\left(\frac{\lambda}{b} + 1\right)}{b^n \Gamma\left(n + \frac{\lambda}{b} + 1\right)} a_0.$$

Notice that although the recurrence equation was valid for $n = 1 : \infty$, the solution, in this form, is valid for $n = 0 : \infty$. Thus

$$y(x; \lambda) = \sum_{n=0}^{\infty} \frac{\Gamma\left(\frac{\lambda}{b} + 1\right)}{b^n \Gamma\left(n + \frac{\lambda}{b} + 1\right)} x^{n+\lambda}.$$

When finding a second solution we need to evaluate $a'_n(\lambda)$. Take the natural logarithm of a_n and differentiate:

$$\ln a_n(\lambda) = \ln \Gamma\left(\frac{\lambda}{b} + 1\right) - \ln \Gamma\left(n + \frac{\lambda}{b} + 1\right) - n \ln b$$

$$\Rightarrow \quad a'_n(\lambda) = a_n(\lambda) \left[\frac{1}{b} \psi\left(\frac{\lambda}{b} + 1\right) - \frac{1}{b} \psi\left(n + \frac{\lambda}{b} + 1\right)\right].$$

Set $\lambda = b$ and use (9.14):

$$a'_n(\lambda) = \frac{1}{b^{n+1}(n + 1)!} [\psi(2) - \psi(n + 2)]$$

$$= \frac{1}{b^{n+1}(n + 1)!} [(-\gamma + H_1) - (-\gamma + H_{n+1})]$$

$$\Rightarrow \quad a'_n(\lambda) = -\frac{1}{b^{n+1}(n + 1)!} (H_{n+1} - 1),$$

since $H_1 = 1$. Therefore, the two independent solutions are

$$y_1(x) = \sum_{n=0}^{\infty} \frac{x^{n+b}}{b^n (n+1)!}$$

and

$$y_2(x) = y_1(x) \ln x - \sum_{n=0}^{\infty} \frac{(H_{n+1} - 1)}{b^{n+1} (n+1)!} x^{n+b}.$$

■ ■ ■

■ **EXAMPLE 9.5** When studying probability, one encounters the integral

$$\mu'_{2n} = \frac{2}{\sqrt{2\pi\sigma^2}} \int_0^{\infty} x^{2n} \exp\left(-\frac{x^2}{2\sigma^2}\right) dx,$$

when computing the $2n^{th}$ moment of a Gaussian random variable. This can be cast in the form of a gamma function by substituting

$$t = \frac{x^2}{2\sigma^2} \quad \Rightarrow \quad dt = \frac{x}{\sigma^2} dx.$$

Thus

$$\mu'_{2n} = \frac{2}{\sqrt{2\pi\sigma^2}} \int_0^{\infty} (2\sigma^2 t)^{(2n-1)/2} e^{-t} \sigma^2 \, dt = \frac{2^n}{\sqrt{\pi}} \sigma^{2n} \int_0^{\infty} t^{n-1/2} e^{-t} \, dt.$$

Using the Gauss duplication formula, (9.10), to eliminate $\Gamma(n + 1/2)$, which is the value of the integral, we find

$$\mu'_{2n} = \frac{(2n)!}{n!} \left(\frac{\sigma^2}{2}\right)^n.$$

■ ■ ■

The following functions are, at least indirectly, related to the gamma function:

(a) **Exponential Integral Function**

$$\text{Ei}(z) := \int_{-\infty}^{z} \frac{e^t}{t} \, dt, \; |\arg(-z)| < \pi.$$

(b) **Error Function**

$$\text{erf}(z) := \frac{2}{\sqrt{\pi}} \int_0^z e^{-t^2} \, dt.$$

(c) **Fresnel Functions**

$$C(z) := \int_0^z \cos\left(\frac{\pi t^2}{2}\right) dt, \quad S(z) := \int_0^z \sin\left(\frac{\pi t^2}{2}\right) dt.$$

(d) **Beta Function**

$$B(x, y) := \int_0^1 t^{x-1}(1 - t)^{y-1}dt, \ \operatorname{Re}(x) \geq 1, \ \operatorname{Re}(y) \geq 1.$$

(e) **Incomplete Gamma Function**

$$\gamma(z; \alpha) := \int_0^\alpha t^{z-1}e^{-t}\, dt, \ \operatorname{Re}(z) > 0, \ |\arg \alpha| < \pi.$$

There are several others. You should consult Hochstadt, Lebedev, Abramowitz & Stegun, or Spanier & Oldham for further details.

9.2.4 *Exercise Set*

1. Verify the following integral representations:

   (a) $\Gamma(z) = \displaystyle\int_0^1 \left(\ln \frac{1}{t}\right)^{z-1} dt.$

   (b) $\Gamma(z) = s^z \displaystyle\int t^{z-1}e^{-st}dt \quad \text{for} \operatorname{Re}(s) > 0.$

   (c) $\Gamma(z) = \displaystyle\int_1^\infty t^{z-1}e^{-t}dt + \sum_0^\infty \frac{(-1)^n}{n!(z + n)}.$

2. If $\Gamma(1.1) = 0.95135$, $\Gamma(1.2) = 0.91817$, and $\Gamma(1.3) = 0.89747$, find the values of $\Gamma(8.1)$, $\Gamma(-6.8)$, $\Gamma(4.3)$, and $\Gamma(2.3)/\Gamma(-0.8)$.

3. If $\ln \Gamma(2 + i) = 0.30434 + 0.48375i$, find $\Gamma(3 + i)$ and $\Gamma(4 + i)$.

4. The beta function is defined by the integral

   $$B(x, y) := \int_0^1 t^{x-1}(1 - t)^{y-1}dt, \ \text{for} \ \operatorname{Re}(x, y) > 0.$$

   In the style of the computation of the value of $\Gamma(1/2)$:

   (a) Form the iterated integral $\Gamma(x)\Gamma(y)$ using s as the integration variable in the first and t in the second.

   (b) Change variables via $s = r \cos^2\theta$ and $t = r \sin^2\theta$.

   (c) Show that the r-integral is $\Gamma(x + y)$.

   (d) In the θ-integral make the substitution $\cos \theta = \sqrt{t}$ to show that

   $$B(x, y) = \frac{\Gamma(x)\Gamma(y)}{\Gamma(x + y)}.$$

5. Use the definition of $B(x, y)$ in the previous problem and an appropriate substitution to show that

(a) $\displaystyle\int_0^{\pi/2} \cos^\alpha\theta\, d\theta = \int_0^{\pi/2} \sin^\alpha\theta\, d\theta = \frac{1}{2}\sqrt{\pi}\,\frac{\Gamma\left(\frac{\alpha+1}{2}\right)}{\Gamma\left(\frac{\alpha}{2}+1\right)}, \quad \mathrm{Re}(\alpha) > -1.$

(b) $\displaystyle\int_0^{\pi/2} \cos^\alpha\theta \sin^\beta\theta\, d\theta = \frac{1}{2}\frac{\Gamma\left(\frac{\alpha+1}{2}\right)\Gamma\left(\frac{\beta+1}{2}\right)}{\Gamma\left(\frac{\alpha+\beta}{2}+1\right)}, \quad \mathrm{Re}(\alpha, \beta) > -1.$

6. Show that $B(a, b) = B(a+1, b) + B(a, b+1)$.

7. Show that

$$\int_0^1 \frac{x^{2n}}{\sqrt{1-x^2}}\, dx = \frac{\sqrt{\pi}}{2}\frac{\Gamma\left(n+\frac{1}{2}\right)}{\Gamma(n+1)}.$$

Use the gamma function to solve each of the following recurrence equations.

8. $(2n+1)a_n + 3a_{n-1} = 0, \quad n = 1:\infty$

9. $3a_n + (2n+1)a_{n-1} = 0, \quad n = 1:\infty$

10. $na_n - (n+2)a_{n-1} = 0, \quad n = 1:\infty$

11. $n(n+1)a_n - 2(n+2)(2n+1)a_n - 1 = 0, \quad n = 1:\infty$

12. $(4n^2 - 1)a_n + (2n^2 + n - 6)a_{n-1} = 0, \quad n = 1:\infty$

13. $(n^2 + 1)a_n - (n^2 - 1)a_{n-1} = 0, \quad n = 1:\infty$

14. $2n(2n+3)(3n - 5)a_n = (n^2 + 4n + 4)^2 a_{n-1}, \quad n = 1:\infty$

15. $n(n-1)a_n - 3(n+3)(4n-3)a_{n-2} = 0, \quad n = 2:\infty$

16. $na_n - (2n+1)(3n-1)a_{n-2} = 0, \quad n = 2:\infty$

17. $(n^2 - 1)a_n + 2(n^2 + 5n + 6)a_{n-2} = 0, \quad n = 2:\infty$

18. $(2n-1)a_n + (12n + 14)a_{n-2} = 0, \quad n = 2:\infty$

19. $na_n - (n+2)a_{n-3} = 0, \quad n = 3:\infty$

20. $a_n + (n^2 + 5n + 6)a_{n-3} = 0, \quad n = 3:\infty$

21. $(2n-1)a_n + na_{n-4} = 0, \quad n = 4:\infty$

22. Show that

$$\frac{\Gamma\left(p + n + \frac{1}{2}\right)}{\Gamma\left(p - n + \frac{1}{2}\right)} = \frac{\left(4p^2 - 1\right)\left(4p^2 - 3\right)\cdots\left(4p^2 - (2n-1)^2\right)}{2^{2n}}.$$

9.3 LEGENDRE POLYNOMIALS

Legendre's equation,

$$(1 - x^2)y'' - 2xy' + \lambda y = 0, \tag{9.15}$$

arises naturally in many partial differential equation models with cylindrical or spherical symmetry, although in the latter situation it appears in a somewhat more complicated form, which we will see at the end of this section.

It can be verified that $x = -1, 1, \infty$ are regular singular points of this equation. When finding a series solution about the ordinary point $x_0 = 0$, using the form $\sum a_k x^k$, we arrive at the recurrence equation

$$a_k = \frac{(k-2)(k-1) - \lambda}{k(k-1)} a_{k-2}, \; k = 2 : \infty, \tag{9.16}$$

with a_0 and a_1 arbitrary. So that we might factor the numerator of (9.16), set $\lambda = \nu(\nu + 1)$. Then we have

$$a_k = -\frac{(\nu - k + 2)(\nu + k - 1)}{k(k-1)} a_{k-2}, \; k = 2 : \infty. \tag{9.17}$$

This is one of the special recurrence equations that steps by two and can be separated into the cases of even and odd k. The general solution can be written in the form

$$y(x) = a_0 \left[1 - \frac{\nu(\nu + 1)}{2!} x^2 + \frac{\nu(\nu - 2)(\nu + 1)(\nu + 3)}{4!} x^4 - \cdots \right]$$

$$+ a_1 \left[x - \frac{(\nu - 1)(\nu + 2)}{3!} x^3 + \frac{(\nu - 1)(\nu - 3)(\nu + 2)(\nu + 4)}{5!} x^5 - \cdots \right]. \tag{9.18}$$

For general values of ν, each series will converge within the unit circle $|x| < 1$, except in the following case, where the radius of convergence will be larger. If $\nu = \ell$, a nonnegative integer, then one of the series in (9.18) will terminate and give a polynomial solution. When ℓ is even, we'll get an even polynomial of degree ℓ, and when ℓ is odd, we'll get an odd polynomial, also of degree ℓ.

The explicit form of the solution of (9.17) when $\nu = \ell$ is best gotten by calculating a_k in the reverse of the usual order; we'll find each a_k, $k < \ell$, in terms of a_ℓ, rather than in terms of a_0 or a_1. Inverting the recurrence equation, we have

$$a_{k-2} = \frac{k(k-1)}{(\ell - k + 2)(\ell + k - 1)} a_k.$$

The first step down is

$$a_{\ell-2} = -\frac{\ell(\ell - 1)}{2(2\ell - 1)} a_\ell,$$

and the next step is

$$a_{\ell-4} = -\frac{(\ell-2)(\ell-3)}{4(2\ell-3)}a_{\ell-2} = (-1)^2\frac{\ell(\ell-1)(\ell-2)(\ell-3)}{2\cdot 4\cdot(2\ell-1)(2\ell-3)}a_\ell.$$

We can write the solution in the form

$$y(x) = a_\ell x^\ell\left[1 - \frac{\ell(\ell-1)}{2(2\ell-1)}\frac{1}{x^2} + \frac{\ell(\ell-1)(\ell-2)(\ell-3)}{2\cdot 4\cdot(2\ell-1)(2\ell-3)}\frac{1}{x^4} - \cdots\right].$$

The general form can be written as

$$y(x) = a_\ell x^\ell\sum_{k=0}(-1)^k\frac{\ell(\ell-1)(\ell-2)\cdots(\ell-2k+1)}{2^k k!(2\ell-1)(2\ell-3)\cdots(2\ell-2k+1)}\frac{1}{x^{2k}}.$$

Both the product in the numerator and that in the denominator can be replaced by factorials (using the Gauss duplication formula), so that we have

$$y(x) = a_\ell\sum_{k=0}(-1)^k\frac{\ell!}{k!}\frac{\ell!(2\ell-2k)!}{(\ell-2k)!(2\ell)!(\ell-k)!}x^{\ell-2k}.$$

We will choose

$$a_\ell = \frac{(2\ell)!}{(\ell!)^2}2^\ell$$

so that everything agrees with standard notation. Then the **Legendre polynomial** of order ℓ can be written in the form

$$P_\ell(x) := \sum_{k=0}(-1)^k\frac{(2\ell-2k)!}{2^\ell k!\,(\ell-k)!\,(\ell-2k)!}x^{\ell-2k}.$$

The series terminates when k reaches the point where the argument of one of the factorials in the denominator is negative. (Remember: The reciprocal gamma function of 0 or a negative integer is defined to be zero.). This will occur when $k = \lfloor \ell/2\rfloor$, where $\lfloor z\rfloor$, called the **floor** of z, is the greatest integer less than or equal to z, which is the same as rounding z *down*. Thus

$$P_\ell(x) := \sum_{k=0}^{\lfloor\ell/2\rfloor}(-1)^k\frac{(2\ell-2k)!}{2^\ell k!\,(\ell-k)!\,(\ell-2k)!}x^{\ell-2k}. \tag{9.19}$$

Some simplification can be gotten by using the identity

$$\left(\frac{d}{dx}\right)^\ell x^{2\ell-2k} = (2\ell-2k)(2\ell-2k-1)\cdots(\ell-2k+1)x^{\ell-2k} = \frac{(2\ell-2k)!}{(\ell-2k)!}x^{\ell-2k},$$

which yields

$$P_\ell(x) = \sum_{k=0}^{\lfloor\ell/2\rfloor}(-1)^k\frac{1}{2^\ell k!\,(\ell-k)!}\left(\frac{d}{dx}\right)^\ell x^{2\ell-2k}$$

$$= \frac{1}{2^\ell \ell!}\left(\frac{d}{dx}\right)^\ell\sum_{k=0}^{\lfloor\ell/2\rfloor}(-1)^k\frac{\ell!}{k!(\ell-k)!}(x^2)^{\ell-k}.$$

But

$$\frac{\ell!}{k!(\ell - k)!} = \binom{\ell}{k}, \text{ the binomial coefficient.}$$

From this we should recognize the binomial expansion of $(x^2 - 1)^\ell$. The end result is called **Rodrigues' formula** for $P_\ell(x)$:

$$P_\ell(x) = \frac{1}{2^\ell \ell!} \left(\frac{d}{dx} \right)^\ell (x^2 - 1)^\ell. \tag{9.20}$$

When one solution of Legendre's equation with $\lambda = \ell(\ell + 1)$ is a polynomial, the other is *not* a polynomial. If we denote the other solution by $Q_\ell(x)$, it can be shown that

$$Q_\ell(x) = \frac{1}{2} P_\ell(x) \log \left| \frac{x + 1}{x - 1} \right| + W_{\ell-1}(x),$$

where $W_{\ell-1}(x)$ is a polynomial of degree $\ell - 1$. The function $Q_\ell(x)$ has branch points at $x = \pm 1$ because of the logarithmic factor.

By way of reference, the first six Legendre polynomials are:

$$P_0(x) = 1, \ P_1(x) = x, \ P_2(x) = \frac{1}{2} \left(3x^2 - 1 \right),$$

$$P_3(x) = \frac{1}{2} \left(5x^3 - 3x \right), \ P_4(x) = \frac{1}{2 \cdot 4} \left(5 \cdot 7x^4 - 2 \cdot 3 \cdot 5x^2 + 1 \cdot 3 \right),$$

$$P_5(x) = \frac{1}{2 \cdot 4} \left(7 \cdot 9x^5 - 2 \cdot 5 \cdot 7x^3 + 3 \cdot 5x \right).$$

Some useful values of the Legendre polynomials are:

$$P_\ell(1) = 1, \ P_\ell(-1) = (-1)^\ell, \ P_{2\ell+1}(0) = 0, \tag{9.21}$$

$$P_{2\ell}(0) = (-1)^\ell \frac{(2\ell - 1)!!}{2^\ell \ell!}. \tag{9.22}$$

The graphs of the first few Legendre polynomials in Figure 9.2 should give you an idea of their general behavior.

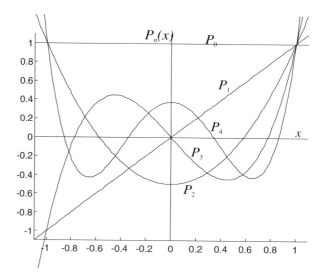

Fig. 9.2   The graphs of the first few Legendre polynomials.

As an alternative, you may want to go back to Chapter 3 to see how the normalized Legendre polynomials were generated from the standard basis $\{1, x, x^2, \ldots, x^n\}$ using the Gram-Schmidt procedure.

9.3.1   *Relations Among the Legendre Polynomials*

There are many other properties of the Legendre polynomials that can be derived. The following recurrence relations are but a few:

$$(\ell + 1)P_{\ell+1}(x) - (2\ell + 1)xP_\ell(x) + \ell P_{\ell-1}(x) = 0, \; \ell = 1 : \infty, \tag{9.23}$$

$$P'_{\ell+1}(x) - xP'_\ell(x) = (\ell + 1)P_\ell(x), \; \ell = 0 : \infty, \tag{9.24}$$

$$xP'_\ell(x) - P'_{\ell-1}(x) = \ell P_\ell(x), \; \ell = 1 : \infty. \tag{9.25}$$

Another fundamental relation involves the integral of a product of Legendre polynomials. To derive it, start by using the identity

$$\left(1 - x^2\right) y'' - 2xy' = \left[\left(1 - x^2\right) y'\right]'$$

to rewrite Legendre's equations of orders ℓ and m

$$\left[\left(1 - x^2\right) P'_\ell(x)\right]' + \ell(\ell + 1)P_\ell(x) = 0,$$

$$\left[\left(1 - x^2\right) P'_m(x)\right]' + m(m + 1)P_m(x) = 0. \tag{9.26}$$

Multiply $(9.26)_\ell$ by $P_m(x)$ and subtract $P_\ell(x)$ times $(9.26)_m$,

$$\left[(1 - x^2)\, P'_\ell(x)\right]' P_m(x) - \left[(1 - x^2)\, P'_m(x)\right]' P_\ell(x)$$
$$+ [\ell(\ell + 1) - m(m + 1)]\, P_\ell(x) P_m(x) = 0.$$

A slight rewrite yields

$$\left[(1 - x^2)\, (P'_\ell(x) P_m(x) - P'_m(x) P_\ell(x))\right]'$$
$$+ (\ell - m)(\ell + m + 1) P_\ell(x) P_m(x) = 0.$$

Now integrate this from -1 to 1 and notice that the integral of the first term involves $1 - x^2$ evaluated between the limits, and hence it is zero. We find

$$(\ell - m)(\ell + m + 1) \int_{-1}^{1} P_\ell(x) P_m(x)\, dx = 0.$$

When $\ell \neq m$, this implies

$$\int_{-1}^{1} P_\ell(x) P_m(x)\, dx = 0. \qquad (9.27)$$

In the notation of Chapter 3 we can say that $\{P_0(x), P_1(x), P_2(x), \ldots\}$ is an orthogonal set on the interval $[-1, 1]$ with weight function $w(x) = 1$. If we compute $\|P_\ell(x)\|$, then we can normalize each function. To find the normalizing constant, go back to recurrence relation (9.23) with ℓ reduced by one:

$$\ell P_\ell(x) - (2\ell - 1)x P_{\ell-1}(x) + (\ell - 1)P_{\ell-2}(x) = 0. \qquad (9.28)$$

Multiply (9.28) by $(2\ell + 1)P_\ell(x)$ and subtract $(2\ell - 1)P_{\ell-1}(x)$ times (9.23); this will cancel out the xP terms, giving us

$$\ell(2\ell + 1)P_\ell^2 + (\ell - 1)(2\ell + 1)P_{\ell-2}P_\ell$$
$$- (\ell + 1)(2\ell - 1)P_{\ell-1}P_{\ell+1} - \ell(2\ell - 1)P_{\ell-1}^2 = 0,$$

which is valid for $\ell = 2 : \infty$. Now integrate from -1 to 1 and use the orthogonality relation to drop the middle two terms, leaving

$$\int_{-1}^{1} P_\ell^2(x)\, dx = \frac{2\ell - 1}{2\ell + 1} \int_{-1}^{1} P_{\ell-1}^2(x)\, dx, \quad \ell = 2 : \infty. \qquad (9.29)$$

Iterating (9.29), we find

$$\int_{-1}^{1} P_\ell^2(x)\, dx = \left(\frac{2\ell - 1}{2\ell + 1}\right) \left(\frac{2\ell - 3}{2\ell - 1}\right) \cdots \left(\frac{5}{7}\right) \left(\frac{3}{5}\right) \int_{-1}^{1} P_1^2(x)\, dx.$$

Since $P_1(x) = x$, the rightmost integral is equal to $1/3$ and

$$\|P_\ell(x)\|_1^2 = \int_{-1}^{1} P_\ell^2(x)\, dx = \frac{2}{2\ell + 1}. \qquad (9.30)$$

You should verify that (9.30) is also valid for $\ell = 1$ and $\ell = 0$.

9.3.2   Exercise Set

1. Use Rodrigues' formula to verify the forms of $P_3(x)$ and $P_4(x)$ stated in the text.

2. Directly show that the Rodrigues' formula representation of $P_\ell(x)$ is a solution of Legendre's equation.

3. Verify the values of the Legendre polynomials given in equations (9.21) and (9.22) of this section.

4. Prove the recurrence equations for the Legendre polynomials given in equations (9.23)–(9.25).

5. In two different ways, show that

$$\int_{-1}^{1} x^k \, P_\ell(x) \, dx = 0, \; k = 0 : \ell - 1.$$

6. The generating function of the set of functions $\{A_n(x)\}$ is defined to be $f(x, t)$ if we can write $f(x, t) = \sum A_n(x) t^n$. The generating function of the Legendre polynomials is $(1 - 2xt + t^2)^{-1/2}$. To prove this write the defining equation

$$\frac{1}{\sqrt{1 - 2xt + t^2}} = \sum_{n=0}^{\infty} A_n(x) \, t^n.$$

   (a) Differentiate both sides of the above equation with respect to t and show that

   $$(x - t) \sum_{n=0}^{\infty} A_n(x) \, t^n = \left(1 - 2xt + t^2\right) \sum_{n=0}^{\infty} n A_n(x) \, t^{n-1}.$$

   (b) Equate coefficients of like powers of t to obtain the recurrence equation

   $$(n + 1)A_{n+1}(x) = (2n + 1)x A_n(x) - n A_{n-1}(x).$$

   Comparing the last equation with equation (9.23), we see that $A_n(x) = P_n(x)$

   (c) Thus infer that $(1 - 2xt + t^2)^{-1/2}$ is the generating function of the Legendre polynomials.

9.4   BESSEL FUNCTIONS

The series solutions of Bessel's equation illustrates many important facets of the method of Frobenius from the previous chapter. These will be studied in some detail. Following that will be a discussion of the properties of the various Bessel functions. Some of the results will be derived, but many will be stated without proof.

9.4.1 *Series Solution of Bessel's Equation*

Bessel's equation of order α was defined to be

$$L[y] := x^2 y'' + x y' + (x^2 - \alpha^2) y = 0. \tag{9.31}$$

We have already seen that $x = 0$ is an RSP and $x = \infty$ is an ISP. Setting $y(x) = \sum a_n x^{n+\lambda}$ in (9.31), we find

$$L[y(x; \lambda)] = \sum \left[(n + \lambda)(n + \lambda - 1) + (n + \lambda) - \alpha^2 \right] a_n x^{n+\lambda} + \sum a_n x^{n+\lambda+2}$$

$$\Rightarrow \quad L[y(x; \lambda)] = \sum (n + \lambda + \alpha)(n + \lambda - \alpha) a_n x^{n+\lambda} + \sum a_n x^{n+\lambda+2}.$$

Shifting the index down by 2 in the second sum, initializing, and pulling out the $n = 0$ and $n = 1$ terms from the first sum yields

$$L[y] = (\lambda + \alpha)(\lambda - \alpha) a_0 x^\lambda + (\lambda + 1 + \alpha)(\lambda + 1 - \alpha) a_1 x^{\lambda+1}$$
$$+ \sum_2^\infty \left[(n + \lambda + \alpha)(n + \lambda - \alpha) a_n + a_{n-2} \right] x^{n+\lambda}.$$

The indicial equation is

$$(\lambda + \alpha)(\lambda - \alpha) a_0 = 0 \quad \Rightarrow \quad \lambda = -\alpha, \alpha. \tag{9.32}$$

Thus when the difference of the roots $\alpha - (-\alpha) = 2\alpha$ is an integer we have those wonderful anomalous cases. This will occur when α is an integral multiple of $1/2$. The secondary equation is

$$(\lambda + 1 + \alpha)(\lambda + 1 - \alpha) a_1 = 0, \tag{9.33}$$

which has two possible solutions. If we take $\lambda = -\alpha$ (from (9.32)), then (9.33) becomes

$$(1 - 2\alpha) a_1 = 0.$$

When $\alpha = 1/2$, then we need not set $a_1 = 0$. Taking $\lambda = \alpha$, (9.33) becomes

$$(1 + 2\alpha) a_1 = 0.$$

When $\alpha = -1/2$, again we need not set $a_1 = 0$, the same as in the case $\alpha = 1/2$.

Since the original differential equation, (9.31), contains α only in the form α^2, $\alpha = \pm 1/2$ are subsumed under a single case, and in each instance we need not take $a_1 = 0$, this is a nonlogarithmic anomalous case, whereby both solutions can be gotten by using the lesser exponent of singularity. When α is an odd multiple of $1/2$, we will be able to obtain a second solution without differentiation with respect to λ.

For the moment, let's assume that α is not an integral multiple of $1/2$. Then the secondary equation leads to $a_1 = 0$.

The recurrence equation is

$$a_n = \frac{-1}{(n + \lambda + \alpha)(n + \lambda - \alpha)} a_{n-2}, \ n = 2 : \infty. \tag{9.34}$$

Because this steps by two and $a_1 = 0$, for all odd n we have $a_n = 0$. We need only consider even $n = 2k$:

$$a_{2k} = \frac{-1}{(2k + \lambda + \alpha)(2k + \lambda - \alpha)} a_{2k-2}, \ k = 1 : \infty. \tag{9.35}$$

We can employ the $\pm \alpha$ symmetry of (9.31) and (9.35) to help us. If we set $\lambda = \alpha$ and find a solution, the other solution can be obtained by replacing α by $-\alpha$ everywhere. So, set $\lambda = \alpha$ in (9.35):

$$a_{2k} = \frac{-1}{2^2 k(k + \alpha)} a_{2k-2}, \ k = 1 : \infty. \tag{9.36}$$

Upon iterating, we find

$$a_{2k} = \frac{(-1)^k \Gamma(\alpha + 1)}{2^{2k} k! \Gamma(k + \alpha + 1)} a_0,$$

which is valid for $k = 0$ because we used the gamma function. A solution by the method of Frobenius is

$$y(x; \lambda) = a_0 \sum_{k=0}^{\infty} (-1)^k \frac{\Gamma(\alpha + 1)}{2^{2k} k! \Gamma(k + \alpha + 1)} x^{2k+\alpha}.$$

If we set $a_0 = 1/2^\alpha \Gamma(\alpha + 1)$, we obtain the series representation of the **Bessel function of the first kind** of order α:

$$J_\alpha(x) = \sum_{k=0}^{\infty} (-1)^k \frac{(x/2)^{2k+\alpha}}{k! \Gamma(k + \alpha + 1)}. \tag{9.37}$$

Therefore, when α is not an integral multiple of $1/2$, the general solution of Bessel's equation is

$$y(x) = c_1 J_\alpha(x) + c_2 J_{-\alpha}(x).$$

When $\mathrm{Re}(a) > 0$, $J_\alpha(x)$ is analytic in the finite complex x-plane, whereas the function $J_{-\alpha}(x)$ is singular at the origin and analytic in the punctured plane $0 < |x| < \infty$, which is an annulus.

9.4.2 Half Integer and Integer Order Bessel Functions

Let's resolve the $\alpha = 1/2$ difficulty by looking at $J_{1/2}(x)$ in some detail rather than starting from the beginning again. Its series representation is

$$J_{1/2}(x) = \sum_{k=0}^{\infty} (-1)^k \frac{(x/2)^{2k+1/2}}{k! \Gamma(k + 3/2)}. \tag{9.38}$$

Rewriting the Gauss duplication formula, equation (9.10), with $n = k + 1$, we have

$$\Gamma(k + 3/2) = \sqrt{\pi} \frac{\Gamma(2k + 2)}{2^{2k+1} \Gamma(k + 1)} = \sqrt{\pi} \frac{(2k + 1)!}{2^{2k+1} k!}.$$

Therefore

$$\begin{aligned}
J_{1/2}(x) &= \frac{1}{\sqrt{\pi}} \sum_{k=0}^{\infty} (-1)^k \frac{2^{2k+1} k!}{2^{2k+1/2} k! (2k + 1)!} x^{2k+1/2} \\
&= \sqrt{\frac{2}{\pi x}} \sum_{k=0}^{\infty} (-1)^k \frac{x^{2k+1}}{(2k + 1)!}.
\end{aligned}$$

We recognize the last power series as that of $\sin x$, and so

$$J_{1/2}(x) = \sqrt{\frac{2}{\pi x}} \sin x. \qquad (9.39)$$

Using similar algebraic manipulation, it can be shown that

$$J_{-1/2}(x) = \sqrt{\frac{2}{\pi x}} \cos x.$$

Since the set $\{J_{1/2}(x), J_{-1/2}(x)\}$ is clearly linearly independent, the problem of half integer α is pretty much laid to rest.

Suppose $\alpha = n$, an integer. Look at $J_{-n}(x)$:

$$J_{-n}(x) = \sum_{k=0}^{\infty} (-1)^k \frac{(x/2)^{2k-n}}{k! \, \Gamma(k - n + 1)}.$$

Now separate the summation into two pieces:

$$J_{-n}(x) = \sum_{k=0}^{n-1} (-1)^k \frac{(x/2)^{2k-n}}{k! \, \Gamma(k - n + 1)} + \sum_{k=n}^{\infty} (-1)^k \frac{(x/2)^{2k-n}}{k! \, \Gamma(k - n + 1)}.$$

In the first summation, the argument of the gamma function is always either 0 or a negative integer. Since $1/\Gamma(0 \text{ or negative integer}) = 0$, the entire first sum vanishes. In the second sum, shift k down by n; i.e., replace k by $k + n$. Then

$$J_{-n}(x) = \sum_{k=0}^{\infty} (-1)^{k+n} \frac{(x/2)^{2k+n}}{(k + n)! \, \Gamma(k + 1)} = (-1)^n \sum_{k=0}^{\infty} (-1)^k \frac{(x/2)^{2k+n}}{k! \, \Gamma(k + n + 1)}.$$

Therefore,

$$J_{-n}(x) = (-1)^n J_n(x). \qquad (9.40)$$

When $\alpha = n$, an integer, we no longer have a pair of linearly independent solutions of Bessel's equation: our two solutions are constant multiples of each other.

To find the second solution corresponding to integral order Bessel functions we have two options:

 i. proceed to the method of Frobenius, or

 ii. introduce the following artifice.

DEFINITION 9.2 *The **Bessel function of the second kind of order** α, also called the **Neumann function of order** α, is defined by*

$$Y_\alpha(x) := \frac{(\cos \alpha\pi)J_\alpha(x) - J_{-\alpha}(x)}{\sin \alpha\pi}. \tag{9.41}$$

For nonintegral α, $Y_\alpha(x)$ is a simple linear combination of the functions $J_\alpha(x)$ and $J_{-\alpha}(x)$. Hence the set $\{J_\alpha(x), Y_\alpha(x)\}$ is linearly independent, and the general solution of Bessel's equation can be written in the form

$$y(x) = c_1 J_\alpha(x) + c_2 Y_\alpha(x). \tag{9.42}$$

Just like $J_{-\alpha}(x)$, $Y_\alpha(x)$ has a singularity at $x = 0$.

9.4.3 *Evaluating $Y_n(x)$*

To evaluate the expression for $Y_\alpha(x)$, we cannot simply put $\alpha = n$ in (9.41) because the denominator is $\sin n\pi = 0$ and the numerator is

$$(\cos n\pi)J_n(x) - J_{-n}(x) = (-1)^n J_n(x) - J_{-n}(x) = 0,$$

by virtue of (9.40). Thus (9.41) is indeterminate for $\alpha = n$, and we must use l'Hôpital's Rule. The limit is

$$Y_n(x) := \lim_{\alpha \to n} Y_\alpha(x) = \frac{\frac{\partial}{\partial \alpha}\left[\cos \alpha\pi\, J_\alpha(x) - J_{-\alpha}(x)\right]_{\alpha=n}}{\frac{\partial}{\partial \alpha}\left(\sin \alpha\pi\right)_{\alpha=n}},$$

which after some differentiation is

$$Y_n(x) = \frac{1}{\pi}\left[\frac{\partial}{\partial \alpha}J_\alpha(x)\right]_{\alpha=n} - (-1)^n \left[\frac{\partial}{\partial \alpha}J_{-\alpha}(x)\right]_{\alpha=n}.$$

The evaluation of these derivatives is complicated by the presence of the gamma function in the series for $J_\alpha(x)$. Several results beyond those presented in Section 9.2 will be needed. For this reason, only the final result will be stated, to wit:

$$Y_n(x) = \frac{2}{\pi}J_n(x)\left(\ln\frac{x}{2} + \gamma\right) - \frac{1}{\pi}\sum_{k=0}^{n-1}\frac{(n-k-1)!}{k!}\left(\frac{x}{2}\right)^{2k-n}$$
$$+ \frac{1}{\pi}\sum_{k=0}^{\infty}(-1)^k\frac{(x/2)^{2k+n}}{k!\,(k+n)!}\left(H_k + H_{k+n}\right), \tag{9.43}$$

where H_k is the kth partial sum of the harmonic series and γ is Euler's constant. The important element to pick out of this horrendous equation is the middle summation. Its $k = 0$ term goes as x^{-n}, and so this term has a pole of order n at the origin. The $\ln(x/2)$ in the first term implies a branch point at the origin. The value $Y_n(0)$ is undefined for any complex n.

Thus equation (9.42) represents the general solution of Bessel's equation for *all* complex α.

9.4.4   Properties of Bessel Functions

The graphs of the first few integral order Bessel functions are given in Figure 9.13.

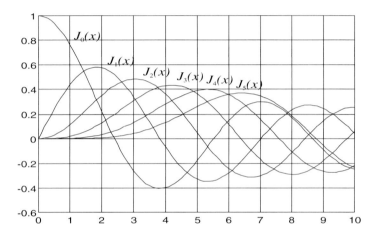

Fig. 9.3   The graphs of the Bessel functions $J_n(x)$ for $n = 0 : 5$.

The somewhat "sinusoidal" behavior of $J_n(x)$ and $Y_n(x)$ stands out, although neither the spacing between zeros nor the maximum height between zeros is constant. The following table lists some of the zeros.

Zeros of the Bessel Functions						
$J_0(x)$	$J_1(x)$	$J_2(x)$	$Y_0(x)$	$Y_1(x)$	$Y_2(x)$	
2.4048	3.8317	5.1356	0.8936	2.1971	3.3842	$3.1416 = \pi$
5.5201	7.0156	8.4172	3.9577	5.4297	6.7938	$6.2832 = 2\pi$
8.6537	10.1735	11.6198	7.0861	8.5960	10.0235	$9.4248 = 3\pi$
11.7915	13.3237	14.7960	10.2223	11.7492	13.2100	$12.5664 = 4\pi$
14.9309	16.4706	17.9598	13.3611	14.8974	16.3790	$15.7080 = 5\pi$

The "amplitude" of the Bessel function oscillations decays approximately like $1/\sqrt{x}$.

Approximate values of the Bessel functions valid near $x = 0$ are obtained from the first terms of their Taylor series:

$$J_0(x) \approx 1, \qquad J_\alpha(x) \approx \frac{x^\alpha}{\Gamma(1+\alpha)}, \qquad J_{-\alpha}(x) \approx \frac{x^{-\alpha}}{\Gamma(1-\alpha)},$$

$$Y_0(x) \approx \frac{2}{\pi}\ln\left(\frac{x}{2}\right), \qquad Y_\alpha(x) \approx \frac{\cot\alpha\pi}{\Gamma(1+\alpha)}x^\alpha + x^{-\alpha}\csc\alpha\pi,$$

$$Y_n(x) \approx -\frac{(n+1)!}{\pi}\left(\frac{x}{2}\right)^{-n}.$$

9.4.5   Recurrence Relations Among the Bessel Functions

Appropriate manipulation of the series representations of the Bessel functions leads to the following recurrence relations, which can be used to generate either higher or lower order Bessel functions from those which are known.

THEOREM 9.1   *For any complex α, we have*

$$\frac{d}{dx}\left(x^{-\alpha}J_\alpha(x)\right) = -x^{-\alpha}J_{\alpha+1}(x), \quad \frac{d}{dx}\left(x^\alpha J_\alpha(x)\right) = x^\alpha J_{\alpha-1}(x). \tag{9.44}$$

Proof   To prove the first, use the series representation of $J_\alpha(x)$:

$$\frac{d}{dx}\left(x^{-\alpha}J_\alpha(x)\right) = \frac{d}{dx}\left[x^{-\alpha}\sum_0^\infty (-1)^k \frac{(x/2)^{2k+\alpha}}{k!\,\Gamma(k+\alpha+1)}\right]$$

$$= \frac{d}{dx}\left[\sum_0^\infty (-1)^k \frac{x^{2k}}{2^{2k+\alpha}\,k!\,\Gamma(k+\alpha+1)}\right].$$

Performing the derivative, we find

$$\frac{d}{dx}\left(x^{-\alpha}J_\alpha(x)\right) = \sum_0^\infty (-1)^k \frac{(2k)\,x^{2k-1}}{2^{2k+\alpha}\,k!\,\Gamma(k+\alpha+1)}$$

$$= \sum_1^\infty (-1)^k \frac{x^{2k+1-2}}{2^{2k+\alpha-1}\,(k-1)!\,\Gamma(k+\alpha+1)}.$$

The last sum begins at $k = 1$ because of the factor of k in the numerator of the previous sum. The strange exponent of x (meaning $2k+1-2$) is suggestive of the following shift of indices $k \leftarrow k+1$ to bring the sum down to a starting value of zero. This last sum is $-x^{-\alpha}J_{\alpha+1}(x)$, as required. $\square$

The other recurrence relation is left to the problems. By taking combinations of these two relations, still others can be derived.

When dealing with problems in wave propagation the following complex variations on our theme are useful:

DEFINITION 9.3 *The* **Bessel function of the third kind of order** α, *also called* **Hankel functions of order** α, *are defined by*

$$H_\alpha^{(1)}(x) := J_\alpha(x) + iY_\alpha(x),$$
$$H_\alpha^{(2)}(x) := J_\alpha(x) - iY_\alpha(x). \tag{9.45}$$

For large $|x|$ we have the following approximations:

$$J_\alpha(x) \approx \sqrt{\tfrac{2}{\pi x}} \cos\left(x - \tfrac{\pi}{2}\alpha - \tfrac{\pi}{4}\right),$$
$$Y_\alpha(x) \approx \sqrt{\tfrac{2}{\pi x}} \sin\left(x - \tfrac{\pi}{2}\alpha - \tfrac{\pi}{4}\right),$$
$$H_\alpha^{(1,2)}(x) \approx \sqrt{\tfrac{2}{\pi x}} \exp\left[\pm i\left(x - \tfrac{\pi}{2}\alpha - \tfrac{\pi}{4}\right)\right].$$

These asymptotic results further validate our experience which indicates a relation between Bessel functions and the functions cosine and sine with the $1/\sqrt{x}$ decrease in amplitude.

9.4.6 *Bessel Functions of More Complicated Arguments*

As if this weren't enough, one often encounters Bessel functions of a complex argument. Replacing x by ix, we get the **modified Bessel's equation**,

$$x^2 y'' + xy' - (x^2 + \alpha^2)y = 0. \tag{9.46}$$

The general solution can be immediately written as

$$y(x) = c_1 J_\alpha(ix) + c_2 Y_\alpha(ix).$$

Looking at the series expansion of $J_\alpha(ix)$,

$$J_\alpha(ix) = \sum_0^\infty (-1)^k \frac{(ix/2)^{2k+\alpha}}{k!\,\Gamma(k+\alpha+1)} = i^\alpha \sum_0^\infty (-1)^k i^{2k} \frac{(x/2)^{2k+\alpha}}{k!\,\Gamma(k+\alpha+1)},$$

we see that $(-1)^k i^{2k} = (-1)^k(-1)^k = +1$. Because of this, it is convenient to introduce the **modified Bessel function** of order α, defined by

$$I_\alpha(x) := \sum_0^\infty \frac{(x/2)^{2k+\alpha}}{k!\,\Gamma(k+\alpha+1)} = i^{-\alpha} J_\alpha(ix), \tag{9.47}$$

and the **Macdonald function** of order α, defined by

$$K_\alpha(x) := \frac{\pi}{2} \frac{(I_{-\alpha}(x) - I_\alpha(x))}{\sin \alpha\pi}, \tag{9.48}$$

with both expressions valid for $|\arg x| < \pi$, in accordance with the branch point at the origin. Then the general solution to the modified Bessel equation (9.46) is given by

$$y(x) = c_1 I_\alpha(x) + c_2 K_\alpha(x)$$

for any value of α.

It can be shown that

$$K_n(x) = \frac{\pi}{2} i^{n+1} \left(J_n(ix) + i Y_n(ix) \right) = \frac{\pi}{2} i^{n+1} H_n^{(1)}(ix),$$

valid for $-\pi < \arg x < \pi/2$ and integral n, thus relating the Macdonald function to the Hankel function of a complex argument (Figure 9.4).

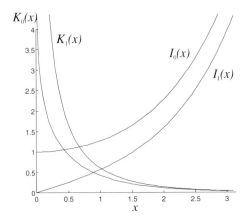

Fig. 9.4 The graphs of the first two modified Bessel functions and the Macdonald functions.

For large $|x|$,

$$I_\alpha(x) \doteq \frac{e^x}{\sqrt{2\pi x}}, \qquad K_\alpha(x) \doteq \frac{e^{-x}}{\sqrt{2\pi x}}.$$

Thus modified Bessel functions are to the exponentials as the regular Bessel functions are to cosine and sine.

9.4.7 The Generalized Bessel Equation

A generalization of Bessel's equation is

$$x^2 y'' + x(a + 2bx^p)y' + [c + dx^{2q} - b(1 - a - p)x^p + b^2 x^{2p}]y = 0. \tag{9.49}$$

It can be shown that the solution has the form

$$y(x) = x^{\left(\frac{1-a}{2}\right)} \exp\left\{ -\left(\frac{b}{p} x^p \right) \right\} Z_\alpha \left(\frac{\sqrt{|d|}}{q} x^q \right), \tag{9.50}$$

where

$$\alpha = \frac{1}{q} \sqrt{\left(\frac{1-a}{2} \right)^2 - c},$$

and where $Z_\alpha(\xi)$ is a shorthand notation for

$$Z_\alpha(\xi) := c_1 J_\alpha(\xi) + c_2 Y_\alpha(\xi) \tag{9.51}$$

when d is positive, and

$$Z_\alpha(\xi) := c_1 I_\alpha(\xi) + c_2 K_\alpha(\xi) \tag{9.52}$$

when d is negative.

If when matching (9.49) with an ODE, we find $p = 0$, then we *must* use $b = 0$ and drop the exponential term $\exp(-bx^p/p)$. We cannot have $q = 0$. Be careful, not all equations can be put into the form of (9.49) (otherwise, we'd see Bessel functions everywhere).

■ **EXAMPLE 9.6** The equation $x^2 y'' + xy' + (k^2 x^2 - \beta^2)y = 0$ arises so frequently that it is worth solving by comparing with (9.49). Matching term by term, we find:

$$x(a + 2bx^p) = x, \quad \text{meaning } p = 0, \ b = 0, \text{ and } a = 1;$$

$$c + dx^{2q} - b(1 - a - p)x^p + b^2 x^{2p} = k^2 x^2 - \beta^2$$

becomes

$$c + dx^{2q} = k^2 x^2 - \beta^2, \quad \text{meaning} \quad d = k^2, \ q = 1, \text{ and } c = -\beta^2.$$

Thus

$$\alpha = \frac{1}{1}\sqrt{\left(\frac{1-1}{2}\right)^2 - (-\beta^2)} = \beta$$

and $\sqrt{|d|}/q = k$. Because $d > 0$, the solution is

$$y(x) = c_1 J_\beta(kx) + c_2 Y_\beta(kx).$$

■ ■ ■

■ **EXAMPLE 9.7** If we want to solve

$$y'' - \frac{2\nu}{x}y' - \gamma^2 y = 0,$$

we must multiply by x^2 to bring it into the form of (9.49):

$$x^2 y'' - 2\nu x y' - \gamma^2 x^2 y = 0.$$

Matching the coefficients of y' and y leads to

$$x(a + 2bx^p) = -2\nu x \qquad \qquad (*)$$
$$c + dx^{2q} - b(1 - a - p)x^p + b^2 x^{2p} = -\gamma^2 x^2. \quad (**)$$

From (*) we have $a = -2\nu$ and $b = 0$, the latter of which eliminates the exponential form in (9.50), so we needn't worry about the value of p. Using these values, (**) simplifies to

$$c + dx^{2q} = -\gamma^2 x^2,$$

so that $c = 0$, $d = -\gamma^2$, and $q = 1$. Then $\sqrt{|d|}/q = \gamma$. Also,

$$\alpha = \frac{1}{q}\sqrt{\left(\frac{1-a}{2}\right)^2 - c} = \frac{1}{1}\sqrt{\left(\frac{1+2\nu}{2}\right)^2 - 0} = \nu + \frac{1}{2}.$$

Because $d < 0$ we should use form (9.52); thus the general solution is

$$y(x) = x^{\nu+1/2}\left(c_1 I_{\nu+1/2}(\gamma x) + c_2 K_{\nu+1/2}(\gamma x)\right).$$

■ ■ ■

■ **EXAMPLE 9.8** Solve

$$x^2 y'' + x^2 y' + \left(\frac{1}{4} - \nu^2\right) y = 0.$$

Solution: Matching, we have

$$x(a + 2bx^p) = x^2, \qquad\qquad (*)$$
$$c + dx^{2q} - b(1 - a - p)x^p + b^2 x^{2p} = \tfrac{1}{4} - \nu^2. \quad (**)$$

From (*) we get $a = 0$, $b = 1/2$, and $p = 1$. Thus (**) becomes

$$c + dx^{2q} + \frac{1}{4}x^2 = \frac{1}{4} - \nu^2.$$

We must choose $c = \tfrac{1}{4} - \nu^2$, $d = -1/4$, and $q = 1$. Because $d < 0$, the solution is

$$y(x) = x^{1/2} e^{-x/2}[c_1 I_\nu(x/2) + c_2 K_\nu(x/2)].$$

■ ■ ■

■ **EXAMPLE 9.9** The equation: $x^2 y'' + x(1 + 3x^2)y' + (2x^4 - 5x^2 + 1)y = 0$ *cannot* be put into the proper form. This is true because

$$x(a + 2bx^p) = x(1 + 3x^2) \quad \Rightarrow \quad a = 1, \ b = 3/2, \text{ and } p = 1.$$

Using these values in the matching of the second term,

$$c + dx^{2q} - \frac{3}{2}(1 - 1 - 1)x + \left(\frac{3}{2}\right)^2 x^2 = 2x^4 - 5x^2 + 1$$

$$\Rightarrow \quad c + 2dx^{2q} + \frac{3}{2}x + \frac{9}{4}x^2 = 2x^4 - 5x^2 + 1,$$

which requires $c = 1$, $d = 1$, $q = 2$, and $(3/2)x + (9/4)x^2 = -5x^2$. The last equation is not valid for all x. ■ ■ ■

As you can see, this approach (when it works!) is considerably easier than the method of Frobenius.

9.4.8 *Applications of Bessel Functions*

Now to some applications with Bessel functions in their solutions.

■ **EXAMPLE 9.10** A massive cable (or chain) is attached to a fixed pivot and allowed to hang freely. Define x to be the distance from the top of the cable, $\rho(x)$ the linear density of the cable, and $T(x)$ the tension as a function of distance x. If the cable is perturbed so that it undergoes small oscillations of frequency $\omega/2\pi$ in a vertical plane with horizontal displacement $u(x)$ (Figure 9.5),

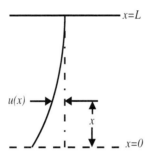

Fig. 9.5 The coordinates for the hanging cable.

then the equation of motion can be shown to be

$$\frac{d}{dx}\left(T(x)\frac{du}{dx}\right) + \rho(x)\omega^2 u = 0.$$

When both the tension T and the density ρ are constant, we have the usual harmonic oscillator equation

$$u'' + k^2 u = 0,$$

where $k^2 := \omega^2/c^2$ and $c^2 := T/\rho$. Unfortunately, this is not a reasonable choice for the parameters T and ρ. If the density is constant, then it is given by $\rho = M/L$, where M is the mass of the chain. The tension $T(x)$ will be the weight of the chain below the reference point at x; hence

$$T(x) = \rho g x.$$

Inserting this into the equation of motion, we arrive at the ODE

$$xu'' + u' + \frac{\omega^2}{g}u = 0.$$

Comparing this with the generalized Bessel equation and discarding the nonphysical part of the solution, Y_α, we have

$$u(x) = cJ_0\left(2\sqrt{\frac{\omega^2 x}{g}}\right).$$

The condition of a fixed pivot point translates to $u(L) = 0$. Applying this condition, we see that

$$J_0\left(2\sqrt{\frac{\omega^2 L}{g}}\right) = 0.$$

Since each Bessel function has infinitely many zeros, there are infinitely many possible frequencies of oscillation ω_n. Using the notation $j_{0,n}$ for the nth zero of the Bessel function $J_0(z)$ allows us to set $2\sqrt{(\omega_n^2 L/g)} = j_{0,n}$, so that we have

$$\omega_n = \frac{1}{2}j_{0,n}\sqrt{\frac{g}{L}}.$$

Thus the lateral displacement in the nth mode of oscillation is

$$u_n(x) = cJ_0\left(j_{0,n}\sqrt{\frac{x}{L}}\right).$$

The quantity $\sqrt{g/L}$ is the value of ω when we have a simple rigid pendulum with all the mass at the bottom. The first mode, $j_{0,1} = 2.4048$, oscillates with frequency

$$f_1 = \frac{\omega_1}{2\pi} = \frac{1.2024}{2\pi}\sqrt{\frac{g}{L}}.$$

Thus, the cable moves with an angular frequency 20% higher than that of the simple rigid pendulum, with a corresponding 17% decrease in the period of oscillation. For the second mode,

$$f_2 = \frac{\omega_2}{2\pi} = \frac{2.7600}{2\pi}\sqrt{\frac{g}{L}}.$$

The higher the mode of oscillation, the larger the angular frequency and the shorter the period. The first several modes are sketched in Figure 9.6.

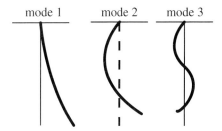

Fig. 9.6   The first three modes of the oscillating cable.

When oscillating in the second mode, the cable has one **node**, or point of no motion. This occurs because the Bessel function solution works off the second zero and has one zero before that. The cable has this single fixed point at $(1.2024/2.7600)^2 = 0.1898$ of the distance from the bottom. Similarly, the third mode has nodes at

$$\left(\frac{1.2024}{4.3268}\right)^2 L = 0.0772L \quad \text{and} \quad \left(\frac{2.7600}{4.3268}\right)^2 L = 0.4069L.$$

Physically generating motion in the first or second modes is not too hard, but getting into higher modes presents some difficulty. The critical problem is one of entanglement. The model used to derive the equation of motion assumed an infinitely flexible cable, meaning that the individual elements of the cable feel no resistance to torsional deformation, which is not very realistic.

As a point of interest, the same equation of motion governs the *rotation* of an infinitely flexible cable about a vertical axis through the pivot point. This motion is more easily displayed. All this should be compared with the simple rigid pendulum which oscillates in one and only one mode. ∎ ∎ ∎

As is usual in mathematics, this problem can be extended by using the more general power model $T(x) = T_0 x^a$ and $\rho(x) = \rho_0 x^b$. Then the equation is

$$x^2 u'' + a x u' + k^2 x^{b-a+2} u = 0.$$

Aside: Not just any values of a and b are allowed, because the tension is the reaction to the weight of the cable below the point in question; i.e.,

$$T(x) = T_0 x^b = \int_0^x \rho(\xi) g \, d\xi = \frac{\rho_0 g}{b+1} x^{b+1}$$

$$\Rightarrow \quad a = b+1 \quad \text{and} \quad T_0 = \frac{\rho_0 g}{b+1}.$$

Thus more general problems of this type of nonuniform chain can be solved in much the same way.

■ **EXAMPLE 9.11** Borelli, Coleman, and Hobson (**Mathematics Magazine 58**, 78–83, March 1985) have looked into a problem originating in Edgar Allan Poe's famous tale "The Pit and the Pendulum." The long and the short of it is that a prisoner is tied to the floor of his cell. Above he detects the ominous presence of a swinging pendulum whose bob is a large scythe (as in very sharp). A later upward glance shows that the length of the pendulum has increased. Not being mathematically inclined he merely relates the event in terms of the horrible conclusion soon to befall him. For us this is a problem that can be accurately modeled by an ODE.

In particular, if we set up our coordinate system as shown in Figure 9.7,

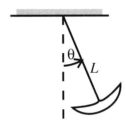

Fig. 9.7

we can write the equations of motion in cylindrical (neglecting any z component) coordinates and the θ component of the gravitational force:

$$m(L\ddot{\theta} + 2\dot{L}\dot{\theta}) = -mg \sin\theta.$$

Assuming small oscillations, so that we can replace $\sin\theta$ by θ, leads to the linear ODE

$$L\ddot{\theta} + 2\dot{L}\dot{\theta} + g\theta = 0.$$

Poe did not tell us the functional dependence of L on time, and so we have no idea how long it will take for the prisoner to reach his doom. Just for argument's sake, let's assume that the blade is being lowered at a constant rate, i.e., $L(t) = mt + b$. The governing equation is then

$$(mt + b)\ddot{\theta} + 2m\dot{\theta} + gh = 0,$$

and it is the long time solution in which we are interested. This is not quite of the form of any well-known equation, but a change of independent variable via $\tau := mt + b$ yields

$$m^2\tau\theta'' + 2m^2\theta' + g\theta = 0,$$

where primes denote derivatives with respect to τ. Fitting this to the generalized Bessel equation allows us to write

$$\theta(t) = t^{-1/2}[c_1 J_1(\xi) + c_2 Y_1(\xi)],$$

where $\xi := (2/m)\sqrt{g\tau}$. We know that for large values of τ the Bessel functions oscillate with amplitudes that decay as $1/\sqrt{\xi}$ which goes as $\tau^{-1/4}$. Taken together with the factor $\tau^{-1/2}$, we see that θ decreases as $\tau^{-3/4}$. This model predicts a decreasing pendulum swing. The total sweep of the pendulum at any given time is $L\theta$, which increases as $\tau \cdot \tau^{-3/4} = \tau^{1/4}$.

An alternative model would have the pendulum length increasing quadratically as $L(t) = mt^2$. This leads to an Euler equation with a decaying solution for θ. The details are left to the reader.   ■ ■ ■

■ **EXAMPLE 9.12** Suppose that we have a long thin uniform elastic rod embedded vertically in concrete with a circular cross section. If the rod is relatively short, we would expect it to remain vertical under small perturbations of its upper end; but if it were much longer than it is wide some form of bending could occur. If there is no bending due to small perturbations, we'll say the rod is stable. The minimum length at which bending occurs is called the **critical length**. Find the critical length of a beam in terms of its geometry and material properties.

Solution: Let L be the length of the rod, R the radius of its assumed circular cross section, w its linear weight density, and E the Young's modulus of the material of which it is made. Choose our coordinates so that the upper end of the vertical rod is the origin O and measure x as the distance down. Let y be the lateral deviation of the rod from the vertical. Take $P(x, y)$ as a point on the rod and $Q(\xi, \eta)$ slightly above P. See Figure 9.8.

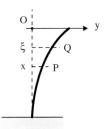

Fig. 9.8

Apply Hooke's Law to the part of the rod above P. In particular, the moment about P of the weight of a differential element $w\,d\xi$ at Q is $w(\eta - y)\,d\xi$. Using the moment of inertia $I = \frac{1}{4}\pi R^4$ and integrating down the rod from O to P, we have

$$EI\frac{d^2y}{dx^2} = \int_0^x w(\eta - y)\,d\xi.$$

Differentiating using Leibniz's Rule, we find

$$EI\frac{d^3y}{dx^3} = [w(\eta - y)]_{\xi=x} - \int_0^x w\frac{dy}{dx}\,d\xi = 0 - w\frac{dy}{dx}x$$
$$\Rightarrow \quad EI\frac{d^3y}{dx^3} + wx\frac{dy}{dx} = 0.$$

The boundary term is zero because $\eta(x) = y$, i.e., it is the point P. The integral is as shown because the integrand is independent of ξ. Using $\gamma^2 := w/EI$, the equation is

$$y'''(x) + \gamma^2 xy'(x) = 0.$$

If we let $v(x) = y'(x)$, we can reduce this to the second order equation

$$v''(x) + \gamma^2 x v(x) = 0.$$

Comparing this with the generalized Bessel equation, we find

$$a = 0, \quad b = 0, \quad p = 0, \quad c = 0, \quad d = k^2, \quad q = \frac{3}{2},$$

and the solution is

$$v(x) = \sqrt{x} \left(c_1 J_{1/3} \left(\frac{2}{3} k x^{3/2} \right) + c_2 J_{-1/3} \left(\frac{2}{3} k x^{3/2} \right) \right).$$

Things are a bit simpler if we replace the Bessel functions by their power series representations. Then, to two terms, we have

$$v(x) = A \left(1 - \frac{k^2 x^3}{6} + \cdots \right) + B \left(x - \frac{k^2 x^4}{14} + \cdots \right)$$

where A and B are related to c_1 and c_2 through k.

Now we must apply the boundary conditions at both ends. Since the upper end is free, there is no bending moment. Thus $y''(0) = v'(0) = 0$. The lower end is embedded vertically, so that $y'(L) = v(L) = 0$. Applying the upper condition we find $A = 0$, which forces $c_1 = 0$. The lower end condition forces

$$J_{-1/3} \left(\frac{2}{3} k L^{3/2} \right) = 0.$$

Once again we face an infinity of roots of this equation, the least of which is 1.8663. Thus we may conclude that

$$\frac{2}{3} k L^{3/2} = 1.8663 \quad \Rightarrow \quad L = \left(7.84 \frac{EI}{w} \right)^{1/3}$$

is the critical length of the rod.   ■ ■ ■

9.4.9   Exercise Set

Use the Chain Rule and/or Product Rule to show the following.

1. $y(x) = c_1 J_\alpha(e^x) + c_2 Y_\alpha(e^x)$ is the general solution of the equation

$$\frac{d^2 y}{dx^2} + \left(e^{2x} - \alpha^2 \right) y = 0.$$

2. $y(x) = \sec x [c_1 J_\alpha(x) + c_2 Y_\alpha(x)]$ is the general solution of

$$\frac{d^2 y}{dx^2} + \left(\frac{1}{x} - 2 \tan x\right)\frac{dy}{dx} - \left(\frac{\alpha^2}{x^2} + \frac{\tan x}{x}\right) y = 0.$$

3. $y(x) = x[c_1 J_\alpha(e^{1/x}) + c_2 Y_\alpha(e^{1/x})]$ is the general solution of

$$x^4 \frac{d^2 y}{dx^2} + \left(e^{2/x} - \alpha^2\right) y = 0.$$

Use the generalized Bessel equation to write the general solution of each of the following equations that can be put into that form:

4. $y'' + \omega^2 y = 0$

5. $y'' + xy = 0$

6. $x^4 y'' + y = 0$

7. $y'' + x^4 y = 0$

8. $3x^2 y'' + xy' + 3x^2 y = 0$

9. $4x^2 y'' + xy' + 4x^2 y = 0$

10. $4x^2 y'' + (64x^4 - 15)y = 0$

11. $x^2 y'' + x(2 - x)y' - xy = 0$

12. $xy'' + (2 - 6x)y' - 6y = 0$

13. $y'' + \beta^2 \gamma^2 x^{2\beta - 2} y = 0$

14. $x^2 y'' - 3xy' + (225 x^{10} - 4)y = 0$

15. $x^2 y'' + (1 - 2n)xy' + n^2(1 - n^2 - x^{2n})y = 0$

16. $4x^2 y'' + 2x(1 + 2x)y' + (x + 1)y = 0$

17. $x^2 y'' + x(3 - 2x^2)y' - (2 + 4x^2)y = 0$

18. $x^2 y'' + 2x(1 + x^2)y' + 3(x^2 - 1)y = 0$

Write the homogeneous linear ODE with solution:

19. $y(x) = x^m \exp(-x^m)[c_1 J_m(x^m) + c_2 Y_m(x^m)]$.

20. $y(x) = \dfrac{1}{x} \exp(-x^2) J_3(4x^5)$.

21. $y(x) = x^3 e^{-x}[c_1 J_1(2x) + c_2 Y_1(2x)]$. Can this solution satisfy the initial conditions $y(0) = 1$ and $y'(0) = 2$?

22. Use the series representation to evaluate

$$\lim_{x \to 0} \sqrt[3]{\pi x}\, J_{-1/3}(2x).$$

Verify each of the following recurrence relations by using the series representations of the Bessel functions:

23. $J_0'(x) = -J_1(x)$

24. $D(x^n I_n(x)) = x^n I_{n-1}(x)$ 25. $D(x^n J_n(x)) = x^n J_{n-1}(x)$

26. By using the Product Rule and Chain Rules of differentiation, verify that the solution of the generalized Bessel equation is as given in equation (9.50).

By using the recurrence relations for the Bessel functions from Theorem 9.1, show the following.

27. $\displaystyle\int J_1(x)\, dx = -J_0(x)$

28. $\displaystyle\int x J_0(x)\, dx = x J_1(x)$

29. $\displaystyle \int xJ_1(x)\,dx = -xJ_0(x) + \int J_0(x)\,dx$

30. $\displaystyle \int x^2 J_0(x)\,dx = x^2 J_1(x) + xJ_0(x) - \int J_0(x)\,dx$

9.5 ORTHOGONAL POLYNOMIALS

The space of real-valued functions continuous on the interval $[a, b]$ is an inner product space when endowed with the weighted inner product

$$\langle f, g \rangle := \int_a^b w(x)f(x)g(x)\,dx, \tag{9.53}$$

where $w(x) \geq 0$ on $[a, b]$, and is equal to zero at most finitely often. We denote this space by $C_w[a, b]$, but we will usually suppress the w. Given the standard basis

$$\mathcal{B}_0 := \{1, x, x^2, x^3, \ldots\},$$

it is a straightforward, albeit tedious, task to apply the Gram-Schmidt algorithm to $\mathcal{B}_0$ to construct an orthonormal set

$$\mathcal{B}_1 = \{\phi_0(x), \phi_1(x), \phi_2(x), \phi_3(x), \ldots\}.$$

By this method $\phi_n(x)$ will be written as a linear combination of $\phi_0(x), \phi_1(x), \ldots, \phi_{n-1}(x)$, and x^n, so that $\phi_n(x)$ is a polynomial of degree n. The set $\mathcal{B}_1$ is called a basis of **orthogonal polynomials**.

When $P_\ell(x)$ is the Legendre polynomial of order ℓ, we saw that

$$\int_{-1}^1 P_\ell(x)P_m(x)\,dx = \frac{2}{2\ell + 1}\delta_{\ell m}. \tag{9.54}$$

Therefore, $\{P_0(x), P_1(x), P_2(x), \ldots\}$ is a basis of $C[-1, 1]$ consisting of orthogonal polynomials.

Of course, as we vary the interval $[a, b]$ and the weight function $w(x)$, we will generate other sets of orthogonal polynomials. As long as $[a, b]$ is finite and $w(x)$ is constant, the algorithm will generate variants of Legendre polynomials, because the change of coordinates

$$t = \frac{2x - (a + b)}{b - a} \tag{9.55}$$

transforms the interval $[a, b]$ into $[-1, 1]$. Aside from varying the weight function $w(x)$, there are only three possible general intervals (to within a transformation of the type given in (9.55)):

(a) $[-1, 1]$, (b) $[0, \infty)$, or

(c) $(-\infty, \infty)$.

For starters, let's concentrate on the first case.

It would be helpful if we could use some of the ideas encountered in the study of Legendre polynomials and extend them to the weighted inner product case. Rather than try to evaluate $\langle \phi_m(x), \phi_n(x) \rangle$, matters can be simplified. The Gram-Schmidt transformation from

$$\mathcal{B}_0 = \{1, x, x^2, \ldots\} \quad \text{to} \quad \mathcal{B}_1 = \{\phi_0(x), \phi_1(x), \phi_2(x), \ldots\}$$

can be represented by a triangular matrix with nonzero diagonal elements; hence it is nonsingular. We can use this matrix to transform back and forth from the ϕ_n's to the x^n's. When evaluating $\langle \phi_m(x), \phi_n(x) \rangle$, we could restrict ourselves to $m < n$ without loss of generality because the real inner product is symmetric. Since the matrix whose entries are $\langle \phi_m(x), \phi_n(x) \rangle = 0$ is triangular, so is its inverse. Then $\langle x^m, \phi_n(x) \rangle$ for all $m < n$, and the two conditions are equivalent. The latter will be much easier to manipulate.

Let's try to generalize Rodrigues' formula. For Legendre polynomials, it is

$$P_\ell(x) = \frac{1}{2^\ell \, \ell!} \left(\frac{d}{dx} \right)^\ell \left(1 - x^2 \right)^\ell, \; \ell = 0 : \infty. \tag{9.56}$$

But comparing (9.54) and (9.56) with the weighted inner product (9.53), we see that to get a complete analogy we'll need a factor of $1/w(x)$ in our generalized version of (9.56) to cancel the $w(x)$ in the integrand of (9.53). Our first try would be

$$\phi_n(x) = \frac{1}{w(x)} \left(\frac{d}{dx} \right)^n [\text{stuff}], \quad n = 0 : \infty.$$

The [stuff] remains to be determined. If $n = 0$, this becomes $\phi_0(x) = [\text{stuff}] / w(x)$, and so we must put $[\text{stuff}] = w(x) [\text{OtherStuff}]$. So that our formula will agree with (9.54) when $w(x) = 1$, put $[\text{OtherStuff}] = (1 - x^2)^n$. We now have a **generalized Rodrigues' formula**:

$$\phi_n(x) = \frac{1}{w(x)} \left(\frac{d}{dx} \right)^n \left[w(x) \left(1 - x^2 \right)^n \right], \; n = 0 : \infty. \tag{9.57}$$

We should immediately ask:

(a) If $\phi_n(x)$ is defined by (9.57), does $\langle x^m, \phi_n(x) \rangle = 0$ for $m = 0 : n - 1$?

(b) Will every function $w(x)$ yield polynomials for the $\phi_n(x)$?

First question first: Use integration by parts m times on the inner product

$$\langle x^m, \phi_n(x) \rangle = \int_{-1}^{1} w(x) x^m \frac{1}{w(x)} \left(\frac{d}{dx} \right)^n \left[w(x) \left(1 - x^2 \right)^n \right] dx$$

$$= x^m \left(\frac{d}{dx} \right)^{n-1} w(x)(1 - x^2)^n \Big|_{-1}^{1}$$

$$- \int_{-1}^{1} m x^{m-1} \left(\frac{d}{dx} \right)^{n-1} \left[w(x)(1 - x^2)^n \right] dx$$

$$= \sum_{0}^{m} (-1)^k m(m - 1) \ldots (m - k + 1) x^{m-k}$$

$$\times \left(\frac{d}{dx} \right)^{n-k-1} \left[w(x)(1 - x^2) \right] \Big|_{-1}^{1}.$$

Since $0 \le k \le m < n$, we have $n - k - 1 \ge 1$. Then every term in the sum has a factor of $1 - x^2$ and will be zero at both endpoints if $w(x)$ is well-behaved there.

Knowing that $\langle x^m, \phi_n(x) \rangle = 0$ for $m = 0 : n - 1$ is not sufficient to guarantee a set of orthogonal polynomials, because the $\phi_n(x)$ may not even be polynomials. Setting $w(x) = \sin(\pi x/2)$ should assure you that not any $w(x)$ will do.

To answer the second question, let's look at the function $\phi_1(x)$, which is supposed to be a polynomial of degree one. From (9.57) we have

$$\phi_1(x) = \frac{w'(x)}{w(x)} \left(1 - x^2 \right) - 2x = ax + b.$$

This is a first order separable ODE that can be rewritten as

$$\frac{d}{dx} \ln w(x) = \frac{(a + 2)x + b}{1 - x^2} = \frac{1}{2} \left[\frac{a + b - 2}{1 - x} - \frac{a - b + 2}{1 + x} \right].$$

After an integration, we find

$$w(x) = (1 - x)^\alpha (1 + x)^\beta, \tag{9.58}$$

where $\alpha = \frac{1}{2}(a + b + 2)$ and $\beta = \frac{1}{2}(a - b + 2)$. Therefore, the most general weight function that leads to a set of orthogonal polynomials on $[-1, 1]$ is given by (9.58). So that $\|\phi_n(x)\|$ will be finite, we must require $\alpha > -1$ and $\beta > -1$.

Using (9.58) in its full generality leads to the **Jacobi polynomials**, which we will not study. Setting $\alpha = \beta = \pm 1/2$ leads to the **Chebyshev polynomials**, which are defined by

$$T_n(x) := \frac{(-1)^n}{(2n - 1)!!} \sqrt{1 - x^2} \left(\frac{d}{dx} \right)^n \left(1 - x^2 \right)^{n-1/2}, \tag{9.59}$$

$$U_n(x) := (-1)^n \frac{(n+1)}{\sqrt{1-x^2}(2n+1)!!} \left(\frac{d}{dx}\right)^n (1-x^2)^{n+1/2}. \qquad (9.60)$$

The $T_n(x)$ are Chebyshev polynomials of the **first kind**, and the $U_n(x)$ are Chebyshev polynomials of the **second kind**. The first few are

$$
\begin{array}{ll}
T_0(x) = 1, & U_0(x) = 1, \\
T_1(x) = x, & U_1(x) = 2x, \\
T_2(x) = 2x^2 - 1, & U_2(x) = 4x^2 - 1, \\
T_3(x) = 4x^3 - 3x, & U_3(x) = 8x^3 - 4x, \\
T_4(x) = 8x^4 - 8x^2 + 1, & U_4(x) = 16x^4 - 12x^2 + 1.
\end{array}
$$

The weight function $(1-x^2)^{-1/2}$ for the $T_n(x)$ gives the lowest weight to points near the origin and the highest weight to those at the ends, $x = \pm 1$, whereas the reverse is true for the $U_n(x)$. The graphs of the Chebyshev polynomials are shown in Figures 9.9.

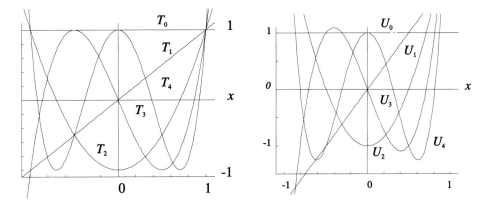

Fig. 9.9 The first five Chebyshev polynomials of the first and second kinds.

An unusual representation of both $T_n(x)$ and $U_n(x)$ is available. In fact,

$$T_n(x) = \cos(n \operatorname{Acos} x) = \operatorname{Re}\left[\left(x + i\sqrt{1-x^2}\right)^n\right], \qquad (9.61)$$

$$U_n(x) = \frac{\sin\left[(n+1)\operatorname{Acos} x\right]}{\sin(\operatorname{Acos} x)} = \operatorname{Im}\left[\frac{\left(x + i\sqrt{1-x^2}\right)^{n+1}}{\sqrt{1-x^2}}\right]. \qquad (9.62)$$

From this, it is clear that in $[-1, 1]$, $T_n(x)$ is zero when

$$x = \cos\left(\frac{(2m+1)\pi}{2n}\right), \quad m = 0 : n - 1. \qquad (9.63)$$

Further, it has extrema at

$$x = \cos\left(\frac{m\pi}{n}\right), \quad m = 0 : n. \qquad (9.64)$$

There are $n + 1$ extrema, $n - 1$ in the interior of $[-1, 1]$ and one at each endpoint.

The Chebyshev polynomials also satisfy the ODE's

$$(1 - x^2)T_n'' - xT_n' - n^2 T_n = 0, \tag{9.65}$$

$$(1 - x^2)U_n'' - 3xU_n' + n(n+2)U_n = 0. \tag{9.66}$$

By using either representation (9.59) or (9.61), it is possible to show that

$$T_{n+1}(x) = 2xT_n(x) - T_{n-1}(x). \tag{9.67}$$

One of the important uses of the Chebyshev polynomials occurs in curve-fitting. A major theorem of numerical analysis tells us the following:

THEOREM 9.2 *Of all polynomials of degree n whose coefficient of x^n is equal to one (usually called* **monic polynomials**), $2^{1-n}T_n(x)$ *oscillates with the minimum maximum amplitude on* $[-1, 1]$.

Proof To prove this result, denote $\hat{T}_n(x) = 2^{1-n}T_n(x)$, which are the monic Chebyshev polynomials. Suppose there is a monic polynomial of degree n, $p_n(x)$, which has smaller minimax amplitude on the interval $[-1, 1]$. The difference

$$d(x) = T_n(x) - p_n(x)$$

must be a polynomial of degree $n - 1$ because both $T_n(x)$ and $p_n(x)$ are monic of degree n (therefore the x^n terms cancel). The $n + 1$ extrema given by (9.64) all have magnitude 2^{1-n} because of the normalization. We assumed that $p_n(x)$ had smaller maximum amplitudes, and so it must be the case that $d(x)$ and $T_n(x)$ have the same sign at the extrema. From (9.61) we see that the extrema of $T_n(x)$ must alternate in sign, so that $d(x)$ must alternate in sign too. As they both must have n sign changes in $[-1, 1]$, we have a contradiction because $d(x)$ was of degree $n - 1$. What if $d(x)$ had the same value as $T_n(x)$ at an extremum? In that case $d(x)$ must have a double root at that point, which again leads to too many zeros. $\quad\square$

Because of this result, the $T_n(x)$ are called **equiripple polynomials**. In digital filter design the $T_n(x)$ are used to design what are called equiripple filters. They are also the optimal choices for minimax error fits to data. When interpolating a function the best choice of the n interpolating points are the zeros of $T_n(x)$, which have been extensively tabulated.

When the interval is $[0, \infty)$ and $w(x) = x^\alpha e^{-x}$, the Gram-Schmidt procedure generates the **Laguerre polynomials** $L_n^\alpha(x)$. They satisfy the orthogonality relation

$$\int_0^\infty x^\alpha e^{-x} L_m^\alpha(x)L_n^\alpha(x)\, dx = (n!)^2 \delta_{mn}. \tag{9.68}$$

The corresponding Rodrigues' formula is

$$L_n^\alpha(x) = \frac{1}{n!} x^{-\alpha} e^x \left(\frac{d}{dx}\right)^n \left(x^{n+\alpha} e^{-x}\right), \quad n = 0 : \infty. \tag{9.69}$$

By employing Leibniz's rule for the derivative of a product we can write part of (9.69) as

$$\left(\frac{d}{dx}\right)^n \left(x^{n+\alpha} e^{-x}\right) = \sum_{k=0}^{n} \binom{n}{k} \left(\frac{d}{dx}\right)^k \left(e^{-x}\right) \left(\frac{d}{dx}\right)^{n-k} \left(x^{k+\alpha}\right);$$

but

$$\left(\frac{d}{dx}\right)^k \left(e^{-x}\right) = (-1)^k e^{-x},$$

and

$$\begin{aligned}
\left(\frac{d}{dx}\right)^{n-k} \left(x^{\alpha+k}\right) &= (n+\alpha)(n+\alpha-1)\cdots(\alpha+k+1)x^{\alpha+k} \\
&= \frac{\Gamma(n+\alpha+1)}{\Gamma(k+\alpha+1)} x^{\alpha+k},
\end{aligned}$$

so that

$$L_n^\alpha(x) = \sum_{k=0}^{n} (-1)^k \frac{\Gamma(n+\alpha+1)}{\Gamma(k+\alpha+1)} \frac{x^k}{k!(n-k)!}. \tag{9.70}$$

The first few Laguerre polynomials for $\alpha = 0$ are:

$$L_0^0(x) = 1, \quad L_1^0(x) = -x + 1, \quad L_2^0(x) = x^2 - 4x + 2,$$

$$L_3^0(x) = -x^3 + 9x^2 - 18x + 6, \quad L_4^0(x) = x^4 - 16x^3 + 72x^2 - 96x + 24.$$

The graphs of the first few Laguerre polynomials are shown in Figure 9.10.

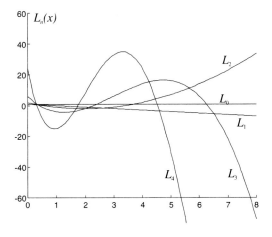

Fig. 9.10 The first five Laguerre polynomials.

The $L_n^\alpha(x)$ can be shown to satisfy the ODE

$$x\left(L_n^\alpha(x)\right)'' + (\alpha + 1 - n)\left(L_n^\alpha(x)\right)' + L_n^\alpha(x) = 0.$$

Extending the interval to $(-\infty, \infty)$ requires a very special weight function because the integral defining the norm of the polynomials must converge, in fact, $\|x^n\|$ must be finite for all $n = 0 : \infty$. Thus, $w(x)$ must approach zero at $\pm\infty$ at least exponentially fast. The weight function $w(x) = \exp(-x^2)$ will guarantee the convergence. The polynomials so generated are the **Hermite polynomials** $H_n(x)$, which satisfy the orthogonality relation

$$\int_{-\infty}^{\infty} e^{-x^2} H_m(x) H_n(x)\, dx = 2^n n! \sqrt{\pi}\, \delta_{mn}. \tag{9.71}$$

The accompanying Rodrigues' formula is

$$H_n(x) = (-1)^n e^{x^2} \left(\frac{d}{dx}\right)^n \left(e^{-x^2}\right), \quad n = 0 : \infty. \tag{9.72}$$

The $H_n(x)$ satisfy the ODE

$$H_n''(x) - 2x H_n'(x) + 2n H_n(x) = 0.$$

The first few Hermite polynomials are given below:

$$H_0(x) = 1, \quad H_1(x) = 2x, \quad H_2(x) = 4x^2 - 2, \quad H_3(x) = 8x^3 - 12x,$$

$$H_4(x) = 16x^4 - 48x^2 + 12, \quad H_5(x) = 32x^5 - 160x^3 + 120x.$$

Their graphs are shown in Figure 9.11.

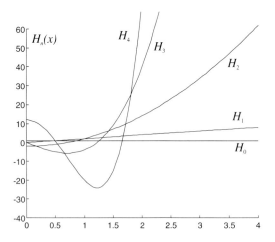

Fig. 9.11   The first five Hermite polynomials.

■ **EXAMPLE 9.13** The one dimensional Schrödinger equation describing the space-time behavior of a particle of mass m and energy E in a potential field $V(x)$ is

$$-\frac{\hbar^2}{2m}\frac{d^2\psi}{dx^2} + V(x)\psi = E\psi,$$

where $\hbar$ is Planck's constant divided by 2π. The potential of a linear harmonic oscillator is $V(x) = \frac{1}{2}m\omega^2 x^2$. If we make the nondimensionalizing substitution

$$z = \sqrt{\frac{m\omega}{\hbar}}x,$$

then the equation can be written as

$$\frac{d^2\psi}{dz^2} + \left(\frac{2E}{\hbar\omega} - z^2\right)\psi = 0.$$

Although $z = 0$ is an ordinary point of this equation, the substitution $\psi(z) = \sum a_n z^n$ leads to a three term recurrence equation, which is not easily solved. As an alternative, set

$$\psi(z) = v(z)\exp(-z^2).$$

Now the equation for $v(z)$ is

$$\frac{d^2v}{dz^2} - 2z\frac{dv}{dz} + 2nv = 0,$$

where n is given by

$$E = \hbar\omega\left(n + \frac{1}{2}\right),$$

which is the relation that will quantize the energy.

  The physical restriction on the wave function is

$$\int_{-\infty}^{\infty} |\psi(x)|^2\, dx < \infty,$$

because $|\psi(x)|^2$ is used as a probability density function; i.e., the probability that a particle lies in the interval $(x, x + dx)$ is $|\psi(x)|^2\, dx$. This restriction can be satisfied if and only if the solutions of the ODE are polynomials. Thus we must have n an integer and the solution for $v(z)$ is a Hermite polynomial. Thus the energy levels are discrete.

  One solution for the wave function in the nth energy level is

$$\psi_n(x) = A_n H_n\left(\sqrt{\frac{m\omega}{\hbar}}x\right)\exp\left(-\frac{m\omega}{2\hbar}x^2\right).$$

The constant A_n can be found from the integral restriction on ψ_n to be

$$A_n = \frac{1}{\sqrt{2^n\, n!}}\left(\frac{m\omega}{\hbar\pi}\right)^{1/4}.$$

Sketches of some of the wave functions are shown in Figure 9.12.

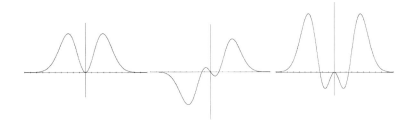

Fig. 9.12 Three different harmonic oscillator wave functions.

The regions near the maximum values of $|\psi(x)|^2$ are the most probable locations for the particle. Although there are points of zero probability, $\psi = 0$, the particle can cross those points in going from one region to another (this phenomenon is called **tunneling**); but it is highly unlikely that a measurement will find a particle near such points. ∎ ∎ ∎

Beyond all this, all sets of orthogonal polynomials can be characterized by a three term recurrence equation

$$\phi_{n+1}(x) - (A_n x + B_n)\,\phi_n(x) + C_n \phi_{n-1}(x) = 0.$$

This turns out to be an extremely powerful tool for summing series of these polynomials because every such series can be made to telescope. This greatly improves one's ability to compute with the orthogonal polynomials. Part of the technique is outlined in the problems, but the interested reader should consult Beckman for more details.

9.5.1 *Exercise Set*

1. Verify the form of the first four Chebyshev polynomials of the first and second kind by using

    (a) Rodrigues' formula in equations (9.59) and (9.60).

    (b) Equation (9.61).

2. Use equation (9.61) to derive equation (9.67).

3. Show that $T_n(1) = 1$ and $T_n(-1) = (-1)^n$.

4. Show that $T_{2n}(0) = (-1)^n$, $T_{2n+1}(0) = 0$, $U_{2n}(0) = (-1)^n$, and $U_{2n+1}(0) = 0$.

5. Show that $T_n(x)$ and $\sqrt{1-x^2}U_{n-1}(x)$ are the two linearly independent solutions of

    $$(1-x^2)y'' - xy' + n^2 y = 0.$$

6. Verify the form of the five Laguerre polynomials given in the text.

7. Show that the Laguerre polynomials satisfy the following recurrence relations.

   (a) $L_n^{\alpha-1}(x) = L_n^\alpha(x) - L_{n-1}^\alpha(x)$.

   (b) $\dfrac{d}{dx} L_n^\alpha(x) = -L_{n-1}^{\alpha+1}(x)$.

   (c) $x L_n^{\alpha+1}(x) = (n + \alpha + 1) L_n^\alpha(x) - (n + 1) L_{n+1}^\alpha(x)$.

8. Verify each of the following identities for the Laguerre polynomials:

   (a) $L_0^\alpha(x) = 1$.

   (b) $L_1^\alpha(x) = \alpha + 1 - x$.

   (c) $L_n^{-n}(x) = (-1)^n \dfrac{x^n}{n!}$.

   (d) $L_n^\alpha(0) = \dbinom{n + \alpha}{n}$.

9. Show that the Laguerre polynomials satisfy the differential equation given in the text.

10. Show that the first five Hermite polynomials are as given in the text.

11. Show that the Hermite polynomials satisfy the following recurrence relations:

   (a) $H_n'(x) = 2n H_{n-1}(x)$.

   (b) $H_{n+1}(x) = 2x H_n(x) - 2n H_{n-1}(x)$.

12. Show that the Hermite and Laguerre polynomials are related by the equations

$$H_{2n}(x) = (-1)^n \, 2^{2n} \, n! \, L_n^{-1/2}(x^2),$$
$$H_{2n+1}(x) = (-1)^n \, 2^{2n+1} \, n! \, L_n^{1/2}(x^2).$$

9.5.2 *Notes and References*

One might argue that special functions belong in the notebooks of nineteenth century mathematicians, but modern research is finding ever more applications for them. Currently, an efficient algorithm available for evaluating π to a large number of decimal places (as in more than 100,000,000) utilizes the theory of the so-called elliptic functions and the arithmetic-geometric mean algorithm. The use of generating functions in modern discrete mathematical models leads to many of the more complicated special functions.

Abramowitz & Stegun is a useful and inexpensive collection of formulas and values, while Spanier & Oldham is an expensive, computer oriented, polychromatic updating of the formulaic and graphical parts of A & S. There are many books devoted exclusively to special functions, some of which are listed below. Most books on ODE's or PDE's contain some material on the properties of some of the special functions.

- Abramowitz & Stegun, *Handbook of Mathematical Functions*: A comprehensive listing of identities and function values.

- Beckman, *Orthogonal Polynomials*: A highly personal approach to the subject.

- Birkhoff & Rota, *Ordinary Differential Equations, 4th ed.*: A good follow-up to the ODE chapters, including proofs of all relevant results.

- Gradshteyn & Ryzhik, *Tables of Integrals, Series, and Products*: An extensive and affordable collection of integrals and formulas for special functions. Many of the integrals *cannot* be done by any of the current computer algebra systems.

- Hochstadt, *The Functions of Mathematical Physics*: A more modern treatment of all the usual functions. Uses complex variable methods freely.

- Lebedev, *Special Functions and Their Applications*: An older book with many applications. Now available in paperback.

- Spanier & Oldham, *An Atlas of Functions*: An up-to-date listing of many ordinary and special functions with computer generated graphs in color. Contains much nonstandard material. Detailed algorithms for approximation are included throughout.

9.6   SUPPLEMENTARY AND COMPLEMENTARY PROBLEMS

1. Show that the double integral of $x^p y^q$ over the triangle bounded by $x + y = 1$ and the coordinate axes has the value
$$\frac{\Gamma(p+1)\,\Gamma(q+1)}{\Gamma(p+q+3)}.$$

2. For positive integral n, write out the forms of the products involving $\Gamma(n)$, $\Gamma(n + 1/3)$, and $\Gamma(n + 2/3)$. Interleave the products and collect powers of 3 to show that
$$\Gamma(3n) = \frac{1}{2\pi} 3^{3n-1/2} \Gamma(n)\,\Gamma(n + 1/3)\,\Gamma(n + 2/3).$$

3. Show that
$$\int_0^\pi \sin\theta_n\,d\theta_n \int_0^\pi \sin^2\theta_{n-1}\,d\theta_{n-1} \cdots \int_0^\pi \sin^n\theta_1\,d\theta_1 = \frac{\pi^{n/2}}{\Gamma\left(\frac{n}{2}+1\right)}.$$

4. (Volume of an n-ball) A particularly simple set of spherical coordinates in n dimensions is given by
$$\begin{aligned}
x_1 &= \rho\cos\theta_1, \\
x_2 &= \rho\sin\theta_1\cos\theta_2, \\
&\vdots \\
x_n &= \rho\sin\theta_1\sin\theta_2\cdots\sin\theta_{n-2}\cos\theta_{n-1},
\end{aligned}$$
where $\theta_k \in [0, \pi]$ for $k = 1 : n - 1$, $\rho \in [0, \infty)$.

(a) Show that the Jacobian transforming from Cartesian to these spherical coordinates is

$$\frac{\partial (x_1, x_2, \ldots, x_n)}{\partial (\rho, \theta_1, \theta_2, \ldots, \theta_{n-1})} = (-\rho)^n \sin {}^n\theta_1 \sin {}^{n-1}\theta_2 \cdots \sin \theta_n.$$

(b) Use part (a) and the result of the previous problem to show that the volume of an n-ball of radius r, $V_n(r)$, is given by

$$V_n(r) = \frac{\pi^{n/2}}{\Gamma\left(\frac{n}{2}+1\right)} r^n.$$

(c) Argue that $V_n(1)$ has a minimum of $8\pi^2/15$ when $n = 5$. [Hint: You may want to look at some numbers.]

(d) Show that

$$\sum_{n=0}^{\infty} V_{2n}(r) = e^{\pi r^2}.$$

5. Take the integral representation of the gamma function in the form

$$\Gamma(z) = \lim_{n \to \infty} \int_0^n t^{z-1} e^{-t} dt,$$

replace e^{-t} by $\left(1 - \frac{t}{n}\right)^n$ within the limit, interchange the limit and the integral, let $t = n\tau$, and integrate by parts n times to show that

$$\Gamma(z) = \lim_{n \to \infty} \frac{n! \, n^z}{z(z+1)(z+2)\cdots(z+n)}.$$

This equation was used as a definition of $\Gamma(z)$ by Gauss.

6. In probability theory, the **probability density function** of a continuous random variable X is a real nonnegative function $f(x)$ whose integral over the real line is 1. The kth **moment** of X is defined to be

$$\mu_k' = E[X^k] := \int_{-\infty}^{\infty} x^k f(x) \, dx.$$

Use the gamma function and/or the beta function to find the kth moment of each of the random variables (rv's) whose probability density functions are given below (they are assumed to be zero outside of the specified range of x):

(a) Gamma random variable,

$$f(x) = \frac{1}{\Gamma(\alpha)} \theta^\alpha x^{\alpha-1} e^{-\theta x}, \ x \geq 0, \ \theta, \alpha > 0.$$

(b) Weibull random variable,

$$f(x) = \alpha \beta x^{\beta-1} e^{-\alpha x^\beta}, \ x \geq 0, \ \alpha, \beta > 0.$$

(c) Beta random variable,

$$f(x) = \frac{1}{B(\alpha, \beta)} x^{\alpha-1}(1-x)^{\beta-1}, \; 0 \le x \le 1, \; \alpha, \beta > 0.$$

(d) Chi-square random variable,

$$f(x) = \frac{1}{2^{\nu/2}\Gamma(\nu/2)} x^{(\nu-2)/2} e^{-x/2}, \; x \ge 0, \; \nu = 1 : \infty.$$

7. The mean of a random variable X is its first moment $\mu := E[X] = \mu_1'$, and its variance is defined to be $\sigma^2 := E\left[(X-\mu)^2\right] = \mu_2' - \mu^2$. Use the results of the previous problem to find the mean and variance of each of the given random variables.

8. Find an integral expression for the second solution to Bessel's equation by setting $y(x) = u(x)J_\alpha(x)$, inserting into the equation, and finding an equation for u. This equation should involve no u term, only u'' and u' terms. Replace u' by v, thus getting a first order linear ODE in v. Solve it. Write the final solution as an indefinite integral of v times $J_\alpha(x)$.

9. Show that

$$J_0(z) = \frac{1}{\pi} \int_0^\pi \cos(z \sin \theta) \, d\theta.$$

10. Show that $y(x) = c_1 J_\alpha(x) + c_2 Y_\alpha(x) + c_3 I_\alpha(x) + c_4 K_\alpha(x)$ is the general solution of the linear homogeneous ODE

$$x^4 y^{(iv)} + 2x^3 y''' - (2\alpha^2+1)x^2 y'' + (2\alpha^2+1)xy' + \left(\alpha^2(\alpha^2-4) - x^4\right)y = 0$$

by considering the product of the Bessel and the modified Bessel operators, i.e.

$$[x^2 D^2 + xD + (x^2 - \alpha^2)][x^2 D^2 + xD - (x^2 + \alpha^2)].$$

11. Multiply the Taylor series expansions of $\exp(-x/2t)$ and $\exp(xt/2)$ to get

$$\exp\left\{\frac{x}{2}\left(t - \frac{1}{t}\right)\right\} = \sum_{j=0}^\infty \sum_{k=0}^\infty \frac{(-1)^k}{j!k!} \left(\frac{x}{2}\right)^{j+k} t^{j-k}.$$

As the sum is over all lattice points in the first quadrant and since the series converges uniformly, we can sum along the diagonals $j - k = n$ for $n = 0 : \infty$. Separate the sum into two parts: on or below the diagonal, in which case put $j = n+k$ and rearrange the sum so you recognize the series representation for $J_n(x)$, above the diagonal as $j - k = -n$, in which case you should recognize terms like $J_{-n}(x)$. Combine both sums to get

$$\exp\left\{\frac{x}{2}\left(t - \frac{1}{t}\right)\right\} = \sum_{n=-\infty}^\infty J_n(x) t^n.$$

Now put $t = e^{i\theta}$ and equate real and imaginary parts of both sides to show that

$$\cos(x \sin \theta) = J_0(x) + 2\sum_{n=1}^\infty J_{2n}(x) \cos 2n\theta,$$
$$\sin(x \sin \theta) = 2\sum_{n=1}^\infty J_{2n-1}(x) \sin(2n-1)\theta.$$

12. Suppose we have the series $\sum a_k \phi_k(x) = f(x)$ summed to n, where the set $\{\phi_k(x)\}$ is a complete orthogonal set (meaning that, in a sense, it is a basis of a linear space of functions). All orthogonal functions satisfy a three term recurrence equation of the form

$$\phi_{k+1}(x) + u_k \phi_k(x) + v_k \phi_{k-1}(x) = 0,$$

where u_k and v_k could be functions of x. Consider three successive terms of the series

$$f(x) = \cdots + a_{k-1}\phi_{k-1}(x) + a_k\phi_k(x) + a_{k+1}\phi_{k+1}(x) + \cdots$$

Set

$$a_k := b_k + u_k b_{k+1} + v_{k+1} b_{k+2}.$$

Show that when this is inserted into the series and summed in the reverse order we have

$$
\begin{aligned}
f(x) = \; & \cdots + \left(b_{k+1} + u_{k+1}b_{k+2} + v_{k+2}b_{k+3}\right)\phi_{k+1}(x) \\
& + \left(b_k + u_k b_{k+1} + v_{k+1}b_{k+2}\right)\phi_k(x) \\
& + \left(b_{k-1} + u_{k-1}b_k + v_k b_{k+1}\right)\phi_{k-1}(x) + \cdots.
\end{aligned}
$$

Rearrange this in terms of the b's to get

$$f(x) = \cdots + b_{k+1}\left(\phi_{k+1}(x) + u_k\phi_k(x) + v_k\phi_k(x)\right) + \cdots.$$

Since the term in the parentheses is zero, the sum has telescoped. All that remains are the first and second terms. Show these are

$$g(x) = b_1\left(\phi_1(x) + u_0\phi_0(x)\right) + b_0\phi_0(x).$$

Use the convention that $a_k = 0$ for $k > n$. Show that the b_k must satisfy the reverse recurrence equations

$$b_n = a_n, \quad b_{n-1} = a_{n-1} - u_{n-1}a_n, \quad b_k = a_k - u_k b_{k+1} - v_{k+1}b_{k+2}.$$

If we start with the value of b_n and work our way down, we can generate all the b's. Show that $\cos nx$ satisfies the three term recurrence relation

$$\cos(k+1)x - 2\cos x \cos(kx) + \cos(k-1)x = 0.$$

Use this to find the value of the sum

$$\sum_{k=0}^{n} a_k \cos kx.$$

13. Orthonormal polynomials satisfy a special three term recurrence equation. If c_n is the coefficient of x^n in $\phi_n(x)$, then

$$\phi_{n+1}(x) - (A_n x + B_n)\phi_n(x) + C_n\phi_n(x) = 0,$$

where $A_n = c_{n+1}/c_n$, $C_n = A_n/A_{n-1}$, and $C_0 = 0$. To prove this write

$$\phi_n(x) = c_n x^n + \cdots$$

and use this to show that

$$\phi_{n+1}(x) - A_n x\phi_n(x) = \sum_{k=0}^{n} \alpha_k x^k = \sum_{k=0}^{n} \beta_k \Phi_k(x),$$

for a suitable choice of α_k and β_k. Use orthonormality to show that

$$\beta_k = -A_n \langle x\phi_n(x), \phi_k(x) \rangle, \quad k \leq n.$$

Argue that this inner product is zero for $k \leq n-2$. This leaves only $\beta_n =: B_n$ and $\beta_{n-1} =: -C_n$, and so the recurrence relation is proven. To get the specific relations among the coefficients, show that

$$C_n = A_n \langle x\phi_n(x), \phi_{n-1}(x) \rangle = A_n \langle \phi_n(x), x\phi_{n-1}(x) \rangle,$$

but

$$x\phi_{n-1}(x) = c_{n-1}x^n + \cdots = \frac{c_{n-1}}{c_n}(c_n x^n + \cdots).$$

Argue that this can be rewritten as

$$x\phi_{n-1}(x) = \frac{1}{A_{n-1}}\left[\phi_n(x) + \sum_{k=0}^{n-1} \gamma_k \phi_k(x)\right].$$

From this infer that $C_n = A_n/A_{n-1}$.

14. This problem will lead to a proof of the **Christoffel-Darboux formula** which is

$$K_n(x, y) := \sum_{k=0}^{n} \phi_k(x)\phi_k(y) = \frac{c_n}{c_{n+1}}\left[\frac{\phi_n(y)\phi_{n+1}(x) - \phi_n(x)\phi_{n+1}(y)}{x - y}\right],$$

where c_n is again the coefficient of x^n in $\phi_n(x)$. Surely $\phi_0(x) = c_0$. Use the Gram-Schmidt procedure to write

$$\phi_1(x) = c_1 x - c_1 c_0^2 \int_a^b xw(x)\, dx.$$

Use these expressions to show that $K_0(x, y)$ is as given. To prove the general expression, use the three term recurrence equation in the form

$$\phi_{n+1}(x) - (A_n x + B_n)\, \phi_n(x) + C_n \phi_n(x) = 0,$$

with $A_n = c_n + 1/c_n$ and $C_n = A_n/A_{n-1}$ to show that

$$K_n(x, y) = \phi_n(x)\phi_n(y) + K_{n-1}(x, y).$$

Iterate this to prove the general result.

Appendix A

MATLAB OPERATIONS AND COMMANDS

A.1 *Algebraic Operations*

+   addition

−   subtraction

∗   multiplication, of scalar or matrices

/   division of scalars

\   left division of a matrix into a vector, e.g., $\mathbf{A}\backslash\mathbf{b}$ solves $\mathbf{A}\mathbf{x} = \mathbf{b}$

^   exponentiation

′   Hermitian conjugate

.∗   Schur-Hadamard product of matrices, entrywise multiplication

./   entrywise division

.^   entrywise exponentiation

A.2 *Commands*

abs : modulus or absolute value

acos : Acos evaluated entrywise

all : returns a 1 if all entries are nonzero and a 0 otherwise

ans : the result of the previous calculation

any : returns a 1 if any entry is nonzero and a 0 otherwise

asin : Asin evaluated entrywise

atan : Atan evaluated entrywise, returning values in $\left[-\frac{\pi}{2}, \frac{\pi}{2}\right]$

atan2(y, x) : Atan of two arguments, returning values in $[-\pi, \pi]$

axis : $[x, y, z]$ specifies the scale of each axis

break : stops a calculation

casesen : toggles the switch case sensitive

chol($\mathbf{A}$) : returns the Cholesky decomposition of a positive definite matrix $\mathbf{A}$

clear x : clears the variable x, or all variables if none are specified

clg : clears the stored graphic

cond($\mathbf{A}$,p) : returns the condition number of a matrix $\mathbf{A}$ in the p norm

conj(z) : returns the complex conjugate of z

cos : returns the cosine evaluated entrywise

delete : deletes

demo : opens the menu for the Matlab demonstration

det($\mathbf{A}$) : returns the determinant of $\mathbf{A}$

diag($\mathbf{A}$,$[k]$) : returns a vector that is the kth diagonal of $\mathbf{A}$ with $k = 0$ if omitted; if the argument is a vector, it returns a square matrix with $\mathbf{A}$ along the kth diagonal

diary : opens a diary file, which records the results of the session

eig($\mathbf{A}$) : returns the eigenvalues of $\mathbf{A}$, and optionally the eigenvectors when used as $[\mathbf{P}, \mathbf{D}] = $ eig($\mathbf{A}$)

eps : machine epsilon, 2^{-52}

eval : evaluates a string command

exist($'Q'$) : returns a 5 if Q is a built-in Matlab function, a 4 if Q is a compiled Simulink function, a 3 if Q is a MEX-file, a 2 if Q or $Q.m$ is the name of a file on disk, a 1 if the variable Q exists in the workspace, and a 0 otherwise

exp : returns the exponential of each entry

eye(n) : $\mathbf{I}_n$

flops : returns the number of floating point operations; flops(0) resets the counter to zero

format compact : suppresses extra carriage returns in the display

format expand : also format loose, returns to unsuppressed carriage returns

format long : sets display to 14 decimal places

format short : sets the display to 6 decimal places

format + : displays a + for a nonzero entry and a blank otherwise

help : prints help menu, or help ## prints help for ##

hilb(n) : returns the Hilbert segment of order n

imag : returns the imaginary part

inf : infinity

inv$(\mathbf{A})$: returns the inverse of $\mathbf{A}$

kron$(\mathbf{A}, \mathbf{B})$: returns the Kronecker product of $\mathbf{A}$ and $\mathbf{B}$

length$(\mathbf{a})$: returns the length of the vector $\mathbf{a}$

load : loads a file saved in Matlab format

log$(\mathbf{A})$: returns the natural logarithm evaluated entrywise

log10$(\mathbf{A})$: returns the common logarithm evaluated entrywise

magic(n) : returns a magic square of order n

max$(\mathbf{A})$: returns the maximum of a vector or the max of each column of a matrix

mean$(\mathbf{A})$: returns the mean of a vector or the mean of each column of a matrix

median$(\mathbf{A})$: returns the median of a vector or the median of each column of a matrix

mesh$(\mathbf{z})$: plots $\mathbf{z}$ over the grid on which it has been defined

meshdom$(\mathbf{x}, \mathbf{y})$: returns a set of ordered pairs at each lattice point as
$[\mathbf{x}, \mathbf{y}] = \mathrm{meshdom}(\mathbf{x}, \mathbf{y})$

min$(\mathbf{A})$: returns the minimum of a vector or the min of each column of a matrix

NaN : not a number

nargin : number of input arguments to a function

nargout : number of output arguments of a function

norm$(\mathbf{a}, p)$: returns the p-norm of $\mathbf{a}$

ones(m, n) : returns an $m \times n$ matrix all of whose entries are 1

ones(n) : returns an $n \times n$ matrix all of whose entries are 1

ones$(\mathrm{size}(\mathbf{A}))$: returns a matrix of 1's the same size as $\mathbf{A}$

orth$(\mathbf{a}, \mathbf{b}, \ldots)$: applies the Gram-Schmidt algorithm to obtain an orthonormal set generated
from the set $\{\mathbf{a}, \mathbf{b}, \ldots\}$

pause(t) : pauses for t seconds, or until a key is pressed if t is omitted

pi : returns the machine value of π

plot : plots the pairs of arguments listed

polyval$(\mathbf{p}, \mathbf{s})$: evaluates the given polynomial $\mathbf{p}$, written as a vector, at the entries of $\mathbf{s}$

prod$(\mathbf{A})$: returns the product of the entries of a vector or the entries of each column of a matrix

qr$(\mathbf{A})$: returns the QR-decomposition of $\mathbf{A}$

quit : exits Matlab

rand(m, n) : returns an $m \times n$ matrix whose entries are random numbers on $[0, 1)$

randn(m, n) : returns an $m \times n$ matrix whose entries are random numbers that are normally distributed with mean 0 and variance 1

rcond$(\mathbf{A})$: returns an estimate of $1/\operatorname{cond}(\mathbf{A})$; r is for **r**eciprocal

real : real part

roots$(\mathbf{p})$: returns the roots of the polynomial $p = p_1 z^{\text{length}(p)} + p_2 z^{\text{length}(p)-1} + \cdots$

rot90$(\mathbf{A}, k)$: rotates the entries of $\mathbf{A}$ $90*k°$ counterclockwise

round : rounds to the nearest integer

rref$(\mathbf{A})$: returns the row-reduced echelon form of $\mathbf{A}$

shg : show last graphic

sign$(\mathbf{A})$: replaces $\mathbf{A}$ by a matrix of the same size with a 1 where an entry is nonzero and a 0 where the entry is zero

sin : sine function evaluated entrywise

size$(\mathbf{A})$: returns a vector $[m, n]$ when $\mathbf{A}$ has m rows and n columns

sort : sorts entries in ascending order; $[\mathbf{y}, \mathbf{k}] = \operatorname{sort}(\mathbf{x})$ returns $\mathbf{y}$ as the sorted entries of $\mathbf{x}$, and $\mathbf{y} = \mathbf{x}(\mathbf{k})$

sqrt$(\mathbf{A})$: returns the square root evaluated entrywise

sum$(\mathbf{A})$: returns the sum of the entries of a vector or the sum of the columns of a matrix

svd$(\mathbf{A})$: singular value decomposition of $\mathbf{A}$

tan : returns the tangent evaluated entrywise

title : title of a graphic

trace(A) : sum(diag(**A**))

tril(A, k) : returns a matrix the same size as **A** but all the entries above the k diagonal are set to zero

triu(A, k) : returns a matrix the same size as **A** but all the entries below the k diagonal are set to zero

what : lists m-files, MAT-files, and MEX-files

who : lists current variable names

whos : lists current variable names, size, and whether they are complex or not

xlabel : label for the horizontal axis

ylabel : label for the vertical axis

zeros(m, n) : in the style of ones(m, n), only returns a matrix of 0's

Appendix B

COMPLEX NUMBERS

Essential to a large portion of work in applied mathematics is a working knowledge of the algebra of complex numbers.

B.1   Complex Algebra

DEFINITION B.1   *The* **set of complex numbers***,* $\mathbb{C}$*, is defined by*

$$\mathbb{C} = \{z = x + iy : x, y \in \mathbb{R}\},$$

where $i^2 = -1$ *and* $\mathbb{R}$ *is the set of real numbers. The real number* x *is called the* **real part** *of* z*, written* $\mathrm{Re}(z)$*, and the real number* y *is the* **imaginary part** *of* z*, written* $\mathrm{Im}(z)$*.*

All the basic algebraic operations with which we are familiar carry over to complex numbers so long as we make the identification $i^2 = -1$ and keep real and imaginary terms separate.

DEFINITION B.2 *Two complex numbers $z_1 = x_1 + iy_1$ and $z_2 = x_2 + iy_2$ are said to be* **equal** *if*

$$x_1 = x_2 \quad and \quad y_1 = y_2.$$

Complex addition *of z_1 and z_2 is defined by*

$$z_1 + z_2 = (x_1 + iy_1) + (x_2 + iy_2) := (x_1 + x_2) + i(y_1 + y_2).$$

Complex multiplication *of z_1 and z_2 is defined by*

$$z_1 z_2 = (x_1 + iy_1)(x_2 + iy_2) := (x_1 x_2 - y_1 y_2) + i(x_1 y_2 + x_2 y_1).$$

It is worth repeating that these are precisely the results one would obtain by performing the usual algebraic operations and reducing powers of i by using the defining equation $i^2 = -1$.

▪ **EXAMPLE B.1** Complete each of the following operations.

(a) $2(3 - 5i) - (4 + 3i) = (6 - 10i) - (4 + 3i) = (6 - 4) + (-10 - 3)i = 2 - 13i.$

(b) $(3 - 2i)(4 + 3i) = 3(4 + 3i) - 2i(4 + 3i) = 12 + 9i - 8i - 6i^2 = 12 + i + 6 = 18 + i.$

(c) $(1 - 4i)(2 + i) - 3i(5i - 4) = (2 - 7i - 4i^2) - (15i^2 - 12i) = (6 - 7i) - (-15 - 12i) = 21 + 5i.$

(d) $(1 - i)^2 = 1 - 2i + i^2 = 1 - 2i - 1 = -2i.$

(e) $(1 + i)^2(2 - 3i)^2 = (1 + 2i + i^2)(4 - 12i + 9i^2) = (2i)(-5 - 12i) = -10i - 24i^2 = 24 - 10i.$

(f) $i^2 = -1$, $i^3 = (i^2)i = -i$, $i^4 = (i^2)^2 = (-1)^2 = 1$, $i^5 = (i^4)i = i$, and this pattern of four numbers repeats. ▪ ▪ ▪

We seek to define division by complex numbers by saying that the reciprocal of z is the complex number $w = z^{-1}$ that is the unique solution to the equation $wz = 1$. Writing $w = a + ib$ and $z = x + iy$, this requirement becomes

$$wz = (ax - by) + i(ay + bx) = 1.$$

Equating the real and imaginary parts we are left with two simultaneous linear equations in the unknowns a and b:

$$ax - by = 1 \quad and \quad ay + bx = 0.$$

It is straightforward to show that the solution exists for $z \neq 0$; it is

$$z^{-1} = \frac{x - iy}{x^2 + y^2}.$$

This result is equivalent to taking $1/(x + iy)$ and multiplying and dividing by $x - iy$. More about that in just a bit.

■ **EXAMPLE B.2** Write each of the following in the form $x + iy$.

(a) $\dfrac{2+i}{1-i} = \dfrac{2+i}{1-i}\dfrac{1+i}{1+i} = \dfrac{2+3i+i^2}{2} = \dfrac{1}{2} + \dfrac{3}{2}i.$

(b) $\dfrac{2+3i}{1-i} + \dfrac{3-3i}{3+4i} = \dfrac{2+3i}{1-i}\dfrac{1+i}{1+i} + \dfrac{3-3i}{3+4i}\dfrac{3-4i}{3-4i}$

$= \dfrac{(2-3)+(3+2)i}{2} + \dfrac{(9-12)-(9+12)i}{25} = -\dfrac{31}{50} + i\dfrac{83}{50}.$ ■ ■ ■

Remember the real and imaginary parts of a complex number are *both* real numbers.

■ **EXAMPLE B.3** Evaluate as indicated.

(a) $\mathrm{Re}(2 - 3i) = 2.$

(b) $\mathrm{Im}(2 - 3i) = -3.$

(c) $\mathrm{Re}(z^{-1}) = \mathrm{Re}\left(\dfrac{x - iy}{x^2 + y^2}\right) = \dfrac{x}{x^2 + y^2}.$

(d) $\mathrm{Im}(z^{-1}) = \dfrac{-y}{x^2 + y^2}.$

(e) $\mathrm{Re}(z^2) = \mathrm{Re}[(x^2 - y^2) + 2ixy] = x^2 - y^2.$

(f) $\mathrm{Im}(z^2) = 2xy.$ ■ ■ ■

DEFINITION B.3 *The* **complex conjugate** *of z, written $\bar{z}$, is defined by*

$$\bar{z} = \overline{(x + iy)} := x - iy. \tag{B.1}$$

Taking the complex conjugate only requires us to change the sign of i everywhere that it appears.

■ **EXAMPLE B.4** Evaluate each of the complex conjugates, as indicated.

(a) $\bar{i} = -i.$

(b) $\overline{(1 - i)} = 1 + i.$

(c) $\overline{(1/i)} = \overline{(-i)} = i.$

(d) $\overline{[(1 + i)^2]} = \overline{(1 + 2i + i^2)} = \overline{2i} = -2i.$ ■ ■ ■

Some obvious properties of complex conjugation are stated in the following theorem.

THEOREM B.1 *For complex z, z_1, and z_2:*

(**CC1**) $\overline{(\bar{z})} = z$.

(**CC2**) $\overline{(z_1 + z_2)} = \bar{z}_1 + \bar{z}_2$.

(**CC3**) $\overline{(z_1 z_2)} = \bar{z}_1 \bar{z}_2$.

(**CC4**) $\overline{(1/z)} = 1/\bar{z}$, *when $z \neq 0$.*   □

The proof is merely a matter of manipulation and will be left to the reader.
If we start with

$$z = x + iy \quad \text{and} \quad \bar{z} = x - iy$$

and treat these as two equations in the two unknowns x and y, we can solve to get

$$x = \text{Re}(z) = \frac{1}{2}(z + \bar{z}), \; y = \text{Im}(z) = \frac{1}{2i}(z - \bar{z}). \tag{B.2}$$

Thus we have explicit formulas for the real and imaginary parts of a complex number that do not depend on the representation of the number.

Using complex conjugation allows us to derive the form of the reciprocal of a complex number quite quickly if we notice that $z\bar{z} = x^2 + y^2$ is a positive real number for nonzero z. Start with $wz = 1$; multiply both sides by $\bar{z}$ to get $wz\bar{z} = \bar{z}$. Then divide by the real quantity $z\bar{z}$ to arrive at

$$w = \frac{1}{z} = \frac{\bar{z}}{z\bar{z}},$$

which you can verify is the same result we derived by using simultaneous linear equations.

The following properties of complex (and real) arithmetic merit listing; any set that has these properties is called a **field**.

THEOREM B.2 *When a, b, and $c \in \mathbb{C}$ (are complex numbers):*

(**Closure**) *then $a + b$ and $ab \in \mathbb{C}$ (closure under $+$ and $\cdot$)*

(**Add1**) $a + b = b + a$ *(addition is commutative)*

(**Add2**) $a + (b + c) = (a + b) + c$ *(addition is associative)*

(**Add3**) $0 \in \mathbb{C}$ *and $a + 0 = 0 + a = a$ (additive identity)*

(**Add4**) $-a \in \mathbb{C}$ *and $a + (-a) = 0$ (additive inverse)*

(**Mult1**) $ab = ba$ *(multiplication is commutative)*

(**Mult2**) $a(bc) = (ab)c$ *(multiplication is associative)*

(**Mult3**) $1 \in \mathbb{C}$ *and $1 \cdot a = a$ (multiplicative identity)*

(Mult4) *If $a \neq 0$, then $a^{-1} \in \mathbb{C}$ and $aa^{-1} = 1$ (multiplicative inverse)*

(Dist) $a(b + c) = ab + ac$ *(multiplication distributes over addition)* $\square$

The proof of the theorem is left to the reader.

When computing powers of sums of complex numbers, it is convenient to employ the Binomial Theorem:

THEOREM B.3 (Binomial Theorem)   *For any complex a, b, and a nonnegative integer n,*

$$(a + b)^n = \sum_{k=0}^{n} \binom{n}{k} a^k b^{n-k} = \sum_{k=0}^{n} \binom{n}{k} a^{n-k} b^k. \tag{B.3}$$

The first sum in equation (B.3) begins with a^0 and goes up to a^n, whereas the second has its terms in the reverse order, starting at a^n and ending at a^0. Properties (Add1) and (Mult1) of the complex field assure us that both sums are indeed the same. The quantity $\binom{n}{k}$ is called the **binomial coefficient**, read "n choose k," and is defined by

$$\binom{n}{k} := \underbrace{\frac{n(n-1)(n-2)\cdots(n-k+1)}{k(k-1)(k-2)\cdots(1)}}_{k \text{ factors, numerator \& denominator}},$$

for any n and positive integers k. We define $\binom{n}{0} := 1$. For positive integer values of n the binomial coefficient can also be written entirely in terms of factorials as

$$\binom{n}{k} = \frac{n!}{k!\,(n-k)!}.$$

■ **EXAMPLE B.5**   Evaluate each of the following binomial coefficients.

$$\binom{6}{2} = \frac{6 \cdot 5}{2 \cdot 1} = 15, \quad \binom{8}{7} = \frac{8 \cdot 7 \cdot 6 \cdot 5 \cdot 4 \cdot 3 \cdot 2}{7 \cdot 6 \cdot 5 \cdot 4 \cdot 3 \cdot 2 \cdot 1} = \frac{8}{1} = 8 = \binom{8}{1},$$

$$\binom{100}{3} = \frac{100 \cdot 99 \cdot 98}{3 \cdot 2 \cdot 1} = 161700,$$

$$\binom{\pi}{4} = \frac{\pi(\pi-1)(\pi-2)(\pi-3)}{4 \cdot 3 \cdot 2 \cdot 1} = 0.04531.$$

■ ■ ■

Some useful properties of the binomial coefficients are listed in the following theorem.

THEOREM B.4   *For nonnegative integers n and k:*

(BinCo1) $\binom{n}{0} = 1, \quad \binom{n}{1} = n.$

(BinCo2) $\dbinom{n}{k} = \dbinom{n}{n-k}.$

(BinCo3) $\dbinom{n}{k} + \dbinom{n}{k+1} = \dbinom{n+1}{k+1}.$ □

There are a whole host of others. The proofs involve little more than manipulating products and will be left to the reader. (BinCo3) allows us to construct Pascal's triangle as shown.

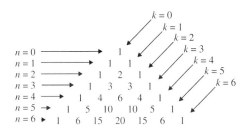

Each row begins and ends with a 1, and each following number is obtained by adding the two numbers on each side from the line above; e.g., $5 = 1 + 4$, $10 = 4 + 6$, $10 = 6 + 4$, $5 = 4 + 1$. To get the coefficient $\binom{n}{k}$, counting from zero, go down n rows and over k steps to the right. Remember, row and column counts start at zero.

Actually applying the Binomial Theorem is straightforward.

■ **EXAMPLE B.6** Expand each of the following.

(a) $(x - 2y)^3 = x^3 + 3x^2(-2y) + 3x(-2y)^2 + (-2y)^3$

$\qquad\qquad = x^3 - 6x^2y + 12xy^2 - 8y^3.$

(b) $(a + b)^5 = a^5 + 5a^4b + 10a^3b^2 + 10a^2b^3 + 5ab^4 + b^5.$

(c) $(3 + 2t^2)^4 = 3^4 + 4 \cdot 3^3(2t^2) + 6 \cdot 3^2(2t^2)^2 + 4 \cdot 3^1(2t^2)^3 + (2t^2)^4$

$\qquad\qquad = 81 + 216t^2 + 216t^4 + 96t^6 + 16t.$ ■ ■ ■

Notice the following:

(a) The power of a goes down by one in each term and the power of b goes up by one.

(b) The sum of the powers of a and b is always n.

(c) The coefficients of each term are just the numbers from the nth row of Pascal's triangle.

■ **EXAMPLE B.7** This example involves a somewhat higher power:

$$
\begin{aligned}
(1+i)^{10} &= 1 + 10i + 45i^2 + 120i^3 + 210i^4 + 252i^5 \\
&\quad + 210i^6 + 120i^7 + 45i^8 + 10i^9 + i^{10} \\
&= 1 + 10i - 45 - 120i + 210 + 252i - 210 - 120i + 45 + 10i - 1 \\
&= (1 - 45 + 210 - 210 + 45 - 1) + i(10 - 120 + 252 - 120 + 10) \\
&= 32i.
\end{aligned}
$$

■ ■ ■

■ **EXAMPLE B.8** Use the Binomial Theorem to find each of the designated terms in the given expansions.

(a) The term with a^7 in the expansion of $(a + b)^{12}$ is

$$
\binom{12}{7} a^7 b^5 = 792 a^7 b^5.
$$

(b) The term with a^{10} in the expansion of $(a^2 - 2a)^7$ is obtained from the general term as given in equation (B.3):

$$
\binom{7}{k} \left(a^2\right)^k (-2a)^{7-k} = (-2)^{7-k} \binom{7}{k} a^{2k+7-k} = (-2)^{7-k} \binom{7}{k} a^{k+7}.
$$

Setting $k + 7 = 10$, we get $k = 3$, and the required term is

$$
\binom{7}{3} \left(a^2\right)^3 (-2a)^4 = 35(-2)^4 a^{10} = 560 a^{10}.
$$

■ ■ ■

The following product, which we encountered when solving for z^{-1}, will be useful in much later work:

$$
z\bar{z} = (x + iy)(x - iy) = x^2 - i^2 y^2 = x^2 + y^2.
$$

Since this is always real and nonnegative, we can unambiguously define:

DEFINITION B.4 *The* **modulus** *of z is the nonnegative number*

$$
|z| := \sqrt{z\bar{z}} = \sqrt{x^2 + y^2}. \tag{B.4}
$$

The following properties of the modulus are easily verified:

THEOREM B.5 *For any complex numbers a and b:*

(Mod1) $|a| \geq 0$, $= 0$ *only if* $a = 0$.

(Mod2) $|ab| = |a| \, |b|$.

(Mod3) $|1/a| = 1/|a|$, *when* $a \neq 0$.

(Mod4) $|a| = |\bar{a}|$.

(Mod5) $|\text{Re}(a)| \leq |a|$, *equality only if* $\text{Im}(a) = 0$.

(Mod6) $|\text{Im}(a)| \leq |a|$, *equality only if* $\text{Re}(a) = 0$. $\qquad\qquad\qquad\square$

Warning: The modulus of a sum is *not* the sum of the moduli.

We can derive an *inequality* relating the modulus of the sum to the sum of the moduli:

$$\begin{aligned} |a+b|^2 &= (a+b)\overline{(a+b)} = a\bar{a} + a\bar{b} + \bar{a}b + b\bar{b} \\ &= |a|^2 + \left(a\bar{b} + \bar{a}b\right) + |b|^2 . \end{aligned} \tag{B.5}$$

The first term in the parentheses is the complex conjugate of the second because

$$\overline{(\bar{a}b)} = \overline{(\bar{a})}\, \bar{b} = a\bar{b}.$$

Using equation (B.2), we have

$$\overline{(\bar{a}b)} + \bar{a}b = 2\,\text{Re}\left(\bar{a}b\right).$$

By virtue of (Mod4) and (Mod6),

$$2\,\text{Re}\left(\bar{a}b\right) \leq 2\,|\bar{a}b| = 2\,|a|\,|b| .$$

Thus (B.5) can be rewritten as the inequality

$$|a+b|^2 \leq |a|^2 + 2\,|a|\,|b| + |b|^2 = (|a| + |b|)^2 .$$

Taking the square root of both sides yields the **Triangle Inequality** for complex numbers:

$$|a+b| \leq |a| + |b| . \tag{B.6}$$

An alternative version involving the difference of complex numbers can be derived using the regular triangle inequality:

$$a = (a-b) + b \quad \Rightarrow \quad |a| \leq |a-b| + |a| \quad \Rightarrow \quad |a| - |b| \leq |a-b| .$$

Interchanging a and b should still leave us with a valid inequality, and so we can combine these to form:

$$||a| - |b|| \leq |a-b| .$$

The original Triangle Inequality, equation (B.6), can be generalized (using mathematical induction) to any finite sequence as

$$\left| \sum_{1}^{N} a_n \right| \leq \sum_{1}^{N} |a_n| .$$

B.2   Polar Form of Complex Numbers

There is a natural correspondence between complex numbers and the polar coordinate representation of points in the plane. Surely, the radial polar coordinate should be

$$r = \sqrt{x^2 + y^2} = |x + iy| = |z| \,.$$

The change of coordinates is

$$x = r\cos\theta, \ y = r\sin\theta,$$

where the analogy to the polar angle is the following.

DEFINITION B.5   *The **principal value of the argument** of z is defined to be*

$$\mathrm{Arg}(z) = \mathrm{Arg}(x + iy) := \theta,$$

where θ is the angle between the positive x-axis and the radius line, taken positive in the counterclockwise direction. The function $\mathrm{Arg}(z)$ *returns values in the range* $(-\pi, \pi]$; *i.e.,*

$$-\pi < \mathrm{Arg}(z) \leq \pi.$$

*The **nonprincipal values of the argument** are*

$$\arg z := \mathrm{Arg}(z) + 2n\pi, \ n = -\infty : \infty, \ n \neq 0;$$

there are infinitely many of these.

Be careful to use the upper case Arg only for the principal value and the lower case arg for the nonprincipal values! When in doubt as to how to determine the angle, locate the point in the complex plane, draw a triangle, and read off the quadrant in which the point lies. Then use the Atan function.

■ **EXAMPLE B.9**   Find each of the following args/Args.

(a) $\mathrm{Arg}(6) = \mathrm{Arg}(212) = \mathrm{Arg}(\pi^e) = 0, \arg(6) = 2n\pi, \mathrm{Arg}(-1) = \pi.$

(b) $\mathrm{Arg}(i) = \mathrm{Arg}(20.56i) = \dfrac{\pi}{2}, \arg i = \dfrac{\pi}{2} + 2n\pi.$

(c) $\mathrm{Arg}(1 + i) = \mathrm{Arg}\left(\dfrac{1+i}{\sqrt{2}}\right) = \dfrac{\pi}{4}, \arg(1 + i) = \dfrac{\pi}{4} + 2n\pi.$

(d) $\mathrm{Arg}(1 - i) = -\dfrac{\pi}{4}, \quad not \quad \dfrac{7\pi}{4}.$

(e) $\arg(1 - i) = -\dfrac{\pi}{4} + 2n\pi,$ of which $\dfrac{7\pi}{4}$ is but one value.

(f) $\mathrm{Arg}(-1 + i) = \dfrac{3\pi}{4}, \arg(-1 + i) = \dfrac{3\pi}{4} + 2n\pi.$ ■ ■ ■

If we write $r = |z|$, $\theta = \text{Arg}(z)$, and the usual polar coordinate transformation $x = r \cos \theta$ and $y = r \sin \theta$, then we have

$$z = |z| (\cos \theta + i \sin \theta).$$ (B.7)

A most amazing relation holds between the right hand side of (B.7) and the exponential function.

THEOREM B.6 (Euler's Formula) *For any complex θ,*

$$e^{i\theta} = \cos \theta + i \sin \theta.$$ (B.8)

$\square$

There are many possible verifications of Euler's Formula in (B.8), but they all involve material beyond this appendix. Suppose all standard theorems of calculus apply to functions of a complex variable. In particular, a theorem in Chapter 2 states that a first order linear differential equation with continuous coefficients and an initial condition has a unique solution. Since

$$\frac{d}{d\theta} e^{i\theta} = i e^{i\theta},$$

and

$$\frac{d}{d\theta} (\cos \theta + i \sin \theta) = -\sin \theta + i \cos \theta = i^2 \sin \theta + i \cos \theta = i (\cos \theta + i \sin \theta),$$

both $e^{i\theta}$ and $\cos \theta + i \sin \theta$ satisfy the linear differential equation $z'(\theta) = iz(\theta)$. Also,

$$e^{i0} = 1 = \cos 0 + i \sin 0,$$

and so they satisfy the same initial condition. Therefore, they are equal because the solution is unique. An alternative argument will be given in a Appendix F using infinite series.

Equation (B.7) can now be rewritten using Euler's formula:

$$z = |z| (\cos \theta + i \sin \theta) = |z| e^{i\theta}.$$ (B.9)

We must use $\theta = \arg z$ rather than $\text{Arg} \, z$ because

$$e^{i2n\pi} = \cos 2n\pi + i \sin 2n\pi = 1,$$

and we cannot distinguish between the different values of $\arg z$ when exponentiated.

The properties of the exponential function (which we assume also hold for complex numbers) lead to some interesting results. For instance,

$$z^n = \left(|z| e^{i\theta} \right)^n = |z|^n e^{in\theta}.$$

Written in nonexponential form using (B.9), this is **de Moivre's Theorem:**

$$[r (\cos \theta + \sin \theta)]^n = r^n (\cos n\theta + i \sin n\theta).$$ (B.10)

We also have

$$z_1 z_2 = \left(r_1 e^{i\theta_1}\right)\left(r_2 e^{i\theta_2}\right) = (r_1 r_2)\, e^{i(\theta_1 + \theta_2)},$$

$$\frac{z_1}{z_2} = \frac{r_1 e^{i\theta_1}}{r_2 e^{i\theta_2}} = \left(\frac{r_1}{r_2}\right) e^{i(\theta_1 - \theta_2)}.$$

A simple application is in order.

■ **EXAMPLE B.10** Compute the value of $(1+i)^{10}$ using the polar notation.

Solution: Since $1+i = \sqrt{2}e^{i\pi/4}$, we have

$$(1+i)^{10} = \left(\sqrt{2}e^{i\pi/4}\right)^{10} = 2^5 e^{i5\pi/2} = 2^5 \left(\cos\frac{5\pi}{2} + i\sin\frac{5\pi}{2}\right) = 2^5 i = 32i.$$

■ ■ ■

B.3   Exercise Set

1. If $a = 2 - i$, $b = -1 + 3i$, $c = 3 - 4i$, $d = 2i$, and $e = -5 + 3i$, use a computer algebra system to write each of the following in the form $x + iy$:

   (a) $a + b$.

   (b) $ac - e$.

   (c) $2a - ic$.

   (d) $ia + 2d$.

   (e) $ab + cd$.

   (f) $\dfrac{a}{b} + \dfrac{c}{d}$.

   (g) $\dfrac{|d - c|}{|d| - |c|}$.

   (h) ade.

   (i) $\dfrac{ab}{d}$.

   (j) b^3.

2. Find the real part, imaginary part, and modulus of each of the following complex numbers:

   (a) $(3 - 4i)^5$.

   (b) $\dfrac{2i}{3 - 2i}$.

   (c) $(1 - i)^3 (1 + i)^6$.

   (d) $i^2 - (\bar{i})^2$.

   (e) $\dfrac{1}{i^3}$.

   (f) $\left(\dfrac{1 - 2i}{1 + 2i}\right)^2$.

   (g) $(2 - 2i)^6 (2 + 2i)^{-5}$.

   (h) $i^3 + i^6 + \cdots + i^{90}$.

   (i) $\dfrac{i(1 + 3i)}{4 - 5i}$.

3. Use the Binomial Theorem to find the coefficient of t^4 in each of the following expansions:

   (a) $(t^2 + 2i)^5$.

   (b) $(2t - 3/t)^8$.

   (c) $(3it - 2\sqrt{t})^8$.

   (d) $(t^{-3/2} - 3t^2)^9$.

4. Prove each of the following binomial coefficient identities.

(a) $\dbinom{n}{k} + \dbinom{n}{k+1} = \dbinom{n+1}{k+1}.$

(b) $\dbinom{-a}{k} = (-1)^k \dbinom{a+k-1}{k}, \quad a > 0.$

(c) $\displaystyle\sum_0^n \dbinom{n}{k} = 2^n.$

5. Find the principal value of the argument (in radians) of each of the following complex numbers:

(a) $\dfrac{1+i}{1-i}.$

(b) $\dfrac{1+i}{-i}.$

(c) $(1+i)^2.$

(d) $\dfrac{i^{21}}{(1-i)^{11}}.$

6. If the modulus and argument are as given, write each of the following complex numbers in Cartesian form, $x + iy$:

(a) $r = 3, \ \theta = \pi.$

(b) $r = 2, \ \theta = -\pi/3.$

(c) $r = 7, \ \theta = 5\pi/6.$

(d) $r = \pi, \ \theta = -619\pi/4.$

(e) $r = 21, \ \theta = 21\pi/2.$

(f) $r = \sqrt{12}, \ \theta = 9\pi/4.$

7. If $a \in \mathbb{R}$ and $m \in \mathbb{C}$

(a) Show that $mz + \bar{m}\bar{z} + a = 0$ is the equation of a line in the complex plane, and find its slope.

(b) If $a \le |m|^2$, what geometric object is represented by the equation

$$z\bar{z} + mz + \bar{m}\bar{z} + a = 0?$$

8. Two complex numbers are defined to be **parallel** if there is a *real* number c such that *either* $z_1 = cz_2$ or $cz_1 = z_2$.

(a) Show by example that both conditions are necessary in the definition, and then show that an equivalent condition is $\operatorname{Im}(z_1 \bar{z}_2) = 0$.

(b) Two complex numbers are defined to be **orthogonal** if

$$|z_1 - z_2|^2 = |z_1|^2 + |z_2|^2.$$

Show that z_1 is orthogonal to z_2 if and only if $\operatorname{Re}(z_1 \bar{z}_2) = 0$.

(c) Show that complex numbers satisfy the **Parallelogram Rule**:

$$|z_1 - z_2|^2 + |z_1 + z_2|^2 = 2|z_1|^2 + |z_2|^2.$$

Appendix C

COMPLEX FUNCTIONS

C.1 Zeros of Functions

DEFINITION C.1 *A function $f(z)$ is said to have a* **zero** *at $z = a$ if $f(a) = 0$. The point $z = a$ will be a* **zero of order** *m if we can write*

$$f(z) = (z - a)^m g(z) \tag{C.1}$$

and $g(a) \neq 0$. If $m = 1$, $z = a$ is said to be a **simple zero.** *When $m = 2$, it is a* **double zero.**

The character of the zeros of a real function tells us a great deal about its graph. If we treat z as a real variable and differentiate (C.1), we find

$$f'(z) = m(z - a)^{m-1} g(z) + (z - a)^m g'(z).$$

When $z = a$ is a simple zero, $m = 1$, and then $f'(a) = g(a) \neq 0$. Thus the graph of $f(z)$ crosses the axis with a nonzero slope when it has a simple zero. But when $z = a$ is a zero of even order, the graph is tangent to the axis and remains either above or below it in a neighborhood of the zero. For zeros of odd order greater than one, the graph crosses the z-axis and is tangent to it at $z = a$.

Furthermore, if the function $f(z)$ has a zero of order m at $z = a$, then the first $m - 1$ derivatives of $f(z)$ will be zero at $z = a$. This will be a useful criterion for determining the order of a zero.

■ **EXAMPLE C.1** Find and classify the zeros of each of the following functions.

(a) The real exponential function has no finite zeros because $e^x = 0$ is equivalent to $x = \ln 0$, which is undefined.

(b) The real function $\sin x = 0$ when $x = n\pi$ for $n = -\infty : \infty$, and all the zeros are simple because the graph of $\sin x$ crosses the axis at nonzero angles, because the derivative of $\sin x$ is nonzero at $x = n\pi$. In fact,

$$\frac{d}{dx} \sin x \bigg|_{x=n\pi} = \cos n\pi = (-1)^n,$$

and so the graph of $\sin x$ crosses the axis at angles of $\pm \pi / 4$.

(c) The real function $\cos x = 0$ when $x = \left(n + \frac{1}{2}\right)\pi$, $n = -\infty : \infty$. These are zeros of order one because

$$\frac{d}{dx}\cos x\bigg|_{\left(n+\frac{1}{2}\right)\pi} = -\sin\left(n + \frac{1}{2}\right)\pi = -(-1)^n \neq 0.$$

■ ■ ■

Now to the simplest class of functions that are of interest.

DEFINITION C.2 *We say $p(z)$ is a **polynomial function of degree** n (the value of the highest power, written $\deg(p)$) if it can be written in the form*

$$p(z) = a_n z^n + a_{n-1} z^{n-1} + \cdots + a_2 z^2 + a_1 z + a_0,$$

when the a_k are complex constants and $a_n \neq 0$, otherwise, $\deg(p) < n$.

Since all the usual rules of algebra carry over to the set of complex numbers $\mathbb{C}$, working with complex polynomials will be no different than working with real polynomials.

The complex field is **algebraically closed**. This means that any polynomial equation of degree n with complex coefficients has n complex roots, counting what are called multiplicities. This result is called the **Fundamental Theorem of Algebra**. The real field is not algebraically closed because the polynomial $p(a) = a^2 + 1$ with real coefficients has no real zeros. The algebraic closure of $\mathbb{C}$ guarantees us that all polynomials can be written as a product of linear terms,

$$p(z) = a_n \left(z - z_1\right)^{m_1} \left(z - z_2\right)^{m_2} \cdots \left(z - z_k\right)^{m_k},$$

where $z_1, z_2, \ldots, z_k$ are the zeros of $p(z)$ and $m_1, m_2, \ldots, m_k$ are the **orders** or **multiplicities** of these zeros. If $p(z)$ can be factored (a tall order at times, even for the best computer algebra system), then all of its zeros can be found. There is no closed form formula for the zeros of higher order polynomials ($n > 4$; in fact, $n = 5$ will test most systems), rather only the methods of trial and error or numerical calculation are available.

In Matlab, polynomials are entered as vectors,

$$p = [a_n, a_{n-1}, \ldots, a_2, a_1, a_0],$$

and **roots**(p) will return a numerical approximation to the roots.

When a polynomial has real coefficients, any complex zeros must occur in conjugate pairs. You can see that this is so by taking the complex conjugate of the polynomial with real coefficients $r(z)$:

$$\overline{r(z)} = \bar{r}(\bar{z}) = r(\bar{z}),$$

where $\bar{r}(z)$ is the polynomial $r(z)$ with all its coefficients replaced by their complex conjugates. If $r(z) = 0$, then we will also have $r(\bar{z}) = 0$.

C.2   Complex Exponential Function

Shifting gears, it is a simple matter to extend the definition of the exponential function to complex z by using Euler's formula,

$$\exp(z) = e^z = e^{x+iy} = e^x e^{iy} = e^x(\cos y + i \sin y). \tag{C.2}$$

It can be shown that all the usual properties of the exponential function remain valid for complex z.

THEOREM C.1   *For any complex numbers z, z_1, z_2, and a:*

(Exp1) $\exp(0) = 1$.

(Exp2) $\exp(z_1 + z_2) = \exp(z_1) \exp(z_2)$.

(Exp3) $\exp(z_1 - z_2) = \exp(z_1)/\exp(z_2)$.

(Exp4) $\exp(az) = (\exp(z))^a$. $\square$

Example C.1(a) can be extended to show that e^z has no finite complex zeros.

■ **EXAMPLE C.2**   Equation (C.2) can be used to greatly simplify the evaluation of some integrals. Usually we would employ integration by parts twice to evaluate

$$\int e^{\alpha t} \cos \beta t \, dt.$$

Instead we'll use $e^{\alpha t} \cos \beta t = \mathrm{Re}\left(e^{(\alpha + i\beta)t}\right)$ and, assuming that all of the standard calculus operations can be applied to integrals of a real variable with complex parameters, we can write

$$\int e^{\alpha t} \cos \beta t \, dt = \mathrm{Re} \left\{ \int e^{(\alpha + i\beta)t} \, dt \right\}$$

This last integral is easily evaluated:

$$\int e^{(\alpha + i\beta)t} dt = \frac{1}{\alpha + i\beta} e^{(\alpha + i\beta)t} = \frac{\alpha - i\beta}{\alpha^2 + \beta^2} e^{(\alpha + i\beta)t}$$
$$= \frac{e^{\alpha t}}{\alpha^2 + \beta^2} \left\{ (\alpha \cos \beta t + \beta \sin \beta t) + i \left(\alpha \sin \beta t - \beta \cos \beta t \right) \right\}.$$

Thus for the price of one simple integration, we have

$$\int e^{\alpha t} \cos \beta t \, dt = \frac{e^{\alpha t}}{\alpha^2 + \beta^2} \left(\alpha \cos \beta t + \beta \sin \beta t \right).$$

For no additional work, we get the imaginary part:

$$\int e^{\alpha t} \sin \beta t \, dt = \frac{e^{\alpha t}}{\alpha^2 + \beta^2} \left(\alpha \sin \beta t - \beta \cos \beta t \right).$$

■ ■ ■

We can use Euler's formula to find roots of complex numbers. Since $\mathbb{C}$ is algebraically closed, the polynomial equation $z^n - a = 0$ should have n complex roots. If we write $a = re^{i\theta}$, then its n n^{th} roots are:

$$a^{1/n} = r^{1/n} \times \begin{cases} \exp\left(i\frac{\theta}{n}\right), \\ \exp\left(i\frac{\theta+2\pi}{n}\right), \\ \exp\left(i\frac{\theta+4\pi}{n}\right), \\ \quad\vdots \\ \exp\left(i\frac{\theta+2\pi(n-1)}{n}\right). \end{cases}$$

There are exactly n of these roots because the next one in the sequence is

$$\exp\left(i\frac{\theta+2n\pi}{n}\right) = \exp\left(i\frac{\theta}{n}\right)\exp(i2\pi) = \exp\left(i\frac{\theta}{n}\right),$$

which is the value with which we started, and after that they continue to repeat. Notice that all the roots are equally spaced about the circle of radius $|z| = r^{1/n}$.

■ **EXAMPLE C.3** Compute all the values of each of the following complex roots.

(a) The cube roots of unity, $1^{1/3}$, are

$$\left\{1 = e^{i0\pi/3}, e^{i2\pi/3}, e^{i4\pi/3}\right\} = \left\{1, \frac{1}{2}\left(-1+i\sqrt{3}\right), \frac{1}{2}\left(-1-i\sqrt{3}\right)\right\}.$$

(b) The square roots of i are

$$i^{1/2} = e^{i\frac{1}{2}\left(\frac{\pi}{2}+2n\pi\right)} = \begin{cases} e^{i\pi/4} = \frac{1}{\sqrt{2}}(1+i) \\ e^{i5\pi/4} = -\frac{1}{\sqrt{2}}(1+i). \end{cases}$$

(c) The fourth roots of -1 are

$$(-1)^{1/4} = e^{\frac{i}{4}(\pi+2n\pi)} = \begin{cases} e^{i\pi/4} = \frac{1}{\sqrt{2}}(1+i), \\ e^{i3\pi/4} = \frac{1}{\sqrt{2}}(-1+i), \\ e^{i5\pi/4} = \frac{1}{\sqrt{2}}(-1-i), \\ e^{i7\pi/4} = \frac{1}{\sqrt{2}}(1-i). \end{cases}$$

■ ■ ■

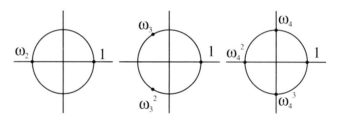

A natural next step is to define the inverse function of $\exp(z)$.

DEFINITION C.3   *The* **natural logarithm** *is the "inverse" of the complex exponential function; i.e.,*

$$z = e^w \quad \text{if and only if} \quad w = \log z \tag{C.3}$$

The notation $\log$ will be reserved for the function of a complex variable and $\ln$ will be used exclusively for the function of a real variable. With this definition, all the usual properties of the logarithm can be shown to hold.

THEOREM C.2   *For any nonzero complex z, z_1, z_2, and a:*

(L1) $\log 1 = 0$.

(L2) $\log(z_1 z_2) = \log(z_1) + \log(z_2)$.

(L3) $\log(z_1/z_2) = \log(z_1) - \log(z_2)$.

(L4) $\log(z^a) = a \log(z)$.   □

The proof is left to the reader. Even with this theorem we will have to be a bit careful. To see that this is so, write

$$z = |z|\, e^{i\arg z},$$

and take $\log$'s of both sides:

$$\log z = \ln |z| + i \arg z,$$

where $\ln$ has been used because $|z|$ is a real quantity. Thus (L2), (L3), and (L4) are to be interpreted modulo 2π. The logarithm "function" has infinitely many possible values for each z. We define the **principal value** of the logarithm by

$$\mathrm{Log}(z) := \ln |z| + i\,\mathrm{Arg}(z).$$

Once again, be careful of the distinction between upper case and lower case letters. We needn't make that distinction for $\ln |z|$ because $|z|$ is real.

■ **EXAMPLE C.4**   Evaluate each of the following logarithms.

(a) $\log(-1) = \ln 1 + i(\pi + 2n\pi) = (2n+1)\pi i$.

(b) $\mathrm{Log}(2i) = \ln 2 + i\dfrac{\pi}{2}$, $\log(2i) = \ln 2 + i\left(\dfrac{\pi}{2} + 2n\pi\right)$.

(c) $\log\left(-1 + i\sqrt{3}\right) = \ln 2 + i\left(\dfrac{2\pi}{3} + 2n\pi\right)$.

(d) $\log(1 + i) = \ln\sqrt{2} + i\left(\dfrac{\pi}{4} + 2n\pi\right) = \dfrac{1}{2}(\ln 2) + i(8n+1)\dfrac{\pi}{4}$.   ■ ■ ■

Using the log function, we can define a **generalized complex exponential** function by

$$a^b = e^{b \log a} = e^{(b_1 + ib_2)(\ln|a| + i \arg a)}$$

$$= e^{(b_1 \ln|a| - b_2 \arg a)} e^{i(b_2 \ln|a| + b_1 \arg a)} \tag{C.4}$$

$$= |a|^{b_1} e^{-b_2 \arg a} \left(\cos(b_2 \ln|a| + b_1 \arg a) + i \sin(b_2 \ln|a| + b_1 \arg a) \right).$$

■ **EXAMPLE C.5** Apply the generalized exponential function to evaluate each of the following.

(a) $i^i = \exp(i \log i) = \exp\left(i \left\{ \ln 1 + i \left(\dfrac{\pi}{2} + 2n\pi \right) \right\} \right) = e^{-(\pi/2 + 2n\pi)}$, which interestingly enough are all *real*.

(b) $(-2)^{1+i} = \exp\left((1+i) \log(-2) \right)$

$$= \exp\left((1+i)(\ln 2 + 1(\pi + 2n\pi)) \right)$$
$$= \exp\left([\ln 2 - (2n+1)\pi] + i[\ln 2 + (2n+1)\pi] \right)$$
$$= 2e^{-(2n+1)\pi} (\cos[\ln 2 + (2n+1)\pi]$$
$$+ i \sin[\ln 2 + (2n+1)\pi])$$
$$= -2e^{-(2n+1)\pi} \left(\cos(\ln 2) + \sin(\ln 2) \right).$$

(c) If $x > 0$ and a is real, then

$$x^{ia} = e^{ia \ln x} = \cos(a \ln x) + i \sin(a \ln x).$$

(d) A combination of polar and Cartesian representations of complex numbers is useful for rewriting (C.4):

$$z^{a+ib} = \left(re^{i\theta} \right)^{a+ib} = r^a e^{ib \ln r} e^{ia\theta} e^{-b\theta}$$
$$= r^a e^{-b\theta} e^{i(b \ln r + a\theta)}.$$

■ ■ ■

C.3   *Complex Trigonometric Functions*

Going back to Euler's formula, we have

$$e^{+i\theta} = \cos\theta + i \sin\theta,$$
$$e^{-i\theta} = \cos\theta - i \sin\theta.$$

We can solve simultaneously to obtain

$$\cos\theta = \frac{e^{i\theta} + e^{-i\theta}}{2}, \qquad \sin\theta = \frac{e^{i\theta} - e^{-i\theta}}{2i}. \tag{C.5}$$

These formulas allow a logical extension of cosine and sine to complex arguments by way of

$$\cos z = \frac{e^{iz} + e^{-iz}}{2}, \qquad \sin z = \frac{e^{iz} - e^{-iz}}{2i}. \tag{C.6}$$

These equations will be taken as the definitions of the cosine and sine of a complex variable. The same thing can be done for the hyperbolic functions:

$$\cosh z = \frac{e^{z} + e^{-z}}{2}, \qquad \sinh z = \frac{e^{z} - e^{-z}}{2}. \tag{C.7}$$

A comparison of (C.6) and (C.7) shows that

$$\begin{aligned} \cosh(iz) &= \cos z, & \cos(iz) &= \cosh z, \\ \sinh(iz) &= i \sin z, & \sin(iz) &= i \sinh z. \end{aligned} \tag{C.8}$$

Equations (C.8) are especially useful because they allow us to extend our trigonometric identities by the replacements $\cos\theta \to \cosh\theta$ and $\sin\theta \to i\sinh\theta$. Thus

$$\cos^2\theta + \sin^2\theta = 1 \quad \text{becomes} \quad \cosh^2\theta + (i\sinh\theta)^2 = 1,$$

or

$$\cosh^2\theta - \sinh^2\theta = 1.$$

Using the formula for the cosine of a sum of angles together with equation (C.8), we have

$$\begin{aligned} \cos z = \cos(x + iy) &= \cos x \cos(iy) - \sin x \sin(iy) \\ &= \cos x \cosh y - i \sin x \sinh y \end{aligned} \tag{C.9}$$

and

$$\sin z = \sin x \cosh y + i \cos x \sinh y. \tag{C.10}$$

C.4 *Exercise Set*

1. Find all the complex zeros and their orders for each of the following polynomials:

(a) $z^2 + (i - 1)z - i$.

(b) $z^2 + iz + 2$.

(c) $z^3 + (1 + i)z^2 + iz$.

(d) $2z^2 - 3iz + 2$.

(e) $z^3 + z^2 + 4z + 4$.

(f) $z^4 + 2z^3 - z^2 - 8z - 12$.

(g) $z^4 - 6z^3 + 13z^2 - 14z + 6$.

(h) $12z^3 - 4z^2 - 3z + 1$.

(i) $2z^5 - z^4 + 4z^3 + 2z - 1$.

(j) $8z^3 - 4z^2 - 10z - 3$.

(k) $z^6 + 3z^4 + 3z^2 + 1$.

(l) $z^3 + (1 + 3i)z^2 + (3i - 2)z - 2$.

2. If $z = x + iy = re^{i\theta}$, find the real part, imaginary part, modulus, and argument of each of the following complex numbers:

(a) z^2.

(b) e^z.

(c) $z^2 + z$.

(d) ze^z.

(e) $z \operatorname{Log}(z)$.

(f) $z \cos z$.

(g) $\dfrac{\sin z}{z}$.

(h) z^z.

(i) $\exp(z^2)$.

(j) z^i.

(k) i^z.

(l) $\dfrac{e^z}{z}$.

3. Find all the zeros and their orders for each of the following functions:

(a) $\cos^2 z$.

(b) $(z^2 - 2z)^3$.

(c) $z^3 \sin z$.

(d) $z \cot z$.

(e) $z \operatorname{Log}(z)$.

(f) $z + i\bar{z}$.

(g) $\sin z (1 - \cos z)^3$.

(h) $\exp(-iz) - \exp(i\bar{z})$.

4. Find all complex numbers a and b for which

(a) a^b is real.

(b) a^b is pure imaginary.

5. Find all values of each of the following complex numbers:

(a) 1^i.

(b) $(1 - i)^{1+i}$.

(c) 2^{-i}.

(d) i^{1+i}.

(e) $(-1 - i)^{i-1}$.

6. For what values of z does $\operatorname{Log}(iz)$ lie in the (a) third quadrant? (b) first quadrant?

7. Find all the cube roots of -1.

8. Find all the cube roots of i.

9. Find all the fourth roots of 1.

10. Find all complex solutions of the following equations:

(a) $\sin z = 0$.

(b) $\cos z = 0$.

(c) $\cos z = \sin z$.

(d) $\sin z = i$.

(e) $e^z = -i$.

(f) $\tan 2z = -1$.

11. Write each of the following in the form $a + ib$ for real a and b:

(a) $\tan(x + iy)$.

(b) $\cosh(x + iy)$.

(c) $\sinh(x + iy)$.

Appendix D

STEP FUNCTIONS AND IMPULSES

D.1 *Step Functions*

We'll start simply by looking at a not very nonstandard function.

DEFINITION D.1 *The* **unit step** *function is defined by*

$$u(x - a) := \begin{cases} 0, & x - a < 0, \\ 1, & 0 \le x - a. \end{cases} \tag{D.1}$$

The graph of the unit step at $x = a$ is quite simple and is shown in Figure D.1.

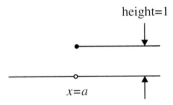

height=1

$x{=}a$

Fig. D.1

The unit step can be generalized to be valid for any real argument by defining

$$u\left(f(x)\right) := \begin{cases} 0, & f(x) < 0, \\ 1, & 0 \le f(x). \end{cases} \tag{D.2}$$

Thus $u(1 - x^2)$ will be nonzero when $0 \le 1 - x^2$ or $|x| \le 1$.

DEFINITION D.2 *We define the* **rectangular window** *from a to b by*

$$w(x; a, b) := u(x - a) - u(x - b). \tag{D.3}$$

- Think of the first step in equation (D.3) as *turning on* at $x = a$ and the second step at $x = b$ as *turning off* the first step (Figure D.2).

$a \qquad b$

Fig. D.2

Any number of steps can be written in this way. For instance, the floor of x, written $\lfloor x \rfloor$, is defined to be the largest integer less than or equal to x. In terms of the step function, we can write the formal expression

$$\lfloor x \rfloor = \sum_{n=1}^{\infty} u(x - n),$$

for nonnegative real x.

We can also construct a half wave rectified sine wave, shown in Figure D.3,

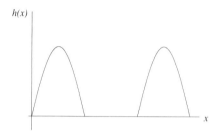

Fig. D.3

by multiplying $\sin x$ by a function that is nonzero only where the sine is nonnegative, which could be $u(\sin x)$. Thus $h(x) = (\sin x)u(\sin x)$ is one possible representation and

$$\sum_{-\infty}^{\infty} (\sin x)\, w(x; 2k\pi, (2k + 1)\pi)$$

is another.

Any function that can be casewise defined in terms of differentiable functions is said to be **piecewise differentiable**. Such a function can be written in terms of unit steps or windows as follows: If $g(x)$ and $h(x)$ are differentiable functions, then

$$f(x) = \left\{ \begin{array}{ll} g(x), & x < a \\ h(x), & a \le x \end{array} \right\} = g(x) + (h(x) - g(x))\, u(x - a) \tag{D.4}$$

will have a jump discontinuity at $x = a$ when $g(a) \ne h(a)$. The interpretation of the step function representation is as follows: $g(x)$ is *turned on* at $-\infty$, and at $x = a$ we *turn on* the difference $(h(x) - g(x))$, which has the effect of *turning off* $g(x)$ and *turning on* $h(x)$.

■ **EXAMPLE D.1** Graph the function

$$f(x) = 1 - (x + 1)u(x + 1) + \frac{1}{2}(x^2 + 2x + 2)u(x + 1) - \frac{1}{2}x^2 u(x - 1).$$

Solution: The function 1 is always turned on. When $x = -1$, we turn on $-(x+1)$ giving us a current total of $1 - (x+1) = -x$ that is turned on. Then at $x = 0$, $\frac{1}{2}(x^2 + 2x + 2)$ is turned on, giving us a total of $1 - (x+1) + \frac{1}{2}(x^2 + 2x + 2) = \frac{1}{2}(x^2 - 2)$. But at $x = 1$, the function $-\frac{1}{2}x^2$ is turned on and the running total is then $1 - (x+1) + \frac{1}{2}(x^2 + 2x + 2) - \frac{1}{2}x^2 = 1$. In tabular form this is

$$x \in (-\infty, -1] : \ f(x) = 1,$$
$$x \in [-1, 0) : \quad f(x) = 1 - (x+1) = -x,$$
$$x \in [0, 1) : \quad f(x) = 1 - (x+1) + \tfrac{1}{2}(x^2 + 2x + 2) = \tfrac{1}{2}(x^2 + 2),$$
$$x \in [1, \infty) : \quad f(x) = 1 - (x+1) + \tfrac{1}{2}(x^2 + 2x + 2) - \tfrac{1}{2}x^2 = 1.$$

The graph of $f(x)$ is drawn in Figure D.4.   ■ ■ ■

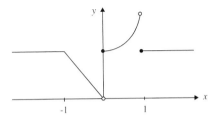

Fig. D.4

■ **EXAMPLE D.2** Suppose a function has the graph shown in Figure D.5.

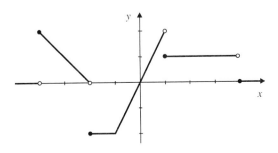

Fig. D.5

Write it in terms of windows and/or unit steps.

Solution: The function can be represented by a sum of functions times unit steps by looking at each segment and using rectangular windows. In the first nonzero segment from $x = -4$ to $x = -2$, it is a straight line from $(-4, 2)$ to $(-2, 0)$ which is $y = -x - 2$. Thus this segment is the window $w(x; -4, -2)$ times $(x + 2)$:

$$-(x + 2)w(x; -4, -2) = -(x + 2)[u(x + 4) - u(x + 2)].$$

The next segment is the constant -2 between $x = -2$ and $x = -1$, so that it is

$$-2w(x; -2, -1) = -2[u(x+2) - u(x+1)].$$

From $x = -1$ to $x = 1$ it is a line from $(0, 0)$ to $(1, 2)$, or $y = 2x$, so that this piece can be written as

$$2xw(x; -1, 1) = 2x[u(x+1) - u(x-1)].$$

Then it becomes constant at $y = 1$ from $x = 1$ to $x = 4$, so that

$$w(x; 1, 4) = u(x-1) - u(x-4)$$

is the appropriate piece. The complete function is

$$
\begin{aligned}
f(x) \;&= -(x+2)w(x; -4, -2) - 2w(x; -2, -1) + 2xw(-1, 1) + w(1, 4) \\
&= [u(x+4) - u(x+2)] - 2[u(x+2) - u(x+1)] \\
&\quad +2x[u(x+1) - u(x-1)] + [u(x-1) - u(x-4)]
\end{aligned}
$$

$$
\begin{aligned}
\Rightarrow f(x) \;= \;&-(x+2)u(x+4) + xu(x+2) + 2(x+1)u(x+1) \\
&+(1 - 2x)u(x-1) - u(x-4).
\end{aligned}
$$

■ ■ ■

All of the piecewise differentiable functions we looked at did include the left endpoint at the jump but did *not* include the right endpoint. What if the situation is reversed? All we need do is use steps that run from right to left instead of left to right. The function $u(1 - x)$ is turned on for $0 \leq 1 - x$ or $x \leq 1$. Thus a window that would include right but not left endpoints between a and $b \ (> a)$ is

$$u(b - x) - u(a - x).$$

D.2 *Generalized Functions*

In many applications of models to real world problems we need to use "functions" with certain pathologies which are not characteristic of our usual set of smooth functions. Nevertheless, these generalized functions, or hyperfunctions, have many properties in common with the more standard functions with which we deal. We will look at only a few of these generalized functions, the impulse function and its derivatives.

Although the unit step $u(x - a)$ is a discontinuous function at $x = a$, it can be considered to be the limit of a sequence of everywhere differentiable real functions. There are several possibilities. One such is

$$\phi_n(x; a) = \frac{1}{2} + \frac{1}{\pi} \operatorname{Atan}\left(n(x - a)\right). \tag{D.5}$$

To see that this is so, think of the range of the Atan function, which is the interval $(-\pi/2, \pi/2)$. As n increases, the argument of the Atan increases in magnitude and the function values get closer to $\pm\pi/2$, depending on whether x is positive or negative. The factor of $1/\pi$ and the added $1/2$ adjust the function to the proper values away from $x = a$. The graphs of some of the functions are sketched in Figure D.6.

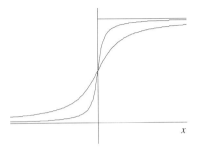

Fig. D.6   The unit step function is a limit of smooth functions.

Not only is each member of the sequence $\phi_n(x; a)$ continuous, but they are also infinitely differentiable for all real x. A reasonable question is, to what do the derivatives converge? The derivative of $u(x - a)$ is surely *not* defined at $x = a$. If we were to attempt to compute it, we would find it to be infinite because there is a finite change in the function at a single point. The associated first derivative sequence $\phi'_n(x; a)$ is

$$\phi'_n(x; a) = \frac{n}{\pi\left(1 + n^2(x - a)^2\right)}. \tag{D.6}$$

As n increases, $\phi'_n(x; a)$ goes to zero when $x \neq a$. But when $x = a$, the sequence grows without bound as $n \to \infty$. Interestingly enough, since this is the derivative of a well-defined function we know that its integral is finite. In fact, the value of the integral is 1.

Define the **Dirac delta function**, or **impulse**, at $x = a$ to be limit of $\phi'_n(x; a)$ as $n \to \infty$, that is,

$$\delta(x - a) = \lim_{n \to \infty} \frac{n}{\pi\left(1 + n^2(x - a)^2\right)}. \tag{D.7}$$

Strictly formally we can express $\delta(x - a)$ as the "derivative" of the standard unit step function $u(x - a)$, i.e.,

$$\delta(x - a) = \frac{d}{dx}u(x - a). \tag{D.8}$$

Even though the unit step is not continuous at $x = a$, the idea of the "derivative" can be made rigorous by extending many of our usual ideas, but that will not be done here.

Several properties of the Dirac delta function can be "derived" using this derivative formalism. Consider

$$\int_{-\infty}^{\infty} f(x)\delta(x - a)\,dx$$

where $f(x)$ is any reasonably smooth function that goes to zero at infinity sufficiently fast to allow its absolute integral $\int |f(x)|\,dx$ to exist. Replace $\delta(x - a)$ by the derivative of $u(x - a)$

and formally perform an integration by parts.

$$\int_{-\infty}^{\infty} f(x) \frac{d}{dx} u(x-a)\, dx = f(x)u(x-a)|_{-\infty}^{\infty} - \int_{-\infty}^{\infty} f'(x)u(x-a)\, dx$$

$$= -\int_{a}^{\infty} f'(x)\, dx = f(x)u(x-a)|_{a}^{\infty} = f(a).$$

Therefore we are left with the unusual formula

$$\int_{-\infty}^{\infty} f(x)\delta(x-a)\, dx = f(a). \tag{D.9}$$

The function $\delta(x-a)$ acts like a *spike* that punches out the value of $f(x)$ at the point $x = a$ where $\delta(x-a)$ is unbounded. If we use $f(x) = 1$, then we get the integral formula

$$\int_{-\infty}^{\infty} \delta(x-a)\, dx = \int_{a-\epsilon}^{a+\epsilon} \delta(x-a)\, dx = 1$$

for any $\epsilon > 0$. The range of integration can be reduced from the whole real line $(-\infty, \infty)$ to $(a - \epsilon, a + \epsilon)$ because $\delta(x-a)$ is zero away from $x = a$. The previous result of equation (D.9) holds over the reduced range of integration as well. Other results will be left to the problems.

The sequence $\phi_n(x; a)$ can be differentiated any number of times, and so it may be reasonable to differentiate $\delta(x - a)$ as many times as we want. We call $\delta(x - a)$ a **generalized function**, or **hyperfunction** (since it is not a function in the usual sense), which can be used to represent the hypothetical point mass and point charges of theoretical physics. Its derivative $\delta'(x - a)$ can be used to represent a "*dipole*." A similar integration by parts argument can be used to show that

$$\int_{-\infty}^{\infty} f(x)\delta'(x-a)\, dx = \int_{a-\epsilon}^{a+\epsilon} f(x)\delta'(x-a)\, dx = -f'(a). \tag{D.10}$$

Because the delta function is unbounded, many authors prefer to think of all equations involving it as being meaningful only when integrated. This avoids the difficulties associated with the limit of the derivative of the sequence $\{\phi_n(x; a)\}$. Since we are doing things purely formally, such niceties can be dispensed with.

The set of all points where a function or generalized function is nonzero is called its **support**. The support of $u(x - a)$ is the interval $[a, \infty)$ and that of $\delta(x - a)$ is the single point $\{a\}$. The set of all points where a generalized function (which is not an ordinary function) is not defined is called its **singular support**. The unit step $u(x - a)$ has no singular support, but the Dirac delta function $\delta(x - a)$ has the single point $\{a\}$ as its singular support.

It can be shown that any generalized function whose singular support is the single point $x = a$ is a finite linear combination of the delta function and its derivatives, i.e.,

$$\sum_{k=1}^{m} a_k \delta^{(k)}(x - a).$$

D.3   *Exercise Set*

1. Sketch the graph of each of the following:

   (a) $a(x) = xu(1 - x) - u(x - 1)$.

   (b) $b(x) = xu(x + 1) + u(x - 1) - 2u(x - 3)$.

   (c) $c(x) = u(\sin x)$.

   (d) $d(x) = (\sin x)u(\sin x)$.

   (e) $e(x) = \ln(x - 1)u(\ln(x - 1))$.

   (f) $f(x) = u(x + 1)u(x - 1)u(2 - x)$.

   (g) $g(x) = x[u(x + 4) - u(x + 3)] - x^2[u(x + 3) - u(x + 1)] - u(x - 2)$.

   (h) $h(x) = e^x u(x + 2) - 2\cosh(x + 2)u(x + 1)$.

   (i) $i(x) = u(x - a)u(b - x) - u(x - a) + u(x - b)$, $a < b$.

2. Write each of the following as a sum of functions times unit steps (all functions are to be understood to be zero other than where they are defined to be nonzero):

   (a) $a(x) = \begin{cases} \sin x, & x < 0, \\ \cos x, & x \geq 0. \end{cases}$

   (b) $b(x) = \begin{cases} x - 1, & x < 0, \\ 1 - x, & x \geq 0. \end{cases}$

   (c) $c(x) = \begin{cases} 3x + 1, & x < -2, \\ x + 12, & -2 \leq x < 1, \\ 2x - 3, & 1 \leq x < 12. \end{cases}$

   (d) $d(x) = \begin{cases} 1 - e^x, & x < 2, \\ e^x + 1, & 2 \leq x < 5, \\ e^{-x} - 1, & 5 \leq x < 6. \end{cases}$

   (e) $e(x) = \begin{cases} 5, & x < -3, \\ 4, & -3 \leq x < 2, \\ 1, & 2 \leq x < 6. \end{cases}$

   (f) $f(x) = \begin{cases} 5, & x \leq -3, \\ 4, & -3 < x \leq 2, \quad \text{Be careful!} \\ 1, & 2 < x \leq 6. \end{cases}$

3. Use the interpretation of the Dirac delta function as the derivative of the unit step within an integration to "prove" the following identities:

(a) $(\delta(g(x)))' = g'(x)\delta'(g(x))$.

(b) $\dfrac{d^2}{dx^2}|x| = 2\delta(x)$.

(c) $\delta(ax + b) = \dfrac{1}{a}\delta\left(x + \dfrac{b}{a}\right)$.

4. Convince yourself of the "validity" of the following limits by showing that the integral of each function in the sequence is 1 and the support of the limit is $\{a\}$:

(a) $\delta(x - a) = \lim\limits_{n\to\infty} \dfrac{n}{\sqrt{\pi}} \exp\left(-n^2(x - a)^2\right)$.

(b) $\delta(x - a) = \lim\limits_{n\to\infty} \dfrac{\sin n(x - a)}{\pi(x - a)}$.

5. If $t, x \in [a, b]$, show that

$$\int_a^b u(s - t)\left(u(x - s) - \frac{x - a}{b - a}\right) ds = \frac{1}{b - a}\left\{ \begin{array}{l} (x - a)(t - b), \;\; x \le t, \\ (t - a)(x - b), \;\; t < x. \end{array}\right.$$

Appendix E

PARTIAL FRACTION EXPANSIONS

Many applications, from integration to inversion of integral transforms, require a detailed analysis of **rational functions**. These are functions of the form

$$f(z) = \frac{N(z)}{D(z)},$$

(E.1)

where $N(z)$ and $D(z)$ are polynomials with no common factors. Additionally, we'll assume $\deg N < \deg D$. If not, we could divide and look at the remainder. By the Fundamental Theorem of Algebra, the denominator can be factored as

$$D(z) = d_n (z - z_1)^{m_1} (z - z_2)^{m_2} \cdots (z - z_k)^{m_k}.$$

(E.2)

We are then guaranteed that we can express $f(z)$ in the fractional form

$$f(z) = \sum_{j=1}^{k} \sum_{n=1}^{m_j} \frac{A_{jn}}{(z - z_j)^n}. \tag{E.3}$$

Although we know that $D(z)$ can always be factored in the form of (E.2), often, it may be more convenient, especially when $D(z)$ has real coefficients, to combine complex conjugate zeros of $D(z)$ into factors like $\left(az^2 + bz + c\right)^k$.

Because there are many possibilities we'll begin with the simplest case.

Case 1: $D(z) = (z - z_1)(z - z_2) \cdots (z - z_n)$, with all z_j distinct. This corresponds to $f(z)$ having only simple poles at $z_1, z_2, \ldots, z_n$. Equation (E.3) takes the far simpler form

$$f(z) = \sum_{j=1}^{n} \frac{A_j}{z - z_j} = \frac{A_1}{z - z_1} + \frac{A_2}{z - z_2} + \cdots + \frac{A_n}{z - z_n}. \tag{E.4}$$

The easiest way to find the values of the A_j's is to multiply both sides of (E.4) by $(z - z_k)$ for some k. Then

$$(z - z_k) f(z) = \sum_{j=1}^{n} A_j \left(\frac{z - z_k}{z - z_j} \right) = A_k + \sum_{\substack{j=1 \\ j \neq k}}^{n} A_j \left(\frac{z - z_k}{z - z_j} \right).$$

The left hand side is indeterminate at $z = z_k$ because of the factor $(z - z_k)$ in both the numerator and denominator, but this is a removable singularity. When $z = z_k$, every term in the rightmost sum is zero, so that

$$A_k = \lim_{z \to z_k} (z - z_k) f(z). \tag{E.5}$$

Equation (E.5) is called the **first Heaviside formula**.

■ **EXAMPLE E.1** Let's go through the entire procedure leading up to (E.5) for

$$\frac{z^2 + z + 1}{z(z + 1)(z - 2)} = \frac{A_1}{z} + \frac{A_2}{z + 1} + \frac{A_3}{z - 2}. \tag{a}$$

To compute A_1, multiply both sides by z:

$$\frac{z^2 + z + 1}{(z + 1)(z - 2)} = A_1 + \frac{A_2 z}{z + 1} + \frac{A_3 z}{z - 2}. \tag{b}$$

Now set $z = 0$ in this equation:

$$\frac{0^2 + 0 + 1}{(0 + 1)(0 - 2)} = A_1 + 0 + 0 \quad \Rightarrow \quad A_1 = -\frac{1}{2}.$$

Here's an easier way to think about the process applied to A_2: Look at the A_2 term in (a). What value of z makes the denominator vanish? $z = -1$. On the left hand side of (a), cover up the factor $(z + 1)$ from the denominator of $f(z)$ (denoted by writing the term undermarked by a two-sided arrow), and then substitute $z = -1$ into the unmarked factors to get the value of A_2:

$$\left. \frac{z^2 + z + 1}{z\underleftrightarrow{(z + 1)}(z - 2)} \right|_{z=-1} = \frac{(-1)^2 + (-1) + 1}{(-1) \cdot (-1 - 2)} = \frac{1}{3} = A_2.$$

To solve for A_3, read off $z = 2$ as the value that makes the denominator of $f(z)$ vanish. Undermark the factor $(z - 2)$ and substitute $z = 2$ into the unmarked factors:

$$\left. \frac{z^2 + z + 1}{z(z + 1)\underleftrightarrow{(z - 2)}} \right|_{z=2} = \frac{2^2 + 2 + 1}{2(2 + 1)\cdot} = \frac{7}{6} = A_3.$$

■ ■ ■

The method described by (E.5) and the minor variant of example E.1 remain unchanged no matter how many factors are in the denominator, whether the z_k's are real or complex.

■ **EXAMPLE E.2** Even problems with complex factors can be handled this way.

$$\frac{2z^2 - z + 5}{(z^2 - 4)(z^2 + 4)} = \frac{2z^2 - z + 5}{(z + 2)(z - 2)(z + 2i)(z - 2i)}$$
$$= \frac{A_1}{z + 2} + \frac{A_2}{z - 2} + \frac{A_3}{z + 2i} + \frac{A_4}{z - 2i};$$

$$A_1 = \frac{2(-2)^2 - (-2) + 5}{\underleftrightarrow{(z + 2)}(-2 - 2)(-2 + 2i)(-2 - 2i)} = -\frac{15}{32},$$

$$A_2 = \frac{2 \cdot 2^2 - 2 + 5}{(2 + 2)\underleftrightarrow{(z - 2)}(2 + 2i)(2 - 2i)} = \frac{11}{32},$$

$$A_3 = \frac{2(-2i)^2 - (-2i) + 5}{(-2i + 2)(-2i - 2)\underleftrightarrow{(z + 2i)}(-2i - 2i)} = \frac{-3 + 2i}{32i} = \frac{2 + 3i}{32},$$

$$A_4 = \frac{2(2i)^2 - (2i) + 5}{(2i + 2)(2i - 2)(2i + 2i)\underleftrightarrow{(z - 2i)}} = \frac{-3 - 2i}{-32i} = \frac{2 - 3i}{32}.$$

We should have expected $A_3 = \bar{A}_4$ because $f(z)$ has real coefficients, and so any complex zeros of its denominator must occur in conjugate pairs. Using this fact would have saved us some arithmetic.

■ ■ ■

Case 2: Multiple roots:

$$D(z) = d_n (z - z_1)^{m_1} (z - z_2)^{m_2} \cdots (z - z_k)^{m_k}$$

with all the z_j's distinct. Once again, the power m_j is called the multiplicity of the zero z_j. Start with the simplest possibility, one repeated root.

(a) $D(z) = (z - z_1)^m$. Then the decomposition is

$$f(z) = \frac{A_1}{z - z_1} + \frac{A_2}{(z - z_2)^2} + \cdots + \frac{A_m}{(z - z_1)^m}. \qquad (E.6)$$

Multiply through by $(z - z_1)^m$:

$$(z - z_1)^m f(z) = A_m + A_{m-1}(z - z_1) + \cdots + A_2(z - z_1)^{m-2} + A_1(z - z_1)^{m-1}.$$

The left hand side $(z - z_1)^m f(z) = N(z)$ now has no singularities, and so it can be expanded in a Taylor series about $z = z_1$. Then

$$A_m \quad = N(z_1),$$

$$A_{m-1} \quad = \frac{1}{1!} \frac{d}{dz} N(z)|_{z=z_1},$$

$$A_{m-2} \quad = \frac{1}{2!} \left(\frac{d}{dz} \right)^2 N(z)|_{z=z_1},$$

$$\vdots \qquad \vdots$$

$$A_1 \quad = \frac{1}{(m-1)!} \left(\frac{d}{dz} \right)^{m-1} N(z)|_{z=z_1}.$$

(b) For the general case,

$$f(z) = \sum_{j=1}^{k} \sum_{k=1}^{m_j} \frac{A_{jk}}{(z - z_j)^k},$$

and we have the result

$$A_{jk} = \frac{1}{(m_j - k)!} \left(\frac{d}{dz} \right)^{m_j - k} [(z - z_j)^{m_j} f(z)]_{z=z_j}, \quad k = 1 : m_j, \ j = 1 : k. \qquad (E.7)$$

Equation (E.7) is called the **second Heaviside formula**. Needless to say, differentiating a large and involved quotient is no bowl of cherries, even when using logarithmic differentiation. Mercifully, computer algebra systems will do all of this for us.

■ **EXAMPLE E.3** Use the second Heaviside formula to evaluate the coefficients in the expansion

$$f(z) = \frac{2z^2 + 3}{z^3(z + 1)} = \frac{A_1}{z} + \frac{A_2}{z^2} + \frac{A_3}{z^3} + \frac{A_4}{z + 1}.$$

Solution: We can use the first Heaviside formula to compute A_4 directly. The value $z = -1$ makes the denominator vanish, so that

$$A_4 = \frac{2(-1)^2 + 3}{(-1)^3 \underleftrightarrow{(z+1)}} = -5.$$

To compute A_1, A_2, and A_3 we'll be forced to use $z^3 f(z)$:

$$A_3 = z^3 f(z)\big|_{z=0} = \frac{2z^2 + 3}{z+1}\bigg|_{z=0} = 3,$$

$$A_2 = \frac{1}{1!}\frac{d}{dz}\left(\frac{2z^2 + 3}{z+1}\right)_{z=0} = \left(\frac{2z^2 + 4z - 3}{(z+1)^2}\right)_{z=0} = -3,$$

$$A_1 = \frac{1}{2!}\frac{d^2}{dz^2}\left(\frac{2z^2 + 3}{z+1}\right)_{z=0} = 5.$$

■ ■ ■

If we want to combine complex conjugate zeros into quadratic terms, then we could factor $D(z)$ as

$$D(z) = d_n\,(z - z_1)^{m_1}\,(z - z_2)^{m_2}\cdots(z - z_\ell)^{m_\ell}\,\times$$
$$\left[(z - a_1)^2 + b_1^2\right]^{n_1}\cdots\left[(z - a_r)^2 + b_r^2\right]^{n_r}$$

where $z_1, z_2, \ldots, z_\ell, a_1, \ldots, a_r, b_1, \ldots, b_r$ are all real. The expansion would take the form

$$f(z) = \sum_{j=1}^{\ell}\sum_{k=1}^{m_j}\frac{A_{jk}}{(z - z_j)^k} + \sum_{j=1}^{r}\sum_{k=1}^{n_j}\frac{B_{jk}z + C_{jk}}{\left[(z - a_j)^2 + b_j^2\right]^k}. \tag{E.8}$$

The A_{jk} can be calculated by the previous methods, but the B_{jk} and C_{jk} cannot. To find them, put everything over a common denominator and equate like powers of z in the resulting numerator. This will result in $2(n_1 + n_2 + \ldots + n_r)$ simultaneous linear equations in as many unknowns to be solved for the B's and C's. Some saving can be effected by setting $z = a_k$ for each k to obtain simpler equations. Nevertheless, the amount of labor (and the usual accompanying errors) can be quite large. One alternative is to stick with the original form (E.2) and use the previous method. Even better, use the computer.

■ **EXAMPLE E.4** Redo the example with complex factors by using the above quadratic expansion of equation (E.8).

Solution: A_1 and A_2 remain unchanged from before;

$$\frac{2z^2 - z + 5}{(z + 2)(z - 2)(z^2 + 4)} = \frac{A_1}{z + 2} + \frac{A_2}{z - 2} + \frac{Bz + C}{z^2 + 4},$$

and they are still $-15/32$ and $11/32$, respectively. Rather than cross-multiplying, set $z = 0$ to get

$$-\frac{5}{16} = -\frac{15}{64} - \frac{11}{64} + \frac{C}{4} \quad \Rightarrow \quad C = \frac{12}{32} = \frac{3}{8}.$$

Now multiply both sides by z and take the limit as $z \to \infty$,

$$0 = -\frac{15}{32} + \frac{11}{32} + B \quad \Rightarrow \quad B = \frac{4}{32} = \frac{1}{8}.$$

Had we formed $A_3(z - 2i) + A_4(z + 2i)$ from example E.2 we would have obtained the numerator of $(z + 3)/8$ also. ∎ ∎ ∎

E.1 Exercise Set

1. Write each of the following rational functions in terms of its partial fraction decomposition:

(a) $\dfrac{2z^2 - 3}{z(z - 1)(z + 2)}$.

(b) $\dfrac{z^2}{(z + 4)(z + 3)(z - 2)(z - 5)}$.

(c) $\dfrac{12}{z^2(z + 1)^2}$.

(d) $\dfrac{z^3 - 6z^2 + 6}{(z^2 + 1)(z^2 - 3z + 2)}$.

(e) $\dfrac{z^4 + z^2 - 12z + 1}{(z^2 - 1)(z^2 - 4)(z^2 - 9)}$.

(f) $\dfrac{z^4 + z^2 - 12z + 1}{(z^2 + 1)(z^2 + 4)(z^2 + 9)}$.

(g) $\dfrac{1}{z(z^2 + 1)}$.

(h) $\dfrac{1}{z^2(z^2 + 1)}$.

2. Use partial fraction expansions to verify the values of the following series:

(a) $\displaystyle\sum_{0}^{\infty} \frac{1}{(2n + 1)(2n + 3)} = \frac{1}{2}$. (b) $\displaystyle\sum_{1}^{\infty} \frac{1}{n(n + 1)(n + 2)} = \frac{1}{4}$.

3. Use partial fractions to evaluate each of the following integrals.

(a) $\displaystyle\int \frac{2z - 5}{z(z+1)(z+4)}\, dz.$

(b) $\displaystyle\int \frac{1}{z^4 - 1}\, dz.$

(c) $\displaystyle\int \frac{z^2 + z + 1}{(z^2 + 1)^2}\, dz.$

(d) $\displaystyle\int \frac{dz}{(z-2)(z-1)(z+3)}.$

Appendix F

INFINITE SERIES

F.1 Convergence

We will begin with a brief discussion of **sequences** of complex functions, denoted by $\{S_n(z)\}$.

■ **EXAMPLE F.1** Each of the following are sequences of complex functions:

$$\{z^n\} = \{z, z^2, z^3, \ldots\}, \quad \{e^{nz}\} = \{e^z, e^{2z}, e^{3z}, \ldots\},$$

$$\{\sin n\pi z\} = \{\sin \pi z, \sin 2\pi z, \sin 3\pi z, \ldots\},$$

$$\left\{\frac{z}{n}\right\} = \left\{z, \frac{z}{2}, \frac{z}{3}, \ldots\right\}, \quad \left\{\frac{z^n}{n}\right\} = \left\{z, \frac{z^2}{2}, \frac{z^3}{3}, \ldots\right\}$$

$$\left\{z + \frac{z^2}{2!} + \frac{z^3}{3!} + \cdots + \frac{z^n}{n!}\right\} = \left\{z, z + \frac{z^2}{2}, z + \frac{z^2}{2} + \frac{z^3}{6}, \ldots\right\}.$$

■ ■ ■

DEFINITION F.1 *We say the sequence $S_n(z)$ **converges** to the function $S(z)$, written $S_n(z) \to S(z)$, for z in $\mathcal{D}$ if for any $\epsilon > 0$ and any z in $\mathcal{D}$ there is a positive integer $N = N(\epsilon, z)$ such that*

$$\text{if } n \geq N \text{ then } |S_n(z) - S(z)| \leq \epsilon \quad \text{for } z \text{ in } \mathcal{D}.$$

*We have **uniform convergence** if the positive integer $N = N(\epsilon)$, i.e., it does not depend on the value of z in $\mathcal{D}$ whenever $\mathcal{D}$ consists of more than one point. We'll speak of uniform convergence on a set of points $\mathcal{D}$.*

It is called uniform convergence because the approximate distance from $S_n(z)$ to $S(z)$ does not depend on z, but rather is the same or "uniform" on $\mathcal{D}$. Were we to graph the limiting function $S(z)$ then an ϵ-width band about $S(z)$ would contain $S_n(z)$ for n large enough. In the case of nonuniform convergence, this band need *not* cover $S_n(z)$ for *all* points z.

The following theorem relates convergence of a sequence to the convergence of its real and imaginary parts.

THEOREM F.1 $S_n(z) \rightarrow S(z)$ *on* $\mathcal{D}$, *if and only if* $\mathrm{Re}\,(S_n(z)) \rightarrow \mathrm{Re}\,(S(z))$ *and* $\mathrm{Im}\,(S_n(z)) \rightarrow \mathrm{Im}\,(S(z))$ *on* $\mathcal{D}$. *Furthermore, if the convergence of* $S_n(z)$ *is uniform, so is the convergence of* $\mathrm{Re}\,(S_n(z))$ *and* $\mathrm{Im}\,(S_n(z))$. $\qquad\square$

Proof   To show that convergence of $S_n(z)$ implies convergence of the real and imaginary parts, all we need are the following inequalities:

$$|\mathrm{Re}[S_n(z) - S(z)]| = |\mathrm{Re}(S_n(z)) - \mathrm{Re}(S(z))| \leq |S_n(z) - S(z)|,$$

$$|\mathrm{Im}[S_n(z) - S(z)]| = |\mathrm{Im}(S_n(z)) - \mathrm{Im}(S(z))| \leq |S_n(z) - S(z)|,$$

which hold by virtue of (Mod4) in of Theorem B.5. The choice of N that suffices for $S_n(z)$ will surely do the trick for both its real and imaginary parts. To go the other way, we can use

$$|S_n(z) - S(z)| \leq |\mathrm{Re}(S_n(z) - S(z))| + |\mathrm{Im}(S_n(z) - S(z))|.$$

$\qquad\square$

■ **EXAMPLE F.2**   If $S_n(z) = \frac{z}{n}$, then we expect $S_n(z) \rightarrow 0$ for any finite z. In fact

$$|S_n(z) - S(z)| = \left|\frac{z}{n} - 0\right| = \frac{|z|}{n} \leq \epsilon$$

whenever $n \geq N$, which is the smallest integer greater than or equal to $|z|/\epsilon$. Since N depends on z, we cannot infer the convergence is uniform. If we restrict our attention to the disc $|z| < R$ for a fixed $R > 0$, then we can choose N to be the smallest integer greater than or equal to R/ϵ, which does not depend on z. Thus $S_n(z)$ converges to zero uniformly in $|z| < R$, but the convergence is not uniform everywhere in the finite complex plane. ■ ■ ■

Our main concern will be infinite series of the form

$$\sum_{n=1}^{\infty} t_n(z)$$

where the notation $t_n(z)$ is used for the nth term of the series.

DEFINITION F.2 *The Nth **partial sum**, $S_N(z)$, of the infinite series is*

$$S_N(z) := \sum_{n=1}^{N} t_n(z).$$

*The infinite series $\sum t_n(z)$ is said to **converge** on $\mathcal{D}$ if the sequence of partial sums $\{S_N(z)\}$ converges on $\mathcal{D}$. The value of the series is then defined as*

$$\sum_{n=1}^{\infty} t_n(z) := \lim_{N \to \infty} S_N(z).$$

*The series **converges uniformly** if the sequence of partial sums converges uniformly. A series is said to **converge absolutely** if $\sum |t_n(z)|$ converges.*

One of the most frequently encountered series is the **geometric series** defined by

$$\sum_{n=0}^{\infty} z^n.$$

Its Nth partial sum is

$$\begin{aligned} S_N(z) &= 1 + z + z^2 + \cdots + z^N = 1 + z \left(1 + z + z^2 + \cdots + z^{N-1} \right) \\ &= 1 + z S_{N-1}(z). \end{aligned}$$

We also have

$$S_N(z) = S_{N-1}(z) + z^N$$

so that

$$S_N(z) = 1 + z \left(S_N(z) - z^N \right).$$

Solving for $S_N(z)$, we find

$$S_N(z) = \frac{1 - z^{N+1}}{1 - z}. \tag{F.1}$$

Equation (F.1) tells us that $S_N(z)$ will converge only for $|z| < 1$, and then

$$\sum_{n=0}^{\infty} z^n = \lim_{N \to \infty} S_N(z) = \lim_{N \to \infty} \left(\frac{1 - z^{N+1}}{1 - z} \right) = \frac{1}{1 - z} \text{ for } |z| < 1. \tag{F.2}$$

For $|z| > 1$ the geometric series *diverges*. The convergence is uniform within the unit circle (which is shorthand for saying the convergence is uniform on any closed bounded set contained within the unit circle).

There is a useful theorem telling how to determine if an infinite series is uniformly convergent, the result is called the **Weierstrass M-Test**.

THEOREM F.2 *If* $|t_n(z)| \leq M_n$ *on a region* $\mathcal{D}$*, where the* M_n *are constants and the series* $\sum M_n < \infty$*, then* $\sum t_n(z)$ *converges uniformly on* $\mathcal{D}$. □

We also have our old friend the **Ratio Test**:

THEOREM F.3 *If the* $t_n(z)$ *are bounded functions in* $\mathcal{D}$ *and*

$$\lim_{n \to \infty} \left| \frac{t_{n+1}(z)}{t_n(z)} \right| = \rho < 1$$

with ρ *constant, then the infinite series* $\sum t_n(z)$ *converges absolutely.* □

■ **EXAMPLE F.3** Test the convergence on $|z| < 1$ of the series

$$\sum_{n=1}^{\infty} \frac{z^n}{n^2}.$$

Solution: Start with

$$|t_n(z)| = \frac{|z|^n}{n^2} \leq \frac{1}{n^2} = M_n.$$

We know that $\sum M_n = \sum \frac{1}{n^2}$ converges by the Integral Test, which says that $\sum_1^{\infty} t_n$ converges if and only if the integral $\int_1^{\infty} t(n) \, dn$ converges, and so we may conclude that $\sum \frac{z^n}{n^2}$ converges uniformly in $|z| < 1$. If we try the Ratio Test

$$\lim_{n \to \infty} \left| \frac{t_{n+1}(z)}{t_n(z)} \right| = |z| \lim_{n \to \infty} \left(\frac{n}{n+1} \right)^2 = |z| < 1.$$

Thus the Ratio Test assures us the convergence is absolute on $|z| < 1$. ■ ■ ■

■ **EXAMPLE F.4** Test the convergence of the series

$$\sum_{n=0}^{\infty} (-1)^n \frac{(z/2)^{2n}}{(n!)^2}.$$

Solution: Applying the Ratio Test, we find

$$\left| \frac{t_{n+1}(z)}{t_n(z)} \right| = \left| \frac{(z/2)^{2n+2} / ((n+1)!)^2}{(z/2)^{2n} / (n!)^2} \right| = \frac{|z/2|^2}{(n+1)^2}$$

and

$$\lim_{n \to \infty} \left| \frac{t_{n+1}(z)}{t_n(z)} \right| = \frac{|z|^2}{4} \lim_{n \to \infty} \frac{1}{(n+1)^2} = 0,$$

for all finite z. Thus the series converges absolutely for all finite z.   ■ ■ ■

Another option available besides the ratio test is the **root test**, wherein we define $\rho = \lim |t_n(z)|^{1/n}$.

THEOREM F.4 *If the $t_n(z)$ are bounded functions in a region $\mathcal{D}$ and we have $\lim |t_n(z)|^{1/n} = \rho < 1$, then $\sum t_n(z)$ converges absolutely.*   □

Both the Ratio and Root Tests give the same conclusion for any series where they both give a conclusion. Generally, when $\rho < 1$ there is convergence, $\rho > 1$ divergence, and for $\rho = 1$ no conclusion may be drawn.

F.2   Rate of Convergence of a Series

Actual numerical summation of a convergent series can be an especially tedious process. Not only do some series converge slowly, but the most notable divergent series, the **harmonic series**, $\sum \frac{1}{n}$, diverges *very slowly*. Define H_N to be the Nth partial sum of this series:

$$H_N := \sum_{n=1}^{N} \frac{1}{n}.$$

Just to give you an idea of how slowly it diverges, the following table lists the number of terms (computed using exact arithmetic) needed to exceed particular values and the amount of computer time needed to compute the partial sum at 0.1 nanosecond per term (this is as fast as the fastest super-computers presently available, 8/94).

$H_N \geq$	N	Computer Time
3	11	1.1 nanosecond
4	31	3.1 nanosecond
5	83	8.3 nanosecond
6	227	22.7 nanosecond
10	12367	0.0012 millisecond
20	2.72×10^8	27.2 millisecond
100	1.5×10^{43}	4.756×10^{26} years
1000	1.1×10^{434}	3.49×10^{416} years

This is highly edifying in light of the fact that the age of the universe (not just the earth, but the *whole universe!*) is estimated to be 10^{10} years.

If we attempt to estimate the value of a convergent series like $\sum \frac{1}{n^2}$ using a microcomputer for evaluating the partial sums of the first N terms, we achieve the following results:

N	S_N
1,000	1.64394 56610
4,000	1.64468 40975
8,000	1.64480 90740
12,000	1.64485 07364
16,000	1.64487 15682
20,000	1.64488 40675
24,000	1.64489 24004
28,000	1.64489 83526
32,000	1.64490 28167

By the other methods, it can be shown that

$$\sum_{n=1}^{\infty} \frac{1}{n^2} = \frac{\pi^2}{6} = 1.64493\ 40668\ldots\ .$$

The accuracy afforded by summing 32,000 terms is not even sufficient for single precision arithmetic.

For comparison, below are several series and the number of terms needed to attain the specified decimal place accuracy in approximating their exact value.

Accuracy	$\sum \frac{1}{n^2}$	$\sum \frac{1}{n!}$	$\sum (.9)^n$	$\sum (.1)^n$
2 decimals	200	5	7	1
10 decimals	2×10^{10}	13	15	3
100 decimals	2×10^{100}	70	46	10
1000 decimals	2×10^{1000}	450	147	31

For further discussion of this and related results, you should read the excellent expository article by R.P. Boas - Partial Sums of Infinite Series, and How They Grow, which appeared in the **American Mathematical Monthly 84**, p.237–258.

It is convenient to talk about the rate of convergence of a sequence or series. Certain sequences grow at the same rate, and others grow at different rates.

DEFINITION F.3 *The sequence a_n is said to be* **big-O** *of b_n, written $a_n = O(b_n)$, if there is a positive constant M such that*

$$|a_n| \leq M\,|b_n|\,.$$

The sequence a_n is said to be **little-o** *of c_n, written $a_n = o(c_n)$, if*

$$\lim_{n \to \infty} \left| \frac{a_n}{c_n} \right| = 0.$$

If $a_n = O(b_n)$, then the elements of the two sequences are about the same size, whereas $a_n = o(c_n)$ means that a_n does not grow as fast as c_n.

■ **EXAMPLE F.5** Each of the following can be verified by taking appropriate limits. $n = O(2n + 5)$, $1/n\ln(n) = o(1/n)$, $n^2 = O(n^2 + pn + q)$, $n^2 = o(n^3)$, $n^2 = O(n(n + 1))$, $1/n^2 = O(1/(n^2 + 1))$. ■ ■ ■

F.3 *Power Series*

DEFINITION F.4 *Any series of the form*

$$\sum_{n=0}^{\infty} a_n \, (z - z_0)^n \, ,$$

*where a_n is a sequence of complex numbers, is said to be a **power series** about $z = z_0$. Any function that can be expanded in a power series that converges in a neighborhood of z_0 is said to be **analytic** at z_0.*

Suppose $f(z)$ is analytic at z_0; then

$$f(z) = \sum_{n=0}^{\infty} f_n \, (z - z_0)^n = f_0 + f_1 \, (z - z_0) + f_2 \, (z - z_0)^2 + \cdots . \qquad \text{(F.3)}$$

Setting $z = z_0$, we find

$$f(z_0) = f_0.$$

Differentiating (F.3), which we assume is valid, and setting $z = z_0$ yields

$$f'(z_0) = f_1.$$

Continuing in this way, we have

$$f^{(n)}(z_0) = n! \, f_n.$$

Thus we have "derived" Taylor's theorem.

THEOREM F.5 (Taylor's Theorem) *If $f(z)$ is analytic near z_0, then*

$$f(z) = \sum_{n=0}^{\infty} \frac{f^{(n)}(z_0)}{n!} (z - z_0)^n \, . \qquad \text{(F.4)}$$

□

Some familiar Taylor series expansions about $z = 0$ follows.

(a) The geometric series: convergence for $|z| < 1$,

$$\frac{1}{1-z} = \sum_{n=0}^{\infty} z^n.$$

(b) The **exponential series**: convergence for all finite z,

$$e^z = \sum_{n=0}^{\infty} \frac{z^n}{n!}.$$

(c) The **cosine series**: convergence for all finite z,

$$\cos z = \sum_{n=0}^{\infty} (-1)^n \frac{z^{2n}}{(2n)!}.$$

(d) The **sine series**: convergence for all finite z,

$$\sin z = \sum_{n=0}^{\infty} (-1)^n \frac{z^{2n+1}}{(2n+1)!}.$$

Using $i^{2n} = (i^2)^n = (-1)^n$ and the above series, we can prove Euler's formula directly:

$$e^{iz} = \sum_{0}^{\infty} \frac{(iz)^n}{n!} = \sum_{even} \frac{(iz)^n}{n!} + \sum_{odd} \frac{(iz)^n}{n!}$$

$$= \sum_{0}^{\infty} \frac{(iz)^{2k}}{(2k)!} + \sum_{0}^{\infty} \frac{(iz)^{2k+1}}{(2k+1)!}$$

$$= \sum_{0}^{\infty} \frac{i^{2k} z^{2k}}{(2k)!} + i \sum_{0}^{\infty} \frac{i^{2k} z^{2k+1}}{(2k+1)!}$$

$$= \sum_{0}^{\infty} (-1)^k \frac{z^{2k}}{(2k)!} + i \sum_{0}^{\infty} (-1)^k \frac{z^{2k+1}}{(2k+1)!}$$

$$\Rightarrow \quad e^{iz} = \cos z + i \sin z.$$

Under certain convergence requirements, the Binomial Theorem is also valid for other than positive integer powers, in which case the sum extends from 0 to ∞.

▪ **EXAMPLE F.6** Apply the Binomial Theorem to the expansion of $(1 - z)^{-1}$.

Solution: Inserting directly into the expansion, we have

$$(1 - z)^{-1} = \sum_{k=0}^{\infty} \binom{-1}{k} (-z)^k.$$

But the binomial coefficient can be expanded to

$$\binom{-1}{k} = \frac{(-1)(-2)(-3) \cdots (-1 - k + 1)}{k!} = \frac{(-1)^k \, k!}{k!} = (-1)^k,$$

so that

$$(1 - z)^{-1} = \sum_{k=0}^{\infty} (-1)^k (-z)^k = \sum_{k=0}^{\infty} z^k,$$

which is our old friend the geometric series, which converges for $|z| < 1$. ▪ ▪ ▪

▪ **EXAMPLE F.7** For a fractional power expansion, we have

$$(1 - z)^{-1/2} = \sum_{k=0}^{\infty} \binom{-\frac{1}{2}}{k} (-z)^k.$$

Once again the binomial coefficient can be rewritten in the form

$$\binom{-\frac{1}{2}}{k} = \frac{\left(-\frac{1}{2}\right) \left(-\frac{3}{2}\right) \left(-\frac{5}{2}\right) \cdots \left(-\frac{1}{2} - k + 1\right)}{k!}$$

$$= \frac{1}{k!} \left(-\frac{1}{2}\right) \left(-\frac{3}{2}\right) \cdots \left(-\frac{(2k - 1)}{2}\right)$$

$$\Rightarrow \quad \binom{-\frac{1}{2}}{k} = (-1)^k \, \frac{1 \cdot 3 \cdot 5 \cdots (2k - 1)}{2^k \, k!}.$$

If we define the **odd semifactorial** by

$$(2k - 1)!! := (2k - 1)(2k - 3)(2k - 5) \cdots 5 \cdot 3 \cdot 1,$$

so that $7!! = 7 \cdot 5 \cdot 3 \cdot 1 = 105$, then

$$(1 - z)^{-1/2} = 1 + \sum_{k=1}^{\infty} \frac{(2k - 1)!!}{2^k \, k!} z^k.$$

▪ ▪ ▪

▪ **EXAMPLE F.8** We can find the power series representation of an analytic function either by direct evaluation of all its derivatives for use in Taylor's Theorem or by manipulating those series that we know.

(a) If we want the power series expansion of $f(z) = (1 - z)^{-2}$, we can use

$$\left(\frac{d}{dz}\right)^n f(z) = \left(\frac{d}{dz}\right)^n (1-z)^{-2} = (n+1)! \, (1-z)^{-(n+2)}.$$

Since $f^{(n)}(0) = (n+1)!$, for $|z| < 1$, we have

$$\frac{1}{(1-z)^2} = \sum_{n=0}^{\infty} (n+1)! \frac{(z-0)^n}{n!} = \sum_{n=0}^{\infty} (n+1) \, z^n$$

as its Taylor series expansion about $z = 0$. On the other hand,

$$\left(\frac{d}{dz}\right)^n f(z) \bigg|_{z=2} = (n+1)! \, (1-2)^{-(n+2)} = (-1)^n \, (n+1)!$$

gives us

$$\frac{1}{(1-z)^2} = \sum_{n=0}^{\infty} (-1)^n (n+1)! \frac{(z-2)^n}{n!} = \sum_{n=0}^{\infty} (-1)^n (n+1) \, (z-2)^n,$$

as its Taylor series expansion about $z = 2$.

(b) To get the Taylor series expansion of $\exp(z^2)$, all we need do is take the series for e^z and replace z everywhere by z^2:

$$e^{z^2} = \sum_{n=0}^{\infty} \frac{\left(z^2\right)^n}{n!} = \sum_{n=0}^{\infty} \frac{z^{2n}}{n!}.$$

■ ■ ■

If we apply the Ratio Test to a power series, we find

$$\rho = \lim_{n \to \infty} \left| \frac{a_{n+1} \, (z - z_0)^{n+1}}{a_n \, (z - z_0)^n} \right| = |z - z_0| \lim_{n \to \infty} \left| \frac{a_{n+1}}{a_n} \right|.$$

Denoting the value of $\lim |a_{n+1}/a_n|$ by L, the criterion for convergence is

$$\rho = |z - z_0| \, L < 1, \quad \text{or} \quad |z - z_0| < \frac{1}{L}.$$

This is the equation of a circle in the complex plane of radius $1/L$ centered at z_0. It is called the **circle of convergence** of the power series. There are only three possibilities for the value of L:

L is (a) infinite,   (b) positive and finite,   or (c) zero.

(a) If $L = \infty$, then the series converges only at the single point z_0, and $f(z)$ is *not* analytic.

(b) If L is finite, then the series converges within the circle of convergence, diverges outside of it, and $f(z)$ is analytic within the circle.

(c) If L is zero, then the series converges everywhere in the finite complex plane. $f(z)$ is called an **entire function** because it is analytic everywhere.

From what we have seen, e^z, $\cos z$, and $\sin z$ are entire functions.

Within its circle of convergence a power series has extremely strong convergence properties.

THEOREM F.6 *Within its circle of convergence, a power series can be differentiated or integrated any finite number of times. Furthermore, the result converges uniformly and absolutely within the same circle of convergence.* □

■ **EXAMPLE F.9** The theorem provides us with another method of finding the power series expansion of $f(z) = (1 - z)^{-2}$. Because

$$\frac{d}{dz}(1 - z)^{-1} = (1 - z)^{-2},$$

its series expansion about $z = 0$ should be the derivative of the geometric series:

$$\frac{1}{(1 - z)^2} = \frac{d}{dz}\sum_{n=0}^{\infty} z^n = \sum_{n=0}^{\infty} nz^{n-1} = \sum_{n=1}^{\infty} nz^{n-1} = \sum_{m=0}^{\infty} (m + 1)\, z^m.$$

The last summation came from a shift in index by one, wherein $n \leftarrow m + 1$, thereby changing the lower summation index. ■ ■ ■

Not all functions are analytic at all points in the complex plane. We need to look at the points where functions are less well behaved. The point z_0 is said to be a **removable singularity** of the function f if $f(z_0)$ is either undefined or defined but not continuous but can be defined so that f is analytic at z_0.

■ **EXAMPLE F.10** Show that each of the following functions has a removable singularity.

(a) $f(z) = z/z$ is undefined at $z = 0$, but if we set $f(0) = 1$, then f becomes analytic with a one term Taylor series.

(b) $g(z) = (\sin z)/z$ is undefined at $z = 0$, but if we set

$$g(0) = \lim_{z \to 0} \frac{\sin z}{z} \overset{\ell}{=} \lim_{z \to 0} \frac{\cos z}{1} = 1,$$

then g is analytic with Taylor series

$$\frac{\sin z}{z} = \frac{1}{z}\sum_{n=0}^{\infty} (-1)^n \frac{z^{2n+1}}{(2n + 1)!} = \sum_{n=0}^{\infty} (-1)^n \frac{z^{2n}}{(2n + 1)!}.$$

The ℓ above the equal sign by the limit indicates that equality was obtained by using l'Hôpital's Rule. ■ ■ ■

DEFINITION F.5 *We say that $f(z)$ has a **pole of order** m, a positive integer, if any of the following equivalent conditions are true:*

(a) $f(z) = g(z)/(z - z_0)^m$, where g is analytic at z_0 and $g(z_0) \neq 0$.

(b) $\lim_{z \to z_0} |(z - z_0)^p f(z)| = \infty$, for $p = 1 : m - 1$.

(c) $1/f(z)$ has a zero of order m at z_0.

*A pole is said to be **simple** if it is of order one, and **double** if it is of order two.*

■ **EXAMPLE F.11**

(a) $\log z$ has a simple pole at $z = 0$, because

$$\lim_{z \to 0} z \log z = \lim_{z \to 0} \frac{\log z}{1/z} \overset{\ell}{=} \lim_{z \to 0} \frac{1/z}{-1/z^2} = - \lim_{z \to 0} z = 0.$$

(b) $(\csc z)/z$ has a double pole at $z = 0$, because

$$z^2 \left(\frac{\csc z}{z} \right) = \frac{z^2}{z \sin z} = \frac{z}{\sin z},$$

which has a removable singularity at $z = 0$. ■ ■ ■

F.4 Exercise Set

1. Find the region of convergence for each of the following series. Determine whether the convergence is uniform and/or absolute:

(a) $\sum n^2 (z - i)^n$.

(b) $\sum \dfrac{(2z + 1 + i)^{2n}}{(2n + 1)!}$.

(c) $\sum \dfrac{n^2 - 1}{n^2 + 1} z^{3n-2}$.

(d) $\sum \left(\dfrac{n}{z} \right)^n$.

(e) $\sum \dfrac{(nz)^n}{n!\sqrt{n}}$.

(f) $\sum e^{-(zn)^2}$.

(g) $\sum z^{\ln n}$.

(h) $\sum (1+i)^n z^{2n}$.

(i) $\sum \dfrac{(1-iz)^n}{n(n+1)(n+2)}$.

(j) $\sum n^z$.

(k) $\sum (-2i)^n \dfrac{z^n}{n(in+1)}$.

(l) $\sum \dfrac{(z-i)^{2n}}{n \ln n}$.

(m) $\sum \dfrac{(3n)!}{(n!)^3} z^{-3n}$.

(n) $\sum (i-2z)^{-n}$.

(o) $\sum z^n e^{inz}$.

(p) $\sum (iz)^{3n}$.

2. If we are given

$$\sum_1^\infty \frac{1}{n^2} = \frac{\pi^2}{6}, \qquad \sum_1^\infty \frac{1}{n^4} = \frac{\pi^4}{90},$$

then by separating the sums into those on even and odd n, find the values of each of the following series:

(a) $\displaystyle\sum_1^\infty \frac{1}{(2k-1)^2}$, (b) $\displaystyle\sum_1^\infty \frac{(-1)^k}{k^2}$, (c) $\displaystyle\sum_1^\infty \frac{1}{(2k-1)^4}$, (d) $\displaystyle\sum_1^\infty \frac{(-1)^k}{k^4}$.

3. By writing in complex form, combining terms, and using the partial sum of a geometric series, show that

$$\frac{1}{2} + \sum_{k=1}^n \cos kt = \frac{\sin\left(n+\frac{1}{2}\right)t}{2\sin\left(\frac{t}{2}\right)}.$$

This sum is of use in the study of the convergence of Fourier series.

4. By writing in complex form, combining terms, and using the partial sums of a geometric series, show that

$$\frac{1}{2} + \sum_1^\infty \left(\frac{r}{a}\right)^n \cos n(\theta-\phi) = \frac{1}{2}\frac{a^2-r^2}{a^2-2ar\cos(\theta-\phi)+r^2}.$$

5. Find all the poles and their orders for each of the following functions:

(a) $\csc 2z$.

(b) $[z(1-\cos z)]^{-2}$.

(c) $\dfrac{z}{\sin^2 2z}$.

(d) $\sin(1/z)$.

(e) $(z^2-1)\tan \pi z$.

(f) $e^{\sec z}$.

(g) $\dfrac{e^z-1}{1-\cos z}$.

(h) $(z^6+3z^4+3z^2+1)^{-3}$.

Appendix G

TABLE OF LAPLACE TRANSFORMS

$f(t) = \mathcal{L}^{-1}\left\{F(s)\right\}$	$F(s) = \mathcal{L}\left\{f(t)\right\}$
$e^{\alpha t} f(t)$	$F(s - \alpha)$
$f'(t)$	$sF(s) - f(0)$
$f^{(n)}(t)$	$s^n F(s) - s^{n-1} f(0) - \cdots - sf^{(n-2)}(0) - f^{(n-1)}(0)$
$\displaystyle\int_0^t f(\tau)\,d\tau$	$\dfrac{F(s)}{s}$
$tf(t)$	$-\dfrac{d}{ds}F(s)$
$t^n f(t)$	$\left(-\dfrac{d}{ds}\right)^n F(s)$
$\dfrac{f(t)}{t}$	$\displaystyle\int_s^\infty F(\sigma)\,d\sigma$
$e^{\alpha t}$	$\dfrac{1}{s - a}$
$e^{\alpha t}\cos\omega t$	$\dfrac{s - \alpha}{(s - \alpha)^2 + \omega^2}$
$e^{\alpha t}\sin\omega t$	$\dfrac{\omega}{(s - \alpha)^2 + \omega^2}$
t^n	$\dfrac{\Gamma(n+1)}{s^{n+1}} = \dfrac{n!}{s^{n+1}}$
$\dfrac{t^{n-1}}{\Gamma(n)} = \dfrac{t^{n-1}}{(n-1)!}$	$\dfrac{1}{s^{n+1}}$
$t\cos\omega t$	$\dfrac{s^2 - \omega^2}{(s^2 + \omega^2)^2}$
$t\sin\omega t$	$\dfrac{2\omega s}{(s^2 + \omega^2)^2}$
$\dfrac{1}{2\omega^3}\left(\sin\omega t - \omega t\cos\omega t\right)$	$\dfrac{1}{(s^2 + \omega^2)^2}$
$\dfrac{1}{2\omega}\left(\sin\omega t + \omega t\cos\omega t\right)$	$\dfrac{s^2}{(s^2 + \omega^2)^2}$
$\cos\omega t - \dfrac{1}{2}\omega t\sin\omega t$	$\dfrac{s^3}{(s^2 + \omega^2)^2}$

Appendix H

ANSWERS

Exercise Set 1.2.5 **Matrix Models**

1. $(Z_1 + Z_2 + 2Z_3) I_1 - Z_1 I_2 - Z_2 I_3 - Z_3 I_4 - Z_3 I_5 = E, -Z_2 I_1 + (Z_1 + Z_2) I_2 = 0,$
$-Z_2 I_1 + (Z_1 + Z_2) I_3 = 0, -Z_3 I_1 + (Z_3 + Z_4) I_4 = 0, -Z_3 I_1 + (Z_3 + Z_5) I_5 = 0.$

Exercise Set 1.3.1 **Matrix Algebra**

1. $\begin{bmatrix} 6 & -1 & 2 \\ 11 & 1+6i & 10 \\ 6-3i & 8 & 6-3i \\ 0 & 1 & -3i \end{bmatrix}$. **3.** $\begin{bmatrix} -2 & -2 & -12+4i & 0 \\ 2 & -2-6i & 4 & -2 \\ -4 & 10 & 8+2i & 4i \end{bmatrix}$.

5. $\begin{bmatrix} -10-2i & 9+2i & -4+3i \\ 14-3i & 6-3i & 3+2i \\ -13+2i & 4-i & 10+4i \\ 2 & -2i & 3+i \end{bmatrix}$. **7.** $4 - 8i$. **9.** $\begin{bmatrix} 1 & 1-i & -1 \\ 0 & 1-2i & -4 \\ 4+i & -2i & -4 \\ -2 & -1+i & 1+i \end{bmatrix}$. **11.** $-51 + 42i$.

13. 19. 15. $1 + i$. **17.** $\begin{bmatrix} -5 & 1 & 1+i \\ 2 & -1-3i & 3 \\ 1-i & 3 & -1 \end{bmatrix}$. **19.** (a)$\mathbf{e}_{(j;n)} \mathbf{e}_{(k;n)}^T = \delta_{jk}$. (b)

$\mathbf{A}\mathbf{e}_{(j;n)} = \mathrm{col}_j(\mathbf{A})$. (c) $\mathbf{e}_{(j;m)}^T \mathbf{A}\mathbf{e}_{(j;n)} = A_{jj}$. (d) $\mathbf{e}_{(j;m)}^T \mathbf{A}\mathbf{e}_{(k;n)} = A_{jk}$.

21. Use $(\mathbf{A}^T \mathbf{A})^T = (\mathbf{A}^T)(\mathbf{A}^T)^T = \mathbf{A}^T \mathbf{A}$, and similarly for the other parts.

23. $\mathrm{tr}(\mathbf{ABC}) = \mathrm{tr}(\mathbf{A}(\mathbf{BC})) = \mathrm{tr}((\mathbf{BC})\mathbf{A}) = \mathrm{tr}(\mathbf{BCA})$, etc. **25.** $\mathbf{A} + \mathbf{B}, \mathbf{AB} + \mathbf{BA}, \mathbf{A}^n,$

$\mathbf{A} + i\mathbf{B}$, and $\mathbf{A} - i\mathbf{B}$ are symmetric. **27.** $\alpha = \frac{1}{n}\mathrm{tr}(\mathbf{A}), \mathbf{S} = \frac{1}{2}\left(\mathbf{A} + \mathbf{A}^T\right) - \alpha\mathbf{I}$ and

$\mathbf{K} = \frac{1}{2}\left(\mathbf{A} - \mathbf{A}^T\right)$. **29.** Component form:

$na^2 + 2a(b-a) + (b-a)^2\delta_{jk} = 2ab + (n-2)a^2 + (a-b)^2\delta_{jk}$. In matrix form this is:

$\mathbf{A}^2 = [2ab + (n-2)a^2]\mathbf{ones}(n) + (a-b)^2\mathbf{I}_n$. **31.** $\mathbf{A}^2 = a^2[(1-a^{2n})/(1-a^2)]\mathbf{A}$. **39.** (a)

$ad - bc = 1 \Leftrightarrow \mathbf{A} = [a, (ac-1)/b; b, c]$.

Exercise Set 1.4.1 **Systems of Linear Equations**

1.(a) is not in rref. (b) is in rref and $\text{null}(\mathbf{B}) = 3$.

$\mathbf{x} = \alpha[1; 0; 0; 0; 0] + \beta[0; -5; 1; 0; 0] + \gamma[0; -2; 0; -1; 1]$. (c) is in rref and $\text{null}(\mathbf{C}) = 2$.

$\mathbf{x} = \alpha[3; -2; 1; 0; 0] + \beta[-5; 2; 0; 1; 1]$. (d) is in rref and $\text{null}(\mathbf{E}) = 3$.

$\mathbf{x} = \alpha[0; 3; 1; 0; 0; 0; 0] + \beta[-2; 2; 0; 1; 0; 0; 0] + \gamma[1; -4; 0; 0; 1; 0; 0]$.

3. $\mathbf{x} = [-\alpha - \beta - 2\gamma; \alpha; 2\beta; \gamma]$. **5.** $\mathbf{x} = [4; 3; 2]$. **7.** $\mathbf{x} = [-\alpha - \beta; \alpha; -\beta; \beta]$.

9. $\mathbf{x} = [-17\alpha + 8\beta + 1.4; -6\alpha - 6\beta + 0.2; 5\alpha; 5\beta]$. **11.** $\mathbf{x} = [1; 2\alpha; \alpha; -3\beta; \beta]$.

13. $\mathbf{x}_1 = [-\alpha - 7\beta + 12\gamma + 12; \alpha; \alpha + 3\beta - 5\gamma - 5; \alpha; \beta; \gamma]$, and the for the second input is

$\mathbf{x}_2 = [-\alpha - 7\beta + 12\gamma + 16; \alpha; \alpha + 3\beta - 5\gamma - 5; \alpha; \beta; \gamma]$. The solution to the homogeneous

system is $\mathbf{x}_0 = [-\alpha - 7\beta + 12\gamma; \alpha; \alpha + 3\beta - 5\gamma; \alpha; \beta; \gamma]$. **15.** (a) $2b - 5c + d = 0$. (b)

$\mathbf{x} = [-1; 1; 0; 0; 0]\alpha + [-11; 0; 12; -4; 3]\beta + \left[\frac{16}{3}; 0; -4; \frac{5}{3}; 0\right]$. **17.** The generalization is

$x_i = \prod_{j \neq i} (a_j - 1)/ \left[a_i \prod_{j \neq i} (a_i - a_j) \right]$. **19.** $w = abcd + 1$, $x = -abc - abd - acd - bcd$,

$y = ab + ac + ad + bc + bd + cd$, $z = -a - b - c - d$. The generalization is $x_1 = 1 + \prod_i a_i$,

$x_2 = -\sum_j \prod_{i \neq j} a_i, \ldots, x_n = (-1)^{n-1} \sum a_i$. **21.** $I_1 = 0.2591 + 0.0118i$,

$I_2 = 0.5785 + 0.0680i$, $I_3 = 2.1737 - 1.5418i$, $I_4 = 0.0801 + 0.0660i$,

$I_5 = 3.9456 - 3.8117i$. **23.** $T_1 = 23.78$, $T_2 = 27.77$, $T_3 = 35.28$, $T_4 = 31.37$, $T_5 = 22.41$,

$T_6 = 18.28$, $T_7 = 14.72$, $T_8 = 18.59$, $T_9 = 19.65$. **25.** Thus all systems with this rref will have

that solution, to within rows of zeros: $\begin{bmatrix} 1 & 0 & 1 & 0 & 0 & 0 & -2 \\ 0 & 1 & -1 & 0 & 0 & -1 & 1 \\ 0 & 0 & 0 & 1 & 0 & -2 & -3 \\ 0 & 0 & 0 & 0 & 1 & -1 & 0 \end{bmatrix}$. **27.** $w = \frac{3(-1+i)z}{(-1+3i)z+4}$.

29. $w = -\frac{1}{z}$. **31.** The matrix $\mathbf{ab}^T$ has each of its rows a multiple of the first row. In fact,

$\mathbf{ab}^T = [a_1 \mathbf{b}^T; a_2 \mathbf{b}^T; \ldots; a_n \mathbf{b}^T]$. **33.** This is a natural for a computer algebra system. To make it

easier to enter, use $a = 10^{-n}$. You'll find: $x_1 = 10^n$, $x_2 = 1 + 10^n$, $x_3 = 2 + 10^n$,

$x_4 = 3 + 10^n$. This will be used in a later section. **35.** $A_{11} = A_{33}$, $A_{12} = 0$, $A_{13} = A_{32}$,

$A_{21} = 0$, $A_{23} = 0$, and $A_{32} = 0$. **37.** $\mathbf{G} = \begin{bmatrix} 1 - \alpha & -\beta \\ 0 & 1 \\ \alpha & \beta \end{bmatrix}$, for any complex α and β.

Exercise Set 1.5.6 **Inverses**

1. $\dfrac{1}{11}\begin{bmatrix} -3i & 5i & -3i \\ 7 & 3 & -4 \\ -6 & -1 & 5 \end{bmatrix}$. **3.** $\dfrac{1}{120}\begin{bmatrix} 20 & 0 & 20 \\ 28 & 12 & 20 \\ 12 & -12 & 0 \end{bmatrix}$. **5.** $\begin{bmatrix} 3 & -5 & -3 \\ -1 & 3 & -2 \\ 0 & -1 & 1 \end{bmatrix}$.

7. $\dfrac{1}{103}\begin{bmatrix} 13 & -8 & 24 & 30 \\ -37 & -1 & 3 & -22 \\ -28 & 41 & -20 & -25 \\ 21 & 5 & 15 & -7 \end{bmatrix}$. **9.** $\begin{bmatrix} 10+i & -2+6i & -3-2i \\ 9-3i & 8i & -3-2i \\ -2+2i & -1-2i & 1 \end{bmatrix}$.

11. $\mathbf{A}=\begin{bmatrix} 1&0&0 \\ 1&1&0 \\ 0&0&1 \end{bmatrix}\begin{bmatrix} 1&0&0 \\ 0&1&0 \\ 1&0&1 \end{bmatrix}\begin{bmatrix} 1&2&0 \\ 0&1&0 \\ 0&0&1 \end{bmatrix}\begin{bmatrix} 1&0&0 \\ 0&1&0 \\ 0&1&1 \end{bmatrix}\begin{bmatrix} 1&0&3 \\ 0&1&0 \\ 0&0&1 \end{bmatrix}\begin{bmatrix} 1&0&0 \\ 0&1&2 \\ 0&0&1 \end{bmatrix}$ **I. 15.** (a)

Multiply both sides by $\mathbf{I}+\mathbf{a}\mathbf{a}^{H}$ and notice that $\mathbf{a}^{H}\mathbf{a}$ is a scalar. (b) Multiply by $\mathbf{I}+\mathbf{a}\mathbf{b}^{H}$ and follow

the same steps as in part (a). (c) $\mathbf{a}=-2\mathbf{u}$ and $\mathbf{b}=\mathbf{u}$ will work. **19.** If $\mathbf{A}^{2}=\mathbf{I}$ and $\mathbf{B}^{2}=\mathbf{I}$, then

$(\mathbf{AB})^{2}=\mathbf{ABAB}$, which need not be the identity unless $\mathbf{A}$ and $\mathbf{B}$ commute. **21.** Use the fact that

$(\mathbf{I}-\mathbf{S})(\mathbf{I}+\mathbf{S})=(\mathbf{I}+\mathbf{S})(\mathbf{I}-\mathbf{S})$. **23.** (a)

$(a+ib)+(c+id)\leftrightarrow[a,b;-b,a]+[c,d;-d,c]=[a+c,b+d;-(b+d),a+c]$

$\leftrightarrow(a+c)+i(b+d)$. Similarly for the product of complex numbers.

25. The $(1,1)$-entry is $\cosh(kL_1)\cosh(kL_2)+\frac{Z_1}{Z_2}\sinh(kL_1)\sinh(kL_2)$, the $(1,2)$-entry is

$Z_2\cosh(kL_1)\sinh(kL_2)+Z_1\cosh(kL_2)\sinh(kL_1)$, the $(2,1)$-entry is

$\frac{1}{Z_1}\sinh(kL_1)\cosh(kL_2)+\frac{1}{Z_2}\cosh(kL_1)\sinh(kL_2)$, and the $(2,2)$-entry is

$\frac{Z_2}{Z_1}\sinh(kL_1)\sinh(kL_2)+\cosh(kL_1)\cosh(kL_2)$. **27.** The $(1,1)$-entry is

$\frac{1}{2}\left\{\left(1+\sqrt{YZ}\right)^{n}+\left(1-\sqrt{YZ}\right)^{n}\right\}$, the $(1,2)$-entry is

$\frac{1}{2}\sqrt{\frac{Z}{Y}}\left(\left(1+\sqrt{YZ}\right)^{n}-\left(1-\sqrt{YZ}\right)^{n}\right)$, the $(2,1)$-entry is

$\frac{1}{2}\sqrt{\frac{Y}{Z}}\left(\left(1+\sqrt{YZ}\right)^{n}-\left(1-\sqrt{YZ}\right)^{n}\right)$, and the $(2,2)$-entry is

$\frac{1}{2}\left\{\left(1+\sqrt{YZ}\right)^{n}+\left(1-\sqrt{YZ}\right)^{n}\right\}$.

Exercise Set 1.6.5 **Determinants**

1. $10 - 46i$. **3.** -30. **5.** 0. **7.** -20. **9.** $\det(a^{j+k}) = 0$. **11.** $-\frac{1}{6}n(n+1)(2n-5)$. **13.** (a)

$z - 2, 1$. (b) $z = -2, 1$. (c) $z = 0, \pm i\sqrt{2}$. **15.** The best way to proceed is by row reduction. Use

the last row as a pivot and for rows $1 : n - 1$ form $(k) - \frac{x_k}{x_n}(1)$. Now form

$(n) - (x_n y_1(1) + x_n y_2(2) + \cdots + x_n y_{n-1}(n-1))$ to sweep out the $1 : n - 1$ entries of the last

row. **17.** even n: $|\mathbf{A}|$ is real, odd n: $|\mathbf{A}|$ is imaginary. When $\mathbf{A}$ is Hermitian, we always have $|\mathbf{A}|$

real. **19.** Just evaluate the determinant.

Exercise Set 1.7.5 **Computer Solutions**

If the "program" is to be a Matlab fragment, then it is, quite simply, x=A\b, r=Ax-b. **7.** The results of

this experiment will prove to be quite interesting.

Exercise Set 1.8.1 **LU-Decomposition**

1. $\begin{bmatrix} 1 & 2 & 3 \\ 4 & 5 & 6 \\ 7 & 8 & 8 \end{bmatrix} = \begin{bmatrix} 1 & 0 & 0 \\ 4 & 1 & 0 \\ 7 & 2 & 1 \end{bmatrix} \begin{bmatrix} 1 & 2 & 3 \\ 0 & -3 & -6 \\ 0 & 0 & -1 \end{bmatrix}$.

3. $\begin{bmatrix} i & 1 & i \\ -i & 2 & i \\ i & 1 & i \end{bmatrix} = \begin{bmatrix} 1 & 0 & 0 \\ -1 & 1 & 0 \\ 1 & 0 & 1 \end{bmatrix} \begin{bmatrix} i & 1 & i \\ 0 & 3 & 2i \\ 0 & 0 & 0 \end{bmatrix}$.

1.9 **Supplementary and Complementary Problems**

1. Symmetric: $2(n + (n-1) + \cdots + 2 + 1) = n(n+1)$; Hermitian:

$n + 2(1 + 2 + \cdots + (n-1)) = n^2$; skew-symmetric:

$0 + 2(1 + 2 + \cdots + (n-1)) = n(n-1)$; skew-Hermitian $n + 2(1 + 2 + \cdots + (n-1))n^2$.

3. There is no equivalent for the anticommutator. **7.** $a_0 = \frac{1}{2}\operatorname{tr}(\mathbf{A})$,

$a_1 = \frac{1}{2}\operatorname{tr}(\operatorname{flipr}(\mathbf{A})) = \frac{1}{2}(A_{12} + A_{21})$, $a_2 = \frac{1}{2i}(A_{21} - A_{12})$, $a_3 = \frac{1}{2}(A_{11} - A_{22})$. **9.** Write

$\mathbf{A}$ in terms of a_0, a_1, a_2, and a_3, as given in problem 7, then find the determinant. **19.** Round:

$\frac{1}{4}(n^2 + 3)$ for n odd and $\frac{1}{4}n(n+2)$ for n even; round and symmetric or round and cross-symmetric

imply round, symmetric, and cross-symmetric: $\frac{1}{2}\lceil\frac{n}{2}\rceil(\lceil\frac{n}{2}\rceil + 1)$. **21.** $\mathbf{A}$ will be invertible under the

Schur-Hadamard product if (a) it is square, and (b) none of its diagonal entries are zero. When will it have a unique inverse? **23.** To see that the Kronecker product is not commutative look at $\mathbf{A} = \mathbf{I}_2$ and $\mathbf{B} = \mathbf{flipr}(\mathbf{A})$. $\mathbf{E} = 1$, the number one. **35.** (b) $\mathbf{adj}\left(\mathbf{adj}(\mathbf{A})\right) = |\mathbf{A}|^{n-2}\,\mathbf{A}$. (c) $\mathbf{adj}(\cdot)$ reduces the rank for $n > 2$; but not for $\mathbf{ones}(2)$. (d) $\det\left(\mathbf{adj}(\mathbf{A})\right) = \left(\det(\mathbf{A})\right)^{n-1}$. (e) $\left(\mathbf{adj}(\mathbf{A})\right)^{-1} = \mathbf{A}/\,|\mathbf{A}|$.

Exercise Set 2.2.1   ODE Models

1. $\ddot{r} = -\frac{GM_e m}{r^2} + \frac{GM_m m}{(R-r)^2}$.   **3.** $\dot{V}_1 = 0$ and $\dot{V}_2 = 0$, with initial conditions $V_1(0) = 200 = V_2(0)$. $\dot{D}_1 = 20\frac{D_2}{V_2}$ and $\dot{D}_2 = 20\frac{D_2}{V_2}$, with initial conditions $D_1(0) = 0$ and $D_2(0) = 200$.

5. $EIy^{(iv)}(x) = -ky(x)$.   **7.** $(L_1 + L_2)\ddot{q} + (R_1 + R_2)\dot{q} + \frac{1}{C_1+C_2}q = E(t)$.   **9.** $\ddot{\theta} + \frac{4k}{m}\theta = 0$.

11. fields to be parallel to the z-axis, $m\dot{v}_1 = qv_2 B$, $m\dot{v}_2 = -qv_1 B$, and $m\dot{v}_3 = E$. fields are orthogonal, we could write $\mathbf{E} = E\mathbf{k}$ and $\mathbf{B} = B\mathbf{i}$. $m\dot{v}_1 = 0$, $m\dot{v}_2 = qBv_3$, and $m\dot{v}_3 = q\,(E - v_2 B)$.

Exercise Set 2.3.4   ODE's

1. specific solution.   **3.** specific solution.   **5.** specific solution.   **7.** general solution.   **9.** specific solution.   **11.** $x'' + 9x = 0$.   **13.** $u'' - u = -s$.   **15.** $y = (t + 1)y' - (y')^3$.   **17.** $u^{(iv)} - 16u = 0$. **19.** nonlinear in both x and y.   **21.** linear, nonhomogeneous, second order.   **23.** nonlinear, second order.   **25.** linear, homogeneous, second order.   **27.** boundary value.   **29.** initial value.   **31.** boundary value.   **33.** $-1 < x + y < 1$.   **35.** $y/x < \tan(1)$.   **37.** all finite t and w.

Exercise Set 2.4.1   Graphical Solutions

1. $x = a$ is stable and $x = -a$ is unstable.   **3.** $x = -a$ is stable, $x = 0$ is semistable, and $x = a$ is unstable.   **5.** $x = 0$ is semistable.

Exercise Set 2.5.4   Numerical Methods

1. If $x(t) = \left(t^2 + \epsilon^2\right)^{-n}$, then $x'(t) = -2nt\left(t^2 + \epsilon^2\right)^{-n-1} = -2ntx^{(n+1)/n}$.

Exercise Set 2.6.4   **First Order ODE's**

1. $x(t) = (t^2 + C) \csc t$. **3.** $r(\theta) = C(1 - b\cos\theta)$. **5.** $y(x) = \tan x - 1 + Ce^{-\tan x}$.

7. $\ln|t^2 - 1| - 3\ln|w| = \ln C \Rightarrow t^2 - 1 = Cw^3$. **9.** $b = \left(\frac{a-1}{a^2}\right) + \frac{1}{a^2}Ce^{-a}$.

11. $c^2\beta + ac + b(c\alpha + 1) = Ke^{c\alpha}$. **13.** $y(\sec x + \tan x) = x - \cos x + 2$.

15. $xy = \exp(x^2 - 1)$. **17.** $9n = 6m + \ln|3m + 1| + C$.

19. $6m - 3n + \ln|3m - 6n + 7| = C$. **21.** $\ln(1 - 2/b) = C - \frac{3}{a}$. **23.** $2tz = 5 - t^2$.

25. $y = \ln(0.5e^{2x} + C)$. **27.** $\ln|ae^y + b| = a(e^x + C)$. **29.** $\ln\left|\frac{y-2}{y}\right| = 2(x - 1)$.

31. $y^2 + \ln(1 - 2x) = C$. **33.** $\tan r + \sec\theta = C$. **35.** $r(1 - \cos\theta) = 1$.

37. $(s^2 - 1)(t - 1) = 2t$. **39.** (a) $Q' = -\lambda Q, Q(0) = Q_0$. (b) $T = \dfrac{\ln 2}{\lambda}$. (c)

$Q(t) = Q_0\left(\frac{1}{2}\right)^{t/T}$. **41.** 46.816 grams. **43.** $r^{3-2\alpha} = (3 - 2\alpha)(4\pi)^{\alpha-1}t + R^{3-2\alpha}$, we must

have $3 - 2\alpha < 0$. **45.** $v_e = \sqrt{\frac{2k}{m\mu}}e^{-\mu/(2R)}$. **47.** $x_{stop} = \frac{mv_0}{k}$. **49.** $t = .09m$. **51.** $t = 27.095$

min. **53.** $y(x) = Cx^{2/3}$. **55.** $I(t) = \frac{aE_0}{R-aL}\left(1 - e^{(-a+R/L)t}\right)$. **57.** As $t \to \infty$ we must have

$I \to \frac{E_0}{R}$. **59.** $t = 460.52$ min.

2.8   **Supplementary and Complementary Problems**

3. $x^2 + 2xy(x) - (y(x))^2 = C$.

5. $\ln|x| + \frac{1}{3}\ln|v| + \frac{1}{3}(v^2 + 2v + 3) + \frac{5\sqrt{2}}{6}\text{Atan}\left(\frac{v+1}{\sqrt{2}}\right) = C$. **9.** $y(t) = \frac{1}{\sqrt{\frac{2}{3}t+Ct^4}}$.

11. $t = \frac{1}{\sqrt{GM}}\left(\frac{1}{2}D^{3/2}\ln\left(\frac{D}{2}\right) - \sqrt{D(R^2 - RD)} - \frac{1}{2}D^{3/2}\ln\left(R - \frac{1}{2}D + \sqrt{R^2 - RD}\right)\right)$.

Exercise Set 3.2.4   **Linear Spaces**

1. Subspace, $\mathcal{B} = \{[2, 1]\}$ and dim $= 1$. **3.** Subspace, $\mathcal{B} = \{x, x^2\}$ and dim $= 2$. **5.** Subspace,

$\mathcal{B} = \{[1, 0; 0, -1], [0, 1; 0, 0], [0, 0; 1, 0]\}$ and dim $= 3$. **7.** Not a subspace. **9.** Not a subspace.

11. $\mathcal{S}_{11} = \{0\}$. **13.** Not a subspace. **15.** Subspace, $\mathcal{B} = \{[1, 1, 2, 1], [2, 1, 1, -1], [-1, -1, 0, 1]\}$

and dim $= 3$. **17.** Subspace, $\mathcal{B} = \{[1, 1, 0, 2], [0, 1, 1, 3]\}$ and dim $= 2$. **19.** Subspace, infinite

dimensional. **21.** Dimension and basis depend on the matrix **B**. **23.** Linearly independent.
25. Linearly dependent. **27.** Linearly dependent; $-\mathbf{a}_1 + 2\mathbf{a}_2 - \mathbf{a}_3 = \mathbf{0}$. **29.** This set is linearly
independent. **31.** Linearly dependent. **33.** The set is linearly dependent. In particular, if the vectors
are denoted by x_k, $k = 1 : 4$, we can read off the linear relation as $4\mathbf{x}_1 + \mathbf{x}_2 - \mathbf{x}_4 = \mathbf{0}$.
35. $c_1\mathbf{0} + c_2\mathbf{x}_2 + \cdots + c_k\mathbf{x}_k = \mathbf{0}$ has a nontrivial solution because c_1 can be anything.

Exercise Set 3.3.1 **Representations of a Vector**

1. $[(x-2)(2x+1)]^{\mathcal{B}} = \left[-\frac{4}{3}; -\frac{5}{3}; 2\right]$.

3. $\left[\begin{bmatrix} a & b \\ c & d \end{bmatrix}\right]^{\mathcal{P}} = \frac{1}{2}[a+d; b+c; i(b-c); a-d]$.

Exercise Set 3.4.4 **Inner Product Spaces**

1. $\|[1,2]\| = \sqrt{5}$, $\|[2,3]\| = \sqrt{13}$, $\|[\pi, e]\| = \sqrt{\pi^2 + e^2}$. **3.** $\|[1, i, -1]\| = \sqrt{3}$,
$\|[1-i, 1+i, 1]\| = \sqrt{5}$, $\|[2, 1, 2]\| = 3$, $\|[2i, 1, -2i]\| = 3$.
5. $\|\sin x\|^2 = \frac{1}{5}\left(e\sin^2 1 - 2e\sin 1\cos 1 + 2e - 2\right)$,
$\|\cos x\|^2 = \frac{1}{5}\left(e\cos^2 1 + 2\sin 1\cos 1 + 2e - 3\right)$, $\|e^{\pm x}\|^2 = \frac{1}{1\pm 2}\left(e^{1\pm 2} - 1\right)$,
$\|2x+3\|^2 = 13e - 5$, $\|1\|^2 = e - 1$. **7.** This is not an inner product because:
$\langle[i,i],[i,i]\rangle = i(i) + 2i(i) + 3i(i) = -6$. **9.** This is an inner product. **11.** Not an inner product.
$\det(\mathbf{A}^2) = 0$ for $\mathbf{A} \neq \mathbf{0}$. **13.** We can be sneaky here. Take $\mathbf{A} = \begin{bmatrix} 1 & 4 & 7 \\ 2 & 5 & 8 \\ 3 & 6 & 9 \end{bmatrix}$. Then $\|\mathbf{A}\|_1 = 18$

and $\|\mathbf{A}\|_\infty = 24$. Now choose $\mathbf{B} = i\mathbf{A}^T = \begin{bmatrix} i & 2i & 3i \\ 4i & 5i & 6i \\ 7i & 8i & 9i \end{bmatrix}$, then $\|\mathbf{B}\|_1 = 24$ and $\|\mathbf{B}\|_\infty = 18$.

I'm sure you can be more inventive than this. **15.** $\|\mathbf{A}\|_E = \sqrt{\text{tr}\left(\mathbf{A}^H\mathbf{A}\right)}$ is not an induced norm
because $\|\mathbf{I}_n\|_E = \sqrt{\text{tr}(\mathbf{I}_n)} = \sqrt{n} \neq 1$, for $n > 1$. **17.** Use $\|\mathbf{x} \pm c\mathbf{y}\|^2 = \langle \mathbf{x} \pm c\mathbf{y}, \mathbf{x} \pm c\mathbf{y} \rangle$
$= \|\mathbf{x}\|^2 \pm c\langle \mathbf{x}, \mathbf{y} \rangle \pm \bar{c}\langle \mathbf{y}, \mathbf{x} \rangle + |c|^2 \|\mathbf{y}\|^2$. **19.** If you start with $\mathbf{u}_1 = \begin{bmatrix} 1 & 0 \\ 0 & 1 \end{bmatrix}$ and proceed in

order, then $\left\{ \begin{bmatrix} 1 & 0 \\ 0 & 1 \end{bmatrix}, \begin{bmatrix} 0 & 0 \\ 1 & 0 \end{bmatrix}, \begin{bmatrix} 0 & 1 \\ 0 & 0 \end{bmatrix}, \begin{bmatrix} 1 & 0 \\ 0 & -1 \end{bmatrix} \right\}$.

Exercise Set 3.5.1 **Fundamental Subspaces**

1. $\mathcal{B}_{\text{null}} = \{[-1; -1; 1; 0; 0], [-1; -1; 0; 1; 1]\}$.

$\mathcal{B}_{\text{row}} = \{[1, 0, 1, 0, 1], [0, 1, 1, 0, 1], [0, 0, 0, 1, -1]\}$. $\text{NullSp}(\mathbf{A}^H) = \{\mathbf{0}\}$.

Exercise Set 3.6.2 **Linear Transformations**

1. Linear, $\ker(T) = \{\mathbf{0}\}$. $\text{im}(T) = \text{Span}\{[1; 2], [-1; 1]\}$. **3.** Linear, $\ker(T) = \text{Span}(\{1, x\})$.

$\text{im}(T) = \text{Span}(\{x^2, x^3, \ldots, x^n\})$. **5.** Linear, $\text{im}(T) = \text{Span}\{x, x^3, x^5, \ldots\}$.

$\ker(T) = \text{Span}\{1, x^2, x^4, \ldots\}$. **7.** Linear, a basis of $\ker(T_7)$ is

$\{[1, -i, 0, 0, 0], [1, 0, -1, 0, 0], [1, 0, 0, -i, 0], [1, 0, 0, 0, -1]\}$. $\text{im}(T_7) = \mathbb{C}$.

9. Linear. $\ker(T_9) = \{\mathbf{0}\}$. $\text{im}(T_9) = \mathbb{C}^n$. **11.** Not linear.

Exercise Set 3.7.1 **Rotations in the Plane and Space**

1. $\begin{bmatrix} \cos\phi\cos\psi - \sin\phi\cos\theta\sin\psi & \sin\phi\cos\psi + \cos\phi\cos\theta\sin\psi & \sin\theta\sin\psi \\ -\cos\phi\sin\psi - \sin\phi\cos\theta\cos\psi & -\sin\phi\sin\psi + \cos\phi\cos\theta\cos\psi & \sin\theta\cos\psi \\ \sin\phi\sin\theta & -\cos\phi\sin\theta & \cos\theta \end{bmatrix}$.

Exercise Set 3.8.1 **Representations of Linear Transformations**

1. With $\{[1, 0, 0], [0, 1, 0], [0, 0, 1]\}$, $[A] = \begin{bmatrix} 1 & -1 & 1 \\ 0 & 1 & -1 \\ 1 & 0 & 1 \end{bmatrix}$. **3.** If we use the standard basis

$$\left\{ \mathbf{E}_{(11)} = \begin{bmatrix} 1 & 0 \\ 0 & 0 \end{bmatrix}, \mathbf{E}_{(21)} = \begin{bmatrix} 0 & 0 \\ 1 & 0 \end{bmatrix}, \mathbf{E}_{(12)} = \begin{bmatrix} 0 & 1 \\ 0 & 0 \end{bmatrix}, \mathbf{E}_{(22)} = \begin{bmatrix} 0 & 0 \\ 0 & 1 \end{bmatrix} \right\},$$

then, $[C] = \begin{bmatrix} 1 & 0 & 1 & 0 \\ 0 & 0 & 1 & 0 \\ 0 & 1 & 0 & 0 \\ 1 & 0 & 0 & -1 \end{bmatrix}$. **5.** $[G] = \begin{bmatrix} 1 & 0 & 0 & 0 & 0 & 0 \\ 0 & 0 & 1 & 0 & 0 & 0 \\ 0 & 0 & 0 & 0 & 1 & 0 \\ 0 & 1 & 0 & 0 & 0 & 0 \\ 0 & 0 & 0 & 1 & 0 & 0 \\ 0 & 0 & 0 & 0 & 0 & 1 \end{bmatrix}$.

7. $\mathbf{D} := \text{diag}(\bar{a}_1, \bar{a}_2, \ldots, \bar{a}_n)$, then $[J] = \underbrace{\begin{bmatrix} \mathbf{D}; \mathbf{D}; \ldots; \mathbf{D} \end{bmatrix}}_{n\text{-such matrices}}^T$.

9. $[T] = \begin{bmatrix} 0 & \pi & 0 & 0 \\ -\pi & 0 & 0 & 0 \\ 0 & 0 & 0 & 0 \\ 0 & 0 & 0 & 0 \end{bmatrix}$. $\mathcal{B}_{\text{ker}} = \{\cos 2x, \sin 2x\}$ and $\mathcal{B}_{\text{im}} = \{\cos x, \sin x\}$.

11. $\|T(\mathbf{x})\|^2 = (\mathbf{Ux})^H (\mathbf{Ux}) = \left(\mathbf{x}^H \mathbf{U}^H\right)(\mathbf{Ux}) = \mathbf{x}^H \left(\mathbf{U}^H \mathbf{U}\right)\mathbf{x} = \mathbf{x}^H \mathbf{Ix} = \mathbf{x}^H \mathbf{x} = \|\mathbf{x}\|^2$.

3.9   **Supplementary and Complementary Problems**

1. $\dim\left(\mathcal{CSC}_n\right) = \left\lceil \frac{n}{2} \right\rceil \left(\left\lfloor \frac{n}{2} \right\rfloor + 1\right)$.

Exercise Set 4.2.4   **Elements of Linear Differential Equations**

5. $m = 1, 2, 3$, or 4.   **7.** $v(t) = e^t - \cos t + 2\sin t$.

9. $y(t) = \cos t - 3\sin t + 5\cosh t + 3\sinh t$.   **11.** linearly independent over $\mathbb{R}$.   **13.** linearly

independent over $(0, \infty)$.   **15.** $\mathbb{R}$.   **17.** linearly independent on $\mathbb{R}$.   **19.** $\mathbb{R} = (-\infty, \infty)$.

21. $(-\infty, -1)$ and $(1, \infty)$ are the largest, but $(-1, 1)$ would also work.   **23.** $(-\infty, 0)$ or $(4, \infty)$. A

smaller interval could be $(0, 4)$.   **25.** The largest such intervals are $(-\infty, -3)$ and $(3, \infty)$, while the

finite ones are $(-3, -1)$, $(-1, 1)$, and $(1, 3)$.

Exercise Set 4.3.2   **Linear Time Invariant ODE's**

1. $y(t) = c_1 + c_2 t + c_3 e^{2t} + c_4 e^{3t}$.   **3.** $y(t) = c_1 e^t + c_2 e^{2t} + A\cosh 3t + B\sinh 3t$.

5. $y(t) = c_1 e^t + c_2 e^{2it} + c_3 e^{3t}$.

7. $y(t) = A_1 \cos t + B_1 \sin t + C e^{2t} + A_2 \cosh(3t) + B_2 \sinh(3t)$.

9. $y(t) = (c_1 + c_2 t + c_3 t^2)e^{et} + (c_4 + c_5 t)e^{3t} + c_6 e^{2et}$.

11. $y(t) = (A_1 + A_2 t)\cosh t + (B_1 + B_2 t)\sinh t + e^{2t}(A_3 \cos 3t + B_3 \sin 3t)$.

13. $y(t) = c_1 e^{-3t} + c_2 e^{-2t} + c_3 e^{-t} + c_4 + (c_5 + c_6 t)e^t + c_7 e^{it} + c_8 e^{2it}$.

15. $y(t) = (A_1 + A_2 t + A_3 t^2 + \cdots + A_m t^{m-1}) + (B_1 + B_2 t + B_3 t^2 + \cdots + B_n t^{n-1})e^t$.

17. $y(t) = -6e^{-2t}$.   **19.** $y(t) = -6e^{-2(t-2)}$.   **21.** $y(t) = e^{-4t}(c_1 \cos 3t + c_2 \sin 3t)$.

23. $y(t) = c_1 e^{3t/2} + c_2 e^{-4t}$.   **25.** $y(t) = c_1 e^{-3t/4}\cosh\left(\frac{\sqrt{41}}{4}t\right) + c_2 e^{-3t/4}\sinh\left(\frac{\sqrt{41}}{4}t\right)$.

27. $u(t) = e^{-t}(c_1 \cos 2t + c_2 \sin 2t)$.   **29.** $w(t) = c_1 e^{4t} + c_2 e^{5t}$.   **31.** $w(t) = c_1 e^{t/3} + c_2 e^{-t}$.

33. $w(t) = (c_1 + c_2 t)e^{t/2}$.   **35.** $x(t) = e^{-2t}(c_1 \cos t + c_2 \sin t)$.   **37.** $x(t) = c_1 e^{-3it} + c_2 e^{2it}$.

39. $y(t) = c_1 e^{-2t} + c_2 e^{-t} + c_3 e^t$. **41.** $y(t) = (c_1 + c_2 t)e^{-3t} + c_3 e^{-2t}$.

43. $y(t) = A_1 \cosh t + B_1 \sinh t + e^{-2t}\left(A_2 \cos(t\sqrt{3}) + B_2 \sin(t\sqrt{3})\right)$.

45. $y(t) = (c_1 + c_2 t + c_3 t^2)e^{-t} + c_4 e^t$.

47. $y(t) = e^{-t/2}[(A_1 + A_2 t)\cos(t\sqrt{3}/2) + (B_1 + B_2 t)\sin(t\sqrt{3}/2)]$.

49. $y(t) = e^{-2t}(A_1 \cos t + B_1 \sin t) + e^{-t}(A_2 \cos t + B_2 \sin t)$.

51. $y(x) = x^{-2}\left(A\cos(\ln x) + B\sin(\ln x)\right)$. **53.** $y(x) = c_1 x^{-1} + c_2 x^{1/3}$.

55. $u(z) = c_1 z^{(1+\sqrt{5})/2} + c_2 z^{(1-\sqrt{5})/2}$. **57.** $u(z) = z^{-1}\left(A\cos(\sqrt{2}\ln z) + B\sin(\sqrt{2}\ln z)\right)$.

59. $u(x) = (c_1 + c_2 \ln x)x^{3/2}$. **61.** $u(z) = c_1 z^{-4} + c_2 z + c_3 z^2$. **63.** $y(t) = -e^{-t} + 2e^{4t}$.

65. $y(t) = 4\cosh 4\,(t - \pi)$. **67.** $w(t) = 2e^{2(t-1)} + e^{4(t-1)}$. **69.** $u(t) = 18te^{3t}$.

71. $u(x) = x + 2/\sqrt{x}$. **75.** $y(x) = \csc ax\,(c_1 \cos bx + c_2 \sin bx)$.

Exercise Set 4.4.3   Free Oscillations

1. $x(t) = 10\cos\left(gt/\sqrt{10}\right)$. **3.** $b = 6.2810$. Also $\delta = 8.747$.

5. $50\left(.99987e^{-6.25t}\cos(499.96t) - 50.0163e^{-6.25t}\sin(499.96t)\right)^2$.

9. $x(t) = \frac{1}{6}h\cos\omega t$. **11.** $\mu = \frac{\pi m}{S}\sqrt{\dfrac{1}{\frac{1}{T_1^2} - \frac{1}{T_2^2}}}$. **13.** $T = 2\pi\sqrt{\dfrac{I_0 + mx^2}{(Mx_0 + mx)g}}$. **15.** $\omega^2 = \frac{k_1 + k_2 + k_3}{m}$.

17. $\omega = \frac{qB}{m}$ and $T = \frac{2\pi m}{qB}$. **19.** When $f = .5$, $c = 6.58$ cycles. When $f = 0.01$, $c = 43.71$

cycles. Since the energy goes as the square of the amplitude, all we need do is take the square root of

the fraction f.

Exercise Set 4.5.3   Nonhomogeneous Equations

1. $y(t) = c_1 e^t + c_2 e^{3t} + 2 + \cos t$. **3.** $v(t) = (c_1 + c_2 t + \ln|t|)e^{-t}$.

5. $y(t) = c_1 \cos t + c_2 \sin t + \sin t \ln|\csc 2t - \cot 2t|$. **7.** $w(t) = c_1 + c_2 t + c_3 e^{-t} + 2t^2$.

9. $w(t) = (c_1 + c_2 t)e^{-t} + 7 - 12\cos 2t - 9\sin 2t$.

11. $x(y) = c_1 y + \frac{c_2}{y}\cos(2\ln|y|) + \frac{c_3}{y}\sin(2\ln|y|) - \frac{3}{25} - \frac{1}{5}\ln|y|$.

13. $x(t) = 1 - e^{-3t} + 2t - 3t^2$. **15.** $g(t) = (c_1 + t)\cos t + (c_2 + \ln|\sec t|)\sin t$.

17. $g(t) = c_1 e^{4t} + c_2 e^{-t} - \frac{1}{34}(5\cos t + 3\sin t)$. **19.** $w(z) = (c_1 + c_2 \ln z)z^{-2} + \frac{1}{4}(\ln z - 1)$.

21. $y(z) = c_1 e^z + c_2 e^{-2z} + 6z e^z + \frac{3}{2}z + \frac{3}{4} - \frac{6}{5}\cos z + \frac{2}{5}\sin z.$

23. $u(z) = c_1 e^{-z}\cos z + c_2 e^{-z}\sin z - \sin z.$ **25.** $w(z) = c_1 z + c_2 z^2 + c_3 z^{-4} + \frac{19}{4}z^{-1} + 2.$

27. $r(\theta) = c_1 e^\theta + c_2 e^{-2\theta} - \frac{1}{2} - \theta + \frac{6}{5}\cos 2\theta - \frac{2}{5}\sin 2\theta.$ **29.** $y(z) = c_1 z^{-2} + c_2 z^2 - \frac{1}{3}z.$

31. $y(x) = c_1 x^{-2} + c_2 x^2 + c_3 x^{-3} + 1 - x + 2\ln x.$

33. $w(u) = c_1 u^{-2} + c_2 u^{-3} + c_3 u^3 + 2\ln u - \frac{3}{4}(u - 4).$

35. $y(z) = \frac{1}{12}z^{-2} + \frac{1}{18}z^3 + \frac{1}{36} - \frac{1}{6}\ln|z|.$ **37.** $y_p(x) = -x.$

39. $(D - 1)^2(D^2 + 1)y(t) = y^{(iv)} - 2y''' + 2y'' - 2y' + y = 1 - 2t + t^2.$

Exercise Set 4.6.3 **Forced Oscillations**

1. Assuming that $x(0) = 0$, the specific solution is $x(t) = v_0 t + \frac{qE}{2m}t^2.$ **3.** $t = \sqrt{\frac{3(L-r)}{g}}.$ **5.** If we

write $\omega^2 := \frac{2k}{m}$, the solution is $x(t) = A\sin(\omega t + \alpha) + \frac{1}{m(\omega^2 - \Omega^2)}(3\cos\Omega t - 4\sin\Omega t).$

Exercise Set 4.7.1 **Boundary Value Green's Functions**

1. $G(x, \xi) = -\frac{1}{L}x_<(L - x_>).$ **3.** $G(x, \xi) = -\frac{\sin\omega x_< \sin\omega(L-x_>)}{\omega\sin\omega L}.$

5. $G(x, \xi) = \frac{\cos\omega(x_< - a)\cos\omega(x_> - b)}{\omega\sin\omega(b-a)}.$ **7.** $G(x, \xi) = -\frac{(\omega\cos\omega(x_< - a) + \sin\omega(x_< - a))\sin\omega(b-x_>)}{\omega^2(\cos\omega(b-a) - \sin\omega(b-a))}.$

9. $G(x, \xi) = \frac{(\omega\cos\omega x_< + \sin\omega x_<)((\sin\omega + \omega\cos\omega)\cos\omega x_> - (\cos\omega - \omega\sin\omega)\sin\omega x_>)}{\omega^3\sin\omega - 2\omega^2\cos\omega - \omega\sin\omega}.$

11. $G(x, \xi) = \frac{1}{2}\left(\ln\left|\frac{1+x_>}{1-x_>}\right| - \ln\left|\frac{1+b}{1-b}\right|\right).$

4.8 **Supplementary and Complementary Problems**

3. $y'' - 3y' + 2y = 0.$ **5.** $(2\cos t\cos 2t + \sin t\sin 2t)y'' + 3(\cos t\sin 2t)y'$

$+ (\cos t(2\cos 2t + 3\sin 2t) + \sin t\sin 2t)y = 0.$ **7.** $\omega^2 t y''' - \omega^3 y'' + \omega^5 t y' - \omega^5 y = 0.$

9. This problem is a test of your knowledge of your CAS. The determinant is so horrible to behold that only the most stout-hearted amongst you will proceed. Only if $a = b$ does any simplification occur.

11. $u''' + 3\pi u'' + 4\pi^2 u' + 2\pi^3 u = 0, u(0) = \pi + 1, u'(0) = -\pi(\pi + 3), u''(0) = \pi^2(\pi + 4).$

13. $u^{(iv)} + 64u = 0, u(0) = 1, u'(0) = 0, u''(0) = -8, u'''(0) = 0.$

15. $4x^2 w'' + 4xw' - w = 0$, with initial conditions $w(1) = 3, w'(1) = \frac{9}{2}.$

17. $x^4 w^{iv} + 4x^3 w''' - 16x^2 w'' + 72w = 0$, $w(1) = 1$, $w'(1) = -3$, $w''(1) = 6$,

$w'''(1) = -51$. **21.** If we write $\frac{1}{\mu} = \frac{1}{m_1} + \frac{1}{m_2}$, then the frequency is $f = \frac{1}{2\pi} \sqrt{\frac{k}{\mu}}$.

21. $L = \ell \frac{m_1 + \sqrt{m_1 m_2}}{m_1 + m_2}$. **22.** $T = \frac{\pi \sqrt{3}}{1 + \frac{a}{r}} \sqrt{\frac{m}{k}}$. **23.** $w^{(iv)} + 2w'' + w = 0$, with initial

conditions $w(0) = 1$, $w'(0) = 0$, $w''(0) = -1$, $w'''(0) = -2$.

25. $y(z) = y_0(z) u(z) = c_1 e^{-\alpha z} \sec z + c_2 e^{\alpha z} \sec z - \frac{1}{\alpha^2 + 4} \sin z$.

Exercise Set 5.3.4 **Laplace Transforms**

1. $\frac{1}{s-2} - \frac{2}{s-1} + \frac{1}{s}$. **3.** $\frac{2}{(s-3)^2} - \frac{1}{s-3}$. **5.** $\frac{s-2}{(s-2)^2 - 9}$. **7.** $\frac{12s}{(s^2+4)^2}$. **9.** $\frac{1}{2}\left[\frac{a}{(s-a)^2 + a^2} - \frac{a}{(s+a)^2 + a^2}\right]$.

11. $\frac{6}{(s+4)^4}$. **13.** $\frac{(s-a)^2 - \omega^2}{((s-a)^2 + \omega^2)^2}$. **15.** $\frac{\pi}{2} - \text{Atan}\left(\frac{s}{\omega}\right)$. **17.** $\frac{1}{2}\left(\frac{1}{s} + \frac{s}{s^2-36}\right)$. **19.** $\frac{6\omega^3}{(s^2+\omega^2)(s^2+9\omega^2)}$.

21. $\frac{2\omega_1 \omega_2 s^2}{[s^2 + (\omega_1 - \omega_2)^2][s^2 + (\omega_1 + \omega_2)^2]}$. **23.** $\frac{1 + (1-s)e^{-\pi s/2}}{s^2 + 1} + \frac{e^{-\pi s/2}}{s}$. **25.** $\frac{2}{s^3} - \frac{3\sqrt{\pi}}{s^{5/2}} + \frac{4}{s^2}$.

27. $\frac{s^5 + 2s^4 + 2(\omega^2 - 1)s^3 + \omega^2(\omega^2 - 6)s - 2\omega^4}{(s^2 + \omega^2)^3}$. **29.** $\frac{1}{s - \ln 2} - \frac{1}{s - \ln 3}$. **31.** $\sqrt{\pi}\left(\frac{3}{4(s+3)^{3/2}} - \frac{1}{(s+3)^{1/2}}\right)$.

33. $\frac{1}{(s-2)^3} + \frac{1}{s^3}$. **35.** $e^{a(a-s)}$. **37.** $\frac{a}{s^2 + a^2} + \frac{a^2 - s^2}{s^2 + a^2}$. **39.** $\frac{1}{2}\left(\frac{1}{s+a} - \frac{s+a}{(s+a)^2 + 4\omega^2}\right)$.

41. $\frac{3}{8s} - \frac{1}{2}\frac{s}{s^2 + \omega^2} + \frac{1}{8}\frac{s}{s^2 + 16\omega^2}$. **43.** $\frac{2}{s^3} - e^{-s}\left(\frac{2}{s^3} + \frac{2}{s^2} + \frac{1}{s} + \frac{\pi/2}{s^2 + (\pi/2)^2}\right)$.

45. $\left(\frac{1}{s} - \frac{2}{s^2}\right) - e^{-2s}\left(-\frac{2}{s^2} - \frac{1}{s}\right)\frac{1}{s}e^{-3s} + e^{-5s}\left(-\frac{\pi}{s^2 + \pi^2} - \frac{1}{s}\right)$.

47. $\frac{1}{s^2 + \pi^2}\left(\pi(1 + e^{-3s}) - (s - \pi)(e^{-s} + e^{-2s})\right)$. **49.** $\frac{1 - e^{-s}}{s^2(1 + e^{-s})}$. **51.** $e^{-3s} \sin 6$. **53.** e^{-4s}.

55. $\frac{1}{s}\left(e^{-4s} - e^{-2s}\right)$. **57.** $\frac{(1 - e^{-s/2})(1 + e^{-3s/2})}{s(1 - e^{-2s})}$. **59.** $\frac{\pi(e^{-s} + 1)}{(s^2 + \pi^2)(1 - e^{-2s})}$. **61.** $2\left(\frac{1}{\sqrt{s+a}} - \frac{1}{\sqrt{s+b}}\right)$.

63. $\frac{1}{s}$. **65.** $\frac{1}{s^2}\frac{e^{-s}}{1 + e^{-s}}$. **67.** $\frac{1 + e^{-\pi s}}{s^2 + 1}\frac{1}{1 - e^{-\pi s}}$.

Exercise Set 5.4.3 **Inverse Transforms**

1. $t + 2\sin t$. **3.** $(1 - t)e^{-4t}$. **5.** $\frac{1}{8}[(3 - t^2)\sin t - 3t\cos t]$. **7.** $\frac{1}{10}(2\sinh t - \sin 2t)$.

9. $e^{-4t}\left(2t - \frac{11}{2}t^2\right)$. **11.** $\frac{1}{b}e^{-at}(b\cos bt - a\sin bt)$. **13.** $6\cosh t - 6\cos t$.

15. $w(t; 0, 2) - w(t; 2, 4)$ extended with period 4. **17.** $2\cosh 3t - 1$.

19. $\frac{1}{2}\left((t - 1)u(t - 1) + (t - 3)u(t - 3)\right)$. **21.** $\delta(t - 2) - 3u(t - 2)$. **23.** $\frac{1}{t}\delta(t - 2)$.

27. $\frac{1}{a^2}\left(e^{at} - (at + 1)\right)$. **29.** $\frac{1}{2!}(t-5)^2 u(t-5)$. **31.** $(t-2)u(t-2) - (t-4)u(t-4)$.

33. $\frac{e^{2t}-e^{-3t}}{2-(-3)}$. **35.** $\frac{1}{(s-1)(s^2+1)}$. **37.** $\frac{1}{2}\left(t^3 - 2(t-1)^3 u(t-1) + (t-2)^3 u(t-2)\right)$.

Exercise Set 5.5.3 **Solving ODE's with Laplace Transforms**

1. $x(t) = \left(1 - e^{-(t-\pi)}\right)u(t-\pi) - \left(1 - e^{-(t-2\pi)}\right)u(t-2\pi)$.

3. $x(t) = \frac{1}{2}\left(1 + 3e^{-2t}\right) - \frac{1}{2}\left(1 - e^{-2(t-1)}\right)u(t-1)$.

5. $x(t) = \frac{1}{4}\left(e^t - e^{-3t}\right) - \frac{1}{12}\left(e^{-(t-1)} + 3e^{t-1} - 4\right)u(t-1)$

$-\frac{1}{36}\left(e^{-3(t-2)} - 9e^{t-2} + 12(t-2) + 8\right)u(t-2)$. **7.** $x(t) = \frac{4}{3}\cosh t + \frac{1}{6}\cosh 2t - \frac{1}{2}$.

9. $x(t) = \frac{1}{16}\cos t + \frac{1}{2}\left(\sin t - t\cos t\right)$.

11. $v(t) = \frac{1}{30}\left(35 - 8e^{3t} - 27e^{-2t}\right) + \frac{e^{-1}}{30}\left(5 + e^{3(t-1)} - e^{-2(t-1)} - 5e^{t-1}\right)u(t-1)$.

13. $y(t) =$

$4e^{-t} - 3e^{-2t} + \frac{1}{2}\left(1 - 2e^{-(t-1)} + e^{-2(t-1)}\right)u(t-1) - \frac{1}{2}\left(1 - 2e^{-(t-2)} + e^{-2(t-2)}\right)u(t-2)$.

15. $x(t) = \frac{1}{15}\left(5e^t - 2e^{-5t} - 3\right)$

$-\frac{1}{30}\left(-6 + 5e^{t-\pi/2} + e^{-5(t-\pi/2)}\right)u(t-\pi/2)$.

17. $x(t) = \sum_{n=1}^{\infty}\sin(t - n\pi)u(t - n\pi) = \sum_{n=1}^{\infty}(-1)^n \sin t \cdot u(t - n\pi)$, a half-wave rectified sine wave.

19. $v(t) = -\frac{1}{\sigma^2+\omega^2}e^{-\sigma(t-T)}\frac{\sin\omega t}{\sin\omega T}\left(1 - e^{-\sigma(T-\tau)}(\cos\omega(T-\tau) + \frac{\sigma}{\omega}\sin\omega(T-\tau))\right) +$

$\frac{1}{\sigma^2+\omega^2}\left(1 - e^{-\sigma(t-\tau)}(\cos\omega(t-\tau) + \frac{\sigma}{\omega}\sin\omega(t-\tau))\right)u(t-\tau)$. **21.** $y(t) = c_2 \sin t$, for any

value of c_2. These boundary conditions do not lead to a unique solution (but then again, nobody said boundary value problems had solutions, no less unique ones.).

23. $y(t) = \left\{\frac{a\omega_2^2}{\omega^2}(1 - \cos\omega t) + \frac{a\omega_2^2}{\omega^2-\Omega^2}(\cos\Omega t - \cos\omega t)\right\} -$

$\left\{\frac{a\omega_2^2}{\omega^2}(1 - \cos\omega(t - 2\pi/\Omega)) + \frac{a\omega_2^2}{\omega^2-\Omega^2}(\cos\Omega(t - 2\pi/\Omega) - \cos\omega(t - 2\pi/\Omega))\right\}u(t -$

$2\pi/\Omega)$. **25.** $x(t) = \frac{F_0}{m\Omega}\frac{1}{\omega^2-\Omega^2}\sin\Omega t\left(1 + 2\sum_{n=1}^{\infty}(-1)^n u(t - n\pi/\Omega)\right)$. The parenthesized

term is a square wave alternating between $+1$ and -1 with period $\frac{2\pi}{\Omega}$. **27.** The model with a constant time lag T follows the equations $\dot{u}_n(t) = k\left(u_{n-1}(t-T) - u_n(t-T)\right)$, $n = 2 : N$, with the same initial conditions as before, $u_n(0) = 0$, $n = 2 : N$. Transforming

$sU_n(s) = ke^{-sT}\left(U_{n-1}(s) - U_n(s)\right)$. Thus

$$U_n(s) = \frac{ke^{-sT}}{s+ke^{-sT}}U_{n-1}(s) = \left(\frac{ke^{-sT}}{s+ke^{-sT}}\right)^{n-1}U_1(s).$$

29. $y(x) = \frac{W_0}{96EIL^3}\left(18\left(\frac{x}{L}\right)^2 - 11\left(\frac{x}{L}\right)^3 + 16\left(\frac{x}{L} - 1\right)^3 u(x - L)\right)$. At the center

$y(L) = \frac{7W_0}{96EIL^3}$.

31. $y(x) = \frac{WL^5}{EI}\left(\frac{5}{256}\left(\frac{x}{L}\right)^2 - \frac{7}{256}\left(\frac{x}{L}\right)^3 + \frac{1}{120}\left(\left(\frac{x}{L}\right)^5 - 2\left(\frac{x}{L} - \frac{1}{2}\right)u\left(x - \frac{L}{2}\right)\right)\right)$.

Exercise Set 5.6.1   **Green's Functions via Transforms**

1. $G(x, \xi) = -\frac{\sin\omega(L-\xi)}{\omega\sin\omega L}\sin\omega x + \frac{1}{\omega}\sin\omega(x - \xi)u(x - \xi)$.

3. $G(x, \xi) = \frac{\cos\omega(x-a)\sin\omega(b-\xi)}{\omega\sin\omega(b-a)} + \frac{1}{\omega}\sin\omega(x - \xi)u(x - \xi)$.

5. $G(x, \xi) = \frac{1}{2\omega(1-\cos\omega)}[(\sin\omega\xi + \sin\omega(1 - \xi))\cos\omega x + \omega(\cos\omega\xi + \cos\omega(1 -$

$\xi))\sin\omega x] + \frac{1}{\omega}\sin\omega(x - \xi)u(x - \xi)$.

7. $G(x, \xi) = \frac{1}{4}(\sinh x + \sin x)\left(\frac{\sin(L-\xi)}{\sin L} - \frac{\sinh(L-\xi)}{\sinh L}\right) - \frac{1}{4}(\sinh x - \sin x)\times$

$\left(\frac{\sinh(L-\xi)}{\sinh L} + \frac{\sin(L-\xi)}{\sin L}\right) + \frac{1}{2}(\sinh(x - \xi) - \sin(x - \xi))u(x - \xi)$.

5.7   Supplementary and Complementary Problems

7. $\int_0^\infty \frac{e^{-\alpha t} - e^{-\beta t}}{t}dt = \ln\left(\frac{\beta}{\alpha}\right)$.   **9.** $\int_0^\infty \frac{\cos(tz)}{1+z^2}dz = \frac{\pi}{2}e^{-t}$.   **13.** $\phi(t) = \frac{\beta}{\beta-1}\left(1 - e^{-(\beta-1)t}\right)$.

Exercise Set 6.2.1   **Multivariate ODE Models**

1. $m_1\ddot{x}_1 + k\left(x_1 + (x_1 - x_2)\right) = 0$, $m_2\ddot{x}_2 + k\left(-(x_1 - x_2) + (x_2 - x_3)\right) = 0$,

$m_3\ddot{x}_3 + k\left(-(x_2 - x_3) + x_3\right) = 0$.   **3.** $2L\dot{I}_1 - L\dot{I}_3 + RI_1 - RI_2 = E(t)$,

$L\dot{I}_2 - RI_1 + 3RI_2 - RI_3 = 0$, $-L\dot{I}_1 + 2L\dot{I}_3 + RI_3 - RI_4 = 0$,

$L\dot{I}_4 - RI_2 - RI_3 + 2RI_4 = 0$.   **5.** Let r_k, $k = 1 : 4$ be the volume of reagent and V_k be the volume of liquid in the kth tank.

$$\dot{\mathbf{r}} = 0.05 \begin{bmatrix} -1 & 1 & 1 & 1 \\ 1 & -1 & 1 & 1 \\ 1 & 1 & -1 & 1 \\ 1 & 1 & 1 & -1 \end{bmatrix} \mathbf{r} + 0.10 \begin{bmatrix} 0 & 0 & 0 & 0 \\ 0 & 1 & 0 & 0 \\ 0 & 0 & 1 & 0 \\ 0 & 0 & 0 & 0 \end{bmatrix} \mathbf{v}.$$

The initial conditions are: $\mathbf{v}(0) = [500; 500; 500; 500]$ liters and $\mathbf{r}(0) = [125; 125; 250; 165]$ liters. We can integrate the volume flow equation to get $\mathbf{v}(t) = [500 + 10t; 500 + 10t; 500; 500]$.

Exercise Set 6.3.3   Systems of Linear ODE's

1. Using $\mathbf{x} = [u; u'; v; v']$, $\mathbf{A} = \begin{bmatrix} 0 & 1 & 0 & 0 \\ 1 & -2 & -2 & 3 \\ 0 & 0 & 0 & 1 \\ 1 & -1 & -3 & -1 \end{bmatrix}$ and $\mathbf{b}(t) = \begin{bmatrix} 0 \\ 0 \\ 0 \\ t \end{bmatrix}$. **3.** Using

$\mathbf{x} = [u; u'; v; v']$, $\mathbf{x}'(t) = \dfrac{1}{2} \begin{bmatrix} 0 & 2 & 0 & 0 \\ -3 & 1 & 1 & -1 \\ 0 & 0 & 0 & 1 \\ 3 & 1 & 1 & 1 \end{bmatrix}$. **5.** $(-\infty, -1)$, $(-1, 0)$, $(0, 1)$, or $(1, \infty)$.

7. $\left(-\infty, -\frac{1}{2}\right)$, $\left(-\frac{1}{2}, \frac{5}{3}\right)$, $\left(\frac{5}{3}, 2\right)$, or $(2, \infty)$.

Exercise Set 6.4.4   The Eigenvalue Problem

1. $(1, [1; 1])$, $(0.2, [11; -5])$. **3.** $\left(\frac{1}{2}\left(1 \pm i\sqrt{3}\right), \left[1 - i; i(1 \mp \sqrt{3})\right]\right)$. **5.** $(-2, [2; 2; 1])$, $(1, [1; 1; 0], [-1; 0; 3])$. **7.** $(5, [1; 2; 2])$, $(2, [2; 1; -2])$, $(-1, [2; -2; 1])$. **9.** $(z + 1, [1; 1; 0])$, $(z - 1, [1; -1; 0])$, $(z, [0; 0; 1])$. **11.** $(a + b, [1; 0; 1])$, $(a - b, [1; 0; -1])$, $(c, [0; 1; 0])$. **13.** $(3, [1; i; 0], [0; 1; 0])$, $(1, [1; -i; 0])$. **15.** $(-4, [6; 5; -24; 20])$, $(1, [1; 0; 1; 0])$, $(0, [-2; 1; 0; 0])$. Thus $\mathbf{A}$ is not diagonalizable. **17.** $(4, [1; 1; 1; 1])$, $(3, [2; 2; 2; 1])$, $(2, [3; 3; 2; 1])$, $(1, [4; 3; 2; 1])$. **19.** $(15, [1; 1; 1; 1])$, $(5, [-1; 0; 0; 1], [0; -1; 1; 0])$, $(-1, [-1; 1; 0; 0])$. $k = 1 : (n - 1)$. **29.** $(\mathbf{a}^T\mathbf{a}, \mathbf{a})$ is an eigenpair and all the other eigenvalues are zero.

Exercise Set 6.5.1   **Jordan Normal Form**

1. $\lambda = 1, 1, 1$; chain $= \{[1; 0; 0], [0; 0; 1], [0; 1; 0]\}$; $\mathbf{J} = \begin{bmatrix} 1 & 1 & 0 \\ 0 & 1 & 0 \\ 0 & 0 & 1 \end{bmatrix}$. **3.** $\lambda = 2, 2, 2$;

chain $= \{[1; 0; 0], [0; 1; 0], [0; -2; 1]\}$; $\mathbf{J} = \begin{bmatrix} 2 & 1 & 0 \\ 0 & 2 & 1 \\ 0 & 0 & 2 \end{bmatrix}$. **5.** $\lambda = 1, 1, 1$;

chain $= \{[1; 1; 3], [-1; -2; 0], [0; 0; 1]\}$; Thus $\mathbf{J} = \begin{bmatrix} 1 & 1 & 0 \\ 0 & 1 & 1 \\ 0 & 0 & 1 \end{bmatrix}$.

Exercise Set 6.6.3   **Solving Autonomous Linear Systems**

1. $\mathbf{x}(t) = c_1 e^t [\cos 2t; \cos 2t + \sin 2t] + c_2 e^t [\sin 2t; \sin 2t - \cos 2t]$.

$\mathbf{X}(t) = e^t \begin{bmatrix} \cos 2t & \sin 2t \\ \cos 2t + \sin 2t & \sin 2t - \cos 2t \end{bmatrix}$. **3.** $\mathbf{x}(t) = c_1 e^t [2; 1] + c_2 e^t \, (t[2; 1] + [1; 0])$.

$\mathbf{X}(t) = e^t \begin{bmatrix} 2 & 2t + 1 \\ 1 & t \end{bmatrix}$. **5.** $\mathbf{x}(t) = e^{-3t}[-2 \cos 4t + \sin 4t; \cos 4t - 3 \sin 4t]$.

$\mathbf{X}(t) = e^{-3t} \begin{bmatrix} -\cos 4t - \sin 4t & -\sin 4t + \cos 4t \\ 2 \cos 4t & 2 \sin 4t \end{bmatrix}$.

7. $\mathbf{x}(t) = e^{-3t}[\cos 2t + 7 \sin 2t; 3 \cos 2t + \sin 2t]$.

$\mathbf{X}(t) = e^{-3t} \begin{bmatrix} 5 \cos 2t & 5 \sin 2t \\ \cos 2t - 2 \sin 2t & \sin 2t + 2 \cos 2t \end{bmatrix}$. **9.** $\mathbf{x}(t) = [-6; 2] e^{-4t}$.

$\mathbf{X}(t) = \begin{bmatrix} -3e^{-4t} & e^{3t} \\ e^{-4t} & 2e^{3t} \end{bmatrix}$. **11.** $\mathbf{x}(t) = e^{6t}[\cos 2t - \sin 2t; -4 \sin 2t]$.

$\mathbf{X}(t) = e^{6t} \begin{bmatrix} \cos 2t + \sin 2t & \sin 2t - \cos 2t \\ 4 \cos 2t & 4 \sin 2t \end{bmatrix}$. **13.** $\mathbf{x}(t) = 2e^{3t}[1; 0] - e^t[1; -1]$.

$\mathbf{X}(t) = \begin{bmatrix} e^{3t} & e^t \\ 0 & -e^t \end{bmatrix}$. **15.** $\mathbf{x}(t) = c_1 e^{4t}[1; 0; 1] + c_2 e^{-2t}[1; 1; 0] + c_3 e^t[1; 1; 1]$.

$\mathbf{X}(t) = \begin{bmatrix} e^{4t} & e^{-2t} & e^t \\ 0 & e^{-2t} & e^t \\ e^{4t} & 0 & e^t \end{bmatrix}$.

17. $\mathbf{x}(t) =$

$$c_1 e^{-2t} \begin{bmatrix} 2 \\ -2 \\ 1 \end{bmatrix} + c_2 e^{-t} \begin{bmatrix} 2\cos t\sqrt{2} + \sqrt{2}\sin t\sqrt{2} \\ -\cos t\sqrt{2} + \sqrt{2}\sin t\sqrt{2} \\ 2\cos t\sqrt{2} \end{bmatrix} + c_3 e^{-t} \begin{bmatrix} 2\sin t\sqrt{2} - \sqrt{2}\cos t\sqrt{2} \\ -\sin t\sqrt{2} - \sqrt{2}\cos t\sqrt{2} \\ 2\sin t\sqrt{2} \end{bmatrix}.$$

$$\mathbf{X}(t) = \begin{bmatrix} 2e^{-2t} & e^{-t}\left(2\cos t\sqrt{2} - \sqrt{2}\sin t\sqrt{2}\right) & e^{-t}\left(2\sin t\sqrt{2} + \sqrt{2}\cos t\sqrt{2}\right) \\ -2e^{-2t} & e^{-t}\left(-\cos t\sqrt{2} + \sqrt{2}\sin t\sqrt{2}\right) & e^{-t}\left(-\sin t\sqrt{2} - \sqrt{2}\cos t\sqrt{2}\right) \\ e^{-2t} & 2e^{-t}\cos t\sqrt{2} & 2e^{-t}\sin t\sqrt{2} \end{bmatrix}.$$

19. $\mathbf{x}(t) = -\frac{2}{3}e^{-t}[4; -4; 1] + \frac{14}{3}e^{2t}[1; -1; 1] + e^{2t}[t; -t-1; t-1].$

$$\mathbf{X}(t) = \begin{bmatrix} 4e^{-t} & e^{2t} & te^{2t} \\ -4e^{-t} & -e^{2t} & (-t-1)e^{2t} \\ e^{-t} & e^{2t} & (t-1)e^{2t} \end{bmatrix}.$$

21. $\mathbf{x}(t) = [2; -3 + \cos 2t + \sin 2t; 2 - \sin 2t - \cos 2t]e^t.$ $\mathbf{X}(t) = e^t \begin{bmatrix} 2 & 0 & 0 \\ -3 & \cos 2t & \sin 2t \\ 2 & \sin 2t & -\cos 2t \end{bmatrix}.$

23. $\mathbf{x}(t) = c_1 e^{3t}[1; 1; 1; 1] + e^{-t}\left(c_2[1; -1; 0; 0] + c_3[1; 0; 0 - 1; 0] + c_4[1; 0; 0; -1]\right).$

$$\mathbf{X}(t) = \begin{bmatrix} e^{3t} & e^{-t} & e^{-t} & e^{-t} \\ e^{3t} & -e^{-t} & 0 & 0 \\ e^{3t} & 0 & -e^{-t} & 0 \\ e^{3t} & 0 & 0 & -e^{-t} \end{bmatrix}.$$

25. $\mathbf{x}(t) = -\frac{1}{80}e^{-4t}[6; 5; -24; -20] + \frac{6}{5}e^t[1; 0; 1; 0] + \frac{1}{16}[-2; 1; 0; 0]$

$+\frac{3}{4}[-2t; t; -2; 1].$ $\mathbf{X}(t) = \begin{bmatrix} 6e^{-4t} & e^t & -2 & -2t \\ 5e^{-4t} & 0 & 1 & t \\ -24e^{-4t} & e^t & 0 & -2 \\ -20e^{-4t} & 0 & 0 & 1 \end{bmatrix}.$

27. $\mathbf{x}(t) = [2(e^{5t} - e^{-5t}); 5e^{3t} - 3e^{-3t}; 4e^{5t} + e^{-5t}; e^{3t} + 3e^{-3t}]$ or

$[4\sinh 5t; 8\sinh 3t + 2\cosh 3t; 3\sinh 5t + 5\cosh 5t; -2\sinh 3t + 4\cosh 3t].$

$$\mathbf{X}(t) = \begin{bmatrix} e^{5t} & -2e^{-5t} & 0 & 0 \\ 0 & 0 & 5e^{3t} & -e^{-3t} \\ 2e^{5t} & e^{-5t} & 0 & 0 \\ 0 & 0 & e^{3t} & e^{-3t} \end{bmatrix}.$$

Exercise Set 6.7.2   **Applications of Linear Systems**

1. $\left(\omega^2 - \omega_p^2\right)\left(\alpha\omega^2 - (\alpha\omega_p^2 + (\alpha - 1)\omega_s^2)\right) = 0$. Thus we still have pure pendulum oscillation, but the spring oscillations have changed. In particular, $\omega = \sqrt{\alpha\omega_p^2 + (\alpha - 1)\omega_s^2}$. As $\alpha \to 0$, we lose our second mass and $\omega \to i\omega_s$, indicating the unreality of this case. As $\alpha \to \infty$, $\omega \to \infty$ and the corresponding period goes to $\omega \to \sqrt{\alpha}\sqrt{\omega_p^2 + \omega_s^2}$. **3.** $\omega^2\left(\omega^2 - \omega_s^2\right)\left(\omega^2 - 3\omega_s^2\right) = 0$.

$(0, [1; 1; 1])$, $(\omega_s^2, [1; 0; -1])$, $(3\omega_s^2, [1; -2; 1])$.

5. $\omega^4 - \left(\frac{f+1}{f+3}\right)\left(1 + \frac{2}{f}\frac{r+L}{r}\right)\frac{g}{L}\omega^2 + \frac{2(1+f)}{f(3+f)}\frac{g}{L}\frac{g}{r} = 0$.

7. $\omega^2 = \omega_1^2$, $\omega^2 = \frac{1}{2}\left(\omega_1^2 + \omega_2^2\right) \pm \frac{1}{2}\sqrt{\omega_1^4 + \omega_2^4 + 6\omega_1^2\omega_2^2}$. As $M \to m$ we have $\omega_2 \to \omega_1$ so these roots become ω_1^2 and the pair $\omega_1^2\left(1 \pm \sqrt{2}\right)$; the negative sign is not physical and must be discarded. As $M \to \infty$, $\omega_2^2 \to 0$ and roots are ω_1^2, ω_1^2, and 0.   **9.**

Exercise Set 6.8.1   **Nonhomogeneous Linear Systems**

1. $\mathbf{x}(t) = c_1[3; 2]e^{-2t} + c_2[2; 1]e^{3t}$. $x_p(t) = e^{3t}[3; 2]e^{-2t} - e^{-2t}[2; 1]e^{3t} = [1; 1]e^t$.

3. $\mathbf{x}_c(t) = c_1[2\cos t - \sin t; \cos t] + c_2[2\sin t + \cos t; \sin t]$.
$$\mathbf{x}_p(t) = \begin{bmatrix} (2t - 1)\cos t - t\sin t \\ t\cos t - \sin t \end{bmatrix}.$$

5. $\mathbf{x}_c(t) = c_1 e^{2t}[\cos 2t; -2\sin 2t] + c_2 e^{2t}[\sin 2t; 2\cos 2t]$. $\mathbf{x}_p(t) = [0; -te^{2t}]$.

7. $\mathbf{x}_c(t) = c_1 e^t[1; 0; 0] + c_2 e^{2t}[1; 1; 0] + c_3 e^{3t}[1; 1; 1]$. $\mathbf{x}_p(t) = \left[t - \frac{1}{6}; \frac{5}{6}; t + \frac{1}{3}\right]$.

9. $\mathbf{x}_c(t) = c_1 e^{2t}[2; 0; 1] + c_2 e^t[0; 1; 0] + c_3 e^{-t}[-1; 0; 1]$. $\mathbf{x}_p(t) = \left[-\frac{3}{2}; t; -\frac{1}{2}\right]e^t$.

$c_1 = 2 = c_2$, $c_3 = -\frac{3}{2}$. **11.** $u(t) = c_1 e^{4t} + c_2 e^{-2t} + 1 - t$, $v(t) = -c_1 e^{4t} + c_2 e^{-2t} + t$.

Exercise Set 6.9.4   **State-Transition Matrix**

1. Distinct eigenvalues λ and μ, $e^{\mathbf{A}t} = \frac{1}{\lambda - \mu}\left((e^{\lambda t} - e^{\mu t})\mathbf{A} + (\lambda e^{\mu t} - \mu e^{\lambda t})\mathbf{I}\right)$. When there are two repeated eigenvalues λ_0 and λ_0, $e^{\mathbf{A}t} = ((1 - \lambda_0 t)\mathbf{I} + t\mathbf{A})e^{\lambda_0 t}$. **3.** The $(1, 1)$-entry is

$\frac{1}{2}\left\{\left(1+\sqrt{YZ}\right)^{n}+\left(1-\sqrt{YZ}\right)^{n}\right\}$, the $(1,2)$-entry is

$\frac{1}{2}\sqrt{\frac{Z}{Y}}\left(\left(1+\sqrt{YZ}\right)^{n}-\left(1-\sqrt{YZ}\right)^{n}\right)$, the $(2,1)$-entry is

$\frac{1}{2}\sqrt{\frac{Y}{Z}}\left(\left(1+\sqrt{YZ}\right)^{n}-\left(1-\sqrt{YZ}\right)^{n}\right)$, and the $(2,2)$-entry is

$\frac{1}{2}\left\{\left(1+\sqrt{YZ}\right)^{n}+\left(1-\sqrt{YZ}\right)^{n}\right\}$. **5.** $\mathbf{C}^{m}=\begin{bmatrix} 1 & 1 & m-1 \\ 0 & 0 & 1 \\ 0 & 0 & 1 \end{bmatrix}$,

$\exp(\mathbf{C}t)=\begin{bmatrix} e^{t} & (t-1)e^{t}+1 & e^{t}-1 \\ 0 & 1 & e^{t}-1 \\ 0 & 0 & e^{t} \end{bmatrix}$. $\sin(\mathbf{C}t)=\begin{bmatrix} \sin t & t\cos t-\sin t & \sin t \\ 0 & 0 & \sin t \\ 0 & 0 & \sin t \end{bmatrix}$.

7. $e^{\mathbf{F}t}=e^{-t}\begin{bmatrix} 1-2\sin t & \cos t+\sin t-1 & 1-\cos t \\ 2(1-\cos t-2\sin t) & 3\cos t+\sin t-2 & 2\cos t-\sin t-2 \\ 2(1-\cos t-\sin t) & 2(\cos t-1) & 2-\cos t+\sin t \end{bmatrix}$.

9. $e^{\mathbf{H}t}=\left(\mathbf{I}+\frac{1}{n}\mathbf{J}\left(e^{ant}-1\right)\right)e^{(b-a)t}$. **11.** $\mathbf{\Phi}(t,0)=e^{6t}\begin{bmatrix} 1-2t & t \\ -4t & 1+2t \end{bmatrix}$.

13. $\mathbf{\Phi}(t,0)=\frac{1}{4}\begin{bmatrix} 8\sinh 4t+4\cosh 4t & -3\sinh 4t \\ 16\sinh 4t & 4\cosh 4t-8\sinh 4t \end{bmatrix}$

$=\frac{1}{8}\begin{bmatrix} 4(3e^{4t}-e^{-4t}) & 3(e^{-4t}-e^{4t}) \\ 16(e^{4t}-e^{-4t}) & 4(3e^{-4t}-e^{4t}) \end{bmatrix}$.

15. $\mathbf{\Phi}(t,0)=\frac{1}{9}\begin{bmatrix} 8e^{-t}+(1-3t)e^{2t} & -4e^{-t}+(4-3t)e^{2t} & 12(e^{2t}-e^{-t}) \\ (8+3t)e^{2t}-8e^{-t} & 4e^{-t}+(3t+5)e^{2t} & 12(e^{-t}-e^{2t}) \\ 2e^{-t}-(3t+2)e^{2t} & -e^{-t}+(1-3t)e^{2t} & 12e^{2t}-3e^{-t} \end{bmatrix}$.

17. $\mathbf{\Phi}(t,0)=\mathbf{X}(t)\mathbf{X}^{-1}(0)=\begin{bmatrix} 3e^{2t}-2e^{t} & 2(e^{2t}-e^{-t}) & 2(e^{t}-e^{2t}) \\ -2e^{5t}+e^{2t}-e^{t} & 2e^{2t}-e^{t} & e^{5t}-2e^{2t}+e^{t} \\ -2e^{5t}+6e^{2t}-4e^{t} & 4(e^{2t}-e^{t}) & e^{5t}-4e^{2t}+4e^{t} \end{bmatrix}$.

$\mathbf{x}(t)=[(2c_1+2)e^{3t}+e^{t}+\frac{1}{2}e^{-2t}(3c_2-6); (c_1+1)e^{3t}+e^{t}+(c_2-2)e^{-2t}]$. **19.** Start with

$\mathbf{\Phi}(t,0)=\frac{1}{2}\begin{bmatrix} 3e^{t}-e^{-t} & e^{-t}-e^{t} \\ 3(e^{t}-e^{-t}) & 3e^{-t}-e^{t} \end{bmatrix}$, $\mathbf{x}_{\mathrm{p}}(t)=\frac{1}{4}\begin{bmatrix} (6t-3)e^{t}+3e^{-t}+t \\ (6t-5)e^{t}+9e^{-t}+2t-1 \end{bmatrix}$.

21. $\mathbf{x}_{\mathrm{p}}(t)=e^{\mathbf{A}t}\begin{bmatrix} \ln|\sin t|-2t+5\ln|\sec t| \\ 2\ln|\sec t| \end{bmatrix}$.

23. $e^{\mathbf{A}t}=\begin{bmatrix} \cos t+\sin t & -\sin t \\ 5\sin t & \cos t-2\sin t \end{bmatrix}$, $\mathbf{x}_{\mathrm{p}}(t)=e^{\mathbf{A}t}\begin{bmatrix} \frac{1}{2}\sin 2t-\frac{1}{4}\cos 2t \\ -3\cos 2t-\left(t-\frac{1}{2}\sin 2t\right) \end{bmatrix}$.

25. $\Phi(t,0) = \dfrac{1}{4}\begin{bmatrix} 2(e^{-t}+e^{3t}) & 0 & e^{3t}-e^{-t} \\ 0 & 4e^{-2t} & 0 \\ 4(e^{3t}-e^{-t}) & 0 & 2(e^{-t}+e^{3t}) \end{bmatrix}$, $\mathbf{x}_p(t) = \begin{bmatrix} e^t + \frac{1}{4}e^{-t} - \frac{5}{4}e^{3t} \\ 2e^t - 2e^{-2t} \\ 3e^t - \frac{5}{2}e^{3t} - \frac{1}{2}e^{-t} \end{bmatrix}$.

27. $\Phi(t,0) = \dfrac{1}{3}\begin{bmatrix} 2e^{2(t-\tau)}+e^{-t+\tau} & 0 & 2(e^{2(t-\tau)}-e^{-t+\tau}) \\ 0 & e^{t-\tau} & 0 \\ e^{2(t-\tau)}-e^{-t+\tau} & 0 & e^{2(t-\tau)}+2e^{-t+\tau} \end{bmatrix}$,

$\mathbf{x}_p(t) = \dfrac{1}{6}\begin{bmatrix} -9e^t + e^{-t} + 8e^{2t} \\ 6te^t \\ -3e^t - e^{-t} + 4e^{2t} \end{bmatrix}$.

Exercise Set 6.10.1 **Initial Value Green's Function**

1. $G(t,\tau) = \frac{\sin\omega(t-\tau)}{\omega}u(t-\tau)$. **3.** $G(t,\tau) = e^{-2(t-\tau)}\sin(t-\tau)u(t-\tau)$.

5. $G(t,\tau) = (-1 + \cosh(t-\tau))\,u(t-\tau)$.

7. $G(t,\tau) = \frac{1}{2}\left(-\sinh(t-\tau) + (t-\tau)\cosh(t-\tau)\right)u(t-\tau)$.

9. $G(t,\tau) = e^{t-\tau}\begin{bmatrix} \cos 2(t-\tau) + \sin 2(t-\tau) & -\sin 2(t-\tau) \\ 2\sin 2(t-\tau) & \cos 2(t-\tau) - \sin 2(t-\tau) \end{bmatrix}u(t-\tau)$.

11. $\mathbf{G}(t,\tau) = \begin{bmatrix} -e^{t-\tau}+e^{4(t-\tau)}+e^{-2(t-\tau)} & e^{t-\tau}-e^{4(t-\tau)} & e^{t-\tau}-e^{-2(t-\tau)} \\ -e^{t-\tau}+e^{-2(t-\tau)} & e^{t-\tau} & e^{t-\tau}-e^{-2(t-\tau)} \\ -e^{t-\tau}+e^{4(t-\tau)} & e^{t-\tau}-e^{4(t-\tau)} & e^{t-\tau} \end{bmatrix}u(t-\tau)$.

13. $\mathbf{G}(t,\tau) = \frac{1}{4}\{e^{3(t-\tau)}\mathbf{ones}(4) + e^{(t-\tau)}[4\mathbf{eye}(4) - \mathbf{ones}(4)]\}u(t-\tau)$.

Exercise Set 6.11.1 **Phase Plane Analysis of Linear Systems**

1. 0 is an unstable spiral. **3.** 0 is an unstable improper node. **5.** degenerate case. **7.** origin is a saddle. Since the eigenvalues are of opposite signs, the origin is a saddle.

Exercise Set 6.12.4 **Introduction to Controllability and Observability**

1. The system is controllable and observable. **3.** controllable and not observable. **5.** controllable and not observable. **7.** controllable and not observable.

Exercise Set 6.13.4 **Solving Linear Systems with Laplace Transforms**

1. $a(t) = 2e^{3t} - e^{2t}$ and $b(t) = e^{3t} - e^{2t}$. **3.** $a(t) = \frac{1}{4}(e^t + (2t-1)e^{3t})$,

$b(t) = \frac{1}{4}(5e^t - (2t+1)e^{3t})$. **5.** $a(t) = -\frac{8}{65}\sin 2t - \frac{5}{312}e^{-3t} - \frac{3}{40}e^{-t} + \frac{3}{40}e^t + \frac{5}{312}e^{3t}$,

$b(t) = \frac{2}{65}(\cos 2t + \sin 2t) + \frac{1}{312}e^{-3t} + \frac{1}{40}e^{-t} - \frac{3}{40}e^{t} + \frac{5}{312}e^{3t},$

$c(t) = -\frac{9}{260}\cos 2t + \frac{7}{130}\sin 2t - \frac{1}{65}e^{-3t} + \frac{1}{15}e^{-t} - \frac{1}{60}e^{2t}.$

7. $\Phi(t,0) = e^t \begin{bmatrix} 1+4t & -4t \\ 4t & 1-4t \end{bmatrix}.$ **9.** $\Phi(t,0) = \begin{bmatrix} e^t & e^t - 1 & (t-1)e^t + 1 \\ 0 & 1 & e^t - 1 \\ 0 & 0 & e^t \end{bmatrix}.$

11. $\exp(\mathbf{A}t) = e^{-t}\begin{bmatrix} 1 - 2\sin t & \cos t + \sin t - 1 & 1 - \cos t \\ 2(1 - \cos t - 2\sin t) & 3\cos t + \sin t - 2 & 2 - 2\cos t + \sin t \\ 2(1 - \cos t - \sin t) & 2(\cos t - 1) & 2 - \cos t + \sin t \end{bmatrix}.$

13. $\mathbf{x}(t) = [-6e^{-2t} + e^t + 6e^{3t}; -4e^{-2t} + e^t + 3e^{3t}].$

15. $\mathbf{x}(t) = \left[4e^{2t} - \frac{3}{2}e^t + \frac{3}{2}e^{-t}; (2+t)e^t; 2e^{2t} - \frac{1}{2}e^t - \frac{3}{2}e^{-t}\right].$

17. $e^{\mathbf{A}t} = \frac{1}{3}\begin{bmatrix} 2e^{2t} + e^{-t} & 0 & 2(e^{2t} - e^{-t}) \\ 0 & 3e^t & 0 \\ e^{2t} - e^{-t} & 0 & e^{2t} + 2e^{-t} \end{bmatrix}.$

6.14 Supplementary and Complementary Problems

5. $\mathbf{A}^{1/2} = \frac{1}{2}\begin{bmatrix} 2+\sqrt{2} & 2-\sqrt{2} & 0 & 0 \\ 2-\sqrt{2} & 2+\sqrt{2} & 0 & 0 \\ 0 & 0 & \sqrt{3}+1 & \sqrt{3}-1 \\ 0 & 0 & \sqrt{3}-1 & \sqrt{3}+1 \end{bmatrix}.$

7. $\omega^2 = \frac{M+m}{M}\frac{g}{L}.$

9. $\omega^2 = 2\omega_s^2, [0;1;0;-1], \omega^2 = 4\omega_s^2, [1;-1;1;-1], \omega^2 = 0, [1;1;1;1].$

Exercise Set 7.4.4 Qualitative Behavior of Nonlinear ODE's

1. $(0,0)$-unstable node, $(0,-4)$-unstable saddle. **3.** $(0,0)$-unstable node, $\left(0,\frac{3}{2}\right)$-unstable saddle,

$(-1,2)$-unstable node.

Exercise Set 8.2.6 Series Solutions about an Ordinary Point

1. SP: $\{-3,3\}, 3, 1, 2.$ **3.** SP: $\{n\pi\}, 0, \pi - 2, \sqrt{(\pi-3)^2 + 4}.$ **5.** SP: $\pm 1, \pm i.$ For $x_0 = 0$:

$R \geq 1.$ For $x_0 = 2, R \geq 1.$ For $x_0 = 3 - 2i, R \geq \sqrt{8}.$ **7.** SP $= \{-5, \pm i\}.$ For $x_0 = 0,$

$R \geq 1.$ For $x_0 = 2, R \geq \sqrt{5},$ For $x_0 = 3 - 2i, R \geq \sqrt{10}.$

9. $2n(n-1)a_n = (n-1)(3n-7)a_{n-1} - (n-4)a_{n-3},$

$y(x) = a_0 + a_1 x - \frac{1}{4}a_1 x^2 + \frac{1}{12}(a_0 - a_1)x^3 + \frac{5}{96}(a_0 - a_1)x^4 + \cdots$. **11.**

$n(n-1)a_n + (n-1)(2n-1)a_{n-1} + (n^2 - 4n + 5)\,a_{n-2} + a_{n-3} = 0$, for $n = 3 : \infty$.

$y_1(x) = 1 - \frac{1}{2}x^2 + \frac{2}{3}x^3 - \frac{23}{24}x^4 + \ldots$, $y_2(x) = x - \frac{3}{2}x^2 + \frac{13}{6}x^3 - \frac{13}{4}x^4 + \cdots$.

13. $y(x) = \sum_{k=0}^{\infty} \frac{x^{2k}}{k!} = \exp\left(x^2\right)$. **15.** $y_1(x) = 1 + \sum_{1}^{\infty}(-1)^k \frac{x^{3k}}{3^k k!(3k-1)(3k-4)\cdots 2}$ and

$y_2(x) = x + \sum_{1}^{\infty}(-1)^k \frac{x^{3k+1}}{3^k k!(3k+1)(3k-2)\cdots 4}$. **17.** $y_1(x) = 1 - x^2$. $y_2(x) = \sum_{0}^{\infty} \frac{x^{2k+1}}{(1-4k^2)}$.

19. $y_1(x) = x$. $y_2(x) = \sum_{n=0}^{\infty}(-1)^{k+1}\frac{x^{2k}}{2k-1}$. **21.** $y_1(x) = x - \frac{8}{3}x^3 + \frac{8}{5}x^5$.

$y_2(x) = 1 + \sum_{1}^{\infty} \frac{(2k+1)(2k-7)(2k-9)\cdots(-3)(-5)}{2^k k!} x^{2k}$. **23.** $y_1(x) = \sum_{k=0}^{\infty}(-1)^k \frac{(2k+2)(2k+1)x^{2k}}{2\cdot 1}$.

$y_2(x) = \sum_{k=0}^{\infty}(-1)^k \frac{(2k+3)(2k+2)x^{2k+1}}{3\cdot 2}$.

25. $y_1(x) = 1 + \sum_{k=1}^{\infty}(-1)^{k+1}\frac{(4k-1)(4k-5)\cdots(7)(3)}{2^k k!(2k-1)} x^{2k}$. $y_2(x) = x$.

27. $y_1(x) = \sum_{0}^{\infty} \frac{1}{4^k k!}x^{2k+1} = x\exp\left(x^2/4\right)$. $y_2(x) = 1 + \sum_{1}^{\infty} \frac{1}{2^k(2k-1)!!}x^{2k}$.

29. $y_1(x) = \sum_{k=0}^{\infty}(-1)^k\left(\frac{2k+3}{3}\right)x^{2k+1}$. $y_2(x) = \sum_{k=0}^{\infty}(-1)^k(k+1)x^{2k}$.

31. $y_1(x) = 1 - 6x^2 + x^4$. $y_2(x) = x - x^3$. **33.** $y_1(x) = x + \frac{5}{12}x^3$.

$y_2(x) = \sum_{k=0}^{\infty}\left(-\frac{1}{4}\right)^k(k+1)\left(\frac{(-1)(-3)}{(2k-1)(2k-3)}\right)x^{2k}$.

35. $y(x) = a_0 + a_1(x-1) - \frac{1}{2}a_1(x-1)^2 - \frac{1}{6}(-a_1 + a_0)(x-1)^3 + \left(\frac{1}{24}a_0 - \frac{1}{8}a_1\right)(x-1)^4$

$+ \left(-\frac{1}{120}a_0 + \frac{1}{20}a_1\right)(x-1)^5 + \cdots$. **37.** $y(x) = a_0 + a_0^2 x + a_0^3 x^2 + a_0^4 x^3 + a_0^5 x^4 + \cdots =$

$a_0\left(1 + a_0 x + (a_0 x)^2 + (a_0 x)^3 + (a_0 x)^4 + \cdots\right)$.

39. $y(x) = \sum_{k=0}^{\infty} \frac{x^{2k+1}}{(2k+1)!}a_1 + \left(a_0 + \sum_{k=1}^{\infty} \frac{x^{2k}}{(2k)!}(a_0 + 1)\right)$.

$y(x) = (c_1 - 1) + c_1 \sum_{k=1}^{\infty} \frac{x^{2k}}{(2k)!} + c_2 \sum_{k=0}^{\infty} \frac{x^{2k+1}}{(2k+1)!}$.

$y(x) = (c_1 - 1) + c_1(\sinh x - 1) + c_2 \cosh x = -1 + c_1 \sinh x + c_2 \cosh x$. $y_p(x) = -1$.

41. SP: $\pm i$. the minimum radius of convergence is $\sqrt{\frac{9}{4} + \left(\frac{3\sqrt{3}}{2} - 1\right)^2}$.

$y(x) = 1 - 5x - 10x^2 + 10x^3 + 5x^4 - x^5 = (x-1)(x^2 - 2x - 1)(x^2 + 6x - 1)$. **43.** To within constant multiples: $\alpha = 0$: $y = 1$; $\alpha = 1$: $y = x$; $\alpha = 2$: $y = 1 - 2x^2$; $\alpha = 3$: $y = 3x - 4x^3$; $\alpha = 4$: $y = 1 - 8x - x^2$.

Exercise Set 8.3.3 Singular Points

1. $x = \pm \frac{1}{2}i$, both are RSP's. **3.** RSP at $x = 2$ and ISP at $x = 0, -2$. **5.** RSP: $0, 1$; ISP: -3.

7. RSP: 0, $\left(n + \frac{1}{2}\right)\pi$ for $n = -\infty : \infty$. **9.** RSP: $0, 1$. **11.** RSP: $0, -1$. $R_{\min} \geq \sqrt{5}$. **13.** RSP at $x = 0$. $2\lambda(\lambda - 1) + 6\lambda + 1 = 2\lambda^2 + 4\lambda + 1 = 0 \Rightarrow \lambda = -1 \pm \frac{1}{2}\sqrt{2}$. **15.** SP: $\pm i$, both RSP; about $x = -i$, $\lambda = 0, 1$; about $x = i$, $\lambda = 0, 1$. **17.** SP: $-2, 0$, both RSP; about $x = -2$, $\lambda = 0, 1$; about $x = 0$, $\lambda = -1, \frac{1}{2}$. **19.** SP: ± 1, both ISP. So no exponents of singularity! **21.** SP: 0 and where $\cos x = 3x$, which will lie between 0 and $\pi/2$. For the RSP at $x = 0$, $\lambda = 1 \pm \sqrt{2}$. At the other RSP we have $\lambda = 0, 1$.

Exercise Set 8.4.3 Method of Frobenius

1. $\lambda = \frac{1}{2}$, $a_n = \frac{2}{2n + 2\lambda - 1} a_{n-1} = \frac{1}{n} a_{n-1} = \frac{1}{n!} a_0 \Rightarrow y(x) = \sum_0^\infty \frac{x^{n+1/2}}{n!} = e^x \sqrt{x}$.

3. $y(x) = c_1 x^{1/3} + c_2 x^{-1/3}$. **5.** $\lambda = \frac{1}{2}, 1$. $y_1(x) = x^{1/2} + \sum_{n=1}^\infty \frac{2^n (n+2)(n+1)}{2 \cdot 1 (2n-1)!!} x^{n+1/2}$. For $\lambda = 1$: $y_2(x) = x + \sum_{n=1}^\infty \frac{(2n+5)(2n+3)}{n!(5 \cdot 3)} x^{n+1}$. **7.** $\lambda = 0, \frac{2}{3}$.

$y_1(x) = 1 + \sum_{k=1}^\infty \left(-\frac{3}{4}\right)^k \frac{x^{2k}}{[k!(3k-1)(3k-3)\cdots(5)(2)]}$.

$y_2(x) = y\left(x; \frac{2}{3}\right) = x^{2/3} + \left(-\frac{3}{4}\right)^k \sum_{k=1}^\infty \frac{x^{2k+2/3}}{[k!(3k+1)(3k-1)\cdots(7)(4)]}$. **9.** $\lambda = 0, \frac{1}{4}$.

$y_1(x) = y(x; 0) = 1 + \sum_{n=1}^\infty \frac{(-3)^n x^n}{n!(4n-1)(4n-5)\cdots(7)(3)}$.

$y_2(x) = y\left(x; \frac{1}{4}\right) = x^{1/4} + \sum_{n=1}^\infty \frac{(-3)^n x^{n+1/4}}{n!(4n+1)(4n-3)\cdots(9)(5)}$. **11.** $\lambda = 0, \frac{3}{2}$.

$y_1(x) = y(x; 0) = \sum_{k=0}^\infty \frac{x^{2n}}{2^n n!} = \exp(x^2/2)$.

$y_2(x) = y\left(x; \frac{3}{2}\right) = x^{3/2} + \sum_{k=1}^\infty \frac{2^k x^{2k+3/2}}{(4k+3)(4k-1)\cdots(9)(5)}$.

13. $y_1(x) = y(x; 0) = 1 + \sum_{n=1}^\infty (-1)^n \frac{(n+2)(n+1)}{2(2n-1)!!} x^n$.

$y_2(x) = y\left(x; \frac{1}{2}\right) = \sum_{n=0}^\infty (-1)^n \frac{(2n+5)(2n+3)}{(5 \cdot 3)2^n n!} x^{n+1/2}$. **15.** $\lambda = -\frac{1}{3}, 3$.

$y_1(x) = y\left(x; -\frac{1}{3}\right) = x^{-1/3} + \sum_1^\infty \left(-\frac{1}{9}\right)^n \left(-\frac{10}{3n-10}\right)(3n+2)(3n-1)\cdots(5)x^{n-1/3}/n!.$

$y_2(x) = x^3.$ **17.** $\lambda = -\frac{1}{2}, 2.$ $y_1(x) = y\left(x; -\frac{1}{2}\right) = x^{-1/2}$

$+ \sum_{n=1}^\infty \frac{(-4)^n x^{n-1/2}}{[(2n-5)(2n-7)\cdots(-1)(-3)]}.$ $y_2(x) = y(x; 2) = \sum_{n=0}^\infty \frac{(-2)^n x^{n+2}}{n!} = x^2 e^{-2x}.$

19. $\lambda = 0, -\frac{1}{2}.$ $y_1(x) = y(x; 0) = 1 + 2x + 3x^2 + \frac{20}{7}x^3 + \frac{5}{3}x^4 + \frac{6}{11}x^5 + \frac{1}{13}x^6.$

$y_2(x) = y\left(x; -\frac{1}{2}\right) = x^{-1/2}.$ **21.** $\lambda = \frac{1}{2}, -2.$ $y_1(x) = y\left(x; \frac{1}{2}\right) = x^{1/2} + \frac{18}{7}x^{3/2} + \frac{11}{7}x^{5/2}.$

$y_2(x) = y(x; -2) = \sum_{n=0}^\infty (-1)^n (n+1)\frac{(-3)(-5)(-7)(-9)}{(2n-3)(2n-5)(2n-7)(2n-9)}x^{n-2}.$ **23.** $\lambda = -\frac{1}{3}, \frac{2}{3},$

$y_1(x) = \sum_{k=0}^\infty \left(-\frac{1}{9}\right)^k \frac{x^{2k-1/3}}{(2k)!} = x^{-1/3}\cos(x/9).$

$y_2(x) = \sum_{k=0}^\infty \left(-\frac{1}{9}\right)^k \frac{x^{2k+1-1/3}}{(2k+1)!} = x^{-1/3}\sin(x/9).$

$y(x) = x^{-1/3}(c_1 \cos(x/9) + c_2 \sin(x/9)).$ **25.** $\lambda = 2.$ $y_1(x) = y(x; 2) = \sum_0^\infty (n+1)x^{n+2}.$

$y_2(x) = y_1(x)\ln|x| - \sum_1^\infty n x^{n+2}.$ **27.** $\lambda = 0, 2.$

$y_1(x) = \sum_{k=0}^\infty \left(-\frac{1}{3}\right)^k \frac{x^{3k}}{k!} = \exp(-x^3/3).$ $y_2(x) = 1 + \sum_{k=1}^\infty (-1)^k \frac{x^{3k+2}}{(3k+2)(3k-1)\cdots(8)(5)}.$

29. $y_2(x) = 2 + 2x + x^2.$ **31.** $y(x) = (c_1 + c_2 \ln x)x^{-1}.$ **33.** $\lambda = 0, 0.$ $y_0(x) = 1.$

$y_2(x) = 1 - 2x + \frac{1}{2}x^2.$ $y_3(x) = 1 - 3x + \frac{3}{2}x^2 - \frac{1}{6}x^3.$ **35.** $\lambda = \pm\frac{1}{2},$

$y_1(x) = \sum_{k=0}^\infty \left(-\frac{1}{4}\right)^k \frac{x^{-(2k+1/2)}}{(2k+1)!}, y_2(x) = \sum_{k=0}^\infty \left(-\frac{1}{4}\right)^k \frac{x^{-(2k-1/2)}}{(2k)!}.$

Exercise Set 8.5.1 **Solution about an Irregular Singular Point**

1. $y(x) = 1 - \frac{1}{3}x^{-2}.$ $a_n = -\frac{(n-2)(n-3)}{n+2}a_{n-2},$ which leads to an increasing sequence and hence a divergent series. You should notice that when we set the separated terms to zero, $a_0 = 0 = a_1$, all the a_n must be zero!!

Exercise Set 9.2.4 **Gamma Function**

3. $\Gamma(3 + i) = 0.96288 + 1.33910i,$ $\Gamma(4 + 1) = 1.54954 + 4.98018i.$

9. $a_n = \left(-\frac{2}{3}\right)^n \frac{\Gamma\left(n+\frac{3}{2}\right)}{\Gamma\left(\frac{3}{2}\right)}a_0.$ **11.** $a_n = 4^n \frac{n+2}{2}\frac{2\Gamma\left(n+\frac{3}{2}\right)}{\sqrt{\pi}n!}a_0.$ **13.** $a_n = 0,$ for $n > 0.$

15. $a_{2k} = \left(\dfrac{4}{3\Gamma\left(\frac{5}{8}\right)}\right) 12^k \dfrac{\left(k+\frac{3}{2}\right)\left(k+\frac{1}{2}\right)\Gamma\left(k+\frac{5}{8}\right)}{k!} a_0;\ a_{2k+1} = \left(\dfrac{\sqrt{\pi}}{\Gamma\left(\frac{9}{8}\right)}\right) 12^k \dfrac{(k+2)(k+1)\Gamma\left(k+\frac{9}{8}\right)}{\Gamma\left(k+\frac{3}{2}\right)} a_1.$

17. $a_{2k} = (-2)^k \dfrac{(k+1)!\left(k+\frac{3}{2}\right)}{\Gamma\left(k+\frac{1}{2}\right)} \dfrac{2}{3}\sqrt{\pi} a_0,\ k=0:\infty;\ a_{2k+1} = \dfrac{(k+2)\Gamma\left(k+\frac{3}{2}\right)}{k!} \dfrac{4}{3\sqrt{\pi}} a_1,\ k=0:\infty.$

19. $a_{3k} = \dfrac{\Gamma\left(k+\frac{5}{3}\right)}{k!\Gamma\left(\frac{5}{3}\right)} a_0;\ a_{3k+1} = \dfrac{(k+1)!\Gamma\left(\frac{4}{3}\right)}{\Gamma\left(k+\frac{4}{3}\right)} a_1;\ a_{3k+2} = \dfrac{\Gamma\left(k+\frac{7}{3}\right)}{\Gamma\left(k+\frac{5}{3}\right)} \dfrac{\Gamma\left(\frac{5}{3}\right)}{\Gamma\left(\frac{7}{3}\right)} a_2.$

21. $a_{4k} = \left(-\dfrac{1}{2}\right)^k \dfrac{k!\Gamma\left(\frac{7}{8}\right)}{\Gamma\left(k+\frac{7}{8}\right)} a_0,\ a_{4k+1} = \left(-\dfrac{1}{2}\right)^k \dfrac{\Gamma\left(k+\frac{5}{4}\right)\Gamma\left(\frac{9}{8}\right)}{k!\Gamma\left(k+\frac{9}{8}\right)\Gamma\left(\frac{5}{4}\right)} a_1,$

$a_{4k+2} = \left(-\dfrac{1}{2}\right)^k \dfrac{\Gamma\left(k+\frac{3}{2}\right)\Gamma\left(\frac{11}{8}\right)}{\Gamma\left(k+\frac{11}{8}\right)\Gamma\left(\frac{3}{2}\right)} a_2,\ a_{4k+3} = \left(-\dfrac{1}{2}\right)^k \dfrac{\Gamma\left(k+\frac{7}{4}\right)\Gamma\left(\frac{13}{8}\right)}{\Gamma\left(k+\frac{13}{8}\right)\Gamma\left(\frac{7}{4}\right)} a_3.$

Exercise Set 9.4.9 **Bessel Functions**

5. $y(x) = x^{1/2} Z_{1/3}\left(\frac{2}{3}x^{3/2}\right)$. **7.** $y(x) = x^{1/2} Z_{1/6}(x^3/3)$. **9.** $y(x) = x^{3/8} Z_{3/8}(x)$.

11. $y(x) = x^{-1/2} e^{x/2} \left(c_1 I_{1/2}(x/2) + c_2 I_{-1/2}(x/2)\right)$

$= e^{-x/2}\left(k_1 \cosh(x/2) + k_2 \sinh(x/2)\right)$. **13.** $y(x) = x^{1/2} Z_{1/2\beta}\left(\frac{1}{2}\gamma x^\beta\right)$.

15. $y(x) = x^n[c_1 I_n(x^n) + c_2 K_n(x^n)]$.

17. $y(x) = x^{-1} \exp(x^2/2)\left(c_1 I_{\sqrt{3}/2}(x^2/2) + c_2 K_{\sqrt{3}/2}(x^2/2)\right)$.

19. $x^2 y'' + x\left(1 + 2m(x^m - 1)\right)y' + \left(m^2(1-m^2) - m^2 x^m(1-x^m)\right) y = 0$. **21.** They cannot satisfy the prescribed initial conditions. **37.** Since $J_0' = -J_1$, an integration of both sides is all you need. **49.** Use the series representation of $J_0(x)$ and integrate term by term.

INDEX